Arguing About Religion

"This collection fits perfectly with the aim of Routledge's 'Arguing About...' series: it brings together excellent essays on central issues in the philosophy of religion, but the topics and essays are fresher and perhaps a bit edgier than those in a 'standard' philosophy of religion anthology. The book is at the same time an accurate representation of the cutting edge of the field at this point and also a challenging, probing, and provocative collection. Highly recommended!"

— John M. Fischer, University of California, Riverside

Arguing About Religion is an ideal collection for students interested in contemporary philosophy of religion and related disciplines. This volume brings together primary readings from over forty of the world's leading philosophers of religion, covering a broad range of issues. Set alongside these works of academic philosophy are excerpts from controversial popular works by Daniel Dennett and Richard Dawkins, in order to introduce the philosophical issues in a way that demonstrates their relevance to everyday life and sets them in the context of contemporary cultural discourse.

The volume is divided into six parts, helping the student get to grips with classic and core arguments. Topics covered include:

Methodological issues in philosophy of religion
God's nature and existence
Evil and divine hiddenness
Providence and interaction
The afterlife
Religion and contemporary life

Featuring lucid general and section introductions and a glossary by volume editor Kevin Timpe, *Arguing About Religion* is an ideal starting point for students coming to philosophy of religion for the first time.

Kevin Timpe is Assistant Professor of Philosophy at the University of San Diego. He is the author of *Free Will: Sourcehood and Its Alternatives,* and the editor of *Metaphysics and God.* His articles have appeared in *Philosophical Studies, Canadian Journal of Philosophy, American Philosophical Quarterly, Faith and Philosophy,* and *Religious Studies.* He also serves as the philosophy of religion editor for the *Internet Encyclopedia of Philosophy.*

Arguing About Philosophy

This exciting and lively series introduces key subjects in philosophy with the help of a vibrant set of readings. In contrast to many standard anthologies which often reprint the same technical and remote extracts, each volume in the *Arguing About Philosophy* series is built around essential but fresher philosophical readings, designed to attract the curiosity of students coming to the subject for the first time. A key feature of the series is the inclusion of well-known yet often neglected readings from related fields, such as popular science, film and fiction. Each volume is edited by leading figures in their chosen field and each section carefully introduced and set in context, making the series an exciting starting point for those looking to get to grips with philosophy.

Arguing About Knowledge
Edited by Duncan Pritchard and Ram Neta

Arguing About Law
Edited by Aileen Kavanagh and
John Oberdiek

Arguing About Metaethics
Edited by Andrew Fisher and Simon Kirchin

Arguing About the Mind
Edited by Brie Gertler and Lawrence Shapiro

Arguing About Art 3rd Edition
Edited by Alex Neill and Aaron Ridley

Arguing About Religion
Edited by Kevin Timpe

Forthcoming titles:
Arguing About Language
Edited by Darragh Byrne and Max Kolbel

Arguing About Metaphysics
Edited by Michael Rea

Arguing About Political Philosophy
Edited by Matt Zwolinski

Arguing About Religion

Edited by
Kevin Timpe

Routledge
Taylor & Francis Group

NEW YORK AND LONDON

First published 2009
by Routledge
711 Third Avenue, New York, NY 10017, USA

Simultaneously published in the UK
by Routledge
2 Park Square, Milton Park, Abingdon, Oxon OX14 4RN

Routledge is an imprint of the Taylor & Francis Group, an informa business

© 2009 Taylor & Francis

Typeset in Joanna by
RefineCatch Limited, Bungay, Suffolk

Library of Congress Cataloging in Publication Data
Arguing about religion / Kevin Timpe, editor.
    p. cm.
   1. Christianity–Philosophy. 2. Religion–Philosophy. I. Timpe, Kevin.
BR100.A64 2009
210–dc22

2008027301

ISBN10: 0–415–98861–6 (hbk)
ISBN10: 0–415–98862–4 (pbk)

ISBN13: 978–0–415–98861–2 (hbk)
ISBN13: 978–0–415–98862–9 (pbk)

Dedication

"None of us could take our eyes off him. He was the most beautiful thing I had ever seen. He was like moonlight."

Anne Lamott, *Operating Instructions*

To Jameson,
Whose gestation and arrival overlapped with those of this volume; who offers hope for the future; and who gives me a glimpse of what it must be to love as God loves.

Contents

Acknowledgements

My great gratitude goes to Kate Ahl at Routledge, who has been a tremendous asset from the moment she approached me about doing this project. At all stages of the volume's production, she has offered invaluable advice and support. Not only is this collection greatly improved from her role in its development, but I would not have been able to complete it without her. Mike Andrews also provided much needed assistance on behalf of Routledge.

Tim Pawl, Chris Callaway, Scott Ragland, Shannon Murphy, and Keith Loftin gave me valuable input and advice on the section introductions. I have also benefitted from the advice of Matt Zwolinski, Tim Pawl, Ryan Nichols, Jennifer Hart Weed, Tully Borland, Mike Rota, Neal Judisch, Lori Watson, Linda Peterson, John Donnelly, and Annie Pirruccello in selecting the readings for this volume. Finally, I would like to thank the students in my Spring 2008 Philosophy of God course at the University of San Diego for letting me try out an early draft of this volume on them. Their feedback and perspective as readers have proven to be quite valuable in putting together a book aimed at their peers.

Permissions Acknowledgements

The editor and publishers wish to thank the following for permission to use copyrighted material:

Blackwell Publishing for Alister McGrath, material from *Dawkins' God: Genes, Memes, and the Meaning of Life* (2004); and Paul Weithman, "Theism, Law, and Politics" in *A Companion to the Philosophy of Religion*, ed. Philip Quinn and Charles Taliaferro (1997) pp. 489–495.

Cambridge University Press for Lynne Rudder Baker, "Persons and the Metaphysics of Resurrection" in *Religious Studies* 43.3 (2007) pp. 333–348, © 2007 Cambridge University Press; Derk Pereboom, "Free Will, Evil, and Divine Providence" in *God and the Ethics of Belief: New Essays in Philosophy of Religion*, ed. Andrew Chignell and Andrew Dole (2005) pp. 77–98, © 2005 Cambridge University Press; Kevin Timpe, "Prayers for the Past" in *Religious Studies* 41.3 (2005) pp. 305–322; and Keith Ward, "Truth and the Diversity of Religions" in *Religious Studies* 26 (1990) pp. 1–18.

The *Christian Scholar's Review* for Alvin Plantinga, "The Reformed Objection to Natural Theology" in the *Christian Scholar's Review* 11:3 (1982), pp. 187–198. Copyright © 1982 by Christian Scholar's Review.

Cornell University Press for Norman Kretzmann, "A General Problem of Creation: Why Would God Create Anything at All?" in *Being and Goodness: The Concept of the Good in Metaphysics and Philosophical Theology,* ed. and trans. Scott MacDonald (1991) pp. 208–228. Copyright © 1991 by Cornell University.

Faith and Philosophy for John Hick, "Religious Pluralism and Salvation" in *Faith and Philosophy* 5 (1998) pp. 365–377; C. Stephen Layman, "God and the Moral Order" in *Faith and Philosophy* 19.3 (2002) pp. 304–316; John Sanders, "Why Simple Foreknowledge Offers No More Providential Control than the Openness of God" in *Faith and Philosophy* 14.1 (1997) pp. 26–40; James Sennett, "Is There Freedom in Heaven" in *Faith and Philosophy* 16.1 (1999) pp. 69–82; and Thomas Talbott, "The Doctrine of Everlasting Punishment" in *Faith and Philosophy* 7.1 (1990) pp. 19–42.

First Things for Phillip Johnson, "Evolution as Dogma: The Establishment of Naturalism" in *First Things* 6 (1990) pp. 15–22.

Houghton Mifflin Harcourt Publishing Company for Richard Dawkins, "Undeserved Respect" and "What's Wrong with Religion? Why Be So Hostile," from *The God Delusion* (2006). Copyright © 2006 by Richard Dawkins. All rights reserved.

InterVarsity Press for William Lane Craig, "The Middle-Knowledge View" in *Divine Foreknowledge: Four Views,* ed. James Beilby and Paul Eddy (2001) pp. 119–143.

The MIT Press for Phillip Kitcher, "Born-Again Creationism" in *Intelligent Design Creationism and Its Critics: Philosophical, Theological, and Scientific Perspectives,* ed. Robert T. Pennock (2002) pp. 257–287. © 2002 Massachusetts Institute of Technology; Robert Pennock, "Why Creationism Should Not Be Taught in the Public Schools" in *Intelligent Design Creationism and Its Critics: Philosophical, Theological, and Scientific Perspectives,* ed. Robert T. Pennock (2002) pp. 755–777. © 2002 Massachusetts Institute of Technology; and Alvin Plantinga, "Creation and Evolution: A Modest Proposal" in *Intelligent Design Creationism and Its Critics: Philosophical, Theological, and Scientific Perspectives,* ed. Robert T. Pennock (2002) pp. 779–791. © 2002 Massachusetts Institute of Technology.

Oxford University Press for Norman Kretzmann, material from *The Metaphysics of Theism* (Clarendon Press, 1997); and David Lewis, "Divine Evil" in *Philosophers Without Gods,* ed. Louise M. Antony (2007) pp. 231–242.

Pearson Education, Inc., Upper Saddle River, NJ, for Wes Morriston, "A Critical Examination of the Kalam Cosmological Argument" in *God Matters: Readings in the Philosophy of Religion,* ed. Raymond Martin and Christopher Bernard (Longman, 2003) pp. 96–108.

Philosophia Christi for Kevin Corcoran, "Dualism, Materialism, and the Problem of Postmortem Survival" in *Philosophia Christi* 4.2 (2002) pp. 411–42. Permission granted by the editors of *Philosophia Christi* (www.philchristi.org).

Ridgeview Publishing Company for William Alston, "The Inductive Argument from Evil and the Human Cognitive Condition" in *Philosophical Perspectives,* 5, Philosophy of Religion (1991) pp. 29–67.

Springer Science+Business Media for Robert P. Lovering, "Divine Hiddenness and Inculpable Ignorance" in the *International Journal for Philosophy of Religion* 56.2 (2004) pp. 89–107.

Taylor and Francis Books for Elliot Sober, "The Design Argument" in *God and Design: The Teleological Argument and Modern Science,* ed. Neil A. Manson (Routledge 2003) pp. 27–54. © 2003 Elliot Sober; William Hasker, material from *Providence, Evil and the Openness of God* (Routledge 2004) pp. 125–143; and Roger Ames, "Death as Transformation in Classical Daoism" in *Death and Philosophy,* eds. Jeff Malpas and Robert C. Solomon (Routledge 1999) pp. 57–71.

The University of Calgary Press for Eleonore Stump, "Dante's Hell, Aquinas's Moral Theory and the Love of God" in the *Canadian Journal of Philosophy* 16 (1986) pp. 181–198.

The University of Hawaii Press for Whitley Kaufman, "Karma, Rebirth, and the Problem of Evil" in *Philosophy East and West* vol. 55, no. 1 (2005) pp. 15–32.

The University of Illinois Press for William Rowe, "The Problem of Evil and Some

Varieties of Atheism" in *American Philosophical Quarterly* 16 (1979) pp. 335–41; Eleonore Stump, "Petitionary Prayer" in *American Philosophical Quarterly* 16 (1979) 81–91; and Michael Murray, "Coercion and the Hiddenness of God" in *American Philosophical Quarterly* 30 (1993) pp. 27–38.

Viking Penguin, a division of Penguin Group (USA) Inc. for Daniel Dennett, "Breaking Which Spell?," "Some Questions About Science," The Evolution of Stewardship," "The Invention of Teen Spirit," "Now What Do We Do?," from *Breaking the Spell: Religion as Natural Phenomena* (2006). © 2006 Daniel C. Dennett.

Wadsworth, a division of Thomson Learning, for Louis Pojman, material from *Philosophy: The Pursuit of Wisdom, 5th Edition* (2006) pp. 127–136.

Westview Press, a member of Perseus Books Group, for Peter van Inwagen, "Necessary Being: The Ontological Argument" in *Metaphysics*, pp. 75–98.

Wm. B. Eerdmans Publishing Company for Timothy O'Connor, "Religious Pluralism" in *Reason for the Hope Within*, ed. Michael J. Murray (1999) pp. 165–182. © 1999 Wm. B. Eerdmans Publishing Co.; Robin Collins, "A Scientific Argument for the Existence of God: The Fine-Tuning Design Argument" in *Reason for the Hope Within*, ed. Michael J. Murray (1999) pp. 47–76. © 1999 Wm. B. Eerdmans Publishing Co.; and Peter van Inwagen, "The Argument from Evil" in *Christian Faith and the Problem of Evil*, ed. Peter van Inwagen (2004) pp. 55–74. © 1994 Wm. B. Eerdmans Publishing Co.

GENERAL INTRODUCTION

PHILOSOPHY OF RELIGION is the philosophical reflection on and examination of the central themes of religion. While philosophy of religion is related to disciplines with a similar subject matter such as theology and religious studies, it is nevertheless distinct. One important way in which philosophy of religion is distinct from theology is that the latter must be done from *within* a particular religious tradition. Philosophy of religion, on the other hand, can be done by those who are not committed to the truth of any particular religion. In fact, many of the leading philosophers of religion are themselves atheists or agnostics. Philosophy of religion is also distinct from religious studies. Religious studies investigates religious beliefs, behaviors, and institutions; but it does not do so primarily by drawing upon the tools, resources, and methodologies of philosophy. Instead, it approaches the subject matter from an interdisciplinary, historical, or anthropological point of view. So philosophy of religion is a study of religion like theology or religious studies. But unlike theology and religious studies, which approach their subject matter by way of a specific religion or by way of historical, anthropological and sociological methods respectively, philosophy of religion approaches religion with an eye to logical analysis and rational consistency.

Philosophy of religion is as old as philosophy itself. One can find, for example, an argument for the existence of an unmoved mover in Aristotle's *Metaphysics*. Throughout its long history, philosophy of religion has informed, and been informed by, all of the major areas of philosophy: metaphysics, epistemology, logic, ethics, political philosophy, philosophy of language, philosophy of science, etc. . . . Because of this, the readings that follow will discuss many issues that are central to these other areas of philosophy: possibility and other modalities, causation, ontology, epistemic justification, rationality, conceptions of the good, political justification, meaning, probability, etc. . . . In fact, many of the readings were selected to highlight the overlap between philosophy of religion and these other areas of philosophy.

A philosophy of religion anthology could be approached in three main ways: as a collection of texts from the history of philosophy, as a collection drawn from contemporary authors, or as a mixture of the two. There is merit in taking a historical or mixed approach. Much of considerable value can be found in historical texts such as Anselm's *Proslogion*, Aquinas' *Summa contra gentiles*, and Hume's *Dialogues Concerning Natural Religion*. And contemporary issues and debates are largely shaped by these, and other, historical works. Nevertheless, I have approached this book exclusively from a contemporary vantage point. The oldest reading in this volume (William Rowe's "The Problem of Evil and Some Varieties of Atheism") was originally published in 1979, and most of the readings appeared within the past decade. My primary reasons for the contemporary focus are twofold. First, the past three decades have been a particularly exciting period for philosophy of religion. William Hasker has described the role of philosophy of religion in philosophy at large before this exciting period, in particular during the first part of the twentieth century, as "less than marginal."[1] During the 1930s, 1940s and 1950s, most philosophy of religion focused on issues related to religious language. During those decades, many thought that statements about the existence of God didn't even rise to the level of being false; it was rather seen as meaningless. During the 1960s, the claim that religious language was devoid of meaning was largely given up, and traditional philosophy of religion (such as that engaged in during much of the medieval and modern periods) made a resurgence. Philosophers turned significant attention to the arguments for and against the existence of God, understanding the divine attributes, and more. The past few decades have been a very exciting time for philosophy of religion as the discipline continues to become more varied and diverse; it also has been one of the most active areas of philosophical scholarship. My second reason for taking a purely contemporary approach in the present volume is related to the first. I hope that these readings will give a snapshot of where various debates central to philosophy of religion currently are, as well as indicate the directions in which the field is headed.

Because of space considerations, I have had to focus on central issues and approaches. For this reason, the volume draws heavily on particular approaches, most notably analytic philosophy and western monotheisms. Many of the articles in particular engage Christianity in particular; this reflects the fact that the majority of philosophers of religion are primarily engaging with the Christian religious tradition. However, most of the arguments that follow would apply equally well to other monotheisms, such as Judaism and Islam. As philosophy of religion continues to diversify, more attention is being given to feminist approaches as well as to eastern, African, and other native religions. But to date the work in these areas is not as developed as it is within the western monotheistic tradition. The present volume thus reflects the current focus of the field.

Philosophy of religion is a complex academic specialization, with its own technical terminology and concepts. But this fact should not dissuade us from thinking long and hard about the topic at hand, for philosophy of religion helps us understand issues of utmost concern—which of the world's diverse religious beliefs are true, whether or not God exists, understanding the existence of evil, the future state of human persons, and how our personal religious beliefs relate to science and politics. In other words, it is worth arguing about religion because religion matters.

Note

1   William Hasker, "Analytic Philosophy of Religion," in William Wainwright, ed., *The Oxford Handbook of Philosophy of Religion* (Oxford: Oxford University Press, 2005), 422. Hasker's article is a wonderful survey of the recent history of philosophy of religion and is highly recommended.

PART 1

Methodological Issues in Philosophy of Religion

INTRODUCTION TO PART 1

MOST GENERALLY, PHILOSOPHY OF RELIGION is the philosophical reflection on and examination of the central themes of religion. Given the diversity of approaches to religion in the world, it is not surprising that philosophy of religion is also disparate in its concerns and approaches. The readings in this section address some of the overarching methodological issues faced in the discipline of philosophy of religion: Can we think about religion without an appeal to revelation? If so, is there something methodologically barring us from believing in God's existence on the basis of reason alone? Do we even need reasons for having the religious beliefs that we do? How do our reasons stack up against those held by others who believe in a different religious tradition? Should we change how we approach philosophy of religion because of the plurality of religious beliefs?

The first two readings explore the role of natural theology in philosophy of religion. According to William Alston,

> *Natural theology* is the enterprise of providing support for religious belief by starting with premises that neither are nor presuppose any religious belief. We begin from the mere existence of the world, or the teleological order of the world, or the concept of God, and we try to show that when we think through the implications of our starting point we are led to recognize the existence of a being that possesses attributes sufficient to identify Him as God.[1]

In "The Nature of Natural Theology," Norman Kretzmann begins by arguing that natural theology can appropriately be considered a branch of philosophy. There is a sense in which natural theology can be part of theology proper, in that it is concerned with exploring the existence and nature of God, as seen in the definition above. But it is also proper, Kretzmann argues, to approach religion philosophically. Kretzmann differentiates "theology from the top down" and "theology from the bottom up." Theology from the top down begins with revelation. Such an approach to theology is confessional in nature in that it takes revealed truths as its starting point. In contrast, theology from the bottom up, or what Kretzmann calls natural theology, avoids appeals to revelation in favor of philosophical argument and analysis. In this way, natural theology aims at rational assessment, like the rest of philosophy. After rejecting a number of objections to natural theology, Kretzmann shows how natural theology is a legitimate starting point for developing a systematic philosophy. He ends by considering the role of arguments for and against the existence of God in natural theology.

Scott MacDonald's "What is Philosophical Theology?" argues that philosophy of religion should not be limited to natural theology, but should also include philosophical theology. By philosophical theology, MacDonald means appropriate philosophical reflection on theological matters. While natural theology is often taken to be the primary task of philosophy of religion and is itself often restricted to attempting to prove truths about the existence and nature of God via reason alone, MacDonald thinks that limiting philosophy of religion to the epistemic task of natural theology results in two unnecessary restrictions. First, it unduly limits the sources and methods for philosophical reflection on God. For example, MacDonald considers the role that testimony can play in justifying one's beliefs. If testimony can provide epistemic justification for non-religious beliefs, then revelation could be a credible source of one's religious beliefs if it could be shown that the testimony of that revelation was reliable. Second, MacDonald thinks that philosophical reflection on theological issues beyond the existence and nature of God is an appropriate goal. While establishing the truth or epistemic justification of beliefs or propositions is part of the task of philosophy, philosophy of religion, like philosophy more broadly, should not be limited to this one epistemic activity. Another task of philosophy is what MacDonald calls "clarification," which he describes as developing, systematizing, and explaining theories regarding ultimate reality. Since this sort of conceptual analysis and systematic investigation is apropos in other areas of philosophy even if one hasn't conclusively argued for the truth of the view under investigation, clarification of theological topics is equally appropriate. It is this broader understanding of philosophy of religion as involving both natural theology and clarification that informs later sections of this book.

The next two readings further explore the epistemic task of natural theology. While it is not surprising that some atheists and agnostics would object to attempting to prove the existence of God via philosophical argument, in "The Reformed Objection to Natural Theology" Alvin Plantinga raises two different religious criticisms of natural theology. The first is that people who believe in the existence of God do not so believe *because of* philosophical arguments of the sort that natural theology attempts to promulgate. Furthermore, Plantinga thinks that such arguments are not needed in order for the theist's belief in the existence of God to be rationally justified. Belief in the existence of God, he suggests, is properly basic—that is, a belief that one is justified in holding even if one has no argument for the truth of that belief. Plantinga concludes by considering and refuting an objection to the thesis that belief in the existence of God is properly basic. According to what Plantinga calls "the Great Pumpkin Objection," if belief in the existence of God were properly basic, then belief in the existence of the Great Pumpkin would also be properly basic. Insofar as it is not rational to believe in the Great Pumpkin without having an argument for his existence, the objection concludes that belief in God's existence is not properly basic.

In "Rational Religious Belief," Richard Swinburne presents a different account of the rationality of beliefs in the existence of God. He begins by differentiating five different kinds of rationality in believing that some proposition p is true, as well as the relationships between these kinds of rationality and the evidence for the truth of p. According to Swinburne, the only kind of rationality for which an individual can be held responsible is rationality$_3$:

Subject S's belief that p is rational$_3$ if and only if p is rendered probable by S's evidence for p and S's evidence for p results from investigation which is in S's view adequate.

Swinburne then turns to investigating whether or not specifically religious beliefs can satisfy this condition for rationality. He argues that there are many sources of evidence for religious beliefs: general features of the universe, the testimony of others, authority, etc. . . . So long as an individual has properly investigated the various sources for her religious beliefs, Swinburne claims that religious beliefs can be rational$_3$. He concludes by exploring why it is important that one's religious beliefs be rationally held.

Assume for the moment that Plantinga and Swinburne are correct, and that at least some religious beliefs, such as the belief in the existence of God, can be rational. One would still have to figure out *which* religious beliefs are among those that it is rational to believe. At this point, one must confront the plurality of religions, for there are many competing religious views in the world, and many of these views contradict each other. How does the plurality and diversity of religious belief affect the rationality of religious belief? The last three readings in this section explore the issue of religious pluralism and its effect on religious belief.[2]

John Hick understands religions as ways to obtain salvation, and in "Religious Pluralism and Salvation" he is concerned with how we should understand the plethora of views regarding not only what salvation is, but also how to achieve it. Hick argues that none of the major world religions are salvifically superior to the others. Instead, he argues that all are different manifestations of some more ultimate ground of salvation. Drawing on the Kantian distinction between the noumenal and phenomenal realms, Hick argues that the ultimate divine reality—which he calls "the Real"—is beyond the grasp of human cognition. The world's various religions are, according to Hick, different but equally valid manifestations of the Real from diverse historical, cultural, and cognitive perspectives. And each of them has developed its own set of answers to the perennial questions of religion. None of these religions has an exclusive hold on truth regarding the Real. Hick thus advocates a version of religious inclusivism in that he thinks that multiple religions have an equally valid claim to truth regarding the ultimate nature of divine reality.

In his "Truth and the Diversity of Religions," Keith Ward argues that Hick's view is philosophically unacceptable. Ward begins with the nature of belief. To believe a proposition is to think that proposition is true. If a particular proposition x is true, then all other propositions which contradict x must be false. In this way, truth-claims are necessarily exclusive. So if an individual has a particular religious belief, say the belief that one and only one God exists, then in order to hold consistent beliefs she needs to think that all contrary religious beliefs, such as the belief that there is no God or the belief that there are many gods, are false. Ward goes on to argue against other central claims defended by Hick—e.g., that the Real is in principle unknowable and the noumenal/phenomenal distinction. Furthermore, he argues, reflection on the plurality of religions shows at most that the claims of multiple religions can be epistemically justified, not that they are all true. The primary lesson to be learned from descriptive religious pluralism, Ward thinks, is not religious inclusivism, but rather religious toleration in which one recognizes that others' religious beliefs may be held for good reasons, even if those beliefs are in fact false.

Timothy O'Connor advances a stronger criticism of evaluative religious pluralism in his aptly named "Religious Pluralism." O'Connor draws the reader's attention to a number of fundamental assumptions that underlie evaluative religious pluralism in order to criticize the view, and advocates instead a version of religious exclusivism. (While O'Connor is primarily arguing for Christian exclusivism, others of differing religious views could equally use his arguments.) He proceeds in two steps. First, he shows that three common arguments against exclusive religious belief all fail:

(i)   the argument that all religious experiences are equally reliable,
(ii)   the argument that exclusive religious belief is immorally arrogant, and
(iii) the argument that there is no objective criterion by which to reasonably select from among competing religious claims.

Even if O'Connor is successful in showing that the pluralist's arguments against exclusivism fail, that by itself doesn't show that evaluative religious pluralism is false. In the second half of this reading, O'Connor argues that evaluative religious pluralism is incoherent in that it leads to contradictory statements both being true (or both being false).

Notes

1 *Perceiving God: The Epistemology of Religious Experience* (Ithaca, NY: Cornell University Press, 1991), 289.
2 It will be helpful, however, to differentiate two different understandings of religious pluralism. First, religious pluralism is sometimes taken to be merely descriptive, in that it points out that there are numerous, and often competing, religious claims. Religious pluralism is also sometimes taken to be the stronger claim that not only are there competing religious claims, but that these competing claims are all equally good in some important philosophical sense. Let us call this latter form evaluative religious pluralism. None of the closing three articles in this section question descriptive religious pluralism. Instead, they all focus on evaluative religious pluralism, with the first author arguing for evaluative religious pluralism and the final two authors arguing against it.

Further Reading

Basinger, David. *Religious Diversity: A Philosophical Assessment* (Burlington, VT: Ashgate Publishing Company, 2002).
Craig, William Lane and J. P. Moreland, eds. *The Blackwell Companion to Natural Theology* (Oxford: Blackwell, 1991).
Davies, Brian. *An Introduction to the Philosophy of Religion* (Oxford: Oxford University Press, 1993).
Geivett, R. Douglas and Brendan Sweetman, eds. *Contemporary Perspectives on Religious Epistemology* (Oxford: Oxford University Press, 1992).

Griffiths, Paul. *Problems of Religious Diversity* (London: Blackwell, 2002).

Helm, Paul. *Faith and Reason* (Oxford: Oxford University Press, 2000).

Hick, John. *An Interpretation of Religion: Human Responses to the Transcendent* (New Haven, CT: Yale University Press, 1989).

Hick, John. *Problems of Religious Pluralism* (New York: St. Martin's Press, 1985).

Plantinga, Alvin. *Warranted Christian Belief* (Oxford: Oxford University Press, 2000).

Swinburne, Richard. *Faith and Reason* (Oxford: Clarendon, 1983).

Zagzebski, Linda. *Rational Faith: Catholic Responses to Reformed Epistemology* (Notre Dame, IN: University of Notre Dame, 1993).

Chapter 1

Norman Kretzmann

THE NATURE OF NATURAL THEOLOGY

In my view a great deal—not all—of theology's traditional subject-matter is really continuous with philosophy's subject-matter, and ought to be integrated with it in practice. Most philosophers who lived before the twentieth century would share that view, and no substantive developments in the last hundred years should have obscured it. In the first three-quarters of this century it surely was obscured, but we may be witnessing a development in which that view is no longer so hard to find among philosophers: as late twentieth-century theologians have been moving away from their traditional subject-matter, philosophers have been moving in.[1] And natural theology, a branch of philosophy, interests me especially, because it provides the traditional and still central means of integrating philosophy with (some of) theology.

Integrating them by means of natural theology amounts to developing within philosophy some of the subject-matter specifically associated with theology. Developing it within philosophy amounts to forgoing appeals to any putative revelation or religious experience as evidence for the truth of propositions, and accepting as data only those few naturally evident considerations that traditionally constitute data acceptable for philosophy generally. That's what makes it *natural* theology. What makes this part of philosophy natural *theology* is, of course, its agenda: investigating, by means of analysis and argument, at least the existence and nature of God and, in a fuller

development, the relation of everything else—especially human nature and behaviour—to God considered as reality's first principle. [. . .]

Natural theology is as old as the rest of philosophy,[2] and the most familiar sort of criticism of it must be almost equally ancient, because it's just the sort that any philosophical undertaking is bound to generate within philosophy itself. The methods of natural theology are analysis and argument, the methods of the rest of philosophy; and, like any other branch of philosophy, natural theology submits its results to rational assessment. The people who constitute the primary audience for natural theology, in this as in any period of the history of philosophy, are philosophers who are willing to assess its results on philosophical grounds. Anyone who in that way develops particular objections to particular arguments of natural theology is simply giving natural theology what it asks for. And, of course, it has had plenty of it. But offering a refutation of an argument for, say, the existence of God is a paradigmatically philosophical objection, which doesn't by itself imply a negative attitude toward the enterprise of natural theology in which the rejected argument arose.

There aren't many philosophical atheists whose atheism explicitly drives part of their philosophical agenda, but, naturally, they can be among the most dedicated challengers of natural theology's results.[3] And sometimes their criticism has been developed to such an extent that it could be taken as a basis for repudiating the entire enterprise on philosophical grounds. In this respect, among others, natural theology resembles metaphysics, which some philosophers have sometimes rejected wholesale. The reason why both disciplines keep rising from their ashes in ever new guises is that their fundamental questions are undeniably and irresistibly there, in the substructure of rational inquiry, demanding yet another attempt at a systematic answer. And so a general philosophical repudiation of either inquiry is likely to be based, too narrowly, on the unsatisfactoriness of a particular set of answers with their supporting arguments, or, less effectively, on the impossibility of pursuing either inquiry by some favoured method or other—for example, those of the natural sciences.

Atheists haven't been the only philosophers to adopt negative attitudes toward natural theology. Philosophers who are theists are, of course, more likely to take an active interest in natural theology, and no doubt they're the only ones who ever engage in it constructively. Those who do so will, naturally, sometimes raise philosophical objections against particular arguments in natural theology, as Aquinas famously does against Anselm's. Religious philosophers may, however, generate or adopt not only philosophical objections to particular arguments; they may also raise religious objections to the whole enterprise of natural theology. There are many kinds of religious objections, a few of which we'll have to sample below, but their general nature and the spirit in which they're often offered can be nicely summed up in Alvin Plantinga's characterization of them: negative religious attitudes toward natural theology look 'a little like the attitude some Christians adopt toward faith healing: it can't be done, but even if it could it shouldn't be' (1983: 63). Philosophers who repudiate natural theology on religious grounds alone do so otherwise than as philosophers, however, and non-philosophical attitudes toward it won't directly concern me. [. . .]

Theology and Philosophy

I'm a philosopher, not a theologian. Even if theologians were inclined to pay any attention to a layman's notions about their field, what I have to say about theology's nature and subject-matter wouldn't contribute anything to the wide-ranging arguments they've been having over those basic issues. My approach is uninfluenced by any consideration of that debate, and is guided simply by the very idea of theology—I mean the idea embedded in the etymology of the word and instantiated more or less fully in the work of just about all dead theologians and most dead philosophers, too, from the pre-Socratics through the seventeenth century at least. Living theologians are of course familiar with the idea, and almost all of them would repudiate it as utterly obsolete.[4]

Broadly speaking, the idea of theology is the idea of a rational investigation of the first principles and most fundamental aspects of reality in general and of human nature and behaviour in particular. That broad characterization could obviously accommodate theology's more readily recognizable, traditional topics: God's existence, God's nature, and the relations to God of all other things, especially human beings. Still, it's likely to seem too broad, leaving theology indistinguishable from philosophy, to which the description seems better suited, even if old-fashioned. But theology and philosophy really are traditionally indistinguishable, broadly speaking. Traditionally, either theology is part of philosophy, or theology and philosophy are two species of the same genus, the very one picked out in that description. I don't know of an established name for that genus, but 'Grandest Unified Theory' strikes me as appropriate.

Obviously, the two-species conception of theology and philosophy must involve a sharper distinction between them than the part–whole conception does. But what essentially differentiates those two species traditionally is really only the starting-points of their investigations, not their goals or their methods or even their subject-matters.[5] Theology, on this view of it as specific-ally different from philosophy, finds data for its version of the Grandest Unified Theory in what it takes to be divinely revealed truths. Starting with what one takes to be divinely revealed truths about the first principles and most fundamental aspects of reality in general and of human nature and behaviour in particular is starting with the conviction that God exists and with some con-ception of God's nature. This non-philosophical 'revealed' theology, then, can be thought of as theology from the top down. Though theology from the top down is specifically different from philosophy, it does share philosophy's goals, generically considered. But the putatively revealed truths it accepts appear to give this the-ology a head start toward those common goals. It's a decidedly unphilosophical head start because, of course, philosophy's data—which traditionally consist of nothing more than what seems boringly obvious to everybody, and only a little even of that—are accepted under con-straints that rigorously rule out revelations. So philosophy from the bottom up might reasonably be thought to be the only kind of philosophy there could be.

On the other hand, there has never been general agreement that theology is exclusively from the top down in this sense of having been handed its data by the central subject of its investigation. Still, theology from the top down, revealed theology, is theology as most people think of it. It's not the theology I'll be focusing on. But I should note in passing that, traditionally, not even revealed theology is unphilosophical in all its developments. It begins, naturally, with 'dogmatic' theology, which extracts relgious doctrine from revelation and codifies doctrine into articles of faith. Dogmatic theology is definitely not philo-sophical—except in the discountable sense that it sometimes uses techniques and standards of analysis and argument that philosophers dis-covered and developed. But dogmatic theology's processing of the raw data of revelation gives rise, traditionally, to 'philosophical' theology, the analytical and argumentative clarification, extension, and defence of the articles of faith. Philosophical theology is what was produced by most medieval theologians, whether or not they would have been happy with that designa-tion, and what is being produced now by many philosophers of religion.[6] Technically and traditionally, philosophical theology is part of revealed theology rather than of philosophy. And it's only philosophical theology, never phil-osophy herself, that can and should be recog-nized under philosophy's old job description of *ancilla theologiae*, theology's maid-servant.[7]

Theology in Philosophy

As for the theology that is not specifically differ-ent from, but part of, philosophy—the 'natural' theology that is at the centre of my interests here—the first thing that should be clear about it is that, as a part of philosophy, it must be theology from the bottom up, in the sense that it must forgo the unphilosophical head start apparently provided by putative revelation and accept as its data only those few naturally evident considerations that traditionally constitute data acceptable for philosophy as a whole. So it seems clear that natural theology's agenda for rational investigation will have the existence of God as its first distinctive item—the first item that marks it off as the theological part of philosophy. If God's existence can be plausibly argued for, its second large-scale topic will be what can be inferred about God's nature; its third, the relation of everything else to God considered as the first principle of reality in general; its fourth, the par-ticular relations of human nature and behaviour to God considered as their first principle.

Because of the difficulties in the first under-taking that distinguishes natural theology from other parts of philosophy, its development as an independent inquiry has typically been stunted, giving it the look of an investigative dead end. It has that look about it largely because most philosophers have held natural theology to standards of argumentation more stringent than those applied in other branches of philosophy, conceiving of it as a narrowly focused enterprise of attempting to develop airtight proofs of the existence, or non-existence, of God. That conception dominated Anglo-American philosophy of religion through at least the first three-quarters of the twentieth century. On the other hand, when natural theology has been fully integrated into the rest of philosophy, it has usually appeared as the culmination of metaphysics, when metaphysics was developed in such a way that the rational investigation of the first principles and most fundamental aspects of reality in general resulted finally in arguments that warranted identifying them, or it, as divine—in, for instance, an argument concluding to the necessity of an ultimate, universal, unmoved mover. When Aristotle calls metaphysics 'theology', he has this sort of culmination of it in view.[8] Purely philosophical metaphysics from the bottom up reaches its traditional top in this integrated natural theology. But even it has been typically, and understandably, limited to sketchy developments of the first three items on natural theology's agenda, the distinctly metaphysical ones.

But suppose we were to take a metaphysically based natural theology—a metaphysics of theism—as the first phase of a systematic presentation of the rest of philosophy. Beginning with the establishment and investigation of what metaphysics has often finally identified as reality's first principle has all the natural appeal of beginning at the real beginning, and it doesn't violate philosophy's strictures against including revealed truths among its data. And suppose we succeed in getting through the first two items on natural theology's agenda, providing philosophically good reasons for thinking that God exists and that God's nature is such that it might be seriously considered as the first principle of reality in general and of human nature and behaviour in particular. Then, in so far as God is the first thing

we argue for and we consider all other things in their relations to God, there's a sense in which we're presenting philosophy from the top down by beginning its presentation with theology from the bottom up. And if the metaphysical tradition was on the right track, and the first principles and most fundamental aspects of reality in general are in some philosophically meaningful sense divine, then from the top down is the most sensible way for philosophy to go, at least as regards the systematic presentation of it.

Philosophy from the top down teaches theism but nevertheless counts as philosophical, because the starting-points and ultimate justifications of its arguments are all accessible to 'natural reason', and because it never uses revealed propositions as more than occasional guides to its agenda.

But if such an enterprise could be made to look feasible and its results illuminating, wouldn't it follow that philosophy from the top down just is natural theology, all the way down? Well, yes—in a way. Philosophy from the top down does look like the metaphysics of theism developed far beyond the very familiar first two items on its agenda. But, after all, if it can be made plausible that the first principles and most fundamental aspects of reality in general are divine, then the subject-matter of the Grandest Unified Theory is God and everything else in relation to God. And in that case the most illuminating systematic presentation of philosophy will be theological—certainly not in the philosophically unacceptable sense of starting from revealed propositions or relying on them to settle arguments, but only in the sense that the part of philosophy called natural theology will be treated as foundational rather than peripheral. [. . .]

The Place of Existence Arguments in Natural Theology

Traditionally, the first item on natural theology's agenda is providing philosophically acceptable evidence in support of the proposition that God exists. For anyone willing to take natural theology seriously, that's a dispiriting prospect. Philosophers have for centuries been raising objections to every known argument for God's existence—a state of affairs that could, by itself, account for natural theology's decline. In such circumstances, can this project get started at all? Obviously it would have to be aborted if there were an airtight proof that God does *not* exist, but there isn't. The argument from evil is indisputably the most plausible candidate for that role, and it has, especially recently, given rise to rejoinders as numerous and at least as powerful as the many versions of the argument. It warrants all the attention it gets, but I think that the amount of attention it's been getting lately excuses me from devoting any time to its consideration here.[9] So, as I see it, starting natural theology is not impossible, just very hard.

While philosophers were finding fault with putative proofs of God's existence, they were, of course, also discovering comparable difficulties in producing proofs of the existence of other minds, for example, or of the reliability of sense-perception.[10] But no philosopher I know of has been dissuaded by such discoveries from undertaking a philosophy of mind or a theory of cognition. That familiar state of affairs has helped to show philosophers that what Aquinas would call 'probable' (rather than 'demonstrative') argumentation must be the norm in philosophy, which includes natural theology. It also helps to account for some recent attempts to show that no philosopher who in those circumstances goes on acknowledging the existence of other minds or the reliability of sense-perception can offer any principled objection to theism based on the state of the evidence for it.[11] But while no sane person can in practice sustain agnosticism regarding consciousness in fellow human beings or regarding the existence of the objects we apparently perceive, very many sane, bright people find no such practical difficulty in setting aside or rejecting the hypothesis that God exists. So even the rare philosopher who thinks that the inconclusiveness of the evidence for God's existence is on a par with the inconclusiveness of the evidence for the existence of physical objects and other persons might reasonably think herself practically justified in believing in bodies and minds other than her own while not believing in God. And *that* familiar state of affairs has helped to motivate the recent upsurge of anti-evidentialism in the epistemology of religious belief, most conspicuously expressed in the thesis of Reformed epistemology that 'it is entirely right, rational, reasonable, and proper to believe in God without any evidence or argument at all'.

Notes

1 Perhaps the fullest, clearest evidence of this development can be found most conveniently in the thriving journal *Faith and Philosophy*, founded in 1984 and associated with the Society of Christian Philosophers.

2 See e.g. Webb 1915; Gerson 1990.

3 For paradigms see Flew 1976; Mackie 1982.

4 See e.g. Kaufman 1989; Stump and Kretzmann 1990 (a reply to Kaufman 1989); also Griffiths 1993; Stump and Kretzmann 1994 (a reply to Griffiths 1993).

5 No theory that leaves God entirely out of consideration could count as theology, and of course plenty of philosophical theories have nothing to do with God. But philosophical theories, too, have often included God as an essential component.

6 Perhaps especially by those associated with the Society of Christian Philosophers.

7 For an excellent account of philosophical theology, see MacDonald 1996. This volume, chap. 2.

8 *Metaphysics* VI 1, 1026a7–23.

9 For important contributions to this literature see e.g. Stump 1985; Adams and Adams 1991; Peterson 1992; Howard-Snyder 1995.

10 For a sophisticated and sensible appraisal of the status of arguments for the existence of God, see Ross 1969: esp. ch. 1, 'Arguments and Proof in Philosophical Theology'.

11 See e.g. Plantinga 1967; also Alston 1991.

References

Adams, Marilyn McCord and Robert Adams, eds. The Problem of Evil (Oxford: Oxford University Press, 1991).

Alston, William. Perceiving God: The Epistemology of Religious Experience (Ithaca, NY: Cornell University Press, 1991).

Flew, Anthony. The Presumption of Atheism (London: Pemberton, 1976).

Gerson, Lloyd. God and Greek Philosophy: Studies in the Early History of Natural Theology (London and New York: Routledge, 1990).

Griffiths, Paul. "Stump, Kretzmann, and Historical Blindness," Faith and Philosophy 10 (1993): 79–85.

Howard-Snyder, Daniel, ed. The Evidential Argument from Evil (Bloomington: Indiana University Press, 1995).

Kaufman, Gordon. " 'Evidentialism': A Theologian's Response," Faith and Philosophy 6 (1989): 35–46.

MacDonald, Scott. "What is Philosophical Theology?" in Peter McEnhill and George Hall, eds., The Presumption of Presence (Edinburgh: Scottish Academic Press, 1996): 61–81.

Mackie, J. L. The Miracle of Theism (Oxford: Clarendon Press, 1982).

Peterson, Michael L., ed. The Problem of Evil (Notre Dame: University of Notre Dame Press, 1992).

Plantinga, Alvin. God and Other Minds (Ithaca, NY: Cornell University Press, 1967).

Plantinga, Alvin. "Reason and Belief in God," in Alvin Plantinga and Nicholas Wolterstorff, eds., Faith and Rationality (Notre Dame: University of Notre Dame Press, 1983).

Ross, James. Philosophical Theology (Indianapolis: Bobbs-Merrill, 1969).

Stump, Eleonore. "The Problem of Evil," Faith and Philosophy 2 (1985): 392–423.

Stump, Eleonore and Norman Kretzmann. "Theologically Unfashionable Philosophy," Faith and Philosophy 7 (1990): 329–339.

Stump, Eleonore and Norman Kretzmann. "Blindingly Obvious Christian Anti-Semitism," Faith and Philosophy 11 (1994): 279–285.

Webb, Clement. Studies in the History of Natural Theology (Oxford: Clarendon Press, 1915).

Chapter 2

Scott MacDonald

WHAT IS PHILOSOPHICAL THEOLOGY?

In this paper I want to explore the role philosophers have to play in Christian theology. The question of the nature and scope of appropriately philosophical reflection on theological matters – what I will call philosophical theology – might seem roughly the same as the very old question of the relation between faith and philosophy or faith and reason. I put my question in these different terms, however, in order to avoid being swamped by a flood of tradition that tempts us with a mistaken assumption. Those who have raised the traditional question of the relation between faith and reason have typically been concerned with whether and to what extent the claims central to Christianity (the claims of faith) are accessible to or certifiable by reason. That is to say, their discussions have tended to focus on the rather narrow issue of whether one can have rational or philosophical grounding or justification for one's belief in God or one's acceptance of some set of theological propositions. Moreover, those discussions often presuppose a quite restricted view of what it is for a proposition to be accessible to or certifiable by reason: when they ask whether a given theological proposition is accessible to reason, they often mean to be asking whether the truth of that proposition can be guaranteed by a certain sort of strict proof or conclusive demonstration.

This tradition of reflection on the relation between faith and reason has attracted an enormous amount of philosophical attention and directed it primarily at a particular sort of natural theology – the project by which reason or philosophy attempts, by its own means, to discover or prove important truths about God. To the extent to which this sort of natural theology has been taken to be successful, it has been judged that reason supports or grounds faith whereas to the extent that it has been supposed to have failed, it has been judged that the domains of faith and reason are distinct and independent. Now, the temptation here is to think that appropriately philosophical reflection on theological matters is exhausted by the sorts of activities and issues representative of this tradition. The sheer weight of this tradition in philosophy since the seventeenth century and the consequent neglect of other models for philosophical theology makes it natural to assume that philosophical theology is coextensive with this kind of natural theology.[1]

If we give in to this temptation, we implicitly agree to two kinds of restrictions on philosophical theology, one limiting the kinds of philosophical activity open to the philosophical theologian, the other limiting the range of issues she can legitimately pursue. First, if philosophical theology is coextensive with natural theology, then its essential activities will be just the same as natural theology's, namely, the discovery and proof of theological truths by reason alone. If we think of philosophical activities concerned with truth and knowledge or justification in general as constituting philosophy's justificatory role, then we can think of the philosophical theologian as restricted to performing this kind of justificatory function for theology.

Second, if philosophical theology is coextensive with natural theology, then insofar as traditional natural theology adopts a narrow view of what constitutes admissible justification or proof, the philosophical theologian will be restricted to theological issues susceptible of proof of that sort. If there are theological truths, for example, that we can know only by means of a supernatural revelation, and if matters knowable only by revelation are not susceptible of the relevant sorts of proof, then theological truths of this sort will fall outside the scope of philosophical theology. Considerations of this sort help to explain why traditional natural theology has focused on the question of God's existence and a narrow range of issues having to do with God's nature – issues constitutive of a generic philosophical theism – leaving aside distinctively Christian theological doctrines such as trinity and incarnation which are typically thought to be accessible only through revelation.

My contention, however, is that it is a mistake to restrict philosophical theology in either of these ways. On the one hand, philosophical activity in general is concerned with much more than establishing the truth or epistemic rationality of certain sets of beliefs, and so I take appropriately philosophical reflection on theological matters to include but not to be restricted to issues about the rationality or justification of faith. In sections 2–3 below I develop and defend this claim by identifying certain important kinds of non-justificatory activity characteristic of philosophy in general and arguing that there is no reason to suppose that these kinds of activity are inappropriate when the objects of investigation are theological matters.

On the other hand, I hold that philosophers can legitimately extend the scope of their theo-

logical reflections beyond the issues associated with traditional natural theology. They can and should be investigating doctrines such as trinity, incarnation, and atonement; they ought to be examining the meaning and implications of biblical and credal claims; they ought to be exploring the distinctively Christian understanding of reality. In short, philosophers ought to be working not only on the so-called preambles to faith but also on issues at the very heart of Christian belief and life. I offer both a negative and a positive argument for this claim. First, in section 1 I examine and reject some well-known reasons for thinking that there is a distinct subset of theological truths in principle inaccessible to reason or to the philosopher. Since the identification of theological truths that are in some way beyond the philosopher's reach depends on a particular conception of natural theology, we will need to look carefully at the nature and scope of that enterprise. If an acceptable conception of natural theology does not provide a basis for a clear distinction between the theological matters that are and those that are not appropriately subjected to philosophical investigation, then there seem to be no good grounds for restricting the range of theological issues open to the philosophical theologian. Second, my argument in sections 2–3, which identifies important non-justificatory tasks essential to philosophical theology, provides positive reasons for thinking that the philosophical theologian can legitimately take up any theological issue she chooses. I argue that it follows from the nature of those tasks that there can be no restriction on the scope of their application.

If I am right about these things, we need to resist the temptation to think of philosophical theology as coextensive with traditional natural theology. Philosophical theology extends well beyond the sort of natural theology that has dominated philosophical reflection on theological matters in modern philosophy, and philosophers can and should be turning their attention to broader theological domains.

1. Natural Theology

If we construe the term 'reason' broadly, as designating both the narrowly intellective capacities and activities that distinguish human beings from other terrestrial creatures and the heterogeneous cognitive functions that are constituted by a mixture of intellective and non-intellective elements (such as sense perception), then we might think of philosophy as the attempt to discover truths or acquire knowledge by means of human reason or, as an older tradition would have put it, by means of the light of nature. It would follow, then, that philosophy directed toward specifically theological matters is just the attempt to discover truths or acquire knowledge about God (or theological matters generally) by those same means. This sort of enterprise, insofar as it depends solely on our natural cognitive resources, is appropriately thought of as natural theology. Natural theology is the attempt to discover and establish truths about God (or theological matters generally) solely on the basis of natural or unaided human reason.

Natural theology contrasts with what we might think of as a non-natural or supernatural theology – an investigation into theological truth that relies at least in part on something not naturally available to us as human beings. This sort of theology might be characterized as revealed theology insofar as the supernatural element on which it relies is something supernaturally revealed to us by God. Revealed theology, then, is not restricted to what is accessible to natural, unaided human reason; it can make use of what is accessible to us only because of special divine aid, namely, a special revelation.

Of course precise characterizations of natural theology and the distinction between natural and revealed theology will require a detailed account of both our natural cognitive resources and the truths that are accessible to and those that exceed them. What is the scope of natural human reason? What data can natural theologians draw on, what methods can they apply to them, and what results can they expect to obtain?

1a. Strict Natural Theology

An influential traditional answer to these questions is based on a model derived from Aristotle's account of demonstrative science. For any distinguishable field of theoretical inquiry, we can think of there being a set of facts or truths that comprise the object of inquiry in that field. Theoretical investigation in that area aims at uncovering and establishing those truths, that is, at attaining knowledge of the relevant object. We can think of the model of demonstrative science as describing the logical structure of a set of truths of this sort and the corresponding epistemic structure of the set of beliefs one has when one has attained theoretical knowledge of it.

On this model, theoretical knowledge is constituted by two sorts of truths: those that are basic or fundamental and those that are in some way dependent on the basic or fundamental truths. Truths of the first sort are facts whose nature is such that they are open to our immediate cognitive gaze. Our knowledge of them consists in our having direct access to or awareness of them. We might call these truths evident: they are self-evident if they are accessible to us in virtue of their being immediately present to our strictly intellective capacities, or evident to sense perception if they are accessible in virtue of their being immediately present to our sensory capacities. When we are directly aware of evident truths in either of these ways, we are epistemically justified in holding them just in virtue of our immediate grasp of their truth. Truths of this sort are epistemically privileged in the sense that one's epistemic justification in holding them is independent of one's justification for any other truths one might happen to hold. For that reason they are not only logically but epistemically basic or fundamental. They are the sort of truths that can suitably ground other sorts of knowledge because they require no epistemic ground beyond themselves.

The second sort of truths constitutive of theoretical knowledge in demonstrative science are non-basic or derivative, those derivable from basic truths by means of demonstrative proofs or deductively valid arguments.[2] These truths are accessible to us by virtue of our capacity for discursive reasoning. Insofar as these are known as conclusions of demonstrative proofs they are epistemically dependent, mediated by our awareness of the truth of the relevant premises and the validity of the relevant inferences. We are inferentially justified in holding these truths by virtue of our having derived them in appropriate ways from truths we are independently and non-inferentially justified in holding.

The model of demonstrative science, then, identifies the capacities of natural human reason relevant to this sort of theoretical inquiry: the intellective and sensory capacities that enable us to be directly aware of certain truths and the capacity for discursive reasoning that enables us to deduce certain truths from others. In identifying these capacities the model specifies the contents and structure of a demonstrative science: it will contain evident truths and truths that stand in the right sort of inferential relation to these.

Conceiving of natural theology as a kind of demonstrative science allows us to characterize it precisely: it consists of truths about God which are either (1) self-evident or evident to sense perception or (2) derived by deductively valid proofs the (ultimate) premises of which are evident in one of these two ways. Thomas Aquinas is perhaps the most famous Christian theologian to develop Aristotle's account of demonstrative science and adapt it to theological inquiry. His famous proofs for the existence of God and his arguments establishing such truths as that God is one, immutable, and eternal – his proofs for what he sometimes calls the preambles of faith – are paradigms of natural theology understood as an Aristotelian demonstrative science.[3] Aquinas's extraordinarily influential

articulation of this sort of model of natural theology and the clear example of its execution that he provides in the opening sections of his two great theological *summae* have made this the dominant and most common conception of that enterprise.[4]

This conception of demonstrative science (and the conception of natural theology as demonstrative science) has great virtues. First, its method – deductive argument – is clear and subject to precise and well-understood standards. As a result, intellectual inquiry that conforms to the model of demonstrative science is open to the sort of rigorous assessment and evaluation crucial to theoretical objectivity. Second, when successful, demonstrative science offers for its results the strongest sort of certification possible. By deriving its conclusions from evident truths by means of necessarily truth-preserving forms of reasoning, a demonstrative science guarantees their truth. When we are in possession of a demonstrative proof, we can be certain of its conclusion and can claim to have conclusively established it.

Demonstrative science's great power, however, is purchased at a price. A demonstrative science possesses the virtues of rigor, objectivity, and certainty only because its criteria for admissible data and methods are very strict: the resources available to demonstrative scientists include only evident truths (their data) and deductive argument forms (their method). For this reason, we might call the sort of natural theology that adopts the restrictions of demonstrative science strict natural theology. Many of those who have raised the question of the relation between faith and reason have wanted to know what propositions of faith (if any) are accessible to or certifiable by strict natural theology.

Now, I do not want to question the possibility or success of the enterprise of strict natural theology; I want only to claim that even if strict natural theology represents an appropriately philosophical manner of reflection on theological matters, it is a mistake to think of it as the only sort of theological reflection open to philosophers. My primary reason for conceiving of philosophical theology as including more than strict natural theology is that philosophical reflection in general is not restricted in the ways identified by the model of demonstrative science. Philosophers, of course, are glad to have conclusive demonstrations when they can get them, but even those who are most sanguine about the general possibility of obtaining them acknowledge the need for other sorts of argument and their work does not come to a halt when strict demonstrations are not forthcoming. Since philosophical reflection in general is not restricted to the search for and construction of strict proofs satisfying the demands of demonstrative science, I see no reason to suppose that philosophical reflection on theological matters must be restricted in that way.

1b. Broad Natural Theology

Philosophers have always recognized the importance of arguments that fall short of the paradigm of demonstrative proof – that is, arguments that carry epistemic weight but in some way fall short of being utterly truth-guaranteeing. Following tradition we might call arguments of this sort dialectical arguments.[5] The criteria constitutive of good or acceptable dialectical arguments will be more generous than those characterizing demonstrative science. On the one hand, dialectic allows as data propositions that we have some appropriate degree of epistemic justification in believing, though they need not be evident either to reason or sense perception. On the other hand, dialectic admits the use of methods of reasoning other than deduction. It allows inductive reasoning broadly conceived – enumerative induction, probabilistic reasoning, argument from analogy, inference to the best explanation, and so on.[6] Of course these specifications of the data and methods of dialectic are imprecise, and we might well find ourselves

disagreeing about what propositions are admissible as data (that is, have an appropriate degree of justification) and whether certain particular inductive arguments are strong or weak. But these disagreements do nothing to show that there are no good dialectical arguments or that philosophers ought not to be engaged in reasoning of this sort. Moreover, quite apart from the justifiability of the use of dialectic in philosophy, it is simply a fact, I think, that few philosophers these days would know how to get on with their work if they were denied the use of what I am calling dialectical methods and arguments.

Now, there is clearly nothing non-natural about the sorts of reasoning allowed by dialectic. Even if we think that we fall short of the paradigm of human reason when we rely on non-demonstrative reasoning, it seems clear that when we do so, we are nevertheless engaged in an activity that is natural to us and for which we require no special extrinsic aid. Given, then, that philosophical activity that relies on dialectic is an enterprise of natural human reason, we ought to acknowledge a corresponding natural theology – dialectical natural theology – that consists in philosophical reflection, of the sort allowed by dialectic, on theological matters. We might call the genus of which strict, demonstrative natural theology and dialectical natural theology are species broad natural theology. The practitioner of broad natural theology will attempt to establish truths or acquire knowledge about God using deductive or non-deductive arguments the premises of which are evident or justified to some appropriate degree. [. . .]

But it differs from strict natural theology (and from some sorts of broad natural theology) in allowing that belief in God can be properly basic, that is, that God's existence can appropriately be included among the starting points or data of natural theology. [. . .]

Hence, even if there is reason to do strict natural theology, there is also reason to recognize a broader natural theology. This seems to me important not only because we need a broad conception of natural theology if we are to account for the variety of appropriately philosophical projects that share the aim of providing epistemic grounding for certain theological propositions but also because it helps us avoid a common mistake in our assessment of arguments in natural theology. It is sometimes supposed that showing that an argument in natural theology fails to be utterly conclusive is sufficient for showing its utter failure. The traditional proofs for God's existence, for example, are sometimes rejected on the grounds that they are not conclusive. But this can be analogous to rejecting certain theoretical claims in physics or certain accounts of historical events just because they have not been established with utter conclusiveness. Objections of this sort are mistaken because epistemic success in many intellectual areas, including natural theology, does not require utter conclusiveness. Only strict natural theology holds that a theological argument's being utterly conclusive is a necessary condition of its being acceptable (and so if an argument in strict natural theology fails to be conclusive, then it ought to be rejected as an instance of strict natural theology), but in broad natural theology, just as in physics and history, it is possible to have good reasons for believing a given proposition even if we lack impeccable evidence. Philosophers working on theological matters, then, ought not to restrict themselves to the overly restrictive enterprise of trying to provide conclusive proofs; that is, they ought to be doing more than what strict natural theology permits them to do.

1c. Natural Theology and Revelation

The strict conception of natural theology provides grounds for a clear distinction between natural and revealed theology. This is because it is essential to revealed theology, insofar as it is based on divine revelation, that its contents are ultimately based on someone's testimony (God's or a divinely authorized agent).

But no proposition whose epistemic grounding essentially involves testimony is either evident or strictly demonstrable. Hence, parts of revelation that are accessible only because they have been revealed are inaccessible to the strict natural theologian and belong exclusively to the domain of revealed theology. If we follow Augustine, Aquinas, and others in thinking of faith as belief based on authority, then we will hold that the contents of revelation are appropriate matters for faith and that the truths accessible only by revelation and not also by strict natural theology are strictly matters of faith.[7]

We lose the grounds for this clear distinction, however, if we adopt a broader conception of natural theology. This is because, unlike demonstrative science, dialectic can make use of arguments that appeal to legitimate authority. As Augustine points out, virtually everything we believe about the past, other parts of the world, and other people's thoughts and attitudes is based on someone's testimony.[8] We typically suppose that we have good reasons for believing things of this sort because we typically suppose we have good reason to accept the testimony on which those beliefs are based. It follows that propositions whose epistemic grounding essentially involves testimony are not eo ipso inaccessible to the philosopher who makes use of dialectic. It is not the case, then, that propositions contained in revelation are in principle off limits to the broad natural theologian just because they rest on testimony: it might turn out that we are epistemically justified in accepting that testimony, and so in accepting those propositions. Perhaps we have, or natural theology can provide, adequate grounds for supposing that the testimony in question is reliable. That is, we might find ourselves in a position to establish, solely on the basis of unaided human reason (broadly construed), the legitimate authority of some body of revelation, and so the truth of any proposition contained in it. [. . .]

Broad natural theology's loosening of the restrictions on the data and methods acceptable in natural theology makes arguments of this sort possible, and so opens natural theology's door to all sorts of issues that have been thought to belong exclusively to theology proper or revealed theology. For example, if the proposition that God was, in Christ, reconciling the world to himself is contained in or derivable from revelation, then given the sorts of considerations I have adduced, the truth of that proposition might be accessible to natural human reason. The same can be said, of course, for any theological proposition or doctrine – including those, such as the doctrine of the trinity, that have been taken to be paradigm examples of truths open only to revealed theology – provided we can identify it as part of divine revelation or derive it by acceptable means from propositions contained in revelation. It follows, then, that it is possible that with respect to their contents, there is no distinction between broad natural theology and revealed theology. That is to say, it is possible that there is no territory open to the practitioner of revealed theology that is not also open to the practitioner of broad natural theology. If there is a principled distinction between the enterprises of revealed and broad natural theology, then, it must be based on something other than the scope or contents of the two enterprises.[9]

The scope of philosophical reflection on theological matters, then, is not restricted to the narrow range of issues open to strict natural theology. Philosophers who undertake the project of broad natural theology may well have access to a wide range of theological matters including, perhaps, much of what is distinctive of and peculiar to Christianity. Moreover, acknowledging that we can put epistemic weight not only on the demonstrations of strict natural theology but also the dialectical arguments of broad natural theology will help us to avoid the confusion of supposing that theological propositions not accessible to strict natural theology are utterly beyond the reach of philosophical reason and incapable of being rationally grounded.

2. Clarification

So far my argument has been that there is more to natural theology than the very narrow enterprise of strict natural theology and that by loosening strict natural theology's restrictions on the data and methods acceptable to natural theology, we lose any clear grounds we might have had for restricting the scope of the natural theologian's investigations. In this section I want to argue that there is more to philosophical theology than natural theology.

Natural theology, whether strictly or broadly conceived, aims at discovering and providing acceptable epistemic support or grounding for theological truths. Strict and broad natural theology differ in their accounts of what constitutes acceptable epistemic support, but in either case the natural theologian is concerned with establishing the truth of certain theological propositions, thereby providing us with epistemic justification for and securing the rationality of our believing them. I will call this the concern for justifying theological truths.[10]

It is not the case, however, that all philosophical activity is concerned primarily with the truth or epistemic justification of a particular theory or set of propositions or beliefs. In order to have a handy way of referring to the sorts of philosophical reflection I want to call attention to here, I will borrow a term from Aquinas's philosophical theology – 'clarification' (*manifestatio*) – and group these different non-justificatory enterprises together under the general heading 'clarification'. A great deal of philosophical activity is concerned not with justifying but with clarifying certain propositions or theories.

I propose to explain what clarification is simply by describing a case in which an ordinary philosopher engages in what I take to be the clarification of a philosophical theory. Imagine a philosopher who works in ethics and is interested in moral realism – the view that there are objective moral facts. She doesn't think moral realism is true (perhaps she doesn't think it is false either) but finds it intriguing and worth investigating. We might say that she takes moral realism as a working hypothesis. She devotes considerable effort to developing that theory in the most sympathetic and sophisticated way she can. Her philosophical agenda includes various kinds of projects, three of which are worth specific mention. First, she gives some attention to analyzing the concepts central to moral realism: she worries, for example, about the correct analysis of the concept of a morally right action and about whether objective moral properties are natural or non-natural. Second, she is interested in the internal coherence and consequences of moral realism: she might be fairly confident that a correspondence theory of moral truth is essential to moral realism; but she might work hard at trying to understand whether it is necessarily committed to a foundationalist moral epistemology or whether it might countenance a coherence theory of justification, or whether moral facts necessarily or only hypothetically provide reasons for acting. Third, she also takes an interest in moral realism's external relations: How does it square with a theistic view of the world? How might it affect a theory of personhood or of rationality? How are moral properties, realistically construed, different from or similar to physical properties construed in that way? In pursuing these kinds of projects our hypothetical moral realist is engaged in the project of clarifying moral realism.

Now, it seems clear that in pursuing this general project, the philosopher I've just described is not primarily concerned with the epistemic justification of moral realism. She is concerned instead with understanding, developing, systematizing, and explaining it. It is possible for her to do all these things without raising the issue of its truth or her justification for holding it. The fact is that a very large part of philosophy has nothing directly to do with the truth or justification of certain theories or propositions. The sort of conceptual analysis and systematic investigation I've described is the stuff of which philosophy is made, and philosophers would not know how to do their jobs if they could not do what our hypothetical moral realist is doing. Philosophers can, do, and must sometimes set aside questions of truth and justification in order to pursue these sorts of tasks.

Now, I see no reason for supposing that any of the techniques and methods appropriate to philosophical reflection in general ought to be excluded from philosophical reflection on specifically theological matters. If moral philosophers, epistemologists, and philosophers of mind (for example) can investigate theories and hypotheses without regard to their epistemic status, then so can philosophers who want to clarify Christian doctrine or some theological working hypothesis. Hence, clarification of theological matters is a legitimate task for the philosopher. Philosophers have not only a justificatory but also a clarificatory role to play in theology.

Moreover, given that the nature of clarificatory activities is such that one can engage in them without regard to the epistemic status of the theories one takes up, it follows that there can be no epistemic restrictions of any sort on the kinds of issues open to philosophical clarification. In fact, it would seem that any theory or doctrine whatsoever (theological or otherwise) is in principle subject to these sorts of activities to some extent. Hence, insofar as philosophical theology encompasses the project of clarification, there can be no restriction on the theological issues and doctrines open to the philosophical theologian.[11] She can legitimately undertake the investigation of not only the question of God's existence and attributes – issues associated with traditional natural theology – but also doctrines such as trinity, incarnation, and atonement – traditional paradigms of doctrines inaccessible to natural reason. When the philosopher takes up these kinds of issues with the aim of articulating and developing them, probing their internal coherence, joint consistency, and systematic connections, and exploring their relations to other theological and non-theological doctrines, she will be engaged in appropriately philosophical reflection on specifically Christian theological matters.

The philosophical project of clarifying Christian doctrine has been largely neglected by modern philosophers, but it was once an integral and fruitful part of philosophical theology. In late antiquity and the Middle Ages, many of the best philosophical minds in the western world devoted large portions of their philosophical energy to that project, and their results – treatises such as Augustine's *De trinitate*, Boethius's treatise on the two natures of Christ, Anselm's *Cur Deus homo*, and most of the thousands of questions, articles, and chapters of later-medieval *summae*, Sentences and biblical commentaries, and disputed questions by the likes of Albert the Great, Aquinas, Bonaventure, and Scotus – are paradigms of philosophical clarification. These thinkers were among the most highly trained philosophers of their day, and their extraordinary philosophical gifts and skills are as clearly displayed in their discussions of trinity, incarnation, and atonement as in their proofs for God's existence or their discussions of issues that we might think of as belonging to philosophy proper. Their work represents an unrivalled commitment to and cultivation of philosophical reflection on theological matters.

Now, one might object that we ought to think of Augustine, Anselm, and Aquinas as they thought of themselves, namely, as theologians rather than philosophers. But this is to miss the point. A great part of their work, including the parts that are most thoroughly and deeply theological in content, are thoroughly and unmistakably philosophical in method and approach, displaying with rigor and sophistication precisely the sorts of activities constitutive of philosophical clarification. This is paradigmatic philosophical theology, and whether we call certain of its practitioners theologians or philosophers makes no difference to the fact that it is the kind of work that manifests and requires appropriately philosophical inclinations, abilities, and skills.

3. The Relation Between Justification and Clarification

Philosophical clarification, then, ought to be and historically has been an important part of philosophical theology distinct from the more widely acknowledged project of natural theology. But one might object here that although the kinds of activities included in the general project of clarification are not themselves concerned with justification, the legitimacy of philosophers' engaging in them depends on their already having relevant justification. In other words, one might hold that philosophers are entitled to undertake clarification of a given theory or proposition only if they are epistemically justified in holding it. If this objection is right, then we have good reason to put off clarification of theological matters until we have in hand a successful natural theology, for we cannot legitimately begin clarifying Christianity unless and until we have established its truth.

Something like this seems to have been the view of those committed to an Aristotelian model of theological investigation. The Aristotelian model requires that systematic theoretical investigation begin by establishing the existence of its subject matter.[12] In conformity with this requirement, Aquinas begins both of his theological summae with strict proofs for the existence of God and only later turns to the project of clarification.

In 'Advice to Christian Philosophers' Alvin Plantinga suggests that a view of this sort is partly responsible for Christian philosophers' neglect of the task of exploring what he calls the Christian perspective.[13] According to Plantinga:

The Christian philosophical community, by virtue of being Christian, is committed to a broad but specific way of looking at humankind and the world and God. Among its most important and pressing projects are systematizing, deepening, exploring, articulating this perspective, and exploring its bearing on the rest of what we think and do. But then the Christian philosophical community has its own agenda.

Plantinga advises Christian philosophers to show more independence and autonomy from the rest of the philosophical world by taking up that agenda. Since the sorts of activities identified in this passage fall under what I am calling the philosophical clarification of theological matters, we can think of Plantinga's advice as an exhortation to Christian philosophers to turn to the project of clarification. But he thinks that because they have made two assumptions, (1) that justification is prior to clarification and (2) that one is justified in one's belief in God only if one has proofs constituting a successful natural theology, many philosophers have concluded that they must pursue natural theology prior to taking up the task of clarification.

> [The Christian philosopher] will think ... that as a philosopher he has no right to [beliefs presupposed by the project of clarification, such as that there is such a person as God] unless he is able to show that it follows from, or is possible, or is justified with respect to premises accepted by all parties to the discussion – theist, agnostic, and atheist alike. Furthermore, he will be half inclined to think he has no right, as a philosopher, to positions that presuppose the existence of God, if he can't show that belief to be justified in this way.[14]

The result has been neglect or postponement of clarification in favor of natural theology.

As Plantinga sees it, the mistake in all of this is in what he takes to be the traditional natural theologian's supposition that we are epistemically entitled to our belief in God only if it's justified by proofs in natural theology – assumption

(2). Plantinga's view is that we can be justified in holding certain of our theological beliefs even without these proofs. "The Christian philosopher quite properly starts from the existence of God, and presupposes it in philosophical work, whether or not he can show it to be probable or plausible with respect to premises accepted by all philosophers, or most philosophers . . ."[15] Christian philosophers can quite properly start from certain of their theological beliefs not because these beliefs needn't have some appropriate epistemic status but because certain of Christian philosophers' theological beliefs have an appropriate epistemic status even in the absence of successful proofs in natural theology. According to Plantinga, then, a Christian philosopher's route to clarification of the Christian perspective needn't go through proofs in natural theology since Christian philosophers already have the epistemic grounding they need.

Now, although Plantinga clearly rejects what he takes to be the traditional natural theologian's account of what constitutes appropriate epistemic justification for theological propositions, he does not challenge the assumption that there must be appropriate epistemic justification grounding the project of theological clarification – assumption (1). That is to say, he does not challenge the view that it is permissible to undertake the project of clarifying Christianity only if one is epistemically justified in one's belief in God. Plantinga's strategy is not to reject that assumption but to show that the conditions it places on the project of clarification can be satisfied even if we have no justification of the sort that might be provided by traditional natural theology. We might say that his idea is to take a short cut to clarification via the non-traditional natural theology he builds around Reformed epistemology.

As I see it, however, we don't need Plantinga's short cut or the more circuitous arguments of traditional natural theology to get us to clarification. This is because it is a mistake to assume that our undertaking the project of clarifying some theory requires us to be antecedently justified in holding it. It seems to me clear that our hypothetical moral philosopher needn't be epistemically justified in believing moral realism or any of the doctrines she presupposes in pursuing its clarification; she can simply assume it and them and get on with her work. She is perfectly entitled to take moral realism as a working hypothesis and to make the further assumptions required to carry out the agenda set by her hypothesis. She can do all of this regardless of whether she's epistemically justified in believing that moral realism is true – in fact, even if she's epistemically justified in believing that moral realism is false. We are entitled to assume all sorts of things in our philosophical work, including things we have no epistemic right to. The same things can be said of our philosophical reflection on theological matters: we are perfectly entitled to take theological beliefs and doctrines as assumptions for the purposes of subjecting them to the process of clarification.

Hence, the philosopher's route to theological clarification need not go through traditional natural theology, Reformed epistemology, or anything else. Philosophers needn't subordinate their clarificatory work in theology to their justificatory responsibilities since the legitimacy of their undertaking the former does not depend on their having discharged the latter.

One might reply here that even if philosophers are sometimes entitled to set aside issues of truth and justification in the way I've described, they are always obligated to take them up again. Qua philosophers, they can't simply leave their castles hanging in the air. Our hypothetical moral realist can always be called upon to defend or discharge her assumptions, and sooner or later we'll want to know from her whether and why she thinks moral realism is true (or false). Hence, we might think that philosophers can only temporarily but not ultimately be exonerated from discharging their epistemic duties.

I don't know whether this conception of the philosopher's epistemic duties is right, but even if it is legitimate to demand that the philosopher sooner or later face up to issues of truth and justification, there are sometimes perfectly good reasons for practicing philosophers to ignore the demand, or at least postpone satisfying it indefinitely. Many issues in philosophy are too important, too complicated, and too difficult. On the one hand, it's unreasonable to wait for the logically most basic issues to be settled before we address other issues (the most fundamental issues, after all, are often the hardest and the least likely to be settled very soon). So we ought to be worrying about how to treat other people and about causal theories of knowledge, for example, whether or not we can on demand provide justification for supposing that there are other people or that there are material objects that can cause perceptions and beliefs in us. We do and should simply make the necessary assumptions and get on with these projects.

On the other hand, there is no guarantee that the results of all our diligent clarificatory work on the basis of our hypotheses and assumptions will be sufficient or of the right sort to allow us to offer consequent justification for what we had previously hypothesized or assumed. Sometimes, of course, the work of clarifying an hypothesis leads us to evidence that confirms it; but there's no reason to suppose that this will always be the case. So philosophers are and need to be providing clarification whether or not they can also provide justification, either antecedently or consequently, and the philosopher who wants to devote her philosophical energy to clarifying some theological hypothesis needs no special dispensation. She needs only to insist that she not be held to any requirements that her colleagues in ethics and epistemology are not subject to.

For all practical purposes, then, the project of clarification is independent of the project of providing justification and just as much as part of the philosophical enterprise. Moreover, given that clarification is independent in this way, philosophers inclined toward the project of clarifying Christianity need not begin with or await the results of any sort of natural theology. They can and should get on with the pressing project of clarification.[16]

4. Philosophical Theology

My view, then, is that the role philosophers have to play in Christian theology encompasses not only the search for truth and justification but also the various analytic and systematic activities I have grouped together under the heading 'clarification'. I think it is natural to use the term 'philosophical theology' to designate this general enterprise, and so I hold that philosophical theology is a genus whose species are natural theology and clarification. The philosopher who works on theological matters – the philosophical theologian – can legitimately undertake any and all of these specific enterprises.

Although philosophical theologians can and should be pursuing both the justification and clarification of Christianity, it is the latter branch of philosophical theology that is in particular need of attention and rehabilitation. In our times, philosophers interested in theological matters have for the most part been preoccupied with the justificatory project, that is, with the epistemic rationality of religious belief, while theologians by and large have lacked the temperament or training necessary for the philosophical work of clarification. Not since the great clarificatory efforts of the later Middle Ages have we seen Christianity subjected to sustained and probing philosophical exploration and cultivation. Christian doctrine and the Christian view of reality it entails constitute an intriguing and intellectually rich domain that begs for and deserves the most careful philosophical scrutiny. Philosophers and philosophically minded theologians need to reclaim these fertile lands, for they have lain fallow much too long.[17]

Notes

1   Two strands of early modern thought seem to me to have been the sources of this tradition. On the one hand, the sort of religious skepticism represented by thinkers such as Hume constituted an aggressive challenge to the rationality of Christianity whereas, on the other, a kind of zealous rationalism of the sort shared by both deists, such as Voltaire, and theists, such as Clarke and Leibniz, was confident of showing that religion – at the very least natural religion – could be given secure rational foundations.

2   Strictly speaking, an Aristotelian demonstrative science admits as derivative truths only those propositions that are derivable by demonstrative syllogisms, which are only one species of deductively valid argument.

3   To my knowledge Aquinas does not use the term 'natural theology', however. He prefers to call his work on the preambles of faith 'divine science'; see his commentary on Boethius's *De trinitate* question 2, article 2 and *Summa theologiae* Ia, question 1. For the history of the term 'natural thology', see Clement C.J. Webb, *Studies in the History of Natural Theology* (Oxford: Clarendon Press, 1915).

4   See, for example, *Summa contra gentiles* Book I, chapters 7–9 and *Summa theologiae* Ia, questions 2–11.

5   Dialectical reasoning is surely as old as philosophy itself. Reflective use of it and explicit consideration of its nature and value seems to have begun with Socrates. Plato and Aristotle, in part reflecting on Socrates's methods, began a long tradition of systematic examination of both the logical and epistemological issues raised by dialectical reasoning. Within that tradition the term 'dialectic' has had a variety of senses, some of them quite narrow. Here I am following that part of the tradition represented by Aquinas who, in the preface to his commentary on Aristotle's *Posterior Analytics*, uses 'dialectic' as the general designation for a kind of reasoning that falls short of the absolute necessity characteristic of demonstration.

6   These requirements on the data and methods of dialectic allow that dialectical reasoning might fall short of demonstrative proof in any of three ways, namely, by (1) having evident premises but lacking

a deductive argument form, (2) having a deductive argument form but lacking evident premises, or (3) lacking both evident premises and a deductive argument form.

7 Aquinas and others have held that the set of truths made available through revelation and the set of truths accessible strict natural theology overlap to some extent. Truths constituting the intersection of the two sets will be matters of faith for the person who accepts them because they have been revealed but not for the person who has proofs for them. See, for example, *Summa contra gentiles* Book I, Chapter 7.

8 See, for example, *De utilitate credendi* ix.22–x.23, xi.25.

9 We might draw the distinction on epistemological grounds, for example, by maintaining that although there may be no theological propositions accessible to revealed theology that are not also accessible to broad natural theology, the practitioner of broad natural theology is required to hold those propositions on certain grounds. The practitioner of broad natural theology can accept a proposition only insofar as she takes it to be an acceptable datum for or grounded by a suitable argument in natural theology. This need not be true of the practitioner of revealed theology, who, we might suppose, can accept a proposition simply because she takes it to be revealed, regardless of whether that belief is adequately grounded. Unlike the natural theologian, the practitioner of revealed theology might pay no attention to the epistemic status of the contents of revelation.

10 Given this characterization of natural theology as concerned with the justification or epistemic rationality of certain theological propositions, we can classify the traditional project of Christian apologetics – the defense of the faith against claims that entail or make likely the falsity of Christianity – as a branch of natural theology. We might think of natural theology as having a constructive and a destructive task: the constructive element providing us with justification for believing certain theological truths and a destructive, apologetic element whose task is to remove any justification we might have had for disbelieving certain theological truths. Aquinas identifies this kind of apologetic task, claiming that we can use philosophy in sacred doctrine to show that arguments putatively contradicting the truths of faith are either impossible or at least not necessary; see In *Boetium De trinitate* Question 2, Article 3, and *Summa contra gentiles* Book I, Chapter 7).

11 Moreover, since the project of clarifying Christian theological propositions presupposes nothing about their epistemic status, philosophers needn't be Christian believers to engage in that project.

12 Aristotle insists that with respect to any object of inquiry the first question to be asked is "Does it exist?" or "Is there such a thing?" (*ei esti?*). This is because any answer to the question "What is it?" (*ti esti?*)—the identification of the thing's essence or nature, on which all genuinely theoretical knowledge is based – presupposes that there is such a thing. See *Posterior Analytics* Book II, Chapters 1–2, 7.

13 "Advice to Christian Philosophers", *Faith and Philosophy* 1 (1984), pp. 253–71.

14 "Advice to Christian Philosophers", p. 271.

15 "Advice to Christian Philosophers", p. 260.

16 "Advice to Christian Philosophers", p. 261.

17 My argument has been that clarification does not require justification and in that sense is independent of it. Claudia Eisen has pointed out to me, however, that the converse is not true. The process of justifying a theory or confirming or disconfirming an hypothesis often requires one to engage to some extent in the project of clarifying the theory or hypothesis. Thus, clarification is not independent of justification in the sense that justification often depends on it.

Chapter 3

Alvin Plantinga

THE REFORMED OBJECTION TO NATURAL THEOLOGY

Suppose we think of natural theology as the attempt to prove or demonstrate the existence of God. This enterprise has a long and impressive history—a history stretching back to the dawn of Christendom and boasting among its adherents many of the truly great thinkers of the Western world. Chief among these is Thomas Aquinas, whose work, I think, is the natural starting point for Christian philosophical reflection, Protestant as well as Catholic. Here we Protestants must be, in Ralph McInerny's immortal phrase, Peeping Thomists. Recently—since the time of Kant, perhaps—the tradition of natural theology has not been as overwhelming as it once was: yet it continues to have able defenders both within and without officially Catholic philosophy.[1]

Many Christians, however, have been less than totally impressed. In particular Reformed or Calvinist theologians have for the most part taken a dim view of this enterprise. A few Reformed thinkers—B. B. Warfield,[2] for example,—endorse the theistic proofs; but for the most part the Reformed attitude has ranged from indifference, through suspicion and hostility, to outright accusations of blasphemy. And this stance is initially puzzling. It looks a little like the attitude some Christians adopt towards faith healing: it can't be done, but even if it could, it shouldn't be. What exactly, or even approximately, do these sons and daughters of the Reformation have against proving the existence of God? What could they have against it? What could be less objectionable to any but the most obdurate atheist?

Proof and Belief in God

Let's begin with the nineteenth century Dutch theologian Herman Bavinck:

> Scripture urges us to behold heaven and earth, birds and flowers and lilies, in order that we may see and recognize God in them. "Lift up your eyes on high, and see who hath created these." Is. 40:26. Scripture does not reason in the abstract. It does not make God the conclusion of a syllogism, leaving it to us whether we think the argument holds or not. But it speaks with authority. Both theologically and religiously it proceeds from God as the starting point.[3]

> We receive the impression that belief in the existence of God is based entirely upon these proofs. But indeed that would be "a wretched faith, which, before it invokes God, must first prove his existence." The contrary, however, is the truth. . . . Of the existence of self, of the world round about us, of logical and moral laws, etc., we are so deeply convinced because of the indelible impressions which all these things make upon our consciousness that we need no arguments or demonstration. Spontaneously,

altogether involuntarily: without any constraint or coercion, we accept that existence. Now the same is true in regard to the existence of God. The so-called proofs are by no means the final grounds of our most certain conviction that God exists: This certainly is established only by faith; i.e., by the spontaneous testimony which forces itself upon us from every side.[4]

According to Bavinck, then, a Christian's belief in the existence of God is not based upon proofs or arguments. By "argument" here, I think he means arguments in the style of natural theology—the sort given by Aquinas and Scotus and later by Descartes, Leibniz, Clarke and others. And what he means to say, I think, is that Christians don't *need* such arguments. Don't need them for what?

Here I think Bavinck means to hold two things. First, arguments or proofs are not, in general, the source of the believer's confidence in God. Typically, the believer does not believe in God on the basis of arguments; nor does he believe such truths as, for example, that God has created the world on the basis of arguments. Secondly, argument is not needed for *rational justification*; the believer is entirely within his epistemic right in believing that God has created the world, even if he has no argument at all for that conclusion. The believer doesn't need natural theology in order to achieve rationality or epistemic propriety in believing; his belief in God can be perfectly rational even if he knows of no cogent argument, deductive or inductive, for the existence of God—indeed, even if there *isn't* any such argument.

Bavinck has three further points. First he means to add, I think, that we *cannot* come to knowledge of God on the basis of argument; the arguments of natural theology just don't work. (And he follows this passage with a more or less traditional attempt to refute the theistic proofs, including an endorsement of some of Kant's fashionable confusions about the ontological

argument.) Secondly, Scripture "proceeds from God as the starting point," and so should the believer. There is nothing by way of proofs or arguments for God's existence in the Bible; that is simply presupposed. The same should be true of the Christian believer then, he should *start* from belief in God, rather than from the premises of some argument whose conclusion is that God exists. What is it that makes those premises a better starting point anyway? And third, Bavinck points out that belief in God relevantly resembles belief in the existence of the self and of the external world—and, we might add, belief in other minds and the past. In none of these areas do we typically *have* proof or arguments, or *need* proofs or arguments.

According to John Calvin, who is as good a Calvinist as any, God has implanted in us all an innate tendency, or nisus, or disposition to believe in him:

"There is within the human mind, and indeed by natural instinct, an awareness of divinity." This we take to be beyond controversy. To prevent anyone from taking refuge in the pretense of ignorance, God himself has implanted in all men a certain understanding of his divine majesty. Ever renewing its memory, he repeatedly sheds fresh drops. Since, therefore, men one and all perceive that there is a God and that he is their Maker, they are condemned by their own testimony because they have failed to honor him and to consecrate their lives to his will. If ignorance of God is to be looked for anywhere, surely one is most likely to find an example of it among the more backward folk and those more remote from civilization. Yet there is, as the eminent pagan says, no nation so barbarous, no people so savage, that they have not a deep-seated conviction that there is a God. So deeply does the common conception occupy the minds of all, so tenaciously does it inhere in the hearts of all! Therefore, since from the beginning of the world there has been no region, no city, in short, no household, that could do without religion, there lies in this a tacit confession of a sense of deity inscribed in the hearts of all.[5]

Indeed, the perversity of the impious, who though they struggle furiously are unable to extricate themselves from the fear of God, is abundant testimony that this conviction, namely, that there is some God, is naturally inborn in all, and is fixed deep within, as it were in the very marrow. . . . From this we conclude that it is not a doctrine that must first be learned in school, but one of which each of us is master from his mother's womb and which nature itself permits no one to forget.[6]

Calvin's claim, then, is that God has created us in such a way that we have a strong propensity or inclination towards belief in him. This tendency has been in part overlaid or suppressed by sin. Were it not for the existence of sin in the world, human beings would believe in God to the same degree and with the same natural spontaneity that we believe in the existence of other persons, an external world, or the past. This is the natural human condition; it is because of our presently unnatural sinful condition that many of us find belief in God difficult or absurd. The fact is, Calvin thinks, one who doesn't believe in God is in an epistemically substandard position—rather like a man who doesn't believe that his wife exists, or thinks she is like a cleverly constructed robot and has no thoughts, feelings, or consciousness.

Although this disposition to believe in God is partially suppressed, it is nonetheless universally present. And it is triggered or actuated by widely realized conditions:

Lest anyone, then, be excluded from access to happiness, he not only sowed in men's minds that seed of religion of which we have spoken, but revealed himself and daily discloses himself in the whole workmanship of the universe. As a consequence, men cannot

open their eyes without being compelled to see him.[7]

Like Kant, Calvin is especially impressed in this connection, by the marvelous compages of the starry heavens above:

Even the common folk and the most untutored, who have been taught only by the aid of the eyes, cannot be unaware of the excellence of divine art, for it reveals itself in this innumerable and yet distinct and well-ordered variety of the heavenly host.[8]

And Calvin's claim is that one who accedes to this tendency and in these circumstances accepts the belief that God has created the world—perhaps upon beholding the starry heavens, or the splendid majesty of the mountains, or the intricate, articulate beauty of a tiny flower—is entirely within his epistemic rights in so doing. It isn't that such a person is justified or rational in so believing by virtue of having an implicit argument—some version of the teleological argument, say. No; he doesn't need any argument for justification or rationality. His belief need not be based on any other propositions at all; under these conditions he is perfectly rational in accepting belief in God in the utter absence of any argument, deductive or inductive. Indeed, a person in these conditions, says Calvin, *knows* that God exists, has knowledge of God's existence, apart from any argument at all.

Elsewhere Calvin speaks of "arguments from reason" or rational arguments:

The prophets and apostles do not boast either of their keenness or of anything that obtains credit for them as they speak; nor do they dwell upon rational proofs. Rather, they bring forward God's holy name, that by it the whole world may be brought into obedience to him. Now we ought to see how apparent it is not only by plausible opinion but by dear truth that they do not call upon God's name heedlessly or falsely. If we desire to provide in the best way for our consciences—that they may not be perpetually beset by the instability of doubt or vacillation, and that they may not also boggle at the smallest quibbles—we ought to seek our conviction, in a higher place than human reasons, judgments, or conjectures, that is, in the secret testimony of the Spirit.[9]

Here the subject for discussion is not belief in the existence of God, but belief that God is the author of the Scriptures; I think it is clear, however, that Calvin would say the same thing about belief in God's existence. The Christian doesn't need natural theology, either as the source of his confidence or to justify his belief. Furthermore, the Christian *ought* not to believe on the basis of argument; if he does, his faith is likely to be unstable and wavering. From Calvin's point of view, believing in the existence of God on the basis of rational argument is like believing in the existence of your spouse on the basis of the analogical argument for other minds—whimsical at best and not at all likely to delight the person concerned.

Foundationalism

We could look further into the precise forms taken by the Reformed objection to Natural Theology; time is short, however; what I shall do instead is tell you what I think underlies these objections, inchoate and unfocused as they are. The reformers mean to say, fundamentally, that belief in God can properly be taken as basic. That is, a person is entirely within his epistemic rights, entirely rational, in believing in God, even if he has no argument for this belief and does not believe it on the basis of any other beliefs he holds. And in taking belief in God as properly basic, the reformers were implicitly rejecting a whole picture or way of looking at knowledge and rational belief; call it *classical foundationalism*. This picture has been enormously popular even

since the days of Plato and Aristotle; it remains the dominant way of thinking about knowledge, justification, belief, faith, and allied topics. Although it has been thus dominant, Reformed theologians and thinkers have, I believe, meant to reject it. What they say here tends to be inchoate and not well-articulated; nevertheless the fact is they meant to reject classical foundationalism. But how shall we characterize the view rejected? The first thing to see is that foundationalism is a *normative* view. It aims to lay down conditions that must be met by anyone whose system of beliefs is *rational*; and here "rational" is to be understood normatively. According to the foundationalist, there is a right way and a wrong way with respect to belief. People have responsibilities, duties and obligations with respect to their believings just as with respect to their (other) actions. Perhaps this sort of obligation is really a special case of a more general moral obligation; or perhaps, on the other hand, it is *sui generis*. In any event there are such obligations; to conform to them is to be rational and to go against them is to be irrational. To be rational, then, is to exercise one's epistemic powers *properly*—to exercise them in such a way as to go contrary to none of the norms for such exercise.

Foundationalism, therefore, is in part a normative thesis. I think we can understand this thesis more fully if we introduce the idea of a *noetic structure*. A person's noetic structure is the set of propositions he believes together with certain epistemic relations that hold among him and these propositions. Thus some of his beliefs may be *based on* other things he believes; it may be that there are a pair of propositions A and B such that he believes *A on the basis of B*. Although this relation isn't easy to characterize in a revealing and non-trivial fashion, it is nonetheless familiar. I believe that the word "umbrageous" is spelled u-m-b-r-a-g-e-o-u-s: this belief is based on another belief of mine, the belief that that's how the dictionary says it's spelled. I believe that $72 \times 71 = 5112$. This belief is based upon several other beliefs I hold—such beliefs as that $1 \times 72 =$

72; $7 \times 2 = 14$; $7 \times 7 = 49$; $49 + 1 = 50$; and others. Some of my beliefs, however, I accept but don't accept on the basis of any other beliefs. I believe that $2 + 1 = 3$, for example, and don't believe it on the basis of other propositions. I also believe that I am seated at my desk, and that there is a mild pain in my right knee. These too are basic for me; I don't believe them on the basis of any other propositions.

An account of a person's noetic structure, then, would include a specification of which of his beliefs are basic and which are non-basic. Of course it is abstractly possible that *none* of his beliefs is basic; perhaps he holds just three beliefs, A, B, and C, and believes each of them on the basis of the other two. We might think this improper or irrational, but that is not to say it couldn't be done. And it is also possible that *all* of his beliefs are basic; perhaps he believes a lot of propositions, but doesn't believe any of them on the basis of any others. In the typical case, however, a noetic structure will include both basic and non-basic beliefs.

Secondly, an account of a noetic structure will include what we might call an index of degree of belief. I hold some of my beliefs much more firmly than others. I believe both that $2 + 1 = 3$ and that London, England, is north of Saskatoon, Saskatchewan; but I believe the former more resolutely than the latter. Here we might make use of the personalist[10] interpretation of probability theory; think of an index of degree of belief as a function $Ps(A)$ from the set of propositions a person S believes or disbelieves into the real numbers between 0 and 1. $Ps(A) = n$, then, records something like the degree to which S believes A, or the strength of his belief that A. $Ps(A) = 1$ proclaims S's utter and abandoned commitment to A; $Ps(A) = 0$ records a similar commitment to not-A; $Ps(A) = .5$ means that S, like Buridan's ass, is suspended in equilibrium between A and not-A. We could then go on to consider whether the personalist is right in holding that a rational noetic structure conforms to the Calculus of Probability.[11]

Thirdly, a somewhat vaguer notion; an account of S's noetic structure would include something like an index of *depth of ingression*. Some of my beliefs are, we might say, on the periphery of my noetic structure. I accept them, and may even accept them quite firmly; but if I were to give them up, not much else in my noetic structure would have to change. I believe there are some large boulders on the top of the Grand Teton. If I come to give up this belief, however (say by climbing it and not finding any), that change wouldn't have extensive reverberations throughout the rest of my noetic structure; it could be accommodated with minimal alteration elsewhere. So its depth of ingression into my noetic structure isn't great. On the other hand, if I were to come to believe that there simply is no such thing as the Grand Teton, or no mountains at all, or no such thing as the state of Wyoming, that would have much greater reverberations. And if, *per impossibile*, I were to come to think there hadn't been much of a past (that the world was created just five minutes ago, complete with all its apparent memories and traces of the past), or that there weren't any other persons, that would have even greater reverberations; these beliefs of mine have great depth of ingression into my noetic structure.

Now classical foundationalism is best construed, I think, as a thesis about *rational* noetic structures. A noetic structure is rational if it could be the noetic structure of a person who was completely rational. To be completely rational, as I am here using the term, is not to believe only what is true, or to believe all the logical consequences of what one believes, or to believe all necessary truths with equal firmness, or to be uninfluenced by emotion; it is, instead, to do the right thing with respect to one's believings. As we have seen, the foundationalist holds that there are responsibilities and duties that pertain to believings as well as to actions, or other actions; these responsibilities accrue to us just by virtue of our having the sorts of noetic capabilities we do have. There are norms or standards for beliefs. To criticize a person as irrational, then, is to criticize her for failing to fulfill these duties or responsibilities, or for failing to conform to the relevant norms or standards. From this point of view, a rational person is one whose believings meet the appropriate standards. To draw the ethical analogy, the irrational is the impermissible; the rational is the permissible.

A rational noetic structure, then, is one that could be the noetic structure of a perfectly rational person. And classical foundationalism is, in part, a thesis about such noetic structures. The foundationalist notes, first of all, that some of our beliefs are based upon others. He immediately adds that a belief can't properly be accepted on the basis of just *any* other belief; in a rational noetic structure, A will be accepted on the basis of B only if B *supports* A, or is a member of a set of beliefs that together support A. It isn't clear just what this supports relation is; different foundationalists propose different candidates. One candidate, for example, is *entailment*; A supports B only if B is entailed by A, or perhaps is self-evidently entailed by A, or perhaps follows from A by an argument where each step is a self-evident entailment. Another and more permissive candidate is probability; perhaps A supports B if B is likely or probable with respect to A. And of course there are other candidates.

More important for present purposes, however, is the following claim: in a rational noetic structure, there will be some beliefs that are not based upon others: call these its *foundations*. If every belief in a rational noetic structure were based upon other beliefs, the structure in question would contain infinitely many beliefs. However things may stand for more powerful intellects—angelic intellects, perhaps—human beings aren't capable of believing infinitely many propositions. Among other things, one presumably doesn't believe a proposition one has never heard of, and no one has had time, these busy days, to have heard of infinitely many propositions. So every rational noetic structure has a foundation.

Suppose we say that *weak* foundationalism is the view that (1) every rational noetic structure has a foundation, and (2) in a rational noetic structure, non-basic belief is proportional in strength to support from the foundations. When I say Reformed thinkers have meant to reject foundationalism, I do not mean to say that they intended to reject weak foundationalism. On the contrary; the thought of many of them tends to support or endorse weak foundationalism. What then do they mean to reject? Here we meet a further and fundamental feature of classic varieties of foundationalism: they all lay down certain conditions of proper or rational basicality. From the foundationalist point of view, not just any kind of belief can be found in the foundations of a rational noetic structure; a belief, to be properly basic (i.e., basic in a rational noetic structure) must meet certain conditions. It is plausible to see Thomas Aquinas, for example, as holding that a proposition is properly basic for a person only if it is self-evident to him (such that his understanding or grasping it is sufficient for his seeing it to be true) or "evident to the senses," as he puts it. By this latter term I think he means to refer to propositions whose truth or falsehood we can determine by looking or listening or employing some other sense—such propositions as

1   There is a tree before me
2   I am wearing shoes

and

3   That tree's leaves are yellow.

Many foundationalists have insisted that propositions basic in a rational noetic structure must be *certain* in some important sense. Thus it is plausible to see Descartes as holding that the foundations of a rational noetic structure don't include such propositions as (1)–(3) but more cautious claims—claims about one's own mental life, for example:

4   It seems to me that I see a tree
5   I seem to see something green

or, as Professor Chisholm puts it,

6   I am appeared greenly to.

Propositions of this latter sort seem to enjoy a kind of immunity from error not enjoyed by those of the former. I could be mistaken in thinking I see a pink rat; perhaps I am hallucinating or the victim of an illusion. But it is at the least very much harder to see that I could be mistaken in believing that I *seem* to see a pink rat, in believing that I am appeared pinkly (or pink ratly) to. Suppose we say that a proposition with respect to which I enjoy this sort of immunity from error is *incorrigible* for me; then perhaps Descartes means to hold that a proposition is properly basic for S only if it is either self-evident or incorrigible for S.

Aquinas and Descartes, we might say, are *strong* foundationalists; they accept weak foundationalism and add some conditions for proper basicality. Ancient and medieval foundationalists tended to hold that a proposition is properly basic for a person only if it is either self-evident or evident to the senses; modern foundationalists—Descartes, Locke, Leibniz and the like—tended to hold that a proposition is properly basic for S only if either self-evident or incorrigible for S. Of course this is a historical generalization and is thus subject to contradiction by scholars, such being the penalty for historical generalization; but perhaps it is worth the risk. And now suppose we say that *classical foundationalism* is the disjunction of ancient and medieval with modern foundationalism.

The Reformed Rejection of Classical Foundationalism

These Reformed thinkers, I believe, are best understood as rejecting classical foundationalism.[12] They were inclined to accept weak foundationalism, I think; but they were completely at odds with the idea that the foundations of a rational noetic structure can at most include propositions that are self-evident or evident to the senses or incorrigible. In particular, they were prepared to insist that a rational noetic structure can include belief in God as basic. As Bavinck put it "Scripture . . . does not make God the conclusion of a syllogism, leaving it to us whether we think the argument holds or not. But it speaks with authority." Both theologically and religiously it proceeds from God as the starting point. And of course Bavinck means to say that we must emulate Scripture here.

In the passages I quoted earlier on, Calvin claims the believer doesn't need argument—doesn't need it, among other things, for epistemic respect-ability. We may understand him as holding, I think, that a rational noetic structure may perfectly well contain belief in God among its foundations. Indeed, he means to go further, and in two separate directions. In the first place, he thinks a Christian *ought* not believe in God on the basis of other propositions; a proper and well formed Christian noetic structure will in *fact* have belief in God among its foundations. And in the second place Calvin claims that one who takes belief in God as basic can nonetheless know that God exists. Calvin holds that one can *rationally accept* belief in God as basic; he also claims that one can *know* that God exists even if he has no argument, even if he does not believe on the basis of other propositions. A weak foundationalist is likely to hold that some properly basic beliefs are such that anyone who accepts them, *knows* them. More exactly, he is likely to hold that among the beliefs properly basic for a person S, some are such that if S accepts them S knows them. A weak foundationalist could go on to say that *other* properly basic beliefs can't be known, if taken as basic, but only rationally believed; and he might think of the existence of God as a case in point. Calvin will have none of this; as he sees it, one needs no arguments to know that God exists.

Among the central contentions of these Reformed thinkers, therefore, are the claims that belief in God is properly basic, and the view that one who takes belief in God as basic can also *know* that God exists.

The Great Pumpkin Objection

Now I enthusiastically concur in these contentions of Reformed epistemology, and by way of conclusion I want to defend them against a popular objection. It is tempting to raise the following sort of question. If belief in God is properly basic, why can't just any belief be properly basic? Couldn't we say the same for any bizarre aberration we can think of? What about voodoo or astrology? What about the belief that the Great Pumpkin returns every Halloween? Could I properly take *that* as basic? And if I can't, why can I properly take belief in God as basic? Suppose I believe that if I flap my arms with sufficient vigor, I can take off and fly about the room; could I defend myself against the charge of irrationality by claiming this belief is basic? If we say that belief in God is properly basic, won't we be committed to holding that just anything, or nearly anything, can properly be taken as basic, thus throwing wide the gates to irrationalism and superstition?

Certainly not. What might lead one to think the Reformed epistemologist is in this kind of trouble? The fact that he rejects the criteria for proper basicality purveyed by the classical foundationalist? But why should *that* be thought to commit him to such tolerance of irrationality? Consider an analogy. In the palmy days of positivism, the positivists went about confidently wielding their verifiability criterion and declaring meaningless much that was obviously meaningful. Now suppose someone rejected a formulation of that criterion—the one to be found in the second edition of A. J. Ayer's *Language, Truth and Logic*, for example. Would that mean she was committed to holding that

7   T' was brillig; and the slithy toves did gyre and gymble in the wabe,

contrary to appearances, makes good sense? Of course not. But then the same goes for the Reformed epistemologist; the fact that he rejects the criteria of Classical Foundationalism does not mean that he is committed to supposing just anything is properly basic.

But what then is the problem? Is it that the Reformed epistemologist not only rejects those criteria for proper basicality, but seems in no hurry to produce what he takes to be a better substitute? If he has no such criterion, how can he fairly reject belief in the Great Pumpkin as properly basic?

This objection betrays an important misconception. How *do* we rightly arrive at or develop criteria for meaningfulness, or justified belief, or proper basicality? Where do they come from? Must one have such a criterion before one can sensibly make any judgments—positive or negative—about proper basicality? Surely not. Suppose I don't know of a satisfactory substitute for the criteria proposed by classical foundationalism; I am nevertheless entirely within my rights in holding that certain propositions are not properly basic in certain conditions. Some propositions seem self-evident when in fact they are not; that is the lesson of some of the Russell Paradoxes.[13] Nevertheless it would be irrational to take as basic the denial of a proposition that seems self-evident to you. Similarly, suppose it seems to you that you see a tree; you would then be irrational in taking as basic the proposition that you don't see a tree, or that there aren't any trees. In the same way, even if I don't know of some illuminating criterion of meaning, I can quite properly declare (7) meaningless, even if I don't have a successful substitute for the positivist's verifiability criterion.

And this raises an important question—one Roderick Chisholm has taught us to ask.[14] What is the status of criteria for meaningfulness, or proper basicality, or justified belief? These are typically universal statements. The modern foundationalist's criterion for proper basicality, for example, is doubly universal:

8   For any proposition A and person S, A is properly basic for S if and only if A is incorrigible for S or self-evident to S.

But how does one know a thing like that? Where does it come from? (8) certainly isn't self-evident or just obviously true. But if it isn't, how does one arrive at it? What sorts of arguments would be appropriate? Of course a philosopher might find (8) so appealing that he simply takes it to be true, neither offering argument for it, nor accepting it on the basis of other things he believes. If he does so, however, his noetic structure will be self-referentially incoherent. (8) itself is neither self-evident nor incorrigible; hence in accepting (8) as basic, the classical foundationalist violates the condition of proper basicality he himself lays down in accepting it. On the other hand, perhaps the philosopher has some argument for it from premises that are self-evident; it is exceeding hard to see, however, what such arguments might be like. And until he has produced such arguments, what shall the rest of us do—we who do not find (8) at all obvious or compelling? How could he use (8) to show us that belief in God, for example, is not properly basic? Why should we believe (8), or pay it any attention?

The fact is, I think, that neither (8) nor any other revealing necessary and sufficient condition for proper basicality follows from obviously self-evident premises by obviously acceptable arguments. And hence the proper way to arrive at such a criterion is, broadly speaking, *inductive*. We must assemble examples of beliefs and conditions such that the former are obviously properly basic in the latter, and examples of beliefs and conditions such that the former are obviously not properly basic in the latter. We must then frame hypotheses as to the necessary and sufficient conditions of proper basicality and test

these hypotheses by reference to those examples. Under the right conditions, for example, it is clearly rational to believe that you see a human person before you: a being who has thoughts and feelings, who knows and believes things, who makes decisions and acts. It is clear, furthermore, that you are under no obligation to reason to this belief from others you hold; under those conditions that belief is properly basic for you. But then (8) must be mistaken; the belief in question, under those circumstances, is properly basic, though neither self-evident nor incorrigible for you. Similarly, you may seem to remember that you had breakfast this morning, and perhaps you know of no reason to suppose your memory is playing you tricks. If so, you are entirely justified in taking that belief as basic. Of course it isn't properly basic on the criteria offered by classical foundationalists; but that fact counts not against you but against those criteria.

Accordingly, criteria for proper basicality must be reached from below rather than above; they should not be presented as *obiter dicta*, but argued to and tested by a relevant set of examples. But there is no reason to assume, in advance, that everyone will agree on the examples. The Christian will of course suppose that belief in God is entirely proper and rational; if he doesn't accept this belief on the basis of other propositions, he will conclude that it is basic for him and quite properly so. Followers of Bertrand Russell and Madalyn Murray O'Hair may disagree; but how is that relevant? Must my criteria, or those of the Christian community, conform to their examples? Surely not. The Christian community is responsible to its set of examples, not to theirs.

Accordingly, the Reformed epistemologist can properly hold that belief in the Great Pumpkin is not properly basic, even though he holds that belief in God is properly basic and even if he has no full fledged criterion of proper basicality. Of course he is committed to supposing that there is a relevant *difference* between belief in God and belief in the Great Pumpkin, if he holds that the former but not the latter is properly basic. But this should be no great embarrassment; there are plenty of candidates. Thus the Reformed epistemologist may concur with Calvin in holding that God has implanted in us a natural tendency to see his hand in the world around us; the same cannot be said for the Great Pumpkin, there being no Great Pumpkin and no natural tendency to accept beliefs about the Great Pumpkin.

By way of conclusion then, the Reformed objection to natural theology, unformed and inchoate as it is, may best be seen as a rejection of classical foundationalism. As the Reformed thinker sees things, being self-evident, or incorrigible, or evident to the senses is not a necessary condition of proper basicality. He goes on to add that belief in God is properly basic. He is not thereby committed, even in the absence of a general criterion of proper basicality, to suppose that just any or nearly any belief—belief in the Great Pumpkin, for example—is properly basic. Like everyone should, he begins with examples; and he may take belief in the Great Pumpkin as a paradigm of irrational basic belief.

Notes

1 See, for example, James Ross, *Philosophical Theology* (Indianapolis: Bobbs-Merrill, 1969), and Richard Swinburne, *The Existence of God* (Oxford: Clarendon Press, 1979).

2 "God," in *Studies in Theology* (New York: Oxford University Press, 1932), pp. 110–11.

3 *The Doctrine of God*, trans. William Hendriksen (Grand Rapids: Eerdmans, 1951). This is a translation of vol. 2 of Bavinck's *Gereformeerde Dogmatiek* (Kampen: Kok, 1918), p. 76.

4 Ibid., p. 78.

5 *Institutes of the Christian Religion*, ed. J. T. McNeill and trans. Ford Lewis Battles (Philadelphia: Westminster Press, 1960), Book I, Chap. iii, sec. 1.

6 *Institutes*, I, iii, 3.

7 *Institutes*, V, v, 1.

8 *Institutes*, V, v, 2.

9 *Institutes*, I, vii, 4.

10 See, for example, Richard Jeffrey's *The Logic of Decision* (New York: McGraw-Hill, 1965).

11 See my paper "The Probabilistic Argument from Evil," *Philosophical Studies* 30 (1979): 21.

12 Here I think they were entirely correct; both ancient and modern foundationalism are self-referentially incoherent. See my paper "Is Belief in God Rational?" [*Rationality and Religious Belief*, ed. C. Delany (South Bend: University of Notre Dame Press, 1979)] p. 26.

13 "Is Belief in God Rational?" p. 22.

14 *The Problem of the Criterion* (Milwaukee: Marquette University Press, 1973).

Chapter 4

Richard Swinburne

RATIONAL RELIGIOUS BELIEF

Some of men's beliefs are true and some are false, and we may assess beliefs on that dimension. But we also assess beliefs on the dimension of rationality. Roughly, a man's belief is a rational belief if he is justified in holding it—for epistemological reasons. There may be various reasons why it is a good thing that a man hold some belief—e.g. that it gives him peace of mind, or prevents him beating up his wife; but the only reasons which concern us here are reasons which concern the likelihood of it being true—these I will call epistemological reasons. We all want to say that men often hold beliefs which are in fact false but which they have no grounds for believing false and are in fact justified in believing. We might say, for example, that the average man of the first century AD held a rational but false belief in holding that the Earth was stationary. However there are various possible kinds of epistemological justification which a man may have for holding beliefs, and I shall need to distinguish five kinds of rationality which beliefs may possess.

A subject S who believes that p will have what I shall call a rational$_1$ belief if and only if his belief that p is probable, given his inductive standards and given his evidence. A subject must believe that a belief of his is rational$_1$ if he is to have that belief but it may not in fact always be rational$_1$. A failure in respect of rationality$_1$ is a failure of internal coherence in a subject's system of beliefs, a failure of which the subject is unaware.

Thus, on the basis of what he has heard in court and outside it, a juryman may hold strong beliefs well-supported by evidence, that (1) the evidence against the prisoner is weak, (2) the police who charged him are intelligent men, (3) the police know far more about the detailed facts than he, the juryman, does, but (4) often police frame suspects. The juryman's inductive standards may be such that (1), (2), and (3) make probable (5), the prisoner is guilty; but (1), (2), (3), and (4) do not make (5) probable. The juryman then comes to believe that (5) is probable, because he forgets the relevance of his belief that (4), in reaching his conclusion. The juryman's belief that (5) is irrational in the first sense of 'rational'.

A subject's beliefs may be rational in that they are internally coherent, and yet we may feel (loosely) that in holding them the subject is not responding to the world in a justifiable way. To attempt to capture what extra we are looking for I define rationality$_2$. A subject S who believes that p has what I shall call a rational$_2$ belief if and only if p is in fact rendered probable by his evidence, and his evidence consists of basic propositions which he is in fact justified in holding with the degree of confidence with which he does hold them. For his belief to be rational$_2$ his belief has to be grounded in those initial propositions which his present experiences (and memories of his past experiences) in fact justify him in holding or prior propositions which considerations

Rational Religious Belief   41

of reason justify him in holding, and to be supported by them in virtue of correct inductive standards. Rationality$_2$ is a matter of conformity to objective standards, which the believer may not recognize and may indeed explicitly deny.

A belief can fail to be rational$_2$ by being grounded in initial propositions which the subject is not justified in holding—e.g. it may be based on a claim to have had a telepathic experience when no conscious experience justified this, or on a claim to have seen a UFO, where the sensations which the subject has had, justify him only in claiming that he has seen a light. Or it may be based on initial propositions about which the subject is excessively over-confident. Or it may fail to be based on initial propositions which the subject, given his experiences, ought to hold.

There are arguments which we can use to show that some man is not justified in holding some initial proposition, with the degree of confidence with which he does hold it, or in failing to hold some initial proposition. To the man who claims telepathic communication, we may attempt to show that what he claims to know telepathically is seldom the case, and hence that he is not justified on a given occasion in having much confidence in initial propositions claiming telepathy. To the man who has excessive confidence in his senses, we can point out how often, when his perceptual judgements can be subjected to objective tests, they fail to be right. Likewise to the man who has too little confidence in his senses, we can point out how often subsequent inquiry showed that what he was hesitant to admit perceiving was in fact there. And so on. But if these arguments are to convince the subject that he has a tendency to hold initial propositions unjustifiably (or not to hold initial propositions which he would have been justified in holding), they must appeal to things which he already accepts, viz. inductive standards and other beliefs which we share with him (e.g. that when many other people in a position to observe report that things are not as he holds, they are right and he is wrong).

Similarly there are arguments which we can use to show that some man is not justified in holding some prior proposition with the degree of confidence with which he does hold it. These arguments would show that he had jumped to the conclusion that the proposition was true without giving enough consideration to whether there was any way in which it could turn out to be false. Thus some man may hold as a prior proposition 'there is no greatest prime number' without ever having thought of the mathematical argument which shows this proposition to be true. We feel that the man should not just believe the proposition without having considered the argument. We can point out to the believer that men who jump too quickly to mathematical conclusions of that complexity often turn out to be wrong.

Arguments to show that a man is not justified in holding basic propositions with the degree of confidence with which he does hold them are arguments to show that he has given to them a wrong prior probability. Note that such arguments are not arguments to show that those propositions are false. A man may include some false proposition among his evidence with perfect rationality—until some good argument is produced to show that it is a false proposition. But the point is that a man may be too hasty in assenting to some proposition on the basis of experience or reason—and we can show him that he is too hasty, and teach him to be more careful in future.

Finally, a belief can fail to be rational$_2$ by not in fact being rendered probable by the subject's evidence, i.e. by his using incorrect inductive standards. Arguments can be used to show that certain inductive standards are the true ones (the true inductive standards being those which license all and only correct inductive judgements). Clearly the starting-point of such investigation is a large set of judgements which seem to the investigator to be indisputably correct; that e_1 makes h_1 probable, but does not make h_2 probable; that e_2 makes h_2 probable, and more probable than h_1; and so on and so forth. As with all investigation we start from what seems to stare us in the face, although allowing for the possibility of later correction. We then seek, using the principle of simplicity, for the most natural extrapolation from those judgements, an extrapolation which would allow that we had made occasional mistakes but no more. Having reached an account of the true principles of induction we then see whether any necessary corrections to our initial particular judgements are ones which seem plausible. In so far as the general account which we reach fails to license judgements which seem, intuitively, to be obviously correct, we must look for another and perhaps more complicated account of the true principles of induction. But it may be that having formulated general principles, these seem so obviously correct to us that we change some particular judgements in the light of them. [. . .]

[A] subject's beliefs are not rational$_2$ if they are not based on evidence which he is justified in holding or if they are not inferred by correct principles, whether or not we are right in our judgements using our own standards about the matter, and whether or not we can convince the subject about this.

A man must believe that his own beliefs are not merely rational$_1$ but rational$_2$. For a man must believe his basic propositions to have (as a result of his experience of the world) the prior probabilities which he ascribes to them, i.e. believes them to have; and unless a man held that his inductive standards were correct, he could not believe that his beliefs were in fact rendered probable by his evidence. But, for all that, a man's beliefs may not in fact be rational$_2$ and we as outsiders may judge that they are not.

Quite obviously, men of past centuries have often had scientific beliefs which were both rational$_2$ and false. A man of the eighteenth century who studied Newton's *Principia* would have been using the inductive standards which we believe to be correct if he judged that on the observational evidence of astronomy and

mechanics which Newton lists, Newton's theory of mechanics was probably true (i.e. that Newton's theory described correctly the behaviour of all material bodies at all points of space and time). He had every reason for believing that the behaviour of planets and moons which Newton cited as evidence was as Newton claimed, and indeed he could have checked it for himself. No other relevant evidence was known. It was only when later evidence turned up in the nineteenth century that men began to doubt the universal applicability of Newton's theory.

The rationality of both rational$_1$ and rational$_2$ beliefs is a matter of the believer's response to present sensations and memories of the past and to apparently self-justifying truths of reason at the time in question. The belief is rational$_1$ if the response satisfies the believer's own standards. The belief is rational$_2$ if the response satisfies correct standards. However, we often feel that although a man is justified in holding a certain belief at some time, he ought to have looked for more evidence or checked his standards more thoroughly at earlier times. Had he done so, he might have beliefs which were better justified, more probable. And so, according to whether the failure at an earlier stage was a failure by the subject's own standards of which he was aware, a failure by the subject's own standards of which he was not aware, or a failure by correct standards, we have three further kinds of irrationality of belief. In so far as these possible failures have been avoided, we have three further kinds of rationality. The subdivision of 'failure by the subject's own standards' into failure of which he was aware and failure of which he was unaware arises when we are concerned with failure in pursuing investigations, because pursuing investigations is something which a man can choose to do or choose not to do. Whereas the only failure by the subject's own standards with which I was concerned before was failure to respond to evidence in the right way at a time; and here there is no category of failure of which the subject is aware, since a man cannot but respond in the way in which the evidence seems to him to point; necessarily a man believes what he believes to be probable on the evidence. Hence the only failure of the type with which I was concerned previously was failure of which the subject was unaware. Here we have both types.

A subject S who believes that p has, I shall say, a rational₃ belief if and only if S's evidence results from past investigation which was in S's view adequate, his inductive standards have been subjected to criticism by S which was in S's view adequate, and S has checked in his view adequately that p is made probable by his evidence. Investigation is adequate if it is adequate for the goal of securing true beliefs.

Examples will illustrate the different ways in which beliefs can fail to be rational₃. First, there may be a culpable failure, of which the subject is aware, to collect enough true, representative, relevant evidence of good quality. Thus, a detective may have a good case against a suspect, whom, on the evidence available at the time of the trial, he justifiably believes to be guilty of murder. But murder is a serious matter and the detective may not, through culpable idleness, have followed up all leads in the past, checked alibis thoroughly, etc. So although it is rational that the detective should hold the belief at the time of the trial, his belief is in a way irrational because it is not backed by enough relevant evidence. Alternatively, the detective may have acquired plenty of evidence but may have looked only for evidence to support his own point of view. Now, in so far as he remains aware that he has done this, necessarily the detective will take into account the bias of the evidence sample. (For if you know that you have not looked for where damaging evidence is most likely to be found, if there is such evidence, you will know that your failure to find it does not give strong support to your theory.) But the detective may now have forgotten how biased his investigation was, and then on the basis of the evidence which he has recorded, justifiably judge that it points to the subject's guilt. There remains however an

element of irrationality in his belief resulting from past failure to investigate—an irrationality which would be compounded if the forgetting of the bias of the investigation was in any way deliberate. The belief may also be irrational₃ in being based on initial propositions, on the reliability of which the subject recognizes that he ought to have checked, e.g. claims to have held telepathic communication. In such a case the subject may recognize, as a result of hearing criticism from others, that he ought to have checked whether what he claims to know telepathically is often, by other criteria, as he claims. The second reason why a belief can fail to be rational₃ is that the subject has formed it by using inductive standards which he recognizes that he has not subjected to proper criticism. Thus, the gambler referred to earlier may realize that other people think him suspicious, and suspect that his method of reaching conclusions about winners of races is unsatisfactory, and yet not have submitted it to a test which he recognizes to be relevant, e.g. not have tested whether it normally works. Or, although he does not recognize such tests to be relevant (i.e. he treats his principle as a primary inductive principle), he may have refused to take account of philosophical criticisms of it (e.g. that it does not cohere with his other inductive principles, and that it ought to do so). The third reason why a belief can fail to be rational₃ is that the subject has culpably failed to check that, given his standards, the belief is made probable by his evidence; he has failed to consider adequately exactly what the evidence does show. A historian may have come to believe some theory on the basis of certain evidence, without having checked whether there were other theories which fitted the evidence equally well and were in fact better supported by it.

For many of our beliefs, however, it surely does not matter whether we look for relevant evidence, or to check their correctness in the other ways. [. . .] It appears that in so far as the rationality of a belief is a matter of whether it results from adequate investigation, it depends on how important it is that the subject should have a correct belief on the matter; or rather, in the case of rationality₃, how important the subject believes it to be that he should have a correct belief on the matter. There are some beliefs which matter because they concern issues about which it is important that I have true beliefs— e.g. whether my house is falling down, whether my daughter has had an accident, whether I owe you an apology or a lot of money, whether the old man next door is ill, whether my chemical experiment will blow up the village, and so on. Yet although my judgement about the importance of the belief is one factor which determines whether it matters that I should investigate the relevant evidence, it is not the only factor. Another factor is my belief, to start with, about probabilities in the field. Granted that it is important that I should have a correct belief about whether my house is falling down, there is only point in my investigating the matter if there is, in my view, some significant non-zero probability that it is falling down and some significant non-zero probability that it is not. If it is virtually certain that it is not falling down . . . there is no point in investigating the matter; and the same holds if it is certain that it is falling down. I do not have to ring up the police to inquire if my daughter has been involved in a road accident if I have no reason to suspect that she has; and so on. I conclude that the importance of investigating is a function of both (a) the subject's beliefs about the importance of true belief in the field, and (b) the subject's beliefs before possible investigation that the issue is far from certain, that the probabilities to start with are not too close to 0 or 1. (a) and (b) of course interact. How close to 0 or 1 is relevant depends on how important is true belief.

Failure to investigate the truth of a proposition is however excusable in so far as (c) the subject believes strongly that no amount of investigation will make any difference to its probability on evidence, will have any effect on showing how likely it is to be true. An issue may be important and the subject have no belief about it, about which he is in any way confident, and yet it would not be irrational₃ of him not to investigate its truth, if he believed it highly probable that no amount of investigation would turn up any new relevant evidence (or show that any mistake had been made in inference). For example, it matters greatly that I shall have a true belief about whether or not a ship on which I am embarking voluntarily in time of war will be blown up by an enemy submarine. Statistics of past enemy successes suggest that there is a probability of 1 in 3 that the ship will be blown up. If, by making a few inquiries, I could discover more relevant evidence, then I should do so; and it would be irrational₃ for me not to. But if I have apparently no possible way of finding out anything further about enemy plans or intentions, there is no point in my trying to do so—I must just take my chance. Adequate investigation of a belief in the subject's view is a matter of his having investigated for such time as the importance of the belief and his initial view of its probability, in his view, requires—given that he does not believe it very probable that investigation will achieve nothing. Just how probable the latter belief has to be to excuse failure to investigate, will of course depend on the exact values, in the subject's view, of the other factors. For a belief about a matter which the subject holds to be of supreme importance, perhaps investigation ought always to be undertaken.

The value of investigation may however be outweighed by the value of doing alternative actions; a man may have a duty to act in some way on the belief in question or to do something unrelated. In that case a man is not culpable for not investigating. Important though it is to check whether my house is falling down, it is even more important to get my family out of it if my present belief is that a collapse is imminent. And important though it may be for the detective to check further on a murder accusation, he ought to postpone such checking if he alone is in a position to save a man from drowning. The value of investigation depends finally on (d)—the subject's beliefs about whether he has other important actions to do, e.g. overriding obligations to fulfil. So, in summary, the value of a subject investigating an issue depends on four beliefs of his: (a) about the importance of the issue, (b) about the closeness to 0 or 1 of the probability of his belief about the issue, (c) about the probability that investigation will achieve something, and (d) about whether he has other more important actions to do. A subject's beliefs are rational₃ if he has investigated them to the extent determined by these factors.

So, my belief that the distance from London to Edinburgh is 400 miles is rational₃ because I believe it to be of little importance whether I have a true belief about the matter. Whereas if I had to bet a considerable sum on the issue, the belief could not in general be rational₃ unless I had gone so far as to look up in an encyclopaedia how far it was. Yet if I believed that there were no encyclopaedias or other sources of information available or that I had no time to investigate because of really pressing rival obligation, then the belief would be rational₃ after all.

Rationality₃ is a matter of the subject's beliefs being backed by investigation which he believed to have been adequate. However, a man can have standards of what is the proper amount of investigation, standards evident in what he says and does on other occasions, judged by which the amount of investigation relevant to a given belief might be inadequate; and yet he might have failed to recognize this. The detective might not have noticed that his investigation of evidence relevant to a particular case was perfunctory, although by his normal standards it was so. Hence we get our fourth kind of rationality. A subject S who believes that p has a rational₄ belief if and only if S's evidence results from past investigation which was by S's own standards adequate, and his inductive standards have been subjected to criticism by S which is by S's own standards adequate, and S has checked

adequately by his own standards that p is made probable by his evidence.

Rationality₃ and rationality₄ are both a matter of whether the belief is backed by investigation adequate in some way by the subject's own outlook. Yet of course subjects may be totally blind to the need for investigation and criticism, and beliefs may be irrational because based on inadequate investigation, although the subject may have considered the investigation sufficient, and it may have been sufficient by his own standards. So we come to a fifth kind of rationality. S's belief that p is a rational₅ belief if and only if S's evidence results from past investigation which was adequate and inductive standards which have been submitted to adequate criticism, and S has investigated adequately whether his evidence makes his belief probable. The detective may have thought that his investigations were adequate, but they may not have been so. He may not have collected enough true representative relevant evidence of good quality. In that case his belief that the prisoner was guilty may be irrational in sense (5), even though it be rational in the other four senses. Again, the superstitious gambler may not have recognized the need to investigate his methods, but the need may exist all the same. In that case his beliefs are irrational in sense (5). It follows from earlier considerations that how much investigation is adequate depends on the importance of the belief at stake; whether it is virtually certain that it is true or virtually certain that it is false; whether or not there is some probability that investigation will achieve results; and whether the subject has other important actions to perform. It depends objectively on these facts—not on the subject's beliefs about them. The point of investigation is that it may give the subject beliefs which are not just fairly probable, but very probable.

It is only irrationality in sense (3) which is culpable irrationality, for it results from the subject neglecting investigative procedures which he recognizes that he ought to pursue. Irrationality in senses (4) and (5) are a matter of objective discrepancy between the subject's actual investigative procedures and either those which he normally recognizes or really adequate investigative procedures; but in so far as the subject does not recognize these discrepancies, no blame attaches to his conduct. Irrationality in sense (1) and (2) arises from a failure to recognize certain things at the time in question—discrepancies within the class of the subject's beliefs in the case of irrationality (1), and unjustified evidence and incorrect standards in the case of irrationality (2). But either you recognize the things in question at the time or you do not; either it strikes you or it does not. Recognizing is coming to believe; and if, as I have argued, belief is a passive matter, so too is recognition. No blame is attachable to you for things that happen to you, only for things that you do.

Men's Evidence for their Religious Beliefs

Having drawn attention to the different kinds of evidence which men have and the different inductive standards which they use to get their beliefs, and the kinds of rationality which are involved therein, I can now apply these general considerations to men's religious beliefs, inquiring what are the structures of men's religious beliefs and when are those beliefs rational. By a man's religious beliefs I understand, very roughly, his beliefs about transcendent reality, including his belief about whether or not there is a God, and his beliefs about what properties God has (what God is like), and what actions he has performed. However, for the sake of simplicity of exposition, I shall in this chapter consider only men's beliefs about whether or not there is a God.

Quite clearly, different men base their religious beliefs on very different kinds of evidence; pieces of evidence which one man treats as quite irrelevant, another man treats as quite crucial for his belief. Some of the evidence which men have, whether or not regarded as of importance, they share with all other men; other of the evidence which men have is available only to some men. To start with, there are apparently necessary truths of reason, in my terminology, prior beliefs, such as the premisses of some ontological argument,—e.g. 'God is a most perfect being'. The religious belief of the occasional philosopher who believes that an ontological argument works is based on such propositions; but the religious beliefs of few other men are grounded here.

Next, there are certain evident general features of the Universe, which all men can recognize but about the evidential force of which they dispute. These constitute initial beliefs in which all men have great confidence. For example, 'there exists a Universe', the starting-point of most versions of the cosmological argument. Or the propositions of experience which occur at the beginning of Aquinas's first three ways—e.g. 'some things in the world are certainly in process of change.'[1] The starting-points of teleological arguments too can be phrased as propositions which all men believe on grounds of experience—e.g. '(almost) all observed natural phenomena conform to scientific laws'. One evident phenomenon which in the past had, and perhaps still has, some importance for men's religious beliefs is the existence of life on earth; others are the existence of conscious beings, and the existence of beings capable of moral choice. All these propositions form grounds for many men's belief that there is a God, for they believe that the phenomena which the propositions report would not occur unless there were a God. Some men may believe that the phenomena in question make certain the existence of God (because the propositions reporting them, possibly together with certain prior propositions, entail the existence of God). Others believe that one or more of the phenomena render the belief that there is a God probable, because they need explaining, and the creative action of God provides such an explanation. Others believe that each of the phenomena adds to the probability that there is a God (confirms this proposition), and that, together with other phenomena yet to be mentioned, they make it probable overall.

The next influence on men's religion is what they are told about history. Many men's religious beliefs are to a lesser or greater extent rooted in beliefs about history, and these latter beliefs depend on initial beliefs as to what they have been told about history. Some of the things which we are told about history, we are told by more than one person (e.g. we read them in books apparently written by different people), and we are told that they are not the subject of serious dispute (or we are told them in such a tone that we infer this)—e.g. that the Christian Church grew in three hundred years from being a small group in Palestine to being the dominant religious group of the Roman Empire, or that all the books of the New Testament came into existence during this period. But many of the things which we are told are the subject of serious dispute and sometimes we may hear rival views about them from different sources; but perhaps more normally we may simply be told that there are views other than those of our source. In this category might come such claims as that St. Mark's Gospel was written before AD 70, that St. Paul's Epistle to the Galatians was written by St. Paul about AD 49, that Jesus lived on earth in the first thirty years AD and was then crucified, that there are diverse accounts of the Resurrection in the New Testament but all agree in the central facts of a physical resurrection. According to the society in which we are brought up, so we are given different pieces of information as indisputable-by-reasonable-men. In one society children may be told as beyond dispute that Jesus was raised physically from the dead, that Jesus was born of a Virgin, or that archaeology has discovered the site of the Garden of Eden. In a second society children may be told that these things are probably so (since serious experts have thus pronounced), although there are cultures where men doubt them. In a third society children may be told that these things are questionable.

On the basis of what they are told, using the testimony principle, men come to have different historical beliefs. These historical beliefs they then use as part of their evidence for belief in God. For example, they argue explicitly, or merely come to believe, that the Gospel records would not be as they are or the Church have had the success it did, unless Jesus had been raised physically. But only God could thus have violated nature; and hence there must be a God. Or they argue that Jesus could not have had his honest character and made the claims he did unless he were a special messenger of God. The pattern of argument here is again that certain things need explaining (certain particular historical facts, this time) and that only the existence and action of God can explain them. Hence they make probable his action.

But the source of the historical beliefs which form the jumping-off ground for these arguments to the best explanation is authority. Among historical beliefs which men come to hold as a result of what they are told, we should include not merely beliefs about matters central to a religious tradition, but beliefs about more local matter—e.g. a local miracle—which also form grounds for some men's beliefs that there is a God. Authority is also of course often a more direct source of religious beliefs. Children are told that there is a God . . . and, at any rate in certain societies and to start with, they believe what they are told, just because they are told it, even if they are also told that there are men who do not believe that there is a God. So either directly or indirectly (via historical claims) authority is a very powerful source of religious belief.

. . . [A]ll men have as a primary inductive principle the testimony principle that what you are told is probably so. Men learn to put various qualifications on the principle in the course of time: that certain men seek to deceive on certain matters; that only certain men are in a position to inform you on certain matters; that certain areas are the subject of such dispute among experts, that nothing can be taken on authority there, etc. But the principle must come first. Basically, men believe what they are told; and it is by assuming that what they are being told is true, that they have come to understand what they are being told. The qualifications are sometimes the result of personal experience: we find that certain particular acquaintances tell us things which by personal investigation we find to be false. Or we may develop for ourselves or at any rate find that our own experience bears out some theory about who is in a position to give us information about different kinds of matter. But more frequently authority itself provides our grounds for believing the qualifications. [. . .]

The evidence which I have listed so far is all evidence which tends to promote the belief that there is a God. Among evidence tending to promote the belief that there is no God there is again evidence varying from the public and certain to the private and not so certain (not so certain in the sense that the believer has less initial confidence in the basic propositions involved). There are prior beliefs that the concept of God contains various incoherences. There are initial beliefs, supported by testimony, of the existence of various kinds and degrees of evil; which men see as rendering improbable the existence of a good creator. There are prior beliefs that the concept of free will is incoherent; and initial beliefs of perceptions which are seen as evidence against human free will (e.g. a man sees the great influence of their environment on the actions of other men); and sometimes men are told on authority that man has no free will. The non-existence of free will is seen as counting against the existence of God for more than one reason, but especially because it would make the existence of evil even more of a difficulty for religion. Then again there is the enormous influence of authority—'Science has proved that everything that happens has a cause other than God', 'Science has proved that miracles do not

happen', 'We know now that the early Church invented a lot of what was written in the Gospels', or even 'Science has proved that there is no God.'

So much for the diversity of evidence about religion, which different men take into account. Each man is aware of some collection of such evidence, and this he assesses, and judges that it makes probable or improbable the existence of God. In so doing he uses certain inductive standards; for it is in virtue of the evidence having certain characteristics that he judges that it makes probable what it does. [. . .]

Rationality$_1$ and Rationality$_2$ of Religious Beliefs

A man's beliefs are rational$_1$ if and only if, given his evidence, they are rendered probable on his own inductive standards. A man's belief that p is irrational$_1$ when he has failed to draw the conclusion, using his general inductive beliefs, that his evidence does not make p probable. So when we see what a man's evidence and inductive standards are, we can conclude with respect to his religious beliefs that they do or do not follow from his evidence, in accordance with those standards.

Suppose, however, a study of a man's inductive behaviour leads us (even when we have taken account of the difficulties mentioned above) to conclude that he is using in all his judgements about religion different standards from those which he uses elsewhere. What then are we to conclude from this about his rationality$_1$? We could say either that none of his judgements about religion are rational$_1$ or that he has one set of inductive standards for arguing about mundane matters and another set for arguing about religious matters, and that there is nothing irrational$_1$ in this. I think that there are cases where it would be right to say the former, and cases where it would be right to say the latter. It would be right to say the latter, for example, if the man explicitly acknowledged the use of different standards, and was consistent in his use of them, and his arguments about religion were never infected by normal standards. He might for example claim that the only test of religious truth was what was written in the Bible, never attempt to justify this claim in ways which used other inductive standards (e.g. never claim that archaeology or prophecy *showed* that the Bible was true), and never use other standards in religious argument; then it would seem right to say that he just did have one set of standards for arguing about religion, and another for arguing about mundane matters; and so wrong to accuse him of being irrational$_1$. For there would be a coherence about his way of arguing, even if we did not like that way of arguing. On the other hand if the subject makes no explicit claim about what are his inductive standards, but simply seems to argue in a different way about religion, only not consistently so, then it seems right to say that his beliefs about religion are not rational$_1$.

A man's belief is rational$_2$ if and only if it is in fact rendered probable by his evidence, and his evidence consists of basic propositions which he is justified in holding with the degree of confidence with which he holds them. Before we can pass judgement on a man for holding beliefs which are irrational$_2$ we need to know what does make what probable, i.e. what are the true inductive standards. We saw earlier the general way in which we can argue to what are the true inductive standards by extrapolating from most of the particular judgements which we make and then seeing whether we are prepared to stick by any particular judgements which do not conform to the resulting standards. It may be that the inductive standards which we naturally extrapolate from our judgements about history, science, and ordinary life, and which we make sufficiently general to have application to the subject-matter of religion, yield different judgements in that field from those which we are initially inclined to make. Those standards might suggest that the existence of the Universe was

some evidence for the existence of God, whereas we judged to start with that it was not—or conversely. We must then just reflect which seems intuitively most obvious—our particular judgement in the religious field, or the general standards extrapolated from other fields. If we conclude that the particular judgement is most evident, then we must modify our account of the true inductive standards. Our account of them may then become more complex by being a conjunction of one set of standards for religious argument, and another set for other fields. Such a set of standards we may well call a split set. I do not believe that anyone who reflects very seriously on the matter is very likely to come down in favour of such a split rationality. For the concepts used for talk in religion, and in particular for talk about God, are concepts which have application in other fields—God, like humans, is said to be 'wise', 'good', 'powerful', etc., even if only analogically so; and so one would expect *somewhat* the same inductive standards for judging that some being is good, wise, or powerful in the two fields. And certainly any attempt to persuade others by rational means that religious claims are true or that they are false must involve inductive standards which the others share; and that means standards which they apply in other fields, for those are the fields in which our inductive judgements coincide with theirs.

This work of discovering the true inductive standards is of course a co-operative one—other people can suggest alternative sets of principles which an individual must test against his own intuitions; and men may argue about which set of principles is the most natural extrapolation from a given set of judgements. The story of such attempts to codify true inductive principles is the story of inductive logic, sometimes known as confirmation theory, and the work is not easy—as is evidenced by the continuing existence over the years of competing accounts in the field. But I see reason for hope that the task of codifying the inductive standards of at any rate civilized contemporary man is a completable one, and those are the inductive standards which are implicit in most of the judgements which we make and which intuitively seem to us to be correct.

The rationality$_2$ of a man's beliefs is not merely a matter of his using correct inductive standards but of his evidence consisting of basic propositions which he is justified in holding with the degree of confidence with which he holds them.

A man's evidence consists of prior propositions and initial propositions. He is justified in believing his evidence if he is justified in believing those propositions with the degree of confidence with which he does believe them. He is justified in believing prior propositions if they seem to him to be true, intuitively, on grounds of reason, and if he is not too hasty in making such a judgement. Thus if a man's religious belief is grounded in an ontological argument (as the religious belief of most men is not), the premises of that argument must be ones which seem evident to the believer and on which he has to some extent reflected to see if there is any possible way in which they could be false. (Men may disagree as to the amount of reflection necessary. We saw earlier how argument on the amount necessary can take place.) The same applies if a man's atheistic belief is grounded in a belief that in some way the concept of God is self-contradictory. If a man's beliefs are based on initial beliefs that someone has told him so-and-so or that he has seen so-and-so, his sensations together with his memories of past experiences have to justify the initial beliefs. He must be neither over- nor under-cautious by true standards in his response (in the light of his memories of his past experiences) to sensations. He must not 'jump to the conclusion' that he is seeing a UFO or a man walk on water, when he is not. Nor must he refuse to believe what stares him in the face. Now a man can only describe things as they seem to him at the time. But over the course of time he can investigate whether the judgements which he makes hesitantly almost always turn out to be correct, or whether those of which he is so confident almost always turn out false. By the success or failure of his judgements he can learn to react to sensations appropriately and can pass judgement on the justifiability of his past initial responses to sensations. Also at a given time, others can investigate what are the sensations (e.g. when he seemed to see a UFO) to which a man was exposed and pass their judgement on whether the report which he gives of his experiences is over- or under-cautious, in the light of what seems to them as a result of their own past experience, to be the right response to those sensations.

In so far as a man believes those basic propositions which his experience justifies him in believing, and comes to believe the further propositions which these warrant on true inductive standards, his beliefs are rational$_2$. Some men claim that their evidence makes it probable that there is a God, and some claim that their evidence makes it probable that there is no God. Which beliefs in this field are rational$_2$ is partly a matter of which basic propositions the believers are justified in believing. For some propositions such as 'there is a Universe' or 'there is evil', which are matters of public knowledge, there is no doubt that all men are justified in believing them. For other basic beliefs about what some agent has seen or been told, argument can take place about whether the agent has believed them with too much or too little confidence. The most controversial issue tends to be whether and by how much by true inductive standards any individual piece of evidence or all a man's evidence put together renders it probable that there is a God. I have discussed here the general principles for showing from what evidence a man ought to make his inductive inferences and what are the inductive standards which he ought to use in reasoning about the existence of God.

Rationality$_3$ of Religious Beliefs

Rationality$_3$, rationality$_4$, and rationality$_5$ are a mater of a belief being backed by adequate earlier investigation. A belief is rational$_3$, you will recall, if it is based on evidence resulting from investigation which was in the subject's view adequate and the subject has subjected his inductive standards to criticism which was in his view adequate, and checked in his view adequately that by them his belief was rendered probable by his evidence. We saw earlier that what constitutes adequate investigation depends on the subject's belief at earlier times about the probability of the hypothesis in question, his belief about the probability of investigation affecting the probability of the conclusion, his belief about the importance of holding a true belief about the hypothesis, and his belief about the importance of other actions which he could be doing. If in past times a man was absolutely certain about the truth of his religious beliefs, then there would have been no need for him to investigate their truth; and those beliefs would automatically be rational$_3$. If, however, he regarded them as dubious or only fairly probable, then, if his beliefs were to be rational$_3$, in so far as he believed the issue important, he ought to have pursued investigations—given that he did not believe that it was more important to do something else or that investigation would achieve nothing. For only if the man pursued investigations would there be any chance of his acquiring beliefs which were very probable.

How a man investigates an issue depends on what he already knows about the field and, in particular, as I stressed earlier, on his beliefs about who are the authorities in the field. To find out the truth about a point of astronomy, the four-year-old will ask his father; the ten-year-old his form teacher, the sixteen-year-old his physics teacher; but the man who already has a Ph.D. in the field will try to persuade some foundation to give him the money to buy equipment which will enable him to find the truth for himself, although, as I stressed earlier, he will need to take for granted results allegedly established by other physicists.

There are fields and cultures where a man has

no idea how to set about investigating further the answer to some question. I so interpret my definition of rationality$_3$ that in that case a man's belief, even though he does not believe that it has a probability close to 1 and even though he has done no investigating, is still rational$_3$. In one way the man does not believe that his investigation has been adequate—for there is more which he believes ought to be done; but in another way he does believe that the investigation has been adequate—for he has done all that he can. Since the definition of rationality$_3$ was designed to pick out the rationality which lies within a man's powers to achieve, I shall say that in such a case a man's beliefs are rational$_3$.

It may sometimes be like that with religion; a man may believe on balance that there is a God but have no idea how to pursue further inquiries. In that case the belief is rational$_3$. Yet the first step which will occur to most people, in this as in all fields, is to consult someone who, they have heard, is an expert. An inquirer may well pursue his inquiries by asking the local priest for the answers and taking them on authority. But in so far as he learns that the subject is a disputed one, it will normally occur to the investigator that he ought to cross-check what the priest says by consulting others. Then he will talk to atheists and gradually assemble the arguments which are supposed to be relevant in the field and begin to see how they stand up to objections.

The investigator will try to acquire more evidence than he had before [. . .] The scope for investigation is endless; one can always go on looking for more evidence and check and recheck the process of utilizing it to form beliefs. All we can do is pursue such inquiries as seem to us adequate within the time at our disposal. The need to pursue investigation is greater, the less the importance of doing other things. In so far as a man has devoted to such investigations the amount of time which he thought to be adequate, and has pursued them honestly, his resulting beliefs will be rational$_3$. If a man's belief that there is a God or that there is no God is rational$_3$, it is established on the basis of as much inquiry as the believer judged it adequate to give to it.

It is noteworthy that the more men seek to have rational$_3$ beliefs about religion (or anything else) and so the more investigation they undertake, the more likely their beliefs are to converge. For the process of investigation will involve a man in learning about the evidence accessible to others and becoming aware of the inductive standards of others and the criticisms which they make of his own standards. Clearly, the greater the sharing of evidence, the closer men will be to having a common basis of evidence whence to make their inference to religious truths. Exposure to each other's inductive standards and criticisms of their own is far more likely to bring them closer together than further apart in their standards. A man must be guided by the truth as he sees it, but the more men investigate the more likely it is that they will see things in the same way.

The rationality$_3$ of a belief is a matter of a man having devoted such time to investigating it as he himself thought adequate. But although a man may think that he has devoted enough time to such investigation, even by his own standards he may not have done. He may have devoted far less time to it than the importance which he believed the matter to have warranted by his normal standards of how much time you ought to devote to investigating things. While believing that religion was a very important matter, he may have devoted far more time to studying football. His resulting belief would then fail to be rational$_4$. For a rational$_4$ belief is one where the believer has by his own standards adequately investigated the evidence, his inductive standards, and the force by them of his evidence.

But whether or not he has followed his own standards, he may not have followed true standards. He may not have devoted the time to religious investigation which the importance of the subject demands. In that case his beliefs will not be rational$_5$. The next chapter will consider the objective factors which determine how much

investigation is needed to obtain rational$_5$ beliefs in the field of religion. This depends, we saw earlier, first, on the importance of having true beliefs in the field. We shall consider how important is true religious belief. Then the rationality$_5$ of men's belief depends on how probable the belief is to start with and how probable it is that investigation will achieve anything. We have already considered how the former issue is to be assessed in considering the rationality$_2$ of a man's religious beliefs. Whether there is a probability that investigation will achieve anything, will depend, as all epistemic probabilities do, on the evidence available to the investigator. But superficially, any subject which men discuss and on which books are written can be investigated, and religion is certainly among those subjects. However, there are arguments in vogue to show that religious inquiry is pointless and these I shall need to assess. Finally, since the rationality$_5$ of a belief depends on the importance of securing a true belief in comparison with other claims on a man's time, I shall need to allude to these. A completely general discussion would not be possible without discussing all a man's obligations, viz. the whole of morality. But there have been down the centuries certain arguments to the effect that men ought to cultivate beliefs identified in advance of investigation—that certain beliefs are desirable for reasons other than that they are likely to be true. These arguments are arguments against cultivating rational$_5$ beliefs at all, for they are arguments against investigating beliefs in a way adequate to secure true beliefs.

The Value of Rational Religious Belief

We have seen that the only kind of rationality in belief for which a man can be held to task is rationality$_3$. For that is the only kind of rationality which is under a man's control. While a man cannot, I argued, help having the beliefs which he has at a given time, he can be held to task for not doing something about his beliefs over a period. He can be held to task for not investigating an area to an extent which he considers adequate, to get more evidence and to see what his evidence shows.

Beliefs are rational$_3$ in so far as they are based on investigation which was, in the believer's view, adequate. If it matters that I have a rational$_3$ belief on some issue, it matters because ensuring that I do have a rational$_3$ belief is all that I can do towards ensuring that I have a rational$_5$ belief, that is, one which is in fact backed by adequate investigation. A belief is rational$_3$ if the believer believes it to be rational$_5$. Ensuring that I have a rational$_5$ belief is all that I can do towards ensuring that I have a true belief. For only by acquiring more evidence which is true, representative, and relevant, by checking my inductive standards and what they show (and not suppressing evidence or distorting inductive standards), can I turn my belief into one which really has a high degree of probability on all my evidence. And ensuring that I have a very probable belief is all that I can do towards ensuring that I have a true belief—for a very probable belief is one which is, very probably true. [. . .]

The Importance of True Belief

If it matters that we have true beliefs, we must seek, we have seen, rational$_5$ beliefs. We must now consider why in general it matters that we should hold true beliefs. [. . .]

The more important is something which I seek, the more important it is that I should have a true belief about how to get it. Hence (given that I am not absolutely certain how to get it or absolutely certain that investigation will not bring me nearer to an answer), the more important it is, if I am to be rational, that I should investigate and investigate for longer how that something is to be attained. If I seek a satisfying career, it is very important that I investigate various possibilities in some detail, so that I reach a well-justified belief about where that satisfaction is to be attained. By contrast, if I seek to relax for a few hours by reading a novel, it would be foolish to devote five hours to reading reviews of possible novels in order to come to a true belief about which will prove the most relaxing. If I have a duty to attain some end, I have a duty to ensure that I have a true belief about how it is to be attained; and the greater the duty to attain the end, clearly the greater the duty to acquire the true belief. If, as a parent, I am under a moral obligation to ensure that my children are happily and well educated, then (subject to the qualifications stated earlier) I am morally obliged to investigate possible schools so that I come to a well-justified belief that a certain school will provide happy and good education. Also if I have a duty to provide knowledge for others (e.g. for my children when they cannot obtain it for themselves), then I have a duty to acquire that knowledge in order to do so—and knowledge involves true belief. I may have such a duty either towards my children and others in my care for whom I have a general duty to provide, or towards those in special need for whom I alone can provide. When men are short of food, the man trained in agricultural biochemistry has some obligation to apply his talents to finding out how they can get more food out of the land. [. . .]

The holding of true beliefs, I have suggested so far, is of importance, moral or other, because beliefs tell us the means by which ends can be achieved. This does not however seem to be the only reason why the holding of true beliefs is important. The holding of true beliefs seems to be valuable in itself, not merely as a means to something else. For true belief is necessary for knowledge and knowledge is valuable in itself, and especially knowledge of things which concern the nature, origin, and purpose of our particular human community; and the nature, origin, and purpose of the Universe itself. Quite obviously, many men seek such knowledge for its own sake, and obviously the only way to attain the knowledge, if you do not already have it, is to investigate with diligence. We feel that individuals who seek such knowledge are doing something worthwhile and that it is a good that they should acquire the knowledge and communicate it to others. [. . .]

The Importance of True Religious Belief

Now let us apply these points about the importance of true, and so of rational₅, belief to religious belief. Which of men's purposes are such that true belief about religious matters will enable them to fulfil them? All men want long-term well-being and deep well-being: that is, they want to be for long in a supremely worthwhile situation doing actions of great value. Hence they need to have true beliefs about how such well-being is to be attained. They are confronted from their own experience with the fact that mundane pleasures, though temporarily satisfying, are not permanently and deeply so. They find from experience—and poets, novelists, and dramatists convince them—that not merely do food and drink, leisure and drugs fail to satisfy at the deepest level; but so do family life, careers in public service, belonging to a local community, having an absorbing hobby, and so on. Also, to all appearances, these pleasures last only the span of a human life—at most some seventy or eighty years. [. . .]

In this situation men hear the proclamation of different religions (in a wide sense of this term) which offer to those who follow their way a deep well-being which lasts for ever. So it is worthwhile investigating which, if any, of them is most likely to provide it. Among the religions which offer such well-being are theistic religions, such as the Christian religion, which claims that there is a God who will give to men a life after death in which those who have been following the religious way will have the Beatific Vision of God which alone will provide that deep and lasting well-being. Investigation into whether or not there is a God would not go all the way towards settling which, if any, religious way will provide lasting well-being, but it would go quite a bit of the way. For if there is a God, being omnipotent, he can provide such well-being and being perfectly good may well choose to do so. If we find it at all probable that there is a God, it becomes worth while investigating further whether he has revealed that such well-being will be provided for those who follow a certain religious way (e.g. the Christian way). On the other hand, if we find that there is no God, clearly the Christian way cannot provide well-being for there will then be no well-being provided by the means which it describes.

A man's reason for investigating which, if any, religious way will lead to deep and lasting well-being need be in no way self-centred. He may be concerned for the well-being of others and, anxious to give men information as to how to secure salvation, devote much time to finding the answer as well as he can.

Does a man have a moral *obligation* to find the way to his own true and lasting well-being? Only, I suggest, if his ability to discover such a way has been given to him and he has accepted this ability on the understanding that he will use it for this purpose. This however hardly applies. If there is a God, he has given men their talents, but he gave them those talents long before they were aware of what they had received and God's purposes in giving them. However, I suggest that some men have a moral obligation to find the way to true and lasting well-being for others. If they have particular talents in this direction (philosophical, psychological, or literary, together with sensitivity to religious claims), I suggest that they have such a prima-facie obligation. To use my earlier example: when men are short of food, the man trained in agricultural biochemistry has some obligation to apply his talents to finding out how they can get more food out of the land. A similar argument applies when men are short of spiritual food. Further, I suggest that anyone who has a responsibility for the upbringing of others has a duty to ensure, if he can, that they know the way to true and lasting well-being, and so has a duty himself to investigate how that is to be attained. This means primarily parents and to a lesser extent teachers;

and of course that means most of us. There is an obligation on most of us to investigate the truth of religion in order to teach our children about whether deep well-being can be obtained, and if so, how. Similarly, of course, if religion is false, the activity of prayer and worship is pointless and certain moral practices are also pointless. A parent's obligations to ensure the well-being of his children will lead him to deter them from such activities if they are pointless, and so there is an obligation on him to find out if they are. With true religious beliefs we will be able to fulfil our moral obligations in the way of educating our children, and from this too it follows that we have an obligation to cultivate rational beliefs about religion.

However, W. K. Clifford in his famous essay 'The Ethics of Belief'[2] seems to me to have carried this kind of argument rather too far. He argues that all our beliefs and the ways in which we acquire them influence others, and for that reason we have a duty to complete rationality in all matters. He writes that 'no man's belief . . . is a private matter which concerns himself alone' and that men who believe 'unproved and unquestioned statements' for their own 'solace and private pleasure' are a perverse influence. Where a man's influence is very obvious and the responsibility is clear, as with a parent towards his children, or a teacher towards his students, or a priest towards his parishioners, this is fair enough. But surely there is a sphere of private morality in which a man may choose what to do even if some others for whom he bears no responsibility who saw what he was doing *might* possibly be led astray thereby. And of course, outside the parent-child context, where rational adults are viewing a man's behaviour, the influence of his bad actions on them, *may* only be to lead them to avoid such actions in future. Clifford seems to have exaggerated a fundamentally good point.

A further reason why it matters to acquire true beliefs about religion, is that religious beliefs themselves have moral consequences. If there is a God and he has made and sustains the world and issued commands to men, men have moral obligations which they would not otherwise have. The grounds for this are as follows. Men ought to acknowledge other persons with whom they come into contact, not just ignore them—and this surely becomes a duty when those persons are our benefactors. We acknowledge people in various ways when we meet them, e.g. by shaking hands or smiling at them, and the way in which we acknowledge their presence reflects our recognition of the sort of individual they are and the kind of relation they have to us. Worship is the only response appropriate to God, the source of all being. Further, if God has given me particular instructions for the use of the Earth, then of course I have a duty to follow these—for if God made the Earth, it is his. (What greater title can one have to property than having created it *ex nihilo*?) And if God has given me instructions as to how to use my life and behave towards my fellows, then I have some duty to obey. A system of morality which recognized no duty of grateful recognition and conformity to the wishes of our benefactors is a pretty poor system of morality. Certainly there may be limits to such obligations; but if there are, if, for example, a command by God to me to murder would impose upon me no obligation to murder, then God being perfectly good would not issue such commands, for it would involve claiming a right which he did not possess. Finally, if God is the source of my being and I have failed to use aright the life which he has given me by rendering to him proper worship and obedience, I ought to seek forgiveness from God for having failed to fulfil my obligations. So, in summary, duties to worship and obey God and seek forgiveness from him are contingent moral duties which would follow, if there is a God, from primary moral duties—to acknowledge people, to please benefactors, and to conform to rules laid down by the owners of property which we use. That particular facts create particular obligations has been recognized in all systems of ethics—this would just be one case of that. Among man's duties is the duty to find out what his duties are. He must therefore find out whether the world is his to use as he pleases, or whether it belongs to someone else; whether he is indebted to anyone for his existence, to whom he owes acknowledgement and service. The duty to pursue religious inquiry is a particular case of the duty to check that we owe nothing to any man.

Finally, in considering the general issue of the importance of true belief, I drew attention to the importance of true belief in itself, as involved in knowledge, especially when it concerns the origin, nature, and purpose of our human community and of the Universe as a whole. If history and physics are of importance for this reason, religious knowledge is obviously of far greater importance. For what more central piece of knowledge could there be about the origin, nature, and purpose of man and the Universe, than whether they depend for their being on a God who made them, or whether the Universe, and all that is in it, and the laws of their operation, just are, dependent upon nothing? A true belief here, whether theistic or atheistic, is of enormous importance for our whole world-view. I suggested that men who had talents in this direction might have an obligation to pursue inquiries, particularly for the benefit of others. That other men should have a true belief about whether or not there is a God, is a good thing in itself; but I cannot see that they have any obligation to cultivate such a belief except in order to fulfil correctly the duties discussed earlier.

Further, not merely is the knowledge that there is a God or that there is no God itself of great value but, if there is a God, being omniscient, he will know all there is to be known about the origin, nature, and purpose of man and the Universe, and also about the worthwhile way for men to live. Some religions (including Christianity) claim that he has provided (e.g. in the Church) more detailed knowledge on these matters and a way of life by which men may grow in that knowledge. If we find that there is some probability that there is a God, then that makes it much more likely that knowledge is to be had in these ways, and so much more worthwhile investigating which, if any, creed or way provides such more detailed knowledge. [. . .]

For the various reasons outlined, it matters greatly that men should have true religious beliefs, and for some of these reasons there is a prima-facie obligation on men to seek such beliefs. It will readily be seen that what goes for the simple belief that there is a God, goes also for beliefs that God has certain properties and that he has done certain actions. Indeed, the belief that there is a God only carries very much in the way of consequence for action about how to seek deep and lasting well-being, or how to worship, or whatever, given further beliefs—e.g. that if there is a God, he wishes to be worshipped in such and such a way, or is to be worshipped for having done such and such actions.

It follows that if a man's beliefs in this field are to be rational$_5$, they will need to be backed up by a significant amount of investigation—unless the man starts with beliefs which are well-nigh certain on his evidence, or it is very probable that investigation in this field will achieve nothing, or he has more important things to do. Some men of course may not realize this. To some men of religious pursuasion it will never even occur that they ought to check up on their beliefs on these important matters. In that case they have rational$_3$ beliefs for they have pursued such investigation as seemed to them adequate—viz. none at all. Nevertheless, I have argued, objectively it is of great importance that men do check up on these beliefs. [. . .]

Notes

1 St. Thomas Aquinas, *Summa Theologiae*, 1a, 2. 3.
2 In his *Essays and Lectures* (1879).

Chapter 5

John Hick

RELIGIOUS PLURALISM AND SALVATION

Let us approach the problems of religious pluralism through the claims of the different traditions to offer salvation—generically, the transformation of human existence from self-centeredness to Reality-centeredness. This approach leads to a recognition of the great world faiths as spheres of salvation; and so far as we can tell, more or less equally so. Their different truth-claims express (a) their differing perceptions, through different religio-cultural "lenses," of the one ultimate divine Reality; (b) their different answers to the boundary questions of origin and destiny, true answers to which are however not necessary for salvation, and (c) their different historical memories.

I

The fact that there is a plurality of religious traditions, each with its own distinctive beliefs, spiritual practices, ethical outlook, art forms, and cultural ethos, creates an obvious problem for those of us who see them, not simply as human phenomena, but as responses to the Divine. For each presents itself, implicitly or explicitly, as in some important sense absolute and unsurpassable and as rightly claiming a total allegiance. The problem of the relationship between these different streams of religious life has often been posed in terms of their divergent belief-systems. For whilst there are various overlaps between their teachings there are also radical differences: is the divine reality (let us refer to it as the Real) personal or non-personal; if personal, is it unitary or triune; is the universe created, or emanated, or itself eternal; do we live only once on this earth or are we repeatedly reborn? and so on and so on. When the problem of understanding religious plurality is approached through these rival truth-claims it appears particularly intractable.

I want to suggest, however, that it may more profitably be approached from a different direction, in terms of the claims of the various traditions to provide, or to be effective contexts of, salvation. "Salvation" is primarily a Christian term, though I shall use it here to include its functional analogues in the other major world traditions. In this broader sense we can say that both Christianity and these other faiths are paths of salvation. For whereas pre-axial religion was (and is) centrally concerned to keep life going on an even keel, the post-axial traditions, originating or rooted in the "axial age" of the first millenium B.C.E.—principally Hinduism, Judaism, Buddhism, Christianity, Islam—are centrally concerned with a radical transformation of the human situation.

It is of course possible, in an alternative approach, to define salvation in such a way that it becomes a necessary truth that only one particular tradition can provide it. If, for example, from within Christianity we define salvation as being forgiven by God because of Jesus' atoning death, and so becoming part of God's redeemed community, the church, then salvation is by definition Christian salvation. If on the other hand, from within Mahayana Buddhism, we define it as the attainment of *satori* or awakening, and so becoming an ego-free manifestation of the eternal Dharmakaya, then salvation is by definition Buddhist liberation. And so on. But if we stand back from these different conceptions to compare them, we can, I think, very naturally and properly see them as different forms of the more fundamental conception of a radical change from a profoundly unsatisfactory state to one that is limitlessly better because rightly related to the Real. Each tradition conceptualizes in its own way the wrongness of ordinary human existence—as a state of fallenness from paradisal virtue and happiness, or as a condition of moral weakness and alienation from God, or as the fragmentation of the infinite One into false individualities, or as a self-centeredness which pervasively poisons our involvement in the world process, making it to us an experience of anxious, unhappy unfulfillment. But each at the same time proclaims a limitlessly better possibility, again conceptualized in different ways—as the joy of conforming one's life to God's law; as giving oneself to God in Christ, so that "it is no longer I who live, but Christ who lives in me" (Galatians 2:20), leading to eternal life in God's presence; as a complete surrender (*islam*) to God, and hence peace with God, leading to the bliss of paradise; as transcending the ego and realizing oneness with the limitless being-consciousness-bliss (*satchitananda*) of Brahman; as overcoming the ego point of view and entering into the serene selflessness of nirvana. I suggest that these different conceptions of salvation are specifications of what, in a generic formula, is the transformation of human existence from self-centeredness to a new orientation, centered in the divine Reality. And in each case the good news that is proclaimed is that this limitlessly

better possibility is actually available and can be entered upon, or begin to be entered upon, here and now. Each tradition sets forth the way to attain this great good: faithfulness to the Torah, discipleship to Jesus, obedient living out of the Qur'anic way of life, the Eightfold Path of the Buddhist dharma, or the three great Hindu *margas* of mystical insight, activity in the world, and self-giving devotion to God.

II

The great world religions, then, are ways of salvation. Each claims to constitute an effective context within which the transformation of human existence can and does take place from self-centeredness to Reality-centeredness. How are we to judge such claims? We cannot directly observe the inner spiritual quality of a human relationship to the Real; but we can observe how that relationship, as one's deepest and most pervasive orientation, affects the moral and spiritual quality of a human personality and of a man's or woman's relationship to others. It would seem, then, that we can only assess these salvation-projects insofar as we are able to observe their fruits in human life. The inquiry has to be, in a broad sense, empirical. For the issue is one of fact, even though hard to define and difficult to measure fact, rather than being settleable by *a priori* stipulation.

The word "spiritual" which occurs above is notoriously vague; but I am using it to refer to a quality or, better, an orientation which we can discern in those individuals whom we call saints—a Christian term which I use here to cover such analogues as arahat, bodhisattva, jivanmukti, mahatma. In these cases the human self is variously described as becoming part of the life of God, being "to the Eternal Goodness what his own hand is to a man"; or being permeated from within by the infinite reality of Brahman; or becoming one with the eternal Buddha nature. There is a change in their deepest orientation from centeredness in the ego to a new centering in the Real as manifested in their own tradition. One is conscious in the presence of such a person that he or she is, to a startling extent, open to the transcendent, so as to be largely free from self-centered concerns and anxieties and empowered to live as an instrument of God/Truth/Reality.

It is to be noted that there are two main patterns of such a transformation. There are saints who withdraw from the world into prayer or meditation and saints who seek to change the world—in the medieval period a contemplative Julian of Norwich and a political Joan of Arc, or in our own century a mystical Sri Aurobindo and a political Mahatma Gandhi. In our present age of sociological consciousness, when we are aware that our inherited political and economic structures can be analyzed and purposefully changed, saintliness is more likely than in earlier times to take social and political forms. But, of whichever type, the saints are not a different species from the rest of us; they are simply much more advanced in the salvific transformation.

The ethical aspect of this salvific transformation consists in observable modes of behavior. But how do we identify the kind of behavior which, to the degree that it characterizes a life, reflects a corresponding degree of reorientation to the divine Reality? Should we use Christian ethical criteria, or Buddhist, or Muslim . . .? The answer, I suggest, is that at the level of their most basic moral insights the great traditions use a common criterion. For they agree in giving a central and normative role to the unselfish regard for others that we call love or compassion. This is commonly expressed in the principle of valuing others as we value ourselves, and treating them accordingly. Thus in the ancient Hindu *Mahabharata* we read that "One should never do to another that which one would regard as injurious to oneself. This, in brief, is the rule of Righteousness" (*Anushana parva*, 113:7). Again, "He who . . . benefits persons of all orders, who is always devoted to the good of all beings, who does not feel aversion to anybody . . . succeeds in

ascending to Heaven" (*Anushana parva*, 145:24). In the Buddhist *Sutta Nipata* we read, "As a mother cares for her son, all her days, so towards all living things a man's mind should be all-embracing" (149). In the Jain scriptures we are told that one should go about "treating all creatures in the world as he himself would be treated" (*Kitanga Sutra*, I.ii.33). Confucius, expounding humaneness (*jen*), said, "Do not do to others what you would not like yourself" (*Analects*, xxi, 2). In a Taoist scripture we read that the good man will "regard [others'] gains as if they were his own, and their losses in the same way" (*Thai Shang*, 3). The Zoroastrian scriptures declare, "That nature only is good when it shall not do unto another whatever is not good for its own self" (*Dadistan-i-dinik*, 94:5). We are all familiar with Jesus' teaching, "As ye would that men should do to you, do ye also to them likewise" (Luke 6:31). In the Jewish Talmud we read "What is hateful to yourself do not do to your fellow man. That is the whole of the Torah" (*Babylonian Talmud*, Shabbath 31a). And in the Hadith of Islam we read Muhammad's words, "No man is a true believer unless he desires for his brother that which he desires for himself" (*Ibn Madja*, Intro. 9). Clearly, if everyone acted on this basic principle, taught by all the major faiths, there would be no injustice, no avoidable suffering, and the human family would everywhere live in peace.

When we turn from this general principle of love/compassion to the actual behavior of people within the different traditions, wondering to what extent they live in this way, we realize how little research has been done on so important a question. We do not have much more to go on than general impressions, supplemented by travellers tales and anecdotal reports. We observe among our neighbors within our own community a great deal of practical loving-kindness; and we are told, for example, that a remarkable degree of self-giving love is to be found among the Hindu fishing families in the mud huts along the Madras shore;

and we hear various other similar accounts from other lands. We read biographies, social histories, and novels of Muslim village life in Africa, Buddhist life in Thailand, Hindu life in India, Jewish life in New York, as well as Christian life around the world, both in the past and today, and we get the impression that the personal virtues (as well as vices) are basically much the same within these very different religio-cultural settings and that in all of them unselfish concern for others occurs and is highly valued. And, needless to say, as well as love and compassion we also see all-too-abundantly, and apparently spread more or less equally in every society, cruelty, greed, hatred, selfishness, and malice.

All this constitutes a haphazard and impressionistic body of data. Indeed I want to stress, not how easy it is, but on the contrary how difficult it is, to make responsible judgments in this area. For not only do we lack full information, but the fragmentary information that we have has to be interpreted in the light of the varying natural conditions of human life in different periods of history and in different economic and political circumstances. And I suggest that all that we can presently arrive at is the cautious and negative conclusion that we have no good reason to believe that any one of the great religious traditions has proved itself to be more productive of love/compassion than another.

The same is true when we turn to the large-scale social outworkings of the different salvation-projects. Here the units are not individual human lives, spanning a period of decades, but religious cultures spanning many centuries. For we can no more judge a civilization than a human life by confining our attention to a single temporal cross-section. Each of the great streams of religious life has had its times of flourishing and its times of deterioration. Each has produced its own distinctive kinds of good and its own distinctive kinds of evil. But to assess either the goods or the evils cross-culturally is difficult to say the least. How do we weigh, for example, the

lack of economic progress, and consequent widespread poverty, in traditional Hindu and Buddhist cultures against the endemic violence and racism of Christian civilization, culminating in the twentieth century Holocaust? How do we weigh what the west regards as the hollowness of arranged marriages against what the east regards as the hollowness of a marriage system that leads to such a high proportion of divorces and broken families? From within each culture one can see clearly enough the defects of the others. But an objective ethical comparison of such vast and complex totalities is at present an unattainable ideal. And the result is that we are not in a position to claim an over-all moral superiority for any one of the great living religious traditions.

Let us now see where we have arrived. I have suggested that if we identify the central claim of each of the great religious traditions as the claim to provide, or to be an effective context of, salvation; and if we see salvation as an actual change in human beings from self-centeredness to a new orientation centered in the ultimate divine Reality; and if this new orientation has both a more elusive "spiritual" character and a more readily observable moral aspect—then we arrive at the modest and largely negative conclusion that, so far as we can tell, no one of the great world religions is salvifically superior to the rest.

III

If this is so, what are we to make of the often contradictory doctrines of the different traditions? In order to make progress at this point, we must distinguish various kinds and levels of doctrinal conflict.

There are, first, conceptions of the ultimate as Jahweh, or the Holy Trinity, or Allah, or Shiva, or Vishnu, or as Brahman, or the Dharmakaya, the Tao, and so on.

If salvation is taking place, and taking place to about the same extent, within the religious systems presided over by these various deities and absolutes, this suggests that they are different manifestations to humanity of a yet more ultimate ground of all salvific transformation. Let us then consider the possibility that an infinite transcendent divine reality is being differently conceived, and therefore differently experienced, and therefore differently responded to from within our different religio-cultural ways of being human. This hypothesis makes sense of the fact that the salvific transformation seems to have been occurring in all the great traditions. Such a conception is, further, readily open to philosophical support. For we are familiar today with the ways in which human experience is partly formed by the conceptual and linguistic frameworks within which it occurs. The basic-ally Kantian insight that the mind is active in perception, and that we are always aware of our environment as it appears to a consciousness operating with our particular conceptual resources and habits, has been amply confirmed by work in cognitive psychology and the sociology of knowledge and can now be extended with some confidence to the analysis of religious awareness. If, then, we proceed inductively from the phenomenon of religious experience around the world, adopting a religious as distinguished from a naturalistic interpretation of it, we are likely to find ourselves making two moves. The first is to postulate an ultimate transcendent divine reality (which I have been referring to as the Real) which, being beyond the scope of our human concepts, cannot be directly experienced by us as it is in itself but only as it appears through our various human thought-forms. And the second is to identify the thought-and-experienced deities and absolutes as different manifestations of the Real within different historical forms of human consciousness. In Kantian terms, the divine noumenon, the Real *an sich*, is experienced through different human receptivities as a range of divine phenomena, in the formation of which religious concepts have played an essential part.

These different "receptivities" consist of conceptual schemas within which various personal, communal, and historical factors have produced yet further variations. The most basic concepts in terms of which the Real is humanly thought-and-experienced are those of (personal) deity and of the (non-personal) absolute. But the Real is not actually experienced either as deity in general or as the absolute in general. Each basic concept becomes (in Kantian terminology) schematized in more concrete form. It is at this point that individual and cultural factors enter the process. The religious tradition of which we are a part, with its history and ethos and its great exemplars, its scriptures feeding our thoughts and emotions, and perhaps above all its devotional or meditative practices, constitutes an uniquely shaped and coloured "lens" through which we are concretely aware of the Real specifically as the personal Adonai, or as the Heavenly Father, or as Allah, or Vishnu, or Shiva . . . or again as the non-personal Brahman, or Dharmakaya, or the Void or the Ground. . . . Thus, one who uses the forms of Christian prayer and sacrament is thereby led to experience the Real as the divine Thou, whereas one who practices advaitic yoga or Buddhist zazen is thereby brought to experience the Real as the infinite being-consciousness-bliss of Brahman, or as the limitless emptiness of *sunyata* which is at the same time the infinite fullness of immediate reality as "wondrous being."

Three explanatory comments at this point before turning to the next level of doctrinal disagreement. First, to suppose that the experienced deities and absolutes which are the intentional objects of worship or content of religious meditation, are appearances or manifestations of the Real, rather than each being itself the Real *an sich*, is not to suppose that they are illusions—any more than the varying ways in which a mountain may appear to a plurality of differently placed observers are illusory. That the same reality may be variously experienced and described is true even of physical objects. But in the case of the infinite, transcendent divine reality there may well be much greater scope for the use of varying human conceptual schemas producing varying modes of phenomenal experience. Whereas the concepts in terms of which we are aware of mountains and rivers and houses are largely (though by no means entirely) standard throughout the human race, the religious concepts in terms of which we become aware of the Real have developed in widely different ways within the different cultures of the earth.

As a second comment, to say that the Real is beyond the range of our human concepts is not intended to mean that it is beyond the scope of purely formal, logically generated concepts—such as the concept of being beyond the range of (other than purely formal) concepts. We would not be able to refer at all to that which cannot be conceptualized in any way, not even by the concept of being unconceptualizable! But the other than purely formal concepts by which our experience is structured must be presumed not to apply to its noumenal ground. The characteristics mapped in thought and language are those that are constitutive of human experience. We have no warrant to apply them to the noumenal ground of the phenomenal, i.e., experienced, realm. We should therefore not think of the Real *an sich* as singular or plural, substance or process, personal or non-personal, good or bad, purposive or non-purposive. This has long been a basic theme of religious thought. For example, within Christianity, Gregory of Nyssa declared that:

The simplicity of the True Faith assumes God to be that which He is, namely, incapable of being grasped by any term, or any idea, or any other device of our apprehension, remaining beyond the reach not only of the human but of the angelic and all supramundane intelligence, unthinkable, unutterable, above all expression in words, having but one name that can represent His proper nature, the single name being "Above Every Name" (*Against Eunomius*, I, 42).

Augustine, continuing this tradition, said that "God transcends even the mind" (*True Religion*, 36:67), and Aquinas that "by its immensity, the divine substance surpasses every form that our intellect reaches" (*Contra Gentiles*, I, 14, 3). In Islam the Qur'an affirms that God is "beyond what they describe" (6:101). The Upanishads declare of Brahman, "There the eye goes not, speech goes not, nor the mind" (*Kena Up.*, 1, 3), and Shankara wrote that Brahman is that "before which words recoil, and to which no understanding has ever attained" (Otto, *Mysticism East and West*, E. T. 1932, p. 28).

But, third, we might well ask, why postulate an ineffable and unobservable divine-reality-in-itself? If we can say virtually nothing about it, why affirm its existence? The answer is that the reality or non-reality of the postulated noumenal ground of the experienced religious phenomena constitutes the difference between a religious and a naturalistic interpretation of religion. If there is no such transcendent ground, the various forms of religious experience have to be categorized as purely human projections. If on the other hand there is such a transcendent ground, then these phenomena may be joint products of the universal presence of the Real and of the varying sets of concepts and images that have crystallized within the religious traditions of the earth. To affirm the transcendent is thus to affirm that religious experience is not solely a construction of the human imagination but is a response—though always culturally conditioned—to the Real.

Those doctrinal conflicts, then, that embody different conceptions of the ultimate arise, according to the hypothesis I am presenting, from the variations between different sets of human conceptual schema and spiritual practice. And it seems that each of these varying ways of thinking-and-experiencing the Real has been able to mediate its transforming presence to human life. For the different major concepts of the ultimate do not seem—so far as we can tell—to result in one religious totality being soteriologically more effective than another.

IV

The second level of doctrinal difference consists of metaphysical beliefs which cohere with although they are not exclusively linked to a particular conception of the ultimate. These are beliefs about the relation of the material universe to the Real: creation *ex nihilo*, emanation, an eternal universe, an unknown form of dependency . . .? And about human destiny: reincarnation or a single life, eternal identity or transcendence of the self . . .? Again, there are questions about the existence of heavens and hells and purgatories and angels and devils and many other subsidiary states and entities. Out of this mass of disputed religious issues let me pick two major examples: is the universe created *ex nihilo*, and do human beings reincarnate?

I suggest that we would do well to apply to such questions a principle that was taught by the Buddha two and a half millennia ago. He listed a series of "undetermined questions" (*avyakata*)— whether the universe is eternal, whether it is spatially infinite, whether (putting it in modern terms) mind and brain are identical, and what the state is of a completed project of human existence (a Tathagata) after bodily death. He refused to answer these questions, saying that we do not need to have knowledge of these things in order to attain liberation or awakening (nirvana); and indeed that to regard such information as soteriologically essential would only divert us from the single-minded quest for liberation. I think that we can at this point profitably learn from the Buddha, even extending his conception of the undetermined questions further than he did—for together with almost everyone else in his own culture he regarded one of our examples, reincarnation, as a matter of assured knowledge. Let us, then, accept that we do not

know whether, e.g., the universe was created *ex nihilo*, nor whether human beings are reincarnated; and, further, that it is not necessary for salvation to hold a correct opinion on either matter.

I am not suggesting that such issues are unimportant. On their own level they are extremely important, being both of great interest to us and also having widely ramifying implications within our belief-systems and hence for our lives. The thought of being created out of nothing can nourish a salutary sense of absolute dependence. (But other conceptions can also nurture that sense.) The idea of reincarnation can offer the hope of future spiritual progress; though, combined with the principle of karma, it can also serve to validate the present inequalities of human circumstances. (But other eschatologies also have their problems, both theoretical and practical). Thus these—and other—disputed issues do have a genuine importance. Further, it is possible that some of them may one day be settled by empirical evidence. It might become established, for example, that the "big bang" of some fifteen billion years ago was an absolute beginning, thus ruling out the possibility that the universe is eternal. And again, it might become established, by an accumulation of evidence, that reincarnation does indeed occur in either some or all cases. On the other hand it is possible that we shall never achieve agreed knowledge in these areas. Certainly, at the present time, whilst we have theories, preferences, hunches, inherited convictions, we cannot honestly claim to have secure knowledge. And the same is true, I suggest, of the entire range of metaphysical issues about which the religions dispute. They are of intense interest, properly the subject of continuing research and discussion, but are not matters concerning which absolute dogmas are appropriate. Still less is it appropriate to maintain that salvation depends upon accepting some one particular opinion or dogma. We have seen that the transformation of human existence from self-centeredness to Reality-centeredness seems to be taking place within each of the great traditions despite their very different answers to these debated questions. It follows that a correct opinion concerning them is not required for salvation.

V

The third level of doctrinal disagreement concerns historical questions. Each of the great traditions includes a larger or smaller body of historical beliefs. In the case of Judaism these include at least the main features of the history described in the Hebrew scriptures; in the case of Christianity, these plus the main features of the life, death, and resurrection of Jesus as described in the New Testament; in the case of Islam, the main features of the history described in the Qur'an; in the case of Vaishnavite Hinduism, the historicity of Krishna; in the case of Buddhism, the historicity of Guatama and his enlightenment at Bodh Gaya; and so on. But although each tradition thus has its own records of the past, there are rather few instances of direct disagreement between these. For the strands of history that are cherished in these different historical memories do not generally overlap; and where they do overlap they do not generally involve significant differences. The overlaps are mainly within the thread of ancient Near Eastern history that is common to the Jewish, Christian, and Muslim scriptures; and within this I can only locate two points of direct disagreement—the Torah's statement that Abraham nearly sacrificed his son Isaac at Mount Moriah (Genesis 22) versus the Muslim interpretation of the Qur'anic version (in Sura 37) that it was his other son Ishmael; and the New Testament witness that Jesus died on the cross versus the Qur'anic teaching that "they did not slay him, neither crucified him, only a likeness of that was shown them" (Sura 4:156). (This latter however would seem to be a conflict between an historical report, in the New Testament, and a theological infer-

ence—that God would not allow so great a prophet to be killed—in the Qur'an.)

All that one can say in general about such disagreements, whether between two traditions or between any one of them and the secular historians, is that they could only properly be settled by the weight of historical evidence. However, the events in question are usually so remote in time, and the evidence so slight or so uncertain, that the question cannot be definitively settled. We have to be content with different communal memories, enriched as they are by the mythic halo that surrounds all long-lived human memories of events of transcendent significance. Once again, then, I suggest that differences of historical judgment, although having their own proper importance, do not prevent the different traditions from being effective, and so far as we can tell equally effective, contexts of salvation. It is evidently not necessary for salvation to have correct historical information. (It is likewise not necessary for salvation, we may add, to have correct scientific information.)

VI

Putting all this together, the picture that I am suggesting can be outlined as follows: our human religious experience, variously shaped as it is by our sets of religious concepts, is a cognitive response to the universal presence of the ultimate divine Reality that, in itself, exceeds human conceptuality. This Reality is however manifested to us in ways formed by a variety of human concepts, as the range of divine personae and metaphysical impersonae witnessed to in the history of religions. Each major tradition, built around its own distinctive way of thinking-and-experiencing the Real, has developed its own answers to the perennial questions of our origin and destiny, constituting more or less comprehensive and coherent cosmologies and eschatologies. These are human creations which have, by their association with living streams of religious experience, become invested with a sacred authority. However they cannot all be wholly true; quite possibly none is wholly true; perhaps all are partly true. But since the salvific process has been going on through the centuries despite this unknown distribution of truth and falsity in our cosmologies and eschatologies, it follows that it is not necessary for salvation to adopt any one of them. We would therefore do well to learn to tolerate unresolved, and at present unresolvable, differences concerning these ultimate mysteries.

One element, however, to be found in the belief-systems of most of the traditions raises a special problem, namely that which asserts the sole salvific efficacy of that tradition. I shall discuss this problem in terms of Christianity because it is particularly acute for those of us who are Christians. We are all familiar with such New Testament texts as "There is salvation in no one else [than Jesus Christ], for there is no other name under heaven given among men by which we must be saved" (Acts 4:12), and with the Catholic dogma *Extra ecclesiam nulla salus* (No salvation outside the church) and its Protestant equivalent—never formulated as an official dogma but nevertheless implicit within the eighteenth and nineteenth century Protestant missionary expansion—no salvation outside Christianity. Such a dogma differs from other elements of Christian belief in that it is not only a statement about the potential relationship of Christians to God but at the same time about the actual relationship of non-Christians to God. It says that the latter, in virtue of being non-Christians, lack salvation. Clearly such a dogma is incompatible with the insight that the salvific transformation of human existence is going on, and so far as we can tell going on to a more or less equal extent, within all the great traditions. Insofar, then, as we accept that salvation is not confined to Christianity we must reject the old exclusivist dogma.

This has in fact now been done by most thinking Christians, though exceptions remain, mostly within the extreme Protestant funda-mentalist constituencies. The *Extra ecclesiam* dogma, although not explicitly repealed, has been outflanked by the work of such influential Catholic theologians as Karl Rahner, whose new approach was in effect endorsed by Vatican II. Rahner expressed his more inclusivist outlook by suggesting that devout people of other faiths are "anonymous Christians," within the invisible church even without knowing it, and thus within the sphere of salvation. The present Pope, in his Encyclical *Redemptor Hominis* (1979), has expressed this thought even more comprehensively by saying that "every man without exception has been redeemed by Christ" and "with every man without any exception whatever Christ is in a way united, even when man is unaware of it" (para. 14). And a number of Protestant theologians have advocated a comparable position.

The feature that particularly commends this kind of inclusivism to many Christians today is that it recognizes the spiritual values of other religions, and the occurrence of salvation within them, and yet at the same time preserves their conviction of the ultimate superiority of their own religion over all others. For it maintains that salvation, wherever it occurs, is Christian salvation; and Christians are accordingly those who alone know and preach the source of salvation, namely in the atoning death of Christ.

This again, like the old exclusivism, is a statement not only about the ground of salvation for Christians but also for Jews, Muslims, Hindus, Buddhists, and everyone else. But we have seen that it has to be acknowledged that the immediate ground of their transformation is the particular spiritual path along which they move. It is by living in accordance with the Torah or with the Qur'anic revelation that Jews and Muslims find a transforming peace with God; it is by one or other of their great *margas* that Hindus attain to *moksha*; it is by the Eightfold Path that Theravada Buddhists come to *nirvana*; it is by *zazen* that Zen Buddhists attain to *satori*; and so on. The Christian inclusivist is, then, by implication, declaring that these various spiritual paths are efficacious, and constitute authentic contexts of salvation, because Jesus died on the cross; and, by further implication, that if he had not died on the cross they would not be efficacious.

This is a novel and somewhat astonishing doctrine. How are we to make sense of the idea that the salvific power of the dharma taught five hundred years earlier by the Buddha is a consequence of the death of Jesus in approximately 30 C.E.? Such an apparently bizarre conception should only be affirmed for some very good reason. It was certainly not taught by Jesus or his apostles. It has emerged only in the thought of twentieth century Christians who have come to recognize that Jews are being salvifically transformed through the spirituality of Judaism, Muslims through that of Islam, Hindus and Buddhists through the paths mapped out by their respective traditions, and so on, but who nevertheless wish to retain their inherited sense of the unique superiority of Christianity. The only outlet left for this sense, when one has acknowledged the salvific efficacy of the various great spiritual ways, is the arbitrary and contrived notion of their metaphysical dependency upon the death of Christ. But the theologian who undertakes to spell out this invisible causality is not to be envied. The problem is not one of logical possibility—it only requires logical agility to cope with that—but one of religious or spiritual plausibility. It would be a better use of theological time and energy, in my opinion, to develop forms of trinitarian, christological, and

soteriological doctrine which are compatible with our awareness of the independent salvific authenticity of the other great world faiths. Such forms are already available in principle in conceptions of the Trinity, not as ontologically three but as three ways in which the one God is humanly thought and experienced; conceptions of Christ as a man so fully open to and inspired by God as to be, in the ancient Hebrew metaphor, a "son of God"; and conceptions of salvation as an actual human transformation which has been powerfully elicited and shaped, among his disciples, by the influence of Jesus.

There may indeed well be a variety of ways in which Christian thought can develop in response to our acute late twentieth century awareness of the other world religions, as there were of responding to the nineteenth century awareness of the evolution of the forms of life and the historical character of the holy scriptures. And likewise there will no doubt be a variety of ways in which each of the other great traditions can rethink its inherited assumption of its own unique superiority. But it is not for us to tell people of other traditions how to do their own business. Rather, we should attend to our own.

Note

This paper was originally delivered as the second Kegley Lecture at California State University, Bakersfield, on February 10th, 1988. For a fuller account of its proposals the reader is invited to see my *An Interpretation of Religion* (New Haven: Yale University Press and London: Macmillan, 1989).

Chapter 6

Keith Ward

TRUTH AND THE DIVERSITY OF RELIGIONS

I will be concerned with only one problem about truth which is raised by the diversity of religions which exist in the world. The problem is this: many religions claim to state truths about the nature of the universe and human destiny which are important or even necessary for human salvation and ultimate well-being. Many of these truths seem to be incompatible; yet there is no agreed method for deciding which are to be accepted; and equally intelligent, informed, virtuous and holy people belong to different faiths. It seems, therefore, that a believing member of any one tradition is compelled to regard all other traditions as holding false beliefs and therefore as not leading to salvation. Since each faith forms a minority of the world's population, all religious believers thus seem committed to saying that most intelligent, virtuous and spiritually devoted people cannot know the truth or attain salvation. This is a problem, because it is in tension with the belief, held by many traditions, that the supremely real being is concerned for the salvation of all rational creatures. How can this be so if, through no fault of their own, most creatures cannot come to know the truth and thereby attain salvation?

Among those who have seen this as a problem and have proposed a philosophical defence of one solution to it, John Hick must take a foremost place. His book, *An Interpretation of Religion* (London, 1989), is a statement of the position which has come to be known as religious pluralism. This major work, filled with illuminating discussions of the phenomena of religious belief and with fresh and lucid insights, is meant to be, not the end of the debate, but an opening up of discussion which might clarify the problem and its solutions further, and might establish a coherent framework for developing inter-faith dialogue and for a credible religious faith held in full awareness of and with full respect for the beliefs of others. My aim is to contribute to this discussion; and I shall do it by using the time-honoured philosophical technique of niggling and irritating criticism of various theses Hick presents. My argument will be that Hick's position is philosophically unacceptable as it stands, though it would be unwise simply to reject it wholesale; and I hope that my attack, such as it is, will be taken as a tribute to the force of the issues Hick places before us.

The pluralistic hypothesis is that religions provide different valid but culturally conditioned responses to a transcendent reality, and offer ways of transcending self and achieving a limitlessly better state centred on that reality. Thus no one tradition possesses a set of absolute and exclusive truths, while all others are delusory and ineffective for salvation. All will, or at least can be, saved by adhering to their own traditions, which purvey differing, but authentic, responses to the ultimately real. All can know the truth and attain salvation in their own traditions; so believers no longer have to condemn all others as mistaken, and no longer have to wonder why their God leaves the majority of creatures in mortal error. Here is an elegant and morally attractive solution of the problem of error in religion; and it is one that has great appeal for those who are reluctant to say that they alone are right and everyone else is wrong.

Nevertheless the hypothesis is riddled with difficulties; and the most obvious one can be put very forthrightly. To believe a proposition is to think that it is true. To think that it is true is to affirm that reality is as it is described by that proposition. Insofar as our affirmations are fallible, it is always possible that reality is not as some proposition asserts it to be. Thus an affirmation by its nature excludes some possible state of affairs; namely, one which would render the proposition false. If an assertion excludes nothing, it affirms nothing. In that sense, all truth-claims are necessarily exclusive.

It immediately follows that, where any truth-claim is made, it is logically possible to make another truth-claim which the first claim excludes. It is logically impossible for all possible truth-claims to be compatible. So it is possible for religious traditions to contain incompatible truth-claims, claims which exclude one another. Since this is a matter of logical possibility, it is a necessary truth that not all possible religious traditions can be equally true, authentic or valid. One can easily construct traditions which are strictly incompatible and of them, at least, pluralism must be false. That is, they will not consist of equally valid concepts of ultimate reality. One does not even need to invent such traditions, since, for example, Satanism and Christianity are fundamentally opposed both morally and factually.

But if this version of pluralism, which we might call 'extreme pluralism', is incoherent, it might nevertheless be the case that many religious traditions, and maybe all the major ones that exist on our planet, do not contain mutually exclusive beliefs, but are equally valid paths of salvation and of authentic experience of

the Real. This is 'hard pluralism'; and it is a contingent hypothesis; whether or not it is true will be a matter for careful investigation. But it certainly looks as though many claims exclude one another. The Buddhist assertion that there is no creator god exclude the Christian assertion that there is one all-perfect creator. The Muslim assertion that Allah has no son excludes the Christian assertion that God has an only-begotten Son. What is the pluralist to do about these *prima facie* incompatible claims?

Hick's strategy is to retreat from discussing particular religious beliefs and to talk instead of 'religion'; to retreat from discussing specific truth-claims and to talk instead of 'religious traditions'. This may seem innocuous, but it can be, and turns out to be, very misleading. It is well-known that definitions of religion are hard to find; and Hick proposes that we regard 'religion' as a family-resemblance concept, so that there is no essential core definition. Yet he is concerned with only one sort of religion or one feature of religious beliefs. He characterizes the central strand of religion with which he is chiefly concerned as 'awareness of and response to a reality that transcends ourselves and our world' (3). Fairly rapidly, he nominalizes the verb 'transcends', and speaks of 'belief in the transcendent', saying that 'most forms of religion have affirmed a salvific reality that transcends human beings and the world' (6). What he is doing is to pick out one class of religious beliefs, or one set of religious phenomena which can be defined in terms of belief in a transcendent salvific reality. There is nothing wrong with that; but it should be noted that it picks out one area of agreement in truth-claims by definition. Faiths which lack that central belief are not going to be counted; conversely, faiths which are counted are assured of a minimal degree of agreement to begin with. They will all agree on something, so they will not be incompatible in all respects. But, so far, this is not really pluralism (the acceptance of very different beliefs as equally valid); it is exclusivism at a relatively abstract and general level (those are excluded who do not believe in one transcendent salvific reality). It is also an acceptance of some truth-claim – the claim that there is such a reality which can bring creatures to a limitlessly good state – as "absolute", or true for everyone, regardless of their point of view or cultural situation.

Even when this area of agreement has been defined, however, there remain many incompatible truth-claims, which notoriously divide religions from each other. Hick's strategy now is to direct our focus of attention away from such particular truth-claims, which he regards as unsettlable and therefore (we shall have to look again at this 'therefore') not necessary for salvation; and to look instead at the 'religious traditions' as totalities 'which mediate the Real' and within which the 'salvific process occurs' (370). The point about a "religious tradition" is that it is not just a collection of truth-claims. Ninian Smart's well-known six-dimensional analysis of religion emphasizes that considerations of truth and falsity concern only one dimension of a much more complex social phenomenon, which includes stories, law codes, social and personal ethical recommendations, ritual practices and techniques of mental training. My own pastoral experience suggests that issues of truth do not loom very large in the life of the average believer, and that one may participate in a tradition for many reasons, including the sort of social relations one finds in it, varieties of aesthetic satisfaction it provides, and the moral and psychological support it provides in times of crisis. Anthropologists and sociologists can provide illuminating accounts of religion and reasons for religious belief without ever raising the issue of truth. Moreover, identical religious assertions can be interpreted in many ways, as conversation with any two Anglican priests soon shows. Thus if one asks the question, 'Can people find resources to help them love others and find meaning in life more or less equally in many traditions?', the answer is obviously going to be affirmative.

Viewed as social phenomena, religious traditions are forms of life which are culturally and ethnically differentiated. Since they contain many possibilities of diverse interpretation, and many dimensions of significance, it becomes apparent that a person will usually belong to such a tradition by birth, and can find within it many resources of meaning and moral teaching. As it seems absurd to say that one culture is 'true' and all others 'false', so the use of the expression 'religious tradition' subtly leads one to say that one cannot compare such traditions for truth; and that therefore one is not to be preferred to the others, except as an expression of cultural imperialism.

It is indeed odd to speak of a whole religious tradition as being true or false, especially when one remembers that people as diverse as Quakers and Tridentine Catholics presumably exist within 'the Christian tradition'. Yet in the end the traditions that exist in the world today go back to particular individuals, known or unknown, who did propound particular beliefs. The 'great traditions' are Scriptural traditions; and the scriptures contain, among many other things, teachings about the nature of reality and the way to salvation. There are particular truth-claims; and even though they can be interpreted variously, one can isolate a particular interpretation and ask of it whether it is true or false. Though the ascension of Jesus into heaven can be interpreted variously, one can ask whether it is true that he physically rose in the air; and there is a correct and precise answer to the question, however hard it is for us to know that answer.

Having isolated traditions which might plausibly be said to believe in one transcendent salvific reality, the hard pluralist then stresses the cultural totality and complexity of such traditions, and suggests that 'we always perceive the transcendent through the lens of a particular religious culture' (8). Since whole cultures cannot reasonably be compared for truth and falsity, recognition of this fact should lead each tradition to 'de-emphasise its own absolute and exclusive claim' (3), and accept that it is one among many ways to knowledge of and union with the transcendent. The correct response to this claim is to refrain from speaking of religio-cultural traditions, with all the problems of boundary-definition that brings with it, and to insist on focusing on particular truth-claims, and on particular interpretations of them, which can be properly assessed for truth and falsity. Then the question is not whether all traditions consti-tute different responses to the transcendent, which covers so many possibilities that it is almost bound to be true in some sense; but whether all specific truth-claims are equally war-ranted by the facts. When the question is put like that, it is obvious that they are not.

The hard pluralist response must now be to accept that disputes about truth, both of histor-ical fact and about human origins and destiny, do exist, both within and between specific parts of diverse religions; but to assert that this is irrelevant both to knowledge of the Real itself and to the completion of the salvific process of moving from selfish egoism to the limit lessly better state of 'Reality-centredness'. There are two parts to this claim, one to do with know-ledge of the Real and one to do with the nature and possibility of salvation. I shall consider each in turn, beginning with the claim that, though disputes about events in the past and future of the world are real enough, when it comes to speaking of the ultimately Real, different beliefs 'constitute different ways in which the same ultimate Reality has impinged upon human life' (373). Moreover, these different ways of impinging are equally veridical for different observers.

Many religious beliefs do speak of a tran-scendent reality; and they do say that this reality is ineffable, or beyond the grasp of human thought. If this is so, it may seem that no humanly formulated truth-claim can apply to it as it really is; so that all claims must be inadequate finite attempts to characterize an infinite reality, and none will be markedly better than any others. But three major difficulties at once arise: if the Real is ineffable, how can one know that it exists? If no truth-claim can apply to it, how can one be entitled to say anything of it? And if this reality is unknowable, how can we know that all claims about it are equally valid, except in the sense that all are completely mis-taken? Hick quotes a number of authoritative sources from a range of religions to show that ineffability is a common characteristic of the ultimately Real. 'The Tao that can be expressed is not the eternal Tao' (*Tao Te Ching*); God is 'incap-able of being grasped by any term' (Gregory of Nyssa); Nirguna Brahman is such that all words fall back from attaining it (Sankara). Inexpress-ibility by any human concepts is certainly a fea-ture of the ultimate object of devotion or striving in many religious traditions. And it may seem a short move from saying that two ideas are of an ineffable reality to saying that they are of the same reality; for what could distinguish two ineffables?

It can easily be seen that this argument is invalid, however. If X is indescribable by me, and Y is indescribable by me, it does not follow that X is identical with Y. On the contrary, there is no way in which X could be identified with Y, since there are no criteria of identity to apply. It is rather like saying, 'I do not know what X is; and I do not know what Y is; therefore X must be the same as Y'. If I do not know what either is, I *ipso facto* do not know whether they are the same or different. To assert identity is thus to commit the quantifier-shift fallacy, of moving from 'Many religions believe in an ineffable Real' to 'There is an ineffable Real in which many religions believe'.

The principle of economy may be appealed to; to identify X and Y, and so have one unknown, is simpler than to keep them distinct. But how do I know that ultimate reality is simple and not complex? The blunt truth is that I am not entitled to assert identity or difference of ineffable objects. Hick says, 'It (the Real *an sich*) cannot be said to be one or many, person or thing, substance or process, good or evil, purposive or non-purposive' (246). But if it cannot be said to be one or many, one is not even entitled to use the singular term 'it'. There may be many unknowns beyond the universe. Hick uses the singular because, he says, 'there cannot be a plurality of ultimates'; but he says in the same paragraph, that there is 'no reason *a priori* why the closest approximation that there is to a truly ultimate reality' may not consist in 'an unrelated plurality'. So I think we must either remain truly agnostic, or confess that the Real can be said to be one; and that is a piece of real and definite knowledge, opposed to all forms of simple polytheism. It is also opposed to at least some forms of Buddhism; as Paul Williams writes of Tibetan Buddhism, which he espouses, 'There is no Being, no Absolute at all'. Many Christians, too, of course, explicitly reject the apophatic doctrine that God is ultimately unknowable, supposing that he is truly known in Christ. So there does not seem to be much hope of uniting all traditions around even the rather short creed of one ineffable reality. They may say there is no such reality; or that there is more than one; or that it is not ineffable.

Suppose, however, one considers those strands of thought which do speak of one transcendent ineffable reality. It is not at all clear that different religions think of that which they say to be ineffable as the same in each case. It is unlikely in the extreme that they simply mean to say, 'As well as everything I have said, there are some things I do not know about, which exist beyond the universe'. This very statement would be self-contradictory, in asserting, 'I know X exists', which entails, 'I know at least one thing about X (that it exists beyond the universe)', at the same time as, 'I know nothing about X'. But ineffability cannot in any case be sensibly interpreted to mean, 'Lack of knowledge'. What I know absolutely nothing about must be, one feels, hardly worth mentioning. One finds a much more positive characterization in, for instance, Aquinas' notion of Divine simplicity, in many ways the

key concept for his interpretation of the Divine. Simplicity is an ontological, not an epistemic, property, for Aquinas. That is, it is not that I do not know what God is; I *do* know that the being of God is such that it contains no distinctions, no parts, no complexity which human concepts could grasp. The Divine being is unlimited, and therefore beyond human comprehension. It is not just unknowable by us – in which case, it might well be internally complex for all we know. On the contrary, we know – thinks Aquinas – that the Divine being is utterly simple; and we know this by an argument from the nature of the world to its ultimately self-sufficient cause.

Now it would seem to follow that if two beings were both simple in this sense, containing no parts or distinctions or properties at all, they would have to be identical. If they were distinct, there would have to be some property, minimally the property of 'not being the same as Y', in virtue of which they were distinct. *Ex hypothesi*, there are no such properties. It might, however, be said in reply that this reality must in any case at least possess the property of 'being identical with itself', of being one and not many, as well as the property of existing – if that is a property. Aquinas perceives this, and it causes him trouble. One possibility is to say that God possesses no property which entails real internal distinctions. But then one could have many simple substances, as atoms were once thought to be; distinguished by some sorts of external relation, as atoms are distinguished by spatial location. Aquinas eliminates this possibility by holding that God is infinite, not being limited by an external relation. And I think it is true that infinity and simplicity together entail that any two beings possessing those properties are identical; i.e. there is only one such possible being.

For Aquinas, then, it is true to say of God that he exists, is one, simple and unlimited in reality. It is Divine simplicity and infinity which renders human concepts, fitted to deal with complex finite objects, incapable of expressing the Divine nature. The essential Divine nature will forever be beyond the grasp of human understanding – that is what ineffability means in the Thomist Christian tradition. It does not mean that nothing at all is known of, or can be truly said of, God. Aquinas asserts that many things can truly, and literally (though analogically) be said of God – that he is good, powerful, knowing and wise, for example (Cf. *Summa Theologiae*; 1a, 13, 2 & 3). What we cannot understand is what his knowledge is like, or what it is like to experience as God experiences. We cannot in this life comprehend the Divine being or be acquainted with it as it essentially is. This is rather like saying that I cannot imagine how bees perceive things, though I know very well that they do. The manner of their perception is beyond my experience or imagination. And, with God, the manner of his essential being will forever be so. We can know that God knows, though we cannot know how he knows, or what it is like for him to know. The traditional doctrine of divine ineffability, as classically formulated by Aquinas, is not that we can know nothing of God; it is that we cannot comprehend what God's essential nature is in itself.

Hick quotes Gregory of Nyssa as saying that God remains 'beyond the reach not only of the human but of the angelic and all supramundane intelligence, unthinkable, unutterable' (*Against Eunomius*, 1: 42). What is significant here is that God is *beyond* or above all human concepts. His proper nature is not just totally other; it is greater than our concepts can reach, not less or such as to render them wholly inappropriate. It is as if we say, 'I know that God is good and wise; but since I also know that he is infinite and simple, I do not know what it is in God's essential nature that makes these terms appropriate'.

How do I know these terms apply to God? For Aquinas, it is by a causal argument from the nature of finite beings to their only wholly adequate cause and foundation. We must say of God that as cause of all, he contains in himself in a greater manner all the perfections to be found

in things. The theistic perception, as Mascall puts it, is 'a genuine apprehension of God as present by immensity at the ontological root of finite beings' (E. L. Mascall, *He Who Is*, 1966: 197). Whatever we think of Aquinas' arguments, he is not portraying the existence of some thing or things of which nothing can be said. He is portraying a being of whom it can truly be said that it is the one perfect cause of all finite things; though if we go on to ask what that being is like outside any relation to us, no adequate description can be given. There is that in God which makes the ascription of goodness to him appropriate; we cannot imagine or describe what it is, for we can only say how it causes God to seem to us (correctly) from our limited viewpoint. I think this is what Aquinas means by saying that terms denoting positive perfections apply properly to God, though not in the sense in which we understand them, i.e. in which we apply them to finite things. We have a positive reason for claiming that we do not know just how these terms apply; the reason is that God, as the adequate cause of all finite things, is simple and infinite. But we also have a positive reason for applying them; namely, that God relates to us as a supremely desirable being who brings us to good by uniting us to himself. We can thus interpret the much-disputed Thomistic *aporia* by saying that what we do not know is the nature of God, as it exists out of any relation to human cognition, though we do know there is such an ineffable nature. We can know that God is not limited in any way, so that finite properties do not, *qua* finite, properly apply to him (we can know 'what he is not'). And we can know what difference the existence of God makes to the experiences and destinies of finite creatures ('how other things are related to him').

I would not wish to be committed to asserting the coherence of Thomas' remarks on ineffability. What I want to bring out is that when he speaks of ineffability, he is not saying that God is such that no terms can be truly affirmed of him – he takes Maimonides to task on this very point (though of course Maimonides too is in no doubt that the assertions of the Hebrew Bible about God are unequivocally true). Thomas is saying that, though we cannot comprehend *how* terms apply to God, because of his simplicity, we can know that they do apply; so that God truly is the omniscient creator of all finite things. Now when Japanese Buddhists in the tradition of Asvaghosa say that Reality is non-dual, they precisely do not mean that this reality can be regarded as personal creator of all. Something is said to be ineffable in both cases; but in Aquinas' case it is the nature of a reality which is quite distinct from that of the finite world; in Asvaghosa's case it is the ultimate nature of the finite world itself. In the Indian philosopher Sankara, we may have yet a different view, that what is ineffable, *nirguna Brahman*, is both different from this illusory finite realm (Nirvana is *not* Samsara) and yet not a substantially distinct reality. In each case, something is said to be ineffable; but that it is *not* precisely the same thing is shown by the disputes on the point between Aquinas and Maimonides, Ramanuja and Sankara, and the followers of Asvaghosa and Nagarjuna respectively.

So the traditional theistic doctrine of ineffability arises from the exploration of the greatness and infinity of God. It presupposes the truth of many descriptive statements; indeed, it entails at least one descriptive statement, namely, that God is ineffable (a proposition which is not self-evident). It can consistently point out the inadequacy of such statements to give anything like a full understanding of God, and their possible misleadingness, if we do take them as implying that God is just like finite cases where such descriptions normally apply. We are aware of our limitations and partialities, of the superficiality of our knowledge, the inadequacy of our grasp of the reality of things. We seek for something unlimited, impartial, with a secure reality and perfection. The Real is not the dependent and transient; it is the wholly independent and enduring; upon it, in some sense, all things depend. The idea of the transcendent is the idea

of supreme reality and value, a reality supremely valuable and a value supremely real. We can postulate that there is such a being, without being able to describe it in any detail. Indeed, the postulate requires that it is beyond our conceptual grasp; we cannot envisage just what or how it is; but we envisage something when we claim that it is supremely real and perfect.

Seeking to defend his view that the Real is radically unknowable, Hick dismisses as 'logical pedantry' the logical point that the Real must at least have the property of 'being able to be referred to' (239). But there is more meat to the point than he admits. For if X has the property of being able to be referred to, this reference must be accomplished either by ostentation or description. Ostentation is ruled out by definition, for an object which transcends the universe. So any reference must be made by description; X must be identified as 'the X which . . .'. Further, if an identifying reference is to have any hope of succeeding, one must be able to pick out X as some sort of substance, process or stuff. It is not enough to say, 'the X which exists beyond the universe', if there may be many such things. One will need to say, 'X is the one and only thing which satisfies the properties . . .'. Hick gives the game away by using the term 'the Real'. For him, X is the one and only thing which is real in the fullest sense (i.e. independent, self-existent, unchanging in its essential nature, unlimited by anything else . . .). This is a description which could only apply to one thing, if it could apply at all. The object is identified descriptively by constructing a notion of a unique sort of reality upon which all others depend. Whether such a reference could ever succeed is another question; but for it even to have meaning, it is apparent that quite a lot of our concepts do need to apply to X.

But these, says Hick, are 'purely formal and logically generated properties'; they are not 'substantial properties', like being good, powerful or wise. Now, he says, the claim to ineffability is that substantial properties do not apply to the being of God beyond the range of human experience. Does this distinction between formal and substantial properties hold? The distinction between form and substance might most naturally be taken as a distinction between what is said and the form in which it is said. Thus the substance, or content, of 'The cat sat on the mat' is whatever is asserted by the utterance of those words. The form is the syntax or grammatical structure of English; noun, verb and predicate; a structure which enables me to say anything at all. Study of the structure will give me no particular content; it is like doing Logic with nothing but ps and qs; I can go on for pages without knowing what I am talking about (perhaps that is not well put; I can set out possible argument-forms without actually uttering an argument).

Now if I say, 'X is to be used as a noun' that could be called a formal property of x; it tells me what sort of term x is, without telling me what real thing x might be. But if I say, 'X is the referent of some noun', I am talking about some actual object, not a term. And I am saying what sort of thing it is; a thing which could be referred to by description, by someone with human conceptual equipment. I am saying, 'This object is such that it can be identified by some human language user'. That may not tell me much about it, but it does have content; it is a synthetic proposition, though it is obvious, in the sense that I would hardly be speaking of the object if it could not be identified, at least in thought. And of course it invites further questions about how it can be identified. We must conclude that the statement 'X is an identifiable object' attributes a substantial property to X, the property of being identifiable; and the more one spells out the manner of identifying it, the more one will say about X. In fact, Hick includes as a formal property the property of being that than which nothing greater can be conceived (246). Far from being purely formal, that property entails (in the concept of 'greatness') the idea of value, of the rationally desirable, and thus of goodness, which he admits to being a substantial property, in at least one clear sense.

Moreover, this is an absolute truth about God. For if it is true from our viewpoint that God is maximally great, then it is true of God that, from our viewpoint, he is maximally great. The distinction which is often made between absolute truths and relative truths is insupportable. An absolute truth is supposed to be one which states what is the case independent of any particular person believing it. A relative truth states what is the case, from the point of view of a particular person; that is, it states what truly appears to be the case to some observer. But if A will truly appear as B to P, then it is true of A that it will appear as B to P. And this truth is absolute; it does not depend upon anybody knowing or believing it; since it may be true even though P never exists. So we know many true things about God; but we also know that much of God transcends our thoughts.

I propose that Hick has seized upon some very difficult and disputed statements of major religious intellectuals; and has taken the doctrine of the *via negativa* out of relation to its complementary doctrine of the *via eminentia*, to produce a new doctrine that the Real *an sich* is wholly unknowable. Then he argues that, since one unknowable is indistinguishable from another, they are all the same. Since all human concepts are bound to be inadequate to the Real, if it is unknowable, and since we have no way of choosing between different descriptions, we must say that all the 'great world faiths embody different perceptions and conceptions of, and correspondingly different responses to, the Real' (240).

When Kant foisted the doctrine of the noumenal realm upon the philosophical world, it was in the form of an undigested remnant of his pre-Critical view that the noumenal, or intelligible world, was the real world, and was knowable by pure intellect, whereas the senses give a confused appearance of this realm of rational spirits. In his Critical doctrine, he confined the intellect strictly to the realm of the senses, and justified the categories as necessary and universal preconditions of the possibility of scientific knowledge. The noumenal lost its theoretical role entirely. It has often been pointed out that a residual inconsistency vitiates Kant's idea of the noumenal, since to say that it exists as the cause of the phenomenal applies the categories beyond the permissible range of cognitive meaning. When this inconsistency is cleared away, Kant can be interpreted as proposing that Reason necessarily constructs an Ideal of a perfect value and reality, to be used as a regulative idea in our practical conduct of life. It has no theoretical validity, and is to be judged by its efficacy in enabling us to live a moral life, or to conceive of the rationality of such a life.

Hick makes a similar move, revealing that the real focus of his concern is not with theoretical truth, but with the 'salvific efficacy' of religions. When he comes to state criteria of assessing religious phenomena, he says that 'the basic criterion is soteriological' (14); that is, efficacy in leading humans from self-centredness to Reality-centredness, most readily observable by growth in love or compassion. Yet, like Kant, he is unable to renounce theoretical claims entirely. This is hardly surprising, since even to say that a limitlessly better state is possible for all is a factual statement about the future, which is presumably experientially accessible in principle. Thus the theistic picture of the universe sees it as 'a creative process leading to a limitlessly good end state in conscious communion with God' (179). This picture can be confirmed beyond rational doubt by conscious experience of that end state. Now there are certainly views which would refute this picture. Any atheistic view or any non-realist religious view would deny the existence of such an end state; so there is no question that some religious views deny precisely what traditional theism asserts. As Hick says, non-realism in religion offers 'a radically different vision' (208) of things, which leaves no place for ultimate cosmic optimism. Samkhya Yogins, Advaitic Vedantins and many Buddhists, both Theravadin and Mahayana, would also deny that the universe is a creative process leading to

an end state; they see the world as an illusory cycle of ills, without beginning or end. And even if the individual can achieve a limitlessly good end state, it will not be one of conscious communion with a perfect creator; it will be entry into the quiescent state of desirelessness, far beyond personhood as we understand it. Assertions made about the nature of the universe and about ultimate human destiny are very different. Is it not obvious that at most one set of such views can be true? And if Hick does not hesitate to exclude non-realist religious views and atheistic views of the world, why should he hesitate to exclude views which take a different view of human destiny, even though they might agree on the existence of a perfect supreme reality?

I think that he has increasingly come to feel, and argues at length in *An Interpretation of Religion*, that we cannot reasonably claim 'that our own form of religious experience ... is veridical whilst the others are not' (235). He allows that virtually every religious tradition has done so; but then proposes the following argument:

1. By something akin to Swinburne's Principle of Credulity, *A* is justified in thinking that what seems to be the case probably is the case, in the absence of strong countervailing reasons. So if *A* seems to apprehend God's presence, she is justified in thinking that God is in fact present, and therefore that God exists.

2. By the principle of universalizability, however, *B* is similarly justified in believing that reality is non-dual, on the basis of her experiences of *samadi* or enlightenment.

3. Since the fact that '*A* is me' is not a relevant reason for giving *A*'s views greater force than *B*'s, it seems that *A* and *B* are equally justified in believing contradictory things.

4. Therefore it is implausible to believe that all religious experience is delusory except one's own.

5.   This suggests the Pluralistic Hypothesis, that different types of religious experience are veridical but partial responses to a reality which cannot be adequately described by any set of beliefs alone.

This argument is plainly invalid. The trouble lies with step (4). A sharp distinction is to be made between justification and truth. I can be justified in believing something false (e.g. that the earth is flat) due to imperfect knowledge. In complex situations, given rather different initial information, people may be justified in believing contradictory things. But contradictory beliefs cannot both be true; so all that follows is that at least one person is justified in believing something false. Hick has already argued that both atheists and theists can be rationally justified in adopting the views of the world they do adopt, given the ambiguous nature of that world. But it does not follow that each must accept the other's view as equally true. The very reverse is the case. If I am rationally justified in believing X; and you are rationally justified in believing not-X; then we are both justified in believing the other to be deluded, or in some other way mistaken.

Now something *does* follow from this about the character of such beliefs. I must admit other believers may have reasons which seem just as strong to them to accept their views as I have to accept mine. Therefore I cannot claim that they are obviously or detectably mistaken. And I cannot seriously claim that my views is obviously or clearly true. So I must admit the equal right of others to exist and hold the views they do. And I must admit the fallibility and theoretical uncertainty of my view. To accept this might in itself be a great advance in religion, but it does not constitute a reason for accepting hard pluralism. It could be a reason for denying any right to believe any view in this area. However, one can argue, as Hick does, that the matter is so important that I am justified in making some choice. It may even be that I must believe something in this area, though it is hard to say how detailed my

beliefs must be. In fact Hick vacillates, sometimes saying that, because conflicting views have so little to choose between them, it is not important to hold such views, and one should concentrate simply on the practical matter of salvation. But at other times (e.g. as between realist and non-realist religious views) he says that it is important to choose a realist and cosmically optimistic view, because only that offers good news to all.

Whichever he says, it is reasonable to claim that our own experiences are veridical whilst all others are not. It is unreasonable to claim anything else. But the situation does not have to have this all-or-nothing character. Surely we do not wish to say that centuries or prayer, meditation, sanctity and devotion in other traditions are founded on illusion? Surely they must be putting people in touch with the real spiritual reality, whatever it is? Hick himself gives the answer: 'There seems to me to be no difficulty in principle in the thought that a person may be correctly experiencing some aspects of reality whilst falsely experiencing others' (220). That is, there may well be something veridical in what great religious traditions experience; but also (very often) something false. He even tells us how to discriminate: we accept some belief as veridical 'because it evokes a confirming echo within our own experience' (220). We reject others because they clash with our experience. There are many echoes of our experience in the religious experiences of others; and we may take these to be veridical. By parity of reasoning, we may think that our own tradition, even our own present experience within that tradition, is liable to contain many mistakes, though we will not know what they are. Humility is certainly in order; it does sound arrogant to say 'my religious experience is perfectly correct; all others are totally false'. But we can say: 'My religious experience is correct in important respects, though it may contain many errors. The experiences of others may contain many veridical elements; but there are important misinterpretations, too'. The veridical elements will be those which seem to echo my own; the errors those which clash with my own; nor will I be able to identify the errors in my own. I can be on the lookout for such errors, and look to other traditions to help me identify them. And I can look for elements other traditions have which may complement, rather than contradict, my own. Thus my beliefs are always revisable; and others may always be capable of disclosing new insights. Yet those beliefs which lie near the core of my belief-system must be given preference over competing beliefs.

Hick does precisely this, of course. He identifies many errors in the Christian tradition – belief in Hell and literal belief in incarnation are just two which he takes to be morally undesirable and rationally insupportable. His core-beliefs are that one should turn from selfish egoism to attain a limitlessly good end-state by some sort of relation to a reality of supreme value; and he is only prepared to accept beliefs which are compatible with these. The suggestion is that any set of beliefs which result in such an endstate is likely to be true; others are not. The trouble is that this criterion is quite unusable, as Hick's discussion makes very clear. Some of the most obviously deluded, restrictive and exclusive belief-systems produce astonishing commitment, assurance, love and self-sacrifice. On the other hand, as Hick points out, the great Scriptural traditions have histories replete with hatred, intolerance and violence; so that none of them emerges as much better than any others, in the long sad history of human fanaticism. It seems, then, that either the suggested criteria of adequacy do not enable us to choose between many different beliefs; or that they are in tension with the criterion of consistency with other well-established knowledge. In this situation, might it not be better to abandon the Kantian *noumenon*, say that we do know something about the Real – namely, that it is an ultimate unity of reality and value – and thus that criteria of adequacy, at this abstract level, are metaphysical

criteria of providing the most intelligible account of the genesis of the universe from an ultimately real and perfect source? Hick tends to dismiss metaphysical speculations, together with particular historical claims, as unsettlable and unnecessary to salvation. But of course his whole book is a metaphysical exploration of what can be intelligibly said about the object of religious faith; and the fact that his version of pluralistic religious realism is unsettlable and highly disputable does not stop him from asserting both its truth and its importance for a correct (non-exclusive) understanding of salvation.

This brings us back to the question, which I deferred earlier, of whether unsettlable beliefs can be necessary for salvation. Hick finds this 'implausible' (369); but it is rendered immediately more plausible by the consideration that the very concept of what salvation is involves beliefs which are theoretically unsettlable in practice. If one asks what is necessary for salvation, one might be asking whether any beliefs are requisite for the final attainment of wholly fulfilled human life. Atheists, of course, will deny that there is any such final attainment, or even any such possible notion as that of a wholly fulfilled life; 'do your own thing' might better be their motto. So the mere acceptance of the concept of a wholly fulfilled life presupposes the very contestable belief that there is a proper goal of human activity. If there is such a consciously attained goal, then one cannot achieve it without having the correct belief about what it is, and how one has come to achieve it. In this sense the possession of some particular beliefs is necessary to salvation. People without those beliefs will not attain salvation, for the simple reason that salvation consists in attaining a state which entails possessing such beliefs; i.e. it entails that one knows what salvation is and that one has attained it. At such a point, of course, one may suppose that religious disputes will finally be settled. As Hick says, 'To participate knowingly in fulfilment would confirm the reality of God beyond the possibility of rational doubt' (179). In other words, at least some important metaphysical claims about the existence and nature of God are settlable by experience in principle.

But one might also ask whether any beliefs are requisite *now* if one is to have a reasonable hope of attaining salvation later, or if one is to be on the right path towards salvation. Different views exist on this question; but Hick seems to me correct in thinking that if there is a God of universal love, he will not make our loss of eternal life dependent merely upon making an honest mistake. So one might suppose that a positive response to whatever seems to be good and true, by a conscience as informed as one can reasonably expect, and a commitment to seek truth and realize goodness, is sufficient to dispose one rightly to salvation. Some beliefs are requisite; but they will depend on particular circumstances, since what one is justified in believing at one time may well be different from what one is justified in believing at another. Nevertheless, if one believes in such a God of love, one will also think that he will eventually bring rational creatures to know what he truly is, so that the search for truth will issue in a specific set of true beliefs sometime. Thus it is misleading, though in one sense true, to say that no metaphysical beliefs are essential to salvation. It may not be essential to your eventual salvation that you hold them now; but it is essential to your actual salvation that you come to hold them. Metaphysics, however difficult and disputable, is important to faith (I don't mean anything very grand by this; just beliefs about the nature of what is ultimately real).

In a recent paper, Hick refers to the 'novel', 'astonishing' and 'bizarre' doctrine that 'the salvific power of the dharma taught five hundred years earlier by the Buddha is a consequence of the death of Jesus'. But one need not deny that the dharma is an effective way of overcoming egoism and attaining inner peace and compassion, when one asserts that it does not bring one into a conscious loving relationship with a personal God. Nor is it bizarre to hold that one can

be brought into such a relationship only by the saving activity of God uniting human nature to himself in the life and death of Jesus, and subsequently in those who come to accept Jesus as Lord and Saviour. It is not that Buddhists attain salvation by the Middle Way, though somehow the efficacy of this way depends on something that had not yet happened. Buddhists do not attain Christian salvation, since their Way does not lead to that personal relationship with God which is salvation. They attain a high degree of compassion and inner peace; and their unselfish devotion to the truth as they see it will surely fit them to receive salvation from a personal God when his saving activity becomes clear to them. There is a salutary reminder here that metaphysics is not what saves us; for Christians, the act of God, establishing creatures in knowledge and love of him, does that. But metaphysics is needed to set out the coherence of the concept of a God who can so act in a world like this.

It may help at this point if we distinguish what we may we may call soft pluralism from hard pluralism. Soft pluralism is the view that the Real can manifest in many traditions, and humans can respond to it appropriately in them. I think this view is defensible and important, and it is certainly different from the view, held by many, that there is only one God, who only reveals himself in one tradition and only saves those who belong to that tradition – the restrictive interpretation of the decree of the Council of Florence, 'Outside the Church there is no salvation'. It is coherent to hold that there is a God who is infinite and beyond human comprehension in his essential nature, who discloses something of that nature, as it stands in relation to us, in many religious traditions. It is coherent to hold that in many (though not all) religious traditions, believers aim to overcome selfish desire in relation to a supreme objective value which promises bliss, knowledge and freedom; and that this does constitute a positive and appropriate response to God, as disclosed to them. It is also coherent to hold that no tradition has the completeness of truth about God; that all contain many revisable and corrigible beliefs, and that we should look to other traditions to complement, correct or reshape our own. This is certainly part of Hick's thesis.

But another form of the thesis is also at work; a thesis both more intolerant of virtually all actual religious traditions and sliding at times into incoherence. The intolerance surfaces in many stringent remarks about the bizarre, primitive and astonishing beliefs held by orthodox believers. The incoherence appears in the claim of hard pluralism that all (or at least all 'great') traditions are equally valid paths to salvation and equally authentic modes of experience of a Real which is a completely unknowable postulate of the religious life. It is the stress on equal validity, equal authenticity and complete unknowability which is incoherent. These three claims constitute an inconsistent triad of propositions, since one cannot assert all of: (1) There is something wholly unknowable; (2) all experiences of it are equally authentic; and (3) all paths to fuller experience of it are equally valid. If (1) is true, (2) and (3) cannot be asserted. Not only is there no way of knowing if they are true; they cannot be true, if they entail (as they do) experiential knowledge of the wholly unknowable. If there are any criteria of authenticity at all, it must be possible to distinguish more and less authentic experiences. But this can only be done by means of some concept of the Real which can be described more or less adequately. Once one has such a concept, there may indeed be experiences which give equally authentic knowledge of it; but that can only be so if those experiences are complementary, not contradictory. That means (as is the case with the often quoted wave–particle duality of light) that competent observers must agree that both of two descriptions of an object can be true, in different conditions of observation. Unfortunately, most Buddhists will not agree that it is true that there is an omnipotent personal agent who brings about changes in history; and most Christians will not agree that

the idea of God is an imaginative projection which needs to be overcome in the recognition of one non-dual reality. Hard pluralism is as strongly falsified as any contingent hypothesis is ever likely to be.

Yet it might be insisted that this situation must be changed. There is another version of pluralism, which might be termed 'revisionist pluralism', which asserts that all the Scriptural traditions need to be radically revised, in consequence of the rise of the natural sciences, of Biblical scholarship and of post-Enlightenment critical thinking in general. The idea of an infallible Scriptural revelation will need to be discarded, and many particular beliefs revised in the light of new knowledge of the world and of human psychology. Now if this is done in all the great Scriptural traditions, one will be much less clear about which beliefs are essential or even central to each tradition; and the revised beliefs may well turn out to be compatible with similarly revised beliefs in other traditions.

If a Buddhist is prepared to regard belief in re-incarnation as a myth, a Christian thinks of the Incarnation as a mistaken fourth-century doctrine, and a Muslim agrees that the Koran is a fallible and morally imperfect document, they might well be able to agree much more than they used to. One can see the Scriptural faiths, defined by their acceptance of infallible revelation (and even the Buddhist scriptures are regarded in that way by many orthodox believers), as belonging to past history just as surely as their tribal predecessors do. Religion can move to a more universal phase, in which insights are selected from many traditions, while most of their differences are relegated to the museum of dead beliefs. I suspect that Hick wishes to commend revisionist pluralism, too. There is much to be said for it; but it cannot be said that it sees all existing traditions as equally valid perceptions of truth. On the contrary, most existing traditions have to be radically purged of error, in the light of the more adequate views of a post-Critical age. It is ironic that this view, which sees the great traditions as 'earlier stages in an evolution of which it is the culmination' is precisely of the type which Hick earlier characterises as unacceptably arrogant (2). Revisionist pluralism makes it own absolute and exclusive claim – it is just true that there is one Reality of supreme value which will bring all creatures to good; and anything which denies this or tries to restrict the ways in which this may happen is false.

Revisionist pluralism is incompatible with hard pluralism, since it denies that unrevised traditions are equally adequate forms of religious truth. It is compatible with soft pluralism, but not entailed by it, since it is possible that one existing tradition characterizes the Real most adequately; that is, that its central truth-claims are more adequately descriptive of the Real than competing alternatives. To the extent that the Real is a personal and active self-disclosing agent, one might think that an existing tradition which claims to have witnessed the self-disclosing acts of this agent is more likely to be adequate than the conclusions of a highly abstract and speculative philosophical hypothesis. But that is a question of the acceptability and coherence of particular conceptions of ultimate reality, which needs to be argued out in detail. One thing is certain, that revisionist pluralism is not in a position to assert moral superiority, greater tolerance or greater impartiality over any particular tradition as such, when traditions are taken as not excluding ultimate salvation for others; since the claims each must make for itself are logically on a par.

Religious believers do not have to suppose that the majority of the human race are excluded from salvation, as long as they have a view which allows for a development of knowledge after death. They are, however, committed to thinking that most people are mistaken in their beliefs about the ultimate nature of reality. That is, after all, not a very surprising thought, though it is a sad one. It should lead to a keen sense of one's own fallibility, a deeper appreciation of the attempts of others to understand human nature and destiny, and a firm stress on the primacy of moral and spiritual practice in religion. These are the leading themes of John Hick's recent work, which he formulates in the pluralist hypothesis. I have suggested that in at least one sense (soft pluralism) his case is persuasive. There are other senses however which, if I am right, are not sustainable. On this, at least, truth is exclusive, and one of us must be wrong.

Chapter 7

Timothy O'Connor

RELIGIOUS PLURALISM

I. Introduction: Tolerance, Relativism, and Pluralism

For many people, the diversity of religious practices and beliefs is a fact of everyday life. When I was an undergraduate, I shared an apartment, at various times, with two Muslims and a Buddhist, among others. In addition, I have had and continue to have friendships with many more people of various religious faiths (as well as those of no faith at all). And such experience is certainly not unusual.

While we have become increasingly exposed to the diversity of religious beliefs that surround us, our culture has at the same time begun to place less emphasis on these very differences. A number of factors have led us in this direction: dismay and regret over religious persecution and cultural imperialism, to name two. But, however exactly we got here, "relativist" and "pluralist" views about religion are all the rage these days, in the academy as well as on the street. Usually, those who hold such "pluralist" views have not thought them through very carefully. Defenders of pluralism will often describe their views with slogans, such as "all religions are true," or "there are many roads to God." (Many appeal to the well-worn Hindu parable of the blind men who touch different parts of the elephant, each mistaking a different part for the whole.) Put in these simplistic terms, it's easy to show that these views are just indefensible. In fact, I'll show later on that there are powerful reasons to reject even the most sophisticated versions of pluralism.

But this offensive strategy is not my main aim here. The reason it is not is this: people today are far less committed to pluralism than they are to the belief that traditional, "absolutist," or "exclusivist" understandings of religious claims are arrogant or irrational or in some other sense unacceptable. According to this way of thinking, it's fine, e.g., to believe that Jesus Christ is *a* way to God, but improper to hold that he is *the* way to God. More radically, it's okay to believe that one has experienced the love of God the Heavenly Father, as long as one doesn't conclude from this that ultimate reality is, "absolutely speaking," a personal being. (For this would imply, e.g., that the Zen Buddhist view of *nirvana*, the pure "such-ness" or ego-less being of ever-changing reality, is false.) One should instead say something more qualified, such as "in my experience, ultimate reality has taken on the appearance of a transcendent, personal being." We are thus admonished not to throw out our Christian beliefs altogether, but to hold them in a way that doesn't "delegitimize" the truths of other religions. Thus, current fashion would urge us to hold our religious beliefs in a way quite different from the way we hold our beliefs about, for example, the physical world. We all think that it is simply true that there are birds and buildings and baseballs. Anyone so mentally impaired as to deny these things is simply wrong. With respect to birds, we might say, we're all exclusivists.

For many people, then, there is a general "air of plausibility" to pluralism in matters of religion, though they don't have any worked-out view on the matter. So, if we were to proceed by arguing against one particular version of pluralism, many would likely think that, while *that* version fails, there is likely some other view that would successfully and coherently describe what they believe. A more promising tack that some contemporary Christian philosophers have taken, and that I will take here, is to root out the fundamental assumptions that lie behind appeals to pluralist doctrines. When this is done, we will see that the reasonableness of the pluralist view vanishes.

I will proceed in two stages. First, in section II, I will show that the main pluralist argument *against* exclusivist Christian belief fail. Second, in section III, I will show that the main arguments in *favor* of the most promising version of pluralism also fails. With that, the critique of pluralism will be complete.

II. Pluralist Objections to "Exclusivist" Christian Belief

Pluralists reject traditional Christianity (where this involves holding beliefs exclusively) in a number of ways. I will take up the three most common of these objections.

A. The "No Difference in Spiritual Fruits" Objection

Unlike many atheists or naturalists, pluralists are not skeptical about religious experience (at least much of it). They're generally happy to admit that a person's religious experiences make it reasonable for him to have the beliefs he does concerning the Ultimate. Let's take me for an example. I have had experiences in which it has seemed to me that my Heavenly Father was in some manner enveloping me, communicating his love for me, and calling me to draw near to him. These are experiences of a kind typical in the Christian tradition, and they have prompted renewal of my commitments to seek deeper and more regular communion with God and to follow the example of Christ in my life. Accordingly, they give me at least some reason to believe that "the Ultimate" is manifested in the Christian tradition as the all-powerful, all-knowing, and loving Creator of all. If *everyone's* experiences were compatible with mine in the sense that they, too, depicted ultimate reality as having the character ascribed to God in the Christian Scriptures, then the reasonable conclusion would be that *that is what ultimate reality is like in itself.*

But, the pluralist points out, there is no such uniformity among religious experiences. And they cannot *all* truthfully represent ultimate reality *in itself*, for they ascribe *incompatible* attributes to it. (It makes no sense to say that ultimate reality, in itself, is both personal and impersonal.) If I conclude instead that my experiences are veridical – God really was present to me, communicating his love, and so forth – while the experiences of Hindus, for example, indicating that ultimate reality is "the blissful universal consciousness of Brahman," are illusory, then I am being *arbitrary*. For there is no objective basis for deciding between these two. In particular, all religions appear to be roughly equal with respect to what the pluralist holds is the common goal of religion: moving from self-centeredness to "Ultimate-Reality-centeredness." This movement is the "spiritual fruit" that comes from sincerely practicing one's faith. We don't all get as far as we'd like, of course. In all traditions, there are few "saints," others in whom there is no discernible change, and a great many more in between. As the pluralist philosopher John Hick has put it, we must, then, "avoid the implausibly arbitrary dogma that religious experience is all delusory with the single exception of the particular form enjoyed by the one who is speaking."[1] The only position, Hick argues, that is both not arbitrary and not completely dismissive of the authenticity of religious experience is the pluralist's.

Recall that, according to the pluralist, many kinds of religious experiences involve legitimate contact with "Ultimate Reality." How then can the pluralist make sense of the contradictory religious beliefs these experiences give rise to (that Ultimate reality is, for example, personal and nonpersonal)? The answer is that pluralists hold that Ultimate Reality *as it really is* is beyond our intellectual grasp – indeed, it utterly *transcends* the categories we apply to it. When we experience it, we conceptualize it in terms of categories that we have available to us (since human beings need to categorize their contact with the Ultimate to make sense of it and respond to it). Numerous categories have been devised for this purpose across cultures, but no particular packaging is necessary. Some forms may be more efficient than others, but there are evidently many forms that get the job done reasonably well.

It may be thought that some religious traditions are in greater agreement with the pluralist regarding the unimportance of creed than Christianity is. When I was a graduate student at Cornell University, the Dalai Lama came and delivered a lecture entitled "Overcoming Our Differences." In the lecture, he stressed themes for which he has become well-known in the U.S. – respect for cultural and religious differences and the centrality of practicing compassion, whatever one's creed. He was quoted in an interview as believing that Buddhism is not the best religion for everyone, and that sincere Christians who find that their faith leads them to act compassionately should by all means continue in it. Is that form of Buddhist teaching, at least, in agreement with Hick on the inessentiality of doctrine? In fact, it is not. According to this Tibetan tradition, it is *essential* to ultimate salvation or liberation that one realizes the truth of the doctrine of emptiness (sunyata). Roughly, on this view, our way of understanding the

world around us is radically illusory. There are no individual objects such as birds and buildings and baseballs (and people!). Reality is a "void," empty of all substance. This recognition is thought to free one from attachment to things and ultimately to lead to liberation from the cycle of rebirth. But such Buddhists recognize that not everyone is ready to understand this teaching. And as this ultimately necessary insight is inextricably bound up with practices (including works of compassion) that *reflect* the cognitive understanding of the doctrine of emptiness, and as good rebirths (which put one in better position to attain it) can be achieved by engaging in them, it may well be best, on the Buddhist scheme of things, for a given individual to set such doctrinal matters aside for a time (or a life or two) in order to cultivate the equally necessary "skillful means."[2] Thus, this form of Buddhist teaching is compatible with a very relaxed attitude about doctrinal religious differences – but only because of its commitment to specific propositions concerning the nature of reality which conflict with those of various other faiths, such as traditional Christianity, and which conflict with the pluralist's conception as well.

Thus, the pluralist's position is at odds with most if not all traditional religions, not just "exclusivist" Christianity. But how should we, as Christians, address the pluralist's no-difference-in-spiritual-fruits objection? The most basic point to make is that the pluralist poses a false choice. The traditional Christian who rejects pluralism is *not* thereby forced to the "arbitrary" claim that Christian experiences of God alone are reliable, while experiences of ultimate reality as mediated by other traditions are wholly illusory. The nature of religious experience and the extent to which its content is shaped by religious tradition are complex subjects, which I cannot explore here. But clearly Christians can allow that non-Christians are capable of experiencing God in some manner, though we will, owing to the teachings of the faith, suppose that some of the very specific claims that are made about God (or the Ultimate) as a result of those experiences are false, stemming from the influence of false religious tenets.[3] For it is integral to Christian teaching that God is Lord of all creation and desires that all should come to him (2 Pet. 3:9). Human beings were made to enjoy him; it is only through the effects of sin that we do not naturally experience his presence as vividly and continuously as one experiences the warmth of the sun on a bright summer day. But sin has not entirely eradicated this natural affinity for our Maker, nor has God abandoned those who have yet to come to understand his purposes and offer of redemption through Christ. None of us can say to what extent our supposed experiences of God are the result of self-delusion or of some unreliable source. Christians themselves are taught to look on their religious experiences with some degree of caution and to test whether any content they have (purporting to reveal something about God's nature or his purposes) are consistent with authoritative teaching. For we, too, are prone to all sorts of pride, dishonesty about our true condition, and susceptibility to social influences, and also to blameless forms of powerful unconscious influences. But as we know that God has not abandoned his people and we are explicitly taught to expect some measure of experience of his gracious presence (at times comforting and at times rebuking), we confidently suppose that much of our apparent experience of God is genuine. God really is intending and causing us to have some measure of heightened awareness of his nature and purposes for us, though there is indeed a degree of processing or "filtering" of "divine input" (which the pluralist supposes entirely shapes the experience), and this distorts, to some extent, what God wants us to understand about himself.

B. The Arrogance Objection

A second and quite common objection to exclusivist religious belief is that it involves arrogance on the part of the believer. If I, as a traditional Christian, suppose that I have come to have true beliefs in such an important matter as religion, where so many other human beings have not, I must think that I am superior to them in some important respect – intellectually or morally. For I have been able to discern the truth in a morally significant matter where so many others have failed.

But, common though this objection is, it is quite unpersuasive. Let us acknowledge at the outset that the Christian Church has not lacked for arrogant people. More particularly, our numbers have included those who have been highly arrogant in just the way the pluralist suggests: people who supposed that Christians have believed rightly where others have not because they are superior intellectually or ethically. This is clearly repugnant. Given the organic unity of the body of Christ, it is one of the many sins we should corporately confess. (Of course, the Church is in no way *special* in this respect: we see this sin in parts of the Church precisely because the Church draws its numbers from the full range of human beings. And humanity does not lack for ample instances of every kind of moral failing, arrogance included.)

But should we think that such arrogance is an inevitable consequence of exclusivist belief? Any one of us can point to exemplary (though still flawed) "exclusivist" Christian brothers and sisters who show no discernible trace of the kind of arrogance highlighted by the pluralist. It is, after all, a basic feature of Christian teaching that faith is a gift of God and that God is specially inclined to call on the poor and those who are "foolish in the eyes of the world." Granted, even this teaching can be (and in some cases, has been) embraced with a perverse kind of pride in one's lowly social or intellectual status. But this need not occur, and often enough it does not.

Furthermore, as Peter van Inwagen has remarked, the pluralist who presses this kind of objection to traditional Christian belief is likely to "find himself surrounded by a lot of broken domestic glass."[4] Why? Because the central idea behind the arrogance objection is one the pluralist is obliged to apply to nonreligious beliefs as well. Perhaps the following best captures this central idea:

> For any belief of yours, once you become aware (a) that others disagree with it and (b) that you have no argument on its behalf that is likely to convince all or most of the reasonable, good-intentioned people who disagree with you, then it would be *arrogant* of you to continue holding that belief.

Now let's think about this principle in light of the pluralist's own views. He embraces this principle while surely being aware that many others think it is false. (I myself disbelieve the principle, but as it would be immodest to point to myself as convincing proof, I'll point instead to the astute and eminently fair-minded editor of this book.) But then, to be consistent, the pluralist should abandon this very principle. Believing the principle in the face of informed disagreement, as the pluralist does, violates the principle. The moral here is that pluralism is no way of escape from the charge of arrogance.

Some quick-thinking pluralist might retreat at this point and conclude that having any kind of view at all (including pluralism) in a climate of disagreement is what is arrogant. But why think that? Isn't it more sensible to suppose that the pluralist has gone overboard? He notes that some exclusivists have held their beliefs in an arrogant fashion, and wrongly concludes that arrogance is an inevitable result of exclusivist belief in the face of disagreement. In any case, the fact that one cannot, as we've just seen, *defend* this claim without falling prey to one's own principle should lead us to reject this pluralist argument.

C. The Irrationality Objection: "Where Reasonable People Differ, the Wise Man Withholds Judgment"

This brings us to a third and most fundamental objection to exclusivism, which, at a first pass, is that since there is no objective basis of *any* sort (experiential or otherwise) for reasonably selecting among religions, preferring some one of them (such as Christianity) above all the rest is irrational. Put this way, however, this argument deserves little sympathy. Following a long line of philosopher-theologians, I myself, for example, hold that a theistic worldview is rationally preferable to any of its rivals, such as philosophical naturalism. I further believe we may reasonably accept the Christian revelation and reasonably prefer it to the going alternatives.

Not surprisingly, most pluralists disagree. But they do not try to engage the thoughtful Christian by pressing the specific grounds for disagreeing on this score – that is, engage in the usual back-and-forth philosophical/theological dialogue with the goal of persuading others of one's own way of understanding things. Instead, they contend that the very fact that relevantly informed, reasonable people of good will disagree with the thoughtful Christian provides a *compelling* basis for withdrawing his acceptance of Christianity as *uniquely* true.

What should the Christian think of this objection? Here the pluralist is perhaps arguing for a "principle of rational belief" which is akin to the principle described in the arrogance objection earlier. Possibly, something like this:

> For any belief of yours, once you become aware both that others disagree with it and that you have no argument on its behalf that is likely to convince all or most of those dissenters that are relevantly informed, reasonable, and of good will, it would be *irrational* of you to continue holding that belief.

But is this really so? One might try to draw an

analogy here to science, where, we are often told, people refrain from belief until the facts come in so as to produce virtual unanimity. But this popular portrayal of the history of scientific practice and belief is a myth. There are numerous instances of scientists vigorously contending for a given theory in the face of highly distinguished opposition. This may take the form of large opposing factions or of even only one scientist defending a position against the rest of the relevant scientific community, a view which in some cases ultimately prevails. Must we say that in all such cases, knowledgeable people who carefully considered the evidence, weighed arguments for competing positions, and came to a particular view were irrational to do so?

Consider the following very recent example. In the 1980s, two researchers named Marshall and Warren uncovered strong evidence that a bacterium known as H. pylori is responsible (in most cases) for making the stomach and intestinal lining vulnerable to the formation of peptic ulcers. When they produced this evidence, the scientific community scoffed at it, in part because it contradicted firm opinion that no bacteria could survive in the half gallon of acid produced by a human stomach. (Marshall went so far as to consume a large quantity of H. pylori. After developing acute ulcers, he then treated himself with an antibiotic that permanently eradicated the problem.) Evidence for the bacterium theory mounted for several years before it was generally accepted. To this day, many who suffer from ulcers are not tested for H. pylori or given the necessary antibiotic.

I take it that this case strongly suggests that the principle of rational belief proposed above is implausible. However, a more reasonable pluralist might argue that the principle does not apply to beliefs of all sorts, but only to religious beliefs (and maybe a few other types of belief) since with these beliefs there is never a convergence of opinion, at least among "experts." This makes religious belief quite different from scientific belief where contested ideas come either to be accepted or rejected, owing to the uncovering of new evidence.

Yet even though there is such a difference between scientific and religious disputes, why exactly should we suppose that it is a *relevant* difference? No doubt, the fact that scientific theories are open to confirmation and disconfirmation in a way that usually leads to consensus, in the end, is a good thing. But why should we think that the fact that scientific theories can be confirmed and disconfirmed in this way makes rational disagreement, in the *absence* of conclusive evidence, acceptable in the scientific case, but not in the religious one?

Some have thought that the absence of decisive empirical testability of religious beliefs shows that they are "meaninglessness." But, again, why should anyone think this? While I haven't the space to explore this matter here, I'll say that I myself don't find the prospects for defending this pluralist principle at all promising. In any case, the reader will note that the argument beginning in the next paragraph applies equally to this restricted version of the irrationality argument.

I have argued that the "principle of rational belief" that seems to lie behind pluralist criticisms of traditional Christian belief is not at all clearly true. But matters get worse for the pluralist critic. One thing all pluralists believe is the thesis of pluralism itself. And this thesis is not something that has been widely agreed upon, even among those who have considered the question. (It has far fewer adherents, for example, than traditional Christianity.) Are not pluralists themselves, then, guilty again of violating their own principle, since they persist in their pluralist beliefs in the face of such honest dissent?[5]

As a final *coup de grace*, it may be noted that this alleged principle of rational belief is prone to turn on *anyone* who endorses it. The principle, you will recall, is this:

For any belief of yours, once you become

aware both that others disagree with it and that you have no argument on its behalf that is likely to convince all or most of those dissenters that are relevantly informed, reasonable, and of good will, it would be *irrational* of you to continue holding that belief.

Now, as with the "arrogance principle" discussed earlier, I know many reasonable people who deny this rationality principle. (I'll again tip my hat towards the distinguished, acutely intelligent editor of this book.) So it seems that anyone who endorses this principle in present intellectual circumstances has good reason to reject it: since reasonable and good-intentioned people disagree about the principle, the principle itself says that the honorable thing to do is not to believe it. It may for all that be *true*, but given the fact that we *don't* all accept it, none of us who are apprised of that fact can *consistently believe* it to be true. And if we cannot *consistently* believe it, we have quite a good reason not to believe it.[6]

The general moral to be drawn here is that we can't avoid making judgments as best we can even where others disagree. Pluralists themselves invariably make highly contentious assumptions about morality and rationality. They can do so, however, only by exempting themselves from their own arbitrary standard.

Clearly, the way to make progress here is not, as the pluralist holds, to pat the exclusivists on the head and declare all the beliefs of the disagreeing parties equally "correct" (though not correct in the way the disagreeing parties *think* they are).

III. Against Pluralism

It is worth noting that my remarks in the previous section, if successful, do not show that pluralism is *false*; rather, they only serve to undercut the arguments that pluralists make against exclusivists. But we may go further, I believe, and provide positive reasons for thinking that the pluralists' own alternative view is defective. To do so, however, we need to have a concrete version of pluralism before us.

A. A Pluralist Picture of Things

Here's one way of telling the pluralist story.[7] Religious beliefs that have formed within major religious traditions such as Christianity are culturally conditioned responses to Ultimate Reality ("the Ultimate"). In itself, the Ultimate is beyond all the categories religious believers apply to it. Many devout persons of every established faith experience the Ultimate, but never as it *really is* (something which is unknowable), but only through one or other of its many manifestations, all of which are conditioned by religious tradition. This is an inevitable consequence of the gulf between this Ultimate Reality and our finite minds. When we come in contact with this Ultimate Reality, our minds actively (though unconsciously) *process* it in a way that makes it understandable *to us*. The result is an experience of the Ultimate by Christians as the Heavenly Father, and by Zen Buddhists as nirvana.

It is important to remember here, as I have hinted at earlier, that the pluralist does not think that the diversity of claims made about the Ultimate shows that those claims are false. This is the point of saying these diverse claims correspond to "authentic manifestations of the Ultimate." Sometimes manifestations are manifestations of deities (Yahweh, Allah, and Krishna) and sometimes of nonpersonal absolutes (the advaitic Hindu Brahman and the Buddhist nirvana). Rather than regarding these different ways of understanding the Ultimate as false, they are viewed as ways in which the Ultimate becomes an actual object of religious worship and pursuit. For we cannot worship the Ultimate "as it really is," since we are intellectually incapable of grasping it in this way. None of the distinctions which structure our religious experience can apply to it, not even as an approximation or by analogy. "As it really is," the Ultimate is neither personal nor impersonal, one nor many, good nor evil.

But though there are many and widely diverse authentic manifestations of the Ultimate, the pluralist is not bound to admit that "anything goes." It would be an embarrassment to the pluralist if, for example, he had to say that the theology of the Branch Davidians or the Aum Shin Rikyo cult is an equally authentic manifestation of the Ultimate. No, only some religious conceptions rightly relate us to the Ultimate. Which ones? Pluralists typically hold that a conception of the Ultimate is "authentic" if it moves adherents from being self-centered to being Reality-centered or to affirming the goodness of ultimate reality.[8]

B. Pluralism as an Explanatory Hypothesis

Pluralists commonly hold that their view is the *simplest hypothesis* that accounts for the diverse forms of religious experience and thought.[9] Thus, we should favor the pluralist hypothesis just as, for example, we favor the simplest available scientific theory capable of providing an account for a wide range of data in a certain domain. However, the supposed explanatory power of pluralism is only superficial. There certainly is a marked simplicity to the pluralist's scheme, but its shortcomings offset this particular virtue by a mile.

Consider, for starters, the relationship that the pluralist supposes exists between the Ultimate "as it really is" and individual human beings. There are at least two very odd features of this relationship, features which undercut the claim that the pluralist hypothesis is the *best explanation* for the diversity of human religious experience. First, *all* the content of religious experience, on this view, is provided by the human experiencer. The only contribution the Ultimate makes to the experience is as some sort of "ultimate source" or "ground" of that experience. But even this way of putting it may suggest too much. For it suggests that the Ultimate *causes* us to have the experience we do. But the pluralist cannot say even this, since putting it this way favor religious

views (such as theism) that conceive of the Ultimate as an entity distinct from the physical universe. On other views, the Ultimate is *simply the physical universe itself*, understood in some special way, and the "relation" between human and the Ultimate involves merely an *insight* that the Ultimate and the universe are *one and the same* in this special way.

Once we see, however, that the pluralist cannot make the very minimal claim that the Ultimate acts as cause of my experience, then the claim that the pluralist hypothesis is even *potentially* explanatory is questionable at best – let alone the claim that the pluralist hypothesis provides the best explanation.

Finally, because the pluralist holds that we can know nothing at all about the nature of the Ultimate "as it really is," the existence of this Ultimate can't do any *more* explanatory work than it does when we say that it is the "ground" of the different forms of religious experience and thought. If we cannot say even that it is active or purposive or even one or many, then we can hardly appeal to it to help us explain, for example, the existence of or order in the universe. So if the only support for the pluralist picture of the Ultimate – its potential to explain the fact of religious diversity – is itself quite weak, as I have argued, then the overall judgment we should make concerning this hypothesis is that it is not a good explanatory hypothesis *at all*.

C. The Incoherence of the Pluralist Picture

So far, I have ignored what, to my mind, is the gravest defect in at least many forms of pluralism, including the one sketched above. And that is that it is demonstrably incoherent. Out of their concern not to "unfairly" favor one religious tradition over another, pluralists usually say not just that we cannot *know* whether the Ultimate is personal or impersonal, active or passive, purposive or purposeless, one or many, etc., but that it is "beyond" these categories altogether. And this is a hard saying indeed. For while certain intellectual quarters encourage people to say such things, the claim is simply unintelligible. Perhaps the best way to make this plain is to proceed in two stages. First, I will give a simple argument for the claim that this sort of pluralist position is unintelligible. I will then note that this initial critique is *too* simple. This will show us that there is one (and only one) basic way of avoiding my critique. The second stage is to note that this way out is not one taken by the pluralist.

Here is the first (overly simple) argument against the intelligibility of pluralism:

> Anyone who asserts the "beyond human categories" kind of pluralism is either in a muddle or has lost the sense of the word "not." For consider the two claims, "The Ultimate is personal" and "The Ultimate is not personal." These are not merely *contraries*, as logicians say, such that at *most* one of them can be true, though it might be that neither is true. (As is the case with the claims, "Tim O'Connor is the greatest living philosopher" and "Michael Murray is the greatest living philosopher." At most one of these is true, but it's also just possible that neither is.) They are logical *contradictories* – it must be that one of them is true and the other is false. If it is false that the Ultimate is personal, then it is true that the Ultimate is not personal. And vice versa. The pluralist wants to assert, however, that it is not true that "the Ultimate is personal" and it is not true that "the Ultimate is not personal." This is simply contradictory (inconsistent), and it is not intelligible that a contradiction be true.

The reason this argument is too simple is that it overlooks a pervasive feature of most of our concepts, which is that they are *vague*. One familiar example of this is our color concepts. Imagine a large array of adjacent color samples, such that the one on the left is clearly red, and the one on the right is clearly orange, and the shades in between constitute a slow transition from red to

orange such that any adjacent two are barely perceptibly different in color. At what point do the red patches end and the orange patches begin? Clearly, if the differences between adjacent shades are subtle enough, there will be no definite answer to this question. There will be a border region such that it will not be (fully or definitely) true that a particular patch in the region is red, nor will it be (fully or definitely) false that it is red, either. Our concept of redness is simply not sharp enough to decide the matter one way or the other.

Now one could claim that personhood, like redness, is a vague concept, admitting borderline cases. And if this were correct, it does not clearly follow from its being not (definitely) true that the Ultimate is personal that it must be (definitely) false that it is personal – that it must be impersonal. And in this way, one might try to escape between the horns of the dilemma.

But the pluralist does not try to escape the simple critique in this way, for doing so would require that the pluralist make some very substantive claims about the nature of the Ultimate, staking out a position that directly competes with each of the major religious outlooks. And this is the very thing the pluralist wants to avoid. No, the typical pluralist's position is more radical than that, and this means that it is also incoherent. There simply is nothing for "being beyond personhood" to mean, if it is neither being utterly impersonal or being somewhere in between personhood and non-personhood. And inconsistency provides as strong a case against a view (in this instance, against pluralism) as one can make.

Maybe, however, there is a middle-of-the-road position available to the pluralist here. The pluralist might say that for any property we wish to ascribe to the Ultimate, it either has that property, or it lacks it, or it is somewhere in between having and lacking it (as some of the colors on the continuum I mentioned earlier might be between "being red" and "being not-red"). Since being one or many, being active or entirely passive, and being identical to or distinct from the physical world are pretty clearly sharp, not vague, divisions, we might feel pushed in one direction or another on properties such as these. (We might say, for example, that the Ultimate is a single, active being distinct from the universe.) But perhaps we're less sure about other attributes, such as personhood. Given disagreement across religious traditions, we could split the difference here. But now however exactly we come down on individual attributes using this procedure, aren't we just being arbitrary? Aren't we simply making our own judgments in at least some cases – thereby *contradicting* some religious tradition or other – and then splitting the difference in others, out of deference to the diversity of opinion, including the ones one has contradicted with respect to other claims? Of all the ways one might come to a developed opinion in religious matters, this seems the *most* arbitrary.

IV. Conclusion

Every age has its unreflectively held assumptions. For the present generation, a vaguely articulated notion of pluralism in relation to religion and morality is one of those assumptions. I hope to have shown that it has a lot less to be said on its behalf than many people suppose. I haven't considered every possible variation on the pluralist theme, but my arguments can, I believe, be generalized.

One less obvious form pluralism takes in our culture is a certain kind of agnosticism (which on its face seems rather different from pluralism). The usual variety is instanced by those who have considered evidence on behalf of various religious beliefs and judge the evidence to be inconclusive. Such people ought to be open to standard apologetical argument. But nowadays, many who profess agnosticism about God or religious claims have not spent a lot of time considering the pros and cons. Instead, they're content to gesture at the widespread disagreement and throw up their hands. ("Who can say?") Five

will get you ten that underlying the view of such a person is the thought that one cannot reasonably have a definite opinion on such matters precisely because there is widespread disagreement. (That's why it's unnecessary to actually look at any arguments in detail.) And this position is unstable in just the way that holding our "principle of reasonable belief" above was seen to be unstable. For it is itself a controversial claim, and so (given what it claims) cannot be consistently held.

In the present climate of opinion, the first task for the contemporary Christian apologist in making the case for Christianity is precisely to convince those he engages of the untenability of this pluralist attitude.

Notes

1 John Hick, *An Interpretation of Religion* (London: Macmillan, 1989), 235.

2 My discussion throughout this paragraph is indebted to Jane Compson's recent article, "The Dalai Lama and the World Religions: A False Friend?" *Religious Studies* 32 (1996): 271–79.

3 In defending this contention, we ought not implausibly to assert as some occasionally do that Christian experiences of God are "self-authenticating" (have a distinguishing mark that guarantees that they're the genuine article) in a manner that other religious experiences are not.

4 See the final few paragraphs of his "Non Est Hick," in *The Rationality of Belief and the Plurality of Faith*, ed. T. Senor (Ithaca: Cornell University Press, 1995), also reprinted in *God, Knowledge, and Mystery* (Ithaca: Cornell University Press, 1995).

5 This point and the one that follows have been made by Alvin Plantinga, in his essay, "A Defense of Religious Exclusivism," in *The Philosophy of Religion: An Anthology*, ed. L. Pojman (Belmont, CA: Wadsworth, 1987), and also reprinted in *The Rationality of Belief.*

6 Thought for the enthusiastic thinker: I have noted that there is no straightforward inconsistency in the circumstance that a principle is *true* even though none of us can consistently (or, therefore, reasonably) believe it. But there would be a special peculiarity to such an unhappy circumstance in its present

application: for how could a true (and if true, importantly true) principle of *rationality* be such that we cannot rationally believe it? In such a case, we would be required to try to form beliefs *in accordance* with the principle – it is by hypothesis *true*, after all – but we could not rationally *reflect* on such practice and form a true belief about the nature of the underlying principle. I take such a bizarre consequence to constitute a "transcendental refutation" of the principle. Away with such intellectual deviltry! Exercise for the enthusiastic and *diligent* thinker: construct a rebuttal (similar to the one given in the text of the irrationality objection) of another pluralist claim – viz., that the fact that religious views are strongly correlated with birthplace and family religion should lead one to doubt their (literal) truth. ("You believe Christianity only because you were raised in a Christian culture and/or home. If you had been born in Saudi Arabia, you would have been a Muslim. Therefore . . .") [A good answer may be found in Alvin Plantinga's "A Defense of Religious Exclusivism." For Hick's reply to this and Plantinga's rejoinder, see their contributions to the symposium on pluralism in the July 1997 issue of *Faith and Philosophy*.]

7 The story I tell (and some of the arguments against any contrasting, "absolutist" religious view, such as that of traditional Christianity) have been developed with greatest care by Professor John Hick, in such works as *An Interpretation of Religion; Disputed Questions in Theology and the Philosophy of Religion* (New Haven: Yale University Press, 1993); "Religious Pluralism," in *A Companion to Philosophy of Religion*, ed. P. Quinn and C. Taliaferro (Cambridge, MA: Blackwell, 1997); and "The Epistemological Challenge of Religious Pluralism," *Faith and Philosophy* (July 1997).

8 See Hick, *Disputed Questions*, 178, 174.

9 See, e.g., Hick, *An Interpretation of Religion*, 248.

God's Existence and Nature

INTRODUCTION TO PART 2

AS SEEN IN A NUMBER of readings in the first part, a central aim of philosophy of religion in general, and natural theology in particular, is proving that God exists or that God doesn't exist on the basis of unaided human reason. There are numerous arguments for the existence of God. Alvin Plantinga, for example, published a paper entitled "Two Dozen (or so) Theistic Arguments." In addition to the more familiar ontological, teleological, and moral arguments, Plantinga also advances lesser known arguments, including the argument from intentionality, the argument from intuition, and the argument from love. Even if after one has considered each individual argument and found it unsatisfactory in some way, it is still possible that all the arguments, together, provide a cumulative case for the existence of God. For this reason, it is helpful to think of the various arguments for the existence of God as interrelated, rather than as standalone entities.

The wide range of arguments can be classified in a number of ways. The most common method of classification differentiates between *a posteriori* arguments and *a priori* arguments. *A posteriori* arguments have at least one premise that is based on some feature of the universe that we know via experience. For example, various versions of the design argument focus on particular facts about the nature of the universe in which we live, such as the exact strength of gravity, the electromagnetic force, or biological facts about living organisms. Similarly, one version of the cosmological argument has a crucial premise that there exists a contingent universe (that is, a universe which does exist but doesn't have to exist). In contrast, *a priori* arguments do not rest on premises known by means of experience. *A priori* arguments for the existence of God instead focus on concepts or principles that can purportedly be known simply by reflection or introspection.

The best known type of *a priori* argument for the existence of God, the ontological argument, is the subject of the first reading in this section. In "Necessary Being: The Ontological Argument," Peter van Inwagen presents and criticizes a historically influential version of the ontological argument, that given by René Descartes. According to Descartes, the concept of God is a being who is perfect in every respect; that is, God has every perfection or great-making property. Consider, then, two piles of gold, one of which is imaginary and the other of which actually exists. Which is better (or greater)? Clearly the pile that exists. For this reason, Descartes claims that actual existence is a perfection. Since God has every perfection, He must actually exist. Van Inwagen then presents Kant's criticism of Descartes' argument, showing how existence cannot be a perfection or great-making property, since existence isn't a property at all. Thus, Descartes' ontological argument fails. Van Inwagen then considers an improved version of the ontological argument according to which existence isn't a perfection, but necessary existence is. While this version of the argument avoids

Kant's criticism, it too fails. Van Inwagen then presents a modal version of the ontological argument, which uses the metaphysics of possible worlds to show that if it is possible that a perfect being (or God) exists, then that being necessarily exists. He then considers a number of challenges to demonstrating the possibility of a perfect being.

The next pair of articles focuses on an *a posteriori* argument for the existence of God, the cosmological argument. Alexander Pruss's "Some Recent Progress on the Cosmological Argument" canvases a number of contemporary versions of the cosmological argument. The general strategy of cosmological arguments is to take a general feature of the world and then argue that the best explanation for that feature is a First Cause, or First Mover. Pruss begins by considering that even if the cosmological argument is successful, further argumentation would be needed to show that the First Cause is God as traditionally conceived by monotheistic religions. Nevertheless, he thinks that a successful cosmological argument would go a considerable distance towards that goal. Many cosmological arguments rely on the Principle of Sufficient Reason (PSR), which holds that all contingently true propositions (such as the proposition that the universes exists) have explanations. If the PSR is true, it could function as a key premise in an argument for the existence of an uncaused First Cause which is the explanation or cause of all contingent things. Pruss considers a number of justifications for the truth of the PSR, concluding that we have good reason to think that it is true. Pruss's contribution concludes with a consideration of cosmological arguments that do not rely on the Principle of Sufficient Reason, but rely instead on weaker explanatory principles. He concludes that the various versions of the cosmological argument give us good reason to think that a God-like being exists.

In "A Critical Examination of the Kalam Cosmological Argument," Wes Morriston investigates in further detail one particular type of cosmological argument, the Kalam cosmological argument. This argument has its origins in Arabic philosophy in the Middle Ages, and has recently been vigorously defended by William Lane Craig, among others. In its simplest version, the Kalam cosmological argument is as follows:

1. Whatever begins to exist has a cause of its existence.
2. The universe began to exist.
3. Therefore, the universe has a cause of its existence.

The first premise of the Kalam cosmological argument is a version of the causal principle discussed by Pruss as an alternative to the PSR, insofar as whatever comes into existence doesn't have to exist, and thus needs an explanation or cause for why it did begin to exist. The second premise has been defended on both philosophical and scientific grounds. The former involves arguments for the conclusion that an infinite past is impossible, while the latter involves big-bang cosmology. Morriston argues against both ways of supporting the second premise. First, he argues that the two philosophical arguments given by Craig for the conclusion that the past couldn't be infinite are unsound. He then argues that big-bang cosmology is consistent with there being an infinite series of big-bangs and big-crunches which, if true, would involve the universe not having begun to exist. Morriston then gives reason to doubt the first premise of the Kalam cosmological argument. He concludes that the Kalam argument is not a successful argument for the existence of God or for creation *ex nihilo.*

The next pair of articles examines another influential type of *a posteriori* argument for the existence of God: design arguments. (Design arguments are also sometimes referred to as teleological arguments, insofar as the purported design provides some goal or *telos.*) Design arguments are empirical arguments for the existence of God which typically begin by identifying some empirical feature of the world and inferring God's existence as the best explanation for the feature in question. Unlike cosmological arguments which tend to focus on a general fact such as the existence of the universe, design arguments focus on more particular properties. In "A Scientific Argument for the Existence of God: The Fine-Tuning Design Argument," Robin Collins uses a number of constants and values in physics to argue that our universe was designed to support life by God. Collins compares three different hypotheses for the apparent design exhibited by the natural world: theism; an atheistic single-universe hypothesis, which holds that there exists only one universe; and an atheistic many-universes hypothesis, which holds that there exists an infinite number of universes which differ in their initial conditions and values for the parameters of physics. According to Collins, the apparent design in our universe is best explained by theism. Such design would not be improbable if theism were true, since the design could be explained by God-qua-designer. On the other hand, the design is quite improbable on the atheistic single-universe hypothesis, since the fine-tuning required for the existence of a universe such as ours is highly improbable on this hypothesis. While the atheistic many-universes hypothesis can account for fine-tuning better than the first atheistic alternative, Collins gives five reasons why the theistic hypothesis should be preferred to the atheistic many-universe hypothesis.

Elliot Sober's "The Design Argument" provides a contrary evaluation of design arguments. Sober approaches design arguments as arguments about likelihood, rather than about objective probabilities. He begins by explaining the nature of likelihood, and the role that it plays in design arguments, arguing that a hypothesis H's likelihood given some observation O is more important for design arguments than the posterior probability of H given O. Likelihood arguments don't purport to tell you which hypothesis to believe; rather, they evaluate how an observation discriminates among competing hypotheses. Sober criticizes extant versions of the design argument on the basis that they assume to know what God's goals for design are, yet do not provide the independent evidence needed to support these crucial assumptions.

Louis Pojman's contribution considers another form of argument for the existence of God: the argument from religious experience. Religious experiences come in a wide variety of forms, but all are understood to involve a subject having some kind of experiential awareness of God or the supernatural. Individuals from diverse religious traditions have claimed to have religious experiences, and such experiences are often taken as justification for belief in the existence of God (or gods). But unlike other experiences, religious experiences are typically private and non-repeatable. Pojman's "A Critique of the Argument from Religious Experience" focuses primarily on two questions:

1.   To what degree, if any, do religious experiences give justification to the subject of that experience for believing in the ontological reality of that which is experienced?

2.   To what degree, if any, does the cumulative witness of religious experience justify the claim that there is a God?

Both of these questions are based on the justification, or reasons, for thinking that something is true (here, that God exists). Pojman differentiates weak justification from strong justification. Weak justification is the justification for the person who has a religious experience to conclude that the object of that experience exists. In contrast, a religious experience provides strong justification for God's existence if it provides evidence of the existence of God for every person. Pojman raises three objections to the claim that religious experiences provide strong justification: one based on the amorphous and varied nature of religious experience, the claim that the justification for the veridicality of religious experience is circular, and the inability for religious experiences to be verified in the same way that ordinary perceptual experiences can be. Taken together, Pojman concludes that religious experience fails to provide strong justification for belief in the existence of God.

The final reading in this section, C. Stephen Layman's "God and the Moral Order," advances a version of the moral argument for God's existence. In general, such arguments have premises about the nature of morality and conclude with the existence of the divine. Layman's version of the moral argument is not intended to prove God's existence by itself; rather, it is intended as part of a larger cumulative case for the existence of God, drawing additional support from other arguments. He also intends his argument to support theism over naturalism, which he defines as the view that everything that exists is material or is dependent on material things, and that these material things are governed by causal laws. Layman's argument can be summarized as follows:

1.   In every actual case one has most reason to do what is morally required.

2.   If there is no God and no life after death, then there are cases in which morality requires that one make a great sacrifice that confers relatively modest benefits.

3.   If in a given case one must make a great sacrifice in order to do what is morally required, but the sacrifice confers relatively modest benefits, then one does not have most reason to do what is morally required.

After clarifying, motivating, and defending each of these premises, Layman shows how they lead to the conclusion that either God exists or there is life after death, or both. He then argues that if there is life after death, it is likely that theism is true. Layman concludes that this version of the moral argument gives some positive support for the existence of God.

Further Reading

Alston, William. *Perceiving God: The Epistemology of Religious Experience* (Ithaca, NY: Cornell University Press, 1991).

Craig, William Lane. *The Kalām Cosmological Argument* (London: The Macmillan Press, 1979).

Craig, William Lane. *The Cosmological Argument from Plato to Leibniz* (London: The Macmillan Press, 1980).

Everitt, Nicholas. *The Non-Existence of God* (London: Blackwell, 2004).

Gale, Richard. *On the Nature and Existence of God* (Cambridge: Cambridge University Press, 1991).

Manson, Neil, ed. *God and Design: The Teleological Argument and Modern Science* (New York: Routledge, 2003).

Oppy, Graham. *Ontological Arguments and Belief in God* (New York: Cambridge University Press, 1995).

Oppy, Graham. *Arguing about Gods* (Cambridge: Cambridge University Press, 2006).

Plantinga, Alvin. *God and Other Minds* (Ithaca, NY: Cornell University Press, 1967).

Pruss, Alexander. *The Principle of Sufficient Reason: A Reassessment* (New York: Cambridge University Press, 2006).

Ratzsch, Del. *Nature, Design and Science* (Albany: SUNY, 2001).

Sobel, Jordan Howard. *Logic and Theism* (New York: Cambridge University Press, 2004).

Swinburne, Richard. *The Existence of God* (New York: Clarendon, 1991).

Wainwright, William, ed. *The Oxford Handbook of Philosophy of Religion* (Oxford: Oxford University Press, 2005).

Chapter 8

Peter van Inwagen

NECESSARY BEING: THE ONTOLOGICAL ARGUMENT

Late in the eleventh century, an archbishop of Canterbury named Anselm wrote a book called the *Proslogium*, which was largely devoted to the exposition of a certain argument for the existence of God. The interesting thing about this argument was that it claimed to show that the non-existence of God was impossible, owing to the fact that any assertion of the non-existence of God must be self-contradictory. This is a very strong claim indeed. To see how strong it is, imagine an atheist named Athelred who is fond of proclaiming to all and sundry that there is no God. If Anselm is right, then every time Athelred issues this proclamation, he contradicts himself; he contradicts himself in just as strong a sense as he would have if he had said, "There is no God . . . *and* there is a God" or "My house is rectangular and has six sides." Anselm did not, of course, contend that the contradiction involved in saying that there is no God is quite as blatant as the contradictions involved in these two statements. (If the contradiction were that easy to spot, no argument would be needed to show that it exists.) But he did contend that this contradiction, though hidden and requiring an argument for its exposure, was a contradiction in the same strong sense as the contradictions involved in these two statements.

It should be obvious that if Anselm is right in his claims for his argument, then this argument provides an answer for the question, Why should there be anything at all? For if the thesis that there is no God is self-contradictory, then it cannot be true. And if there were nothing at all, then that thesis would be true. If Anselm's argument shows that there has to be a God, then it shows that there cannot be nothing at all. It is true that it does not show that there has to be a physical universe like the one we observe around us, and thus it does not answer the question why there should be such a universe. But the question, Why should there be anything at all? is not the same question as, Why should there be a physical universe? The conclusion of Saint Anselm's argument, moreover, is not irrelevant to the latter question, since, if there is a God, then this God no doubt has a great deal to do with the fact that there is a physical universe.

Anselm's argument was almost immediately attacked by one Gaunilo, a Benedictine monk, and theologians and philosophers have been attacking it ever since. About two hundred years after Anselm's time, in the late thirteenth century, the argument was declared invalid by Saint Thomas Aquinas, and almost everyone has followed his lead in declaring it invalid. Indeed, philosophers and theologians have not only mostly regarded the argument as invalid but have also mostly regarded it as obviously, scandalously, and embarrassingly invalid. This judgment was nicely summed up by the nineteenth-century German philosopher Arthur Schopenhauer, who called the argument a "charming joke."

And what is this notorious argument? Actually, rather than examine Anselm's argument, we shall render our task considerably easier if we look at an argument devised about five hundred years later—at roughly the time the Pilgrims were landing at Plymouth Rock—by Descartes. Descartes's argument (which is much easier to state and to follow than Anselm's) and Anselm's argument are generally considered to be different "versions" of the same argument: each is customarily described as a version of "the ontological argument."[1]

Descartes's argument goes something like this:

If we look within ourselves, we find that we possess the concept of a perfect being. [Descartes identifies the concept of a perfect being with the concept of God and therefore regards his argument as a proof of the existence of God. But since the existence of God is not our primary concern at the moment—our primary concern is the question why there is anything at all—let us ignore this aspect of Descartes's argument. We shall simply avoid the word 'God' and the question whether the concept of a perfect being is the same as the concept that we customarily associate with this word.] That is, we find the concept of a being that is perfect in every respect or, as we may say, possesses all perfections. But existence itself is a perfection, since a thing is better if it exists than if it does not exist. But then a perfect being has to *exist*; it simply wouldn't be perfect if it didn't. Existence is a part of the *concept* of a perfect being; anyone who denied that a perfect being had the property existence would be like someone who denied that a triangle had the property three-sidedness. Just as three-sidedness is a part of the concept of a triangle—the mind cannot conceive of triangularity without also conceiving of three-sidedness—existence is a part of the concept of a perfect being: the mind cannot conceive of perfection without also conceiving of existence.

Now if this argument of Descartes is correct, then it provides us with an answer to the question, Why is there anything at all? If Descartes is right, then it is impossible for there to be no perfect being, just as it is impossible for there to be a triangle that does not have three sides. And if it is impossible for there to be no perfect being, then it is impossible for there to be nothing at all, since the existence of a perfect being is the existence of something.

The faults that have been ascribed to the ontological argument are many and various. One might, for example, raise the question why existence should be regarded as a "perfection." What's so wonderful about existence? one might wonder. After all, many people seem to think that they can improve their lot by suicide—that is, by electing non-existence. But it is generally conceded, or was until rather recently, that one of the faults of the ontological argument is so grievous that it is the only one that the critic of the argument need mention. This fault, or alleged fault, is best known in the formulation of Immanuel Kant. Kant's diagnosis of the argument's chief fault can be stated as follows:

Whatever else a perfection may be, any perfection must be a property—or feature, attribute, or characteristic—of things. But existence is not a property of things. 'Existence' is not one item in the list of the properties of (for example) the Taj Mahal, an item that occurs in addition to such items as 'white', 'famous for its beauty', 'located in the city of Agra', and so on. Rather, when we specify certain properties and say that something having those properties *exists*, all we are saying is that something has those properties. Suppose, for example, that the following are the properties that everyone agrees the poet Homer had if he existed: he was a blind, male Ionian poet of the eighth century B.C. who wrote all or most of the epic poems we know as the *Iliad* and the *Odyssey*. Call this collection of properties H. Now suppose that there are two classical scholars, one of whom thinks that Homer existed and one of whom thinks Homer was legendary (the two great epics that are supposedly his compositions having been pieced together over a long period from the work of many anonymous poets). It would be wrong—in fact, it would be absurd—to describe the disagreement of these two scholars by saying that the former thinks that someone had the collection of properties H and, in addition, the property of existence while the latter agrees that someone had the collection of properties H but goes on to assert that this person lacked the property of existence. No, it's just that the former scholar thinks that someone had all of (or at least most of) the properties in the set H and that the latter thinks that no one had all of (or even very many of) them. This case illustrates the sense in which existence is not a property.[2] But if existence is not a property, it cannot be an ingredient in a concept. A concept is really no more than a list of properties, the properties that a thing must have to fall under that concept. For example, the concept of a dog is just the list of properties that a thing must have to count as a dog. (The list of properties enumerated a few sentences back spells out the concept associated with the description 'the poet Homer'.) What Descartes has done is to treat existence as if it were the kind of thing that could be an ingredient in a concept. If one does this, however, one opens the door to all sorts of evident absurdities. Here is an example of such an absurdity. Define an 'egmount' as an existent mountain made entirely of gold: to be an egmount, a thing must (a) be a mountain, (b) be made entirely of gold, and (c) exist. It is obviously a part of the concept of an egmount that an egmount *exists*: it says so on the label, as it were. But, as everyone knows, there are no

egmounts. The ontological argument is this same absurdity in a (thinly) disguised form.

Although this refutation of the ontological argument was "standard" for almost two hundred years, it cannot be regarded as satisfactory. The problem is not so much that Kant says anything that is definitely wrong. The difficulty is rather as follows. It is possible to construct an argument very similar to Descartes's argument—an argument that just obviously ought to be invalid for the same reason as Descartes's argument—that does not treat existence as a property. And it is possible to point to a rather obvious defect that is shared by the two arguments. It will be obvious when we have done this that the shared defect is what is really or fundamentally wrong with Descartes's argument and that the Kantian refutation of the argument is at best a point about a peripheral fault in the argument.

Let us consider the idea of *necessary existence*. A thing has necessary existence if it would have existed no matter what, if it would have existed under any possible circumstances. An equivalent definition is this: A thing has necessary existence if its non-existence would have been impossible. And by "impossible" we mean *absolutely* impossible: if *x* is a necessary being, then the non-existence of *x* is as impossible as a round square or a liquid wine bottle. It is obvious that you and I do not possess necessary existence: we should never have existed if our respective sets of parents happened never to have met, and that is certainly a "possible circumstance." Moreover, it is clear that the same point applies to Julius Caesar and the Taj Mahal. As to the latter, it would not have existed if the beloved wife of a certain Mogul emperor had not died young. And even an object that has, by everyday standards, a really impressive grip on existence—Mount Everest, say—lacks necessary existence: Mount Everest would not have existed if the Indian subcontinent had not drifted into contact with Asia. The very sun would not have existed if certain random density distributions in the pre-stellar nebulae had not led to the gravitational contraction of a particular grouping of hydrogen atoms into a radiating body. For all we know, even the physical universe might not have existed—either because whatever it was that caused the universe to come into existence ten or fifteen thousand million years ago failed to produce any universe at all or because this unknown factor produced some different universe.

These reflections make it clear that necessary existence is a property, in just the sense that mere existence is not (if Kant is right) a property. It is true that it may not be a *possible* property. Perhaps it is a property like *being both round and square* or *being a liquid wine bottle* or *being a prime number that is larger than all other prime numbers* that nothing could possibly have. (It is certainly hard to think of an uncontroversial example of something that has necessary existence.) The important point for present purposes is that necessary existence cannot be said not to be a property at all or at least not because of considerations like those that Kant adduces to show that existence is not a property. It seems clear that whatever may be the case with mere existence, necessary existence *can* be an ingredient in a concept. In fact, many philosophers and theologians have held that necessary existence is a part of the concept of God—and other philosophers and theologians have denied that necessary existence is a part of the concept of God. Now let us consider an argument that is like Descartes's ontological argument, except that 'necessary existence' is substituted for 'existence' throughout. The argument would look something like this:

- A perfect being has all perfections.
- Necessary existence is a perfection.
  Hence, A perfect being has necessary existence.
- Whatever has necessary existence has existence.
  Hence, A perfect being has existence.

- Whatever has existence exists.
  Hence, A perfect being exists.

It is interesting to note that in one way, at least, this argument is more plausible than Descartes's actual argument. We saw above that it is not quite clear why one should assume that existence is a perfection. But there seems to be no such problem about necessary existence. A being (like you and me and Caesar and the Taj Mahal and the sun and perhaps even the physical universe) that lacks necessary existence will typically depend for its own existence on the prior operations of other beings, and probably these operations will involve a large element of sheer *chance*. But a being that has necessary existence is not dependent on the vagaries of chance, for its existence is absolutely inevitable. Necessary existence is, therefore, a most impressive property—the same can hardly be said for existence: the lowliest worm and the most ephemeral subnuclear resonance *exist*—and anything that possesses it is a most impressive being. It is for this very reason that many philosophers and theologians have wanted to include necessary existence among the attributes of God. It therefore seems very plausible to hold that necessary existence should be an item in any list of "perfections."

Be that as it may, the new version of Descartes's argument is obviously invalid, and it looks very much as if it were invalid for much the same reason as the original version. Recall the example of the egmount. We can easily construct a similar example that is addressed to the revised argument. Let us define a "negmount" as a *necessarily* existent golden mountain. If the revised version of the argument is valid, then (or so it would seem) so is the following argument. Let us call the three properties that occur in this definition (necessary existence, being made of gold, and being a mountain) the "negmontanic properties." We may now argue:

- A negmount has all negmontanic properties.

- Necessary existence is a negmontanic property.

  Hence, A negmount has necessary existence.
- Whatever has necessary existence has existence.

  Hence, A negmount has existence.
- Whatever has existence exists.

  Hence, A negmount exists.

But the conclusion of this argument is obviously false. There is no negmount. In fact, it can plausibly be argued that not only is the conclusion false but it couldn't *possibly* be true. A mountain, whatever it may be made of, is a physical object, and it is very hard to see how a physical object could possibly be necessarily existent. Even if necessary existence is possible for some sorts of things, a physical object is composed of parts, and it would not have existed if those parts had never come together. But there is no need to argue about this subtle point. The same conclusion can be reached in a way that allows no evasion. Let a "nousquare" be a necessarily existent round square. If the above argument is valid, then an exactly parallel argument proves the existence of a necessarily existent round square—and hence of a round square.

It is clear, therefore, that the above argument is *not* valid. But wherein does its invalidity lie? Not, apparently, where Kant says, for the argument does not assume that existence is a property, and Kant has provided no reason that should lead us to say that necessary existence cannot figure as an ingredient in a concept. (The concept of a negmount seems to me to be a perfectly good example of a concept, albeit it is not a very useful concept.) What is wrong with the negmount argument is very simple: its first premise—'A negmount has all negmontanic properties'—is ambiguous. That is, it could have either of two meanings:

- Anything that is a negmount has all of the negmontanic properties.

- There is a negmount that has all of the negmontanic properties.

(The former of these statements is true whether or not there are negmounts. It simply says that a thing does not count as a negmount unless it has all of the negmontanic properties. The latter statement, of course, cannot be true unless there is a negmount.) The ambiguity is rooted in two quite different functions performed by the indefinite article. To say "A public official is sworn to uphold the law" is to say that anyone who is a public official is sworn to uphold the law, an assertion that, in principle, could be true even if there were no public officials. To say "A public official was arraigned in Superior Court today" is to say that there *is* a public official who was arraigned in Superior Court today. (Descartes's original statement of his argument was in Latin, which has no word corresponding to 'a' and 'an'. But there is a corresponding ambiguity in Latin.)

Because the first premise of the negmount argument is ambiguous, "it" is not really one argument at all, but two arguments jumbled together. When we disentangle the jumble, we find that one of these arguments proceeds from the premise that anything that is a negmount has all of the negmontanic properties to the conclusion that anything that is a negmount exists; the other proceeds from the premise that there is a negmount having all of the negmontanic properties to the conclusion that there is a negmount that exists. Neither of these two arguments should convince anyone that there is a negmount.

As to the first argument, its premise is clearly true, but its conclusion—anything that is a negmount exists—is true whether or not any negmounts exist (just as 'Anything that is a unicorn has a single horn' is true whether or not there are any unicorns). As to the second argument, its conclusion obviously implies that there is a negmount (an existent negmount, if that adds anything to the assertion that there is a negmount), but this was asserted by the premise—there is a negmount that has all of the negmontanic properties—and it is no news that one can derive the conclusion that there is a negmount from the assumption that there is a negmount. Such plausibility as the original negmount argument had derived from the fact that because the two arguments were run together, it looked as if we had an argument that had the impressive conclusion of the second argument and the innocent premise of the first.

All of these points apply, with very minor adjustments, both to Descartes's ontological argument and to the revised version of his argument (the one that appeals to the notion of necessary existence rather than to simple existence). Let us consider the revised version. When the first premise of the argument is properly disambiguated, we have two arguments:

- Anything that is a perfect being has all perfections.
- Necessary existence is a perfection.
  Hence, Anything that is a perfect being has necessary existence.
- Whatever has necessary existence has existence.
  Hence, Anything that is a perfect being has existence.
- Whatever has existence exists.
  Hence, Anything that is a perfect being exists.

- There is a perfect being that has all perfections.
- Necessary existence is a perfection.
  Hence, There is a perfect being that has necessary existence.
- Whatever has necessary existence has existence.
  Hence, There is a perfect being that has existence.
- Whatever has existence exists.
  Hence, There is a perfect being that exists.

The first of these two arguments proceeds from an obvious premise to a trivial conclusion. The second argument has a non-trivial conclusion, but this conclusion is, essentially, the first premise. Those who grant the first premise of the second argument hardly need the other premises; they can make do with a much simpler argument:

- There is a perfect being that has all perfections.
  Hence, There is a perfect being.

But this argument has—to say the least—little persuasive force. And it should by now be clear that neither Descartes's ontological argument nor our revision of it is any better. Such persuasive force as these arguments have is due simply to the fact that each of them is a jumble of two arguments; in each case, one of the two has an obviously true premise and the other has an interesting conclusion.

It would seem that Descartes's attempt to prove that the non-existence of a perfect being is impossible is a failure and that it therefore cannot be of any help in our inquiry into why there should be anything at all. (Without going into the details of the matter, I will record my conviction that the earlier argument of Saint Anselm is also a failure.) This does not mean, however, that the ontological argument is of no relevance to our inquiry, for it may be that there are other versions of the ontological argument that are not guilty of the fallacy of ambiguity that was the downfall of Descartes's argument. And recent researches in the philosophy of modality (the philosophy of necessity and possibility) do indeed seem to have produced an argument that it is reasonable to call a version of the ontological argument and which does not exploit a hidden ambiguity or commit any other logical fallacy.

This argument, which is usually called the modal ontological argument, is best presented in terms of "possible worlds." This notion may be explained as follows. We have said "the World" is the totality of everything that there is. But it is obvious that the World might be different—indeed that it might always have been different—from the way it is. There might be fewer cats or more dogs. There might never have been any cats or dogs at all (if, say, evolution had taken a slightly different course). Napoleon might have lost the battle of Austerlitz or won the battle of Waterloo. As we saw in our discussion of the notion of a necessary being, the sun— perhaps even the physical universe—might never have existed. A list of the ways things might have been different (which is the same as a list of the ways the World might have been different) could go on and on without any discernible limit. By a possible world, we mean simply a complete specification of a way the World might have been, a specification that is so precise and definite that it settles every single detail, no matter how minor.[3] If we assume that everything that there is or could be is subject to the flow of time—almost certainly not a wise assumption—we could say that a possible world is a complete history-and-future that the World might have (or might have had), one whose completeness extends to every detail.

In order to make full use of the concept of a possible world, we need the idea of *truth in a given possible world* and we need the idea of *existence in a given possible world*. While various technical accounts of these ideas are available, we shall be content with an intuitive or impressionistic account of them. A few examples should suffice. If in a given world *x* there are no dogs—if that is how *x* specifies things: that there are no dogs—then in *x* dogs do not exist, and it is true in *x* that there are no dogs, and the proposition (assertion, statement, thesis) that there are no dogs is true in *x*. If in a given possible world *y* Napoleon won the battle of Waterloo, then it is true in *y* that Napoleon won the battle of Waterloo, and the proposition that Napoleon won the battle of Waterloo is true in *y*. And, of course, Napoleon must *exist* in *y*, for one cannot win a battle if one does not exist. But there are possible worlds in which Napoleon was never born

(or even conceived) and in those possible worlds he does not exist.

Once we have the notion of a proposition's being true in a possible world, we can say what it is for a proposition to be *possibly true* and for a proposition to be *necessarily true*. A proposition is possibly true if it is true in *at least one* possible world, and necessarily true if it is true in *all* possible worlds.

The possible world that specifies the way the World really *is* is called *the actual world*. A more formal definition is this: a possible world *w* is the actual world just in the case that something is true in *w* if and only if it is—without qualification—true.[4] It is important not to confuse the actual world with the World. The actual world is a mere specification, a description of a way for things to be. It has only the kind of abstract reality that belongs to a story or a scenario or a computer program. The World, however, is not a description of a way for things to be: it is, so to speak, the things themselves. If it is an individual, it has you and me and every other individual as parts. If it is not an individual but a mere collection, it is at least the collection of all of the individuals. It is the features of the World that make one of the possible worlds the one that is actual, just as it is the geographical features of the earth that make some maps accurate or correct and other maps inaccurate or incorrect. It is the features of the World that make *one* of the ways for things to be the way that things are.

It is not necessary to make use of the concept of a possible world in presenting the "modal ontological argument," but it is advisable, since the English grammatical constructions that are used in formulating modal reasoning are sources of much ambiguity, and this ambiguity can cause arguments that are logically invalid to look as if they were valid.[5] The easiest and most elegant way to avoid these ambiguities is to carry on discussions that involve modal reasoning in terms of possible worlds.

In order to state the modal ontological argument, we need two notions: the notion of a necessary being and the notion of something's having a property (feature, attribute, characteristic) essentially.

We have already met the notion of necessary existence in our discussion of Descartes's ontological argument. A necessary *being* is simply a being that possesses necessary existence. But we may define this concept very simply in terms of the concept of a possible world: a necessary being is a being that exists in all possible worlds (and necessary existence is the property of existing in all possible worlds). Beings that are not necessary are called *contingent*. That is, a contingent being is simply a being that exists in some but not all possible worlds. You and I and every object of our experience are, no doubt, contingent beings. You, for example, do not exist in any possible world in which you were never conceived (and this would certainly seem to be a possible state of affairs).

The concept of the essential possession of a property is this: a thing has a property essentially just in the case that that property is a part of the thing's nature, so inextricably entwined with the thing's being that it could not exist if it did not have that property. We may explain this notion in possible-worlds language as follows: for a thing *x* to have a given property essentially is for *x* to have that property in every possible world in which *x* exists. It should be emphasized that this is a definition, not a recipe. It tells us what the essential possession of a property is, but it does not give us a method for determining whether a particular property is in fact possessed essentially by a particular thing.

Consider you, for example, and the property of humanity, or being human. Obviously you *have* this property—you *are* human—but do you have it *essentially*? Is being human so "inextricably entwined with your being" that you could not exist without being human? Are you a human being in every possible world in which you so much as exist? This is a metaphysical question, and a very controversial one. Philosophers disagree about the answer to this question

because they disagree about what *you* are, and, as a consequence, they disagree about what you could have been. But for our present purposes it will not be necessary to have any uncontroversial examples of the essential possession of a property (which is fortunate, for there are few if any examples that are uncontroversial); it is enough that we understand what is meant by the essential possession of a property. It will sometimes be useful to have a term to oppose to 'essentially' in discussion of the possession of a property by a thing. If a thing has a property but does not have it essentially, we say that it has that property *accidentally*.

The ontological argument is, or claims to be, a proof that a perfect being exists. And what is a perfect being? A perfect being, Descartes tells us, is a being that possesses all perfections. But now let us raise a question that is not settled by this formula. When we say that a perfect being possesses all perfections, do we mean that a perfect being possesses all perfections essentially or could a being be a perfect being if, although it indeed had every perfection, it had some or all of its perfections only accidentally? In order to see more clearly what is at stake in this question, let us look at a particular perfection. We may not be sure exactly which properties are perfections, but it seems reasonable to suppose that wisdom is among them. If this is not right, however, it will make no difference to our argument, which—with one exception, as we shall see—does not make any assumptions about which properties are perfections. We choose wisdom only to have something to use as a reasonably plausible example of a perfection.

Let us consider two (equally) wise beings, one of which has its wisdom essentially and the other of which has its wisdom only accidentally. This means that while one of the two beings would have been wise no matter what (as long as it managed to exist at all), the other might have been unwise. The nature of the former being is incompatible with unwisdom, and the nature of the latter is compatible both with wisdom and with unwisdom. Although it is a matter of necessity that the former is wise, given that it exists, it is, speaking metaphysically, an *accident* that the latter is wise. The latter's wisdom is, so to speak, a gift of the circumstances in which that being happens to exist, and that gift would not have been conferred by other sets of circumstances, circumstances in which that being might have found itself. (This is certainly the way most of us look at the wisdom of human beings. If Alice is, as we all agree, wise, we do not suppose that it follows from the undisputed fact of her wisdom that she would have been wise if she had been raised among people who provided her with no examples of wisdom or if she had been raised in grinding poverty that left her with no leisure for reflection. And we should probably agree that she would definitely *not* have been wise if she had, as a small child, suffered brain damage that left her with severely diminished mental capacities.)

Now—we continue to assume for the sake of the illustration that wisdom is a perfection—which of our two beings is a better candidate for the office of perfect being? The example seems to offer fairly strong support for the thesis that the essential possession of a perfection brings a being closer to the status of "perfect" than does the merely accidental possession of that same perfection. Let us therefore say that a perfect being is a being that possesses all perfections and, moreover, possesses those perfections essentially and not merely accidentally—of its own nature, and not merely as a gift of circumstance.

And what properties are perfections? As we said, we shall make only one assumption about this. We shall assume that *necessary existence* is a perfection. And this does not seem to be an implausible assumption. As we said in our discussion of Descartes's ontological argument, a being that has necessary existence is not dependent on the vagaries of chance, for its existence is absolutely inevitable. Is not "just happening to exist" a disqualification for the office of "perfect

being"? Must we not, therefore, count necessary existence as a perfection?

That necessary existence is a perfection is one of the premises of the modal ontological argument. The argument has only one other premise: that a perfect being is possible—or, equivalently, that a perfect being is not *impossible*. And such a premise must in some sense be required by any argument for the existence of anything, since an impossible being—a round square, say, or a liquid wine bottle—by definition cannot exist. Here, then, is the modal ontological argument:

- A perfect being (that is, a being that possesses all perfections essentially) is not impossible.
- Necessary existence is a perfection.[6]
  Hence, A perfect being exists.

Our first task will be to show that this argument is logically valid—that is, that its conclusion (that a perfect being exists) follows logically if its two premises are granted. Our next task will be to see whether the two premises *should* be granted. And this will come down to the task of seeing whether the first premise (that a perfect being is not impossible) should be granted, for we have already said about as much as there is to be said on the question whether necessary existence is a perfection.

We proceed to show that this argument is valid. It will be easiest to display the reasoning behind the modal ontological argument diagrammatically. Let us suppose (just to keep the diagram manageable; our argument in no way depends on how many possible worlds there are) that there are exactly four possible worlds, which we shall call One, Two, Three, and Four. We shall represent each possible world by a circle. And let us represent the assertion that, in a given possible world, there exists something that has a given property by placing inside the circle that represents that possible world a symbol that represents that property. For example, if 'W' represents wisdom, then the figure

Four   (W)

represents the assertion that in Possible World Four there exists something that is wise. And let us represent the assertion that a given possible world is actual by placing the symbol '<' to the right of the circle that represents that possible world. (We shall call this symbol the 'actuality cursor', since it will be useful to think of it as a movable "pointer.") Thus, the figure

Two   ( )   <

represents the assertion that Possible World Two is the actual world, and the figure

One   (W)   <

represents the assertion that Possible World One is actual and contains something wise. By a *world-diagram* we mean a diagram that satisfies two conditions: first, the diagram must contain a circle representing each possible world, and, secondly, the diagram must contain the actuality cursor (the symbol '<'), placed to the right of exactly one of the circles. (The second condition corresponds to the fact that exactly one possible world is actual.)

In addition to these two "required" features, a world-diagram may also have the following "optional" feature: it may contain any number of symbols representing properties, these symbols being placed inside any or all of the circles.

Given our assumption that there are just the four possible worlds One, Two, Three, and Four, the following figure is a world-diagram:

One   (W)
Two   ( )
Three   ( )   <
Four   (W)

A world-diagram tells us which possible worlds there are and which of them is the actual world; it may also tell us whether, in various of those possible worlds, there are things having certain specified properties. The above diagram represents the assertion that there are exactly four possible worlds, One, Two, Three, and Four, that Three is the actual world, and that in worlds One and Four there is something wise.

A world-diagram is said to be "correct in" a given possible world if (and only if) every assertion represented in the diagram is true in that possible world. The above diagram is correct in Possible World Three if it is true in Three that there exist exactly the four possible worlds displayed in the diagram, that Possible World Three is the one that is actual, and that in two of the other worlds, One and Four, there is something that is wise.

Let us now see how world-diagrams can help us with the question whether the conclusion of the modal ontological argument follows from its two premises. Let us assume for the sake of argument that both of the premises of the modal ontological argument are true and see whether we can deduce its conclusion from this assumption. The first premise tells us that a perfect being, a being having all perfections essentially, is possible, and that is the same thing as saying that in at least one possible world there exists a being who has all perfections essentially. Let us arbitrarily assume that such a being exists in Possible World Two—that Two is the possible world, or one of the possible worlds, in which there is a perfect being. Our arbitrary choice of Possible World Two as a "starting point" can do no harm since, according to the premise whose truth we have assumed, a perfect being must exist either in One or in Two or in Three or in Four (or else in more than one of these four possible worlds), and we shall see that the reasoning that we are about to examine would lead to the same conclusion no matter which possible world we took as our starting point.

Let us use the symbol 'P' to stand for the

property of being a perfect being (that is, the property of having all perfections essentially), and let us suppose that a certain inhabitant of Possible World Two, William, is set the task of drawing a world-diagram that shows how the property P is, as we might say, distributed among the four possible worlds. William, let us suppose, knows that there is a perfect being in Two, and he therefore begins drawing his diagram as follows:

Two   (P)   <

Why does William place the actuality cursor to the right of the circle representing Possible World Two? Well, we are imagining William's constructing his diagram in Possible World Two, and it is true in Possible World Two that Possible World Two is the actual world. (In general, it is true in any given possible world that *that* possible world is the actual world—just as it is true in any story that everything in that story is true.)

Now how is William to fill in the rest of the world-diagram he is constructing? William, we may imagine, reasons as follows. "Let's see . . . I know that there is a perfect being. Suppose I call that being—or one of them if there is more than one—'X'. X has all perfections, and one perfection is necessary existence. Therefore, X exists in all possible worlds. Moreover, I know that X has all perfections essentially. That is, I know that X has all perfections in every possible world in which X exists. I can infer that there is something in every possible world—namely X—that has the property P. Therefore, the following world-diagram

One   (P)
      (P)   <
Three   (P)
Four   (P)

correctly represents the distribution of the property P among the various possible worlds."

Let us assume for the moment that the reasoning that we have attributed to William is correct. Then—given the truth of our two premises—it follows that the world-diagram William has drawn is correct in Possible World Two. Can we infer from this anything about which world-diagrams are correct in the other three possible worlds? We certainly cannot infer that *this* world-diagram is correct in any other possible world, for this diagram tells us that Possible World Two is the actual world, and that proposition is, as we have seen, true only in Two. But suppose that we make just one change in William's diagram; suppose that we take the actuality cursor and "slide it down a notch," so that it is placed beside the circle representing Possible World Three:

One   (P)
Two   (P)
Three   (P)   <
Four   (P)

The revised diagram says that Possible World Three is the actual world. This assertion is true in Possible World Three. Does it follow from the assumption that William's diagram is correct in Two that the revised diagram is correct in Three? The following general principle of modal reasoning would justify this conclusion:

> If a world-diagram is correct in the possible world *x*, then the diagram obtained from it by moving the actuality cursor until it is beside the circle representing the possible world *y* is correct in the possible world *y*.

This principle seems intuitively very plausible. All it really says is that the "inner" or intrinsic features of a given possible world are features that world has from the perspective of all the possible worlds. It could be summed up in the following slogan: the only thing that changes from possible world to possible world is which possible world is actual. But this slogan is ambiguous, for there is a sense in which lots of other things "change from possible world to possible world": who won the battle of Waterloo, the population of Russia, whether I exist—in fact, everything that could be different. A more cautious way to put the thought the slogan is intended to convey is this: The only thing about a possible world x that can "change" or "look different" when x is "viewed from" various possible worlds (including x itself) is whether x is actual.

Thus, the only feature of the whole set of possible worlds that two possible worlds "disagree" about is which member of that set is the actual world. (They must, of course, disagree about at least this much, since it is true in each possible world that it is the actual world. Our principle says that this is all they disagree about.) We have, in fact, already assumed this principle, or something very much like it. We assumed it when we were describing William's reasoning. William, we remember, reasoned (in part) as follows: "I can infer that there is something in every possible world—namely X—that has the property P. Therefore, the following world-diagram

    One   ⓟ
    Two   ⓟ   <
    Three   ⓟ
    Four   ⓟ

correctly represents the distribution of the property P among the various possible worlds." But what—a carping critic might ask—allows us to assume that William, having reached the conclusion that something in every possible world had the property P, would go on to draw the world-diagram displayed above? Why shouldn't he go on to draw, say, the following diagram?

    One   ⓟ
    Two   ⓟ   <
    Three   ⓟ

"But we are assuming that there are four possible worlds, and a world-diagram, by definition, contains circles representing all of the possible worlds." True, the carping critic replies, but it does not follow from the assumption that there are four possible worlds, Possible World Two among them, that in *Possible World Two* there are four possible worlds. That would only follow if we assumed that Possible World Two was the actual world (in which case what was true would be true in Two) or at least that the possible worlds that exist from the point of view of Two are the same ones that exist from the point of view of the actual world. But suppose that (say) Possible World Four is the actual world and that, according to Possible World Two, there are only the three possible worlds One, Two, and Three. How do we know that the following world-diagram isn't correct in Four?

    One   ⓟ
    Two   ⓟ
    Three   ⓟ
    Four   ◯   <

If this diagram is indeed correct in Possible World Four, then it might well be that there is no perfect being in Four (which, remember, is the actual world) even though it is true in Two that a perfect being exists in all possible worlds—for it might just be that from the point of view of Possible World Two, there is no such possible world as Four. And this shows that the conclusion of the modal ontological argument does not follow from its premises; for all we know we are in just the situation we have imagined: a perfect being is *Possible* because it exists in a certain possible world, but it does not in fact exist because the possible world that is in fact the actual world does not exist—even as a possibility—from the point of view of the world in which the perfect being exists.

Here ends the carping critic's carping. What the critic is suggesting is, in effect, that what is possible is not fixed and necessary: certain things that are in fact possible might not have been even possible. For example, if Possible World Four does not exist from the point of view of Possible World Two, this means—given that Four is the actual world—that the way things are might not even have been possible. The critic is in fact suggesting that what is possible and impossible might have been different. And this does not seem to be a very plausible notion.

At any rate, it does not seem to be very plausible if by "possible and impossible" we understand those things that are possible and impossible "in themselves," as opposed to those things that are possible and impossible in relation to other things. Perhaps some examples will make the proposed distinction clearer. It is now impossible for anyone to own a passenger pigeon; that is because passenger pigeons are now extinct. It was impossible for anyone to fly to the moon in 1930; that was because the relevant technology had not yet been invented. Such impossibilities as these we might call conditional impossibilities, since their impossibility is conditional on something that might have been different: *if* passenger pigeons had not become extinct (as they might well not have), it *wouldn't* be impossible to own one; if the pace of technological development since the beginning of the industrial revolution had been considerably more rapid (as presumably it might have been), it *wouldn't* have been impossible to fly to the moon in 1930. One might even argue that, although it is in fact impossible to travel at 400,000 kilometers per second, it wouldn't have been impossible if the speed of light were twice what it is, and that the speed of light could have been—in some sense of 'could have been'—twice what it is. But the impossibility of a round square or a liquid wine bottle is not conditional on anything; such things are simply, without qualification, impossible. This kind of impossibility we may call *intrinsic* impossibility, and we may say that what is not intrinsically impossible is intrinsically possible.

It seems very plausible to suppose that although what is conditionally impossible may

be different in different possible worlds, what is intrinsically impossible (and intrinsically possible) is the same in all possible worlds. A round square is intrinsically impossible, and it would have been intrinsically impossible no matter what: not only is there no possible world in which there are round squares, but there is no possible world in which it is true that there *could be* round squares. A sixty-meter-high marzipan statue of Lassie is intrinsically possible, and it would have been intrinsically possible no matter what: not only is there a possible world in which there is a sixty-meter-high marzipan statue of Lassie, but there is no possible world in which it is true that there *couldn't be* a sixty-meter-high marzipan statue of Lassie.

I said above that our principle rules out the critic's objection. This is not difficult to see. If the above world-diagram were indeed correct in Possible World Four, as suggested, then the "three-world" diagram would not be correct in Two; instead—the principle says—the following diagram would be correct in Two:

One   Ⓟ
Two   Ⓟ   <
Three   Ⓟ
Four   ◯

Let us assume that our plausible principle is indeed correct. The *actual* existence of a perfect being now follows easily. One of the four possible worlds must be actual, and it does not make any difference (in the matter of the validity of the modal ontological argument) which of them it is, since, in each of them, a world-diagram obtained from the figure

One   Ⓟ
Two   Ⓟ
Three   Ⓟ
Four   Ⓟ

by an appropriate placement of the actuality cursor is correct. (The world-diagram obtained by placing the actuality cursor on the top line of the figure is correct in Possible World One, and so on.) Therefore, no matter which of the four worlds the actual world is, a perfect being exists in the actual world. (It should now be evident that our argument did not depend on our simplifying assumption that there were just four possible worlds. And neither did it depend on our arbitrary choice of Possible World Two as our "starting point": if we had begun by assuming that a perfect being existed in One or in Three or in Four, we should have got the same result.)

Have we therefore proved the existence of a perfect being? If we have, then we have answered the question, Why should there be anything at all? If there has to be a perfect being—and the modal ontological argument claims to show not only that there is a perfect being, but that there *has to be* one—then it is impossible for there to be nothing at all. But the modal ontological argument rests on two premises and a principle of modal inference. And at least one of these three things is far from evident: that a perfect being is not impossible. Our argument perhaps shows that the concept of a perfect being is in an important way unlike the concept of a lion or a unicorn. It is not impossible for there to be unicorns,[7] but there are none. If there were no lions, it would nevertheless be possible for there to be lions, and lions, despite their possibility, would not exist. A perfect being, however, is not like that: if a perfect being is so much as intrinsically possible—like a unicorn, and unlike a liquid wine bottle—then a perfect being really does exist. But is a perfect being possible?

This is a question that we cannot evade, for there can be no presumption in favor of possibility. It may be that in many areas of thought and inquiry one is entitled to assume that a certain concept is possible—not self-contradictory, not intrinsically impossible—in the absence of a specific argument for its impossibility, rather as, under Common Law, a person is to be presumed innocent of a charge till proved guilty. But this cannot be a presumption in any area of inquiry in which modal reasoning like that which we have been considering is employed. This contention is easily demonstrated by the fact that such a presumption of possibility would lead to contradictory results.

To see that this is a fact, consider the concept of a "knowno": the concept of a being who knows that there is no perfect being. There would seem to be no reason, on the face of it, to suppose that there being a knowno is an intrinsically impossible state of affairs, like there being a liquid wine bottle. But consider. If a knowno is not intrinsically impossible, then there is a knowno in some possible world. But then there is a possible world in which there is no perfect being, since, if someone knows something, then what that person knows is true. And, as we have seen, if a perfect being is possible, then there exists a perfect being in every possible world. It follows that if a knowno is possible, then a perfect being is impossible—and it also follows that if a perfect being is possible, then a knowno is impossible.

We have, therefore, a pair of concepts—the concept of a perfect being and the concept of a knowno—that is such that either is possible if and only if the other is impossible. We know, therefore, that one of these concepts is possible and the other impossible. But, at present, we have no grounds for saying of either of the two concepts that it is the one that is the possible one. But if we adopted the general rule "A concept is to be assumed to be possible in the absence of a specific argument for its impossibility," we should have to assume both of these concepts to be possible, and we know that it is false that they are both possible. (It is interesting to note that we cannot consistently adopt the Common Law principle "A person is to be presumed innocent of a charge till proved guilty" if we know that either Alice or Bertram murdered Clara but have no reason to think that Alice murdered her and no reason to think that Bertram murdered her. The best we can do in such a case if we want to be logically consistent is not to assume that Alice is guilty and not to assume that Bertram is guilty.)

If we wish to evaluate the modal ontological argument, therefore, there is no alternative to attempting to find some specific argument for the conclusion that the concept of a perfect being is possible or else some specific argument for the conclusion that a perfect being is impossible.

How shall we do this? Well, how, in general, do we go about finding out whether a concept is possible? The most reliable way of showing that a concept is possible is to show that is has *instances*. That is, the most reliable way of showing that the concept of a dog is possible is to show that there are dogs; the most reliable way of showing that the concept of a unicorn is possible is to show that there are unicorns, and so on. But this method will not help us to find out whether the concept of a perfect being is possible, since we do not know whether there are any perfect beings. (Or, if some among us do know that there is a perfect being, or do know that there is no perfect being, this knowledge is certainly not *common* knowledge, and it is not, therefore, knowledge that we can appeal to in presenting a metaphysical argument that is not addressed to any particular group of people.)

What other methods are there? There is always the method of abstract metaphysical argument. The seventeenth-century metaphysician G. W. Leibniz claimed to have discovered a metaphysical argument demonstrating the possibility of a perfect being. (Leibniz, a very acute modal reasoner, saw that any successful version of the ontological argument must include a proof that a perfect being was not impossible.) His reasoning was as follows. A perfect being is a being who has all perfections and thus is possible if all perfections are consistent with one another. And every perfection is a "simple, positive property." (A simple property is one that is not a complex that includes simpler properties, as *being both red and round* is a complex

that includes both *being red* and *being round*. A positive property is a property that is not negative: *being red* and *being round* are positive properties, and *not being red* and *being non-round* are negative properties.) And all simple, positive properties are consistent with one another, since the only way for two properties to be inconsistent is for one to be the negation of the other (example: *not being red* is the negation of *being red*) or for one to be a complex that includes the negation of the other or the negation of a property included in the other (example: *being round and not red* is inconsistent with both *being red* and *being hard and red*).

Leibniz held that most of our everyday adjectives stood for elaborate complexes of simple, positive properties and their negations. This is what makes it possible for, say, 'hard' and 'soft' to denote incompatible properties; a complete analysis of hardness and softness would show that there is some simple, positive property F such that one of them includes F and the other includes the negation of F. It obviously follows from this analysis of inconsistency that no simple, positive properties are inconsistent with one another, and, if every perfection is indeed a simple, positive property, it follows that a being who has all perfections is possible. (It does not, however, follow that a perfect being, in our sense of the term, is possible, for we have defined a perfect being as a being who has all perfections *essentially*. To reach the further conclusion that a perfect being, in our sense, was possible, we should need some further premise, such as 'If a property is a perfection, then the property of having *that* property essentially is also a perfection'. An instance of this general thesis would be: If wisdom is a perfection, then *having wisdom essentially* is also a perfection.)

There are a great many problems with Leibniz's argument. I will mention only one of them. It is by no means clear that the idea of a simple, positive property makes any sense. Let us look just at the idea of a positive property (remarks similar to those that follow apply to the idea of a simple property). Consider the property *not having parts*. This would seem to be a pretty good example of a negative property, being obviously the negation of the property *having parts*. But suppose we call the property of not having parts 'simplicity', as Leibniz himself did. (He in fact regarded it as one of the perfections, and thus as a simple, positive property.) Then we can call the property of having parts 'non-simplicity', and, if we do our thinking in this terminology, it looks as if non-simplicity is the negative property, being the negation of simplicity. This case suggests that properties are not negative or positive *in themselves* and that the belief that they are is a mistaken inference from the fact that properties can have names that have negative or positive forms—sometimes both a negative and a positive name for one and the same property. There is a good deal more to this issue, however, and Leibniz would have a lot to say in reply to what I have said. In this brief passage I have tried only to give a rough idea of why I regard Leibniz's argument for the possibility of a perfect being as unsatisfactory.

If we find it difficult to show that the concept of a perfect being is possible, this could be because that concept is in fact impossible. If this were true, is there any way in which it might be demonstrated? It is sometimes possible to show that a concept is impossible by showing that some sort of impossibility can be deduced from the proposition that that concept applies to something. For example, we can show that the concept of a round square is impossible by pointing out that if there were a round square it would have corners (since it is square) and would also *not* have corners (since it is round).

The Anglo-American philosopher J. N. Findlay once claimed to be able to show that an impossibility could be derived from the concept of a perfect being. His argument was that a perfect being must be a necessary being, and that an impossibility follows from the concept of a necessary being. An impossibility follows from the concept of a necessary being, Findlay

argues, because if there were a necessary being, there would have to be at least one necessarily true existential proposition, and necessarily true existential propositions are impossible. (An existential proposition is a proposition that asserts the existence of something, a proposition of the form "There is an *x*" or "There exists an *x*" or "An *x* exists.") And necessarily true existential propositions are impossible because necessary truths are just those truths that owe their status as truths to the meanings of words. (For example, it is necessarily true that all nuns are female; but the necessity of all nuns' being female is due simply to the fact that 'female' is a part of the meaning of the word 'nun': we simply don't apply the word 'nun' to males—not even to members of religious orders—for 'nun' simply *means* 'woman belonging to a religious order, membership in which implies vows of poverty, chastity, and obedience'.)

Now it is obviously impossible (the argument continues) for there to be a true existential proposition that owes its truth to the meanings of words. It may be a consequence of the meanings of the word A and the word B that whatever A applies to, B applies to also—as with 'nun' and 'female'. But it can never be a consequence simply of the meaning of the word A that A applies to anything. We may give to 'nun' or 'aardvark' or 'molybdenum' whatever meanings we like, but these meanings will never guarantee that there is anything to which these words apply. But for there to be a necessary existential proposition, there would have to be a word or words whose meaning guaranteed that they applied to something, and this, as we have seen is impossible.

To retrace the steps of the argument: there can be no such thing as a necessary existential proposition, so there can be no such thing as a necessary being, so there can be no such thing as a perfect being. And, therefore, the modal ontological argument has a false premise: that a perfect being is not impossible. And, therefore, the modal ontological argument is a failure, and we are still without an answer to the question, Why should there be anything at all?

The main problem with Findlay's argument lies in the theory of necessary truth that it appeals to. Why should we accept the thesis that all necessary truths are due to the meanings of words and the consequent judgment that there can be no necessary existential propositions? This theory was almost universally accepted by English-speaking philosophers at the time at which Findlay wrote (1948).[8] It was widely, if not universally, regarded as a theory that philosophical investigation had shown to be true. As of the time of this writing, however, it has become merely a part of the history of philosophy. A great many philosophers of logic and language currently working would argue that the proposition 'The atomic number of iron is 26' is necessarily true and that its truth is not due to the meanings of words. They would argue that this proposition is necessarily true because the atomic structure of an element is of its very essence and that no matter how much some possible metal might superficially resemble iron, unless the nuclei of the atoms that composed it contained twenty-six protons, it would simply not *be* iron. And yet, these philosophers would argue, it is not a part of the meaning of the word 'iron' that it apply only to a substance that is a chemical element having the atomic number 26—not, at least if something can be a part of the meaning of a word only if a person who knows the meaning of that word knows that it is (as, for example, someone who knows the meaning of the word 'nun' knows that a nun has to be female).

That this is so is evident from such facts as the following: lots of people who have no idea that there is such a concept as "atomic number" know the meaning of the word 'iron' perfectly well; Queen Elizabeth I meant by the word 'iron' just what you and I mean by it, even though she died long before the advent of modern chemistry (lots of English words have changed their meanings since the sixteenth century, but 'iron' is not one of them); the Latin word 'ferrum' means exactly what the English word 'iron' means, even though Latin ceased to be a living language a thousand years or more before the advent of modern chemistry.

We should note, however, that even if these philosophers are right, it does not follow that there can be necessary existential propositions, for 'The atomic number of iron is 26' is not an existential proposition: if the currently popular theory I have sketched is right, this proposition states one of the essential characteristics of iron, but it does not say that there *is* any iron. But it does at least follow from this theory that the account of necessary truth on which Findlay bases his conclusion that there can be no necessary existential propositions is mistaken. And there are propositions that many philosophers would say were necessary existential propositions. Mathematics provides many plausible examples of necessary existential propositions, such as 'There exists a number that can be expressed in more than one way as the sum of two cubes'. It is true that the mathematical examples provide only cases of necessary propositions that assert the existence of universals, such as numbers. Still, they tend to undermine Findlay's position, since his argument and its conclusion are very general. His argument proceeds from premises about the nature of language, and its conclusion should hold for any proposition, regardless of its subjectmatter. His conclusion would therefore appear to be refuted by examples of necessary existential propositions no matter what their subject-matter. If his argument were sound, it should show that there could not be necessary existential propositions even in mathematics.

If this much is correct, however, it does not show that there could be a necessarily existent *individual thing*. Perhaps it is only universals like numbers that can be necessarily existent. And a perfect being would certainly have to be an individual thing. Findlay's argument may be refuted by the observation that it proves too

much (that there could not be necessarily existent universals), but even if this is granted,
it has no tendency to show that his stated conclusion—the impossibility of a perfect being—is
wrong. I know of no argument that purports
to show that there could not be a necessarily
existent individual thing, with the exception of
Findlay-style arguments for the conclusion that
there could not be a necessarily existent *anything*.
Such an argument would have to show that the
two properties *being necessarily existent* and *being an
individual thing* were inconsistent with each other,
and I can see no way of constructing even a
plausible candidate for such an argument.

It is interesting to note that if these two properties are *not* inconsistent, then there is in fact a
necessarily existent individual thing. This can be
shown by a simplified version of the reasoning
that we used to show the validity of the modal
ontological argument:

If a necessarily existent individual thing is
possible, then there is a necessarily existent
individual thing in some possible world.
Since that individual thing is necessarily
existent in that possible world, it is true in
that possible world that it, that very individual
thing, exists in all possible worlds. It follows
that it is true in every possible world that that
thing exists in all possible worlds, since
"nothing changes from possible world to
possible world but which possible world is
actual." Moreover, it seems evident that the
property *being an individual thing* is essential to
whatever has it; if something is an individual
thing, then it could not have been a universal
or a mere collection or a stuff or any other
kind of non-individual thing. Therefore, this
being not only exists in every possible world
but is also an individual thing in every
possible world. And there is thus a necessarily
existent individual thing in every possible
world, including, of course, whichever world
is the actual world. Therefore, there actually is
a necessarily existent individual thing.

This argument, which we may call the minimal
modal ontological argument, shows that the
reasoning that underlies the modal ontological
argument does not really have anything to do
with the concept of a perfect being. What this
reasoning really shows is that, for any set of
properties whatever, if it is possible for there
to be a thing that is necessarily existent and has
all of these properties essentially, then there
actually is something that is necessarily existent
and has all of these properties essentially. (A perfect being is a being that has all perfections and
has them essentially; a perfect being is thus a
being that is necessarily existent—necessary
existence being a perfection—and has a certain
set of properties essentially.) It is interesting
to note that the minimal modal ontological
argument will do as well as the modal ontological argument itself for our purposes. (Our
question is, Why is there something rather than
nothing? and any individual thing is a "something.") It is free from logical error if and only
if the modal ontological argument itself is
free from logical error, and its controversial
premise—a necessarily existent individual thing
is possible—is true if the corresponding premise
of the modal ontological argument is true. I say
'if' and not 'only if' because the proposition
that a perfect being is possible entails that a
necessarily existent individual thing is possible,
but the reverse entailment does not hold, or at
least does not obviously hold. A perfect being
has to be a necessarily existent individual thing,
but a necessarily existent individual thing does
not have to be a perfect being, or does not obviously have to be a perfect being. It looks as if the
premise of the minimal modal ontological
argument might well be easier to investigate
than the premise of the modal ontological
argument. And the conclusion of the minimal
modal ontological argument suffices for our
present purposes, since we are investigating the
question, Why should there be anything (i.e.,
any individual thing) at all?

Let us therefore turn our attention to the

minimal modal ontological argument and ask whether its premise is true; that is, whether a necessarily existent individual thing is possible; that is, whether the properties *existing necessarily* and *being an individual thing* are compatible. It does not seem possible to deduce any formal contradiction from the assumption that there is a necessarily existent individual thing.

Nevertheless, these two properties may well be incompatible. It is hard to believe that the two properties *being a solid sheet of iron* and *being as transparent as glass* are compatible, but there is no way of deriving a formal contradiction from the proposition 'There is a solid sheet of iron that is as transparent as glass'. On the other hand, the two properties may well be compatible. How can one know? I am at a loss to answer this question. In general, there are only two "foolproof" ways to discover whether two properties are compatible. One knows that two properties are compatible if one knows that there is in fact something that has both of them. And one knows that two properties are incompatible if one can deduce a formal contradiction from the assumption that something has both of them. As I have said, I know of no way to apply the latter method in the case of necessary existence and individuality. And as to the former method, if I knew how to show that there was a necessarily existent individual thing, I should have no need of the minimal modal ontological argument, since I should know that its conclusion—that there is a necessarily existent individual thing— was true independently of the minimal modal ontological argument.

If we cannot show that a necessarily existent individual thing is possible, then we certainly cannot show that a perfect being is possible, since a perfect being is a being that is a necessarily existent individual thing *and* has various other properties—such as wisdom and goodness and unlimited power (or whatever the perfections other than necessary existence may be). And while there might in theory be a proof that a perfect being was impossible that did not prove

that a necessarily existent individual thing was impossible—a proof, say, that wisdom was a perfection, together with a proof that wisdom was incompatible with necessary existence—no one has in fact proposed such a proof and no such proof suggests itself. All the proofs of the thesis that a perfect being is impossible that have ever been proposed are (supposed) proofs of the impossibility of necessary existence. It would seem, therefore, that the long history of the ontological argument, from Saint Anselm to the present day, is at best inconclusive. Every version of the argument either contains some logical error or other or else depends upon a premise whose claim to truth we are unable to adjudicate. And, therefore, we have not found an answer to the question, Why should there be anything at all?

There is, nevertheless, one valuable lesson we have learned from our study of the ontological argument. If we could show that there was a necessary being, a necessarily existing individual thing, we should have an answer to our question. For if there were a necessary being, then it would be impossible for there to be nothing. And if we could show that it was impossible for there to be nothing, that, surely, would count as an answer to our question.

Is there any approach to the question whether there is a necessary being other than *via* the ontological argument? There is indeed. It has often been suggested that if there were no necessary being there could not be any beings at all. If this "if" statement could be shown to be true, we could combine it with the obvious truth that there is something to show that there is a necessary being.

Notes

1 The label 'ontological argument' seems first to have been applied to Anselm's and Descartes's arguments by Kant in the eighteenth century. The word 'ontological' is derived from the Greek word for 'being' or 'existence'.

2   What Kant actually says is that existence is "a logical but not a real predicate (Prädikat)." I believe that the idea he intended to express by this formula is more or less the idea I have expressed in the text by the words "Existence is not a property".

3   Or perhaps it would be better to say, "a complete specification of a way a World might have been," for it may be that the World is a full-fledged individual thing, as opposed to a mere collection, and that if things had been sufficiently different, that individual thing would not have existed at all, and some other individual thing—either a part of the World or some individual thing that does not exist at all—would have been the World.

4   What allows us to speak of the actual world here? Why can't there be two possible worlds that specify the way things really are? Well, those two possible worlds, being, by definition, completely specific, would have to agree in all details—otherwise at least one of them would get the way things really are wrong. If, according to one of the two possible worlds, the number of Douglas fir trees in Canada is odd and according to the other it is even, then it can't be that both possible worlds get the way things really are right, for, as things really are, the number of Douglas firs in Canada is either odd or even. But if the two possible worlds agree on *everything*, in what sense are they *two* possible worlds, two *different* specifications of how things are? Does it make sense to speak of two specifications of the features of, say, a house that are the same in every detail and yet are two different specifications? At any rate, I am going to make this true by definition: if x and y are possible worlds, and if x and y agree in every detail, then x and y are one and the same possible world.

5   Consider, for example, the sentence, 'If the Pythagorean Theorem has been proved, then it can't be false'. This could mean either 'The following is impossible: that the Pythagorean Theorem be proved and also be false' or 'If the Pythagorean Theorem has been proved, then the following is impossible: that the Pythagorean Theorem be false'.

6   The logically sophisticated will be aware that this premise must be read as saying that not only is the property of existing necessarily in fact a perfection but that this property would exist and would be a perfection no matter what. But few would want to deny that if there is such a property as necessary existence, and if the property of necessary existence is a perfection, then this property would exist no matter what and would be a perfection no matter what.

7   At any rate, it is possible for there to be animals that are shaped the way the unicorns of legend are supposed to be shaped. The American philosopher Saul Kripke has, however, presented interesting and plausible arguments for the conclusion that no possible animal would really count as a *unicorn* and that unicorns are therefore impossible.

8   But it was by no means a recent invention. Hume, for example, wrote, "Whatever we conceive as existent, we can also conceive as non-existent. There is no being, therefore, whose non-existence implies a contradiction." (*Dialogues Concerning Natural Religion*, XI. The *Dialogues* were first published in 1779, three years after Hume's death.)

Chapter 9

Alexander R. Pruss

SOME RECENT PROGRESS ON THE COSMOLOGICAL ARGUMENT

1. Introduction

In the first chapter of Romans, Paul tells us that the power and deity of God are evident from what he has created. One reading of this is that there is an argument from the content of what has been created. Thus, the Book of Wisdom, which may well have been the source of Paul's ideas here, says that "from the greatness and beauty of created things their original author, by analogy, is seen" (13:5, New American Bible). This is a kind of teleological or design argument. But one might also argue cosmologically instead from general features of the universe, such as the fact that there is a universe at all, or that there are contingent states of affairs, or that there is motion. Alternately, one might argue from something extremely specific, but where the details do not matter, such as the conjunction of all contingent facts.

The general strategy of cosmological arguments is to take a grand feature of the world, and then argue, abstracting from much of its specific content, that the best or only possible explanation is a First Cause, an entity that stands at the head of a causal chain leading to the occurrence of the grand feature. Typically, the grand feature is something the opponent will not challenge. Instead, opponents tend to ask:

1   Does the grand feature actually have an explanation?

2   Can there be an explanation not involving a First Cause?

3   Need the First Cause be God?

Recent discussion has particularly focused on the first two questions, and I wish to primarily focus on the first question myself in this paper. But first a few words about progress on the second and third question, in reverse order.

2. Need the First Cause be God?

The third of the questions presents the "gap problem"—how to go from a First Cause to theism.

In the first part of the *Summa Theologiae*, St. Thomas Aquinas gives a series of elaborate arguments that the First Cause must be a necessary being that is utterly simple and with no potentiality. The necessity part of the argument is adopted by a number of contemporary cosmological arguers. After all, if the First Cause were just a contingent being, then asking for the explanation of the First Cause's existence would seem to be just as reasonable as asking for the explanation of the existence of the universe.

From simplicity and complete actuality, Aquinas argues that the necessary being is perfect in every way, and derives enough of the attributes of God that there is no difficulty identifying the First Cause with God. I find a number of St. Thomas's arguments here to be quite powerful, and they have not been sufficiently studied by contemporary philosophers of religion. However, they are very heavy on controversial metaphysics, and there is virtue in finding arguments that do not rely on so much controversial metaphysics.

Perhaps the most obvious question to ask is whether the First Cause needs to be a person at all. If we accept Richard Swinburne's (1968) division of explanations into the personal, where we explain by invoking the agency of a free person, and the scientific, where we explain by means of initial conditions and laws of nature, then we have a good argument for the personhood of the First Cause, given necessary existence. For, arguably, the initial conditions and laws in scientific explanations are always contingent. And indeed a number of cosmological arguments do conclude to a necessarily existing First Cause, or to a First Cause that otherwise has a status, such as atemporality or immutability, that the conditions entering into scientific explanations lack.

If Swinburne's division is exhaustive, then we have made some progress. After all, a necessarily existing, or even just atemporal or immutable, person is already rather God-like, and typical atheists deny the existence of any such person. Of course one might object that even though all our explanations are personal or scientific, nonetheless another kind of explanation can be given. But in the search for explanation, a known type of explanation is surely to be epistemically preferred to an unknown one, so we at least get an inductive argument for the existence of a God-like being. I think there is one kind of explanation, constitutive explanation, that Swinburne misses—the knife is hot holds because the molecules in it have high kinetic energy (the kinetic energy is heat, and not the cause of the heat). However, arguably, the ultimate explanations of contingent states of affairs have to be causal, not constitutive, since we can always query why a constituting contingent state of affairs holds.

Robert Koons (1997) has combined the cosmological and teleological arguments. Once we know that this universe has a cause, it becomes plausible that the wondrous combination of complexity and order that is found in it is there by design, i.e., that the cause is a person who planned for this. Moreover, this complexity and order is so great that this must be a person of very high intelligence, and we might argue that the person has at least a certain kind of attunement to the good and the beautiful. Hence, we solve part of the gap problem by using the design argument.

Finally, in the case where the feature to be explained is the sum total of all contingent facts about this world and the cosmological argument is one that can be run in every possible world, Jerome Gellman (2000) has come up with a very clever argument that the First Cause is omnipotent. Here is a simple version. Let N be the aggregate of all necessary beings that are persons. In every possible world, a cosmological argument to a necessarily existing First Cause can be run. This First Cause must be a part of N. On the assumption that if a part counts as the cause of something, so does the whole (albeit in virtue of the part), at least as long as the effect is distinct from that whole, we can argue that N is itself a First Cause in every possible world. But to be the First Cause in every possible world is to be capable of initiating a chain of causes leading to any possible world, and this is very close to omnipotence.

If we could establish the existence of an all-powerful, highly intelligent and necessarily existing First Cause of the universe, we would have accomplished much. It might not be enough to justify us in concluding that the God of Western monotheism exists, but perhaps the rest of the gap could be bridged by a reasonable faith or other arguments, like those of Aquinas.

3. Can There be an Explanation Not Involving a First Cause?

There are historically two ways that this question has been asked. First, we might ask whether there can be a non-causal ultimate explanation, namely, a non-causal ultimate explanation of one of these highly general states of affairs such as the existence of contingent facts. Second, Hume (1907) has asked whether a causal explanation could not be given by means of a *chain* of non-ultimate causes, a chain that does not have a first element.

Recent defenders of non-causal ultimate explanations invoke either laws of nature or metaphysical principles but no *entities*. Perhaps there is some law of nature that states that universes of such-and-such a sort have such-and-such a probability of coming into existence. One way to try to counter this kind of an answer is to use Koons' (1997) solution to the gap problem here again: the complexity and order of our universe is such that, granting that there is an explanation, it is unlikely that random processes yield this explanation. Rescher (2000), on the other hand, invokes the principle that everything must be for the best. (In his view, this is also why God exists.) But of course, such a Leibnizian view raises the problem of evil in a particularly virulent way.

More generally, one might worry about the coherence of an explanation that involves no entities. On such an explanation, the fact that does the explaining is literally not a fact *about* anything. Can there be facts that are not about anything?

When my daughter was three years old, I had asked whether something non-substantival, such as sleep (I cannot remember the exact example I used), was a thing. She told me that it was "not a thing", but also was "not imaginary". This is presumably the answer the defender of explanations without entity will give. The principle or law of nature that is invoked in the explanation is not a thing, but also not imaginary. But such a

philosopher faces a more serious conceptual problem than the one I presented my daughter with. For while sleep is not a thing, a reason sleep is not imaginary is that there are things—people and animals—that sleep. But the principles or laws in question were supposed to explain the existence of contingent things, and hence cannot presuppose it. Nor can these principles or laws be given reality by being descriptions of the behavior of necessary beings, since the point of positing them was to get away from explanation in terms of necessary beings.

Moreover, if no thing's existence or state is reported in the explaining fact, how can the fact do any explaining? The old adage *ex nihilo nihil fit* seems deeply appropriate here. And one of the few things more absurd than the idea that something might come from (not necessarily in a temporal sense) nothing is the idea that something might come from nothing *and yet be explained*.

Hume's objection, on the other hand, posited lots of entities as explanations. Suppose that the fact that the cosmological arguer seeks the explanation of is the existence of the universe, understood as the aggregate of all contingent beings. Hume will present the following scenario: Each contingent being has its cause in another contingent being *ad infinitum*. Now, each contingent being's existence has been explained. Hume (1907, p. 120) accepts the principle that when each part of a whole has been explained, the whole has been explained, and so we have allegedly explained the existence of the universe.

Hume's principle that to explain the parts is to explain the whole fails, however, in cases where the parts are explained by other parts. Here is a simple counterexample. As the whole, take the flight of a cannon-ball that was shot out of a cannon at noon, the flight including all the states between noon and the landing, excluding both. As the parts, take the momentary states of the cannon-ball. We can explain any one of these states by reference to the laws and an earlier state. You want to know why the cannon-ball had the state it did four seconds after noon? It is because it had such and such a state two seconds after noon which by the laws of nature led to its having the posited state four seconds after noon. Why did it have the state it did one second after noon? Because it had such and such a state half a second after noon. Thus, any of the states of the cannon-ball after noon can be explained by another state of the cannon-ball after noon. Hume's principle thus entails that the whole flight of the cannon-ball can be explained by *itself* together with the laws of nature, without any mention of the cannon's being fired. This is absurd and so Hume's principle is false.

4. The Principle of Sufficient Reason

The most powerful objection to the cosmological argument is to the assumption that there is an explanation at all for the feature of the world that the arguer starts with. To avoid being *ad hoc*, the cosmological arguer needs a principle here, and this usually takes the form of the Principle of Sufficient Reason (PSR) or a special case or variant of it. The PSR that I defend (Pruss, 2006) holds that all contingently true propositions have explanations.

At one point Leibniz says that the existence of God cannot be proved without the PSR (a strange claim given that he liked the ontological argument), but he never to my knowledge either gives an argument for this claim or offers a convincing positive reason to believe the PSR. Aquinas makes use of the somewhat weaker Causal Principle (CP) that holds that every contingent event or thing has a cause. The PSR and the CP are generally considered necessary truths by their defenders.

A strategy for philosophically inclined atheists, ever since Hume, is simply to deny the PSR that is used in a cosmological argument. A standard positive Humean argument is that we could imagine something coming into existence *ex nihilo*, and hence something could come into

existence *ex nihilo*, contrary to the PSR. Of course, the inference from imaginability to possibility here is dubious, but I think there is at least a defeasible inference available.

But the idea of "imagining" something coming into existence for no cause at all is a bit odd. It is easy to imagine a brick without imagining a cause for it. But how do I actually imagine the causelessness of a brick? Do I maybe imagine a bunch of vacuum and a brick popping into existence? I am not sure I can even imagine vacuum. I can imagine a region of space that looks empty, but a room full of air also looks empty, and so my imagining does not seem to distinguish a vacuum from airlessness. I suppose I might somehow mentally insist on every kind of reality being absent from the region of space I am imagining: there are no solids, no liquids, no gases, no fields, etc. But remember I am supposed to be doing this in imagination. How amenable to imagination electromagnetic fields or their absence is unclear. Moreover, I need to imagine the lack of invisible entities of a sort that I had never thought about, that I could never imagine, for to imagine an empty region of space is to imagine it empty of *them* as well.

And even if I should ever manage to perform this feat of imagination and imagine a region of space that was empty but a brick popped into existence in the middle of it, the content of my imagination would not be sufficient to imply that I have imagined a brick popping into existence *ex nihilo*, but only that I have imagined a brick popping into existence that has no *a prior cause in that region of space*. But the exercise was to imagine a brick that has no cause at all. And here, I suspect, we have gone beyond the limits of imagination. We can imagine a brick in an empty region of space and we can ensure that we are not positively imagining for it a cause elsewhere in space, but to say that this is a causeless brick, we must go beyond imagination—we must actually verbally *suppose* the imagined brick to have no cause elsewhere. And our ability to verbally *suppose* something seems no evidence for its metaphysical possibility. Indeed, mathematicians constantly *suppose* impossibilities to disprove them by *reductio ad absurdum*.

There are three other prominent objections to the PSR. The first is that there is insufficient reason for the theist to accept the PSR. This is, in effect, a challenge for the defender of the PSR to produce an argument for it. The second is Schopenhauer's "taxi cab objection", sophisticated versions of which have been offered by authors like Rowe (1975) and van Inwagen (1983, pp. 202–204). Once the PSR has been used to arrive at God, it is dismissed like a cab we no longer need, instead of being used to query why God exists or why God created what he did, which would lead to a vicious regress. The third is free will and unexplainable quantum facts.

I will quickly sketch four ways one might justify the PSR or at least the CP. Then, I will respond to the taxi cab objection. I will have talked about free will while talking about the taxi cab objection. The quantum case can be dismissed fairly quickly, since the following logically possible proposition is compatible with all empirical observations and if true makes quantum mechanics logically compatible with the PSR (this isn't the only way of doing so): In the case of each physically indeterministic event, a supernatural being chooses how that event will go.

I will end by sketching four ways of weakening the PSR which nonetheless may suffice for the purposes of cosmological arguments.

5. Four Justifications of Belief in the PSR or the CP

I. The PSR is Self-Evident

To use an example that apparently Nicholas Rescher once gave, when an airplane crashes, we do not accept the verdict: "The airplane crashed for no reason at all." If that is what the investigators came up with, we would charitably understand them as saying that they did not know what the reason for the crash is. Quite possibly the PSR is self-evident. If so, then its opponents are perverse or deluded. Or maybe they just do not understand the PSR. That may be, but just saying that it is so is not going to be any dialectical use.

A somewhat better strategy might be to point out that even the PSR's opponents make use of the PSR in their everyday and philosophical pursuits. Their denial of it in the case of the grand explanatory questions, like why there are contingent beings, may be *ad hoc* and driven by a desire to remain atheists.

II. Why Does the PSR Hold for Everyday Events?

Almost nobody seriously doubts (Richard Swinburne is the only exception I know of) that the PSR holds almost always for macroscopic events like airplanes crashing and lightbulbs turning on, that rocks placed somewhere stay there unless they have a cause to move, and that bricks do not pop into existence *ex nihilo*. But why does the PSR hold at least most of the time even in such a restricted context? This is a perfectly legitimate request for explanation. The simplest explanation is that the PSR is a metaphysical principle holding of necessity. This is not a viciously circular invocation of the PSR, but an innocent application of inference to the best explanation.

The main alternate explanation that will be offered is that the laws of nature, especially the conservation laws, are such as to entail that the PSR holds almost all the time for macroscopic events. But whether this alternate explanation succeeds depends on substantial questions about laws. The inference to best explanation argument for the PSR works best on one account of laws: the Aristotelian one. On this account, the laws of nature are grounded in the essences and powers of finite, non-divine substances. But if so, then how can the laws of nature prevent a brick from popping into existence in a vacuum? What essences and powers are keeping the brick from having such a cause-less beginning? Certainly not the essences and powers of the hypothetical brick, since these do not in fact exist. Is it the essences and powers of other entities? But a power to prevent the coming into existence of a new entity, *ex nihilo*, seems at least a little odd.

We can imagine a non-divine substance that can blow a brick to smithereens once the brick comes into existence and maybe even a non-divine substance that could utterly annihilate a brick. But how would such a substance go about preventing the brick from coming into existence? Maybe it could take up some of the spaces where the brick would have come into existence, but we were supposing a brick coming into existence in a vacuum.

III. Cartesian Demons

This argument is inspired by Plantinga's self-defeatingness argument against naturalistic evolution (see Beilby, 2002). Consider the following plausible principle:

(*)   Suppose there is a proposition p that is not epistemically unlikely and that is such that p implies that almost all of our apparent knowledge is false. Then this fact about p is a defeater for all or almost all of our knowledge.

It had better be unlikely that almost of our apparent knowledge is false—else our knowledge is defeated. Note that there are three ways for a proposition not to be unlikely: it might be likely, or it might have inscrutable or indefinable probability.

By definition, an entity is "my Cartesian demon" if and only if this entity is supernatural and brings it about that almost all of what I think I know consists of false propositions. Now if the CP is false, then no objective probability can be assigned to my Cartesian demon's coming into existence *ex nihilo* at my concep-

tion. How could one assign probabilities to non-spatial beings coming into existence *ex nihilo* for no reason? Hence the coming into existence of such a demon is not objectively unlikely. But if I know that something is not objectively unlikely and, furthermore, it is something against which I have no evidence, then I should likewise say it is not epistemically unlikely. Hence, denying the CP yields a defeater for almost all of my apparent knowledge. In fact, it is clear that unless I think the CP is likely true, I have such a defeater. Believing that I do not in fact have a defeater for almost all of my knowledge commits me to holding that the CP is likely true.

IV. The Nature of Possibility

I could have failed to contribute to this volume, but could not have become the number seven. What makes these claims true?

One of the most prominent answers to questions like this is David Lewis's (1986). What makes it true to say that I could have failed to contribute to this volume is that there really exists a physical universe where someone relevantly like me does not contribute to a volume relevantly like this one. There is a universe with the Greek gods, too, Lewis explicitly says. Indeed, all possible universes, namely, maximal spatiotemporally connected aggregates, exist. Lewis's is a philosophically courageous answer, but one that leads to absurdities. A simple one is this. Even for a deontologist, there are cases in ethics where consequentialistic considerations are key. When choosing between two morally similar charities to which to donate money, the crucial question can sometimes be which of them will help the greater number of people. But if all possible universes exist, then whichever option I choose, a counterpart of me in another world will choose the other option, and in the totality of reality, the net result will be the same. Hence the consequentialistic reasoning is undercut.

The second answer, given by Robert Adams (1974) and Alvin Plantinga (1974) and others, is that modal truths are primitive truths about a Platonic realm. On the Adams version, propositions are Platonic entities, which have properties like possibility or necessity. This answer is unsatisfactory because it fails to explain why these facts about the Platonic realm are connected with this world as they are. What connection does the fact that some Platonic propoisiton has the Platonic property of impossibility have with the curious absence of square circles in this room? Or why is it that whenever anybody has the concrete ability to do A, the Platonic proposition that she does A has the property of possibility?

This last question suggests an alternative account. After all, for a lot of possibility claims we can say very easily what makes them possible. Indeed, there is an embarrassment of riches here. That I might not have contributed to this volume is made true by a driver's ability to murder me while I am on a sidewalk, by my ability to decide to go for a swim in the Brazos instead, and by the ability of my wife to obtain and dose me with chloroform to prevent my writing this chapter. Anything that can prevent an event makes it true that possibly the event does not happen. Likewise, anything that can cause an event makes it true that possibly the event happens.

What if in fact all of modality is like that? Generalizing, the view would be something like this. A non-actual event E is possible provided there is (in the timeless sense—this thing might be in the past) something (an event or substance) that can cause E, or providing that there is something that can cause something that can cause E, or providing that there is something that can cause something that can cause something that can cause E, and so on. More generally, an event E is possible provided either E is actual or there exists something that has the ability to initiate a chain of causes capable of leading to E.

It is clear then why modality is connected with the stuff around us, since possibility is grounded in the powers of things in the world. Dually, impossibility is grounded in the powerlessness of things in the world: it is impossible for there to be square circles because nothing has the power to cause a square circle. Moreover, we have some hope at least of making a little bit of progress on the obvious epistemological problems facing the Lewisian and Platonic views. For we experience the powers of things, at least in their activation, and can form scientific theories about a number of them. I can be most sure that something is possible if I can sketch a causal story for it.

But this Aristotelian account of modality entails the PSR. To see this, I will show that the account implies:

(**) Necessarily, if p is a contingently false proposition, then it is not possible for it to be the case that both p is true and there is no explanation why p is true.

Suppose I have established this. Let p be a contingently true proposition. Then there is some possible world w at which p is false. Apply (**) at w. The conclusion is that at w it is the case that it is not possible that p is both true and unexplained. But by the axiom S5 of modal logic, what is not possible at w is not possible at the actual world. Hence it is not possible that p is true but does not have an explanation. Since p is in fact true, it has an explanation. Q.E.D.

Let's prove (**). Take a contingently false proposition p. Suppose for a *reductio* that it is possible that p is true and unexplained. By the Aristotelian account of possibility, there would be something that can initiate a causal chain leading to its both being the case that p is true and that it is unexplained. But the causal chain would then explain p, and hence p would not be unexplained. Thus, p would and would not be unexplained upon conclusion of this causal chain, which is absurd and impossible.

The Aristotelian account of modality is arguably the best account of modality we have, and it entails the PSR. Hence we have good reason to think the PSR is true. And if the PSR is true, then a necessarily existing supernatural being exists.

6. The Taxi Cab Objection

Take a typical cosmological argument, say one that accepts the full PSR, notes that it is a contingent fact that this universe exists, and proposes God's creative decision as an explanation. We can now ask two questions. The first is why God exists. The defender of the argument can say that God is a necessary being. Then, one can either say that the PSR applies only to contingent propositions or that God's existence is explained by its necessity.

But the more serious question is why God has created this universe. Let U be a description of those contingent aspects of this universe that God is responsible for. Consider the claim:

(E)   a necessarily existing God freely chose to create a universe satisfying U.

Then, according to the cosmological argument, a universe satisfying U exists because of E. But E itself is a contingent claim, since it reports the contingent decision of a necessary being, and hence unless we dismiss the PSR like a cab we no longer need, we need to say that E itself has an explanation. But since E is contingent, its explanation had better be a contingent fact as well. Hence, a vicious regress ensues.

In the past, Richard Gale and I have defended a claim that in this context would say that E is self-explanatory (Gale and Pruss, 1999). But there is also another solution, and one that now appears superior. God has a reason for his choice to create a universe satisfying U. We do not know this reason, but can speculate that it has something to do with the kinds of values that a universe satisfying U instantiates. Leibniz, for instance, thought that these values were some-

thing like *optimal balance of diversity and unity*. Different kinds of universes have different values. Some are more diverse, some involve less suffering, some contain more courage, some have fewer erring persons in them, etc. A number of these values are incommensurable—the value of knowledge is neither greater nor lesser than the value of courage, but different. When God chooses one universe over another, it is because of the values that the one universe exemplifies. Had he created a universe with just a single particle, it might have been because it exemplified maximal simplicity.

Let V be the collection of values that the universes described by U satisfy. We can then say that God freely chose to create a universe satisfying U because

(F)   God appreciated the values in V and knew that the universes satisfying U had these values.

Now God, being essentially all-knowing and all-good, must appreciate all values and must know what universes satisfy them. Hence we have explained E in terms of a necessary proposition—that God appreciated certain values and knew what universes satisfied them.

What is puzzling about F as an explanation is that F would have held even had God freely chosen to create a universe not satisfying U. Of course, had God freely chosen to a create a universe not satisfying U, it would not have been because of F, but because of a similar proposition F* to the effect that God appreciated the values in some V* and knew that the universes satisfying some U* had these values. The fact that F would have held even had God not created a U-type universe is not a problem. In general, an explaining proposition need not entail the explained fact—this is clear in the case of statistical explanation, for instance. Our proposition F is necessarily true but only contingently explanatory.

Now one may try to run the regress

differently. Why is it that F explains E, one might ask? But the answer is simple: F explains E because of the conceptual fact that appreciating the value of an outcome is a reason for choosing to produce the outcome, and when this reason is acted on, it is explanatory of the action. But why, we may ask, did God act on these values? Again, an easy answer: because they impressed him.

But why act on *these* values rather than other values? Here two answers can be given. Arguably, "p rather than q" is not a proposition, and the PSR applies only to propositions. Alternately, we can say that God acted on V rather than V* precisely because he was impressed by V. Had he acted on V* rather than V, it would have been because he was impressed by V*. Granted, he was impressed by both. But that does not affect my claim. In the case of a closely contested tug of war, even an indeterministic one, we could say that the winning side won because of that side's effort, whereas had the other side won, we would have explained that victory in terms of the effort on that side (cf. Kane, 2002).

Of course, I cannot say what the values in V are. For that we may need Revelation. But the PSR never claimed that the explanations were knowable. But in any case the regress is stopped and the taxi cab objection is answered.

7. Alternatives to the PSR

A different strategy for defending the cosmological argument is to use something weaker than the PSR. The advantage is two-fold. First, the weaker proposition may appeal to a wider audience, and, second, it will be subject to fewer objections. So let me quickly sketch four of the options available.

I. White's (1979) Inference to Only Explanation

Here is a version of David White's argument. It is plausible that the best explanation is true. But it is even more plausible that if one can show that at most one explanation is possible and if that one explanation cannot be shown to be false, then we should accept that explanation. Only the action of a God-like being can explain the existence of the universe. We cannot show that such a being does not exist. Ergo, such a being exists. Note that an opponent of the PSR will presumably accept the principle of only explanation as at best a defeasible one, but the argument will still have value.

II. Taylor's (1974, Chapter 10) PSR for Positive States of Affairs

Every actual contingent *positive* state of affairs has an explanation. This is all we need for a cosmological argument: There must be an explanation of the conjunction of all actual contingent positive states of affairs. This explanation surely involves the causal efficacy of something the existence of which will also be a positive state of affairs, and at the pain of vicious circularity this entity whose causal efficacy is involved will not be contingent. Moreover, it turns out that Taylor's PSR restricted to positive states of affairs, seen as a necessary truth, implies the full PSR for contingent states of affairs. For we can first explain all actual positive contingent states of affairs with Taylor's PSR. If N is an actual negative state of affairs, then not-N is a positive state of affairs, and we can explain N as follows: there is no explanation of not-N, and hence not-N cannot hold by Taylor's PSR. Thus we can explain all positive contingent facts. It is plausible that once all negative and all positive contingent facts have been explained, all of contingent reality has been explained.

Note, however, that the typical opponent of the full PSR will object to Taylor's version as well.

III. *Gale and Pruss's* (1999) *Weak PSR*

Necessarily, if *p* is a contingent true proposition, then it is possible that *p* has an explanation. It turns out that the Weak PSR entails the full PSR. The proof depends on supposing *p* is a contingent, true, unexplained proposition and then applying the Weak PSR to the proposition *p*&(*p* has no explanation), to conclude absurdly that it is possible to simultaneously explain why both *p* holds and why *p* has no explanation. Whether an argument based on the Weak PSR is any better off epistemically than an argument based on the PSR, and whether the plausibility of the Weak PSR provides any additional evidence for the PSR, is an open question.

IV. *The Restricted PSR*

One reason to object to the full PSR is because one may think that there are some truths that just cannot have an explanation. For instance, van Inwagen (1983) thinks that the conjunction of all contingent true propositions is like that. Someone else might think that a report of a free choice is like that. The Restricted PSR is meant to be a principled way of avoiding all such objections: Every proposition that can have an explanation does have an explanation, where a proposition "can have an explanation" provided that there is some possible world at which it holds and has an explanation.

One might think that the Restricted PSR is insufficient for a cosmological argument because an atheist could simply insist that the general fact that the cosmological argument seeks an explanation for is in fact inexplicable. But this is incorrect. I will show how a cosmological argument based on the Restricted PSR can be run by showing how the argument would work in a very tiny universe. Suppose then that there are only three contingent entities in existence: a donkey, a cat and a pig. Consider the proposition that there exist at least three animals. This is a proposition that surely *can* have an explanation.

For there is a possible world where there is a God, angel, ghost or evolutionary process that produces three animals.

Thus, by the Restricted PSR, even in our tiny three-contingent-entity world there is an explanation of why there are at least three animals. Plausibly, an explanation of an existential fact like that must involve the causal efficacy of some being. This being is not one of the three animals, nor any combination of them, since none of these three beings and no combination of them is capable of explaining its own existence. Hence the fact must be explained by the causal efficacy of some being that is not one of these three. Since these three were all the contingent beings in existence, the fact must be explained by the causal efficacy of a non-contingent, and hence necessary, being. The argument generalizes to all universes whose entities can be divided up into a set of qualitative types with only a finite number of entities falling into each type. Our world is probably like that.[1]

8. Conclusions

The last fifty years of analytic philosophy have focused our attention on three critical questions about cosmological arguments. Each of these questions can receive a plausible answer from a defender of the cosmological argument. Moreover, a cumulative case argument can be run from the number of different principles on which a cosmological argument can be based. There is thus good reason, even on the basis of the cosmological argument alone, to suppose that a God-like being exists.

Note

1   In discussion, Dean Zimmerman has, however, come up with an objection to arguments like this. We can find a different explanation of why there are at least three animals without making any use of causes. Let's give names to our three animals: Bottom, Felix and Porky. Then we can explain why

there are at least three animals as follows: *there exist Bottom, Felix and Porky, each of whom is a distinct animal.* Whether we should accept this as a genuine explanation is unclear, but if we do then the argument has been blocked. One might, however, also try to modify the Restricted PSR as follows to get around the Zimmerman worry: every proposition p that can have a *causal* explanation in fact does have a causal explanation.

Bibliography

Adams, Robert M. (1974). "Theories of Actuality." *Noûs* 8: 211–31.

Beilby, James K. (2002). *Naturalism Defeated? Essays on Plantinga's Evolutionary Argument Against Naturalism.* Ithaca NY: Cornell University Press.

Gale, Richard M. and Pruss, Alexander R. (1999). "A New Cosmological Argument", *Religious Studies* 35: 461–476.

Gellman, Jerome (2000). "Prospects for a Sound Stage 3 of Cosmological Arguments." *Religious Studies* 36: 195–201.

Hume, David (1907). *Dialogues Concerning Natural Religion.* Edinburgh: Blackwood and Sons.

Kane, Robert (2002). "Free Will: Ancient Dispute, New Themes." In: J. Feinberg and R. Shafer-Landau (eds.), *Reason and Responsibility.* Stamford CT: Wadsworth, pp. 499–512.

Koons, Robert C. (1997). "A New Look at the Cosmological Argument." *American Philosophical Quarterly* 34: 193–212.

Lewis, David (1986). *On the Plurality of Worlds.* Malden MA: Blackwell.

Plantinga, Alvin (1974). *The Nature of Necessity.* Oxford: Clarendon.

Pruss, Alexander R. (2006). *The Principle of Sufficient Reason: A Reassessment.* Cambridge: Cambridge University Press.

Rescher, Nicholas (2000). *Nature and Understanding: The Metaphysics and Method of Science.* Oxford: Clarendon.

Rowe, William L. (1975). *The Cosmological Argument.* Princeton: Princeton University Press.

Swinburne, Richard G. (1968). "The Argument from Design." *Philosophy* 43: 199–212.

Taylor, Richard C. (1974). *Metaphysics.* 2nd ed. Englewood Cliffs, NJ: Prentice Hall.

van Inwagen, Peter (1983). *An Essay on Free Will.* Oxford: Oxford University Press.

White, David E. (1979). "An Argument for God's Existence." *International Journal for Philosophy of Religion* 10: 101–115.

Chapter 10

Wes Morriston

A CRITICAL EXAMINATION OF THE KALAM COSMOLOGICAL ARGUMENT

The *kalam*[1] cosmological argument has two parts. The first part attempts to show that there is a First Cause of the universe. It can be conveniently summarized as follows:

(1) Everything that begins to exist has a cause of its existence.
(2) The universe began to exist.
(3) Therefore, the universe has a cause of its existence.

The second (and much less straightforward) part of the argument tries to show that the cause of the universe is a very powerful person—something like the God of classical theism. Only a personal cause, it is said, could have produced a universe with a temporal beginning.

In "Philosophical and Scientific Pointers to Creation *ex Nihilo*"[2], William Lane Craig strongly defends both parts of the *kalam* argument. Believing that premise 1 above is so obviously true that no sane person could doubt it, he concentrates most of his attention on premise 2, offering two philosophical arguments against the possibility of an infinite past. He also points to "scientific confirmation" of the claim that the universe has a beginning. Finally, Craig briefly presents the second part of the *kalam* argument, arguing (1) that the cause of the universe must be eternal, and (2) that an eternal cause of something that begins to exist could only be a person.

In the present essay, I shall raise a number of objections to both parts of the *kalam* argument. I shall try to show (1) that they depend heavily on the two philosophical arguments against the infinite past; (2) that neither of the philosophical arguments against the infinite past is successful; (3) that when it is applied to events happening at the very first moment of time, premise 1 is much more problematic than Craig realizes; (4) that the argument provides no evidence for creation *out of nothing*; and (5) that Craig's argument for the claim that the first cause is a person cannot be sustained in the context of the sort of theism that he himself wishes to defend.

1. First Philosophical Argument Against the Infinite Past

If the series of past events had no beginning, then the past would consist in an infinite series of events, all of which have actually happened. Is this possible? Craig thinks that it isn't. An infinite series of past events would be an actually infinite set of events, and he believes that there cannot be an actual infinite in reality.

To convince us that this is so, Craig asks us to imagine a library containing infinitely many books, numbered from zero onwards. Such a library would have some very peculiar properties. For example, one could add infinitely many books to such a library without increasing the number of books in the library. One could remove the first three books, and the library would not have any fewer books. One could even remove every other book, and it would not have any fewer books. Craig thinks it is obvious that such a library could not exist in reality. Even God could not create a library with infinitely many books.

Let's pause for a moment, and try to see what is going on. Why would the library not have any more books, no matter how many were added to its collection? Why would it have no fewer books even if every other book were removed? The reason is that there is a "one-to-one correspondence" between the set of books in the library before and the set of books after the change.

To see how this works, suppose that all the odd-numbered books have been removed. We can map the collection of books after their removal onto the total collection as follows. Let book #0 after the change correspond to book #0 before the change, book #2 after to book #1 before, book #4 after to book #2 before, and so on . . . There is then a one-to-one correspondence between the set of books *before*, and the set of books *after* the removal of all the odd-numbered books.

Now according to the *Principle of Correspondence*, as its mathematicians call it,

PC If two sets can be placed in one-to-one correspondence, they must have the same number of elements.

It follows that there are no *fewer* books after the removal of all the odd-numbered ones.

Craig thinks this is absurd—there ought to be more odd-and-even numbered books altogether than even-numbered alone. So he concludes that there is something wrong with the whole idea of an infinite collection. Such collections simply cannot exist in reality.

Craig's argument at this point assumes the truth of a general principle that is worth stating explicitly. He calls it "*Euclid's maxim*" (after Euclid's fifth axiom).[3]

EM A whole is greater than any of its parts.

Given PC and EM, Craig thinks he can show that there are no actually infinite sets. For suppose there were. Then its members could be placed in one-to-one correspondence with a mere part (a "proper subset"[4]) of itself. By PC, it would then follow that the set has no more members than its part, contrary to EM.

As Craig sees it, both the Principle of Correspondence and Euclid's maxim are intuitively plausible. Both are obviously true of all finite sets. We get into trouble only when we try to apply them to infinite sets. So the reasonable thing to do is simply to deny that there are any actually infinite sets in reality. And since the series of past events exists in reality, Craig concludes that there cannot be infinitely many past events. The past must have a beginning—a very first event before which there were no others.

How strong is Craig's argument against the possibility of an actual infinite? The first thing to see is that Euclid's maxim about wholes and parts says nothing about the *number* of elements in a set. At most, it entails that *taken as a whole,* a set is *greater* than a mere *part* (a "proper subset") of itself. This is important, because Craig's argument turns on the claim that an infinite set would *not* be "greater" than its parts, and because (as we are about to see) there is a perfectly straightforward sense in which an infinite set *is* greater than any one of its proper subsets, even those that also have infinitely many members.

Craig's own example will make this clear. There is an obvious sense in which his imaginary library is "greater" than any of its parts, and this is so even though it does not have a greater *number* of books than some of its parts. For instance, the library as a whole is "greater" ("larger") than the part of the library containing only books numbered 3 and higher *simply in virtue of the fact that it contains books numbered 0, 1, and 2 as well as all the higher numbered books.* This is all by itself a perfectly legitimate sense of the word "greater"—one that is logically independent of the question, "What is the *number* of books in the two sets?"

There is, then, a fairly intuitive sense in which any set—even an infinite one—is "greater" than any of its parts. Not because the *number* of elements in the greater set is necessarily larger than the number of elements in the lesser one—but merely in virtue of the fact that it "contains" all the elements in the lesser set plus some others that the lesser one does not contain. That, all by itself, and without any reference to the *number* of elements in either set, is sufficient to make one "greater" than the other. When the word "greater" is understood this way, Craig's infinite library does *not* violate the principle that the "whole" is greater than its "part."

So EM by itself will not get Craig's argument off the ground. His argument requires something like the following principle:

EM*   A set must have a greater *number* of elements than any of its proper subsets.

Now everyone would agree that while EM* is true of finite sets, it cannot be true of infinite sets. But what should we conclude from this? That there can't be any infinite sets? Or merely that while EM* is true of finite sets, but not of *all* sets?

How can we decide? Craig's appeal to the allegedly "absurd" properties of an actually infinite set won't settle the issue, since the "absurdity" of those properties depends on the necessary truth of EM*.

It seems that we have arrived at an impasse. Craig thinks it is obvious that something like EM* must be true of all sets, and that an actual infinite is therefore impossible. His opponents think that an actual infinite is possible, and that EM* is therefore true only of finite sets. Is there any way to decide who is right?

One way to break the impasse would be to ask whether we know of any sets that really do (or could) have infinitely many members. Several candidates have been proposed.[5] I'll present just one of them.

Consider a finite chunk of spatial extension. It can, as we all know, be divided into subregions, each of which can again be divided into smaller subregions, and so on *ad infinitum*. It seems, then, that within any region of space, there are infinitely many subregions.

Craig is well aware of this objection. His answer is that space is not composed of points.[6] It follows that there are no natural boundaries within a given chunk of space, so that the various subregions do not exist as subregions until a division is actually made (at least in thought). Since we never arrive at a point at which all possible divisions have already been made (we can always—at least in principle—divide again), Craig thinks the number of subregions is only *potentially* infinite. It follows that we do not after all have a good example of an actual infinite existing in reality.

I think Craig is wrong about this. While it is true that we cannot actually make an infinite number of subdivisions within a region of space, it doesn't follow that the subregions are not *there* prior to any possible division. Nor does the lack of natural boundaries within a region of space settle this issue in Craig's favor. What follows from the absence of natural boundaries is only that the infinitely many subregions do not exist *apart from a specified way of dividing things up.*

It is not difficult to come up with a specification relative to which the number of coexistent subregions is infinite. Unlike actually dividing a thing a given number of times, the specification for so dividing it doesn't have to be provided one step at a time—it can be given all at once. Just as we can specify the set of natural numbers all at once by the single rule, "starting with one, add one to the previous sum *ad infinitum*," so too I suggest that we can specify all the subregions of a given region R of space *relative to the rule*, "starting with R divide the results of the previous division by half *ad infinitum*." We don't have to rely on *natural* points of division within R to apply this rule to R. Nor do we need to *complete* the series of divisions in order to know that, *relative to this rule,* there is an *actual*—and not merely a potential—infinity of subregions.[7]

2. Second Philosophical Argument Against the Infinite Past

Craig has a second philosophical argument against the infinite past. Even if infinitely many things could exist at the same time, Craig thinks that the series of past events could not be actually infinite. He summarizes this argument as follows.

(a) The series of events in time is a collection formed by adding one member after another.

(b) A collection formed by adding one member after another cannot be actually infinite.

(c) Therefore, the series of events in time cannot be actually infinite.[8]

Probably no one will want to deny the first premise. It just says that in any temporal series of events, the members of the series happen successively, one after the other. One event passes by, then another, and so on, up until the last event in the series. But what about the second premise? Why can't a collection formed in this step-by-step way have infinitely many members? Craig's answer is that an infinite collection could never be completed. No matter how many members have been added to the collection, you could always add one more. No matter how many events have "gone by," the number of past events is only finite. We never arrive at infinity.

The second premise is obviously true of any series *having a temporal beginning*. Consider, for example, the series of years that began exactly one hundred years ago. One hundred of its members have passed by. The hundred and first is on its way. But no matter how many years are added, only finitely many years will have passed by. The collection will never be a completed infinity.

But what about a series *having no temporal beginning*? Why couldn't there be a series of years in which there is no first year? It's true that in such a series we never "arrive" at infinity, but that is only because infinity is, so to speak, "always already there." At every point in the series, infinitely many years have already passed by.

Craig thinks this is impossible. If infinitely many years must have passed by before a given year, then that year could never arrive. Craig illustrates his point as follows:

. . . suppose we meet a man who claims to have been counting from eternity, and now he is finishing: −5, −4, −3, −2, −1, 0. Now this is impossible. For, we may ask, why didn't he finish counting yesterday or the day before or the year before? By then an infinity of time had already elapsed, so that he should have finished. The fact is, we could never find anyone completing such a task because at any previous point he would have already finished.[9]

This is not a good argument. It confuses "having counted infinitely many numbers" with "having counted all the negative numbers up to zero." The man has indeed always already completed the first of these tasks; but he has not completed the second one until he arrives at zero. When he arrived at −1 he had completed a different task—that of counting all the members in the series < . ., −n, . ., −2, −1 >. When he arrived at −2, he had completed yet another task—that of counting all the members in the series, < . ., −n, . ., −3, −2 >. And so on.

No doubt there *could* have been a beginningless count ending in zero at any time in the infinite past. But Craig gives no good reason for thinking that there *must* have been one or that the infinite counter in his example would have to be the person who had completed it. Consequently, it seems to me that our objection to Craig's defense of premise *b* remains undefeated. This premise holds true for any series *having a beginning*—if you *start out* on an infinite series, you will never complete it. But that tells us nothing at all about whether a *beginningless* series of events is possible.

3. Hasn't God Always Existed?

But suppose Craig is right, and the past does have a beginning. You might wonder how long he thinks *God* has existed. Since God does not begin to exist, mustn't He have existed forever? And wouldn't that be an actual infinite of the very sort that Craig says is impossible? Craig's explanation is interesting.

> God was timeless prior to creation, and He created time along with the world. From that point on God places Himself within time so that He can interact with the world He has created. [198]

This might seem incoherent. If God exists *prior* to creation, mustn't He exist at a *time* prior to creation? How, then, can He be *timeless* prior to creation? Craig's answer is that God is causally, but not temporally, prior. He has the kind of "priority" that any cause has over its effect. Let me explain.

Craig believes that it is possible for a cause and its effect to occur simultaneously. For example, it might be thought that the pressure of a man's posterior on a cushion causes the depression in the cushion, even though these states of affairs obtain simultaneously. But even in cases like this, the causal relation is asymmetrical—the cause is the source of the effect, and not the other way around. In that sense, the cause is "prior" to its effect.

This is how we must understand Craig's claim that God is timeless "prior" to the creation of time. Insofar as he is the *creator* of time, God is "causally prior" to time itself. And this is so even though there is (obviously enough) no time prior to the creation of time. "Prior to" (apart

from) the creation of time and the universe, God is timeless.

On the other hand, Craig also insists that in creating time God "places Himself within time so that He can interact with the world He has created." Even though God—*as* creator of the universe and time—is timeless, Craig insists that God's life in relation to the world He creates has temporal duration. God's life in time, so to speak, begins with creation. Subsequent to creation, God has a past and that past has a beginning, since it began with the creation of time and the universe.

There is a small but extremely important qualification that Craig does not mention in "Philosophical and Scientific Pointers to Creation *ex Nihilo*." He wants to leave open the *possibility* that time began prior to the creation of the physical universe. This may surprise you, since the four "prominent astronomers" whose words Craig quotes with so much approval in this essay assert that it is "meaningless" to "ask what happened before the big bang."[10] This might lead one to suppose that Craig agrees that it is meaningless to suggest that there was a time prior to the creation of our physical universe. But this is not his considered view. In another essay, he writes:

> . . . [S]uppose that God led up to creation by counting, "1, 2, 3, . . ., fiat lux!" In that case the series of mental events alone is sufficient to establish a temporal succession prior to the commencement of physical time at t = 0. There would be a sort of metaphysical time based on the succession of contents of consciousness in God's mind prior to the inception of physical time. Thus, it is meaningful to speak both of the cause of the Big Bang and of the beginning of the universe.[11]

In this scenario, the physical time of the universe is created at t = 0 when God says, "fiat lux" ("let there be light"). But the creation of physical time happens within a more fundamental kind of time—"metaphysical time," as Craig calls it. This more fundamental temporal series also has a beginning, however. For expository purposes, Craig usually operates on the assumption that it is created along with physical time. But in the passage quoted above he acknowledges another possibility—that of a temporal series of events leading up to creation. In Craig's imaginary illustration, metaphysical time begins on the count of "one," and whole series of events between that first moment and the creation of the universe occurs prior to the first moment of physical time.

The nature of metaphysical time and its relation to physical time are large and difficult questions, lying well beyond the scope of this essay.[12] But for reasons that will become apparent in the next section, it is important to see that Craig does allow for the possibility of a series of events that are prior—in metaphysical time—to the beginning of our universe.

4. Scientific Confirmation

In sections 1 and 2 I tried to show that Craig's two philosophical arguments against the possibility of an infinite past are unsuccessful. But you might think this doesn't matter very much, since scientists have shown that the universe very likely *did* have a beginning—that it almost certainly began with a very big "bang" about fifteen billion years ago. So doesn't Craig's argument get all the backing it needs even if the two philosophical arguments against the possibility of an infinite past are unsound?

Unfortunately, things are not that simple. What the scientific considerations show is only that our physical universe very likely had a beginning. What, if anything, happened before the beginning of our universe—and even whether or not there was any "before"—is not settled by the scientific evidence. Discoveries in the empirical sciences have not ruled out the possibility that our universe is the product of events that occurred at a time prior to the beginning of our space-time.

It may occur to you to object that it makes no sense to speak of a time prior to the beginning of space-time, since it is created along with the universe. But this point is of no use to Craig, since, as we saw at the end of the previous section, he thinks there is another more fundamental kind of time—*metaphysical* time—that does not depend on the existence of our universe. So on Craig's own view, there at least *could* have been a series of events occurring in metaphysical time prior to the beginning of our universe.

This is important, because it means that we have to take into account the logical possibility of a temporal series of causes and effects prior to the beginning of the universe. Perhaps the universe was produced by something else, which in turn was produced by something else, and so on *ad infinitum*. The scientific considerations do not rule this out. To block the possibility of such a regress, Craig must rely on his philosophical arguments against the infinite past. If those arguments are unsound, then the beginning of our universe might (for all Craig has shown) be merely the most recent in a beginningless series of causes and effects.

One much discussed version of this possibility is the so-called "oscillating universe" hypothesis. On this hypothesis, the universe expands and then contracts. Each cycle begins with a "big bang," and ends in a "big crunch." And that's how it is throughout a possibly infinite past.

Craig thinks there is more than enough scientific evidence to refute the oscillating universes hypothesis. For example, he points out that there isn't enough dark matter to reverse the expansion of the universe and bring about a "big crunch."[13] But even if this is correct, it tells us only that the pattern of oscillation is not going to *continue*. It tells us nothing about what, if anything, *preceded* the big bang. Why think that in the previous cycle—if there was one—there was no more dark matter than in ours? Why even think it must have been governed by the same physical laws as ours?

Now Craig would undoubtedly point out that there is no empirical support for saying that the preceding cycles contained more dark matter than ours. For that matter, he could point out that there is no empirical support for any sort of infinite series of past causes and effects. This is undoubtedly true. On the other hand, unless Craig's arguments against the infinite past are better than I think they are, an infinite series of causes and effects in metaphysical time remains one of the logical possibilities. And even if it lacks empirical support, it is not obvious that it has any *less* going for it than Craig's hypothesis—that of a timeless person who somehow managed to create time and put itself into time. One should not overlook the possibility that none of our hypotheses about the origin of the universe is especially likely to be true. Perhaps we just don't have enough to go on to choose among the logical possibilities, and the right thing to say is that we simply do not know how or why the universe came into existence.

5. Must the Beginning Have a Cause?

But suppose it is granted that the past is finite, and that there is a very first event in the series of events leading up to the present. For simplicity's sake, let us assume that this first event coincides with the beginning of our universe.

This brings us to our next question. Is premise 1 of the *kalam* argument true? Must everything that begins to exist—even the very first event in the history of time—have a cause? Craig thinks it is unnecessary to give a lengthy defense of this claim. "Does anyone in his right mind," he asks, "really believe that, say, a raging tiger could suddenly come into existence uncaused, out of nothing, in this room right now?"[14] Probably no one does. Craig then invites us to apply this "intuition" to the beginning of the universe, and conclude that it too must have a cause.

But surely this is much too quick. Of course, no one thinks a tiger could just spring into exist-

ence "in this room right now." But before we jump to conclusions, we need to ask *why* this is so. What makes this so obvious? Is it, as Craig seems to suppose, that all normal persons believe the first premise of the *kalam* argument, and then apply it to the case of the tiger? Call that the *top-down* explanation. Or is it rather that we have a lot of experience of animals (and other middle-sized material objects), and we know that popping up like that is just not the way such things come into existence? Call that the *bottom-up* explanation.

The bottom-up explanation takes note of the fact that we are dealing with a familiar *context*—one provided by our collective experience of the world in which we live and of the way it operates. It is our background knowledge of that context—our empirical knowledge of the natural order—that makes it so preposterous to suppose that a tiger might pop into existence uncaused. We *know* where tigers and such come from, and that just isn't the way it happens.

Now contrast the situation with regard to the beginning of time and the universe. There is no familiar law-governed context for it, precisely because there is nothing (read, "there is not anything") prior to such a beginning. We have no experience of the origin of worlds to tell us that *worlds* don't come into existence like that. We don't even have experience of the coming into being of anything remotely analogous to the "initial singularity" that figures in the big bang theory of the origin of the universe. The intuitive absurdity of tigers and the like popping into existence out of nowhere does not entitle us to draw quick and easy inferences about the beginning of the whole natural order.

However, Craig thinks it is, if anything, even *more* obvious that the universe (and time) could not have come into existence uncaused. His reason seems to be that prior to the beginning of an uncaused universe, there would be absolutely nothing. Immediately following the tiger passage quoted above, he writes, "If prior to the existence of the universe, there was absolutely nothing—no God, no space, no time—how could the universe possibly come to exist?"[15] Craig thinks this is a straightforward application of the medieval principle that "nothing comes from nothing" (*ex nihilo nihil fit*)—a principle he believes to be so obviously true that no one could sincerely deny it. In another place, he writes:

> . . . if originally there were absolutely nothing—no God, no space, no time—then how could the universe possibly come to exist? The truth of the principle *ex nihilo, nihil fit* is so obvious that I think we are justified in foregoing an elaborate defense of the argument's first premiss.[16]

Let's think about this a bit. It sounds rather as if Craig is saying that if there existed a *situation* in which there was absolutely nothing, then—in that situation—nothing could come into existence. This is nonsense. "Nothing at all" is not a weird sort of "something." It is not a situation "in" which something else "can" or "cannot" come to be. "Nothing" just means "not anything."

What else could Craig mean when he says that "if originally there were absolutely nothing" nothing could come into existence? Perhaps he means no more than this:

(NA) If there had not been anything, then there would not have been anything.

NA is undoubtedly true. If there were "not anything"—*not even time*—then there would not be anything—not even a "coming-into-existence" of the universe. But I doubt if this can be all that Craig has in mind, since nothing of interest follows from so trivial a claim.

It is not surprising, therefore, that Craig sometimes slips into talking as if the issue were whether something could "spring into existence" out of a *temporally prior situation* in which there is nothing at all. In the following passage, for example, he writes:

. . . virtually no one ever challenges the premiss that if *in the past* nothing existed then nothing would exist now. . . . The old principle ex nihilo nihil fit appears to be so manifestly true that a sincere denial of this axiom is well-nigh impossible.[17]

Since there can hardly be a *past* state of affairs in which there is *no time*, it looks as if Craig here understands the principle, *ex nihilo nihil fit*, to mean something like the following.

(NT) If, at a given time, there were nothing at all (apart from time itself), then at no later time could anything begin to exist.

But this won't give Craig what he wants, since even if it is true, NT does not entail that the first event—the event before which there was no time—must have a cause.

If neither NA nor NT provides what is needed here, is there anything else Craig might mean by his frequent repetition of the phrase, "from nothing, nothing comes"? I think there is. I suspect that at bottom this is merely a confusing way of saying that whatever begins to exist must have a cause (something "from" which it "comes"). But if that's all it comes to, then the great medieval principle is merely a restatement of premise 1 of the *kalam* argument, and provides no additional support for it. Certainly it tells us nothing useful about the beginning of the whole natural order—or about the need for a cause at a time prior to which there is no time.

There may also be something to be said *against* the claim that there could be a cause of the whole temporal order of events. Many philosophers hold that causes must precede their effects in time. If they are right, then it follows straightaway that a first event *could not* have a cause.

The nature of causation is another large and difficult issue that lies beyond the scope of this essay, but it is interesting to observe that some of the very philosophers Craig cites as favoring his own causal principle also hold that causes must precede their effects in time. For example, David Hume's famous analysis of the causal relation explicitly includes this requirement. And in the very passage quoted by Craig, C. D. Broad says that he cannot believe that anything could begin to exist "without being caused by something else which existed *before and up to* the moment when the thing in question began to exist."[18] This is obviously inconsistent with Craig's account of creation, since according to that account, there is no time prior to the very first event. Its cause cannot therefore have existed "before and up to the moment" at which it occurred.

I am not sure what Hume and Broad and the rest would say if they thought time had a beginning. Would they (like Craig) conclude that some causes do not precede their effects in time? Or would they simply say that a first event (unlike all later ones) could not have a cause? I won't try to settle that issue here. But it is important to see that in order to get the *kalam* argument off the ground, Craig must take controversial positions on a number of highly debatable issues having to do with the nature of time and of causation. Contrary to what Craig supposes, therefore, a sane adult may have sincere—and quite reasonable—doubts about the scope of premise 1 of the *kalam* argument.

6. Creation out of Nothing?

As the title "Philosophical and Scientific Pointers to Creation *ex Nihilo*" suggests, Craig believes he can show, not merely that the universe was created *by* a person, but that it was created *out of* nothing. His argument for the second of these claims appeals to a version of the big bang theory according to which the universe emerged from an infinitely dense particle that exploded some fifteen billion years ago.

This event that marked the beginning of the universe becomes all the more amazing when one reflects on the fact that a state of "infinite density" is synonymous with "nothing." There can be no object that possesses infinite density, for if it had any size at all, it would not be *infinitely* dense. Therefore, as astronomer Fred Hoyle points out, the big bang theory requires the creation of matter from nothing. This is because as one goes back in time, he reaches a point at which, in Hoyle's words, the universe was "shrunk down to nothing at all." Thus, what the big bang model requires is that the universe had a beginning and was created out of nothing.[19]

The argument Craig presents in this passage can be summarized as follows.

(a) According to the big bang theory, the universe was created out of an infinitely dense particle.

(b) There can be no object having infinite density.

(c) So "infinite density" is synonymous with "nothing."

(d) Therefore, the big bang theory entails that the universe was created out of nothing.

This argument is extremely confused. For one thing, step *c* of the argument is obviously false. "Infinite density" is not synonymous with "nothing," and the "initial singularity" that figures in the big bang theory is not simply nothing at all. A mere *nothing* could not explode, as the infinitely dense particle is supposed to have done. And even if it lacks spatial and temporal spread, the initial singularity has other properties. For starters, it has the property of "being infinitely dense." It is therefore a quite remarkable *something*, and not a mere nothing.

But this is not all. If premise *b* is true—if it is really true that "there can be no object that possesses infinite density," then this version of the big bang theory is simply false, since it says that there once was such an object.

So far, then, it appears that the big bang model of the origin of our universe provides no support for the claim that the universe was created *out of nothing*. Elsewhere, however, Craig explains his position somewhat differently.

On such a model the universe originates *ex nihilo* in the sense that at the initial singularity it is true that *There is no earlier space-time point* or it is false that *Something existed prior to the singularity*.[20]

In this passage, Craig does not deny that an infinitely dense particle could exist. Nor does he make the mistake of saying that the "initial singularity" is a mere "nothing." What he says instead is that nothing *preceded* the initial singularity *in time*, and this is somehow supposed to show that the initial singularity was created out of nothing. The argument goes like this:

(e) The initial singularity exists at the earliest point of space-time.

(f) There is no time prior to the earliest point in space-time.

(g) Therefore, there was nothing temporally prior to the initial singularity.

(h) So the initial singularity must have been created out of nothing.

There are at least two problems with this argument. For the reasons already given in section 3 above, I do not think the big bang theory entails the truth of premise f. Even it is granted that space-time begins at the initial singularity, it does not follow that *metaphysical* time begins with the first moment in space-time. Recall that on Craig's view, God *could have* created time long before creating the space-time of our universe. It follows that there *could have been* something prior to the earliest point in space-time (t = 0), in which case premise f would be false. Premise f *may* be true anyway—metaphysical time and space-time *could have* begun together. But since the big bang theory says nothing about metaphysical time, Craig cannot consistently claim that the big bang theory shows this to be so.

But suppose that the first moment of metaphysical time does coincide with t = 0 in the space-time of our universe. That still doesn't give us creation *ex nihilo*. What follows is only that the universe wasn't created out of something *that existed at a time earlier than* t = 0. So step h of the argument does not follow from step g without an additional premise:

(i) If there was nothing temporally prior to the initial singularity, then it must have been created out of nothing.

But why think this additional premise is true? Why couldn't the initial singularity be created out of something that exists timelessly? Whether this is possible depends on what sorts of things exist outside of time. According to Craig we know that God, the first cause of the universe exists outside time "prior" to creating the universe. But why suppose that God is the only being who exists outside time? Why couldn't there also have been a timeless "stuff" that God formed into a universe?

Craig thinks he can rule out this possibility on the ground that physical matter and energy are temporal in nature. But why suppose that these are the only possible "stuffs" out of which God might have made the universe? It's true that we are not acquainted with any timeless "stuffs" that could have played this role. But we don't encounter any timeless persons either, and Craig has no trouble with that idea. So why couldn't there also have been a timeless material "stuff" for God to work with?

I am not putting this forward as a particularly likely hypothesis. It seems to me that we simply don't have enough to go on to decide what (if anything) God (if he exists) might have made the universe out of. As a wise philosopher once said, "Our line is too short to fathom such abysses."[21] What I am sure of is that the big bang theory does not settle the issue in favor of creation *ex nihilo*.

7. Must the First Cause be a Person?

Our final topic is Craig's argument for saying that the First Cause of the universe must be a person. It is a difficult argument, and Craig's presentation of it is brief. It seems to go something like this.

We know that the cause of the beginning of the universe (or whatever the first event was) must be eternal. Otherwise it would be one of the things that begins to exist, and would be just as much in need of a cause as the universe.

Now natural causes—"mechanical" causes, as Craig sometimes calls them[22]—are *sufficient* for their effects. They produce their effects as soon as all the relevant conditions are in place. It follows that if this sort of cause had no beginning, its effect could not have a beginning either. For example, Craig says, if the temperature is cold enough for long enough, whatever water happens to be around must have turned to ice. So if there had always been water and the temperature had *always* been below zero, all the water would *always* have been frozen.

The general point is that if a cause is sufficient for its effect, and the cause is eternal, then the effect must be eternal too. So if it had that sort of eternal cause the universe would have to be eternal too.

Craig thinks he has shown that the universe isn't eternal—that it has a beginning. How then, he asks, can it have an eternal cause? We have just seen that it couldn't have an eternal "mechanical" cause. But what other sort of eternal cause might there be?

Craig thinks there is another familiar sort of cause that provides the answer to this question. In addition to mechanical causes that automatically produce their effects, he says that there are *personal* causes. Individual persons are free agents who have the power to cause all sorts of things. But they don't have to do so and can exist fully without producing the various effects they are capable of causing.

Suppose, for example, that a man is seated. The man can, at any time, decide to stand up. But he can also choose to remain seated. He has the power to decide either way—it is entirely up to him to determine when or even whether to stand up. If he does decide to stand, then he, and he alone, is the *cause* of his decision. Unlike a merely mechanical cause, the man can exist fully without exercising his power to produce the various effects of which he is the cause.

This is quite a controversial claim. Many philosophers believe that the true cause of a person's decision is not simply the person, but various other psychological factors at work within the person—his beliefs and values and preferences, and that these in turn are the product of other causes. Unlike these philosophers, Craig claims that a person—and not something else happening within the person—is the sole cause of his own decisions. In *exactly the same situation*, with *exactly the same ongoing desires and beliefs*, our seated man could decide either to stand up or to remain seated.

Let's suppose, at least for the sake of argument, that Craig is right about this. It follows that there are at least two radically different kinds of causation in the world. On the one hand, there are mechanical causes that cannot help bringing about their effects; and on the other hand, there are personal causes with the power to bring about various effects, but who are free to determine just how and when and whether they will exercise that power.

Against this theoretical background, we can see why Craig thinks the First Cause must be a person. How is it, he asks, that the cause of the universe is eternal, even though the universe is not? We have already seen that an eternal mechanical cause could have only an eternal effect. But what about an eternal personal cause? Craig thinks that an eternal person could cause a temporal effect. Here is his explanation.

> . . . a man sitting from eternity may will to stand up; hence, a temporal effect may arise from an eternally existing agent. Indeed, the

agent may will from eternity to create a temporal effect, so that no change in the agent need be conceived.[23]

Suppose, then, that the cause of the universe is an eternal person. It does not follow that the universe is eternal—since the personal cause of the universe could have "willed from eternity" to produce a universe with a beginning in time. Craig thinks this is the only possible way to explain why the universe is not eternal: "The only way to have an eternal cause but a temporal effect would seem to be if the cause is a personal agent who freely chooses to create an effect in time."[24]

There are a number of difficult issues here. Does personal causation work the way Craig thinks it does? Or is causation by a person always analyzable in terms of other things happening within the person? Is personal causation the only alternative to mechanical causation? Or might there be some other type of "eternal cause" that wouldn't necessarily produce an eternal effect? I won't pursue these questions further here, but there is another objection to Craig's argument that I would like to develop. To see how this line of criticism goes, we need to back up a bit and take a close look at the way persons are related to the things they cause.

When a person stands up, he makes his body move. But he does that by producing another kind of change in himself—a mental change. He *decides* that now is the time to get up—he forms the intention to get up right away—and it is this mental change that is the immediate cause of the changed position of his body. Granted that a person can sit on a bench for a long time without deciding to get up, once his decision to "get up now" is made, it normally produces its effect straightaway—faster even than a temperature below zero freezes water.

So how does it work with God and creation? Apparently, God must *choose* to create, or nothing will happen. It is God's choosing to create that is the immediate cause of the beginning of the universe. God chooses to create a universe, and the universe comes into being.

You might think that God's choosing is a mental *change* in God. God thinks it over, *and then* decides to create. But Craig denies that this is so.

> By "choose" I do not mean God changes His mind. I mean God intends from eternity to create a world in time.[25]

It is not hard to see why Craig wouldn't want to say that "choosing to create" is a *change* in God. Craig's God is omniscient. He can't arrive at decisions the way you and I do, because He always already knows what He is going to do. (You aren't *arriving at* a decision about what to do if you *already know* what you are going to do.) So naturally Craig concludes that God's decision to create is eternal—that He "intends from eternity to create a world."

But this creates a different problem for Craig's account of creation. We have seen that God's decision to create is the immediate cause of the universe. But now we learn that God's decision to create is eternal. So how, on Craig's principles, can we avoid the conclusion that the universe is just as eternal as God's decision to create it?

To be sure, Craig also says, "God chooses from eternity to create a world *with a beginning*."[26] But it is hard to see how this is possible. You will recall that Craig's argument for saying that the first cause must be a person assumes that:

(a) An eternal sufficient cause must have an eternal effect.

But presumably Craig doesn't think God needs any help getting the universe going. So it is natural to suppose that:

(b) God's will to create "a world with a beginning" is *sufficient* to produce it.

But we have just learned that:

(c) God's will to create "a world with a begin-ning" is eternal.

From these three premises, it follows that:

(d) "A world with a beginning" is eternal.

This conclusion is obviously absurd. A "world with a beginning" cannot be eternal. So, since *d* follows from premises *a*, *b*, and *c*, one of them must be false. But which? Craig's answer appears to be that *b* is false.

> I am inclined simply to deny that God's eter-nally willing to create the universe, properly understood, is sufficient for the existence of the universe . . .[27]

How could this be? Surely Craig doesn't think God could fail to accomplish what he "eternally wills"! Here is his explanation:

> . . . [I]t is insufficient to account for the ori-gin of the universe by citing simply God, His timeless intention to create a world with a beginning, and His power to produce such a result. There must be an exercise of His causal power in order for the universe to be cre-ated. . . . [We must] differentiate between God's timeless intention to create a temporal world and God's undertaking to create a tem-poral world.[28]

Craig here distinguishes God's eternal will to create a world from his actually exercising the power to do what He thus wills—His eternal intention to create from His "undertaking" to carry out this intention. God's "undertaking" to create the universe is presumably sufficient for the existence of the universe, and the universe begins to exist "as soon as" God "undertakes" to create it. But this doesn't make the universe eter-nal because the "undertaking" (unlike the ori-ginal intention) is not eternal. Since God puts Himself into time when He "undertakes" to

create the universe, His "undertaking" to create occurs at the very first moment of time. It is, so to speak, the very first of the events that God causes.

But surely this only pushes the question back to the relation between God's eternal will and His "undertaking" to execute His prior inten-tion. If God's will to create is sufficient for His undertaking to create, then on Craig's principles the undertaking must be eternal, in which case, once again, the universe must be eternal. Craig must therefore deny, not only that God's eternal will is sufficient for the existence of the universe, but also that it is sufficient for His *undertaking* to create the universe. Is this at all plausible?

I don't think so. It is easy enough to see that the will of a merely human person is often not sufficient for his actually undertaking to do what he intends to do. There are at least two reasons for this. You and I can intend to do something at a *later time*, but not until that time comes will we *undertake* to do anything about our earlier inten-tion. This afternoon, for example, I plan to go to a certain store to buy some vitamins. I have not—yet—undertaken to do so, because the time I have selected for this activity has not yet arrived. But even when the proper time does arrive, I may change my mind and not go. This is the second reason for saying that a human per-son's will is not sufficient for his actually under-taking to do what he has willed. Human beings have wills that are changeable and inconstant. Sometimes they even suffer from *weakness* of will, and fail to do what they (perhaps sincerely) intended to do, even when it is long past the time for action.

It is obvious that neither of these explanations of the gap between willing and undertaking can be applied to the sort of God Craig believes in— a God who is omnipotent, omniscient, and timeless. An omnipotent being cannot suffer from weakness of will. An omniscient being cannot change its mind. And a time-less being cannot meaningfully be said to "delay" undertaking to carry out its intentions.

So it is very hard indeed to see how God's eternal will to create can fail to be sufficient for His undertaking to do so, in which case it is also sufficient for the beginning of the universe. On Craig's principles, therefore, it ought to follow that the universe is eternal.

8. Conclusion

I have tried to show that the *kalam* argument is not a successful argument for the existence of God or for creation *ex nihilo*. This does not mean, of course, that I have a better theory of the origin of the universe on offer. My own view is that we simply don't know enough to draw firm conclusions about such matters. It is fun to speculate, but we cannot hope to come up with answers that any honest, reasonable, and well-informed person would be bound to accept. Most of us have different and somewhat conflicting intuitions about time and eternity, causation and agency, about the nature of personhood, and about many other matters. It is an illusion to suppose that there is a single obviously correct way of sorting it all out. That is why the history of philosophy is, and will continue to be, a history of contest and controversy . . . and fun.[29]

Notes

1 So called in recognition of the Islamic philosophers who first developed this argument for the existence of God. The word "*kalam*" is Arabic for "speech" or "discourse," but it became the name of a school of Islamic theology that flourished in the middle ages.

2 William Lane Craig, "Philosophical and Scientific Pointers to Creation *ex Nihilo*," in R. Douglas Geivett and Brendan Sweetman, eds., *Contemporary Perspectives on Religious Epistemology*, (New York and Oxford: Oxford University Press, 1992), 185–200.

3 William Lane Craig (with Quentin Smith), *Theism, Atheism, and Big Bang Cosmology*, (Oxford: Oxford University Press, 1993), 23ff.

4 A set *A* is a proper subset of a set *B* if every element of *A* is an element of *B*, but not every element of *B* is an element of *A*.

5 Here are some other candidates. (1) Euclidean space contains an infinity of nonoverlapping sub-regions. Space may not be Euclidean, but it could have been. So an actual infinite is at least possible. (2) There are infinitely many natural numbers. If they are real, then the set of natural numbers is an actual infinite. (3) Craig thinks the future is infinite, and that there is a complete set of facts known to God about this infinite future. He argues that this is a merely potential infinite, on the ground that the future is not "real." This is quite a controversial claim—but even it is granted, it might still seem that Craig is committed to thinking that the set of *facts* about the future is actually infinite. Naturally, Craig has things to say about these candidates for an actual infinite, but limitations of space prevent a full treatment of the issue here.

6 See William Lane Craig and Michael Tooley, *A Classic Debate on the Existence of God* (http://www.leaderu.com/offices/billcraig/docs/craig-tooley0.html)

7 For a more thorough treatment of Craig's argument against the possibility of an actual infinite, see Wes Morriston, "Craig on the Actual Infinite," *Religious Studies* 38 (2002), 147–166.

8 "Philosophical and Scientific Pointers to Creation *ex Nihilo*," 190.

9 "Philosophical and Scientific Pointers to Creation *ex Nihilo*," 189–90.

10 This is the view of the four "prominent astronomers" whom Craig quotes so approvingly. See "Philosophical and Scientific Pointers to Creation *ex Nihilo*," 192.

11 "The Origin and Creation of the Universe: A Response to Adolf Grünbaum," *British Journal for the Philosophy of Science* 43 (1992), 233–240.

12 For more on Craig's view of these matters, see his *Time and Eternity: Exploring God's Relationship to Time* (Wheaton, III: Crossway Books, 2001).

13 Actually, the most recent speculation has it that there is enough "dark matter," but that this is more compensated for by the presence of something called "dark energy." There is, so they say, enough dark energy to resist the pull of gravity, and keep the universe expanding indefinitely. If this is right, then our universe is not going to collapse in a "big crunch."

14 Craig, "the Existence of God and the Beginning of

the Universe," *Truth Journal*, v. 3 (http://www.iclnet.org/clm/truth/3truth11.html)

15   *Reasonable Faith: Christian Truth and Apologetics*, 93.

16   "The Existence of God and the Beginning of the Universe." My emphasis.

17   *Theism, Atheism, and Big Bang Cosmology*, 58–59. My emphasis.

18   "Philosophical and Scientific Pointers to Creation *ex Nihilo*," 196. My emphasis.

19   *Ibid.*, 192.

20   "The Ultimate Question of Origins: God and the Beginning of the Universe," *Astrophysics and Space Science* 269–270 (1999), 723–740.

21   David Hume, *Enquiry Concerning the Human Understanding*, section vii, part i.

22   "The Existence of God and the Beginning of the Universe."

23   "The Existence of God and the Beginning of the Universe."

24   *Ibid.*

25   "Philosophical and Scientific Pointers to Creation *ex Nihilo*," 197.

26   *Ibid.*, 197.

27   Must the Beginning of the Universe Have a Personal Cause?: A Rejoinder," *Faith and Philosophy* 19 (2002), 94–105.

28   *Ibid.*

29   I would like to take this opportunity to thank Barbara Morriston, who read an earlier draft of this paper and made many helpful suggestions.

Chapter 11

Robin Collins

A SCIENTIFIC ARGUMENT FOR THE EXISTENCE OF GOD
The Fine-Tuning Design Argument

I. Introduction

The Evidence of Fine-Tuning

Suppose we went on a mission to Mars, and found a domed structure in which everything was set up just right for life to exist. The temperature, for example, was set around 70° F and the humidity was at 50 percent; moreover, there was an oxygen recycling system, an energy gathering system, and a whole system for the production of food. Put simply, the domed structure appeared to be a fully functioning biosphere. What conclusion would we draw from finding this structure? Would we draw the conclusion that it just happened to form by chance? Certainly not. Instead, we would unanimously conclude that it was designed by some intelligent being. Why would we draw this conclusion? Because an intelligent designer appears to be the only plausible explanation for the existence of the structure. That is, the only alternative explanation we can think of – that the structure was formed by some natural process – seems extremely unlikely. Of course, it is *possible* that, for example, through some volcanic eruption various metals and other compounds could have formed, and then separated out in just the right way to produce the "biosphere," but such a scenario strikes us as extraordinarily unlikely, thus making this alternative explanation unbelievable.

The universe is analogous to such a "biosphere," according to recent findings in physics. Almost everything about the basic structure of the universe – for example, the fundamental laws and parameters of physics and the initial distribution of matter and energy – is balanced on a razor's edge for life to occur. As the eminent Princeton physicist Freeman Dyson notes, "There are many . . . lucky accidents in physics. Without such accidents, water could not exist as liquid, chains of carbon atoms could not form complex organic molecules, and hydrogen atoms could not form breakable bridges between molecules"[1] – in short, life as we know it would be impossible.

Scientists call this extraordinary balancing of the parameters of physics and the initial conditions of the universe the "fine-tuning of the cosmos." It has been extensively discussed by philosophers, theologians, and scientists, especially since the early 1970s, with hundreds of articles and dozens of books written on the topic. Today, it is widely regarded as offering by far the most persuasive current argument for the existence of God. For example, theoretical physicist and popular science writer Paul Davies – whose early writings were not particularly sympathetic to theism – claims that with regard to basic structure of the universe, "the impression of design is overwhelming."[2] Similarly, in response to the life-permitting fine-tuning of the nuclear resonances responsible for the oxygen and carbon synthesis in stars, the famous astrophysicist Sir Fred Hoyle declares that

> I do not believe that any scientists who examined the evidence would fail to draw the inference that the laws of nuclear physics have been deliberately designed with regard to the consequences they produce inside stars. If this is so, then my apparently random quirks have become part of a deep-laid scheme. If not then we are back again at a monstrous sequence of accidents.[3]

A few examples of this fine-tuning are listed below:

1   If the initial explosion of the big bang had differed in strength by as little as one part in 10^{60}, the universe would have either quickly collapsed back on itself, or expanded too rapidly for stars to form. In either case, life would be impossible. (As John Jefferson Davis points out, an accuracy of one part in 10^{60} can be compared to firing a bullet at a one-inch target on the other side of the observable universe, twenty billion light years away, and hitting the target.)[4]

2   Calculations indicate that if the strong nuclear force, the force that binds protons and neutrons together in an atom, had been stronger or weaker by as little as five percent, life would be impossible.[5]

3   Calculations by Brandon Carter show that if gravity had been stronger or weaker by one part in 10^{40}, then life-sustaining stars like the sun could not exist. This would most likely make life impossible.[6]

4   If the neutron were not about 1.001 times the mass of the proton, all protons would have decayed into neutrons or all neutrons would have decayed into protons, and thus life would not be possible.[7]

5   If the electromagnetic force were slightly stronger or weaker, life would be impossible, for a variety of different reasons.[8]

Imaginatively, one could think of each instance of fine-tuning as a radio dial: unless all the dials are set exactly right, life would be impossible. Or, one could think of the initial conditions of the universe and the fundamental parameters of physics as a dart board that fills the whole galaxy, and the conditions necessary for life to exist as a small one-foot wide target: unless the dart hits the target, life would be impossible. The fact that the dials are perfectly set, or that the dart has hit the target, strongly suggests that someone set the dials or aimed the dart, for it seems enormously improbable that such a coincidence could have happened by chance.

Although individual calculations of fine-tuning are only approximate and could be in error, the fact that the universe is fine-tuned for life is almost beyond question because of the large number of independent instances of apparent fine-tuning. As philosopher John Leslie has pointed out, "Clues heaped upon clues can constitute weighty evidence despite doubts about each element in the pile."[9] What is controversial, however, is the degree to which the fine-tuning provides evidence for the existence of God. As impressive as the argument from fine-tuning seems to be, atheists have raised several significant objections to it. Consequently, those who are aware of these objections, or have thought of them on their own, often will find the argument unconvincing. This is not only true of atheists, but also many theists. I have known, for instance, both a committed Christian Hollywood filmmaker and a committed Christian biochemist who remained unconvinced because of certain atheist objections to the argument. This is unfortunate, particularly since the fine-tuning argument is probably the most powerful current argument for the existence of God. My goal in this chapter, therefore, is to make the fine-tuning argument as strong as possible. This will involve developing the argument in as objective and rigorous a way as I can, and then answering the major atheist objections to it. Before launching into this, however, I will need to make a preliminary distinction.

A Preliminary Distinction

To develop the fine-tuning argument rigorously, it is useful to distinguish between what I shall call the *atheistic single-universe hypothesis* and the *atheistic many-universes hypothesis*. According to the atheistic single-universe hypothesis, there is only one universe, and it is ultimately an inexplicable, "brute" fact that the universe exists and is fine-tuned. Many atheists, however, advocate another hypothesis, one which attempts to explain how the seemingly improbable fine-tuning of the universe could be the result of chance. We will call this hypothesis the *atheistic many-worlds hypothesis*, or the *atheistic many-universes hypothesis*. According to this hypothesis, there exists what could be imaginatively thought of as a "universe generator" that produces a very large or infinite number of universes, with each universe having a randomly selected set of initial conditions and values for the parameters of physics. Because this generator produces so many universes, just by chance it will eventually produce one that is fine-tuned for intelligent life to occur.

Plan of the Chapter

Below, we will use this distinction between the atheistic single-universe hypothesis and the atheistic many-universes hypothesis to present two separate arguments for theism based on the fine-tuning: one which argues that the fine-tuning provides strong reasons to prefer theism over the atheistic single-universe hypothesis and one which argues that we should prefer theism over the atheistic many-universes hypothesis. We will develop the argument against the atheistic single-universe hypothesis in section II below, referring to it as the *core argument*. Then we will

answer objections to this core argument in section III, and finally develop the argument for preferring theism to the atheistic many-universes hypothesis in section IV.

II. Core Argument Rigorously Formulated

General Principle of Reasoning Used

The Principle Explained

We will formulate the fine-tuning argument against the atheistic single-universe hypothesis in terms of what I will call the *prime principle of confirmation*. The prime principle of confirmation is a general principle of reasoning which tells us when some observation counts as evidence in favor of one hypothesis over another. *Simply put, the principle says that whenever we are considering two competing hypotheses, an observation counts as evidence in favor of the hypothesis under which the observation has the highest probability (or is the least improbable).* (Or, put slightly differently, the principle says that whenever we are considering two competing hypotheses, H_1 and H_2, an observation, O, counts as evidence in favor of H_1 over H_2 if O is more probable under H_1 than it is under H_2.) Moreover, the degree to which the evidence counts in favor of one hypothesis over another is proportional to the degree to which the observation is more probable under the one hypothesis than the other.[10] For example, the fine-tuning is much, much more probable under theism than under the atheistic single-universe hypothesis, so it counts as strong evidence for theism over this atheistic hypothesis. In the next major subsection, we will present a more formal and elaborated rendition of the fine-tuning argument in terms of the prime principle. First, however, let's look at a couple of illustrations of the principle and then present some support for it.

Additional Illustrations of the Principle

For our first illustration, suppose that I went hiking in the mountains, and found underneath a certain cliff a group of rocks arranged in a formation that clearly formed the pattern "Welcome to the mountains, Robin Collins." One hypothesis is that, by chance, the rocks just happened to be arranged in that pattern – ultimately, perhaps, because of certain initial conditions of the universe. Suppose the only viable alternative hypothesis is that my brother, who was in the mountains before me, arranged the rocks in this way. Most of us would immediately take the arrangements of rocks to be strong evidence in favor of the "brother" hypothesis over the "chance" hypothesis. Why? Because it strikes us as extremely *improbable* that the rocks would be arranged that way by chance, but *not improbable* at all that my brother would place them in that configuration. Thus, by the prime principle of confirmation we would conclude that the arrangement of rocks strongly supports the "brother" hypothesis over the chance hypothesis.

Or consider another case, that of finding the defendant's fingerprints on the murder weapon. Normally, we would take such a finding as strong evidence that the defendant was guilty. Why? Because we judge that it would be *unlikely* for these fingerprints to be on the murder weapon if the defendant was innocent, but *not unlikely* if the defendant was guilty. That is, we would go through the same sort of reasoning as in the above case.

Support for the Principle

Several things can be said in favor of the prime principle of confirmation. First, many philosophers think that this principle can be derived from what is known as the *probability calculus*, the set of mathematical rules that are typically assumed to govern probability. Second, there does not appear to be any case of recognizably good reasoning that violates this principle. Finally, the principle appears to have a wide range of applicability, undergirding much of our reasoning in science and everyday life, as the examples above illustrate. Indeed, some have even claimed that a slightly more general version of this principle undergirds all scientific reasoning. Because of all these reasons in favor of the principle, we can be very confident in it.

Further Development of Argument

To further develop the core version of the fine-tuning argument, we will summarize the argument by explicitly listing its two premises and its conclusion:

- *Premise 1.* The existence of the fine-tuning is not improbable under theism.
- *Premise 2.* The existence of the fine-tuning is very improbable under the atheistic single-universe hypothesis.
- *Conclusion:* From premises (1) and (2) and the prime principle of confirmation, it follows that the fine-tuning data provide strong evidence to favor the design hypothesis over the atheistic single-universe hypothesis.

At this point, we should pause to note two features of this argument. First, the argument does not say that the fine-tuning evidence proves that the universe was designed, or even that it is likely that the universe was designed. In order to justify these sorts of claims, we would have to look at the full range of evidence both for and against the design hypothesis, something we are not doing in this chapter. Rather, the argument merely concludes that the fine-tuning strongly *supports* theism *over* the atheistic single-universe hypothesis.

In this way, the evidence of the fine-tuning argument is much like fingerprints found on the gun: although they can provide strong evidence that the defendant committed the murder, one could not conclude merely from them alone that the defendant is guilty; one would also have to look at all the other evidence offered. Perhaps, for instance, ten reliable witnesses claimed to see the defendant at a party at the time of the shooting. In this case, the fingerprints would still count as significant evidence of guilt, but this evidence would be counterbalanced by the testimony of the witnesses. Similarly the evidence of fine-tuning strongly supports theism over the atheistic single-universe hypothesis, though it does not itself show that, everything considered, theism is the most plausible explanation of the world. Nonetheless, as I argue in the conclusion of this chapter, the evidence of fine-tuning provides a much stronger and more objective argument for theism (over the atheistic single-universe hypothesis) than the strongest atheistic argument does against theism.

The second feature of the argument we should note is that, given the truth of *the prime principle of confirmation*, the conclusion of the argument follows from the premises. Specifically, if the premises of the argument are true, then we are guaranteed that the conclusion is true: that is, the argument is what philosophers call *valid*. Thus, insofar as we can show that the premises of the argument are true, we will have shown that the conclusion is true. Our next task, therefore, is to attempt to show that the premises are true, or at least that we have strong reasons to believe them.

Support for the Premises

Support for Premise (1)

Premise (1) is easy to support and fairly uncontroversial. One major argument in support of it can be simply stated as follows: *since God is an all good being, and it is good for intelligent, conscious beings to exist, it is not surprising or improbable that God would create a world that could support intelligent life.* Thus, the fine-tuning is not improbable under theism, as premise (1) asserts.

Support for Premise (2)

Upon looking at the data, many people find it very obvious that the fine-tuning is highly improbable under the atheistic single-universe hypothesis. And it is easy to see why when we think of the fine-tuning in terms of the analogies offered earlier. In the dart board analogy, for example, the initial conditions of the universe and the fundamental parameters of physics are thought of as a dart board that fills the whole galaxy, and the conditions necessary for life to exist as a small one-foot wide target. Accordingly, from this analogy it seems obvious that it would be highly improbable for the fine-tuning to occur under the atheistic single-universe hypothesis – that is, for the dart to hit the target by chance.

Typically, advocates of the fine-tuning argument are satisfied with resting the justification of premise (2), or something like it, on this sort of analogy. Many atheists and theists, however, question the legitimacy of this sort of analogy, and thus find the argument unconvincing. For these people, the appendix to this chapter offers a rigorous and objective justification of premise (2) using standard principles of probabilistic reasoning. Among other things, in the process of rigorously justifying premise (2), we effectively answer the common objection to the fine-tuning argument that because the universe is a unique, unrepeatable event, we cannot meaningfully assign a probability to its being fine-tuned.

III. Some Objections to Core Version

As powerful as the core version of the fine-tuning argument is, several major objections have been raised to it by both atheists and theists. In this section, we will consider these objections in turn.

Objection 1: More Fundamental Law Objection

One criticism of the fine-tuning argument is that, as far as we know, there could be a more fundamental law under which the parameters of physics must have the values they do. Thus, given such a law, it is not improbable that the known parameters of physics fall within the life-permitting range.

Besides being entirely speculative, the problem with postulating such a law is that it simply moves the improbability of the fine-tuning up one level, to that of the postulated physical law itself. Under this hypothesis, what is improbable is that of all the conceivable fundamental physical laws there could be, the universe just happens to have the one that constrains the parameters of physics in a life-permitting way. Thus, trying to explain the fine-tuning by postulating this sort of fundamental law is like trying to explain why the pattern of rocks below a cliff spell "Welcome to the mountains, Robin Collins" by postulating that an earthquake occurred and that all the rocks on the cliff face were arranged in just the right configuration to fall into the pattern in question. Clearly this explanation merely transfers the improbability up one level, since now it seems enormously improbable that of all the possible configurations the rocks could be in on the cliff face, they are in the one which results in the pattern "Welcome to the mountains, Robin Collins."

A similar sort of response can be given to the claim that the finetuning is not improbable because it might be *logically necessary* for the parameters of physics to have life-permitting values. That is, according to this claim, the parameters of physics must have life-permitting values in the same way 2 + 2 must equal 4, or the interior angles of a triangle must add up to 180 degrees in Euclidian geometry. Like the "more fundamental law" proposal above, however, this postulate simply transfers the improbability up one level: of all the laws and parameters of physics that conceivably could have been logically necessary, it seems highly improbable that it would be those that are life-permitting.[11]

Objection 2: Other Forms of Life Objection

Another objection people commonly raise to the fine-tuning argument is that as far as we know, other forms of life could exist even if the parameters of physics were different. So, it is claimed, the fine-tuning argument ends up presupposing that all forms of intelligent life must be like us. The answer to this objection is that most cases of fine-tuning do not make this presupposition. Consider, for instance, the case of the fine-tuning of the strong nuclear force. If it were slightly smaller, no atoms could exist other than hydrogen. Contrary to what one might see on *Star Trek*, an intelligent life-form cannot be composed merely of hydrogen gas: there is simply not enough stable complexity. So, in general the fine-tuning argument merely presupposes that intelligent life requires some degree of stable, reproducible organized complexity. This is certainly a very reasonable assumption.

Objection 3: Anthropic Principle Objection

According to the weak version of the so-called *anthropic principle*, if the laws of nature were not fine-tuned, we would not be here to comment on the fact. Some have argued, therefore, that the fine-tuning is not really *improbable or surprising* at all under atheism, but simply follows from the fact that we exist. The response to this objection is to simply restate the argument in terms of our existence: our existence as embodied, intelligent beings is extremely unlikely under the atheistic single-universe hypothesis (since our existence requires fine-tuning), but not improbable under theism. Then, we simply apply the prime principle of confirmation to draw the conclusion that *our existence* strongly confirms theism over the atheistic single-universe hypothesis.

To further illustrate this response, consider the following "firing squad" analogy. As John Leslie points out, if fifty sharpshooters all miss me, the response "if they had not missed me I wouldn't be here to consider the fact" is not adequate. Instead, I would naturally conclude that there was some reason why they all missed, such as that they never really intended to kill me. Why would I conclude this? Because my continued existence would be very improbable under the hypothesis that they missed me by chance, but not improbable under the hypothesis that there was some reason why they missed me. Thus, by the prime principle of confirmation, my continued existence strongly confirms the latter hypothesis.[12]

Objection 4: The "Who Designed God?" Objection

Perhaps the most common objection that atheists raise to the argument from design, of which the fine-tuning argument is one instance, is that postulating the existence of God does not solve the problem of design, but merely transfers it up one level. Atheist George Smith, for example, claims that

> If the universe is wonderfully designed, surely God is even more wonderfully designed. He must, therefore, have had a designer even more wonderful than He is. If *God* did not require a designer, then there is no reason why such a relatively less wonderful things as the universe needed one.[13]

Or, as philosopher J.J. C. Smart states the objection:

> If we postulate God in addition to the created universe we increase the complexity of our hypothesis. We have all the complexity of the universe itself, and we have in addition the at least equal complexity of God. (The designer of an artifact must be at least as complex as the designed artifact). . . . If *the theist can show the atheist that postulating God actually reduces the complexity of one's total world view, then the atheist should be a theist.*[14]

The first response to the above atheist objection is to point out that the atheist claim that the designer of an artifact must be as complex as the artifact designed is certainly not obvious. But I do believe that their claim has some intuitive plausibility: for example, in the world we experience, organized complexity seems only to be produced by systems that already possess it, such as the human brain/mind, a factory, or an organism's biological parent.

The second, and better, response is to point out that, at most, the atheist objection only works against a version of the design argument that claims that all organized complexity needs an explanation, and that God is the best explanation of the organized complexity found in the world. The version of the argument I presented against the atheistic single-universe hypothesis, however, only required that the fine-tuning be more probable under theism than under the atheistic single-universe hypothesis. But this requirement is still met even if God exhibits tremendous internal complexity, far exceeding that of the universe. Thus, even if we were to grant the atheist assumption that the designer of an artifact must be as complex as the artifact, the fine-tuning would still give us strong reasons to prefer theism over the atheistic single-universe hypothesis.

To illustrate, consider the example of the "biosphere" on Mars presented at the beginning of this paper. As mentioned above, the existence of the biosphere would be much more probable under the hypothesis that intelligent life once visited Mars than under the chance hypothesis. Thus, by the prime principle of confirmation, the existence of such a "biosphere" would constitute strong evidence that intelligent, extraterrestrial life had once been on Mars, even though this alien life would most likely have to be much more complex than the "biosphere" itself.

The final response theists can give to this objection is to show that a supermind such as God would *not* require a high degree of unexplained organized complexity to create the universe. Although I have presented this response elsewhere, presenting it here is beyond the scope of this chapter.

IV. The Atheistic Many-Universes Hypothesis

The Atheistic Many-Universes Hypothesis Explained

In response to the theistic explanation of fine-tuning of the cosmos, many atheists have offered an alternative explanation, what I will call the atheistic many-universes hypothesis. (In the literature it is more commonly referred to as the *many-worlds hypothesis*, though I believe this name is somewhat misleading.) According to this hypothesis, there are a very large – perhaps infinite – number of universes, with the fundamental parameters of physics varying from universe to universe.[15] Of course, in the vast majority of these universes the parameters of physics would not have life-permitting values. Nonetheless, in a small proportion of universes they would, and consequently it is no longer improbable that universes such as ours exist that are fine-tuned for life to occur.

Advocates of this hypothesis offer various types of models for where these universes came from. We will present what are probably the two most popular and plausible, the so-called *vacuum fluctuation* models and the *oscillating big bang* models. According to the vacuum fluctuation models, our universe, along with these other universes, were generated by quantum fluctuations in a preexisting superspace.[16] Imaginatively, one can think of this preexisting superspace as an infinitely extending ocean full of soap, and each universe generated out of this superspace as a soap bubble which spontaneously forms on the ocean.

The other model, the oscillating big bang model, is a version of the big bang theory. According to the big bang theory, the universe came into existence in an "explosion" (that is, a "bang") somewhere between ten and fifteen billion years ago. According to the *oscillating* big bang theory, our universe will eventually collapse back in on itself (what is called the "big crunch") and then from that "big crunch" will arise another "big bang," forming a new universe, which will in turn itself collapse, and so on. According to those who use this model to attempt to explain the fine-tuning, during every cycle, the parameters of physics and the initial conditions of the universe are reset at random. Since this process of collapse, explosion, collapse, and explosion has been going on for all eternity, eventually a fine-tuned universe will occur, indeed infinitely many of them.

In the next section, we will list several reasons for rejecting the atheistic many-universes hypothesis.

Reasons for Rejecting the Atheistic Many-Universes Hypothesis

First Reason

The first reason for rejecting the atheistic many-universes hypothesis, and preferring the theistic hypothesis, is the following general rule: *everything else being equal, we should prefer hypotheses for which we have independent evidence or that are natural extrapolations from what we already know.* Let's first illustrate and support this principle, and then apply it to the case of the fine-tuning.

Most of us take the existence of dinosaur bones to count as very strong evidence that dinosaurs existed in the past. But suppose a dinosaur skeptic claimed that she could explain the bones by postulating a "dinosaur-bone-producing-field" that simply materialized the bones out of thin air. Moreover, suppose further that, to avoid objections such as that there are no known physical laws that would allow for such a mechanism, the dinosaur skeptic simply postulated that we have not yet discovered these laws or detected these fields.

Surely, none of us would let this skeptical hypothesis deter us from inferring the existence of dinosaurs. Why? Because although no one has directly observed dinosaurs, we do have experience of other animals leaving behind fossilized remains, and thus the dinosaur explanation is a *natural extrapolation* from our common experience. In contrast, to explain the dinosaur bones, the dinosaur skeptic has invented a set of physical laws, and a set of mechanisms that are *not* a natural extrapolation from anything we know or experience.

In the case of the fine-tuning, we already know that minds often produce fine-tuned devices, such as Swiss watches. Postulating God – a supermind – as the explanation of the fine-tuning, therefore, is a natural extrapolation from what we already observe minds to do. In contrast, it is difficult to see how the atheistic many-universes hypothesis could be considered a natural extrapolation from what we observe. Moreover, unlike the atheistic many-universes hypothesis, we have some experiential evidence for the existence of God, namely religious experience. Thus, by the above principle, we should prefer the theistic explanation of the fine-tuning over the atheistic many-universes explanation, everything else being equal.

Second Reason

A second reason for rejecting the atheistic many-universes hypothesis is that the "many-universes generator" seems like it would need to be designed. For instance, in all current worked-out proposals for what this "universe generator" could be – such as the oscillating big bang and the vacuum fluctuation models explained above – the "generator" itself is governed by a complex set of physical laws that allow it to produce the universes. It stands to reason, therefore, that if these laws were slightly different the generator probably would not be able to produce any universes that could sustain life. After all, even my bread machine has to be made just right in order to work properly, and it only produces loaves of bread, not universes! Or consider a device as simple as a mousetrap: it requires that all the parts, such as the spring and hammer, be arranged just right in order to function. It is doubtful, therefore, whether the atheistic many-universe theory can entirely eliminate the problem of design the atheist faces; rather, at least to some extent, it seems simply to move the problem of design up one level.[17]

Third Reason

A third reason for rejecting the atheistic many-universes hypothesis is that the universe generator must not only select the parameters of physics at random, but must actually randomly create or select the very laws of physics themselves. This makes this hypothesis seem even more farfetched since it is difficult to see what possible physical mechanism could select or create laws.

The reason the "many-universes generator" must randomly select the laws of physics is that, just as the right values for the parameters of physics are needed for life to occur, the right set of laws is also needed. If, for instance, certain laws of physics were missing, life would be impossible. For example, without the law of inertia, which guarantees that particles do not shoot off at high speeds, life would probably not be possible.[18] Another example is the law of gravity: if masses did not attract each other, there would be no planets or stars, and once again it seems that life would be impossible. Yet another example is the *Pauli Exclusion Principle*, the principle of quantum mechanics that says that no two fermions – such as electrons or protons – can share the same quantum state. As prominent Princeton physicist Freeman Dyson points out,[19] without this principle all electrons would collapse into the nucleus and thus atoms would be impossible.

Fourth Reason

The fourth reason for rejecting the atheistic many-universes hypothesis is that it cannot explain other features of the universe that seem to exhibit apparent design, whereas theism can. For example, many physicists, such as Albert Einstein, have observed that the basic laws of physics exhibit an extraordinary degree of beauty, elegance, harmony, and ingenuity. Nobel prize-winning physicist Steven Weinberg, for instance, devotes a whole chapter of his book *Dreams of a Final Theory*[20] explaining how the criteria of beauty and elegance are commonly used to guide physicists in formulating the right laws. Indeed, one of the most prominent theoretical physicists of this century, Paul Dirac, went so far as to claim that "it is more important to have beauty in one's equations than to have them fit experiment."[21]

Now such beauty, elegance, and ingenuity make sense if the universe was designed by God. Under the atheistic many-universes hypothesis, however, there is no reason to expect the fundamental laws to be elegant or beautiful. As theoretical physicist Paul Davies writes, "If nature is so 'clever' as to exploit mechanisms that amaze us with their ingenuity, is that not persuasive evidence for the existence of intelligent design behind the universe? If the world's finest minds can unravel only with difficulty the deeper workings of nature, how could it be supposed that those workings are merely a mindless accident, a product of blind chance?"[22]

Final Reason

This brings us to the final reason for rejecting the atheistic many-universes hypothesis, which may be the most difficult to grasp: namely, neither the atheistic many-universes hypothesis (nor the atheistic single-universe hypothesis) can at present adequately account for the improbable initial arrangement of matter in the universe required by the second law of thermodynamics. To see

this, note that according to the second law of thermodynamics, the entropy of the universe is constantly increasing. The standard way of understanding this entropy increase is to say that the universe is going from a state of order to disorder. We observe this entropy increase all the time around us: things, such as a child's bedroom, that start out highly organized tend to "decay" and become disorganized unless something or someone intervenes to stop it.

Now, for purposes of illustration, we could think of the universe as a scrabble-board that initially starts out in a highly ordered state in which all the letters are arranged to form words, but which keeps getting randomly shaken. Slowly, the board, like the universe, moves from a state of order to disorder. The problem for the atheist is to explain how the universe could have started out in a highly ordered state, since it is extraordinarily improbable for such states to occur by chance.[23] If, for example, one were to dump a bunch of letters at random on a scrabble-board, it would be very unlikely for most of them to form into words. At best, we would expect groups of letters to form into words in a few places on the board.

Now our question is, Could the atheistic many-universes hypothesis explain the high degree of initial order of our universe by claiming that given enough universes, eventually one will arise that is ordered and in which intelligent life occurs, and so it is no surprise that we find ourselves in an ordered universe? The problem with this explanation is that it is overwhelmingly more likely for local patches of order to form in one or two places than for the whole universe to be ordered, just as it is overwhelmingly more likely for a few words on the scrabble-board randomly to form words than for all the letters throughout the board randomly to form words. Thus, the overwhelming majority of universes in which intelligent life occurs will be ones in which the intelligent life will be surrounded by a small patch of order necessary for its existence, but in which the rest of the universe is disordered. Consequently, even under the atheistic many-universes hypothesis, it would still be enormously improbable for intelligent beings to find themselves in a universe such as ours which is highly ordered throughout.[24]

Conclusion

Even though the above criticisms do not definitively refute the atheistic many-universes hypothesis, they do show that it has some severe disadvantages relative to theism. This means that if atheists adopt the atheistic many-universes hypothesis to defend their position, then atheism has become much less plausible than it used to be. Modifying a turn of phrase coined by philosopher Fred Dretske: these are inflationary times, and the cost of atheism has just gone up.

V. Overall Conclusion

In the above sections I showed there are good, objective reasons for claiming that the fine-tuning provides strong evidence for theism. I first presented an argument for thinking that the fine-tuning provides strong evidence for preferring theism over the atheistic single-universe hypothesis, and then presented a variety of different reasons for rejecting the atheistic many-universes hypothesis as an explanation of the fine-tuning. In order to help one appreciate the strength of the arguments presented, I would like to end by comparing the strength of the *core* version of the argument from the fine-tuning to what is widely regarded as the strongest atheist argument against theism, the argument from evil.

Typically, the atheist argument against God based on evil takes a similar form to the core version of the fine-tuning argument. Essentially, the atheist argues that the existence of the kinds of evil we find in the world is very improbable under theism, but not improbable under atheism. Thus, by the prime principle of confirmation, they conclude that the existence of evil

provides strong reasons for preferring atheism over theism.

What makes this argument weak in comparison to the core version of the fine-tuning argument is that, unlike in the case of the fine-tuning, the atheist does not have a significant objective basis for claiming that the existence of the kinds of evil we find in the world is highly improbable under theism. In fact, their judgment that it is improbable seems largely to rest on a mistake in reasoning. To see this, note that in order to show that it is improbable, atheists would have to show that it is *unlikely* that the types of evils we find in the world are necessary for any morally good, greater purpose, since if they are, then it is clearly not at all unlikely that an all good, all powerful being would create a world in which those evils are allowed to occur. But how could atheists show this without first surveying all possible morally good purposes such a being might have, something they have clearly not done? *Consequently, it seems, at most the atheist could argue that since no one has come up with any adequate purpose yet, it is unlikely that there is such a purpose.* This argument, however, is very weak, as I will now show.

The first problem with this atheist argument is that it assumes that the various explanations people have offered for why an all good God would create evil – such as the free will theodicy – ultimately fail. But even if we grant that these theodicies fail, the argument is still very weak. To see why, consider an analogy. Suppose someone tells me that there is a rattlesnake in my garden, and I examine a portion of the garden and do not find the snake. I would only be justified in concluding that there was probably no snake in the garden if either: i) I had searched at least half the garden; or ii) I had good reason to believe that if the snake were in the garden, it would likely be in the portion of the garden that I examined. If, for instance, I were randomly to pick some small segment of the garden to search and did not find the snake, I would be unjustified in concluding from my search that there was probably no snake in the garden. Similarly, if I were blindfolded and did not have any idea of how large the garden was (e.g., whether it was ten square feet or several square miles), I would be unjustified in concluding that it was unlikely that there was a rattlesnake in the garden, even if I had searched for hours with my rattlesnake-detecting dogs. Why? Because I would not have any idea of what percentage of the garden I had searched.

As with the garden example, we have no idea of how large the realm is of possible greater purposes for evil that an all good, omnipotent being could have. Hence we do not know what proportion of this realm we have actually searched. Indeed, considering the finitude of our own minds, we have good reason to believe that we have so far only searched a small proportion, and we do not have significant reason to believe that all the purposes God might have for allowing evil would be in the proportion we searched. Thus, we have little objective basis for saying that the existence of the types of evil we find in the world is highly improbable under theism.

From the above discussion, therefore, it is clear that the relevant probability estimates in the case of the fine-tuning are much more secure than those estimates in the probabilistic version of the the atheist's argument from evil, since unlike the latter, we can provide a fairly rigorous, objective basis for them based on actual calculations of the relative range of life-permitting values for the parameters of physics. . . . *Thus, I conclude, the core argument for preferring theism over the probabilistic version of the atheistic single-universe hypothesis is much stronger than the atheist argument from evil.*[25]

Notes

1   Freeman Dyson, *Disturbing the Universe* (New York: Harper and Row, 1979), 251.

2   Paul Davies, *The Cosmic Blueprint: New Discoveries in Nature's Creative Ability to Order the Universe* (New York: Simon and Schuster, 1988), 203.

3   Fred Hoyle, in *Religion and the Scientists* (1959);

quoted in *The Anthropic Cosmological Principle*, ed. John Barrow and Frank Tipler (Oxford: Oxford University Press, 1986), 22.

4   See Paul Davies, *The Accidental Universe* (Cambridge: Cambridge University Press, 1982), 90–91. John Jefferson Davis, "The Design Argument, Cosmic 'Finetuning,' and the Anthropic Principle," *The International Journal of Philosophy of Religion* 22 (1987): 140.

5   John Leslie, *Universes* (New York: Routledge, 1989), 4, 35; *Anthropic Cosmological Principle*, 322.

6   Paul Davies, *Superforce: The Search for a Grand Unified Theory of Nature* (New York: Simon and Schuster, 1984), 242.

7   Leslie, *Universes*, 39–40.

8   John Leslie, "How to Draw Conclusions from a Fine-Tuned Cosmos," in *Physics, Philosophy and Theology: A Common Quest for Understanding*, ed. Robert Russell et al. (Vatican City State: Vatican Observatory Press, 1988), 299.

9   Leslie, "How to Draw Conclusions," 300.

10 For those familiar with the probability calculus, a precise statement of the degree to which evidence counts in favor of one hypothesis over another can be given in terms of the odds form of Bayes's Theorem: that is, $P(H_1/E)/P(H_2/E) = [P(H_1)/P(H_2)] \times [P(E/H_1)/P(E/H_2)]$. The general version of the principle stated here, however, does not require the applicability or truth of Bayes's Theorem.

11 Those with some training in probability theory will want to note that the kind of probability invoked here is what philosophers call *epistemic probability*, which is a measure of the rational degree of belief we should have in a proposition . . . Since our rational degree of belief in a necessary truth can be less than 1, we can sensibly speak of it being improbable for a given law of nature to exist necessarily. For example, we can speak of an unproven mathematical hypothesis – such as Goldbach's conjecture that every even number greater than 6 is the sum of two odd primes – as being probably true or probably false given our current evidence, even though all mathematical hypotheses are either necessarily true or necessarily false.

12 Leslie, "How to Draw Conclusions," 304.

13 George Smith, "The Case Against God," reprinted in *An Anthology of Atheism and Rationalism*, ed. Gordon Stein (Buffalo: Prometheus Press, 1980), 56.

14 J. J. C. Smart, "Laws of Nature and Cosmic Coincidence," *The Philosophical Quarterly* 35 (July 1985): 275–76, italics added.

15 I define a "universe" as any region of space-time that is disconnected from other regions in such a way that the parameters of physics in that region could differ significantly from the other regions.

16 Quentin Smith, "World Ensemble Explanations," *Pacific Philosophical Quarterly* 67 (1986): 82.

17 Moreover, the advocate of the atheistic many-universes hypothesis could not avoid this problem by hypothesizing that the many universes always existed as a "brute fact" without being produced by a universe generator. This would simply add to the problem: it would not only leave unexplained the fine-tuning or our own universe, but would leave unexplained the existence of these other universes.

18 Leslie, *Universes*, 59.

19 Dyson, *Disturbing the Universe*, 251.

20 Chapter 6, "Beautiful Theories."

21 Paul Dirac, "The Evolution of the Physicist's Picture of Nature," *Scientific American* (May 1963): 47.

22 Davies, *Superforce*, 235–36.

23 This connection between order and probability, and the second law of thermodynamics in general, is given a precise formulation in a branch of fundamental physics called *statistical mechanics*, according to which a state of high order represents a very improbable state, and a state of disorder represents a highly probable state.

24 See Lawrence Sklar, *Physics and Chance: Philosophical Issues in the Foundation of Statistical Mechanics* (Cambridge: Cambridge University Press, 1993), chapter 8, for a review of the nontheistic explanations for the ordered arrangement of the universe and the severe difficulties they face.

25 This work was made possible in part by a Discovery Institute grant for the fiscal year 1997–1998.

Chapter 12

Elliott Sober

THE DESIGN ARGUMENT

The design argument is one of three main arguments for the existence of God; the others are the ontological argument and the cosmological argument. Unlike the ontological argument, the design argument and the cosmological argument are *a posteriori*. And whereas the cosmological argument could focus on any present event to get the ball rolling (arguing that it must trace back to a first cause, namely God), design theorists are usually more selective.

Design arguments have typically been of two types – *organismic* and *cosmic*. Organismic design arguments start with the observation that organisms have features that adapt them to the environments in which they live and that exhibit a kind of *delicacy*. Consider, for example, the vertebrate eye. This organ helps organisms survive by permitting them to perceive objects in their environment. And were the parts of the eye even slightly different in their shape and assembly, the resulting organ would not allow us to see. Cosmic design arguments begin with an observation concerning features of the entire cosmos – the Universe obeys simple laws, it has a kind of stability, its physical features permit life and intelligent life to exist. However, not all design arguments fit into these two neat compartments. Kepler, for example, thought that the face we see when we look at the moon requires explanation in terms of intelligent design. Still, the common thread is that design theorists describe some empirical feature of the world and argue that this feature points towards an explanation in terms of God's intentional planning and away from an explanation in terms of mindless natural processes.

The design argument raises epistemological questions that go beyond its traditional theological context. As William Paley (1802) observed, when we find a watch while walking across a heath, we unhesitatingly infer that it was produced by an intelligent designer. No such inference forces itself upon us when we observe a stone. Why is explanation in terms of intelligent design so compelling in the one case, but not in the other? Similarly, when we observe the behavior of our fellow human beings, we find it irresistible to think that they have minds that are filled with beliefs and desires. And when we observe non-human organisms, the impulse to invoke mentalistic explanations is often very strong, especially when they look a lot like us. When does the behavior of an organism – human or not – warrant this mentalistic interpretation? The same question can be posed about machines. Few of us feel tempted to attribute beliefs and desires to hand calculators. We use calculators to help us add, but they don't literally figure out sums; in this respect, calculators are like pieces of paper on which we scribble our calculations. There is an important difference between a device that *we* use to help us think and a device that *itself* thinks. However, when a computer plays a decent game of chess, we may find it useful to explain and predict its behavior by thinking of it as having goals and deploying strategies (Dennett 1987b). Is this merely a useful fiction, or does the machine really have a mind? And if we think that present-day chess-playing computers are, strictly speaking, mindless, what would it take for a machine to pass the test? Surely, as Turing (1950) observed, it needn't look like us. In all these contexts, we face the problem of other minds (Sober 2000a). If we understood the ground rules in this general epistemological problem, that would help us think about the design argument for the existence of God. And, conversely, if we could get clear on the theological design argument, that might throw light on epistemological problems that are not theological in character.

What is the Design Argument?

The design argument, like the ontological argument, raises subtle questions about what the logical structure of the argument really is. My main concern here will not be to describe how various thinkers have presented the design argument, but to find the soundest formulation that the argument can be given.

The best version of the design argument, in my opinion, uses an inferential idea that probabilists call the *likelihood principle* (LP). This can be illustrated by way of Paley's (1802) example of the watch on the heath. Paley describes an observation that he claims discriminates between two hypotheses:

(W) O_1: the watch has features $G_1 \ldots G_n$.
   W_1: the watch was created by an
      intelligent designer.
   W_2: the watch was produced by a
      mindless chance process.

Paley's idea is that O_1 would be unsurprising if W_1 were true, but would be very surprising if W_2 were true. This is supposed to show that O_1 favors W_1 over W_2; O_1 supports W_1 more than it

supports W_2. Surprise is a matter of degree; it can be captured by the concept of conditional probability. The probability of observation (O) given hypothesis (H) – $Pr(O|H)$ – represents how unsurprising O would be if H were true. LP says that comparing such conditional probabilities is the way to decide what the direction is in which the evidence points:

(LP) Observation O supports hypothesis H_1 more than it supports hypothesis H_2 if and only if $Pr(O|H_1) > Pr(O|H_2)$.

There is a lot to say on the question of why the likelihood principle should be accepted (Hacking 1965; Edwards 1972; Royall 1997; Forster and Sober 2003); for the purposes of this essay, I will take it as a given.

We now can describe the likelihood version of the design argument for the existence of God, again taking our lead from one of Paley's favorite examples of a delicate adaptation. The basic format is to compare two hypotheses as possible explanations of a single observation:

(E) O_2: the vertebrate eye has features
      $F_1 \ldots F_n$.
   E_1: the vertebrate eye was created by an
      intelligent designer.
   E_2: the vertebrate eye was produced by a
      mindless chance process.

We do not hesitate to conclude that the observations strongly favor Design over Chance in the case of argument (W); Paley claims that precisely the same conclusion should be drawn in the case of the propositions assembled in (E).[1]

Clarifications

Several points of clarification are needed here concerning likelihood in general and the likelihood version of the design argument in particular. First, I use the term "likelihood" in a technical sense. Likelihood is not the same as probability. To say that H has a high likelihood, given observation O, is to comment on the value of $Pr(O|H)$, not on the value of $Pr(H|O)$; the latter is H's *posterior probability*. It is perfectly possible for a hypothesis to have a high likelihood and a low posterior probability. When you hear noises in your attic, this confers a high likelihood on the hypothesis that there are gremlins up there bowling, but few of us would conclude that this hypothesis is probably true.

Although the likelihood of H (given O) and the probability of H (given O) are different quantities, they are related. The relationship is given by Bayes's theorem:

$$Pr(H|O) = Pr(O|H) \cdot Pr(H)/Pr(O).$$

$Pr(H)$ is the hypothesis' *prior probability* – the probability that H has before we take the observation O into account. From Bayes's theorem we can deduce the following:

$$Pr(H_1|O) > Pr(H_2|O) \text{ if and only if}$$

$$Pr(O|H_1) \cdot Pr(H_1) > Pr(O|H_2) \cdot Pr(H_2).$$

Which hypothesis has the higher posterior probability depends on how their likelihoods are related, but also on how their prior probabilities are related. This explains why the likelihood version of the design argument does not show that Design is more probable than Chance. To draw this further conclusion, we would have to say something about the prior probabilities of the two hypotheses. It is here that I wish to demur (and this is what separates me from card-carrying Bayesians). Each of us perhaps has some subjective degree of belief, before we consider the design argument, in each of the two hypotheses (E_1) and (E_2). However, I see no way to understand the idea that the two hypotheses have *objective* prior probabilities. Since I would like to restrict the design argument as much as possible to matters that are objective, I will not represent it as an argument concerning which hypothesis

is more probable. However, those who have prior degrees of belief in (E_1) and (E_2) may use the likelihood argument to update their subjective probabilities. The likelihood version of the design argument says that the observation O_2 should lead you to increase your degree of belief in (E_1) and reduce your degree of belief in (E_2).

My restriction of the design argument to an assessment of likelihoods, not probabilities, reflects a more general point of view. Scientific theories often have implications about which observations are probable (and which are improbable), but it rarely makes sense to describe them as having objective probabilities. Newton's law of gravitation (along with suitable background assumptions) tells us that the return of Halley's comet was to be expected, but what is the probability that Newton's law is true? Hypotheses have objective probabilities when they describe possible outcomes of a chance process. But as far as anyone knows, the laws that govern our universe were not the result of a chance process. Bayesians think that *all* hypotheses have probabilities; the position I am advocating sees this as a special feature of *some* hypotheses.[2]

Not only do likelihood considerations leave open what probabilities one should assign to the competing hypotheses; they also don't tell you which hypothesis you should believe. I take it that belief is a dichotomous concept – you either believe a proposition or you do not. Consistent with this is the idea that there are three attitudes one might take to a statement – you can believe it true, believe it false, or withhold judgment. However, there is no simple connection of the matter-of-degree concept of probability to the dichotomous (or trichotomous) concept of belief. This is the lesson I extract from the lottery paradox (Kyburg 1961). Suppose 100,000 tickets are sold in a fair lottery; one ticket will win and each has the same chance of winning. It follows that each ticket has a very high probability of not winning. If you adopt the policy of believing a proposition when it has a high probability, you will believe of each ticket that it will not win. However, this conclusion contradicts the assumption that the lottery is fair. What this shows is that high probability does not suffice for belief (and low probability does not suffice for disbelief). It is for this reason that many Bayesians prefer to say that individuals have *degrees* of belief. The rules for the dichotomous concept are unclear; the matter-of-degree concept at least has the advantage of being anchored to the probability calculus.

In summary, likelihood arguments have rather modest pretensions. They don't tell you which hypotheses to believe; in fact, they don't even tell you which hypotheses are probably true. Rather, they evaluate how the observations at hand discriminate among the hypotheses under consideration.

I now turn to some details concerning the likelihood version of the design argument. The first concerns the meaning of the intelligent design hypothesis. This hypothesis occurs in (W_1) in connection with the watch and in (E_1) in connection with the vertebrate eye. In the case of the watch, Paley did not dream that he was offering an argument for the existence of *God*. However, in the case of the eye, Paley thought that the intelligent designer under discussion was God Himself. Why are these cases different? The bare bones of the likelihood arguments (W) and (E) do not say. What Paley had in mind is that building the vertebrate eye and the other adaptive features which organisms exhibit requires an intelligence far greater than anything that human beings could muster. This is a point that we will revisit at the end of this essay.

It is also important to understand the nature of the hypothesis with which the intelligent design hypothesis competes. I have used the term "chance" to express this alternative hypothesis. In large measure, this is because design theorists often think of chance as the alternative to design. Paley is again exemplary. *Natural Theology* is filled with examples like that of the vertebrate eye. Paley was not content to describe a few cases of delicate adaptations; he wanted to make sure that even if he got a few details wrong, the weight of evidence would still be overwhelming. For example, in Chapter 15 he considers the fact that our eyes point in the same direction as our feet; this has the convenient consequence that we can see where we are going. The obvious explanation, Paley (1802: 179) says, is intelligent design. This is because the alternative is that the direction of our eyes and the direction of our gait were determined by chance, which would mean that there was only a 1/4 probability that our eyes would be able to scan the quadrant into which we are about to step.

I construe the idea of chance in a particular way. To say that an outcome is the result of a *uniform chance process* means that it was one of a number of *equiprobable* outcomes. Examples in the real world that come close to being uniform chance processes may be found in gambling devices – spinning a roulette wheel, drawing from a deck of cards, tossing a coin. The term "random" becomes more and more appropriate as real-world systems approximate uniform chance processes. As R.A. Fisher once pointed out, it is not a "matter of chance" that casinos turn a profit each year, nor should this be regarded as a "random" event. The financial bottom line at a casino is the result of a large number of chance events, but the rules of the game make it enormously probable (though not certain) that casinos end each year in the black. All uniform chance processes are probabilistic, but not all probabilistic outcomes are "due to chance."

It follows that the two hypotheses considered in my likelihood rendition of the design argument are not exhaustive. Mindless uniform chance is one alternative to intelligent design, but it is not the only one. This point has an important bearing on the dramatic change in fortunes that the design argument experienced with the advent of Darwin's (1859) theory of evolution. The process of evolution by natural selection is not a uniform chance process. The process has two parts. Novel traits arise in individual organisms "by chance"; however, whether they then disappear from the population or increase in frequency and eventually reach 100 percent representation is anything but a "matter of chance." The central idea of natural selection is that traits which help organisms survive and reproduce have a better chance of becoming common than traits that hurt. The essence of natural selection is that evolutionary outcomes have *unequal* probabilities. Paley and other design theorists writing before Darwin did not and could not cover all possible mindless natural processes. Paley addressed the alternative of uniform chance, not the alternative of natural selection.[3] [. . .]

Showing that Design is more likely than Chance leaves it open that some third, mindless, process might still have a higher likelihood than Design. This is not a defect in the design argument, so long as the conclusion of that argument is not overstated. Here the modesty of the likelihood version of the design argument is a point in its favor. To draw a stronger conclusion – that the Design hypothesis is more likely than *any* hypothesis involving mindless natural processes – one would have to attend to more alternatives than just Design and (uniform) Chance.[4]

I now want to draw the reader's attention to some features of the likelihood version of the design argument (E) concerning how the observation and the competing hypotheses are formulated. First, notice that I have kept the observation (O_2) conceptually separate from the two hypotheses (E_1) and (E_2). If the observation were simply that "the vertebrate eye exists," then since (E_1) and (E_2) both entail this proposition, each would have a likelihood of unity. According to LP, this observation does not favor Design over Chance. Better to formulate the question in terms of explaining the properties of the vertebrate eye, not explaining why the eye exists. Notice also that I have not formulated the design hypothesis as the claim that God exists; this existence claim says nothing about the putative

designer's involvement in the creation of the vertebrate eye. Finally, I should point out that it would do no harm to have the design hypothesis say that God created the vertebrate eye; this possible reformulation is something I'll return to later.

Other Formulations of the Design Argument, and Their Defects

Given the various provisos that govern probability arguments, it would be nice if the design argument could be formulated deductively. For example, if the hypothesis of mindless chance processes entailed that it is *impossible* that organisms exhibit delicate adaptations, then a quick application of *modus tollens* would sweep that hypothesis from the field. However much design theorists might yearn for an argument of this kind, there apparently are none to be had. As the story about monkeys and typewriters illustrates, it is *not* impossible that mindless chance processes should produce delicate adaptations; it is merely very *improbable* that they should do so.

If *modus tollens* cannot be pressed into service, perhaps there is a probabilistic version of *modus tollens* that can achieve the same result. Is there a Law of Improbability that begins with the premise that $Pr(O|H)$ is very low and concludes that H should be rejected? There is no such principle (Royall 1997: Ch. 3). The fact that you won the lottery does not, by itself, show that there is something wrong with the conjunctive hypothesis that the lottery was fair and a million tickets were sold and you bought just one ticket. And if we randomly drop a very sharp pin onto a line that is a thousand miles long, the probability of its landing where it does is negligible; however, that outcome does not falsify the hypothesis that the pin was dropped at random.[5]

The fact that there is no probabilistic *modus tollens* has great significance for understanding the design argument. The logic of this problem is essentially comparative. To evaluate the design hypothesis, we must know what it predicts and compare this with the predictions made by other hypotheses. The design hypothesis cannot win by default. The fact that an observation would be very improbable if it arose by chance is not enough to refute the chance hypothesis. One must show that the design hypothesis confers on the observation a higher probability, and even then the conclusion will merely be that the observation *favors* the design hypothesis, not that that hypothesis *must be true*.

In the continuing conflict (in the USA) between evolutionary biology and creationism, creationists attack evolutionary theory, but never take even the first step in developing a positive theory of their own. The three-word slogan "God did it" seems to satisfy whatever craving for explanation they may have. Is the sterility of this intellectual tradition a mere accident? Could intelligent design theory be turned into a scientific research program? I am doubtful, but the present point concerns the logic of the design argument, not its future prospects. Creationists sometimes assert that evolutionary theory "cannot explain" this or that finding (e.g. Behe 1996). What they mean is that certain outcomes are *very improbable* according to the evolutionary hypothesis. Even this more modest claim needs to be scrutinized. However, even if it were true, what would follow about the plausibility of creationism? In a word – *nothing*.

It isn't just defenders of the design hypothesis who have fallen into the trap of supposing that there is a probabilistic version of *modus tollens*. For example, the biologist Richard Dawkins (1986: 144–6) takes up the question of how one should evaluate hypotheses that attempt to explain the origin of life by appeal to strictly mindless natural processes. He says that an acceptable theory of this sort can say that the origin of life on Earth was somewhat improbable, but it cannot go too far. If there are N planets in the Universe that are "suitable" locales for life to originate, then an acceptable theory of the origin of life on Earth must say that that event had a probability of at least 1/N. Theories that say that terrestrial life

was less probable than this should be rejected. This criterion may look plausible, but I think there is less to it than meets the eye. How does Dawkins obtain this lower bound? Why is the number of planets relevant? Perhaps he is thinking that if 1/N is the actual frequency of life-bearing planets among "suitable" planets (i.e. planets on which it is possible for life to evolve), then the true probability of life's evolving on Earth must also be 1/N. There is a mistake here, which we can uncover by examining how actual frequency and probability are related. With a small sample size, it is perfectly possible for these quantities to have different values (consider a fair coin that is tossed three times and then destroyed). However, Dawkins is obviously thinking that the sample size is very large, and here he is right that the actual frequency provides a good estimate of the true probability. It is interesting that Dawkins tells us to reject a theory if the probability it assigns is too low, but why doesn't he also say that it should be rejected if the probability it assigns is too high? The reason, presumably, is that we cannot rule out the possibility that Earth was not just suitable but *highly conducive* to the evolution of life. However, this point cuts both ways. Even if 1/N is the probability of a randomly selected suitable planet having life evolve on it, it still is possible that different suitable planets might have different probabilities – some may have values greater than 1/N while others may have values that are lower. Dawkins' lower bound assumes a *priori* that the Earth was above average; this is a mistake that might be termed the "Lake Wobegon Fallacy."

Some of Hume's (1779) criticisms of the design argument in his *Dialogues Concerning Natural Religion* depend on formulating the argument as something other than a likelihood inference. For example, Hume at one point has Philo say that the design argument is an argument from analogy, and that the conclusion of the argument is supported only very weakly by its premises. His point can be formulated by thinking of the design arguments as follows:

Watches are produced by intelligent design.

Organisms are similar to watches to degree p.

p[================================

Organisms were produced by intelligent design.

Note that the letter "p" appears twice in this argument. It represents the degree of similarity of organisms and watches, and it represents the probability that the premises confer on the conclusion. Think of similarity as the proportion of shared characteristics. Things that are 0 percent similar have no traits in common; things that are 100 percent similar have all traits in common. The analogy argument says that the more similar watches and organisms are, the more probable it is that organisms were produced by intelligent design.

Let us grant the Humean point that watches and organisms have relatively few characteristics in common (it is doubtful that there is a well-defined totality consisting of all the traits of each, but let that pass). After all, watches are made of metal and glass, and go "tick tock"; organisms metabolize and reproduce and go "oink" and "bow wow." This is all true, but entirely irrelevant, if the design argument is a likelihood inference. It doesn't matter how similar watches and organisms are overall. With respect to argument (W), what matters is how one should explain the fact that watches are well adapted for the task of telling time; with respect to (E), what matters is how one should explain the fact that organisms are well adapted to their environments. Paley's analogy between watches and organisms is merely heuristic. The likelihood argument about organisms stands on its own (Sober 1993).

Hume also has Philo construe the design argument as an inductive argument, and then complain that the inductive evidence is weak. Philo suggests that for us to have good reason to think that our world was produced by an intelligent designer, we would have to visit other worlds and observe that all or most of them were produced by intelligent design. But how many

other worlds have we visited? The answer is − not even one. Apparently, the design argument is an inductive argument that could not be weaker; its sample size is zero. This objection dissolves once we move from the model of inductive sampling to that of likelihood. You don't have to observe the processes of intelligent design and chance at work in different worlds to maintain that the two hypotheses confer different probabilities on the observations.

Three Objections to the Likelihood Argument

There is another objection that Hume makes to the design argument, one that many philosophers apparently think is devastating. Hume points out that the design argument does not establish the attributes of the designer. The argument does not show that the designer who made the Universe, or who made organisms, is morally perfect, or all-knowing, or all-powerful, or that there is just one of him. Perhaps this undercuts some versions of the design argument, but it does not touch the likelihood argument we are considering. Paley, perhaps responding to this Humean point, makes it clear that his design argument aims to establish the *existence* of the designer, and that the question of the designer's *characteristics* must be addressed separately.[6] Does this limitation of the design argument make the argument trivial? Not at all − it is *not* trivial to claim that the adaptive contrivances of organisms are due to intelligent design. This supposed "triviality" would be big news to evolutionary biologists.

The likelihood version of the design argument consists of two premises − Pr(O|Chance) is very low and Pr(O|Design) is higher. Here O describes some observation of the features of organisms or some feature of the entire cosmos. The first of these claims is sometimes rejected by appeal to a theory that Hume describes under the heading of the Epicurean hypothesis. This is the monkeys-and-typewriters idea that if there are a finite number of particles that have a finite number of possible states, then, if they swarm about at random, they will eventually visit all possible configurations, including configurations of great order.[7] Thus, the order we see in our universe, and the delicate adaptations we observe in organisms, in fact had a high probability of eventually coming into being, according to the hypothesis of chance. Van Inwagen (1993: 144) gives voice to this objection and explains it by way of an analogy. Suppose you toss a coin twenty times and it lands heads every time. You should not be surprised at this outcome if you are one among millions of people who toss a fair coin twenty times. After all, with so many people tossing, it is all but inevitable that some people should get twenty heads. The outcome you obtained, therefore, was not improbable, according to the chance hypothesis.

There is a fallacy in this criticism of the design argument, which Hacking (1987) calls "the Inverse Gambler's Fallacy." He illustrates his idea by describing a gambler who walks into a casino and immediately observes two dice being rolled that land double-six. The gambler considers whether this result favors the hypothesis that the dice had been rolled many times before the roll he just observed or the hypothesis that this was the first roll of the evening. The gambler reasons that the outcome of double-six would be more probable under the first hypothesis:

Pr(double-six on this roll | there were many rolls) > Pr(double-six on this roll | there was just one roll).

In fact, the gambler's assessment of the likelihoods is erroneous. Rolls of dice have the *Markov property*: the probability of double-six on this roll is the same (1/36), regardless of what may have happened in the past. What is true is that the probability that a double-six will occur *at some time or other* increases as the number of trials is increased:

Pr(a double-six occurs sometime | there were many rolls) > Pr(a double-six occurs sometime | there was just one roll).

However, the *principle of total evidence* says that we should assess hypotheses by considering *all* the evidence we have. This means that the relevant observation is that *this* roll landed double-six; we should not focus on the logically weaker proposition that a double-six occurred *sometime*. Relative to the stronger description of the observations, the hypotheses have identical likelihoods.

If we apply this point to the criticism of the design argument that we are presently considering, we must conclude that the criticism is mistaken. There is a high probability (let us suppose) that a chance process will sooner or later produce order and adaptation. However, the relevant observation is not that these events occur at some time or other; but that they are true here and now – *our* universe is orderly and the organisms here on Earth are well adapted. These events *do* have very low probability, according to the chance hypothesis, and the fact that a weaker description of the observations has high probability on the chance hypothesis is not relevant (see also White 2000).[8]

If the first premise in the likelihood formulation of the design argument – that Pr(O | Chance) is very low – is correct, then the only question that remains is whether Pr(O | Design) is higher. This, I believe, is the Achilles' heel of the design argument. The problem is to say how probable it is, for example, that the vertebrate eye would have features $F_1 \ldots F_n$ if the eye were produced by an intelligent designer. What is required is not the specification of a single probability value, or even a range of such. All that is needed is an argument that shows that this probability is indeed higher than the probability that Chance confers on the observation.

The problem is that the design hypothesis confers a probability on the observation only when it is supplemented with further assumptions about what the designer's goals and abilities would be if he existed. Perhaps the designer would never build the vertebrate eye with features $F_1 \ldots F_n$, either because he would lack the goals or because he would lack the ability. If so, the likelihood of the design hypothesis is zero. On the other hand, perhaps the designer would want to build the eye with features $F_1 \ldots F_n$ and would be entirely competent to bring this plan to fruition. If so, the likelihood of the design hypothesis is unity. There are as many likelihoods as there are suppositions concerning the goals and abilities of the putative designer. Which of these, or which class of these, should we take seriously?

It is no good answering this question by assuming that the eye was built by an intelligent designer and then inferring that he must have wanted to give the eye features $F_1 \ldots F_n$ and that he must have had the ability to do so since, after all, these are the features we observe. For one thing, this pattern of argument is question-begging. One needs *independent* evidence as to what the designer's plans and abilities would be if he existed; one can't obtain this evidence by *assuming* that the design hypothesis is true (Sober 1999). Furthermore, even if we assume that the eye was built by an intelligent designer, we can't tell from this what the probability is that the eye would have the features we observe. Designers sometimes bring about outcomes that are not very probable given the plans they have in mind.

This objection to the design argument is an old one; it was presented by Keynes (1921) and before him by Venn (1866). In fact, the basic idea was formulated by Hume. When we behold the watch on the heath, we know that the watch's features are not particularly improbable on the hypothesis that the watch was produced by a designer who has the sorts of *human* goals and abilities with which we are familiar. This is the deep and non-obvious disanalogy between the watchmaker and the putative maker of organisms and universes. We are invited, in the latter case, to imagine a designer who is radically different from the human craftsmen we know about. [. . .]

The upshot of this point for Paley's design argument is this: *Design arguments for the existence of human (and human-like) watchmakers are often unproblematic; it is design arguments for the existence of God that leave us at sea.*

I began by formulating the design hypothesis in argument (E) as the claim that an intelligent designer made the vertebrate eye. Yet, I have sometimes discussed the hypothesis as if it asserted that God is the designer in question. I don't think this difference makes a difference with respect to the objection I have described. To say that some designer or other made the eye is to state a disjunctive hypothesis. To figure out the likelihood of this disjunction, one needs to address the question of what each putative designer's goals and intentions would be.[9] The theological formulation shifts the problem from the evaluation of a disjunction to the evaluation of a disjunct, but the problem remains the same. Even supposing that God is omniscient, omnipotent, and perfectly benevolent, what is the probability that the eye would have features $F_1 \ldots F_n$ if God set his hand to making it? He *could* have produced those results if he had wanted. But why think that this is what he *would* have wanted to do? The assumption that God can do anything is part of the problem, not the solution. An engineer who is more limited would be more predictable.

There is another reply to my criticism of the design argument that should be considered. I have complained that we have no way to evaluate the likelihood of the design hypothesis, since we don't know which auxiliary assumptions about goal/ability pairs we should use. But why not change the subject? Instead of evaluating the likelihood of Design, why not evaluate the likelihood of various conjunctions – (Design & GA_1), (Design & GA_2), etc.? Some of these will have high likelihoods, others will have low, but it will no longer be a mystery what likelihoods these hypotheses possess. There are two problems with this tactic. First, it is a game that two can play. Consider the hypothesis that the vertebrate eye was created by the mindless process of electricity. If I simply get to invent auxiliary hypotheses without having to justify them independently, I can simply stipulate the following assumption – if electricity created the vertebrate eye, the eye must have features $F_1 \ldots F_n$. The electricity hypothesis is now a conjunct in a conjunction that has maximum likelihood, just like the design hypothesis. This is a dead end. My second objection is that it is an important part of scientific practice that conjunctions be broken apart (when possible) and their conjuncts scrutinized (Sober 1999, 2000b). If your doctor runs a test to see whether you have tuberculosis, you will not be satisfied if she reports that the conjunction "you have tuberculosis & auxiliary assumption 1" is very likely while the conjunction "you have tuberculosis & auxiliary assumption 2" is very unlikely. You want your doctor to address the first *conjunct*, not just various *conjunctions*. And you want her to do this by using a test procedure that is *independently* known to have small error probabilities. Demand no less of your theologian.

The Relationship of the Organismic Design Argument to Darwinism

Philosophers who criticize the organismic design argument often believe that the argument was dealt its death blow by Hume. True, Paley wrote after Hume, and the many Bridgewater Treatises elaborating the design argument appeared after Hume's *Dialogues* were published posthumously. Nonetheless, for these philosophers, the design argument after Hume was merely a corpse that could be propped up and paraded. Hume had taken the life out of it.

Biologists often take a different view. Dawkins (1986: 4) puts the point provocatively by saying that it was not until Darwin that it was possi-

ble to be an intellectually fulfilled atheist. The thought here is that Hume's skeptical attack was not the decisive moment; rather, it was Darwin's development and confirmation of a substantive scientific explanation of the adaptive features of organisms that really undermined the design argument (at least in its organismic formulation). Philosophers who believe that theories can't be rejected until a better theory is developed to take its place often sympathize with this point of view.

My own interpretation coincides with neither of these. As indicated above, I think that Hume's criticisms largely derive from an empiricist epistemology that is too narrow. However, seeing the design argument's fatal flaw does not depend on seeing the merits of Darwinian theory. True, LP says that theories must be evaluated comparatively, not on their own. But for this to be possible, each theory must make predictions. It is at this fundamental level that I think the design argument is defective.

Biologists often present two criticisms of creationism. First, they argue that the design hypothesis is untestable. Second, they contend that there is plenty of evidence that the hypothesis is false. Obviously, these two lines of argument are in conflict. I have already endorsed the first criticism, but I want to say a little about the second. A useful example is Stephen Jay Gould's (1980) widely read article about the panda's thumb. Pandas are vegetarian bears who have a spur of bone (a "thumb") protruding from their wrists. They use this device to strip bamboo, which is the main thing they eat. Gould says that the hypothesis of intelligent design predicts that pandas should not have this inefficient device. A benevolent, powerful, and intelligent engineer could and would have done a lot better. Evolutionary theory, on the other hand, says that the panda's thumb is what we should expect. The thumb is a modification of the wrist bones found in the common ancestor that pandas share with carnivorous bears. Evolution by natural selection is a tinkerer; it does not design adaptations from scratch, but modifies pre-existing features, with the result that adaptations are often imperfect.

Gould's argument, I hope it is clear, is a likelihood argument. I agree with what he says about evolutionary theory, but I think his discussion of the design hypothesis falls into the same trap that ensnared Paley. Gould thinks he knows what God would do if He built pandas, just as Paley thought he knew what God would do if He built the vertebrate eye. But neither of them knows this. Both help themselves to *assumptions* about God's goals and abilities. However, it is not enough to make assumptions about these matters; one needs independent evidence that these auxiliary assumptions are true. Paley's problem is also Gould's.

Anthropic Reasoning and Cosmic Design Arguments

Evolutionary theory seeks to explain the adaptive features of organisms; it has nothing to say about the origin of the Universe as a whole. For this reason, evolutionary theory conflicts with the organismic design hypothesis, but not with the cosmic design hypothesis. Still, the main criticism I presented of the first type of design argument also applies to the second. I now want to examine a further problem that cosmic design arguments sometimes encounter.[10]

Suppose I catch 50 fish from a lake, and you want to use my observations O to test two hypotheses:

O: All the fish I caught were more than ten inches long.

F_1: All the fish in the lake are more than ten inches long.

F_2: Only half the fish in the lake are more than ten inches long.

You might think that LP says that F_1 is better supported, since

(1) $Pr(O \mid F_1) > Pr(O \mid F_2)$.

However, you then discover how I caught my fish:

(A1) I caught the 50 fish by using a net that (because of the size of its holes) can't catch fish smaller than ten inches long.

This leads you to replace the analysis provided by (1) with the following:

(2) $Pr(O \mid F_1 \& A_1) = Pr(O \mid F_2 \& A_1) = 1$.

Furthermore, you now realize that your first assessment, (1), was based on the erroneous assumption that

(A0) The fish I caught were a random sample from the fish in the lake.

Instead of (1), you should have written

$Pr(O \mid F_1 \& A_0) > Pr(O \mid F_2 \& A_0)$.

This inequality is true; the problem, however, is that (A_0) is false.

This example, from Eddington (1939), illustrates the idea of an *observational selection effect* (an OSE). When a hypothesis is said to render a set of observations probable (or improbable), ask what assumptions allow the hypothesis to have this implication. The point illustrated here is that the procedure you use to obtain your observations can be relevant to assessing likelihoods.[11]

One version of the cosmic design argument begins with the observation that our universe is "fine-tuned." That is, the values of various physical constants are such as to permit life to exist, and, if they had been even slightly different, life would have been impossible. I'll abbreviate this fact by saying that "the constants are right." A design argument can now be constructed, one that claims that the constants being right should be explained by postulating the existence of an intelligent designer, one who wanted life to exist and who arranged the Universe so that this would occur (Swinburne 1990a). As with Paley's organismic design argument, we can represent the reasoning in this cosmic design argument as the assertion of a likelihood inequality:

(3) Pr(constants are right | Design) > Pr(constants are right | Chance).

However, there is a problem with (3) that resembles the problem with (1). Consider the fact that

(A_3) We exist, and if we exist the constants must be right.

We need to take (A_3) into account; instead of (3), we should have said:

(4) Pr(constants are right | Design & A_3) = Pr(constants are right | Chance & A_3) = 1.0.

That is, given (A_3), the constants must be right, regardless of whether the Universe was produced by intelligent design or by chance.

Proposition (4) reflects the fact that our observation that the constants are right is subject to an OSE. Recognizing this OSE is in accordance with a *weak anthropic principle* – "what we can expect to observe must be restricted by the conditions necessary for our presence as observers" (Carter 1974: 291). The argument involves no commitment to *strong anthropic principles*. For example, there is no assertion that the correct cosmology must entail that the existence of observers such as ourselves was inevitable; nor is it claimed that our existence explains why the physical constants are right (Barrow 1988; Earman 1987; McMullin 1993)

Although this point about OSEs undermines the version of the design argument that cites the fact that the physical constants are right, it does not touch other versions. For example, when Paley concludes that the vertebrate eye was produced by an intelligent designer, his argument cannot be refuted by claiming that:

(A_4) We exist, and if we exist vertebrates must have eyes with features $F_1 \ldots F_n$.

If (A_4) were true, the likelihood inequality that Paley asserted would have to be replaced with an equality, just as (1) had to be replaced by (2) and (3) had to be replaced by (4). But, fortunately for Paley, (A_4) is false. However, matters change if we think of Paley as seeking to explain the modest fact that organisms have at least one adaptive contrivance. If this were false, we would not be able to make observations; indeed, we would not exist. Paley was right to focus on the details; the more minimal description of what we observe does not sustain the argument he wanted to endorse.

The issue of OSEs can be raised in connection with other cosmic versions of the design argument. Swinburne writes that "the hypothesis of theism is that the Universe exists because there is a God who keeps it in being and that laws of nature operate because there is a God who brings it about that they do" (1990b: 191). Let us separate the *explananda*. The fact that the Universe exists does *not* favor Design over Chance; after all, if the Universe did not exist, we would not exist and so would not be able to observe that it does.[12] The same point holds with respect to the fact that the Universe is law-governed. Even supposing that lawlessness is possible, could we exist and make observations if there were no laws? If not, then the lawful character of the Universe does not discriminate between Design and Chance. Finally, we may consider the fact that our universe is governed by one set of laws, rather than another. Swinburne (1968) argues that the fact that our universe obeys *simple* laws is better explained by the hypothesis of Design than by the hypothesis of Chance. Whether this observation is also subject to an OSE depends on whether we could exist in a universe obeying alternative laws.

Before taking up an objection to this analysis of the argument from fine-tuning, I want to summarize what it has in common with the fishing example. In the fishing example, the source of the OSE is obvious – it is located in a device outside of ourselves. The net with big holes insures that the observer will make a certain observation, regardless of which of two hypotheses is true. But where is the device that induces an OSE in the fine-tuning example? There is none; rather, it is the observer's own existence that does the work. But, still, the effect is the same. Owing to the fact that we exist, we are bound to observe that the constants are right, regardless of whether our universe was produced by chance or by design.

Leslie (1989: 13–4, 107–8), Swinburne (1990a: 171), and van Inwagen (1993: 135, 144) all defend the fine-tuning argument against the criticism I have just described that appeals to the idea of an OSE. Each mounts his defense by describing an analogy with a mundane example. Here is Swinburne's rendition of an analogy that Leslie presents:

> On a certain occasion the firing squad aim their rifles at the prisoner to be executed. There are twelve expert marksmen in the firing squad, and they fire twelve rounds each. However, on this occasion all 144 shots miss. The prisoner laughs and comments that the event is not something requiring any explanation because if the marksmen had not missed, he would not be here to observe them having done so. But of course, the prisoner's comment is absurd; the marksmen all having missed is indeed something requiring explanation; and so too is what goes with it – the prisoner's being alive to observe it. And the explanation will be either that it was an accident (a most unusual chance event) or that it was planned (e.g., all the marksmen had been bribed to miss). Any interpretation of the

anthropic principle which suggests that the evolution of observers is something which requires no explanation in terms of boundary conditions and laws being a certain way (either inexplicably or through choice) is false.

(Swinburne 1990a: 171)

First, a preliminary clarification – the issue isn't whether the prisoner's survival "requires explanation" but whether this observation provides evidence as to whether the marksmen intended to spare the prisoner or shot at random.[13]

My response to Swinburne takes the form of a dilemma. I'll argue, first, that if the firing squad example is analyzed in terms of LP, the prisoner is right and Swinburne is wrong – the prisoner's survival does not allow him to conclude that Design is more likely than Chance. However, there is a different analysis of the prisoner's situation, in terms of the *probabilities* of hypotheses, not their *likelihoods*. This second analysis concludes that the prisoner is mistaken; however, it has the consequence that the prisoner's inference differs fundamentally from the design argument that appeals to fine-tuning. Each horn of this dilemma supports the conclusion that the firing squad example does nothing to save this version of the design argument.

So let us begin. If we understand Swinburne's claim in terms of LP, we should read him as saying that

(L_1)   Pr(the prisoner survived | the marksmen intended to miss) > Pr(the prisoner survived | the marksmen fired at random).

He thinks that the anthropic principle requires us to replace this claim with the following irrelevancy:

(L_2)   Pr(the prisoner survived | the marksmen intended to miss & the prisoner survived) =

Pr(the prisoner survived | the marksmen fired at random & the prisoner survived) = 1.

This equality would lead us to conclude (Swinburne thinks mistakenly) that the prisoner's survival does not discriminate between the hypotheses of Design and Chance.

To assess Swinburne's claim that the prisoner has made a mistake, it is useful to compare the prisoner's reasoning with that of a bystander who witnesses the prisoner survive the firing squad. The prisoner reasons as follows: "Given that I now am able to make observations, I must be alive, whether my survival was due to intelligent design or chance." The bystander says the following: "Given that I now am able to make observations, the fact that the prisoner is now alive is made more probable by the design hypothesis than it is by the chance hypothesis." The prisoner is claiming that he is subject to an OSE, while the bystander says that he, the bystander, is not. Both, I submit, are correct.[14]

I suggest that part of the intuitive attractiveness of Swinburne's claim that the prisoner has made a mistake derives from a shift between the prisoner's point of view to the bystander's. (L_1) is correct and involves no OSE if it expresses the bystander's judgment; however, it is flawed, and needs to be replaced by (L_2), if it expresses the prisoner's judgment. My hunch is that Swinburne thinks the prisoner errs in his assessment of likelihoods because we bystanders would be making a mistake if we reasoned as he does.[15]

The basic idea of an OSE is that we must take account of the procedures used to obtain the observations when we assess the likelihoods of hypotheses. This much was clear from the fishing example. What may seem strange about my reading of Swinburne's story is my claim that the prisoner and the bystander are in different epistemic situations, even though their observation reports differ by a mere pronoun. After the marksmen fire, the prisoner thinks "I exist" while the bystander thinks "he exists"; the

bystander, but not the prisoner, is able to use his observation to say that Design is more likely than Chance, or so I say. If this seems odd, it may be useful to reflect on Sorenson's (1988) concept of *blindspots*. A proposition p is a blindspot for an individual S just in case, if p were true, S would not be able to know that p is true. Although some propositions (e.g. "nothing exists," "the constants are wrong") are blindspots for everyone, other propositions are blindspots for some people but not for others. Blindspots give rise to OSEs; if p is a blindspot for S, then if S makes an observation to determine the truth value of p, the outcome must be that not-p is observed. The prisoner, but not the bystander, has "the prisoner does not exist" as a blindspot. This is why "the prisoner exists" has an evidential significance for the bystander that it cannot have for the prisoner.[16]

I now turn to a different analysis of the prisoner's situation. The prisoner, like the rest of us, knows how firing squads work. They always or almost always follow the orders they receive, which is almost always to execute someone. Occasionally, they produce fake executions. They almost never fire at random. What is more, firing squads have firm control over outcomes; if they want to kill (or spare) someone, they always or almost always succeed. This and related items of background knowledge support the following *probability* claim:

(P_f) Pr(the marksmen intended to spare the prisoner | the prisoner survived) > Pr(the marksmen intended to spare the prisoner).

Firing squads rarely intend to spare their victims, but the survival of the prisoner makes it very probable that his firing squad had precisely that intention. The likelihood analysis led to the conclusion that the prisoner and the bystander are in different epistemic situations; the bystander evaluates the hypotheses by using (L_1), but the prisoner is obliged to use (L_2). However, from the point of view of probabilities, the prisoner and the bystander can say the same thing; both can cite (P_f).

What does this tell us about the fine-tuning version of the design argument? I construed that argument as a claim about likelihoods. As such, it is subject to an OSE; given that we exist, the constants have to be right, regardless of whether our universe was produced by Chance or by Design. However, we now need to consider whether the fine-tuning argument can be formulated as a claim about probabilities. Can we assert that

> (P_u)   Pr(the Universe was created by an intelligent designer | the constants are right) > Pr(the Universe was created by an intelligent designer)?

I don't think so. In the case of firing squads, we have frequency data and our general knowledge of human behavior on which to ground the probability statement (P_f). But we have neither data nor theory on which to ground (P_u). And we cannot defend (P_u) by saying that an intelligent designer would ensure that the constants are right, because this takes us back to the likelihood considerations we have already discussed. The prisoner's conclusion that he can say nothing about Chance and Design is mistaken if he is making a claim about probabilities. But the argument from fine-tuning can't be defended as a claim about probabilities.

The rabbit/duck quality of this problem merits review. I've discussed three examples – fishing, fine-tuning, and the firing squad. If we compare fine-tuning with fishing, they seem similar. This makes it intuitive to conclude that the design argument based on fine-tuning is wrong. However, if we compare fine-tuning with the firing squad, they seem similar. Since the prisoner apparently has evidence that favors Design over Chance, we are led to the conclusion that the fine-tuning argument must be right. This shifting gestalt can be stabilized by imposing a

formalism. The first point is that OSEs are to be understood by comparing the *likelihoods* of hypotheses, not their *probabilities*. The second is that it is perfectly true that the prisoner can assert the *probability* claim (P_f). The question, then, is whether the design argument from fine-tuning is a likelihood argument or a probability argument. If the former, it is flawed because it fails to take account of the fact that there is an OSE. If the latter, it is flawed, but for a different reason – it makes claims about probabilities that we have no reason to accept; indeed, we cannot even *understand* them as objective claims about nature.[17]

A Prediction

It was obvious to Paley and to other purveyors of the organismic design argument that, if an intelligent designer built organisms, that designer would have to be far more intelligent than any human being could ever be. This is why the organismic design argument was for them an argument for the existence of *God*. I predict that it will eventually become clear that the organismic design argument should never have been understood in this way. This is because I expect that human beings will eventually build organisms from non-living materials. This achievement will not close down the question of whether the organisms we observe were created by intelligent design or by mindless natural processes; in fact, it will give that question a practical meaning, since the organisms we will see around us will be of both kinds.[18] However, it will be abundantly clear that the fact of organismic adaptation has nothing to do with whether God exists. When the Spanish conquistadors arrived in the New World, several indigenous peoples thought these intruders were gods, so powerful was the technology that the intruders possessed. Alas, the locals were mistaken; they did not realize that these beings with guns and horses were merely *human* beings. The organismic design argument for the existence of God embodies the same mistake. Human beings in the future will be the conquistadors, and Paley will be our Montezuma.[19]

Notes

1 Does this construal of the design argument conflict with the idea that the argument is an *inference to the best explanation*? Not if one's theory of inference to the best explanation says that observations influence the assessment of explanations in this instance via the vehicle of likelihoods.

2 In light of the fact that it is possible for a hypothesis to have an objective likelihood without also having an objective probability, one should understand Bayes's theorem as specifying how the quantities it mentions are related to each other, *if all are well defined*. And just as hypotheses can have likelihoods without having (objective) probabilities, it is also possible for the reverse situation to obtain. Suppose I draw a card from a deck of unknown composition. I observe (O) that the card is the four of diamonds. I now consider the hypothesis (H) that the card is a four. The value of $Pr(H|O)$ is well defined, but the value of $Pr(O|H)$ is not.

3 Actually, Paley (1802) *does* consider a "selective retention" process, but only very briefly. In Chapter 5 (pp. 49–51) he explores the hypothesis that a random process once generated a huge range of variation, and that this variation was then culled, with only stable configurations surviving. Paley argues against this hypothesis by saying that we should see unicorns and mermaids if it were true. He also says that it mistakenly predicts that organisms should fail to form a taxonomic hierarchy. It is ironic that Darwin claimed that his own theory *predicts* hierarchy. In fact, Paley and Darwin are both right. Darwin's theory contains the idea that all living things have common ancestors, while the selection hypothesis that Paley considers does not.

4 Dawkins (1986) makes the point that evolution by natural selection is not a uniform chance process by way of an analogy with a combination lock. This is discussed in Sober (1993: 36–9).

5 Dembski (1998) construes the design inference as "sweeping from the field" all possible competitors, with the effect that the design hypothesis wins by default (i.e. it never has to make successful predictions). As noted above, Paley, Arbuthnot,

and other design theorists did not and could not refute all possible alternatives to Design; they were able to test only the alternatives that they were able to formulate. For other criticisms of Dembski's framework, see Fitelson *et al.* (1999).

6 Paley (1802) argues in Chapter 16 that the benevolence of the deity is demonstrated by the fact that organisms experience more pleasure than they need to (p. 295). He also argues that pain is useful (p. 320) and that few diseases are fatal; he defends the latter conclusion by citing statistics on the cure rate at a London hospital (p. 321).

7 For it to be certain that all configurations will be visited, there must be infinite time. The shorter the time frame, the lower the probability that a given configuration will occur. This means that the estimated age of the Universe may entail that it is very improbable that a given configuration will occur. I set this objection aside in what follows.

8 It is a standard feature of likelihood comparisons that O_s sometimes fails to discriminate between a pair of hypotheses, even though O_w is able to do so, when O_s entails O_w. You are the cook in a restaurant. The waiter brings an order into the kitchen; someone ordered bacon and eggs. You wonder whether this information favors the hypothesis that your friend Smith ordered the meal, or that your friend Jones did. You know the eating habits of each. Table 12.1 gives the probabilities of four possible orders, conditional on the order having come from Smith and conditional on the order having come from Jones.

The fact that the customer ordered bacon and eggs does not discriminate between the two hypotheses (since $0.3 = 0.3$). However, the fact that the customer ordered bacon favors Smith over

Table 12.1 Probabilities of four possible orders, conditional on who orders

	Smith's probabilities	Jones's probabilities
bacon and eggs	0.3	0.3
bacon without eggs	0.4	0.2
eggs without bacon	0.2	0.1
neither bacon nor eggs	0.1	0.4

Jones (since $0.7 > 0.5$), and so does the fact that the customer ordered eggs (since $0.5 > 0.4$).

9 Assessing the likelihood of a disjunction involves an additional problem. Even if the values of $\Pr(O|D_1)$ and $\Pr(O|D_2)$ are known, what is the value of $\Pr(O|D_1$ or $D_2)$? The answer is that it must be somewhere in between. But exactly where depends on further considerations, since $\Pr(O|D_1$ or $D_2) = [\Pr(O|D_1) \cdot \Pr(D_1|D_1$ or $D_2)] + [\Pr(O|D_2) \cdot \Pr(D_2|D_1$ or $D_2)]$. If either God or a super-intelligent extraterrestrial built the vertebrate eye, what is the probability that it was God who did so?

10 To isolate this new problem from the one already identified, I'll assume in what follows that the design hypothesis has built into it auxiliary assumptions that suffice for its likelihood to be well defined.

11 This general point surfaces in simple inference problems like the ravens paradox (Hempel 1965). Does the fact that the object before you is a black raven confirm the generalization that all ravens are black? That depends on how you gathered your data. Perhaps you sampled at random from the set of *ravens*; alternatively, you may have sampled at random from the set of *black ravens*. In the first case, your observation confirms the generalization, but in the second it does not. In the second case, notice that you were bound to observe that the object before you is a black raven, regardless of whether all ravens are black.

12 Similarly, the fact that there is something rather than nothing does not discriminate between Chance and Design.

13 There is a third possibility – that the marksmen intended to kill the prisoner – but for the sake of simplicity (and also to make the firing-squad argument more parallel with the argument from fine-tuning), I'll ignore this for most of my discussion.

14 The issue, thus, is not whether (L_1) or (L_2) are true (both are), but which one an agent should use in interpreting the bearing of observations on the likelihoods of hypotheses. In this respect the injunction of the weak anthropic principle is like the principle of total evidence – it is a pragmatic principle, concerning which statements should be used for which purposes.

15 In order to replicate in the fine-tuning argument the difference between the prisoner's and the bystander's points of view, imagine that we observe through a telescope another universe in which the constants are right. We bystanders can use this observation in a way that the inhabitants of that universe cannot.

16 Notice that "I exist," when thought by the prisoner, is *a priori*, whereas "the prisoner exists," when thought by the bystander, is *a posteriori*. Is it so surprising that an *a priori* statement should have a different evidential significance than an *a posteriori* statement? I also should note that my claim is that the proposition "I am alive" does not permit the prisoner to conclude that Design is more likely than Chance. I do not say that there is no proposition he can cite after the marksmen fire that discriminates between the two hypotheses. Consider, for example, the observation that "no bullets hit me." This favors Design over Chance, even after the prisoner conditionalizes on the fact that he is alive. Notice also that if the prisoner were alive but riddled with bullets, this would not so clearly make Design more likely than Chance.

17 The hypothesis that our universe is one among many has been introduced as a possible explanation of the fact that the constants (in our universe) are right. A universe is here understood to be a region of space-time that is causally closed. See Leslie (1989) for discussion. If the point of the multiverse hypothesis is to challenge the design hypothesis, on the assumption that the design hypothesis has already vanquished the hypothesis of chance, then the multiverse hypothesis is not needed. Furthermore, in comparing the multiverse hypothesis and the design hypothesis, one needs to attend to the Inverse Gambler's Fallacy discussed earlier. This is not to deny that there may be other evidence for the multiverse hypothesis; however, the mere fact that the constants are right in our universe is not evidence that discriminates between the three hypotheses in contention.

18 As Dennett (1987a: 284–5) observes, human beings have been modifying the characteristics of animals and plants by *artificial selection* for thousands of years. However, the organisms thus modified were not created by human beings. Recall that I formulated the design argument as endorsing a

hypothesis about how organisms were brought into being. This is why the work of plant and animal breeders, *per se*, does not show that the design argument should be stripped of its theological trappings.

19 I am grateful to Martin Barrett, Nick Bostrom, David Christensen, Ellery Eells, Branden Fitelson, Malcolm Forster, Daniel Hausman, Stephen Leeds, Lydia McGrew, Williams Mann, Roy Sorenson, and Richard Swinburne for useful comments. Thanks also to the members of the Kansas State University Philosophy Department for a very stimulating and productive discussion of this chapter.

References

Arbuthnot, J. (1710) "An argument for Divine Providence, taken from the constant regularity observ'd in the births of both sexes," *Philosophical Transactions of the Royal Society of London* 27: 186–90.

Barrow, J. (1988) *The World within the World*, Oxford: Clarendon Press.

Behe, M. (1996) *Darwin's Black Box*, New York: Free Press.

Carter, B. (1974) "Large number coincidences and the anthropic principle in cosmology," in M.S. Longair (ed.) *Confrontation of Cosmological Theories with Observational Data*, Dordrecht: Reidel, pp. 291–8.

Darwin, C. (1964 [1859]) *On the Origin of Species*, Cambridge, Massachusetts: Harvard University Press.

Dawkins, R. (1986) *The Blind Watchmaker*, New York: Norton.

Dembski, W. (1998) *The Design Inference*, Cambridge: Cambridge University Press.

Dennett, D. (1987a) "Intentional systems in cognitive ethology – the 'panglossian paradigm' defended," in *The Intentional Stance*, Cambridge, Massachusetts: MIT Press, pp. 237–86.

—— (1987b) "True believers," in *The Intentional Stance*, Cambridge, Massachusetts: MIT Press, pp. 13–42.

Dick, S. (1996) *The Biological Universe – the Twentieth-Century Extraterrestrial Life Debate and the Limits of Science*, Cambridge: Cambridge University Press.

Earman, J. (1987) "The SAP also rises – a critical examination of the anthropic principle," *American Philosophical Quarterly* 24: 307–17.

Eddington, A. (1939) *The Philosophy of Physical Science*, Cambridge: Cambridge University Press.

Edwards, A. (1972) *Likelihood*, Cambridge: Cambridge University Press.

Fisher, R.A. (1957 [1930]) *The Genetical Theory of Natural Selection*, 2nd edn, New York: Dover.

Fitelson, B., Stephens, C., and Sober, E. (1999) "How not to detect design – a review of W. Dembski's *The Design Inference*," *Philosophy of Science* 66: 472–88, available online at http://philosophy.wisc.edu/sober.

Forster, M. and Sober, E. (2003) "Why likelihood?" in M. Taper and S. Lee (eds) *The Nature of Scientific Evidence*, Chicago: University of Chicago Press, available online at http://philosophy.wisc.edu/forster.

Gould, S. J. (1980) *The Panda's Thumb*, New York: Norton.

Hacking, I. (1987) "The Inverse Gambler's Fallacy: The argument from design. The anthropic principle applied to Wheeler universes," *Mind* 96: 331–40.

—— (1965) *The Logic of Statistical Inference*, Cambridge: Cambridge University Press.

Hempel, C. (1965) "Studies in the logic of confirmation," in *Aspects of Scientific Explanation and Other Essays in the Philosophy of Science*, New York: Free Press.

Hume, D. (1990 [1779]) *Dialogues Concerning Natural Religion*, London: Penguin.

Keynes, J. (1921) *A Treatise on Probability*, London: Macmillan.

Kyburg, H. (1961) *Probability and the Logic of Rational Belief*, Middletown, Connecticut: Wesleyan University Press.

Leslie, J. (1989) *Universes*, London: Routledge.

McMullin, E. (1993) "Indifference principle and anthropic principle in cosmology," *Studies in the History and Philosophy of Science* 24: 359–89.

Paley, W. (1802) *Natural Theology, or, Evidences of the Existence and Attributes of the Deity, Collected from the Appearances of Nature*, London: Rivington.

Royall, R. (1997) *Statistical Evidence – a Likelihood Paradigm*, London: Chapman & Hall.

Sober, E. (2000a) "Evolution and the problem of other minds," *Journal of Philosophy* 97: 365–86.

—— (2000b) "Quine's two dogmas," *Proceedings of the Aristotelean Society*, supplementary volume 74: 237–80.

—— (1999) "Testability," *Proceedings and Addresses of the American Philosophical Association* 73: 47–76, available online at http://philosophy.wisc.edu/sober.

—— (1993) *Philosophy of Biology*, Boulder, Colorado: Westview Press.

Sorenson, R. (1988) *Blindspots*, Oxford: Oxford University Press.

Stigler, S. (1986) *The History of Statistics*, Cambridge, Massachusetts: Harvard University Press.

Swinburne, R. (1990a) "Argument from the fine-tuning of the Universe," in. J. Leslie (ed.) *Physical Cosmology and Philosophy*, New York: Macmillan, pp. 160–79.

—— (1990b) "The limits of explanation," in D. Knowles (ed.) *Explanation and Its Limits*, Cambridge:

Cambridge University Press, pp. 177–93.

—— (1968) "The argument from design," *Philosophy* 43: 199–212.

Turing, A. (1950) "Computing machinery and intelligence," *Mind* 59: 433–60.

van Inwagen, P. (1993) *Metaphysics*, Boulder, Colorado: Westview Press.

Venn, J. (1866) *The Logic of Chance*, New York: Chelsea.

White, R. (2000) "Fine-tuning and multiple universes," *Nous* 34: 260–76.

Chapter 13

Louis P. Pojman

A CRITIQUE OF THE ARGUMENT FROM RELIGIOUS EXPERIENCE

Encounters with God

The heart of religion is and always has been experiential. Encounters with the super-natural, a transcendent dimension, the Wholly Other are at the base of every great religion. Abraham hears a Voice that calls him to leave his family in Haran and venture out into a broad unknown, thus becoming the father of Israel. Abraham's grandson, Jacob, wrestles all night with an angel and is transformed, gaining the name "Israel, prince of God." While tending his father-in-law's flock, Moses is appeared to by "I am that I am" (Yahweh) in the burning bush and ordered to deliver Israel out of slavery into a land flowing with milk and honey. Isaiah has a vision of the Lord "high and exalted, and the train of his robe filled the temple" of heaven. In the New Testament, John, James, and Peter behold Jesus gloriously transformed on the Mount of Transfiguration and are themselves transformed by the experience. After the death of Jesus, Saul is traveling to Damascus to persecute Christians, when he is met by a blazing light and hears a Voice, asking him why he is persecuting the Lord.[1] Changing his name to Paul, he becomes the leader of the Christian missionary move-ment. The Hindu experiences the Atman (soul) as the Brahman (God), "That art Thou," or beholds the glories of Krishna. The Advaitian Hindu merges with the One, as a drop of water merges with the vast ocean. The Buddhist merges with Nirvana or beholds a vision of the Buddha.[2] Allah reveals his holy word, the Koran, to Mohammed. Joan of Arc hears voices calling on her to save her people, and Joseph Smith has a vision of the angel Moroni calling him to do a new work for God.

Saints, mystics, prophets, ascetics, and com-mon believers—of every creed, of every race, in every land, and throughout recorded history—have undergone esoteric experiences that are hard to explain but impossible to dismiss as mere nonsense. Common features appear to link these otherwise disparate experiences to one another, resulting in a common testimony to this Other-ness, a *consensus mysticum*. Rudolf Otto characterizes the religious (or "numinal" spiritual) dimension in all of these experiences as the "mysterium tre-mendum et fascinans."[3] Religion is an unfathom-able mystery, *tremendum* ("to be trembled at"), awe-inspiring, *fascinans* ("fascinating"), and mag-netic. To use a description from Søren Kierke-gaard, religious experience is a "sympathetic antipathy and an antipathetic sympathy" before a deep unknown.[4] Like looking into an abyss, it both repulses and strangely attracts.

An Analysis of Religious Experience

What, then, is the problem with religious experience? If I say that I hear a pleasant tune, and you listen and say, "Yes, I hear it now too," we have no problem; but if you listen carefully and don't hear it, you might well wonder whether I am really hearing sounds or only imagining that I am. Perhaps we could bring in others to check out the matter. If they agree with me, well and good; but if they agree with you and don't hear the sounds, then we have a problem. Perhaps, we could bring in an audiometer to measure the decibels in the room. If the meter confirms my report, then it is simply a case of my having better hearing than you and the rest of the witnesses; but if the meter doesn't register at all, assuming that it is in working order, we would then have good evidence that I am only imagining the sounds. Perhaps, I need to change my claim and say, "Well, I seem to be hearing a pleasant tune."

One problem is that religious experience is typically private. You have the sense of God forgiving you or an angel speaking to you, but I, who am in the same room with you, neither hear, nor see, nor feel anything unusual. You are praying and suddenly feel transported by grace and sense the unity of all reality. I, who am sitting next to you, wonder at the strange expression on your face and ask you if something is wrong. Perhaps your brain is experiencing an altered chemical or electrical state?

Yet, religious experiences of various types have been reported by numerous people, from dairymaids like Joan of Arc to mystics like Teresa of Avila and St. John of the Cross. They cannot be simply dismissed without serious analysis.

There are two levels of problem here: (1) To what degree, if any, is the subject of a religious experience justified in inferring from the psychological experience (the subjective aspect) to the existential or ontological reality of that which is the object of the experience (the objective aspect)? (2) To what degree, if any, does the cumulative witness of those undergoing religious experience justify the claim that there is a God or transcendent reality?

Traditionally, the argument from religious experience has not been one of the "proofs" for God's existence. At best, it has confirmed and made existential what the proofs conveyed with icy logic. Some philosophers, such as C. D. Broad (1887–1971), as well as contemporary philosophers, such as Richard Swinburne and Gary Gutting, believe that the common experience of mystics is *strong justification* or evidence for all of us for the existence of God.[5] Others, such as William James (1842–1910), believe that religious experience is sufficient evidence for the subject himself or herself for the existence of a divine reality, but only constitutes a possibility for the nonexperiencer. That is, religious experience grants us only *weak justification*. Religious skeptics, like Walter Stace (1886–1967) and Bertrand Russell (1872–1970), doubt this and argue that a subjective experience by itself is never a sufficient warrant for making an existential claim (of an object existing outside oneself). It is a fallacy to go from the psychological experience of X to the reality of X.

There are two main traditions regarding religious experience. One, which we can call *mystical*, posits the unity of all reality or the unity of the subject with its object (the mystic is absorbed in God, becomes one with God, etc.). The second type of religious experience can be called simply *religious experience* in order to distinguish it from the mystical. It does not conflate the subject with the object but is a numinal experience wherein the believer (or subject) experiences the presence of God or an angel or Christ or the Holy Spirit, either speaking to or appearing to the experient or forgiving him or her. While in prayer, believers often experience a sense of the presence of God or the Holy Spirit.

Many psychological explanations of religious experience cast doubt on its validity. One of the most famous is the Freudian interpretation. Sigmund Freud said that it was the result of the projection of the father image within oneself. The progression goes like this. When you were a child, you looked upon your father as a powerful hero who could do everything, meet all your needs, and overcome the normal obstacles that hindered your way at every step. When you grew older, you sadly realized that your father was fallible and very finite, indeed, but you still had the need of the benevolent, all-powerful father. So, subconsciously you projected your need for that long-lost parent onto the empty heavens and invented a god for yourself. Because this is a common phenomena, all of us who have successfully "projected daddy onto the big sky" go to church or synagogue or mosque or whatever and worship the illusion on our favorite holy day. But it is a myth. The sky is empty, and the sooner we realize it, the better for everyone.

This is one explanation of religious experience and religion in general. It is not a disproof of God's existence, simply an hypothesis. Even if it is psychologically true that we tend to think of God like a powerful and loving parent, it could still be the case that the parental relationship is God's way of teaching us about himself—by analogy.

In his classic on the subject, *Varieties of Religious Experience* (1902), James describes what he considers the deepest kind of religious experience, mystical experience, a type of experience that transcends our ordinary, sensory experience and that cannot be described in terms of our normal concepts and language. It is "ineffable experience." The experient realizes that the experience "defies expression, that no adequate report of its content can be given in words. It follows from this that its quality must be directly experienced; it cannot be imparted or transferred to others."[6] And yet it contains a noetic quality, a content. It purports to convey truth about the nature of reality, namely, that there is a unity of all things and that unity is spiritual, not material. It is anti-naturalistic, pantheistic, and optimistic. Two other characteristics are predicated to this state. Mystical states are *transient*—that is, they cannot be sustained for long—and they are *passive*—that is, the mystic is acted upon by divine deliverance, grace. We can prepare ourselves for the experience, but it is something that happens to us, not something that we do.

James is cautious about what can be deduced

from mystic experience. Although mystic states are and ought to be absolutely authoritative over the individuals to whom they come, "no authority emanates from them which should make it a duty for those who stand outside of them to accept their revelations uncritically." But their value is that they provide us a valid alternative to the "non-mystical rationalistic consciousness, based on understanding and the senses alone. They open up the possibility of other orders of truth, in which, so far as anything in us vitally responds to them, we may freely continue to have faith."

Broad goes even further than James. In his book *Religion, Philosophy, and Psychical Research* (1930), he likens the religious sense to an ear for music. There are a few people on the negative end who are spiritually tone deaf and a few on the positive end who are the founders of religion, the Bachs and Beethovens. In between are the ordinary followers of religion, who are like the average musical listener, and above them are the saints, who are likened to those with a very fine ear for music.

The chief difference is that religion, unlike music, says something about the nature of reality. Is what it says true? Does religious experience lend any support to the truth claims of religion? Is religious experience "veridical," and are the claims about "the nature of reality which are an integral part of the experience, true or probable?" Broad considers the argument from mystical agreement:

1   There is an enormous unanimity among the mystics concerning the spiritual nature of reality.

2   When there is such unanimity among observers as to what they take themselves to be experiencing, it is reasonable to conclude that their experiences are veridical (unless we have good reason to believe that they are deluded).

3   There are no positive reasons for thinking that mystical experiences are delusive.

4   ∴. It is reasonable to believe that mystical experiences are veridical.

Premise 3 is weak, for there is evidence that mystics are neuropathic or sexually repressed. Broad considers these charges, admits some plausibility in them, but suggests that they are not conclusive. Regarding the charge of neuropathology, he urges that "one might need to be slightly 'cracked' in order to have some peep-holes into the super-sensible world"; with regard to sexual abnormality, it could simply be the case that no one who was "incapable of strong sexual desires and emotions could have anything worth calling religious experience."

His own guarded judgement is that, given what we know about the origins of religious belief and emotions, there is no reason to think that religious experience is "specially likely to be delusive or misdirected," so that religious experience can be said to offer us strong justification for a transcendent reality.

Gutting develops Broad's strong-justification thesis further, arguing that religious experience "establishes the existence of a good and powerful being concerned about us, and [this] justifies a central core of religious belief."[7] On this basis, he argues that the essential validity of religion is vindicated. However, like Broad, he finds that this sort of justified belief "falls far short of the claims of traditional religions and that detailed religious accounts are nearly as suspect as nonreligious accounts. The heart of true religious belief is a realization that we have *access* to God but only minimal reliable *accounts* of his nature and relation to us." Gutting develops three criteria that veridical religious experiences must meet: They must be repeatable, be experienced by many in many diverse climes and cultures, and issue forth in morally better lives.

But in arguing for the strong-justification thesis, Gutting seems to me to have gone too far. A strong justification makes it rationally obligatory for everyone to believe in the conclusion of an argument, in this case, that God exists. A weak justification only provides rational support for those who have an "of-God" experience (or already accept the worldview that made such experiences likely). Gutting believes that he has given a strong justification for religious belief, sufficient to establish the existence of God, but there are reasons to suppose that the argument from religious experience offers, at best, only weak justification.

A Critique of the Strong-Justification Thesis

Three criticisms of the strong thesis are the following:

1   Religious experience is too amorphous and disparate for us to generalize from in the way Gutting would have us do. That is, there are many varieties of religious experiences, which seem mutually contradictory or vague, so that it is not clear whether we can give the proper criteria necessary to select "of-God" experiences as veridical or having privileged status.

2   Justification of belief in the veridicality of religious experience is circular, so that the belief in it will rest on premises that are not self-evident to everyone. In effect, all assessment of the veridicality of such experience depends on background beliefs.

3   When taken seriously as a candidate for veridical experience, religious experience has the liability of not being confirmed in the same way that perceptual experience is. That is, although religous experience may sometimes be veridical, it cannot be checked like ordinary perceptual experience, nor can we make predictions on account of it. This indicates that it cannot be used as an argument for the existence of God in the way that Gutting uses it.

Let us look closer at these counterarguments.

Religious Experience is Amorphous and Varied

Religious experience is amorphous and too varied to yield a conclusion with regard to the existence of God. Consider the various types of religious experiences, most of which can be documented in the literature:

1   S senses himself absorbed into the One, wherein the subject-object distinction ceases to hold.
2   One senses the unity of all things and that she is nothing at all.
3   The Buddhist monk who is an atheist senses the presence of the living Buddha.
4   One senses the presence of God, the Father of our Lord Jesus Christ.
5   The Virgin Mary appears to S (in a dream).
6   The Lord Jesus appears to Paul on the road one afternoon, though no one else realizes it but him.
7   One senses the presence of Satan, convincing him that Satan is the highest reality.
8   Achilles is appeared to by the goddess Athene, whom he believes to be descended from Zeus's head. She promises that he will win the battle on the morrow.
9   Allah appears to S and tells him to purify the land by executing all infidels (e.g., Jews and Christians) whose false worship corrupts the land.
10   A guilt-ridden woman senses the presence of her long-deceased father, assuring her that he has forgiven her of her neglect of him while he was aging and dying.
11   A mother senses the presence of the spirit of the river, telling her to throw back her deformed infant because it belongs to the river and not to her.
12   One senses the presence of the Trinity and understands how it could be that the three persons are one God, but he cannot tell others.
13   One senses the presence of the demiurge who has created the universe but makes

no pretense to be omnipotent or omnibenevolent.
14   An atheist senses a deep infinite gratitude for the life of his son without in the least believing that a god exists (George Nakhnikian's personal example).
15   An atheist has a deep sense of nothingness in which she is absolutely convinced that the universe has manifested itself to her as a deep void.

The problem for those who would strongly justify the practice of religious experience—that is, show that we are rationally obligated to believe the content of the experience—is to differentiate the valid interpretations from the invalid. Which of these experiences are valid? That is, do any of these guarantee the truth of the propositions contained in the experience? For the believer or experient, each is valid for him or her, but why should the nonexperient accept any of these reports? And why should the experient continue to believe the content of the report himself after it is over and after he notes that there are other possible interpretations of it or that others have had mutually contradictory experiences? It would seem that they cancel each other out. Note the disparity of different types of "nonphysical" or religious experiences in the preceding list. There is not even any consensus that there is one supreme being, who is benevolent. Experiences 1 through 3 do not involve a divine being at all. Contrary to what Gutting says about the virtual universality of god experiences, the branches of Buddhism and Hinduism (in experiencing Nirvana) have religious experiences without experiencing a god. Furthermore, experience 7 supposes that the supreme being is evil, and experience 13 denies omnibenevolence. Experiences 14 and 15 have all the self-authenticating certainty of a religious experience but involve a conviction that no God exists. Do we understand how to distinguish genuine religious experiences from "spiritually" secular ones like experience 14? Why should we believe that the testimony of "of-God" experients is veridical, but not the other types (e.g., 1–3, 7–9, 11, 13, and 15) that are inconsistent with it? The very private nature of religious experience should preclude out being hasty in inferring from the psychological state to the reality of the object of the experience.

Gutting recognizes the diversity of religious experiences but fails to realize how troublesome this is for his thesis. He tries to find a core in these experiences to the effect that there is a "good and powerful non-human being who cares about us."[8] Gutting admits that we can't derive very much from "of-God" experiences, only that there is a being who is more powerful than us, very powerful and very good. But even if his argument were to show this, would it be sufficient as a definition of "God"? What would be the difference between this and experience 13, Plato's finite demiurge, or experience 10, the guilt-ridden woman's sense of her father, who presumably was both mentally and physically more powerful than she? (He was Arthur Conan Doyle, a genius and pugilist.) How would this show that there is a God, whom we should worship? How would this differ from ancestor worship or polytheism? Or a visitor from outer space? All of these could be "powerful, good, nonhuman, and caring for us." Why should we prefer the "of God" experiences to the "of-a-supreme-devil" experiences? Gutting rejects the notion of self-authentication as the guarantee for the veridicality of these religious experiences,[9] but if this is so, how does the experient tell the difference between the non-human being who cares for her and one who only pretends to care? And how does one reidentify the being who has appeared to him in a nonsensory form?

Religious Experience is Circular

Justification of belief in religious experience is circular, so that the belief in it will rest on premises that are not self-evident to everyone. If I am right about the difficulties in singling out "of-God" experiences from other deeply felt experiences, it would seem that we can only justify belief in the content of religious experience through circular reasoning, by setting forth hypothetical assumptions that we then take as constraints on the experience itself. For example, we suppose that God's ways are mysterious and beyond finding out, and so we are ready to accept our fellow believer's testimony of a deep "of-God" experience. A polytheist in East Africa already believes that the hippopotamus-god appears to women with deformed children in dreams, asking for them back and so credits his wife with a veridical experience when she reports that she has had such an encounter in a dream.

It would seem, then, that whether or not our interpretations of religious experience are justified depends on our background beliefs and expectations. Our beliefs appear to form a network, or web, in which all our beliefs are variously linked and supported by other beliefs. Some beliefs (call them "core beliefs"—e.g., my belief that $2 + 2 = 4$ or that there are other minds or that I am not now dreaming) are more centrally located and interconnected than other beliefs. If our core beliefs fall, our entire noetic structure is greatly affected, whereas some beliefs are only loosely connected to our noetic structure (e.g., my belief that the Dodgers will win the pennant this year or that it is better to have an IBM PC computer than a Macintosh). Similarly, religious people and nonreligious people often differ by having fundamentally different propositions at or near the center of their noetic structure. The religious person already is predisposed to have theistic-type religious experiences, whereas the nonreligious person is not usually so disposed (in the literature, Christians have visions of Jesus; Hindus, of Krishna; Buddhists, of Buddha; ancient Greeks, of Athene and Apollo; etc.). If you had been brought up in a Hindu culture, wouldn't you be more likely to have Hindu religious experiences than a Christian type? Would there be enough in common for you to decide that both really converged to a common truth?

All experiencing takes place within the framework of a worldview. Certain features of the worldview may gradually or suddenly change in importance, thus producing a different total picture, but there is no such thing as neutral evaluation of the evidence. As we have noted, what we see depends to some degree on our background beliefs and expectations. The farmer, real estate dealer, and the artist looking at the same field do not see the same field. Neither do the religious person and the atheist see the same thing when evaluating other people's religious experience.

It might be supposed that we could agree on some criteria of assessment in order to arrive at the best explanatory theory regarding religious experience, and there are, of course, competing explanations. There are Freudian, Marxian, and naturalist accounts that, suitably revised, seem to be as internally coherent as the sophisticated theist account. For one account to win our allegiance, it would be necessary for that account to win out over all others. To do this, we would have to agree on the criteria to be met by explanatory accounts. But it could turn out that there are competing criteria, so that theory A would fulfill criteria 1 and 2 better than theories B and C; but B would fulfill criteria 3 and 4 better than the others, whereas C might have the best overall record without fulfilling any of the criteria best of all. It could be a close second in all of them. At this point, it looks like the very formulation and preference of the criteria of assessment depend on the explanatory account that one already embraces. The theist may single out *self-authentication* of the "of-God" experience, but why should that convince the atheist who suspects that criterion in the first place? It seems that there is no unambiguous, noncircular consensus of a hierarchy of criteria.

Gutting is confident of a core content that would be experienced (1) repeatedly, (2) by many, and (3) in such a way that these will be led to live better moral lives.[10] But why should this convince a naturalist who already has a coherent explanation of this phenomena? Plato's "noble lie" (a lie that is useful to achieve social harmony) presumably would have had the same effect, but it still is a lie. Even if we took a survey and discovered that the "of-God" experiences were common to all people, what would that in itself prove? We might still have grounds to doubt its veridicality. As Richard Gale notes, mere unanimity or agreement among observers is not a sufficient condition for the truth of what is experienced:

> Everybody who presses his finger on his eyeball will see double, everybody who stands at a certain spot in the desert will see a mirage, etc. The true criterion for objectivity is the Kantian one: An experience is objective if its contents can be placed in a spatiotemporal order with other experiences in accordance with scientific laws.[11]

Gale may go too far in limiting objectivity to that which is accessible to scientific laws, but his negative comments about unanimity are apposite.

Let me illustrate this point in another way. Suppose Timothy Leary had devised a psychogenic pill that had this result: Everyone taking it had a "deep religious experience" exactly similar to that described by the Western theistic mystics. Would this be good evidence for the existence of God? Perhaps some would be justified in believing it to be. We could predict the kinds of religious experience atheists would have upon taking the pill. But suppose, further, that upon taking two of the same pills, everyone had a deep religious experience common only to a remote primitive tribe: sensing the presence of a pantheon of gods, one being a three-headed hippopotamus who created the lakes and rivers of the world but didn't care a bit about people. The fact that there was complete agreement about what was experienced in these states hardly *by itself* can count for strong evidence for the truth of the existential claims of the experience. It would be likely that theists took the experience to be veridical until they had a double dosage, and it would be likely that the tribes people believed the double dosage to be veridical until they took a single dosage. Doesn't this indicate that it is our accepted background beliefs that predispose us to accept or reject that which fits or doesn't fit into our worldview?

Religious Experience Cannot Be Confirmed

When taken seriously as candidates of veridical experience, religious experience fails in not being confirmed in the same way that perceptual experience is. There is, however, one criterion of assessment that stands out very impressively in the minds of all rational people (indeed, it is one of the criteria of rationality itself) but that is unduly ignored by proponents of the argument from religious experience, like Gutting. It is the Achilles' heel (if anything is) of those who would place too much weight on religious experience as *evidence* for the content of religion. This is the complex criterion of *checkability—predictability* (I link them purposefully). The chemist who says that Avogadro's law holds (i.e., equal volumes of different gases at the same temperature and pressure contain an equal number of molecules) predicts exactly to what degree the inclusion of certain gases will increase the overall weight of a gaseous compound. Similarly, if, under normal circumstances, we heat water to 100°C, we can predict that it will boil. If you doubt my observation, check it out yourself. After suitable experiment, we see these propositions confirmed in such a way as to leave little room for doubt in our minds about their truth. After studying some chemistry, we see that they play a role in a wider network of beliefs that are mutually supportive. The perceptual beliefs force themselves on us.

This notion of predictability can be applied to social hypotheses as well. For instance, an orthodox Marxist states that if his theory is true, capitalism will begin to collapse in industrialized countries. If it doesn't, we begin to doubt Marxism. Of course, the Marxist may begin to revise her theory and bring in *ad hoc* hypotheses to explain why what was expected didn't occur, but the more *ad hoc* hypotheses she has to bring to bear in order to explain why the general thesis isn't happening, the weaker the hypothesis itself becomes. We come to believe many important propositions through experiment, either our own or those of others whom we take as authoritative (for the moment at least). With regard to authority, the presumption is that we could check out the propositions in question if we had time or need to do so.

How do we confirm the truth of religious experience? Does it make any predictions that we could test now in order to say, "Look and see, the fact that X occurs shows that the content of the religious experience is veridical"? How do we check on other people's religious experiences, especially if they purport to be nonsensory perceptions?

The checkability factor is weak in Gutting's account. He claims that we have a duty to believe simply on the report of others, not on the basis of our own experience or any special predictions that the experient would be able to make. But, if the Bible is to be believed, this wasn't always the case, nor should it be today. We read in 1 Kings 18 that to convince the Israelites that Yahweh, and not Baal, was worthy of being worshipped, Elijah challenged the priests of Baal to a contest. He proposed that they prepare a bullock and call on Baal to set fire to it. Then he would do the same with Yahweh. The priests failed, but Elijah succeeded. Convincing evidence! Similarly, at the end of Mark, we read of Jesus telling his disciples that "signs shall follow them that believe; in my name shall they cast out devils; they shall speak with new tongues; they shall take up serpents; and if they drink any deadly thing, it shall not hurt them; they shall lay hands on the sick, and they shall recover" (Mark 16:17,

18). Some believers doubt whether this text is authentic, and others seek to explain it away (e.g., "Jesus only meant his apostles and was referring to the apostolic age"), but if a religion is true, we might well expect some outward confirmation of it, such as we find in Elijah's actions at Mt. Carmel or in Jesus' miracles. The fact that religions experience isn't testable and doesn't yield any non-trivial predictions surely makes it less reliable than perceptual experience.

Not only doesn't religious experience usually generate predictions that are confirmed, but it sometimes yields false predictions. An example is an incident that happened to me as a student in an evangelical Christian college. A group of students believed that the Bible is the inerrant Word of God and cannot contain an untruth. Now the Gospel of Matthew 18:19 records Jesus as saying that "if two of you shall agree on earth as touching anything that they shall ask, it shall be done for them of my Father which is in heaven," and Matthew 17:20 tells of faith being able to move mountains: "Nothing shall be impossible for you." Verses in Mark confirm this, adding that God will answer our prayer if we pray in faith and do not doubt. So, one night several believers prayed through the entire night for the healing of a student who was dying of cancer. They prayed for her in childlike faith, believing that God would heal her. As morning broke, they felt the presence of God among them, telling them that their prayer had been answered. As they left rejoicing and were walking out of the room, they received the news that the woman had just died.

It is interesting to note that none of the participants lost faith in God over this incident. Some merely dismissed it as one of the mysteries of God's ways, others concluded that the Bible wasn't to be taken literally, and still others concluded that they hadn't prayed hard enough or with enough faith. But as far as the argument for the veridicality of the content of religion is concerned, this has to be taken as part of the total data. How it weighs against empirically success-ful prayers or times when the content of the experience was confirmed, I have no idea, and I think Gutting hasn't either. But unless we do, it is hard to see how the argument from religious experience could be used as strong evidence for the existence of God *to anyone else except those who had the experiences*. As James concludes about mystical states (one form of religious experience), whereas those having the experience have a right to believe in their content, "no authority emanates from them which should make it a duty for those who stand outside of them to accept their revelations uncritically."

Let me close with an illustration of what might be a publicly verifiable experience of God, one that would be analogous to the kind of perceptual experience by which we check scientific hypotheses. What if tomorrow morning (8 AM CST) there were a loud trumpet call and all over North America people heard a voice speak out, saying, "I am the Lord, your God, speaking. I have a message for you all. I am deeply saddened by the violence and lack of concern you have for one another. I am calling upon all nations to put aside nuclear weapons. This same message is being delivered to all other nations of Earth at different times today. I want you to know that I will take all means necessary to prevent a nuclear war and punish those nations who persist on the mad course on which they are now embarked. I love each one of you. A few signs will confirm this message. Later today, while speaking to Israel and the Arab states, I will cause an island, which is intended as a homeland for the Palestinians, to appear west of Lebanon in the Mediterranean. I will also cause the Sahara desert to become fruitful in order to provide food for the starving people in that area. But I will have you know that I will not intervene often in your affairs, I making this exception simply because it is an emergency situation."

Imagine that all over the world the same message is conveyed during the next twenty-four hours and the predictions fulfilled. Would your religious faith be strengthened by such an event?

The question is, Why don't religious experiences like this happen? If there is a God, why does he seem to hide from us? Why doesn't God give us more evidence? I leave this question for you to reflect on.

Summary

Religious experience is at the core of the religious life. Throughout the ages, in virtually every culture, people have reported deeply religious, even mystical, experiences that have confirmed their beliefs and added meaning to their lives. Yet problems surround the phenomena: There are discrepancies between accounts, they tend to be amorphous and varied, and they seldom are verified.

Notes

1   "Now as he journeyed, Saul approached Damascus, and suddenly a light from heaven flashed about him. And he fell to the ground and heard a voice saying to him, 'Saul, Saul, why do you persecute me?' And he said, 'Who are you, Lord?' And he said, 'I am Jesus whom you are persecuting; but rise and enter the city, and you will be told what you are to do.' The men traveling with him stood speechless, hearing the voice but seeing no one. Saul arose from the ground; and when his eyes were opened, he could see nothing; so they led him into Damascus" (Acts 9).

2   Here is an illustration of Buddhist meditation:

> Of one who has entered the first trance the voice has ceased; of one who has entered the second trance reasoning and reflection have ceased; of one who has entered the third trance joy has ceased; of one who has entered the fourth trance the inspiration and expiration have ceased; of one who has entered the realm of the infinity of space the perception of form has ceased; of one who has entered the realm of the infinity of consciousness the perception of the realm of the infinity of space has ceased; of one who has entered the realm of nothingness the perception of the realm of the infinity of consciousness has ceased. [*Samyutta-Nikaya* 36:115, in *Buddhism in Translation*, ed. Henry C. Warren (New York: Atheneum, 1973), 384.]

3   Rudolf Otto, *The Idea of the Holy* (Oxford: Oxford University Press, 1958).

4   Søren Kierkegaard, *The Concept of Dread* (Princeton, NJ: Princeton University Press, 1939).

5   C. D. Broad, *Religion, Philosophy, and Psychical Research* (London: Routledge & Kegan Paul, 1930); Richard Swinburne, *The Existence of God* (Oxford: Clarendon Press, 1979); and Gary Gutting, *Religious Belief and Religious Skepticism* (Notre Dame, IN: University of Notre Dame Press, 1982).

6   James, op. cit., 371. Here is another testimony reported by James:

> I remember the night, and almost the very spot on the hilltop, where my soul opened out, as it were, into the Infinite, and there was a rushing together of the two worlds, the inner and the outer. I stood alone with Him who had made me, and all the beauty of the world, and love, and sorrow, and even temptation. I did not seek Him, but felt the perfect unison of my spirit with His. The darkness held a presence that was all the more felt because it was not seen. I could not any more have doubted that He was there than that I was. I felt myself to be, if possible, the less real of the two. (p. 67)

7   Gutting, op. cit.

8   Ibid., 113.

9   Ibid., 145.

10   Ibid., 152.

11   Richard Gale, "Mysticism and Philosophy," *Journal of Philosophy* (1960).

Chapter 14

C. Stephen Layman

GOD AND THE MORAL ORDER

I argue that three theses about the moral order are defensible, that they do not beg the question of God's existence, and that they support theism over naturalism. The three theses are:

1   In every actual case, one has most reason to do what is morally required. (One has most reason to do act x if and only if the strongest relevant reasons favor doing x.)

2   If there is no God and no life after death, then there are cases in which morality requires that one make a great sacrifice that confers relatively modest benefits (or prevents relatively modest harms).

3   If in a given situation one must make a great sacrifice in order to do what is morally required, but the sacrifice confers relatively modest benefits (or prevents relatively modest harms), then one does not have most reason to do what is morally required.

("Sacrifice" is here used in a technical way to indicate a permanent and uncompensated loss of something that is in the agent's long-term best interests.) After arguing for these three theses, I claim that since theism can accommodate them and naturalism cannot, theism has a theoretical advantage over naturalism.

Skepticism about the value of moral arguments for theism is widespread among philosophers. But I maintain that there is a conjunction of theses about the moral order that increases the probability of theism. None of these theses begs the question of God's existence and each is, I believe, plausible upon reflection.

Prior to stating my argument, a number of preliminaries are in order. First, in this paper "God" means "an almighty and wholly good being." By "theism" I mean simply the view that God exists. I assume that a wholly good being is

perfectly loving. I also assume that God would not order reality in such a way that being moral would disadvantage agents in the long run. And I assume that "the long term" likely involves life after death, given theism.[1]

Second, I do not think the moral argument I am advancing can stand alone. Hence, in putting it forward, I assume either that other theistic arguments provide some significant support for the existence of God or that belief in God is properly basic.[2] Thus, I claim merely that my moral argument makes a positive contribution to a larger, rational case for (or defense of) theism.

Third, the argument I wish to advance is primarily an attempt to show that a certain body of evidence supports theism over *naturalism*. By "naturalism" I mean roughly the view that (a) whatever exists is material or dependent (causally or by supervenience) on material things and (b) material things are entirely governed by natural laws. There is no God according to the naturalist and no life after death. When we die, our bodies decay, and we cease to exist.

Fourth, my argument is designed to appeal to those who believe that there are irreducibly moral facts. I assume, for example, that it is a moral fact that *it is wrong to torture people for fun*. Some individuals or groups may deny or ignore this fact, but it remains a fact. (Analogously, it is fact that the earth is round, and this remains a fact even though it is denied by the Flat Earth Society.) In saying that there are *irreducibly* moral facts, I mean that the facts in question cannot correctly be identified with non-evaluative or non-normative facts, such as merely psychological or sociological facts. To illustrate, the fact that *murder is wrong* cannot be identified with the fact that *most humans disapprove of murder*.[3]

Fifth, my argument is meant to appeal to those who accept a fairly traditional understanding of what is morally right and wrong. I shall simply assume, for example, that lying, stealing, and killing are generally wrong, though I shall not beg any questions about cases commonly regarded as allowable exceptions. For instance, I shall assume that it is generally wrong to intentionally kill a human being, but I shall not beg any questions about the usual range of possible exceptions, e.g., killing in self-defense. Of course, some moral theorists reject what I here call a "fairly traditional understanding of what is right and wrong." To illustrate, some act-utilitarians find killing, stealing, and lying permissible in many situations in which these acts are traditionally considered wrong. In my opinion, ethical theories that justify killing, stealing, and

lying in a much wider range of cases than is traditionally allowed are, for that very reason, highly problematic; but I shall not argue that case here. I can only say that those who reject a fairly traditional view about the wrongness of killing, stealing, and lying need read no further, for this paper is unlikely to be of any interest to them.

Sixth, in this paper, locutions such as "This is a moral duty" or "This is a moral requirement" express not merely *prima facie* moral duties but *ultima facie* moral duties. That is, when I say that an act is a moral duty (or that it is morally required), I mean that, in the situation in question, the act is what one morally ought to do *all things considered*. For example, if I say that one is morally required *not to steal* in a certain situation, I do not mean simply that there are some moral considerations against stealing that may be outweighed by other moral considerations in favor of stealing; rather I mean that, taking all morally relevant factors into account, one ought not to steal in that situation.

Seventh, I shall frequently use the locution "x has most reason to do y." A person has "most reason" to do something, in my sense, when the weightiest or strongest reasons favor doing that thing. So, if an agent has most reason to do act A, then taking all relevant reasons into account (e.g., prudential, moral, and aesthetic reasons), they on balance favor performing A. And I assume that "the balance of reasons" is not a merely subjective notion; agents can make mistakes in weighing up reasons for and against an action. For example, in my view, a person who thinks that moral requirements are typically outweighed by personal whims would be making a grave mistake.

Finally, I shall use the word "sacrifice" in a somewhat technical way to indicate *a permanent, net loss of something that is in the long-term best interests of the agent*. So, for present purposes, the word "sacrifice" indicates a permanent loss to the agent, not a temporary one; moreover, it indicates a loss that is not "made up for" in the long run. Of course, as the term is ordinarily used, sacrifices are often temporary and/or compensated, so let me provide some examples of a sacrifice in my sense. Suppose, for the sake of illustration, that there is no life after death, and hence that this earthly life is the only one we've got. On this supposition, if one gave up one's eyesight permanently and this loss was not compensated in any way, then one would have made a sacrifice in my sense of the term, indeed a great sacrifice. Similarly, if a person who is not poor were to give up all of her material goods, and this loss was not compensated in any way, she would have made a sacrifice in my sense of the term, presumably a great one.

I. The Argument Briefly Stated

In this section I will state my argument. My intent is to summarize the basic intuitions that give the argument its plausibility. In the next section I will consider some important objections to the argument and amplify some key points.

My argument has three main premises.[4] Premise (1) is this: *In every actual case one has most reason to do what is morally required.* In other words, in every actual case, if a person is morally required to do some act, then (taking all relevant reasons into account) the balance of reasons favors performing that act. Why think (1) is true? Consider an actual case in which someone has performed an action that you initially find quite puzzling or odd. Then imagine that you become convinced that in performing the action the person was doing his or her moral duty. The act was morally required. Would you not assume that the action was fully justified on this basis? Most of us would and most moral theorists (theist or non-theist) would agree. If an act is my moral duty, then I have overriding reason to perform it. In short, premise (1) is part of our pre-theoretical conception of morality. And thus, if we take an Aristotelian approach to philosophy, (1) is among the appearances to be saved.

We can, however, say a bit more in favor of

(1): If one does not always have most reason to do what is morally required, then why should one be moral? In a given case, considerations of prudence, aesthetics, and/or etiquette may conflict with moral considerations and one faces the question, "How should one act?", where the "should" is not moral but may be interpreted along the following lines: "Which alternative course of action is backed by the strongest or weightiest reasons?" And if we grant that a certain course of action X is backed by the strongest or weightiest reasons, then from a rational point of view X should be done. Moreover, if we agree that the best reasons sometimes favor immoral actions, and yet we give our full allegiance to morality, then our allegiance to morality is irrational in the sense that it involves acting on inferior reasons. But I presume that most of my readers give morality their full allegiance and do not regard this allegiance as involving such irrationality. So, I assume that my readers will find themselves strongly inclined to accept (1).

Before going on, however, I should point out that premise (1) is *not* the claim that one has most reason to do what is morally required in every *logically possible* case. In other words, I have not claimed that (1) is a necessary truth, I have merely claimed that it is true. And I shall soon describe some *logically possible* cases or situations in which it seems to me that the agent would not have most reason to do what is morally required. I regard these cases as *merely* logically possible— I myself do not think that cases combining all of the relevant features occur in the actual world. However, those who are convinced that there is no God and no life after death may be inclined to regard cases of the relevant type as actual, and this may raise questions about premise (1). I shall return to this matter in section II, but for now I will simply make three assertions: (a) since we are discussing an argument for God's existence, I take it that the non-existence of God is not properly assumed in evaluating the truth of my premises, (b) I hope to show that each of my three main premises is either embedded in our pre-theoretical conception of morality or defensible via argument (or both), and (c) my overall strategy is to argue that theism has a theoretical advantage over naturalism because theism can accommodate my three main premises while naturalism cannot.

Premise (2) is as follows: *If there is no God and no life after death, then there are cases in which morality requires that one make a great sacrifice that confers relatively modest benefits (or prevents relatively modest harms).* The following case—let us call it the "Ms. Poore case"—is offered in support of premise (2). Suppose Ms. Poore has lived many years in grinding poverty. She is not starving, but has only the bare necessities. She has tried very hard to get ahead by hard work, but nothing has come of her efforts. An opportunity to steal a large sum of money arises. If Ms. Poore steals the money and invests it wisely, she can obtain many desirable things her poverty has denied her: cure for a painful (but nonfatal) medical condition, a well-balanced diet, decent housing, adequate heat in the winter, health insurance, new career opportunities through education, etc. Moreover, if she steals the money, her chances of being caught are very low and she knows this. She is also aware that the person who owns the money is very wealthy and will not be greatly harmed by the theft. Let us add that Ms. Poore rationally believes that if she fails to steal the money, she will likely live in poverty for the remainder of her life. In short, Ms. Poore faces the choice of stealing the money or living in grinding poverty the rest of her life. In such a case, I think it would be *morally wrong* for Ms. Poore to steal the money; and yet, assuming there is no God and no life after death, failing to steal the money will likely deny her a large measure of personal fulfillment, i.e., a large measure of *what is in her long-term best interests.*[5]

I believe that the Ms. Poore case offers intuitive support for premise (2). However, some may reject (2) on the grounds that *virtue is its own reward,* and hence we are *necessarily* compensated for our *morally required* losses because moral virtue is a great enough benefit to those who possess it

to compensate fully for any losses it entails. Now, I do not doubt that virtue is a benefit to those who possess it. But the suggestion that *perfect* virtue is *necessarily* a great enough benefit to its possessor to compensate fully for any loss it entails strikes me as highly implausible. Consider the following thought experiment.[6] Imagine two people, Mr. Gladwin and Ms. Goodwin. Mr. Gladwin is a morally lukewarm person who happens to be regarded as a paragon of virtue. He is admired by most people, prosperous, loved by his family and friends, and enjoys his life very much. Ms. Goodwin on the other hand is genuinely virtuous—honest, just, and pure in heart. Unfortunately, because of some clever enemies, Ms. Goodwin is widely regarded as wicked. She is in prison for life on false charges. Her family and friends, convinced that she is guilty, have turned against her. She subsists on a bread and water diet. Leaving God out of the picture for the moment, which of these two people is better off? Which is more fulfilled assuming there is no God? Surely it is Gladwin, not Goodwin. And note that even if virtue is of value for its own sake, it isn't the *only* thing of value.[7] In particular, freedom is valuable too. Suppose the warden agrees to release Ms. Goodwin if and only if she commits one morally wrong act. Perhaps her accounting skills enable her to help steal some money for the warden. Now, it seems to me that if there is no God and no life after death, it could easily be in Ms. Goodwin's long-term best interest to act immorally in this sort of case. The choice is roughly between life-long misery and an action that is immoral but produces relatively modest harms. So, it does not seem *necessarily* true that the rewards of *perfect* virtue compensate for the rewards of wrongdoing; nor does it seem *necessarily* true that being *perfectly* virtuous is in the agent's long-term best interest. I conclude that the cases of Ms. Poore and Ms. Goodwin provide strong intuitive support for (2).

The above cases also help to support premise (3): *If in a given case one must make a great sacrifice in order to do what is morally required, but the sacrifice confers* relatively modest benefits (or prevents relatively modest harms), then one does not have most reason to do what is morally required. Further support for this third premise comes from the following principle: *It is always and necessarily prudent to act so as to promote one's long-term best interests.* And therefore, making a great sacrifice (where a sacrifice is an *uncompensated* giving-up of something that is in one's long-term best interests) is not prudent. Premise (3) makes explicit what the cases of Ms. Poore and Ms. Goodwin strongly suggest, namely, that *when considerations of prudence and morality clash, if the prudential considerations are truly momentous while the results of behaving immorally are relatively minor, then morality does not override prudence.*

There are, I recognize, multiple barriers to the acceptance of (3). I shall make two brief comments here and leave more technical issues for the next section. First, it may be helpful to note that if God exists, there will be no genuine conflicts between prudence and morality. The reason is this: to act immorally is to sin; to sin is to alienate oneself from God; and it is never in one's long-term best interests to alienate oneself from God. Accordingly, the situation envisioned in the antecedent of premise (3) could not be actual if God exists, for in doing one's moral duty one prevents a very great harm to oneself, namely, alienation from God.

Second, it might be claimed that (a) acting immorally even just once will ruin one's character and (b) to ruin one's character is to incur a great loss; hence, one always has most reason to act morally. The problem with this objection to premise (3) is that (a) is manifestly false. For one's character can be summed up in terms of traits (e.g., being fair, being responsible, being wise, being loving, etc.), each trait being a tendency to act in a certain way. But many or even most people can do something wrong *in what they regard as a rare special case* without thereby altering significantly the basic behavioral tendencies associated with their traits of character.[8]

We have, then, three premises, each of which is plausible on reflection and none of which begs

the question of God's existence. Let us now examine the logic of the situation:

> Premise 1. In every actual case, one has most reason to do what is morally required.
>
> Premise 2. If there is no God and no life after death, then there are cases in which morality requires that one make a great sacrifice that confers relatively modest benefits (or prevents relatively modest harms).
>
> Premise 3. If in a given case one must make a great sacrifice in order to do what is morally required, but the sacrifice confers relatively modest benefits (or prevents relatively modest harms), then one does not have most reason to do what is morally required.

Premises (2) and (3) imply the following sub-conclusion:

> 4. If there is no God and no life after death, then in some cases one does not have most reason to do what is morally required.

But (4) and (1) combine to yield:

> 5. "There is no God and no life after death" is false, i.e., either God exists or there is life after death (or both).

Given (5), one can still avoid the conclusion that God exists by arguing that there would be (or at least might well be) a life after death in *which the best interests of morally virtuous persons are realized* even if God does not exist. This move is not, however, open to the naturalist. So, let us consider some objections that, if correct, would prevent us from arriving at step (5).

II. Objections and Replies

Objection 1. Your argument presupposes that, on pain of irrationality, one needs some non-moral or prudential reason to do what is morally required; but this presupposition is false. In fact, to be genuinely morally virtuous, one must do the morally right thing simply because it is right. Those who do the right thing for an ulterior, prudential reason are, from a moral point of view, substandard.

Reply. My argument does not involve this presupposition. Granted, from the moral standpoint, one should do the right thing for moral reasons. But what if there are possible situations in which the weightiest reasons favor doing something *besides* what's morally required? On the assumption that agents can find themselves in such situations, it would seem that agents are rationally justified in doing something other than what's morally required. So, I'm not suggesting people should behave morally for ulterior motives, I'm raising the question whether they "should" behave morally at all in certain hypothetical situations. (The "should" in scare quotes does not express the dictates of morality, but the dictates of rationality, i.e., what one *should* do is what one has the weightiest reasons to do). Let me elaborate briefly.

Assuming that conflicts between morality and prudence occur, I agree that moral reasons *can* outweigh prudential ones. For example, suppose ten children will die a very painful death if I don't help them, but helping them will produce a very slight *net* decrease in the satisfaction of my long-term best interests. Such cases are not actual, in my view, but if they do occur, then it seems clear to me that the moral reasons would outweigh the conflicting prudential ones. And so, in such cases, I would have most reason to act morally even though prudence runs contrary to morality.

What I question is the rationality of doing what's morally required if the gains (for all affected) are relatively minor and the long-term disadvantages to the agent are momentous. In such hypothetical cases it seems to me that the strongest reasons do not back morality. Thus, my argument draws attention to the fact that certain

metaphysical views are demoralizing, in the sense that they make acting on weaker reasons the price of moral virtue in some instances. It may be useful to illustrate this point with a rather far-fetched metaphysical view: Suppose a very powerful Deity is in control of the universe but the Deity particularly delights in ensuring that those who do their duty for duty's sake fare very poorly as compared to the self-serving phonies, the morally lukewarm, and the wicked. And suppose the free agents are well aware of these grim metaphysical facts. In such a situation it seems to me that the free agents would often lack overriding reason to do their moral duty. Again, my point is not that people should do the right things to get a reward; rather, my point is that in certain hypothetical situations people lack overriding reason to do the right thing.

Objection 2. The cases you describe in support of premises (2) and (3) are bound to be taken by the naturalist as evidence against premise (1). Also, by attacking or qualifying the thesis that *virtue is its own reward,* you have undermined the only ground a naturalist has for accepting (1). Thus, although your premises may be logically consistent, your argument is dialectically flawed; in effect you give the naturalist good reason to reject premise (1).[9]

Reply. First of all, my moral cases (i.e., Ms. Poore, Ms. Goodwin) provide evidence against premise (1) *only* on the assumption that there is no God and no life after death. But one can hardly make this assumption and give the argument an open-minded run for its money; it is after all an argument for God's existence! So, if the naturalist regards my moral cases as evidence against (1), the naturalist is begging the question, and the dialectical error is on the naturalist's side.

Second, I doubt that many people accept (1) on the grounds that *virtue is its own reward.* I doubt that (1) is typically accepted on the basis of an argument at all. Rather, when certain questions are posed, we simply find that we are presupposing (1). To illustrate, consider an (admittedly contrived) moral theory: *one is always morally required to do what is best for others.*[10] On this theory, the agent's interests are irrelevant to morality—the agent must do what is best for others regardless of the cost to himself. But suppose a significant sacrifice on my part would only marginally improve someone else's lot, e.g., Sue's minor headache can somehow be relieved if I give up my annual two-week vacation. This moral theory seems to demand that I give up my vacation. Well, why not accept this theory of morality? One good reason seems to be this: it fails to give self-interest its due, and thus yields a situation in which *alleged* moral requirements are overridden by self-interest. The point, of course, is not that self-interest does override morality, but rather that the overridingness of moral reasons is presupposed in our moral theorizing. And of course, we bring this presupposition to our moral theorizing because it is deeply embedded in our pre-theoretical conception of morality.[11]

Third, the appeal to *virtue is its own reward* is not the only possible defense of premise (1). As noted previously, if (1) is false, then immoral actions are sometimes backed by reasons as strong as (or stronger than) those backing the moral alternative. But if immoral actions are sometimes backed by reasons as strong as (or stronger than) those backing the moral alternative, then the institution of morality lacks rational authority. That is, the system of morality does not a have blanket endorsement from the rational point of view—only parts of it do. And even if those parts are very large, this consequence is not something most of us can readily accept.

Objection 3. Some moral theorists, in company with Kant and R.M. Hare, claim that moral reasons necessarily or by definition override all others.[12] If such views are correct, then premise (3) must be false. For if moral reasons necessarily override all other kinds of reasons, then there can be no situation in which one lacks most reason to act morally; but (3) presupposes that such situations are possible.

Reply. No dictionary defines "morality" in terms of overridingness. So, those who *define* moral reasons as overriding ones are offering a *theory* and we need evidence for the theory. Similarly, the claim that moral reasons *necessarily* override all others is not obvious, and it won't do to argue for it in an inductive fashion by citing cases. The problem with such an inductive approach is that it runs afoul of the very sorts of cases that serve as the focus of this paper. The hypothetical cases described in section I cast doubt on the claim that "It is *necessarily* true that moral reasons are overriding." So, the situation seems to be that most of us find ourselves believing that, in every actual case, moral reasons are overriding; but—unless we take for granted certain highly controversial metaphysical theses (see the response to objection 5 below)—we lack good reason to think that "Moral reasons are overriding" is a *necessary* truth.

Objection 4. Kantians argue that *whenever an agent acts immorally, she acts on a maxim that she cannot consistently will to be universal law.* But it is irrational to act on a maxim one cannot consistently will to be universal law; hence, one always has most reason to act morally; therefore, premise (3) is false.

Reply. My reply is twofold. First, the Kantian thesis is in fact highly dubious. Consider the case of Ms. Poore. How should we describe the maxim she is acting on? Presumably along the following lines: *Whenever I find myself in a circumstance in which (a) I am very poor but not destitute, (b) I can easily steal a large sum of money with impunity from a very rich person, (c) I will doom myself to enduring and wretched poverty by not stealing, and (d) I will inflict little harm by stealing, I shall steal.* Why can't Ms. Poore consistently will this maxim to be universal law? The clauses of the maxim ensure that it can be applied only rarely. And I see no conceptual difficulties regarding theft (or the institution of private property) if we contemplate a world (similar to the actual world but) in which all relevantly situated persons act in accord with the maxim. And although Ms. Poore might not like to have money stolen from her if she were rich, she might nevertheless be *willing* to have anyone in her current circumstances act in accord with the stated maxim, and willing to take a chance on being stolen from in the event that she herself should become rich. Perhaps a few Kantians (certainly not Kant himself) will agree with all this and adopt a revisionist morality that allows stealing (lying, etc.) in the cases I've described. But since such revisionism runs contrary to my settled judgment of the cases, I do not think it provides the naturalist with a cost-free response to my argument.

Second, suppose we grant that *if one acts immorally, one acts on a maxim one cannot consistently will to be universal law.* Does it follow logically that one has most reason to be moral? Not clearly. For one may have very strong reasons to make a special exception in one's own case. And even if making a special exception in one's own case is always immoral, it may sometimes be rational.[13] One can imagine Ms. Poore saying, "Even if I cannot consistently will that all possible agents in my situation commit theft, the fact is relatively few people will ever be in my situation and in this case there's just too much at stake for me personally in doing the moral thing."

Objection 5. Not only naturalists but many theists must reject your argument, namely, those theists, very common in the Christian tradition, who hold that God exists necessarily, is necessarily perfectly morally good, and is necessarily omnipotent. Let us call these theists "classical theists." According to classical theists, it is not logically possible for there to be a situation in which an agent makes a great sacrifice (which involves a permanent and uncompensated loss of something in the agent's long-term best interests) in order to do something morally required. For a perfectly good and omnipotent Deity would not set up a moral order in which doing one's duty is contrary to one's long-term best interests. Moreover, such a Deity exists in every possible world and is perfectly good and omnipotent in every possible world, according to the classical theist. Hence, your argument

countenances situations that are simply not possible according to the classical theist.

Reply. First, since I am arguing for God's existence, it would hardly be dialogically appropriate for me to begin by assuming that God cannot fail to exist. Moreover, the classical theist herself can grant the possibility that God doesn't exist *for the sake of the argument.* So, I don't think my argumentative strategy is necessarily in conflict with classical theism.

Second, the classical theist should accept all three of my premises: Premise (2) obviously has an impossible antecedent given classical theism ("If there is no God . . ."). Hence, by a familiar principle of modal logic, classical theists should regard (2) as a necessary truth. Premise (3) is also necessarily true given classical theism, for reasons alluded to in objection 5: A perfectly good God would never set up a moral order in which doing one's duty is contrary to one's long-term best interests and such a God exists in every possible world, according to the classical theist. Hence, the situation envisaged in the antecedent of (3) is impossible, and (3) itself is necessary. Finally, classical theists should accept premise (1), but deny my claim that (1) is contingent. Since immoral behavior is sin, sin alienates one from God, and alienation from God undermines personal fulfillment, I presume prudence never trumps morality if God exists. Hence, one always has most reason to act morality, if God exists. Moreover, God exists in every possible world according to the classical theist (and is both perfectly good and omnipotent in every possible world). Of course, this way of arguing for the *necessity* of premise (1) is not available to the naturalist or indeed to any type of non-theist.

III. Completing the Argument

If my argument up to this point is any good, then it has given some support to step (5), i.e., the thesis that either God exists or there is life after death (or both). However, (5) could be true even if God does not exist; for it may be that there is no God but there is a life after death in which the best interests of the morally virtuous are realized. So, in this section I wish to complete my moral argument for theism by defending the following premise:

6. It is likely that if there is a life after death in which the long-term best interests of the morally virtuous are realized, then God exists.

If premise (6) is defensible, then if it is conjoined with premises (1) through (3), we have an argument that lends positive support to theism. In defending (6), I shall rely on two assumptions. First, I shall assume that there is no life after death given naturalism. Second, I shall assume that the two best theories of the afterlife centrally involve either theism or reincarnation.

Given that reincarnation occurs, each person's soul is transferred to another body at some time after death. So, given reincarnation, there is life after death. And given the doctrine of karma, one's degree of moral virtue determines one's circumstances in the next life. Indeed, if the law of karma governs the universe, the more nearly one lives up to the demands of morality, the better one's circumstances in the next life.[14] Thus, the traditional Hindu doctrines of reincarnation and karma combine to yield a cosmic moral order.

Of course, a doctrine of reincarnation could be combined with theism, but we are here concerned with versions of reincarnation that are in logical competition with theism, i.e., views that deny the existence of any sort of personal Deity. And it seems to me that such views are self-undermining, for the complexity of the moral order they postulate provides good evidence of an Intelligent and Moral Designer. Consider: given that reincarnation and karma hold in the absence of any Deity, the universe is governed not only by physical laws but by impersonal moral laws. These moral laws must be very complicated, for they have to regulate the connection between each soul's moral record in one life and that soul's total circumstances in its next life, including which body it has and the degree of happiness (and/or misery) it experiences. Accordingly, these laws must somehow take into account every act, every intention, and every choice of every moral agent and ensure that the agent receives nothing less than his or her just deserts in the next life. Now, the degree of complexity involved here is not only extraordinarily high, it is also complexity that serves a moral end, namely, justice. Such complexity can hardly be accepted as a brute fact. *Highly complex order serving a moral end* is a phenomenon that legitimates appeal to an intelligent cause. And if the order is on a scale far surpassing what can reasonably be attributed to human intelligence, the appeal to divine intelligence is surely justified. Thus, the moral order postulated by nontheistic reincarnation provides evidence for theism.[15]

To sum up, even if reincarnation occurs in accordance with the principle of karma, the nature of the postulated moral order lends support to theism. Therefore, it seems likely that if there is a life after death in which the ultimate fulfillment of the morally virtuous is realized, then God exists. And this thesis, together with the argument of section 1, provides at least some positive support for the proposition that God exists.[16]

Notes

1   Here is a sketch of an argument linking theism and life after death: A wholly loving God would care deeply about the fulfillment of human creatures and would not leave human creatures frustrated and unfulfilled if he is able to provide the means of fulfillment. Yet, as virtually everyone will admit, in this earthly life, the deepest yearnings of human beings are not fulfilled, and many human beings have led lives characterized by frustration. An almighty God is surely able to provide the means of fulfillment by providing human creatures with a

form of existence after death in which their deepest yearnings can be satisfied. So, if God exists, life after death seems likely.

2 A belief is *properly basic* if it does not need to be based on other beliefs in order to be rational or warranted. Note that, even if belief in God is properly basic, arguments for God's existence are not necessarily rendered pointless; for even when a proposition is already known or rationally believed, independent lines of support can still have a significant confirming role. For a defense of the thesis that belief in God can be properly basic, see Alvin Plantinga, "Reason and Belief in God," in Alvin Plantinga and Nicholas Wolterstorff, eds., *Faith and Rationality* (New York: University of Notre Dame Press, 1983), 16–93 and Alvin Plantinga, *Warranted Christian Belief* (New York: Oxford University Press, 2000), 167–198.

3 Though I shall not discuss the issue in this paper, I believe that severe problems result from the denial of moral facts. See David Brink, "Moral Realism and the Sceptical Argument from Disagreement and Queerness" *Australasian Journal of Philosophy* 62 (1984): 111–125. This article is anthologized in Louis Pojman, ed., *Ethical Theory: Classical and Contemporary Readings*, second edition (Belmont, CA: Wadsworth, 1995), 469–476. For a well-known rejection of moral facts, see J.L. Mackie, *Ethics: Inventing Right and Wrong* (New York: Penguin Books, 1977), 15–49. I should also note that my assumption that moral facts cannot be identified with non-evaluative (or non-normative) facts is incompatible with certain (I think rather extreme) versions of the divine command theory, e.g., versions claiming that *moral wrongness* is identical with *being forbidden by an all powerful being*. On the other hand, my assumption is compatible with divine command theories that identify *moral wrongness* with *being forbidden by a morally good or loving Deity*.

4 My premises are partly inspired by a quartet of theses discussed in David O. Brink, "A Puzzle About the Rational Authority of Morality," ed. James E. Tomberlin, *Philosophical Perspectives*, 6 Ethics, 1992 (Atascadero, CA: Ridgeview Publishing Company, 1992), 1–26.

5 In discussing this case with various philosophers, I have found that certain ways of elaborating the case make it more convincing to some. (A) For example, to some it might make a difference if Ms. Poore steals the money partly to enrich the lives of her children (e.g., by providing them with better clothing, food they enjoy, etc). I welcome such elaborations, but with this proviso: it is essential that the elaborations not be such as to give Ms. Poore a moral duty that plausibly overrides her duty not to steal. For example, if she steals the money to pay for expensive surgery needed to save the life of one of her children, it would be at least plausible to suppose that her duty to preserve life overrides her duty not to steal. I have presented the case simply as one in which *momentous prudential concerns compete with the moral duty not to steal.* (B) Details about Ms. Poore's emotional life can make a difference in how one responds to the case. For example, if she is going to be wracked with literally unending and intense guilt for stealing the money, then it presumably is not to her advantage to steal it. But there is no need to suppose that Ms. Poore has this type of sensitivity. We may imagine her to be a person who is clear-headed, who realizes that she is in a very special sort of moral situation, and who is not going to berate herself for performing the action that is backed by the strongest reasons.

6 This thought experiment is borrowed in its essentials from Richard Taylor, "Value and the Origin of Right and Wrong," in Louis Pojman, ed., *Ethical Theory: Classical and Contemporary Readings* (Belmont, California: Wadsworth, 1989), 115–121. For some interesting, brief reflections on the difficulty of showing that it is in everyone's best interest to be virtuous, see Bernard Williams, *Ethics and the Limits of Philosophy* (Cambridge, Massachusetts: Harvard University Press, 1985), 43–45. Also see, Peter Singer, *Practical Ethics* (London: Cambridge University Press, 1979), 201–220.

7 Thus I leave open the disputed question whether the virtues are good merely as means to an end, e.g., that being fair is not good for its own sake, but good as a means to harmonious and rewarding relationships with others.

8 For an interesting set of reflections confirming the main point of this paragraph, see Christine M. Korsgaard, *The Sources of Normativity* (New York: Cambridge University Press, 1996), 102–103. ("You may know that if you always did this sort of thing your identity would disintegrate, . . ., but you

also know that you can do it just this once without any such result," p. 102.)

9   I am indebted to Eleonore Stump for helping me to phrase this objection in a clear fashion.

10 The example is borrowed from Sarah Stroud, "Moral Overridingness and Moral Theory," *Pacific Philosophical Quarterly* 79 (1998), 170–189.

11 Here perhaps is the place to note that some ethicists have rejected the thesis that moral requirements always override all other considerations. See, for example, Philippa Foot, "Are Moral Considerations Overriding?" in *Virtues and Vices* (Berkeley and Los Angeles: University of California Press, 1978), pp. 181–188. The argumentation in Foot's essay seems to me unconvincing, however. For example, Foot points out that people who care about morality will sometimes say things of this sort, "It was morally wrong to do X but I *had to* do X to avoid disaster for myself, my family, or my country." But it seems to me that this sort of statement does not prove even that the speaker believes that the moral reasons are overridden by other reasons. After all, a smoker may say, "I know that the best and strongest reasons favor not smoking, but I *had to* light up anyway." Notoriously, we humans often feel we "have to" do things that are backed by inferior reasons.

12 For a helpful discussion of conceptions of morality and overridingness, see Richard Swinburne, *Responsibility and Atonement* (Oxford: Clarendon Press, 1989), 9–33.

13 See, e.g., Philippa Foot, "Morality as a System of Hypothetical Imperatives," in *Virtues and Vices and Other Essays in Moral Philosophy* (Los Angeles, CA: University of California Press, 1978), 157–173.

14 According to traditional Hindu thought, if one is *perfectly* moral, one deserves *moksha* (salvation), i.e., deliverance from *samsara* (the cycle of birth and death). This deliverance is generally equated with a kind of oneness with ultimate reality.

15 The main point of this paragraph is borrowed from Robin Collins, "Eastern Religions," in Michael J. Murray, ed., *Reason for the Hope Within* (Grand Rapids, MI: Eerdmans, 1999), 206.

16 I wish to thank Terence Cuneo, Jeanine Diller, Paul Draper, Evan Fales, Peter Forrest, Douglas Geivett, Phillip Goggans, Kenneth Einar Himma, Daniel Howard-Snyder, Robert Koons, Mark Murphy, Stephen Porter, and Eleonore Stump for thoughtful comments on various earlier drafts of this paper.

PART 3

Evil and Divine Hiddenness

INTRODUCTION TO PART 3

WHILE THE READINGS IN THE PREVIOUS section focused on presentations and criticisms of influential arguments for the existence of God, the readings in this section focus on arguments which have as their conclusions the claim that God doesn't exist. In particular, the readings focus on versions of the problem of evil (sometimes also called the argument from evil) and the problem of divine hiddenness (or the argument from hiddenness).

Despite widespread reference to "the problem of evil," there is no single argument or problem deserving of this phrase at the expense of others. Rather, there are a plethora of arguments that fall under the scope of this phrase. As Peter van Inwagen notes in his recent book on the topic,

> The word 'evil' when it occurs in phrases like "the argument from evil" or 'the problem of evil' means 'bad things'. What, then, is the problem of evil; what is the problem of bad things? It is remarkably hard to say. . . . I think the reason is this: there are really a lot of different problems, problems intimately related to one another but nevertheless importantly different from one another, that have been lumped together under the heading 'the problem of evil'. The phrase is used to refer to this family of problems collectively. . . . Any attempt to give a precise sense of the term 'the problem of evil', any attempt to identify it with any "single, reasonably well-defined" philosophical or theological problem, or any single, reasonably well-defined problem of any sort, runs afoul of this fact.[1]

It is common, however, to differentiate two general versions of the argument from evil; these are commonly referred to under the titles the "logical problem of evil" and the "evidential problem of evil."

Versions of the logical problem of evil (sometimes also called the deductive problem of evil) attempt to show that there is a logical inconsistency between the existence of evil and the existence of an omnipotent, omniscient, omnibenevolent God. A simplified version of the argument is as follows:

1   God, if He exists, is omnipotent or all-powerful.
2   God, if He exists, is omniscient or all-knowing.
3   God, if He exists, is omnibenevolent or all-good.
4   If an omnipotent, omniscient, omnibenevolent God existed, then there would be no evil.
5   Evil exists.
6   Therefore, God does not exist.

The logical problem of evil has historically been very influential. Versions of it can be found as far back as Epicurus (341–270 B.C.), and one can find proponents of it throughout every period of philosophy.

Recently, however, the argument has come under considerable scrutiny; it is now widely agreed that the logical problem of evil is a failure because there is no logical contradiction between the existence of a perfect being and the existence of evil. That there is no logical contradiction can be shown by telling a story that, if that story were true, would show why evil could exist even if an all-perfect God also existed. Such stories are commonly referred to as "defenses." Defenses aim to give a morally sufficient reason God could have for allowing evil to exist. (In contrast, theodicies aim to give the actual reason God has for allowing evil.) It is common for defenses (and theodicies) to claim that the greater good served by God's allowing evil is the good of agents having free will; for this reason, such defenses are called "free will defenses."

The first reading of this section, Peter van Inwagen's "The Argument from Evil," presents a version of the free will defense that is, as he puts it, "true for all we know." According to van Inwagen, the reason there is evil in the world is that it is a great good for rational beings to have free will. But if God creates such beings with free will, then not even God can ensure how that free will is used. "Having this power of free choice, some or all human beings misuse it and produce a certain amount of evil. But free will is a sufficiently great good that its existence outweighs the evils that result from its abuse" (215). Since the existence of evil is justified by a greater good, it is not gratuitous and thus does not count against the existence or goodness of God. Such is the heart of van Inwagen's defense. Furthermore, in order to show that the logical problem of evil fails, van Inwagen's story need not actually be true; it must merely be possibly true insofar as *if it were true*, it would demonstrate that both God and evil could co-exist, thereby showing that the two are not contradictory.

The second reading, Whitley Kaufman's "Karma, Rebirth, and the Problem of Evil," addresses the problem of evil from the perspective of Indian religions. Kaufman neither defends nor argues for karma and reincarnation, but instead presupposes them to construct a version of the free will defense which claims that all of the evils an individual suffers in this life can be explained by that person's moral failings in previous lives. He then considers a number of objections to this argument, concluding that the eastern doctrine of karma ultimately fails as a defense for all evils.

Suppose for the moment that some version of the free will defense is true, and that as a result God is justified in allowing evil in the world as a result of the good of our having free will. This, by itself, doesn't seem to account for all the evil in the world insofar as it is difficult to see how some evils could be the result of misused free will. Consider, for the moment, the more than 80,000 people who died in an earthquake in China on May 12, 2008. Or consider the 300 million deaths resulting from smallpox in the twentieth century, or the countless billions of animals who have suffered in evolutionary history. Such evils are called natural evils, and are contrasted with moral evils, which do result from the misuse of free will. What we see, then, is that even if the free will defense shows a reason God could have for allowing moral evils, it doesn't address natural evils. And the existence of natural evils could serve as a premise in an argument for the non-existence of God. In "Natural Evil and the

Possibility of Knowledge," Richard Swinburne tries to extend the free will defense to account not only for moral evils, but also for natural evils. Swinburne argues that in order for agents to exercise their free will in a morally significant way, those agents must have knowledge of the nature and effects of their actions. According to Swinburne, natural evils are needed for humans to have the requisite knowledge. If there were no natural evils, then humans would not be able to exercise their free will; but since having free will is such a great good, the existence of natural evils is not gratuitous. Swinburne thus extends the free will defense to cover natural evils as well.

Largely as a result of defenses of the above sort, most proponents of the problem of evil now focus on another version of the problem, known as the evidential (or inductive) problem of evil. Even if the logical problem of evils fails, that is if the existence of God and evil are logically compatible, the amounts and kinds of evil we see in the world may still give us reason or evidence to believe in the nonexistence of God. The third reading in this section, William Rowe's "The Problem of Evil and Some Varieties of Atheism," advances the evidential problem of evil by considering particular cases of evil which give rational grounds for rejecting the existence of God. In doing so, Rowe articulates and defends a view he calls "friendly atheism," according to which "some theists are rationally justified in holding to theism" even if there are sufficient grounds for one to rationally deny the non-existence of God. In "The Inductive Argument from Evil and the Human Cognitive Condition," William Alston argues that given the limitations on human cognitive capacities, the evidential argument for evil doesn't establish the irrationality of belief in God's existence. According to Alston, even *apparently gratuitous* cases of suffering and evil do not give us good reason to deny the existence of God insofar as our cognitive capacities are too limited for us to have good reason for thinking that *if* God did have a morally sufficient reason for allowing these evils, we would know about it. If Alston's evaluation of our epistemic situation with regard to these evils is correct, then the fact that we have no idea why God might allow these evils gives us no evidence in favor of his non-existence.

The final three readings of this section address the issue of divine hiddenness. A number of philosophers have used the apparent hiddenness of God to argue against His existence. One version of the argument from hiddenness is as follows:

1   If God were to exist, then He would want everyone to believe in Him and would not hide His existence from anyone. Instead, he would provide everyone with sufficient evidence of His existence.
2   There are people who do not believe in the existence of God because they do not have sufficient evidence of His existence.
3   Therefore, the fact that the existence of God is hidden from some people proves that He does not exist.

Many philosophers of religion think of the argument for hiddenness as a version of the argument from evil insofar as God's being hidden from individuals is an evil that God would have no morally justifiable reason for allowing. However, in "The Hiddenness of God," Peter van Inwagen shows that while the problem of evil and the problem of hiddenness are related, it is a confusion to treat them as synonymous—for either problem could arise independently of the other. According to van Inwagen, it could be the case that God is hidden even if there is no evil. Furthermore, it is possible that there would be evil in the world even if everyone were to believe in God. Since the problem of evil and the problem of hiddenness are to this degree independent of each other, the two problems are not identical. After differentiating the problem of hiddenness from the problem of evil, van Inwagen expands the free will defense to cover the argument from divine hiddenness as well as the argument from evil.

In contrast to van Inwagen, Michael Murray thinks that the problem of hiddenness can be viewed as a version of the problem of evil. In his "Coercion and the Hiddenness of God," Murray aims to develop not just a defense for divine hiddenness, but a theodicy. While Murray's argument has similarities with van Inwagen's free will defense, Murray claims that free will is the actual reason God has for remaining hidden from some individuals. He argues that in order for individuals to be significantly free, certain antecedent conditions must be met. Among these antecedent conditions is the absence of coercion, since compulsion by another in the context of a threat undermines free will. Murray differentiates a number of factors that contribute to coercion, including the likelihood of the threatened punishment and the severity of that punishment. Since those who do not believe in God are threatened with a very severe punishment, God can avoid coercing people to believe in Him only by minimizing the epistemic immanence of the threat. But minimizing the epistemic immanence involves not making His existence too evident; it is for this reason, Murray claims, that justifies God's remaining hidden.

In the final reading of this section, "Divine Hiddenness and Inculpable Ignorance," Robert Lovering builds upon Murray's line of reasoning to develop an argument for the non-existence of God. Lovering agrees with Murray that if God exists and were *not* hidden, individuals would not have the ability to develop morally significant characters given the threat of coercion. But, according to Lovering, coercion is not the only factor that undermines individuals' ability to develop their morally significant character. Non-culpable ignorance (i.e., ignorance for which the agent isn't blameworthy) also undermines moral character. Lovering then argues that if God exists and *is* hidden from individuals, those individuals lack the ability to develop morally significant characters for reasons of non-culpable ignorance. Since Lovering thinks that it is true that individuals do have the ability to develop morally significant characters, he concludes that God does not exist.

Note

1 *The Problem of Evil* (New York: Oxford University Press, 2006), 4.

Further Reading

Adams, Marilyn McCord. *Horrendous Evils and the Goodness of God* (Ithaca, N.Y.: Cornell University Press, 1999).
Howard-Snyder, Daniel, ed. *The Evidential Argument from Evil* (Bloomington and Indianapolis: Indiana University Press, 1996).

Howard-Snyder, Daniel, and Paul K. Moser, eds. *Divine Hiddenness: New Essays* (Cambridge: Cambridge University Press, 2002).

Mackie, John L. "Evil and Omnipotence," *Mind* 64 (1955): 200–212.

Peterson, Michael L., ed. *The Problem of Evil: Selected Readings* (Notre Dame, IN: University of Notre Dame Press, 1992).

Plantinga, Alvin. *God, Freedom, and Evil* (Grand Rapids, MI: Wm. B. Eerdmans Publishing Company, 1974).

Rowe, William L., ed. *God and the Problem of Evil* (Malden, MA: Blackwell, 2001).

Schellenberg, J. L. *Divine Hiddenness and Human Reason* (Ithaca, NY: Cornell University Press, 2006).

Swinburne, Richard. *Providence and the Problem of Evil* (Oxford: Clarendon Press, 1998).

Trakakis, Nick. "What No Eye Has Seen: The Skeptical Theist Response to Rowe's Evidential Argument from Evil," *Philo* 6 (2003): 263–279.

van Inwagen, Peter. *The Problem of Evil* (Oxford: Oxford University Press, 2006).

van Inwagen, Peter, ed. *Christian Faith and the Problem of Evil* (Grand Rapids, MI: Wm. B. Eerdmans Publishing Company, 2004).

Chapter 15

Peter van Inwagen

THE ARGUMENT FROM EVIL

By the argument from evil, I understand the following argument (or any argument sufficiently similar to it that the two arguments stand or fall together): We find vast amounts of truly horrendous evil in the world; if there were a God, we should not find vast amounts of horrendous evil in the world; there is, therefore, no God.

One might suppose that no argument was exempt from critical examination. But it is often asserted, and with considerable vehemence, that it is extremely wicked to examine the argument from evil with a critical eye. Here, for example, is a famous passage from John Stuart Mill's *Three Essays on Religion*:[1]

We now pass to the moral attributes of the Deity. . . . This question bears a very different aspect to us from what it bears to those teachers of Natural Theology who are encumbered with the necessity of admitting the omnipotence of the Creator. We have not to attempt the impossible problem of reconciling infinite benevolence and justice with infinite power in the Creator of a world such as this. The attempt to do so not only involves absolute contradiction in an intellectual point of view but exhibits to excess the revolting spectacle of a jesuitical defense of moral enormities. (p. 179)

And here is a second example. The following poem occurs in Kingsley Amis's novel *The Anti-Death League*[2] (it is the work of one of the characters), and it puts a little flesh on the bones of Mill's abstract Victorian indignation. It contains several specific allusions to just those arguments that Mill describes as jesuitical defenses of moral enormities. Its literary effect depends essentially on putting these arguments, or allusions to them, into the mouth of God.

To a Baby Born without Limbs

This is just to show you who's boss around
  here.
It'll keep you on your toes, so to speak,
Make you put your best foot forward, so to
  speak,
And give you something to turn your hand to,
  so to speak.
You can face up to it like a man,
Or snivel and blubber like a baby.
That's up to you. Nothing to do with Me.
If you take it in the right spirit,
You can have a bloody marvelous life,
With the great rewards courage brings,
And the beauty of accepting your LOT.
And think how much good it'll do your Mum
  and Dad,
And your Grans and Gramps and the rest of
  the shower,
To be stopped being complacent.
Make sure they baptize you, though,

In case some murdering bastard
Decides to put you away quick,
Which would send you straight to LIMB-o,
  ha ha ha.
But just a word in your ear, if you've got one.
Mind you, DO take this in the right spirit,
And keep a civil tongue in your head about
  Me.
Because if you DON'T,
I've got plenty of other stuff up My sleeve,
Such as leukemia and polio
(Which, incidentally, you're welcome to any
  time,
Whatever spirit you take this in).
I've given you one love-pat, right?
You don't want another.
So watch it, Jack.[3]

I am not entirely out of sympathy with writers like Mill and the fictional author of the poem in Amis's novel. There is one sort of position on God and evil toward which the intellectual scorn of Mill (I'll presently discuss his moral scorn) seems entirely appropriate. I have in mind the idea that – in the most strict and literal sense – evil does not exist. Now it might seem surprising that anyone would say this. Consider the following passage from *The Brothers Karamazov*:

> By the way, a Bulgarian I met lately in Moscow . . . told me about the crimes committed by Turks and Circassians in all parts of Bulgaria through fear of a general rising of the Slavs. They burn villages, murder, outrage women and children, they nail their prisoners by the ears to the fences, leave them so till morning, and in the morning they hang them. . . . These Turks took a pleasure in torturing children, too; cutting the unborn child from the mother's womb, and tossing babies up in the air and catching them on the points of their bayonets before their mothers' eyes. . . .[4]

How can anyone listen to stories like this and say that evil does not exist? Their idea, if I understand it, is something like this. An event like the Turkish massacres in Bulgaria *would* be an evil if it constituted the entire universe. But, of course, no such event does. The universe as a whole contains no spot or stain of evil, but it looks to us human beings as if it did because we view it from a limited perspective. Perhaps an aesthetic analogy will help us to understand this rather obscure idea. (I owe this analogy to Wallace Matson.) Many pieces of music that are of extreme beauty and perfection contain short discordant passages that would sound very ugly if they were played all by themselves, outside the musical context in which the composer intended them to occur. (Bach's *Well-Tempered Clavier* is an example.) But these passages are not ugly in their proper musical context; they are not the kind of passage Rossini was referring to when he said, "Wagner has lovely moments but awful quarters of an hour." Seen, or rather heard, in the context of the whole, they are not only not ugly but are essential elements of the beauty and perfection of that whole. The idea I am deprecating is that the horrors and atrocities of our world are analogous to these discordant passages. The *loci classici* of this idea are Leibniz's *Theodicy* and the following well-known lines from Pope's "Essay on Man" (Epistle I, ll. 289 et seq.):

> All nature is but art unknown to thee,
> All chance, direction which thou canst not see;
> All discord, harmony not understood;
> All partial evil, universal good;
> And, spite of pride, in erring reason's spite,
> One truth is clear, Whatever is, is right.

I don't see how anyone could believe this. It seems to me to be a wholly fantastic thesis. Do not misunderstand this statement. I wish to distance myself from the vulgar slander that ascribes moral insensibility (or downright wickedness) to Pope – a slander about which I'll have more to say in a moment. For my part, I accuse him only of intellectual error. But the intellectual error is of enormous magnitude – comparable to the intellectual error of, say, the astronomer Percival Lowell, who believed that Mars was covered with canals or to Descartes's belief that cats and dogs are unconscious automata. If we think of soldiers making mothers watch while they throw their babies in the air and catch them on the points of their bayonets, or of the ancient Mesopotamian practice of Moloch – of throwing living infants into a furnace as a sacrifice to Baal – or of a child born without limbs, we shall, I hope, find it impossible to say that evil is not real. Bad things really do happen, and anyone who, like Pope, says that we call certain things bad only because we don't see them *sub specie aeternitatis* is in grave error. One might as well say that if we could only observe pain from God's point of view, we'd see that it doesn't hurt.

If anyone takes the Leibniz/Pope line on the reality of evil, then, I think, that person deserves some of the scorn that Mill and Amis so eloquently express. I insist, however, that the scorn should be intellectual rather than moral. Given what Pope believed, he is guilty of no moral error; but his intellectual error is profound and not to be imitated.

In any case, the scorn of Mill and the other writers I've alluded to is not directed only at those who deny the reality of evil. This scorn is poured on anyone who is unwilling to admit, without further argument, that the evils of this world entail the non-existence of a good and omnipotent God. And when they imply that all such people, all people who are not immediately converted to atheism by the argument from evil in its simplest form, are morally defective, they go too far – they go *far* too far – and I must accuse them of intellectual dishonesty.

Thinking clearly about God and evil is *hard*. Thinking clearly for an extended period about any topic is hard. It is easier to pour scorn on those who disagree with you than actually to address their arguments. (It was easier for Voltaire to caricature Leibniz's arguments and to

mock the caricature than actually to address them. And so he wrote *Candide*. And of all the kinds of scorn that can be poured on someone's views, moral scorn is the safest and most pleasant (most pleasant to the one doing the pouring). It is the safest kind because, if you want to pour moral scorn on someone's views, you can pretty much take it for granted that most people will regard it as unanswerable; you can take it as *certain* that everyone who is predisposed to agree with you will believe that you have made an unanswerable point. You can pretty much take it for granted that your audience will dismiss any attempt your opponent in debate makes at an answer as a "rationalization" – that great contribution of modern depth-psychology to intellectual complacency and laziness. Moral scorn is the most *pleasant* kind of scorn to deploy against those who disagree with you because a display of self-righteousness – moral posturing – is a pleasant action whatever the circumstances, and it is nice to find an excuse for it. No one can tell me that Mill wasn't enjoying himself when he wrote the words, "exhibits to excess the revolting spectacle of a jesuitical defense of moral enormities." (Perhaps he was enjoying himself so much that his attention was diverted from the question, "What would it be to exhibit a revolting spectacle in moderation?")

To people who avoid having to defend the argument from evil by this sort of moral posturing, I can only say, "Come off it." These people are, in point of principle, in exactly the same position as those defenders of law and order who, if you express a suspicion that a man accused of abducting and molesting a child has been framed by the police, tell you with evident disgust that molesting a child is a horrible crime and that you're defending a child molester.

Having defended the moral propriety of critically examining the argument from evil, I will now do just that. The argument presupposes, and rightly, that two features God is supposed to have are "non-negotiable": that he is omnipotent and morally perfect. That he is omnipotent means that he can do anything that doesn't involve an intrinsic impossibility. Thus, God, if he exists, can change water to wine, since there is no intrinsic impossibility in the elementary particles that constitute the water in a cup being rearranged so as to constitute wine. But even God can't draw a round square or cause it both to rain and not to rain at the same place at the same time or change the past because these things are intrinsically impossible. To say that God is morally perfect is to say that he never does anything morally wrong – that he could not possibly do anything morally wrong. If God exists, therefore, and if you think he's done something morally wrong, you must be mistaken: either he didn't do the thing you think he did, or the thing he did that you think is morally wrong isn't. Omnipotence and moral perfection are, as I said, non-negotiable components of the idea of God. If the universe was made by an intelligent being, and if that being is less than omnipotent (and if there's no other being who is omnipotent), then the atheists are right: God does not exist. If the universe was made by an omnipotent being, and if that being has done even one thing that was morally wrong (and if there isn't another omnipotent being, one who never does anything morally wrong), then the atheists are right: God does not exist. If the Creator of the universe lacked either omnipotence or moral perfection, and if he claimed to be God, he would be either an impostor (if he claimed to be omnipotent and morally perfect) or confused (if he conceded that he lacked either omnipotence or moral perfection and claimed to be God anyway).

To these two "non-negotiable" features of the concept of God, we must add one other that doesn't call for much comment: God, if he exists, must know a great deal about the world he has created. Now it is usually said that God is *omniscient* – that he knows *everything*. But the argument from evil doesn't require this strong assumption about God's knowledge – it requires only that God know enough to be aware of a significant amount of the evil that exists in the

world. If God knew even the little that you and I know about the amount and extent of evil, that would be sufficient for the argument.

Now consider those evils God knows about. Since he's morally perfect, he must desire that these evils not exist – their non-existence must be what he *wants*. And an omnipotent being can achieve or bring about whatever he wants. So if there were an omnipotent, morally perfect being who knew about these evils – well, they wouldn't have arisen in the first place, for he'd have prevented their occurrence. Or if, for some reason, he didn't do that, he'd certainly remove them the instant they began to exist. But we observe evils, and very long-lasting ones. So we must conclude that God does not exist.

How much force has this argument? Suppose I believe in God and grant that the world contains vast amounts of truly horrible evil. What might I say in reply? I should, and do, think that the place to begin is with an examination of the word 'want'. Granted, in some sense of the word, the non-existence of evil must be what a morally perfect being *wants*. But we often don't bring about states of affairs we can bring about and want. Suppose, for example, that Alice's mother is dying in great pain and that Alice yearns desperately for her mother to die – today, and not next week or next month. And suppose it would be easy for Alice to arrange this – she is perhaps a doctor or a nurse and has easy access to pharmaceutical resources that would enable her to achieve this end. Does it follow that she will act on this ability that she has? It is obvious that it does not, for Alice might have *reasons* for not doing what she can do. Two obvious candidates for such reasons are: she thinks it would be morally wrong; she is afraid that her act would be discovered and that she would be prosecuted for murder. And either of these reasons might be sufficient, in her mind, to outweigh her desire for an immediate end to her mother's sufferings. So it may be that someone has a very strong desire for something and is able to obtain this thing, but does not act on this desire – because he has reasons for not doing so that seem to him to outweigh the desirability of the thing. The conclusion that evil does not exist does not, therefore, follow *logically* from the premises that the non-existence of evil is what God wants and that he is able to bring about the object of his desire – since, for all logic can tell us, God might have reasons for allowing evil to exist that, in his mind, outweigh the desirability of the non-existence of evil. But are such reasons even imaginable? What might they be?

Suppose I believe I know what God's reasons for allowing evil to exist are, and that I tell them to you. Then I have presented you with what is called a *theodicy*. This word comes from two Greek words that mean 'God' and 'justice'. Thus, Milton, in *Paradise Lost*, tells us that the purpose of the poem is to "justify the ways of God to men" – 'justify' meaning 'exhibit as just'. If I could present a theodicy, and if those to whom I presented it found it convincing, I'd have a reply to the argument from evil. But suppose that, although I believe in God, I *don't* claim to know what God's reasons for allowing evil are. Is there any way for someone in my position to reply to the argument from evil? There is. Consider this analogy.

Suppose your friend Clarissa, a single mother, left her two very young children alone in her flat for over an hour very late last night. Your Aunt Harriet, a maiden lady of strong moral principles, learns of this and declares that Clarissa is unfit to raise children. You spring to your friend's defense: "Now, Aunt Harriet, don't go jumping to conclusions. There's probably a perfectly good explanation. Maybe Billy or Annie took ill, and she decided to go over to St. Luke's for help. You know she hasn't got a phone or a car and no one in that neighborhood of hers would come to the door at two o'clock in the morning." If you tell your Aunt Harriet a story like this, you don't claim to know what Clarissa's reasons for leaving her children alone really were. And you're not claiming to have said anything that shows that Clarissa really is a good mother. You're claiming only to show that the fact Aunt Harriet has adduced doesn't prove that she isn't one; what you're trying to establish is that for all you and Aunt Harriet know, she had some good reason for what she did. And you're not trying to establish only that there is some remote possibility that she had a good reason. No lawyer would try to raise doubts in the minds of the members of a jury by pointing out to them that for all they knew his client had an identical twin, of whom all record had been lost, and who was the person who had actually committed the crime his client was charged with. That may be a possibility – I suppose it *is* a possibility – but it is too remote a possibility to raise real doubts in anyone's mind. What you're trying to convince Aunt Harriet of is that there is, as we say, *a very real possibility* that Clarissa had a good reason for leaving her children alone; and your attempt to convince her of this consists in your presenting her with an example of what such a reason *might* be.

Critical responses to the argument from evil – at least responses by philosophers – usually take just this form. A philosopher who responds to the argument from evil typically does so by telling a story, a story in which God allows evil to exist. This story will, of course, represent God as having reasons for allowing the existence of evil, reasons that, if the rest of the story were true, would be good ones. Such a story philosophers call a *defense*. A defense and a theodicy will not necessarily differ in content. A defense may, indeed, be verbally identical with a theodicy. The difference between a theodicy and a defense is simply that a theodicy is put forward as true, while nothing more is claimed for a defense than that it represents a real possibility – or a real possibility given that God exists. If I offer a story about God and evil as a defense, I hope for the following reaction from my audience: "Given that God exists, the rest of the story might well be true. I can't see any reason to rule it out."

A defense cannot simply take the form of a story about how God brings some great good out of the evils of the world, a good that out-weighs those evils. At the very least, a defense will have to include the proposition that God was *unable* to bring about the greater good without allowing the evils we observe (or some other evils as bad or worse). And to find a story that can plausibly be said to have this feature is no trivial undertaking. The reason for this lies in God's omnipotence. A human being can often be excused for allowing, or even causing, a certain evil if that evil was a necessary means, or an unavoidable consequence thereof, to some good that outweighed it – or if it was a necessary means to the prevention of some greater evil. The eighteenth-century surgeon who operated without anesthetic caused unimaginable pain to his patients, but we do not condemn him because (at least if he knew what he was doing) the pain was an unavoidable consequence of the means necessary to some good that outweighed it – such as saving the patient's life. But we should not excuse a present-day surgeon who had anesthetics available and who neverthe-less operated without using them – not even if his operation saved the patient's life and thus resulted in a good that outweighed the horrible pain the patient suffered.

A great many of the theodicies or defenses that one sees are insufficiently sensitive to this point. Many undergraduates, for example, if they are believers, seem inclined to say something like the following: if there were no evil, no one would appreciate – perhaps no one would even be aware of – the goodness of the things that *are* good. You know the idea: you never really appreciate health till you've been ill, you never really understand how great and beautiful a thing friendship is till you've known adversity and known what it is to have friends who stick by you through thick and thin – and so on. Now the obvious criticism of this defense is so immediately obvious that it tends to mask the point that led me to raise it. The immediately obvious criticism is that this defense may be cap-able of accounting for a certain amount of, for example, physical pain, but it certainly doesn't account for the degree and the duration of the pain that many people are subject to. But I have brought up the "appreciation" defense – which otherwise would not be worth spending any time on – to make a different point. It is not at all evident that an omnipotent creator would need to allow people really to experience *any* pain or grief or sorrow or adversity or illness to enable them to appreciate the good things in life. An omnipotent being would certainly be able to provide the knowledge of evil that human beings in fact acquire by bitter experience of real events in some other way. An omnipotent being could, for example, so arrange matters that at a certain point in each person's life – for a few years dur-ing his adolescence, say – that person have very vivid *nightmares* in which he is a prisoner in a concentration camp or dies of some horrible disease or watches his loved ones being raped and murdered by soldiers bent on ethnic cleans-ing. It seems evident to me that the supposed good (the capacity for the appreciation of good things) that some say is a consequence of the evils of the world could (if it exists) be equally well achieved by this means. And it is indisput-able that a world in which horrible things occurred only in nightmares would be better than a world in which the same horrible things occurred in reality, and that a morally perfect being ought to prefer a world in which horrible things were confined to dreams to a world in which they existed in reality. The general point this example is intended to illustrate is simply that the resources of an omnipotent being are unlimited – or are limited only by what is intrin-sically possible – and that a defense must take account of these unlimited resources.

There seems to me to be only one defense that has any hope of succeeding, and that is the so-called free-will defense. In its simplest, most abstract, form, the free-will defense goes as follows:

God made the world and it was very good. An

indispensable part of the goodness he chose was the existence of rational beings: self-aware beings capable of abstract thought and love and having the power of free choice between contemplated alternative courses of action. This last feature of rational beings, free choice or free will, is a good. But even an omnipotent being is unable to control the exercise of the power of free choice, for a choice that was controlled would *ipso facto* not be free. In other words, if I have a free choice between x and y, even God cannot ensure that I choose x. To ask God to give me a free choice between x and y and to see to it that I choose x instead of y is to ask God to bring about the intrinsically impossible; it is like asking him to create a round square, a material body that has no shape, or an invisible object that casts a shadow. Having this power of free choice, some or all human beings misuse it and produce a certain amount of evil. But free will is a sufficiently great good that its existence outweighs the evils that results from its abuse; and God foresaw this.

The free-will defense immediately suggests several objections. The two most pressing of them are these:

How could anyone possibly believe that the evils of this world are outweighed by the good inherent in our having free will? Perhaps free will is a good and would outweigh a certain amount of evil, but it seems impossible to believe that it can outweigh the amount of physical suffering (to say nothing of other sorts of evil) that actually exists.

Not all evils are the result of human free will. Consider, for example, the Lisbon earthquake or the almost inconceivable loss of life produced by the hurricane that ravaged Honduras in 1997. Such events are not the result of any act of human will, free or unfree.

In my view, the simple form of the free-will defense I have presented is unable to deal with either of these objections. The simple form of the free-will defense can deal with at best the existence of *some* evil – as opposed to the vast amount of evil we actually observe – and the evil with which it can deal is only that evil that is caused by the acts of human beings. I believe, however, that more sophisticated forms of the free-will defense do have interesting things to say about the vast amount of evil in the world and about those evils that are not caused by human beings. Before I discuss these "more sophisticated" forms of the free-will defense, however, I want to examine an objection that has been raised against the free-will defense that is so fundamental that, if valid, it would refute any elaboration of the defense, however sophisticated. This objection has to do with the nature of free will. There is a school of thought – Hobbes, Hume, and Mill are its most illustrious representatives – whose adherents maintain that free will and determinism are perfectly compatible: that there could be a world in which the past determined a unique future and the inhabitants of which were nonetheless free beings. Now if this school of philosophers is right, the free-will defense fails, for if free will and determinism are compatible, then an omnipotent being can, contrary to the central premise of the free-will defense, create a person who has a free choice between x and y and ensure that that person choose x rather than y. Those philosophers who accept the compatibility of free will and determinism defend their thesis as follows: being free is being free to do what one wants to do; prisoners in a jail, for example, are unfree because they want to leave and can't. The man who desperately wants to stop smoking but can't is unfree for the same reason – even though no barrier as literal as the bars of a cage stands between him and a life without nicotine. The very words 'free will' testify to the rightness of this analysis, for one's will is simply what one wants, and a free will is just exactly an unimpeded will. Given this account of free will, a Creator who wants to give me a free choice between x and y has only to arrange the components of my body and my environment in such a way that the following two 'if' statements are both true: if I were to want x, I'd be able to achieve that desire, and if I were to want y, I'd be able to achieve *that* desire. And a Creator who wants to ensure that I choose x, rather than y, has only to implant in me a fairly robust desire for x and see to it that I have no desire at all for y. And these two things are obviously compatible. Suppose, for example, that there was a Creator who had put a woman in a garden and had commanded her not to eat of the fruit of a certain tree. Could he so arrange matters that she have a free choice between eating of the fruit of that tree and not eating of it – and also *ensure* that she not eat of it? Certainly. To provide her with a free choice between the two alternatives, he need only see to it that two things are true: first, that if she wanted to eat of the fruit of that tree, no barrier (such as an unclimbable fence or paralysis of the limbs) would stand in the way of her acting on that desire, and, secondly, that if she wanted *not* to eat of the fruit, nothing would force her to act contrary to *that* desire. And to ensure that she not eat of the fruit, he need only see to it that not eating of the fruit be what she desires. This latter end could be achieved in a variety of ways; the simplest, I suppose, would be to build into her psychological makeup a very strong desire to do whatever he tells her to and a horror of disobedience – a horror like that experienced by the acrophobe who is forced to approach the edge of a cliff – and then to instruct her not to eat of the fruit. If all this is indeed correct, it would seem that an omnipotent being could both grant its creatures free will and ensure that they never bring any evil into the world by the abuse of it. And, of course, if *that* is true, the free-will defense fails.

But how plausible is this account of free will? Not very, I think. It certainly yields some odd conclusions. Consider the lower social orders in

Aldous Huxley's *Brave New World*, the "deltas" and "epsilons." These unfortunate people have their deepest desires chosen for them by others – by the "alphas" who make up the highest social stratum. What the deltas and epsilons primarily desire is to do what the alphas (and the "beta" and "gamma" overseers who are appointed to supervise their labors) tell them. This is their primary desire because it is imposed on them by prenatal and postnatal conditioning. (If Huxley were writing today, he might have added genetic engineering to the alphas' list of resources for determining the desires of their slaves.) It would be hard to think of beings who better fitted the description 'lacks free will' than the deltas and epsilons of *Brave New World*. And yet, if the account of free will that we are considering is right, the deltas and epsilons are exemplars of beings with free will. Each of them is always doing exactly what he wants, after all, and who among us is in that fortunate position? What he wants is to do as he is told by those appointed over him, of course, but the account of free will we are examining says nothing about the *content* of one's desires: it requires only that there be no barrier to acting on them. The deltas and epsilons are not very intelligent, and are therefore incapable of philosophizing about their condition, but the alphas' techniques could as easily be applied to highly intelligent people. It is interesting to ask what conclusions such people would arrive at if they reflected on their condition. If you said to one of these highly intelligent slaves, "Don't you realize that you obey your master only because your desire to obey him was implanted in you by prenatal conditioning and genetic engineering," he would, I expect, reply by saying something like this: "Yes, and a good thing, too, because, you see, they had the foresight to implant in me a desire that my desires be so formed. I'm really very fortunate: I'm not only doing exactly what I want, but I want to want what I want, and I want what I want to be caused by prenatal conditioning and genetic engineering." Despite the fact that (I freely confess) I do not have a philosophically satisfactory account of free will, I can see that this person hasn't got it. Therefore, I contend, the atheist's attempt to show that the story that constitutes the free-will defense is false rests on a false theory about the nature of free will. Now my argument for the falsity of this theory is, I concede, inconclusive. (If it were conclusive, it would convince Hobbes and Hume and Mill and their fellow "compatibilists" that their account of free will was wrong. And experience shows that most compatibilists who hear and understand this argument are unmoved by it.) But let us remember the dialectical situation in which this inconclusive argument occurs. That is, let us remember who is trying to prove what. The atheist has opened the discussion by trying to prove the non-existence of God; the alleged proof of this conclusion is the argument from evil. The theist responds by producing the free-will defense and contends that this defense shows that evil does not prove the non-existence of God. The atheist's rejoinder is that the story called the free-will defense is false and that its falsity can be demonstrated by reflection on the nature of free will. The theist replies that the atheist has got the nature of free will wrong, and he offers a philosophical argument for this conclusion (the "Brave New World" argument), an argument that perhaps falls short of being a proof but has nevertheless seemed fairly plausible to many intelligent people. When we add up all the pluses and minuses of this exchange, it seems that the free-will defense triumphs in its limited sphere of application. When we think about it, we see that, for all the atheist has said, the story called the free-will defense *may well be true* – at least given that there is a God. One cannot show that a story involving creatures with free will is false or probably false by pointing out that the story would be false if a certain theory about free will were true. To show that, one would also have to show that the theory of free will that one has put forward was true or probably true. And the atheist hasn't shown that his theory of free will, the "no barriers" theory, is

true or probably true, for the objections to the atheist's theory of free will that I have set out show that this theory faces very serious problems indeed.

The atheist's most promising course of action, I think, is to admit that the free-will defense shows that there might, for all anyone can say, be a certain amount of evil, a certain amount of pain and suffering, in a world created by an all-powerful and morally perfect being, and to stress the amounts and the kinds of evil that we find in the world as it is. The world as it is, I have said, contains vast amounts of truly horrendous evil (that's the point about amounts), and some of the kinds of evil to be found in the world as it is are not caused by human beings – wholly unforeseeable natural disasters, for example (that's the point about kinds). Can any elaboration of our simple version of the free-will defense take account of these two points in any very plausible way?

Let me suggest some elaborations toward this end. The reader must decide whether they are plausible. The free-will defense as I've stated it suggests – though it does not entail – that God created human beings with free will, and then just left them to their own devices. It suggests that the evils of the world are the more or less unrelated consequences of uncounted millions of largely unrelated abuses of free will by human beings. Let me propose a sort of plot to be added to the bare and abstract free-will defense I stated above. Consider the story of creation and rebellion and the expulsion from paradise that is told in the first three chapters of Genesis. Could this story be true – I mean literally true, true in every detail? Well, no. It contradicts what science has discovered about human evolution and the history of the physical universe. And that is hardly surprising, for it long antedates these discoveries. The story is a re-working – with much original material – by Hebrew authors (or, as I believe, a Hebrew author) of elements found in many ancient Middle Eastern mythologies. Like the *Aeneid*, it is a literary refashioning of materials originally supplied by legend and myth, and it retains a strong mythological flavor. It is possible, nevertheless, that the first three chapters of Genesis are a mythico-literary representation of actual events of human pre-history. The following is consistent with what we know of human pre-history. Our current knowledge of human evolution, in fact, presents us with no particular reason to believe that this story is false. (Here and there in the story, the reader will encounter various philosophical *obiter dicta*, asides to the reader thoughtfully provided by the omniscient narrator – myself.)

For millions of years, perhaps for thousands of millions of years, God guided the course of evolution so as eventually to produce certain very clever primates, the immediate predecessors of *Homo sapiens*. At some time in the last few hundred thousand years, the whole population of our pre-human ancestors formed a small breeding community – a few hundred or even a few score. That is to say, there was a time when every ancestor of modern human beings who was then alive was a member of this tiny, geographically tightly knit group of primates. In the fullness of time, God took the members of this breeding group and miraculously raised them to rationality. That is, he gave them the gifts of language, abstract thought, and disinterested love – and, of course, the gift of free will. He gave them the gift of free will because free will is necessary for love. Love, and not only erotic love, implies free will. The essential connection between love and free will is beautifully illustrated in Ruth's declaration to her mother-in-law Naomi:

And Ruth said, Entreat me not to leave thee, or to return from following after thee: for whither thou goest, I will go; and where thou lodgest, I will lodge: thy people shall be my people and thy God my God: where thou diest, will I die, and there will I be buried; the Lord do so to me, and more also, if aught but death part thee and me.

(Ruth 1:16–17)

It is also illustrated by the vow I made when I was married:

I, Peter, take thee, Elisabeth, to be my wedded wife, to have and to hold from this day forward, for better for worse, for richer for poorer, in sickness and in health, to love and to cherish, till death us do part, according to God's holy ordinance; and thereto I plight thee my troth.

God not only raised these primates to rationality – not only made of them what we call human beings – but also took them into a kind of mystical union with himself, the sort of union that Christians hope for in heaven and call the Beatific Vision. Being in union with God, these new human beings, these primates who had become human beings at a certain point in their lives, lived together in the harmony of perfect love and also possessed what theologians used to call preternatural powers – something like what people who believe in them today call paranormal abilities. Because they lived in the harmony of perfect love, none of them did any harm to the others. Because of their preternatural powers, they were able somehow to protect themselves from wild beasts (which they were able to tame with a word), from disease (which they were able to cure with a touch) and from random, destructive natural events (like earthquakes), which they knew about in advance and were able to avoid. There was thus no evil in their world. And it was God's intention that they should never become decrepit with age or die, as their primate forbears had. But, somehow, in some way that must be mysterious to us, they were not content with this paradisal state. They abused the gift of free will and separated themselves from their union with God.

The result was horrific: not only did they no longer enjoy the Beatific Vision, but they now faced destruction by the random forces of nature, and were subject to old age and natural death. Nevertheless, they were too proud to end their rebellion. As the generations passed, they drifted further and further from God – into the worship of false gods (a worship that sometimes involved human sacrifice), inter-tribal warfare (complete with the gleeful torture of prisoners of war), private murder, slavery, and rape. On one level, they realized, or some of them realized, that something was horribly wrong, but they were unable to do anything about it. After they had separated themselves from God, they were, as an engineer might say, "not operating under design conditions." A certain frame of mind became dominant among them, a frame of mind latent in the genes they had inherited from a million or more generations of ancestors. I mean the frame of mind that places one's own desires and perceived welfare above everything else, and which accords to the welfare of one's immediate relatives a subordinate privileged status, and assigns no status at all to the welfare of anyone else. And this frame of mind was now married to rationality, to the power of abstract thought; the progeny of this marriage were the continuing resentment against those whose actions interfere with the fulfillment of one's desires, hatreds cherished in the heart, and the desire for revenge. The inherited genes that produced these baleful effects had been harmless as long as human beings had still had constantly before their minds a representation of perfect love in the Beatific Vision. In the state of separation from God, and conjoined with rationality, they formed the genetic substrate of what is called original sin or birth-sin: an inborn tendency to do evil against which all human efforts are vain. We, or most of us, have some sort of perception of the distinction between good and evil, but, however we struggle, in the end we give in and do evil. In all cultures there are moral codes (more similar than some would have us believe) and the members of every tribe and nation stand condemned not only by alien moral codes but by their own. The only human beings who consistently do right in their own eyes, whose consciences are always clear, are those

who, like the Nazis, have given themselves over entirely to evil, those who say, in some twisted and self-deceptive way, what Milton has his Satan say explicitly and clearly: "Evil, be thou my Good."

When human beings had become like this, God looked out over a ruined world. It would have been just for him to leave human beings in the ruin they had made of themselves and their world. But God is more than a God of justice. He is, indeed, more than a God of mercy – a God who was merely merciful might simply have brought the story of humanity to an end at that point, like someone who shoots a horse with a broken leg. But God is more than a God of mercy: he is a God of love. He therefore neither left humanity to its own devices nor mercifully destroyed it. Rather, he set in motion a rescue operation. He put into operation a plan designed to restore separated humanity to union with himself. This defense will not specify the nature of this plan of atonement. The three Abrahamic religions, Judaism, Christianity, and Islam, tell three different stories about the nature of this plan, and I do not propose to favor one of them over another in telling a story that, after all, I do not maintain is true. This much must be said, however: the plan has the following feature, and any plan with the object of restoring separated humanity to union with God would have to have this feature: its object is to bring it about that human beings once more love God. And, since love essentially involves free will, love is not something that can be imposed from the outside, by an act of sheer power. Human beings must choose freely to be reunited with God and to love him, and this is something they are unable to do of their own efforts. They must therefore cooperate with God. As is the case with many rescue operations, the rescuer and those whom he is rescuing must cooperate. For human beings to cooperate with God in this rescue operation, they must know that they need to be rescued. They must know what it means to be separated from him. And what it means to be separated from God is to live in a world of horrors. If God simply "canceled" all the horrors of this world by an endless series of miracles, he would thereby frustrate his own plan of reconciliation. If he did that, we should be content with our lot and should see no reason to cooperate with him. Here is an analogy. Suppose Dorothy suffers from angina, and that what she needs to do is to stop smoking and lose weight. Suppose her doctor knows of a drug that will stop the pain but will do nothing to cure the condition. Should the doctor prescribe the drug for her, in the full knowledge that if the pain is alleviated, there is no chance that she will stop smoking and lose weight? Well, perhaps the answer is yes. The doctor is Dorothy's fellow adult and fellow citizen, after all. Perhaps it would be insufferably paternalistic to refuse to alleviate Dorothy's pain in order to provide her with a motivation to do what is to her own advantage. If one were of an especially libertarian cast of mind, one might even say that someone who did that was "playing God." It is far from clear, however, whether there is anything wrong with *God's* behaving as if he were God. It is at least very plausible to suppose that it is morally permissible for God to allow human beings to suffer if the result of suppressing the suffering would be to deprive them of a very great good, one that far outweighed the suffering. But God does shield us from *much* evil, from a great proportion of the sufferings that would be a natural consequence of our rebellion. If he did not, all human history would be at least this bad: every human society would be on the moral level of Nazi Germany. But, however much evil God shields us from, he must leave in place a vast amount of evil if he is not to deceive us about what separation from him means. The amount he has left us with is so vast and so horrible that we cannot really comprehend it, especially if we are middle-class Americans or Europeans. Nevertheless, it could have been much worse. The inhabitants of a world in which human beings had separated ourselves from God and he had

then simply left them to their own devices would regard our world as a comparative paradise. All this evil, however, will come to an end. At some point, for all eternity, there will be no more unmerited suffering. Every evil done by the wicked to the innocent will have been avenged, and every tear will have been wiped away. If there is still suffering, it will be merited: the suffering of those who refuse to cooperate with God's great rescue operation and are allowed by him to exist forever in a state of elected ruin – those who, in a word, are in hell.

One aspect of this story needs to be brought out more clearly than I have. If the story is true, much of the evil in the world is due to chance. There is generally no explanation of why *this* evil happened to *that* person. What there is is an explanation of why evils happen to people without any reason. And the explanation is: that is part of what being separated from God means: it means being the playthings of chance. It means living in a world in which innocent children die horribly, and it means something worse than that: it means living in a world in which innocent children die horribly *for no reason at all*. It means living in a world in which the wicked, through sheer luck, often prosper. Anyone who does not want to live in such a world, a world in which we are the playthings of chance, had better accept God's offer of a way out of that world.

Here, then, is a defense. Do I believe it? Well, I believe parts of it and I don't disbelieve any of it. (Even those parts I believe do not, for the most part, belong to my faith; they merely comprise some of my religious opinions.) I am not at all sure about "preternatural powers," for example, or about the proposition that God shields us from much evil and that the world would be far worse if he did not. The story I have told is, I remind you, only supposed to be a defense. It is not put forward as a theodicy, as a statement of the real truth of the matter, as I see it, about the co-presence of God and evil in the world. I contend only that this story is – given that God exists – true for all we know. And I certainly don't see any very compelling reason to reject any of it. In particular, I don't see any reason to reject the thesis that God raised a small population of our ancestors to rationality by a specific action on, say, June 13, 116,027 B.C. – or on some such particular date. It is not a discovery of evolutionary biology that there are no miraculous events in our evolutionary history. It *could* not be, any more than it could be a discovery of meteorology that the weather at Dunkirk on those fateful days in 1940 was not due to a specific and local divine action. Anyone who believes either that the coming-to-be of human rationality or the weather at Dunkirk had purely natural causes must believe this on philosophical, not scientific, grounds. In fact the case for this is rather stronger in the case of the genesis of rationality, for we know a lot about how the weather works, and we know that the rain clouds at Dunkirk are the sort of thing that *could* have had purely natural causes. We most assuredly do not know that rationality could have arisen through natural causes – or, at any rate, we do not know this unless there is some philosophical argument that shows that *everything* has purely natural causes. And this is because everyone who believes that human rationality could have had purely natural causes believes this solely on the basis of the following argument: Everything has purely natural causes; human beings are rational; hence, the rationality of human beings could have had purely natural causes because it in fact did.

Suppose, then, for the sake of argument, that the defense I have presented is a true story. Does it justify the evils of the world? Or put the question this way. Suppose there were an omnipotent and omniscient being and that this being acted just as God has acted in the story I have told.

Could any moral case be made against the actions of this being? Is there any barrier to saying that this being is not only omnipotent and omniscient but morally perfect as well? In my view, it is not self-evident that there is no barrier to saying this – but it is not self-evident that there is a barrier, either. The defense I have presented, the story I have told, should be thought of as the beginning of a conversation. If there is anyone who maintains that the story I have told, even if it is true, does not absolve a being who acts as I have supposed God to act from serious moral criticism, let that person explain why he or she thinks this is so. Then I, or some other defender of theism, can attempt to meet this objection, and the objector can reply to the rejoinder and . . . but so philosophy goes: philosophy is argument without end. As J. L. Austin said – also speaking on the topic of excuses – here I leave and commend the subject to you.

Notes

1   London: Longmans, Green, 1875.

2   New York: Harcourt, Brace & World, 1966.

3   In the poem as it is printed in the novel there are (for reasons of the plot, as they say) several illiteracies (e.g., "whose" for "who's" in l. 1). I have "corrected" them – with apologies to Martin Amis, in whose opinion they are an important part of the intended effect of the poem on the reader (that is, the effect Kingsley Amis intended the poem to have on readers of *The Anti-Death League*). For Martin Amis's argument for this conclusion (and the poem without my officious corrections), see his memoir *Experience* (New York: Hyperion, 2000), p. 188.

4   From Chapter 4 ("Rebellion") of Book V. Ivan is speaking. It is very nearly obligatory for writers on the problem of evil to quote something from this chapter.

Chapter 16

Whitley R. P. Kaufman

KARMA, REBIRTH, AND THE PROBLEM OF EVIL

According to the seed that's sown
So is the fruit ye reap therefrom.
Doer of good will gather good,
Doer of evil, evil reaps.
Sown is the seed, and thou shalt taste
The fruit thereof.

Samyutta Nikaya[1]

The doctrine of karma and rebirth represents perhaps the most striking difference between Western (Judeo-Christian and Islamic) religious thought and the great Indian religious traditions (Hindu, Buddhist, Jain). To be sure, Western theology also makes use of a retributive explanation of evil in which an individual's suffering is accounted for by his previous wrongdoing. But given the obviously imperfect correlation between sin and suffering in an individual's lifetime, Western religions have resorted to other explanations of suffering (including, notoriously, that of Original Sin). However, Indian thought boldly combines this retributionism with the idea of multiple human incarnations, so that all suffering in this life can be explained by each individual's prior wrongdoing, whether in this or in a prior life, and all wrongdoing in the present life will be punished in either this or a future life. In this way, Indian thought is able to endorse a complete and consistent retributive explanation of evil: all suffering can be explained by the wrongdoing of the sufferer himself. As Ananda Coomaraswamy declares, in answer to the question "Who did sin, this man or his parents, that he was born blind?": "The Indian theory replies without hesitation, *this man*."[2]

It is frequently claimed that the doctrine of karma and rebirth provides Indian religion with a more emotionally and intellectually satisfying account of evil and suffering than do typical Western solutions to the problem of evil. Thus, for Max Weber, karma

> stands out by virtue of its consistency as well as by its extraordinary metaphysical achievement: It unites virtuoso-like self-redemption by man's own effort with universal accessibility of salvation, the strictest rejection of the world with organic social ethics, and contemplation as the paramount path to salvation with an inner-worldly vocational ethic.[3]

Arthur Herman, in his classic *The Problem of Evil and Indian Thought*, similarly asserts the superiority of karma to all Western theodicies: "Unlike the Western theories, . . . the doctrine of rebirth is capable of meeting the major objections against which those Western attempts all failed" (Herman 1976, p. 287).[4] Michael Stoeber also claims that the Indian idea of rebirth is "more plausible" than traditional Christian ideas such as purgatory (Stoeber 1992, p. 167). And the karma doctrine appears to be increasing in popularity in the West as well, perhaps because of these perceived advantages.

However, despite these and similar enthusiastic endorsements, karma as a theodicy has still received comparatively little critical analysis in comparison with the scrutiny to which dominant Western ideas such as Original Sin or free will have been subjected. Paul Edwards contrasts the "devastating critical examination" to which Christian and Jewish tenets have been subjected with the lack of any "similarly detailed critique of reincarnation and the related doctrine of Karma" by Western philosophers (Edwards 1996, p. 7).[5] A bibliography of theodicy writings between 1960 and 1991 lists over four thousand entries, but only a half dozen or so of these specifically address karma.[6] In this essay I would like to make a gesture toward filling in this gap. Whereas Edwards' work concentrates on the metaphysical and scientific critique of Karma, I will limit my discussion to the specific question of whether a karma-and-rebirth theory, even if true, could solve the problem of evil. That is, can it provide a satisfactory explanation of the (apparent) unfairness, injustice, and innocent suffering in the world? I will argue here that the doctrine, in whatever form it is proposed, suffers from serious limitations that render it unlikely to provide a satisfactory solution to the problem of evil.

Preliminary Qualifications

Let me state at the outset my limited purposes in this essay. This is not an exercise in doctrinal exegesis or historical comparative anthropology; such issues are not my concern and are outside my competence in any case. Nor do I do intend to enter into the debate about the textual sources of the karmic doctrine (e.g., whether they first appear in the Upanishads, or whether there are precursors in the Brahmanas), or the question of the extent of the influence of the karma doctrine in contemporary Indian thought.[7] Rather, my method will be to examine a simplified, idealized version of the karma-and-rebirth doctrine, one abstracted as far as possible from particular historical or doctrinal questions.

Such an approach will not be without controversy. Many writers have, in fact, doubted whether karma is meant to function as a theodicy, or indeed whether Indian thought should be taken as recognizing a "problem of evil" in anything like its Western formulation. Wendy O'Flaherty points to the "widespread" belief that Indians do not recognize the problem of evil, or even that "there is no concept of evil at all in India" (O'Flaherty 1980, p. 4). Arthur Herman makes the extraordinary claim that Indian thought is not much interested in the theodicy question precisely because the karma doctrine provides a fully satisfactory explanation of evil:

> since the rebirth solution is adequate for solving the theological problem of evil, this undoubtedly explains why the problem was never of much concern to the classical Indian, and why theodicy, as a philosophical way of life, was practically unknown to them. (p. 288).

However, O'Flaherty's *The Origins of Evil in Hindu Mythology* amply demonstrates the falsity of the claim that theodicy is solely a Western concern. She shows how Western scholars have "overlooked" the presence of the problem of evil in Indian thought by focusing on systematic philosophy and theology rather than mythology and folk tradition; in fact, "myths of theodicy are perennial in India" (p. 6).

Still, there remains the question of whether it is appropriate to use such doctrines as karma as solutions to the peculiarly Western formulation of the theodicy problem, structured as an inconsistent triad (God is omnipotent, God is good, and yet there is evil in the world). Thus, Charles Keyes points out that many writers have been uneasy with characterizing karma as a theodicy, because this presupposes the idea of a benevolent, omnipotent deity that is "uncharacteristic of South Asian religions" (Keyes 1983, p. 167). However, it would be a great mistake to insist on an unnecessarily narrow formulation of the problem of evil, in particular one that assumes an ethical monotheist religion. In fact, there is no reason to restrict the problem to monotheist religions, or to theist religions, or even to religions at all. As Susan Neiman points out, "nothing is easier than stating the problem of evil in nontheist terms" (Neiman 2002, p. 5); she cites, for example, Hegel's insistence that the real is identical to the rational. The problem of evil in its broadest question simply asks such universal human questions as "Why do the innocent suffer and the wicked flourish?" "Why is not the world better ordered and more just?" "Why is there suffering and death at all in the universe?" One might call this the "existential" problem of evil in contrast to the "theological" problem, and it is one that is shared by all people and all religions. And to this broader existential problem of evil, karma clearly does function as a purported solution. As Keyes explains, karma is a "theory of causation that supplies reasons for human fortune, good or bad, and that can at least in theory provide convincing explanations for human misfortune" (p. 167).

There is yet one further question regarding my approach. Even granting that karma serves as a theodicy of some sort, is it appropriate to treat it as a rigorous and systematic theoretical explanation of all evil in the world? That is, does karma constitute a "theory" in the sense of a fully developed philosophical or theological account of the presence of evil?[8] Scriptural references to the doctrine are notoriously vague and obscure and require substantial filling in (e.g.,

the epigraph given above). In part this obscurity is deliberate; the Upanishads in places suggest that the doctrine is deliberately kept secret and esoteric (e.g., Brihad-Aranyaka Upanished 3.2.13). In part this obscurity is due to the gradual evolution of the doctrine from the idea of efficacy of the sacrifice to the idea of efficacy of virtuous action in general, and to the effects extending beyond the lifetime. As Chapple (1986) points out, there is no intrinsic connection between the idea of karmic causation and that of rebirth or reincarnation (except that without the rebirth idea karma would not constitute a plausible theodicy). And the karma doctrine constitutes only one element of a very complex system of Indian thought, so that it is hard to know whether karma ought to be treated as a complete and systematic theodicy on its own. For this reason, Francis Clooney (1989) has attacked the notion of abstracting the theory from its historical, cultural, and doctrinal context (what he calls the culture's "frames of reference").

However, the evidence that the theory can be treated as a self-contained theory on its own terms is precisely that modern defenders have done so. For the idea of karma is brilliant in its simplicity and straightforwardness. As Clooney characterizes it, the basic idea is simply that "people suffer because of their past deeds in this and previous lives, and likewise enjoy benefits based on past good deeds" (p. 530). The attraction of the idea is obvious: each person makes his own fate, and all suffering happens for a reason. There is no arbitrary or meaningless suffering in the world. Moreover, even if one is miserable in this life, one can look forward to happiness in future lives, if one does one's duty. The tremendous intellectual and emotional power of this theory no doubt accounts for its wide popularity over the ages.

Hence, my project here is to evaluate karma as a complete, systematic theory of the origins and explanation of human suffering. This view of karma is just what has attracted such Western thinkers as Max Weber, who praised the doctrine for its consistency, and Peter Berger, who characterizes the theory as the "most rational" type of theodicy: "every conceivable anomy is integrated within a thoroughly rational, all-embracing interpretation of the universe" (Berger 1967, p. 65). Arthur Herman singles out for praise the consistency and completeness of the theory (p. 288). Karl Potter is impressed by the "carefully worked-out theory concerning the mechanics of karma and rebirth" (Potter 1980, p. 248). And M. Hiriyanna equally defends karma as a systematic explanation of all events in the world: "the doctrine extends the principles of causation to the sphere of human conduct and teaches that, as every event in the physical world is determined by its antecedents, so everything that happens in the moral realm is preordained" (Hiriyanna 1995, p. 46).[9]

It is this modern development of karma as systematic theodicy (whatever its historical antecedents) that I propose to examine and critique here. As Bruce Reichenbach argues, even if we have no way of knowing what historically was the problem that karma was originally intended to meet, the progressive development of the theory was no doubt motivated by a desire "rationally to account for the diversity of circumstances and situations into which sentient creatures were born, or for the natural events experienced during one's lifetime which affected one person propitiously and another adversely" (Reichenbach 1990, p. 63, see also p. 13).[10] The attraction of the karma doctrine over time is, as Reichenbach says, "its alleged explanatory power in this regard which has gained for it adherents through the centuries" (ibid.). I propose, then, to examine the doctrine of karma as developed in the modern period into a complete and systematic explanation of human suffering. Hence, my focus will be on modern commentators and secondary sources rather than on scriptural origins, and I will analyze the doctrine of karma in its rationalized and simplified form; the particular details, or alternative formulations of the doctrine, will

not be noted unless they appear relevant to the theodicy question.[11]

I will restrict my analysis in particular to the issue of whether karma provides a morally satisfactory solution to the problem of evil. There are, of course, serious physical and metaphysical issues involved as well in evaluating karma, including the idea that there is a causal mechanism by which deeds in one's past life affect events in future lives, that the soul (or some entity independent of the physical body) is the bearer of individual identity, that the soul can inhabit different bodies at different times and does not die with the body's death, that it can act wholly independent of the body, and that it is the bearer of moral responsibility (as well as personal identity) across time. Paul Edwards provides a careful critique of such issues in his *Reincarnation*. The present essay, in contrast, considers karma not as a metaphysics but solely as a theodicy: we will ask simply whether, even on these assumptions, the theory can explain the presence in the world of human suffering and misery. In the end, the purpose of this essay is not to evaluate the relative merits of one religion over another, but rather to explore one of the most intriguing conceptual possibilities in the theodicy debate: whether suffering can be wholly (or even mostly) explained and justified as the result of individual wrongdoing.

Karma as Systematic Theodicy: Five Moral Objections

The advantages of the karma theory are obvious and I will not dwell on them here. It is repeatedly pointed out, for example, that it can explain the suffering of innocent children, or congenital illnesses, with which Western thought has great difficulty. It is further argued that it is a more profoundly just doctrine, in that the fact of multiple existences gives the possibility of multiple possibilities for salvation—indeed, that in the end there can be universal salvation. This is again in contrast to the Western tradition, in which there is only one bite at the apple; those who fail in this life are doomed to eternal perdition. However, the doctrine as a whole is subject to a number of serious objections. Here I will present five distinct objections to the rebirth doctrine, all of which raise serious obstacles to the claim that rebirth can provide a convincing solution to the Problem of Evil. I do not claim this to be an exhaustive list, nor do I claim that everyone will agree with each of them. However, I think that they are serious enough as to require at the very least a fuller and more detailed defense of karma as theodicy than has so far been given.

The Memory Problem

An oft-raised objection to the claim of prior existences is the utter lack of any memory traces of previous lives. Both Paul Edwards and Bruce Reichenbach point out the oddity that all of us have had long, complex past lives, yet none of us have any recollection of them at all. More often, this objection is raised to cast doubt on whether we did in fact have any past lives at all. But my concern here is the *moral* issue raised by this deficiency: justice demands that one who is being made to suffer for a past crime be made aware of his crime and understand why he is being punished for it. Thus, even Christmas Humphreys in his vigorous defense of karma concedes the "injustice of our suffering for the deeds of someone about whom we remember nothing" (Humphreys 1983, p. 84). A conscientious parent explains to his child just why he is being punished; our legal system treats criminal defendants in just the same way. Would not a compassionate deity or a just system make sure the guilty party knows what he has done wrong? It is true that one's belief that all crime is eventually punished might serve a disciplinary function even where one is not aware just what one is being punished for at the time. However, the fact that the sufferer can never know just what crime he is being punished for at a given time, that the system of meting out punishments is so random

and unpredictable, constitutes a violation of a basic principle of justice.

Moreover, the memory problem renders the karmic process essentially useless as a means of moral education. Yet, strikingly, it is regularly claimed by adherents that one of the great virtues of karma and rebirth is precisely that "the doctrine presupposes the possibility of moral growth" and that rewards and punishments "constitute a discipline of natural consequences to educate man morally."[12] For example, suppose I am diagnosed with cancer: this must be a punishment for something I have done wrong— but I have no idea what I did to deserve this, or whether it occurred yesterday, last week, or infinitely many past lives ago. For that matter, I might be committing a sin right now—only I will not know it is a sin, because the punishment might occur next week, next year, or in the next life.[13] Radakrishnan suggests that retaining memory could be a hindrance to our moral development, since it would bring in memories of lower existences in the past (see Minor 1986, p. 32). But even if this is occasionally true, it is hardly plausible to say it is better *never* or even rarely to remember past deeds or lives; acknowledging past mistakes is in general an important (even essential) educating force in our lives. Yet none of us does remember such past events, nor is there definitive evidence that anyone has *ever* recalled a past life.[14]

The memory problem is particularly serious for the karmic doctrine, since most wrongs will be punished in a later life, and most suffering is the result of wrondoing in prior existences. (Recall that the theory is forced into this position in order to explain the obvious fact that most misdeeds do *not* get automatically punished in this world, and most suffering is not obviously correlated with wickedness.) How, then, can it be said that the doctrine promotes moral education? It is not an answer to say that our knowledge of moral duties can come from elsewhere, from religious scripture, for example. For the point is that the mechanism of karma itself is poorly designed for the purposes of moral education or progress, given the apparently random and arbitrary pattern of rewards and punishments. If moral education were truly the goal of karma and rebirth, then either punishment would be immediately consequent on sin, or at least one would have some way of knowing what one was being punished (or rewarded) for.

In fact, the difficulty is not merely one of moral education. It has been pointed out that the total lack of memory renders the theory more of a *revenge* theory than a retributive one—and hence morally unacceptable.[15] That is, it suggests that justice is satisfied merely because satisfaction has been taken on the perpetrator of the crime, ignoring completely a central moral element of punishment: that the offender where possible be made aware of his crime, that he acknowledge what he has done wrong and repent for it, that he attempt to atone for his crime, and so forth. As such the rebirth theory fails to respect the moral agency of the sinner in that it is apparently indifferent to whether or not he understands that what he has done is wrong. As Reichenbach rightly points out, the lack of memory prevents one from undergoing the moral process involved in repentance for one's crimes and even attempted rectification for them (p. 95).[16] Further, as Francis Clooney recognizes, the lack of memory of prior lives undermines the pastoral effectiveness of karma as providing comfort to the sufferer: "little comfort is given to the suffering person who is usually thought not to remember anything of the culprit past deeds" (p. 535). A vague assurance that one must have done unremembered terrible deeds in the past is hardly satisfactory.[17]

The Proportionality Problem

The rebirth solution to the Problem of Evil purports to explain every ill and benefit of this life by prior good or bad conduct. To be a morally adequate solution it must presuppose as well (although this is rarely stated explicitly) a proportionality principle—that the severity of suffering be appropriately proportioned to the severity of the wrong. But herein lies a problem: given the kinds and degrees of suffering we see in this life, it is hard to see what sort of sins the sufferers could have committed to deserve such horrible punishment. Think of those who slowly starve to death along with their family in a famine; those with severe depression or other mental illness; those who are tortured to death; young children who are rendered crippled for life in a car accident; those who die of incurable brain cancer; those burned to death in a house fire. It is difficult to believe that every bit of this kind of suffering was genuinely earned. One may grant that we as finite humans are not always in a position to judge what is just or unjust from God's perspective; nevertheless, the point of the rebirth theory is precisely to make suffering comprehensible to us as a form of justice. Indeed, belief in karma might make us tend to enact even more brutal and cruel penalties (e.g., torturing to death) if we try to model human justice on this conception of what apparently counts as divine justice.

The evidence from our own practices is that in fact we do not consider such punishments morally justified. For example, capital punishment is considered excessive and inappropriate as punishment even for a crime as serious as rape. Yet according to the karma theory every one of us without exception is condemned to "capital punishment," that is, inevitable physical death, even apart from the various other sufferings we have to endure. An eye-for-an-eye version of the rebirth theory holds that if one is raped in this life it is because one must have been a rapist in a past life, and what could be fairer than that whatever harm one caused to others will be caused to you later? But it is hard to believe that we are all subject to death because we have all been murderers in a past life. Moreover, this answer simply will not work for most diseases (one cannot "cause" another to have Parkinson's or brain cancer). (It also leads to an infinite regress problem, on which see below). It is certainly hard to stomach the notion that the inmates of Auschwitz and Buchenwald did something so evil in the past that they merely got what was coming to them—but the rebirth theory is committed to just this position.[18]

Nor does the idea of the "pool of karmic residues" solve this problem: it is equally hard to believe that even an enormous accumulation of past bad acts could justify the horrible suffering of this world, or indeed that fairness would allow all one's lesser wrongs to accumulate and generate a single, horrible punishment rather than smaller punishments over a longer period. Indeed, it raises the question of fairness of the mechanism: why would some people be punished separately for each individual wrong, while others are punished only all at once and horribly (further undermining the possibility of moral education, one might note)?

The Infinite Regress Problem

In order to explain an individual's circumstances in the present life, karma refers to the events of his prior life. But in order to explain the circumstances of that prior life, we need to invoke the events of his previous life—and so on, ad infinitum. The problem is quite general: how did the karmic process begin? What was the first wrong? Who was the original sufferer? This familiar objection points out that rebirth provides no solution at all, but simply pushes the problem back.[19] And the response typically given by defenders of rebirth is quite inadequate: they claim that the process is simply beginningless (*anādi*), that the karmic process extends back infinitely in time.[20] But this is no answer at all; indeed, it violates a basic canon of rationality, that the "explanation" not be equally as problematic as the problem being explained.[21] Thus, explains Wendy O'Flaherty: "Karma 'solves' the problem of the origin of evil by saying that there is no origin. . . . But this ignores rather than solves the problem" (p. 17).

Roy Perrett has responded to this criticism by arguing that the doctrine of karma satisfactorily explains each individual instance of suffering, and it is unreasonable to demand that it give an "ultimate explanation" of the origin of suffering. After all, he says, "explanation has to come to an end somewhere" (Perrett 1985, p. 7). However, the fallacy in this argument can be illustrated by analogy. Consider the "theory" that the world is supported on the back of an elephant, which in turn rests on the back of a tortoise. Now if this is to be an explanatory account of what supports the world, it only begs the question: what supports the tortoise? A famous (probably apocryphal) exchange between Bertrand Russell and an anonymous woman goes as follows:

WOMAN: The world rests on the back of a giant turtle.
RUSSELL: What does the turtle rest on?
WOMAN: Another turtle.
RUSSELL: What does it rest on?
WOMAN: Another turtle.
RUSSELL: What does it rest on?

The discussion goes on this way for quite some time, until the woman becomes exasperated and blurts out: "Don't you see, Professor Russell, it's turtles *all the way down!*"[22] It will hardly do for the woman to claim that, as her solution explains how the world is supported in each individual instance, she need not worry about the infinite regress. This solution is the equivalent of borrowing money in order to pay off a debt: a solution that merely postpones the problem is no solution at all.[23]

It is also noteworthy that the denial of a beginning to the process sidesteps the question of divine responsibility for the beginning of evil in the world. If there is a creator, then why is he not responsible for the misdeeds of his creations? There is no easy answer to this question, but neither can it be avoided altogether. Christianity has long been criticized for its doctrine of the Fall of Man and Original Sin for these same reasons. I do not claim here that the Christian solution succeeds, but only that the Indian solution does not evade these difficulties, either.

The Problem of Explaining Death

If rebirth is to account for all human suffering, it must, of course, explain the paradigmatic case of innocent suffering: death itself. But the problem here is that in the typical rebirth theory death seems not to be presented as punishment for wrong, but rather is *presupposed* as the mechanism by which karma operates. That is, it is through rebirth that one is rewarded or punished for one's past wrongs (by being born in high or low station, healthy or sickly, etc.). But there can be no rebirth unless there is death. So even if one is moving up in the scale of karma to a very high birth for one's great virtue, one must still undergo death. This would appear to undermine the moral justification for (arguably) the greatest of evils, death itself. For in most versions of the theory death is not even taken as something that needs explaining, but is rather assumed as simply the causal process by which karma operates. Indeed, one might well ask why *everyone* is mortal; why are there not at least some who have been virtuous enough to live indefinitely? Did we all commit such terrible wrongs right away that we have always been subject to death? Typically, though, death and rebirth are not themselves morally justified but simply taken as the neutral mechanism of karma (see, e.g., Humphreys, p. 22).

There are several ways one might try to get around this problem. Max Weber suggests that the finiteness of good deeds in our life accounts for the finiteness of our life span.[24] But this entails a quite different karmic system, one in which one is punished not for positive misdeeds, but for the lack of infinitely many good deeds. It also seems to suggest that we are morally required to be infinitely good to avoid death—a rather implausible moral demand on us and one that undermines the moral justification of karma

to be a fair system of rewards and punishments (one might ask why we are not rewarded with infinitely long life for not committing "infinite evil"). Moreover, there is a troublesome hint of circularity in Weber's solution: it seems odd to say that the finiteness of our life span derives from the finiteness of our goodness; to do infinitely much good one apparently needs an infinitely long life.

Another possible solution is simply to deny that death is indeed an evil, since it is the means by which one reaches greater rewards in life. But this is hardly satisfying, for there is no reason at all that death needs to be the mechanism by which one attains one's rewards: why not simply reward the person with health, wealth, and long life, without having to undergo rebirth in the first place? Karma certainly does not need death and rebirth: as soon as one accumulates sufficient merit, one could be instantly transformed into a higher state of existence. Further, this solution simply resorts to denial of the commonsense fact that death usually involves a terrible and often physically painful disruption of one's existence, including the separation from all one's loved ones and from all that one holds dear.

A different strategy might be to say that the ultimate reward is indeed escape from death, the release from the cycle of *saṃsāra* or rebirth, as many Indians believe. The trouble with this solution is, to put it colloquially, that it throws out the baby with the bathwater. The problem of evil arises not because life itself is an unmitigated evil, but because it contains such a strange mixture of good and evil. Karma implies that all of the good in life—health, wealth, happiness—is due to our good deeds. Why, then, is not perfect goodness rewarded with a perfectly good earthly life (one without death, pain, sickness, poverty, etc.)? If the idea that the ultimate goal is escape from life itself, it simply goes too far.[25] The idea of Nirvāṇa in Indian thought is often identified with release from not only the evil in life, but from all aspects of life, the good and the bad.[26]

But to say that life itself (not just the bad aspects of it) is the problem cannot be a solution to the problem of evil, but rather an admission of failure to solve it. For why is life bad, full of suffering and misery, rather than good? It is also an implausible claim, since experience shows that life can be very good indeed, so why is it not good all the time?

The Free Will Problem

The karma solution is often presented as the ideal solution that respects free moral agency: one determines one's own future by one's present deeds. In fact, as is often pointed out, karma is paradoxically both a fatalist and a freewill theory. For Keyes, karma "manages to affirm and deny human responsibility at the same time" (p. 175); Walli tries to account for this peculiarity by interpreting karma in two stages: in the early stages of existence it is fatalistic, but later it becomes a "moral force" (Walli 1977, p. 328). It is often noted that, despite the promise of control over one's destiny, in practice the doctrine of karma can often result instead in an attitude of fatalistic pessimism in the believer. Thus, Berger argues that by legitimating the conditions of all social classes, karma "constitutes the most thoroughly conservative religious system devised in history" (p. 65).

Karma is also praised as a freewill theory on the grounds that it gives the individual multiple (infinitely many?) chances to reach salvation in future lives. However, it is not clear whether the multiple-life theory in fact constitutes an advantage over Christian doctrine. Since in Christianity the individual has but one life in which to earn salvation, this entails a high degree of moral importance to one's life (especially given that death could come at any time). In contrast, for karma there is no such urgency, for all mistakes and misdeeds can be rectified in the fullness of future lives. The significance of a particular lifetime, let alone a particular action, is radically diminished if the "life of the individual is only

an ephemeral link in a causal chain that extends infinitely into both past and future" (Berger, p. 65). Again, this could encourage fatalism, a sense that one's choice here and now does not matter much in the greater scheme of things.

But a deeper problem is whether the doctrine of karma can in fact be squared at all with the existence of free moral agency. The difficulty can be illustrated with the following example. Consider the potential terrorist, who is deciding whether to draw attention to his political cause by detonating a bomb in a civilian area. How are we to reconcile the automatic functioning of karma with the man's choice? The karma solution must face a dilemma here. There is either of the following possibilities:

(1) Karma functions in a determinate and mechanical fashion. Then, whomever the terrorist kills will not be innocent but deserving of their fate. From the terrorist's perspective, if he is the agent of karma his action is no more blameworthy than that of the executioner who delivers the lethal injection. Indeed, no matter what evils he does in the world, he can always justify them to himself by saying he is merely an agent for karma, carrying out the necessary punishments for these "wicked" people. Alternatively, it may be that his potential victims do not deserve to die this way, in which case the man must be determined not to kill them. In either case, freedom of the will (supposedly a virtue of the karma theory) is absent.

(2) The other possibility might be countenanced as a way to preserve freedom of the will. Perhaps it really is up to the terrorist to choose whether to kill his victims. Indeed, let us say that he has the potential to create genuine evil: to kill innocent, undeserving civilians. But now the problem is that a central, indeed crucial, tenet of the karma theory has been abandoned: that *all suffering* is deserved and is justified by one's prior wrongful acts. For now we have admitted the genuine possibility of gratuitous evil, innocent suffering—just what the theory was designed to deny. One could, of course, suggest that such

gratuitous suffering will eventually be fully compensated for in a future life. But this, as Arthur Herman recognizes, would be a theory very different from that of karma. It would be a doctrine that asserts that all suffering will be *compensated* for (eventually) rather than holding that all suffering is *justified* (i.e., by one's misdeeds). Herman rightly rejects this alternative version of the theory as a recompense, not a karma, theory (p. 213).[27]

This dilemma also undermines the idea of karma as a predictive, causal law (a status often asserted for it). Further, either horn of the dilemma undermines the moral-education function of karma as well (see Herman, p. 215). In (1) one cannot learn because one apparently cannot do wrong. In (2) if one suffers, one can never know if it is because one has done wrong or because of the gratuitous harm caused by the wrongdoing of others. Similarly, if one enjoys success one can never know if it is because of one's merits or because it is payback for the gratuitous evil one suffered earlier.

Reichenbach (p. 94) suggests a way in which some defenders of the doctrine of karma have tried to evade this difficulty and preserve the reality of free will: by asserting that karma explains only evil that is not caused by wrongful human choices (i.e., karma is a theory of "natural evil" rather than of "moral evil"). But this strategy is troublesome. First, there are innumerable cases where the categories of moral-versus-natural evil seem to break down: harm caused or contributed to by human negligence (negligent driving of a car, failing to make buildings earthquake proof); harm that was not directly caused but that was anticipated and could have been prevented (starvation in Africa); harm caused in cases of insanity or diminished mental capacity; harm caused while in a state of intoxication (drunk driving); and so forth. In such cases it is doubtful that we could draw a clear distinction between moral and natural evil, but the strategy fails if one cannot draw such a line. Moreover, the great comforting and consoling function of

the karma doctrine is gone: one cannot be sure whether or not one's suffering is retribution for past wrong, and one cannot even know which of one's sufferings are punishments for one's prior wrongs and which are not. Even more importantly, this strategy represents not so much a solution to the difficulty as a wholehearted concession to the radical limitations of the theory, an admission that enormous amounts of suffering cannot be explained or justified in terms of just punishment for past wrongs. One can no longer be sure whether the circumstances one is born into (e.g., poverty) are the result of one's previous sins or of someone else's wrongdoing. This revised explanation of moral evil presumes that suffering can be random, inexplicable, meaningless, freely chosen without regard to the victim's deserts, while the explanation of natural evil presumes that all suffering is explicable and justified. One might wonder whether the explanations of moral and natural evil are now so much at such cross-purposes that the rebirth theory as a whole loses its coherence.

Thus, the dilemma seems to show that karma is simply not consistent with the genuine possibility of free moral choice. The basic problem here is the deep tension (even incompatibility) between the causal determinism implicit in the karma doctrine and the ideal of free moral responsibility, which makes one fully responsible for one's actions. Most commentators never successfully reconcile the two, if indeed they can be reconciled. An example is Hiriyanna, who insists that "everything that happens in the moral realm is preordained," but that this is fully consistent with human freedom, by which he means "being determined by oneself" (pp. 46–47 and n. 23). It is not clear how one can escape this contradiction. The more one insists on human freedom, the less are events in the world subject to karmic determination.[28]

The difficulty is even worse for the interpretation of karma that extends the idea of causal determinism to one's character or disposition in future lives. Thus, someone who does evil will inherit in the next life not only lowly circumstances but also a wicked, malevolent disposition; those who have a good disposition owe it to their good deeds in previous lives. Now even one's character and moral choice are influenced, even determined by, one's past lives; this threatens to do away with free moral choice altogether. And once one has a wicked disposition, it is a puzzle how one can escape spiraling down into further wrongdoing, or at best being permanently stuck at a given moral level, if karma has already determined one's moral character. (The problem is exaggerated even further if one accepts the view that particularly bad people become animals; how could one ever escape one's animal state, since animals do not appear to be capable of moral choice at all?)[29]

There is in the end a fatalistic dilemma for the theory. Either the karma theory is a complete and closed causal account of evil and suffering or it is not. That is, either the present state of affairs is fully explained causally by reference to prior events (including human actions) or it is not. If it is fully explained, then there can be no progress or indeed no change at all in the world. Past evil will generate present evil, and present evil will in turn cause equivalent future evil. There is no escape from the process. Alternatively, if there is the possibility of change, then karma must no longer be a complete causal account. That is, it fails as a systematic theory and therefore cannot in fact solve the problem of evil, since there must be evil in the world for which it cannot account.

Karma and the Verifiability Problem

There is one final matter that I think has significant moral relevance in this debate: the charge that the rebirth (or preexistence) doctrine is objectionable because it is *unverifiable* (or unfalsifiable).[30] Whatever happens is consistent with the theory; no fact could apparently falsify it. Whatever the terrorist does is (as Humphreys insists) simply the determination of karma. Further, one has no capacity effectively to predict the future

by this theory. Even if one has done wrong (assuming that there are precise guidelines for what counts as wrongdoing, a difficult assumption in a world of moral dilemmas), one has no way of knowing just what the punishment will be, or when it will occur, in this life or the next. A remarkable example of the willing endorsement of the advantages of unfalsifiability is made by Arthur Herman in defending karma:

> Thus no matter how terrible and awe-inspiring the suffering may be, the rebirth theorist can simply attribute the suffering to previous misdeeds done in previous lives, and the puzzle is over. Extraordinary evil is solved with no harm done to the majesty and holiness of deity.[31]

Another defender of karma and transmigration also unwittingly demonstrates the problem with such theories. He claims that the evidence for transmigration is provided by the law of karma itself (i.e., the law of moral cause and effect), since without the transmigration of souls, karma would be an inadequate solution to the Problem of Evil.[32] Such a justification is transparently circular: it presupposes that the karma solution is true in order to defend it.

Now, one might fairly doubt whether, in general, religious claims can meaningfully be held to the same standards of empirical verification as scientific claims. Nonetheless, the virtue of testability and falsifiability is that it provides a check against all of the familiar human biases: dogmatism, ethnocentrism, and so on. This is a particular problem for the karma theory, since the very unfalsifiability of the doctrine can be used to rationalize the status quo or justify oppression or unfairness on the grounds that their suffering is punishment for their prior wrongs (for they would simply have to pay their debt later). It is widely acknowledged that the repressive caste system in India lasted so long in large part because the doctrine of karma encouraged Indians to accept social oppression as the mechanical workings of karma. Hiriyanna remarkably presents it as an *advantage* of the karma theory that in India sufferers cannot blame God or their neighbors for their troubles, but only themselves (even if their neighbors are indeed unjustly oppressing them).[33] Human fallibility being what it is, the idea that all suffering is due to a previous wrongful action provides a great temptation to rationalize the status quo with reference to unverifiable claims about one's past wrongs. This is surely too great a price to pay for whatever pastoral comfort such fatalistic reassurance provides.

Conclusion

I conclude that the doctrine of karma and rebirth, taken as a systematic rational account of human suffering by which all individual suffering is explained as a result of that individual's wrongdoing, is unsuccessful as a theodicy. Even if this conclusion is correct, however, it does not follow that the doctrine must be wholly discarded for purposes of theodicy. As I mentioned earlier, it is far from clear whether karma should be interpreted in the rationalistic manner of Max Weber and Peter Berger. Francis Clooney argues that the Vedānta rejects rationalism and "believes that reason working alone is eventually confronted with insoluble problems" (p. 545). Perhaps the doctrine of karma should not be taken in a literalistic sense as a system of "moral accounting," but rather be understood figuratively, as pointing to the higher mysteries of Indian religion such as the ultimate unity of *ātman* (the individual self) and *brahman* (the ground of being). In rejecting the rationalist account of karma as a theodicy, I leave it as an open and important question whether a mystical interpretation of the doctrine might be a better way to approach the profound mystery of human suffering.

Notes

1 Cited in Keyes, p. 262.

2 Coomaraswamy 1964, p. 108. The reference, of course, is to John 9:2, in which Jesus rejects the retributive explanation of a man's blindness.

3 Weber 1947, p. 359.

4 In the second edition, Herman backs off this claim, and says that he now thinks that the traditional problem of evil is "insolvable" (p. viii).

5 I do not, however, necessarily mean to endorse his claim that the critique of Christian and Jewish thought has been "devastating."

6 Whitney 1998.

7 On which there is enormous disagreement. See, for example, Creed 1986, p. 10 (karma is "not central to the modern Hindu philosophical curriculum"), and Walli 1977, p. 277 (the "entire structure of Indian culture" is "dominated" by the idea of karma).

8 See Karl Potter's defense of treating karma as a "theory" (pp. 243 ff.).

9 Even Wendy O'Flaherty says she has "come to have more respect for the internal consistency and usefulness of the karma theory as a theodicy" (1976, Preface to the paperback edition).

10 Not all modern defenders of karma would accept this version of the doctrine. Robert Minor (1986) describes how the modern Indian philosophers Sri Aurobindo and Radakrishnan develop alternative interpretations, both rejecting the idea of karma as a juridical and hedonistic concept, that is, as dispensing sorrow and suffering as punishment for wrongdoing.

11 For example, a rebirth theory that does not allow for rebirth in animals may be unable to account for animal suffering, and hence may perhaps be objectionable on the grounds that it cannot explain all suffering. See, for example, the Chandogya Upanishad (rebirth in a dog's or pig's womb) and the Brihadaranyaka Upanishad (rebirth as an insect). See also Minor, p. 34 (for Radakrishnan, Vedic claims about human rebirth as animals or plants should be taken only metaphorically).

12 Hiriyanna, p. 49; see also Stoeber, p. 178. John Hick has pointed to a related problem: if karma is an effective system of moral education, then why do we not see steady moral progress through the ages? (Hick 1976, p. 320). Herman, too, acknowledges that payback cannot be deferred, lest it undermine the possibility of learning (p. 215).

13 Even worse for the theory of karma is the idea that a punishment might be due to a "pool" of accumulated karma from the past (see Reichenbach, p. 78), making it even more difficult to know whether I am being punished for a specific sin or a collection of many sins.

14 Various defenses are given for the apparent lack of memory. Yogis are said to remember past lives, but it is hard to verify such a claim, and in any case the problem is that *everyone* ought to remember. Sometimes it is said that in the time between lives we will recall all our past sins, but again this is hard to verify and doesn't answer the problem of why karma does not allow us to remember them here and now. For a discussion of some of these problems, see Edwards, pp. 233 ff., and Herman, pp. 255 ff. See also Reichenbach, p. 160, and Humphreys' cryptic solution (the brain forgets, but the "inner mind" remembers [p. 56]). John Hick lists some literature of purported recollections of past lives (1990, p. 132). Edwards critiques such claims (chap. 7).

15 See, for example, Nayak, quoted in Stoeber, p. 178.

16 It might also be noted that for theories of personal identity that make persistence of memory essential to personal identity, the lack of memory would indicate that the person being punished is not the same person who committed the wrong.

17 A closely related further problem is, of course, that karma violates the legal principle "nulla poena sine lege": no penalty (punishment) without a law clearly identifying in advance that the conduct is wrong, and just what the penalty is for violating it.

18 Remarkably, just such a claim was recently made by an ultra-orthodox rabbi in Jerusalem, who declared that the victims of the Nazi Holocaust were killed because they were reincarnations of sinners and had to atone for their sins.

19 See, for example, Watts 1964, p. 38; Hick 1976, pp. 309, 314; Hick 1990, p. 139; and O'Flaherty 1976, p. 17.

20 See Herman, p. 263, and Hiriyanna, pp. 47, 198. The latter's "solution" is even worse: he denies that it would even be possible to solve this problem, since we cannot conceive of a first action before one's character is formed. But instead of recognizing that this undermines the karma solution, he inexplicably thinks that the impossibility of solving the regress problem is a defense of karma. See also Herman, p. 285 (the Vedas do indicate an ultimate beginning).

21 Indeed, according to this infinite-regress explanation, every wrong is *preceded* as well as followed by suffering, so it is not clear on what basis one can say which is cause and which is effect.

22 John Locke cynically relates a similar story in an attack on the philosophical notion of "substance", which he thought had no explanatory value. He mentions the "Indian philosopher" who, in trying to explain what supports the world, had he "but thought of this word *Substance*, he needed not to have been at the trouble to find an Elephant to support it, and a Tortoise to support his Elephant: The word Substance would have done it effectually" (John Locke, *Essay Concerning Human Understanding*, bk. 2, chap. 13, par. 19).

23 Roy Perrett argues that the objection is based on an "over-stringent conception of explanation" (p. 9), and that, while "individual instances of suffering are explicable by reference to karma, the fact that suffering exists in our world at all . . . is just a brute fact" (p. 7). And this, Perrett suggests, is "perfectly reasonable," since all explanations have to come to an end somewhere. However, it is surely implausible to construct a theodicy that answers the question "why is there suffering" by saying: "it is just a brute fact."

24 Weber 1964, p. 145.

25 See Hick 1976, pp. 321, 437.

26 Hiriyanna, p. 69.

27 See also Reichenbach, p. 17.

28 Humphreys' analysis of an analogous dilemma, whether to aid a sufferer, is not particularly helpful: "the help or withholding of it is just as much his karma as his present sufferings": "one can't interfere with karma" (pp. 65–66).

29 Augustine raises a further objection, pointing to a man who is mentally retarded (a "moron") but is of high moral character: "How will they be able to attribute to him a previous life of so disgraceful a character that he deserved to be born an idiot, and at the same time of so highly meritorious character as to entitle him to a preference in the award of the grace of Christ over many men of the acutest intellect?" ("On the Merits and Forgiveness of Sins," chap. 32, in Augustine 1984).

30 A problem raised both by Paul Edwards (1996) and Bruce Reichenbach (1990).

31 Herman, p. 287.

32 Hiriyanna, p. 47.

33 Ibid., p. 48 (although he does not specifically mention caste). See Humphreys, p. 55 (the condition of cripples and dwarfs can be justified by their sins).

References

Augustine. 1984. *The City of God.* Translated by Henry Bettenson. New York: Penguin Books.

Berger, Peter. 1967. *The Sacred Canopy.* Garden City: Doubleday.

Chapple, Chris. 1986. *Karma and Creativity.* Albany: State University of New York Press.

Clooney, Francis. 1989. "Evil, Divine Omnipotence, and Human Freedom: Vedanta's Theology of Karma." *Journal of Religion* 69: 530–548.

Coomaraswamy, Ananda. 1964. *Buddha and the Gospel of Buddhism.* New York: Harper and Row.

Creed, Austin. 1986. "Contemporary Philosophical Treatments of Karma and Rebirth." In Ronald Neufeldt, ed., *Karma and Rebirth.* Albany: State University of New York Press.

Edwards, Paul. 1996. *Reincarnation: A Critical Examination.* New York: Prometheus Books.

Herman, Arthur. 1976. *The Problem of Evil in Indian Thought.* Delhi: Motilal Banarsidass.

Hick, John. 1976. *Death and Eternal Life.* New York: Harper and Row.

——. 1990. *Philosophy of Religion.* New Jersey: Prentice-Hall.

Hiriyanna, M. 1995. *The Essentials of Indian Philosophy.* Delhi: Motilal Banarsidass.

Humphreys, Christmas. 1983. *Karma and Rebirth.* London: Curzon Press.

Keyes, Charles. 1983. "Merit-Transference in the Karmic Theory of Popular Theravada Buddhism." In *Karma,* edited by Charles Keyes and Valentine Daniel. Berkeley: University of California Press.

Minor, Robert. 1986. "In Defense of Karma and Rebirth: Evolutionary Karma." In Ronald Neufeldt, ed., *Karma and Rebirth.* Albany: State University of New York Press.

Neiman, Susan. 2002. *Evil in Modern Thought.* Princeton: Princeton University Press.

O'Flaherty, Wendy Doniger. 1976. *The Origins of Evil in Hindu Mythology.* Berkeley: University of California Press.

Perrett, Roy. 1985. "Karma and the Problem of Suffering." *Sophia* 24: 4–10.

Potter, Karl H. 1980. "The Karma Theory and Its Interpretation in Some Indian Philosophical Systems." In Wendy O'Flaherty, *Karma and Rebirth in Classical Indian Traditions.* Berkeley: University of California Press.

Prabhupāda, A. C. Bhaktivedanta Swami. 1972. *The Bhagavad-Gītā as It Is.* Los Angeles: Bhaktivedanta Book Trust.

Reichenbach, Bruce. 1990. *The Law of Karma.* Honolulu: University of Hawai'i Press.

Sivananda, Swami. 1985. *Practice of Karma Yoga.* Himalayas, India: Divine Life Society; Dist. Tehri-Garwhal, U.P.

Stoeber, Michael. 1992. *Evil and the Mystics' God.* Toronto: University of Toronto Press.

Walli, Koshelya. 1977. *Theory of Karman in Indian Thought.* Bharata Mahisha.

Watts, Alan. 1964. *Beyond Theology.* New York: Vintage Books.

Weber, Max. 1947. *Essays in Sociology.* Translated by Gerth and Mills. London: K. Paul, Trench, Trubner.

——. 1964. *The Sociology of Religion.* Translated by Ephraim Fischoff. Boston: Beacon Press. (Original publication date in German: 1922.)

Whitney, Barry, ed. 1998. *Theodicy: An Annotated Bibliography on the Problem of Evil, 1960–1991.* Bowling Green: Philosophy Documentation Center.

Chapter 17

Richard Swinburne

NATURAL EVIL AND THE POSSIBILITY OF KNOWLEDGE

The Need to Know about the Effects of our Actions, Good and Bad

For humans to have a choice between doing good and doing bad, we need to have true beliefs about the effects of our actions, for the goodness or badness of an action is so often a matter of it having good or bad effects. It is bad to kick other people because it will hurt them, good to give the starving food because that will enable them to stay alive. And so on. So if God is to give us the choice between good and bad, he must give us, or allow us to acquire, true beliefs about the effects of our actions—beliefs in which we have enough confidence to make it matter how we choose. We need a whole sheaf of strong true beliefs with respect to many different actions, about what effects will follow from them. How is God to give us these beliefs? The argument of this chapter is that God cannot give us true beliefs about the effects of our actions (good and bad) without providing natural processes (in which humans are not involved) whereby those effects (good and bad) are produced in a regular way—or rather he cannot do this without depriving us of considerable other benefits. Natural evil is needed to give us the true beliefs without which we could not have a free choice between good and bad.[1] [. . .]

Let us distinguish between the necessary truths of morality, and the contingent truths which follow therefrom when factual information about the effects and circumstances of actions is added. It is (plausibly) a necessary moral truth that it is wrong to give money to beggars if they will spend it only on drugs which kill. It is a matter of fact that certain beggars will spend money only on drugs which kill. It follows that it is a contingent moral truth that it is wrong to give money to those particular beggars. Now I do not know of any good reason to suppose that experience is necessary either for the possession or for the acquisition of concepts or knowledge of necessary truths or their interconnection. Someone has a concept to the extent to which he can conceive what it would be like for it to have application, and to the extent to which he can recognize that it does apply. And someone can see what is involved in its application (i.e. know necessary truths which concern it) without ever having observed its application. Someone might be born with an ability to conceive what it would be like for something to be red or green and to recognize red and green objects, even if he has never observed such; and this ability would enable him to recognize as a necessary truth that nothing can be red and green all over. The same applies to the necessary truths of morality. Someone might know what wrong was when the world as yet contained none, and he might know which actions were wrong and which states of affairs were bad before ever they had occurred. Our moral knowledge is not acquired in this way but there is no reason why that of some human agent should not be. God could ensure that humans were given moral concepts and a deep imagination which would enable them to comprehend necessary truths about their application without their having any experience of harsh moral realities. We could know that it is good to feed anyone starving even if we knew of no one who was starving; that torturing in order to extort belief in a creed is wrong, even if no one had ever done it. However, I argued earlier that although humans could acquire moral knowledge without experience, there was, nevertheless, a certain value in their acquiring it through experience.

My concern here is not with knowledge of necessary moral truths, but with the factual knowledge of the effects of our actions (the effects being described in non-morally loaded terms, e.g. just as pain or death) and so with the nature of our actions (e.g. as causing pain or killing) which we need in order to know the contingent moral truths, e.g. that certain particular actions are wrong (because they do have those effects). How is God to make such knowledge available to us? The argument of this chapter is that while God might be able to give moderately well-justified knowledge of the effects of our actions, good and bad, without too great a cost, he could not allow us to learn what the effects are, let alone to choose to seek such knowledge, without providing natural processes (in which humans are not involved) whereby those effects (good and bad) are produced in a regular way—or rather he could not do this without depriving us of a very considerable other benefit. Natural evil is needed to give us the choice of whether to acquire knowledge of the good and bad effects of our actions, and indeed in order to allow us to have very well-justified knowledge at all.

God could perhaps implant in us strong true beliefs about the effects of our actions; or make us such that we gradually find ourselves with more and more such beliefs as time goes by,

beliefs which open up more and more possible actions for us. We could start life with beliefs that crying causes adults to feed one, and kicking the bedclothes off causes one to be cooler (and perhaps we do start life with those beliefs; however, I write "perhaps" because it may be that when babies want food or want to be cooler, they just cry or kick without having a belief that these actions will have the desired effects). And then as we get older we could find ourselves with more and more complicated beliefs about the effects of actions. Wondering how to hurt someone, I could find myself believing strongly that kicking him, or telling others about the misdemeanours of his youth, would in different ways hurt him. I could perhaps find myself believing strongly, for no reason at all, that setting light to hydrogen will cause an explosion, and that giving money to Oxfam will relieve starvation, whereas spending it on buying books will not have this effect.

If we are to have the opportunity of doing an action of any complexity over time, we will need to have beliefs at each time as to which subactions in the particular circumstances of the time will contribute to the total action. In order to have the choice of sailing round the world, I will need to find myself at each stage with a true belief about which actions (tacking, going about, taking this course rather than that) will produce the sought-after result. And I will need to find myself with beliefs about the effects of my actions on others of the crew. All that could happen. I could find myself with the relevant beliefs. They might even be probabilistic beliefs —that if I pull the sail in further there is a 30 per cent chance that the boat will capsize. These beliefs, combined with the moral beliefs about which effects are good and which effects are bad, would then allow us to choose between doing good and doing bad. Beliefs need never come through experience of what we or others have done in the past or observed to happen in the natural world, or others have told us; let alone as the result of our constructing a complicated scientific theory on the basis of many observations.

Would these spontaneously arising beliefs amount to knowledge? [. . .] These beliefs would not be nearly as strongly justified and so amount as obviously to knowledge, as beliefs based on observation of what has happened in the past and extrapolation therefrom. My belief B that if I set light to hydrogen there will be an explosion is far better justified if it is not a basic belief, but justified by many beliefs to the effect that I have observed that when I have set light to hydrogen in the past (or it has accidentally caught light) there has been an explosion. [. . .]

An intermediate position is possible. B might not be justified by my beliefs about the past explosions which I have observed, but simply by (true and justified) beliefs to the effects that I have always found in the past that my basic beliefs about effects of my actions have subsequently proved true. But if I have always done actions with effects of a certain kind—e.g. actions whose short-term effects concern only myself, or the physical well-being of those close to me, or actions such that I have basic beliefs only about their good effects—there will remain a doubt about whether my basic beliefs about the effects of actions with effects of other kinds are equally trustworthy.

If a belief that my action will have a certain effect is to be as well justified as possible, it will need to be backed up by beliefs that in the past actions of just that type have had that kind of effect; or that the immediate result which the action consists in bringing about has had that kind of effect in the past. What I mean by the latter is this. Every human action done by means of the body consists in bringing about some bodily movement or immediate effect in the environment, which in time has more distant effects. If I move my hand (intentional action), this consists of my bringing about the motion of my hand; if I open the door, this consists of my bringing about the door being open. The latter events—the hand moving or the door being open—I shall call

results of my actions of moving my hand or opening the door; they are events which could be produced by non-intentional causes. My belief that if I light hydrogen it will explode will for its strongest justification depend on beliefs that in the past when I (or others) have lit hydrogen it has exploded; or our beliefs that in the past when hydrogen has caught light accidentally it has exploded. By the Principle of Honesty, such justifying beliefs must in general be true.

So if my beliefs about some contemplated action having a bad effect are to be as well justified as possible, this will in general require there having been similar actions, or events not produced intentionally, producing similar bad effects in the past, which I can observe (or others can tell me about) and I can take account of. Given that it is good that our actions shall be guided by our beliefs, it is good that we should have beliefs as well justified as possible. For in so far as there is a justified doubt about which effects our actions will have, we can evade the moral force of a choice between good and bad on the ground that it is not certain which effects our actions will have. The less certain the effects, the less serious the choice. If there is a doubt about whether smoking causes cancer, it is less evidently a bad thing to smoke. To be well justified our beliefs need to be backed up by experience. It may not be a necessary truth that all knowledge (of matter of contingent fact) comes from experience of similar matters, but it is a necessary truth that it is better justified and so will give a firmer basis for action if it does.

But yes, perhaps, with this rather important qualification, we could simply find ourselves with knowledge of the effects of our actions, well enough justified to provide a basis for considerable moral choice of which effects to cause. As described it would not be a knowledge based on any understanding of how the world worked: I could just find myself with the knowledge that to make this arm movement after this leg movement would enable me to sail round the world; but I would not know how wind and tide and sail interact to make this possible. I could find myself with knowledge about such matters also. Yet such knowledge would not be knowledge which I acquired by learning, let alone knowledge that I chose to have and was prepared to sacrifice much to get. Knowledge would be ours unchosen.

Although I have done my best to describe this situation as one where humans would have something amounting to knowledge (even if not knowledge as well justified as possible), it is difficult for me to avoid the feeling that my best is not good enough. Could mental attitudes of mine really be described even as beliefs, let alone knowledge, about the geography and history and science of the world if they did not result from experience, argument, challenge, falsification? The mental attitudes which guided my behaviour in the absence of such empirical backing seem more like instincts or hunches. Is that quality of reason which we value so much in humans really present at all in this situation? If it is not, the need for natural evil will be even stronger than I am representing.

What, however, we could not do in this supposed situation of innate knowledge is to learn from experience, to discern by observing its unintended consequences that some action of ours caused good or bad of some new kind and so to learn that by doing a similar action we could cause good or bad. Above all, we could not choose to seek new knowledge by thinking, searching, and asking—knowledge of what we can do and can bring about by our actions, as well as theoretical knowledge of the structure of the world.

The greatness of human (and to a lesser extent, animal) reason consists not only in having knowledge, but in acquiring it and changing one's beliefs in the light of evidence. And it is a great good for humans that we should have the free choice of whether to exercise our reason in finding out deep theoretical truths about the universe—how big it is, how old it is, what it is made of, whether God sustains it, and so on—as

well as important factual truths about the human race and those close to us. And it is good also that we should have the choice of whether or not to extend our power over others and the world; and extending that power involves acquiring knowledge of which present actions will lead to humans being killed or fed, being educated or depressed, going to Mars or living beneath the ocean. Not to have the choice of extending our knowledge of such matters is not to have the choice of helping or harming people in new ways; and to refuse to exercise the former choice is not merely to refuse to acquire the power to help or harm, but to risk helping or harming through the consequences of our actions of which we are still unaware. Free choice without knowledge of effects is empty, and a significant kind of free choice is the choice of seeking knowledge of how to bring about different effects.

Learning Involves the Operation of Natural Processes Producing Good and Bad

Creatures who are to learn how to produce some distant effect must have a limited repertoire of basic actions that they can do at will; and learning will consist of discovering that some basic actions done in certain circumstances will have certain effects. Thereby we learn to produce those effects. [. . .] If God is to allow me to choose to acquire knowledge of how to travel to Mars or to kill millions of people, he must allow me to learn which immediate states of affairs (which could be results of my bodily movements) will lead to those effects. He must allow me to learn in which circumstances will the depression of a button lead to a rocket going to Mars, and in which circumstances will it lead to nuclear explosions which will kill millions of people.

Much acquisition of knowledge comes from being told by others, that is from testimony. But a belief of mine acquired by testimony will only amount to knowledge if my informant or someone from whom he acquired his belief via a chain of informants had a belief amounting to knowledge, whose strong justification was of a different kind. And if the chain of testimony is too long, the justification which it produces for the resulting beliefs will be very much less. The human race as a whole must learn in a different way.

All knowledge of the future is knowledge either of what natural processes will bring about or of what agents will bring about intentionally (or both, if intentions are moulded by natural processes, or if they mould those processes). Someone may infer to a future event either by regarding what will happen as to be produced by a natural process or as to be produced intentionally. So knowledge that my action A, which consists in bringing about some result C, will have a further consequence E, will be knowledge either that natural processes dictate that C brings about E, or knowledge that some other agent on observing C will bring about E intentionally. Knowledge that putting cyanide in a man's drink will kill him is knowledge of a natural process—that cyanide kills; and knowledge that you will visit me today when you have promised to visit me is knowledge of intentional agency.

If God is to give to humans a range of actions with consequences bad and good, he must ensure that human actions have these consequences, either as a result of a natural process which he implants in the world, or as a result of his direct intentional action. And if the human agent is to learn about those consequences, he must learn about them either by discerning the natural process or by discovering God's intention. God could allow me to learn the consequences of my action by allowing me to ask him what he will bring about if I do the action. I might ask him, "How can I kill John?" And then I might hear in my ear or see on the screen the English words "If you shoot John, he will die". But if I regard my actions as having the consequences they do in virtue of some other agent

intentionally making the actions have those consequences, I must regard that agent as in control of my life; and not merely my life, but, since he determines the effect of my actions on others, as in control of their lives too. I must regard him as in control of the Universe, at least locally. And I must regard him as perfectly good. For his local freedom of operation to determine what happens is (to all appearances) absolute, and so therefore is his local knowledge of what will happen. And so, as the simplest hypothesis, I must regard him as knowledgeable also in other fields, including morality, and free in other fields; and so as knowing the good, and, not being distracted by temptation from pursuing it, as perfectly good. Under those circumstances I could indeed discover the consequences of my actions, and know whether they are ones which I believe good or ones which I believe bad. But I would regard my every movement as overseen by an all-knowing and perfectly good being, i.e. a God. And this would be no mere balance-of-probability belief. It would be an evident belief which guided every action of mine. That . . . would make the choice between good and bad impossible, given that we have certain good desires.

So, to preserve our serious choice between good and bad, God must implant in nature a system of natural causal processes and let us learn what they are. I understand by a natural process one in which a cause of a given kind produces an effect of another kind in a regular way either with natural necessity or with natural probability. Natural processes are predictable processes; and if they are to be of any use to humans for prediction, the regularities must be of a simple recognizable kind. The a priori principles of what is evidence for what . . . have the consequence that the strongest evidence for the claim that Cs bring about Es will come from past observations of Cs being followed by Es in varied conditions. If in the past mustard seeds being put in the ground and watered has always been followed by the appearance of mustard seedlings, then very probably the implanting and watering of mustard seeds causes the appearance of mustard seedlings. So the basic way in which God can allow us to acquire knowledge of natural processes, that Cs cause Es, is by providing us many instances of the successions involved under different conditions. He will implant in the world many instances of Cs being followed by Es under different conditions; and allow us to reach our knowledge by reflecting on these observations, or—making it a choice which involves more effort by us—allow us to search for and eventually find such evidence. Once we have this knowledge of causal succession, then we know that if we produce a C as an immediate effect of a bodily movement, thereby we cause an E. Observing many mustard seed–seedling successions, we come to know that the way to produce mustard seedlings is to sow mustard seeds. We can make this kind of inference without automatically needing to suppose that God causes the system of natural processes (although, I believe and have argued elsewhere, the operation of natural processes does in fact provide an important part of a cumulative case for belief in God). And this of course is the way in which we do come to learn about the effects of our actions, and see any beliefs about this we already have as strongly justified.

We (i.e. humans in general) learn that eating toadstools causes stomach pain by seeing people eat toadstools and then suffer pain. We learn that alcohol makes people unsteady drivers by seeing people have many drinks and then drive unsteadily, and so on. And we choose whether to acquire such knowledge, by choosing to search for and find observational evidence from which we infer such causal processes. These observations open up a range of possible actions, good and bad, which would not otherwise be available. Once we learn that eating toadstools causes stomach pain, we then have open to us the opportunity to cause others to suffer stomach pain (by feeding them with toadstools), to allow others (e.g. children) to be exposed to the risk of stomach pains

(by allowing them to gather toadstools without warning them of the possible effects), or to prevent others from incurring this risk. These opportunities would not have been available without the knowledge; observation of natural processes producing pain provides that knowledge. We know that rabies causes a terrible death. With this knowledge we have the possibility of preventing such death (e.g. by controlling the entry of pet animals into Britain), or of negligently allowing it to occur or even of deliberately causing it. Only with the knowledge of the effects of rabies are such possibilities open to us. That knowledge is provided by observations of various people suffering subsequently to being bitten by dogs and other animals with rabies in various circumstances. Or, again, how are humans to have the opportunity to stop future generations contracting asbestosis, except through knowledge of what causes asbestosis? We can choose to obtain that knowledge through laborious study of records which show that persons in contact with blue asbestos many years ago have died from asbestosis thirty years later.

Our study of nature may reveal processes with which we cannot interfere, but whose further consequences we may learn to avoid by learning where and when they will occur. We may come to learn when comets will appear, volcanoes erupt, or earthquakes strike, without (yet) being able to initiate or prevent these; but whose further consequences we may be able to influence. Knowledge of when and where earthquakes are likely to occur gives us the opportunity deliberately to cause, negligently to risk, or, alternatively, intentionally to prevent suffering and death caused by earthquakes, e.g. by taking the risk of building on areas subject to earthquake, or by making the effort to mobilize the human race to avoid in future the consequences of a major earthquake.

The claim that a particular future C will cause an E will be justified by past observations, paradigmatically of past Cs being followed by Es. Our a priori inductive criteria reveal that such a claim is better justified if it is based on many recent purported observations of Cs in many different circumstances being followed invariably by Es. Observations remote in time may have been mis-recorded or have occurred under circumstances different in some way from those holding in the present which affects the causal sequence in some crucial way. The more observations there are in different circumstances, the better the evidence that the sequence of Cs being followed by Es is a genuine causal sequence, not a mere occasional regularity. The observations might concern, not Cs and Es, but many very different sequences which provide substantial but indirect evidence for a general scientific theory of which it is a remote consequence that a C will be fol-lowed by an E. But the less similar is the evidence to the kind of phenomena predicted, (because of the greater probability of alternative explan-ations of the evidence) the greater the doubt must be whether the sophisticated scientific the-ory really works for Cs and Es; and that will require to be checked out by looking at pheno-mena very similar to those predicted. Our know-ledge of the future consequences of our actions is better justified in so far as it comes from many recent observations in similar circumstances.

So sure knowledge that if I take frequent large doses of heroin I shall die must come from observations of frequent heroin intake being fol-lowed by death. And many recent observations under different conditions provide the surest knowledge possible. There could be a compli-cated scientific theory of which it was a remote consequence that heroin would have this effect. The theory would be confirmed by it being a simple theory which yielded true predictions of the consequences of taking other, chemically similar drugs, perhaps tested sometimes on ani-mals rather than humans. The remoteness of the theory, and its never having been tested with respect to heroin on humans, would, however, make its prediction about the effect of heroin on me much less well evidenced. And that some drug causes pain is hardly likely to be even

remotely evidenced, except via observation of other drugs causing pain or other unpleasant sensations (so different are sensations from other things). Pain there must be which is observed if we are to have knowledge of when our actions will cause pain.

The events by far the most important for the moral significance of actions which bring them about are mental events, i.e. experiences of sen-tient beings. As noted earlier in this book, actions are paradigmatically good in so far as they pro-mote pleasurable and knowledge-deepening and friendship-deepening experiences; bad in so far as they promote pain, ignorance, and poverty of imagination and understanding. Most sure knowledge of the experience to be caused by some natural process is to be had through having experiences oneself of what followed from past occurrences of the process. One knows best just what it feels like to be burnt by having been burnt oneself in the past. But the public behaviour of others also produces strong evidence about their experiences. And if we have actually observed others being burnt, we shall know quite a lot about what it feels like to be burnt. A person's knowledge is, however, less securely based if the observations which support a theory are not their own, but ones known only through the testimony of others; and that, of course, is the most usual case. My justification for believing that heroin causes death is that everyone says that observers report (via television programmes and newspapers) that many who have taken large doses of heroin have died quickly there-after. This evidence, though good evidence, is always open to the possibility of lying or exag-geration; or, where description of experiences is involved, lack of adequate vocabulary for the purpose.

So I conclude this complicated discussion thus: if God is to allow us to acquire knowledge by learning from experience and above all to allow us to choose whether to acquire know-ledge at all or even to allow us to have very well-justified knowledge of the consequences of our actions—knowledge which we need if we are to have a free and efficacious choice between good and bad—he needs to provide natural evils occurring in regular ways in consequence of natural processes. Or rather, he needs to do this if he is not to give us too evident an awareness of his presence.

Knowledge Provided by Animal Suffering

The suffering which provides knowledge is not confined to humans. The higher animals acquire knowledge by normal induction, knowledge of where to obtain food, drink, and fellowship; and also knowledge of the causes of pain, loss of health, and loss of life. Seeing the suffering, disease, and death of others in certain circumstances, they learn to avoid those circumstances. And not merely do they observe and infer passively, but many animals actively seek knowledge: they look for food, spy out the land for predators, put their feet gingerly on possibly unsafe surfaces, etc. The lower animals of course avoid many situations and do many actions instinctively; but in those cases they cannot be said to be doing the action or avoiding the situation through very well-justified knowledge of its consequences. We have noted that acting in the light of such knowledge is a good thing even if the agent does not have free will; and so too, I suggest, is actively searching for knowledge.

It is a great good that animals are not mere digestion machines with pleasurable sensations attached to the digestive process; but that they struggle to get food, save themselves and their offspring from predators and natural disasters, seek mates over days, and so on. But they can only do these things with some knowledge of the consequences of their actions, and they could only acquire this by learning and seeking (as opposed to being born with it) and it could only amount to very well-justified knowledge, if it is derived from experience of the actions of others, of the unintended effects of their own

actions, and of the effects of natural processes. Languageless animals could not acquire knowledge by being told (by God or anyone else). They can acquire knowledge only by learning from experience. Other animals must suffer if some animals are to learn to avoid suffering for themselves and their offspring. If deer are to learn how to help prevent their offspring from being caught in fires, some fawns have to be caught in fires for the deer to see what happens. If gazelle are to learn to avoid being killed by tigers, they have at least to have been mauled themselves or seen others mauled. Otherwise it will all reasonably seem a game. There will not be any difference between playing "tig" with tigers and playing "tig" with other gazelles. And then animals will be deprived of the possibility of serious and heroic actions.

The suffering of animals provides us, as well as themselves, with much knowledge; though since they are only somewhat, not totally, like ourselves, the knowledge which the suffering provides is a less sure guide to what we would suffer in certain circumstances than would be the suffering of humans; but still it is quite a good guide. Indeed, a great deal of our knowledge of the disasters for humans which would follow some actions comes from study of the actual disasters which have befallen animals. The bad states which have naturally befallen animals provide a huge reservoir of information for humans to acquire knowledge of the choices open to them, a reservoir which we have often tapped: seeing the fate of sheep, humans have learnt of the presence of dangerous tigers; seeing the cows sink into a bog, they have learnt not to cross that bog, and so on. (And alas humans have for a long time chosen to increase their knowledge of the effects of actions by deliberately doing things to animals which might cause them to suffer. They have discovered the effects of drugs or surgery or unusual circumstances on humans by deliberately subjecting animals to those drugs or surgery or circumstances. Before putting humans into space, we put animals into space and saw what happened to them. Now I certainly do not think that humans had the right to do many such things. My only point here is to illustrate the claim that animal suffering, however caused, often provides valuable knowledge for humans.)

And as regards very long-term consequences of changes of circumstances, environment, or climate, the story of animal evolution provides our main information. Human history so far is too short to provide knowledge of the very long-term consequences of our actions; and yet we are doing things which may have a considerable effect on the constitution of the atmosphere (e.g. on whether there is still an ozone layer), on the balance of nature (e.g. on whether there are many vertebrates on Earth other than humans), and on the climate. And we may discover how to make some very big changes to the Earth and its surroundings, e.g. alter the Earth's magnetic field, drive the Earth nearer to the sun or further away from it. And so on. We need information about the long-term effects of all these actions. There is a lot of information to be gleaned from pre-hominid history on all these matters, for climate, magnetic field, and balance of nature have changed often over the past 300 million years and if we learn more about their effects on animals we shall avoid many disasters ourselves. But those effects must include suffering, in virtue of the similarities of animals to ourselves. If there were not these similarities, the information would not show what would happen to us. To take but one more and very strong example: biologists are beginning to acquire the power to cause much good or ill by inducing various genetic mutations. Human history does not provide the data which will give them any knowledge of the consequences of their actions. Their surest knowledge of those consequences will come from a study of the evolutionary history of the consequences in animals of various naturally occurring mutations.

In addition to these detailed bits of information, the story of pre-human nature "red in tooth and claw" already provides one very general bit of information crucially relevant to our possible choices. For suppose that animals had come into existence at the same time as humans, and always in situations where humans could save them from any suffering. Naturally it would then seem a well-confirmed theory that (either through act of God or nature) suffering never happens to animals except such as humans can prevent. So we would seem not to have the opportunity to do actions which would cause suffering to present-day animals let alone later generations of animals of a subsequently unpreventable kind, or the opportunity to prevent such suffering. We simply would not (and rightly would not) seriously consider the possibility that some of our actions might have enormous and subsequently unpreventable long-term bad consequences. As evidence of this claim of mine, I point out that hardly anybody ever did consider such matters before the nineteenth century. It is difficult to get back into a pre-Darwinian way of thought, but if you do, you do not (and rightly do not) take seriously the possibility of our actions having long-term effects on nature. The story of evolution tells us that the causation or prevention of long-term suffering is indeed within our power; such suffering can happen because it has happened. The story of pre-human evolution reveals to humans just how much the subsequent fate of animals and humans is in our hands—for it will depend on the environment which we form for them, and their genes, which we may cause to mutate.

We may not know exactly when and where the past natural evils occurred, but the mere knowledge that suffering of a certain type occurred to certain kinds of creatures under certain conditions provides us with very good reason to avoid actions which may produce those conditions. Indeed all past evils of which we know provide knowledge of past events, and, more strikingly, since all natural evils occur as a result of largely predictable natural processes (there are no kinds of natural evil which occur in a totally random way), all such knowledge helps to build up knowledge of the natural processes which we can utilize to produce or prevent future evils. All past and present human and animal natural evils of which we know thus contribute to the widening of human choice when we learn about them. And (except at an undesirable cost) we could not learn, and especially choose to learn, without them.

Note

1 I first advocated the defence from the need for knowledge in "Natural Evil", *American Philosophical Quarterly*, 15 (1979), 295–301; and developed it more fully in *The Existence of God* (rev. edn., Clarendon Press, 1991), chs. 9, 10, and 11 (see esp. ch. 11); and in "Knowledge from Experience and the Problem of Evil", in W. J. Abraham and S. W. Holtzer (eds.), *The*

Rationality of Religious Belief (Clarendon Press, 1987). It has come in for quite a bit of criticism. See David O'Connor, "Swinburne on Natural Evil", *Religious Studies*, 19 (1983), 65–73; Eleonore Stump, "Knowledge, Freedom, and the Problem of Evil", *International Journal for the Philosophy of Religion*, 14 (1983), 49–58; Paul K. Moser, "Natural Evil and the Free Will Defence", *International Journal for the Philosophy of Religion*, 15 (1984), 49–56. In my elaboration of it here I seek to defend it against these criticims. Those familiar with this discussion will recognize that I have amended the defence considerably in the light of these criticisms. It is no longer in the form of the need for natural evil if we are to have knowledge of the consequences of our actions; but in the form of the need for natural evil if we are to have very well-justified knowledge, and the opportunity to learn from experience and to choose to seek new knowledge.

Chapter 18

William L. Rowe

THE PROBLEM OF EVIL AND SOME VARIETIES OF ATHEISM

This paper is concerned with three inter-related questions. The first is: Is there an argument for atheism based on the existence of evil that may rationally justify someone in being an atheist? To this first question I give an affirmative answer and try to support that answer by setting forth a strong argument for atheism based on the existence of evil.[1] The second question is: How can the theist best defend his position against the argument for atheism based on the existence of evil? In response to this question I try to describe what may be an adequate rational defense for theism against any argument for atheism based on the existence of evil. The final question is: What position should the informed atheist take concerning the rationality of theistic belief? Three different answers an atheist may give to this question serve to distinguish three varieties of atheism: unfriendly atheism, indifferent atheism, and friendly atheism. In the final part of the paper I discuss and defend the position of friendly atheism.

Before we consider the argument from evil, we need to distinguish a narrow and a broad sense of the terms "theist," "atheist," and "agnostic." By a "theist" in the narrow sense I mean someone who believes in the existence of an omnipotent, omniscient, eternal, supremely good being who created the world. By a "theist" in the broad sense I mean someone who believes in the existence of some sort of divine being or divine reality. To be a theist in the narrow sense is also to be a theist in the broad sense, but one may be a theist in the broad sense—as was Paul Tillich—without believing that there is a supremely good, omnipotent, omniscient, eternal being who created the world. Similar distinctions must be made between a narrow and a broad sense of the terms "atheist" and "agnostic." To be an atheist in the broad sense is to deny the existence of any sort of divine being or divine reality. Tillich was not an atheist in the broad sense. But he was an atheist in the narrow sense, for he denied that there exists a divine being that is all-knowing, all-powerful and perfectly good. In this paper I will be using the terms "theism," "theist," "atheism," "atheist," "agnosticism," and "agnostic" in the narrow sense, not in the broad sense.

I

In developing the argument for atheism based on the existence of evil, it will be useful to focus on some particular evil that our world contains in considerable abundance. Intense human and animal suffering, for example, occurs daily and in a great plenitude in our world. Such intense suffering is a clear case of evil. Of course, if the intense suffering leads to some greater good, a good we could not have obtained without undergoing the suffering in question, we might conclude that the suffering is justified, but it remains an evil nevertheless. For we must not

The Problem of Evil and Some Varieties of Atheism

confuse the intense suffering in and of itself with the good things to which it sometimes leads or of which it may be a necessary part. Intense human or animal suffering is in itself bad, an evil, even though it may sometimes be justified by virtue of being a part of, or leading to, some good which is unobtainable without it. What is evil in itself may sometimes be good as a means because it leads to something that is good in itself. In such a case, while remaining an evil in itself, the intense human or animal suffering is, nevertheless, an evil which someone might be morally justified in permitting.

Taking human and animal suffering as a clear instance of evil which occurs with great frequency in our world, the argument for atheism based on evil can be stated as follows:

1   There exist instances of intense suffering which an omnipotent, omniscient being could have prevented without thereby losing some greater good or permitting some evil equally bad or worse.[2]

2   An omniscient, wholly good being would prevent the occurrence of any intense suffering it could, unless it could not do so without thereby losing some greater good or permitting some evil equally bad or worse.

3   There does not exist an omnipotent, omniscient, wholly good being.

What are we to say about this argument for atheism, an argument based on the profusion of one sort of evil in our world? The argument is valid; therefore, if we have rational grounds for accepting its premises, to that extent we have rational grounds for accepting atheism. Do we, however, have rational grounds for accepting the premises of this argument?

Let's begin with the second premise. Let s_1 be an instance of intense human or animal suffering which an omniscient, wholly good being could prevent. We will also suppose that things are such that s_1 will occur unless prevented by the omniscient, wholly good (OG) being. We might be interested in determining what would be a *sufficient* condition of OG failing to prevent s_1. But, for our purpose here, we need only try to state a *necessary* condition for OG failing to prevent s_1. That condition, so it seems to me, is this:

Either (i) there is some greater good, G, such that G is obtainable by OG only if OG permits s_1[3],

or (ii) there is some greater good, G, such that G is obtainable by OG only if OG permits either s_1 or some evil equally bad or worse,

or (iii) s_1 is such that it is preventable by OG only if OG permits some evil equally bad or worse.

It is important to recognize that (iii) is not included in (i). For losing a good greater than s_1 is not the same as permitting an evil greater than s_1. And this because the *absence* of a good state of affairs need not itself be an evil state of affairs. It is also important to recognize that s_1 might be such that it is preventable by OG *without* losing G (so condition (i) is not satisfied) but also such that if OG did prevent it, G would be lost *unless* OG permitted some evil equal to or worse than s_1. If this were so, it does not seem correct to require that OG prevent s_1. Thus, condition (ii) takes into account an important possibility not encompassed in condition (i).

Is it true that if an omniscient, wholly good being permits the occurrence of some intense suffering it could have prevented, then either (i) or (ii) or (iii) obtains? It seems to me that it is true. But if it is true then so is premise (2) of the argument for atheism. For that premise merely states in more compact form what we have suggested must be true if an omniscient, wholly good being fails to prevent some intense suffering it could prevent. Premise (2) says that an omniscient, wholly good being would prevent the occurrence of any intense suffering it could, unless it could not do so without thereby losing some greater good or permitting some evil equally bad or worse. This premise (or something not too distant from it) is, I think, held in common by many atheists and nontheists. Of course, there may be disagreement about whether something is good, and whether, if it is good, one would be morally justified in permitting some intense suffering to occur in order to obtain it. Someone might hold, for example, that no good is great enough to justify permitting an innocent child to suffer terribly.[4] Again, someone might hold that the mere fact that a given good outweighs some suffering and would be lost if the suffering were prevented, is not a morally sufficient reason for permitting the suffering. But to hold either of these views is not to deny (2). For (2) claims only that if an omniscient, wholly good being permits intense suffering *then* either there is some greater good that would have been lost, or some equally bad or worse evil that would have occurred, had the intense suffering been prevented. (2) does not purport to describe what might be a *sufficient* condition for an omniscient, wholly good being to permit intense suffering, only what is a *necessary* condition. So stated, (2) seems to express a belief that accords with our basic moral principles, principles shared by both theists and nontheists. If we are to fault the argument for atheism, therefore, it seems we must find some fault with its first premise.

Suppose in some distant forest lightning strikes a dead tree, resulting in a forest fire. In the fire a fawn is trapped, horribly burned, and lies in terrible agony for several days before death relieves its suffering. So far as we can see, the fawn's intense suffering is pointless. For there does not appear to be any greater good such that the prevention of the fawn's suffering would require either the loss of that good or the occurrence of an evil equally bad or worse. Nor does there seem to be any equally bad or worse evil so connected to the fawn's suffering that it would have had to occur had the fawn's suffering been prevented. Could an omnipotent, omniscient

being have prevented the fawn's apparently pointless suffering? The answer is obvious, as even the theist will insist. An omnipotent, omniscient being could have easily prevented the fawn from being horribly burned, or, given the burning, could have spared the fawn the intense suffering by quickly ending its life, rather than allowing the fawn to lie in terrible agony for several days. Since the fawn's intense suffering was preventable and, so far as we can see, pointless, doesn't it appear that premise (1) of the argument is true, that there do exist instances of intense suffering which an omnipotent, omniscient being could have prevented without thereby losing some greater good or permitting some evil equally bad or worse?

It must be acknowledged that the case of the fawn's apparently pointless suffering does not *prove* that (1) is true. For even though we cannot see how the fawn's suffering is required to obtain some greater good (or to prevent some equally bad or worse evil), it hardly follows that it is not so required. After all, we are often surprised by how things we thought to be unconnected turn out to be intimately connected. Perhaps, for all we know, there is some familiar good outweighing the fawn's suffering to which that suffering is connected in a way we do not see. Furthermore, there may well be unfamiliar goods, goods we haven't dreamed of, to which the fawn's suffering is inextricably connected. Indeed, it would seem to require something like omniscience on our part before we could lay claim to *knowing* that there is no greater good connected to the fawn's suffering in such a manner that an omnipotent, omniscient being could not have achieved that good without permitting that suffering or some evil equally bad or worse. So the case of the fawn's suffering surely does not enable us to *establish* the truth of (1).

The truth is that we are not in a position to prove that (1) is true. We cannot know with certainty that instances of suffering of the sort described in (1) do occur in our world. But it is one thing to *know* or *prove* that (1) is true and quite another thing to have *rational grounds* for believing (1) to be true. We are often in the position where in the light of our experience and knowledge it is rational to believe that a certain statement is true, even though we are not in a position to prove or to know with certainty that the statement is true. In the light of our past experience and knowledge it is, for example, very reasonable to believe that neither Goldwater nor McGovern will ever be elected President, but we are scarcely in the position of knowing with certainty that neither will ever be elected President. So, too, with (1), although we cannot know with certainty that it is true, it perhaps can be rationally supported, shown to be a rational belief.

Consider again the case of the fawn's suffering. Is it reasonable to believe that there is some greater good so intimately connected to that suffering that even an omnipotent, omniscient being could not have obtained that good without permitting that suffering or some evil at least as bad? It certainly does not appear reasonable to believe this. Nor does it seem reasonable to believe that there is some evil at least as bad as the fawn's suffering such that an omnipotent being simply could not have prevented it without permitting the fawn's suffering. But even if it should somehow be reasonable to believe either of these things of the fawn's suffering, we must then ask whether it is reasonable to believe either of these things of *all* the instances of seemingly pointless human and animal suffering that occur daily in our world. And surely the answer to this more general question must be no. It seems quite unlikely that *all* the instances of intense suffering occurring daily in our world are intimately related to the occurrence of greater goods or the prevention of evils at least as bad; and even more unlikely, should they somehow all be so related, that an omnipotent, omniscient being could not have achieved at least some of those goods (or prevented some of those evils) without permitting the instances of intense suffering that are

supposedly related to them. In the light of our experience and knowledge of the variety and scale of human and animal suffering in our world, the idea that none of this suffering could have been prevented by an omnipotent being without thereby losing a greater good or permitting an evil at least as bad seems an extraordinary absurd idea, quite beyond our belief. It seems then that although we cannot *prove* that (1) is true, it is, nevertheless, altogether *reasonable* to believe that (1) is true, that (1) is a *rational belief*.[5]

Returning now to our argument for atheism, we've seen that the second premise expresses a basic belief common to many theists and nontheists. We've also seen that our experience and knowledge of the variety and profusion of suffering in our world provides *rational support* for the first premise. Seeing that the conclusion, "There does not exist an omnipotent, omniscient, wholly good being" follows from these two premises, it does seem that we have *rational support* for atheism, that it is reasonable for us to believe that the theistic God does not exist.

II

Can theism be rationally defended against the argument for atheism we have just examined? If it can, how might the theist best respond to that argument? Since the argument from (1) and (2) to (3) is valid, and since the theist, no less than the nontheist, is more than likely committed to (2), it's clear that the theist can reject this atheistic argument only by rejecting its first premise, the premise that states that there are instances of intense suffering which an omnipotent, omniscient being could have prevented without thereby losing some greater good or permitting some evil equally bad or worse. How, then, can the theist best respond to this premise and the considerations advanced in its support?

There are basically three responses a theist can make. First, he might argue not that (1) is false or probably false, but only that the reasoning given in support of it is in some way *defective*. He may do this either by arguing that the reasons given in support of (1) are in *themselves* insufficient to justify accepting (1), or by arguing that there are other things we know which, when taken in conjunction with these reasons, do not justify us in accepting (1). I suppose some theists would be content with this rather modest response to the basic argument for atheism. But given the validity of the basic argument and the theist's likely acceptance of (2), he is thereby committed to the view that (1) is false, not just that we have no good reason for accepting (1) as true. The second two responses are aimed at showing that it is reasonable to believe that (1) is false. Since the theist is committed to this view I shall focus the discussion on these two attempts, attempts which we can distinguish as "the direct attack" and "the indirect attack."

By a direct attack, I mean an attempt to reject (1) by pointing out goods, for example, to which suffering may well be connected, goods which an omnipotent, omniscient being could not achieve without permitting suffering. It is doubtful, however, that the direct attack can succeed. The theist may point out that some suffering leads to moral and spiritual development impossible without suffering. But it's reasonably clear that suffering often occurs in a degree far beyond what is required for character development. The theist may say that some suffering results from free choices of human beings and might be preventable only by preventing some measure of human freedom. But, again, it's clear that much intense suffering occurs not as a result of human free choices. The general difficulty with this direct attack on premise (1) is twofold. First, it cannot succeed, for the theist does not know what greater goods might be served, or evils prevented, by each instance of intense human or animal suffering. Second, the theist's own religious tradition usually maintains that in this life it is not given to us to know God's purpose in allowing particular instances of suffering. Hence, the direct attack against premise (1) cannot succeed and violates basic beliefs associated with theism.

The best procedure for the theist to follow in rejecting premise (1) is the indirect procedure. This procedure I shall call "the G. E. Moore shift," so-called in honor of the twentieth century philosopher, G. E. Moore, who used it to great effect in dealing with the arguments of the skeptics. Skeptical philosophers such as David Hume have advanced ingenious arguments to prove that no one can know of the existence of any material object. The premises of their arguments employ plausible principles, principles which many philosophers have tried to reject directly, but only with questionable success. Moore's procedure was altogether different. Instead of arguing directly against the premises of the skeptic's arguments, he simply noted that the premises implied, for example, that he [Moore] did not know of the existence of a pencil. Moore then proceeded indirectly against the skeptic's premises by arguing:

> I do know that this pencil exists.
> If the skeptic's principles are correct I cannot know of the existence of this pencil.
> ∴ The skeptic's principles (at least one) must be incorrect.

Moore then noted that his argument is just as valid as the skeptic's, that both of their arguments contain the premise "If the skeptic's principles are correct Moore cannot know of the existence of this pencil," and concluded that the only way to choose between the two arguments (Moore's and the skeptic's) is by deciding which of the first premises it is more rational to believe—Moore's premise "I do know that this pencil exists" or the skeptic's premise asserting that his skeptical principles are correct. Moore concluded that his own first premise was the more rational of the two.[6]

Before we see how the theist may apply the G. E. Moore shift to the basic argument for atheism, we should note the general strategy of the shift. We're given an argument: p, q, therefore, r. Instead of arguing directly against p, another argument is constructed—not-r, q, therefore, not-p—which begins with the denial of the conclusion of the first argument, keeps its second premise, and ends with the denial of the first premise as its conclusion. Compare, for example, these two:

I. p   II. not-r
   q   q
   —   ———
   r   not-p

It is a truth of logic that if I is valid II must be valid as well. Since the arguments are the same so far as the second premise is concerned, any choice between them must concern their respective first premises. To argue against the first premise (p) by constructing the counter argument II is to employ the G. E. Moore shift.

Applying the G. E. Moore shift against the first premise of the basic argument for atheism, the theist can argue as follows:

not-3. There exists an omnipotent, omniscient, wholly good being.
2. An omniscient, wholly good being would prevent the occurrence of any intense suffering it could, unless it could not do so without thereby losing some greater good or permitting some evil equally bad or worse.
therefore,
not-1. It is not the case that there exist instances of intense suffering which an omnipotent, omniscient being could have prevented without thereby losing some greater good or permitting some evil equally bad or worse.

We now have two arguments: the basic argument for atheism from (1) and (2) to (3), and the theist's best response, the argument from (not-3) and (2) to (not-1). What the theist then says about (1) is that he has rational grounds for

believing in the existence of the theistic God (not-3), accepts (2) as true, and sees that (not-1) follows from (not-3) and (2). He concludes, therefore, that he has rational grounds for rejecting (1). Having rational grounds for rejecting (1), the theist concludes that the basic argument for atheism is mistaken.

III

We've had a look at a forceful argument for atheism and what seems to be the theist's best response to that argument. If one is persuaded by the argument for atheism, as I find myself to be, how might one best view the position of the theist. Of course, he will view the theist as having a false belief, just as the theist will view the atheist as having a false belief. But what position should the atheist take concerning the *rationality* of the theist's belief? There are three major positions an atheist might take, positions which we may think of as some varieties of atheism. First, the atheist may believe that no one is rationally justified in believing that the theistic God exists. Let us call this position "unfriendly atheism." Second, the atheist may hold no belief concerning whether any theist is or isn't rationally justified in believing that the theistic God exists. Let us call this view "indifferent atheism." Finally, the atheist may believe that some theists are rationally justified in believing that the theistic God exists. This view we shall call "friendly atheism." In this final part of the paper I propose to discuss and defend the position of friendly atheism.

If no one can be rationally justified in believing a false proposition then friendly atheism is a paradoxical, if not incoherent position. But surely the truth of a belief is not a necessary condition of someone's being rationally justified in having that belief. So in holding that someone is rationally justified in believing that the theistic God exists, the friendly atheist is not committed to thinking that the theist has a true belief. What he is committed to is that the theist has rational grounds for his belief, a belief the atheist rejects and is convinced he is rationally justified in rejecting. But is this possible? Can someone, like our friendly atheist, hold a belief, be convinced that he is rationally justified in holding that belief, and yet believe that someone else is equally justified in believing the opposite? Surely this is possible. Suppose your friends see you off on a flight to Hawaii. Hours after take-off they learn that your plane has gone down at sea. After a twenty-four hour search, no survivors have been found. Under these circumstances they are rationally justified in believing that you have perished. But it is hardly rational for you to believe this, as you bob up and down in your life vest, wondering why the search planes have failed to spot you. Indeed, to amuse yourself while awaiting your fate, you might very well reflect on the fact that your friends are rationally justified in believing that you are now dead, a proposition you disbelieve and are rationally justified in disbelieving. So, too, perhaps an atheist may be rationally justified in his atheistic belief and yet hold that some theists are rationally justified in believing just the opposite of what he believes.

What sort of grounds might a theist have for believing that God exists? Well, he might endeavor to justify his belief by appealing to one or more of the traditional arguments: Onto-logical, Cosmological, Teleological, Moral, etc. Second, he might appeal to certain aspects of religious experience, perhaps even his own religious experience. Third, he might try to jus-tify theism as a plausible theory in terms of which we can account for a variety of phenom-ena. Although an atheist must hold that the the-istic God does not exist, can he not also believe, and be justified in so believing, that some of these "justifications of theism" do actually rationally justify some theists in their belief that there exists a supremely good, omnipotent, omniscient being? It seems to me that he can.

If we think of the long history of theistic belief and the special situations in which people are sometimes placed, it is perhaps as absurd to think that no one was ever rationally justified in believing that the theistic God exists as it is to think that no one was ever justified in believing that human beings would never walk on the moon. But in suggesting that friendly atheism is preferable to unfriendly atheism, I don't mean to rest the case on what some human beings might reasonably have believed in the eleventh or thir-teenth century. The more interesting question is whether some people in modern society, people who are aware of the usual grounds for belief and disbelief and are acquainted to some degree with modern science, are yet rationally justified in accepting theism. Friendly atheism is a signifi-cant position only if it answers this question in the affirmative.

It is not difficult for an atheist to be friendly when he has reason to believe that the theist could not reasonably be expected to be acquaint-ed with the grounds for disbelief that he (the atheist) possesses. For then the atheist may take the view that some theists are rationally justified in holding to theism, but would not be so were they to be acquainted with the grounds for dis-belief—those grounds being sufficient to tip the scale in favor of atheism when balanced against the reasons the theist has in support of his belief.

Friendly atheism becomes paradoxical, how-ever, when the atheist contemplates believing that the theist has all the grounds for atheism that he, the atheist, has, and yet is rationally justified in maintaining his theistic belief. But even so excessively friendly a view as this perhaps can be held by the atheist if he also has some reason to think that the grounds for theism are not as tell-ing as the theist is justified in taking them to be.[7]

In this paper I've presented what I take to be a strong argument for atheism, pointed out what I think is the theist's best response to that argu-ment, distinguished three positions an atheist might take concerning the rationality of theistic belief, and made some remarks in defense of the position called "friendly atheism." I'm aware that the central points of the paper are not likely to be warmly received by many philosophers.

Philosophers who are atheists tend to be tough-minded—holding that there are no good reasons for supposing that theism is true. And theists tend either to reject the view that the existence of evil provides rational grounds for atheism or to hold that religious belief has nothing to do with reason and evidence at all. But such is the way of philosophy.[8]

Notes

1 Some philosophers have contended that the existence of evil is *logically inconsistent* with the existence of the theistic God. No one, I think, has succeeded in establishing such an extravagant claim. Indeed, granted incompatibilism, there is a fairly compelling argument for the view that the existence of evil is logically consistent with the existence of the theistic God. (For a lucid statement of this argument see Alvin Plantinga, *God, Freedom, and Evil* (New York, 1974), pp. 29–59.) [*Philosophy of Religion: Selected Readings*, Third Edition, pp. 259–84.] There remains, however, what we may call the *evidential* form—as opposed to the *logical* form—of the problem of evil: the view that the variety and profusion of evil in our world, although perhaps not logically inconsistent with the existence of the theistic God, provides, nevertheless, *rational support* for atheism. In this paper I shall be concerned solely with the evidential form of the problem, the form of the problem which, I think, presents a rather severe difficulty for theism.

2 If there is some good, G, greater than any evil, (1) will be false for the trivial reason that no matter what evil, E, we pick the conjunctive good state of affairs consisting of G and E will outweigh E and be such that an omnipotent being could not obtain it without permitting E. (See Alvin Plantinga, *God and Other Minds* [Ithaca, 1967], p. 167.) To avoid this objection we may insert "unreplaceable" into our premises (1) and (2) between "some" and "greater." If E isn't required for G, and G is better than G plus E, then the good conjunctive state of affairs composed of G and E would be *replaceable* by the greater good of G alone. For the sake of simplicity, however, I will ignore this complication both in the formulation and discussion of premises (1) and (2).

3 Three clarifying points need to be made in connec-tion with (i). First, by "good" I don't mean to exclude the fulfillment of certain moral principles. Perhaps preventing s_1 would preclude certain actions prescribed by the principles of justice. I shall allow that the satisfaction of certain principles of justice may be a good that outweighs the evil of s_1. Second, even though (i) may suggest it, I don't mean to limit the good in question to something that would *follow in time* the occurrence of s_1. And, finally, we should perhaps not fault OG if the good G, that would be lost were s_1 prevented, is not actually greater than s_1, but merely such that allowing s_1 and G, as opposed to preventing s_1 and thereby losing G, would not alter the balance between good and evil. For reasons of simplicity, I have left this point out in stating (i), with the result that (i) is perhaps a bit stronger than it should be.

4 See Ivan's speech in Book V, Chapter IV of *The Brothers Karamazov*.

5 One might object that the conclusion of this paragraph is stronger than the reasons given warrant. For it is one thing to argue that it is unreasonable to think that (1) is false and another thing to conclude that we are therefore justified in accepting (1) as true. There are propositions such that believing them is much more reasonable than disbelieving them, and yet are such that *withholding judgment* about them is more reasonable than believing them. To take an example of Chisholm's: it is more reasonable to believe that the Pope will be in Rome (on some arbitrarily picked future date) than to believe that he won't; but it is perhaps more reasonable to suspend judgment on the question of the Pope's whereabouts on that particular date, than to believe that he will be in Rome. Thus, it might be objected, that while we've shown that believing (1) is more reasonable than disbelieving (1), we haven't shown that believing (1) is more reasonable than withholding belief. My answer to this objection is that there are things we know which render (1) probable to the degree that it is more reasonable to believe (1) than to suspend judgment on (1). What are these things we know? First, I think, is the fact that there is an enormous variety and profusion of intense human and animal suffering in our world. Second, is the fact that much of this suffering seems quite unrelated to any greater goods (or the absence of equal or greater evils) that might justify it. And,

finally, there is the fact that such suffering as is related to greater goods (or the absence of equal or greater evils) does not, in many cases, seem so intimately related as to require its permission by an omnipotent being bent on securing those goods (the absence of those evils). These facts, I am claiming, make it more reasonable to accept (1) than to withhold judgment on (1).

6 See, for example, the two chapters on Hume in G. E. Moore, *Some Main Problems of Philosophy* (London, 1953).

7 Suppose that I add a long sum of numbers three times and get result x. I inform you of this so that have pretty much the same evidence I have for the claim that the sum of the numbers is x. You then use your calculator twice over and arrive at result y. You, then, are justified in believing that the sum of the numbers is *not* x. However, knowing that your calculator has been damaged and is therefore unreliable, and that you have no reason to think that it is damaged, I may reasonably believe not only that the sum of the numbers is x, but also that you are justified in believing that the sum is not x. Here is a case, then, where you have all of my evidence for p, and yet I can reasonably believe that you are justified in believing not-p—for I have reason to believe that your grounds for not-p are not as telling as you are justified in taking them to be.

8 I am indebted to my colleagues at Purdue University, particularly to Ted Ulrich and Lilly Russow, and to philosophers at The University of Nebraska, Indiana State University, and The University of Wisconsin at Milwaukee for helpful criticisms of earlier versions of this paper.

Chapter 19

William P. Alston

THE INDUCTIVE ARGUMENT FROM EVIL AND THE HUMAN COGNITIVE CONDITION

i

The recent outpouring of literature on the problem of evil has materially advanced the subject in several ways. In particular, a clear distinction has been made between the "logical" *argument against the existence of God* ("atheological argument") from evil, which attempts to show that evil is logically incompatible with the existence of God, and the "inductive" ("empirical", "probabilistic") argument, which contents itself with the claim that evil constitutes (sufficient) empirical evidence against the existence of God. It is now acknowledged on (almost) all sides that the logical argument is bankrupt, but the inductive argument is still very much alive and kicking.

In this paper I will be concerned with the inductive argument. More specifically, I shall be contributing to a certain criticism of that argument, one based on a low estimate of human cognitive capacities in a certain application. To indicate the point at which this criticism engages the argument, I shall use one of the most careful and perspicuous formulations of the argument in a recent essay by William Rowe (1979).

1   There exist instances of intense suffering which an omnipotent, omniscient being could have prevented without thereby losing some greater good or permitting some evil equally bad or worse.

2   An omniscient, wholly good being would prevent the occurrence of any intense suf-

fering it could, unless it could not do so without thereby losing some greater good or permitting some evil equally bad or worse.

3   There does not exist an omnipotent, omniscient, wholly good being (p. 336).

Let's use the term "gratuitous suffering" for any case of intense suffering, E, that satisfies premise 1, that is, which is such that an omnipotent, omniscient being could have prevented it without thereby losing some greater good or permitting some evil equally bad or worse.[1] 2 takes what we might call the "content" of 1 (losing a greater good or permitting some worse or equally bad evil) as a necessary condition for God to have a sufficient reason for permitting E. E's being gratuitous, then, is the contradictory of the possibility of God's having a sufficient reason to permit it, and equivalent to the impossibility of God's having a sufficient reason for permitting it. I will oscillate freely between speaking of a particular case of suffering, E, being gratuitous, and speaking of the impossibility of God's having a sufficient reason for permitting E. I shall call a proponent of an inductive argument from evil the "critic".

The criticism I shall be supporting attacks the claim that we are rationally justified in accepting 1, and it does so on the grounds that our epistemic situation is such that we are unable to make a sufficiently well grounded determination that 1 is the case. I will call this, faute de mieux, the *agnostic* thesis, or simply *agnosticism*. The criticism claims that the magnitude or complexity of the question is such that our powers, access to data, and so on are radically insufficient to provide sufficient warrant for accepting 1. And if that is so, the inductive argument collapses.[2]

How might one be justified in accepting 1? The obvious way to support an existential statement is to establish one or more instantiations and then use existential generalization. This is Rowe's tack, and I don't see any real alternative. Thus Rowe considers one or another case of suffering and argues, in the case of each, that it instantiates 1. I will follow him in this approach. Thus to argue that we cannot be justified in asserting 1, I shall argue that we cannot be justified in asserting any of its instantiations, each of which is of the form

1A.   E is such that an omnipotent, omniscient being could have prevented it without thereby losing some greater good or permitting some evil equally bad or worse.

In the sequel when I speak of being or not being justified in accepting 1, it must be remembered that this is taken to hang on whether one is, or can be justified, in accepting propositions of the form 1A. [. . .]

ii

Before setting out the agnostic thesis in more detail and adding my bit to the case for it, let me make some further comments about the argument against which the criticism is directed and variants thereof.

A. The argument is stated in terms of intense suffering, but it could just as well have appealed to anything else that can plausibly be claimed to be undesirable in itself. Rowe focuses on intense suffering because he thinks that it presents the greatest difficulty for anyone who tries to deny a premise like 1. I shall follow him in this, though for concision I shall often simply say "suffering" with the "intense" tacitly understood.

B. Rowe doesn't claim that all suffering is gratuitous, but only that some is. He takes it that even one case of gratuitous suffering is incompatible with theism. I go along with this assumption (though in E, I question whether Rowe has succeeded in specifying necessary and sufficient conditions for gratuitousness, and for God's having a sufficient reason for permitting suffering). As already noted, Rowe does not argue for 1 by staying on its level of unspecificity; rather he takes particular examples of suffering and argues in the case of each that it is gratuitous; from there it is a short step of existential generalization to 1. In (1979) and subsequent papers Rowe focuses on the case of a fawn trapped in a forest fire and undergoing several days of terrible agony before dying (hereinafter "Bambi"). In (1988) he adds to this a (real life) case introduced by Bruce Russell (1989), a case of the rape, beating, and murder by strangulation of a 5-year-old girl ("Sue") by her mother's boyfriend. Since I am specifically interested in criticizing Rowe's argument I will argue that we are not justified, and cannot be justified, in judging these evils to be gratuitous. It will turn out that some of my discussion pertains not to Rowe's cases but to others. I will signal the reader as to how to understand the dummy designator, "E", in each part of the paper.

C. The argument deals with a classical conception of God as omnipotent, omniscient and perfectly good; it is designed to yield the conclusion that no being with those characteristics exists. I shall also be thinking of the matter in this way. When I use "God" it will be to refer to a being with these characteristics.

D. There are obvious advantages to thinking of the inductive argument from evil as directed against the belief in the existence of God as God is thought of in some full blown theistic religion, rather than as directed against what we may call "generic theism". The main advantage is that the total system of beliefs in a religion gives us much more to go on in considering what reasons God might possibly have for permitting E. In other terms, it provides much more of a basis for distinguishing between plausible and implausible theodicies. I shall construe the argument as directed against the traditional Christian belief in God.[3] I choose Christianity for this purpose because (a) I am more familiar with it than other alternatives, as most of my readers will be, and (b) most of the philosophical discussions of the problem of evil, both historically and currently, have grown out of Christian thought.

E. Rowe does not claim to know or to be able to prove that 1 is true. With respect to his fawn example he acknowledges that "Perhaps, for all we know, there is some familiar good outweighing the fawn's suffering to which that suffering is connected in a way we do not see" (1979, p. 337). He only claims that we have sufficient rational grounds for believing that the fawn's suffering is gratuitous, and still stronger rational grounds for holding that at least some of the many cases of suffering that, so far as we can see, instantiate I actually do so.[4] Not all of Rowe's fellow atheologians are so modest, but I will concentrate my fire on his weaker and less vulnerable version. [. . .]

iii

Clearly the case for 1 depends on an inference from "So far as I can tell, p" to "p" or "probably, p". And, equally clearly, such inferences are sometimes warranted and sometimes not. Having carefully examined my desk I can infer "Jones' letter is not on my desk" from "So far as I can tell, Jones' letter is not on my desk". But being ignorant of quantum mechanics I cannot infer "This treatise on quantum mechanics is well done" from "So far as I can tell, this treatise on quantum mechanics is well done". I shall be contending that our position vis-a-vis 1 is like the latter rather than like the former. [. . .]

iv

Now, at last, I am ready to turn to my central project of arguing that we cannot be justified in accepting 1A. As already noted, I will be emphasizing the fact that this is a negative existential claim. It will be my contention that to be justified in such a claim one must be justified in excluding all the live possibilities for what the claim denies to exist. What 1A denies is that there is any reason God could have for permitting it. I will argue that we are not, and cannot, be justified in asserting that none of these possibilities are realized. I will draw on various theodicies to compile a (partial) list of the reasons God might conceivably have for permitting E. That will provide me with a partial list of the suggestions we must have sufficient reason to reject in order to rationally accept 1. Note that it is no part of my purpose here to develop or defend a theodicy. I am using theodicies only as a source of *possibilities* for divine reasons for evil, possibilities the realization of which the atheologian will have to show to be highly implausible if his project is to succeed.

Since I am criticizing Rowe's argument I am concerned to argue that we are not justified in asserting 1A for the particular kinds of suffering on which Rowe focuses. And we should not suppose that God would have the same reason for permitting every case of suffering.[5] Hence it is to be expected that the reasons suggested by a given theodicy will be live possibilities for some cases of evil and not others. I am, naturally, most interested in suggestions that constitute live possibilities for divine reasons for permitting Bambi's and Sue's suffering. And many familiar theodicies do not pass this test. (This is, no doubt, why these cases were chosen by Rowe and Russell.) Bambi's suffering, and presumably Sue's as well, could hardly be put down to punishment for sin, and neither case could seriously be supposed to be allowed by God for the sake of character building. [. . .]

I shall first consider theodical suggestions that

seem clearly not to apply to Bambi or Sue. Here I shall be thinking instead of an adult sufferer from a painful and lengthy disease (fill in the details as you like) whom I shall call "Sam". Having argued that we are not in a position to exclude the possibility that God has reasons of these sorts for permitting Sam's suffering, I shall pass on to other suggestions that do constitute genuine possibilities for Bambi and/or Sue.

v

I begin with a traditional theme, that human suffering is God's punishment for sin. Though it hardly applies to Bambi or Sue, it may be a live possibility in other cases, and so I will consider it. The punishment motif has tended to drop out of theodicies in our "soft-on-criminals" and "depravity-is-a-disease" climate, but it has bulked large in the Christian tradition.[6] If often draws the criticism that, so far as we can see, degree or extent of suffering is not nicely proportioned to degree of guilt. Are the people of Vietnam, whose country was ravaged by war in this century, markedly more sinful than the people of Switzerland, whose country was not? But, remembering the warnings of the last section, that does not show that this is never God's reason for permitting suffering, and here we are concerned with a particular case, Sam. Let's say that it seems clear, so far as we can tell, that Sam's suffering is not in proportion to his sinfulness. Sam doesn't seem to have been a bad sort at all, and he has suffered horribly. Can we go from that to "Sam's suffering was not a punishment for sin," or even to "It is reasonable to suppose that Sam's suffering was not a punishment for sin". I suggest that we cannot.

First, we are often in a poor position to assess the degree and kind of a certain person's sinfulness, or to compare people in this regard. Since I am thinking of the inductive argument from evil as directed against Christian belief in God, it will

be appropriate to understand the punishment-for-sin suggestion in those terms. Two points about sin are particularly relevant here. (1) Inward sins—one's intentions, motives, attitudes—are more serious than failings in outward behavior.[7] (2) The greatest sin is a self-centered refusal or failure to make God the center of one's life. (2) is sharply at variance with standard secular bases for moral judgment and evaluation. Hence the fact that X does not seem, from that standpoint, more wicked than Y, or doesn't seem wicked at all, does nothing to show that God, on a Christian understanding of God, would make the same judgment. Because of (1) overt behavior is not always a good indication of a person's condition, sin-wise. This is not to say that we could not make a sound judgment of a person's inner state if we had a complete record of what is publicly observable concerning the person. Perhaps in some instances we could, and perhaps in others we could not. But in any event, we rarely or never have such a record. Hence, for both these reasons our judgments as to the relation between S's suffering and S's sinfulness are usually of questionable value.

Second, according to Christianity, one's life on earth is only a tiny proportion of one's total life span. This means that, knowing nothing about the immeasurably greater proportion of Sam's life, we are in no position that deny that the suffering qua punishment has not had a reformative effect, even if we can see no such effect in his earthly life.[8] [. . .]

vi

I have led off my survey of theodical suggestions with the punishment motif, despite the fact that it is highly controversial and the reverse of popular. Nor would I want to put heavy emphasis on it were I constructing a theodicy. I have put my worst foot forward in order to show that even here the critic is in no position to show that Sam's suffering is not permitted by God for this reason. If the critic can't manage even this, he will presumably be much worse off with more plausible suggestions for divine reasons, to some of which I now turn.

One of the most prominent theodical suggestions is that God allows suffering because He is interested in a "vale of soul making". He takes it that by confronting difficulties, hardships, frustrations, perils, and even suffering and only by doing this, we have a chance to develop such qualities of character as patience, courage, and compassion, qualities we would otherwise have no opportunity to develop. This line has been set forth most forcefully in our time by John Hick in *Evil and the God of Love* (revised edition, 1978), a book that has evoked much discussion. To put the point most generally, God's purpose is to make it possible for us to grow into the kind of person that is capable of an eternal life of loving communion with Himself. To be that kind of person one will have to possess traits of character like those just mentioned, traits that one cannot develop without meeting and reacting to difficulties and hardships, including suffering. To show that E would not be permitted by God, the critic has to show that it does not serve the "soul-making" function.

To get to the points I am concerned to make I must first respond to some standard objections to this theodicy. (1) God could surely just create us with the kind of character needed for fellowship with Himself, thereby rendering the hardships and suffering unnecessary. Hick's answer is that what God aims at is not fellowing with a suitably programmed robot, but fellowship with creatures who freely choose to work for what is needed and to take advantage of the opportunity thus engendered. God sees the realization of this aim for some free creatures,[9] even at the cost of suffering and hardship for all, as being of much greater value than any alternative, including a world with no free creatures and a world in which the likes of human beings come off the assembly line pre-sanctified. As usual, I am not concerned to defend the claim that this is the way things are, but only to claim that we are in

no position to deny that God is correct in this judgment. . . .

(2) "If God is using suffering to achieve this goal. He is not doing very well. In spite of all the suffering we undergo, most of us don't get very far in developing courage, compassion, etc." There are two answers to this. First, we are in no position to make that last judgment. We don't know nearly enough about the inner springs of peoples' motivation, attitudes, and character, even in this life. And we know nothing about any further development in an after-life. Second, the theism under discussion takes God to respect the free will of human beings. No strategy consistent with that can guarantee that all, or perhaps any, creatures will respond in the way intended. Whether they do is ultimately up to them. Hence we cannot argue from the fact that such tactics often don't succeed to the conclusion that God wouldn't employ them. When dealing with free creatures God must, because of self-imposed limitations, use means that have some considerable likelihood of success, not means that cannot fail. It is amazing that so many critics reject theodicies like Hick's on the grounds of a poor success rate. I don't say that a poor success rate could not, under any circumstances, justify us in denying that God would permit E for the sake of soul making. If we really did know enough to be reasonably sure that the success rate is very poor *and* that other devices open to God would be seen by omniscience to have a significantly greater chance of success, *then* we could conclude that Hick's line does not get at what God is up to. But we are a very long way indeed from being able to justifiably assert this.

We cannot take the kind of reason stressed by Hick to be a live possibility for the Bambi and Sue cases. The former is much more obvious than the latter, but even in the latter case Sue has no chance to respond to the suffering in the desired way, except in an after life, and it strains credulity to suppose that God would subject a 5-year old to *that* for the sake of character building in the life to come. Hence once more, and until further notice, we will stick with Sam.

Let's stipulate that Sam's suffering does not appear, on close examination, to be theistically explainable as aimed by God at "soul-making". He seems already to have more of the qualities of character in question than most of us, or the amount of suffering seems to be too much for the purpose, or to be so great as to overwhelm him and make character development highly unlikely. And so our best judgment is that God wouldn't be permitting his suffering for that reason. But that judgment is made in ignorance of much relevant information. Perhaps a more penetrating picture of Sam's spiritual condition would reveal that he is much more in need of further development than is apparent to us from our usual superficial perspective on such matters. Since we don't see his career after death, we are in a poor position to determine how, over the long run, he reacts to the suffering: perhaps if we had that information we would see that this suffering is very important for his full development. Moreover, we are in a poor position, or no position, to determine what is the most effective strategy for God to use in His pursuit of Sam. We don't know what alternatives are open to God, while respecting Sam's freedom, or what the chances are, on one or another alternative, of inducing the desired responses. We are in a poor position to say that this was too much suffering for the purpose, or to say how much would be just right. And we will continue to be in that position until our access to relevant information is radically improved.

Thus we cannot be justified in holding that Sam's suffering is not permitted by God in order to further His project of soul-making. There is an allied, but significantly different theodical suggestion by Eleonore Stump concerning which I would make the same points. Briefly, and over-simply, Stump's central suggestion is that the function of natural evil in God's scheme is to bring us to salvation, or, as she likes to put it, to contribute to the project of "fixing our wills",

which have been damaged by original sin. Natural evil tends to prod us to turn to God, thereby giving Him a chance to fix our wills.

> Natural evil—the pain of disease, the intermittent and unpredictable destruction of natural disasters, the decay of old age, the imminence of death—takes away a person's satisfaction with himself. It tends to humble him, show him his frailty, make him reflect on the transience of temporal goods, and turn his affections towards other-worldly things, away from the things of this world. No amount of moral or natural evil, of course, can *guarantee* that a man will seek God's help. If it could, the willing it produced would not be free. But evil of this sort is the best hope, I think, and maybe the only effective means, for bringing men to such a state.
>
> (Stump, 1985, p. 409)

Objections will be raised somewhat similar to those that have been made to Hick. A perfectly good God wouldn't have let us get in this situation in the first place. God would employ a more effective technique.[10] There's too much suffering for the purpose. It is not distributed properly. And so on. These will [be] answered in the same way as the analogous objections to Hick. As for Sam, if we cannot see how his suffering was permitted by God for the reason Stump suggests, I will do a rerun of the parallel points concerning Hick's soul making suggestion. [. . .]

If we were to try to decide whether Sam's suffering is permitted by God for any of these reasons, we would be in a poor position to make a negative judgment for reasons parallel to those brought out in the discussion of Hick. Given the limits of our access to the secrets of the human heart and the course of the after life, if any, we are, in many instances, in no position to assert with any confidence that this suffering does not have such consequences, and hence that God does not permit it (at least in part) for the sake of just those consequences.

vii

[. . .] Moreover, remember that our topic is not the possibilities for future human apprehensions, but rather what an omniscient being can grasp of modes of value and the conditions of their realization. Surely it is eminently possible that there are real possibilities for the latter that exceed anything we can anticipate, or even conceptualize. It would be exceedingly strange if an omniscient being did not immeasurably exceed our grasp of such matters. Thus there is an unquestionably live possibility that God's reasons for allowing human suffering may have to do, in part, with the appropriate connection of those sufferings with goods in ways that have never been dreamed of in our theodicies. Once we bring this into the picture, the critic is seen to be on shaky ground in denying, of Bambi's or Sue's suffering, that God could have any patient-centered reason for permitting it, even if we are unable to suggest what such a reason might be.[11]

This would be an appropriate place to consider Rowe's argument that we can be justified in excluding the possibility that God permits one or another case of suffering in order to obtain goods of which we have no conception. In his latest article on the subject (1988) Rowe claims that the variant of 1 there put forward:

Q. No good state of affairs is such that an omnipotent, omniscient being's obtaining it would morally justify that being in permitting E1 or E2 (p. 120).[12]

can be derived probabilistically from:

P. No good state of affairs we know of is such that an omnipotent, omniscient being's obtaining it would morally justify that being's permitting E1 or E2 (p. 121).

I have been arguing, and will continue to argue, that Rowe is not justified in asserting P, since he is not justified in supposing that none of the particular goods we have been discussing provide God with sufficient reason for permitting the suffering of Bambi and Sue. But even if Rowe were justified in asserting P, what I have just been contending is that the argument from P to Q does not go through. In defending the argument Rowe says the following.

> My answer is that we are justified in making this inference in the same way we are justified in making the many inferences we constantly make from the known to the unknown. All of us are constantly inferring from the A's we know of to the A's we don't know of. If we observe many A's and all of them are B's we are justified in believing that the A's we haven't observed are also B's. If I encounter a fair number of pit bulls and all of them are vicious, I have reason to believe that all pit bulls are vicious.
>
> (1988, pp. 123–24)

But it is just not true that Rowe's inference from known goods to all goods is parallel to inductive inferences we "constantly make". Typically when we generalize from observed instances, at least when we are warranted in doing so, we know quite a lot about what makes a sample of things like that a good base for general attributions of the properties in question. We know that temperamental traits like viciousness or affectionateness are often breed-specific in dogs, and so when a number of individuals of a breed are observed to exhibit such a trait it is a good guess that it is characteristic of that breed. If, on the other hand, the characteristic found throughout the sample were a certain precise height or a certain sex, our knowledge indicates that an inference that all members of that breed are of that height or of that sex would be foolhardy indeed. But, as I have been arguing, an inference from known goods lacking J to all goods (including those we have never experienced and even those of which we have no conception) is unlike both the sorts just mentioned in the way they resemble one another, viz., our possession of knowledge indicating which characteristics can be expected to be (fairly) constant in the larger population. We have no background knowledge that tells us the chances of J's being a "goods-specific" characteristic, one that can reasonably be expected to be present in all or most goods if it is found in a considerable sample. Hence we cannot appeal to clearly warranted generalizations in support of this one. Rowe's generalization is more like inferring from the fact that no one has yet produced a physical theory that will unify relativity and quantum mechanics, to the prediction that no one will ever do so, or inferring, in 1850, from the fact no one has yet voyaged to the moon that no one will ever do so. We have no way of drawing boundaries around the total class of goods; we are unable to anticipate what may lie in its so-far-unknown sub-class, just as we are unable to anticipate future scientific developments and future artistic innovations. This is not an area in which induction by simple enumeration yields justified belief.[13]

viii

It is now time to move beyond the restriction on divine reasons to benefits to the sufferer. The theodical suggestions we will be discussing from here on do not observe this restriction. [. . .]

From now on I will be considering possible divine reasons that extend beyond benefit to the sufferer. [. . .] The theodicies to be considered now will give us more specific suggestions for Bambi and Sue.

I will begin with the familiar free will theodicy, according to which God is justified in permitting creaturely wickedness and its consequences because he has to do so if he is bestow on some of his creatures the incommensurable privilege of being responsible agents who have, in many areas, the capacity to choose between alternatives as they will, without God, or anyone or anything else (other than themselves),

determining which alternative they choose. The suggestion of this theodicy is that it is conceptually impossible for God to create free agents and also determine how they are to choose, within those areas in which they are free. If He were so to determine their choices they would, ipso facto, not be free. But this being the case, when God decided to endow some of His creatures, including us, with free choice, He thereby took the chance, ran the risk, of our sometimes or often making the wrong choice, a possibility that has been richly realized. It is conceptually impossible for God to create free agents and not subject Himself to such a risk. Not to do the latter would be not to do the former. But that being the case, He, and we, are stuck with whatever consequences ensue. And this is why God permits such horrors as the rape, beating, and murder of Sue. He does it not because that particular wicked choice is itself necessary for the realization of some great good, but because the permission of such horrors is bound up with the decision to give human beings free choice in many areas, and that (the capacity to freely choose) is a great good, such a great good as to be worth all the suffering and others evils that it makes possible.[14] [. . .]

Thus we may take it to be a live possibility that the maintenance of creaturely free will is at least part of God's reason for permitting wrongdoing and its consequences. But then the main reason one could have for denying that this is at least part of why God would allow the attack on Sue is that God could, miraculously or otherwise, prevent any one incipient free human action without losing the value of human free will. Clearly a divine interference in normal human operations in this one instance is not going to prevent even Sue's attacker from being a free moral agent in general, with all that that involves. This point is supported by the consideration that, for all we know, God does sometimes intervene to prevent human agents from doing wicked things they would otherwise have done, and, so the free will theodicist will claim, even if that is the case we do enjoy the incommensurable value of free choice. We can also think of it this way. It is perfectly obvious that the scope of our free choice is not unlimited. We have no effective voluntary control over, e.g., our genetic constitution, our digestive and other biological processes, and much of our cognitive operations. Thus whatever value the human capacity for free choice possesses, that value is compatible with free choice being confined within fairly narrow limits. But then presumably a tiny additional constriction such as would be involved in God's preventing Sue's attacker from committing that atrocity would not render things radically different, free-will-wise, from what they would have been without that. So God could have prevented this without losing the good emphasized by this theodicy. Hence we can be sure that this does not constitute a sufficient reason for His not preventing it.

To be sure, if God were to act on this principle in every case of incipient wrongdoing, the situation would be materially changed. Human agents would no longer have a real choice between good and evil, and the surpassing worth that attaches to having such a choice would be lost. Hence, if God is to promote the values emphasized by the free will theodicy. He can intervene in this way in only a small proportion of cases. And how are these to be selected? I doubt that we are in a position to give a confident answer to this question, but let's assume that the critic proposes that the exceptions are to be picked in such a way as to maximize welfare, and let's go along with that. Rowe's claim would then have to be that Sue's murder was so horrible that it would qualify for the class of exceptions. But that is precisely where the critic's claims far outrun his justification. How can we tell that Sue falls within the most damaging n% of what would be cases of human wrongdoing apart from divine intervention? To be in a position to make such a judgment we would have to survey the full range of such cases and make reliable assessments of the deleterious consequences of

each. Both tasks are far beyond our powers. We don't even know what free creaturely agents there are beyond human beings, and with respect to humans the range of wickedness, past, present, and future, is largely beyond our ken. And even with respect to the cases of which we are aware we have only a limited ability to assess the total consequences. Hence, by the nature of the case, we are simply not in a position to make a warranted judgment that Sue's case is among the n% worst cases of wrongdoing in the history of the universe. No doubt, it strikes us as incomparably horrible on hearing about it, but so would innumerable others. Therefore, the critic is not in a position to set aside the value of free will as at least part of God's reason for permitting Sue's murder.

ix

[. . .] Next I want to consider a quite different theodicy that also sees God's reasons for permitting suffering in terms of benefits that are generally distributed, viz., the appeal to the benefits of a lawlike natural order, and the claim that suffering will be an inevitable byproduct of any such order. I choose the exposition of this theodicy in Bruce Reichenbach in Evil and a Good God (1982).

> . . . creation, in order to make possible the existence of moral agents . . . had to be ordered according to some set of natural laws (p. 101).

The argument for this is that if things do not happen in a lawlike fashion, at least usually, agents will be unable to anticipate the consequences of their volitions, and hence will not be able to effectively make significant choices between good and evil actions. Reichenbach continues:

> Consequently, the possibility arises that sentient creatures like ourselves can be negatively affected by the outworkings of these laws in

nature, such that we experience pain, suffering, disability, disutility, and at times the frustration of our good desires. Since a world with free persons making choices between moral good and evil and choosing a significant amount of moral good is better than a world without free persons and moral good and evil, God in creating had to create a world which operated according to natural laws to achieve this higher good. Thus, his action of creation of a natural world and a natural order, along with the resulting pain and pleasure which we experience, is justified. The natural evils which afflict us—diseases, sickness, disasters, birth defects—are all the outworking of the natural system of which we are a part. They are the byproducts made possible by that which is necessary for the greater good (100–01).

This is a theodicy for natural evil, not for the suffering that results from human wickedness. Hence it has possible application to Bambi, but not to Sue, and possible application to any other suffering that results from natural processes that are independent of human intentional action.

Let's agree that significant moral agency requires a natural lawful order. But that doesn't show that it is even possible that God had a sufficient reason to allow Bambi's suffering. There are two difficulties that must be surmounted to arrive at that point.

First, a natural order can be regular enough to provide the degree of predictability required for morally significant choice even if there are exceptions to the regularities. Therefore, God could set aside the usual consequences of natural forces in this instance, so as to prevent Bambi's suffering, without thereby interfering with human agents' reasonable anticipations of the consequences of their actions. So long as God doesn't do this too often, we will still have ample basis for suppositions as to what we can reasonably expect to follow what. But note that by the same line of reasoning God cannot do this too

often, or the desired predictability will not be forthcoming. Hence, though any one naturally caused suffering could have been miraculously prevented. God certainly has a strong prima facie reason in each case to refrain from doing this; for if He didn't He would have no reason for letting nature usually take its course. And so He has a possible reason for allowing nature to take its course in the Bambi case, a reason that would have to be overridden by stronger contrary considerations.

This means that in order to be justified in supposing that God would not have a sufficient reason to refrain from intervening in this case, we would have to be justified in supposing that God would have a sufficient reason to make, in this case, an exception to the general policy. And how could we be justified in supposing that? We would need an adequate grasp of the full range of cases from which God would have to choose whatever exceptions He is going to make, if any, to the general policy of letting nature take its course. Without that we would not be in a position to judge that Bambi is among the n% of the cases most worthy of being miraculously prevented.[15] And it is abundantly clear that we have and can have no such grasp of this territory as a whole. We are quite unable, by our natural powers, of determining just what cases, or even what kinds of cases, of suffering there would be throughout the history of the universe if nature took its course. We just don't know enough about the constituents of the universe even at present, much less throughout the past and future, to make any such catalogue. And we could not make good that deficiency without an enormous enlargement of our cognitive capacities. Hence we are in no position to judge that God does not have sufficient reason (of the Reichenbach sort) for refraining from interfering in the Bambi case.[16]

But all this has to do with whether God would have interfered with the natural order, as it actually exists, to prevent Bambi's suffering. And it will be suggested, secondly, that God could have instituted a quite different natural order, one that would not involve human and animal suffering, or at least much less of it. Why couldn't there be a natural order in which there are no viruses and bacteria the natural operation of which results in human and animal disease, a natural order in which rainfall is evenly distributed, in which earthquakes do not occur, in which forests are not subject to massive fires? To be sure, even God could not bring into being just the creatures we presently have while subjecting their behavior to different laws. For the fact that a tiger's natural operations and tendencies are what they are is an essential part of what makes it the kind of thing it is.[17] But why couldn't God have created a world with different constituents so as to avoid subjecting any sentient creatures to disease and natural disasters? Let's agree that this is possible for God. But then the critic must also show that at least one of the ways in which God could have done this would have produced a world that is better on the whole than the actual world. For even if God could have instituted a natural order without disease and natural disasters, that by itself doesn't show that He would have done so if He existed. For if that world had other undesirable features and/or lacked desirable features in such a way as to be worse, or at least no better than, the actual world, it still doesn't follow that God would have chosen the former over the latter. It all depends on the overall comparative worth of the two systems. Once again I am not concerned to argue for Reichenbach's theodicy, which would, on the rules by which we are playing, require arguing that no possible natural order is overall better than the one we have. Instead I merely want to show that the critic is not justified in supposing that some alternative natural order open to God that does not involve suffering (to the extent that we have it) is better on the whole. [. . .]

Before leaving this topic I want to emphasize the point that, unlike the theodicies discussed earlier the natural law theodicy bears on the question of animal as well as human suffering. If the value of a lawful universe justifies the suffering that results from the operation of those laws, that would apply to suffering at all levels of the great chain of being.

X

I have been gleaning suggestions from a variety of theodicies as to what reasons God might have for permitting suffering. I believe that each of these suggestions embody one or more sorts of reasons that God might conceivably have for some of the suffering in the world. And I believe that I have shown that none of us are in a position to warrantedly assert, with respect to any of those reasons, that God would not permit some cases of suffering for that reason. Even if I am mistaken in supposing that we cannot rule out some particular reason, e.g. that the suffering is a punishment for sin, I make bold to claim that it is extremely unlikely that I am mistaken about all those suggestions. Moreover, I have argued, successfully I believe, that some of these reasons are at least part of possible divine reasons for Rowe's cases, Bambi and Sue, and that hence we are unable to justifiably assert that God does not have reasons of these sorts for permitting Rowe-like cases.

However that does not suffice to dispose of Rowe's specific argument, concerned as it is with the Bambi and Sue cases in particular. For I earlier conceded, for the sake of argument, that (1) none of the sufferer-centered reasons I considered could be any part of God's reasons for permitting the Bambi and Sue cases, and (2) that non-sufferer-centered reasons could not be the whole of God's reasons for allowing any case of suffering. This left me without any specific suggestions as to what might be a fully sufficient reason for God to permit those cases. And hence showing that no one can be justified in supposing that reasons of the sort considered are not at least part of God's reasons for one or another case of suffering does not suffice to show that no one can be justified in supposing that God could have no sufficient reason for permitting the Bambi and Sue cases. And hence it does not suffice to show that Rowe cannot be justified in asserting 1.

This lacuna in the argument is remedied by the point that we cannot be justified in supposing that there are no other reasons, thus far unenvisaged, that would fully justify God in permitting Rowe's cases. That point was made at the end of section vii for sufferer-centered reasons, and it can now be made more generally. Even if we were fully entitled to dismiss all the alleged reasons for permitting suffering that have been suggested, we would still have to consider whether there are further possibilities that are undreamt of in our theodicies. Why should we suppose that the theodicies thus far excogitated, however brilliant and learned their authors, exhaust the field? The points made in the earlier discussion about the impossibility of anticipating future developments in human thought can be applied here. Just as we can never repose confidence in any alleged limits of future human theoretical and conceptual developments in science, so it is here, even more so if possible. It is surely reasonable to suppose that God, if such there be, has more tricks up His sleeve than we can envisage. Since it is in principle impossible for us to be justified in supposing that God does not have sufficient reasons for permitting E that are unknown to us, and perhaps unknowable by us, no one can be justified in holding that God could have no reasons for permitting the Bambi and Sue cases, or any other particular cases of suffering.[18]

This last point, that we are not warranted in supposing that God does not have sufficient reasons unknown to us for permitting E, is not only an essential part of the total argument against the justifiability of 1. It would be sufficient by itself. Even if all my argumentation prior to that point were in vain and my opponent could definitively rule out all the specific suggestions I have put forward, she would still face the insurmountable task of showing herself to be justified in supposing that there are no further possibilities for sufficient divine reasons. That point by itself would be decisive.

Notes

1   The term "gratuitous" is used in different ways in the literature. Lately it has sprouted variations (Hasker, 1992). My use of the term is strictly tied to Rowe's 1.

2   In (1979) Rowe considers this criticism. He says of it: "I suppose some theists would be content with this rather modest response . . . But given the validity of the basic argument and the theist's likely acceptance of (2), he is thereby committed to the view that (1) is false, not just that we have no good reasons for accepting (1) as true" (338). No doubt, the theist is committed to regarding (1) as false, at least on the assumption that it embodies necessary conditions for God's having sufficient reason for permitting suffering . . . But Rowe does not explain why he thinks that showing that we are not justified in asserting 1 does not constitute a decisive reason for rejecting his argument.

3   The qualifier "traditional" adheres to the restrictions laid down in D and excludes variants like process theology. Admittedly, "traditional Christianity" contains a number of in-house variants, but in this paper I will appeal only to what is common to all forms of what could reasonably be called "traditional Christianity".

4   Rowe does not often use the term "justified belief", but instead usually speaks of its being *rational* to hold a belief. I shall ignore any minor differences there may be between these epistemic concepts.

5   Hence the very common procedure of knocking down theodical suggestions, one by one, by pointing out, in the case of each, that there are evils it does not cover, will not suffice to make the critic's case. For it may be that even though no one divine reason covers all cases each case is covered by some divine reason.

6   It is often dismissed nowadays on the grounds that it presupposes a morally unacceptable theory of punishment, viz., a retributive conception. But it need not make any such presupposition; whatever the rationale of punishment, the suggestion is that (in some cases) God has that rationale for permitting

suffering. Though it must be admitted that the "retributive" principle that *it is intrinsically good that persons should suffer for wrongdoing* makes it easier to claim that suffering constitutes justifiable punishment than a reformatory theory does, where a necessary condition for the justification of punishment is the significant chance of an improvement of the punishee. For purposes of this discussion I will not choose between different theories of punishment.

7 I don't mean to suggest that a person's inner sinfulness or saintliness cannot be expected to manifest itself in behavior. Still less do I mean to suggest that one could be fully or ideally living the life of the spirit, whatever her outward behavior.

8 Rowe writes: "Perhaps the good for which *some* intense suffering is permitted cannot be realized until the end of the world, but it certainly seems likely that much of this good could be realized in the lifetime of the sufferer . . . In the absence of any reason to think that O [God] would need to postpone these good experiences, we have reason to expect that many of these goods would occur in the world we know" (1986, 244–45). But why suppose that we are entitled to judge that justifying goods, if any, would be realized during the sufferer's earthly life, unless we have specific reasons to the contrary? Why this initial presumption? Why is the burden of proof on the suggestion of the realization of the goods in an after-life? Rowe doesn't say, nor do I see what he could say.

9 Actually, Hick is a universalist and believes that all free creatures will attain this consummation; but I do not take this thesis as necessary for the soul making theodicy.

10 Stump gives her answer to this one in the passage quoted.

11 There is, to be sure, a question as to why, if things are as I have just suggested they may be. God doesn't fill us in on His reasons for permitting suffering. Wouldn't a perfectly benevolent creator see to it that we realize why we are called upon to suffer? I acknowledge this difficulty; in fact it is just another form taken by the problem of evil. And I will respond to it in the same way. Even if we can't see why God would keep us in the dark in this matter, we cannot be justified in supposing

that God does not have sufficient reason for doing so.

12 El is Bambi's suffering and E2 is Sue's suffering. There are, of course, various differences between Q and 1. For one thing, Q, unlike 1 makes reference to God's being morally justified. For another, Q has to do with God's *obtaining* particular goods, apparently leaving out of account the cases in which cooperation from human free choice is required. However, these differences are not germane to the present point.

13 Cf. the criticism of Rowe's move from P to Q in Christlieb (1992). Note too that Rowe restricts his consideration of the unknown to "good states of affairs" we do not know of. But, as is recognized in my discussion, it is an equally relevant and equally live possibility that we do not grasp ways in which good states of affairs we know of are connected with cases of suffering so to as to provide God with a reason for permitting the latter. Both types of unknown factors, if realized, would yield divine reasons for permitting suffering of which we are not cognizant.

14 The reader may well wonder why it is only now that I have introduced the free will theodicy, since it has such an obvious application to Sue's case. The reason is that I wanted at first to focus on those suggestions that confined the rationale of suffering to benefit to the sufferer.

15 There are also questions as to whether we are capable of making a reasonable judgment as to which cases from a given field have the strongest claim to being prevented. Our capacity to do this is especially questionable where incommensurable factors are involved, e.g., the worth of the subject and the magnitude of the suffering. But let this pass.

16 The reader will, no doubt, be struck by the similarity between this problem and the one that came up with respect to the free will theodicy. There too it was agreed that God can occasionally, but only occasionally, interfere with human free choice and its implementation without sacrificing the value of human free will. And so there too we were faced with the question of whether we could be assured that a particular case would be a sufficiently strong candidate for such interference that God would have sufficient reason to intervene.

17 Reichenbach, 110–11.

18   For Rowe's objection to this invocation of the possibility of humanly unenvisaged divine reasons for
permitting suffering, and my answer thereto, see
the end of section vii.

References

Adams, Marilyn McCord, "Redemptive Suffering: A
Christian Approach to the Problem of Evil", in
Rationality, Religious Belief, and Moral Commitment, ed.
R. Audi & W. J. Wainwright (Ithaca, NY: Cornell U.
Press, 1986).

Adams, Robert M., "Must God Create the Best?", in *The
Virtue of Faith and Other Essays in Philosophical Theology*
(New York: Oxford University Press, 1987).

Ahern, M. B., *The Problem of Evil* (London: Routledge &
Kegan Paul, 1971)

Christlieb, Terry, "Which Theisms Face an Evidential
Problem of Evil?", *Faith and Philosophy*, (1992).

Fitzpatrick, F. J., "The Onus of Proof in Arguments
about the Problem of Evil", *Religious Studies*, 17
(1981).

Hasker, William, "The Necessity of Gratuitous Evil",
Faith and Philosophy, (1992).

Hick, John, *Evil and the God of Love*, rev. ed. (New York:
Harper & Row, 1978).

Keller, James, "The Problem of Evil and the Attributes of
God", *Int. Journ. Philos Relig.*, 26 (1989).

Kripke, Saul A., "Naming and Necessity", in *Semantics of
Natural Language*, ed. Donald Davidson & Gilbert
Harman (Dordrecht: D. Reidel Pub. Co., 1972).

Plantinga, Alvin, *The Nature of Necessity* (Oxford: Clarendon Press, 1974).

Reichenbach, Bruce, *Evil and a Good God* (New York:
Fordham U. Press, 1982).

Rowe, William L., "The Problem of Evil and Some
Varieties of Atheism", *Amer. Philos. Quart.*, 16, no. 4
(October, 1979).

Rowe, William L., "The Empirical Argument from
Evil", in *Rationality, Religious Belief, and Moral Commitment*,
ed. R. Audi & W. J. Wainwright (Ithaca, NY: Cornell
U. Press, 1986).

Rowe, William L., "Evil and Theodicy", *Philosophical
Topics*, 16, no. 2 (Fall, 1988).

Russell, Bruce, "The Persistent Problem of Evil", *Faith
and Philosophy*, 6, no. 2 (April, 1989).

Stump, Eleonore, "The Problem of Evil", *Faith and
Philosophy*, 2, no. 4 (Oct., 1985).

Stump, Eleonore, "Providence and Evil", in *Christian
Philosophy*, ed. Thomas P. Flint (Notre Dame, IN: U. of
Notre Dame Press, 1990).

Tracy, Thomas F. "Victimization and the Problem of
Evil", *Faith and Philosophy*, (1992).

Wykstra, Stephen, "The Humean Obstacle to Evidential
Arguments from Suffering: On Avoiding the Evils of
'Appearance' ", *Int. Journ. Philos. Relig.*, 16 (1984).

Chapter 20

Peter van Inwagen

THE HIDDENNESS OF GOD

I will begin by laying out an argument for your consideration:

If God existed, that would be a very important thing for us human beings to know. God, being omniscient would know that this would be an important thing for us to know, and, being morally perfect, he would act on this knowledge. He would act on it by providing us with indisputable evidence of his existence. St Paul recognized this when he in effect said (Rom. 2: 18–23) that the blasphemies of the pagans were without excuse because God *had* provided humanity with indisputable evidence of his existence—simply by placing humanity in a world in which, to quote a text we can be sure Paul approved of, the heavens declare the glory of God and the firmament showeth his handiwork. But Paul was wrong to think we had such evidence. It's quite obvious that we don't have it and never have had it, for the unprejudiced know that the heavens are quite silent about the glory of God and that the firmament displays nothing of his handiwork. And, therefore, the absence of evidence for the existence of God should lead us to become atheists, and not merely agnostics.

This argument is in some ways very similar to the global argument from evil.[1] It contends that if there were a God, the world would, owing to his moral perfection, his knowledge, and his power, have certain observable features; it

contends, moreover, that the world can be seen not to have these features; it concludes that God does not exist. In a way, it is an argument from evil, for, if God *does* exist, then a rational creature's being ignorant of his existence is an evil. It might also be said that this argument stands to a famous theological problem called "the problem of the hiddenness of God" or "the problem of divine hiddenness" as the argument from evil stands to the problem of evil. But if the problem of the hiddenness of God is indeed a famous theological problem, it is not so famous a theological problem as the problem of evil, and perhaps not everyone will be familiar with the problem of the hiddenness of God, or will even have heard of it.[2] I will, therefore, take some time to lay out this problem. As is the case with the problem of evil, the problem of the hiddenness of God is more often referred to than precisely stated. Theologians often refer to this problem as if it were perfectly clear what it was, but their writings on the subject do not always make it wholly clear what the problem is. In some writers, it is hard to distinguish the problem of the hiddenness of God from the problem of evil. The writers I am thinking of introduce the problem of the hiddenness of God with reflections along the following lines. The world is full of terrible things, and we observe no response from God when these terrible things happen: the heavens do not rain fire on the Nazis, the raging flood does not turn aside just before it sweeps away the peaceful village, the paralyzed child remains paralyzed.

Nevertheless, I think it is possible to make an intuitive distinction between what is naturally suggested by the words "the problem of divine hiddenness" and what is naturally suggested by the words "the problem of evil". I think I can imagine worlds in which it would not be right or natural by anyone's lights to say that God was "hidden" but in which evil was as much a problem for theists as it is in the actual world.

Imagine, for example, that to every Jew who was to perish in the Holocaust there had come, a few weeks before his or her death, a vision of a seraph, a being of unutterable splendor, who recited Psalm 91 in Hebrew—and then vanished. The doomed recipients of these visions, comparing notes, found that the visions were remarkably consistent. Learned Jews understood the seraph's words perfectly. Less learned Jews recognized the psalm and understood bits and pieces of it, just as they would have if they had heard it recited in a synagogue. Others, less learned still, recognized the language as biblical Hebrew, and said things like, "It sounded like poetry—maybe a psalm". A few wholly secularized Jews did not even recognize the language, but gave an account of the visual aspect of the apparition consistent with everyone else's, and said that the apparition spoke to them in a language they did not understand. (But those victims of the Holocaust who were not Jews according to the Law but were Jews according to the Nazi Race Laws did not experience the vision at all; some of them, however, experienced other visions, of a kind I will describe in a moment.) There were, then, these visions, but that was all. Nothing else happened: not a single life was saved, not a single brutal incident was in any way mitigated. With the exception of the visions, the Holocaust proceeded exactly as it did in the actual world. And let us further imagine that many other victims of horrendous evil in our imaginary world, victims of horrendous

evils throughout all its recorded history, have received, shortly before their final suffering and death, analogous or comparable "signs" in the form of visions incorporating religious imagery—every victim, in fact, who belonged to any cultural tradition that provided religious images he could recognize and interpret. It would seem that in this imaginary world, the problem of evil is no less pressing than it is in ours, but "the problem of the hiddenness of God" does not arise. Or at least we can say this: if the existence of the visions is generally known among the inhabitants of the imaginary world, writers of the sort who in our world speak of "the hiddenness of God" will not use that phrase (they will perhaps speak instead of the "passivity of God").

The problem of evil and the problem of the hiddenness of God are, therefore, not identical. But is the latter essentially connected with suffering and other forms of evil? Would, or could, this problem exist in a world without suffering? I think that trying to answer this question will help us understand what the problem is. Let us imagine a world without suffering—not a world in which everyone enjoys the Beatific Vision, but a world that is as much like our world (as it is at present) as the absence of suffering permits. I will call such a world a "secular utopia", because my model for this world is just that future of alabaster cities undimmed by human tears that secularists yearn for.

In the world I imagine, human beings are benevolent, and nature is kind. There is no physical pain, or very little of it (just enough to remind people to take care not to damage their extremities). There is no premature death, whether by violence, accident, or disease. There are, in fact, no such things as violence and disease, and accidents are never very serious. (The inhabitants of this world all enjoy a vigorous old age and die peacefully in their sleep when they are well over 100 years old—and the fear of death is unknown.) No one is a cripple or mentally retarded or mentally unbalanced or even mildly neurotic. There is no racial prejudice or prejudice of any sort. No one is ugly or deformed. Everyone is provided with all the physical necessities and comforts of life—but great wealth and luxury are as unknown as poverty. Consumer goods are produced in a way that does no violence to nature: the human and non-human inhabitants of the world live in perfect harmony.[3] Everyone has interesting and rewarding work to do, and this work is appropriately rewarded with respect and, if appropriate, admiration. No one covets anyone else's possessions. There is no lying or promise breaking or cheating or corruption—there is in fact nothing for anyone to be corrupt *about*, for there are no laws and no money, and there is essentially no government. If there is any unhappiness in this world, it arises only in cases like these: Alfred has fallen in love with Beatrice, but Beatrice is in love with Charles; Delia has devoted her life to proving Goldbach's Conjecture, and Edward has published a proof of it when Delia had a proof almost within her grasp. And even in such cases, everyone involved behaves with perfect rationality and complete maturity, thereby keeping the resulting unhappiness to an irreducible (and usually transient) minimum.

Now let us suppose that in this world, as in ours, some people believe in God—in a necessarily existent, omniscient, omnipotent, omnipresent creator and sustainer of the world. (The inhabitants of our invented world would have trouble grasping the concept "moral perfection"—but, if you could get them to understand it, the theists among them wouldn't hesitate to ascribe moral perfection to God.) And, as in our world, some people believe that there is no such being. Could someone in this world, perhaps one of its atheists, raise the problem of divine hiddenness? I think so. I think we can imagine a dialogue in which the problem is raised, a dialogue "purer" than any that could be imagined to take place in our world, purer because neither of the participants has ever known or heard of any horrendous evil.

Atheist. This God of yours—why does he hide himself? Why doesn't he come out in the open where we can see him?

Theist. Your question doesn't make any sense. God is omnipresent. That is, he is totally present everywhere and locally present nowhere. A thing is locally present in a place (that is, a region of space) if it occupies or takes up or fills that place. And God occupies neither any particular place (as does a cat or a mountain) nor all places (as the luminiferous aether would, if it existed). He is totally present everywhere in that the totality of his being is reflected in the sustaining power that keeps every spatial thing everywhere in the physical universe in existence from moment to moment. Similarly, we might say that Rembrandt is locally present nowhere in "Aristotle Contemplating a Bust of Homer" and totally present everywhere in this painting. (But the analogy is imperfect, since the three-dimensional objects and spatial relations "in" the painting are fictional, illusory, or imaginary, whereas the ones in the physical universe are—of course—real.) Only a locally present thing can reflect light, and thus only a locally present thing can be visible. Only a locally present thing can exclude other things from the space it occupies, and thus only a locally present thing can be tangible. And only a visible or tangible thing can "show itself". Someone who wants God to "show himself" just doesn't understand the concept of God. Asking for that is like demanding that Rembrandt "show himself" in a painting. The complaint "I can't find God anywhere in the world" is as misplaced as the complaint "I can't find Rembrandt anywhere in 'Aristotle Contemplating a Bust of Homer' ".[4]

Atheist. Well, if he can't show himself by being present in the world, why can't he show himself by his effects on some of the things that *are* present in the world?

Theist. You haven't been listening. Everything in the world is his "effect". He "shows himself by his effects" in the world just as Rembrandt "shows himself by his effects" in his paintings.

Atheist. That sounds good, but I wonder if it's anything more than words. What I want is not "general effects" but, if I may coin a phrase, "special effects". Given your picture of God's relation to the world, everything will look just the same whether there is a God or not—wait, stop, don't tell me that that's like saying that one of Rembrandt's paintings will look the same whether there is a Rembrandt or not! I couldn't bear it. Let me put the problem this way. I have bought one of the modal telescopes invented by the great metaphysicist Saul Kripke, and I have looked into other possible worlds. In one of them I caught a glimpse of the following argument, in a book by a man named Thomas Aquinas (evidently a sound atheist like myself):

Objection 2. It is, moreover, superfluous to suppose that what can be accounted for by a few principles has been produced by many. But it seems that everything we see in the world can be accounted for by other principles, without supposing God to exist. For all natural things can be accounted for by one principle, which is nature; and all voluntary things can be accounted for by one principle, which is human reason or will. Hence, there is no need to suppose that a God exists.

[ST I, q. 2, art. 3]

Surely this argument is unanswerable? Surely one should not believe in the existence of an unobservable entity unless its existence is needed to explain some observed phenomenon?

Theist. So what you are looking for is a particular event, an event that is not caused by any human action, whose occurrence resists any natural or scientific explanation, and which is evidently the work of someone trying to send human beings a message or signal whose con-

tent is that there is such a being as God. How about the stars in the sky rearranging themselves to spell out "I am who am"? [Exod. 3: 14] Would that be satisfactory?

Atheist. It would.

Theist. You don't want much, do you? But it happens I can supply something of the sort you want. My own religion is called Julianism, after its founder, Julia, the great prophetess and author of *The Book of Julia* and the forty volumes of sermons we call *The Words of Julia.* Julia's message was so important that God granted her three times a natural span of life, as a sign of his special favor and to ensure that her teachings would have a chance to put down deep roots. Julia lived 326 years. And every physiologist agrees that it is physiologically impossible for a human being to live 326 years. Therefore, Julia's preternaturally long life must have been a sign from God.

Atheist. Well, that would be pretty impressive if it actually happened. But when did Julia live, and how do you Julianists know that she really did live that long?

Theist. Julia lived about 2,000 years ago. We know of her long life and lots of other things about her because the facts of her biography are carefully set out in the Holy Records of the Julian Church, which originally derive from the testimony of eyewitnesses.

Atheist. Forgive me if I'm skeptical. Even if we discount the possibility of some mixture of fraud and simple factual error on the part of your "eyewitnesses", we must concede that stories can become distorted as they pass from mouth to mouth. As stories are passed from one teller to another, people unconsciously fill in or change minor details in the story. These minor distortions can accumulate, and, given long enough, the accumulation of minor distortions can change a story till it's no longer really the same story. We know that this happens. Just last month, there was a rumor in Neapolis of a terrible tragedy somewhere in Asia—a woman had actually lost a finger in an industrial accident! The whole town was in an uproar. But when the dust settled, it turned out that what had really happened was that the Asian woman had got her finger badly mauled in a piece of machinery while she was day-dreaming. The finger, of course, healed perfectly within a week. Now since we know from experience that stories can become distorted in this fantastic way—the very idea of someone's losing a finger!—and since we know from experience that no one in our modern record-keeping era has lived even 150 years, the most reasonable thing to suppose is that, although Julia may indeed have lived to be remarkably old, she certainly did not live to be 326; the reasonable thing to suppose is that what experience tells us often happens happened this time (that is, the story grew in the telling; it certainly had plenty of time to grow), and that what experience tells us never happens did not happen.[5]

Theist. What you are saying seems to come down to this. You contend that if God is to make his existence credible to human beings, he must cause some particular, unmistakable sign to occur somewhere in the world of space and time. But when you hear a story of some event that would have been such a sign if it had actually occurred, you refuse, on general epistemological grounds, to believe the story.

Atheist. My position is not so extreme as that, or so unreasonable as you make it sound. Take your first, hypothetical example. If the stars in the sky were suddenly rearranged so as to spell out 'I am who am', I'd believe in the existence of God then, all right.[6] That would be a good, clear case of what I'd call "God's coming out of hiding". In such a case, God would be making it evident to human beings that Reality contained another intelligence than human intelligence—and not just any non-human intelligence, but an intelligence grand enough to be a plausible candidate for the office "God". And, obviously, this—or something along the same lines—is what such

a grand intelligence would do if it wanted us to believe in it. If, *per impossibile*, the figures in a Rembrandt painting were conscious beings and aware of (and only of) the objects in their little two-dimensional world, what reason could they have for believing in Rembrandt but something he put specially into the painting that was not a part of the natural order of things in the painting (his signature, perhaps). If he didn't do that, how could he blame the denizens of the painting for not believing in him?

Theist. Let me make two points. First, these signs you want God to place in the world would have to recur periodically, or, after a few generations had passed, people like you would say that the stories about the signs had grown in the telling—perhaps from the seed of an astronomical prodigy that, remarkable as it was, had some purely natural explanation. Secondly, even the "I am who am" story wouldn't make the existence of *God* evident to a sufficiently determined skeptic—for even the (apparent) rearrangement of the stars could be the work of a lesser being than God. We can imagine no sign that would *have* to be the work of a necessary, omnipresent, omnipotent being. Any sign one might imagine could be ascribed to a contingent, locally present being whose powers, though vastly greater than ours, were finite. I should expect that someone like you would say that if two hypotheses explain the data equally well, and if they are alike but for the fact that one of them postulates an unobservable *infinite* being and the other an unobservable *finite* being, one should always prefer the latter hypothesis, since it does the same explanatory work as the former, but is, literally, infinitely weaker.

Atheist. Well, perhaps you're right when you say that to be convincing the signs would have to recur periodically. I don't see why I shouldn't ask for that, and I don't see that it will weaken my argument if I do. And the more I think about it, the more inclined I am to accept your second point as well. Your argument has convinced me of something you didn't foresee: that you theists have invented a being whose existence no one could possibly rationally believe in, since the hypothesis that he exists is necessarily infinitely stronger than other hypotheses that would explain any possible observations equally well. And if you haven't invented him, if he really does exist, even *he* couldn't provide us—or any other finite beings he might create—with evidence that would render belief in him rational. If he exists, he should approve of me for not believing in him, and disapprove of you for believing in him.

Let us at this point leave our dialogue and the secular utopia in which it was imagined to occur, and return to the real world. The lesson of the dialogue is that in a world that lacks any real suffering, the problem of the hiddenness of God is a purely epistemological problem, or a cluster of epistemological problems: can one rationally believe in God in a world devoid of signs and wonders?[7] Under what conditions would it be rational to believe a story that reports signs and wonders? Could any possible sign or wonder or series of signs and wonders make it reasonable to believe in a necessarily existent, omnipresent, omnipotent Creator and Sustainer of the world of locally present things?

These epistemological questions obviously have the same force in the real world as in our secular utopia. The most pointed of them, the one I wish to discuss, is this: Why does God not show us that he exists by providing us with signs and wonders? Anyone who thinks that this question has no answer can present an argument for the non-existence of God whose premise is the absence of signs and wonders. We have seen a simple version of this argument. Here is a more careful version of the argument—a version that turns on one component of knowledge, belief, rather than knowledge itself:

1   If God exists, he wants all finite rational beings to believe in his existence.

2   If every finite rational being observed signs and wonders of the right sort, every finite rational being would believe in God.

3   There is, therefore, something that God could do to ensure that every finite rational being believed in his existence.

4   If God wants all finite rational beings to believe in his existence and there is something he can do to bring this about, he will do something to bring it about.

5   But not all finite rational beings believe in God.
    Hence,

6   God does not exist.

I will make two observations about this argument, which I will call the doxastic argument. First, it is not formally valid, but it could easily be made so, and it hardly seems plausible to suppose that any of the premises that would have to be added to make the argument formally valid would be false. If there is any defect in this argument, it must be that one or more of the premises of the argument as I have stated it are false. And these premises seem to be, to say the least, plausible. It is certainly true that not all people believe in God. Although no one is likely to dispute this premise, I want to make it clear that widespread unbelief is almost certainly not a recent thing, even in officially Christian cultures. Here are some remarkable words, written by one Peter of Cornwall, Prior of Holy Trinity, Aldgate, around the year 1200:

> There are many people who do not believe that God exists, nor do they think that a human soul lives on after the death of the body. They consider that the universe has always been as it is now and is ruled by chance rather than by Providence.[8]

If this was the best God could do in twelfth-century England, it would seem that he just wasn't trying! (And, obviously, he hasn't done any better since.)

My second observation is that some might find this argument more persuasive if 'rational belief' were substituted for 'belief' in it. If this substitution is made, the first two premises of the argument read:

If God exists, he wants all finite rational beings to believe rationally in his existence.

If every finite rational being observed signs and wonders of the right sort, every finite rational being would believe in God rationally.

I am not sure which version of the argument is the more persuasive, but I mean my remarks to apply equally to either.

Now how should the theist respond to this argument? I propose that the theist's response be strictly parallel to Theist's response to the global argument from evil. That is, that the theist should attempt to tell a story that has the following logical consequences:

The world was created and is sustained by a necessary, omnipresent, omniscient, omnipotent, morally perfect being—that is, by God. There are rational beings in this world, and God wants these beings, or some of them at some times, to believe in his existence. The world is devoid of signs and wonders—of "special effects". Or if the world contains any such events, they are so rare that very few people have actually observed one or even encountered anyone who claims to have observed one. (In the latter case, among those people whom God wants to believe in his existence are many of the people who are distant in space and time from any of the very rare signs and wonders.)

And I propose that the doxastic argument should be judged a failure just in the case that the theist is able to tell a story with these consequences such that an audience of ideal agnostics (who have been presented with the doxastic argument and have been trying to decide whether it is convincing) will respond to it by saying, "Given that God exists, the rest of that story may well be true. I don't see any reason to rule it out." And, of course, we require that this reaction be achieved in the presence of an ideal atheist who does everything possible to block this reaction, everything possible to defend the truth of the premises of the argument against the doubts raised by the theist's story. We may as well call such a story what we called stories that played an analogous role in relation to the argument from evil: we may as well call it a defense. The term is appropriate enough because God is, once more, in the dock—the charge being that he has not presented us with indisputable evidence in the form of signs and wonders in the important matter of his existence—and the theist is the counsel for the defense. We may remember at this point the famous story of Lord Russell's reply to a woman at a London dinner party (or an American undergraduate— the story comes in various versions) who had asked him what he would say to God on the Day of Judgment (if, contrary to his expectations, there should be such a day): "Lord, you gave me insufficient evidence."[9] Russell's indignant postmortem protest is one formulation of the accusation that the God in the dock faces. How should counsel for the defense reply?

In discussions of the global argument from evil, the kernel of every defense is a *reason* (or a set of reasons), God's reason or reasons for permitting the existence of evil. So it should be with discussions of the doxastic argument: the kernel of every defense should be a reason or reasons, God's reason or reasons for not providing the human species with ubiquitous signs and wonders, despite the fact that he thinks it very important that they believe in his existence.

I will try to present such a defense. This defense will build upon the expanded freewill defense that I had Theist present in our discussion of the argument from evil. The essential idea of that defense was that the elimination of all evil from the world by an enormous congeries of local miracles would frustrate God's plan of atonement, his plan for reuniting separated humanity with himself. The essential idea of the defense I shall present in response to the doxastic argument is that ubiquitous signs and wonders would also frustrate God's plan of atonement.

I begin with an observation. Note that the proposition

God wants people to believe in his existence

does not entail the proposition

God wants people to believe in his existence—*and* he does not care why anyone who believes in him has this belief.

The former proposition, in fact, is consistent with the proposition that God would regard the following list as presenting three states of affairs in order of decreasing value:

1 Patricia believes, for reason A, that God exists.
2 Patricia believes that God does not exist.
3 Patricia believes, for reason B, that God exists.

It is, for example, consistent with God's wanting Patricia to believe in him that he regard (1) as a good state of affairs, (2) as a bad state of affairs, and (3) as a bad state of affairs that is *much* worse than (2). (And this would be consistent with reason B's being an epistemically unobjectionable reason for belief in God: reason B might be, from the point of view of someone interested only in justification or warrant, a perfectly good reason for believing in the existence of God.) And this is no idle speculation about a logical possibility. Most theists hold that God expects a good deal more from us than mere belief in his existence. As James says in his epistle, "You believe in the one God—that is creditable

enough, but the demons have the same belief, and they tremble with fear" (2: 19).[10] God expects a complex of things, of which belief in his existence is a small (although essential) part. It is certainly conceivable that someone's believing in him for a certain reason (because, say, that person has witnessed signs and wonders) might make it difficult or even impossible for that person to acquire other features God wanted him or her to have.

Can we make this seem plausible? Let us wander a bit, and look at some examples and analogies. Let us consider a second New Testament text. Remember the story of the rich man in Hell in chapter 16 of Luke's Gospel. The rich man, who had in life treated the poor with contemptuous neglect, is in Hell (for that very reason), and petitions Abraham (who is somehow able to converse with him across a "great gulf") that a messenger should be sent to his still living brothers, who also have starving beggars at their sumptuous gates, to warn them to mend their ways before it is too late. Abraham replies, "If they do not hear Moses and the Prophets, neither will they be persuaded though one rose from the dead." A very striking parable, but can its message really be true? That is, can it be true that witnessing a miracle, even a very personal and pointed miracle, would have no effect on the character of values of someone who witnessed it, no effect on the type of person he or she is? In order that our imaginations may not be distracted by the quaint literary devices of an old book, let us imagine a parable for our own time. This parable has two central characters. The first is the Russian strategist whose contribution to his country's cause in Afghanistan was the clever idea of placing powerful bombs disguised as bright shiny toys in the vicinity of unreliable villages. This man dies (in bed, of course) and receives an appropriate reward in the afterlife. He begs Abraham to be allowed, after the fashion of Marley's ghost,[11] to be allowed to appear to his living brother (who is, let us say, the general whose forces carried out the distribution of the "toys" in the Afghan countryside) and warn him of what awaits him. In this case the petition is granted. He appears to his brother and says to him, "Listen, brother, we were wrong. There is a God and there is a judgment. I am in Hell because of the terrible things I did. Repent and change your life and avoid my unhappy fate." What would the result be?

I would suppose that the best result one could hope for would be this—and remember, we're talking about someone who distributed anti-personnel bombs disguised as toys. This is a man who, in the words of the Wisdom of Solomon, had made a covenant with death: that is, who had, in his own mind, traded eternal extinction after death for the privilege of behaving any way he liked, with impunity, during life.[12] Such a man could only regard what his brother told him as bad news—as a bad child who was told that Santa Claus would bring him no toys if he behaved according to his normal inclinations would regard this information as bad news. The general's reaction would, or so it seems to me, be articulable along these lines: "All right, it seems I was badly out in my calculations. The nature of the universe is entirely different from what I thought it was. It has a personal creator, a being of such great power that it is hopeless to oppose his will. This being has some rules, and the penalty for disobeying them is terrible, and it seems that these rules are, are to put it mildly, inconsistent with the kind of life I want to live. It seems that if I kill and maim Afghan children and their families in order to curry favor with my political bosses, I'll be subjected to eternal torment. This is the worst news of my life; all my plans have to be rethought. Well, I'd better get on with it. What I have to do is to figure out how to obey these damned rules in a way that will require a minimum modification of my goals in life." (Or, at least, that's one way the general might react. Another possibility would be simple rebellion. The infernal debate in Pandaemonium in Book II of *Paradise Lost*, which is a debate about the best way to conduct a rebellion against an authority whose power is immeasurably greater than one's own, lays out various possibilities that the general might want to consider.) If the general resolves to modify his behavior and his goals in response to be the bad news he has received from his dead brother, it is far from clear that even this resolution could be expected to last very long. The effect of hell-fire sermons—on those who are affected by them at all—is in general a repentance and an attempt at amendment of life that are transitory indeed. I shouldn't be surprised if our general would, before too long, find some way to convince himself that his vision of his brother was some sort of illusion, perhaps a transient psychotic episode, and to push it out of his mind altogether. But whether he does or doesn't continue to believe that the miracle he witnessed was real, it's not going to produce any change in his behavior that God would be interested in. It's not going to cause him to realize that the world is a horrible place and to seek a way out of this horrible world. It's not going to make of him a man who believes that the world is a horrible place *because* human beings are separated from God, and that the world can be healed only if humanity is reunited with God. It's not going to convince him that *he* is a moral horror, and that his only hope of being anything else is to be united with God in bonds of love. No, he likes things just the way they are—or just the way they seemed to be before the visitation. He doesn't think the world is a horrible place, although he no doubt realizes that it's a horrible place for many *other* people. But other people are of interest to him only as instruments. His only objection to the world as he perceived it before the visitation was that he didn't enjoy enough power in it, a deficiency he was devoting every minute of his waking life to correcting.

I would generalize this contention. If God were to convince us of his existence by ubiquitous miracles, this would contribute nothing to his plan of atonement. And it seems to me likely that it would interfere with it. If I were an atheist or agnostic who witnessed such things as the following:

The stars in the skies spell out 'I am who am';

A voice heard in the thunder tells us that there is a God and that we had better mend our ways;

Microscopic examination of grains of sand reveals that each of them carries the inscription "Made by God" (this amusing example is due to John Leslie);

I suppose I should conclude that God existed— or at least that some being I should probably refer to as 'God' existed. (It isn't clear that I'd conclude that a being who was God, properly speaking, existed; for, as I had my characters in the story of the secular utopia point out, any series of miraculous events can always be explained by postulating a finite being of great power and knowledge.) But I should also probably infer that this being's main project for me was this: he wanted me to believe in his existence, and, no doubt, to behave in some way that would be a natural consequence of this new piece of knowledge. And this isn't really what God wants at all. From the point of view of theism, or at least from the point of view of the theistic religions—Judaism, Christianity, and Islam—it is indeed true that God wants us human beings to believe in his existence,[13] but, like many truths, this truth can be very misleading if it is asserted out of context. I want my wife to believe in my existence; if I say this, I say something true; but it's not a thing I would ever say outside a philosophical example. What I want is for my wife and me to stand in a certain complex set of relations that, as a matter of fact, have her believing in my existence as an essential component or logical consequence. If my marriage were destroyed, if this complex set of relations ceased to obtain, she would no doubt still believe in my existence, but that, by itself, would be of no value to me. And God does not place any

particular value on anyone's believing in his existence, not *simpliciter*, not by itself. What he values is, as I noted earlier, a complex of which belief in his existence is a logical consequence. . . . Is it not possible, does it not seem plausible, that if God were to present the world with a vast array of miracles attesting to the existence of a personal power beyond nature, this action would convey to us the message that what he desired of us was simply that we should believe in his existence?—and nothing more?— or nothing more than believing in his existence and taking account of it as one important feature of reality, a feature that has to be factored into all our practical reasoning? If that is so, then the vast array of miracles would not only be useless from God's point of view, but positively harmful, a barrier to putting his plan of reconciliation into effect.

If it is hard to see what I am getting at here, perhaps a sort of analogy will help. There are *many* propositions God wants everyone to accept that people don't generally accept, or haven't generally accepted in the course of human history. One of them would be "Women are not intellectually, emotionally, or spiritually inferior to men." But if God wants everyone to accept this proposition, everyone at all times and in all places, why has he not (as Russell might have asked) provided us with *more evidence* for it? Why doesn't a voice from a whirlwind or a burning bush inform everyone of its truth on their eighteenth birthday? Why isn't every woman born with a tastefully small but clearly legible birthmark that says (perhaps in the native language of her parents) "Not intellectually, emotionally, or spiritually inferior to men"? If God had done any of these things, he'd have vastly changed the course of human history. There would have been no sexism, no male domination, no clitoral circumcision, no prostitution, no sexual slavery, no foot-binding or purdah or suttee. So why hasn't God "provided us with more evidence"? Part of the answer, I think, is that he has already given us all the evidence we need or should ever have needed to be convinced—to *know*—that women are not the intellectual, emotional, or spiritual inferiors of men. And this is, simply, the evidence that is provided by normal human social interaction. Another part of the answer is that it would be useless for him to do this if his purpose were a real transformation of the attitude of fallen male humanity toward women. The best that such "external" evidence could produce would be a sort of sullen compliance with someone else's opinion—even if that "someone else" were God. (If you doubt this, consider how a present-day radical feminist would be likely to respond if it suddenly came to pass that male babies began to be born with scientifically inexplicable birthmarks that spelled out "The superior sex" and female babies began to be born with scientifically inexplicable birthmarks that spelled out "The inferior sex".) What is really needed to eliminate sexism is not sullen compliance forced on one by evidence that has no natural connection with life in the human social world. What is needed is natural conviction that proceeds from our normal cognitive apparatus operating on the normal data of the senses. Sexism will be really eliminated (as opposed to repressed) only when everyone, using his normal cognitive capacities, applying them to the data of everyday social interaction, believes in the intellectual, emotional, and spiritual equality of the sexes in the same way in which everyone now believes in the equality of the auditory and visual capacities of the sexes. And might it not be that miraculous evidence for the equality of the sexes would actually interfere with our capacity to come to a belief in the equality of the sexes in the right way? If most men at most times (and perhaps most women, too) have believed that men were superior to women—and they have—they have managed to do this in a world in which they were positively swimming in evidence to the contrary. Something, therefore, must have been wrong with their ability to process the data of everyday experience. They must have been epistemically defective (and not innocently so like the natural philosophers who believed that heavy bodies fell faster than light ones,[14] but culpably epistemically defective, like Holocaust deniers). Might it not be that external, miraculous evidence for the equality of the sexes would simply raise such emotional barriers, such waves of sullen resentment among the self-deceived, that there would be no hope of their gradually coming to listen to what their senses were saying to them in the course of ordinary human social interaction? If there is, as St Paul has said, a natural tendency in us to see the existence and power and deity of the maker of the world in the things around us (Rom. 2: 20), and if many people do not see this because they do not want to see it, is it not possible that grains of sand bearing the legend "Made by God" (or articulate thunder or a rearrangement of the stars bearing a similar message) would simply raise such emotional barriers, such waves of sullen resentment among the self-deceived, that there would be no hope of their eventually coming to perceive the power and deity of God in the ordinary, everyday operations of the things he has made?

Notes

1 This argument does not appeal to the validity of "Absence of evidence is evidence of absence" as a general epistemological principle. And that is to its credit, for that principle is wrong: we have no evidence for the existence of an inhabited planet in the galaxy M31, but that fact is not evidence for the non-existence of such a planet. For a discussion of this principle and arguments for the non-existence of God that appeal to it, see my essay "Is God an Unnecessary Hypothesis?" If the present argument appeals to any general epistemological principle, it is this rather obvious one: If a proposition is such that, if it were true, we should have evidence for its truth, and if we are aware that it has this property, and if we have no evidence for its truth, then this fact, the fact that we have no evidence for its truth, is (conclusive) evidence for its falsity.

2 Those who wish to learn more about the problem of the hiddenness of God should consult Daniel

Howard-Snyder and Paul K. Moser's *Divine Hiddenness: New Essays*. The present lecture is an expanded version of my own contribution to that volume, "What is the Problem of the Hiddenness of God?"

3   Those who think that the sufferings of non-human animals that are unrelated to the acts of human beings are relevant to "the problem of the hiddenness of God" should feel free to imagine that our invented world is one in which beasts in the state of nature never suffer. As I said in the previous lecture, it is not easy to imagine in any detail a biologically rich world without animal suffering unless one imagines it as a world of ubiquitous miracles—a world in which, for example, fawns are always miraculously saved from forest fires. The imaginer who has recourse to a vast array of miracles had better take care to make them "unnoticeable" (at least in those epochs and places in which there are human beings to notice them), for if the ubiquitous miracles were *obviously* miracles, this would defeat our purpose in trying to imagine a utopia in which "the problem of the hiddenness of God" could be raised.

4   I can imagine someone in the actual world (a reader of this book) protesting, "This metaphysical argument confuses the God of the Philosophers with the God of Abraham, Isaac, and Jacob. For the prophet Isaiah says (45: 15), 'Verily, thou art a God that hidest thyself, O God of Israel, the Saviour' ". In my view, however, Isaiah is simply calling attention to the fact that God has revealed himself to the Hebrews alone, and not to the great nations of Egypt and the Fertile Crescent. (In the Vulgate, incidentally, Isa. 45: 15 is rendered as "Vere, tu es Deus absconditus, Deus Israel, Salvator". This is the source of the phrase 'Deus absconditus'—'the hidden God'—that often occurs in discussions of the problem of the hiddenness of God.)

5   This argument is, of course, modeled on the central argument of Hume's unjustly celebrated essay "Of Miracles" (*An Enquiry concerning Human Understanding*, sect. X).

6   Atheist's statement is reminiscent of a famous statement of Norwood Russell Hanson's ("What I Don't Believe", 322):

I'm not a stubborn guy. I would be a theist under some conditions. I'm open-minded. . . . Okay.

Okay. The conditions are these: Suppose, next Tuesday morning, just after breakfast, all of us in this one world are knocked to our knees by a percussive and ear-shattering thunderclap. Snow swirls, leaves drop from trees, the earth heaves and buckles, buildings topple, and towers tumble. The sky is ablaze with an eerie silvery light, and just then, as all of the people of this world look up, the heavens open, and the clouds pull apart, revealing an unbelievably radiant and immense Zeus-like figure towering over us like a hundred Everests. He frowns darkly as lightning plays over the features of his Michelangeloid face, and then he points down, *at me*, and explains for every man, woman, and child to hear: "I've had quite enough of your too-clever logic chopping and word-watching in matters of theology. Be assured Norwood Russell Hanson, that I do most certainly exist!"

7   By 'signs and wonders' I mean "visible" miracles, events that are on the face of it contraventions of the natural order of things. ("The raising of a house or ship into the air is a visible miracle. The raising of a feather, when the wind wants ever so little of a force requisite for that purpose, is as real a miracle, though not so sensible with regard to us" (Hume, "Of Miracles," n.) 1.) To use this biblical term in this sense is by no means an anachronism. "Law of nature" may be a modern concept (it would have been difficult indeed to explain to anyone in the ancient world what Hume meant when he said that the raising of a feather by the wind might be a violation of the natural order—if the wind *did* raise the feather, how could it have wanted, to any degree, a force requisite to that purpose?; what could that *mean*?), but people in biblical times were well aware that the truth of certain reports would entail the existence of violations of the natural order, for those reports are reports of things that "just don't happen". See, e.g., the reaction of Porcius Festus, procurator of Judea, to Paul's confession of faith before King Agrippa (Acts 26: 24). Festus was a first-century man of affairs, not a post-Newtonian philosopher, but his reaction to Paul's speech evidence a position that is as "Humean" as those differences from Hume permit: it is more reasonable to believe that Paul is

mad than it is to believe what he says, for the kinds of things that Paul has described are kinds of things that just don't happen—and a learned man's being driven mad by his great learning *is* a thing that has been known to happen.

8 These words are from a manuscript that, as far as I know, is unpublished. They are quoted in Robert Bartlett, *England under the Norman and Angevin Kings*. I take them from a review of the book by John Gillingham. Here is a second quotation from the book by the reviewer: "simple materialism and disbelief in the afterlife were probably widespread, although they leave little trace in sources written by clerics and monks". (No page citations are given in the review.)

9 In the "American undergraduate" version, Russell went on to say: "Then God will say to me, 'Good for you, Bertie; you used the mind I gave you. Enter into the Kingdom of Heaven.' And you, young man, you he will send straight to Hell."

10 This is the translation of the Jerusalem Bible. Here is a more literal translation: "Do you believe that God is one? You do well. The demons also believe, and they shudder."

11 Is there any evidence that *A Christmas Carol* was influenced by Luke 16? I should like to know.

12 Wisd. 1: 16–2: 11. The phrase "they have made a covenant with death" occurs in Isaiah (28: 15), but in that verse, I believe, a different sort of covenant is intended.

13 "For whoever would draw near to God must believe that he exists (*hoti estin*) and that he rewards those who seek him" (Heb. 11: 6, RSV). Note that the first conjunct is (logically) redundant: one who believes that God rewards those who seek him *ipso facto* believes that God exists. Note also that even the more inclusive belief—that God rewards those who seek him—is represented as having merely instrumental value: what is of intrinsic value is drawing near to God.

14 If Descartes's account of intellectual error was right, this epistemic defect wasn't innocent, for it involved an abuse of free will (but I don't suppose that his account was right).

Chapter 21

Michael J. Murray

COERCION AND THE HIDDENNESS OF GOD

> But if I go to the east, he is not there;
> if I go to the west I do not find him.
> When he is at work in the north, I do not see him;
> when he turns to the south, I catch no glimpse of him.
> —Job 23:8–9

I

The sentiments expressed by Job in the above epigram are ones that have been expressed by the sophisticated atheist as well as the typical church-goer. Most of us, in fact, have wondered at one time or another why it is that God does not reveal Himself in some dramatic fashion if He actually exists. Yet, while this question is widely entertained, it has received surprisingly little attention in the philosophical literature. In addition to puzzling many theists, the fact of divine hiddenness has prompted some non-theists to challenge the theist to provide some explanation for God's apparent silence. The problem they have raised can be roughly stated as follows: If, as most theists claim, belief in God is essential to ultimate human fulfillment, one would expect that God would provide us with unambiguous evidence for His existence. However, such evidence is not forthcoming. Therefore, it is unlikely that the theist's God exists.

The atheist Norwood Russell Hanson makes this case against the theist as follows in his essay "What I Do Not Believe":

. . . 'God exists' *could* in principle be established for all factually—it just happens not to be, certainly not for everyone! Suppose, however, that next Tuesday morning, just after breakfast, all of us in this one world are knocked to our knees by a percussive and ear-shattering thunderclap. Snow swirls; leaves drop from the trees; the earth heaves and buckles; buildings topple and towers tumble; the sky is ablaze with an eerie, silvery light. Just then, as all the people of this world look up, the heavens open the clouds pull apart-revealing an unbelievably immense and radiant-like Zeus figure, towering above us like a hundred Everests. He frown darkly as lightning plays across the features of his Michelangeloid face. He then points down— *at me!*—and explains, for every man and child to hear:

'I have had quite enough of your too-clever logic-chopping and word-watching in matters of theology. Be assured, N. R. Hanson, that I most certainly do exist.'

. . . Please do not dismiss this as a playful,

irreverent Disney-oid contrivance. The conceptual point here is that if such a remarkable event were to occur, I for one should certainly be convinced that God does exist. That matter of fact would have been settled once and for all time. . . . That God exists would, through this encounter, have been confirmed for me and for everyone else in a manner every bit as direct as that involved in any non-controversial factual claim.[1]

Hanson's point, of course, is that since God has not produced such a theophany, we not only lack good evidence that such a God exists, but that this heavenly silence actually inveighs against God's existence. The argument is made even more forcefully by Nietzsche in the following section:

A god who is all-knowing and all powerful and who does not even make sure his creatures understand his intention—could that be a god of goodness? Who allows countless doubts and dubities to persist, for thousands of years, as though the salvation of mankind were unaffected by them, and who on the other hand holds out the prospect of frightful consequences if any mistake is made as to the nature of truth? Would he not be a cruel god if he possessed the truth and could behold mankind miserably tormenting itself over the truth?—But perhaps he is a god of goodness notwithstanding—and merely *could* express himself more clearly! Did he perhaps lack the intelligence to do so? Or the eloquence? So much the worse! For then he was perhaps also in error as to that which he calls his "truth", and is himself not so very far from being the "poor deluded devil"! Must he not then endure almost the torments of Hell to have to see his creatures suffer so, and go on suffering even more through all eternity, for the sake of knowledge of him, and *not* be able to help and counsel them, except in the manner of a deaf and dumb man making all kinds of

ambiguous signs when the most fearful danger is about to befall on his child or his dog? . . . All religions exhibit traces of the fact that they owe their origin to an early, immature intellectuality in man—they all take astonishingly *lightly* the duty to tell the truth: they as yet know nothing of a *Duty of God* to be truthful towards mankind and clear in the manner of his communications.[2]

The challenge to the theist is to explain this heavenly silence.

II

In order to understand the nature of the problem of divine hiddenness it is important to ask exactly what the objector to theism finds problematic here. The real problem, as I see it, is the fact that the hiddenness of God seems to be closely tied to disbelief. For most Christian theists, disbelief is a form of sin, possibly the most damaging form. As a result, the problem appears to reduce to the fact that God's self-imposed obscurity seems to be indirectly, or possibly directly, responsible for an important form of evil.[3] The atheists challenge, then, amounts to this: why has God established conditions, or at least allowed conditions to prevail, which seem to lead to the occurrence of a significant amount of evil, especially evil of such a grave sort? Seen in this way, the problem is similar to a number of others which fall under the traditional problem of evil. One might thus be led to consider, first, whether or not the hiddenness of God might simply be treated as a species of the problem of evil and thus be resolved by appealing to certain traditional theodicies regarding this problem. What I intend to show here is that certain traditional theodicies do seem to provide some interesting resolutions to the problem of God's hiddenness. I will begin in this section with a discussion of the traditional free-will defense and show how it can be brought to bear on this vexing problem.

Briefly, a free-will theodicy claims that the

existence of free-will causes, allows, or presupposes the possibility of certain evils. However, there are two distinct species of free-will theodicies, both of which I will make use of in the course of this discussion. The first type of free-will theodicy argues that one of the consequences of endowing creatures with free-will is that these beings have the option to choose evil over good. As a result, it is impossible that God actualize a world such that there are both free beings and also no possibility of these beings undertaking evil actions. I call theodicies of this type *consequent free-will theodicies*. They are "consequent" in the sense that evil is to be accounted for in terms of conditions that arise as a consequence of the existence of free-will in our world. It is this sort of theodicy that is most often invoked by theists in order to account for the existence of moral evil in the world.

However, the type of free-will theodicy I am going to be concerned with first is somewhat different. The theodicy that is important here argues that there are certain *antecedent* conditions that must necessarily hold or fail to hold if beings endowed with freedom are to be able to exercise this freedom in a morally significant manner. For example, Swinburne, and others, have argued that any world which is such that free beings can exercise their freedom in a morally significant manner must also be a world in which there are stable natural regularities of some sort. If this were not the case, it is argued, free creatures could never come to understand that there are regular connections between their undertakings and the consequence of their undertakings. So, for example, if there were no stable natural regularities, firing a gun at another person's head at point-blank range may, on one occasion, give them a haircut, whereas on another occasion it may kill them. But it seems clear that one could not be said to be morally responsible for their actions if they had no way of knowing that their undertaking, in this case firing the gun, would have the undesirable consequence of taking another life. As a result, free creatures

must be created in a world in which such stable connections between undertakings and the consequences of undertakings obtain. And it seems plausible to suppose that such a world requires a set of stable natural regularities to insure the stability of this very connection. It is only when we can be assured that, for example, gun-firings result in certain predictable consequences, that we can be responsible for the outcomes of such actions.

However, the argument continues, the existence of stable natural laws may also lead to other events which result in natural evil, for example, hurricanes, earthquakes, and so on. Thus, if one can argue that there is come overriding reason why God should create a world with beings that are free and also able to exercise that freedom in a morally significant fashion, then the existence of these laws which give rise to natural evil are justified.

This argument strategy thus contends that certain antecedent conditions must obtain if free creatures are to be able to exercise their freedom in the most robust sense. And since there is good reason for creating creatures who can exercise their freedom in this fashion, there is good reason to create the necessary antecedent conditions which would allow for such exercising of freedom. One can then argue that even though certain evil states of affairs might result from these antecedent conditions obtaining, such is necessary if God is going to be able to bring about the greater good of actualizing a world in which free creatures can exercise their freedom in a thoroughly robust manner.

Clearly, theodicies of this sort differ from theodicies of the consequent type in that they argue that there are certain antecedent conditions which are requisite for free beings to be able to exercise their freedom and that such conditions may incidentally lead to certain other evil states of affairs. However, it is argued, the circumstances for which these antecedent conditions are necessary are sufficiently good to justify the evil which arises as a result of their obtaining. I will refer to this class of theodicies as *antecedent free-will theodicies*.

In addition to arguing that certain conditions must *obtain* for free creatures to be able to exercise their freedom, it can also be shown that certain conditions must *fail to obtain* if free beings are to be able to exercise their freedom in a morally significant manner. Specifically, it appears that one cannot act freely when one is in the condition of *compulsion by another in the context of a threat*. Under conditions that I will specify below, it seems clear that fully robust and morally significant free-will cannot be exercised by someone who is compelled by another in the context of a threat. Further, I will argue that if God does not remain "hidden" to a certain extent, at least some of the free creatures He creates would be in the condition of being compelled in the context of a threat and, as a result, such creatures could not exercise their freedom in this robust, morally significant manner.

It seems at least *prima facie* plausible to claim that morally significant freedom cannot be exercised by an individual who is being told to perform a certain action in the context of a significant threat, say, hand over his money to one holding a gun to his head and threatening to shoot. The threatened individual is compelled by another in such a way that morally significant free-will cannot be exercised. This claim, however, is certainly not uncontroversial. Adequately defending this position would require a separate treatment on the nature of coercion and its relation to freedom, a task too great given the limitations of this essay. However, a few things need to be said here about the relationship between a significant threat and freedom. First of all, I am certainly not claiming that freely willed acts are metaphysically impossible in the context of a significant threat. There is even no *physical* impossibility involved in the case of one refusing to comply with the demands of the robber described above. But if this is so, what is going on in cases where we are threatened?

There are at least three alternative answers.

The first possibility is that we *are* free in such cases but that under the circumstances no rational person would choose to act contrary to the demands of the threatener. We might say, further, that as a result of the threat, our ability to rationally deliberate about alternatives is blocked because the threatener has brought it about that there can only be one rational choice. If we look at the matter in this way what is surrendered in such cases is the *deliberative* or *reasoned* exercise of freedom. On this account the external threat of an intentional agent has limited the rational possibilities of action to just one. And in such circumstances, one may hold, we are not able to fully exercise our freedom.[4]

The second thing one might say is that we are not free at all. It is a common view amongst libertarians that a free action requires that neither metaphysically necessary truths, the history of the world, nor the laws of nature prevent us from choosing between more than one option. One might hold, however, that there are cases in which certain operative psychological laws make only one alternative *psychologically* possible. When such laws are operative we are in a state where we cannot view physically possible alternative courses of action as legitimate possibilities for action for us at that time. In such cases, these psychological laws make it the case that one psychologically could not choose to fail to act in accordance with the threateners demands. As a result, in cases such as these the libertarian might legitimately hold that we are not free in the most fundamental sense.

Finally, one might argue that what is not possible in these threat contexts, is free actions that are *morally significant*. One adopting this approach might argue that freedom has not been lost here because the threatened can consider the alternatives and choose what, in that instance, is the most rational course of action. What the threat does provide, however, are excuses for the behavior—excuses which suffice to relieve the threatened of moral responsibility for the action committed.[5] Traditional Christian theists often argue that it is not only freedom, but morally significant freedom which is desirable for free creatures. Plantinga argues, for example, that the moral significance of the free actions is important because God desires to increase the diversity and amount of good in His creation. One way to accomplish this is to create free beings who can exercise this freedom in a morally significant manner, thus creating a world containing *moral good* in addition to just, say, metaphysical goodness, the sort of goodness that attaches to something mere existence or being. If this is correct, one might argue that praise and blame are not justified in the context of significant threats because such threats provide adequate moral excuses for the behavior performed. Suppose that the individual being robbed in the case described above, call him Barney, had been sent by his friend, Fred, to make a deposit to Fred's savings account. On his way to drop off the deposit, Barney is stopped by our robber and promptly hands over the cash. In such a case it seems clear that we would not feel that Barney is morally culpable for giving up the money as we would if he were simply to hand it to some passerby. The fact that there was a significant threat provides an excuse which is sufficient to make Barney no longer morally culpable for an act he would have been responsible for had the significant threat not been present. Because praise or blame are not justifiably imputed in such cases of compulsion it would appear that although freedom *simpliciter* is not eliminated, the moral significance of the action performed is.

Whichever interpretation one wishes to place on such cases of compulsion, the fact remains that the prospect of being in such circumstances is quite unsavory. If one thinks that such threats make the threatened unable to act freely, then threatening destroys freedom. But even if one concludes that the threatened is still free, there is still something defective about the activity of the threatened in such a case. Whatever this defect might be explains why we legislate against such coercive behavior and do not allow robbers to

excuse their action by claiming that they do nothing wrong since the victim "gave his money over freely." For the purposes of this essay I will not argue for any of these three views about the relationship between threats and freedom. Instead I will simply note that such cases do put the threatened in an unsavory position, one which in some way interferes with their exercising morally-significant freedom in a fully robust manner.

III

There is, however, an ambiguity regarding exactly what constitutes a "significant threat." Not just any threat counts as a compelling one since, for example, one would not feel compelled to hand their money over to a robber who simply threatened to call them a dirty word. What would be helpful is a list of necessary and sufficient conditions which would suffice to clarify exactly what constitutes a threat significant enough to eliminate the possibility of morally significant, rational freedom. Unfortunately, the subject matter here does not allow for such precision. However, there are certain factors which jointly determine "threat significance." Below I will discuss these factors in an effort to provide a clearer picture of how threats give rise to compulsion and how this compulsion affects the exercise of morally significant free-will.

The three factors that are important for my analysis are what I will call *threat strength, threat imminence,* and *wantonness of the threatened*. By threat strength I mean the degree to which the threatened person feels the consequences of the threatened to be harmful to him. By threat imminence I mean the degree to which the threatened perceives that the threat will inevitably follow given that the conditions for the threatened consequences being enacted are met. The notion of "inevitably follows" is ambiguous here and intentionally so. Below I will explain that this notion must be carefully unpacked since the notion of threat imminence is multi-faceted.

Finally, by wantonness of the threatened I have in mind a characteristic of the individual threatened to disregard personal well-being in the fact of threats to his freedom. My claim is that the degree of compulsion is *directly proportional* to threat strength and imminence and *inversely proportional* to wantonness. I will now discuss these conditions in more careful detail.

It should be obvious that the degree of compulsion is directly proportional to the degree of threat strength. The degree to which I feel compelled to do an act that I would not otherwise do (say, to give all my money to a stranger) would be much greater if the threatener held a gun to my back than if he threatened to call me a dirty word if I failed to comply with his wish.

It is more difficult to see exactly how threat imminence relates to compulsion simply because it is less easy to characterize. By examining a few cases I think it will become clear that the notion of the consequences of a threat "inevitably following" when the threatened fails to satisfy the conditions of a threat must be cashed out in more than one way. There are, in fact, at least three distinct senses of threat imminence which must be distinguished for my purposes.

The first type of threat imminence is what I will call *probabilistic* threat imminence. Consider the standard robber case above in which I am threatened with being shot if I fail to hand over my wallet to the thief. In this case I would consider it highly probable that the thief would shoot me if I failed to comply with the conditions of the threat. As a result, the probabilistic threat imminence would be high in this case. However, consider another case in which certain prisoners are allowed to spend recreation time in an enclosed prison yard. Surrounding the yard are high barbed wire fences which are periodically punctuated by guard towers. The prisoners have been told that the guards have orders to shoot if any of the prisoners attempt to escape. As a result we have a case which, in important respects, is similar to the standard robber case. Most importantly, in both cases the threatened

individuals are under a threat of the same strength, namely, being shot if the conditions of the threat are not satisfied. However, in the prison-yard case, a prisoner might be more tempted to attempt to escape because he might feel that there is some significant probability that the threat would not be successfully carried out because, for example, the guards might miss him at that distance, or because they may fail to see him since they are so busy watching the other prisoners. Thus, in this case the degree of compulsion is somewhat lower than in the standard robber case because the *probability* that the threat will be carried out is somewhat less even though the threat strength is identical.

The second type of threat imminence is what I call *temporal* threat imminence. With this type of threat imminence, compulsion is greater in those cases in which the threat will be carried out with more temporal immediacy, once the conditions of the threat have not been met. To show this consider the standard robber case once again. In such a case the temporal threat imminence is high since I know that if I fail to comply with the robber's demands I will be shot on the spot. Compare this, however, to a case in which the robber tells me that he has a blow gun with darts which he will shoot at me if I fail to hand over my money. Furthermore, the robber tells me that these darts contain a poison which has no antidote and will lead to my certain death in fifty years. In the former case, compulsion is higher because the *temporal imminence* of the threat is greater.[6] Differing degrees of temporal threat imminence may also explain phenomena such as the fact that some individuals choose to eat high fat foods which they know, in the long run, are very likely to cause, say, fatal arteriosclerosis, while these same individuals would not ingest antifreeze, which although quite sweet tasting, is very likely to be immediately fatal. Ingesting both types of substances makes death likely; but ingesting high fat foods makes death likely sometime in the future, whereas ingesting ethylene glycol makes death immediately likely.

Finally, there is *episternic* threat imminence. This type of imminence is also quite difficult to characterize but it is one with which I believe that we are all familiar. It is this third type of imminence that explains why we believe that massive advertising campaigns are effective in reducing the incidence of smoking or drinking and driving. In both of these cases it seems that few engaging in the behaviors really believe that it is not bad for them; they are usually quite well aware that they are so. Clearly, then, the purpose of such advertising campaigns is not to inform the individuals engaging in these behaviors that they are bad for them. What then is their purpose? It can only be to make the fact that these behaviors are dangerous more *epistemically forceful*. Somehow, by repeating the message over and over we become more powerfully aware of just how harmful such behaviors potentially are. As a result, the more epistemically forceful the danger is, the more likely we are to not act in such a way. Likewise, when we are discussing compulsion, the more epistemically imminent a threat, the more compelled the threatened individual will fee.

However, these two factors of strength and imminence alone are not sufficient to explain compulsion by another in the context of a threat completely. This is evident when we look again at our prison-yard case. Why, one might wonder, do certain prisoners try to escape, while others in similar circumstances do not, even though threat strength and imminence are the same for all prisoners? Assuming that none of them wishes to remain in prison, why do they not all try to escape? This question points to the need for a third factor, and this factor is the wantonness of the threatened. Again, this factor is difficult to define precisely. However, it does seem clear that different individuals under the same threat and with the same degree of threat imminence can feel compelled to different degrees depending on a certain internal character trait which can be described as incorrigibility or threat indifference. This trait can be roughly characterized as a feeling of indifference for one's well-being in cases where that well-being is threatened should there be a refusal to submit to the terms of some restriction on one's freedom.

These, then, are the factors which must be taken into account when we consider the degree to which a threat prevents the exercise of robust morally significant freedom. While it is surely impossible to quantify these characteristics in order to define exactly what constitutes a threat which overwhelms freedom, it can be said that the degree to which freedom is compromised is directly proportional to threat strength and imminence and inversely proportional to wantonness.

IV

One feature of the major Western theistic traditions is that they seem to involve the issuing of both temporal and eternal threats for disobedience to the divine will. Passages from, for example, the Hebrew and Christian scriptures, such as the following, represent both aspects of this threatened punishment:

A man who remains stiff-necked after many rebukes will suddenly be destroyed—without remedy.

(Prov. 29:1)

and

But because of your stubbornness and your unrepentant heart you are storing up wrath against yourself for the day of God's wrath.

(Rom. 2:5)

As a result, those who are aware of such threats and are convinced of their veracity are in a state where their freedom is at risk. What this creates, simply, is some degree of compulsion by another in the context of the threat. Specifically, it is compulsion by God in the context of a threat of both temporal and eternal punishment. Consequently, on the picture painted by these traditions, God has issued threats, both temporal and eternal, which will be carried out if one fails to submit to Him, in action or belief, in certain ways.[7] Here I will focus particularly on the Christian tradition and the notion of a threat contained therein.

Since these appear to be quite significant threats, the theist must provide some explnation for how this threat can be mitigated so as to prevent the compromising of human freedom. To do this, one of the three factors of compulsion must be mitigated in some way. I will now look at each one to see where the force of compulsion could be averted.

Certainly, with regard to the factor of threat strength, the threat posed by the prospect of eternal damnation is equal to the strongest imaginable threat. One, of course, might wonder why God does not simply eliminate the threat of hell for disobedience and in doing so eliminate or severely limit the threat strength and thus the compulsion. This is an interesting question but not one I will address here. My goal here is to determine whether the traditional, orthodox Christian position can be reconciled with the fact that God does not reveal himself in the manner Hanson might wish. Since the existence of hell is, I take it, a presumption of the traditional Christian view, I will take it for granted at this point. By doing so, however, we also preclude the possibility of mitigating compulsion by attenuating threat strength.

As a result, unless one of the other two factors can be appropriately controlled, it would seem that morally significant exercise of human free-will would be precluded. What about wantonness? It is unlikely that this factor will provide what is required to avoid the consequence of compulsion which eliminates free-will. The reason for this is that it seems likely that the development and functioning of traits such as wantonness is something which falls within the domain of the freedom of the individual. To

attempt to argue for this claim in any complete way would lead into the complex psychological question of whether such personality traits in general are acquired by heredity, environment or elements of individual free choice. Another area that would need to be addressed is how we develop character traits relating to wantonness. Aristotelian views on the development of virtues by the willful cultivation of habits of right-acting, for example, would support the view I hold above in my claim that wantonness is a factor that God cannot manipulate if He desires to preserve free-will. As a result, my claim is that if God were to preserve human free-will, manipulating this element of the picture would not be an option.

This leaves us with the possibility of controlling the degree of threat imminence. Let's begin by looking at *probabilistic* threat imminence. This condition seems to provide little help since, on the Christian story, it is nothing less than certain that the threat will be carried out if the conditions of the threat are not met.

What about *temporal* threat imminence? Clearly this condition has some relevance to our case since carrying out the threat does not follow immediately upon failure to obey the conditions of the threat. There is no trap door to hell that opens upon one's first sin or willful failure to assent to the Christian plan of redemption. Yet merely reducing the temporal imminence of the threat does not appear to be sufficient guarantee that creature's freedom is not compromised by divine compulsion. Given the strength of the threat involved it does not seem that merely delaying the carrying out of the threat temporally is sufficient to mitigate compulsion. If it were, it appears that we should be content to say that God could appear in the sky, *à la* Hanson, issuing the relevant temporal and eternal threats, and yet not have the actions of free creatures be compelled by the issuing of such threats. Yet, it seems that the actions of such free creatures clearly *would be* compelled if they were to be confronted by such obvious threats.

We are left then with *epistemic* threat imminence as the final factor which can be attenuated
if God desires to preserve the exercise morally
significant freedom by creatures. My claim is
that the hiddenness of God is required in order
for free beings to be able to exercise their freedom in a morally significant manner given the
strength of the threat implied by knowledge of
the threat implicit in the traditional Christian
story. If God revealed his existence in a more
perspicuous fashion we would be in a situation
very much like the one in the standard robbery
case, i.e., strong threat strength and strong threat
imminence such that the level of wantonness of
most, if not all, individuals would not significantly diminish their feeling compelled to act in
accordance with the demand of the threatener.
However, if God desires that there be individuals
with free-will who can use it in morally significant ways, then He must decrease the threat
imminence of eternal and temporal punishment
and He, in fact, does so by making the existence
of the threat epistemically ambiguous. It is this
epistemic ambiguity that we call the problem of
the hiddenness of God.

This may make it clear why God does not, say,
open the sky and give a world-wide, unambiguous proclamation of his existence. However, it
does not seem to explain why there is *the particular
degree* of divine hiddenness that there is. An
objector may reply here that God may not be able
to "open the sky" without the loss of morally
significant freedom on the part of humans; yet,
must that also mean that merely one more unit
of divine manifestation in the world would cause
the fabric of significant moral freedom to collapse? The answer is no. What this argument is
intended to provide is a response to the question
of why God does not provide a grand, universal
display of general revelation.[8] But why then does
God provide the fairly low general level of revelation that he does? Since God is concerned with
preserving the freedom of each individual, the
level of general revelation must be such as not to
preclude the possibility of anyone's exercising

his or her free-will in a morally significant fashion. Since threat strength is constant, God must
tailor the degree of general revelation to the
individual most likely to be compelled by a
threat, namely, the least wanton individual. If
this is correct, the degree of threat imminence,
and consequently the degree of divine manifestation in the world, must be appropriately mod-
erated. And, the degree of moderation here is
likely to be great, with the result that the amount
of unambiguous general revelation that God can
provide is likely to be fairly minimal.

V

It will be helpful here to consolidate the ground
that has been covered up to this point. What has
been shown is that with respect to the general
revelation that God gives for his existence, there
are tight constraints on the amount which can be
provided, given God's desire to preserve the
morally significant exercise of human freedom.
Showing this in itself would alone be of quite
some interest, if indeed I have achieved it, simply
because it answers a number of theistic critics
who hold that God should "part the heavens and
show Himself." However, the solution offered
above does not answer the whole question with
respect to the hiddenness of God because it does
not address the possibility that God could supplement his general revelation by individual
revelation that would be such that each individual is maximally aware of God's existence to
the extent possible *for that individual* without such
revelation impugning the possibility of the exercise of free-will. If, for example, as Calvin taught,
there is a sense of the divine, or *sensus divinitatus*, in
each of us, making us aware of the divine presence, why is God not able to make up the lack of
general revelation at an individual level and
thereby avoid the difficulty of having to cater to
the least common denominator with respect to
wantonness?

It is this question which emphasizes the limitations of the antecedent free-will theodicy I

have chosen and shows why it is unable to handle the entire problem of the hiddenness of God. What this theodicy lacks, however, can be supplemented by a consequence free-will theodicy combined with a second theodicy, i.e., an Augustinian-style punishment theodicy. In what remains I will explain how such theodicies would apply in this case although I will not develop them in any detail since others have reviewed such theodicies and their application in this context.[9]

Let us assume that it is correct that God does supplement general revelation through a *sensus divinitatus* which provides each individual with knowledge of God yielding a maximal threat imminence without thereby eliminating the possibility for the morally significant exercise of that individual's free will. How could one then account for the hiddenness of God? The consequence free-will theodicy claims that part of the hiddenness of God can be accounted for as a result of some act which prevents the individual from interpreting this revelation properly or giving the properly interpreted evidence the appropriate epistemic weight.[10] As a result, one might argue that one source of God's hiddenness is that free individuals can turn away from the less ambiguous internal evidence that God has provided for his existence. These theories are sometimes characterized as "human-defectiveness" approaches to the hiddenness of God.

Not only does the corruptness of human nature contribute to the hiddenness of God, but it also seems clear that the Jewish and Christian traditions represents God, in some cases, as veiling His existence and "hardening" the epistemic capacity that is normally used to understand the revelation He gives. This hardening is usually a punishment which results from some form of moral disobedience. As such, this explanation for the hiddenness of God can be subsumed under the punishment theodicy which claims that some evil (in this case, some divine hiddenness) is the result of justified punishment for sin.[11]

The view that humans can orient themselves in such a way as to make divine revelation less readily understood, either by a direct act or as a result of cultivating a sinful character, as well as the claim that God sometimes withdraws revelation or the ability to properly interpret revelation, combine to give a potential solution to the problem of "individual" divine hiddenness. These supplement the earlier argument as to why God's general revelation is as ambiguous as it is by showing that even if individual revelation were originally intended to be at its maximum, while still allowing morally significant employment of free-will, it may still be the case that divine hardening as punishment for sin and/or a self-induced human blindness with regard to divine revelation may cause one to find divine exposure non-compelling.

VI

In a recent essay on the subject of divine hiddenness, Robert McKim argues that even if the theist can give an account which successfully explains why a theistic God would remain hidden, the fact of divine hiddenness still yields some lessons which militate against the claims of many of these particular traditions.[12] In particular. McKim argues that divine hiddenness shows us 1) that "the fact of divine hiddenness gives us reason to doubt that it is very important that we should believe."[13] and 2) that whatever theistic beliefs we do hold should not be held dogmatically.[14] Thus even if the theist can explain the hiddenness of God, she cannot explain why belief, and *a fortiori* dogmatic belief, is so highly valued by the theistic traditions.

McKim defends the first claim by arguing that if belief were important, our circumstances would surely have been more conducive to it. However, he adds the qualification that if divine hiddenness is explained in terms of human defectiveness, then it is still consistent for the theist to hold that belief is extremely important. This is so since hiddenness, in such a case, is explained not by the fact that God fails to make Himself evident (in virtue of the fact that faith is not of a high relative importance to God), but simply that free creatures have done something to impede their ability to appropriately understand or interpret the divine manifestation that has been provided. However, these human defectiveness theories would also have to explain how these defects account for the *extent* of divine hiddenness. If they do not adequately do so, we can assume that God could have been more evident than He is by, say, putting forth a better effort, and in fact would do so if belief were of high relative importance. But since human defectiveness theories cannot explain the degree of hiddenness in this way, the theist ought to remain sceptical about the paramount importance of belief.

What if the theist were to respond as follows? What God values is not only belief but a number of other things as well. Amongst these is the existence of a world which has on balance the greatest amount of moral good with respect to moral evil. In creating such a world, God must create beings who are capable of bringing about moral good, i.e., creatures that have significant moral freedom. Of course, as I have argued above, achieving this goal requires that God remain hidden in a substantial way. As a result, while theistic belief (and possibly also acting in a manner obedient to divine commands) is important, in addition to being the prime requisite for the fulfillment of a free and rational creature, there are other things God values, such as the goodness of the world he actualizes. Thus, belief in a world where God attempts to maximize this value will not be as easy (or better, belief will not be forced) as it might be if God did not hold these other values in creating.

McKim might respond to this in a manner similar to his response above. We can imagine him saying something on the order of, "Of course one can make that claim, but in doing so you once again demonstrate that belief is not that important. What is important is freedom, both

regarding action and belief, while the actual attainment of belief takes the back seat to these values." But this response fails to show that belief is of secondary importance. What it shows is that belief or action in accordance with the divine will *simpliciter* is not what God values. The theist may hold that what God values is belief and action which contribute to the moral goodness of the world. So, what is ultimately valued is a world containing the greatest balance of moral good with respect to moral evil, and in such a world both believing and acting in a certain manner (namely, a free manner) are what suffice to yield this goal. As a result, belief and right action are not subservient to freedom, it is just that they lack value when had in the absence of freedom.

But what about McKim's second claim that the theist should not be overly confident about specific claims concerning the nature of God? Does divine hiddenness entail such a consequence? McKim argues that divine hiddenness entails that our knowledge of the divine nature will be obscure at best. If we lack access to unambiguous evidence on the question of whether or not God exists, is it not also reasonable to assume that we would have no better access to the particular nature of that divine being? And if we answer "yes" to this question should we not also be cautious about being dogmatic concerning the claims of particular traditions about the divine nature?

In proposing this move it appears that McKim has simply become confused about exactly what divine hiddenness amounts to. Nothing in the account elucidated above entails that there are not demonstrably certain means for acquiring knowledge about the divine nature. While many of the Western theistic traditions could endorse the present account of divine hiddenness, many of these traditions also contend that the deliverances of natural theology can provide one with a substantial amount of even certain knowledge about the divine nature. What God cannot do is make this knowledge, and its supporting evidence, so epistemically forceful that they compel belief or behavior.

What McKim seems to have errantly assumed in making his case is that divine hiddenness amounts to the claim that there is no way for one to come to discover, in any demonstrative way, answers to questions about the nature and existence of God. But God need not be hidden in such a profound manner. All that is required is that the demonstrative evidence for God's existence be sufficiently obscured so that it does not compel belief or behavior in accordance with the perceived divine standard. Consequently, it does not appear that either of the lessons McKim takes from the fact of divine hiddenness actually follow.

Conclusion

The paper has argued that it is possible to view the problem of the hiddenness of God as a species of the problem of evil and to apply relevant theodicies for evil to this problem. In particular, it seems that to preserve the exercise of robust, morally significant free-will, God cannot provide grand-scale, firework displays in an effort to make His existence known. Further, free creatures may hinder attempts by God to reveal Himself on a more individual basis by human defectiveness understood in terms of willful rejection of revelatory evidence. Finally, the fact that God sometimes utilizes "hardening of hearts" as a means of punishment for sins provides another explanation for the fact that evidence for God's existence appears to be ambiguous at best. While the solution sketched here is open to amendment as other theodicies may be developed or adapted to apply to this problem, invoking these three theodicies itself goes far towards providing a coherent response to the problem of the hiddenness of God.[15]

Notes

1 Norwood Russell Hanson, *What I Do Not Believe And Other Essays* (New York: Humanities Press, 1971), pp. 313–14.

2 Friedrich Nietzsche, *Daybreak*, trans. R. J. Hollingdale (Cambridge: Cambridge University Press, 1982), pp. 89–90. I thank Leon Galis for this quote.

3 In fact, disbelief may be the worst form of evil since its presence can, according to traditional Christian theism, lead to one's being eternally damned.

4 A couple of qualifications are worthy of note here. First, I say "the external threat of an intentional agent" by which I hope to exclude a) cases where the threat is self-imposed ("If I eat one more piece of cake, I will starve myself for a week") or b) cases where I am limited in my choices merely by the physical circumstances surrounding my choice. As an example of this latter situation consider a case in which I, dressed in shorts, T-shirt, and with bare feet head to the door to go play basketball. Upon opening the door I find that there is a blizzard outside. To strengthen the case imagine that I also have a disposition towards frostbite of which I am aware and about which I am concerned. In such a case it seems that I am limited to just one rational option— turn around and head back inside. But in such cases we do not feel that our freedom has been inhibited as it is when the robber holds a gun to our back. This means one of two things: either i) that what makes the robber a case of coercion is the fact that an *intentional agent* knowingly limits our rational options to just one or b) that I am in error here and that our freedom is equally restricted in both cases. Regardless of which is correct, I do not believe it detracts from the central thesis of the essay.

5 However, this point itself is not at all free from controversy. Some have surely defended this alternative way of looking at action in contexts of a threat. For example, Ian Tipton agrees that acts performed under compulsion are ones for which the agent cannot be held responsible (see *The Handbook of Western Philosophy* (New York: Macmillan, 1988), p. 500. However, the issue is not quite as simple as I make it out here. Aristotle, in Book III Chapter I of the *Ethics*, recognizes the difficulties involved in such cases. Whether or not the action should be considered to

have moral import depends on both the strength of the threat and on *what the threatened is being asked to do*. If the threat is sufficiently strong we do not hold the threatened morally responsible for the action, generally. However, there are some cases where one is held morally responsible no matter how strong the threat is; Aristotle gives the example in which one is threatened with death if he does not kill his mother. Under these circumstances, says Aristotle, the threatened is still morally culpable if he gives in to the threat and commits matricide, so there is some principle here that requires us to balance off the strength of the threat on the one hand with the gravity of what the thereatened is being asked to do on the other hand. When the severity of the action being demanded of the one threatened reaches a certain threshold, no threat will excuse the performance of that action by the threatened. While all this seems true, however, it is not, I believe, of much import for the thesis of this essay.

6   Some have objected to this illustration of the role of temporal imminence since, they argue, the difference between the standard case and the blow-gun case is really a matter of threat strength. In the robber case I stand to lose the remainder of my life if I fail to comply whereas in the blowgun case I will still be able to live most of the rest of my life, missing only little of it. Thus, what I stand to lose in the robber case is much greater and that is why I feel compelled in that case. This may be so, but I believe that other cases can be constructed which make the temporal imminence feature much more salient. To show this consider the following two cases. In the first case a would-be robber tells me that if I fail to hand over my money he has an extremely powerful cattle-prod which will deliver a shock so severe that, while it will not kill me, will cause me extreme pain as well as a short but painful two week hospital stay. In this case I suspect that failure to comply with the threat will lead to an immediate shock-experience. Compare this to a case in which the would-be robber tells me that he has a delayed-action cattle prod which delivers the same shock but the shock that it delivers is such that I will not actually experience the shock sensation and two week disability for fifty years. It seems to me that the result is the same here, namely, that

the degree to which I feel compelled is greater in the case with the higher temporal imminence.

7   I put the matter this way so as not to take a stand on the relation between performing good works, faith, and salvation.

8   By general revelation I have in mind revelation given to all, or a very large number of, individuals.

9   Robert McKim summarizes these approaches in his essay, "The Hiddenness of God," *Religious Studies*, vol.26 (1990), pp. 141–61. There he cites the arguments of Marylin Adams, John Hick, Terence Penelhum, and William Alston.

10   This type of explanation seems to be employed by Paul and Jesus in the following passages: "The wrath of God is being revealed against all the godlessness and wickedness of men who *suppress the truth in unrighteousness* . . ." (Romans 1:18), and, "For the people's heart has become calloused; they hardly hear with their ears, and they have closed their eyes. Otherwise they might see with their eyes, hear with their ears, understand with their hearts and turn, and I would heal them" (Matthew 13:15). In such passages it seems that humans are represented as being able to dispose themselves in such a way as to depreciate the epistemic value of divine revelation whether internal or external.

11   Passages such as the following indicate instances when such hardening occurred: "[Because the Israelites worshipped the golden calf] God turned away and gave them over to the worship of heavenly bodies . . ." (Acts 7:42), and, "But my people would not listen to me; Israel would not submit to me. So I gave them over to their stubborn hearts to follow their own devices" (Psalm 81:11–12).

12   Robert McKim, "The Hiddenness of God."

13   *Ibid.*, p. 157.

14   *Ibid.*, pp. 159–60.

15   An earlier version of this paper was read in 1991 at the Society of Christian Philosophers, Midwest Division Regional Meeting held at Central College in Pella, Iowa. I am indebted to A. A. Howsepian, and Trenton Merricks for helpful and insightful comments and criticism on earlier drafts of this essay. I especially thank Thomas V. Morris for encouraging me to pursue this topic further and for voluminous comments on countless earlier drafts.

Chapter 22

Robert P. Lovering

DIVINE HIDDENNESS AND INCULPABLE IGNORANCE

I. Introduction

The topic of God's hiddenness has recently become popular among philosophers of religion again, a resurgence largely due to J. L. Schellenberg's provocative and illuminating treatise on it entitled *Divine Hiddenness and Human Reason.* In *Divine Hiddenness,* Schellenberg argues that the weakness of evidence for God's existence is not merely a sign that God is hidden; rather, "it is a revelation that God does not exist."[1] Schellenberg summarizes his argument in the following way:

1   If there is a God, he is perfectly loving.
2   If a perfectly loving God exists, reasonable nonbelief does not occur.
3   Reasonable nonbelief occurs.
4   No perfectly loving God exists.
5   There is no God.[2]

Schellenberg's argument has inspired numerous philosophers of religion to examine the topic of God's hiddenness more carefully. One such philosopher, Michael J. Murray, provides a "soul-making" defense of God's hiddenness in the recently released *Divine Hiddenness: New Essays.*[3] Briefly, Murray argues that if God were not hidden, then at least some of us would lose something many theists deem a (very) good thing: the ability to develop morally significant characters. In the following, I examine Murray's

soul-making defense and argue that it not only fails to defend adequately God's hiddenness, it produces (ironically) an argument for the nonexistence of God.

II. Murray's Soul-Making Defense

Murray summarizes his soul-making defense of God's hiddenness in the following way:

> [O]ne of the reasons that God must remain hidden is that failing to do so would lead to a loss of morally significant freedom on the part of creatures. The reason, in brief, is that making us powerfully aware of the truth of God's existence would suffice to coerce (at least many of us) into behaving in accordance with God's moral commands. Such awareness can lead to this simply because God's presence would provide us with over-powering incentives which would make choosing the good ineluctable for us. . . . Our fear of punishment, or at least our fear of the prospect of missing out on a very great good, would compel us to believe the things that God has revealed and to act in accordance with them. But in doing this, God would have removed the ability for self-determination since there are no longer good and evil courses of action between which creatures could freely and deliberately choose. Thus we would all be compelled to choose in

accordance with the divine will and would all thereby become conformed to the divine image. However, a character wrought in this fashion would not be one for which we are responsible since it does not derive from morally significant choosing. It has instead been forced upon us.[4]

Though the preceding summary is relatively straightforward, a few clarifications are required if one is to understand properly Murray's soul-making defense.

First, when Murray claims that "we" would be coerced to choose in accordance with the divine will, that "our" fear of punishment would compel "us" to believe the things that God has revealed and to act in accordance with them, he is not claiming that *all* human beings would be so coerced. Rather, he is merely asserting that at least *some* human beings would be, as is made clear when he states that "making us powerfully aware of the truth of God's existence would suffice to coerce (*at least many of*) us into behaving in accordance with God's moral commands."[5] Thus, Murray's soul-making defense of God's hiddenness does not hinge upon whether *all* human beings would be coerced to choose in accordance with the divine will were God to reveal himself, but whether at least *some* would. Throughout the paper, then, propositions such as "If God is not hidden, then we do not have the ability to choose and cultivate morally significant characters" should be understood in terms of this qualification.

Second, by "morally significant freedom" Murray means a particular kind of libertarian freedom, i.e., freedom entailing the ability to choose freely between courses of action. Murray reminds us that "theists have, at least of late, lain a great deal of explanatory weight on the need to preserve creaturely freedom."[6] For example, some have attempted to explain or justify the presence of evil in our world by appealing to the great good of a world in which beings have libertarian freedom. Yet, according to Murray, libertarian freedom *simpliciter* does not adequately explain or justify the presence of evil in our world, for "there seems to be no reason why God could not create a world with libertarian free beings who are incapable of doing evil."[7] What's important, then, is a particular *kind* of libertarian freedom, viz., *morally significant* freedom: freedom entailing the ability to choose freely to do good and evil.[8] As one can see, morally significant freedom entails not only that there *are* good and evil courses of action available from which we may choose freely, but that we have the ability to take these courses of action.

According to Murray, theists have often argued that morally significant freedom "is a good (indeed, a very good) thing," and this is because it gives one the opportunity to develop a morally significant character and, in turn, to become either lover or imitator of God, or one who "worships and serves the creature rather than the creator."[9] But, as Murray writes, "Developing characters which have moral significance requires that they be chosen and cultivated *by their bearers*" (emphasis mine).[10] In other words, *we* must be responsible for the choice and cultivation of our characters if they are to be morally significant; and "this can only be done if creatures are first given the sort of morally significant freedom we have been discussing heretofore."[11] That is, this can be done only if there are good and evil courses of action available from which we may choose freely and we have the ability to take these courses of action. Morally significant freedom, then, is a necessary condition for having the ability to choose and cultivate morally significant characters.

Moreover, Murray holds that God desires that we have the ability to develop morally significant characters. And given that having morally significant freedom is a necessary condition for this ability, God must remain hidden – failing to do so "would lead to a loss of morally significant freedom on the part of creatures."[12] Murray's defense of God's hiddenness, then, includes the following two premises:

(P1) We have the ability to develop morally significant characters; and,

(P2) If God is not hidden, then we do not have the ability to develop morally significant characters.[13]

Third, though Murray does not delve deeply into metaethics, there are at least two metaethical positions that underlie Murray's defense of God's hiddenness. First, according to Murray, there is (at least) a correlative relationship which holds between morality and God's commands at all times. In other words, that which is morally good is correlative to that which God commands us to do, and that which is morally evil is correlative to that which God commands us to refrain from doing. To see that this is the case, consider his aforementioned claims that:

> making us powerfully aware of the truth of God's existence would suffice to coerce (at least many of us) into *behaving in accordance with God's moral commands* (emphasis mine); and,

> such awareness can lead to this simply because God's presence would provide us with overpowering incentives which would make *choosing the good* ineluctable for us (emphasis mine).

It should be emphasized, however, that this view regarding the relation between morality and God's commands entails neither horn of Euthyphro's dilemma, and that the ground of morality goes unstated. Even so, Murray clearly holds that the moral status of actions – particularly whether actions are morally good or morally evil – is *not* determined by what human beings *believe* to be the moral status actions. This is demonstrated by the fact that, according to Murray, morality is correlative to God's commands, and God's commands do not always coincide with the moral beliefs of human beings. Indeed, if God's commands *did* always coincide with the moral beliefs of human beings, then soul-

making would be superfluous, for we would already be imitators of God. Hence, Murray's defense of God's hiddenness entails that the moral status of actions is *not* determined by what human beings believe to be the moral status of actions. This is the second metaethical position that underlies Murray's defense of God's hiddenness. Both of these metaethical positions play an important role in my response to Murray and, thus, are noteworthy.

Finally, by "coerced" or "compelled" behavior Murray means behavior resulting from the loss of morally significant freedom to overpowering incentives. One can think of these incentives as consisting of either threats or offers, Murray maintains, though he often uses examples drawn from cases of coercion via threats. In the following, Murray explains what it means to be coerced via a threat:

> It should be obvious that not just any incentives will suffice to overwhelm our desires for contrary courses of action. The incentive must be sufficiently strong that it outweighs the desires I have for those things which are inconsistent with acting in accordance with it. Let's say that a desired course of action, A_1, renders competing desired courses of action, $A_2 - A_n$, ineligible when A_1 is sufficiently compelling that it makes it impossible for me reasonably to choose $A_2 - A_n$ over A_1. We can then say that an individual, P, is *coerced* to do some act, A, by a threat when a desire is induced by a threat, which desire is sufficiently compelling that it renders every other course of action except A ineligible for P.[14]

An example of coerced behavior, according to Murray, is that of handing over one's money while being robbed at gunpoint.[15] We are asked to consider a mugger who sticks the barrel of the gun in Murray's back and demands that he (Murray) hand over his money or else be shot. Murray states that, in such a situation, he would indeed hand over his money and his doing so would be the result of coercion. Vis-à-vis Murray's analysis of coerced behavior, this example satisfies the conditions under which we can say that Murray is coerced since presumably every other course of action *except* handing over the money is ineligible for him. That is, it is impossible for him reasonably to take any other course of action except that of handing over his money.

With these clarifications out of the way, a more developed capitulation of Murray's soul-making defense of God's hiddenness is in order. Murray holds that:

(P1)   We have the ability to develop morally significant characters.

He also holds that God is pleased with those who freely choose courses of action He commands us to take (morally good courses of action) and rewards them with a very great good (eternal bliss).[16] And God is displeased with those who freely choose courses of action He commands us to refrain from taking (morally evil courses of action) and punishes them with a very great evil (eternal damnation).[17] If God were not hidden, then we would be informed of the courses of action He has commanded us to take as well as those He has commanded us to refrain from taking – that is, we would be informed of which courses of action are morally good and which are morally evil. Accordingly, we would be informed of those courses of action that please and displease God as well as their correlative consequences. As a result, some of us would strongly desire to choose to behave in accordance with God's commands – we would strongly desire to choose to do good – in an attempt to please Him and thereby obtain eternal bliss and/or avoid eternal damnation.[18] Our strong desire to choose to behave in accordance with God's commands would be sufficiently compelling to render every other course of action ineligible (unreasonable) for us. At least

some of us, then, would be coerced into choosing to act in accordance with God's commands, i.e., into choosing to take morally good courses of action. Thus, at least some of us would lose morally significant freedom. And in losing morally significant freedom, we would no longer be able to choose freely and cultivate our characters. That is, we would lose the ability to develop morally significant characters, for morally significant freedom is a necessary condition for having that ability. Hence,

(P2)   If God is not hidden, then we do not have the ability to develop morally significant characters.

The ability to develop morally significant characters is a (very) good thing, and God desires that we have it. Thus,

(C)   God is hidden.

III. Morally Significant Characters and Inculpable Ignorance of the Moral Status of Actions

Murray's soul-making defense of God's hiddenness is quite compelling for at least two reasons. First, many of us agree with Murray that we have the ability to develop morally significant characters and that having this ability is a (very) good thing. Second, given the conception of God with which Murray is concerned, it seems he is entirely correct in holding (P2).

There is, however, a significant defect in Murray's defense: though being coerced is *one* way to lose the ability to develop a morally significant character, it's certainly not the *only* way. Another way to lose the ability to develop a morally significant character is through inculpable ignorance of the moral status of actions. In order to see that this is the case, we need to analyze more deeply what it means to develop morally significant characters.

Recall Murray's claim that the development

of characters which have moral significance requires that they be "chosen and cultivated by their bearers." In other words, *we* must be responsible for the choice and cultivation of our characters if they are to be morally significant; and this can only be done only if we have morally significant freedom. Moreover, choosing and cultivating one's character involves, among other things, choosing among numerous courses of action – particularly those that are morally good or morally evil as opposed to those that are morally neutral – and acting in accordance with those choices. Thus, developing morally relevant characters can be done only if there are morally good and morally evil courses of action available from which we may choose freely and we have the ability to take these courses of action – that is, only if we have morally significant freedom.

Though Murray fails to develop significantly the kind of metaphysic that explains exactly *how* choosing freely among morally good and morally evil courses of action and acting in accordance with those choices contributes to one's development of a morally significant character, the picture he seems to paint is as follows: If one chooses freely to take a morally good course of action, then goodness is (somehow) instantiated in[19] one's character through that choice; and if one chooses freely to take a morally evil course of action, then badness is (somehow) instantiated in one's character through that choice. And, I would add, if one chooses freely to take a morally neutral course of action – one that is neither morally good nor morally bad – then neither goodness nor badness is instantiated in one's character through that choice.

It seems, however, that choosing freely among morally good and morally evil courses of action and acting in accordance with those choices, though necessary, is not *sufficient* for the development of a morally significant character.[20] For consider the case of Smith, who consistently chooses freely courses of action that are morally good, yet he erroneously and inculpably believes

of himself that he consistently chooses courses of action that are morally neutral. Should our considered judgment be that goodness is instantiated in Smith's character in virtue of his consistently choosing freely morally good courses of action? That is, should we believe that Smith is a good person in virtue of his consistently choosing freely morally good courses of action? It seems not. Rather, it seems that Smith's consistently choosing freely morally good courses of action instantiates goodness in his character only if he *intends* to choose morally good courses of action and to act in accordance with that choice. And he cannot intend to choose morally good courses of action if he is inculpably ignorant of the moral status of the courses of action he takes.

Likewise, suppose Jones consistently chooses freely morally evil courses of action, yet she erroneously and inculpably believes of herself that she consistently chooses courses of action that are morally neutral. Should our considered judgment be that badness is instantiated in Jones's character in virtue of her consistently choosing freely morally evil courses of action? That is, should we believe that Jones is a bad person in virtue of her consistently choosing freely morally evil courses of action? It seems not. Rather, it seems that Jones's consistently choosing freely morally evil courses of action instantiates badness in her character only if she *intends* to choose morally evil courses of action and to behave in accordance with that choice. And she cannot intend to choose morally evil courses of action if she is inculpably ignorant of the moral status of the courses of action she takes.

If the preceding is correct, then another necessary condition for developing morally significant characters is that we *intend* to choose the morally good or morally evil courses of action that are freely chosen and acted upon.[21] This explains the considered judgment that (at least some) goodness is instantiated in the character of someone who intentionally chooses what he erroneously and inculpably believes is a morally good course of action, even though the chosen course of action is morally neutral or even morally evil.[22] Likewise, it explains the considered judgment that (at least some) badness is instantiated in the character of someone who intentionally chooses what he erroneously and inculpably believes is a morally evil course of action, even though the chosen course of action is morally neutral or even morally good.[23] Thus, in addition to the condition that has already been discussed as necessary for the development of morally significant characters, viz., morally significant freedom, which entails not only that there are morally good and morally evil courses of action available from which we may choose freely, but that we have the ability to take these courses of action, it seems that we need to add a second necessary condition, namely, that we intend to choose the morally good or morally evil courses of action that are freely chosen and acted upon. And intending to choose morally good or morally evil courses of action cannot be done if we are inculpably ignorant of the moral status of actions.

IV. A Reply to Murray

The ability to develop a morally significant character can be lost, then, in at least two ways: by being coerced into taking a particular course of action or by being inculpably ignorant of the moral status of courses of actions. In his defense of God's hiddenness, Murray suggests that if God were not hidden, then some of us would lose the ability to develop morally significant characters through divine coercion, and this would be bad. However, what Murray fails to recognize is that if God is hidden, then some of us lose the ability to develop morally significant characters through inculpable ignorance of the moral status of actions. And this, presumably, is equally bad.

Due to God's hiddenness, some human beings exhibit inculpable nonbelief in God's existence and, in turn, believe they must rely solely on their own cognitive capacities (as opposed to relying additionally upon divine revelation) in order to determine whether certain courses of action can even be morally good or morally evil, let alone determining which (if any) are. In doing so, some of these individuals, through no fault of their own, reject the view that some courses of action can be morally good or morally evil, i.e., they become moral nihilists. Like many reflective, prominent contemporary and historical theists and nontheists alike, these individuals believe that if God does not exist, moral nihilism is true. These moral nihilists find the antecedent to be (strongly) supported by God's hiddenness; thus, they find the consequent to be (strongly) supported as well. Furthermore, qua moral nihilists, they do not believe that morally good and morally evil courses of action are among the possible courses of action from which they may choose. Rather, they hold that all courses of action are, in my terms, morally neutral. Accordingly, when these moral nihilists choose a course of action, they do not believe that the chosen course of action may be either morally good or morally evil. A fortiori, when they choose a course of action, they do not intend to choose one that is morally good or morally evil. Hence, even on the assumption that moral nihilism is false and that some courses of action are morally good or morally evil (as Murray holds), the moral nihilists in question are not able to develop morally significant characters. For, as stated previously, a necessary condition for developing morally significant characters is that we must intend to choose the morally good or evil courses of action that are chosen. But these moral nihilists do not intend to choose morally good or morally evil courses of action since they are inculpably ignorant of the fact that some courses of action are morally good or morally evil. Thus, when these moral nihilists choose a course of action that they erroneously and inculpably believe is morally neutral, though as a matter of fact it is morally good, goodness is not thereby instantiated in their characters. That is, they are not good (or at least better) persons in virtue of their unintentionally choosing a morally good course of action. For goodness to be instantiated in their characters, they must *intend* to choose a morally good course of action. But, qua moral nihilists, this they do not – indeed, *cannot* – do.

Due to God's hiddenness, then, some human beings exhibit inculpable nonbelief in God's existence and, through no fault of their own, embrace moral nihilism. In doing so, these individuals are inculpably ignorant of the fact that some courses of action are morally good or morally evil. In turn, they do not intend to choose morally good or morally evil courses of action. Consequently, even when they *do* unintentionally choose morally good or morally evil courses of action, they are not able to develop morally significant characters through those choices, for a necessary condition for the development of morally significant characters is that we intend to choose the morally good or morally evil courses of action that are freely chosen and acted upon. In short, if God is hidden, then some of us lose our ability to develop morally significant characters through inculpable ignorance of the moral status of actions. Thus,

> (P3)   If God is hidden, then we do not have the ability to develop morally significant characters.

If the preceding is correct, then God's hiddenness is no more compatible with our ability to develop morally significant characters than His nonhiddenness. Indeed, God's hiddenness brings about the very thing He is allegedly trying to avoid. And this (ironically) produces an argument for the nonexistence of God. Specifically, (P1), (P2), and (P3) – when conjoined with the tautology (P4) Either God is hidden or God is not hidden – entail that God does not exist via reductio. Assume God exists. Tautologically, either God is hidden or God is not hidden. If the former, then we do not have the ability to develop morally significant characters. Likewise, if the latter, then we do not have the ability to

develop morally significant characters. Both of these entailments contradict (P1), the premise stating that we *do* have the ability to develop morally significant characters. Our original assumption that God exists, then, must be false. Thus, God does not exist.

V. Possible Objections

In addition to the defense of (P3) provided above, one way we may attempt to establish the plausibility of (P3) is by determining if there are any grounds for rejecting it. Given that Murray already explicitly embraces (P1) and (P2), and undoubtedly would embrace (P4) as well, it seems that finding grounds for rejecting (P3) will be precisely what Murray will want to do. In the following, I discuss two objections to (P3), the second of which is the most promising and, thus, is the focus of the large majority of this section.

The Argument from Natural Revelation

One way Murray may attempt to reject (P3) is to challenge my tacit assumption that human beings who exhibit inculpable nonbelief in God's existence and, in turn, believe they must rely solely on their own cognitive capacities to decide issues of morality do *not*, in fact, rely upon divine revelation. Murray might contend that even these nonbelievers rely upon a particular kind of divine revelation, viz., *natural* revelation: the divine disclosure of truths (moral or otherwise) through the natural order. Specifically, Murray might argue that, given natural revelation, even human beings who exhibit inculpable nonbelief in God's existence and believe they must rely solely on their own cognitive capacities to decide issues of morality rely upon divine revelation.

The problem with this objection is that even if one grants that God *is* revealing truths to us through the natural order, it does not follow that we will recognize them as such. So the question isn't whether these truths are actually being revealed through nature, but whether individuals who exhibit inculpable nonbelief in God's existence based on His hiddenness – individuals who believe they must rely *solely* on their own cognitive capacities to decide issues of morality – *recognize them as such*. Needless to say, many of these nonbelievers do not, and presumably this is explained by the fact that they are relying solely on their own cognitive capacities to decide issues of morality, *including the issue of whether some moral truths are revealed by God through the natural order*. And, as we have seen, their belief that they must rely solely on their own cognitive capacities to decide issues of morality is rooted in their inculpable nonbelief in God's existence based on God's hiddenness. So even if we grant that natural revelation occurs, it does not follow that individuals who exhibit inculpable nonbelief in God's existence based on His hiddenness rely upon it in deciding issues of morality.

Indeed, one might argue that some of the aforementioned inculpable nonbelievers not only *do* not, but *cannot* recognize divine disclosure of truths (moral or otherwise) through the natural order as such. For recognizing divine disclosure of truths as such involves, among other things, assenting to propositions such as, "God exists and is disclosing divine truths to me." But the notion that someone who exhibits inculpable nonbelief in God's existence could, at the same time, believe that God exists and is disclosing moral truths to him is absurd. So it is not even clear that the moral nihilists of above, for example, *could* recognize divine disclosures of truths.

The Argument from Disanalogy

Perhaps the most promising way Murray may attempt to reject (P3) is by finding a significant disanalogy between losing the ability to develop morally significant characters through divine coercion and losing the ability to develop morally significant characters through inculpable

ignorance of the moral status of actions. Specifically, he might argue that in the case of losing the ability to develop morally significant characters through divine coercion, the loss is *absolute*, meaning that the coerced individual *never* has the opportunity to develop a morally significant character since there are no times at which she is not coerced to take the morally good course of action. But in the case of the individual losing the ability to develop morally significant characters through inculpable ignorance of the moral status of actions, the loss is *not* absolute, meaning that the inculpably ignorant individual *sometimes* has the opportunity to develop a morally significant character since there are moments at which she is either culpably ignorant or informed of the moral status of actions. With this in mind, Murray might argue that with regard to the inculpably ignorant moral nihilist, though at times she is inculpably ignorant of the moral status of actions, it is unreasonable to believe that there are *no* times at which she is either culpably ignorant or informed of the moral status of actions. And if this is the case, then her loss of the ability to develop a morally significant character through inculpable ignorance is not absolute, as it is in the case of divine coercion. At least some of the time, then, the moral nihilist has the ability to develop a morally significant character, whereas this is not the case with divinely coerced individuals. And this, Murray might contend, is a significant disanalogy between the two cases.

Though such an objection appears to be fairly strong, there are a number of problems with it.

First, it is not clear that it *is* unreasonable to believe that there are no times at which the moral nihilist is either culpably ignorant or informed of the moral status of actions. So long as the moral nihilist finds moral nihilism to be more reasonable than the alternatives, the most reasonable courses of action for her to take are those that accord with moral nihilism. And so long as she is concerned with choosing the most reasonable courses of action, she will act in accordance with moral nihilism and, in turn, lack the ability to develop a morally significant character. Of course, Murray may point out that it's unlikely that she will *always* be concerned with and choose the most reasonable courses of action and, in turn, act in accordance with moral nihilism. Even if this is the case, however, unless she is somehow culpable for failing to choose the most reasonable courses of action, her deviance from moral nihilism would not immediately entail the ability to develop a morally significant character. Moreover, it seems equally unlikely that the divinely coerced individual will *always* be concerned with and choose the most reasonable courses of action and, in turn, act in accordance with God's commands. So if the likelihood of always being concerned with and choosing the most reasonable courses of action counts against the case of the moral nihilist, it should count equally against the case of the divinely coerced individual.

Second, even if we grant that there are times at which the moral nihilist has the opportunity to develop morally significant characters since she is either culpably ignorant or informed of the moral status of actions, it is reasonable to believe that, in some cases, these times are few and far between. And if the ratio is significantly disproportional, as it is reasonable to believe that it is in many cases, then, for all intents and purposes, she loses the ability to develop a morally significant character. In other words, though she does not lose her ability to develop a morally significant character *absolutely*, she does so *almost absolutely*. And though there may be a *conceptual* difference between losing the ability to develop morally significant characters *absolutely* and losing it *almost absolutely*, there does not seem to be a significant *practical* difference. And Murray's defense clearly hinges upon the practical implications of God's hiddenness, for integral to it is the relationship between God's hiddenness and our *ability to develop* morally significant characters. Hence, though inculpable ignorance of the moral status of actions based on God's hiddenness may not result in the *absolute* loss of the ability to develop morally significant characters, it is likely that, in some cases, it results in the *almost absolute* loss of such an ability, and this renders Murray's defense of God's hiddenness significantly weaker. For not only does this alleged significant disanalogy between losing the ability to develop morally significant characters through divine coercion and losing the ability to develop morally significant characters through inculpable ignorance of the moral status of actions fail to undermine (P3), it suggests that God's hiddenness is the result of unreasonable obstinacy. For, when one takes into account all the individual and societal problems that result from God's hiddenness, problems that may very well be avoided were God to refrain from hiding Himself (e.g., religious intolerance and wars, severe confusion [moral and otherwise], deep feelings of insignificance, etc.), God's hiding Himself in the name of preserving the mere *conceptual* distinction between the absolute and almost absolute loss of the ability to develop morally significant characters appears to be unduly stubborn.

Finally, the claim that the loss of the ability to develop morally significant characters through divine coercion is absolute rests upon Murray's contention that it is impossible for the divinely coerced individual reasonably to take any other course of action except that of obeying God's commands. In other words, obeying God's commands in an attempt to obtain eternal bliss and/or avoid eternal damnation is the only reasonable course of action. But this contention is dubitable at best, for there seem to be numerous grounds for believing that alternative courses of action are not only reasonable but, in some cases, *more* reasonable than obeying God's commands, *even if* disobedience results in the loss of eternal bliss and/or the procuring of eternal damnation.

The first ground for believing that there are reasonable alternatives to obeying some of God's commands is that God's commands are often quite controversial. For example, God is reported to have commanded genocide, the subjugating of women to men, the stoning to death of homo-sexuals, of unruly children, of adulterers, etc. Some of us find such commands to be so objectionable that disobedience to these commands is a reasonable if not *more* reasonable alternative to obedience, even if disobedience results in the loss of eternal bliss and/or the procuring of eternal damnation. In the spirit of Mill, some of us might hold that if a God who commands these objectionable courses of action can sentence us to eternal damnation for disobedience to them, then to eternal damnation we will go.

Of course, Murray may respond by suggesting that God would not command such courses of action, since each is morally evil. There is, however, a significant problem with such a response: God's not commanding such courses of action in virtue of the fact that they are morally evil is difficult to reconcile with Murray's view that God damns eternally those who live lives of total disobedience to His commands. Take the case of stoning the adulterer. Presumably, such an action is morally evil in virtue of its injustice: the adulterer does not *deserve* to be *killed* for his adulterous activity. Since stoning the adulterer is unjust and thereby morally evil, God (allegedly) would not command it. With this in mind, we might wonder whether one who lives a life of total disobedience to God's commands deserves *eternal damnation*. Many theists and nontheists alike believe one does not – imposing this "maximal" punishment, as Murray describes it, would be unjust and thereby morally evil.[24] If this is correct, and if Murray is correct in holding that God would not *command* morally evil courses of action, then presumably God would not *take* the morally evil course of action of imposing this maximal and eternal punishment on one who lives a life of total disobedience. And if this is the case, then Murray's defense of God's hiddenness is severely undermined. For, according to it, our fear of eternal damnation would coerce us to obey God's commands. But if we have reason to believe that God would not damn us eternally, then we have reason to reject the claim that some

of us would be divinely coerced through fear of eternal damnation.[25]

The second ground for believing that there are reasonable alternatives to obeying some of God's commands is that, given the prima facie badness of coercion (a view Murray seems to embrace), there is prima facie reason to *resist* being coerced.[26] For example, in the case of being robbed at gunpoint, there is reason for one not to comply with the robber, and that is the fact that he is attempting to *coerce* one into handing over one's money, and coercion is prima facie bad. Of course, this reason for noncompliance is overridden by other considerations, such as the goodness of preserving one's life. But we can think of cases in which resistance to coercion based on the prima facie badness of coercion is *not* overridden by other considerations, even that of the goodness of preserving one's life. Take the case of slavery. The life of a slave is dominated by coercion, and surely resistance to further coercion on the basis of its prima facie badness, at least for some slaves, is not overridden by other considerations (even the goodness of preserving one's life). In such cases, disobedience, even on pain of death, is a reasonable (albeit unfortunate) alternative to continued obedience. Indeed, even if the slave is coerced to take only morally good courses of action, resistance to further coercion on the basis of its prima facie badness is, for some, a reasonable alternative to continued obedience and existence. Ceteris paribus, disobedience to God's commands might be deemed a reasonable alternative to obedience in virtue of the fact that God's commands are coercive in nature, *even* if one is coerced to take only morally good courses of action *and* disobedience leads to eternal damnation.

Murray might object to the preceding by attempting to establish a significant disanalogy between the case of the slave and that of the divinely coerced individual. Specifically, he might suggest that the slaveholder does not have the authority to coerce the slave (i.e., the slaveholder's authority is illegitimate), while God does have the authority to coerce His subjects (i.e., God's authority is legitimate). Most would agree with Murray that the slaveholder's authority to coerce the slave is illegitimate, and the justification for this would be something along the following lines: To say that someone has legitimate authority over others is to say that the one with the authority has the *right* (morally speaking) to coerce them. And the slaveholder does not have such a right, for rights are grounded in sound moral principles, and the moral principle or set of principles from which the slaveholder presumes to have the right to coerce is unsound.[27] God's right to coerce his subjects, on the other hand, *is* derived from a sound moral principle or set of principles; thus, God has legitimate authority to coerce His subjects.

Even if one grants that the slaveholder's authority is illegitimate and that God's right to coerce his subjects is derived from a sound moral principle or set of principles, one might ask what the sound moral principle or set of principles from which God derives His legitimate authority is. One candidate, presumably, is something like the following: "If P creates X, then P has legitimate authority over X." Such a moral principle, however, is vulnerable to counterexamples. For example, if Smith creates a human being via intercourse, it does not immediately follow that Smith has legitimate authority over that human being.[28] Or, if Smith is a bioengineer and creates a human being through cloning, it does not immediately follow that Smith has legitimate authority over that human being. What, then, is the sound moral principle or set of principles from which God's legitimate authority is derived? Suffice it to say that this needs to be addressed before the disanalogy between the slave and the divinely coerced individual is rendered plausible.

The final ground for believing that there are reasonable alternatives to obeying some of God's commands is that God is allegedly *mysterious* — as some theists say, "His ways are not our ways."

Based on God's mysteriousness, it may be reasonable to believe that the alleged correlative relationship between morality and God's commands does *not* hold at all times. Specifically, it may be reasonable to hold that, in some cases, rather than commanding us to do that which is morally good, God commands us to do that which is morally evil. After all, He is reported to have commanded Abraham to do what many of us find to be especially evil — viz., to kill unjustly his own son Isaac — though He apparently had no intention of allowing Abraham to fulfil His command. And many theists appeal to the mystery of God's ways, among other things, in an attempt to explain this troubling command. With God's mysteriousness in mind, then, some of us may reasonably believe that, in some cases, God commands us to do that which is morally evil though He does not intend for us to fulfill His command. Hence, not fulfilling God's command through disobedience may be a reasonable alternative to obedience.

To the preceding, Murray may respond in one of two ways. First, he may respond by arguing that God's mysteriousness isn't so, well, *mysterious* such that His commands, *when revealed via His non-hiddenness*, would be so interpretively flexible. But what reason might Murray have for believing this? It's certainly not true a priori. And he cannot claim to have first-person empirical evidence to support such a claim (remember, God is supposed to be *hidden*). Nor can he rely upon the first-person empirical accounts of Moses, Abraham, and the like, to whom God has allegedly submitted commands. For either God's submitting commands to them was done in such a way as to be an instantiation of *nonhiddenness*, which flies in the face of Murray's original claim that God *must* remain hidden; or it was done in such a way as to be an instantiation of hiddenness and, thus, will not serve as evidence for claims about the interpretive flexibility of the commands of a *nonhidden* God. It seems, then, that the view that God's mysteriousness isn't *so* mysterious such that His commands, when revealed via His nonhiddenness, would be so interpretively flexible is speculative at best.

Second, Murray may respond by denying that God is mysterious. But whether something or someone is mysterious, I submit, is fundamentally determined by or relative to the individual. For example, I might find the idea that some infinite sets are larger than others to be mysterious, while Cantor may not. And it would be odd to say that one of us is incorrect, that there is an objective truth to the matter. Instead, it seems more accurate to say that whether the notion of different sizes of infinite sets is mysterious is person relative. Likewise, whether God is mysterious is person relative.[29] If this is correct, then even if Murray rejects the view that God is mysterious, others may embrace it without contradiction. In turn, such individuals may reasonably believe that, at times, this mysterious God commands us to do that which is morally evil though He does not intend for us to fulfill such commands. Hence, for them, disobedience to God's command, particularly when they or their loved ones have much to gain from it, may be a reasonable alternative to obedience.

The assumption that the divinely coerced individual does not have reasonable alternatives to obeying God's commands, then, is highly dubitable. For there seem to be numerous grounds for believing that the alternatives to obeying God's commands are not only reasonable but, in some cases, *more* reasonable than obeying His commands, even if disobedience results in the loss of eternal bliss and/or the procuring of eternal damnation.

To conclude: an attempt to reject (P3) by finding a significant disanalogy between losing the ability to develop morally significant characters through divine coercion and losing the ability to develop morally significant characters through inculpable ignorance of the moral status of actions, though perhaps not hopeless, faces significant difficulties.

VI. Conclusion

In his defense of God's hiddenness, Murray suggests that if God were not hidden, then some of us would lose the ability to develop a morally significant character through divine coercion, and this, in turn, would be bad. I have argued that Murray fails to recognize that if God is hidden, then some of us lose our ability to develop a morally significant character through inculpable ignorance of the moral status of actions. And this, presumably, is equally bad. God's hiddenness, then, is no more compatible with our ability to develop morally significant characters than His nonhiddenness. And this (ironically) produces an argument for the nonexistence of God. Specifically, (P1), (P2), and (P3) – when conjoined with the tautology (P4) – entail that God does not exist via reductio.[30]

Notes

1   J. L. Schellenberg, *Divine Hiddenness and Human Reason* (Ithaca, New York: Cornell University Press, 1993), 1.

2   Ibid., 83.

3   *Divine Hiddenness: New Essays*, eds. Daniel Howard-Snyder and Paul K. Moser (Cambridge: Cambridge University Press, 2002).

4   Michael J. Murray, "Deus Absconditus," in *Divine Hiddenness: New Essays*, 63 and 68.

5   Ibid., 63, emphasis mine.

6   Ibid., 63.

7   Ibid., 64.

8   Ibid., 65.

9   Ibid., 63 and 65.

10 Ibid., 65.

11 Ibid., 65.

12 Ibid., 63.

13 For practical purposes, I have chosen to state (P2) as an indicative conditional rather than as a subjunctive or counterfactual conditional, though there is no major difference between the two since, in this case, we are dealing with present-tense conditionals. As Graham Priest states, there is no major difference between "If I shoot you, you will

die" and "If I were to shoot you, you would die." See Graham Priest, *An Introduction to Non-Classical Logic* (Cambridge: Cambridge University Press, 2001), 12.

14 Ibid., 70. Whether a desire induced by a threat is *sufficiently compelling* to coerce P depends on at least three factors: (1) threat strength, (2) threat imminence, and (3) threat indifference. And, according to Murray, the degree to which the desire compels P to act in accordance with the threat "is directly proportional to the first two and inversely proportional to the third." See "Deus Absconditus," 70–71.

15 Ibid., 70. See also Michael J. Murray, "Coercion and the Hiddenness of God," in *Philosophy of Religion: The Big Questions*, Eleonore Stump and Michael J. Murray, eds. (Oxford: Blackwell, 1999), 244.

16 Murray, "Deus Absconditus," 67.

17 Some may object to my seeming caricature of the way God doles out punishments and rewards. Exactly how God goes about calculating who has acted in accordance with His will enough such that he deserves the very great good and who has not acted in accordance with His will enough such that he deserves the very great evil escapes me, and I do not intend to figure it out, as such is beyond the scope of this paper. I am only trying to state succinctly Murray's view that, at the end of the day (or, perhaps more appropriately, at the end of one's earthly life) God rewards some for behaving in accordance with His will and punishes others for not behaving in accordance with His will.

18 Murray, "Deus Absconditus," 67 and 75.

19 "Contributed to" or "conferred upon" may be preferable. But in the absence of a more rigorous metaphysic supplied by Murray, I cannot decide among them nonarbitrarily. Hence, I will stick with "instantiated in."

20 The following discussion is the result of careful consideration of an insightful objection raised by an anonymous referee.

21 The relation between intention and moral character is supported by deontologists such as Kant, among others. Of course, consequentialists (particularly utilitarians) reject this alleged relation between intention and moral character. But given the conception of God with which Murray is working, a God whose commands are typically understood in terms of duties and not consequences, it will not help Murray to reject the aforementioned relation by embracing a consequentialist moral theory.

22 For example, suppose Brown knows that terrorists have planted numerous bombs in supermarkets and have rigged soda machines in their respective parking lots to serve as detonators, and that radical philanthropists have planted cash dispensers in numerous supermarkets and have rigged soda machines in their respective parking lots to serve as activators. The next person to purchase a soda from one of the bomb-detonating soda machines will detonate a bomb in a supermarket, thereby killing scores of innocent human beings, while the next person to purchase a soda from these cash-dispensing soda machines will activate the cash dispensers, thereby lavishing enormous amounts of cash on the shoppers inside. Assuming that killing scores of innocents in this way is morally evil, the next person to purchase a soda from the bomb-detonating machines will take a morally evil course of action, while, assuming that lavishing enormous amounts of cash on the shoppers inside is a morally good course of action, the next person to purchase a soda from the cash-dispensing machines will take a morally good course of action. Suppose further that Brown relishes good deeds, and attempts to purchase a soda from what he erroneously and inculpably believes to be a cash-dispensing soda machine with the intention of dispensing enormous amounts of cash on the shoppers inside, and instead purchases a soda from a bomb-detonating soda machine. That is, Brown intends to choose a morally good course of action, but is inculpably ignorant of the fact that he is taking a moral evil course of action. Upon purchasing a soda from the machine, a bomb detonates which, to Brown's horror, kills scores of innocent human beings in the supermarket. Should our considered judgment be that Brown's taking this morally evil course of action fails to instantiate goodness, or worse, instantiates *badness* in his character? I think not. Rather, the fact that his intention was to choose what he believed erroneously and inculpably was a morally good course of action instantiates (at least some) goodness in his character.

23 Suppose that Jones also knows that terrorists have planted numerous bombs in supermarkets and have rigged soda machines in the parking lots to serve as detonators. However, unlike Brown, Jones does not know that radical philanthropists have planted cash dispensers in a number of other supermarkets and have rigged soda machines in their respective parking lots to serve as activators. Suppose further that Jones relishes evil deeds, and attempts to purchase a soda from what he believes to a bomb-detonating soda machine with the intention of killing scores of innocents in the supermarket, but instead purchases a soda from a cash-dispensing soda machine. That is, Jones intends to choose a morally evil course of action, but is inculpably ignorant of the fact that he is taking a moral good course of action. Upon purchasing a soda from the machine, the cash dispenser activates which, to his horror, lavishes enormous amounts of cash on the shoppers inside. Should our considered judgment be that Jones's taking this morally good course of action fails to instantiate badness, or worse, instantiates *goodness* to his character? I think not. Rather, the fact that his intention was to choose what he believed erroneously and inculpably was a morally evil course of action instantiates (at least some) badness in his character.

24 Murray, "Deus Absconditus," 75.

25 Of course, Murray may argue that one who lives a life of total disobedience to God's commands does indeed deserve eternal damnation; thus, it would not be morally evil for God to impose this punishment on such individuals. Let it suffice for now that I find such a view to be highly implausible and, for that reason and others, I will not address it here.

26 I am grateful to Paul Studtmann for pointing this out to me.

27 Presumably, the moral principle upon which the slaveholder rests his right to coerce his slaves would be, roughly: "It is morally permissible to subjugate the interests of certain human beings to those of others on the basis of their race."

28 Suppose Joe's means to creating that human being involved rape. Surely he does not have legitimate authority over the human he created.

29 Indeed, presumably God does not find Himself to be mysterious, while others do.

30 Thanks to Paul Studtmann for his invaluable comments. Without his input, this paper would be a mere shadow of what it is today.

PART 4

Providence and Interaction

INTRODUCTION TO PART 4

NEARLY EVERY THEISTIC religion includes, as one of its commitments, a belief in divine providence. Thomas Flint encapsulates the doctrine of divine providence as the claim that "the events of our world, no matter how chaotic or disturbing they might appear, unfold precisely according to the plan established by our all-knowing and loving sovereign."[1] But how exactly divine providence works, and its exact scope, are questions of considerable philosophical debate. Does God control everything that happens, down to the very last detail? Is the world guaranteed to end up exactly as God wishes, or is there a chance that God's ultimate plan for creation can be thwarted? How does free will fit into God's providence? Or can it? The readings in this section address these issues.

The first five readings in this section each articulate and defend one of the leading models of divine providence, with a particular eye toward how providence relates to human free actions. The strongest account of divine providence is one called "theological determinism." According to theological determinism, God's willing an event to happen is necessary and sufficient for that event's occurring. The first part of theological determinism (i.e., "God's willing an event to happen is necessary for that event occurring") means that no event happens without God's willing that particular event's to happen. The second part of this doctrine (i.e., "God's willing an event to happen is sufficient for that event's occurring") means that nothing else is needed in addition to God's will for an event to happen. In other words, if God wills a particular event, nothing else can prevent that event from occurring. If theological determinism is true, then either there are no free human actions (because God doesn't will there to be any), or whatever free human actions that do exist are also determined by God to happen. This latter option involves a view known as theological compatibilism, according to which a human action's being free is compatible with God's determining the individual in question to do that very action. (Compatibilism is distinct from incompatibilism, according to which it is not possible for a human action to be both free and determined to happen by God. Those incompatibilists who believe that there are free human actions, and thus that not all things are determined by God, are called libertarians and are often said to believe in "libertarian free will.") While many philosophers in general are compatibilists, most theistic philosophers of religion are incompatibilists for reasons which deal with the problem of evil. As seen in the previous section's readings, the free will defense claims that it is possible that God's reason for allowing moral evils is the greater good of our having free will. But if compatibilism were true, it would be possible for God to determine us to always use our free will in such a way that we never commit moral evil; that is, we could have the good of having free will without the moral evil that free will makes possible. If this were the case, then God would need to have some reason other than the good of our having free will which justifies the moral evil in the world. While incompatibilism thus makes it easier for the theist to respond to the problem of evil, it comes at a cost with respect to the doctrine of divine providence. If it is not possible for humans to be both free and determined, then God relinquishes some of His providential control over the world by creating human agents with free will.

In his "Free Will, Evil, and Divine Providence," Derk Pereboom advances a version of theological determinism, holding that God's will is the sufficient cause of everything in creation. However, given that he is also an incompatibilist, Pereboom is forced to deny that humans are free and morally responsible agents. Such a position can be found throughout the history of Christian theology and philosophy, but is usually thought to have unacceptable consequences. Pereboom argues that the consequences for religious belief of denying human free will are not as problematic as they are often claimed to be. For example, Pereboom argues that since humans are not free and responsible agents, no human deserves to be punished for the sins that he or she commits. Since no one is deserving of punishment, Pereboom suggests that no one will be punished with an eternity in hell. (We will return to the issue of hell in the readings in the following section.) Furthermore, he argues that while God is the cause of sin, God has a morally justifiable reason for causing sin—just as readings in the previous section argued that God has a morally justifiable reason for allowing moral or natural evils. Pereboom concludes his argument by embracing skeptical theism, which is the view that given our finite cognitive capacities, it is not surprising that we are unable to understand how God's providential plan is compatible with His goodness. Nevertheless, he is confident that there is such a plan, and that humans can take comfort in knowing that everything that happens is determined to happen as a part of God's plan for His creation.

The second reading of this section, William Lane Craig's "The Middle-Knowledge View," defends a view called Molinism, named after a sixteenth-century Spanish Jesuit, Luis de Molina. Molinists embrace a libertarian view of free will, one in which an agent's free actions cannot be determined by another agent, including God. Nevertheless, Molinists defend a robust account of divine providence on the basis of God's "middle knowledge." To better understand this distinctive feature of Molinism, let us first differentiate God's natural knowledge from His free knowledge. God's natural knowledge is His pre-volitional knowledge of necessary truths. For example, God knows that it is a necessary truth that all bachelors are unmarried, even prior to His decision to create anything (including any bachelors). God's free knowledge, on the other hand, is His post-volitional knowledge of contingent truths; God can know that it is a contingent truth that Lloyd is, as a matter of fact, a bachelor, but only after His volition to bring Lloyd into existence. Most accounts of God's knowledge include both natural and free knowledge. What is unique to Molinism is its holding that in addition to natural and free knowledge, God also has middle knowledge. Like His natural knowledge, God's middle knowledge is pre-volitional; but like His free knowledge, it is knowledge of contingent truths. In terms of providence, the most important object of God's middle knowledge is His knowledge of what are called "counterfactuals of creaturely freedom." A counterfactual of creaturely freedom is a contingent proposition about how a creature would freely act in a particular situation. Such propositions have the following form:

If agent *A* were in circumstances *C*, *A* would freely do *X*.

Since such counterfactuals are pre-volitional, God doesn't determine which of these propositions are true and which ones are false. By knowing prior to His creative decree how creatures would in fact freely act, God can know which creatures, and which initial circumstances, to create in order to achieve His purpose. To take a simple example, suppose that the following counterfactuals of creaturely freedom are true:

If Lloyd were in circumstance *C*, he would freely choose to love God.

If Lloyd were in circumstance *D*, he would freely choose not to love God.

If Randie were in circumstance *C*, he would freely choose not to love God.

If God's providential plan includes at least one creature who freely loves Him, God can achieve this goal by choosing to create Lloyd in circumstance *C* on the basis of His middle knowledge. God's foreknowledge—His knowledge of what *will* happen—is therefore a function of His middle knowledge and His initial creative act. Once God creates, He knows exactly how everything will unfold via His natural, middle, and free knowledge.

It is widely thought that Molinism is the strongest account of divine providence available to the incompatibilist. However, many philosophers of religion think that Molinism is false because God does not or cannot have middle knowledge. Many philosophers deny that God's foreknowledge is based on middle knowledge; rather, God foreknows things by having direct knowledge of the actual future. This view is called "the simple foreknowledge view." Others, however, reject divine foreknowledge, whether that foreknowledge be simple or based on middle knowledge. William Hasker's "The Openness of God" opens with an argument that foreknowledge of either variety is incompatible with libertarian free will. Since Hasker thinks that humans do have free will as understood by libertarians, he concludes that it is impossible for God (or anyone else) to have foreknowledge of free actions. Hasker defends open theism, a view according to which God knows everything that can be known. Open theism derives its name from holding that the future is genuinely open, both in terms of being contingent and unknowable. Since it is impossible for anyone to foreknow free actions, God doesn't foreknow how His creation will freely act. Furthermore, since God lacks exhaustive foreknowledge, He does not know in advance how His creation will turn out. More specifically, God takes a risk in creating free agents since He cannot know how those agents will freely act, and thus cannot ensure that they will act according to His divine plan. Open theists thus believe in a weaker form of divine providence than do theological determinists or Molinists.

The next two readings focus on what, if any, providential benefit exhaustive foreknowledge would lead to. According to open theists, while God does not have exhaustive foreknowledge, He does have exhaustive knowledge of the present and probabilistic knowledge of the future. It might initially seem that having exhaustive knowledge of the present *and* the future would allow God to exercise a greater degree of providential control over His creation than would the kind of knowledge open theists think God possesses. In "Why Simple Foreknowledge Offers No More Providential Control than the Openness of God," John Sanders elaborates an argument hinted at in the previous reading by Hasker, which is that even if God were to have exhaustive foreknowledge, it would be providentially useless. Sanders differentiates two models of simple foreknowledge: complete simple foreknowledge and incremental simple foreknowledge. According to the complete simple foreknowledge view, God knows the whole future all at once, while according to the incremental model God knows the future incrementally or sequentially. Through a careful consideration of seven cases of divine providence, Sanders argues that simple foreknowledge understood along either model would be of no benefit in the exercise of God's providential control.

David Hunt's "The Providential Advantage of Divine Foreknowledge," which appears in this volume for the first time, argues that Sanders' conclusion is mistaken. After making clear the theological stakes of the debate, Hunt argues for the providential utility of foreknowledge. He does this by first describing an example in which foreknowledge *prima facie* would enable God to secure a result He couldn't secure otherwise. Building on this example, Hunt then argues that Sanders' case against complete simple foreknowledge is flawed in virtue of his failure to distinguish consistently between the temporal and explanatory orders. The temporal order in cases of foreknowledge is clear; in order to be a case of foreknowledge, God's knowledge of an event must occur prior in time to that event. But in such cases, the explanatory ordering is reversed: it is the fact that the event will occur in the future that explains why God foreknows that the event will occur. When one pays proper attention to the difference between these two orders, Sanders' argument against the providential usefulness of complete simple foreknowledge is unsound. Hunt then turns his attention to incremental simple foreknowledge, arguing that while Sanders recommends this as the most promising account of foreknowledge, it is transparently reducible to present knowledge insofar as God accesses his foreknowledge in exactly the same explanatory order as the God of open theism.

The final three readings in this section deal not with general accounts of divine providence, but instead focus on particular actions in which God's providential control is expressed. Norman Kretzmann's article focuses on the most general question of divine providence, namely why did God choose to create something over which to exercise His providential care? (Note, the question isn't "why did God create *this* rather than *that*?", but "why did God choose to create *something* versus choosing *not to create*?") In "Why Would God Create Anything at All?," Kretzmann traces two competing lines of response to this very general question. According to the first, which he calls the necessitarian explanation, God creates because His nature compels Him to in some way. According to the second explanation, the libertarian explanation, God creates not because He has to, but simply because He freely chooses to do so. After examining the thought of a number of historically influential philosophers such as Plato, Augustine, Aquinas, and Bonaventure, Kretzmann shows the tension between these two lines of explanation. He ultimately endorses a Dionysian principle that goodness is necessarily self-diffusive, and thus that God necessarily creates out of the fullness of His own goodness.

The final two readings in this section focus on God's providential care for the world as reflected in His response to petitionary prayers. The world's major monotheisms all affirm that petitionary prayers can be causally efficacious, that is, that God's answers to such prayers are one of the ways in which He exercises providential control over creation. In "Petitionary Prayer," Eleonore Stump presents an argument that God never answers prayer because there is an inconsistency between God's goodness and the efficacy of petitionary prayer. The heart of the argument can be presented in the form of a dilemma: either the prayed for state of affairs is good or not good. If the former, an essentially good God would bring about that state of affairs even if it was not prayed for. If, on the other hand, the prayed for state of affairs is not good, God would not answer such prayers because of His essential goodness. Either way, it's not the case that God brings about some state of affairs merely as an answer to prayer. Stump then goes on to show how this argument is mistaken, and that an essentially good God could have a justifying reason for bringing about some good states of affairs only as an answer to a petitionary prayer. The justifying reason Stump gives is the good of having a close relationship between humans and God, and that by giving some goods only as the result of prayer God can contribute to this closeness.

Finally, in "Prayers for the Past," I argue that if Stump is correct that petitionary prayers can be causally efficacious, then petitionary prayers for the past can also be efficacious on some accounts of divine providence. That is, it is possible for God to answer a prayer even before that prayer is made. After defining the criteria for what I call past-directed impetratory prayers, I show how such prayers can be efficacious on a number of theological views, including Molinism and the simple foreknowledge view. Such prayers, however, cannot be causally efficacious if open theism is true because this view of divine providence denies that God has the kind of knowledge needed for efficacious past-directed impetratory prayers.

Note

1   Thomas Flint, "Two Accounts of Divine Providence," in Thomas V. Morris, ed., *Divine and Human Action* (Ithaca, NY: Cornell University Press, 1988), 569.

Further Reading

Basinger, David. *The Case for Freewill Theism: A Philosophical Assessment* (Downers Grove, IL: InterVarsity Press, 1996).

Craig, William Lane. *Divine Foreknowledge and Human Freedom* (Leiden: E.J. Brill, 1990).

Fischer, John Martin, ed. *God, Freedom, and Foreknowledge* (Stanford, CA: Stanford University Press, 1989).

Flint, Thomas. *Divine Providence: The Molinist Account* (Ithaca, NY: Cornell University Press, 1998).

Hasker, William. *God, Time, and Knowledge* (Ithaca, NY: Cornell University Press, 1989).

Hasker, William. *Providence, Evil, and the Openness of God* (New York: Routledge, 2004).

Hasker, William, David Basinger, and Eef Dekker, eds. *Middle Knowledge: Theory and Applications* (Oxford: Peter Lang, 2000).

Helm, Paul. *The Providence of God* (Downers Grove, IL: InterVarsity Press, 1993).

Hunt, David. "Simple Foreknowledge and Divine Providence." *Faith and Philosophy* 10:3 (1993): 394–414.

Morris, Thomas V., ed. *Divine and Human Action* (Ithaca, NY: Cornell University Press, 1988).

Zagzebski, Linda. *The Dilemma of Freedom and Foreknowledge* (New York: Oxford University Press, 1991).

Chapter 23

Derk Pereboom

FREE WILL, EVIL, AND DIVINE PROVIDENCE

Traditional theists in our environment, and Christians in particular, tend to endorse libertarianism about free will, according to which we have the free will required for moral responsibility, free will of this sort is incompatible with determinism, and determinism is false. Divine determinism is nonetheless well-represented in the history of traditional theism – and by "divine determinism" I mean to specify the position that God is the sufficient active cause of everything in creation, whether directly or by way of secondary causes such as human agents. This position is either obviously or arguably held by Augustine, Luther, Calvin, Descartes, Spinoza, Leibniz, and Schleiermacher, among others. Yet despite the historical prominence of this view, there is an obvious and compelling reason for rejecting it. The consequence that God is the sufficient active cause of all the evils that occur threatens to make divine determinism unconscionable from the very outset. Now if an available alternative were the position that we have libertarian free will, that God is not omnipotent, and that there are evil forces in the universe, other than mere willings, against which God needs to *struggle*, then one can see why rejecting the determinist perspective would seem attractive. Yet even if this Zoroastrian alternative remains the de facto position of some, it is outside the bounds of traditional Christian, Jewish, and Islamic orthodoxy. But affirming libertarianism while retaining a commitment to

divine omnipotence, while attractive indeed, is not obviously and decisively superior to certain options open to the divine determinist. At least so I shall argue.

For some theists, an important motivation for accepting the libertarian view of free will has been that the doctrine of eternal damnation is difficult to reconcile with determinism, and divine determinism in particular. In addition, libertarianism also promises a solution to the problem of evil, and this yields another motivation. However, libertarianism has also been thought to pose a threat to divine providence, God's beneficent governance of the world. But this last problem would be solved by Molinism, according to which God can know what every possible libertarian free creature would choose in every possible circumstance, and then with this knowledge, God is able to direct the course of history with precision.[1] Indeed, it would seem that all things considered, from the point of view of theological desirability – setting aside considerations of plausibility – libertarianism supplemented by Molinism is without equal. But both libertarianism and Molinism are controversial positions. What if they were, in the last analysis, false? Is the fate of Christian theism tied to the truth of these two positions? One possibility that appears to be gaining currency is that libertarianism is true and Molinism is false, and as result divine providence is relatively weak; Thomas Flint calls this position 'openism.' But what if libertarianism itself is false, and I don't think we can take for granted that it isn't. Would Christianity thereby be rendered implausible?

Moral Responsibility and Theism

The most prominent trend in traditional Calvinism, and more broadly, in the Augustinian strain in Christianity, maintains a strong doctrine of divine providence. In the hands of some, the development of this doctrine includes the claim that God determines everything that occurs in creation. At the same time, another prominent trend in traditional Calvinism and Augustinianism has it that human beings are morally responsible for their sinful actions, and that they deserve punishment – even eternal damnation – by virtue of having acted sinfully. Together, these doctrines strongly suggest a theological compatibilism between moral responsibility and divine determinism. This theological compatibilism has historically been a concern to those raised in traditions. From Molina and Arminius on, the most common avenue of disagreement has been to adopt a libertarian view of free will. (From here on, the term 'free will' shall refer to libertarian free will, unless otherwise noted.) But another option, typically only hinted at, is to endorse hard determinism or a similar position, according to which determinism is true and as a result we are not morally responsible for our actions.[2]

A serious misgiving one might have about this view is that it would undermine the notions of sin, guilt, repentance, forgiveness, and gratitude so central to the ethical framework of traditional theistic religions. But there are good reasons to think that this worry is ultimately unfounded. What is claimed to be incompatible with determinism is moral responsibility. For an agent to be *morally responsible for an action* is for it to belong to the agent in such a way that she would deserve blame if the action were morally wrong, and she would deserve credit or perhaps praise if it were morally exemplary. The desert at issue

here is basic in the sense that the agent, to be morally responsible, would deserve the blame or credit just because she has performed the action, and not, for example, by virtue of consequentialist considerations. It is commonly supposed that moral responsibility is an absolutely central ethical notion, so that morality itself stands or falls with it. In my view, this is a misconception.

First of all, note that being morally responsible is distinct from *behaving responsibly*, that is, behaving morally, and from *taking responsibility* for something – making a sincere commitment to a task in one's community, for example, or to care for someone. It is also different from the legitimacy of holding oneself and others *morally accountable*, where this amounts to the legitimacy of demanding that agents explain how their decisions accord with the moral point of view, and that they consider what their decisions reveal about their moral character and dispositions. The notions of behaving responsibly, taking responsibility, and moral accountability are independent of moral responsibility, and can survive without it.

Furthermore, absence of moral responsibility is compatible with our actions being good and bad, or right and wrong. By ordinary intutions, the actions of a small child can be good or bad, right or wrong, before she qualifies as morally responsible. A legal analogy also indicates why this might be so. Suppose that someone has unbeknownst to you slipped a drug into your seltzer that makes you compulsively speed in your car – so much so that it causally determines you to speed. Suppose that an officer stops you as you are speeding on the freeway. Even if you are not blameworthy for speeding in this case, what you were doing was manifestly legally wrong. By analogy, moral wrongdoing is also consistent with the absence of blameworthiness. Even if an agent is not blameworthy for lying, it can still be wrong for him to lie.

But denying moral responsibility might be thought to threaten the attitudes of guilt and repentance, since these attitudes would seem to presuppose that we are blameworthy for what we have done. Here there is much at stake, for these attitudes lie at the core of the traditional theistic conception of the formation of moral and religious character, and of what it is to have the right relationship with God. Without guilt and repentance, an agent would be incapable of restoring relationships damaged because she has done wrong. She would be kept from re-establishing her moral integrity and the kind of relationship with God that these changes make possible. For other than the attitudes of guilt and repentance we would seem to have no psychological resources that can play these roles. But giving up on moral responsibility would appear to undermine guilt because this attitude essentially involves the belief that one is blameworthy for something one has done. Moreover, if guilt is undermined, the attitude of repentance would also seem threatened, for feeling guilty is not implausibly required for motivating repentance.

However, imagine that you behave immorally, but because you do not believe that you are morally responsible, you deny that you are blameworthy. Instead, you agree that you have done wrong, you are saddened your having behaved immorally, and you thoroughly regret what you have done. In addition, because you are committed to moral improvement, you resolve not to behave in this way in the future, and you seek the help of others in sustaining your resolve. None of this is threatened by giving up moral responsibility. Indeed, I suspect that given what is ordinarily meant by a sense of guilt, since moral sadness and regret are not undermined, the sense of guilt would thereby still count as legitimate.

Forgiveness might appear to presuppose that the person being forgiven is blameworthy, and if this is so, it would indeed be undermined if one gave up moral responsibility. But forgiveness has central features that would be unaffected, and they are sufficient to sustain the role forgiveness as a whole typically has in good relationships. Suppose a friend repeatedly mistreats you, and

because of this you have resolved to end your relationship with him. However, he then apologizes to you, in such a way that he thereby signifies that he believes he has done wrong, that he wishes he had not mistreated you, and that he is sincerely committed to refraining from the offensive behavior in the future. Because of this you decide to renew rather than to end the friendship. None of this conflicts with giving up moral responsibility. The aspect of forgiveness that is undercut by the denial of moral responsibility is the willingness to disregard deserved blame or punishment. But if we were not morally responsible and did not believe we were, we would no longer need the willingness to overlook deserved blame and punishment to have good relationships.

Gratitude might well presuppose that those to whom one is grateful are morally responsible for beneficial acts, and for this reason gratitude would be threatened. At the same time, certain aspects of this attitude would not be imperilled, and I contend that these aspects can play the role gratitude as a whole has in good relationships. Gratitude involves, first of all, thankfulness towards someone who has acted beneficially. True, being thankful toward someone often involves the belief that she is praiseworthy for an action. But at the same time one can also be thankful to a toddler for some kindness, even though one does not believe she is morally responsible. Even more, one can be thankful to a friend whose beneficent actions proceed from deeply held commitments. The aspect of thankfulness could be retained even if the presupposition of praiseworthiness is rejected. Gratitude also typically involves joy occasioned by the beneficent act of another. But a rejection of moral responsibility fully harmonizes with being joyful and expressing joy when others are considerate or generous in one's behalf. Such expression of joy can bring about the sense of goodwill often brought about by gratitude, and so in this respect, abandoning moral responsibility does not produce a disadvantage.

What has traditionally been the greatest difficulty for divine determinism is the consequence that God is the cause of sin. Libertarians can hold that God does not cause sin at all (in the sense of actively bringing it about), but instead that free creatures cause it. Divine determinists have tried to avoid God's being the cause of sin by distinguishing different ways in which God determines our decisions, but I find all such attempts that I have encountered unpersuasive. A few, such as William Mann, advocate accepting all of the consequences (given compatibilist presuppositions) of the claim that God is the cause of sin.[3] Now both theistic compatibilists and hard determinists face this difficulty. But in an important respect the problem is worse for compatibilism, for this position is threatened not only with the claim that God deterministically causes sin, but that God deterministically causes our blameworthiness and our being deserving of punishment. Of these, the hard determinist need countenance only that God causes sin, and not also our blameworthiness and our deserving punishment. For the hard determinist, sin has more of the features of natural evil than usually supposed, and as a result God's causing sin is much more like God's causing natural evil as it is typically conceived.

Salvation

Libertarian free will might seem to provide an especially crucial advantage to Christian theism in the area of soteriology. For the most widespread view as to how Christ's suffering, death and resurrection save us is the standard substitutionary atonement theory, and it must be relinquished if moral responsibility is denied. On this theory, we deserve extensive punishment just by virtue of our sinful actions, and Christ, by his suffering and death, bears this punishment in our place. But if we do not deserve even blame, let alone punishment, just by virtue of our sinful behavior, then an essential component of this theory is false. One should note that this substitutionary theory has familiar problems of its own – even without concerns about free will the retributive theory of punishment is not without its difficulties,[4] and the notion that retributive justice allows one person's punishment to count for another's is difficult to reconcile with ordinary moral intuitions. Moreover, other theories of Christ's atonement are consistent with this view. Among them is Abelard's moral example theory, according to which Christ's obedience unto death serves as a motivating example for us to emulate. On Jürgen Moltmann's view, through Christ's suffering and death, God manifests solidarity with us in our worst sufferings, thereby identifying with us in our most difficult and painful experiences.[5] As far as I can see, nothing in this position depends crucially on our being morally responsible. Or consider Richard Swinburne's position, according to which the perfect life of Christ is a gift that God gives us so that we can pay the compensation we owe for our wrongdoing. It is not at all clear that any feature of this view conflicts with the denial of free will and moral responsibility.[6]

Historically, perhaps the most effective reason for rejecting any sort of divine determinism, and endorsing instead libertarian free will is the unconscionability of God's damning people to hell after determining them to sin. But another response is Schleiermacher's – to maintain the divine determinism and accept instead the doctrine of universal salvation.[7] Indeed, the best reading of the texts of the Christian scriptures might well be on the side of universalism. Here are a number of passages that count in its favor:

1   *Romans* 5:18. Therefore just as one man's trespass led to condemnation for all, so one man's act of righteousness leads to justification and life for all.

2   *Romans* 11:32. For God has imprisoned all in disobedience so that he may be merciful to all.

3   *I Corinthians* 15:22. For as all die in Adam, so all will be made alive in Christ.

4   *Colossians* 1:19–20. For in him [Christ] all the fullness of God was pleased to dwell, and through him God was pleased to reconcile to himself all things, whether on earth or in heaven, by making peace through the blood of his cross.

Universalism is an option for the Christian who is a divine determinist, and in my view it is far from obvious that on the whole the scriptural texts count against this position.[8]

The Free Will Theodicy

A potential drawback for the rejection of libertarianism is that it rules out the free will theodicy, which is often thought to be the most powerful defense we have of divine goodness in the face of evil. The free will theodicy in systematized form dates back at least to early Christianity and perhaps to Zoroastrianism, and remains the most prominent of all theodicies. On the most common version, God had the option of creating or refraining from creating libertarian significantly free beings – beings with libertarian free will that can make choices between right and wrong. A risk incurred by creating such beings is that they might freely choose evil and the choice be unpreventable by God. Benefits include creatures having moral responsibility for their actions and being creators in their own right. Since the benefits outweigh the risks, God is morally justified in creating such significantly free beings, and he is not culpable when they choose wrongly.

But how plausible is this as a theodicy for the most horrible evils? If it isn't very plausible, perhaps not much is relinquished by accepting a view that rules it out. A familiar problem is that many of the more horrible evils would not seem to be or result from freely willed decisions. People being injured and dying as a result of earthquake, volcanic eruptions,

diseases – including mental illnesses that give rise to unfree immoral choices – would not seem to result from freely willed decisions, and for this reason are standardly classified as *natural* as opposed to *moral* evils. But a further objection, raised by several critics, is that even if we have free will of the libertarian sort, and many of our choices are freely willed in this libertarian sense, the consequences of those decisions are preventable by God. In general, evil consequences are preventable effects of freely willed decisions.[9] Or, God might intervene earlier on in the process. Given the nature of libertarian free will, short of killing them or disabling their wills, God might not have been able to prevent the Nazi leadership from deciding to perpetrate genocide, but God could have nonetheless prevented or limited the genocide, by, say, rendering the Nazi guns, trains, and gas chambers ineffective. One answer to this is Richard Swinburne's, that if God were to regularly prevent such evils in this way, then we would not fully understand the kinds of consequences our decisions could have, and this would have considerable disvalue. But, one might argue, God might have intervened earlier yet in the process, by, for example, healing the bad effects of childhood abuse and trauma. Or rather than intervening, God might have designed us so that we were not nearly as vulnerable to experiences of this sort, and, more generally, less vulnerable to the kinds of psychological problems that play a role in motivating evil decisions.

Swinburne has developed a thorough response to these sorts of objections. He argues that it is not just freely willed decision *tout court* that has the relevantly high intrinsic value, but two characteristics in addition: freely willed decision's accomplishing what the agent intended – what he calls *efficacious* free will, and freely willed decision's adjudicating between good and evil options each of which genuinely motivate the agent – *serious* free will, in his terminology. Swinburne contends that it is serious and efficacious free will that has the intrinsic value high enough to justify God in sometimes not preventing the decidedly evil consequences of immoral decisions. His account is significant, for it does not avoid a proposal for the kind of value free will must possess to sustain the role in theodicy that so many believe it has. In his view, first of all, "the very fact of the agent having a free choice is a great good for the agent; and a greater good the more serious the kind of free will, even if it is incorrectly used." Moreover, an agent "is an ultimate source in an even fuller way if the choices open to him cover the whole moral range, from the very good to the very wrong." And indeed, "an agent who has serious and efficacious free will is in a much fuller way an ultimate source of the direction of things in the world" than one who does not.[10] Furthermore, in preparation for his theodicy, Swinburne contends that:

> It is a good for us if our experiences are not wasted but are used for the good of others, if they are the means of a benefit which would not have come to others without them, which will at least in part compensate for those experiences. It follows from this insight that it is a blessing for a person if the possibility of his suffering makes possible the good for others of having the free choice of hurting or harming them . . . and of choosing to show or not show sympathy.[11]

To illustrate the import of these claims for theodicy, Swinburne discusses the example of the slave trade from Africa in the eighteenth century. About this practice he writes, in what is by now a well-known passage:

> But God allowing this to occur made possible innumerable opportunities for very large numbers of people to contribute or not to contribute to the development of this culture; for slavers to choose to enslave or not; for plantation-owners to choose to buy slaves or not and to treat them well or ill; for ordinary

white people and politicians to campaign for its abolition or not to bother, and to campaign for compensation for the victims or not to bother; and so on. There is also the great good for those who themselves suffered as slaves that their lives were not useless, their vulnerability to suffering made possibile many free choices, and thereby so many steps towards the formation of good or bad character.[12]

One problem for this line of thought is that it finds itself in opposition to strongly ingrained moral practice when horrible evil is at issue. First, as David Lewis points out, for us the evil-doer's freedom is a weightless consideration, not merely an outweighed consideration.[13] When the slave traders come to take your children, and you are contemplating violent resistance, we do not expect you to consider the value of the slave traders' efficacious but immoral free will, which would be high indeed if value of this sort could have the role in justifying God's allowing the slave trade that Swinburne suggests it does. Moreover, if he is right, then when twenty slave traders have freely decided to try to take your children, ten times as much value of the sort he describes would be at stake as when there are only two, and there would be that much more reason not to resist. Moreover, all else being equal, there would be significantly less reason to harm in self-defense an opponent who appears to have free will then one who is known to be mentally ill and incapable of free decisions.[14] None of this has a role in our ordinary moral practice.[15]

A further problem for the free will theodicy is occasioned by Swinburne's view that to choose freely to do what is right one must have a serious countervailing desire to refrain from doing what is right instead, strong enough that it could actually motivate a choice so to refrain.[16] Swinburne thinks that this point supports the free will theodicy, since it can explain why God allows us to have desires to do evil, and, by extension, why God allows choices in accord with those desires.

But this claim rather serves to undermine the force of the free will theodicy as an explanation for many horrible evils. For we do not generally believe that the value of a free choice outweights the disvalue of having desires to perform horribly evil actions, especially if they are strong enough to result in action. For example, the notion that it is more valuable than not for people to have a strong desire to abuse children for the reason that this gives them the opportunity to choose freely not to do so has no purchase on us. Our practice for people with desires of this sort is to provide them with therapy to diminish or eradicate such desires. We have no tendency to believe that the value of making a free decision not to abuse a child made in struggle against a desire to do so carries any weight against the proposal to provide this sort of therapy. Furthermore, were we to encounter someone with a strong desire to abuse children but who nevertheless resisted actively seeking do so, we would not think that his condition has more value overall than one in which he never had the desire to abuse children in the first place. Moreover, I daresay that a significant proportion of people alive today – well over 90% – has neither intentionally chosen a horrible evil nor had a genuine struggle with a desire to do so – they have never, for instance, tortured, maimed, or murdered, nor seriously struggled with desires to do so. But we do not think that their lives would have been more valuable had they possessed such desires even if every struggle against them had been successful. Thus it is questionable whether God would allow such desires in order to realize the value of certain free choices. This aspect of Swinburne's theodicy may have some credibility with respect to evils that are not horrible, but much less, I think, when it comes to horrible evils. Here I would like to emphasize that if we thought free will did in fact have the proposed degree of intrinsic value, our moral practice would be decidedly different from what it is now – in ways that, given our moral sensibilities, we would find very disturbing.

I should note that some versions of the free will theodicy do not essentially require the libertarian version of free will. For example, Eleonore Stump argues that suffering from moral and natural evil contributes to a humbling recognition of oneself as having a defective will, which in turn can motivate one to turn to God to fix the defect in the will.[17] The defect in the will is that one has a bent towards evil, so that one has a diminished capacity to will what one ought to will. Now, as far as I can see, no feature of this account demands libertarian free will, nor even a notion of free will of the sort required for moral responsibility. Indeed, hard determinism can accommodate the causal process that Stump specifies. Nothing about this process, as she describes it, requires an indeterministic conception of free will, nor does it require that the agent be morally responsible, in this case praiseworthy, for turning to God on the occasion of suffering.

The Retributive Punishment Theodicy

Another traditional theodicy that potentially requires libertarian free will is that God brings about or allows evil as punishment for sin. Now no feature of hard determinism per se rules out a deterrence theory or a moral education theory of punishment, but retributivism, as it is usually conceived, would be precluded. What is lost as a result? It is implausible to think that in William Rowe's example, the five-year-old girl deserves to be punished by being raped and beaten by virtue of anything she has done.[18] Does an ordinary person, never having committed a serious crime, and who is not in any other respect an extraordinary sinner, deserve to suffer from a lengthy painful and fatal disease as punishment for the wrongs he has done?[19] Our judicial system would regard punishment of this sort for *serious crimes* as monstrous. Imagine if we were to punish *murderers* by inducing such suffering – who would find that conscionable?

Someone might reply that since each of us

deserves an eternity of torture, *a fortiori* each of us also deserves suffering of this sort. But because it is doubtful that anyone genuinely understands why we all might deserve punishment of this degree as a matter of retributive justice alone, this line of thought does not promise a plausible theodicy. Let me emphasize that even thinking of ordinary people as deserving a long and painful disease, for example, would constitute a serious revision in our moral practice, for in that practice sympathy without reservation is the appropriate response.[20]

Doing and Allowing

The libertarian view would appear to enjoy a considerable advantage precisely in making possible a theodicy for the consequences of freely willed evil decisions. For it need only grant that God allows these consequences, while divine determinism seems constrained to accept that God actively brings them about. When one envisions some particularly egregious past horror, it might be especially difficult to accept that God actively brought it about. I find it very difficult to reconcile myself to such particular claims. But is it any easier to reconcile oneself to the claim that God *allows* that specific horror? Suppose that you are subjected to abuse by someone who hates you. If the abuser had libertarian free will, then even though God did not actively bring about the decision to abuse you, God nevertheless allowed the consequences of this decision to occur while at the same time having the power to prevent them. In the divine determinist view, by contrast, God actively brings about these consequences. Factoring in providence, on the libertarian view, God allows the abuse to occur in order to realize a greater good, while on the determinist view, God actively brings it about in order to realize a greater good.

One should first note that while it is often held that actively bringing about or *doing* evil is prima facie morally worse than merely *allowing* evil, of course it is not as if allowing evil is

generally morally permissible. Rather, in comparing the libertarian and determinist theological conceptions on this issue, the important question is this. Supposing that on the libertarian position God is justified in allowing evil consequences for the sake of some greater good, would it be morally worse for God actively to bring them about for the sake of that good? The answer to this question depends at least in part on the nature of the good to be realized. In some cases God might well be justified in allowing the evil consequences, but not in actively bringing them about. By analogy, a parent might justifiably allow a child to play with matches, foreseeing that he might well incur a slight burn as a result, while it would be wrong for the parent to actively bring about that burn.[21] But consider, for instance, the purported good of retributively justified punishment where the evil consequences in question are actively brought about by agents other than God who are not appropriate authorities for inflicting the punishment at issue. If these evils are to be justified as retributive punishment, it would actually seem *better* for God actively to bring them about than merely to allow these other agents to do so. By analogy, if Lee Harvey Oswald did in fact kill John F. Kennedy, and if Oswald did deserve the death penalty, it would have been better for an appropriate authority to administer the penalty than for that authority to allow Jack Ruby to kill him. Assuming that God is an appropriate authority for punishment, it would then be better that God actively bring about some punishment than merely allow a person who is not an appropriate authority to do so.

Consider, furthermore, the good of soulbuilding that John Hick discusses.[22] Suppose God knew that someone's character would be significantly improved morally if he suffered in a certain way, and that God were justified in allowing the person to suffer on such grounds. Wouldn't God then also be justified in actively bringing about the suffering on those grounds? An apt analogy would seem to be that of say, Civil War surgery. Suppose the doctor knows that the patient will not survive unless he undergoes painful surgery. It is clearly not morally worse for the doctor to actually perform the surgery himself than it would be for him to allow another doctor to perform it.

Now indeed the intrinsic value of serious and efficacious free will would not be realizable if God actively caused rather than merely allowed the consequences of evil free decisions. But several key goods could be realized whether God actively brought about or merely allowed the suffering required for those goods, and for them it would appear at least as good for God to bring about the suffering as to allow it.

Skeptical Theism

What position on the problem of evil is open to the divine determinist? A non-retributive punishment theodicy is available, as is a modified form of the soul building theodicy, as well as a version of Alvin Plantinga's theodicy according to which sin and suffering are required for the greater good of the incarnation and atonement.[23] But rather than advocate a full-fledged theodicy, I prefer to side with skeptical theism, developed in recent times by Stephen Wykstra and William Alston, among others.[24] Skeptical theism claims that due to the limitations of our cognitive capacities, the nature of the good is or might well be beyond our understanding to such a degree that we should not expect to understand how it is that God's governance of the universe accords with divine goodness. Various problems for skeptical theism have been raised. To my mind an especially serious one is that it might occasion further skeptical analogues and consequences that we would want to avoid. I shall argue that one main version of this threat is especially serious for possible goods that essentially involve libertarian free will, but not for certain possible goods that are independent of this sort of free will.[25]

The version of this challenge to skeptical theism on which I want to focus has been advanced by Bruce Russell, and it claims that this view will have skeptical consequences for our moral practice.[26] If the theist claims that there are goods not fully understood by us that could not have been realized had God prevented various horrible evils, and that God might well be justified in allowing these evils in order to realize those goods, then there might well be situations in which we fail to prevent evils of these kinds where we do no wrong. In fact, we may on some such occasions be obligated not to prevent these evils. Or at very least, on certain occasions we might have to give serious consideration to reasons not to prevent those evils when ordinary moral practice would not give serious consideration to such reasons. Let us call this *the challenge from skeptical consequences for morality*.

Now Alston, Daniel Howard-Snyder, and Michael Bergmann have replied to this objection by claiming in effect that in morally justifying our actions, we are limited to goods that we understand, while the possible goods the skeptical theist is adducing are at least to some degree beyond our understanding.[27] But this does not seem right; our moral justifications should not be limited to goods we understand — as Russell in fact argues. Let me amplify Russell's contention. Consider first an analogy to the skeptical theist's situation that features only human agents.[28] Fred assists doctors in a clinic that specializes, among other things, in a painful bone disease. He is careful to note what the doctors do to help the patients. Suppose that Fred has excellent reason to trust the doctors as thoroughly competent. The clinic stocks morphine as a pain killer, and Fred knows that if morphine were administered to the bone disease patients, their acute pain would be relieved. But the doctors never, in his experience, have given morphine to patients suffering from this disease, even though they, in his experience, have given it to other patients in the clinic. Fred has no inkling why they do not administer the morphine to the bone disease patients. However, for all he knows, they might have given it to such patients in certain circumstances in the past, although he has no reasonable guess as to frequency, and he has no idea of what these circumstances might be. One day, due to a hurricane, all the doctors are away from the clinic, but Fred is there. A patient is suffering from the bone disease, and Fred has the opportunity to administer morphine. It would seem that he has some significant moral reason not to do so.

Now consider the skeptical theist's analogous situation. Sue, a doctor, knows that there have been thousands of cases of people suffering horribly from disease X. She is a skeptical theist who believes that God is justified for the sake of goods beyond her ken in not preventing these thousands of cases of suffering (she trusts God in a way analogous to the way in which Fred trusts the bone specialists). Suppose that her belief in God is rational, and also that her belief regarding the God-justifying goods is rational. In addition, for all she knows, God in the past might have prevented people from suffering from this disease under certain circumstances, although she has no reasonable guess as to how often God might have done this, and he has no idea of what these circumstances might be. Now a drug that cures disease X has just been developed, and Sue is deciding whether to administer it. Sue's situation seems similar to Fred's: it would seem that insofar as Sue is rational in believing that God has significant moral reason to allow thousands of people to suffer from disease X, she has significant moral reason not to administer the drug that cures disease X – even if in the last analysis she should administer the drug because the reasons she has to heal the sick and to relieve suffering are stronger.[29]

Stump raises an objection of this sort as a possible rejoinder to her "fixing the will" theodicy. She says "someone might object . . . that this solution to the problem of evil prohibits us from any attempt to relieve human suffering and in fact suggests that we ought to promote it, as the means to man's salvation." In reply, she argues that

Because God can use suffering to cure an evil will, it does not follow that we can do so also. God can see into the minds and hearts of human beings and determine what sort and amount of suffering is likely to produce the best results; we cannot . . . Furthermore, God as parent creator has a right to, and a responsibility for, painful correction of his creatures, which we as sibling creatures do not have. Therefore, since all human suffering is prima facie evil, and since we do not know with any high degree of probability how much (if any) of it is likely to result in good to any particular sufferer on any particular occasion, it is reasonable for us to eliminate the suffering as much as we can. At any rate, the attempt to eliminate suffering is likely to be beneficial to our characters, and passivity in the face of others' suffering will have no such good effects.[30]

The analogy between Fred and Sue casts some doubt on some of these contentions. In Stump's view, the evil will can be cured through both moral and natural evil. To the extent that we are capable of bringing about moral evil and preventing natural evil, it would seem that we can indeed help to bring about the suffering that would cure the will. Moreover, our duty not to produce but rather to prevent suffering is in a sense not absolute; a doctor might actually be obligated actively to bring about suffering if it is required for the sake of a great enough medical good. And even if we do not know with any high degree of probability whether suffering is likely to be beneficial, this fact would not all by itself remove the obligation to take this consideration seriously in moral deliberation. Still, as we shall now see, in a skeptical theist account, the good Stump adduces has an advantage over those that require libertarian free will.

There is a continuum of possible God-justifying goods that potentially serve the aims of skeptical theism, ranging from goods of which we haven't the least knowledge, through those of which we have some but nevertheless incomplete knowledge. As I have argued, skeptical theism does suggest a general threat to ordinary moral practice. However, of those goods of which we have some inkling, some would yield a more substantial threat than others. Consider the skeptical theist's claim that the following hypothesis is true for all we know: The intrinsic value of serious and efficacious free will justifies God in allowing certain horrible evils – whose point we cannot otherwise see. Weight given to this hypothesis would pose a clear and immediate threat to our moral practice. For we would have reasonable beliefs as to where this intrinsic value is to be found and how to secure it, and this would then give rise to certain prima facie obligations. For example, we could have a reasonable belief as to whether a slave trader was freely willing his aims, and we would have a prima facie obligation to take the intrinsic value of his serious and efficacious free will into consideration in deciding what to do by way of defense against him. But again, as Lewis remarks, the value of free will is now a weightless consideration for us, and thus we would face a disruptive effect on our moral practice.

Consider, in addition, the skeptical theist's claim that the following hypothesis is true for all we know: The value of retributive punishment justifies God in allowing certain horrible evils, whose point we cannot otherwise see. Suppose a skeptical theist were to suggest the hypothesis that ordinary people suffer from painful diseases as retribution for sinful inner lives.[31] It might well be that we are in no epistemic condition to tell whether any ordinary person's inner life merits suffering of this kind. But weight given to this hypothesis would give rise to reasons to abandon the unreserved sympathy we have for ordinary people who suffer from painful diseases. This, again, would constitute a clear and immediate threat to our moral practice.

But there are skeptical theist hypotheses regarding other goods of which we have some inkling, which would not yield such a clear and immediate threat, and the reasons are epistemic. Stump's proposal is a case in point. As she herself points out, it would never be reasonably clear to us when suffering would have the beneficial effect of motivating the agent to turn to God, nor how much would be required to have this effect. So in this case the undermining threat to our moral practice would not be clear and immediate. The good of our identifying with God in suffering that Marilyn Adams discusses is like this as well. We would be completely in the dark, I would think, whether someone would be able to re-envision her suffering as point of identification with God.[32] The same is true for the good of the incarnation and atonement that Plantinga adduces. Suppose we believed that God might well allow evils as a requirement for the atonement in particular, the purpose of which is to reconcile the world to God. We would have very limited knowledge as to where or to what degree such evils would be required. So on the assumption that this hypothesis is true, the threat of our moral practice being undermined is not clear and immediate. It must be acknowledged that even if for these sorts of goods the threat to moral practice is not clear and immediate, the prospect of realizing these goods might still occasion some loss of resolve to prevent suffering.[33] However, here a consideration raised by Swinburne, William Alston and Steve Layman is pertinent, that the difference in powers and in authority between God and us, or facts about God's relation to us that derive from these differences, might have significant consequences for the justification of allowing or bringing about suffering.[34] For example, given God's epistemic capacities relative to ours, there are goods for the sake of which God's allowing or bringing about evil might well be justified while our doing the same would not. Accordingly, I would draw the following tentative conclusion: skeptical theism that adduces goods essentially involving libertarian free will gives rise to an especially serious version of the challenge from skeptical consequences for morality, while this is not the case for several prominent examples of goods that do not essentially involve free will.

Divine Providence

Does divine determinism undermine the comfort and the meaning in life that a belief in divine providence potentially provides? The understanding that everything that happens is causally determined by God in accord with a divine plan for the world could indeed be a comfort to us. A problem one might raise for this conception is that any individual person would be participating in that plan without freely willing that participation – where freely willing participation includes not only choosing it without being determined to do so, but also adequately understanding in advance what one is participating in. But there is reason to hold that believing one has a role in a great divine plan, even if one does not freely will one's participation, could provide comfort in one's suffering and a sense of meaning for one's life. It is well known that during the early years of the Civil War, Abraham Lincoln's leading purpose was to preserve the Union, and not to end slavery.[35] But later he began to waver on this issue, and, what is more, to have a sense that God had a purpose for the war that he, Lincoln, did not initially have. A few years into the war he wrote:

> I am almost ready to say this is probably true – that God wills this contest, and wills that it shall not end yet. By his mere quiet power, on the minds of the now contestants, he could have either saved or destroyed the Union without a human contest. Yet the contest began. And having begun, He could give the final victory to either side any day. Yet the contest proceeds.[36]

And then in 1864 we find Lincoln saying:

> I claim not to have controlled events, but confess plainly that events have controlled me.

Now, at the end of three years's struggle the nation's condition is not what either party, or any man, devised or expected. God alone can claim it. Whither it is tending seems plain. If God now wills the removal of a great wrong, and wills also that we of the North as well as you of the South shall pay fairly for our complicity in that wrong, impartial history will find there in new cause to attest and revere the justice and goodness of God.[37]

One's sense is that Lincoln's conception of the Civil War as a key component in God's plan to end slavery in the United States reconciled Lincoln to the evils of that struggle and gave it immense significance for him, despite the fact that he did not initially choose to fight the war for the reasons he came to believe God had for ordaining it, and thus even though at first he did not freely participate in the divine plan as he later conceived it.

But what about the suffering that God's plan might involve – suffering that given divine determinism, none of us endorse with free will? Would one's conviction that everything that happens is determined in accord with that plan nevertheless provide adequate comfort in suffering? According to the Stoic view, God determines everything that happens in accord with the good of the whole universe, and the nature of this good is incompletely understood on our part.[38] There is an all-encompassing divine plan, neither whose nature nor means of realization we understand very well if at all, but yet we can know that everything that happens is determined by God with an aim to the realization of that plan. One can reconcile oneself to the suffering in one's life by abandoning one's merely personal concerns – that is, one's ordinary human aspirations for personal survival, happiness, and success – by identifying with these divine aims. Descartes, in a letter to Chanut, eloquently expresses the Stoic idea (that is, if we take his reference to free will to be compatibilist). In this excerpt, he sets out "the path one ought to follow to arrive at the love of God:"

> But if . . . we heed the infinity of his power, through which he has created so many things, of which we are the least part; the extension of his providence that makes him see in one thought alone everything that has been, is, shall be, and could be; the infallibility of his decrees which, although they do not disturb our free will, nevertheless cannot in any fashion be changed; and finally, if, on the one hand, we heed our insignificance, and if, on the other hand, we heed the grandeur of all created things, by noting the manner in which they depend on God and by considering them in a fashion that has a relationship to his omnipotence . . . meditation upon all this so abundantly fills the man who hears it with such extreme joy that, realizing he would have to be abusive and ungrateful toward God to wish to occupy God's place, he thinks himself as already having lived sufficiently because God has given him the grace to reach such knowledge, and willingly and entirely joining himself to God, he loves God so perfectly that he desires nothing more in the world than that God's will be done. That is the reason he no longer fears either death, or pains, or disgraces, because he knows that nothing can happen to him save what God shall have decreed; and he so loves this divine decree, esteems it so just and so necessary, knows he ought so entirely to depend upon it, that even when he awaits death or some other evil, if *per impossibile* he could change that decree, he would not wish to do so. But if he does not refuse evils or afflictions, because they come to him from divine providence, he refuses still less all the goods or licit pleasures one can enjoy in this life, because they too issue from that providence; and accepting them with joy, without having any fear of evils, his love renders him perfectly happy.[39]

In Descartes's understanding, if one's love for God were of the right sort, one's identification with the aims of God would be so thorough that even if one could, one would not refuse one's own death or other personal suffering, since one understands them as proceeding from the decree of God.

In the Stoic conception, we should align ourselves with the divine perspective so that we will enjoy equanimity no matter what happens, even if the divine plan conflicts with the good as conceived from one's personal point of view. This vision seems a little glassy-eyed; one might doubt whether such a reason is sufficient to motivate many of us. As Thomas Nagel remarks, normally "one is supposed to behold and partake of the glory of God, for example, in a way in which chickens do not share in the glory of *coq au vin*."[40] To consider an extreme case, if one believed in divine determinism and in eternal damnation then one's comfort and sense of meaning might well be compromised, certainly in the case of the person who was convinced that he himself was eternally damned, but even for the believer who feels assured of his salvation. For then God's care for the universe would allow for God's deterministically causing the lives of certain persons to be endlessly miserable. The comfort that might result from believing that everything that happens is determined by a being with this sort of character would not, in my estimation, be unequivocal.

However, what if the point of the divine plan were to reconcile everything – including every person – to God. The Christian scriptures state that this will happen through the incarnation and atonement of Christ. So what if –

> Ephesians 1:8–10: [God] has made known to us in all wisdom and insight the mystery of his will, according to his purpose which he set forth in Christ as a plan for the fulness of time, to unite all things in him, things in heaven and things on earth?

And what if for each of us:

> Romans 8:18: Our present sufferings are not worth comparing with the glory that will be revealed in us?

Then God would not determine any of us to a life of endless misery. Moreover, what if, as Marilyn Adams suggests, God is in the end good to every person by insuring each a life in which all of the suffering experienced contributes to a greater good within that very life?[41] Then it might even be, as Plantinga states it, that God would know that if I were able to make the decision whether to accept the suffering, and knew enough about the divine plan, and had the right affections, then I myself would accept the suffering.[42] Then each of us would say, by analogy with Lincoln on the Civil War, that the suffering was worth the result even if we did not in fact freely endorse either the suffering or the result.

Conclusion

So it may be that traditional theistic religion does not require libertarian free will. It might be that Molinism is theologically preferable, but I believe that there is a deterministic perspective that is not decidedly worse. At least, given our limited cognitive capacities and our lack of ability to understand divine purposes, we should not be confident in judging that the deterministic perspective is decidedly worse. It is indeed difficult for us to believe that God brings about the horrors of this world, but it is perhaps no less difficult to believe that God merely allows them, especially if, as I have argued, it is implausible that the goods that essentially involve free will can justify God's allowing these evils. But if we focused instead on the good that the traditional theistic religions view as the goal of history, then, despite initial appearances, a deterministic conception of the plan for realizing that good might well turn out to be as attractive as a Molinist alternative.[43]

Notes

1 Luis de Molina, *Liberi Arbitrii cum Gratiae Donis, Divina Praescientia, Providentia, Praedestinatione et Reprobatione Concordia* (1595); tr (of Part IV) A.J. Freddoso, *On Divine Foreknowledge: Part IV of the Concordia* (Ithaca: Cornell University Press, 1988). For an excellent exposition and defense of Molina's position, see Thomas Flint, *Divine Providence* (Ithaca: Cornell University Press, 1988).

2 Perhaps Friedrich Schleiermacher had hard determinist views, at least early in his career. I was made aware of this possibility by Andrew Dole's "Schleiermacher's Early Essay on Freedom" a paper he presented at a conference of the Society for Christian Philosophers in Bloomington, Indiana, in September 2002. The manuscript version of Schleiermacher's essay has no title. It was originally published in excerpted form in Wilhelm Dilthey's *Leben Schleiermachers* under the title "Über die Freiheit des Menschen". In the *Friedrich Schleiermacher: Kritische Gesamtausgabe* (Berlin: Walter De Gruyter, 1983) it appears as "Über die Freiheit" (KGA 1.1, 1984, pp. 217–357), which has been translated into English as *On Freedom* (Edwin Mellen Press, 1992),

3 William Mann, "God's Freedom, Human Freedom, and God's Responsibility for Sin," in *Divine and Human Action*, ed. Thomas V. Morris (Ithaca: Cornell University Press, 1988), pp. 182–210.

4 For my view on retributivism, see my *Living Without Free Will* (Cambridge: Cambridge University Press, 2001), pp. 159–61. In this book I develop my more general perspective on free will and moral responsibility.

5 Jürgen Moltmann, *The Crucified God* (New York: Harper and Rowe, 1974).

6 Richard Swinburne, *Responsibility and Atonement* (Oxford: Oxford University Press, 1989).

7 Friedrich Schleiermacher, *The Christian Faith*, ed. Mackintosh and Stewart (Philadelphia: T&T Clark, 1928), pp. 550–1.

8 See Keith De Rose's "Universalism and the Bible," on his website, http://pantheon.yale.edu/~kd47.

9 Steven Boër, "The Irrelevance of the Free Will Defense," *Analysis* (1975), pp. 110–12; J. L. Mackie, "Evil and Omnipotence," *Mind* 64 (1955), pp. 200–12.

10 Richard Swinburne, *Providence and the Problem of Evil* (Oxford: Oxford University Press, 1999), pp. 82–9.

11 Richard Swinburne, *Providence and the Problem of Evil*, p. 103.

12 Richard Swinburne, *Providence and the Problem of Evil*, p. 245.

13 David Lewis, "Evil for Freedom's Sake," *Philosophical Papers* 22 (1993), pp. 149–72, at p. 155.

14 Mark Moyer made this point in conversation.

15 When this paper was presented at Yale University, Swinburne argued that only God has the authority to allow people to suffer intensely in order to secure the intrinsic value of free will, drawing on the analogy of parents and children. However, there is at least no epistemic problem here for us. There are epistemic reasons that non-doctors should refrain from performing painful operations on patients in order to secure medical goods. Non-doctors usually don't know enough to be successful at realizing medical goods by such means. But there is no analogous problem for allowing or causing people to suffer for the sake of securing the intrinsic value of serious and efficacious free will, for all adult human beings can typically understand well enough where that value is to be had, and how to secure it.

16 Swinburne actually makes a stronger claim than this: see his *Providence and the Problem of Evil*, pp. 85–6.

17 Eleonore Stump, "The Problem of Evil," *Faith and Philosophy* 2 (1985), pp. 392–418.

18 William Rowe, "The Evidential Argument Argument from Evil: A Second Look," in *The Evidential Argument from Evil*, Daniel Howard-Snyder, ed. (Indianapolis: Indiana University Press, 1996), pp. 262–85.

19 For an opposing perspective, see William Alston, "The Inductive Argument from Evil and the Human Cognitive Condition," *Philosophical Perspectives* 5 (1991), pp. 27–67; reprinted in *The Evidential Argument from Evil*, Daniel Howard-Snyder, ed. (Indianapolis: Indiana University Press, 1996), pp. 97–125, section V.

20 This general issue is raised in the ninth chapter of the Gospel of John, which begins as follows:

> John 9:1–3. As he walked along, he saw a man blind from birth. His disciples asked him, "Rabbi, who sinned, this man or his parents, that he was born blind?" Jesus answered, "Neither this man nor his parents sinned; he was born blind so that God's works might be revealed in him."

21 Thanks to Andrew Chignell for this point and example.

22 John Hick, *Evil and the God of Love*, 2nd ed. (New York: Harper and Rowe, 1978).

23 Alvin Plantinga, "Supralapsarianism or O Felix Culpa," ms.

24 See, for example, Stephen J. Wykstra, "The Human Obstacle to Evidential Arguments from Suffering: On Avoiding the Evils of 'Appearance,' " *International Journal for Philosophy of Religion* 16 (1984), pp. 73–94, and "Rowe's Noseeum Arguments from Evil," *The Evidential Argument from Evil* pp. 126–150; also William Alston's "The Inductive Argument from Evil and the Human Cognitive Condition." These skeptical theist accounts were occasioned by William Rowe's "The Problem of Evil and Some Varieties of Atheism," *American Philosophical Quarterly* 16 (1979), pp. 335–41. Immanuel Kant developed a version of this strategy in his late essay "On the Miscarriage of all Philosophical Trials in Theodicy," of which an English translation appears in *Kant: Religion within the Boundaries of Mere Reason and Other Writings*, Allen Wood and George di Giovanni, eds. (Cambridge: Cambridge University Pres, 1998); see my "Kant on God, Evil, and Teleology," *Faith and Philosophy* 13 (1996), pp. 508–33.

25 I discuss skeptical theism in more detail in "The Problem of Evil," in *The Blackwell Guide to the Philosophy of Religion*, ed. William E. Mann (Oxford: Blackwell Publishing, 2004), pp. 148–70, at pp. 159–6.

26 Bruce Russell, "Defenseless," in *The Evidential Argument from Evil*, pp. 193–205, at pp. 197–8.

27 Michael Bergmann, "Skeptical Theism and Rowe's New Evidential Argument from Evil," *Nous* 2000, Daniel Howard-Snyder, "The Argument From Inscrutable Evil," in *The Evidential Argument from Evil*, pp. 286–310, at pp. 292–3.

28 I present an example of this sort in "The Problem of Evil," op. cit., pp. 164–5.

29 Thanks to David Christensen, Michael Bergmann, and Daniel Howard-Snyder for discussions that

helped formulate this example and that influenced what follows.

30 Eleonore Stump, "The Problem of Evil," pp. 412–3.

31 See William Alston, "The Inductive Argument from Evil and the Human Cognitive Condition," Section V.

32 Marilyn Adams, *Horrendous Evils and the Goodness of God* (Ithaca: Cornell University Press, 1999).

33 Thanks to Andrew Dole for prompting this clarification.

34 Richard Swinburne, *Providence and the Problem of Evil*, p. 243; the comment by Steve Layman is in Daniel Howard-Snyder's "The Argument from Inscrutable Evil," p. 292; William Alston, "Some (Temporarily) Final Thoughts," in *The Evidential Argument from Evil*, pp. 311–32, at p. 321.

35 Lincoln wrote to Horace Greeley: "My paramount object in this struggle is to save the Union, and is not either to save or destroy slavery. If I could save the Union without freeing any slave I would do it, and if I could save it by freeing some of the slaves I would do it; and if I could save it by freeing some and leaving others alone I would also do that. What I do about slavery, and the colored race, I do because it helps to save the Union." (In Stephen B. Oates, *With Malice Towards None: The Life of Abraham Lincoln* (New York: New American Library, 1977), p. 340.)

36 Stephen B. Oates, *With Malice Towards None*, p. 343.

37 Stephen B. Oates, *With Malice Towards None*, p. 416. Lincoln wrote in the Second Inaugural Address of 1865:

If we shall suppose that American slavery is one of those offenses which, in the providence of God, must needs come, but which, having continued through His appointed time, He now wills to remove, and that He gives to both North and South this terrible war as the woe due to those by whom the offense came, shall we discern therein any departure from those divine attributes which the believers in a living God always ascribe to Him? Fondly do we hope, fervently do we pray, that this mighty scourge of war may speedily pass away. Yet, if God wills that it continue until all the wealth piled by the bondsman's two hundred and fifty years of unrequited toil shall be sunk, and until every drop of blood drawn with the lash shall be paid by another drawn with the sword, as was said three thousand years ago, so still it must be said "the judgments of the Lord are true and righteous altogether."

38 I discuss these issues in "Stoic Psychotherapy in Descartes and Spinoza," *Faith and Philosophy* 11, (1994), pp. 592–625.

39 (AT = *Oeuvres de Descartes*, edited by Ch. Adam and P. Tannery (revised edition, Paris: Vrin/C.N.R.S., 1964–76.) The translation is from John J. Blom, *Descartes, His Moral Philosophy and Pyschology* (New York: NYU Press, 1978), pp. 206–7.

40 Thomas Nagel, "The Absurd," in *Mortal Questions*, (Cambridge: Cambridge University Press, 1979), p. 16.

41 Marilyn Adams, *Horrendous Evils and the Goodness of God*, p. 55.

42 Alvin Plantinga, "Supralapsarianism or *O Felix Culpa*," ms.

43 This paper benefitted from questions and comments at the conference at Yale University at which it was first presented, and from discussions at the University of San Francisco and at the University of Minnesota, Morris. Thanks in addition to Michael Bergmann, David Christensen, Mark Moyer, Daniel Howard-Snyder, Andrew Chignell and Andrew Dole for helpful commentary.

Chapter 24

William Lane Craig

THE MIDDLE-KNOWLEDGE VIEW

The climax of Charles Dickens's wonderful classic *A Christmas Carol* comes when Scrooge, shaken by the scenes shown him by the Spirit of Christmas Yet to Come, pleads, "Answer me one question. Are these the shadows of the things that Will be, or are they shadows of things that May be, only?"[1] The ghost does not speak a word in answer to Scrooge.

And with good reason! For had the spirit responded, "These shadows are merely scenes of things that could be," Scrooge might well have breathed a sigh of relief and gone on with his life as before. "After all," he might quite rightly reflect, "almost anything *could* happen! No need to lose sleep about that!" On the other hand, if the spirit had told him candidly, "No, these shadows are not scenes of things that will be" (as we know to be true from the story's end), then Scrooge might have felt no cause for alarm at all, since none of what he had witnessed would in fact come to pass. In that case, he might not have been led to repent and change his life.

Scrooge's problem was that he was asking the wrong question; he had failed to exhaust the alternatives. For between what *could* be and what *will* be lies what *would be*. What the spirit was revealing to Scrooge was what *would* happen if Scrooge did not repent and change. The spirit was not exhibiting mere possibilities (it was *possible* that Scrooge would sell his business and open a flower stand in Covent Garden, but who cares about that?), nor was he showing Scrooge what was in fact going to happen (Dickens assures us that Tiny Tim did *not* die). Rather the spirit was warning Scrooge that if he did not repent, all these terrible things would come to pass.

In philosophical terminology, the spirit was revealing to Scrooge a bit of *counterfactual* knowledge. Counterfactuals are conditional statements in the subjunctive mood: for example, "If I were rich, I would buy a Mercedes"; "If Barry Goldwater had been elected president, he would have won the Vietnam War"; and "If you were to ask her, she would say yes." Counterfactuals are so called because the antecedent or consequent clauses are typically contrary to fact: I am not rich, Goldwater was not elected president, and the U.S. did not win the Vietnam War. Nevertheless, sometimes the antecedent and/or consequent is true. For example, your friend wants to ask the girl of his dreams for a date and, emboldened by your reassurance that "If you were to ask her, she would say yes," does ask her and she does say yes.

Counterfactual statements make up an enormous and significant part of our ordinary language and are an indispensable part of our decision making: For example, "If I pulled out into traffic now, I wouldn't make it"; "If I were to ask J. B. for a raise with his mood, he'd tear my head off"; "If we sent the Third Army around the enemy's right flank, we would prevail."

Clearly life-and-death decisions are made daily on the basis of the presumed truth of counterfactual statements.

The Doctrine of Middle Knowledge

Christian theologians have typically affirmed that in virtue of his omniscience, God possesses counterfactual knowledge. He knows, for example, what would have happened if he had spared the Canaanites from destruction, what Napoleon would have done had he won the Battle of Waterloo, and how Jones would respond if I were to share the gospel with him. Not until Friedrich Schleiermacher and the advent of modern theology did theologians think to deny God knowledge of true counterfactuals. Everyone who had considered the issue agreed that God has such knowledge.

What theologians did dispute, however, was, so to speak, *when* God has such counterfactual knowledge. The question here did not have to do with the moment of time at which God acquired his counterfactual knowledge. For whether God is timeless or everlasting throughout time, in neither case are there truths that are unknown to God until some moment at which he discovers them. As an omniscient being, God must know every truth there is and so can never exist in a state of ignorance. Rather the "when" mentioned above refers to the point in the *logical* order concerning God's creative decree at which God has counterfactual knowledge.

This idea of a logical order with regard to God's decrees is a familiar one to Reformed theologians. For although all God's decrees occur at once rather than sequentially, there is a logical order among the decrees. For example, infralapsarians say that God decreed Christ's death on the cross in order to remedy humanity's fall into sin, so that logically God's decree of the cross comes after his decree of the fall. By contrast, supralapsarians say that God's primary aim for humankind was redemption via the cross, and therefore he decreed the fall in order to have

something to redeem humans from. On this scheme, the decree of the cross is logically prior to the decree of the fall. Thus even though it was agreed on all hands that God's decrees occur all at once, theologians debated how they were to be logically arranged.

A similar dispute existed among post-Reformation theologians with respect to the place of God's counterfactual knowledge. Everybody agreed that logically prior to God's decree to create a world, God has knowledge of all necessary truths, including all the possible worlds he might create. This was called God's *natural knowledge*. It gives him knowledge of what *could* be. Moreover, everyone agreed that logically subsequent to his decree to create a particular world, God knows all the contingent truths about the actual world, including its past, present and future. This was called God's *free knowledge*. It involves knowledge of what *will* be. The disputed question was where one should place God's counterfactual knowledge of what *would* be. Is it logically prior to or posterior to the divine decree?

Catholic theologians of the Dominican order held that God's counterfactual knowledge is logically *subsequent* to his decree to create a certain world. They maintained that in decreeing that a particular world exist, God also decreed which counterfactual statements are true. Logically prior to the divine decree, there are no counterfactual truths to be known. All God knows at that logical moment are the necessary truths, including all the various possibilities.

At that logically prior moment God knows, for example, that there is a possible world in which Peter denies Christ three times, and another possible world in which Peter affirms Christ, and yet another world in which it is Matthew who denies Christ three times, and so on. God picks one of these worlds to be actual, and thus subsequent to his decree it is true that Peter will deny Christ three times. Moreover, God knows this truth because he knows which world he has decreed. Not only so, but in decreeing a particular world to be real, God also decrees which counterfactuals are true. Thus he decrees, for example, that if Peter had instead been in such-and-such circumstances, he would have denied Christ two times. God's counterfactual knowledge, like his foreknowledge, is logically posterior to the divine creative decree.

By contrast, Catholic theologians of the Jesuit order inspired by Luis de Molina maintained that God's counterfactual knowledge is logically *prior* to his creative decree. This difference between the Jesuit Molinists and the Dominicans was no mere matter of theological hair-splitting! The Molinists charged that the Dominicans had in effect obliterated human freedom by making counterfactual truths a consequence of God's decree, for on the Dominican account it is God who determines what each person will do in whatever circumstances he finds himself. By contrast, the Molinists, by placing God's counterfactual knowledge prior to the divine decree, made room for creaturely freedom by exempting counterfactual truths from God's decree. In the same way that necessary truths like $2 + 2 = 4$ are prior to and therefore independent of God's decree, so also counterfactual truths about how creatures would freely choose under various circumstances are prior to and independent of God's decree.

Not only does the Molinist view make room for human freedom, but it affords God a means of choosing which world of free creatures to create. For by knowing how persons would freely choose in whatever circumstances they might be in, God can—by decreeing to place just those persons in just those circumstances —bring about his ultimate purposes through free creaturely decisions. Thus, by employing his counterfactual knowledge, God can plan a world down to the last detail and yet do so without annihilating creaturely freedom, since what people would freely do under various circumstances is already factored into the equation by God. Since God's counterfactual knowledge lies logically in between his natural knowledge and his free knowledge, Molinists called it God's *middle knowledge*.

On the Dominican view, there is one logical moment prior to the divine creative decree at which God knows the range of possible worlds that he might create; then he chooses one of these to be actual. On the Molinist view, there are two logical moments prior to the divine decree: first, the moment at which he has natural knowledge of the range of possible worlds, and second, the moment at which he has knowledge of the proper subset of possible worlds that, given the counterfactuals true at that moment, are feasible for him to create. The counterfactuals which are true at that moment thus serve to delimit the range of possible worlds to worlds feasible for God.

For example, there is a possible world in which Peter affirms Christ in precisely the same circumstances in which he in fact denied him. But given the counterfactual truth that if Peter were in precisely those circumstances he would freely deny Christ, then the possible world in which Peter freely affirms Christ in those circumstances is not feasible for God. God could *make* Peter affirm Christ in those circumstances, but then his confession would not be free.

Thus on the Molinist scheme, we have the following logical order:

Moment 1: . . . O O O O O O O . . .
Natural knowledge: God knows the range of possible worlds.

Moment 2: . . .   O   O   O   . . .
Middle knowledge: God knows the range of feasible worlds.

Divine creative decree

Moment 3:   O
Free knowledge: God knows the actual world.

Arguments for Middle Knowledge

Why should one think that the Molinist scheme is correct? Two lines of argument—theological and philosophical—may be adduced in support of the Molinist position. Let us consider each in turn. [. . .]

Theological Arguments

The strongest arguments for the Molinist perspective are theological. Once one grasps the concept of middle knowledge, one will find it astonishing in its subtlety and power. Indeed, I would venture to say that it is the single most fruitful theological concept I have ever encountered. In my own work, I have applied it to the issues of Christian particularism, perseverance of the saints and biblical inspiration.[2] Thomas Flint has used it to analyze infallibility; and Del Ratzsch has used it to explore evolutionary theory.[3] An article begs to be written on a Molinist perspective of quantum indeterminacy and divine sovereignty. With respect to the concerns of this book, middle knowledge provides an illuminating account of divine foreknowledge and providence.

Divine Foreknowledge

The doctrine of divine foreknowledge raises two questions: First, is divine foreknowledge compatible with future contingents? And second, how can God know future contingents? Though I think that acceptable answers to these questions are available to the defender of simple foreknowledge, it is worth laying out a Molinist perspective as well.

The Compatibility of Divine Foreknowledge and Future Contingents

With respect to the first question, it must be the case that divine foreknowledge and future contingents (in particular, human free acts) are compatible for the simple reason that Scripture teaches both.[4] When so-called openness theologians dispute this compatibility, their denial is clearly driven not by biblical exegesis but by a philosophical argument derived from ancient Greek fatalism and dressed in theological guise; biblical exegesis is being bent to support a conclusion already determined by philosophical considerations. This is ironic since these same theologians loudly decry the polluting influence of Greek philosophical thought upon the biblical tradition. In fact, it is they themselves who have been seduced by philosophical reasoning of Greek provenance, which was stoutly resisted by the early church fathers. If openness theologians are not convinced by the proffered solutions to fatalism, then it is the better part of intellectual humility simply to confess that one lacks the philosophical insight to solve the problem (cf. Ps 139:6) and hold the biblical doctrines in tension rather than deny the Scripture's clear teaching that God does know the future.[5]

So what is the argument that allegedly demonstrates the incompatibility of divine foreknowledge and human freedom? Letting x stand for any event, the basic form of the argument is as follows:

1 Necessarily, if God foreknows x, then x will happen.
2 God foreknows x.
3 Therefore, x will necessarily happen.

Since x happens necessarily, it is not a contingent event. In virtue of God's foreknowledge, everything is fated to occur.

The problem with the above form of the argument is that it is just logically fallacious. What is validly implied by (1) and (2) is not (3) but (3'):

3' Therefore, x will happen.

The fatalist gets things all mixed up here. It is correct that in a valid, deductive argument the premises necessarily imply the conclusion. The conclusion follows necessarily from the premises; that is to say, it is impossible for the premises to be true and the conclusion to be false. But the conclusion itself need not be necessary. The fatalist illicitly transfers the necessity of the *inference* to the conclusion *itself*. What necessarily follows from (1) and (2) is just (3'). But the fatalist in his confusion thinks that the conclusion is itself necessarily true and so winds up with (3). In so doing he simply commits a common logical fallacy.

The correct conclusion, (3'), is in no way incompatible with human freedom. From God's knowledge that I shall do x, it does not follow that I must do x but only that I shall do x. That is in no way incompatible with my doing x freely.

Undoubtedly, a major source of the fatalist's confusion is his conflating *certainty* with *necessity*. In the writings of contemporary theological fatalists, one frequently finds statements which slide from affirming that something is *certainly* true to affirming that something is *necessarily* true. This is sheer confusion. Certainty is a property of persons and has nothing to do with truth, as is evident from the fact that we can be absolutely certain about something that turns out to be false. By contrast, necessity is a property of statements or propositions, indicating that a proposition cannot possibly be false. We can be wholly uncertain about statements that are, unbeknownst to us, necessarily true (for example, some complex mathematical equation or theorem). Thus, when we say that some statement is "certainly true," this is but a manner of speaking indicating that we are certain the statement is true. People are certain; propositions are necessary.

By confusing certainty and necessity, the fatalist makes his logically fallacious argument deceptively appealing. For it is correct that from (1) and (2) we can be absolutely certain that x will come to pass. But it is muddle-headed to think that because x will certainly happen then x will necessarily happen. We can be certain, given God's foreknowledge, that x will not fail to

happen, even though it is entirely possible that x fail to happen. Event x could fail to occur, but God knows that it will not. Therefore, we can be sure that it will happen—and happen contingently.

Contemporary theological fatalists recognize the fallaciousness of the above form of the argument and therefore try to remedy the defect by making (2) also necessarily true:

1. Necessarily, if God foreknows x, then x will happen.
2'. Necessarily, God foreknows x.
3. Therefore, x will necessarily happen.

So formulated, the argument is no longer logically fallacious, and so the question becomes whether the premises are true.

Premise (1) is clearly true. It is perhaps worth noting that this is the case not because of God's essential omniscience or inerrancy but simply in virtue of the definition of "knowledge." Since knowledge entails true belief, anybody's knowing that x will happen necessarily implies that x will happen. Thus, we could replace (1) and (2') with the following:

1*. Necessarily, if Smith truly believes that x will happen, then x will happen.
2*. Necessarily, Smith truly believes that x will happen.

And (3) will follow as before. Therefore, if any person ever holds true beliefs about the future (and surely we do, as we smugly remind others when we say, "I told you so!"), then, given the truth of (2), fatalism would also follow from merely human beliefs, a curious conclusion!

Indeed, as ancient Greek fatalists realized, the presence of any agent at all is really superfluous to the argument. All one needs is a true, future-tense statement to get the argument going. Thus, we could replace (1) and (2') with this:

1**. Necessarily, if it is true that x will happen, then x will happen.

2**   Necessarily, it is true that x will happen.

And we shall get (3) as our conclusion. Thus, philosopher Susan Haack quite rightly calls the argument for theological fatalism "a needlessly (and confusingly) elaborated version" of Greek fatalism, and she says that the addition of an omniscient God to the argument constitutes a "gratuitous detour" around the real issue, which is the truth or falsity of future-tense statements.[6]

In order to avoid the above generalization of their argument to all persons and to mere statements about the future, theological fatalists will deny that the second premise is true with respect to humans or mere statements, as it is for God. They will say that Smith's holding a true belief or some future-tense statement's being true is not necessary in the way that God's holding a belief is necessary.

That raises the question as to whether (2') is true. At face value, (2') is obviously false. Christian theology has always maintained that God's creation of the world is a free act, that God could have created a different world—in which x does not occur—or even no world at all. To say that God necessarily foreknows any event x implies that this is the only world God could have created and thus denies divine freedom.

But theological fatalists have a different sort of necessity in mind when they say that God's foreknowledge is necessary. They are talking about *temporal necessity*, or the necessity of the past. Often this is expressed by saying that the past is unpreventable or unchangeable. If some event is in the past, then it is now too late to do anything to affect it. It is in that sense necessary. Since God's foreknowledge of future events is now part of the past, it is now fixed and unalterable. Therefore, it is said, (2') is true.

But if (2') is true in that sense, then why are not (2*) and (2**) true as well? The theological fatalist will respond that Smith's belief's being true or a future-tense statement's being true is not a fact or an event of the past, as is God's holding a belief.

But such an understanding of what constitutes a fact or event seems quite counterintuitive. If Smith believed in 1997 that "Clinton will be impeached," was it not a fact that his belief was true? If Smith held that same belief today, would it not be a fact that his belief is no longer true (since Clinton has left office)? If Smith's belief changes from being true to being false, then surely it was a fact that it was then true and is a fact that it is now false. The same obviously goes for the mere statement "Clinton will be impeached." This statement once had the property of being true and now has the property of being false. In any reasonable sense of "fact," these are past and present facts.

Indeed, a statement's having a truth value is plausibly an event as well. This is most obvious with respect to statements like "Flight 4750 to Paris will depart in five minutes." That statement is false up until it is five minutes prior to departure, it becomes true at five minutes till departure, and then it becomes false again immediately thereafter. Other statements' being true may be more long-lasting events, like "Flight 4750 to Paris will depart within the next hour." Such a statement's being true is clearly an event on any reasonable construal of what constitutes an event.

No theological fatalist whom I have read has even begun to address the question of the nature of facts or events which would make it plausible that Smith's truly believing a future-tense statement and a future-tense statement's being true do not count as past facts or events. But then we see that theological fatalism is not inherently theological at all. If the theological fatalist's reasoning is correct, it can be generalized to show that every time we hold a true belief about the future or every time a statement about the future is true, then the future is fated to occur—surely an incredible inference!

Moreover, we have the best of reasons for thinking that (2') is defective in some way: namely, fatalism posits a constraint on human freedom that is unintelligible. For the fatalist admits that the events God foreknows may be causally indeterminate; indeed, they could theoretically be completely uncaused, spontaneous events. Nevertheless, such events are said to be somehow constrained. But by what? Fate? What is that but a mere name? If my action is causally free, how can it be constrained by God's merely knowing about it?

Sometimes fatalists say that God's foreknowledge places a sort of logical constraint on my action. Even though I am causally free to refrain from my action, there is some sort of logical constraint upon me, rendering it impossible for me to refrain. But insofar as we can make sense of logical constraints, these constraints are not analogous to the sort of necessitation imagined by the theological fatalist. For example, given the fact that I have already played basketball at least once in my life, it is now impossible for me to play basketball for the first time. I am thus not free to go out and play basketball for the first time. But this sort of constraint is not at all analogous to theological fatalism. For in the case we are envisioning, it is within my power to play basketball or not. Whether or not I've played before, I can freely execute the actions of playing basketball. It's just that if I have played before, my actions will not *count* as playing for the first time. By contrast, the fatalist imagines that if God knows that I shall not play basketball, then even though I am causally free, my actions are mysteriously constrained so that I am literally unable to walk out onto the court, dribble and shoot. But such noncausal determinism is utterly opaque and unintelligible.

The argument for fatalism must therefore be unsound. Since (1) is clearly true, the trouble must lie with (2'). And (2') is notoriously problematic. For the notion of temporal necessity to which the fatalist appeals is so obscure a concept that (2') becomes a veritable mare's nest of philosophical difficulties. For example, since the necessity of (1) is logical necessity and the necessity of (2') is temporal necessity, why think that such mixing of different kinds of modality is valid? If the fatalist answers that logical necessity

entails temporal necessity, so that (1) can be construed merely in terms of temporal necessity, then how do we know that such necessity is passed on from the premises to the conclusion in the way that logical necessity is? Indeed, since *x* is supposed to be a future event, how *could* it be temporally necessary? And even if *x* is temporally necessary, how do we know that this sort of necessity is incompatible with an action's being free? So long as a person's choice is causally undetermined, it is a free choice even if that person is unable to choose the opposite of that choice.[7] So even if *x* were temporally necessary, such that not-*x* cannot occur, it is far from obvious that *x* is not freely performed or chosen.

All of the above problems arise even if we concede (2') to be true. But why think that this premise is true? What is temporal necessity anyway, and why think that God's past beliefs are now temporally necessary? Theological fatalists have never provided an adequate account of this peculiar modality. I have yet to see an explanation of temporal necessity according to which God's past beliefs are temporally necessary that does not reduce to either the *unalterability* or the *causal closedness* of the past.

But interpreting the necessity of the past as its unalterability (or unchangability or unpreventability) is clearly inadequate, since the future, by definition, is just as unalterable as the past. To *change* the future would be to bring it about that an event which will occur will not occur, which is self-contradictory. It is purely a matter of definition that the past and future cannot be changed, and no fatalistic conclusion follows from this truth. We need not be able to *change* the future in order to *determine* the future. If our actions are freely performed, then it lies within our power to determine what the course of future events will be, even if we do not have the power to change the future.

Fatalists will insist that the past is necessary in the sense that we do not have a similar ability to determine the past. Nonfatalists may happily concede the point: backward causation is impossible. But the past's causal closedness does not imply fatalism. For freedom to refrain from doing as God knows one will do does not involve backward causation.

Here we come to the Molinist solution to theological fatalism. The Molinist is quite glad to admit that nothing I can do now will cause or bring about the past. But he will insist that it does lie within my power to freely perform some action *a*, and if *a* were to occur, then the past would have been different than it in fact is. Suppose, for example, that God has always believed that in the year 2000 I would accept an invitation to speak at the University of Regensburg. Up until the time arrives I have the ability to accept or refuse the invitation. If I were to refuse the invitation, then God would have held a different belief than the one he in fact held. For if I were to refuse the invitation, then different counterfactual propositions would have been true, and God would have known this via his middle knowledge. Neither the relation between my action and a corresponding counterfactual proposition about it, nor the relation between a true counterfactual proposition and God's believing it, is a causal relation. Thus, the causal closedness of the past is irrelevant. If temporal necessity is merely the causal closedness of the past, then it is insufficient to support fatalism.

To my knowledge, no fatalist has explicated a conception of temporal necessity that does not amount to either the unalterability or the causal closedness of the past. Typically, fatalists just appeal gratuitously to some sort of "Fixed Past Principle" to the effect that it is not within my power to act in such a way, and that if I were to do so, then the past would have been different— which begs the question. On analyses of temporal necessity that are not reducible to either the unalterability or the causal closedness of the past, God's past beliefs always turn out *not* to be temporally necessary.[8] The Molinist accounts for this in terms of God's middle knowledge, which infallibly tracks true counterfactual propositions concerning our free choices.

Thus, the argument for theological fatalism is unsound. The doctrine of middle knowledge helps to make the compatibility of divine foreknowledge and human freedom perspicuous.

The Basis of Divine Foreknowledge of Future Contingents

What, then, about the second question raised by divine foreknowledge, namely, the basis of God's knowledge of future contingents? Detractors of divine foreknowledge sometimes claim that because future events do not exist, they cannot be known by God. The reasoning seems to go as follows:

1   Only events that actually exist can be known by God.
2   Future events do not actually exist.
3   Therefore, future events cannot be known by God.

Now (2) is not uncontroversial. A good many physicists and philosophers of time and space argue that future events do exist. They claim that the difference between past, present and future is merely a subjective matter of human consciousness. For the people in the year 2015, the events of that year are just as real as the events of our present year are for us; and for those people, it is we who have passed away and are unreal. On such a view God transcends the four-dimensional space-time continuum, and thus all events are eternally present to him. It is easy on such a view to understand how God could therefore know events that to us are in the future.

Nevertheless, I do think that such a four-dimensional view of really faces insuperable philosophical and theological objections, which I have discussed elsewhere.[9] Therefore, I am inclined to agree with (2) of the above argument. So the question becomes whether there is good reason to think that (1) is true.

In assessing the question of how God knows which events will transpire, it is helpful to distinguish two models of divine cognition: the *perceptualist* model and the *conceptualist* model. The perceptualist model construes divine knowledge on the analogy of sense perception. God looks and sees what is there. Such a model is implicitly assumed when people speak of God's "foresee-ing" the future or having "foresight" of future events. The perceptualist model of divine cogni-tion does run into real problems when it comes to God's knowledge of the future, for, since future events do not exist, there is nothing there to perceive.

By contrast, on a conceptualist model of div-ine knowledge, God does not acquire his know-ledge of the world by anything like perception. His knowledge of the future is not based on his "looking" ahead and "seeing" what lies in the future (a terribly anthropomorphic notion in any case). Rather God's knowledge is self-contained; it is more like a mind's knowledge of innate ideas. As an omniscient being, God has essen-tially the property of knowing all truths; there are truths about future events; thus, God knows all truths concerning future events.

Middle knowledge can help us understand how God knows truths about the future. Divine foreknowledge is based on God's middle know-ledge of what every creature would freely do under any circumstances and on his knowledge of the divine decree to create certain sets of circumstances and to place certain creatures in them. Given middle knowledge and the divine decree, foreknowledge follows automatically as a result.

Of course, the skeptic may ask how God knows counterfactuals concerning human free choices if those choices do not exist. Molinists could respond either that God knows the indi-vidual essence of every possible creature so well that he knows just what each creature would do under any set of circumstances he might place him in, or that God, being omniscient, simply discerns all the truths there are and, prior to the divine decree, there are not only necessary truths but counterfactual truths, and therefore

God possesses not only natural knowledge but middle knowledge as well.

So long as we are not seduced into thinking of divine foreknowledge on the model of percep-tion, it is no longer evident why knowledge of future events should be impossible. A con-ceptualist model along the lines of middle know-ledge furnishes a perspicuous basis for God's knowledge of future contingents.

Thus, both with respect to the problem of theological fatalism and the question of the basis of divine foreknowledge, the Molinist doctrine of middle knowledge provides an illuminating account of God's foreknowledge.

Divine Providence

The Molinist account of divine providence is even more stunning than its account of divine foreknowledge. Here its superiority to the doc-trine of simple foreknowledge emerges. [. . .]

If we take the term *foreknowledge* as encom-passing middle knowledge, then we can make perfect sense of God's providential control over a world of free agents. For via his middle know-ledge, God knew exactly which persons, if members of the Sanhedrin, would freely vote for Jesus' condemnation; which persons, if in Jerusalem, would freely demand Christ's death, favoring the release of Barabbas; what Herod, if king, would freely do in reaction to Jesus and to Pilate's plea to judge him on his own; and what Pilate himself, if holding the prefecture of Palestine in A.D. 27, would freely do under pres-sure from the Jewish leaders and the crowd. Knowing all the possible circumstances, persons and permutations of these circumstances and persons, God decreed to create just those circum-stances and just those people who would freely do what God willed to happen. Thus, the whole scenario, as Luke insists, unfolded according to *God's plan*. This is truly mind-boggling. When one reflects that the existence of the various circum-stances and persons involved was itself the result of a myriad of prior free choices on the part of these and other agents, and these in turn of yet other prior contingencies, and so on, then we see that only an omniscient mind could providentially direct a world of free creatures toward his sovereignly established ends. [. . .]

Now what account of divine providence can be given in the absence of middle knowledge? Advocates of divine openness freely admit that without middle knowledge, a strong doctrine of divine providence becomes impossible. But such a viewpoint can make no sense whatsoever of scriptural passages such as those cited above. I am bewildered that partisans of this camp can deny divine foreknowledge while claiming to be biblical, when, as seen above, "foreknowledge" is part of the very *vocabulary* of the New Testament. Nor can it be said that God's plan was hit upon by him late in the game, once he could reasonably guess what the relevant agents would do. [. . .]

The Augustinian-Calvinist perspective interprets the above passages to mean that foreknowledge is based upon foreordination: God knows what will happen because he makes it happen. Aware of the intentions of his will and his almighty power, God knows that all his purpose shall be accomplished. But this interpretation inevitably makes God the author of sin, since it is he who moved Judas, for example, to betray Christ, a sin that merits the hapless Judas everlasting perdition. But how can a holy God move people to commit moral evil and, moreover, how can these people then be held morally responsible for acts over which they had no control? The Augustinian-Calvinist view seems, in effect, to turn God into the devil.

The proponent of simple foreknowledge can make no good sense of God's providentially planning a world of free creatures. For logically prior to the divine decree, God has natural knowledge of all the possible scenarios, but he does not have knowledge of what would happen under any circumstances. Thus, logically posterior to the divine decree, God must consider himself extraordinarily lucky to find that this

world happened to exist. ("What a break!" we can imagine God saying to himself, "Herod and Pilate and all those people each reacted just perfectly!") Actually, the situation is such worse than that, for God had no idea whether Herod or Pilate or the Israelite nation or the Roman Empire would even exist posterior to the divine decree. Indeed, God must be astonished to find himself existing in a world—out of all the possible worlds he could have created—in which mankind falls into sin and he himself enters human history as a substitutionary sacrificial offering to rescue them! Of course, I am speaking anthropomorphically here; but the point remains that without middle knowledge, God cannot know prior to the creative decree what the world would be like. If the defender of simple foreknowledge goes on to say that God's foreordination of future events is based upon his simple foreknowledge, then this trivializes the doctrine of foreordination, making it a fifth wheel that carries no load since, as we have seen, the future by definition cannot be changed. Once God knows that an event really is future, there is nothing more left to do; foreordination becomes a redundancy. Surely, there is more substance to the biblical doctrine of foreordination than the triviality that God decrees that what will happen will happen!

Thus of the options available, the Molinist approach provides by far the most elucidating account of divine providence. It enables us to embrace divine sovereignty and human freedom without mysticism or mental reservation, thereby preserving faithfully the biblical text's affirmation of both these doctrines. We therefore have powerful theological motivation for adopting the Molinist perspective.

Philosophical Arguments

Finally, I think that we also have good philosophical grounds for thinking that a doctrine of middle knowledge is correct. We may argue as follows:

1   If there are true counterfactuals of creaturely freedom, then God knows these truths.

2   There are true counterfactuals of creaturely freedom.

3   If God knows true counterfactuals of creaturely freedom, God knows them either logically prior to the divine creative decree or only logically posterior to the divine creative decree.

4   Counterfactuals of creaturely freedom cannot be known only logically posterior to the divine creative decree.

From (1) and (2) it follows logically that

5   Therefore, God knows true counterfactuals of creaturely freedom.

From (3) and (5) it follows that

6   Therefore, God knows true counterfactuals of creaturely freedom either logically prior to the divine creative decree or only logically posterior to the divine creative decree.

And from (4) and (6) it follows that

7   Therefore, God knows true counterfactuals of creaturely freedom logically prior to the divine creative decree

which is the essence of the doctrine of divine middle knowledge.

Let us say a word in defense of each of the argument's premises. The truth of (1) is required by the definition of omniscience:

(O)   For any agent x, x is omniscient $=_{def}$. For every proposition p, if p, then x knows that p and does not believe not-p.

What (O) requires is that any agent is omniscient if and only if he knows all truths and believes no falsehoods. This is the standard definition of omniscience. It entails that if there are counterfactual truths, then an omniscient being must know them.

Opponents of divine foreknowledge have suggested revisionary definitions of omniscience so as to be able to affirm that God is omniscient even as they deny his knowledge of future contingents (and counterfactuals of creaturely freedom).[10] William Hasker's revisionist definition is typical:

(O′)   God is omniscient $=_{def}$. God knows all propositions which are such that God's knowing them is logically possible.

Revisionists then go on to claim that it is logically impossible to know propositions about future contingents, as shown by the argument for theological fatalism, and so God may count as omniscient despite his ignorance of an infinite number of true propositions.

As it stands, however, (O′) is drastically flawed. It does not exclude that God believes false propositions as well as true ones. Worse, (O′) actually requires God to know false propositions, which is incoherent as well as theologically unacceptable. For (O′) requires that if it is logically possible for God to know some proposition p, then God knows p. But if p is a contingently false proposition, say, *There are eight planets in the sun's solar system*, then there are possible worlds in which p is true and known by God. Therefore, since it is logically possible for God to know p, he must actually know p, which is absurd.

What the revisionist really wants to say is something like this:

(O″)   God is omniscient $=_{def}$. God knows only and all true propositions which are such that it is logically possible for God to know them.

Unlike (O′), (O″) limits God's knowledge to a certain subset of all true propositions.

The fundamental problem with all such

revisionary definitions of omniscience as (O″) is that any adequate definition of a concept must accord with our intuitive understanding of the concept. We are not at liberty to "cook" the definition in some desired way without thereby making the definition unacceptably contrived. Definition (O″) is guilty of being "cooked" in this way. For intuitively, omniscience involves knowing all truth, yet according to (O″) God could conceivably be ignorant of infinite realms of truth and yet still count as omniscient. The only reason why one would prefer (O″) to (O) is because one has an ulterior motivation to salvage the attribute of omniscience for a cognitively limited deity rather than to deny outright that God is omniscient. Definition (O″) is therefore unacceptably contrived.

A second problem with (O″) is that it construes omniscience in modal terms, speaking, not of knowing all truth, but of knowing all truth which is knowable. But omniscience, unlike omnipotence, is not a modal notion. Roughly speaking, omnipotence is the capability of actualizing any logically possible state of affairs. But omniscience is not merely the *capability* of knowing only and all truths; it *is* knowing only and all truths. Nor does omniscience mean knowing only and all knowable truths, but knowing only and all truths, period. It is a categorical, not a modal, notion.

Third, the superiority of (O″) over (O) depends on there being a difference between a truth and a truth that is logically possible to know. If there is no difference, then (O″) collapses back to the general definition (O) and the revisionist has gained nothing. What is a sufficient condition for a proposition to be logically knowable? So far as I can see, the only condition is that the proposition be true. What more is needed? If revisionists think that something more is needed, then we may ask them for an example of a proposition that could be true but logically impossible to know. A proposition like "Nothing exists" or "All agents have ceased to exist" comes to mind; but on traditional theism

these propositions are not possibly true, since God is an agent whose nonexistence is impossible. Unless the revisionist can give us some reason to think that a proposition can be true yet unknowable, we have no reason to adopt (O″). It seems that the only intrinsic property that a proposition must possess in order to be logically knowable is truth.

The revisionist will claim at this point that true future contingent propositions are logically impossible for God to know, since if he knows them, then they are not contingently true, as shown by the fatalistic argument.[11] But here the revisionist commits a logical howler. He reasons that for any future-tense proposition *p* it is impossible that God know *p* and *p* be contingently true; therefore, if *p* is contingently true, it is not possible that God knows *p*. But such reasoning is logically fallacious. What follows is merely that God does not know *p*, not that it is impossible that God knows *p*. Thus, even *granted* the fatalist's false premise (that it is impossible that God know *p* and *p* be contingently true), it does not follow from *p*'s contingent truth that *p* is such that it is logically impossible for God to know *p*. Therefore, even on the defective definition (O″) proposed by the revisionist, God turns out not to be omniscient, since *p* is a true proposition that, so far as we can see, is logically possible for God to know, and yet God does not know *p*. Thus, the theological fatalist must deny divine omniscience and therefore reject God's perfection—a very serious theological consequence, indeed.

So with regard to the first premise of our philosophical argument, omniscience requires that if there are true counterfactuals of creaturely freedom, God must know them.

Premise (2) asserts that there are true counterfactuals of creaturely freedom. This premise does not require us to believe that all counterfactuals about creatures' free acts are either true or false. But it does seem plausible that counterfactuals of the following from are either true or false (letting *p* be any person, *A* some action and

C any set of circumstances including the whole history of the world up until the point of decision):

(CCF)   If P were in C, P would freely do A.

It is counterfactuals of this form that we dignify with the title "counterfactuals of creaturely freedom."

We have every reason to think that there are true counterfactuals of creaturely freedom. In the first place, it is plausible, as I say, that counterfactuals of the form (CCF) are true or false. For once the circumstances are fully specified, any ambiguity which might cause us to doubt that the counterfactual has a truth value is removed. And it is plausible that in many cases P would freely do A in C, just as the counterfactual states. Second, we ourselves often know the truth of such counterfactuals. For example, if I were to offer my wife a plate of chocolate-chip cookies and a plate of liver and onions, I know which one she would choose as surely as I know almost anything! A little reflection reveals how pervasive and indispensable such counterfactual truths are to rational conduct and planning. We base our very lives upon their truth or falsity. [. . .]

The most common objection urged against the truth of counterfactuals of creaturely freedom is the so-called grounding objection. The basic complaint here is that there is nothing to make such counterfactuals true (since they are supposed to be true logically prior to God's creative decree and even now are usually contrary-to-fact); but without a ground of their truth, they cannot be true.

Thomas Flint, an eminent defender of middle knowledge, has rightly observed that the grounding objection is, in the minds of many philosophers, the principal obstacle to endorsing a Molinist perspective.[12] It is therefore all the more remarkable that this objection is virtually never articulated or defended in any depth by its advocates. No anti-Molinist to my knowledge has yet responded to Alvin Plantinga's simple retort: "It seems to me much clearer that some counterfactuals of freedom are at least possibly true than that the truth of propositions must, in general, be grounded in this way."[13] What Plantinga understands—and what the grounding objectors generally do not—is that behind the grounding objection sticks a theory about the relationship of truth and reality that is both subtle and controversial and that needs to be articulated, defended and applied to counterfactuals of creaturely freedom if the grounding objection is to have any force. Anti-Molinists have not even begun to address these issues.

The theory presupposed by the grounding objection is a particular construal of truth as correspondence known among contemporary philosophers as the theory of truth-makers.[14] According to a view of truth as correspondence, a statement is true if and only if reality is as that statement describes. In order to identify the reality corresponding to a true statement, one typically employs the method of disquotation: the statement "Snow is white," for example, is true if and only if snow is white. During the revival of the correspondence theory of truth in the early part of the twentieth century, philosophers such as Bertrand Russell and Ludwig Wittgenstein maintained that there must exist not only truth-bearers (whether these be sentences or thoughts or propositions or what have you) which have the property of being true and so corresponding with reality, but also something in reality in virtue of which the sentences or propositions are true. This interpretation of the correspondence theory was taken up again in the 1980s as the theory of truth-makers.

A truth-maker may be defined as *that in virtue of which a sentence or proposition is true*. Immediately we see the potentially misleading connotations of the term *truth-maker*. The word *making* suggests a causal relation involving some concrete object, but truth-makers are not normally so conceived by their advocates. Instead truth-makers are typically construed to be abstract realities like "facts" or "states of affairs"—more often than not, the fact stated as the truth conditions of a proposition, as disclosed by disquotation. Thus, what makes the statement "Snow is white" true is the fact that snow is white or the state of affairs of snow's being white. Such abstract entities do not stand in causal relations. This invalidates at a single swoop the crude construal of the grounding objection expressed in Robert Adams's demand, "Who or what does cause them [counterfactuals of creaturely freedom] to be true?"[15] The question is inept because the relation between a proposition and its truth-maker is not a causal relation.

The grounding objector seems to think that in order to be true, counterfactuals of creaturely freedom must have truth-makers that either are or imply the existence of physical objects. But this assumption seems quite unwarranted, since we can think of other types of possibly true propositions whose truth-makers neither are nor imply physical objects. For example:

1 No physical objects exist.
2 Dinosaurs are extinct today.
3 All ravens are black.
4 Torturing a child is wrong.
5 Napoleon lost the Battle of Waterloo.
6 The U.S. president in 2070 will be a woman.
7 If a rigid rod were placed in uniform motion through the ether, it would suffer a Lorentz-FitzGerald contraction.

Statement 1 could be true and statement 2 is true, yet they preclude truth-makers that imply the relevant physical objects, such as dinosaurs. Statement 3 is a universal statement which does not apply just to any ravens that happen to exist and so cannot be made true just by any existing ravens' being black. Statement 4 is a value judgment which implies neither that children do exist nor that any are actually tortured. Statements 5 and 6 are true tensed statements about persons who no longer or do not yet exist and so cannot have such persons among their truth-makers.

Finally, statement 7 is a true counterfactual about the ether of nineteenth-century physics, which does not exist. These statements reveal just how naive an understanding grounding objectors have of the notion of truth-makers. For if these statements have truth-makers, their truth-makers are not physical objects out there in the world but are abstract entities like states of affairs or facts.

Now, as I say, it is a matter of debate whether true propositions do have truth-makers. In a recent critique, Greg Restall demonstrates that given the customary axioms of truth-maker theory, it follows that every true proposition is made true by every truth-maker there is, so that, for example, "Grass is green" is made true by snow's being white. In the understatement of the year, Restall muses, "This is clearly not acceptable for any philosophically discriminating account of truthmakers."[16] Truth-maker theorists typically deny the doctrine of *truth-maker maximalism*, the doctrine that every true statement has a truth-maker. I have yet to encounter an argument for the conclusion that counterfactuals of creaturely freedom cannot be among those types of truths lacking a truth-maker. Indeed, when one reflects on the fact that they are *counterfactual*, then such statements seem prime candidates for that type of statement which is true without any truth-maker.

If there are, on the other hand, truth-makers for counterfactuals of creaturely freedom, then the most obvious and plausible candidates are the facts or states of affairs disclosed by the disquotation principle. Thus, what makes it true that "If I were rich, I would buy a Mercedes" is the fact that if I were rich I would buy a Mercedes. Just as there are tensed facts that now exist even though the objects and events they are about do not (as illustrated by statements 5 and 6 above), so there are counterfacts that actually exist even though the objects and events they are about do not. If counterfactuals of creaturely freedom have truth-makers, then it is in virtue of these facts or states of affairs that the corresponding propositions are true. And since these counter-facts are not the result of God's decree, they exist even logically prior to God's decree to create any physical objects.

In short, I concur with Plantinga in saying that I am far more confident that there are true coun-terfactuals of creaturely freedom than I am of the theory which requires that they have truth-makers. And if they do, then no reason has been given why these cannot be the facts or states of affairs that are stated as their truth conditions.

Premise 3 of our philosophical argument for middle knowledge states logically exhaustive alternatives for an omniscient deity and so must be true: Counterfactuals of creaturely freedom are known by God either prior to his decree or only after his decree.

Finally, (4) must be true because if counter-factuals of creaturely freedom were known only after the divine decree, then it is God who deter-mined what every creature would do in every circumstance. Augustinian-Calvinist thinkers bear witness to the truth of this premise in their affirmation of compatibilist theories of crea-turely freedom. They thereby testify that God's all-determining decree precludes libertarian freedom, which is the sort of freedom with which we are here concerned. Thus, if God knows counterfactual truths about us only pos-terior to his decree, then there really are no coun-terfactuals of creaturely freedom. If there are such counterfactuals, they must be true logically prior to the divine decree.

Given the truth of the premises, the conclu-sion follows that prior to his creative decree God knows all true counterfactuals of creaturely freedom, which is to say that he has middle knowledge, Q.E.D.

Conclusion

In conclusion, while not explicitly taught by the biblical text, the doctrine of divine middle know-ledge is certainly compatible with it, which can-not be said of at least some of its competitors. . . .

Moreover, we have good theological and philo-sophical grounds for affirming middle know-ledge. Theologically, middle knowledge enables us to explain both the compatibility of divine foreknowledge with future contingents as well as the basis of divine foreknowledge and, more importantly, to provide an intelligible account of God's providence over a world of free crea-tures. Philosophically, omniscience by definition entails knowledge of all truth and, since counter-factuals of creaturely freedom are true logically prior to God's creative decree, they must there-fore by known by God at that logical moment. Therefore, we should affirm that God has middle knowledge.

Notes

1 Charles Dickens, *A Christmas Carol and Other Stories*, The Modern Library (New York: Random House, 1995), p. 97.

2 On Christian particularism, see William Lane Craig, " 'No Other Name': A Middle Knowledge Pers-pective on the Exclusivity of Salvation Through Christ," *Faith and Philosophy* 6 (1989): 172–88. On perseverance of the saints, see William Lane Craig, " 'Lest Anyone Should Fall': a Middle Knowledge Perspective on Perseverance and Apostolic Warn-ings," *International Journal for Philosophy of Religion* 29 (1991): 65–74. On biblical inspiration, see William Lane Craig, " 'Men Moved by the Holy Spirit Spoke from God' (2 Peter 1:2): A Middle Knowledge Perspective on Biblical Inspiration," *Philosophia Christi* 1 (1999): 45–82.

3 Thomas P. Flint, "Middle Knowledge and the Doctrine of Infallibility," in *Philosophy of Religion*, vol. 5 of *Philosophical Perspectives*, ed. Jas. E. Tomberlin (Atascadero, Calif.: Ridgeway, 1991), pp. 373–93; Del Ratzsch, "Design, Chance and Theistic Evolution," in *Mere Creation*, ed. William Dembski (Downers Grove, Ill.: InterVarsity Press, 1998), pp. 289–312.

4 See D. A. Carson, *Divine Sovereignty and Human Responsi-bility: Biblical Perspectives in Tension*, New Foundations Theological Library (Atlanta: John Knox, 1981).

5 For a discussion of the biblical data pertinent to divine foreknowledge, see William Lane Craig, *The*

Only Wise God (Grand Rapids, Mich.: Baker, 1987), part 1.

6 Susan Haack, "On a Theological Argument for Fatalism," *Philosophical Quarterly* 24 (1974): 158.

7 See Harry Frankfurt, "Alternative Possibilities and Moral Responsibility," *Journal of Philosophy* 66 (1969): 829–39; Thomas V. Morris, *The Logic of God Incarnate* (Ithaca, N.Y.: Cornell University Press, 1986), 151–52. Morris imagines a man with electrodes secretly implanted in his brain who is presented with the choice of doing either A or B. The electrodes are inactive so long as the man chooses A; but if he were going to choose B, then the electrodes would switch on and force him to choose A. In such a case the man is unable to choose B, but his choosing A is still entirely free, since the electrodes do not function at all when he chooses to do A. For an application of the scenario to theological fatalism see David P. Hunt, "On Augustine's Way Out," *Faith and Philosophy* 16 (1999): 3–26.

8 See, e.g., Alfred J. Freddoso, "Accidental Necessity and Logical Determinism," *Journal of Philosophy* 80 (1983): 257–78.

9 See my companion volumes *The Tensed Theory of Time: A Critical Examination*, Synthese Library 293 (Dordrecht, Holland: Kluwer Academic Publishers, 2000) and *The Tenseless Theory of Time: A Critical Examination*, Synthese Library 294 (Dordrecht, Holland: Kluwer Academic Publishers, 2000).

10 For the following definition see William Hasker, "A Philosophical Perspective," in *The Openness of God: A Biblical Challenge to the Traditional Understanding of God*, ed. Clark Pinnock et al. (Downers Grove, Ill.: Inter-Varsity Press, 1994), p. 136.

11 Ibid., pp. 147–48.

12 Thomas P. Flint, *Divine Providence: The Molinist Account*, Cornell Studies in the Philosophy of Religion (Ithaca, N.Y.: Cornell University Press, 1998), p. 123.

13 Alvin Plantinga, "Reply to Robert Adams," in *Alvin Plantinga*, ed. Jas. E. Tomberlin and Peter Van Inwagen, Profiles 5 (Dordrecht, Holland: Reidel, 1985), p. 378.

14 See the seminal article by Kevin Mulligan, Peter Simons and Barry Smith, "Truth-Makers," *Philosophy and Phenomenological Research* 44 (1984): 287–321.

15 Robert Adams, "Plantinga on the Problem of Evil," in *Alvin Plantinga*, ed. Jas. E. Tomberlin and Peter Van Inwagen, Profiles 5 (Dordrecht, Holland: Reidel, 1985), p. 232. Compare William Hasker's demand, "Who or what is it (if anything) that brings it about that these propositions are true?" (William Hasker, "A Refutation of Middle Knowledge," *Noûs* 20 [1986]: 547).

16 Greg Restall, "Truthmakers, Entailment and Necessity," *Australasian Journal of Philosophy* 74 (1996): 334. Restall offers an account of truth-makers involving abstract entities to solve this problem, but in doing so he leaves his truth-makers undefined. This result only underscores how ham-fisted a handling of truth-makers is presupposed by grounding objectors to middle knowledge.

Chapter 25

William Hasker

THE OPENNESS OF GOD

God is not remote, closed off and self-contained. Rather, God is open to us his creatures, to the world he has made, and to the future. We in turn need to be open toward God and toward the future he is creating for us. These are the central themes of "open theism," which was introduced to the religious public by the book, *The Openness of God*.[1] Various elements in this conception of God have been extensively discussed by such philosophers as Peter Geach, J. R. Lucas and Richard Swinburne,[2] but the appearance of open theism as a general theological perspective is quite recent.[3] [. . .]

If God is not all-determining, as the Calvinists think, if he does not possess middle knowledge, as urged by the Molinists, if he does not possess "simple foreknowledge" of the actual future, and if, like us, he experiences the passage of time moment by moment and not all at once in the "eternal now," then it follows ineluctably that God's knowledge of the future, incomparably greater though it is than any knowledge we could possess, is not the complete, certain and infinitely detailed knowledge posited by most of the theological tradition. [. . .] What remains is to work out the implications of this.

What, then, are the implications of this view of God for our understanding of providence?[4] According to the open view of God, God is strictly omnipotent, in that *he is able to do anything which is logically possible and consistent with God's morally perfect nature*. It is worth stressing that God as so

conceived is in no way deficient in power as compared with God as viewed by Calvinism.[5] We hold that God is completely capable of creating a universe, every detail of whose history is solely determined by his sovereign decree. But it seems to us that a wise and good God would not want—and in fact, has not chosen—to create a universe such as this. We in turn would ask the Calvinist, "Is God as you conceive him unable to create a world in which there are free creatures who voluntarily enter into a relationship of love and friendship with him? Or does he prefer a world in which he alone monopolizes control, leaving nothing to be decided by his creatures? And why should we think that he would prefer a world like that?"

God is also omniscient, in that *he knows everything that logically can be known*. We believe, however, that it is logically impossible for God to have foreknowledge of creaturely actions that are truly free. (An argument for this will be given below.) Note, however, that God has a vast amount of knowledge about the probabilities that free choices will be made in one way rather than another. To be sure, God could have created a world in which he would have full foreknowledge of every detail, simply by creating a world in which everything that happens is fully controlled by his sovereign decrees. But it seems to us that God found such a world less desirable—less appealing to his creative goodness—than a world which contains genuinely free creatures.

We believe that the open view of God has important advantages over alternative views (such as Calvinism and Molinism) in conceiving our personal relationship with God. God knows an immense amount about each one of us—far more, in fact, than we know about ourselves—but he does not, because he cannot, plan his actions toward us on the basis of a prior knowledge of how we will respond. That is to say: he is not a manipulator, relating to us by "pressing the right buttons" to get the exact response he desires to elicit. And this means that God is a risk-taker; in expressing his love toward us, he opens himself up to the real possibility of failure and disappointment. God doesn't, of course, "need" us in all of the ways we need one another, but he does genuinely and deeply care about us; he is saddened when we reject his love and rejoices when one of us turns to him in repentance and faith.

We believe that the open view of God is substantially better off than alternative views in dealing with the problem of evil. According to this view God knows that evils will occur, but he has not for the most part specifically decreed or incorporated into his antecedent plan the individual instances of evil. Rather, God's governance of the world is primarily in terms of *general strategies*, strategies which are, as a whole, ordered for the good of the creation, but whose detailed consequences are not foreseen or intended by God prior to the decision to adopt them. As a result of this, we are able to abandon the difficult doctrine of "meticulous providence,"[6] and to admit the presence in the world of particular evils, God's permission of which is not the means of bringing about any greater good or preventing any equal or greater evil. And this, we believe, is an important advantage for our view as compared with others.

Criticisms of the openness-of-God theory typically claim that God as we conceive him would be unable to do the kinds of things that Scripture represents God as doing. One such complaint deals with the subject of prophecy

—if God doesn't know everything about the future, how can he tell us about it? Obviously a full discussion of this topic is beyond our present scope (and also beyond my competence), so I must limit myself to a few summary remarks. We have available to us three different ways of understanding biblical prophecies, consistent with God's openness to the future. Some prophecies—perhaps more than have generally been so recognized[7]—are conditional on the actions of human beings. Others are predictions based on existing trends and tendencies, while still others are announcements of what God himself intends to bring about irrespective of the choices made by creaturely agents. We believe (though I cannot argue here in detail[8]) that these approaches can lead one to a satisfying understanding of the phenomena of biblical prophecy.

We will take time to consider here just one more objection against the open view of God. It is sometimes asserted that God as we conceive him would not be able to ensure the fulfillment of his plan even in the most general respects. If every single human being has it in her power to accept or reject God's offer of salvation, and if God has no advance knowledge of how a person will respond, then it would be possible for every person without exception to reject salvation—and if this were to occur, there would be no "people of God," no Church, and a key element in God's plan would be frustrated. As things actually stand, to be sure, this has not happened, but it could have happened; that it has not, is attributable to nothing but "God's luck."

To answer this fully, we should have to know exactly what methods and resources are available to God in his providential governance of the world. But this is something we certainly do not know, and cannot expect to know—and without it, any answer to the objection must be based on speculation. We certainly should not underestimate the tremendous resourcefulness of God in adapting his responses to human actions —even willful and disobedient human actions— so as to achieve his wise and loving purposes. But even if it is possible, in the open view of God, for all human beings without exception to reject salvation, still this might be overwhelmingly improbable—so improbable that the risk of such an outcome is negligible. Consider a parallel: According to modern physics, there is a finite probability that all of the oxygen in a room should concentrate itself in a small volume, leaving the rest of the room devoid of oxygen and unable to sustain life. But the probability of this happening is so minute that rational persons can and do disregard the possibility in conducting their lives; I am completely confident that not a single one of my readers goes about with bottled oxygen in order to protect himself in the event of such an occurrence! So why should our inability to show how God can logically guarantee that humans will respond to his love constitute a serious objection?

I will bring this discussion to a close by calling some arguments to your attention. First, let us consider an argument for the claim that comprehensive divine foreknowledge and human free will are logically inconsistent. The idea, roughly, is this: If God knows already what will happen in the future, then God's knowing this is part of the past and is now fixed, impossible to change. And since God is infallible, it is completely impossible that things will turn out differently than God expects them to. But this means that the future event God knows is also fixed and unalterable, and it cannot be true of any human being that they are both able to perform a certain action and able not to perform that action. If God knows they are going to perform it, then it is impossible that they fail to perform it—so, they do not have a free choice whether or not to perform it. There are dozens of different versions of this argument; one of my favorites concerns a certain Clarence, known to be addicted to cheese omelets. Will Clarence have a cheese omelet for breakfast tomorrow morning, or won't he? The argument proceeds as follows:

1 It is now true that Clarence will have a cheese omelet for breakfast tomorrow. (Premise.)

2 It is impossible that God should at any time believe[9] what is false, or fail to believe anything that is true. (Premise: divine omniscience.)

3 God has always believed that Clarence will have a cheese omelet tomorrow. (From 1,2.)

4 If God has always believed a certain thing, it is not in anyone's power to bring it about that God has not always believed that thing. (Premise: the unalterability of the past.)

5 Therefore, it is not in Clarence's power to bring it about that God has not always believed that he would have a cheese omelet for breakfast. (From 3,4.)

6 It is not possible for it to be true both that God has always believed that Clarence would have a cheese omelet for breakfast, and that he does not in fact have one. (From 2.)

7 Therefore, it is not in Clarence's power to refrain from having a cheese omelet for breakfast tomorrow. (From 5,6.) So Clarence's eating the omelet tomorrow is not an act of free choice. (From the definition of free will.)[10]

What this argument shows is that it is logically impossible that God should have foreknowledge of a genuinely free action. It follows from this that if there are actions which are free in the libertarian sense, it is logically impossible for God to know in advance how such actions will turn out. And in the light of our definition of omniscience, God's failure to know what logically cannot be known in no way detracts from God's omniscience. As soon as these truths become available, God will be the first to know them! (On the other hand, the definition of omniscience given in step 2 of the argument above is faulty, because it fails to allow for the possibility of truths which are intrinsically unknowable.)

Since it is out of the question to address all of the alternatives to the open view, my final two arguments will be directed primarily at what may be the most commonly accepted approach to these matters, the theory of "simple fore-knowledge." This theory accepts libertarian free will (unlike Calvinism), and rejects middle knowledge, but holds that God has complete and certain knowledge of the actual future.

Clearly there are reasons for the popularity of such an approach. It avoids the immense theo-logical difficulties of Calvinism, and the logical and metaphysical perplexities of Molinism, yet it upholds what many perceive to be the irreducible minimum for an adequate doctrine of omniscience and foreknowledge. I maintain, however, that the advantages of this theory are less than meet the eye. In particular, there are *no benefits whatever* for our understanding of divine providence, of God's action in the world, from the affirmation of simple foreknowledge. Let me explain why. Suppose God knows, in exhaustive detail, exactly what the situation on the earth will be as of a particular future date—say, April 11, 2013. Suppose, also, that there is something about that situation that displeases God—something he would wish to make otherwise. Could God not then act, at some time prior to the date in question, so as to bring about a situation on April 11, 2013, that is more in accord with his purposes? A little reflection will show this thought to be incoherent. For the future God knows is, by supposition, the *actual* future for that date; the supposition that God then acts so that what he knows to be the actual future is in fact not the actual future makes no sense at all. Reflec-tion on this and similar scenarios will lead us to see that it is *impossible that God should use a foreknowledge derived from the actual occurrence of future events to deter-mine his own prior actions in the providential governance of the world.* If simple foreknowledge did exist, it would be useless.[11]

Let me add a couple of comments concerning the application of this argument. First, notice that it applies equally to simple foreknowledge and to the doctrine of divine timelessness. The argument makes no use of the fact that God knows the future *before* it occurs; the difficulty arises from the circularity in which knowledge of a later event is the basis for God's action at a time prior to the event in question. Thus the knowledge of the future possessed by a timeless God, like that of a God with simple foreknowledge, would be providentially useless.

The second point is one which, I now realize, has not been stressed sufficiently in previous dis-cussions of this argument. Included among the range of divine actions which, according to the argument, could not be based on foreknowledge of events still to come, is the action of inspiring a prophet to predict the future.[12] The giving of a prophecy is just as much an action as the caus-ing of a plague, and can have effects that are equally great; indeed, the prophets were inspired to speak as they did precisely in order to cause their hearers to act in ways they otherwise would not have. So any problem about prophecy that may exist for the open view applies also to sim-ple foreknowledge and divine timelessness. To gain relief from such problems (if relief is really needed), your only recourse is to turn to Molinism or Calvinism.

The final argument I will present is targeted specifically at those of you who accept most fea-tures of the open view, but can't bring yourselves to give up simple foreknowledge. You hold, as we do, that God is temporal and genuinely responsive. And you believe, like us but unlike Thomas Aquinas, that God's compassion really is compassion and not just compassionate actions carried out against a divine emotional back-ground of imperturbable tranquility. But for whatever reason, you balk at giving up total div-ine foreknowledge. Let me say, first of all, that we openness-of-God believers regard you already as much more an ally than an opponent. What unites us truly is far more important than what divides us; in this context, the debate over foreknowledge and free will comes to seem more a fascinating logical conundrum than a fundamental theological watershed. Still, the difference remains, and we would like to persuade you to come the rest of the way and join us. The previous argument shows that your view doesn't confer some of the benefits you may have supposed; the argument I'm about to present exhibits a positive advantage of the open view of God.

An important characteristic of the open view is that it takes seriously what we may term the "emotional life of God"—in Abraham Heschel's term, the divine "pathos." To be sure, a flatly literal reading of the biblical descriptions of God's emotions is implausible; surely there is much here of anthropomorphism—or, more precisely, "anthropopathism." Nevertheless, when we read that "As a father pities his children, so the LORD pities those who fear him" (Ps. 103:13), we take this for a true description of the inner life of God. Now I submit that many of these descriptions exhibit the following two characteristics:

1   The emotion ascribed to God is connected with, and appropriate to, the particular situation of the human beings to whom God is related;

2   the emotion would be profoundly different if we assumed it to be informed by a definite prior knowledge of the situation's outcome.

To take a single example, consider the well-loved parable of the Prodigal Son. As we know, the "waiting father" in the parable represents God, and the father's longing for his son's return—an experience to which many a human parent can relate—represents the heavenly Father's longing for the return of an estranged sinner. And then the son appears, and "while he was yet at a distance, his father saw him and had compassion, and ran and embraced him and kissed him" (Luke 15:20). The father's joy at this reunion is crucial for the parable as a whole. As Richard Rice observes, "the thrill of recovery is quite

different from the satisfaction of a predictable achievement . . . Losing something of value can inflict enormous pain. We feel the threat of permanent deprivation. The uncertainty as we search or wait to get it back can be agonizing. And then, if we're fortunate, the moment of recovery brings a rush of surprise, relief and joy" (*Openness*, p. 41). Now let's try retelling the parable on the assumption that the father possesses foreknowledge of the outcome—he knows just when, where and how his son will reappear. The father is still unhappy over his son's absence, of course; to lose him from the family even for a limited time is a sad affair. But the father is spared any deep anxiety, nor will he stand day after day peering out in the hope that his son will reappear. Instead, on the appointed day he checks the calendar, glances at the sundial and instructs the family retainer to break out the chariot: "Sonny will be showing up real soon now." The whole emotional content of the parable is profoundly altered.

I wouldn't expect this argument to have force for a classical theist like Anselm or Aquinas. For them, all references to divine emotions are a mere manner of speaking, a way of communicating in terms of human-like emotions some distant reflection of the truth about a God who in reality is far above that sort of thing. But if, like me, you think God really does have an emotional life, then you may also feel you have some stake in being able to say that the emotions attributed to God in Scripture are emotions he really experience. If that is what you want, the open view of God can give it to you—and so far as I can see, it is the only view that can. [. . .]

The God Who Takes Risks

What exactly would it mean for God to take risks? Let me put it like this: *God takes risks if he makes decisions that depend for their outcomes on the responses of free creatures in which the decisions themselves are not informed by knowledge of the outcomes.*[13] For if he does this, the creatures' decisions may be contrary to God's wishes, and in this case God's intentions in making those decisions may be at least partly frustrated. If on the other hand God's decisions are always guided by full knowledge of how the creatures will respond, he takes no risks even though some of the creaturely responses may be unfavorable. The unfavorable responses, in this case, are simply part of the "cost of doing business"; in incurring these costs God was not taking any risk, but was merely accepting what he knew in advance would be the mixed results from his decision.

But if this is what it means for God to take risks, what is it that determines whether God's actions are risky or risk-free? There is a surprisingly simple answer to this question: *God is a risk-taker if he endows his creatures with libertarian freedom; otherwise not.*[14] By "libertarian freedom" is meant freedom such that the agent who makes a choice is really able, under exactly the same circumstances, to choose something different than the thing that is in fact chosen. The choices in question, then, are not causally determined to occur as they do; libertarian freedom is inherently indeterministic. This means that there is *nothing whatever* that predetermines which choice will be made, until the creature actually is placed in the situation and makes the decision. God may know in advance how the creature will *probably* decide, but he cannot make his own decision in the light of the creature's *actual* decision.

It needs to be said, however, that this rather simple answer suffices only if another possible theory, that of divine middle knowledge, is excluded. According to the theory of middle knowledge, there is a vast array of propositions that are known to God, generally termed "counterfactuals of freedom." These propositions state, with regard to each actual or possible free creature, what that creature would freely (in the libertarian sense) decide to do, in any possible situation of free choice with which that creature might be confronted. And given this knowledge, God is able to make his decisions in full knowledge of exactly how the creatures will respond,

even though the creaturely decision is free in the libertarian sense and thus not causally determined. Once again, the element of risk is completely eliminated.

In my view, the theory of middle knowledge cannot be true, because the truths God is alleged to know—the "counterfactuals of freedom"—simply do not exist to be known. As Paul Helm says, "the circumstances [of a libertarian free choice] never ensure one determinate freely-chosen outcome; they provide only the conditions for the free choice of one of several outcomes. Hence God cannot . . . use his knowledge of what a free creature would do under certain circumstances to achieve a desired end" (p. 59). The reason God cannot do this is that there simply is no such truth to be known; insofar as an agent is genuinely free, there *are* no true counterfactuals stating what the agent would definitely (as opposed to probably) do under various possible circumstances.

Having said this much, let me acknowledge that the subject of middle knowledge is complex and difficult, and a full treatment of it would need to be much more extensive than can be attempted here.[15] Having rejected middle knowledge as impossible, I will say no more about it in this chapter. And this returns us to the position previously stated: God is a risk-taker if he endows his creatures with libertarian freedom; otherwise not. This connection, furthermore, suggests a pair of useful labels for the positions under discussion: the view that affirms divine risk-taking may be termed *free-will theism*; whereas the contrary view can be described as *theological determinism*.

Thus far we have been discussing freedom for human beings, but what about the freedom of God? Are God's decisions free in the libertarian sense? One might expect that a view bearing the label "free-will theism," would attribute libertarian freedom to God as well as to creatures, and this expectation is not disappointed. But what of theological determinism? Does this theory also consider God as being free in the libertarian sense? This is not always so clear; theological determinists like to speak of the "freedom of God," but it may not be immediately evident what sort of freedom they have in mind. A little reflection, however, suggests that theological determinists also must attribute libertarian freedom to God—at least, they must do so if they wish to be orthodox Christians. For if God is not free in this sense, then the divine act of creation must be somehow necessitated by the nature of God; the creation will then be *necessary for God*, and not a free and gracious act as the Christian tradition has affirmed it to be.[16]

So free-will theism and theological determinism do not differ with regard to the freedom of God. Freedom is, of course, only one divine attribute among many, and the two views will indeed differ with regard to some divine attributes. But these differences are less than many suppose. For example: the *power* of God, the essential divine attribute of omnipotence, will not be different for the two views: in either case, it can truly be said that God is able to do anything that is neither self-contradictory nor in conflict with God's perfect nature.[17] To be sure, the *extent of the exercise* of divine power may in a sense be somewhat greater for the deterministic view, in that on this view there are fewer kinds of events that God does not actively control.[18] But this difference does not concern God's essential omnipotence, but rather the sort of universe God has freely decided to create in which to exercise his omnipotence. A universe containing genuinely free creatures is one in which God has generously decided that there shall be certain events that are *not* positively controlled by him, namely the free choices of the creatures.

Some readers may be surprised to learn that free-will theism and theological determinism do not differ with regard to the *essential omniscience* of God. The reason this is especially surprising is that free-will theism, when held consistently, entails that God does not have comprehensive fore-knowledge of future free actions.[19] Yet this does not imply any difference in God's essential

nature from that which is posited by theological determinism. To see this, consider once again God's situation as he contemplates whether or not to create a universe, and, if he does create, what sort of universe to create. Among God's choices, both views will concede, is the choice whether or not to endow his creatures with libertarian free will.[20] Both views, furthermore, will recognize the following truth: If God creates persons with libertarian freedom, he will not have exhaustive knowledge of the future, whereas if he creates no such persons, he will have exhaustive knowledge of the future.[21] Both possibilities are consistent with God's perfect nature, and therefore with his essential omniscience, which is no different for free-will theism than for theological determinism. As in the case of omnipotence, the difference does not concern the essential divine attribute but rather the sort of universe God has freely chosen to create.

But what sort of universe *has* God created? Or rather, what sort of universe is it reasonable for us to think he has created? One important bit of evidence here concerns our *experience* of being free agents. According to John Searle:

> [I]f there is any fact of experience that we are all familiar with, it's the simple fact that our own choices, decisions, reasonings, and cogitations seem to make a difference to our actual behaviour. There are all sorts of experiences that we have in life where it seems just a fact of our experience that though we did one thing, we feel we know perfectly well that we could have done something else. We know we could have done something else, because we chose one thing for certain reasons. But we were aware that there were also reasons for choosing something else, and indeed, we might have acted on those reasons and chosen that something else.[22]

A striking fact about this quotation is that Searle is himself a determinist, one who feels that this experience of freedom must ultimately be illusory! Nevertheless, he testifies that this is indeed how we experience our lives to be. Now, it must be admitted that Searle, and other determinists, are right in holding that our "experience of freedom" does not *prove* that we are free, because there could be determining causes of our actions of which we are unaware. But unless there are compelling reasons to think this experience is illusory, we must acknowledge that it gives us a strong *reason*, though not absolute proof, to think that we really do possess free will just as libertarians say we do.

But in this chapter we are raising the question of free will primarily from the perspective of God's decision about what sort of world to create. As a start on answering the question, I am going to ask my readers to join me in a thought experiment. Imagine yourself, then, as a prospective parent shortly before the birth of your first child. And suppose that someone has offered you the following choice: On the one hand, the child will be one that, without any effort on your part, will always and automatically do and be exactly what you want it to do and be, no more and no less. The child will have no feeling of being constrained or controlled; nevertheless, it will spontaneously carry out your wishes on any and every occasion. Or on the other hand, you can choose to have a child in the normal fashion, a child that is fully capable of having a will of its own and of resisting your wishes for it, and even of acting against its own best interests. You will have to invest a great deal of effort in its education, wishing for the best, but without any advance guarantee of success. And there is the risk, indeed the near-certainty, that the child will inflict on you considerable pain and suffering, as you strive to help the child become all that he or she can be and ought to be. Which do you choose?

Such a choice is admittedly deeply subjective, and it may well be that some readers will choose the first alternative, to have a child that is always and automatically in compliance with their wishes for it. (And if you have chosen that way, I probably have little hope of persuading you to accept the view of God as a risk-taker.) It is my hope, however, that many readers—perhaps even a strong majority—will agree with me in saying that it is far better to accept the challenge of parenting a child with a will of its own, even at the price of pain and possible heartbreak, than to opt for an arrangement in which the child's choices will all really be my choices made for it, its life a pale reflection of mine lived through the child.

The friends of a risk-free providence may charge me with excessive anthropomorphism in this analogy. It is anthropomorphic, but so is the Bible, in its portrayal of God as a loving Father—for instance, in the parable of the Prodigal Son. And it is difficult to see the point of such portrayals, unless one is permitted to make some inferences from the character and conduct of good human parents to that of the divine Parent. Helm has opened the door to such analogies by arguing (in favor of the no-risk view) that genuine personal relationships are compatible with a certain amount of constraint, manipulation and pressure, and that close relationships typically involve a high degree of predictability by each other of the partners' behavior. I agree with all of this, but with the following proviso: the better the relationship is, the more mature the partners become in their dealings with each other, the less need there is for either pressure or manipulation. After nearly forty years of marriage, my wife and I know each other reasonably well. We seldom attempt to pressure or manipulate each other, and while we can often anticipate each other's responses we are still quite capable of surprising each other—and thank God for that! The notion that one partner in a relationship could exercise complete, unilateral control over the other and yet the relationship remain a genuinely personal one, strikes me as unconvincing in the extreme.

Our considerations to this point have been in a sense *a priori*, in that we have paid little or no attention to the actual character of the world God has created. As we turn to consider the way the world is, we cannot help but be struck by the troubling prevalence of sin, evil and suffering. A theory of providence must reckon with these facts, and they create formidable problems for any such theory. It seems, however, that the difficulties for the no-risk view are especially severe.

One such difficulty concerns the issue of responsibility for sin and moral evil. Given the assumptions of the no-risk view, are human sinners truly responsible for their evil actions? And how does God escape being responsible for moral evil—from being, as some have said, the "author of sin"? In responding to this, theological determinists stress the obscure and mysterious nature of the relationship between human and divine willing. As Helm says, "The basic question . . . has to do with the very nature of the division and connection between divine and human reality" (p. 162). That this relation is obscure and mysterious (whatever one's theory of providence) no one should deny. This obscurity should not, however, lead us to neglect or overlook what is clearly implied about the relationship by the no-risk theory. Here is one such implication: *God himself is the sufficient cause of all events, including sinful human actions, in that he deliberately and without constraint establishes the causal conditions that of necessity lead to these events and actions.* That God is in this sense the "cause of sin" simply cannot be denied by theological determinists.

There are certain explanations and clarifications that need to be made here. God is not, in this view, the *sole* cause of all worldly events, as has sometimes been claimed. The creatures serve as "secondary causes," and their causality, though needing to be sustained by God in his conserving activity, is genuine and distinct from that of God himself. Furthermore, God's causal involvement in worldly events is different for different classes of events. In particular, God's relation to morally evil actions is not the same as his relation to good actions (see pp. 168–171,

190–191). It is often said in this connection that God "permits" evil actions to occur, but does not cause them to occur. But this language of permission can easily become evasive and misleading. No doubt, in this view, God "permits" evil actions without actively assisting them in the way that he assists good actions through his gracious influence. Nevertheless, *the evil actions are the necessary consequence of causes that were deliberately created by God with full knowledge of what their results would be.* God's involvement may be less direct than in the case of good actions, but it is no less decisive. In the end it is simply incoherent for the no-risk view to deny that God is the cause of sin. As Helm states, his view "does not, in the final analysis, attribute certain evils to the human will and certain others to natural causes; rather, all are finally attributed to the divine reason and will" (p. 198).

How then is the human responsibility for sin and evil to be preserved? At this point Helm embraces "divine compatibilism," a view that agrees with the "compatibilist" account of free will that holds that free and responsible actions need not be causally undetermined, so long as they are not the result of compulsion. This view is a fairly common one in contemporary philosophy, and it has been developed with considerable sophistication. Helm's "divine compatibilism" adds to this secular view the claim that "if compatibilism is true, the fact that it is God who ordains those factors which determine human agency, and that the factors are not determined in a purely natural or secular way, is not an *additional* difficulty for compatibilism" (p. 174).

For some of us, the suggestion that theological determinism suffers "only" from the same difficulties that afflict compatibilism in a secular setting is a weak recommendation at best. Nevertheless, it is true that compatibilism is a widely held philosophical view, and the fact that theological determinism can avail itself of this support is of some benefit to the latter. But is it really the case that supposing God to be the ultimate cause of all human actions creates no additional difficulty?[23] When we think of responsibility in a secular context, we will be thinking primarily of responsibility *to society*, whether this is expressed through the law or through more informal means. Now whatever the natural causes of human behavior are thought to be, it is clear that society exerts, at best, very limited control over them. And on the other hand, it is unavoidable that some sort of sanctions will be applied to those who act destructively, since without this the maintenance of social order would be impossible. So in this context the assignment of responsibility to causally determined actions makes some sense, even if the conceptual situation remains murky.

In the theistic context, however, things are much different. God is not the unfortunate onlooker forced to put up with behavior determined by forces over which he has little control. On the contrary, it is God himself who has ordained those very forces with full knowledge of their consequences. Nor is God faced with the need to impose penalties as the only means by which he can maintain order; instead, he could simply have refrained from setting up the causal chains that led to the behavior in the first place. The picture we have, then, is of God, with full knowledge and deliberation, intentionally creating a situation in which human beings act in morally abhorrent ways and then punishing those humans for that behavior, while remaining all the while beyond reproach himself. [. . .]

Let us now place on one side the issue of responsibility, and ask instead a more general question: What shall we take God's attitude to be, toward the world he has created and the sin and evil it contains? From the no-risk view of providence, we obtain the following answer: *God is entirely pleased with the world exactly as it is; there is no single fact he would wish to alter in any respect.* This may, on first glance, seem somewhat surprising, but the reasoning leading to this conclusion is quite compelling. For consider, on the no-risk view, the situation of God prior to creation, as he is

deciding what sort of world to bring into existence.[24] God holds before his mind every possible scenario for world-history—all the different "possible worlds," as philosophers say—and selects the very one that he finds most satisfying and most in tune with his creative purposes. Then he proceeds to put that scenario into effect, and of course there is no possibility whatever that the actual result will differ in any respect from that envisioned prior to creation. Since God in his wisdom has selected the "best of all possible worlds" (or one of the best, in case there are several tied for that distinction), he cannot fail to be entirely delighted with the course actually taken by his creation.

There is, to be sure, a small qualification that is needed at this point. We need not suppose that, on the no-risk view, every single fact in the universe is exactly as God would prefer it to be, *if he were to consider that fact in isolation from its context in creation as a whole.* So it may be that, for instance, some episode of sexual child-abuse is not the thing God would most prefer, considered simply as an isolated fact. But of course, God's evaluation of events is *not* as isolated facts, but precisely in the broader context of which they form a part. And considered in the broadest possible context, not only that instance of child abuse but every other crime and atrocity is *exactly what God desires for it to be.*

And this brings us to one of the divine attributes on which the risk-taking and no-risk views differ. The no-risk view is committed to the traditional doctrine of *divine impassibility*, which holds that God is, of necessity, completely free from negative emotions, but lives his life in a continual state of bliss and serenity. Sometimes metaphysical reasons are given for this doctrine, but we are now able to see a rather direct connection between divine impassibility and the basic assumptions of the no-risk theory. Since God has selected exactly the world-history he desires, and obtains precisely what he has selected, it would be simply unintelligible to suppose that God experiences aversion, anger, or disappointment over the actual course of events. He has chosen the best, and the best is what happens, so how could he be less than supremely happy with the result?

Nevertheless, the implications of impassibility in this context are deeply troubling. *How can God be so delighted with the actual course of events*, we may ask, in view of the enormity of the evils that continually occur? And what becomes of the biblical teaching that God hates sin, that he is angry with oppressors, and feels compassion for innocent sufferers? "As a father pities his children, so the LORD pities those who fear him" (Ps. 103:13)—are we to understand that this is not, after all, a truthful account of God's mind and heart? Professor Helm recognizes that the Bible presents God's emotional life—the divine pathos, as it has been termed by Abraham Heschel[25]—in a far different light. If we were to take various biblical statements at face value, he acknowledges, "we should be committed to maintaining that God has a rich, ever-changing emotional life" (p. 51). He takes it for granted that we would not want to maintain this—but the implications of the contrary doctrine of divine impassibility are soul-chilling. Consider, above all, the biblical teaching that the Lord is "not wishing that any should perish, but that all should reach repentance" (II Peter 3:9). How can this be, when what the Lord truly desires is precisely what actually happens— including the fact that, as Scripture attests, some persons do indeed fail to repent and thus perish everlastingly? The no-risk view has an answer for this, but it is a very troubling answer. The no-risk view distinguishes two different senses of the will of God, sometimes termed the "revealed will" (the will of God as declared in Scripture) and the "will of God's good pleasure" which is the will that determines what actually takes place (see p. 131). So what God actually desires to happen is that some do indeed perish eternally, never reaching the repentance that would open them to God's love and forgiveness. But for some reason his revealed will, as portrayed in the Bible,

is quite the opposite of this.[26] Readers must decide for themselves whether this is an acceptable answer, one that presents to us the loving God who disclosed himself to us in Jesus.

The view that sees God as a risk-taker rejects the doctrine of impassibility as one that lacks biblical warrant and has no very impressive support from any other quarter. And in doing so, it is enabled to take seriously the biblical representation of God's emotional involvement with the world he has created. God is described as alternately comforting, indignant, triumphal, furious, grief-stricken, tender, threatening—the range of emotive responses is very wide. We need not deny that there is in these descriptions a measure of anthropomorphism; nevertheless, free-will theism will take them as an essentially truthful rendition of the inner life of God. The acknowledgment of negative emotions in God goes hand-in-hand with the view of God as a risk-taker. This view is able to take with full seriousness the anger of God against sin, and also the ecstatic joy that God experiences when, as in the parable of the Prodigal Son, one of his lost children returns to the fold. In escaping from the dark paradoxes of theological determinism, and freeing us to take seriously the pervasive biblical witness to God's emotional involvement with us his creatures, the view of God as a risk-taker stakes out a strong claim to being the best and most attractive version of Christian theism.[27]

Notes

1 Clark Pinnock, Richard Rice, John Sanders, William Hasker and David Basinger, *The Openness of God: A Biblical Challenge to the Traditional Understanding of God* (Downers Grove, Ill.: InterVarsity, 1994).

2 See Peter Geach, *Providence and Evil* (New York, N.Y.: Cambridge University Press, 1977); J. R. Lucas, *The Future* (Cambridge, Mass.: Blackwell, 1989); and Richard Swinburne, *The Coherence of Theism* (Oxford: Oxford University Press, 1977; revised edition 1993).

3 See Clark Pinnock and Robert Brow, *Unbounded Love:*

A Good News Theology for the 21st Century (Downers Grove, Ill.: InterVarsity Press, 1994); David Basinger, *The Case for Freewill Theism: A Philosophical Assessment* (Downers Grove, Ill.: Inter-Varsity Press, 1996); Gregory Boyd, *God at War: The Bible and Spiritual Conflict* (Downers Grove, Ill.: InterVarsity Press, 1997); John Sanders, *The God Who Risks: A Theology of Divine Providence* (Downers Grove, Ill.: InterVarsity Press, 1998). John B. Cobb, Jr. and Clark H. Pinnock, eds, *Searching for an Adequate God: A Dialogue Between Process and Free Will Theists* (Eerdmans: Grand Rapids, 2000) offers an extended comparison between open theism and process theism.

4   In the next few pages I draw extensively from *Openness*, pp. 147–154.

5   In this part of the discussion I use "Calvinism" as a shorthand for theological determinism, while recognizing that historically not all theological determinists are Calvinists and not all who call themselves Calvinists are theological determinists. Edward Wierenga has objected to this usage, on the ground that "J. T. McNeil's *The History and Character of Calvinism* . . . is not primarily a history of the doctrine of theological determinism!" (See Wierenga's review of *The Openness of God*, *Faith and Philosophy* 14:2 (1997), p. 252 n.2.) This is undoubtedly true, but the popular tendency to identify "Calvinism" with the doctrines of election and predestination is hardly without basis. Arminius, after all, agreed with the Synod of Dordt about practically everything except those doctrines, but apparently all that agreement is not enough to constitute him a "Calvinist" in good standing!

6   This term is taken from Michael Peterson, *Evil and the Christian God* (Grand Rapids, Mich.: Baker, 1982); see especially pp. 79–99. Meticulous providence is best defined as the view that "every single instance of evil that occurs is such that God's permitting either that specific evil or some other equal or greater evil is necessary for some greater good that is better than anything God could have brought about without permitting the evil in question" (*Openness*, p. 146). Peterson does not commit himself on the issue of foreknowledge, but his theodicy overall is highly congruent with the open view of God.

7   Usually only unfulfilled prophecies are identified as conditional, as a way of explaining why they were not fulfilled. But it is extremely plausible to suppose that many fulfilled prophecies were also conditional. See in this connection Jeremiah 18:7–10.

8   Some additional material is found in *Openness*, pp. 50–53.

9   The term "believe" is used here instead of "know" for technical philosophical reasons; it does not imply that God's "beliefs" are tentative or uncertain.

10 William Hasker, *God, Time, and Knowledge* (Ithaca: Cornell University Press, 1989) (paperback edition 1998), p. 69.

11 David Hunt has attempted to answer this argument, but I do not believe he succeeds. (See David P. Hunt, "Divine Providence and Simple Foreknowledge," *Faith and Philosophy* 10: 394–414. Also, Tomis Kapitan, "Providence, Foreknowledge, and Decision Procedures," 415–420; David Basinger, "Simple Foreknowledge and Providential Control," 421–427, and David P. Hunt, "Prescience and Providence: A Reply to My Critics," 428–438.) In my view, the only way to avoid the argument would be to straightforwardly accept the possibility of circular explanations. Hunt hints that he might possibly be willing to do this (p. 413 n.5), but so far he has not pursued this possibility.

12 Prophecy is alluded to in this connection in *God, Time, and Knowledge*, p. 58. But the point is not strongly emphasized, and could easily be missed by a reader.

13 This formulation is adapted from William Hasker, *God, Time, and Knowledge* (Ithaca: Cornell University Press, 1989), p. 197. Also, Paul Helm, *The Providence of God* (Downers Grove, Ill.: InterVarsity Press, 1994), p. 41. (Page references throughout this chapter are to Helm's book, unless otherwise noted.)

14 A minor qualification is needed here: Even without libertarian freedom, providence could be somewhat risky if the world includes genuinely uncaused events such as are postulated in the usual interpretation of quantum mechanics. Advocates of a risk-free providence will hold that such physically undetermined events, if they exist, are directly controlled by God.

15 Middle knowledge is discussed in Chapter 2 of *God, Time, and Knowledge*; see also William Hasker, "Middle

Knowledge: A Refutation Revisited," in *Faith and Philosophy* 12:2 (April 1995), pp. 223–236. By far the best recent defense of middle knowledge is Thomas Flint's *Divine Providence: The Molinist Account* (Ithaca, N.Y.: Cornell University Press, 1998).

16 Consider in this regard Helm's criticism of panentheism, because on that view "the universe does not depend for its existence on the free choice of God, but is an inevitable emanation of his goodness" (p. 73).

17 This is the point that is overlooked (or sometimes, one fears, deliberately suppressed) by those who equate free-will theism with process theism.

18 It should be noted, however, that theological determinism also recognizes acts not directly controlled by God, namely morally evil actions.

19 For argument, see Hasker, *God, Time, and Knowledge,* Chapters 4–7.

20 Some theological determinists would dispute this, holding that "free will" as understood by libertarians is an incoherent notion. Helm does not take this line (see p. 55), and it is difficult to see how such a view could be sustained, given the need to attribute libertarian freedom to God.

21 This point rests on the assumption, which I accept, that God, God's knowledge, and God's actions are temporal. If God is timelessly eternal, then he will have timeless knowledge even of the future actions of free creatures. But this makes no difference to the question whether providence is risky or risk-free. (See *God, Time, and Knowledge,* pp. 176–177.)

22 John Searle, *Minds, Brains, and Science* (Cambridge, Mass.: Harvard University Press, 1984), pp. 87–88.

23 Helm replies to an argument by Antony Flew, himself a compatibilist, to the effect that the assignment of responsibility to the human agent breaks down if God is the ultimate cause (see pp. 175–176). In what follows, I attempt to sharpen and reinforce Flew's argument.

24 Here and elsewhere the temporal language in describing God's decisions as viewed by the no-risk view is a concession for ease of understanding; on this view, God's creative decisions are taken outside of the time-sequence.

25 Heschel writes, "God does not simply command and expect obedience; He is also moved and affected by what happens in the world and he reacts accordingly. Events and human actions arouse in Him joy or sorrow, pleasure or wrath. He is not conceived as judging facts, so to speak, 'objectively,' in detached impassibility. He reacts in an intimate and subjective manner, and thus determines the value of events" (Abraham J. Heschel, *Between God and Man: An Interpretation of Judaism,* ed. Fritz A. Rothschild (New York, N.Y.: The Free Press, 1959), p. 116).

26 Helm points out that the risk-taking view also must distinguish multiple senses of God's will, for evil actions are at least *permitted* by God, and therefore are in some sense willed by him (p. 132). This may be so (though the slide from "permits" to "wills" could be questioned), but it hardly raises the troubling questions that arise from the two-wills doctrine described in the text.

27 For a readily accessible discussion of the view that God is a risk-taker, see Clark Pinnock *et al., The Openness of God: A Biblical Challenge to the Traditional Understanding of God* (Downers Grove, Ill.: InterVarsity Press, 1994). The most extensive presentation to date is John Sanders, *The God Who Risks: A Theology of Divine Providence* (Downers Grove, Ill.: InterVarsity Press, 1998).

Chapter 26

John Sanders

WHY SIMPLE FOREKNOWLEDGE OFFERS NO MORE PROVIDENTIAL CONTROL THAN THE OPENNESS OF GOD

Does a God with simple foreknowledge (SF) possess greater providential control than a God with present knowledge (PK)? It is claimed by the proponents of SF that a deity lacking such knowledge would not be able to provide the sort of providential aid commonly thought by theists to be given by God. To see whether this is the case I first distinguish two different versions regarding how God's foreknowledge is accessed according to simple foreknowledge. These two versions are then utilized to examine seven separate areas of divine providence to asses the utility of simple foreknowledge. I conclude that SF affords no greater providential control than PK.

Introduction

According to the theory of simple foreknowledge God has direct vision of all future events. God does not cause all these events to happen, nor is his knowledge inferred from what has happened in the past. Rather, God has direct noninferential apprehension of the future. The foreknowledge God has of what creatures with libertarian freedom will do is *dependent* on, and logically subsequent to, what the creatures actually decide to do.[1] That is, what the creatures decide affects what God knows the future to be. "Once" God decided to create this world then God apprehended all that would ever happen—right down to the movements of quarks—in this world.

For the openness of God model, God has only present knowledge of what free creatures do and only possesses "foreknowledge" of the specific actions he determines to do in the future. God knows all that has happened and all that is happening—right down to the movements of quarks—and may infer or believe that certain things will occur in the future. But God does not *know* the future actions of free creatures. Moreover, even how and if some of the divine intentions will be actualized are not known in a hard sense since they depend upon God's reaction to human decisions.[2] In the openness model God is understood to be responsive to the creatures he made. There is a give-and-take dynamic between God and his creation.

Some people are attracted to the element of divine responsiveness in the openness model but find two significant problems with the openness theory. First, they understand the nature of biblical prophecy to imply that God has foreknowledge of the future. If God has SF then, it is claimed, he can predict the future through his prophets. Second, they believe the open God model implies too much divine risk in providence such that God cannot guarantee the end from the beginning. A God lacking omniprescience cannot meet the challenges of the future. David Hunt claims that "divine control will be hamstrung and God's purposes jeopardized if events can ever catch Him by *surprise*, or find Him *unprepared*, or force Him to *react* after the fact to patch things up. . . . the kind of providential control expected of a theistic God is possible only on the assumption of foreknowledge."[3] Both of these problems are overcome, it is claimed, if God possesses SF.

Theologian Jack Cottrell maintains that SF is a key element in God's providential control over the world. He says,

> Because it is by this means that God can allow man to be truly free in his choices, even free to resist his own special influences, and at the same time work out his own purposes infallibly. For if God foreknows all the choices that every person will make, he can make his own plans accordingly, fitting his purposes around these foreknown decisions and actions. . . . Acts 2:23 is a perfect illustration of the way God works through his foreknowledge. . . . On the one hand, God had predetermined that Jesus would die as a propitiation for the sins of the world; this was his own unconditional plan for saving the world. On the other hand, the details of *how* this would be accomplished were planned in relation to God's foreknowledge of the historical situation and of the character and choices of men such as Judas.[4]

These are strong claims for the providential benefits of SF. Before examining the validity of these claims, I think it important to distinguish two different versions of how God's foreknowledge is accessed. SF is commonly explained as God "seeing the whole at once" and thus, knowing all that will happen. In this way God atemporally *learns* all at once everything that his free creatures will do. For example, God previsioned before the creation of the world my birth, sibling rivalries, marriage, adoption of children, writing this paper, etc. What God previsioned, moreover, included all the details

leading up to and surrounding all these events— right down to the number of hairs on my head at any given moment. This vision of God happens all at once and even though he knows things will occur in sequence God does not acquire the knowledge in sequence. God simply sees the whole at once. I shall coin the term "Complete Simple Foreknowledge" (CSF) for this version of SF.

Unfortunately, CSF has a difficult time explaining how God can intervene in what he foresees will happen. The problem arises because of the fact that what God previsions is what will *actually* occur. Divine foreknowledge, by definition, is always correct. If what will actually happen is, for example, the holocaust, then God knows it is going to happen and cannot prevent it from happening since his foreknowledge is never mistaken. Furthermore, if what God has foreseen is the *entire* human history *at once*, then the difficulty is to somehow allow for God's intervention into that history since, presumably, his prevision did not include his own actions.[5] For example, if God sees Abraham's birth, life and death all at once then how does God interject the test of the binding of Isaac (Gen. 22) into Abraham's life? How does God see God's own actions in Abraham's life which would alter Abraham's life and consequently change God's foreknowledge? Even more seriously, if God sees all of human history and the sin involved in it, but not his own actions, then this foreknowledge does not include any redemption from sin and God cannot save the creatures he is about to create. Hunt is correct that a God "with total foreknowledge . . . is equipped to make maximally informed decisions—but there is nothing left to be decided."[6] In this state of affairs there is no room for any providential activity if God sees the whole at once.[7] This raises the specter of deism which is unacceptable for orthodox theists.

Not surprisingly some believers in SF have sought a different explanation of God's direct apprehension of the future, one that allows for God to act providentially. In this version God timelessly accesses the future *in sequence* or *incrementally*.[8] That is, not in a temporal sequence, but in what might be called an explanatory order.[9] God sort of atemporally rolls the tape of the future up to a certain point and then stops it in order to interject his own actions into the tape and then rolls the tape further to see what his creatures will do in response to his actions. Then God again decides what he will do and then rolls the tape further. Hence, there is a logical sequence or order of dependence in the way God comes to access his foreknowledge. In this version God still learns the future, atemporally of course, but he learns it in sequence. As a result God can weave his own actions into the flow of human history. I shall coin the term "Incremental Simple Foreknowledge" (ISF) to designate this view.

Does the theory of SF provide better support for the doctrine of providence than the openness model? I propose to examine seven different, but related, aspects of the doctrine of providence to see what benefits, if any, SF has over PK.

Providential Uses of SF

1. Creation and Sin

Some people believe that a God with SF could have prevented the free creatures from committing evil. Since God did not prevent sin from happening, God is ultimately responsible. John Hick takes this line when he says it is "hard to clear God from ultimate responsibility for the existence of sin, in view of the fact that He chose to create a being whom He foresaw would, if He created him, freely sin."[10] Lorenzo McCabe, a nineteenth century Methodist theologian who wrote two lengthy treatments on foreknowledge, said that "a being who the Creator foreknew would be disobedient should not be created. . . . How easy for omnipotence to prevent the existence of those who, as his omniscience foresaw, would choose to be disobedient."[11] Cottrell gives the background for

this sort of providential control when he says, "It is *foreknowledge* that enables God to maintain complete control of his world despite the freedom of his creatures. God *knows* the future; it is not open or indefinite for him. This gives God the genuine option of either permitting or preventing men's planned choices, and prevention is the ultimate control."[12]

But can a God with CSF prevent sinners from being born or prevent certain evil choices? No, for the simple reason that if what God *foreknows* is the *actual* world then God foreknows the births, lives and deaths of actual sinners. Once God has foreknowledge he cannot change what will happen for that would make his foreknowledge incorrect. If God foreknows (has actual knowledge) that Adam will freely choose to mistrust God, then God cannot intervene to prevent Adam from this mistrust. Hence, God can see the evil coming before he creates the world but is powerless to prevent it. William Hasker is correct when he says,

> [I]t is clear that God's foreknowledge cannot be used either to *bring about* the occurrence of a foreknown event or to *prevent* such an event from occurring. For what God foreknows is *not* certain antecedents which, unless interfered with in some way, will *lead* to the occurrence of the event; rather, it is *the event itself* that is foreknown as occurring, and it is contradictory to suppose that an event is *known* to occur but then also is *prevented* from occurring. In the logical order of dependence of events, one might say, by the "time" God knows something will happen, it is "too late" either to *bring about* its happening or to *prevent* it from happening.[13]

The proponent of SF may appeal to Incremental Simple Foreknowledge (ISF) in an attempt to rescue providential control. Thus, God roles the tape forward and learns (prior to creation) that Adam is succumbing to temptation—but does not role the tape far enough to see whether he actually sins or not. At this point God may press the pause button on his remote and decide to intervene in order to buttress Adam's flagging trust. Will God's efforts be successful? To find out God roles the tape forward to see how Adam will respond.[14] If Adam chooses to continue to trust God then the temptation is overcome. If he fails to trust God then sin enters the world. Regardless, once God sees the actual future choice of the creature he is powerless to prevent it. Prior to the actual choice being made God can seek to persuade Adam to trust God, but once God knows that Adam will fail to trust God then it is too late for God to prevent the sin.

It must be remembered that a God with SF (either CFS or ISF) does not have middle knowledge and so cannot "try out" alternative scenarios in order to ascertain which one will achieve his objective in preventing Adam from sinning.[15] A God with SF knows what will occur in the actual world once he decides to create this world. But God does not know before he decides to create this particular world what sorts of decisions and actions a world containing individuals with libertarian freedom will freely choose to do if created. Consequently, a God with SF is no less a risk taker than a God with PK, for he could only gamble that a desirable state of affairs would actually come about. Hence, God is open to being surprised or disappointed by what he discovers will come about. Thus, a God with SF might "luck out" in that his free creatures never, in fact, decide to sin. But in this case there is no providential advantage for a God with SF over a God with PK. In fact, the way God providentially interacts with the world would be explained the same way in both models.

2. Election

What of all those God foreknew would never exercise saving faith in him and thus are not part of the elect of salvation? Can God decide not to create them? James Mill, the father of John Stuart Mill, thought so. "Think of a being," he says,

"who would make a hell, who would create the race with the infallible foreknowledge that the majority of them were to be consigned to horrible and everlasting torment."[16] Mill believed this a serious objection to the existence of the Christian God.

Although this charge may carry some weight against theological determinism it does not apply to SF because it misunderstands the nature of foreknowledge. Early church fathers such as Justin Martyr and Origen set forth a view of election, much later taken up by Arminius, which sought to use SF without divine determinism.[17] In their view God uses his foreknowledge to see which individuals will freely come to faith in Christ and God then decides to elect these people for eternal salvation. Hence, God's election is dependent on, and logically subsequent to, the choice of the creatures even though God's election of them is temporally prior to creation. God atemporally *responds* to the free choices of his creatures.[18]

A God with SF takes risks in creating a world with libertarian freedom since it was possible, before God decided to create and had no foreknowledge of the actual world, that no single human being would love God. This is as true for the theory of SF as for PK. Even with SF God gains no more providential control over who is saved than a God with PK. Hence, even a God with SF could, once he decided to create, have learned through his foreknowledge that no humans would ever freely come to love him in response to his love for them. As it has, in fact, turned out the actual world does, I believe, contain a number of people who respond in faith to the divine love. But, it must be remembered, this is not due to any providential use of his foreknowledge. One could say that God "lucked out," or one could say that God was confident and courageous enough to create a world where this tragic possibility existed but thankfully did not obtain.[19] Perhaps God had enough confidence in his ability to love the creatures and in his planned incarnation into human history that the risk was, from the divine point of view, worth taking if not minimal.

3. Guidance and Protection

It is often assumed that a God with SF would be in a maximally informed position to offer guidance and protection to those who petition him in prayer. For instance, say Mandie asks God whether she should marry Matthew or Jim, believing that God knows what is best for her and will advise her accordingly. In fact, Mandie may believe, with C. S. Lewis,[20] that a God with CSF knew of her prayer beforehand and so has prearranged things (perhaps even prior to her birth) in such a way that her request will be providentially answered. Mandie initiates her request in good faith believing that since God knows the future he can help her. She believes, for instance, that God knows whether Jim will be loving or abusive towards her. Perhaps God knows that Jim will turn out to be a drug dealer and quite abusive while Matthew will be a very loving person.[21] Mandie believes that God would, in this case, give her the guidance to marry Matthew. The problem is that if God knows that she will actually marry Jim and be quite unhappy, then it is useless for God to give her the guidance to marry Matthew. It would be incoherent to claim that God, knowing the actual future and on the basis of this knowledge, changes it so that it will not be the actual future. Of course, God might foreknow that Jim will be a wonderful husband for Mandie. Even so, it is not because God brought it about. A God who already knows the future cannot answer such prayers.

Furthermore, a God with CSF not only knows the "big" decisions Mandie will make, such as whom she will marry, but all the "little" ones leading up to and surrounding them as well. Hence, God knows all the details of her life as well as that of Jim's. If God sees that Mandie will be a very impatient person in the future God cannot act to bring it about that she become more patient than he foreknew. That is, God

cannot work to improve her character so that it falsifies his knowledge of what he knew her character would be like. If God acts at all in her life it will, presumably, make an impact on her and so change her if ever so slightly. But if God foreknows that such changes will never come about in her life then God is prohibited, by his foreknowledge, from acting in her life to improve her character.

Perhaps we can again salvage SF from such dreadful conclusions by appealing to ISF. In this way God only accesses his foreknowledge up to the point where Mandie invokes God for guidance as to whom she should marry—but does not yet know whom she will actually marry. At this juncture God is free to advise her, but his advice is limited to what he actually knows at present and what God surmises regarding the sorts of husbands Matthew and Jim might become. Remember, at this point in the tape God does not yet know the full development of their character traits. God may have very good beliefs about such matters which are virtually (always?) correct. Yet, if this is the case then the advice a God with ISF is able to give Mandie is no different from the advice a God with PK is able to give.

The same is true concerning prayers for protection. If God knows that I will be seriously injured in an auto accident on this particular trip, then no prayer for "travelling mercies" can alter this situation. Consequently, prayers for protection would be useless and any divine interventions prohibited. Only if God does not yet know the outcome of my journey can a prayer for safe traveling be coherent within the model of SF.[22] If God decides to act in response to my prayer it cannot be based on his foreknowledge. Hence, this situation is no different from asking a God with PK for safety in traveling.

4. Divine Repentance and Alternative Plans in the Divine-Human Dialogue

It is commonly thought that a God with CSF cannot "change his mind" and will have no need of resorting to alternative plans in his inter-actions with humans. The biblical texts speaking of divine repentance or alternative plans are taken to be simple anthropomorphisms. Thus one's view of foreknowledge deeply impacts the way one reads the biblical text. The story of Exodus 32 is a good case in point. In this story Moses has been up on the mountain for quite some time receiving the covenant from God. The people of Israel fashion and worship a golden calf which arouses the divine anger against their idolatry. God tells Moses to leave him alone so that he may destroy the people and begin his plan of human redemption over again—this time starting with Moses. Moses, however, does not agree with this "plan B" and so does not leave God alone. Instead, he intercedes for the people giving God three reasons why he should not carry out his threat. In response God "changed his mind (Hebrew *Nacham*) about the disaster that he planned to bring on his people" (32:14, *NRSV*).

How does the theory of CSF interpret such texts? Throughout history many philosophers have thought that since God knew the future it was literally impossible for God to change his mind or *respond* to his creatures in any way.[23] Hence, Exodus 32:14 and the numerous other texts referring to divine repentance and alterna-tive plans were interpreted to mean that from the *human* perspective God changed his mind, but God always knew he was not going to do what was threatened. Why, then, would God issue such threats? Some have suggested it is to teach Moses just how much Moses cared for the people of Israel.

More problematic are texts such as 1 Samuel 2:30 where God revokes a promise made to the priest Eli and his household. "Therefore the LORD God of Israel declares: 'I promised that your family and the family of your ancestor should go in and out before me forever'; but now the LORD declares: 'Far be it from me; for those who honor me I will honor, and those who despise me shall be treated with contempt.' "

God had made what appeared to be an unconditional promise to Eli for a perpetual priesthood; now, however, God responds to the sin of Eli's sons by reneging on that promise. But if God always knew that he would never fulfill that promise then it is a serious question whether God made the promise with integrity.

ISF affords a way out of this problem. By employing ISF, we can understand the text to mean that God genuinely intended to fulfill the promise because he did not know, "when" he made the promise, the future sins of Eli's sons. Once God "looked ahead" into the future then he learned of their sins and could then revoke the promise without being accused of mendacity. This interpretation of SF allows for God to change his mind, resort to a "plan B" and truly be responsive to his creatures. A big plus for this view is that we are allowed to read the biblical texts in a more straightforward way—as God entering into genuine give-and-take relations with his creatures. Again, however, we see that such an interpretation is identical to how the openness model would explain such texts.

5. Can God be Mistaken?

Many people have thought that the divine perfec-tion ruled out any possibility of God being wrong in any judgment. If God has knowledge rather than beliefs about the future then, of course, he cannot be mistaken about anything. Boethius said that "God sees everything in advance and cannot be deceived in any way."[24] Augustine agreed saying, "Whoever says that anything can happen otherwise than as God has foreknown it, is attempting to destroy the divine foreknowledge with the most insensate impiety."[25] Francis Beckwith has recently argued that a God with PK would base prophetic utter-ances not on his knowledge of the future but, rather, on his exhaustive knowledge of the past and present. He rejects this notion because "this means that it is within the realm of possi-bility that God could make a mistake about the future."[26] If God can be mistaken about what will happen in the future then divine prophecies may be in doubt.

These thinkers seem to affirm CSF where God accesses his knowledge of the future "all at once." In this version it is correct that God could never be mistaken about the future. But the major objection to this version, as was mentioned above, is that it seems to render problematic any divine intervention into the history God foresees. Before leaving CSF it may be instructive to see how it would interpret a biblical text where one of God's predictions is called into question.

The narrative of Moses' dialogue with God at the burning bush is fascinating because Moses suggests the possibility that God might be mistaken. In Exodus chapter three God seeks to enlist Moses in the divine service. Moses is reluctant, however, and gives God five reasons why he is not the right man for the job. In 3:16–22 God instructs Moses to gather the elders of Israel together and inform them of their impending liberation. Moreover, God explicitly says (v. 18) that the leaders will believe Moses. Perhaps Moses' understanding of divine foreknowledge was inadequate for he replies to God, "But suppose they do not believe me or listen to me?" (4:1). God responds by giving Moses a "sign" to perform before the elders—his rod turns into a serpent. God then declares that the purpose of this sign is "so that they may believe that the LORD . . . has appeared to you." (4:5). God then gives Moses a second sign—his skin becomes cancerous and is then healed (4:6–7). Amazingly, God then says, "If they will not believe you or heed the first sign, they may believe the second sign. If they will not believe even these two signs or heed you" (4:8–9) then here is a third sign.

According to CSF Moses' question is ridiculous for God knows precisely what will happen in the future and if God says it then that is the way it is going to be. Moses' understanding of divine foreknowledge is erroneous (a genuine possibility). The passage should be interpreted to mean that God condescended to Moses' frailty

and "played along" with him in order to give Moses greater confidence to undertake his mission. God knew they would believe but perhaps God also knew that they would only believe on the witness of the signs and so it is important for Moses to make this sort of request. The question remains, however, whether this interpretation does full justice to the statements "if they will not believe you."[27]

On the other hand, if we go with ISF where God accesses his knowledge of the future incrementally then we arrive at the astonishing conclusion that God could indeed be mistaken about the future. For in this view God does not know, at the time he is speaking with Moses, whether or not the elders will actually believe Moses. God may have a very good idea of their predisposition to believe but the possibility remains that God could be mistaken. Hence, on this view Moses' question is quite appropriate and so are the signs given to Moses. Furthermore, the language of the biblical text retains its prima facie integrity. Yet, it must be acknowledged that this interpretation is in full agreement with a PK reading of the text.

But this raises the *possibility* that some of God's predictions may be mistaken. Beckwith argues that the "test of a prophet" in Deuteronomy 18:22 expressly rules out such a possibility: "If a prophet speaks in the name of the LORD but the thing does not take place or prove true, it is a word that the LORD has not spoken."[28] If God says something will come to pass and it does not then the divine faithfulness and trustworthiness of the prophets is called into question. The biblical writers wrestled with this issue, particularly regarding the divine repentance. In this regard, philosopher J. R. Lucas and biblical scholar Terence Fretheim agree that these are, indeed, "failed" prophecies precisely because God is the sort of God who changes his mind in response to prayers and contrition.[29] In fact, Jonah includes this idea in his creedal statement: Yahweh is a "gracious God and merciful, slow to anger, and abounding in steadfast love, and ready to relent (Hebrew *Nacham*) from punishing" (4:2). Both

ISF and openness of God models are logically consistent with the notion of divine repentance and God being "mistaken". Of course, in a strict sense God would only be mistaken if he said a certain event would happen for sure and it did not come about. So long as God's "failed" predictions are understood in the sense of, "God believed this would happen but it did not," then there may be no mistake here at all.

6. Predictive Prophecy

It is commonly thought that one of the strongest values of a God with SF is that he can know the actual future and so is able to inform his prophets beforehand what precisely will happen. This is thought to give evidence of divine revelation, accreditation to the prophet and, perhaps, influence the hearers of the prophecy to live their lives in accordance with the divine will.

Biblical texts where God is said to "declare the end from the beginning" (Isaiah 46:10) or specific predictions of events which then came about (e. g. Jesus' prediction of Peter's denial in Luke 22:31–4) are usually given as evidence that God has SF. Such texts can, of course, be explained by the other views of divine omniscience and do not necessitate SF as an interpretation.[30]

There is a logical difficulty which makes this particular understanding of predictive prophecy problematic with both CSF and ISF. As has already been shown CSF cannot be used as the means by which God predicts the future for the simple reason that, if God sees history "all at once" and, presumably, his actions were not foreseen, then God never foresees any prophets making predictions given by God.

Moreover, it is probably clear by now why ISF cannot be used to predict (in the strong sense) the future. It must be remembered that explaining SF as a logical sequence implies that God does not know precisely what is going to happen after the event he is foreseeing. If God learns as he previsions the future then it becomes impossible for God to interject something based

on his knowledge of the future into the chemistry of past events which would alter his knowledge of what actually occurred in the past. For instance, if God foresees the whole of Jesus' life, he has not yet (logically speaking) foreseen the destruction of the Jerusalem temple in 70 A.D. Once God previsions the events of 70 A.D. it is "too late" for God to go back and reveal through Jesus a prediction about this event during the life of Jesus for God never foresaw Jesus uttering such a prediction.

If God knows all the details and causal antecedents leading up to event Z and his prediction of event Z based on ISF was not part of this foreknowledge, then ISF is useless for predicting the future. For God to make a prediction of Z prior to the occurrence of Z would, presumably, change the course of history and alter some of the details which God foresees. Let us say that God looks ahead and sees that the Babylonian invasion will happen and then God decides to reveal to Jeremiah that it will occur in the future. At a minimum, Jeremiah will now know something which he did not know when God first previsioned Jeremiah's life and words. That is, God "now" knows (logically) that he will provide to Jeremiah a prediction of event Z at time A, a future event which neither God nor Jeremiah knew about when God first previsioned time A since it was not part of his original foreknowledge. This would imply a change in the divine foreknowledge rendering the original foreknowledge incorrect.

Perhaps an illustration will help. Rajesh, wishing to make some money, may believe that a God with ISF would be in a position to inform him who will win the next Super Bowl and, if God should inform him, he could place his bet accordingly. Unfortunately, once God has "rolled the tape" up to the point where Rajesh makes his request, God does not yet know who the winner will be. And as God continues to prevision the future he does not foresee his answer to Rajesh until after he previsions which team actually wins the next Super Bowl. By this time, however, it is too late for Rajesh to place his bet and it is "too late" for God to alter the past. This is the converse of the problem raised above in connection to divine guidance and miracles. In those cases the problem was that once God knows what will happen he cannot change it. In this case, once God knows the "past" (as he previsions it sequentially) he cannot change it.

A God with ISF could, however, inform Rajesh which team he *believes* will win the next Super Bowl based upon his exhaustive knowledge of all the details available to his prevision at the time Rajesh makes his request. Of course, such a "prediction" will be no different from the sort of help a God with PK could give him.

7. The Guarantee of the Success of God's plans

It is felt by some proponents of SF that a key value is its ability to guarantee, from before creation, that God's plans would be successful. David Clark asserts that "foreknowledge could put God in a position to promise, with integrity, at the beginning of history, that good will overcome evil."[31] Clark believes that a weakness of the openness model is its inability to guarantee that God will ultimately eliminate evil. He claims that a God with PK cannot, while a God with SF can, affirm that God shall conquer evil triumphantly at the end of history while yet granting libertarian freedom by which humans sometimes resist the divine will.[32] He goes on to argue that a God with only PK is not in a position to guarantee, prior to creation, that anyone would come to faith. "Would anyone believe? One could say that God is infinitely resourceful and would have started another line like Seth's or called out another Noah. Yet how could God know that Plan C would work any better than failed Plans A and B? Could God with integrity promise that Seed would overcome Serpent (Genesis 3:15)? Or would it have been more correct for God to say, 'I hope to do everything I can so that Seed will strike Serpent's heel?' "[33] Clark feels that redemption itself is threatened if

God lacks foreknowledge—there is too much risk involved otherwise.

Does either version of simple foreknowledge alleviate the risk of creating creatures with libertarian freedom? It has already been shown that SF does not make creation and providence any less risky than PK. Does SF enable God to promise from the beginning that his redemptive plans will succeed? No, for the claim that God uses SF to predict the future (guarantee success) was shown to fail. Does SF allow God to know which of plans A or B or C will succeed? No, as David Basinger correctly responds: "A God with [SF] does know what will occur in the *actual* world—including what humans with indeterministic freedom will freely choose to do. . . . But this means, of course, that before God's creative decision was made, he did not know with respect to any creative option containing individuals with indeterministic freedom what such individuals would freely choose to do if actualized. Thus, he, like a God with PK, could only 'gamble' on the fact that a desirable state of affairs would come about."[34]

"Once" God decides to create this world, then a God with SF can "look ahead" to see whether anyone with libertarian freedom will come to faith. But if nobody ever trusts God then what God foreknows is that his plans have failed. If some people do exercise faith in God then God foreknows, from the beginning, that his efforts will meet with success. But the reason for the success is not the divine foreknowledge. Rather, the reason is that humans freely decided to trust God. Moreover, as has been shown, God cannot use this foreknowledge to predict the future and so a God with SF is not in a position to guarantee success from the beginning. Consequently, a God with SF has no more ability to guarantee the success of his plans than does a God with PK.

Conclusion

If this analysis is correct, then SF (either CSF or ISF) affords God no greater providential control in these seven areas than does PK. CSF appears to stymie divine involvement and, though ISF allows for divine responsiveness to his creatures and enables us to read the biblical texts of divine-human dialogue in a more straightforward manner, it results in explanations essentially identical to the openness model. In passing, it should be noted that the problems encountered in constructing a coherent account of the providential use of SF are also problems for the doctrine of divine timeless knowledge. Keith Ward has argued that the appeal to timelessness gives "the illusion of control" but actually does not enhance providence at all.[35] Finally, those who make the common claim that SF is useful for providence have not given a plausibile account of how this is so. If the supposed values of SF for providence are illusory, then the reasons for affirming it are greatly reduced. In which case, the "live options" regarding the use of omniscience for providential interaction with creatures with indeterministic freedom are narrowed to either molinism or openness.

My preference is to develop an understanding of divine providence from a PK view of omniscience where God only foreknows what he, himself determines to do. If God is the risk taker which the openness of God view affirms then some serious rethinking is in order concerning how God exercises providence. Nevertheless, according to the openness model God is supremely loving, wise, good, knowledgeable, and powerful. Hence, God can offer us the greatest possible guidance and protection he can given the sort of world he chose to create. This God is able to respond to us, dialogue with us and supply mercy and grace in time of need (Heb 4:16).[36]

Notes

1 Indeterministic freedom is assumed throughout this essay.

2 God may intend to perform a certain action at a particular time unless conditions are such that an alternate plan is warranted. There are some things (e. g. the incarnation) which God decrees unilaterally apart from any consideration of human action. Hence, I make a distinction between absolute and conditional decrees by God.

3 David P. Hunt, "Divine Providence and Simple Foreknowledge," *Faith and Philosophy* 10, 3 (July, 1993), pp. 394–5.

4 Jack Cottrell, *What the Bible Says About God the Ruler* (Joplin, MO: College Press Publishing, 1984), pp. 208–9. It seems that what Cottrell is actually describing is closer to Middle Knowledge than SF.

5 If a God with CSF possesses foreknowledge of his own actions, then the problem is to explain how the foreknowledge can be the *basis* for the actions when it already *includes* the actions. As William Hasker says in his *God, Time, and Knowledge* (Ithaca, NY: Cornell University Press, 1989), p. 63, "[I]t is impossible that God should use a foreknowledge derived from the actual occurrance of future events to determine his own prior actions in the providential governance of the world." See also note seven below.

6 Hunt, "Divine Providence," p. 408.

7 This problem holds unless, of course, one wishes to say that God sees his own actions in his foreknowledge (which, it seems, SF needs to affirm). God would then know what he is going to do before he makes up his mind and God would be unable to plan, anticipate or decide (see Eleanore Stump and Norman Kretzman, "Eternity" *Journal of Philosophy*, 78, no. 8 [August, 1981]: 446). Unfortunately, this calls the divine freedom and omnipotence into question making God a prisoner of his omnipresence (see J. R. Lucas, "Foreknowledge and the Vulnerability of God," in Godfrey Vesey ed., *The Philosophy in Christianity* [New York: Cambridge University Press, 1989], p. 126).

8 William P. Alston suggests this possibility in his "Divine-Human Dialogue and the Nature of God," *Faith and Philosophy* 2, no. 1 (Jan. 1985), p. 17; Hunt hints at it in his "Divine Providence and Simple Foreknowledge," p. 412; and William Hasker clearly explains it in his *God, Time, and Knowledge*, pp. 57–9.

9 All time related terms used in this discussion are meant in a logical rather than temporal fashion. After all, an atemporal deity does not literally have "fore" knowledge.

10 John Hick, *Evil and the God of Love*, revised ed. (New York: Harper and Row, 1978), p. 69.

11 Lorenzo McCabe, *The Foreknowledge of God* (Cincinnati, OH: Cranston and Stowe, 1887), p. 364. See also his *Divine Nescience of Future Contingencies a Necessity* (New York: Phillips and Hunt, 1862). Though verbose McCabe's two books contain many of the same arguments being used by contemporary defenders of PK.

12 Cottrell, *God the Ruler*, p. 214. I do not understand how Cottrell can consistently maintain both that the future is closed for God and that God is able to alter that same future.

13 Hasker, *God, Time, and Knowledge*, pp. 57–8. Keith Ward makes the same point in his *Rational Theology and the Creativity of God* (New York, Pilgrim Press, 1982), p. 152.

14 The tape metaphor may, itself, be deceiving since it assumes the future is available to be known. That is, even if God should stop the tape the rest of the future is there to be known and if God knows it is there to be known, then it is difficult to understand how God's actions would change anything. Consequently, ISF may not be a legitimate alternative to CSF. I owe thus observation to a referee of this journal.

15 Although writers such as McCabe and Cottrell do not refer to middle knowledge, at times it seems they have something like it in mind. Actually, I believe many proponents of SF need middle knowledge to warrant their claims. But then, SF will have been forfeited. Interestingly, Arminius affirmed a version of middle knowledge. See *The Writings of James Arminius*, 3 vols., trans. James Nichols (Grand Rapids: Baker, 1956), 1:248 and Richard A. Muller, *God, Creation, and Providence in the Thought of Jacob Arminius* (Grand Rapids, Baker, 1991), 154–7.

16 Quoted in McCabe, *Foreknowledge of God*, p. 25.

17 See my "Historical Considerations," in Clark Pinnock et al., *The Openness of God: A Biblical Challenge to the Traditional Understanding of God* (Downers Grove, IL: InterVarsity Press, 1994), pp. 72–75, 91.

18 If God responds in this way, then election is a bilateral choosing and not a unilateral act of God. Moreover, if as God looks ahead in history he does not yet know whether, for instance, Saul will come to faith in Jesus, then it makes sense for God to encourage him towards salvation. But if God already knows that Saul will never come to faith, then what does this make of God's attempts to convert him? Are such attempts genuine? It could be argued that God makes genuine efforts to save those he knows will never actually come to faith, but whatever reasons one adduces for such divine actions, it will not be for the benefit of Saul. McCabe, (*Foreknowledge of God*, p. 353), asks, "Is it possible to conceive of God's putting forth efforts with that burning earnestness which the urgent necessities of the case demand, in order to snatch from everlasting death an endangered moral agent when he is absolutely certain that that agent is going forward to endless perdition?"

19 Phillip Yancy and G. K. Chesterton both assert that God was "courageous" in creating this sort of world. See Yancy, "Cosmic Combat," *Christianity Today* 38, no. 14 (Dec. 12, 1994), p. 21.

20 C. S. Lewis, "On Special Providences" in *Miracles* (New York: Macmillan, 1974), pp. 180–7.

21 Some proponents of SF speak as though God had gaps in his foreknowledge. For instance, they sometimes speak as though God knows exactly what sort of person Abe will become while God does not know whether Abe and Mandie actually get married. But if God knows Abe's future character then he would also know whether or not they got married. See, for example, David Hunt, "Divine Providence and Simple Foreknowledge," p. 409.

22 I am not here addressing the issue of how libertarian freedom affects what God does or does not do in answer to such prayers. I am only examining how such prayers make sense within the theory of SF.

23 See my "Historical Considerations," in Clark Pinnock et. al., *The Openness of God*, pp. 69–91. For some Medieval Jewish philosophical reflections on the matter see Seymour Feldman, "The Binding of Isaac: A Test-Case of Divine Foreknowledge," in Tamar Rudavsky, *Divine Omniscience and Omnipotence in Medieval Philosophy: Islamic, Jewish and Christian Perspectives* (Boston: D. Reidel, 1985), pp. 105–133.

24 Boethius, *The Consolation of Philosophy*, 5.3.

25 Augustine, *On Free Will*, 3.2.4.

26 Beckwith, "Limited Omniscience and the Test For a Prophet: A Brief Philosophical Analysis," *Journal of the Evangelical Theological Society* 36, mo. 3 (Sept. 1993), p. 359.

27 Three times the text says that God gives the signs for the benefit of the leaders of Israel—not for Moses' benefit (at least, not for his benefit alone). Moreover, God says, if they do not believe you. Terence Fretheim discusses divine uses of "if" in the Hebrew Bible and concludes they are genuine conditionals for God. God's response to Moses' question indicates that not even God knew for sure the people would believe. See his *The Suffering of God: An Old Testament Perspective* (Philadelphia: Fortress, 1984), pp. 47–9 and *Exodus, Interpretation* (Louisville, KY: John Knox, 1991), p. 68. In addition, CSF does not allow such divine-human dialogue to take place at all which leads back to the same problem discussed in note number 4 above.

28 It seems that Beckwith reads this verse as a sort of philosophical principle—a timeless truth—removed from its cultural context and insufficiently nuanced with other texts related to the issue. For instance, in the book of Jonah the prophet announces doom upon the city of Ninevah which never comes about. Elijah foretold judgment upon king Ahab which never came to pass (texts which Beckwith does not address). In both stories there is no conditional element in the foretold doom. If Beckwith's understanding of the test of a prophet is correct then both Jonah and Elijah gave false prophecies. I suggest the verse be understood as a guiding rule (rather than a universal principle) which does not override the divine freedom to modify the divine judments in favor of mercy should God choose to do so.

29 See J. R. Lucas, *The Future* (Cambridge, MA: Basil Blackwell, 1989), pp. 222–3, and his "Foreknowledge and the Vulnerability of God," p. 119; Terence Fretheim, "Prayer in the Old Testament," in Paul Sponheim ed., *A Primer on Prayer* (Philadelphia: Fortress, 1988), p. 59 and his *The Suffering of God*, pp. 45–59.

30 For instance, PK can interpret these texts as referring to acts that God has decided to perform

(which is what Is 46:10 explicitly goes on to say!) and so no foreknowledge is involved. Jesus' prediction of Peter's denial can be explained by proponents of PK as an instance where Jesus knew his disciples and the situation so well that he could make such a statement—though it was most likely a conditional one which could have been falsified. See Pinnock, *The Openness of God* pp. 50–3 and McCabe's two works cited above which deal in depth with this issue. Admittedly, more work needs to be done in explaining these types of texts by the proponents of PK.

Problematic, and commonly overlooked by proponents of SF, are the numerous occasions where biblical predictions either do not come to pass at all (e. g. Jonah and 2 Kings 20) or not in the exact way they were foretold (e. g. Gen 27:27–40 where Jacob's blessing is qualified by Esau's blessing; Gen 37:6–10 where Joseph's parents never bow down to him; and Acts 21:11 where it is predicted, incorrectly, that the Jews will deliver Paul over to the Gentiles). Presumably a God with SF would not err in predicting the future in any details.

31 David K. Clark, "A Response to *The Openness of God*," unpublished paper given at the Evangelical Philosophical Society, November 18, 1994 in Chicago, p. 7.

32 Clark, *Ibid.*, pp. 4–5.

33 Clark, *Ibid.*, p. 7.

34 David Basinger, "Divine Knowledge and Divine Control: A Response to Gordon and Sadowsky," *Religious Studies*, 26, no. 2 (June, 1990), p. 274.

35 Ward, *Rational Theology*, pp. 162–3. Ward observes that the real issue is the necessity of divine omnipotence for a temporal deity can easily control every present and future situation if he so decides.

36 I would like to thank William Hasker, David Basinger and the referees of this journal for making some helpful suggestions on an earlier draft of this paper.

Chapter 27

David P. Hunt

THE PROVIDENTIAL ADVANTAGE OF DIVINE FOREKNOWLEDGE

Classical Theism is committed not just to divine *omniscience* but also to exhaustive *foreknowledge*: for everything that happens, there was no time at which God didn't know that it would happen.[1] If God is an unexcellably perfect being, one compelling reason for attributing to him exhaustive knowledge of the future is that this would make him *smarter* than he would be if he lacked it. This reason has force in the logic of perfect being theology whether or not such foreknowledge would endow God with any further advantage—for example, by equipping him to do things he couldn't do if he lacked such knowledge.

Of course this reason for ascribing exhaustive foreknowledge to God presupposes that this attribute is coherent and, if coherent, that it doesn't conflict with more important desiderata. Divine foreknowledge has in fact been challenged on both scores. The controversy centers on God's knowledge of *future contingents*: propositions about the future whose truth isn't determined by anything that has *already* happened, but only by what happens *later*. (Example: tomorrow I come to a fork in the road and it's genuinely open to me to go left or right; suppose I in fact go right; then relative to today, when my going right at that fork is still future, the statement *I will go right when I come to that fork in the road* expresses a future contingent.) If there are future contingents and these are (while future) *neither true nor false*, there cannot be such a thing as truly

exhaustive foreknowledge, for some of the future (the contingent part) will be unknowable.[2] And if a world with future contingents is the kind of world a perfectly good God prefers (perhaps because this is a precondition for the good of libertarian free agency) and foreknowing such facts would leave them *noncontingent*, then it's arguable that God would be more excellent for *not* knowing them, even if there are such truths to be known; for God would then be in a position to create a better world (one with genuine future contingencies) than if he knew everything in advance.[3] Both of these challenges are subjects of ongoing debate. Classical Theists, of course, must hold that both challenges fail, while so-called "Open Theists," who deny exhaustive foreknowledge, are convinced that one or both succeed.

What is at stake in this debate? Certainly there are *logical* and *metaphysical* issues at stake. Does the Law of Excluded Middle apply to propositions about the future? In what sense is the past (now) *necessary*? Can free agency exist in the absence of alternative possibilities? There is a vast literature on such questions, and I don't propose to add to it here.

What I would like to explore instead are the *theological* stakes. What are these? One issue that is not at stake is divine perfection: the debate isn't over whether God is maximally great, but whether maximal greatness includes exhaustive foreknowledge.[4] What *does* seem to be at stake theologically is the issue raised in the first paragraph: whether foreknowledge would endow God with any "further advantage." Open Theists are at pains to deny that exhaustive foreknowledge would render God more capable than if he lacked it. This is the thesis argued in the selection by John Sanders (this volume, chapter 26), and it's the thesis that I mean to dispute.

What could be more useful than knowing the future? Action is future-oriented, and the success of our actions depends on how events unfold. What's going to happen to the stock market over the next few days? If only I knew! Is my tennis opponent about to rush the net? Then a lob would be in order. Will George be in the audience tomorrow? Then I'd better spend some time anticipating the objections he will surely raise. Will Sue show up as promised to drive me to the airport? If not, it would be nice to know now, so I can order a cab; if I wait to find out, it may be too late.

The claim by Sanders and other Open Theists that foreknowledge would nevertheless be useless is rather surprising. There appear to be a number of worries here, which don't always get clearly distinguished. The cleanest way to proceed, given the immense confusion surrounding this topic, is to describe a single case—the simpler the better—in which foreknowledge prima facie enables God to secure a result he couldn't secure without it. We can then see how this case compares with Sanders' own characterization of the Classical Theist's position and whether his objections to the providential utility of divine foreknowledge raise any genuine difficulties for it.[5]

Let's begin the construction of this simple scenario with a single contingent event, an event that can be foreknown by the God of Classical Theism but not by the God of Open Theism. Call this event "E". Next, God must actually know that E will occur. Let "K(E)" designate God's knowledge of E. Finally, God must put this knowledge to use by doing something. Call this divine action

"A". E, K(E), and A are the three constituents of our simple scenario for the providential employment of divine foreknowledge.

In constructing this scenario, I followed the logical or explanatory order of its three constituents. E *explains* K(E); in other words, the fact that E will occur explains why God knows that E will occur. (This distinguishes "simple foreknowledge," the subject of Sanders' essay, from other models of divine foreknowledge—see the beginning of the next section, page 377.) Moreover, K(E) *explains* A: God's knowledge that E will occur explains why God does A. (If it doesn't, K(E) is idling.) In sum, God does A *because* he knows that E will occur, and he knows that E will occur *because* E will in fact occur.

An interesting question is whether, in addition to specifying the explanatory relations that *do* obtain in this scenario, it is also important to specify that a certain explanatory relation does *not* obtain, namely, that *A does not explain* E. If God's action A *did* help explain why event E occurs, we would appear to have an explanatory circle on our hands: A because K(E), because E, because A. Whether such explanatory circles are possible is a difficult question. I'm not sure that they aren't possible—the philosopher David Lewis, for example, maintained that they are *inexplicable* but nevertheless *possible*.[6] Still, providential scenarios that generate explanatory circles would raise serious concerns that are best avoided. Let's therefore stipulate that A does *not* explain E.[7]

A further question is how this scenario embodies providential utility. For divine foreknowledge to be useful, God must have some objective—call it "O"—which his foreknowledge puts him in a better position to achieve than if he lacked that knowledge. The limit case is where, given his foreknowledge, God knows *exactly* what to do to *guarantee* that O is achieved. When O depends in part on the libertarianly free actions of agents other than God, however, this ideal of providential control will often be out of reach, and divine foreknowledge will show its providential utility only by providing God information that *increases the likelihood* of O coming about. In keeping with the simplicity of our scenario, let's suppose God's objective O is simply this: that he shall have done A, if E will occur. Our scenario then embodies the limit case in which, given his foreknowledge of E, God knows exactly what to do (namely, A) to guarantee the achievement of O. Near the end of the paper, after we've spent some time thinking as clearly as we can about this simple scenario, I will introduce a probabilistic version involving another free agent and we can see whether this raises any additional difficulties that haven't already been dealt with.[8]

The last thing we need to do is assign times to the three constituents in the scenario. K(E), of course, must *precede* E in time; otherwise it won't amount to foreknowledge and the scenario won't capture the providential advantage that an omniprescient deity is supposed to have over one who lacks exhaustive knowledge of future contingents. As for A, it must come *after* (or at least *no earlier than*) K(E), since God does A *because* of K(E). But A must also *precede* E; otherwise God's performance of A could be informed by a knowledge of E acquired *after* the occurrence of E, and that's a knowledge that would be available to the God of Open Theism as well as the God of Classical Theism. The temporal order, then, is this: K(E) at T1, A at T2, E at T3, where T1<T2<T3. In contrast, the logical or explanatory order, as outlined two paragraphs earlier, is this: E at T3, K(E) at T1, A at T2.

Call this scenario "The Basic Schema." Because The Basic Schema is so abstract and, well, *schematic*, it might be helpful to the reader to have in mind a more concrete case that exemplifies The Basic Schema. Suppose, then, that Satan challenges God to a game of rock-paper-scissors. Satan realizes, of course, that he's taking on *the Supreme Being*, and he's understandably concerned that he may not face a level playing field. In particular, he fears that if he and God declare at the same time T, there might be no lag in God's knowledge of and reaction to what Satan declares, so that if Satan declares, e.g., "paper" at T, God will know this at T and can declare "scissors" at T. Satan won't have a chance under such conditions. Satan therefore asks that God go first; but in order that the playing field be genuinely leveled, and not stacked in Satan's favor, God is to make his declaration of rock, paper or scissors *mentally*, revealing it only after Satan declares.[9] (The Father of Lies is confident that the Father of Truth won't deceive him when it comes time to reveal what he declared!) God agrees to this handicap and the game commences. Unfortunately for Satan, in correcting for God's unexcellably quick reflexes, he overlooked God's foreknowledge of future contingents. Knowing beforehand what Satan will declare, God is able to win every round.

The foregoing scenario is a clear instance of The Basic Schema. Consider a round in which Satan declares rock. Then E=Satan's declaring rock, K(E)=God's foreknowing that Satan will declare rock, and A=God's (mentally) declaring paper. The explanatory order is the one just given, while the temporal order is God's foreknowing at T1 that Satan will declare rock, God's (mentally) declaring paper at T2, and Satan's declaring rock at T3. O=God's winning the game. K(E) is providentially useful because God's chances of achieving O, given K(E), are 100%, whereas his chances without it are no better than 50% (perhaps a bit higher, given God's superlative knowledge of Satan's psychology and past choices).[10]

Here then is an instance of The Basic Schema—call it "The Game"—in which a God with exhaustive knowledge of future contingents appears to enjoy a clear advantage over a God who lacks such knowledge. We must now turn to Sanders' reasons for holding that, appearances to the contrary notwithstanding, there can be no such cases.

Sanders begins his critique of the providential utility of divine foreknowledge by distinguishing "two different versions of how God's foreknowledge is accessed." (p. 363) Both are versions of so-called "simple foreknowledge." Simple foreknowledge (or SF) is a knowledge of the contingent future that is not arrived at by inference from other things that God knows. In particular, it does not rest on God's knowledge of his own intentions for the future (which wouldn't help him know what other agents will do), or his knowledge of deterministic connections between the past and future (which won't give him access to the *contingent* future), or his "middle knowledge" of so-called "counterfactuals of freedom" (a providentially rich resource whose coherence is a matter of considerable controversy. Rather, in SF God can "see" what is temporally distant (the future as well as past) in something like the way that we can see what is spatially distant. And just as, when we see things truly, our visual information depends on, and is explained by, what we see, so God's knowledge of future events is explanatorily dependent on those events: he believes that an event will occur *because* it will occur; it doesn't occur *because* he believes it will occur. It was to accommodate this feature of simple foreknowledge that the Basic Schema was set up so that K(E) is explanatorily dependent on E.

On the first version of "how God's foreknowledge is accessed," which Sanders labels "Complete Simple Foreknowledge" (or CSF), God takes in the entire future "at once." Sanders briefly elaborates: "though he knows things will occur in sequence God does not acquire the knowledge in sequence. God simply sees the whole at once." (p. 363) Sanders dismisses this version of divine foreknowledge in short order, on the ground that "there is no room for any providential activity if God sees the whole at once." (p. 363) The second version of how God accesses his foreknowledge is "Incremental Simple Foreknowledge" (or ISF), in which God "accesses the future *in sequence* or *incrementally*." ISF provides a better understanding of simple foreknowledge than does CSF, Sanders maintains, inasmuch as it appears to allow God to "weave

his own actions into the flow of human history" (p. 364). For this reason, it's ISF whose providential resources Sanders compares with those of Open Theism throughout the remainder of his essay.

Sanders' dismissal of CSF's providential possibilities occupies just one paragraph. He evidently thinks that its problems are so obvious that a single paragraph is all that's necessary; he also evidently thinks that Classical Theists will readily agree that ISF provides a superior model of simple foreknowledge, so that lingering over CSF is wasted effort. In fact, the whole argument of Sanders' paper turns on this one paragraph. We'll need to pay it more attention than Sanders does.

Why exactly does Sanders think that CSF has no room for God's providential activity? There appear to be two reasons offered in this paragraph. The first has to do with "the fact that what God previsions is what will *actually* occur." So consider some future event E (Sanders' example is the Holocaust); God, given CSF, "knows it is going to happen and cannot prevent it from happening since his foreknowledge is never mistaken." In other words, were God to act so that E, a future event foreknown by God, does *not* happen, his foreknowledge would be mistaken; but that's obviously impossible; so God can't act so that E doesn't happen. The same argument applies to any future event, since a God with CSF knows all such events. Therefore God can't prevent *anything* from happening. So much the worse for divine providence, if CSF provides the right account of how God accesses his knowledge of the future.

There are at least a couple of problems with this first reason for dismissing CSF. The first is that *prevention* isn't the only point to providential intervention. Consider The Game. God doesn't use his foreknowledge to *prevent* something he foreknows from happening; rather, he uses his foreknowledge to *bring about* something, namely, his declaring paper. So CSF's alleged uselessness for preventative purposes doesn't warrant the conclusion that it is useless *simpliciter*.

The second problem is that Sanders' argument doesn't work against "preventative providence" in the first place. What is it to prevent some event E from occurring? Prevention doesn't involve doing something ("preventing it") to some actually existing event; after all, if the event exists, you didn't prevent it! Rather, preventing E means (roughly) doing something A which is such that E *does not* occur, where E *would have* occurred if one had not done A. In The Game, for example, God not only makes providential use of his foreknowledge by *bringing about* his declaration of paper; he also makes providential use of his foreknowledge by *preventing* Satan from winning the game. What God prevents here (Satan's victory) is not, of course, to be found either among future events or among the things that God foreknows; if it were, he didn't succeed in preventing it! Rather, God prevents Satan's winning the game because he does something—declaring paper—which is such that Satan does *not* win the game, whereas Satan *would have* won (or tied) if God hadn't declared paper.

In sum, Sanders draws the wrong moral from God's foreknowing "what will *actually* occur." Because this is indeed the *actual* future, it not only provides the material for God's foreknowledge; it also includes all the results of any providential actions (whether productive or preventative) that God undertakes. Far from defeating his providential aspirations, foreknowledge provides a record of God's providential successes.

So much for Sanders' first reason for dismissing CSF. His second reason is more complex. He introduces it this way: "if what God has foreseen is the *entire* human history *at once*, then the difficulty is to somehow allow for God's intervention into that history since, presumably, his prevision did not include his own actions" (p. 363). This reason contains both (i) an assumption and (ii) a difficulty alleged to rest on that assumption. Let's begin with (i).

(i) CSF is supposed to be God's knowing *all*

of the future *at once*. It is surprising, then, to find Sanders claiming that what God knows "at once" is *not* in fact all of the future: God's own future actions are not included. *Complete* Simple Foreknowledge turns out to be a misnomer. Since Sanders has already appropriated this name for his "gappy" version of simple foreknowledge, we'll need to introduce a new name—"*Really* Complete Simple Foreknowledge"—for the view that what God knows "at once" does indeed include *all* of the future. The more important question, though, is *why* Sanders thinks that CSF should be qualified in this way. There is nothing in the main text, other than the word "presumably," that so much as recognizes this question, let alone answers it. Such reasons as Sanders has for ignoring Really Complete Simple Foreknowledge are relegated to two endnotes.

In the first, endnote 5, he writes: "If a God with CSF possesses foreknowledge of his own actions, then the problem is to explain how the foreknowledge can be the *basis* for the actions when it already *includes* the actions." But this "problem" is wholly an artifact of the careless way in which Sanders refers to "the foreknowledge" and "the actions." *Which* foreknowledge, and *which* actions? Certainly God couldn't make foreknowledge of his *own* action A the "basis" for that very action A; but there's no reason why he couldn't use foreknowledge of *other* events as the basis for A. In The Game, for example, God doesn't use his foreknowledge that he is going to declare paper as the basis for his decision to declare paper. ("Why did you declare paper?" one of the angels asks. "Because I foreknew that I would declare paper," God replies. What kind of reason is that?) Instead, God uses his foreknowledge that *Satan is going to declare rock* as the basis for his decision to declare paper. Endnote 5 is just confused about how God would make providential use of simple foreknowledge.

The second, endnote 7, raises a different difficulty: if CSF includes God's own actions, "God would then know what he is going to do before he makes up his mind and God would be unable to plan, anticipate or decide." How so? Sanders doesn't tell us. As it happens, I have written extensively on this subject and have much to say about it, but Sanders' silence regarding the reasons behind his claim leaves it unclear how best to proceed. Since it's impossible to engage Sanders' reasons without knowing what they are, I will simply summarize what I think is the right view of the matter and leave it at that. While there is little doubt that Sanders' claim that God couldn't make up his mind if he already knew what he's going to do has some intuitive appeal, I believe that the intuition will dissipate upon further reflection.[11] There is a good theoretical reason why this is so. Foreknowledge of one's own actions involves endorsement of the declarative proposition *I will do A*, while planning and deciding are oriented toward endorsement of the optative proposition *Would that I might do A*.[12] These are different propositions, and endorsement of the first proposition does not logically pre-empt endorsement of the second.[13] A time traveler, for example, who has just returned from witnessing his own future suicide, may (sadly) be prepared to endorse the declarative proposition *I will kill myself* while not yet being ready to endorse the optative proposition *Would that I might kill myself*, because he does not (yet) will that he shall kill himself. For this reason, it is in principle possible to acquire the intention to perform an action (say, by deliberating) while already knowing that one will perform that action. Since this is possible, Sanders has failed to show that a God who already knows what he is going to do would be unable to do it in a planful and intentional manner.[14]

I see no reason, then, to join Sanders in his assumption that CSF does not include foreknowledge of God's own actions. Let's now turn to the difficulty that Sanders raises for CSF, given his understanding of it.

(ii) Sanders is clear in his statement of the difficulty: "if what God has foreseen is the *entire* human history at *once*," where this did not include his own actions, "then the difficulty is to somehow allow for God's intervention into that history." What is not clear is what exactly Sanders takes this difficulty to be. Sanders' reference to "God's own actions in Abraham's life which would alter Abraham's life and consequently change God's foreknowledge" suggests an answer. Start with God's Complete Simple Foreknowledge, understood not as *Really* Complete Simple Foreknowledge but as containing gaps into which God's own actions can be inserted. *Can* God interject his actions into these gaps, thereby making a contribution to history? Apparently not; if God were to do this, it would *make a difference* to history, consequently *changing his foreknowledge*. Once his CSF informs him of the entire and detailed course of human history, it's *too late* for him to do anything about it.

Let me make three points in response. First, the foregoing argument doesn't provide any reason to think that God couldn't interject his actions into history so long as they *make no difference* to what happens. But wouldn't such interventions, by making no difference, be non-providential, and thus irrelevant to the present issue? That depends on what counts as *making a difference*. Sanders appears to believe that God's providential acts, inserted into the gaps in his CSF where there are placeholders for his own actions, would "make a difference" by *changing* the surrounding events and his foreknowledge of them ("alter Abraham's life and consequently change God's foreknowledge"). Of course that is impossible. But this doesn't mean that a God with CSF can't intervene in history so as to "make a difference;" it only means that Sanders is operating with an incoherent concept of "making a difference." No one can make a difference to what happens by *changing* the future. Recall what was said earlier about *prevention*. You don't prevent an event by taking an event and then preventing it. Likewise you don't make a difference to the future by taking the future and then making a difference to it. You make a difference to the future, not by changing it, but by doing something that *brings it about*, where a different future would have obtained if you *hadn't* done that thing.

Second, Sanders' argument appears to be relevantly similar to fatalistic arguments like the following:

> Either I will be struck by a car while crossing this busy road, or I will not; if I will be struck by a car, any precautions I take will be ineffective; if I will not be struck by a car, any precautions I take will be superfluous; so taking precautions while crossing this road is either ineffective or superfluous, and hence pointless; so I might as well throw caution to the wind.

The Stoics called this the "Lazy Argument" because anyone taken in by it would become terminally lazy about their actions. There are many things to be said about this argument, but I will limit myself to just one comment, which seems most relevant to the argument offered by Sanders. The Lazy Argument does not take into account my actions, only their outcome: either I will be struck by a car, or I won't be struck by a car. The claim is that I can't act, at least in any way that would "make a difference" to the outcome: what I do will be either ineffective or superfluous, and in any case pointless. What this overlooks is that the outcome—that I'm hit or not hit by a car—may obtain *because* of my actions in taking or not taking precautions. Likewise, given a set of historical outcomes foreknown by God, these may obtain *because* of any interventions made by God. There are no grounds here for divine laziness.

Finally, let's think about the force of such terms as "already," "at once," and "too late." On CSF, God "already" knows all of the future, "at once," making it "too late" to do anything about it. These are *temporal* terms that can also be used to indicate the *logical* or *explanatory* order of things. Which sense do they have here? Take the temporal sense. Then it's undoubtedly true that God,

in the Basic Schema, "already" (i.e., temporally prior to the occurrence of E at T3) knows that E will occur, because he foreknows it at T1; but then it's *not* too late in the temporal sense to do something about E: God has all the time between T1 and T3! So Sanders must intend such terms to indicate the logical or explanatory ordering of God's foreknowledge and providential efforts (something he explicitly confirms in endnote 9). But then it *isn't* true that God "already" (i.e., explanatorily prior to the occurrence of E at T3) knows that E will occur, for God's foreknowledge of E is *explanatorily subsequent* to E. Nor is it true that what God "already" knows, in light of his CSF, makes it "too late" for him to do anything about the future. Simple foreknowledge implies only that God's knowledge of everything is "already" in place in the temporal sequence, not that it is "already" in place in the explanatory sequence. Whether it is also already in place in the explanatory order depends on the details of the case. In The Game, God's knowledge that Satan will declare rock is "already" in place, in both the temporal and the explanatory sequence, when God decides what to declare at T2; it is then "too late" for God to make a difference to Satan's declaration of rock. But God's foreknowledge that the angels will throw a hosannafest in heaven at T4 to celebrate his victory over Satan is *not* "already" in place, in the explanatory sequence, as God decides what to do at T2, though it *is* in place in the temporal sequence. It is therefore *not* "too late" for God to do something at T2 that makes a difference to what happens in heaven at T4, despite God's already knowing at T1 how things will turn out. Sanders' critique of CSF, on which God's foreseeing "the *entire* human history *at once*" precludes "God's intervention into that history," is undermined by his failure to distinguish consistently between the temporal and explanatory orders.

To conclude our discussion of what Sanders has to say about CSF in that all-important paragraph of his paper: Sanders has given us no good reason to understand CSF as restricted (that is, as anything other than *Really* Complete Simple Fore-knowledge), and no good reason to think that CSF (whether restricted or unrestricted) does not allow for, let alone enhance, divine providential control. Our initial judgment that divine foreknowledge contributes toward God's providential control in The Game is not affected in any way by the supposition that God is accessing the future via CSF, nor is it shaken by any of the objections to CSF that it's possible to tease out of Sanders' brief discussion.

Let's now turn to ISF, Sanders' preferred version of how God accesses his simple foreknowledge. On this version, as you may recall, God "accesses the future *in sequence* or *incrementally*." Sanders hastens to add that God does not do this "in a temporal sequence, but in what might be called an explanatory order." This sounds promising, especially given the way these two sequences were run together in Sanders' discussion of CSF.

As a helpful model of how ISF works, Sanders introduces the notion of a "tape of the future" that God can play. God's *possessing* the tape presumably models his *having* simple foreknowledge; his *viewing* the tape then models his *accessing* his foreknowledge. Let's see how this would work in The Game. At T1 God has in his possession a tape depicting everything that will happen. A God with CSF would somehow view the contents of the tape "at once," but the ISF God views its contents in their explanatory order. In The Game this order begins at T3, when Satan makes a libertarianly free decision, undetermined by anything that preceded it, to declare rock. If God is to have this information at T1, it appears that he will need to fast-forward the tape to T3, where he views Satan's declaring rock. He can then rewind to T1 and let it play forward to T2, where God inserts his winning declaration of paper. (As I read Sanders here, God doesn't reach T2 in the explanatory sequence and just *find* the scene in which he declares paper. That scene is not already on the tape. Rather, when God reaches T2 there is a blank tract of tape waiting for

him; he presses *Record* and *adds* that scene to the tape.)

At least this is how things would look if one takes seriously Sanders' claim that the ISF God accesses the future "not in a temporal sequence, but in . . . an explanatory order." When we turn to Sanders' own elaboration of the tape model, however, things look rather different:

> God sort of atemporally rolls the tape of the future up to a certain point and then stops it in order to interject his own actions into the tape and then rolls the tape further to see what his creatures will do in response to his actions. Then God again decides what he will do and then rolls the tape further. (p. 364)

Despite Sanders' remark that God views the tape "sort of atemporally," it is hard to know how to read this as anything other than God (atemporally) accessing the future *in its temporal order*. This reading is confirmed when Sanders applies this model later in the paper. Consider, for example, the story of Rajesh, who petitions God for information about the next winner of the Super Bowl.

> Unfortunately, once God has "rolled the tape" up to the point where Rajesh makes his request, God does not yet know who the winner will be. And as God continues to pre-vision the future he does not foresee his answer to Rajesh until after he previsions which team actually wins the next Super Bowl. By this time, however it is too late for Rajesh to place his bet . . . (p. 369)

Every scene God views on this account, he reaches with the *Play* button; he never fast-forwards or rewinds. While Sanders had claimed that the ISF God accesses events in their explanatory order, there isn't the slightest effort here to follow the explanatory rather than temporal sequence. Or if the Rajesh narrative *does* take events in their explanatory order, it can only be because the explanatory order *is* the temporal order. But in that case, ISF can't possibly capture the providential use of simple foreknowledge, since the latter requires that the two orders *diverge*.

Suppose God were to access his foreknowledge in The Game by following Sanders' recipe above. At T1 God has in his possession a tape of the future, including future contingents (except his own actions). This means that he *has* something not possessed by the God of Open Theism. But what advantage does this give him? To find out, we need to follow him as he accesses the tape. So he rolls the tape forward to T2, at which point he's required, under the rules of the game he's playing with Satan, to make a mental declaration of rock, paper or scissors. What does he do? If only he had a fast-forward button so he could peek ahead at Satan's declaration! Without it, he's stuck making a guess: *scissors*. He rolls the tape forward to discover Satan declaring rock. Ouch! He must now stop the tape so he can reveal that he had chosen scissors. No sooner has he pressed *Play* again than he observes a wave of disappointment passing through the assembled host; he immediately presses *Stop* so he can insert a reassuring word. The next round begins . . .

It is hard to see why any defender of simple foreknowledge would be drawn to ISF, as Sanders puts it through its paces. It's true that God knows the future, and he does it in such a way that it remains possible for him to act in and make a difference to history. But God gets no providential advantage out of his "preview of coming attractions" at T1 that he couldn't get by simply waiting until T2, T3, etc., and acting on the *present knowledge* (PK) available to him at that time. ISF, as Sanders deploys it, "results in explanations essentially identical to the openness model." (p. 371)

Sanders' paper is devoted to showing that simple foreknowledge provides God with no more providential control than he would have under Open Theism. Sanders' principal argument for this conclusion is spread out over the pages of his essay, as he applies SF and PK to seven different areas of divine providence. This argument is fundamentally flawed because Sanders has mistakenly rejected CSF in favor of ISF, and ISF has been set up from the beginning as a model of SF under which God accesses his foreknowledge in exactly the same explanatory order as the God of Open Theism. The Basic Schema for the providential use of divine foreknowledge requires that God's providential action A be explained by his knowledge of something E that happens *later*; this is precisely what ensures God's victory in The Game. It's no wonder, when this requirement is ignored, that SF comes out providentially equivalent to PK. Reviewing Sanders' comments under the seven areas of divine providence would simply recapitulate, seven times over, the flawed understanding of SF that he develops so quickly in the first two or three pages of his paper.

Threading through his discussion of these seven areas, but especially in the seventh, "The Guarantee of the Success of God's Plans," is a second argument for the conclusion that simple foreknowledge provides God no more providential control than SF. Unlike Sanders' flawed analysis of SF, crucial to his first argument, this argument rests on something true: "a God with SF is not in a position to guarantee success from the beginning." (p. 370) At least this is true when the success of God's plans depends on what other agents with libertarian freedom choose to do, rather than when (as in The Game) it depends only on what God does. Let me illustrate with a variation on The Game. Suppose Satan again proposes to God a game of rock-paper-scissors, but this time God demurs. "Consider my servant Job," God suggests. Satan does consider him and agrees to a match, with God along as Job's coach. God again accesses his simple foreknowledge of Satan's future declarations and reveals it to Job. God wants Job to win—that's O—but access to Satan's future moves provides no guarantee. Job might doubt, misconstrue, or ignore God's leading; he might pridefully attempt to do it on his own; he might even throw the game to Satan just to frustrate God. In cases such as these, involving free agents other than himself, SF does not guarantee that God will get exactly the results that he wants.

So Sanders is certainly right that SF does not come with any guarantes. "Consequently," he continues, "a God with SF has no more ability to guarantee the success of his plans than does a God with PK." (p. 370) The argument appears to be this:

> SF cannot guarantee that God's plans will be successful.
> PK cannot guarantee that God's plans will be successful.
> Therefore, SF provides God *no more* providential control than PK.

This is of course a fallacious argument, as should be evident by comparison with the following:

> Gathering evidence cannot guarantee that a detective will solve the case.
> Consulting Tarot cards cannot guarantee that a detective will solve the case.
> Therefore, gathering evidence provides the detective *no better* method for solving the case than consulting Tarot cards.

Sanders' argument against the providential benefits of simple foreknowledge is no more successful than this argument against the investigative benefits of evidence-gathering.

SF *does not* claim to provide as much providential control as Calvinism or Molinism, which deploy truly impressive resources (theological determinism and middle knowledge, respectively). SF is a contender only because these heavyweights may be subject to disqualification, on the grounds that they fail to accommodate robust free agency. With this possibility in mind, the match-up between SF and PK becomes more important. The question is whether SF can secure *more* providential control than is available with PK alone.

The fact that neither PK nor SF comes with a providential guarantee is irrelevant. The question concerns their *relative* usefulness. Who is in a better position to coach Job in a game of rock-paper-scissors played against Satan? A God who knows what Satan is going to declare but cannot guarantee Job's victory because Job might not act on the knowledge God shares with him? Or a God who doesn't have the knowledge to share in the first place? Neither one has a guarantee; but the answer should be obvious.

Notes

1 A couple of comments on this opening statement are in order. First, Classical Theists would maintain that foreknowledge isn't something in *addition to* omniscience; foreknowledge is just omniscience with respect to the future, making it redundant to say that some being has omniscience *and* foreknowledge. But not everyone agrees with Classical Theists on this score. Many Open Theists, including John Sanders, maintain that God lacks exhaustive foreknowledge but is still omniscient, because the foreknowledge God lacks does not correspond to *truths of which God is ignorant* but to *gaps in what is now true about the future.* For God to be omniscient is for God to know all truths; where there are no truths to be known, God's ignorance doesn't count against his omniscience. It is therefore important to point out that Classical Theism is committed not just to divine omniscience—Open Theists also understand themselves to be upholders of divine omniscience—but also to exhaustive foreknowledge, which Open Theists deny.

The second comment is that this formulation is deliberately neutral between two different ways that Classical Theists have understood divine omniscience: as the knowledge at every moment of all truths by a God who is in time but without beginning and end; and as the timeless knowledge of all truths by a God who is *not* in time. On the latter understanding, God does not literally possess foreknowledge: since he does not exist in time, he obviously does not exist at earlier times, and so does not know *then* what will happen later. Nevertheless, he can be said to have foreknowledge of what will happen after a particular time T inasmuch as he knows timelessly all that is future relative to T.

2   This is Sanders' own position. For a recent defense by three fellow Open Theists, see Rhoda, Boyd & Belt, "Open Theism, Omniscience, and the Nature of the Future," *Faith and Philosophy* 23 (2006), pp. 432–59.

3   This is the classic problem of divine foreknowledge v. human freedom, discussed by most of the great Christian philosophers beginning with St. Augustine. William Hasker is an example of an Open Theist who rejects exhaustive foreknowledge on the ground that future contingents cannot be foreknown; see his *God, Time, and Knowledge* (Ithaca: Cornell University Press, 1989), especially chapter 10.

4   The principal reason one might worry that the Open Theist position on divine foreknowledge threatens God's maximal greatness is that it weakens omniscience. But virtually all Open Theists, Sanders included, affirm divine omniscience; I think, moreover, that they're entitled to do so, at least insofar as their position rests on denying that there are any true future contingents—see the first comment in endnote 1.

5   In my "Divine Providence and Simple Foreknowledge," *Faith and Philosophy* 10 (July 1993), pp. 396–416, I distinguish two kinds of problems for the providential use of simple foreknowledge, which I term the "Metaphysical Problem" and the "Doxastic Problem." It's not clear where Sanders' critique falls relative to these two problems, making a test case all but indispensable as a way of clarifying the exact nature of his concerns.

6   David Lewis, "The Paradoxes of Time Travel," *American Philosophical Quarterly* 13 (April 1976), pp. 145–52.

7   Some critics of simple foreknowledge argue that one can't just banish these concerns by stipulation. William Hasker, for example, maintains that an explanatory circle is unavoidable so long as A precedes E in time, while Michael Robinson argues that the mere *possibility* that a given scenario might generate an explanatory circle is grounds for rejecting that scenario. Hasker's is the classic version of what I call the "Metaphysical Problem" in my "Divine Providence and Simple Foreknowledge" (*op. cit.*), while Robinson's is a modal version of that problem. Hasker's argument may be found in his *God, Time, and Knowledge, op. cit.*, chapter 3, and my reply in "Divine Providence and Simple Foreknowledge." Robinson's argument may be found in his "Divine Providence, Simple Foreknowledge, and the 'Metaphysical Principle'," *Religious Studies* 40 (Dec. 2004), pp. 471–483; immediately following, in the same issue, is my "Providence, Foreknowledge, and Explanatory Loops: A Reply to Robinson," *Religious Studies* 40 (Dec. 2004), pp. 485–491. So the issue itself is an important one that can't simply be dismissed. Nevertheless, it can be ignored in the context of the present paper, on a couple of grounds. First, the providential test case I'm in the process of constructing is arguably immune to the sorts of worries pushed by Hasker and Robinson. Second, Sanders himself does not push this particular worry in his paper, at least in any clear and unequivocal fashion—and my job is to figure out and respond to what is worrying Sanders.

8   This is the Job scenario on pp. 382–383.

9   The idea that the odds could ever be *stacked against* a truly omnipotent being may strike some readers as oxymoronic. But games have *rules*, and so long as God's omnipotence does not equip him to do the logically impossible and he plays by the rules, it's not inconceivable that he might lose: it all depends on the game. (Even Thomas Aquinas, whose theistic credentials are beyond dispute, would agree that an omnipotent God cannot win a game of chess in which he's *already been checkmated*.)

10   I'm assuming that the game continues for a number of rounds. God's chances of winning a *particular round* of the game, unguided by simple foreknowledge, are closer to 33%, since there are always three possible moves open to him, one of which wins, one of which loses, and one of which ties.

11   It's also unclear that divine agency must involve God's *making up his mind* about what to do in the first place. So that's another point in Sanders' argument about which we'd need to hear more. Since I happen to think that simple foreknowledge wouldn't frustrate divine agency even if the latter *did* involve God's making up his mind, this is the defense that I briefly pursue in the main body of the text.

12   The optative mood is related to the subjunctive and

conveys the speaker's wish or hope. Here it is used to express the speaker's practical commitment to a course of action rather than theoretical commitment to a future-contingent truth.

13 Alternatively, these are different propositional *attitudes* toward the same propositional *content*, and adopting the one attitude toward that content does not mean that one has thereby adopted the other attitude toward that content—whether one does so may be left as further business.

14 For much fuller statements of this approach, see my "Omniprescient Agency," *Religious Studies* 28 (September 1992), pp. 351–369; "Divine Providence and Simple Foreknowledge," *op. cit.*; "Prescience and Providence: A Reply to My Critics," *Faith and Philosophy* 10 (July 1993), pp. 430–440; "The Compatibility of Omniscience and Intentional Action: A Reply to Tomis Kapitan," *Religious Studies* 32 (March 1996), pp. 49–60; and "Two Problems with Knowing the Future," *American Philosophical Quarterly* 34 (April 1997), pp. 273–85.

Chapter 28

Norman Kretzmann

WHY WOULD GOD CREATE ANYTHING AT ALL?

1. Introduction

Judaism, Christianity, and Islam agree that God is the absolutely perfect being who created the world. There's something puzzling about that description. Why would an absolutely perfect being create anything at all?

The general explanation of creation being asked for in that question must lie along either one of two divergent lines. The starting points of those two lines can be represented in two rudimentary answers to the question: one, "Because it is a consequence of his nature"—the beginning of a necessitarian line—and the other, "Because he freely chooses to do so"—the libertarian line of explanation. Explanations lying along the necessitarian line will try to show that an absolutely perfect being is essentially productive. And so the necessitarian line entails that there cannot be a state of affairs consisting of an absolutely perfect being's existing all by itself. On the other hand, libertarian explanations deny that God is essentially productive and insist that God could have been absolutely perfect without being a creator. Such libertarian explanations may or may not go on to try to say why God freely chooses to create.

Much of my understanding of this issue stems from medieval Christian philosophers. They generally adopted libertarian explanations of creation, at least partly because they had interpreted the data of Scripture as requiring that sort of account (in, for example, Psalms 134/135:6, James 1:18, and Revelation 4:11).[1] But, of course, Scripture wasn't the only constraint on their explanations. There was also Christian theology with all its inherent Greek philosophy, some of which plainly had a tendency to produce explanations that lay along the necessitarian line. These were exemplified most flagrantly in the neo-Platonist emanationism that had been taken over by medieval Islamic philosophers, and their writings were well known to thirteenth- and fourteenth-century Christian theologians. This apparent difference between the biblical data and the philosophy in Christianity is one important source of tension in medieval Christian explanations of creation.

I want to begin uncovering the explanations and the tension in them by raising some simple questions about creation as Augustine raised them.[2]

2. Creation and Volition

In the beginning God created the heaven and the earth. Why? In one of his treatises on Genesis, Augustine says, "Anyone who asks 'Why did God make heaven and earth?' should be given this answer: 'Because he willed it.' "[3] That answer isn't quite as empty as it sounds. Part of Augustine's purpose in giving the answer "Because he willed it" is to bring out the special significance of the ex nihilo aspect of creation as he sees it: "For when it is said that God produced [the world] out of nothing (ex nihilo), all that's meant is that there wasn't anything *from* which he might have produced [it]; and yet he did produce [it], [simply] *because he willed*."[4] The obvious significance of the ex nihilo doctrine is the denial of any independently pre-existing stuff out of which God made the world, but Augustine is extending the scope of the doctrine beyond matter to motive. If creation is out of nothing, then the volition to create not only uses nothing but also derives from nothing. The fullest possible explanation for creation ex nihilo appears to be the volition of the omnipotent creator.

Still, Augustine's empty-sounding answer is bound to prompt most people to ask a second question, as he realizes. "Anyone who [then] asks *why* God *willed* to make the world is looking for a cause of God's will. But every cause has an effect (*efficiens est*), and everything that has an effect is greater than what is effected [by it]. But nothing is greater than God's will."[5] "God's will," he says in another place, "is the cause of heaven and earth and is therefore greater than heaven and earth. Now anyone who asks 'Why did God *will* to make heaven and earth?' is looking for something greater than God's will; but he cannot find anything greater than that."[6]

Those two passages together strongly suggest that Augustine's position on explaining creation is not simply libertarian but voluntarist, denying the possibility of any meaningful search for a general explanation of creation beyond "God *willed* it." But there are two features of those passages that leave the voluntarism looking half-baked. In the first place, there is no good reason why Augustine's cause-greater-than-effect principle couldn't be weakened to a more plausible cause-at-least-as-great-as-effect principle. On that weaker, more plausible principle, everything he says would be compatible with a case in which something as great as God's will played a causal role in God's volition to create. And there are promising candidates for that causal role among other aspects of God's own nature (and

of course only among them). An explanation of God's volition to create as caused by some other aspect of his nature is theoretically possible, and it would leave this apparent voluntarism compatible with the necessitarian line of explanation, as we'll see.

In the second place, Augustine's voluntarism here seems to stem from his view that the only explanation that could count as an answer to "Why did he will it?" would be an explanation in terms of the kind of causation involved in creation itself, as if the question were "What is related to God's will as his will is related to creation?" God's will is the external agent cause of creation. But no necessitarian explanation that might derive from or be compatible with Christian theology could have any tendency to lead to an account in which God's will is causally determined by an external agency. The only threat Augustine is protecting God's autonomy from is an unimaginable threat. And in taking that overly protective stance he appears to be blocking a kind of further inquiry that would ordinarily be the most appropriate basis for asking "Why?" about any act of any will—an inquiry into the internal sources of it, the reason, motive, or purpose of the volition. Sources altogether internal to an agent who is, as God is, altogether invulnerable to passions pose no threat to the agent's autonomy.

3. Motivation for the Volition to Create

But there is a simpler and even more convincing sort of reason for not taking Augustine's voluntarism in these passages at face value. In many of his other discussions of creation, perhaps most, Augustine himself neither sounds like a voluntarist nor allows voluntarism to block his own attempt to explain God's volition. In commenting on Psalms 134/135:6, "All things whatsoever that he willed, he made" (*omnia quaecumque voluit, fecit*), Augustine begins by observing that God was "not compelled" to make anything, that "the cause of all the things he made is his will." Then he contrasts God's case with ours in this respect: "You make a house because if you didn't, you'd be without shelter; need (*necessitas*) compels you to make a house, not free will," and similarly as regards your clothing and food— "All these you make because of need. God made [whatever he made] because of goodness; he needed nothing that he made. And that's why [it says] 'all things whatsoever that he *willed*, he made.' "[7] In the light of what we've already seen Augustine saying, it's no surprise to find him here implying still more clearly that God's volition to create is an instance of *free* will; nor is it surprising to see God described as self-sufficient. As Augustine puts it elsewhere, "Where there is no needfulness (*indigentia*), there is no need (*necessitas*); where there is no lack (*defectus*), no needfulness. But there is no lack in God; therefore, no need."[8] What is surprising about the passage contrasting human making with divine making is that (human) actions willingly performed for good reasons are denied inclusion under "free will." After all, no one is absolutely necessitated even in the getting of food, shelter, and clothing. The contrast Augustine points out is not really between unfree and free actions but rather between actions performed out of self-interest and actions performed out of "goodness." And that contrast leaves us with a further question. We expect goodness to be ascribed to God, but just how is God's goodness supposed to constitute his motive or reason for doing what he has no need to do? As regards human actions, if we say that one was performed out of self-interest and the other out of goodness, we might very well mean that the second action was altruistic. But altruism is not the aspect of goodness Augustine points to as an explanation of God's act of creation.

His primary basis for associating creation with goodness is pretty clearly in the Genesis story itself, where the basis explicitly provided is an observation not about the nature of the creator but about the nature of the creation. In Genesis the same thing is said specifically six times about the work of the six days, "God saw that it was *good*,"[9] and then more emphatically regarding the whole: "God saw every thing that he had made, and, behold, it was *very good*."[10] From these appraisals it appears to follow that the production of good was God's intention, and in general the motivation for an agent whose intention is the production of good is the agent's goodness. Augustine generously develops this sort of explanation of God's volition in another of his discussions of Genesis 1: " 'God saw that it was good'—What meaning can be assigned to those words that appear everywhere [in this chapter] other than approval of a finished product skilfully wrought, that is, wrought with the skill that is the wisdom of God? But God wasn't previously so ignorant that he could only discover that his work was good when it was complete. Far from it! Nothing he created would have been created if he hadn't known it very well beforehand. Therefore, when he sees that a thing is good—a thing he wouldn't have made at all if he hadn't seen it was good before he made it— he is teaching us, not learning for himself, that it is good. . . . And in fact there were three main points concerning the work of creation that had to be reported to us and that it was right for us to know: *who* made it, *how*, and *why*. So what Scripture says is: 'God said "Let there be light"; and there was light. And God saw that the light was good.' So if we ask '*Who* made it?', the answer is 'It was God.' If we ask '*How*?', the answer is 'God said "Let it be"; and it was.' If we ask '*Why*?', the answer is 'Because it is *good*.' Nor is there any originator more excellent than God, any skill more effective than God's word, any purpose better than that something good should be created by a good God."[11]

When Augustine does open the door to explanations of creation, he opens it wide. But for all its detail, that passage gives us next to nothing by way of an answer to Augustine's second question. Why does God will to create the world? Because he is good and knows it to be good. Augustine says he's shown God's purpose in creating, but we're left wanting to know *why* a perfectly good God would create any world, even one he knows to be very good. What could be the *point* of it? Augustine plausibly treats the goodness God finds in the newly created world as aesthetic rather than moral, and Revelation 4:11 suggests that God created for his own pleasure. But such an explanation seems incompatible with the concept of an absolutely perfect being (who cannot want entertainment) besides being rife with new problems of its own.

That third general question, about the point of creation, may not have been asked (or answered) by Augustine, but it certainly did exercise later medieval philosophers. The first suggestion of the kind of answer to it the medievals took most seriously is found not in Genesis, but in Plato's creation story. But before moving explicitly to the Greek side of the Christian heritage, I want to suggest that we have already seen both the biblical and the metaphysical sides, the Jewish and the Greek sides of this heritage in Augustine's treatments of creation. In his voluntarist mood, his insistence on God's absolute self-sufficiency and on the primacy and absolute independence of God's volition represents one prominent (libertarian) strain in Greek thought, whereas his expansive, informal account of the who, how, and why of creation is biblical with hardly a trace of philosophy in it.

4. Plato's Explanation of Creation

The basis for an answer to our third question and the classical starting point for necessitarian explanations of creation is this passage in Plato's *Timaeus*: "Let us now give *the reason why* the maker made becoming, and the universe. He was *good*, and in him that is good no envy ever arises regarding anything. Being devoid of envy, he wanted everything to be *like himself*, as far as possible. . . . God desired that everything should be *good* and nothing evil, as far as possible. . . . For him who is most good it *neither was nor is*

permissible to do anything other than what is most beautiful."[12]

The stories of creation in Genesis and the *Timaeus* are enough alike that Augustine wondered whether Plato had not plagiarized his from Moses.[13] But there are at least four noticeable relevant differences between them. In the first place, Plato's world maker, the Demi-urge, is not omnipotent and is not creating the world out of nothing, but is merely shaping and ordering matter that is already in existence. That is what gives Plato's denial of envy in him its point,[14] and that is why it would be impossible in this context even to attempt a radical voluntarism in which the existence of the world has no explanation beyond the maker's volition. Second, in the *Timaeus* the primary, explicit ascription of goodness is to the maker, not to the world he makes—although that world is described in the end as "most beautiful." Third, we are offered the beginning of an account of the point of creation: the production of something as much like the good creator as created things can be. Finally, although the *Timaeus* passage explains the origin of the world in terms of an agent's action, it also includes a strong suggestion that that action is a consequence of the agent's nature. The suggestion is that the making of the world, or at least the character of the world that gets made, is *not* a result of the maker's free choice: "For him who is most good it neither was nor is *permissible* to do *anything other* than what is most beautiful."

Whatever Plato himself may have intended by this, the later Platonists, who influenced medieval thought far more than Plato did directly, strengthened this line of explanation, arguing (as we'll see) that it is part of the essence of goodness to give rise to being and goodness—in other words, that the existence of a world is an inevitable consequence of God's perfect goodness rather than the result of a freely chosen action of his. Medieval Christian philosophers were deeply influenced and sometimes attracted by that part of their Greek heritage even when they were convinced that it had to be repudiated. Thomas Aquinas's accounts of creation strike me as providing a paradigm of that sort of tension in Christian thought.

5. Libertarian and Necessitarian Strains in Aquinas

Is God free to choose whether or not to create? Aquinas's official answer to that question is an emphatic, unqualified yes: "one must hold, without any doubt, that God produced creatures in existence by a free choice of his will, without any natural necessity."[15] But I believe that his conceptions of God, goodness, creation, and choice entail a negative reply.[16] It seems to me that he resolutely adopted the libertarian line but was drawn to and sometimes even expressed a necessitarian line. I think that the necessitarian and libertarian strains in Aquinas's account of creation might be reconciled, but I don't think he reconciled them. And so I see no way of avoiding the inconsistency (or, at least, ambivalence) in Aquinas's account as it stands.

I begin with the libertarian position, the one Aquinas explicitly adopts. It is part of his concept of God that God has freedom of choice.[17] But God's volition is not entirely characterized by free choice, since "God *necessarily* wills his own being and his own goodness, and he *cannot* will the contrary."[18] In keeping with Aquinas's understanding of divine simplicity, God's goodness, like everything else properly ascribable to God himself, is simply God himself conceived of by us in a particular way. Conceived of as goodness, God himself is recognized by Aquinas as the universal, unique, ultimate *final* cause: "the ultimate end is God himself, since he is the highest good."[19] In willing his own goodness, therefore, God is willing the one universal natural end, regarding which no choice is possible. And so Aquinas recognizes that some aspects of God's activity can be both necessitated and volitional although, of course, not both necessitated and freely chosen.

Nevertheless, even God's willing his nature (and existence) is not, according to Aquinas, incompatible with every sort of freedom: "in respect of its principal object, which is its own goodness, the divine will does have necessity—not, of course, the necessity of constraint, but the necessity of natural order, which is not incompatible with freedom."[20] That this freedom compatible with the necessity of natural order is not freedom of choice is clear from Aquinas's restricted assignment of choice to only one aspect of the action of God's will: "since God wills himself as the end but other things as things that are for the end, it follows that in respect of himself he has *only* volition, but in respect of other things he has *selection*. Selection, however, is always accomplished by means of free choice. Free choice, therefore, is suited to God."[21] And the term "free choice," he makes clear, "is used in respect of things one wills *not* necessarily, but of one's own accord."[22]

So Aquinas appears to be an incompatibilist regarding freedom of choice, but he recognizes another kind of freedom in volition that is compatible with the necessity of natural order—*willingness*, it might be called. This state of willing freely although necessarily is not hard to exemplify in ordinary circumstances. A human being is susceptible to emotions necessarily, essentially. But if his positive attitude toward this susceptibility is just what it would have been if he had freely chosen an inner life characterized by emotions from among available relevant possibilities and had found that it measured up to his expectations, then he wills susceptibility to emotions freely though necessarily. I call that state "willingness" because it seems more natural to describe such a person as being willingly susceptible to emotions than as willing that susceptibility. In God's case, then, willingness, not freedom of choice, characterizes the divine will "in respect of its principal object, which is its own goodness."

Since God's freedom of choice is essentially connected with his willing of things other than himself, it is, on this view, associated solely with creation in some way or other. Ascribing *any* free choice to God conceived of as eternal, simple, and purely actual, is obviously not easy, even when its objects are restricted to things other than God. Of course, Aquinas recognizes that difficulty, taking up and rejecting many putative reasons for asserting that God wills *everything* he wills under the necessity of natural order.[23] But one obstacle in the way of exempting creation from the necessity of natural order was, I think, never dealt with satisfactorily by Aquinas.[24] This obstacle is located in the divine attribute of goodness, which we have already seen presented (by Plato and by Augustine) as essentially associated with creation.

The essence of goodness is an aspect of the essence of God, who is, Aquinas says, "goodness itself, not merely good."[25] The particular locus of the obstacle in goodness is its essential self-diffusiveness, brought out in a neo-Platonist principle Aquinas often appeals to, sometimes attributing it to Dionysius: *Goodness is by its very nature diffusive of itself and (thereby) of being.*[26] I think this Dionysian Principle, the root of which can be discerned in the *Timaeus* passage, expresses an important truth about goodness, most obviously about the goodness of agents, which is the only kind at issue here. (There is no obvious inconsistency in the notion of knowledge that is unexpressed, never shared by the agent who possesses it even if he is omnipotent, but there is inconsistency in the notion of goodness that is unmanifested, never shared, even though united with omnipotence.)[27] The use Aquinas makes of the Dionysian Principle on many occasions suggests that he, too, considers it to be important and true, at least most of the time.[28] But, of course, the principle also looks as if it must give rise to a necessitarian line of explanation of creation, one in which creation would be a natural consequence of God's nature in its perfect goodness,[29] or in which God's goodness would be understood to cause his volition to create, somewhat as our nature causes our volition for

happiness.[30] And the fact that the volition to create, like the volition for happiness, is governed by the necessity of natural order would in no way militate against its being done with the freedom of willingness, even though not with the freedom of choice.[31]

Aquinas, as we've seen, is explicitly opposed to such a line of explanation. Nevertheless, he sometimes writes in a way that indicates that he does see God's creating as an instance of the natural self-diffusion of goodness, as in this passage, where he is discussing not creation itself but God's goodness: "The communication [or sharing] of being and goodness proceeds from goodness. This is indeed evident both from the nature of the good and from its definition. . . . But that diffusion is suited to God, since he is the cause of being for other things."[32] If that diffusion is no more than "suited to God" (*competit Deo*), it sounds as if God could conceivably not be characterized by it, or as if he could turn it on or off, in which case the essential diffusiveness of goodness would pose no threat to God's having a free choice whether or not to create. But it seems Aquinas has no right to the convenient weakness of "suited to," the same expression he sometimes uses in associating free choice with God.[33] God is perfect goodness itself, and goodness is *essentially*—from its nature and from its definition—diffusive of itself and being. Doesn't it follow that the volition to create is a consequence of God's nature?

As more pointed evidence that it does, consider this passage in which Aquinas is discussing God's willing the existence of things other than himself, and notice in it the echoes of the *Timaeus*: "every agent, to the extent to which it is in act and perfect, produces something like itself. Thus this, too, pertains to the nature of the will, that the good which anyone has he communicates to others as much as possible. And it pertains above all to the divine will, from which every perfection is derived in virtue of a kind of likeness."[34]

If perfect goodness is an aspect of God's essence, and self-diffusiveness is essential to goodness, it looks as if creation has got to be an inevitable consequence of God's nature—unless the diffusion of goodness can somehow be completely accounted for within the divine nature. The passages we have just been considering, like almost all those in which Aquinas is relying on the Dionysian Principle, speak of the communication of the divine goodness to other things. But in the earliest of his three big theological works (and only there, as far as I know) he presents the following intriguing argument for the plurality of the divine Persons in the triune God: "As Dionysius says, . . . the good is communicative of itself. But God is good in the highest degree; therefore, God will communicate himself in the highest degree. But he does not communicate himself in the highest degree in creatures, because they do not receive *all* his goodness. Therefore, there must be a *perfect* communication, resulting in his communicating all his goodness [with] another. But that cannot be in a diversity of essence; therefore, there must be more than one distinct [Person] in the unity of the divine essence."[35] I think this Trinitarian application of the principle deserves further consideration in its own right, but it cannot by itself dispel the principle's tendency to initiate a necessitarian account of creation. For even if the Son's being begotten by the Father and the Holy Spirit's proceeding from the Father and the Son can be considered an essential intrinsic diffusion of goodness and being, in the Christian theology to which Aquinas subscribes it is the *triune* God that is characterized as "goodness itself, not merely good."[36] And so even when the plurality of the divine Persons has been explained on this basis, the essential self-diffusiveness of goodness as an aspect of the essence of the triune God remains in force, calling for *extrinsic, volitional* diffusion, or creation. Although God's will is the total cause of creation, in bringing it about that something besides God exists, his will, it seems, does not freely choose but acts, willingly, in a way necessitated by the natural order, the relevant aspect of which in this case is the diffusiveness of goodness and being that is essential to goodness itself, God's own essence.

Aquinas's principal strategy for avoiding that necessitarian, Platonist, perhaps heretical outcome[37] is to rely on his own novel interpretation of the Dionysian Principle, an interpretation that strikes me as counterintuitive. He proposes that the diffusiveness essential to goodness be understood not as "the operation of *efficient* causation" but as having *solely* "the status of *final* causation."[38] This attempt to introvert the principle has nothing to recommend it as an interpretation. For one thing, drawing of the sort essential to final causation is *contrary* to diffusing. Of course, goodness has an attractive as well as a productive side, but the principle is an expression of the *productive* side of goodness, as Aquinas's predecessors unanimously recognized.[39] It seems wrongheaded to propose reading it as expressing *exclusively* the *attractive* side of goodness. More important, Aquinas's final-causation-only proposal leaves him with no explanation at all of God's willing the existence of other things. The diffusiveness of goodness conceived of as final causation can't be extended to the drawing of anything other than God himself toward it unless there *is* something else. But in the case in which God, perfect goodness, exists alone, why *would* God will to cause anything else to begin to exist?

Is Aquinas headed toward voluntarism regarding creation, then? That way out might seem firmly closed to him by his own emphatic repudiation of what he calls "the *error* of certain people who said that all things depend on the simple divine volition, without any reason."[40] But there are crucial passages in which it becomes clear that he perceives that sort of voluntarism to be mistaken mainly in its universality, in its claiming that "*all* things depend on the simple divine volition, without any reason." On one occasion when Aquinas considers the question "whether any cause can be assigned to divine volition," he answers that "in *no* way does God's volition have a cause." But he has to deal with the objection that "if God's volition has no cause, it follows that all the things that are made depend on his simple volition and have no other cause, which is absurd." His rejoinder to this objection certainly does sound like voluntarism regarding creation: "Since God wills effects to occur on account of causes, any effects that presuppose some other effect do not depend on God's volition alone, but on something else [as well]. But the *first* effects depend on the divine volition *alone*."[41] And yet it is an ambivalent voluntarism, as can be seen from an earlier passage in the same Question: "Since God wills things other than himself only *because* of the end which is his own goodness, as was said, it does not follow that anything *else* moves his will *except* his own goodness."[42]

Despite the occasional flashes of voluntarism in Aquinas's discussions of creation, I think he is committed to providing some explanation of God's volition to create. But he is aware of the difficulty of doing so in view of the apparently closed system constituted by God as perfect will drawn to God as perfect goodness. His libertarian explanation of the volition to create begins with claims that look like the beginning of the necessitarian line: "in willing himself God also wills other things,"[43] and "God wills himself and other things in one act of will."[44] Aquinas recognizes that someone could well infer from statements of this sort that God therefore wills all other things necessarily, as he wills himself; but Aquinas rejects that inference on the grounds of God's self-sufficiency: "since the divine goodness can be without other things and, indeed, nothing is added to it by means of other things, there is in him no necessity to will other things in virtue of the fact that he wills his own goodness."[45]

No matter how much detail I added to this account of Aquinas's position, it would in the end still be dominated by these two opposing forces: Platonist self-diffusiveness and Aristotelian self-sufficiency.[46] The rift in Aquinas's account of creation seems to be the widening of a crack in his characterization of God, a crack that runs not between the Jewish and the Greek elements in Christian theology, but between two main strands within Greek philosophy itself. The tension between necessitarian and libertarian explanations of creation in Aquinas is a tension between aspects of Platonism and Aristotelianism, respectively. He seems to me to have deliberately committed himself to the Aristotelian side despite his marked tendency to think along the Platonist line, as in this argument for God's willing things other than himself: "To the extent to which something has the perfection of a power, its causality is extended to more things and over a wider range. . . . But the causality of an end consists in the fact that other things are desired because of it. Therefore, the more perfect and the more willed an end is, the more the will of the one willing the end is extended to more things by reason of that end. But the divine essence is most perfect in the essential nature of goodness and of end. *Therefore*, it will diffuse its causality as much as possible to many things, so that many things will be willed *because* of it— and especially by *God*, who wills it [the divine essence] perfectly in respect of all its power."[47]

But nowhere else have I seen him weave the Platonist and Aristotelian strands together so neatly as in this passage: "Speaking absolutely, he [God] of course does not will them [things other than himself] necessarily . . . because his goodness has *no need* of things that stand in an ordered relationship to it, and the manifestation of it can be appropriately accomplished in various ways.[48] *And so there remains for him a free judgment for willing this one or that one*, just as in our own case."[49] As I read this passage, it comes very close to saying what I think Aquinas *should* say about God's need to create something: that goodness does require things other than itself as a manifestation of itself, that God therefore necessarily though altogether willingly wills the being of something other than himself, and that the free choice involved in creation is confined to the selection of which possibilities to actualize for the purpose of manifestation. But even if we can occasionally find

Aquinas thinking Platonist thoughts, he interrupts them often enough with Aristotelian pronouncements, such as "the divine goodness is complete in itself, even if no creature were to exist,"[50] or "It is not necessary, if God wills that his own goodness be, that he will that other things be produced by him."[51]

I once suggested a way of getting rid of the inconsistency or ambivalence in Aquinas's account of creation, along the following lines.[52] Aquinas's "necessity of natural order, which is not incompatible with freedom," could simply be extended to cover God's willing the existence of something or other besides himself. We could then agree with Aquinas that "God cannot will that he not be good and, consequently, that he not be understanding or powerful or any of those things which the essential nature of his goodness includes,"[53] granting as well that this necessity of willing is not incompatible with one sort of freedom, the sort I called "willingness."[54] But I would then want to go on to urge, in accordance with the Dionysian Principle, that God's bringing into existence something other than himself is among "those things which the essential nature of his goodness includes." Although it couldn't be said on the basis of this revision that God is *free to choose* whether or not to create, it could consistently be said that God *freely, although necessarily, wills* the existence of something besides himself.

6. Goodness, Trinity, and Creation in Bonaventure

I still think that suggestion is on the right track. But since making it I have looked at Bonaventure's answer to the question why God created anything at all. Bonaventure's answer strikes me as extending and en-riching the line of thought I took in attempting to repair Aquinas's account.[55]

Bonaventure was born a few years earlier than Aquinas, but the two of them were colleagues and almost exact contemporaries; both were appointed to chairs of theology in the University of Paris on the same day in 1256, and both died in 1274. In their explanations of creation they used virtually the same elements and principles, but their results were quite different in ways that seem to reflect a difference in their intellectual backgrounds, which has at least a little to do with the fact that Aquinas was a Dominican and Bonaventure a Franciscan. The inconsistency or ambivalence in Aquinas's account stems, I've been saying, from his decided commitment to Aristotelian self-sufficiency in his conception of God combined with his hesitant appreciation of the insight and explanatory power of the Dionysian Principle, or Platonist self-diffusion as a basic characterization of God. Bonaventure managed to unify those ingredients, I think, partly because he was, like many other Franciscans, an Augustinian Platonist whose attitude toward Aristotelianism was never warmer than guarded tolerance. I don't have any evidence that Bonaventure's explanations of creation were written with Aquinas's in mind, but at least some of them could have been, and they often read as if they were. Whatever the historical relationship between the two may have been, I present Bonaventure's views in the light of our discussion of Aquinas, and so I'm not much concerned with preserving the order in which Bonaventure developed or presented his position.

I begin with sketchy remarks about being and goodness.[56] We've already seen being and goodness linked together in the Dionysian Principle: Goodness is essentially diffusive of itself and (thereby) of being. The basic ancient and medieval thesis connecting being and goodness, fully subscribed to by Aquinas, can be conveniently expressed, to begin with, as the claim that the two terms "being" and "goodness" are alike in their reference but different in their senses—that they are like the terms "evening star" and "morning star" in referring to one and the same entity despite their different senses. Bonaventure wholeheartedly adopts this analysis and insightfully identifies the single referent of "being" and "goodness" as God himself, distinguishing their two senses in terms of the dominant Old and New Testament conceptions of God: "The one mode [of contemplating the invisible and eternal things of God] looks primarily and essentially to God's *being*, and says that God's foremost name is 'He Who Is.' The other mode looks to God's *goodness*, and says that his foremost name is this very '*Goodness*.' The first approach looks more to the Old Testament, which stresses *the unity of the divine essence*, for it was said to Moses: 'I Am Who Am.'[57] The second approach looks to the New Testament, which reveals *the plurality of [the divine] Persons* . . . Christ, our Teacher, . . . attributes to God the name 'Goodness' as belonging to him essentially and exclusively, for he says: '*No one is good but only God.*' "[58] There's no mystery about why Bonaventure would associate God's Old Testament name with divine unity, or the plurality of the divine Persons with the New Testament, but how, exactly, is the name "Goodness" supposed to reveal the plurality? Since the New Testament was seen as the completion and interpretation of the Old, in Bonaventure's view the concept of being has to be completed and understood in terms of goodness. And since he fully accepts the Dionysian Principle, he can be said to begin with what he takes to be the New Testament conception of God as essentially *dynamic* in his self-diffusiveness. Bonaventure thus naturally employs the Dionysian Principle as his primary explanatory device in accounting for God's nature or activity. Thus the account of the plurality of the divine Persons in terms of the essential diffusiveness of goodness, which, as we saw, Aquinas considered only peripherally, early in his career, becomes the centerpiece of Bonaventure's mature account: "Good is said to be self-diffusive; therefore, the highest good is that which diffuses itself the most. Now, diffusion cannot stand as the highest unless it is intrinsic yet active, substantial yet personal, essential yet voluntary, necessary yet free, perfect yet unceasing." I am interrupting the passage here to point out that the first adjective in each

pairing is more readily associated with static self-sufficiency, or the *being* side of the being-goodness relationship, whereas the second adjective brings out dynamic self-diffusion, or the *goodness* side. *Static*: intrinsic, substantial, essential, necessary, perfect; *dynamic*: active, personal, voluntary, free, unceasing. "Thus, in the supreme good, there must be from all eternity an actual and consubstantial producing, the producing of a hypostasis as noble as the One who produces by way of both generation and spiration. So, there is produced an Eternal Principle, who is an eternal Co-producer. And thus, there is the producing of one Beloved and one Co-beloved, of one Engendered and one Spirated. So, in all, there are the Father, the Son, and the Holy Spirit. Otherwise, this good would not be supreme, since it would not be *supremely* self-diffusive."[59]

In Bonaventure's system the full diffusion of goodness constitutive of the triune nature of God is a necessary concomitant of perfect goodness, divine Fatherhood being characterized as *fontalis plenitudo*, the full, unstinting flowing of a spring.[60] This feature of Bonaventure's dynamic conception of God seems to have been directly repudiated by Aquinas in a characterization of divine Fatherhood that could hardly contrast more sharply with Bonaventure's. After affirming that "innascibility," signified by the name "unbegotten," is proper to God the Father, Aquinas deals with some attempts to give positive content to these negative terms: "Some people say that innascibility . . . considered as a property of the Father is not spoken of only negatively, but that either it means that the Father is from no one and is the source of others, or it means universal authority, or even *fontalis plenitudo*. But that is evidently not true. . . . Primary and simple things are designated by negations, as when we say that a point is that which has no part."[61] In this later, presumably more representative, treatment of divine Fatherhood by Aquinas it is hard to see even the basis for the plurality of Persons, let alone a source of creation.

Bonaventure's contrasting treatment of the Trinity as the primary, supreme instance of self-diffusiveness takes it to be simply the indispensable first stage of the diffusion of goodness that proceeds into creation. "Because [God] is most perfect, he is of the highest goodness; *because* he is of the highest goodness, he wills to produce *many* things and to communicate himself."[62] And this volition, as we've already seen Bonaventure noting, is "essential yet voluntary, necessary yet free."[63] "In God the essential nature of productive diffusion occurs in this way: his being is supremely good; therefore, it supremely diffuses itself."[64]

The supreme diffusion, as we've seen, is the generation and spiration resulting in the plurality of the divine Persons. The diffusion that is creation is immeasurably feebler in its effect, but in its cause it is the divinely willed manifold manifestation of the full being and goodness of the triune God. In keeping with the motive of divine manifestation, the creature of the first day is light, the paradigmatic material representation of self-diffusing being, as had been pointed out by Robert Grosseteste, who was second only to Augustine as the philosophical teacher of the Franciscans, including Bonaventure: "Light of itself diffuses itself in every direction, so that a sphere of light as great as you please is engendered instantaneously from a point of light."[65] As for the immeasurable disparity between the divine Persons and creatures, "diffusion is utterly final (*ultimata*) in that the [perfectly good, omnipotent] producer gives everything he *can* give. But a creature cannot receive everything that God can give. And so, just as a point adds nothing to a line—nor do a million points—a creature's goodness adds nothing to the creator's goodness."[66] "The temporal diffusion [of goodness] in a creature is only like a center or a point in respect of the immensity of the eternal goodness. That is why a diffusion greater than creation can be conceived of, the one in which the diffusing [goodness] does communicate its whole substance and nature to

another. Therefore, there would not be a highest good if it could lack that diffusiveness really or conceptually."[67]

I've been providing evidence of Bonaventure's reliance on the *efficient* causality inherent in goodness, as expressed in the Dionysian Principle. Aquinas, at least in his most systematic pronouncements, relied instead on the Aristotelian conception of the good as the universal object of desire, the ultimate *final* cause. But Bonaventure also recognized and relied on the Aristotelian conception, in keeping with the altogether sensible neo-Platonist tradition, which included *both* these aspects, the Platonic and the Aristotelian, the productive and the attractive, in its account of the essence of goodness.[68] As Bonaventure puts it, "The reason why causality is attributed to the will is that the *essence* (*ratio*) *of causing, both efficient and final, is goodness*. For the good is said to be diffusive, *and* the good is that for the sake of which all things [are and act]. But an efficient cause does not actually produce an effect except for the sake of an end. Therefore, that which expresses the conjoining of an efficient source with an end explains the actual occurrence of causing. But volition is the act in accordance with which a good is turned toward (*reflectitur supra*) a good, or goodness. Therefore, it is volition that unites an efficient cause with an end. . . . And that is why we attribute causality to God under the aspect of will."[69]

7. Conclusion

Aquinas, like Bonaventure and most other medieval theologians, saw the structure and the history of the world as a cosmic cycle willed by God, the manifold manifestation of his goodness in the procession of creatures from him and the return of creatures to him. Given that world view and the concept of God as perfect goodness personified, could there be an explanatory mechanism more apt than the neo-Platonist dual-aspect conception of goodness, suggesting the circulation of all created good from the heart of goodness and back again? Bonaventure took full advantage of this dual-aspect conception. Aquinas, who knew it well and sometimes tried it out, in the end left it to one side, leaving himself with a one-sided orthodox Aristotelian conception that seems to have given him more trouble than help.[70]

Notes

1 Psalms 134/135:6: "All things whatsoever that he willed he made, in heaven and in earth, in the seas and all deep places." James 1:18: "Of his own will begat he us. . . ." Revelation 4:11: "thou hast created all things, and for thy pleasure they are and were created."

2 My discussion of Augustine was substantially complete in 1986, when I presented an earlier version of this article as a lecture in an NEH Summer Institute on the philosophy of religion. Teske 1988 contains a good discussion of material precisely relevant to issues I discuss here, including some material not cited here. It should be consulted by anyone interested in further research into Augustine's position on these issues. I am grateful to Scott MacDonald for calling my attention to Teske's article.

3 *De Genesi contra Manichaeos* I.ii.4 (PL 34.175).

4 *Ad Orosium* i.3 (PL 42.671).

5 *De diversis quaestionibus* LXXXIII q. 28 (PL 40.18).

6 *De Genesi contra Manichaeos* I.ii.4 (PL 34.175).

7 *Ennarationes in Psalmos* CXXXIV. 10 (PL 37.1745).

8 *De diversis quaestionibus* LXXXIII q. 22 (PL 40.16).

9 Genesis 1:4, 10, 12, 18, 21, 25. There is no specific appraisal of the work of the second day; vv. 10 and 12 both concern the work of the third day.

10 Genesis 1:31.

11 *De civitate Dei* XI.21. See Teske 1988, p. 247, for more texts to this effect.

12 *Timaeus* 29E–30B.

13 *De civitate Dei* XI.21.

14 Teske 1988, pp. 249 and 251–53, provides several striking passages in which Augustine in his accounts of creation is careful to deny that the creator could be envious. Plato's denial of envy in the Demi-urge seems connected with the world maker's intention to produce something as much

like himself as possible. Augustine's denial of envy in God is connected with God's permitting anything besides himself to exist *at all*.

15 *DP* III. 15c. The question is "whether things proceeded from God by a necessity of nature or by a choice of will."

16 I have argued this in Kretzmann 1983b.

17 See, e.g., *SCG* I.88: "QUOD IN DEO EST LIBERUM ARBITRIUM."

18 *SCG* I.80 (n. 676).

19 *SCG* I.74 (n. 636).

20 *DV* XXIII.4c.

21 *SCG* I.88 (n. 732).

22 *SCG* I.88 (n. 730).

23 See, e.g., *DV* XXIII.4; XXIV.3.

24 See, e.g., his rejoinders to objections 1, 5, 12, and 14 in *DP* III.15. (Obj. 12 is in n. 27 below, his rejoinder to it in n. 28 below; obj. 1 and his rejoinder are in n. 29 below, obj. 14 and his rejoinder in n. 30 below.)

25 *SCG* I.38 (n. 310).

26 "Dionysius," or pseudo-Dionysius, is the otherwise unidentified author of four Christian neo-Platonist treatises and ten letters dating from the sixth century. These works had special authority during the Middle Ages, when they were thought to have been written by the Athenian Dionysius mentioned in Acts 17:34 as having been converted by Saint Paul's sermon on Mars Hill. On the history of this principle see esp. Peghaire 1932; also Kremer 1965.

27 This point is brought out well in *DP* III.15. obj. 12: "In II Timothy 2:13 it says 'God remains faithful and cannot deny himself.' But since he himself is his goodness, he would deny himself if he denied his goodness. And he would deny his goodness if he did not diffuse it by sharing it, for that is a *proprium* of goodness." (See n. 28 below for Aquinas's rejoinder.)

28 See the list in Peghaire 1932, p. 19*, nn. 45 and 46, and scattered references in subsequent notes in his article. Aquinas's rejoinder to the objection quoted in n. 27 above contains one of his rare rejections of the Dionysian Principle: "If God were to deny his goodness in such a way as to do something contrary to his goodness, or something in which his goodness was not expressed, it would follow, *per impossibile*, that he would deny himself. But that

would not follow even if he did not share his goodness at all, for it would be no loss at all to goodness if it were not shared."

29 See, e.g., DP III.15.obj.1: "Dionysius says [*De divinis nominibus* IV], 'Just as our sun, neither reasoning nor choosing, but by its very being illuminates with its light all things willing to share it, so the divine goodness by its essence sheds its rays of goodness proportionally for all existing things.' But the sun, illuminating without choice and reason, does this by a necessity of nature. Therefore, God also produces creatures by a necessity of nature in sharing his goodness." Aquinas's rejoinder: "Dionysius's simile must be understood as having to do with the *universality* of the diffusion; for the sun pours its rays onto all bodies, not distinguishing one from another, and so does the divine goodness. But [the simile] is not understood as having to do with a privation of will." If the objection had focused exclusively on the absence of *choice*, Aquinas would not have been able to characterize it as suggesting a privation of *will* in God's sharing of goodness.

30 See, e.g., DP III.15.obj.14: "Everyone who wills wills his ultimate end of necessity, as a human being of necessity wills to be happy. But the ultimate end of the divine will is the sharing of his goodness, for he produces creatures in order to share his goodness. Therefore, God wills this of necessity, and so of necessity he produces." Aquinas's rejoinder: "The ultimate end is not the sharing of goodness, but rather the divine goodness itself; it is out of love for it that God wills to share it. For he does not act because of his goodness as if desiring what he does not have, but as if wanting to share what he has, because he acts not out of desire for the end, but out of love for the end."

31 In DP XV.3, Aquinas's reply is made up of four arguments intended to support his very strong libertarian thesis, which insists that creation proceeds from "a free choice of his will . . . with no natural necessity." But the first, third, and fourth arguments conclude only that creation proceeds from will rather than from nature. As we have seen, Aquinas clearly distinguishes between volition and free choice, and so showing that creation proceeds from will is not yet to show that it proceeds from free choice. Furthermore, by his own lights, the

dichotomy between will and nature (or natural necessity) invoked in these conclusions is a false dichotomy; some of what God wills he wills with "the necessity of natural order." The conclusion of the second argument does mention choice: "The fact that he established a creature in this [or that] determinate degree [of inequality] was a consequence of a choice of will, not of natural necessity." This conclusion concerns not creation generally, however, but the creation of some universe in particular, and, as we will see, there are good reasons for supposing that free choice can operate as regards *what* to create even if not as regards *whether* to create. (Cf. the article cited in n. 16 above and the immediately following essay in this volume.)

32 SCG I.37 (n. 307).

33 See, e.g., SCG I.88 (n. 732), quoted on p. 216 above.

34 ST Ia.19.2c.

35 *Super Sent.* I, d. 2, q. 1, a. 4, s.c.

36 SCG I.38 (n. 310); see p. 217 above. In at least one place, in a work written after *Summa contra gentiles* and around the time he was beginning *Summa theologiae* (1265–67), Aquinas himself makes this identification very emphatically: "That which is per se one itself, which is God, unknown and supersubstantial (i.e., above every substance), and which is the good itself (i.e., the very essence of goodness), and which is itself that which is (i.e., per se being itself)—namely, the triune unity itself, in which, I maintain, there are no degrees, all three being at once and equally God, and *at once and equally the good itself* (the Son is no 'shadow of goodness,' as Origen and Arius said)—that, I say, we can neither speak nor think of, considered as it is in itself. For in this present life we cannot see the very essence of God, which is unity in trinity" (*In librum beati Dionysii De divinis nominibus expositio*, c. 1, l. iii, n. 81).

37 At least nineteenth-century Catholic orthodoxy is clearly opposed to this outcome: "If anyone should not confess that the world and all the things contained in it, both spiritual and material, are produced ex nihilo by God as regards their entire substance, or should say that God did not create by a volition free from every necessity but created as necessarily as he necessarily loves himself, or should deny that the world was established for the

glory of God, let him be anathema" (First Vatican Council [1870], sessio III, canones "de deo rerum omnium creatore" 5; Denzinger 1976, n. 3025). I do not know of any earlier pronouncement as explicit as this, but William Anglin called my attention to the condemnation of Abelard at the Council of Sens for maintaining that God could not do otherwise than he does (Denzinger 1976, n. 726).

38 *DV* XXI. 1.ad4.

39 See Peghaire 1932, pp. 6*, 9*, 12*, 15*, and 17*.

40 *SCG* II.24 (n. 1008).

41 *ST* Ia.19.5.ad3.

42 *ST* Ia.19.2.ad2.

43 *SCG* I.75 (n. 639).

44 *SCG* I.76 (n. 647).

45 *SCG* I.81 (n. 683).

46 As presented, e.g., in *Metaphysics* XII.9 (1074b15–34).

47 *SCG* I.75 (n. 644).

48 My translation here follows the Leonine edition (Thomas Aquinas 1970–76): "*bonitas eius his quae ad ipsam ordinantur non indiget, et eius manifestatio convenienter pluribus modis fieri potest.*" The version of this passage in the Marietti edition (Thomas Aquinas 1931) is even more in line with my own interpretation, supporting the translation "*except as a* manifestation *of it, which* can be appropriately accomplished in various ways" (*bonitas eius his quae ad ipsam ordinantur, non indiget nisi ad manifestationem, quae convenienter pluribus modis fieri potest*). The Busa edition (Thomas Aquinas 1980c) presents precisely the same reading as the Marietti, a reading not even included in the Leonine's critical apparatus. I am grateful to Peter

van Veldhuizen for first calling my attention to the discrepancy between the Leonine and Marietti editions.

49 *DV* XXIV.3c.

50 *DV* XXIII.4c.

51 *SCG* II.28 (n. 1054).

52 See Kretzmann 1983b.

53 *DV* XXIII.4c.

54 See p. 390 above.

55 For much relevant, helpful information, see Keane 1975.

56 For more detail, see Eleonore Stump and Norman Kretzmann, "Being and Goodness" (Chapter 4 in this volume).

57 Exodus 3:14.

58 Mark 10:18 and Luke 18:19. *IMD* V.2.

59 *IMD* VI.2.

60 *In Sent.* I, d. 27, p. 1, a. un., q. 2.

61 *ST* Ia.33.4.ad1.

62 *In Sent.* II, d. 1, p. 2, a. 1, q. 1.

63 P. 395 above.

64 *CH* XI.11.

65 *De luce seu de inchoatione formarum*; Robert Grosseteste 1912, 51.11–13.

66 *CH* XI.11.

67 *IMD* VI.2. For further discussion of Bonaventure on the Trinity, see Kretzmann 1989a and 1989b.

68 See, e.g., Dionysius, *De divinis nominibus* I.5, IV.4.

69 *In Sent.* I, d. 45, a. 2, q. 1, resp.; cf. ad 2.

70 I am grateful to William Haines, Scott MacDonald, William Mann, and, especially, Eleonore Stump for very helpful comments on earlier drafts of this paper.

Chapter 29

Eleonore Stump

PETITIONARY PRAYER

Ordinary Christian believers of every period have in general taken prayer to be fundamentally a request made of God for something specific believed to be good by the one praying. The technical name for such prayer is "impetration;" I am going to refer to it by the more familiar designation "petitionary prayer." There are, of course, many important kinds of prayer which are not requests; for example, most of what is sometimes called "the higher sort of prayer" – praise, adoration, thanksgiving – does not consist in requests and is not included under petitionary prayer. But basic, common petitionary prayer poses problems that do not arise in connection with the more contemplative varieties of prayer, and it is petitionary prayer with its special problems that I want to examine in this paper.

Of those problems, the one that has perhaps been most discussed in the recent literature is the connection between petitionary prayer and miracles. For instance, if one believes in divine response to petitionary prayer, is one thereby committed to a belief in miracles? But as much as possible I want to avoid this issue (and several others involving petitionary prayer[1]) in order to concentrate on just one problem. It is, I think, the problem stemming from petitionary prayer which has most often occurred to ordinary Christian believers from the Patristic period to the present. Discussion of it can be found, for example, in Origen's third-century treatise on prayer,[2] in various writings of Aquinas,[3] and, very recently, in a book by Keith Ward.[4]

Put roughly and succinctly, the problem comes to this: is a belief in the efficacy and usefulness of petitionary prayer consistent with a belief in an omniscient, omnipotent, perfectly good God? It is, therefore, a problem only on certain assumptions drawn from an ordinary, orthodox, traditional view of God and of petitionary prayer. If one thinks, for example, as D. Z. Philipps does,[5] that all "real" petitionary prayer is reducible to the petition "Thy will be done," then the problem I want to discuss evaporates. And if one thinks of God as the unknowable, non-denumerable, ultimate reality, which is not an entity at all, as Keith Ward does,[6] the problem I am interested in does not even arise. The cases which concern me in this paper are those in which someone praying a petitionary prayer makes a specific request freely (at least in his own view) of an omniscient, omnipotent, perfectly good God, conceived of in the traditional orthodox way. I am specifying that the prayers are made freely because I want to discuss this problem on the assumption that man has free will and that not everything is predetermined. I am making this assumption, first because I want to examine the problem on the assumption that man has free will and Christian believers, and I think their understanding of the problem typically includes the assumption that man has free will, and secondly because adopting the opposite view enormously complicates the attempt to understand and justify petitionary prayer. If all things are predetermined – and worse, if they are all predetermined by the omnipotent and omniscient God to whom one is praying – it is much harder to conceive of a satisfactory justification for petitionary prayer. One consequence of my making this assumption is that I will not be drawing on important traditional Protestant accounts of prayer such as those given by Calvin and Luther, for instance, since while they may be thoughtful, interesting accounts, they assume God's complete determination of everything.

I think that I can most effectively and plausibly show the problem which interests me by presenting a sketchy analysis of the Lord's Prayer. It is a prayer attributed to Christ himself, who is supposed to have produced it just for the purpose of teaching his disciples how they ought to pray. So it is an example of prayer which orthodox Christians accept as a paradigm, and it is, furthermore, a clear instance of petitionary prayer. Consequently, it is a particularly good example for my purposes. In what follows, I want to make clear, I am not concerned either to take account of contemporary Biblical exegesis or to contribute to it. I want simply to have a look at the prayer – in fact, at only half the prayer – as it is heard and prayed by ordinary twentieth-century Christians.

As the prayer is given in Luke 11, it contains seven requests. The last four have to do with the personal needs of those praying, but the first three are requests of a broader sort.

The first, "Hallowed be thy name," is commonly taken as a request that God's name be regarded as holy.[7] I am not sure what it means to regard God's name as holy, and I want to avoid worries about the notion of having attitudes towards God's *name*. All the same, I think something of the following sort is a sensible interpretation of the request. The common Biblical notion of holiness has at its root a sense of strong separateness.[8] And it may be that to regard God's

name as holy is only to react to it very differently from the way in which one reacts to any other name – and that could happen because it seems specially precious or also (for example) because it seems specially feared. On this understanding of the request, it would be fulfilled if everyone (or almost everyone) took a strongly emotional and respectful attitude towards God's name. But it may be that this is too complicated as an interpretation of the request, and that to regard God's name as holy is simply to love and revere it. In that case, the request is fulfilled if everyone or almost everyone regards God's name very reverentially. And there are New Testament passages which foretell states of affairs fulfilling both these interpretations of the request – prophesying a time at or near the end of the world when all men fear or love God's name, and a time when the inhabitants of earth are all dedicated followers of God.[9]

The second request in the Lord's Prayer is that God's kingdom come. Now according to orthodox Judaeo-Christian beliefs, God is and always has been ruler of the world. What then does it mean to ask for the advent of his kingdom? Plainly, there is at least some sense in which the kingdom of heaven has not yet been established on earth and can be waited and hoped for. And this request seems to be for those millennial times when everything on earth goes as it ought to go, when men beat their swords into plowshares (Isaiah 2: 4) and the wolf dwells at peace with the lamb (Isaiah 11: 6, 65: 25). This too, then, is a request for a certain state of affairs involving all or most men, the state of affairs at the end of the world prophesied under one or another description in Old and New Testament passages (cf., e.g., Revelation 21: 1–4).

And it seems closely related to the object of the third request, "Thy will be done on earth as it is in heaven." There is, of course, a sense in which, according to Christian doctrine, God's will is always done on earth. But that is the sense in which God allows things to happen as they do (God's so-called "permissive will"). God permits certain people to have evil intentions, he permits certain people to commit crimes, and so on, so that he wills to let happen what does happen; and in this sense his will is always done. But in heaven, according to Christian doctrine, it is not that God permits what occurs to occur, and so wills in accordance with what happens, but rather that what happens happens in accordance with his will. So only the perfect good willed unconditionally by God is ever done in heaven. For God's will to be done on earth in such a way, everyone on earth would always have to do only good. This request, then, seems to be another way of asking for the establishment of God's kingdom on earth; and it also seems linked with certain New Testament prophecies – there will be a "new earth," and the righteous meek will inherit it (cf., e.g., Matthew 5: 5 and Revelation 5: 10 and 21: 1–4).

What I think is most worth noticing in this context about all three of these first requests of the Lord's Prayer is that it seems absolutely pointless, futile, and absurd to make them. All three seem to be requests for the millenium or for God's full reign on earth. But it appears from New Testament prophecies that God has already determined to bring about such a state of affairs in the future. And if God has predetermined that there will be such a time, then what is asked for in those three requests is already sure to come. But, then, what is the point of making the prayer? Why ask for something that is certain to come whether you beg for it or flee from it? It is no answer to these questions to say, as some theologians have done,[10] that one prays in this way just because Jesus prescribed such a prayer. That attempt at an answer simply transfers responsibility for the futile action from the one praying to the one being prayed to; it says nothing about what sense there is in the prayer itself. On the other hand, if, contrary to theological appearances, the things prayed for are not predetermined and their occurrence or non-occurrence is still in doubt, could the issue possibly be resolved by someone's asking for

one or another outcome? If Jimmy Carter, say, (or some other Christian) does not ask for God's kingdom to come, will God therefore fail to establish it? Or will he establish it *just because* Jimmy Carter asked for it, though he would not have done so otherwise? Even Carter's staunchest supporters might well find it frightening to think so; and yet if we do not answer these questions in the affirmative, the prayer seems futile and pointless. So either an omniscient, omnipotent, perfectly good God has predetermined this state of affairs or he hasn't; and either way, asking for it seems to make no sense. This conclusion is applicable to other cases of petitionary prayer as well. To take just one example, suppose that Jimmy Carter prays the altruistic and Christian prayer that a particular atheistic friend of his be converted and so saved from everlasting damnation. If it is in God's power to save that man, won't he do so without Jimmy Carter's prayers? Won't a perfectly good God do all the good he can no matter what anyone prays for or does not pray for? Consequently, either God of his goodness will save the man in any case, so that the prayer is pointless, or there is some point in the prayer but God's goodness appears impugned.

We can, I think, generalize these arguments to all petitionary prayer by means of a variation on the argument from evil against God's existence.[11] (The argument that follows does not seem to me to be an acceptable one, but it is the sort of argument that underlies the objections to petitionary prayer which I have been presenting. I will say something about what I think are the flaws in this argument later in the paper.)

1   A perfectly good being never makes the world worse than it would otherwise be if he can avoid doing so.

The phrase "than it would otherwise be" here should be construed as "than the world would have been had he not brought about or omitted to bring about some state of affairs." In other words, a perfectly good being never makes the world, in virtue of what he himself does or omits to do, worse than it would have been had he not done or omitted to do something or other. *Mutatis mutandis*, the same remarks apply to "than it would otherwise be" in (4) and (7) below.

2   An omniscient and omnipotent being can avoid doing anything which it is not logically necessary for him to do.

3   ∴ An omniscient, omnipotent, perfectly good being never makes the world worse than it would otherwise be unless it is logically necessary for him to do so. (1, 2)

4   A perfectly good being always makes the world better than it would otherwise be if he can do so.

5   An omniscient and omnipotent being can do anything which it is not logically impossible for him to do.

6   ∴ An omniscient, omnipotent, perfectly good being always makes the world better than it would otherwise be unless it is logically impossible for him to do so. (4, 5)

7   It is never logically necessary for an omniscient, omnipotent, perfectly good being to make the world worse than it would otherwise be; it is never logically impossible for an omniscient, omnipotent, perfectly good being to make the world better than it would otherwise be.

8   ∴ An omniscient, omnipotent, perfectly good being never makes the world worse than it would otherwise be and always makes the world better than it would otherwise be. (3, 6, 7)

This subconclusion implies that unless the world is infinitely improvable, either the world is or will be absolutely perfect or there is no omniscient, omnipotent, perfectly good being. In other words, (8) with the addition of a pair of premises –

(i)   The world is not infinitely improvable

and

(ii)   It is not the case that the world is or will be absolutely perfect (i.e. there is and always will be evil in the world) –

implies the conclusion of the argument from evil. That is not a surprising result since this argument is dependent on the argument from evil.[12]

9   What is requested in every petitionary prayer is or results in a state of affairs the realization of which would make the world either worse or better than it would otherwise be (that is, than it would have been had that state of affairs not been realized).

It is not always clear whether a petitionary prayer is requesting just an earthly state of affairs, or God's bringing about that earthly state of affairs. So, for example, when a mother prays for the health of her sick son, it is not always clear whether she is requesting simply the health of her son or God's restoration of the health of her son. If we can determine the nature of the request on the basis of what the one praying desires and hopes to get by means of prayer, then at least in most cases the request will be just for some earthly state of affairs. What is important to the mother is simply her son's getting well. For a case in which the request is for God's bringing about some earthly state of affairs, we might consider Gideon's prayer concerning the fleece, discussed below. In any event, I intend "state of affairs" in this argument to range broadly enough to cover both sorts of cases.

10   ∴ If what is requested in a petitionary prayer is or results in a state of affairs the realization of which would make the world worse than it would otherwise be, an omniscient, omnipotent, perfectly good being will not fulfill that request. (8)

11   ∴ If what is requested in a petitionary prayer is or results in a state of affairs the realization of which would make the world better than it would otherwise be, an omniscient, omnipotent, perfectly good being will bring about that state of affairs even if no prayer for its realization has been made. (8)

It might occur to someone here that what is requested in at least some petitionary prayers is that God bring about a certain state of affairs *in response to the particular petitionary prayer being made*. In such cases, of course, it is logically impossible that God bring about what is requested in the petitionary prayer in the absence of that petitionary prayer. It is not clear to me that there are such cases. The familiar entreaties such as "Hear the voice of my supplications" (Psalm 28: 2) in the Psalms seem to me not to be cases of the relevant sort, because they seem to be an elaborate "Please" rather than anything influencing the nature of what is requested in the prayer. Perhaps one of the best candidates for such a case is Gideon's prayer about the fleece: "If you will save Israel by my hand, as you have said, I will put a fleece of wool on the floor and if the dew is on the fleece only and it is dry on all the earth, then I will know that you will save Israel by my hand, as you have said" (Judges 6: 36–7; cf. also 6: 39). Gideon here is requesting that God give him a sign by means of the fleece of wool. Does his prayer amount to a request that God produce dew only on the fleece and not on the surrounding ground, or does it come to a request that God do so in response to Gideon's prayer? If there are cases in which the request implicitly or explicitly includes reference to the prayer itself, then in those cases the inference from (8) to (11) is not valid; and such cases ought simply to be excluded from consideration in this argument.

12   ∴ Petitionary prayer effects no change. (9, 10, 11)

There is, of course, a sense in which the offering of a prayer is itself a new state of affairs and accompanies or results in natural, psychological changes in the one praying, but step (12) ought to be understood as saying that no prayer is itself efficacious in causing a change of the sort it was designed to cause. An argument which might be thought to apply here, invalidating the inference to the conclusion (13), is that prayer need not effect any change in order to be considered efficacious, provided the offering of the prayer itself is a sufficient reason in God's view for God's fulfillment of the prayer.[13] In other words, if, for certain reasons apart from consideration of a prayer for a state of affairs S, God has determined to bring about S, a prayer for S may still be considered to be efficacious if and only if God would have brought about S just in response to the prayer for S. But I think that even if this view is correct, it does not in fact invalidate the inference to (13). There is a difference between being efficacious and having a point. This argument about the efficacy of prayer seems to assume that not all answers to prayer will be of the overdetermined type. And as long as a believer is not in a position to know which states of affairs are divinely determined to occur regardless of prayers, there is some point in petitionary prayer – any given case may be one in which God would not have brought about the desired state of affairs without prayer for it. But if it is the case for every fulfilled prayer that God would have brought about the desired state of affairs without the prayer, it does seem that there is no point in petitionary prayer, except for those cases (which I think must at best form a very small minority) in which the real object of the one praying a petitionary prayer is not so much to see the realization of the state of affairs he is requesting as to have some influence on or contact with the Deity by means of petitionary prayer; and such cases may then simply be excepted from the conclusion of the argument.

13   ∴ Petitionary prayer is pointless. (12)

The basic strategy of this argument is an attempt to show that there is an inconsistency between God's goodness and the efficacy of petitionary prayer; but it is possible to begin with other divine attributes and make a case for a similar inconsistency, so that we can have other, very different arguments to the same conclusion, namely, that petitionary prayer is pointless. Perhaps the most formidable of such alternative arguments is the one based on God's immutability, an argument the strategy of which can be roughly summarized in this way. Before a certain petitionary prayer is made, it is the case either that God will bring about the state of affairs requested in the prayer or that he will not bring it about. He cannot have left the matter open since doing so would imply a subsequent change in him and he is immutable. Either way, since he is immutable, the prayer itself can effect no change in the state of affairs and hence is pointless. Even leaving aside problems of foreknowledge and free will to which this argument (or attempted objections to it) may give rise, I think that orthodox theology will find no real threat in the argument because of the doctrine of God's eternality. However problematic that doctrine may be in itself, it undercuts arguments such as this one because it maintains God's atemporality.[14] My thirteen-step argument against petitionary prayer is, then, not the only argument rejecting petitionary prayer on theistic principles, but it (or some argument along the same lines) does, I think, make the strongest case against petitionary prayer, given Christian doctrine.

The premise that is most likely to appear false in the argument, at first reading, is (9) because one is inclined to think that there are many petitionary prayers which, if they are granted, would not make the world either better or worse than it would otherwise be. Such a view might be accommodated without damaging the argument simply by weakening (9) and the conclusion: many petitionary prayers, and surely the most important ones, are such that if fulfilled they make the world either a better or a worse place. But I think it is possible to argue plausibly for (9) in the strong form I have given it. Take, for instance, the case of a little boy who prays for a jackknife. Here, we might think we have an example of a petitionary prayer the fulfillment of which makes the world neither better nor worse. But, on the one hand, if the little boy has prayed for a jackknife, surely he will be happier if he gets it, either because he very much wants a jackknife or because God has honored his request. Consequently, one could argue that fulfilling the request makes the world better in virtue of making the one praying happier. Or, on the other hand, if we think of the little boy's prayer for a jackknife from God's point of view, then we see that fulfillment of the prayer involves not just the little boy's acquiring a jackknife but also God's bringing it about in answer to prayer that the little boy acquire a jackknife. Fulfilling the prayer, then, will have an influence on at least the little boy's religious beliefs and perhaps also on those of his parents and even on those of the people in his parents' community. One might argue that the influence in this case would be deleterious (since it is conducive to wrong views of the purpose of prayer and of relationship with God), and consequently that fulfilling this prayer would make the world a worse place than it would otherwise be. So I think it is possible to argue plausibly that the fulfillment of even such a prayer would make the world either a worse or a better place.

Christian literature contains a number of discussions of the problem with petitionary prayer and various attempts to solve it. For the sake of brevity, I want to look just at the proposed solution Aquinas gives. It is the most philosophically sophisticated of the solutions I know; and in the wake of the twentieth-century revival of Thomism, it is the solution adopted by many theologians and theistic philosophers today.[15] Thomas discusses problems of petitionary prayer in his Sentence commentary and in the *Summa contra gentiles*,[16] but the clearest exposition of his views is in the question on prayer in the *Summa theologiae*, where he devotes an entire article to showing that there is sense and usefulness in petitionary prayer.[17] The basic argument he relies on to rebut various objections against the usefulness of prayer is this. Divine Providence determines not only what effects there will be in the world, but also what causes will give rise to those effects and in what order they will do so. Now human actions, too, are causes. "For," Thomas says, "we pray not in order to change the divine disposition but for the sake of acquiring by petitionary prayer what God has disposed to be achieved by prayer."[18]

Perhaps the first worry which this argument occasions stems from the appearance of theological determinism in it: God determines not only what effects there will be but also what the causes of those effects will be and in what order the effects will be produced. It is hard to see how such a belief is compatible with freedom of the will. In the preamble to this argument, however, Thomas says he is concerned not to deny free will but, on the contrary, to give an account of prayer which preserves free will. So I want simply to assume that he has in mind some distinction or some theory which shows that, despite appearances, his argument is not committed to a thorough-going determinism, and I am going to ignore any troubles in the argument having to do with the compatibility of predestination or foreknowledge and free will.

For present purposes, what is more troublesome about this argument is that it does not provide any real help with the problem it means to solve. According to Thomas, there is nothing absurd or futile about praying to God, given God's nature, because God has by his providence arranged things so that free human actions and human prayers will form part of the chain of cause and effect leading to the state of the world ordained in God's plan. And so, on Thomas's view, prayer should not be thought of as an attempt to get God to do something which he would not otherwise do but rather as an effort to produce an appropriate and preordained cause which will result in certain effects since God in his providence has determined things to be so. Now surely there can be no doubt that, according to Christian doctrine, God wants men to pray and answers prayers; and consequently it is plain that God's plan for the world includes human prayers as causes of certain effects. The difficulty lies in explaining how such a doctrine makes sense. Why should prayers be included in God's plan as causes of certain effects? And what sense is there in the notion that a perfect and unchangeable God, who disposes and plans everything, fulfills men's prayers asking him to do one thing or another? Thomas's argument, I think, gives no help with these questions and so gives no help with this problem of petitionary prayer.

This argument of Thomas's is roughly similar in basic strategy to other traditional arguments for prayer[19] and is furthermore among the most fully developed and sophisticated arguments for prayer, but it seems to me inadequate to make sense of petitionary prayer. I think, then, that it is worthwhile exploring a sort of argument different from those that stress the connection between God's omniscience or providence and men's prayers. In what follows I want to offer a tentative and preliminary sketch of the way in which such an argument might go.

Judaeo-Christian concepts of God commonly represent God as loving mankind and wanting to be loved by men in return. Such anthropomorphic talk is in sharp contrast to the more sophisticated-sounding language of the Hellenized and scholastic arguments considered so far. But a certain sort of anthropomorphism is as much a part of Christianity as is Thomas's "perfect being theology,"[20] and it, too, builds on intricate philosophical analysis, beginning perhaps with Boethius's attempt in *Contra Eutychen et Nestorium* to explain what it means to say of something that it is a person. So to say that God loves men and wants to be loved in return is to say something that has a place in philosophical theology and is indispensable to Christian doctrine. Throughout the Old and New Testaments, the type of loving relationship wanted between man and God is represented by various images, for example, sometimes as the relationship between husband and wife, sometimes as that between father and child. And sometimes (in the Gospel of John, for instance) it is also represented as the relationship between true friends.[21] But if the relationship between God and human beings is to be one which at least sometimes can be accurately represented as the love of true friendship, then there is a problem for both parties to the relationship, because plainly it will not be easy for there to be friendship between an omniscient, omnipotent, perfectly good person and a fallible, finite, imperfect person. The troubles of generating and maintaining friendship in such a case are surely the perfect paradigms of which the troubles of friendship between a Rockefeller child and a slum child are just pale copies. Whatever other troubles there are for friendship in these cases, there are at least two dangers for the disadvantaged or inferior member of the pair. First, he can be so overcome by the advantages or superiority of his "friend" that he becomes simply a shadowy reflection of the other's personality, a slavish follower who slowly loses all sense of his own tastes and desires and will. Some people, of course, believe that just this sort of attitude towards God is what Christianity wants and gets from the best of its adherents; but I think that such a belief goes counter to the spirit of the Gospels, for example, and I don't think that it can be found even in such intense mystics as St Teresa and St John of the Cross. Secondly, in addition to the danger of becoming completely dominated, there is the danger of becoming spoiled in the way that members of a royal family in a ruling house are subject to. Because of the power at their disposal in virtue of their connections, they often become tyrannical, willful, indolent, self-indulgent, and the like. The greater the discrepancy in status and condition between the two friends, the greater the danger of even inadvertently overwhelming and oppressing or overwhelming and spoiling the lesser member of the pair, and if he is overwhelmed in either of these ways, the result will be replacement of whatever kind of friendship there might have been with one or another sort of using. Either the superior member of the pair will use the lesser as his lackey, or the lesser will use the superior as his personal power source. To put it succinctly, then, if God wants some kind of true friendship with men, he will have to find a way of guarding against both kinds of overwhelming.

It might occur to someone to think that even if we assume the view that God wants friendship between himself and human beings, it does not follow that he will have any of the problems just sketched, because he is omnipotent.[22] If he wants friendship of this sort with men, one might suppose, let him just will it and it will be his. I do not want to stop here to argue against this view in detail, but I do want just to suggest that there is reason for thinking it to be incoherent, at least on the assumption of free will adopted at the beginning of this paper, because it is hard to see how God could bring about such a friendship magically, by means of his omnipotence, and yet permit the people involved to have free will. If he could do so, he could make a person freely love him in the right sort of way, and it does not seem reasonable to think he could do so.[23] On the face of it, then, omnipotence alone does not do away with the two dangers for friendship that I sketched above. But the institution of petitionary prayer, I think, can be understood as a safeguard against these dangers.

It is easiest to argue that petitionary prayer serves such a function in the case of a man who prays for himself. In praying for himself, he makes an explicit request for help, and he thereby acknowledges a need or a desire and his dependence on God for satisfying that need or desire. If he gets what he prayed for, he will be in a position to attribute his good fortune to God's doing and to be grateful to God for what God has given him. If we add the undeniable uncertainty of his getting what he prays for, then we will have safeguards against what I will call (for lack of a better phrase) overwhelming spoiling. These conditions make the act of asking a safeguard against tyrannical and self-indulgent pride, even if the one praying thinks of himself grandly as having God on his side.

We can see how the asking guards against the second danger, of oppressive overwhelming, if we look for a moment at the function of roughly similar asking for help when both the one asking and the one asked are human beings. Suppose a teacher sees that one of his students is avoiding writing a paper and is thereby storing up trouble for himself at the end of the term. And suppose that the student *asks* the teacher for extra help in organizing working time and scheduling the various parts of the work. In that case I think the teacher can without any problem give the student what he needs, provided, of course, that the teacher is willing to do as much for any other student, and so on. But suppose, on the other hand, that the student does not ask the teacher for help and that the teacher instead calls the student at home and simply presents him with the help he needs in scheduling and discipline. The teacher's proposals in that case are more than likely to strike the student as meddling interference, and he is likely to respond with more or less polite variations on "Who asked you?" and "Mind your own business." Those responses, I think, are healthy and just. If the student were having ordinary difficulties getting his work done and yet docilely and submissively accepted the teacher's unrequested scheduling of his time, he would have taken the first step in the direction of unhealthy passivity towards his teacher. And if he and his teacher developed that sort of relationship, he could end by becoming a lackey-like reflection of his teacher. Bestowing at least some benefits only in response to requests for them is a safeguard against such an outcome when the members of the relationship are not equally balanced.

It becomes much harder to argue for this defense of prayer as soon as the complexity of the case is increased even just a little. Take, for example, Monica's praying for her son Augustine. There is nothing in Monica's praying for Augustine which shows that *Augustine* recognizes that he has a need for God's help or that *he* will be grateful if God gives him what *Monica* prays for. Nor is it plain that *Monica's* asking shields Augustine from oppressive overwhelming by God. So it seems as if the previous arguments fail in this case. But consider again the case in which a teacher sees that a student of his could use help but does not feel that he can legitimately volunteer his help unasked. Suppose that John, a friend of that student, comes to see the teacher and says, "I don't know if you've noticed, but Jim is having trouble getting to his term paper. And unless he gets help, I think he won't do it at all and will be in danger of flunking the course." If the teacher now goes to help Jim and is rudely or politely asked "What right have you got to interfere?," he'll say, "Well, in fact, your friend came to me and *asked* me to help." And if John is asked the same question, he will probably reply, "But I'm your friend; I had to do *something*." I think, then, that because John asks the teacher, the teacher is in a position to help with less risk of oppressive meddling than before. Obviously, he cannot go very far without incurring that risk as fully as before; and perhaps the most he can do if he wants to avoid oppressive meddling is to try to elicit from Jim in genuinely uncoercive ways a request for help. And, of course, I chose Monica and Augustine to introduce this case because, as Augustine tells it in the *Confessions*, God responded to Monica's fervent and continued prayers for Augustine's salvation by arranging the circumstances of Augustine's life in such a way that finally Augustine himself freely asked God for salvation.

One might perhaps think that there is something superfluous and absurd in God's working through the intermediary of prayer in this way. If Jim's friend can justify his interference on the grounds that he is Jim's friend and has to do *something*, God can dispense with this sort of petitionary prayer, too. He can give aid unasked on the grounds that he is the *creator* and has to do something. But suppose that Jim and John are only acquaintances who have discussed nothing more than their schoolwork; and suppose that John, by overhearing Jim's phone conversations, has come to believe that all Jim's academic troubles are just symptoms of problems he is having with his parents. If John asks the teacher to help Jim with his personal problems, and if the teacher begins even a delicate attempt to do so by saying that John asked him to do so, he and John could both properly be told to mind their own business. It is not the *status* of his relationship or even the depth of his care and compassion for Jim which puts John in a position to defend himself by saying "But I'm your friend." What protects John against the charge of oppressive meddling is rather the degree to which Jim has freely, willingly, shared his life and thoughts and feelings with John. So John's line of defense against the charge of oppressive meddling can be attributed to God only if the person God is to aid has willingly shared his thoughts and feelings and the like with God. But it is hard to imagine anyone putting himself in such a relation to a person he believes to be omnipotent and good without his also *asking* for whatever help he needs.

Even if the argument can be made out so far, one might be inclined to think that it will not be sufficient to show the compatibility of God's goodness with the practice of petitionary prayer. If one supposes that God brought Augustine to Christianity in response to Monica's prayers, what is one to say about Augustine's fate if Monica had not prayed for him? And what does this view commit one to maintain about people who neither pray for themselves nor are prayed for? It looks as if an orthodox Christian who accepts the argument about petitionary prayer so far will be committed to a picture of this sort. God is analogous to a human father with two

very different children. Both Old and New Testaments depict God as doing many good things for men without being asked to do so, and this human father, too, does unrequested good things for both his children. But one child, who is healthy and normal, with healthy, normal relations to his father, makes frequent requests of the father which the father responds to and in virtue of which he bestows benefits on the child. The other child is selectively blind, deaf, dumb, and suffering from whatever other maladies are necessary to make it plausible that he does not even know he has a father. Now either there are some benefits that the father will never bestow unless and until he is asked; and in that case he will do less for his defective child, who surely has more need of his help than does the healthy child. Or, on the other hand, he will bestow all his benefits unasked on the defective child, and then he seems to make a mockery of his practice with the normal child of bestowing some benefits only in response to requests – he is, after all, willing to bestow the same benefits without being asked. So it seems that we are still left with the problem we started with: either God is not perfectly good or the practice of petitionary prayer is pointless. But suppose the father always meets the defective child's needs and desires even though the child never comes to know of the existence of his father. The child knows only that he is always taken care of, and when he needs something, he gets what he needs. It seems to me intuitively clear that such a practice runs a great risk, at least, of making the defective child willful and tyrannical. But even if the defective child is not in danger of being made worse in some respects in this situation, still it seems plain that he would be better off if the father could manage to put the child in a position to know his father and to frame a request for what he wants. So I think a good father will fulfill the child's needs unasked; but I think that he can do so without making a mockery of his practice of bestowing benefits in response to requests only if putting the child in a position to make requests is among his first concerns.

And as for the question whether God would have saved Augustine without Monica's prayers, I think that there is intermediate ground between the assertion that Monica's prayers are necessary to Augustine's salvation, which seems to impugn God's goodness, and the claim that they are altogether without effect, which undercuts petitionary prayer. It is possible, for example, to argue that God would have saved Augustine without Monica's prayers but not in the same amount of time or not by the same process or not with the same effect. Augustine, for instance, might have been converted to Christianity but not in such a way as to become one of its most powerful authorities for centuries.[24]

With all this, I have still looked only at cases that are easy for my position; when we turn to something like a prayer for Guatemala after the earthquake – which begins to come closer to the sort of petitions in the first half of the Lord's Prayer – it is much harder to know what to say. And perhaps it is simply too hard to come up with a reasonable solution here because we need more work on the problem of evil. Why would a good God permit the occurrence of earthquakes in the first place? Do the reasons for his permitting the earthquake affect his afterwards helping the country involved? Our inclination is surely to say that a good God must in *any case* help the earthquake victims, so that in this instance at any rate it is pointless to pray. But plainly we also have strong inclinations to say that a good God must in any case prevent earthquakes in populated areas. And since orthodox Christianity is committed to distrusting these latter inclinations, it is at least at sea about the former ones. Without more work on the problem of evil, it is hard to know what to say about the difference prayer might make in this sort of case.

I think it is worth noticing, though, that the first three requests of the Lord's prayer do not run into the same difficulties. Those requests seem generally equivalent to a request for the kingdom of God on earth, that state of affairs in which, of their own free will, all men on earth are dedicated, righteous lovers of God. Now suppose it is true that God would bring about his kingdom on earth even if an individual Christian such as Jimmy Carter did not pray for it. It does not follow in this case, however, that the prayer in question is pointless and makes no difference. Suppose no one prayed for the advent of God's kingdom on earth or felt a need or desire for those millennial times strongly enough to pray for them. It seems unreasonable to think that God could bring about his earthly kingdom under those conditions, or if he could, that it would be the state of affairs just described, in which earth is populated by people who *freely* love God.[25] And if so, then making the requests in the first half of the Lord's Prayer resembles other, more ordinary activities in which only the effort of a whole group is sufficient to achieve the desired result. One man can't put out a forest fire, but if everyone in the vicinity of a forest fire realized that fact and on that basis decided not to try, the fire would rage out of control. So in the case of the opening petitions of the Lord's Prayer, too, it seems possible to justify petitionary prayer without impugning God's goodness.

Obviously, the account I have given is just a preliminary sketch for the full development of this solution, and a good deal more work needs to be done on the problem. None the less, I think that this account is on the right track and that there is a workable solution to the problem of petitionary prayer which can be summarized in this way. God must work through the intermediary of prayer, rather than doing everything on his own initiative, for man's sake. Prayer acts as a kind of buffer between man and God. By safeguarding the weaker member of the relation from the dangers of overwhelming domination and overwhelming spoiling, it helps to promote and preserve a close relationship between an omniscient, omnipotent, perfectly good person and a fallible, finite, imperfect person. There is, of course, something counter-intuitive in this notion that prayer acts as a buffer; prayer of all sorts is commonly and I think correctly said to have as one of its main functions the production of closeness between man and God. But not just any sort of closeness will result in friendship, and promoting the appropriate sort of closeness will require inhibiting or preventing inappropriate sorts of closeness, so that a relationship of friendship depends on the maintenance of both closeness and distance between the two friends. And while I do not mean to denigrate the importance of prayer in producing and preserving the appropriate sort of closeness, I think the problem of petitionary prayer at issue here is best solved by focusing on the distance necessary for friendship and the function of petitionary prayer in maintaining that distance.

As for the argument against prayer which I laid out at the start of the paper, it seems to me that the flaw lies in step (7), that it is never logically necessary for God to make the world worse than it would otherwise be and never logically impossible for him to make the world better than it would otherwise be. To take a specific example from among those discussed so far, orthodox Christianity is committed to claiming that the advent of God's kingdom on earth, in which all people freely love God, would make the world better than it would otherwise be. But I think that it is not possible for God to *make* the world better in this way, because I think it is not possible for him to *make* men *freely* do anything.[26] And in general, if it is arguable that God's doing good things just in virtue of men's requests protects men from the dangers described and preserves them in the right relationship to God, then it is not the case that it is always logically possible for God to make the world better and never logically necessary for him to make the world worse than it would otherwise be. If men do not always pray for all the good things they might and ought to pray for, then in some cases either God will not bring about some good thing or he will do so but at the expense of the good wrought and preserved by petitionary prayer.

It should be plain that there is nothing in this analysis of prayer which *requires* that God fulfill every prayer; asking God for something is not in itself a sufficient condition for God's doing what he is asked. Christian writings are full of examples of prayers which are not answered, and there are painful cases of unanswered prayer in which the one praying must be tempted more to the belief that God is his implacable enemy than to the sentimental-seeming belief that God is his friend. This paper proposes no answer for these difficulties. They require a long, hard, careful look at the problem of evil, and that falls just outside the scope of this paper.

And, finally, it may occur to someone to wonder whether the picture of God presented in this analysis is at all faithful to the God of the Old or New Testaments. Is this understanding of God and prayer anything that Christianity ought to accept or even find congenial? It seems to me that one could point to many stories in either the Old or New Testament in support of an affirmative answer – for example, Elijah's performance on Mount Carmel (1 Kings 18), or the apostles' prayer for a successor to Judas (Acts 1: 24–6). But for a small and particularly nice piece of evidence, we can turn to the story in the Gospel of Luke which describes Jesus making the Lord's Prayer and giving a lecture on how one is to pray. According to the Gospel, Jesus is praying and in such a way that his disciples see him and know that he is praying. One of them makes a request of him which has just a touch of rebuke in it: teach us to pray, as *John* taught *his* disciples to pray (Luke 11: 1). If there is a note of rebuke there, it seems just. A religious master should teach his disciples to pray, and a good teacher does not wait until he is asked to teach his students important lessons. But Jesus is portrayed as a good teacher of just this sort in the Gospel of Luke.[27] Does the Gospel, then, mean its readers to understand that Jesus would not have taught his disciples how to pray if they had not requested it? And if it does not, why is Jesus portrayed as waiting until he is asked? Perhaps the Gospel means us to understand[28] that Jesus does so just in order to teach by experience as well as by sermon what is implicit throughout the Lord's Prayer: that asking makes a difference.[29]

Notes

1   For a good recent account of the problem of petitionary prayer and miracles, see Robert Young, "Petitioning God," *American Philosophical Quarterly*, 11 (1974), pp. 193–201. Other issues I intend to avoid include Peter Geach's worries about prayer for events in the past in *God and the Soul* (London, 1969), pp. 89ff., and about "certain tensed propositions about the divine will . . . in connexion with prayer" (*God and the Soul*, p. 97).

2   Eric George Jay, *Origen's Treatise on Prayer* (London, 1954), vols V–VI, pp. 92–103.

3   Most notably, *Summa theologiae*, 2a–2ae, 83, 1–17; *Summa contra gentiles*, I.III. 95–6; *In IV. Sent.*, dist. XV, q. 4, a. I.

4   *The Concept of God* (New York, 1974), pp. 221–2. Ward introduces the problem only as an embarrassment for what he calls "Thomistic" theology. Cf. my review in *The Philosophical Review*, 86 (1977), pp. 398–404.

5   *The Concept of Prayer* (New York, 1966), pp. 112ff.

6   Cf. *The Concept of God*, pp. 62, 101, 111, and 185.

7   Cf., for example, the similar understanding of this petition in two very different theologians: Augustine, *Homilies on the Gospels*, Serm. 6; and Calvin, *Institutes of the Christian Religion*, III. xx. 41.

8   The most common Old Testament word for "holy" and its correlates is some form of "kādash," the basic, literal meaning of which is separation, withdrawal, or state of being set apart; cf. Gesenius, *A Hebrew and English Lexicon of the Old Testament*. In the New Testament, the most frequently used word is "hagiazō" and its correlates, the basic meaning of which also includes the notion of being separate and being set apart; cf. Thayer, *A Greek–English Lexicon of the New Testament*, and Arndt and Gringich, *A Greek–English Lexicon of the New Testament and Other Early Christian Literature*.

9   Cf., e.g., Isaiah 2: 2–21, 45: 23, and 65: 23; Matthew 24; Mark 13; Luke 21; and Revelation 6: 15–17.

10   See, for example, Martin Luther, *Large Catechism*, pt. III. 169. Luther's argument for prayer has more force in the context of the catechism than it does in the context of a philosophical discussion, because Luther's purpose there is the practical one of blocking what he understands as believers' *excuses* for not praying.

11   My approach to the argument from evil, which underlies the following argument, owes a good deal to Carl Ginet and Norman Kretzmann.

12   There is a noteworthy difference between (ii) and the premise ordinarily supplied in its stead in arguments from evil, namely, (ii′) "There is evil in the world." The difference suggests a way to develop an alternative or at least an addition to the standard free will defense against the argument from evil.

13   See Terence Penelhum, *Religion and Rationality* (New York, 1971), pp. 287–92.

14   Norman Kretzmann and I examine the concept of eternity in ancient and medieval metaphysics and theology in our forthcoming book on that subject, attending particularly to the usefulness of the concept in resolving certain problems in rational theology.

15   See, for example, the articles on prayer in the *Dictionnaire de Théologie Catholique* and *The New Catholic Encyclopedia*.

16   See *In IV. Sent.*, dist. XV, q.4, a. 1, and *Summa contra gentiles*, I. III. 95–6.

17   See 2a–2ae, q. 83, a.2.

18   See reply, a.2. "*Non enim propter hoc oramus ut divinam dispositionem immutemus: sed ut id impetremus quod Deus disposuit per orationes sanctorium implendum.*"

19   Cf., e.g., Origen, op. cit., and Augustine, *City of God*, Bk V, ix.

20   Plainly, a good deal of skillful work is needed to weave such anthropomorphism and scholastic theology into one harmonious whole. The problem is, of course, given lengthy, detailed treatment in various scholastic writings, including Thomas's *Summa theologiae*.

21   See especially John 15: 12–15.

22   I want to avoid detailed discussion of the various controversies over omnipotence. For present purposes, I will take this as a rough definition of omnipotence: a being is omnipotent if and only if he can do anything which it is not logically

impossible for him to do and if he can avoid doing anything which it is not logically necessary for him to do.

23 Controversy over this point is related to the more general controversy over whether or not it is possible for an omnipotent, omniscient, perfectly good God to create men who would on every occasion freely do what is right. For a discussion of that general controversy and arguments that it is not possible for God to do so, see Alvin Plantinga's *God and Other Minds* (Ithaca, 1967), pp. 132–48; I am in agreement with the general tenor of Plantinga's remarks in that section of his book.

24 I have presented the case of Monica and Augustine in a simplified form in order to have an uncomplicated hard case for the view I am arguing. As far as the historical figures themselves are concerned, it is plain that Monica's overt, explicit, passionate concern for her son's conversion greatly influenced the course of his life and shaped his character from boyhood on. It is not clear whether Augustine would have been anything like the man he was if his mother had not been as zealous on behalf of his soul as she was, if she had not prayed continually and fervently for his salvation and let him know she was doing so. Augustine's character and personality were what they were in large part as a result of her fierce desire for his espousal of Christianity; and just his knowledge that his beloved mother prayed so earnestly for his conversion must have been a powerful natural force helping to effect that conversion. In this context the question whether God could have saved Augustine without Monica's prayers takes on different meaning, and an affirmative answer is much harder to give with reasoned confidence.

25 See n. 23 above.

26 See n. 23 above.

27 See, for example, the lessons taught in the two incidents described in Luke 21: 1–6.

28 I have used awkward circumlocutions in this paragraph in order to make plain that it is not my intention here to make any claims about the historical Jesus or the intentions of the Gospel writer. I am not concerned in this paper to do or to take account of contemporary theories of Biblical exegesis. My point is only that the story in the Gospel, as it has been part of ordinary Christian tradition, lends itself to the interpretation I suggest.

29 In writing this paper, I have benefited from the comments and criticisms of John Boler, Norman Care, and Bill Rowe. I am particularly indebted to my friend Norman Kretzmann for his thorough reading and very helpful criticism of the paper. And I am grateful to John Crossett, from whom I have learned a great deal and whose understanding of philosophical problems in Christian theology is much better than my own.

Chapter 30

Kevin Timpe

PRAYERS FOR THE PAST

Introduction

Consider the following scenario. Allison is an agent with libertarian free will. While watching the evening news, she learns that there is currently a tornado touching down in western Ohio, leaving a path of devastation and destruction in its wake. Allison's father lives in the path of the storm. As she runs to the phone to call him, she offers a prayer that he not be hurt or killed by the tornado. Allison thinks that God might hear her prayer and, as a result, intervene in such a way as to protect her father from harm.[1]

Scenarios such as this are common, wherein a person petitions God to bring about a certain state of affairs. All three of the world's major monotheistic religions affirm that petitionary prayers can be causally efficacious in bringing about certain states of affairs. Dealing with petitionary prayer from a Christian perspective, David Basinger distinguishes three senses in which petitionary prayer can be causally efficacious.

1   Petitionary prayer can beneficially affect the petitioner herself.
2   Petitionary prayer can beneficially affect people who are aware that petitions are being made on their behalf.
3   Petitionary prayer affects whether or not God directly intervenes in the world.[2]

While I do not intend to downplay the significance of the first two ways in which a petitionary prayer might be causally efficacious, it is only the third of these three senses that presently concerns me.[3] Thus, in what follows, I will leave aside the ways in which petitionary prayer affects either the one praying or those who are aware that prayers are being offered on their behalf, concentrating only on issues related to the third sense of a prayer's efficaciousness.

Basinger elaborates the third way that prayer can be causally efficacious as follows: 'God has granted us the power to decide whether to request his assistance and . . . at times the decision we make determines whether we receive the help desired. . . . Divine activity is at times dependent on our freely offered petitions.'[4] According to Basinger, the heart of the Christian's belief in petitionary prayer is the belief that 'they ask him to bring about some state of affairs which they believe may not occur without divine intervention'.[5] Peter Geach makes a similar claim regarding petitionary prayer when he says that 'Christians, who rely on the word of their Master, are confident that some prayer is impetratory: that God gives us some things, not only *as* we wish, but *because* we wish.'[6] Let us call a petitionary prayer 'impetratory' if God's granting of the petition is due, at least in part, to the petition offered.

Returning to the scenario described above, then, let us say that Allison's prayer for her father is imperatory if God keeps him from harm at least in part as a result of her prayer. As I mentioned above, many theists think that such situations are relatively common. But let us slightly change the details of the story. Consider then the following modified scenario. Allison is watching the morning news, and learns that a tornado touched down in western Ohio the previous evening, leaving a path of devastation and destruction in its wake. The news anchor reports that seventeen homes were destroyed by the tornado, and that one individual was killed. Allison's father lives in the area affected by the storm. As she runs to the phone to call him, she offers a prayer that he not have been the one killed in the tornado. Even though she knows that the state of affairs she is praying about is already in the past, and that thus it is already a fact whether or not her father was killed, Allison thinks that her prayer might be efficacious in the same way that prayers for future states of affairs can be.

The difference between Allison's prayer in the original scenario and her prayer in the modified scenario has to do with the temporal relationship between the offering of the prayer and the state of affairs the prayer is aimed at helping to bring about. The former, or 'future-directed' prayers, are more familiar to us; these are the sorts of petitions that many religious individuals make on a regular basis. And most philosophers of religion are willing to grant that such prayers can be impetratory.[7] But what of prayers similar to the one in the modified scenario? What are we to make of 'past-directed' prayers in which the prayer is offered at a time later than the state of affairs it petitions God to bring about? It is clearly possible for a person to pray such a prayer. But the question regarding whether such a prayer can be impetratory still remains. If we take the similarities between the two scenarios seriously, we might be tempted to think that both prayers are impetratory. However, we may be hesitant to think that prayers for the past can be impetratory for reasons dealing with the dir-

ection of time and causal chains. Can we make sense of past-direction impetrations without having to embrace backward causation?

Let us call prayers such as Allison's prayer in the modified scenario 'past-directed impetratory prayers', or PIPs.[8] Such prayers are 'past-directed' insofar as they are prayers aimed at bringing about a state of affairs that is already past for the one praying; they will be impetratory if they contribute to God bringing about the state of affairs petitioned for. Let us define PIPs as follows:

PIP = $_{df}$ A petitionary prayer that meets the following four criteria:

(i) the prayer is offered by an agent A at time t_2;

(ii) the prayer requests that God bring about some state of affairs S at time t_1 (where t_1 is prior to t_2);

(iii) the prayed-for state of affairs S is brought about by God, at least in part, as a result of A's prayer; that is, God's knowledge of A's prayer is one of the reasons He has for bringing S about; and

(iv) God desires to bring about S only if A prays for S, such that if A had not prayed for S, then God would not have brought it about.[9]

What is one to make of PIPs? Can such prayers exist?

The first thing to note is that, despite the intuition that a response needs to follow a request if the response is to be a result of the request, there is some reason to think that this intuition is in fact false. If the intuition were to turn out to be true, then it would be impossible for PIPs to be efficacious. But is such an intuition really true? Eleonore Stump, for one, thinks that it is false, even for human agents. To see this, she asks us to consider the following example:

If at 3 o'clock, a mother prepares a snack for her little boy because she believes that when he gets home at 3.30 he will ask for one, it does not seem unreasonable to describe her as preparing the food because of the child's request, even though in this case the response is earlier than the request.[10]

Later in this paper, I give reason for thinking that mere belief about the future (even if such belief happens to be true) is not enough to save the sort of responsiveness needed for impetratory prayers. However, I think that the moral of Stump's story can be salvaged if the mother not only *believes* that the child will make the request, but if she also *knows* that he will.[11] And, according to many views in philosophical theology, God does have such knowledge of what free agents will do.

The second thing to notice is that a PIP is not a request that God *now* do something about the past. The advocate of PIPs need not join Descartes in thinking that God can change the past once it has come about.[12] Rather, past-directed prayers, as I understand them, are requests for God to *have done* something at a time prior to the time of the prayer.[13] As Gerald Taylor puts the point,

> Any present prayer that our son *has not* drowned must be interpreted as a prayer that he *should not have* drowned two hours earlier if the logical absurdities of changing the past are to be avoided. When we pray that he *has* survived the disaster, what we ask is that our son *was* not drowned two hours ago, that he *was* able to reach a lifeboat, and perhaps that he *is* on a lifeboat at this very moment. We do not ask that God *now* make our son *to have been* on a lifeboat, or *now* set in motion a chain of events which will culminate in our son *having reached* a lifeboat two hours earlier. For any prayer which asks that something *now* be done with respect to the past is necessarily self-contradictory, and thus incoherent.[14]

What this quotation from Taylor shows us is that PIPs are not obviously incoherent in the way

that one might initially think. But this is not enough to establish the claim that PIPs *are* coherent. There may be other reasons to reject such prayers.

In this paper, I aim to show how certain views in philosophical theology can intelligibly defend the existence of PIPs. I am not the first to have done so. For example, in his treatment of the relationship between prayer and providence at the end of *Miracles*, C.S. Lewis writes:

> The event [in question] has already been decided – in a sense it was decided "before all worlds". But one of the things taken into account in deciding it, and therefore one of the things that really cause it to happen, may be this very prayer that we are now offering. Thus, shocking as it may sound, I conclude that we can now at noon become part causes of an event occurring at ten o'clock [in the morning]. . . . My free act [of prayer] contributes to the cosmic shape. That contribution is made in eternity or 'before all worlds'; but my consciousness of contributing reaches me at a particular point in the time-series.[15]

I will further show how one's view regarding PIPs depends on other issues in philosophical theology, namely the mode of God's knowledge of human free actions and the related issue of God's relationship to time. It should be noted that I am in no way commenting on either the intelligibility or plausibility of the views of God and His knowledge I deal with below. I am instead interested in whether these views can make sense of PIPs on their own terms. Of course, if any of these views are incoherent or false (as some have claimed), then it does not matter if they can make sense of PIPs. But the latter, not the former, is my concern in this paper. However, before I turn my attention to these matters, I first address a general objection raised against PIPs that is claimed to be independent of these issues.

Geach's Objection

In *God and the Soul*, Peter Geach defends the claim that petitionary prayers can be impetratory. But the does not think that past-directed prayers can be. He considers C.S. Lewis's defence of PIPs mentioned above. Geach correctly captures the thrust of Lewis's position: 'Lewis argues that God timelessly sees the whole pattern of events in time and the whole pattern is subject to God's will: so God can shape an event that comes earlier to fit in with a prayer that comes later.'[16] However, according to Geach, to say of a prayer that 'God brought about situation S because of X's prayer' is incompatible with the claim that 'God would have brought about situation S regardless of X's praying or not praying'.[17] As we saw above, to affirm that God brought about S because of the petition in question is simply to say that the petition was impetratory. And if S would not have come about had X not prayed, then it must be the case, Geach thinks, that S is contingent: 'if we are to be justified in saying that a state of affairs S came about from somebody's impetratory prayer, then at the time of the prayer S must have had two-way contingency: it could come about, it could come about, it could also not come about'.[18] So far, so good.

However, Geach immediately continues that 'the first and most obvious conclusion from this is that there can be no impetratory prayer in regard to things already past at the time of the prayer'.[19] It looks, then, like Geach has something of the following sort in mind. Since S is two-way contingent, that is, it either could come about or not, it is not possible for the time of S to be prior to the time of the prayer. But how exactly is Geach using the notion of 'two-way contingency' in this argument? When Geach first introduces the term, it sounds as if he might be using it as it is standardly employed in contemporary metaphysics: a state of affairs is contingent if and only if it is included in some possible worlds and precluded by others. But the contingency of a state of affairs, thus

understood, is unaffected by whether or not that state of affairs has already been realized. So Geach must have something else in mind. Perhaps we can infer how he understands the contingency at issue from what else he says. He writes, 'It is irrelevant that a past issue was contingent, if we know that it is now decided and there is no longer any contigency about it.'[20]

As I mentioned above, the contingency of a state of affairs, as standardly understood in terms of possible worlds, is not affected by its time. If a state of affairs was contingent, then it remains so. What then does Geach mean by 'contingent'? I think one can see the answer to this question by taking seriously the idea implicit in Geach's statement that there can be a state of affairs that *was* contingent but no longer *is* contingent. Thus, we might think that a state of affairs is contingent at a time t only if there is something that can be done at (or after) t to either bring it about or to prevent its being brought about. This understanding of contingency is to be contrasted with what is often referred to as either accidental necessity, necessity *per accidens* or temporal necessity. What Geach needs for his objection to PIPs, though, is not merely that S, the prayed for state of affairs, is not necessary in the strict sense, but also the stronger claim that S must not be accidentally necessary at the time of the request. However, if this is what Geach intends, then it hard to see how he is not merely begging the question against the possibility of PIPs rather than arguing against their possibility.[21]

One might hope for help from Geach's further comment that 'the contingency of what we may sensibly pray for arises because it is foolish to try and obtain by prayer what is either impossible or inevitable'.[22] The question then becomes whether Geach is using 'impossible' and 'inevitable' synonymously. If he is, then the state of affairs prayed for will be neither, since, as shown above, the state of affairs will not be impossible in virtue of its being contingent. On the other hand, if Geach does think there is a difference between the two, it is hard to figure out what it is. Consider an analogous case regarding the future. He cannot mean inevitable to be that 'whatever will happen will happen', since that is tautologically true and of no help to his argument. Even if whatever will happen will happen, this does not mean that whatever will happen *must* happen. Likewise, to say of the past that it is inevitable is only to say that the past *is* what it is, not that it *must have been* the way it is. Thus, I conclude that Geach's objection to PIPs fails. There is no reason at this point to think that PIPs are impossible. Of course, not having a reason to think something impossible does not entail that it is possible. In the following sections, I try to show how PIPs are possible according to various views regarding God's knowledge and His relation to the world.

Simple Foreknowledge

Let us start with what I take to be the easiest case. One view in philosophical theology holds that God is a temporal being and necessarily has complete and infallible foreknowledge of all future events, including the actions of free agents, and that He uses this knowledge to exercise His providential control over creation. Let us call this the 'simple-foreknowledge' view.[23] So, for example, God knows at t_1 that Allison will freely do some action at t_2 (where t_2 is later than t_1), such as decide to adopt a puppy from the animal shelter.[24] According to the simple-foreknowledge view, it is in virtue of what Allison will do at t_2 that God has true beliefs prior to t_2 about Allison and her action at t_2.

If this is the case, then it is easy to see how the simple-foreknowledge view can account for PIPs. Suppose that Allison prays at time t_2 that God bring about some state of affairs S at time t_1. As we saw before, this need not be understood as supposing that God, at t_2, brings it about that S occurred at an earlier time t_1, which would require genuine backward causation. Rather, the defender of PIPs can grant that the past is now

unalterable if we understand the situation as one in which God knows at or prior to t_1, via His foreknowledge, that Allison will make the petition in question at t_2 and, on the basis of this knowledge, decides to intervene in the world and bring about S at t_1. As Geoffrey Brown notes,

> Causation is, of course, normally understood as a transitive relation, and so it is true that in this case P at t was a cause of S at t_1. But the way in which this is brought about (via the foreknowledge of God) is such that, provided we can accept the credibility of divine foreknowledge, there is less oddity in this account than in one which introduces 'direct' backward causation.[25]

If agents like Allison have libertarian freedom and God has foreknowledge of their free actions, then agents like Allison have counterfactual power over God's beliefs. Suppose again that Allison does some action A at t_2. As we have seen, according to the simple-foreknowledge view, God knows at t_1 that Allison will do A at t_2. But what if, contrary to our assumption, Allison does not do A at t_2? In such a scenario, it is not the case that Allison at t_2 would have caused God to have a false belief at t_1. This would be impossible, for if God is essentially omniscient, as the proponents of the simple-foreknowledge view traditionally assume, then God cannot have false beliefs. Rather, Allison would have caused God to have (at t_1) different beliefs than He actually had (again, at t_1). Given her libertarian freedom, Allison could have done something such that, had she done it, God would have had different beliefs than He actually did have.[26] Insofar as the proponent of the simple-foreknowledge view is committed to free agents having counterfactual power over certain of God's beliefs, she can use this power to explain the efficacy of PIPs.[27]

However, even granting counterfactual power over God's beliefs, there may be a worry lurking nearby.[28] Let us assume that state of affairs S obtained at t_1. If Allison does not pray at t_2 that

God bring about S, then S cannot be the result of God granting Allison's prayer. But if God knows at t_1 that Allison will offer the prayer in question, is Allison's future prayer impetratory? One might think that, since S has already obtained, it does not matter whether or not Allison offers the prayer. This, however, does not necessarily follow. Since we are assuming that God has foreknowledge of what Allison will do at t_2, whether her prayer will be impetratory given that S obtained at t_1 depends on whether the following conditional is true:

4   If it was not the case that Allison would offer the prayer at t_2, then God would not have brought about S at t_1.

If (4) is false, and God would have brought about S regardless of what Allison will do at t_2, then even if she does offer the prayer, it fails to satisfy criterion (iv) of PIPs given above. In such a case, Allison's prayer is indeed irrelevant to the obtaining of S. However, on the other hand, if (4) is true, then God only brought about S because of what Allison would do in the future, and her prayer could still be impetratory. Like her counterfactual power over God's beliefs, if we assume that S has already obtained, Allison has counterfactual power over whether God brings about S because of her impetratory prayer or for another reason. But her having this additional sort of counterfactual power is no more objectionable than the type of counterfactual power required for the simple-foreknowledge view to be true in the first place.

This presentation of the simple-foreknowledge view is brief and incomplete, and I have not attempted to defend the view from various objections that have been raised to it in the literature. What I have shown is how this view, if coherent, can explain the efficacy of PIPs. If God has foreknowledge of free agents' future actions, then one can defend the claim that God brought about a state of affairs in the past relative to the petitioner partly as a result of her petition.

Eternalism

The second position in philosophical theology I want to consider is what I will call 'eternalism'. Unlike the simple-foreknowledge view, which asserts that God is a temporal being, the hallmark of eternalism is the claim that God is an atemporal being, outside of time as well as space. Eternalism is the view implicit in C. S. Lewis's discussion of PIPs mentioned earlier. Speaking of God, Lewis writes that 'To Him all the physical events and all the human acts are present in an eternal Now'.[29] Classically defended by, among others, Boethius and Aquinas, eternalism holds that God has 'the complete possession all at once of illimitable life'.[30] Since an eternal entity is atemporal, there is no past or future *within* the life of such an entity; nor can any temporal event or entity be past or future with respect to such a life. Nevertheless, an eternal being can have knowledge of temporal entities. As Aquinas puts the point, 'God's vision is measured by eternity, which is all at once; consequently, all times and everything done in them is subject to his sight.'[31] For this reason, Aquinas claims that God knows things that for us are future in the same way that He knows things that for us are past: both are equally present to God in his eternity. 'From the standpoint of eternity, every time is present, co-occurrent with the whole of infinite atemporal duration.'[32] While a full treatment of eternalism is beyond the scope of the present paper, there is one objection to eternalism that, if sound, would render prayer to an atemporal, and thus simple, God irrelevant.

One might think that if God is atemporal, then it is impossible for Him to interact with temporal entities. But if it is impossible for God to interact with temporal entities, then God cannot respond to a petitionary prayer made by a temporal entity. Eleonore Stump, in her insightful article on petitionary prayer, considers this sort of objection in a particularly poignant way:

Before a certain petitionary prayer is made, it

is the case either that God will bring about the state of affairs requested in the prayer or that he will not bring it about. He cannot have left the matter open since doing so would imply a subsequent change in him and he is immutable. Either way, since he is immutable, the prayer itself can effect no change in the state of affairs and hence is pointless.[33]

Walter Wink raises the same objection in this manner:

> Before that unchangeable God, whose whole will was fixed from all eternity, intercession is ridiculous. There is no place for intercession with a God whose will is incapable of change. What Christians have too long worshiped is the God of Stoicism, to whose immutable will we can only surrender ourselves, conforming our wills to the unchangeable will of deity.[34]

If this objection holds, then the eternity and subsequent immutability of God would entail that God *cannot* respond to petitionary prayers. Defenders of eternalism, however, think that this sort of objection to their view misses the mark. Aquinas, for example, clearly held that God was both atemporal and simple, yet maintained that not all petitionary prayer is done in vain,[35] and Stump has discussed the flaw in this objection at length.[36]

Assuming then that the defender of eternalism is correct that it is possible for an eternal and simple God to respond to temporal beings, eternalism can also account for PIPs. Consider a scenario characterized as follows:

(i)   Allison prays at t_2 that God bring about state of affairs S at time t_1.
(ii) God is eternal is the ways described above.
(iii) God is nevertheless able to respond to prayers offered by temporal agents.
(iv) In this case, God is both willing and able to bring about S at time t_1, and does so in response to Allison's prayer at t_2.[37]

(v)   Had Allison not prayed at t_2, God would not have brought about S at t_1.

(ii) and (iii) will be true if eternalism is true and if the position has the resources to respond to the objection raised earlier. (iv) and (v) are possibly true if there are impetratory prayers, and will be true if the prayer at issue is, in fact, an impetratory prayer. Like me here stipulate that (iv) and (v), as well as (i), are true. It seems that (i) through (v) jointly establish that Allison has impetrated an eternal and simple God. But, if this is the case, notice that these five characterizations say nothing about the temporal relationship between t_2 (the time of Allison's prayer) and t_1 (the time of the prayed-for state of affairs). While t_2 could be prior to t_1 (with the implication that the prayer is a future-directed impetration), on the assumption of divine eternity, no contradiction or absurdity is introduced by the temporal priority of t_1 over t_2. As with the simple-foreknowledge view, eternalism can account for the efficacy of PIPs.

Molinism

The next position in philosophical theology to consider is Molinism. Molinism has been the subject of much scholarship in the philosophy of religion in the past few decades. Molinism, most generally, is an attempt to explain how it is that God can retain providential control over a creation that contains libertarian free agents. So, for example, suppose that God, as part of His providential plan, wants Allison to perform a particular action, X. If Allison is free in the way described by libertarians, then how can God make sure that she freely does X? According to Molinists, the answer is found in God's middle knowledge (*scientia media*), more specifically in His knowledge of counterfactuals of creaturely freedom, or CCFs. A CCF is a statement about what a free creature would freely do in a particular situation, such as the following:

5   If in circumstance C, Allison will freely do action X.

So in order to be assured that Allison will freely do X, God must simply make sure that she is in circumstance C. It is via this knowledge of true CCFs that Molinists explain the compatibility of creaturely freedom and divine governance. God can ensure that Allison does X without violating her freedom by seeing to it that she finds herself in C.

With this overview of Molinism in mind, it should be apparent how the Molinist will account for petitionary prayers for the past. Thomas P. Flint develops a Molinist account of PIPs in his book *Divine Providence*. Flint claims there that prayers for past events are defensible because the counterfactuals based upon them are eternally true (or false) and known to God via His middle knowledge. Modifying Flint's example to accord with the case of Allison used in this paper, consider Allison's situation when she hears the news report of the tornado near her father's house the night before. Allison is uncertain whether her father was hurt, or even killed, by the tornado. Let us again call the state of affairs that is Allison's father being unhurt by the tornado, S. Let us further assume that S obtains, that is, that her father was not hurt in the storm. And while there are many factors that might influence Allison's decision to pray for her father – such as her love for him, her desire to spend the next holiday with him – if Allison is in fact uncertain as to his current health, then it cannot be among her motivations for praying. In other words, even if S had not obtained, there is no reason to think that her decision to pray would have been any different.

It looks then like some parts of the circumstances Allison finds herself in are relevant to her decision to pray for her father's safety, while others are not. Let us call those parts of the circumstances that are counterfactually relevant to Allison's decision to pray, R. R will include, among other things, her belief in a God that listens and responds to prayers, her love for her father, etc. Members of R are those parts of the circumstances that 'it is reasonable to think that her activity wouldn't have been exactly the same had they not been present'.[38] Let us call those parts of the circumstances that are not counterfactually relevant to Allison's free decision, T. Members of T might include the fact that Allison is currently wearing a green striped shirt, or the fact that her dog is currently sleeping on her bed, or the fact that Franklin Pierce was the fourteenth president of the United States. T will include lots of states of affairs. But on the assumption that Allison is unaware that her father is currently safe, that is, that she is unaware of S, presumably S will also be a member of T, rather than R.

The conjunction of R and T is then the complete circumstance in which Allison finds herself. Let us assume that in this complete circumstance, Allison decides to pray for the safety of her father. In other words, let us assume that the following CCF is true:

6   [(Allison is in R) and T] → Allison prays for the safety of her father.

Since the conjunction of R and T is the complete circumstance Allison is in, (6) is a CCF and, if true, would be know by God via His middle knowledge. If, as we assumed above, T includes all those circumstances that make no difference to her decision to pray, the following condition will also be true:

7   [(Allison is in R) and ∼ T] → Allison prays for the safety of her father.

Like (6), (7) is also an element of God's middle knowledge. (6) and (7) together entail:

8   (Allison is in R) → Allison prays for the safety of her father.

Since (8) is a contingent truth entailed by two

elements of God's middle knowledge, it too is something that God knows via His middle knowledge. Thus,

9   [(Allison is in R) → Allison prays for the safety of her father] ⇒ God has middle knowledge that [(Allison is in R) → Allison prays for the safety of her father].

But (8) also entails that

10   (Allison is in R) → [(Allison is in R) → Allison prays for the safety of her father].

(9) and (10) together entail that:

11   Allison prays in R → [God has middle knowledge that (Allison is in R → Allison prays for the safety of her father)].

In other words, if it is in fact true, as we have been assuming, that Allison prays in R, then God knows via His middle knowledge that she would so pray if in R. And if God has such knowledge, then assuming that He knows that Allison will be in R, He can use that knowledge of the true counterfactual expressed by (10) to bring about the safety of Allison's father as a result of her future prayer.[39]

Openism

The final position I want to consider is called 'open theism' or 'openism'.[40] As others have noted, however, this is a very misleading title because perhaps the most distinctive tenet of the view is not a claim directly about either God or His attributes, but rather about the existence or nonexistence of certain true propositions.[41] The view is not the claim, as some of its opponents would suggest, that there are truths that God does not know, such as what Allison will do fifty years from now. Rather, the view is a claim that neither of the following propositions is now true:

12   Allison will freely do A fifty years from now.

13   Allison will freely refrain from doing A fifty years from now (either by doing something other than A or by doing nothing at all).

If neither of these propositions is now true, then it is not a limitation of God's omniscience to say that He does not know which one is true, much in the same way that it is not a limitation of God's omnipotence that He cannot do something that is logically impossible to do (again, Descartes' view notwithstanding). As such, the view presently under consideration is a view about what there is to be known; the view is thus compatible with the traditional understanding of omniscience according to which God knows all and only true propositions.

According to openism, God is a temporal being and knows at a particular time, via His omniscience, all and only the propositions that are true at that time. Let us say that a presently contingent future proposition is a proposition about the future whose truth-value is not determined by any presently existing objects, states of affairs, or events. Cases of agents' free actions in the future will be examples of such presently contingent future propositions.[42] Since presently contingent future propositions do not *now* have a determinate truth-value, such propositions are not among the objects of God's knowledge.

How does one understand petitionary prayers on the model of openism? That agents like Allison are presently making petitions, or have made petitions in the past, is something that God can know and use in His providential control of the world. So some prayers could be impetratory. But what of PIPs? Along the lines of openism, Terence Penelhum suggests perhaps past-oriented prayers can be impetratory:

> In giving men freedom of choice, God makes it genuinely *uncertain* what they will do, and in consequence (since men's actions are

uncertain before they happen) even He does not know what their actions will be before they do them. Yet the fact that Jones's doing A rather than B is never *certain* before it happens does not show that his doing A is *no more likely* than his doing B before it happens. If this is true, there is nothing absurd about the suggestion that the laws of nature incorporate answers to likely prayers. And since it seems necessarily true that more likely things happen than unlikely ones, we have a good reason for expecting that a majority of likely prayers will in fact be offered and can thus be provided for.[43]

Penelhum, like the openist, thinks that the most God can know of future actions is the probability of their occurrence.[44] Furthermore, Penelhum thinks that this knowledge is sufficient for God to be responsive to prayers. Unfortunately such a suggestion will not work for an account of past-directed prayers.

Consider the case that God knows at t_1 that it is likely that Allison will pray at t_2 for God to bring about a state of affairs, S. Let us further suppose that God does bring about S at t_1. On the chance (no matter how miniscule) that Allison does not make the petition at t_2, then God could not have brought about S, even in part, because of Allison's prayer, since there is no such prayer. Furthermore, even if Allison does make the petition in question, God could not have brought about S, even in part, because of her petition at t_2, because prior to t_2 there was no fact of the matter about what she would do at t_2, and condition (iii) of the definition of PIPs is violated.

Thus, if God is a temporal being, and if one rejects God having foreknowledge of the future (either through having simple foreknowledge or through the conjunction of His middle knowledge and creative act) as the openist does, then it appears that one cannot defend the efficacy of PIPs. The most that can be said is that God brings about state of affairs S because of His belief that an agent *might* or *probably* or *in all likelihood* will pray

at some point in the future that God bring S about. Insofar as this fails to meet the definition of PIPs given above, openism cannot account for the efficacy of past-directed impetratory prayers.

A Further Implication

Gerald Taylor objects to a defence of PIPs given by Michael Dummett as follows:

> The problem which Dummett faces is that he is unable to explain how the casual efficacy of a present retrospective prayer becomes located in the past. . . . On Dummett's analysis, we must simply accept, without any hope of explanation, the fact that the causal efficacy of a present retrospective prayer is located in the past.[45]

I have argued in the previous pages that a number of views in philosophical theology can account for PIPs, and have shown how such prayer can be causally efficacious in a way that presumably Taylor thinks Dummett has not. Whether a view can account for such prayers depends on its understanding of God's knowledge of free actions, which in turn is related to God's relationship to time.

Such a conclusion will, no doubt, strike many as peculiar. Nevertheless, I think that the above discussion is also suggestive of what many will take to be an even more startling claim. Most defenders of PIPs restrict PIPs to cases where the praying agent does not know what the outcome of the state in question is. That is, Allison does not know at time t_2 (the time of the prayer) whether or not S obtained earlier at t_1. Eleonore Stump, for example, only wants to consider PIPs where the praying agent does not know whether God has already brought about the state of affairs in question.[46] Similarly, Flint writes that 'where we are genuinely unsure whether the prayed-for event occurs, though, praying often seems appropriate, whether the event be in the future or in the past. . . . Of course, were we certain concerning the occurrence of the past event in question, things might be different.'[47] But it seems to me that the above discussion gives us reason to question this limitation. Might it not be possible for a prayer for the past to be efficacious in whatever way petitionary prayers are even if the agent knows that the outcome for which she is praying has already happened? Can Allison's prayer for her father only be efficacious if she does not know whether he was hurt or not? What if she instead already knows his status?

There is clearly one sense in which it does not make sense to pray for the past if one already knows how it turned out: cases where one knows that the desired state of affairs has not obtained. C. S. Lewis approached this topic in this way:

> If we can reasonably pray for an event which must in fact have happened or failed to happen several hours ago, why can we not pray for an event which we know *not* to have happened? e.g. pray for the safety of someone who, as we know, was killed yesterday. What makes the difference is precisely our knowledge. The known event states God's will. It is psychologically impossible to pray for what we know to be unobtainable: and if it were possible the prayer would sin against the duty of submission to God's known will.[48]

I am less certain than Lewis is as to what is 'psychologically impossible' for us to do. Such a prayer would definitely be irrational (though, I would note, we do lots of irrational things). Stump has similarly described such a prayer as absurd: 'It is obviously absurd to pray in 1980 that Napoleon win at Waterloo when one knows what God does not bring about at Waterloo.'[49] Regardless of whether it is possible for an agent to make such a prayer, what is clear to me is that it is not possible for such a prayer to be impetratory. Consider the following situation: at t_2, Allison is deliberating whether to petition God

to bring about some state of affairs SA at t_1. If Allison knows that S did not obtain, then she should also know that her prayer for S, should she decide to make it, cannot be impetratory. If God does not bring about S, then *a fortiori* He did not bring about S as a result of Allison's prayer. So a prayer for a previous state of affairs S cannot be impetratory if one knows that S did not obtain.

But what about cases where the state of affairs Allison is considering petitioning for 'tracks', so to speak, what she knows already occurred? Can Allison's prayer that God bring about S help bring about S even if she knows that S already happened? Again, Stump suggests that such a prayer would be absurd: 'The only appropriate version of that prayer is "Let Napoleon have lost at Waterloo", and for one who knows the outcome of the battle more that a hundred and fifty years ago, that prayer is pointless and in that sense absurd.'[50] Stump, I believe, is mistaken here. Why think that a prayer that otherwise would have not been pointless is made to be so simply by the addition of the praying subject's knowledge that the result was already granted?

To see that such a prayer could be impetratory, consider again the simple-foreknowledge view. Assume that Allison will pray at t_2 that her father be spared from the tornado at t_1. Given His omniscience, God knows this prior to t_2 and can thus bring about the safety of her father at t_1. So long as Allison prays that God bring about S, and God is able and willing to bring about S, then it does not matter whether or not Allison already knows that S obtained (that is, so long as what God foreknows is that Allison will pray for S even though she already knows that S obtained). And a similar conclusion will be reached on both eternalism and Molinism.[51] So it looks like a past-directed prayer can be efficacious even if the one praying knows that the prayed-for state of affairs has already obtained. This is a stronger, and more counterintuitive, conclusion that has been reached by other defenders of PIPs.

At this point, one might object that if the

praying subject knows the desired result has already obtained, then she no longer has any motivation for offering the prayer.[52] Suppose that Allison knows that her father was not hurt or killed in the tornado. She might think to herself, 'Wait, even if I don't pray, my father will be safe from the tornado – God's not going to change the past because I don't pray. My prayer is clearly not needed on this score. And given that, it would be more worthwhile for me to do something else with my time, such as pray for something else, or just thank God for bringing it about he is safe.'

I agree with the objector that Allison's not praying that God protect her father will not cause it to be the case that her father is hurt (since he already was not, in fact, injured). It is further true that knowing that her father is safe might undercut Allison's motivation to pray that God keep her father safe. But this does not mean that such a prayer, if offered, cannot be impetratory. There is no reason to think that God cannot answer a petitionary prayer that is offered by an individual who does not have sufficient motivation for making that prayer. If Allison has reason to believe that God is the sort of deity who responds to petitionary prayers and that it is good for her to make such prayers, then she may have reason for offering a prayer for a state of affairs that she knows has already obtained. And, as we have seen above, there is reason to think that, on certain views in philosophical theology, such prayers can actually be efficacious.[53]

Notes

1 It is not my intention in this paper to defend the claim that petitionary prayers *are* efficacious. Since my concern is with whether prayers about the past can be efficacious in the same way that prayers for the future are, I simply assume here that some petitionary prayers *are* efficacious. I am also not addressing *why* God might require prayer in order to intervene when it seems that He could intervene apart from the petition.

2 David Basinger *The Case for Free Will Theism* (Downers Grove IL: InterVarsity Press, 1996), 105f.

3 In a previous paper, I criticized accounts of prayer according to which petitionary prayer is efficacious in only the first two senses. See Kevin Timpe 'Toward a process philosophy of petitionary prayer', *Theology & Philosophy*, 12 (2000), 397–418.

4 Basinger *The Case for Free Will Theism*, 106, 108.

5 *Idem* 'Why petition an omnipotent, omniscient, wholly good God?', *Religious Studies*, 19 (1983), 25–42, 25. Petitionary prayers will differ from other merely necessary causal factors in that prayers, as a free action of agents possessing libertarian freedom, are beyond the direct control of God, whereas presumably the other necessary causal factors are not.

6 Peter Geach *God and the Soul* (London: Routledge & Kegan Paul, 1969), 87. Furthermore, as Geach notes, 'to say that God brought something about *because* of a man's prayers is not at all to say that, once the prayer had been said, God could not but grant them'; *ibid*.

7 Where they differ is *how* such prayers are causally efficacious.

8 Geach calls such prayers 'ex post facto' prayers (Geach *God and the Soul*, 90), and Michael Dummett calls then 'retrospective prayers' in 'Bringing about the past', *The Philosophical Review*, **73** (1964), 338–359.

9 This later clause means that overdetermined and necessary state of affairs cannot be the results of PIPs. Furthermore, God's desire to bring about certain states of affairs only as the result of petitions will be closely connected with His reasons for responding to petitionary prayers in the first place.

10 Eleonore Stump *Aquinas* (London: Routledge, 2003), 154.

11 If Stump does have knowledge, rather than mere belief, in mind here, then there may be an inconsistency between this illustration and what I say later about openism, for openism denies that anyone can have knowledge of what agents will freely do in the future. But I think that there is good reason to think that the mother does not have knowledge in such a case. Insofar as the mother is not an omniscient agent, it is extremely plausible that her belief will be the same regardless of whether the

child actually does make the request. If he does not, then her belief will not track the truth. But if she has the same belief whether or not he makes the request, then even in the case where he does make the request, her belief will not track the truth in the way required for knowledge.

12 Geoffrey Goddu has recently argued that it is logically possible that we can change the past. See his 'Time travel and changing the past: (or how to kill yourself and live to tell the tale)', *Ratio*, **16** (2003), 16–32.

13 For a discussion of this point and its relation to causation, see Gerald Gilmore Taylor 'Dummett on retrospective prayer'. *Franciscan Studies*, **50** (1990), 309–323.

14 *Ibid.*, 319. I should state that I, unlike Taylor here, am not willing to say that backward causation is 'necessarily self-contradictory'. I do not here defend the claim that backward causation is possible; rather what I want to defend in this paper is the weaker claim that PIPs can be explained without the need for backward causation. Of course, if backward causation is possible, then it would provide another way of understanding PIPs.

15 C. S. Lewis *Miracles* (New York NY: Collier Books, 1947), 179f. I return to the conception of eternity that Lewis's defence of PIPs presupposes in a later section.

16 Geach *God and the Soul*, 90. Part of Geach's objection is to Lewis's endorsement of the doctrine of divine eternity. For a defence of the doctrine of divine timelessness that shows where Geach's objection is mistaken, see Eleonore Stump *Aquinas*, particularly ch. 4.

17 Geach *God and the Soul*, 88.

18 *Ibid.*, 89.

19 *Ibid.*, 89.

20 *Ibid.*, 93f.

21 Geoffrey Brown has independently come to a similar criticism of Geach: "If he is not denying *contingency*, in the ordinary sense, to past states of affairs, but only means that there is nothing which can now be done which can form part of their causal nexus, then the argument boils down to no more than a flat denial of what Lewis is affirming [i.e. the possibility of PIPs]. What looked like a premise supporting the negation of Lewis's thesis now appears as a mere unsupported contradiction of

that thesis. Geach is (trivially) correct in holding that a prayer can only be a cause of a state of affairs if it is uttered in circumstances which permit it to enter into a causal nexus of that event: but what those circumstances are is precisely the point of disagreement. ... One is tempted to think [as Geach apparently does that] "If God has already made up his mind and acted, then it makes no difference whether I pray now or not". But this ignores the very point at issue: that on Lewis's view, God's mind *has* been made up *taking into account* what I am about to do – I may not know this yet myself, but God does, *and always did*"; Geoffrey Brown 'Praying about the past', *The Philosophical Quarterly*, 35 (1985), 83–86, 84. Despite my general agreement with Brown's evaluation of Geach's argument, my treatment of PIPs differs from his in two ways. First, whereas Brown discusses PIPs from only one theological perspective, in the present paper I relate such prayers to a number of philosophical positions. Second, at the end of the present paper I show how my account of PIPs has a stronger conclusion than that reached by Brown.

22 Geach *God and the Soul*, 94.

23 The simple-foreknowledge view should be distinguished from the stronger claim that it is in virtue of God's knowledge that free agents like Allison do what they do, that is, that God's knowledge causes Allison's actions. It is hard to see on this stronger view, often called 'theological determinism', or 'Augustianism,' how an agent could be free in a libertarian sense.

24 In this paper, I intend to remain agnostic about how God knows what He knows, though I will speak at times in terms of God knowing propositions to be true. For an argument that God has *de re* but not *de dicto* knowledge, see William Alston 'Does God have beliefs?', in *Divine Nature and Human Language: Essays in Philosophical Theology* (Ithaca NY: Cornell University Press, 1989), 178–193. For an argument that God has *de dicto* as well as *de re* knowledge, see William Hasker 'Yes, God has beliefs!', *Religious Studies*, 24 (1988), 385–394.

25 Brown 'Praying about the past', 85.

26 See George Mavrodes 'Prayer', in E. Craig (ed.) *Routledge Encyclopedia of Philosophy* (London: Routledge, 2000), http://www.rep.routledge.com/article/K070SECT2: 'The divine foreknowledge may

anticipate human action in the order of time, but it cannot substitute for that action, in the sense of making it irrelevant whether the action is actually done. For if the action were not done, then the divine knowledge would have been different from what is actually was. This applies to prayer as much as to anything else."

27 The debate regarding the hard fact/soft fact distinction is also relevant here, as the simple foreknowledge view depends upon free agents having the type of counterfactual power over God's beliefs that is typical of soft facts. If one sides with the opponents of the hard fact/soft fact distinction and thinks that counterfactual power over God's beliefs involves backward causation, then one is likely to believe that the simple foreknowledge view requires backward causation to affirm the efficacy of PIPs. I believe that one can maintain the hard fact/soft fact distinction, though I do not argue for that conclusion here. For a recent argument against counterfactual power over God's beliefs, see Alan G. Padgett 'Divine foreknowledge and the arrow of time: on the impossibility of retrocausation', in G. Ganssle and D. Woodruff (eds) *God and Time: Essays on the Divine Nature* (Oxford: Oxford University Press, 2002), 65–74.

28 An anonymous referee for *Religious Studies* suggested this worry.

29 Lewis *Miracles*, 177.

30 Boethius 'The consolation of philosophy', in H. Stewart, E. Rand, and S. Tester (eds) *The Theological Tractates and the Consolation of Philosophy* (London and Cambridge, MA: Harvard University Press, 1973), 422.5–424.21.

31 Thomas Aquinas *Disputed Questions on Truth*, J. McGlynn (tr.) (Chicago IL: H. Regnery Co., 1952), q. 12.6.

32 Stump *Aquinas*, 143.

33 Idem 'Petitionary prayer', in E. Stump and M. Murray (eds) *Philosophy of Religion: The Big Questions* (Malden MA: Blackwell Publishers, 1999), 358.

34 Walter Wink *Engaging the Powers: Discernment and Resistance in a World of Domination* (Minneapotis MN: Fortress Press, 1992), 301.

35 Thomas Aquinas *Summa Theologiae*, Fathers of the English Dominican Province (tr.), Ia, IIae, q. 83.

36 Stump *Aquinas*, 115ff.

37 Note that God is bringing it about that S occurs at t_1, not that God is bringing it about at t_1 that S occurs. Since, according to (ii) God is atemporal, it does not make sense to say that one of God's actions occurs at a time; rather, it is accurate to say that the one of the effects of God's eternal and timeless act of willing occurs at a time.

38 Thomas P. Flint *Divine Providence: The Molinist Account* (Ithaca NY: Cornell University Press, 1998), 245.

39 God could either ensure that Allison finds herself in R by weakly actualizing R via His knowledge of other CCFs, or by strongly actualizing R.

40 Gregory A. Boyd's *Satan and Problem of Evil: Constructing a Trinitarian Warfare Theodicy* (Downers Grove IL: InterVarsity Press, 2001) is a very interesting and thorough, though philosophically inconsistent, defence of one openist's view.

41 Two other central tenets of openism are the belief that humans (and perhaps other agents) have libertarian free will, and the belief that God is also a temporal being (*contra* eternalism). However, insofar as these other tenets are also thought true by one of more of the other positions canvassed here, I take the tenet about the extension of truth to be the primary demarcation of openism.

42 There will also be presently contingent future propositions that do not involve the action of free agents. Propositions dealing with whether particular atoms of a radioactive isotope will degrade at a particular time in the future are also examples of presently contingent future propositions. According to openism, God does not know the truth-value of any presently contingent future proposition (since they do not *now* have a truth-value to be known), and not just those regarding free human actions.

43 Terence Penelhum *Religion and Rationality* (New York NY: Random House, 1971), as quoted in Robert Young 'Petitioning God', *American Philosophical Quarterly*, 11 (1974), 200.

44 It is for this reason that Penelhum and openism differ from the example given from Stump in the first section of this paper.

45 Taylor 'Dummett on retrospective prayer', 320.

46 Stump 'Petitionary prayer', 365, n. 1.

47 Flint *Divine Providence*, 230.

48 Lewis *Miracles*, 180.

49 Stump *Aquinas*, 505, n. 78.

50 *Ibid.*

51   Actually, the Molinist account of PIPs given above will need to be reworked, since the presentation given there assumes ignorance (i.e. it assumes that Allison's knowledge belongs to T rather than R). I think that a Molinist account of PIPs can be worked out even if the agent's knowledge regarding S belongs to R rather than T, though I will leave it to the reader to reconstruct the counterfactuals involved.

52   Various versions of this objection have been raised by Mike Murray, Mike Rota, Matt Zwolinski, and an anonymous referee for *Religious Studies*.

53   I would like to thank Mike Murray, Mike Rota, Lincoln Stevens, and two anonymous referees for *Religious Studies* who provided valuable comments and criticisms on earlier versions of this paper. A preliminary draft was read to the Philosophy Department at the University of San Diego, where I benefited from many insightful questions. The writing of this paper was made possible by a fellowship from the Center for the Philosophy of Religion at the University of Notre Dame.

PART 5

The Afterlife

INTRODUCTION TO PART 5

THE MAJORITY OF THE WORLD'S major religions believe in life, of some sort or other, after death. But there is considerable disagreement about the nature of the afterlife. Christianity, Islam, and some forms of Judaism believe, for instance, in the resurrection of the physical body, while Hinduism and Buddhism endorse reincarnation or rebirth.

The first three readings in this section examine various philosophical accounts of life after death. The nature of life beyond the grave depends on the nature of the human person whose life it will be. The two most common accounts of the nature of human persons, and their relationship with their physical bodies, are materialism and dualism. Materialism is the view that the person is identical with her physical body (or a part of her physical body), while dualism is the view that there is more to the person than just her physical body. Some dualists hold that persons are immaterial substances—such as souls—which are numerically distinct from their bodies, while others hold that persons are composed of both a physical substance and a non-physical substance. Dualists of both sorts think that persons are able to interact with their physical bodies (though they have both been criticized for failing to account for *how* this interaction takes place). At death, the causal interaction between a person and her body is severed. Some argue that dualists are able to account for resurrection with the re-establishment of causal interaction with the material body. In this way, some think that dualist accounts of postmortem resurrection are relatively unproblematic. It is harder to see how materialists, who hold that human persons are essentially material objects, can account for resurrection since the physical body undergoes decay and decomposition upon death.

The first reading in this section, Kevin Corcoran's "Dualism, Materialism, and the Problem of Postmortem Survival," challenges this perceived advantage for dualism. Corcoran argues that despite appearances, dualism offers no advantage over materialism when it comes to the problem of resurrection insofar as resurrection requires sameness of physical body—i.e., the resurrection of the numerically same body as existed before bodily death. Both views thus must provide an account of how one and the same material object (the physical body in the case of the dualist, and the physical person in the case of the materialist) can exist, cease to exist at death, and come back into existence in the future. One option would be reassembly—the person (or body) comes back into existence when its parts are brought back together. But Corcoran argues that resurrection by reassembly does not accord with the persistence conditions of human persons. He ends by suggesting an account of resurrection based on causal relations between the original and resurrected individual.

Lynne Rudder Baker's "Persons and the Metaphysics of Resurrection" also develops and defends a materialist account of the human person, which she calls the constitution view, and then shows how such an account provides for the possibility of resurrection. On the constitution view, human persons are not identical with their physical bodies, but are instead constituted by them. According to Baker, two conditions are necessary and jointly sufficient for a thing, X, to be a human person:

(i) X must have a "first-person perspective" and
(ii) X must be constituted by a particular type of physical thing, namely a human body.

The first condition ensures that X is a *person*, while the second condition ensures that X is a *human* person. After explaining the nature of both the first-person perspective and the constitution relation, Baker turns toward the nature of the resurrection. She claims the Christian account of the resurrection involves three features. First, resurrection requires sameness of person: the numerically same individual must exist after resurrection as existed prior to death. Second, resurrection is necessarily physical, even though post-resurrection bodies are different from pre-death bodies. Third, resurrection is not a natural process, but instead requires a miracle. Any acceptable Christian account of the resurrection must thereby show how it is metaphysically possible for the very same person to exist before and after physical death despite the difference between the physical bodies involved. Baker then compares seven different metaphysical accounts of resurrection with respect to these three characteristics. While Corcoran argued that dualism has no advantage over materialism in accounting for the resurrection, Baker argues that a certain materialist view—the constitution view—has the advantage over dualism.

Roger Ames' "Death as Transformation in Classical Daoism" explores issues of death from a different perspective, that of classical Chinese philosophy. In contrast to many western religions that see death as inexorably connected with sin and as something to be avoided, classical Chinese thought considers death inseparable from life. The world is eternal and in constant flux, and the cycle of life to death to life again is a necessary transformation that is to be affirmed and embraced. On this view, death is neither unnatural nor something to be avoided. In fact, death is beneficial insofar as death makes novelty and progress possible. Death is to be anticipated rather than feared, since it makes life "deliciously anticipatory and inconclusive." Ames locates this approach to death in both Daoism and Confucianism, two of the leading religions in Chinese thought. Aims furthermore draws our attention to the inherently social aspect of Chinese culture and religion. Because of this social emphasis, being forgotten or exiled from one's community is worse than physical death, and being remembered is more important than being alive. Thereby, Chinese religion places a heavy emphasis on genealogical continuity, ancestor worship, and proper respect for the dead.

The final four readings in this section explore the nature of the afterlife in a different way by focusing on the concepts of heaven and hell. While belief in heaven and hell are usually reserved for those religions which accept resurrection, considerable recent philosophical interest has been stimulated by the issues involved. Particular attention has been given to the relationship between the nature of the afterlife and the nature of God, as well as to the relationship between an individual's free will and where they end up in the afterlife. The first reading, David Lewis' "Divine Evil," uses the traditional understanding of hell as a place of eternal punishment for the insubordinate to advocate a version of the problem of evil. Rather than focusing on evils that God fails to prevent, Lewis takes aim at a particular evil that God is said to perpetrate Himself: the eternal damnation of sinners. Lewis argues that there is no amount of earthly wrongdoing that could justify an infinite amount of punishment and suffering. Insofar as injustice is contrary to moral goodness, an essentially morally perfect God could not send an individual to hell for all eternity. Let us call this version of the problem of evil "the problem of hell." Lewis then argues that the free will defense is an inadequate response to the problem of hell. First, he argues that incompatibilist accounts of free will are not superior to compatibilist accounts. As seen earlier in Part 3, if compatibilism were true, then the existence of free will does not provide God with a morally sufficient reason for allowing evil, including the evil of damnation—for if compatibilism were true, then God could prevent evil without removing freedom by simply determining agents always to make good choices. For those who think that incompatibilist construals of free will are superior to their compatibilist counterparts, Lewis provides a number of reasons for thinking that not even the misuse of incompatibilist freedom would justify eternal damnation. He then argues for a conception of universalism according to which God redeems all but rewards individuals differently. This allows God to treat individuals as they deserve, while still maintaining that none deserve to be the recipient of damnation. Whether such a view is consistent with Christian theology, Lewis leaves for others to adjudicate. Lewis concludes with a consideration of whether it is appropriate to admire Christian believers, given the evils perpetrated by the God these believers worship.

In "The Doctrine of Everlasting Punishment," Thomas Talbott argues from a theistic perspective that any version of theism which includes the belief that some individuals will suffer an eternity of torment and suffering in hell is necessarily false. According to Talbott, since one of God's essential attributes is omnibenevolence, God is bound by His goodness to insure that no person suffers eternal damnation, and thus that universalism is true. It will be helpful in understanding Talbott's view, however, to differentiate two versions of universalism: contingent universalism and necessary universalism. According to contingent universalism, while it is logically possible that some are eternally damned, all are as a matter of contingent fact saved. Necessary universalism, on the other hand, claims that it is a necessary truth that none are eternally damned. Talbott argues for necessary universalism, and proceeds by differentiating a number of different species of theism: conservative theism, hard-hearted theism, moderately conservative theism, and biblical theism. (The rhetorical force of this last title will not be lost on many readers.) Each of these forms of theism agrees that there exists both evil and an omniscient and omnipotent God; where they differ is in terms of other claims they also embrace. Conservative theism, for example, holds that while God loves every created person, some of those persons will be eternally damned because at some point God will withdraw His grace from them. Talbott argues that conservative theism is contradictory, and that there is no way to reconcile God's love for all people with His damning of any. Hard-hearted theism denies that

God loves all created persons; instead, it maintains that God loves only some. Those who are damned are those who God does not love, and there is no contradiction between God's nature and their damnation. Nevertheless, Talbott argues that hardhearted theism is necessarily false, since love for only some is incompatible with God's essential lovingkindness. According to moderately conservative theism, while God desires the salvation of all, that desire might be frustrated if some individuals freely choose damnation over salvation. Talbott claims that such a choice is incoherent and that, even if it were coherent, God would have a good reason for preventing people from making such a choice by overriding their free will. The only remaining alternative is that it is necessarily the case that none will be eternally damned in hell. Talbott concludes that this view, "biblical theism" in his terminology, is the only viable form of theism.

Eleonore Stump's "Dante's Hell, Aquinas's Moral Theory, and the Love of God" defends a version of the position that Talbott calls moderately conservative theism by trying to show how eternal damnation is logically compatible with God's essential omnibenevolence. Building upon the work of the medieval philosopher Thomas Aquinas, Stump argues that everything that exists, or has being, is good to some degree or other. Evil, on the other hand, is the lack of goodness (or being) that a thing ought to have in virtue of the kind of thing it is. Because humans are supposed to be virtuous, they are evil to the degree that they are vicious. However, even the most vicious of persons are good to some degree or other because they still have being. Stump then argues that part of what it means to love another is to desire what is good for the other. Insofar as union with God is good for those whom God loves, God will seek their union with Him in heaven. To be in union with God, a person must make certain free choices: she must freely will only what is in accord with God's will. However, it is not within the power of even an omnipotent agent to make a person freely will anything, and so God is not able to determine that all will find union with Him in heaven. Some, unfortunately, will make bad choices and develop vicious habits or second natures. Stump then argues that God has two options for what to do with those who choose not to be reconciled with Him. He could either annihilate them or place them in hell, where their second natures can enjoy as much fulfillment—as much being and goodness—as they are capable of. Insofar as their annihilation would involve the removal of whatever being and goodness they still possess, God's goodness prevents Him from annihilating the damned. Thus, according to Stump, it is divine love and respect for free will that are at the heart of the traditional view of hell.

The final reading of this section explores the relationship between free will and the redeemed in heaven. Accounts of the nature of heaven have traditionally included two claims: (i) the redeemed in heaven have free will, and (ii) the redeemed in heaven are no longer capable of sinning. These two claims appear to be in tension, for how could God ensure that the redeemed never sin without vitiating their free will? This question is what James Sennett calls "the dilemma of heavenly freedom" (512). In his "Is There Freedom in Heaven?" Sennett attempts to reconcile the freedom of the redeemed in heaven with their inability to sin. One way to resolve the tension would be to embrace compatibilism, holding that God can determine that the redeemed freely never choose to sin. But Sennett is not willing to embrace compatibilism of this sort because he thinks that an agent cannot be free if she is determined to act as she does by something outside of herself. Instead, Sennett defends a view he calls "proximate compatibilism," according to which free will is compatible with agents' being determined to act as they do by their moral character so long as they freely formed that moral character in way that was not itself determined. In other words, agents can use their free will to form their moral characters in such a way that they are then determined to act in certain ways by their characters. Provided that they enjoyed libertarian freedom when they formed their moral character in this way, Sennett thinks this sort of self-imposed determinism does not rule out free will. It is along precisely these lines that Sennett understands heavenly freedom; after death, the redeemed in heaven are determined by their own freely formed character in such a way that it is no longer possible for them to choose to sin. The redeemed in heaven have formed their character through free actions in such a way that while their later willings are constricted by their moral character, those constricted willings are nonetheless free.

Further Reading

Adams, Marilyn McCord. "Hell and the God of Justice," *Religious Studies* 11 (1975): 433–447.

Adams, Marilyn McCord. "The Problem of Hell: A Problem of Evil for Christians," in Eleonore Stump, ed., *Reasoned Faith* (Ithaca, NY: Cornell University Press, 1993), pp. 301–327.

Baker, Lynne Rudder. *Persons and Bodies: A Constitution View* (Cambridge: Cambridge University Press, 2000).

Corcoran, Kevin, ed. *Soul, Body, and Survival: Essays on the Metaphysics of Human Persons* (Ithaca, NY: Cornell University Press, 2001).

Corcoran, Kevin. *Rethinking Human Nature: A Christian Materialist Alternative to the Soul* (Ada, MI: Baker Academic, 2006).

Crockett, William, ed. *Four Views on Hell* (Grand Rapids, MI: Eerdmans Publishing Co, 1997).

Kvanvig, Jonathan. *The Problem of Hell* (New York: Oxford University Press, 1993).

Swinburne, Richard. "A Theodicy of Heaven and Hell," in Alfred J. Freddoso, ed., *The Existence and Nature of God* (Notre Dame, IN: University of Notre Dame Press, 1983), pp. 37–54.

Talbott, Thomas. *The Inescapable Love of God* (Upublish.com, 1999).

Walls, Jerry. *Hell: The Logic of Damnation* (Notre Dame, IN: University of Notre Dame Press, 1992).

Walls, Jerry. *Heaven: The Logic of Eternal Joy* (Oxford: Oxford University Press, 2002).

Chapter 31

Kevin J. Corcoran

DUALISM, MATERIALISM, AND THE PROBLEM OF POSTMORTEM SURVIVAL

Does dualism have any obvious advantage over materialism when it comes to postmortem survival? It would seem so. After all, it seems bodies peter out and eventually cease to exist. And on any plausible materialist account of persons, one's body is necessary for one's own existence. So the materialist, it seems, has quite a story to tell about how a body that peters out and ceases to exist can somehow turn up in the New Jerusalem. Or if the materialist happens to believe in immediate resurrection, then she's got to tell some whopper of a story about how a body that has apparently died nevertheless continues to live. I say the story must be a whopper because often the corpse is right before our eyes. How then can a *dead* body be enjoying any kind of meaningful *resurrection* existence? Dualists don't have such problems. Or do they?

This paper falls into two parts. In the first part of the paper I show why it is plausible to believe that Christian dualists are no better off when it comes to making sense of the afterlife than their materialist siblings. For it is plausible to believe that the Christian dualist, whether she realizes it or not, faces one of the very same challenges as the Christian materialist; namely, that of accounting for how a body that apparently falls apart and ceases to exist can nevertheless put in an appearance in the Heavenly City. In the second part of the paper I take up the challenge of providing just such an account. I begin with a presentation of the standard reassembly view of

resurrection and suggest ways of defending that view against two common objections. I then offer what I take to be a plausible account of the persistence conditions for human bodies; one which, at least on the face of it, seems to conflict with the reassembly view. I go on to offer reasons for believing that this account of the persistence conditions for human bodies is compatible with intermittent existence and also, therefore, compatible with belief in resurrection of the body, even it should turn out that resurrection is not possible via reassembly. I close with a consideration of a non-gappy account of survival for friends of immediate resurrection. If I am correct in my diagnosis of Christian dualists, namely, that they face one of the very same challenges as their materialist brothers and sisters, then the discussion of resurrection that follows cannot be summarily dismissed as only of parochial interest.[1]

Dualism and Postmortem Survival

We are all familiar with Descartes' dualism. According to Descartes, properties can be divided into those that are mental (e.g., being in pain, desiring an ice cream cone or believing some proposition) and those that are physical (e.g., having a certain weight, shape and mass). That is dualism about *properties*. Cartesian dualism is property dualism *plus*. What Cartesian dualism adds to property dualism is a claim about substance. Cartesian dualism follows from accepting property dualism together with the claim that a single thing can exist having properties of only *one* sort. Hence, the Cartesian dualist claims that there must be *two* fundamental kinds of *substance*—unextended, thinking substance (soul) and unthinking, extended substance (body). The appropriate bearers of mental properties are unextended, thinking substances (souls or minds) and the appropriate bearers of physical properties are unthinking, extended substances (bodies). Descartes famously argued that he is essentially a thinking thing. And if that is so, then Descartes is an immaterial soul or mind.

On the Cartesian dualist view, although it is true of me now that I am in some sense inextricably bound up with this particular body, my existence does not depend on my possessing either this or any other body (i.e., I could exist in a disembodied state). Why did Descartes think that? Well, according to Descartes, it is the fundamentally dissimilar natures of souls and bodies that accounts for this. Descartes notes that there is, for example, nothing in the nature of soul that requires for its existence the existence of a body. Nor is there anything in the nature of body that requires for its existence the existence of a soul or mind. To be a soul is to be simple, unextended and thinking. To be a body is to be complex, unthinking and extended. Thus Descartes reckoned it *possible* for the one kind of substance to exist without the other, and the other to exist without the one. It is easy to see, therefore, why, coupled with traditional theism, postmortem survival is no problem at all for Cartesian souls.

Cartesian dualism is not, of course, the only kind of anthropological dualism. A relatively new kid on the dualist block is *emergent dualism*. William Hasker has done the most to get this view on the map in his excellent book *The Emergent Self*.[2] *Emergent* dualism is, as its name suggests, a species of emergence. The basic idea behind emergentism in the philosophy of mind is that consciousness and mentality do not appear until physical systems reach a sufficiently high level of configurational complexity. Just as liquidity and solidity are features that require matter to be suitably arranged before they are manifested, so too with consciousness and the mental. So according to emergentism in the philosophy of mind, the appearance of mentality is dependent on a physical system (i.e., a brain) of appropriate complexity.

Hasker's original contribution is to claim that consciousness cannot be an emergent *property* of the organisms that exhibit it. Why? For one thing consciousness is normally experienced as unified and this cannot be accounted for by attributing it to the brain. The reason is that the brain itself is not an additional *thing* over and above the constituent parts that make it up. The brain is, in philosophical jargon, a "mereological sum" (i.e., an aggregate of parts). The problem is that none of the parts of the brain enjoy a unified conscious experience. But if the parts of the brain are not conscious and the "brain" is nothing over and above the parts that make it up, *what* then enjoys unified conscious experience? Hasker claims that we need a *substance* to account for unified conscious experience and that it is an emergent *soul* or *subject* (i.e., in the case of human beings, a *person*) that enjoys conscious experience. What about an afterlife? Well, Hasker claims that just as it is possible for God to maintain a magnetic field in existence after the demise of its source of generation, so too is it possible for God to maintain a person in existence even after the body that generated the person peters out and ceases to exist. Given theism, therefore, emergent dualism is also compatible with belief in an afterlife.[3]

I claimed earlier that it is plausible to believe that Christian dualists have one of the very same problems when it comes to postmortem survival as their materialist siblings. We are now in a position to see why. While both Cartesian dualism and emergent dualism, for example, are compatible with belief in an afterlife neither Hasker nor any Cartesian dualist that I am familiar with has offered an account of the Christian doctrine of *resurrection* of the body. Yet it is plausible to believe that it is precisely that doctrine that needs to be addressed by *Christian* dualists. For none of the ecumenical creeds of the Church confesses belief in a doctrine of "soul survival." The Christian doctrine has been understood as the doctrine of bodily *resurrection*. Contemporary dualists seem to have forgotten this in a way that our ancient dualist ancestors did not. Most, if not all, orthodox Christian theologians of the early church were anthropological *dualists*. And it was these dualist-minded theologians who struggled in systematic ways to make sense of the Christian doctrine of *bodily* resurrection.[4] Telling a story of how a body that apparently suffered a martyr's death can be numerically the same as a body that enjoys resurrection life is not the special preoccupation of twenty-first century Christian materialists. This has been, at least until very recently, a concern for dualists too.

Thomas Aquinas, for example, believed that what accounts for the fact that a body once dead can nevertheless enjoy resurrection life is the further fact that the human soul continues to exist, temporarily disembodied, between death and resurrection. That soul, Thomas believed, organizes both the matter that composed the body before death and the matter that will compose the body after death. Same soul; therefore, same body.

Thomas's view of the soul, however, is not without difficulties. Some of the difficulties center on Thomas's ambiguous use of the term "soul," using it sometimes in the sense of a particular *thing* and at other times in the sense of "form" or kind of "state" a body is in. There are additional difficulties raised for Thomas's view by the apparent cognitive life of nonhuman animals, which does *not* require an immaterial soul for its explanation. One wonders why, then, the cognitive life of human animals requires such a soul. Perhaps most important, however, is how, given the rest of Thomas's metaphysics of

substance, a soul can plausibly be said to survive the death of the body. In any case, unlike contemporary dualists, Thomas recognized the need to provide an account of the resurrection of the body. And like the dualists who preceded him, his view seeks to account for the *numerical sameness* of the resurrection and earthly body. In fact, it is plausible to believe that providing an account of the identity between the resurrected and earthly body is constitutive of an account of *resurrection* of the body. For the Christian doctrine is not the doctrine of *reincarnation* or the doctrine of the *acquisition* of some body or other, any more than it is the doctrine of *soul survival*. Consider, for example, I Corinthians 15:42b–43a, where we read: "So will it be with the resurrection of the dead. The body that is sown is perishable, it is raised imperishable; it is sown in dishonor, it is raised in glory; it is sown in weakness, it is raised in power; it is sown a natural body, it is raised a spiritual body" (NIV). It is reasonable to believe that it is numerically the *same* body which exists before and after death, although after death that body is glorified and radically changed. For this reason, I think providing an account of the sameness of resurrected and earthly bodies ought to be of interest to *all* Christian philosophers, dualists no less than materialists.[5] Moreover, given the fact that the Christian tradition has historically understood the doctrine of resurrection as involving numerically the same body, any putatively Christian view of the afterlife that departs from tradition at least owes us an explanation for why we should understand the doctrine in a way that explicitly or implicitly departs from that tradition.

The Problem in Plain Terms

In case anyone has missed it, here's the problem that it is plausible to believe Christian philosophers face, both dualists and materialists. How can some body that exists in the resurrection life be numerically the same as (say) George Washington's body? It doesn't matter if you're an animalist who believes that George Washington is identical with his body, a constitutionalist who believes that George Washington is essentially constituted by his body (even if not identical with it) or a Cartesian dualist who believes that George Washington is an unextended, simple soul only contingently joined to his body. If George Washington's *body*, which existed in 1770, exists in the hereafter, then a physical object numerically identical with George Washington's body exists in the hereafter. But how can that be? There appear to be obviously good reasons for denying that George Washington's body could exist in the hereafter. Even if his body survived for sometime as a fairly well preserved corpse, chances are it has undergone radical decay over the years and has long since passed out of existence. How can a physical object that exists in the hereafter be numerically identical with a physical object that has either radically decayed or passed out of existence under more gruesome circumstances? The following is one attempt to answer just these questions.

A. Resurrection by Reassembly

There are two broad views of resurrection of the body, and each is open to both materialists *and* dualists. There are "gappy" views of the resurrection and "non-gappy" views. I am going to present what I think are defensible versions of each. Before I do that, however, I want to consider a common version of the gappy view, a version I do not find persuasive. The version I have in mind is also historically the most dominant view of resurrection. According to it resurrection is by *reassembly*.[6] The standard account of resurrection by reassembly secures the numerical sameness of the earthly and resurrected body, but, even though some of the most popular objections against it can be met it is still plausible to believe that the view suffers from a serious, if not fatal, flaw. First, the view.

The reassembly view of resurrection is the view that our dualist ancestors seem to have favored. On this view, what happens when God resurrects a human body is that God gathers together all of the smallest bits (the atoms, say) that compose a body at death and reassembles them and causes them to be propertied and related in exactly the way those atoms were propertied and related at the time of death. The resulting object, on this view, is the previously existing body. Lest resurrection by reassembly be facilely rejected, it ought to be noted that there are analogies to this view in common experience. When my camera is taken in for repairs, thoroughly dismantled, cleaned and later reassembled, what we are inclined to say is that the camera returned to me is numerically the same as the camera I took in for repairs. True, the camera did not persist through its disassembly and cleaning, but its constituent parts did. The camera received after repairs, on this view, is the same as the camera taken in for repairs because it has all the same parts propertied and related in exactly the same way. On the reassembly view of resurrection, so too with human bodies.

There are, as I have mentioned, several objections to the standard reassembly view of resurrection. First, suppose your body becomes the tasty morsel of a cannibal and that some of the atoms that made up your body at death are also part of his or her body at death. How can God see to it that *both* you *and* the cannibal get reassembled, since now the very atoms in question have *two* equal claimants?[7] It would seem that God cannot resurrect both of you since *some* of the atoms that composed your body at death composed the cannibal's body at death, and in order for God to resurrect either of you God must reassemble *all* of the atoms that belonged to your respective bodies at death. So the fact of atom sharing seems to tell against resurrection by reassembly.

The defender of reassembly is not without a response. For atom sharing only prevents God from *simultaneously* resurrecting you and the cannibal. It does not prevent God from *first* resurrecting one of you *and then*, after the resurrected body has sloughed off the requisite atoms, God using those very same atoms to resurrect or reassemble the other body.[8] So atom sharing does not *preclude* resurrection; it just makes it necessary that resurrection be temporally staggered.

Whatever the problems with a temporally staggered resurrection, there is also this further problem with the reassembly view. Consider once again our camera. I suggested earlier that gathering all of the camera's parts and reassembling them—placing them in the same pre-cleaning-relations to each other—would result in numerically the same camera. But there is a very relevant disanalogy when it comes to the sorts of changes a human body can suffer without loss of identity and the sorts of changes a camera can suffer without loss of identity. For example, suppose you take your camera in for repairs and all or nearly all of the parts of the camera are replaced. Now surely the camera you receive after repairs is not the same as the camera you took in for repairs. The persistence conditions for cameras, we might say, do not tolerate complete or nearly complete part replacement. Such is not the case, however, with human bodies. Human bodies are constantly sloughing off old bits and taking on new ones. In fact the atoms that composed your body twenty years ago are not the same as the atoms that compose your body today.[9] And this presents a problem for the reassembly view of resurrection. Peter van Inwagen puts it like this. Imagine that God were to take all of the atoms that composed your body at age ten and reassembled them, placing the living human body that results right next to you. Van Inwagen wants to know who has your body, you or the reassembled ten year old? Or imagine that 2,000 years from now God reassembles all of the atoms that composed your body at the age of eighteen and also reassembles all of the atoms that composed your body at the moment of you death at (say) age ninety. Which is you? It would seem that either both are or neither is. Since you can't be two things it must be the case that neither is you. What does this show? It seems to

show that *sameness of bits* is not among the persistence conditions for human bodies. In other words, while it is plausible to believe that gathering all of the parts that composed your pre-repair camera and reassembling them will result in numerically the same camera, such is not the case with human bodies. Gathering all of the atoms that composed your body at any stage of its past career, and reassembling them, will not result in numerically the *same* body. And if the defender of resurrection by reassembly insisted that what is required for resurrection are the atoms that compose the body *at death*, then there would seem to be no principled reason for privileging *those* atoms. Why not the atoms that composed one's body at age eighteen or thirty? Why the atoms that compose one's body at death?

One possible answer to these two questions is suggested by the following examples. If you and I are watching a tennis match and four sets into it the match must be postponed for a day because of rain we would not reckon the match that commences the next day a *continuation* of the match we were watching a day earlier if when it commences it does so in the first game of the first set. But if the match commences *where it left off the previous day* we would reckon it a continuation.[10] Likewise, with some artifacts. Take our camera. Even if all of a camera's parts that had been replaced over a ten-year period were to be recombined to compose a camera we would not reckon the newly assembled camera numerically the same camera as I bought ten years ago. Why? Because many of us have the intuition that the parts composing a thing *at its "last" moment*, together with their properties and relations, are necessary for that object's reappearance. If a camera is dismantled and reassembled out of the parts that composed it *at the time it was dismantled*, those parts being propertied and related just as they were at the time of dismantling, we would reckon the reassembled camera numerically the *same* camera. So when it comes to resurrection by reassembly there is the intuition for why we should prefer the atoms that composed one's body at death and not the ones that composed one's body at age eighteen or thirty.

Aside from particular worries peculiar to this line of response it is the larger issue of the persistence conditions for bodies that leads me ultimately to reject the standard reassembly view of resurrection. Persistence conditions for things of a certain kind tell us what sorts of changes things of that kind can undergo without ceasing to exist. For example, the persistence conditions for bananas are such that a banana can persist through color changes (the same banana can be green on Tuesday, and yellow on Friday) but it cannot persist through changes that render it an ingredient in banana bread.

B. The Persistence of Bodies

Let me now offer what I take to be a plausible account of the persistence conditions for human bodies, as this will help to set in sharp relief what I take to be the problem with the standard reassembly view of resurrection. First, it would help to get clear on what I mean by *human body*. By the words *human body* I mean, for starters, to pick out that kind of entity usually associated with the words *physical organism of the species homo sapiens*. Thus understood, what the term *human body* picks out is to be distinguished from the mass of cell-stuff that constitutes it. One but not the other is a mere *mass* or aggregate. And a mass just is a mereological sum. Therefore, the one but not the other is able to survive material part replacement.

So by *body* I mean to refer to a living animal and by *human body* I mean to refer to a living animal or organism of the species *homo sapiens*. Peter van Inwagen has described organisms this way: organisms, says van Inwagen, are "things that are composed of objects whose activities constitute lives,"[11] where by "life" van Inwagen means a special sort of self-directing biological event. This view of physical organisms suggests the following criterion of identity:

If x and y are physical organisms, then x is identical with y if and only if x and y are constituted by (sets of) physical simples whose activities constitute the same continued life.

What then are the persistence conditions for bodies? There are good reasons for denying that spatiotemporal continuity is sufficient for the survival of physical organisms. For it seems possible that an evil genius could totally annihilate a body during a certain interval of time and that God could replace it with a newly created molecular duplicate during precisely the same interval, and in precisely the same place as the place occupied by the original body at the time of its annihilation. The picture is that of the gradual top down annihilation of one body and the simultaneous replacement of it with a numerically distinct duplicate, the replacement body exactly filling the human body shaped receptacle created by the annihilated body. In other words, the same interval of time would mark the *end* of one body's existence and the *beginning* of a duplicate's existence, while the spatial region originally filled by the annihilated body would come to be wholly filled by a body numerically distinct from it. This *seamless* replacement of one body with another seems to suggest that spatiotemporal continuity is not sufficient for the persistence of bodies.[12]

But if spatiotemporal continuity is not sufficient for the persistence of bodies, is it nevertheless *necessary* for their persistence? Perhaps not, for some philosophers have called to our attention that spatiotemporal continuity is normally merely a consequence of persistence and not its ground.[13] What is absent in the simple spatiotemporal continuity criterion of persistence is any mention of the role of *causation*. If the computer monitor before me has persisted into the present then its existence in the immediate past must be *causally* relevant to its existence now. So too with human bodies. If a human body sitting before me at 9:00 a.m. is not causally connected with one that was sitting before me at 8:59 a.m.

then it is plausible to think that the human body before me at 9:00 a.m. is not a *continuation* of the body that was before me at 8:59 a.m., but rather is a numerically distinct replacement, even if there is spatiotemporal continuity between the 9:00 a.m. and 8:59 a.m. bodies and even if the bodies are phenomenologically indistinguishable.

Causal considerations, therefore, seem especially pertinent to the giving of persistence conditions for material objects of any sort. Of course the kinds of causal dependencies relating an object at earlier and later stages of its career will very likely differ according to the kind of object whose career we are tracing. Different kinds of persisting things will have different persistence conditions. What it is in virtue of which a *human body* persists is different from what it is in virtue of which a *table* persists. But even so, it is causal considerations that are relevant to the persistence of each.[14]

When it comes to the persistence of bodies I suggest the following:

> If an organism O that exists some time in the future is the same as an organism P that exists now, then the (set of) simples that compose P now must be causally related to the (set of) simples that will compose O in the future.

Let's specify further that the relation must be of the *immanent* causal and life preserving variety. In fact, we can name this condition on the persistence of bodies the *Immanent Causal Condition* (ICC). In immanent causation, a state x of thing A brings about a consequent state y in A itself, whereas in cases of causation of the sort we normally think of a thing A brings about state-changes in a numerically distinct thing, B. For example, the state or event of the rock's hurtling through the air brings about state changes in the window it hits. ICC makes it a requirement on the persistence of an organism that *immanent* causal relations hold among the different stages of an organism's career.[15] We can put it this way:

> A human body B that exists in the future is the same as a human body A that exists now just in case the temporal stages leading up to B are immanent causally connected to the temporal stage of A now.[16]

C. Back to Reassembly

We are now in a position to see what is problematic about the standard reassembly view of resurrection; namely, it seems to conflict with the ICC for the persistence of bodies. While it is true, on the standard reassembly view, that the atoms in the resurrected body *are the way they are* because the atoms in the body just before death *were the way they were*, it's not the case that the two stages of the "body's" existence are *immanent* causally related. Instead, on the standard reassembly view, the causal chain runs through God. God reassembles the original bits based on their arrangement at death. My concern with the standard reassembly view of resurrection, then, is not that it requires *gaps* in a thing's existence. My concern is that it seems to fail to meet the immanent causal requirement for the persistence of bodies.

It has lately been suggested by Dean Zimmerman that a certain kind of reassembly view may in fact be compatible with the immanent causal requirement for persistence. After all, what the requirement rules out is that there be some state or event, which is both present during the temporal gap during which the body is not present *and* which is itself *causally sufficient* for the later stage of the body's existence. That requirement, however, would not be violated if God were to issue a decree of the following form: "Let there be a resurrected body that is composed of the same parts, propertied and related just the same way, as the parts that composed George Washington's body at his death," followed by the appearance of said body. God's decree, in other words, though causally *necessary* for the reappearance of George Washington's body is not causally *sufficient* for its appearance and, therefore, would not transgress the immanent causal requirement.[17]

While I agree that the divine decree or "back-tracking" version of the reassembly view could be made compatible with ICC, I find Zimmerman's own version problematic. I would suggest that so long as the parts that compose the post-gap body are the way they are at least partly in virtue of the *causal contribution* of the pre-gap parts (and their properties and relations), then such a view can succeed. However, I would also suggest that there are aesthetic reasons for preferring a view of the resurrection that involves God on the front of end of the gap, perhaps even at the beginning of creation, bestowing on the simples that compose bodies a capacity for passing on causal "umph" across temporal gaps and issuing a general decree, also at the beginning of creation, to the effect that when the requisite conditions obtain that capacity is exercised. Such a view would be preferable to any reassembly view according to which the mere presence of the parts of a body (and their properties and relations) at death are, together with God's decree, causally sufficient for the reappearance of the body after death (à la Zimmerman). So although the standard reassembly view of resurrection may be at odds with the immanent causal condition on the persistence of bodies it is possible to construct an alternative that isn't.

But let us suppose for the sake of argument that resurrection is *not* possible via reassembly. Would it be possible at all? It is reasonable for the Christian to believe that the answer is "yes." But how? In answering this question we will see why it is plausible for the Christian to believe that resurrection is compatible with gappy existence even if, as we suppose, it is not possible via reassembly.

D. God and the Gap

The belief that a necessary and sufficient condition for the persistence of bodies is that earlier and later stages of its existence stand in immanent causal relations places certain constraints on just how resurrection can go. How can one maintain that a single body can begin to exist, cease to exist and then, if resurrection is true, begin again to exist? That's a nice question!

It seems to me that, in the absence of a fully worked out account, a perfectly sensible reply for the Christian is simply to plead ignorance. She might just say this: We know from revelation that God promises resurrection. And experience seems to teach us that bodies cease to exist. Now given a philosophical commitment to ICC, if some future body is going to be numerically the same body as one that previously existed but ceased, then the two stages of that body's career are going to have to stand in immanent causal relations to one another. But doesn't that require that immanent causal relations can cross a temporal gap? Yes, it does. Well, is it reasonable to believe they can? The Christian believer has reason to think so. In fact, here's an argument to that conclusion.

1   Bodies cease to exist.
2   The scriptures teach that my body is going to be raised.
3   The Immanent Causal Condition for the persistence of bodies is true.
4   Therefore, immanent causal relations can cross temporal gaps.

Assuming that a requirement for my body to exist after ceasing is that its stages be immanent causally related, it *must be* true that immanent causal relations can cross gaps! The challenge for the Christian who embraces ICC (dualist or materialist), is to seek to understand just how that might work. But regardless, insofar as she believes the argument is sound it provides the Christian with good reason for believing that gappy existence is compatible with a plausible principle of bodily persistence, even if it should be the case that surviving such a gap is not possible via reassembly.

E. Non-Gappy Survival: Fissioning of Causal Paths

But suppose you believe that the scriptures teach immediate or non-gappy survival. Suppose, in fact, you believe that a single thing cannot have *two* beginnings, that a thing cannot begin to exist, cease to exist, and then *begin again* to exist. How can there be a body in heaven numerically the same as a body I watch die if there's no such thing as gappy existence?

In different places Dean Zimmerman and I have argued that one answer to this question lies in the fissioning of causal paths. It seems possible that the causal paths traced by the simples caught up in the life of my body just before death can be made by God to fission such that the simples composing my body then are causally related to two different, spatially segregated sets of simples.[18] One of the two sets of simples would immediately cease to constitute a life and come instead to compose a corpse, while the other would continue to constitute a body in heaven.[19] In other words, the set of simples along one of the branching paths at the instant after fission fails to perpetuate a life while the other set of simples along the other branch does continue to perpetuate a life. If this is at least possible, as it seems, then we have a view of survival compatible with the claim that human bodies cannot enjoy gappy existence.

This view of immediate survival, like most others in the neighborhood, does not come without a price. At least part of the cost involves giving up the assumption that *material* continuity is necessary for the persistence of physical objects. Moreover, whereas we may be willing to allow physical organisms in particular to gradually replace some or all of the matter that constitutes them, we may not be willing to allow for an all-at-once replacement like that entailed by the fissioning of causal paths view of survival. We may think that's too high a price to pay. However, insofar as what ultimately matters for the persistence of organisms is the holding of immanent causal relations between any two stages of an organism's career, giving up the assumption about *material* continuity is not a cost incurred by the view, but rather an entailment of it.

There is a more serious metaphysical problem with the fissioning of causal paths view of survival, however; namely, it seems to violate what has come to be called "the only *x* and *y*" principle. According to this principle, whether or not some objects *x* and *y* compose some concrete individual F should have nothing to do with events involving numerically distinct objects spatiotemporally segregated from F. But in the account of immediate resurrection just suggested it looks as though whether or not a body persists into the afterlife has everything to do with what happens to the other fission product, namely, that it immediately perish. I have answered this charge elsewhere in some detail and so won't take it up here, except to say that I think there are good reasons for believing that it can never be the case that there be a competitor for identity with my body.[20] In any case, for reasons having mostly to do with biblical interpretation I find the teaching of scripture to be more in tune with intermittent existence.[21] But if your interpretation of scripture leads you to believe in immediate survival, then I recommend the fissioning of causal paths view as a coherent way to secure numerical sameness of body.

Concluding Thoughts

When I talk to Christian dualists about the afterlife I am frequently met with something like the following response: "Wow, am I ever glad I'm a dualist! I mean, whatever the problems with dualism, at least we dualists don't need any wacked-out metaphysical prestidigitation in order to make sense of postmortem survival." If the issue is simply one of postmortem survival, then I admit that dualists have a much easier time accommodating such a doctrine. But if one is both a dualist and a Christian, then it's plausible to believe that such an individual has at least one of the very same problems as Christian materialists, namely, how to make sense of the Christian doctrine of resurrection of the body. I have suggested one way a Christian, dualist or materialist, might provide a non-gappy account of that doctrine and also offered reasons for believing that a gappy account of survival is compatible with a plausible condition on the persistence of human bodies.[22]

Notes

1 I assume in this paper a three-dimensionalist account of material objects. Therefore, what I go on to say will be of only limited relevance for friends of four-dimensionalism. For a discussion of my problems with a four-dimensionalist view of persons see my "Persons, Bodies and the Constitution Relation," *Southern Journal of Philosophy* 37 (1999): 1–20.

2 William Hasker, *The Emergent Self* (Ithaca, NY: Cornell University Press, 1999).

3 Although compatible with belief in an afterlife, I find Hasker's account implausible. There are some things not even God can do! Among them, I would argue, is keeping a magnetic field in existence even after its generating source is destroyed. This is not a failure on God's part. It just seems plausible to believe that a necessary condition for the survival of a magnetic field is that its generating source survive. So too with persons. It seems plausible to believe that if Hasker's emergentist view is correct, then in order for me to survive my body must survive.

4 For fascinating reading on the importance of bodily continuity and numerical sameness in patristic and medieval reflections on the resurrection see Caroline Walker Bynum's *The Resurrection of the Body in Western Christianity, 200–1336* (New York: Columbia University Press, 1995).

5 I say this in full recognition that it is, surprisingly, a minority view. Apparently most contemporary philosophers of religion do not think the claim that the resurrection body is numerically the same as the premortem, earthly body is even plausible.

See, for example, Bruce Reichenbach's *Is Man the Phoenix?* (Grand Rapids, MI: Eerdmans, 1978). "The language of resurrection is misleading when it suggests that the very thing which died will be raised again . . . [this] seem[s] generally contrary to any factual possibility, given the disintegration of bodies upon death and the dispersal of their constituent elements" (181). See also John Hick's *Death and Eternal Life* (New York: Harper and Row, 1976). "A human being is by nature mortal and subject to annihilation at death. But in fact God, by an act of sovereign power, either sometimes or always resurrects or reconstitutes or recreates him—not however as the identical physical organism that he was before death" (279, emphasis mine). And John Cooper, although he does not come right out and say it, seems to think that the resurrection bodies we human beings will enjoy in the afterlife are not the same numerical bodies we had in our pre-resurrection existence. See his *Body, Soul and Life Everlasting* (Grand Rapids, MI: Eerdmans, 1989), 185–95.

6 See Bynum, *The Resurrection of the Body*.

7 At issue is not cannibalism as such, but the fact of part-sharing. We could suppose that the atoms that compose your body at death eventually become part of the earth which, in turn, become part of the chicken which, in turn become part of someone else's body at the time of his or her death. Same problem.

8 My colleague Del Ratzch pointed this out to me.

9 If you are inclined to object to this comparison on the grounds that the example of the camera was an all-at-once replacement of parts, whereas the replacement of atoms in humans occurs over time, I later offer reasons for thinking that a human being *can* survive (where a camera *cannot*) an all-at-once replacement of parts.

10 For a defense along these lines see David B. Hershenov, "The Metaphysical Problem of Intermittent Existence and the Possibility of Resurrection," *Faith and Philosophy* 20 (2003): 24–36.

11 Peter van Inwagen, *Material Beings* (Ithaca, NY: Cornell University Press, 1990), 92.

12 The idea of "smooth" replicas or "immaculate" replacements can be credited either to Sydney Shoemaker, "Identity, Properties, and Causality," *Midwest Studies in Philosophy* 4 (1979): 321–42,

reprinted in Sydney Shoemaker, *Identity, Cause and Mind* (Cambridge: Cambridge University Press, 1984), 234–60; or David Armstrong, "Identity Through Time," in *Time and Cause*, ed. Peter van Inwagen (Dordrecht: D. Reidel, 1980), 67–78.

13 See for example David Armstrong's "Identity Through Time," 76.

14 See Chris Swoyer, "Causation and Identity," *Midwest Studies in Philosophy* 9 (1984): 593–622.

15 Such stages need not be thought of as temporal parts of the persisting organism; like the life lived by an organism, they need only be thought of as events. Thus, following Zimmerman, we can define "temporal stage of an organism" as follows: "*s* is the temporal stage at t of an organism O = def. there is a set R of all the intrinsic properties and internal relations O has at t, and *s* is the event of O's exemplifying R at t." See his "Immanent Causation," in *Philosophical Perspectives*, vol. 11, and also his "The Compatibility of Materialism and Survival," *Faith and Philosophy* 16 (1999): 194–212. Zimmerman offers the definition of "temporal-stage" for objects in general; I have taken the liberty to make the relevant substitutions so that the definition applies to organisms in particular.

16 For more on the notion of immanent causation see Zimmerman's "Immanent Causation." For a definition of "temporal-stage," see previous footnote.

17 Such a view has been suggested by Dean Zimmerman, "The Compatibility of Materialism and Survival: The 'Falling Elevator' Model," *Faith and Philosophy* 16 (1999): 194–212.

18 Dean Zimmerman was the first to suggest this view in a paper presented at the Pacific Division APA meeting in 1994. I take up the view in my "Persons and Bodies," *Faith and Philosophy* 15 (1998): 324–40, and Zimmerman develops it further in "The Compatibility of Materialism and Survival: The 'Falling Elevator' Model."

19 We will assume not only that persons are essentially persons, but that being alive or conscious is a necessary condition for human personhood. Therefore, there is after the fissioning only one possible candidate for a person-constituting object since the surviving corpse is not a living organism and so not capable of subserving consciousness.

20 See my "Physical Persons and Postmortem Survival without Temporal Gaps," in *Soul, Body and Survival*, ed. Kevin Corcoran, (Ithaca, NY: Cornell University Press, 2001), 201–17.

21 For a very nice discussion of the relevant biblical data see Joel B. Green's "Eschatology and the Nature of Humans: A Reconsideration of Pertinent Biblical Evidence."

22 I wish to thank the Tuesday afternoon philosophy colloquium at Calvin College, the Council for Christian Colleges and Universities and the following individuals: Rebecca DeYoung, Hud Hudson, Trenton Merricks, Christina Van Dyke, and Dean Zimmerman.

Chapter 32

Lynne Rudder Baker

PERSONS AND THE METAPHYSICS OF RESURRECTION

'But what, then, am I?', Descartes famously asked. Although many of us today reject Descartes's equally famous answer – 'I am an immaterial mind' – Descartes was right, I believe, to identify himself with a thinking thing, a thing who 'doubts, understands, affirms, denies, wills, refuses, and which also imagines and senses'.[1] But neither an immaterial mind nor a material brain is the thing that thinks. The thing that thinks is the person. Just as your legs and feet are the limbs by means of which you walk, you the person – not your legs and feet – are the walker; so too the brain is the organ by means of which you think, but you the person – not your brain – are the thinker.

Where Cartesians see a relation between minds and bodies, I see a relation between persons and bodies. Understanding 'person' to refer to entities like you and me, it is obvious that persons exist. And just as clearly there are bodies. So, the important philosophical question – whose answer cannot be read off neurophysiology or scientific psychology – is this: What is a person? What is the relation between a person and her body?[2]

On the answer that I shall propose – I call it 'the constitution view' – persons are not identical to their bodies, nor to parts of their bodies (e.g. brains), nor to their bodies plus something else (e.g. immaterial souls). In 'logical space' there is room for another possibility, which I shall develop and defend. I shall explore the idea that a person is constituted by a body, where constitution is not identity. On such a constitutional account of persons and bodies, it is necessary that human persons are embodied; but it is not necessary that they have the bodies that they in fact have. Thus, the view that I shall develop shares with the Cartesian dualist the claim that persons are not identical to their bodies (I could have a different body from the one that I do have), and it shares with the classical materialist the claim that, necessarily, human persons are embodied. After setting out this constitution view, I shall turn to the metaphysics of resurrection.

First, let me comment on the term 'human being'. Some philosophers use 'human being' to denote a biological kind.[3] Others use it to denote a partly psychological kind.[4] I use 'human being' in the latter way, to name a partly psychological kind, a human person. All human persons are human beings, and vice versa.

The Constitution View of Human Persons

What makes a human person a *person* is having what I'll call a 'first-person perspective'. What makes a human person *human* is being constituted by a human body.

A first-person perspective is the defining characteristic of all persons, human or not.[5]

From a (robust) first-person point of view, one can think about oneself as oneself and think about one's thoughts as one's own. In English, we not only use first-person pronouns to refer to ourselves 'from the inside' so to speak (e.g. 'I'm happy') but also to attribute to ourselves first-person reference (e.g. 'I wonder whether I'll be happy in ten years'). The second occurrence of 'I' in 'I wonder whether I'll be happy in ten years' directs attention to the person *per se*, without recourse to any name, description, or other third-person referential device to identify who is being thought about. The first-person perspective opens up a distinction between thinking of oneself in the first person and thinking of oneself in the third person. Once someone can make this distinction, she can think of herself as a subject in a world of things different from herself. And since human persons are necessarily embodied, a person can think of her body, as well as her thoughts, from her first-person perspective.

A being may be conscious without having a first-person perspective. Non-human primates and other higher animals are conscious, and they have psychological states like believing, fearing, and desiring. They have points of view (e.g. 'danger in that direction'), but they cannot conceive of themselves as the subjects of such thoughts. They can not *conceive of* themselves in the first person. (We have every reason to think that they do not wonder how they will die.) So, being conscious, having psychological states like beliefs and desires, and having a point of view are not sufficient conditions for being a person.

To be a person – whether God, an angel, a human person, or a Martian person – one must have a first-person perspective. *Person* is a non-biological genus, of which there may be several species: human, divine, bionic, Martian, etc. It is in virtue of having a first-person perspective that an entity is a person. So, what makes something a person is not the 'stuff' it is made of. It does not matter whether something is made of organic material or silicon or, in the case of God, no

material 'stuff' at all. In short, *person* is an ontological kind whose defining characteristic is a first-person perspective.

Babies are not born with the kind of *robust* first-person perspective that I have been describing, but they are born with what I call 'rudimentary first-person perspectives': they are sentient; they imitate; they behave in ways which require attribution of beliefs and desires to explain. An organism comes to constitute a person when it develops a *rudimentary* first-person perspective, provided that the organism is of a kind that normally develops a robust first-person perspective. Human babies are persons in virtue of having rudimentary first-person perspectives and of being members of the human species. Members of the human species – unlike non-human animals who may also have rudimentary first-person perspectives – normally develop robust first-person perspectives as they mature and learn a language. A human organism that has a rudimentary or a robust first-person perspective at time t constitutes a person at time t.[6]

At the other end of human life, a person who becomes demented still has a first-person perspective. Patients who are severely mentally handicapped (e.g. with late Alzheimer's disease) still can conceive of themselves as 'I'. If you think that you don't exist (Cotard's syndrome), you have a first-person perspective. Your existence on earth comes to an end with the *permanent and irretrievable* loss of the ability to think of yourself from the first person. As long as it is physically possible for a patient (even in a coma) to regain the ability to think of herself in the first-person way, there is a person. When the physical possibility of that ability is forever lost (as in the case of Terry Schiavo), but the brain stem is still functioning, then there is no person there, but only an organism.

A first-person perspective is the basis of all self-consciousness. It makes possible an inner life, a life of thoughts that one realizes are one's own. The appearance of first-person perspectives in a world makes an ontological difference in that world: a world populated with beings with inner lives is ontologically richer than a world populated with no beings with inner lives. But what is ontologically distinctive about being a person – namely, a first-person perspective – does not have to be secured by an immaterial substance like a soul.

Human persons differ from non-bodily or immaterial persons (if there are any) in that human persons are not just pure subjects; they do not exist unembodied. So, myself includes my body. And persons' bodies are the objects of first-person reference. If Smith wonders whether she has cancer, she is wondering about her body from a first-person perspective. She is not wondering whether there is a malignant tumour in some particular body identified by a third-person demonstrative pronoun or description; she is wondering whether there is a malignant tumour in her own body, considered as herself. This is different from wondering about a material possession, say. If Smith wonders whether her car will run, she wonders about a particular car, which she identifies by a description or a third-person demonstrative reference. Without a third-person way to think about the car, she could not wonder about its battery. But if Smith is wondering how she will die, she can think of her body as her own without recourse to any name or description or second- or third-person demonstrative pronoun. And reference without recourse to the familiar third-person devices is the mark of first-person reference.

Human persons – who, like all persons, have first-person perspectives – are distinguished from other kinds of persons in that human persons are constituted by human bodies that are the objects of their first-person thoughts. A human person is a person who is constituted by a human body during some part of her existence. (I say 'is constituted by a human body during some part of her existence' to avoid issues raised by the Incarnation. The orthodox Christian view is that the eternal second person of the Trinity is identical with Jesus Christ, who is both fully human and fully divine. How this could be so is ultimately a mystery that requires special treatment far beyond the scope of this paper.)

Putting that issue aside, a human person is constituted by a biological entity – an organism, a member of the species homo sapiens – that is physically able to support first-person intentional states.[7] (It is up to neuro-scientists, not philosophers, to determine the biological conditions under which a human being is able to support first-person intentional states.)

A human person – Smith, say – must have a biological body that she can think about in a first-person way. Smith can think of a biological body in the first-person way if she can entertain thoughts about that body without aid of a name, or description, or third-person pronoun. Even if she is totally paralysed, Smith has a first-person relation to her body if she can entertain the thought, 'I wonder if I'll ever be able to move my legs again'. To put it differently, Smith can think of a biological body in the first-person way if she can conceive of its properties as her own. For example, Smith's thoughts about how photogenic she (herself) is, or her worries about her (own) state of health – thoughts that she would express with first-person pronouns – make first-person reference to her body as her own. Since a body constitutes a person, a first-person reference to one's body is ipso facto a first-person reference to oneself.

So, what makes a particular body Smith's, rather than someone else's, is that it is the body that Smith can think of and refer to in a first-person way, 'from the inside'. The body to which Smith has a first-person relation is the body some of whose parts she (normally) can move without moving anything else, the body that she tends when she is in pain, and the body that expresses her intentional states. States like pain, longing, sadness, hope, fear, frustration, worry, effort, and joy as well as states like believing, desiring, and intending are expressed through posture, facial expression, sounds, and other bodily motions.

The body that expresses Smith's intentional states is the body to which Smith has a first-person relation. Smith's first-person relation to her body at t does not imply that Smith is actually thinking of her body at t; indeed, Smith may believe at t that she is disembodied. The body to which Smith has a first-person relation is the body whose sweaty hands manifest the fact that Smith is nervous, and the body whose stomach's being tied in knots expresses the fact that Smith is frightened, or the body that would move if Smith carried out her decision to leave the room. Smith's body at time t distinguishes Smith from all other persons at t. What distinguishes me now from all other coexisting persons – even physical and psychological replicas of me, if there are any – is that at this time, I have a first-person relation to this body and to no other; and any replica of me at this time has a first-person relation to some other body, but not to this one.

The body to which I have a first-person relation constitutes me. But what is constitution? Elsewhere,[8] I have a more rigorous account of the relation of constitution, but the general idea of constitution is this: when various things are in various circumstances, new things – new kinds of things, with new causal powers – come into existence. Every concrete object is of (what I call) a primary kind. A thing has its primary-kind property essentially. So, kind membership (or species membership) is not contingent. The relation of constitution unites things of different primary kinds, and hence things with different essential properties. For example, a human organism is essentially a member of the human species; a person essentially has a first-person perspective.[9] A human person is a person constituted by a human organism.

Constitution is everywhere: pieces of paper constitute dollar bills; strands of DNA constitute genes; pieces of cloth constitute flags; pieces of bronze constitute statues. Constitution is never identity: the piece of cloth that constituted the first Union Flag could exist in a world without nations; hence that piece of cloth could exist

without constituting a flag, and the first Union Flag is not identical to the piece of cloth that constituted it. Similarly, the piece of bronze that constituted Myron's statue 'Discobolus' could have existed in a world without art; hence that piece of bronze could have existed without constituting a statue.[10]

The non-identity of persons and bodies may be seen in another way – in a way that has no parallel for statues. Despite the similarities between persons and statues, there is a major difference between them: Persons have bodies that change drastically over the course of a person's life, but pieces of marble that constitute statues change very little. To put it the other way around: if the piece of marble that constitutes Michelangelo's 'David' were to change significantly, the statue 'David' would no longer exist; but Smith's body alters radically while Smith endures.

Leaving aside the analogy between persons and statues, consider another argument against the person/body identity theory, based on criteria for individuating bodies and persons. Criteria of individuation may be vague, but they are not totally elastic. Smith's body is a human body in virtue of being a member of the species *homo sapiens*. What makes something a human body are its biological properties; its career may be followed from beginning to end without respect to whether or not it is any person's body. Similarly, its persistence conditions are independent of whether or not it is any person's body. The identity of a human body is independent of whether it is Smith's or any other person's body.[11]

In the natural course of things, our organic bodies undergo full atomic replacement over some years, and we person survive this total replacement without interruption in mental functioning. It seems possible that we could equally survive gradual replacement of organic cells by bionic cells – until finally the body that sustains us is no longer an organic body. Exactly how much replacement of parts a human body may undergo and still remain a *human* body is somewhat vague, but if a body is mostly made up of inorganic material and is not sustained by organic processes, it is not a member of the species *homo sapiens*. The non-organic body that ends up constituting Smith now is a different body from the organic body that was a member of the species *homo sapiens*.

Consider the organic body that Smith was born with. Call it 'OB'. Suppose that the organs of OB were totally replaced over a period of time by bionic parts, until what remained was a fully bionic, non-biological body that resembled OB in appearance, that moved in ways indistinguishable from OB, that emitted sounds that we took to be English sentences that reported memories of things that had happened to Smith, and indeed that we took to be professions that this person was Smith. Is the bionic body the same body as Smith's biological body OB? No. OB was a carbon-based body that was a member of the species *homo sapiens*. The bionic body is not a member of any biological species. Would Smith still exist? Of course. Otherwise Smith's possessions and property should be taken from the bionic-body-Smith and distributed to Smith's heirs. After the organ replacement, Smith would still exist but would no longer by constituted by OB; rather, Smith would be constituted by a bionic body. (I really do not like bizarre thought-experiments, but I think that we are actually close to bringing this thought experiment to fruition. There are now devices implanted in brains that allow paralysed people to operate computers by their thoughts, cochlear implants allow deaf people to 'hear', and so on. Moreover, it's easy to imagine billionaires seeking 'whole-body' replacements to prevent ageing.)

The point is that this is a realistic example that shows that a single person may be constituted by different bodies at different times: Smith had a first-person relation to a biological body at one time, and to a bionic body at a later time, and a biological body is essentially organic, and is not numerically identical to any bionic body. Note

that spatio-temporal continuity in general does not signal sameness of entity: Very slowly, atoms could be added or taken away from Smith's biological body until it was indistinguishable from a turnip or a bookcase. In that case, it would no longer be the same body, and presumably Smith would no longer be with us. Indeed, there may be a period of time during which it is indeterminate whether there is a human body or not. I have argued elsewhere that everything that we encounter in the natural world comes into existence gradually; hence, everything that we interact with has vague temporal boundaries.

To sum up: on the constitution view, a human person is constituted by a particular biological body, but the person is not identical to the body. What distinguishes persons from all other beings is that they have first-person perspectives essentially. The persistence conditions of a human person are determined by the property in virtue of which she is a person – viz. the property of having a first-person perspective: a human person could cease to have an organic body without ceasing to exist. But she could not cease to be a person without ceasing to exist.

On the constitution view, then, a human person and the organic body that constitutes her differ in persistence conditions without there being any actual physical intrinsic difference between them. The persistence conditions of animals – all animals, human or not – are biological; and the persistence conditions of persons – all persons, human or not – are not biological.

On the Metaphysics of Resurrection

All the great monotheistic religions – Judaism, Christianity, and Islam – have doctrines of an afterlife. These are religious doctrines, whose grounding in scripture and tradition leaves open how they should be understood metaphysically. I want to focus on the Christian doctrine of resurrection, and to find the best metaphysics to support it.

To begin, consider three features that characterize the Christian view of resurrection.

First, identity: the very same person who exists on earth is to exist in an afterlife. Individuals exist after death, not in some undifferentiated state merged with the universe, or with an eternal mind, or anything else. Not only is there to be individual existence in the resurrection, but *the very same individuals* are to exist both now and after death. 'Survival' in some weaker sense of, say, psychological similarity is not enough. The relation between a person here and now and a person in an afterlife must be identity.

Second, embodiment: resurrection requires some kind of bodily life after death. Post-mortem bodies are different from pre-mortem bodies in that they are said to be 'spiritual', 'incorruptible', or 'glorified'. Even if there is an 'intermediate state' between death and a general resurrection, in which the soul exists disembodied, those who live after death will ultimately be embodied, according to Christian doctrine.

Third, miracle: life after death, according to Christian doctrine, is a gift from God. Christian doctrine thus contrasts with the Greek idea of immortality as a natural property of the soul. The idea of miracle is built into the Christian doctrine of life after death from the beginning. Since resurrection, if it occurs, is miraculous, we cannot expect a full philosophical account or explanation of it. There will always be some mystery left. The best that we can hope for is a metaphysics consistent with and congenial to the doctrine.

The task for a metaphysics of resurrection is to present a view of human persons whose persistence conditions allow, by means of a miracle, for post-mortem as well as pre-mortem life. The best that metaphysics can do is to show how resurrection is metaphysically possible. That is, any candidate for a metaphysics of resurrection must conceive of human persons in such a way that it is metaphysically possible (even if physically impossible) that one and the same person whose earthly body is corruptible may also exist with a post-mortem body that is incorruptible. That is the task. I shall argue that the constitution view fares better than its competitors in fulfilling that task.

There are a number of candidates for a metaphysics of resurrection:

1   Immaterialism: sameness of person is sameness of soul both before and after death.
2   Animalism: sameness of person is sameness of living organism before and after death.
3   Thomism: sameness of person is sameness of body/soul composite before and after death.
4   The memory criterion, according to which pre- and post-mortem persons are the same person if and only if they are psychologically continuous.
5   The soul-as-software view, according to which sameness of person is analogous to sameness of software.
6   The soul-as-information-bearing-pattern view, according to which sameness of person is sameness of pattern of information.
7   The constitution view, which I explained earlier.

Let's consider each of these.

Immaterialism

Although souls in this world are linked to brains, there is no contradiction, according to Richard Swinburne, in the soul's continuing to exist without a body. Indeed, the soul is the necessary core of a person which must continue if a person is to continue.[12] Since, on Swinburne's view, no natural laws govern what happens to souls after death, there would be no violation of natural law if God were to give to souls life after death, with or without a new body. Swinburne solves the problem of personal identity for this world and the next by appeal to immaterial souls.

There is a metaphysical problem with immaterialism: in virtue of what is a soul the same
soul both before and after death? Perhaps the
best answer is that souls are individuated by
having a 'thisness' or haecceity. This is an
intriguing suggestion that I cannot pursue here.
An haecceity view, if otherwise satisfactory, may
well be suitable as a metaphysics of resurrection – if it did not leave dangling the question
of why resurrection should be bodily.

However, I believe that immaterialism should
be rejected. My reason for rejecting immaterialism has less to do with resurrection than with
the natural world. Immaterial souls just do not fit
with what we know about the natural world. We
human persons evolved by natural selection
(even if God actualized this world on the basis of
His foreknowledge of the outcome). Immaterial
souls would simply stand out as surds in the
natural world.

Someone may object: 'If you dismiss immaterial souls on the grounds that they would be
surds, then you should dismiss resurrection too.
Resurrected persons would surely be surds if
immaterial souls are.' This objection can be met:
My opposition to souls concerns their putative
existence in the natural world. Resurrected persons, by contrast to immaterial souls, would not
be surds in the natural world, because resurrection is not part of the natural order in the first
place. Resurrection involves miracles, and miracles require God's specific intervention. We
human persons – who, as I mentioned, evolved
by natural selection – are part of the natural
order, but immaterial souls are not. At least, I do
not see how immaterial entities (unlike first-
person perspectives, whose evolutionary roots
can be seen in chimpanzees) could have evolved
by natural selection.

Animalism

According to animalism, a human person is identical to a human animal. Therefore, animalists
hold, a human person has the same persistence
conditions as a human animal. If animalism is
correct, then the story about Smith's having a
biological body at one time and a distinct bionic
body at another time is incoherent: on the animalist conception, no human person can have
numerically distinct bodies at different times. I
believe that this disqualifies animalism as part of
a metaphysics of resurrection. Here's why.

If any sort of animalism is true, then a human
person has her human body essentially. Her
body changes cells, size, and shape, but the
human person is nothing but that (changing)
body. If her body went permanently out of existence, then that person would go permanently
out of existence. Here is a simple argument to
show that a biological body is not identical to a
resurrection body.

Let h be your human biological body, the one
that you have now. Let b be your spiritual body,
the one that you have in the resurrection. Then:

1 h is corruptible.
2 b is incorruptible.
3 Whatever is corruptible is essentially
   corruptible.

So,

4 $h \neq b$.

Both the second and third premises may seem
open to challenge. Consider the second premise.
Someone may hold that resurrection bodies are
not really incorruptible; they remain corruptible,
but God just prevents them from actual decay.[13] I
have a couple of responses.

First, the suggestion that your resurrection
body is the same body as your corruptible
earthly body raises the well-known problems of
reassembly of earthly bodies that, prior to resurrection, have burned to ashes or decayed or
been eaten by animals.[14] I have been convinced
by Peter van Inwagen that God could not restore
a particular body by reassembling the particles formerly in the body.[15] And the other

suggestions about how an earthly body could survive to be a resurrection body without reassembly (Dean Zimmerman's and Van Inwagen's)[16] seem to me much less plausible than the constitution view.

The next response to the claim that resurrection bodies are not incorruptible comes from Paul, who in I Corinthians 15, calls resurrection bodies 'incorruptible' or 'imperishable' or 'spiritual', depending on the translation. In *The New English Bible*, Paul says: 'What I mean, my brothers, is this: flesh and blood can never possess the kingdom of God, and the perishable cannot possess immortality' (I Corinthians 15.50). Although I am leery of proof-texts, Paul's words clearly suggest that resurrection bodies are not identical to earthly bodies – despite the tradition to the contrary. So, I stand by the second premise: resurrection bodies are incorruptible.

Now consider the third premise. You may think that God, in His omnipotence, could transform a corruptible body into an incorruptible body. I agree. But the transformation would be what Aristotle and Aquinas call a substantial change. The incorruptible body would not be identical to the corruptible body from whence it came. Why not? A corruptible body has different persistence conditions from an incorruptible body. A corruptible body would go completely out of existence under different circumstances from an incorruptible body. Since things have their persistence conditions essentially, a single body cannot change its persistence conditions; so, a single body cannot be corruptible at one time and incorruptible at another time.[17]

To put it another way: earthly bodies are organisms, and organisms are essentially carbon-based. Anything that is carbon-based is corruptible. So, anything that is incorruptible is not carbon-based, and is not an organism, not a human biological body. Since resurrection bodies are incorruptible, they are not carbon-based and hence not identical to organisms, human biological bodies.

God could transform your human body into a resurrection body in the same way that He transformed Lot's wife into a pillar of salt. The pillar of salt, which is not organic, is not identical to Lot's wife's body, which is essentially organic. (Nor, of course, is the pillar of salt identical to Lot's wife.) Nothing that is a pillar of salt is identical to Lot's wife's body. Similarly, if God changed your human biological body into a resurrection body, the resurrection body would not be identical to your human biological body. So, if animalism (or Thomism, for that matter) is true, you would not exist in the resurrection.

If my argument here is correct, then no view of human persons (like animalism or Thomism) that construes a person's corruptible body to be essential to her is consistent with the doctrine of bodily resurrection.

Thomism

Thomism takes over Aristotle's notion of a human being as a substance for which the body supplies the matter and the soul supplies the form. According to Thomas, then, a human being is a composite of a rational soul (form) and a body (matter). The human being is a substance; the rational soul is not – it is a substantial form that nonetheless can 'subsist' on its own. Before the general resurrection, people who have died are in an 'intermediate state', during which the human being (the substance) does not exist. What continues through the intermediate state is the rational soul that subsists (disembodied) until reunited with the body, at which time the human being is recovered.

I think that there are two difficulties with Thomism, considered as a metaphysics of resurrection. The first is the same as with animalism: Thomas requires that a person's resurrection body be numerically identical to his or her earthly body. But (as we just reflected) resurrection bodies and earthly biological bodies have different persistence conditions, and are thus not numerically identical.

The second difficulty is how to individuate disembodied souls. In the case of immaterialism, we could appeal to haecceities, because according to immaterialism, the soul itself is a substance. But according to Thomas, the soul is not a substance. Disembodied souls are individuated by the bodies that they long for and desire to be reunited with. Smith's soul is the one that longs for and desires reunion with a certain body. But what makes a body (mere potency, the matter of which the soul is the form) the body that Smith's soul longs for? It can only be that Smith's soul longs for 'it'. But since the body is mere potency, there is no 'it' for Smith's soul to long for. Hence, what makes a soul Smith's soul cannot be the body that it longs for. As Caroline Bynum says, 'God can make the body of Peter out of the dust that was once the body of Paul'.[18] If this is the case, then disembodied souls cannot be individuated at a time by their yearning for certain bodies – because the identity of the body (Smith's, say) will depend upon the identity of the soul. It is difficult to see how Aquinas can combine the Aristotelian view that matter individuates with his view that the soul is a substantial form that can 'subsist' – and experience God – apart from a body.

Let me pause here and say that I realize that there is scriptural basis for the view that resurrection bodies will be identical to human biological bodies. There are puzzling metaphors in I Corinthians 15 and in II Corinthians 5, as well as the post-resurrection appearances of Jesus, in which he still seems to have his wounds. On the other hand, the fact that he can walk through locked doors and disappear into thin air may lead us to suppose that resurrection bodies are not identical to human biological bodies. But I don't think that such passages wear their meanings on the sleeve.

The Memory Criterion, the Soul-as-Software View, and the Soul-as-Information-Bearing-Pattern View

These may be considered together. The memory criterion is familiar from Locke (and his Scottish opponents). What I am calling the soul-as-software view takes seriously a computer metaphor: the soul is software to the hardware of the brain; if persons are identified with souls (software), they can be 're-embodied, perhaps in a quite different medium', as D.M. Mackay put it.[19] Another materialistic view of the soul (this one from Polkinghorne) conceives of the soul as an 'information-bearing pattern, carried at any instant by the matter of my animated body'.[20] At death, God will remember the patterns and 'its instantiation will be recreated by him' when at the resurrection.[21]

These views share a widely recognized defect: the duplication problem. The problem is that two people (B and C, say) may both be psychologically continuous with (or run the same software, or exhibit the same information-bearing pattern as) a single earlier person, A. If B and C bear exactly the same relationship to A, and if B and C are distinct, then the relation that they both bear to A cannot be identity. A cannot be identical with two distinct objects, and it would be arbitrary to suppose that A is identical to one but not the other. Identity is a one–one relation, but person A's (quasi-)memories, software, information-bearing pattern, etc., could be transferred to more than one person. So, sameness of (quasi-)memories, software, or information-bearing pattern cannot suffice for sameness of person. To avoid this problem, defenders of the memory criterion and the like usually add the (ad hoc) requirement that there be no duplication.

However, there is a theological argument, suggested in conversation by my colleague Gareth B. Matthews, that supporters of the memory criterion etc. need not worry about duplication and need not appeal to ad hoc stipulations.

I'll call the argument 'the Matthews argument'. The premises of this argument are explicitly religious. They appeal to God's necessary attributes – viz. that God is essentially just – and to the notion of a judgment after death. If God is essentially just and God judges everyone, then it is metaphysically impossible for God to let a person A branch into persons B and C.

The reason that it would be metaphysically impossible for A to branch into B and C is this. Assume that everyone except Christ deserves punishment. God is essentially just and judges everyone. Suppose that person A branched into persons B and C: both B and C had A's (quasi-)memories (caused in the right way etc.). Whom does God punish? If God punished B but not C, or C but not B, then God would not be essentially just: B and C are related to A in exactly the same way; it is impossible to be just and to judge B and C differently. On the other hand, if God punished both B and C, then there would be twice the punishment that A deserved, and again God would not be essentially just. Either way, supposing that B and C both had A's (quasi-) memories (caused in the right way), violates God's essential justice in judgment. Since God is essentially just, if A deserves punishment, it is metaphysically impossible for B and C both to have A's (quasi-)memories. So, God's essential justice rules out the metaphysical possibility that A could have a duplicate in the afterlife.

The Matthews argument relies on weighty theological assumptions; but it does rescue the memory criterion from the duplication problem. And it works equally well to save the soul-as-software view and the soul-as-information-bearing-pattern view. So, if the memory criterion (or the soul-as-software view, or the soul-as-information-bearing-pattern view) could be developed in ways that avoid other problems (besides the duplication problem), any of them would be suitable candidates for a metaphysics of resurrection.

The Constitution View

Now let me turn to the constitution view, according to which sameness of pre- and post-mortem person is sameness of first-person perspective. In the first place, the constitution view avoids some of the pitfalls of the other candidates for a metaphysics of resurrection. Since human persons are essentially embodied, the constitution view avoids the problem of individuating disembodied souls – a problem that afflicts Thomism. Since a person's identity depends on her first-person perspective, the constitution view avoids the problem of the numerical identity of corruptible and incorruptible bodies – a problem that afflicts both animalism and Thomism.

Still, the constitution view is not home free. What is needed is a criterion for sameness of first-person perspective over time. In virtue of what does a resurrected person have the same first-person perspective as a certain earthly person who was born in, say, 1800? In my opinion, there is no informative non-circular answer to the question: 'In virtue of what do person P_1 at t_1 and person P_2 at t_2 have the same first-person perspective over time?' It is just a primitive, unanalysable fact that some future person is I; but there is a fact of the matter nonetheless.

We can see this by means of an argument from providence. Now, according to the traditional doctrine of providence, God has two kinds of knowledge – free knowledge and natural knowledge. God's free knowledge is knowledge of contingent truths, and His natural knowledge is knowledge of logical and metaphysical necessities. (I'm disregarding the possibility of middle knowledge here.) Again, according to the traditional doctrine of providence, the obtaining of any contingent state of affairs depends on God's free decree. Whether the person with resurrected body 1, or body 2, or some other body, is Smith is a contingent state of affairs. Therefore, which if any of these states of affairs obtains depends on God's free decree. No immaterial soul is needed for there to be a fact of the matter as to whether Smith is the person with resurrected body 1. All that is needed is God's free decree that brings about one contingent state of affairs rather than another. If God decrees that the person with body 1 have Smith's first-person perspective, then Smith is the person with body 1.[22] So, there is a fact of the matter as to which, if any, of the persons in the resurrection is Smith, even if we creatures cannot know it. On the Christian idea of providence, it is well within God's power to bring it about that a certain resurrected person is identical to Smith.[23]

Notice that the argument from providence provides for the metaphysical impossibility of Smith's being identical to both the person with body 1 and the person with body 2 in the resurrection. For it is part of God's natural knowledge that it is metaphysically impossible for one person to be identical to two persons. And according to the notion of God's natural knowledge, what is metaphysically impossible is not within God's power to bring about. Hence, there is no threat from the duplication problem. Indeed, this argument from providence may be used to support, not only the constitution view, but also immaterialism, the soul-as-software view, the soul-as-information-bearing-pattern view, and the memory criterion, to guarantee a fact of the matter about which person is you in the resurrection. The only views of persons that receive no aid from the argument from providence are those (like animalism and Thomism) that require that incorruptible resurrection bodies be identical to corruptible biological bodies.

The Relative Merits of the Constitution View

The constitution view can deliver the benefits of immaterialism and Thomism without having to postulate immaterial souls, which would be surds in the natural world. In light of the Matthews argument, the memory criterion, the soul-as-software view, and the soul-as-information-bearing-pattern view may be saved from the duplication problem, but none of these is really a fully developed metaphysical theory. The constitution view of persons is superior in that it is integrated into a comprehensive unified view of the natural world.

But the real advantage of the constitution view, at least for Christians, is over animalism. In contrast to animalism, the constitution view does not take being a person to be just a contingent and temporary property of beings that are fundamentally non-personal (organisms). On animalism, being a person has no ontological significance at all.

Indeed, on the animalist view, our having first-person perspectives (or any mental states at all) is irrelevant to the kind of being that we are. But the Christian story cannot get off the ground without presuppositions about first-person perspectives. On the human side, without first-person perspectives, there would be no sinners and no penitents. Since a person's repentance requires that she realize that she herself has offended, nothing lacking a first-person perspective could possibly repent. On the divine side, Christ's atonement required that Christ suffer, and an important aspect of his suffering was his anticipation of his death (e.g. the agony in the Garden of Gethsemane); and his anticipation of his death would have been impossible without a first-person perspective. This part of Christ's mission specifically required a first-person perspective. What is important about us (and Christ) according to the Christian story is that we have first-person perspectives.

Also, of course, there is Genesis 2.26, according to which God said: 'Let us make man in our image, after our likeness'. A natural reading of this verse is that we were made to be persons, to be capable of reflective thought about ourselves – in short, to have first-person perspectives. On the animalist view, our first-person perspectives are just contingent features of us. On the constitution view, they are essential to us.

Given how important the first-person perspective is to the Christian story, Christians have good reason to take our having first-person perspectives to be central to the kind of being that we are. Hence, Christians have good reason to endorse the constitution view.[24]

Notes

1 René Descartes *Meditations on First Philosophy*, Donald A. Cress (tr.) (Indianapolis IN: Hackett Publishing Co., 1979), 19.

2 Peter van Inwagen has argued that many philosophical uses of 'her body' are nonsensical. 'Philosophers and the words "human body" ', in Peter van Inwagen (ed.) *Time and Cause* (Dordrecht: Reidel, 1980), 283–299. Michael Tye offers a rebuttal in 'In defense of the words "human body" ', *Philosophical Studies*, 38 (1980), 177–182. I take a human organism to be a kind of body. Wherever I use the term 'human body,' the reader may substitute the term 'human organism'. My concern is with the relation between human persons and human organisms (i.e. human bodies).

3 E.g. John Perry says that 'human being' 'is a purely biological notion; John Perry 'The importance of being identical', in Amelie Oksenberg Rorty (ed.) *The Identities of Persons* (Berkeley CA: University of California Press, 1976), 70.

4 E.g. Mark Johnston says: ' '[H]uman being' names a partly psychological kind, whereas "human organism" . . . names a purely biological kind'; Mark Johnston 'Human beings', *Journal of Philosophy*, 84 (1987), 64.

5 I give an account of the conditions under which something has a first-person perspective in Lynne Rudder Baker *Persons and Bodies: A Constitution View* (Cambridge: Cambridge University Press, 2000).

6 For details on the idea of a rudimentary first-person perspective, as well as a defence of the idea based on evidence from developmental psychology, see Lynne Rudder Baker 'When does a person begin?', *Social Philosophy and Policy*, 22 (2005), 25–48.

7 Unlike David Wiggins, I do not distinguish between an animal and an animal body. In David Wiggins *Sameness and Substance* (Oxford: Basil Black-

well, 1980), 187, he says, '[M]y claim is that by *person* we mean *a certain sort of animal*.' Then, he distinguishes the animal (that I supposedly am) from the body (that supposedly constitues it). On the other hand, I think that an animal *is* (identical to) a body of a special self-sustaining and self-organizing sort, and I distinguish the animal/body from the person. Also, I take an animal to be a member of its species whether it is alive or dead. How could an animal lose species-membership on dying? It simply becomes a dead member of its species. See Fred Feldman *Confrontations with the Reaper* (New York NY: Oxford University Press, 1992).

8 'Unity without identity: a new look at material constitution', in Peter A. French and Howard K. Wettstein (eds) *New Directions in Philosophy*, Midwest Studies in Philosophy 23, (Malden MA: Blackwell Publishers, Inc., 1999), 144–165. For a related view, see Wiggins, *Sameness and Substance*.

9 Here I am not talking about entities that are human organisms or persons derivatively. An entity x has F derivatively only if x has F in virtue of its constitution-relations. See Baker *Persons and Bodies*, ch. 2.

10 For detailed arguments against the view that Discobolus and that piece of bronze that constituted it are identical (contingently or necessarily), see Lynne Rudder Baker 'Why constitution is not identity', *The Journal of Philosophy*, 94 (1997), 599–622.

11 Moreover, since organisms do not lose their membership in their species at death, a human body remains a human body whether alive or dead. In an ordinary, non-violent death, one and the same human body persists through the change: it is first alive, and then it is dead.

12 Richard Swinburne *The Evolution of the Soul* (Oxford: Oxford University Press, 1997), 146.

13 This is a suggestion of David Hershenov's. Hershenov defends a reassembly conception of resurrection.

14 But see David B. Hershenov 'The metaphysical problem of intermittent existence and the possibility of resurrection', *Faith and Philosophy*, 20 (2003), 89–100, and his 'Van Inwagen, Zimmerman, and the materialist conception of resurrection', *Religious Studies*, 38 (2002), 11–19.

15 Peter van Inwagen 'The possibility of resurrection', in *International Journal for Philosophy of Religion, 9*

(1978), repr. in Paul Edwards (ed.) *Immortality* (New York NY: Macmillan, 1992), 242–246.

16   Dean Zimmerman 'The compatibility of materialism and survival: the "falling elevator" model', *Faith and Philosophy*, 16 (1999), 194–212, and Van Inwagen 'The possibility of resurrection'.

17   Although I am not considering four-dimensionalism here, a four-dimensionalist may hold that a single person could have corruptible temporal parts during part of her existence and incorruptible temporal parts during another part of her existence. Although so far, your temporal parts are all corruptible, after your death, God could make an incorruptible body and freely decree it to be a temporal part of your body. Then, in the sense that a four-dimensionalist construes 'same body' – i.e. as being a sequence of temporal parts – you would have (or rather, be) the same body in the resurrection that you have now. Perhaps so, but there are other reasons beyond the scope of this paper for Christians to reject four-dimensionalism.

18   Caroline Walker Bynum *The Resurrection of the Body in Western Christianity* (New York NY: Columbia University Press, 1995), 260.

19   D. M. MacKay 'Brain science and the soul', in Richard L. Gregory (ed.) *The Oxford Companion to the Mind* (Oxford: Oxford University Press, 1987), 724–725.

20   John Polkinghome *The Faith of a Physicist: Reflections of a Bottom-Up Thinker* (Minneapolis MN: Fortress Press, 1996), 163.

21   *Ibid.*, 163.

22   Stephen T. Davis *Risen Indeed: Making Sense of the Resurrection* (Grand Rapids MI: Eerdmans Publishing Co., 1993), 119–121.

23   The idea of haecceity we find in Duns Scotus seems to offer another possibility: God knows our haecceities in this life, but we do not.

24   This paper was presented as a plenary address at the Society of Christian Philosophers meeting at San Diego University in Feburary, 2006. I am very grateful to the SCP and to Gareth B. Matthews and David B. Hershenov for reading drafts of this paper and for making helpful comments.

Chapter 33

Roger T. Ames

DEATH AS TRANSFORMATION IN CLASSICAL DAOISM

The Unreality of Death

One familiar way of thinking about death is to deny it. There has been a thick strain of such denial in the narrative of Western culture. In the 'received' Plato,[1] we begin from the assumption of an eternal and immutable formal order – the Realm of Forms. We then confine death by defining it as a kind of change that attends only the material aspect within the Realm of Appearance. In this Platonic model, the enduring identity of the human being – the immortal soul – is guaranteed by its affinity to what is Real. The particular human being might 'die' in the sense of undergoing accidental changes, but her essential 'human being-ness' is underwritten by the immutable 'form' of the human being, and its relationship with a tran-scendent principle that, in the interpretation of the Church Fathers, becomes the creator deity. Such a world view establishes life and death as dualistic categories in the sense that life stands independent and unaffected by death. The analogy is that life and death are as God and world, where the latter category is a temporary and imperfect reflection of the former. The human experience is stabilized and provided a cultural horizon by metaphysical and super-natural assumptions such as an immortal soul and a realm beyond.

Essential change in this 'One behind the many' model, were it possible, would be cata-clysmic. Friedrich Nietzsche, in his well-known 'Madman' passage, recounts the catastrophic consequences of rejecting the underlying formal principle of order in our killing of God:

'Where has God gone?' he cried. 'I shall tell you. *We have killed him* – you and I. We are all his murderers. But how have we done this? How were we able to drink up the sea? Who gave us the sponge to wipe away the entire horizon? What did we do when we unchained this earth from its sun? Whither is it moving now? Whither are we moving now? Away from all suns? Are we not perpetually falling? Backward, sideward, forward, in all directions? Is there any up or down left? Are we not straying as through an infinite nothing? Do we not feel the breath of empty space? Has it not become colder? Is more and more night not coming on all the time? Must not lanterns be lit in the morning? . . .'[2]

To kill God would not only eclipse Plato's sun and place the responsibility for inventing those values needed to illuminate the human experience on our own shoulders, but would further require that we come to terms with the reality and inevitability of our own deaths, a realization that, for Nietzsche, would have a salubrious effect on the energy with which we live our lives.[3]

The Correlativity of Life and Death

An alternative, perhaps less familiar attitude toward death pervasive in classical Chinese philosophy, particularly the Daoist tradition, that has had an impact on Sinitic cultures broadly down to the present day is the opposite: to affirm death.[4] This affirmation of death is captured in the *Zhuangzi*'s rather cryptic assertion:

> He who is able to take 'nothing' as his head, 'life' as his backbone, and 'death' as his buttocks, he who understands that life and death, existing and perishing, are one continuous unit – I would be his friend.[5]

An interpretation of this passage must begin from the observation that, unlike some representative texts in the classical Western tradition, the *Theogony*, *Timaeus* and Genesis, there is a marked absence of cosmogonic mythology in the classical Chinese sources. Where there are initial beginnings, a reasonable inference is that there will be final ends. Death, then, is the end of life.

The dominant assumption in classical China, by contrast, is that the energy of transformation is not invested in some external efficient principle that stands independent of its creature, but rather that this energy for change resides within the world itself. The world is autogenerative and 'self-so-ing (*ziran* 自然)', without initial beginning and without presumptive end. If there is an 'ontological' assumption here, it is that the cosmos is an ever condensing and expanding field of psycho-physical energy (*qi* 氣) that undergoes its own process of ceaseless transformation. In such a world, 'things' are radically situated. And situation has priority over agency. Sometimes called *qi*, sometimes called *dao* 道, sometimes called *ziran* 自然 – this field of experience is the locus from which agency is abstracted. Because the world is processional and because its creativity is *ab initio* rather than *ex nihilo* – a creativity expressed across the careers of its constitutive phenomena – phenomena are never either atomistically discrete nor complete. The *Zhuangzi* recounts:

> With the ancients, understanding had gotten somewhere. Where was that? Its height, its extreme, that to which no more could be added was this: some of them thought that there had never begun to be things. The next lot thought that there are things, but that there had never begun to have boundaries among them . . .[6]

In contrast to the "two-world" metaphysical model of the Platonic-cum-Christian cultural dominant, the classical Chinese tradition is a 'this-world' theory in which change and temporality are not to be denied. It is a 'this-world' rather than a 'one-world' theory because it is an unbounded process, and since we are inextricably embedded within it, there is no objective viewpoint outside of it from which it can be quantified or made into an object.

Within such a world, this notion of the correlativity of life and death is anything but mystical or obscure. Quite simply, life and death have no separate status. The absence of cosmogonic thinking means that life and death are not distinguished as events distinct from the normal, more gradual processes of change. In the *Zhuangzi*'s philosophical reflections on death – a theme that commentators such as Fukunaga Mitsuji and Angus Graham take to be its major contribution[7] – it 'naturalizes' the process of dying by locating it among the other operations of nature familiar in everyday lives:

> The sun rises in the eastern quarter only to set in the distant western reaches, and all of the myriad things take their bearings from it. Those things with eyes and feet can only get their work done by relying upon it; they come out with it and disappear with it. The myriad things are all the same – relying on something they die, and relying on something they come to life. Having once received my present

form, I persist and wait for it to be used up. On the model of other things, I move day and night without a break, never knowing where it all ends.[8]

Like 'up and down' or 'left and right', life and death are correlative categories which depend upon each other for explanation. They are thus merely explanatory rather than ontological categories required to describe a relative persistence within an unrelenting process of transformation. The formal aspect of order does not depend upon or appeal to metaphysical assumptions, but is discernible as the continuous patterns in the everyday world around us. It is a sense of order that is persistent while always being attended by an indeterminate aspect – it is at once a presencing and a dying away. The sun rises and the sun sets, yet always on a new day. And the previous day fades away. There is regularity as each set of waves emerges and falls, yet each wave in each set has its own distinct character. And the previous wave recedes from the shoreline. There is a pattern of granulation on each piece of wood, and yet each piece has its own unique signature. And it grows only to wither away.

Formal order in such a world does not stand behind and independent of our experience as stabilizing metaphysical principles or assumptions. Rather, order is the sometimes-persisting sometimes-receding traces left by the inscription of a continuous and complex pathway as we advance along it. Order, far from overcoming and defeating chaos, is in partnership with it in producing usually familiar yet always novel experiences.

The Unremarkability of Death

David Keightley, in his reflections on the meaning and value of death in classical China, generally allows that death was perceived as 'unproblematic'.[9] Of course, he is not claiming that the end of life was not approached with some trepidation. He means rather that death was not considered unnatural, perverse or horrible. Chinese 'natural' death is contrasted with the enormity of death in the Judaeo-Christian tradition, where mortality is conceived as divine punishment meted out for human hubris and disobedience. While there is an uneasiness manifested in visions of the 'Yellow Springs', a name for the netherworld, there is a marked absence of the morbidity and gloom that we associate with the Greek, Roman and medieval European conceptions of death.[10] There is a preponderant emphasis in the classical Chinese world view on 'life', with relatively little attention given over to the tragedy and poignancy of death familiar in classical Western sources. This emphasis on life is not only Daoist, but can be illustrated by such canonical texts as the Confucian *Analects*:

> Jilu asked about serving the gods and the spirits of the dead, but the Master replied: 'If you are not yet able to serve other people, how can you serve the spirits of the dead?' He then asked about death, but the Master replied, 'If you do not yet understand life, how can you understand death?'[11]

Rather than a gruesome and morbid portrayal of death, there is the Chinese tolerance of death as a relatively unremarkable aspect of the human experience. Behind this, there is a recognition that life could not be what it is if it were not for the anticipation of death. Without death in its broadest sense, life would be static, transparent, predictable and tedious. Death is the indeterminate aspect that makes process, change, complexity and novelty possible. It can be understood as a positive, enabling presence rather than a negative, disabling absence. Death does not inhibit or subvert life, but stimulates and drives it, making it more intense and poignant.

In explanation of this relatively accepting Chinese attitude, Keightley observes that 'ancestor worship and the endurance of the lineage served to render the loss of the individual more palatable'.[12] And further,

> Given the lack of divine animus, of immanent man-god hostility, it was natural that death in China should not have been regarded as an affront to mortals to the degree that it was in Mesopotamia and Greece; rather it was part of the inevitable and harmonious order.[13]

Certainly the cultivated awareness of continuity that is fostered by the cultural superstructure was an important factor in making death less terrifying than it would be otherwise.

Death as Life

The primacy of continuity in thinking about the transition from life in the here-and-now to life in the netherworld is not simply a philosophical insight. In her analysis of the conception of death in ancient China, Kang Yunmei points out the affinity that Zhuangzi's 'transformation of things (wuhua 物化)' has with the stories that abound in the popular mythology of this early period.[14] This notion of continuity is further evidenced in the popular religious practices with the perception of the afterlife as simply an extension of this world. This extension is usually described in terms of the hun 魂 and the po 魄 – a person's heavenly and earthly spiritual aspects. The assumption is that the hun's departure signals the very moment of death, while the earthly po remains to lead a life similar to our own, within the social hierarchies and with all of the attendant problems that we must face. At the moment of death, the focus is on trying through prescribed ritual practices to persuade the hun to return to the body of the deceased. Attention then turns to the anticipated 'life' of the po. While types of talisman would be included among the funerary objects to provide the hun direction on its usually vaguely conceived journey, most of the tomb furnishings would be surrogate lodgings, servants, animals, and the

chattel necessary to go about the business of the day. The tomb over time evolved in imitation of the houses of the living. Favourite articles of clothing, household items, and even drafts of preferred manuscripts, have frequently been found in the excavated tombs.[15]

Routine memorial observances for the deceased include the replenishing of foodstuffs, 'banking' a netherworld currency for the departed by burning it, and the provisioning of all the other daily goods needed to pay taxes and resolve anticipated problems in the land of the dead. While life on the other side was perceived as similar to this side, the passage from life in this world to the next would often entail a process of apotheosization – the deceased would take on superhuman powers that could be called upon for the benefit of their living descendants.[16] This was true not only generally with institutionalized ancestor worship in which the lineage ancestors become a focus of deference, but was further evidenced in more specific instances in which temples would be built to celebrate local cultural heroes.

Most importantly, the observance of religious practices, in seeking to propitiate the spirits of the dead, established a communication link between the world of the living and its extension into the world of the dead. The manipulation of this link was clearly directed at achieving happiness in the here and now, with the quality of future life in the netherworld as only a secondary consideration. Just as popular religion in China tended to be human-centred rather than god-centred, the objective of such practices was the welfare of the living first, and more incidentally, the benefit of the dead. To take care of one's dead was an encouragement for them to take care of you; to fail to take care of one's dead could bring them back as a hostile influence on one's own fortunes.

Mu-chou Poo makes two interesting points with respect to this relationship between the living and the dead.[17] First, the living mourned their dead, but were persuaded that the breach between life and death was sufficiently wide that no further direct contact with one's deceased kinsmen was desirable. Second, there was more reason for the lower strata of society to be concerned about the conditions of the netherworld because they did not have descendants who had the wherewithal to provide for them first in the initial burial arrangements and then later in the regular sacrificial offerings. In the late Warring States and early Han periods, social mobility became increasingly a matter of personal merit. Achieved social status and material comforts would affect the enthusiasm with which persons were inclined to view their prospects, both while living and after death.

At the end of the day, the living, through ritual observances and sacrifice, had a measure of power in dealing with death that gave them a certain sense of control. This is not to diminish the importance death occupied in popular religious practices nor to suggest that it was in any way ignored in the classical Chinese corpus. As observed above, a compelling argument can and has been made that coming to terms with death is a central concern of both the *Zhuangzi* and the *Daodejing*. Before turning to explore these central Daoist texts, we need to examine the language of death – the cluster of terms used to define this experience within Chinese culture broadly.

The Language of Death

The term, *si* 死 is usually translated as 'death'. The Han dynasty *Shuowen* 說文 lexicon defines *si* paronomastically – that is, by phonetic and semantic association – as *si* 澌 meaning 'to drain dry', underscoring the sense of 'expiring' or 'using up' that is usually entailed in the Chinese notion of a natural death. Typically, the correlative term for *si* is *sheng* 生, 'to be born, to live, to grow', where *sheng* occupies the dominant position in the binomial, 'life and death 生死'. *Si* has a positive aspect, meaning 'natural end'. So when the *Daodejing* 42 announces that violent

people '*bu de qi si* 不得其死', it means that these persons 'do not meet their *natural end*' rather than that they 'do not die'. They certainly do die, and sooner than they would have if they conducted themselves better.

A second recurrent term is *wang* 亡, which has as its primary meaning 'to depart, to flee, to escape' and then by extension, 'to perish'. The *Shuowen* defines *wang* explicitly as *tao* 逃, 'to flee', with a range of meaning including 'to be exiled' and 'to disappear'. The Duan Yucai 段玉裁 commentary adds that *wang* is a 'combined meaning (*huiyi* 會意) character', connoting the 'entering (*ru* 入)' into a remote and concealed place. Duan Yucai argues that the original meaning of *wang* is 'to flee', and that its association with death is an extension of this meaning: 'to lose' and then 'to die'. He suggests that when a filial child cannot endure the death of his parents, he suspects they have simply quit the place. In correlative pairing, *wang* occurs in dyadic apposition with 'to dwell, to be among, to preserve' (*cun* 存), 'to have' (*you* 有), and 'to get' (*de* 得), with *wang* always being the subordinate member.

Death in the *Daodejing*

Important for understanding *wang* 亡 is its cognate relationship with *wang* 忘, 'to forget', a relationship made explicit in the *Daodejing*. There is a strong sense that real dying occurs when one is forgotten. In a cultural tradition in which persons are understood to be irreducibly social, constituted by the pattern of roles and rituals of their lives' narratives, the answer to the question: what is lost? and what is left? is important. As long as a person is remembered, he or she has a place and a life. The emphasis on genealogical continuity, the ethic of filiality, the cultural requisite of returning the body to the ancestors intact, the elaborate structure of Chinese funerary rites, and the role of ancestor worship as the primary religious observance, are all an expression of this social memory. On the other hand, 'not being around', 'being exiled', and 'disappearing' are all ways of dying while still being otherwise alive. Hence, the interchangeability of 'to perish' *wang* 亡 and 'to be forgotten' *wang* 忘 is found in alternative readings of *Daodejing* 33:

不失其所者久
死而不亡（忘）者壽

Not losing one's place is to be long enduring,
Dying and yet not perishing (not being forgotten) is to be long lived.

Wang 忘 – 'being forgotten' – is a textual variant found on the Mawangdui manuscripts for the *wang* 亡 found in the received redactions. The acceptability of the variant *wang* 忘 here would suggest that 'perishing' and 'being forgotten' amount to the same thing, and that the line can be read either way.[18]

In looking at death in classical Daoism, *Daodejing* 50 is frequently cited:

出生入死，生之徒，十有三，死之徒，
十有三，
人之生，亦之於死地、亦十有三。
夫何故。以其生生之厚。

In the process of coming out in life and returning in death,
    The travellers on the path of life are about a third,
    The travellers on the path of death are about a third,
    And those who have life
    But who shift over to the path of death
    Are also about a third.
    How so?
    Because of their excessive care for life.

In the world that this classical Daoist text reports on, people can be expected to divide up into three fairly equal groups: those who live out their natural lives, those who because of disease, famine, war, or some other unfortunate circumstance succumb to death along the way, and finally those who would belong to the first group, but because of their excessive preoccupation with staying alive, join the second in meeting with a premature end. Excess is dangerous, and thus the sage 'spurns the extreme, spurns the extravagant, and spurns the excessive'. Life and death, like all of the correlative relationships which organize our world, such as long and short, high and low, difficult and easy, old and young, and so on, are continuous and mutually entailing, so that being hung up on one at the expense of the other introduces an abnormality that challenges the natural balance and cadence of life. As the *Daodejing* 75 states, it is 'simply that one who does not seek after life is superior to one who prizes it'.

Death in the Zhuangzi

The *Zhuangzi* moves in the same direction as the *Daodejing*, emphasizing the continuity between and the interdependence of life and death. But *Zhuangzi* goes beyond the mere acceptance of death. Since each moment is attended by a presencing and an absencing, by an emerging novelty and a dying away, to abstract the dying away aspect from this continuing process as 'death' and to consider the emerging aspect independent of it as 'life' confounds our experience in this world – it is a nonsense. The argument of the *Zhuangzi* is simple: the very reasons we have for being attached to one aspect are the same reasons we must appreciate the other. The problem is not death, but our fear of death, a fear that is unwarranted:

How do I know that to delight in life isn't being muddle-headed? And how do I know that to despise death is not the feeling of someone lost in his youth being unable to find his way back? Madame Li was the child of a border guard at Ai. When the state of Jin first captured her, tears flowed until her robes were sopping wet. It was only when she had reached the King's quarters, shared his bed and eaten of his fine domesticated meats, that she regretted her tears. How do I know that the dead do not regret that they had once had longings for life?[19]

Within this world, death is equated with the process of transformation itself. As the *Zhuangzi* says explicitly:

For one who realizes the enjoyments of Heaven, his life is travelling with Heaven, and his death is the transformation of things 其死也物化.[20]

Once we have accepted the intuitively powerful assumption that we transform rather than disappear, the *Zhuangzi* wants to take us one rather large step further. One of the prejudices that this text repeatedly challenges is our uncritical assumption that in this process of ceaseless change (*wuhua* 物化), it is better to remain in our human form than to become something else:

Before long, Master Lai fell ill. Wheezing and panting, he was on the brink of death. His wife and children gathered about him and wept. Master Li, having gone to enquire after him, scolded them, saying: "Get away! Don't impede his transformations!"

Leaning against the door, Master Li talked with him, saying: "Extraordinary, these transformations! What are you going to be made into next? Where are you going to be sent? Will you be made into a rat's liver? Or will you be made into an insect's arm? . . ."

Now if a great ironsmith were in the process of casting metal, and the metal leapt about saying: "I must be forged into an Excalibur sword!" the great ironsmith would certainly consider it to be an inauspicious bit of metal.

If once having been cast in the human form, I were to whine: "Make me into a human being! Make me into a human being!", the transformer of things would certainly take me to be an inauspicious

person. Once we take the heavens and earth to be a giant forge and transformation to be the great ironsmith, where ever I go is just fine. Relaxed I nod off and happily I awake.[21]

For the *Zhuangzi*, not only is the fear of death unwarranted, it is death as transformation that makes life deliciously anticipatory and inconclusive. Around each corner is the possibility of ever new and exciting experiences.

Not long thereafter, Ziyu fell ill, and Zisi went to ask after him. "Extraordinary!" said Ziyu, "The transformer of things continues to make me all gnarly and bent. He hunches me up so badly that my vital organs are above my head while my chin is buried in my bellybutton. My shoulders are higher than my crown, and my hunchback points to the heavens. Something has really gone haywire with the *yin* and *yang* vapors!" . . .

"Do you resent this?" asked Zisi.

"Indeed no," replied Ziyu, "What's to resent? If in the course of things it transforms my left arm into a clock, I'll use it to tell the time of day. If it goes on to transform my right arm into a crossbow bolt, I'll use it to shoot me an owl for roasting. If it then transforms my buttocks into wheels and my spirit into a horse, I will ride about on them without need of further transportation . . . What's to resent?"[22]

The *Zhuangzi* locates the possibility of assuming a human form within the larger process of transformation. There is real comfort and indeed even a religious awe in the recognition that assuming the form of one kind of thing gives way to becoming another in a ceaseless adventure. Such a recognition also stimulates empathetic feelings and compassion for other creatures in a shared environment. It encourages an existential appreciation of the 'very now' by relocating the dying away in every moment and by redefining 'life' as 'life-and-death'. Zhuangzi's counsel is: rather than wishing to be one thing as opposed to another, enjoy the ride.

Kang Yunmei suggests that the famous butterfly story really has as its subtext Zhuangzi's dying out of one kind of life and his transformation into another.[23] This interpretation is certainly reinforced by another lesser known anecdote which tells a similar story but in much greater detail:

> Liezi was having his lunch by the side of the road when he spied a hundred year old skull. Spreading back the reeds, he pointed at it and said: 'Is it only you and I who know that we have never experienced either life or death? Should you then be anxious, and should I be glad?'
>
> Within the seeds of things there is something that triggers them off. In water, seeds become amoeba, and at the water's edge they become a kind of seaweed. When they grow on a hillside, they become a hill-slipper grass, and when this grass is fertilized it becomes crow-foot grass. The roots of the crow-foot grass become beetle larva, and its blades become butterflies. Shortly the butterflies undergo a metamorphosis to become those insects which live under the stove and shed their skins – they are called house crickets. These house crickets after a thousand days become birds, and they are called 'dried leftover bones' birds. The spittle of these birds becomes *simi* bugs which become vinegar flies. *Yilu* bugs are born from the vinegar flies, and *huangkuang* grubs are born from *jiuyou* insects. Gnats are born from fireflies, and when sheep's groom grass grows beside bamboo that has not sprouted for some time, it produces *chingning* bugs. *Chingning* bugs give birth to leopards which give birth to horses which in turn give birth to human beings. In due time, human beings revert to what triggered them off. All of the myriad things come out from what triggers them off and revert back to it.[24]

This passage uses specific plants and beasties familiar in their own specific time and place to describe the animated and linear process of transformation. One thing leads to another. Through the patterns of association that the reader brings to this everyday world, these various kinds of living things provide a bottomless resource out of which all things in proper sequence emerge. The 'something that triggers them off (ji 機)' is the indeterminate aspect that drives the ongoing reconstrual of the world around us.

Perhaps the best known anecdote on death in the entire classical corpus is Zhuangzi's response to the death of his own wife of a lifetime:

> Zhuangzi's wife had died. Huizi went to offer his condolences, only to find Zhuangzi squatting on his heels, beating on a clay pot, and singing. Huizi admonished him, saying, 'She has shared your home, raised your children, and grown old with you. Not weeping at her passing is more than enough, but beating on a pot and singing – this is too much!'
>
> Zhuangzi replied, 'Not so. When she first died, how could I not grieve like anyone would? But on looking back into her beginnings, I saw that she originally had no life, and not only was she without life, she had no bodily form, and not only was she without bodily form, she had no qi. Scattered amidst the muddle and confusion, a change occurred and there emerged her qi, the qi changing, she emerged in bodily form, and her bodily form changing, she emerged alive. Now, she has changed again, and has died. This is but to travel together with the passage of the four seasons from one to the next. When she was on the point of taking her repose in the great mansion of the world, I was in a state, trailing after her bawling and howling, but it then occurred to me that this was a failing on my part to understand her circumstances, so I gave it up.'[25]

When we consider that religion in classical China as in Greece was constituted of solemn observances – orthopraxis rather than orthodoxy, what people *do* rather than what they *believe* – the parody of the funeral wailing by beating on an overturned pot becomes doubly serious as a kind of religious defilement. As we have observed, in the natural (rather than 'supernatural' or metaphysical) cosmology presupposed in classical China and expressed through this anecdote, the priority of process and change over stasis and form is assumed. This priority of process and change guarantees the irreversibility of order, defeats any globalizing assertions, and makes absolute predictability precarious. It is the conditions of this process that has provided Zhuangzi with a wife who has been unique and exciting. And the focus on cosmology rather than ontology places the onus on 'how' things hang together productively (*he* 和) rather than on 'what' they really are. The question for Zhuangzi is not: what is her death? Rather, it is: how do we dispose ourselves so that we can continue to flourish within this process of transformation?

Zhuangzi, in reflecting on the 'loss' of his wife, discovers that he has not really lost her at all. Her continuing participation in the process of change is guaranteed, and his mourning for her death becomes the celebration of her life. Even more important than this realization, however, is the notion that life and death are both contributory aspects of the process. What has made this wife a unique and cherished companion is dependent upon the mutuality of both change and persistence in the human experience. Every moment must at once be a living and a dying in order for the process to be vibrant and productive.

This inseparability of death and uniqueness is reiterated with some poignancy after Huizi, Zhuangzi's favourite interlocutor, has left this life:

Zhuangzi was in a burial procession when he passed the tomb of Huizi. Turning around to address those following him, he said to them: "There was a man of Ying who, when finding a piece of mortar on the tip of his nose as thick as a fly's wing, would get Carpenter Rock to swipe it off with his blade. Carpenter Rock wielded his axe like the wind, and doing as he was told, would cut the bit of mortar away cleanly without injury to the nose. And the whole time the man of Ying would stand there without batting an eye."

"Lord Yuan of Song heard of this, and summoning Carpenter Rock to him, said, "Try to do this on me.""

"Carpenter Rock replied, "As for me, I once was able to swipe the mortar off with my blade, but it has been some time now since my target died.""

"Since Huizi died, I too have had no one as a target, no one to really talk with!"[26]

Huizi, a person of an analytical, positivistic bent, appears in several anecdotes throughout the *Zhuangzi* as a rather straight and humourless target of Zhuangzi's many ripostes. In this particular reverie, Zhuangzi acknowledges that his own repartee – his ability to wield his wit like the wind – has been dependent upon his relationship with Huizi, who could stand his always logical ground without batting an eye. Death has made Huizi one of a kind, because in Huizi's absence, there is no one who can take his place. Zhuangzi cannot carry the philosophical conversation on alone. Is there resentment in this passage? Such would be out of keeping with the spirit of the *Zhuangzi* as a whole. Rather than resentment, there is in fact a profound appreciation for the process that has made it all possible.

As we have seen, the *Zhuangzi* emphatically rejects the notion that having a human form is preferable to any other. This is perhaps the theme on which the text must be most persuasive because it threatens what most people take to be an uncritical value.

Zhuangzi was on his way to Chu, when he spied an empty skull which, though dried and parched, had its shape. Turning it over with his carriage whip, he addressed it with his questions. 'Sir, was it that, being greedy for life you were led astray, and so have come to this pass? Or was it that, being caught up in the fall of your kingdom, you suffered the executioner's axe, and so have come to this pass? Or was it that, having done some wicked deed, you were mortified at having made your parents and family heirs to your disgrace, and so have come to this pass? Or was it that, suffering the misery of hunger and cold, you have come to this pass? Or was it that, having lived out your full complement of seasons, you have come to this pass?'

On finishing his monologue, Zhuangzi laid hold of the skull and, cradling his head on it, went off to sleep. In the middle of the night, the skull came in a dream, and said to him, 'What you were saying sounds like the prattle of a philosopher. Your words are all about being enmeshed in the world of the living; the dead have none of this. Would you like me to tell you about what it means to be dead?'

'By all means' said Zhuangzi.

The skull replied, 'For we the dead there are neither rulers above nor subjects below, and there is none of work brought on with the four seasons. Contentedly we take the heavens and earth as our playground. Even the pleasure of a king sitting on his throne does not surpass it'.

Zhuangzi did not believe him, and so asked him, 'If I called on the Magistrate of Life to bring your body back to life, to restore your bones, flesh, and skin, and to return you to your hometown to be with your parents, family, and neighbors, would you want this?'

The skull frowned with annoyance, saying 'How could I abandon the pleasures of a king sitting on his throne to again take on the toil and travail of life in the human world!'[27]

Zhuangzi apparently took this theme of 'the transformation of things (wuhua)' to heart, for when it was time for him to die, he upbraided his followers for assuming that sumptuous funeral trappings were able to enhance a not necessarily unfortunate transition from one form into another – what others might call the passage from life into death:

Zhuangzi was on the verge of death, and his disciples were thinking of preparing a lavish burial for him. Zhuangzi said to them, "I have the heavens and earth for my inner and outer coffins, the sun and moon for my jade discs, the constellations of stars for my pearls, and the myriad things for my grave gifts. These burial furnishings are fully prepared for me – how can you add to them?"

The disciples replied, "We are afraid that the crows and kites will feed on you, sir."

"Above ground I'll be eaten by the crows and kites," Zhuangzi said, 'and below ground I'll be eaten by the ants and mole-crickets. What is your bias in taking from one to give to the other?"[28]

As we have seen, a familiar refrain in the *Zhuangzi* passages that deal with death is the good-humoured expectation that death opens one up to assume a vast range of possible shapes and forms, and that far from privileging the human form, one is best to take them as they come. There is nothing of the pathetic fallacy in this tradition that makes something exceptional about becoming human. The text is devoted to stories of ageing adherents of Daoist ideas embracing the process of change with the firm conviction that its continuity and novelty requires one to esteem death in the same degree that one would exalt life.

Notes

The translations of the classical texts are by the author; other published translations have sometimes been referenced for the sake of comparison. The references to *Zhuangzi* are to the *Chuang Tzu*: Harvard-Yenjing Insitute Sinological Index Series, Supplement 20, Peking, 1947.

1 In fairness to Plato, it is necessary to distinguish between the 'received' Plato as metaphysician and abstract formist, a product of Christianization and twentieth-century scientism, and the much more interesting Plato as mythologer, playwright, artist that is being rehabilitated in our present moment.

2 R. J. Hollingdale (trans.), *The Nietzsche Reader*, London, Penquin, 1977, pp. 202–3.

3 See the essay by Graham Parkes in this same volume for a discussion of Nietzsche's attitude toward death.

4 Again, see the examples of Japanese philosophers referenced by Parkes, and their affinity with early Daoism.

5 *Zhuangzi* 17/6/46; cf. A. C. Graham (trans.), *Chuang-tzu: The Inner Chapters*, London, George Allen & Unwin, 1981, p. 87 (hereafter Graham, *Chuang-tzu*).

6 *Zhuangzi* 5/2/40 and commentary on it in 63/23/58; cf. Graham, *Chuang-tzu*, pp. 54 and 104 respectively.

7 See A. C. Graham, *Disputers of the Tao: Philosophical Argument in Ancient China*, La Salle, Ill., Open Court, 1989, pp. 202–4. He observes 'Nothing in his unusual sensibility is more striking than the lyrical, ecstatic tone in which he writes of death.' See also A. C. Graham, *Chuang-tzu*, pp. 23–4 and his *Studies in Chinese Philosophy and Philosophical Literature*, Albany, State University of New York Press, 1990, pp. 295–6, and Fukunaga Mitsuji, *Sōshi*, Tokyo, Asashi Shinbun Chugoku kotensen series, 1966, commentary on chapter 6.

8 *Zhuangzi* 55/21/19; cf. Graham, *Chuang-tzu* p. 168.

9 David Keightley, 'Early Civilization in China: Reflections on How it Became Chinese', in Paul S. Ropp (ed.), *Heritage of China: Contemporary Perspectives on Chinese Civilization*, Berkeley, University of California Press, 1990, p. 33.

10 A. C. Graham, *Disputers of the Tao*, p. 203, makes this same point. *Zhuangzi*'s discussion of confronting death 'is quite without the morbidity of the stress on corruptibility in the late-Medieval art of Europe, which reminds of the horrors of mortality for the good of our souls'.

11 *Analects* 11/12.

12 Keightley, 'Early Civilization', p. 33.

13 Ibid., p. 34.

14 Kang Yunmei, *Zhongguo gudai siwanguan zhi tanjiu* (An Exploration of the Ancient Chinese View of Death), Taibei, National Taiwan University History and Chinese Literature Series No. 85, 1994, chapter 2.

15 Mu-chou Poo, 'Immortality, Soul, and the Netherworld', in *In Search of Personal Welfare: A View of Ancient Chinese Religion*, Albany, State University of New York Press, 1997, chapter 7; and Michael Loewe, 'Services to the dead', in *Chinese Ideas of Life and Death: Faith, Myth and Reason in the Han Period (202 BC – AD 220)*, London, George Allen & Unwin, 1982, chapter 11.

16 Mu-chou Poo, *Personal Welfare*, pp. 214–15.

17 Ibid., pp. 172–9.

18 See Robert G. Henricks (trans.), *Lao-tzu: Tao-te Ching*, New York, Ballentine, 1989, p. 274 n. 162.

19 *Zhuangzi* 6/2/78; cf. Graham, *Chuang-tzu*, p. 59.

20 *Zhuangzi* 34/13/14; cf. Graham, *Chuang-tzu*, p. 260.

21 *Zhuangzi* 17/6/53; cf. Graham, *Chuang-tzu*, p. 88.

22 *Zhuangzi* 17/6/47; cf. Graham, *Chuang-tzu*, p. 88.

23 Kang Yunmei, *Zhongguo gudai siwangguan zhi tanjiu*, pp. 21–2.

24 *Zhuangzi* 47/18/40; cf. Graham, *Chuang-tzu*, p. 184.

25 *Zhuangzi* 46/18/15; cf. Graham, *Chuang-tzu*, pp. 123–4.

26 *Zhuangzi* 66/24/48; cf. Graham, *Chuang-tzu*, p. 124.

27 *Zhuangzi* 46/18/22; cf. Graham, *Chuang-tzu*, pp. 124–5.

28 *Zhuangzi* 90/32/47; cf. Graham, *Chuang-tzu*, p. 125.

Chapter 34

David Lewis

DIVINE EVIL

A Neglected Argument

Standard versions of the argument from evil concern the evils God fails to prevent: the pain and suffering of human beings and non-human animals, and the sins people commit. The most ambitious versions of the argument claim that the existence of evil is logically incompatible with the existence of an omnipotent, omniscient, and completely benevolent deity. More-cautious approaches maintain that the existence of pain and sin ought to make us skeptical about any such deity. Or that the extent of the suffering in the millions of years of sentient life on Earth gives us strong reason to think no such deity exists. Or that particular cases of extreme anguish and human cruelty make belief in this sort of deity irrational. And so on.

In my view, even the most ambitious version succeeds conclusively. There is no evasion, unless the standards of success are set unreasonably high. Those who try to escape the conclusion have to insist that no use can be made of disputable premises, however antecedently credible those premises may be.[1] But philosophers can and do dispute anything. Some, for example, are prepared to argue about the law of non-contradiction. The faithful who claim that the strong argument from evil leaves open a bare possibility—the sort of possibility only a philosopher could cherish—gain a victory in name only.

What interests me here, however, is a simpler argument, one that has been strangely neglected. The standard versions, I said, focus on evil that God fails to prevent. But we might start instead from the evils God himself perpetrates. There are plenty of these, and, in duration and intensity, they dwarf the kinds of suffering and sin to which the standard versions allude.

For God, if we are to believe an orthodox story, has prescribed eternal torment as a punishment for insubordination. There are, of course, disagreements about what it takes to be insubordinate. Some say that the mere fact of not believing in him is enough to mark you out. Others think that you must violate one of the divine commandments. However the test is set up, it is clear that there is some complex of psychological attitudes and actions that suffices for damnation.

The orthodox story is explicit about the temporal scale of the punishment: it is to go on forever. Many of those who tell the orthodox story are also concerned to emphasize the quality of the punishment. The agonies to be endured by the damned intensify, in unimaginable ways, the sufferings we undergo in our earthly lives. So, along both dimensions, time and intensity, the torment is infinitely worse than all the suffering and sin that will have occurred during the history of life in the universe. What God does is thus infinitely worse than what the worst of tyrants did. However clever they were at prolonging the agonies of their victims, their tortures killed fairly quickly. God is supposed to torture the damned forever, and to do so by vastly surpassing all the modes of torment about which we know.

Although those who elaborate the orthodox account are sometimes concerned with the fit between crime and punishment, there is no possibility of a genuine balance.[2] For the punishment of the damned is infinitely disproportionate to their crimes. Even the worst of this-worldly offenders is only capable of inflicting a finite amount of suffering. However many times that offender endures the exact agony he caused, there will still be an infinite number of repetitions to come. Moreover, in each of these repetitions, the torment will be intensified and extended across all possible modes.

This is to assume, of course, that the damned have committed some crime. If the orthodox story supposes only that they fail to believe in God, then the injustice is even more palpable. Alice the agnostic may live a life full of charity and good works, notable for its honesty, fairness, and loving care of those around her. If lack of faith suffices for damnation, then the divine reward will be an eternity of the most exquisite agony.

Varieties of Theism

So I think the usual philosophical discussions of the problem of evil are a sideshow. We seem to strain at the gnat and swallow the camel. Why is this?

Many will say that what I have called the "orthodox story" is a cartoon theism. Real, grownup theists believe something much more sophisticated. The standard versions of the argument from evil prove attractive to philosophical unbelievers because they are taken to deploy only uncontroversial premises, the sorts of premises grownup theists can be expected to have to grant.

I reply that this overlooks two important points. First, the neglected argument does apply against mainstream versions of theism preached all around us. There is a strong case for claiming that the overwhelming majority of Christians and Muslims, both in North America and the rest of the world, are committed to the "orthodox story." There are many passages in the New Testament (and in the Koran) that tell, or presuppose, that story, if they are read at face value.[3]

Second, the reply fails to appreciate how difficult it is to avoid the "orthodox story" while simultaneously retaining the distinctive doctrines of Christianity. To evade the neglected argument, you must contend that prominent passages of scripture should not be read literally. Perhaps there are alternative ways of reading the idea of God's punishment or understanding torment. But we need to hear not just that there *are* such ways but *what* they are.

I concede that the neglected argument doesn't apply against deism. If you simply hold that there is an omniscient, omnipotent, completely benevolent deity but have no views about his plans for rewarding and punishing people in any hereafter, then you can save your energies to defend against the more familiar problems of evil. But, I shall suggest, you will have to acknowledge that your doctrine isn't Christianity.

There are several ways in which you might try to elaborate a more substantial theism. Perhaps you think that talk of *judgment* and of *punishment* isn't to be taken literally. Maybe what happens in this life is that people make choices. Some choose salvation, and others damnation. Those who are damned receive what they have chosen. But if damnation is torment, or if it is a state for which eternal torment is an apt metaphor, then trouble recurs. For if we suppose that the alleged choice is ill informed and irrevocable, then God does evil. He places people in a situation in which they must make a judgment that binds them for eternity, and he knows that some will be so inadequately informed that they will opt for an eternity of torment (or for a state for which torment is an apt metaphor). It is hard to distinguish between God and the parent who equips the nursery with sharp objects galore and plenty of matches, fuses, and dynamite. Moreover, it is very difficult to see how our actual choices could be anything except ill informed. For the world in which we live is one in which we have scanty evidence about any hereafter of potential torment, and one in which those who tell tales about God's judgments and punishments offer incompatible suggestions about what should be done to avoid torment. On many versions of Christianity, of course, our lack of evidence is an integral part of the divine plan, for it is supposed that the greatness of faith consists in the ability to trust in the absence of—or even in the teeth of—the evidence.[4]

Things would be different if those who are damned are stubborn, persisting in their choice even when fully informed. What would these people be like? They must prefer a state of torment (literal or metaphorical) to the alternative of salvation. Why do they see subordinating themselves to God as worse? Perhaps because they set supreme value on their own independence. But, if God is genuinely worthy of our worship, then to be fully informed is to recognize all the attributes that make this so. It is hard to recognize how resistance could survive an eternity of demonstrations of the divine magnificence.

Even if we suspend doubts about the possibility of stubbornness in the face of full information, we can still ask why God fails to prevent damnation. This returns us to the familiar versions of the argument from evil. A standard explanation is on offer: incompatibilist freedom is of supreme value. It is alleged that even an omnipotent, omniscient, and completely benevolent deity who wished to create a world in which incompatibilist freedom was found might have to allow for the existence of stubborn beings who chose eternally to remain in torment.

I reply in two parts. First, I question the supreme value of incompatibilist freedom. Imagine two worlds. In one of these, actions are produced by psychological states, themselves caused by prior psychological conditions and by the pressures of the environment, those conditions and environments in turn being caused by earlier circumstances, all in accordance with the conditions philosophers introduce to allow for compatibilist freedom. In the second world, just the same actions are performed, but in accordance with your favorite incompatibilist account. Why should we think of the second world as a great advance on the first? In what, precisely, does its superiority reside?

If you are inclined to think, as I do, that there is no superiority to be found, you will not be satisfied with the thought that God may have to allow some people who eternally choose damnation. You will think that God could have settled for a world with compatibilist freedom and that he could have set things up so as to keep his creatures out of trouble. So, to escape the problem, theists will have to explain why the value of incompatibilist freedom is so great that it outweighs the extraordinary torment endured by those who continue forever to resist.

Yet even if we allow that incompatibilist freedom is a great value, it's still worth asking why God has arranged things in the way we find them. He could leave incompatibilist freedom intact while doing far more luring and urging than he does. Assuming we have to make a choice, why must it be made through a glass darkly? Once again, God seems negligent, at best.

Instead of substituting our free choice for God's judgment and punishment, theists may contend that we should reinterpret the notion of torment. Lurid anecdotes about unquenchable fire, sulfur, and brimstone are not to be taken literally. Damnation simply consists in the state of being insubordinate to God.[5] This proposal depends on supposing that torment is an apt metaphor for insubordination.

I deny that it is. Contented atheist that I am, my state of alienation from the deity is not one for which torment is an apt metaphor. Christians may respond that this judgment is shallow: From my mundane perspective, I may judge myself happy enough in my denial of God. Once I am fully informed, however, I will appreciate the grossness of my swinish satisfaction, and torment will be an apt description of my insubordinate condition.

Now familiar troubles arise. Suppose, first, that my state of insubordination is unmodifiable: insubordinate on Earth, insubordinate eternally. Then indeed, I can envisage my eternal separation from God as being one of great anguish, as I come to appreciate the glorious bliss that is forever beyond my reach. But, as before, I have been placed in a dangerous situation, one in which my eternal prospects were determined by a choice I was forced to make in ignorance. Once again, I have been treated unjustly.

A second possibility is that I can make amends in the hereafter. When acquainted with the divine greatness and the divine plan, I accede and subordinate myself to God. Now, it seems, the metaphor dissolves. My state of insubordination is remedied, and I am no longer in torment. Perhaps the response will be that my torment endures because of the memory of my past insubordination. But why should the memory cause me more than a pang, if I rightly see myself as insubordinate because of ignorance and as remedying my insubordination in light of the facts? I might come to applaud those who made the correct choice from the earthly perspective, but it would be hard to justify chiding myself so severely that it would amount to anything like torment. Furthermore, if the memory *does* serve as a source of torment, then, once again, God has failed to prevent evil by permitting me to hazard my eternal felicity in a state of radically incomplete knowledge.

The charge was that the neglected argument depended on a cartoon version of the hereafter. I reply that the strategy of reading the scriptures non-literally either fails to take torment as an apt metaphor for the state of damnation or else reinstates the problem. If the texts (and the doctrines drawn from them) are not radically misleading, then God remains as a source of divine evil.

But the strategy has exposed another possibility: what if everyone repents and is saved?

Universal Salvation

It is plainly possible for God to avoid perpetrating evil. He might not punish anyone. Or, perhaps, he might just administer ordinary finite punishments, designed, in some way, to change the psychological condition of those who had resisted him.

I find the option of limited punishment mysterious. Presumably there is some great end that God has designed his creation to achieve, an end that is furthered by the repentance of those who had failed the earthly test. An obvious rejoinder, from those of us who find no great value in incompatibilist freedom, is that God could have saved himself the trouble of limited punishment by setting up the causal conditions so that the resisters didn't go astray to begin with. Even if we acquiesce in the supreme value of incompatibilist freedom, however, inflicting torment seems quite unnecessary. An omnipotent God could be expected to convert resisters by other means—displays of magnificence, for example. If it is suggested that these are not guaranteed to do the trick, that the resistance may persist, then it should also be noted that, under the conditions of incompatibilist freedom, punishment also comes without any guarantee of repentance. Why should sticks work better than carrots?

The idea of limited punishment supposes that God is disposed to punish his creatures so long as they remain insubordinate. If one of us resists eternally, then that person will suffer eternal torment. But perhaps this never happens. All of us may eventually knuckle under. We come to love Big Brother. We find the ministry of love irresistible. Yet this only diminishes the force of the neglected argument. God retains the disposition to punish those who resist, and to punish them eternally if they resist forever. In other words, even if he never inflicts the infinite torment, he is prepared to do so. He is ready to perpetrate evil far in excess of the sum total of pain, suffering, and cruelty manifested in the created universe. Divine evil continues to exist in the cast of the divine will.

Some Christians are universalists. They maintain that God saves all of us. This happens not because everyone eventually falls into line, but because God isn't disposed to punish any of his creatures. Now God is genuinely exempt from divine evil. He neither causes the infinite torment nor has any disposition to do so.

Is universalism really a Christian option? Can Christians afford to deny divine evil? Christianity, properly so-called, requires a redemption. At its heart is the claim that Jesus was born to save us from something. The condition from which we have been redeemed must be truly horrible. What can be horrible enough except for eternal torment?

Finite torment, perhaps. But for the sacrifice of Christ, God would have had to purify each of us individually, and that would have involved significant torment in the hereafter. God envisaged two possible scenarios. In the first, sinful humanity is unredeemed and all of us must be punished before achieving union with the deity. In the second, the crucifixion serves to cleanse us from our state of sin, and no punishment after death is needed. Because God has no wish to punish any of us, he chose the second.

But this apology fails. If each of us can be saved without punishment under the second scenario, then there is no differentiation between those who acknowledge the sacrifice of Christ and those who scoff, between the most devout saints and the greatest sinners. All of us can instantly be forgiven and brought into the bliss of salvation. If that were so, then there would be no need for punishment in the first scenario. The choice is between universal acceptance without the sacrifice of Christ and universal acceptance with that sacrifice. There is no redemption, no distinguishing the faithful from the insubordin-

ate. Alternatively, if salvation is made possible for all by the death of Christ, but some who fail to appreciate this act of redemption need further cleansing in order to be saved, then we return to the idea of limited punishment. Universalism cannot be sustained.

Orthodox Christians think that the sufferings of Jesus give all of us a second chance but that some of us don't avail ourselves of the opportunity. The redemption works for all of us by freeing us from the stain of sin (part of our human condition), but it doesn't provide instant salvation for all. That's why Christian theologians, and Christian preachers everywhere, emphasize the importance of faith, of following the precepts of Christ, and so on.[6] If everyone wins without regard to performance, not only do all these doctrines drop away, but so too does the rationale of the earthly life. If even the most-wicked of people can be immediately forgiven without punishment, then there is no point to our life of trial in the vale of tears.

So if there's a redemption, there'll have to be a distinction between those who take advantage of it and those who don't. What happens to those who don't? According to universalism, they are not to be punished. God will place them in some condition without perpetrating divine evil.

One possible condition would be nonexistence. Those who take advantage of the sacrifice of Christ, the faithful, are called to salvation. The rest of us simply die.[7] You might worry, perhaps, that this is something of a waste. Couldn't God have done better by increasing the fraction of those who would rise to the opportunity? Once again, the theist is likely to sing the praises of incompatibilist freedom. A world with fewer who are saved and more who depart into eternal sleep is better than one in which the ratio of sleepers to saved is decreased (even to zero), if the decrease is purchased by exchanging incompatibilist freedom for its compatibilist counterpart. Even granting that, it seems appropriate to worry about the justice for individuals. Imagine a happy atheist, one for whom the earthly life goes well. From the standpoint of eternity, we might (and God presumably does) observe a life truncated. Our atheist didn't turn to Christ, and so bodily death came as the end. Overall, however, we can see the life in positive terms because of the success of its mundane phase (its only phase as it turns out). The trouble is that other atheists (as well as agnostics and heathen worshippers) have earthly lives that are not so wonderful; some of them indeed endure sufferings that are, by our mundane standards, excruciating (although, of course, their pains are nothing in comparison with those inflicted in the orthodox story with which we started). From the eternal perspective, this life looks like an utter mistake, for its only phase is utterly dreadful. By bringing this person into being, God has brought about divine evil.

The universalist Christian might reply that my assessment is wrong. God creates someone who turns out to suffer horribly. Bodily death comes as the end because, despite having the opportunity for faith, the atheist failed to turn to Christ; the resistance was free (in the incompatibilist sense). Arguments we have met before apply here too. Why is this type of freedom of such great value? Why does that freedom compensate this individual for the horrible suffering? Why not make the inducements to faith a bit stronger?

I think universalists have a better reply. The afterlife is a more heterogeneous affair than people have thought. The point of our earthly lives isn't to divide us into two groups, one to live forever in unimaginable bliss, the other to suffer unimaginable torment. Instead of being tried, we simply discover who we are. Some, perhaps the most fortunate, find out that they are people for whom the adoration of the deity is the highest form of rapture; they appreciate Christ's sacrifice and are summoned to the presence of God. Others resist the Christian message and develop different ideals for their lives. They are assigned to places in the afterlife that realize those ideals for them. Atheist philosophers, perhaps, discover themselves in an eternal seminar

of astonishing brilliance. Each of us finds an appropriate niche.[8]

This fantasy allows the sufferings of our mundane lives to be redeemed. Not all of us are destined for Christian salvation, for God's eternal Sabbath, but everyone will receive a well-adapted reward.[9] God does not treat all of us alike. But there is no divine evil.

Redemption is taken to consist in making available to some, those who freely turn to Christ, the highest form of bliss. We are freed from sin, not so that we avoid the terrors of eternal damnation but so that we have the chance of gaining the most wonderful reward. We are as much freed for as freed from. But as I read the scriptures, the fantasy involves ignoring (or denying) crucial texts. It underplays the importance of sin.[10] And, of course, it passes very lightly over the references to the torments of the damned.

Most Christians follow a version of the religion that is committed to divine evil, evil perpetrated by God. Most, therefore, fall afoul of the neglected argument. Perhaps some do not. Perhaps some are inclined to accept the universalist fantasy I have just outlined. Can that count as a genuine style of Christianity? I shall leave that for the theologians to decide.

Can We Admire the Believers?

Many Christians appear to be good people, people worthy of the admiration of those of us who are non-Christians. From now on let us suppose, for simplicity's sake, that these Christians accept a God who perpetrates divine evil, one who inflicts infinite torment on those who do not accept him. Appearances notwithstanding, are those who worship the perpetrator of divine evil themselves evil?

Consider Fritz. Fritz is a neo-Nazi. He admires Hitler. Fritz's admiration of an evil man suffices, we might think, to make Fritz evil.

But perhaps this is too quick. Fritz's evil character, we might say, arises not from his admiration for Hitler but from his willingness to behave in the same way. Simply admiring Hitler isn't enough. One must also be disposed to emulate Hitler's deeds; and if this disposition is present, one is evil, whether or not the admiration remains.

Modest Fritz is not so disposed. He thinks himself unworthy. "Great deeds are reserved for great men," he says. (Compare: "Vengeance is mine," saith the Lord.[11]) Fritz wouldn't even beat up a defenseless weakling—not even with a dozen of his mates at his side. He might even go so far as to restrain them. "This is the Führer's work, not ours," he argues. Fritz knows very clearly what Hitler would want done. Even though he admires Hitler, he does not do it.

Fritz is evil, it seems, simply because it is evil to admire someone who is evil. Or more exactly, it is evil to admire someone evil in full recognition of the characteristics and actions that express their evil. Evil is contagious, transmitted by clear-eyed admiration.

Some worshippers of the perpetrator are obviously evil. They relish contemplating the torment of the damned. Some of them even think that delight in the eternal sufferings of worldly sinners will be a component of the bliss of the saved.[12] Like Fritz, they may think that inflicting such suffering, or even any suffering at all, is beyond their humble station. They are glad that the perpetrator has instituted a division of labor. Their part is to forgive those who insult them, to turn the other cheek. They are happy in the thought that, by doing so, they will heap coals of fire on the heads of their enemies.[13]

Many other Christians are not like this at all. They are sincerely compassionate; they genuinely forgive their enemies. Yet they knowingly worship the perpetrator. Perhaps they do not like to think about it, but they firmly believe that, in the hereafter, their God will consign people they know, some of whom they love, to an eternity of unimaginable agony. Moved by this thought, they do whatever they can to urge others to join them in faith. Their deep sympathy with the unbelievers is expressed in efforts to persuade others to play by the rules the perpetrator has set. In worshipping the perpetrator, however, they acquiesce in those rules. They are well aware that many will not fall in line with the rules. They think that, if that happens, the perpetrator will be right to start the eternal torture. They endorse the divine evil. And that's bad enough.

Among those of us who do not worship the perpetrator, there are many who admire worshippers of the perpetrator. We admire some of our neighbors, recognizing their honesty, fairness, kindness, courage, and so forth. We admire religious people famed for their selflessness, their courage, or their scholarship—Mother Teresa, Father Murphy, Jean Buridan.[14] Yet we know that they worship the perpetrator. Moreover, since they worship the perpetrator, endorsing his judgments about the propriety of eternal torment for some (including us), the perpetrator's evil extends to them. They admire evil and are tainted by it. In admiring them, we too admire evil. Does the evil spread by contagion to us?

What of those who admire those who admire those who worship the perpetrator? Are they too infected? If admiration transmits evil, then so do chains of admirers of arbitrary length. Eventually, almost every living person will be infected. It is almost impossible to avoid being hooked up to a chain that will terminate, possibly at a very long distance, in admiration of the perpetrator. Ecumenicism only makes matters worse. The more we are prepared to be tolerant in religious matters, the more we'll be prepared to overlook the details of others' theological views; the more we'll focus on their exemplary behavior toward those around them; as more admire the perpetrator's admirers, there will be more people for others to admire, and the contagion will spread.

This will occur even if, someday, there are no more worshippers of the perpetrator, even if nobody remembers the perpetrator, even if nobody remembers anyone who worshipped the perpetrator, even if nobody remembers anyone who remembered worshippers of the perpetrator. The only ones to escape will be the committed misanthropes. Leaving aside those who find nothing admirable in humanity, everyone will be tainted with divine evil.

The conclusion is absurd. It is also depressing. How can it be morally permissible to be tolerant of others and to appreciate their worth? What saves us from chains of contagion?

Perhaps what saves us is that sometimes those who admire are not well enough informed. If Fritz did not know about Hitler's evil deeds, thinking of the Führer only as a strong and patriotic leader who was restoring morale, then the misguided admiration would not mark Fritz as evil. Similarly, if I admire a worshipper of the perpetrator, recognizing that the worshipper appreciates the divine commitment to eternal torment, and if you admire me, not knowing of my admiration of the worshipper but recognizing my (occasional) good deeds, then the taint of divine evil does not spread from me to you. You are in the dark about the source of the evil in me. Like Fritz, you are an innocent. And, perhaps, your ignorance is far less culpable than his.

Admiration, we might suppose, is a bit more selective than the examples suggest. We don't just give it or withhold it. We admire people for particular qualities; sometimes we admire them despite perceived defects. I may admire the worshipper because he does so much for the poor and the sick. If I admire the worshipper despite his endorsement of the perpetrator, I place great weight on qualities that are genuinely good. You may admire me because you take me to be responding to that good. You do not know of my knowledge of the worshipper's acquiescence in the perpetrator's rules, and my decision to give that relatively little weight in my overall assessment. If you did know that, you might have second thoughts about me; you might not admire me after all. So the chain of contagion would be broken.

It is possible, then, to limit the spread of divine evil. Chains of contagion can be broken because admirers are often not fully informed about the attitudes of those they admire, because admiration can be a selective matter, a response to particular qualities. This is probably how things work in actuality. We are not all tainted with evil.

A residual difficulty remains. What of the worshippers themselves? And what attitude should we non-believers have toward our Christian friends? Can they avoid contagion? Can we admire them and not be infected?

If our friends believe the universalist fantasy, there's no problem. They don't worship a perpetrator, and we can freely admire them. But I suspect that the vast majority are more orthodox. They genuinely think that their God will commit those who do not accept him to eternal torment. They may prefer not to dwell on the point, but when they consider it, they accept his judgment. Of course, they do not see this as divine evil. Instead they talk of divine justice and the fitting damnation of sinners. If Fritz is clear about Hitler's actual deeds, he will tend to use similar locutions. He won't talk about evil and genocide but will praise the proper purification of the highest form of culture and the justified wiping out of a disease.

Modest Fritz isn't disposed to persecute the Jews in his neighborhood. Nor are our Christian friends inclined to rain suffering and humiliation upon us. Yet if Hitler, or one of his appropriate representatives were there, beside Fritz and his mates and the potential Jewish victim, Fritz would approve of the persecution's being carried out by the proper authorities. So, too, with the worshippers. If the day of judgment were to arrive now, and they were to stand by and observe God's decision to punish us—their unbelieving friends—they would endorse it. Perhaps they would grieve for the fact that the punishment was prescribed for us; they would be full of regrets that we had not listened to their warnings and urgings; perhaps they would blame themselves for not having done more. But, in the end, they would worship the perpetrator; they would label divine evil as divine justice.

Can we absolve them of evil for their collaboration? We might try to recall the many good things they do, the sufferings they alleviate, the comforts they bring. There is plenty to throw into the balance in their favor. We can admire their compassion, their perseverance, their self-lessness. But can we admire them, despite their preparedness to worship the perpetrator?

The balance seems to tilt in the negative direction. For, as the original neglected argument makes clear, the evil that God causes is infinitely greater than the entire sum of mundane suffering and sin. It is infinitely intense, and it lasts forever. However much pain our friends forestall or relieve, it is infinitesimal in comparison with the torment inflicted on a single individual who receives God's damnation. Yet they are willing to testify to the perpetrator's rightness in passing so severe a sentence. They are prepared to go on worshipping.

Overall, it seems, our evaluation must be negative. They are like the tyrant whose many small contributions to his subjects' welfare pale in contrast to the monstrous repression he will countenance. If we think of them as clear-headed, as fully aware of the character of their commitments in worshipping the perpetrator, we cannot excuse them.

But most of us do, at least most of the time. Are we too conniving at the divine evil? Probably not, precisely because the neglected argument is neglected. The magnitude of the torment isn't taken seriously. We dodge the consequence by keeping it all in soft focus, consoling ourselves with the thought that hellfire and brimstone are mere conceits, that grownup theists have gotten beyond the cartoon scenarios. That is probably the stance most favored by those who worship the perpetrator; starting from their trust in God, they suppose that there must be some nice version of the story, one that will not literally end with billions of damned souls writhing in eternal agony. Can they articulate a nice version that retains the distinctive ideas of Christianity?

Non-believers have been able to excuse their religious friends on the grounds that they are probably not clear-headed about the commitments of their worship. We can think of them as good people who have not seen the perpetrator's dark side. In bringing the problem of divine evil to their attention, I am presenting them with a choice they have previously avoided. Ironically, I may be making it impossible for myself to admire many whom I have previously liked and respected.

Notes

1. See, for example, Alvin Plantinga, *God, Freedom, and Evil* (Grand Rapids, MI: Eerdmans, 1977).

2. Dante's *Inferno* tries to match punishments to crimes and sins. The torment is immeasurably worse than the evil produced by the sinner. Yet the entire arrangement is set up—as the sign at the entrance announces—in the service of what claims to be divine justice, and even love.

3. For a sample, see Matthew 11:20–24, 13:47–50, 18:1–10, 25:31–46; Mark 9:42–49; Luke 10:13–15, 16:19–31, 17:20–37; Romans 12:14–21; 2 Thessalonians 1:5–10; Hebrews 6:7–8, 10:26–31, 12:18–29; James 5:1–3; 2 Peter 2:4–22; Jude 13, 23; *Revelation passim.* Qur'an Suras 82–85, 87–89.

4. Søren Kierkegaard, *Fear and Trembling.*

5. Although Christians are sometimes inclined to offer this identification, unbelievers can find it difficult to grasp. Is the idea that actively opposing God's will is a form of damnation? Or that having the disposition to oppose constitutes damnation? In either case, I'll argue, it's very hard to see why this state should prove painful, or why, if it were painful, the person damned wouldn't change his attitude.

6. See Paul's letters, Romans in particular.

7. Perhaps there could be a version of Christianity emphasizing the Gospel of John and the uncontroversially Pauline letters that adopted this view. In these Christian texts, salvation and eternal life are usually contrasted with a vaguely characterized state of death. I shall leave it to Christian theologians to

decide whether the sorts of passages cited in note 3 can simply be jettisoned.

8   This is the mirror image of the vision of the afterlife offered in a favorite story of the late Sidney Morgenbesser. According to that vision, we find ourselves after death studying Talmud; for some that's heaven, for others hell.

9   Augustine, *City of God* XXII, 30.

10 See Romans, chs. 7–12.

11 Romans 12:19.

12 Most obviously, Tertullian. "You are fond of spectacles; expect the greatest of all spectacles, the last and eternal judgment of the universe. How shall I admire, how laugh, how rejoice, how exult, when I behold so many proud monarchs and fancied gods groaning in the lowest abyss of darkness; so many magistrates, who persecuted the name of the Lord, liquefying in fiercer fires than they ever kindled against the Christians; so many sage philosophers blushing in red-hot flames, with their deluded scholars." Interestingly, this passage is quoted both by Gibbon (*Decline and Fall of the Roman Empire*, ch. XV) and by Nietzsche (*Genealogy of Morals*, essay 3).

13 Romans 12:20.

14 Father John Murphy was a courageous leader in the Wexford battles of the Uprising of 1798. He is much celebrated in popular song.

Chapter 35

Thomas Talbott

THE DOCTRINE OF EVERLASTING PUNISHMENT

I. Introduction

As anyone familiar with recent work on the problem of evil knows, the argument that theism is self-contradictory because evil is itself inconsistent with the existence of God has been remarkably unsuccessful; no one, it seems, has managed to deduce a contradiction from doctrines essential to theism, and Alvin Plantinga's proof of consistency,[1] whether successful in every detail or not, remains a formidable obstacle to any *deductive* argument of the relevant kind. But even if theism in general is consistent—and I believe it is—it does not follow that all forms of theism, or even that the most popular forms, are likewise consistent. Take those popular forms of theism that include the traditional doctrine of hell, the doctrine of everlasting punishment. As John Hick has observed, "misery which is eternal and therefore infinite would constitute the largest part of the problem of evil";[2] and evil of that kind is indeed, I believe, inconsistent with the existence of God. Accordingly, in this paper, I shall examine the traditional doctrine of hell and the various ways in which theists have tried to square this doctrine with other doctrines essential to Christian theism. I shall conclude that *any* form of theism that includes the traditional doctrine of hell, even one that tries to preserve consistency by denying the universal love of God, is in fact logically inconsistent.

By the doctrine of hell I mean the doctrine that, as punishment for their sin, God will consign some persons to a place of everlasting torment from which there will be, very simply, no hope of escape; I mean the doctrine that some of the very ones whom God has commanded us to love, if Christian theology is correct, are thus destined to be, in Peter Geach's horrifying expression, "irretrievably miserable."[3] So far as I can tell, not a single passage in the Bible would require a believer to accept such a doctrine and the whole thrust of the New Testament is inconsistent with it; but that does not seem to be the majority opinion, even among philosophers. According to Geach, "if the Gospel account [of Christ's teaching] is even approximately correct, then it is *perfectly clear* [my emphasis] that according to that teaching many men are irretrievably lost."[4] And Richard Swinburne, another proponent of the traditional doctrine, also seems to rely on the words of Jesus:

> It seems to me that the central point of New Testament teaching is that an eternal fate is sealed, at any rate for many, at death, a good fate for the good and a bad fate for the bad. This appears to be the main point of such parables as the sheep and the goats.[5]

But if the main point of this parable were really that the fate of many bad persons is sealed at death, and a bad fate at that, it is strange that the gospel writer should employ a word, kolasis, that always implies *remedial* punishment, never retribution; as one Greek scholar, William Barclay, observes, "in all Greek secular literature, *kolasis* is never used of anything but remedial punishment."[6] Beyond that is the more fundamental question of how we should understand the words of Jesus, as the gospels have recorded them. Even a superficial reading of the gospels reveals one point very clearly: Jesus steadfastly refused to address in a systematic way abstract theological questions, especially those concerning the age to come. His whole manner of expressing himself, the incessant use of hyperbole and riddle, of parable and colorful stories, was intended to awaken the spiritual imagination of his disciples and to leave room for reinterpretation as they matured in the faith; it was not intended to provide final answers to their theological questions. As Swinburne himself points out, moreover, Jesus never intended for anyone to take the details of his parables literally;[7] the details merely provided a colorful background for the main point. And as I read the parable of the sheep and the goats, the main point has nothing to do with final judgment or the ultimate fate of the wicked; the main point is simply that "as you did it [i.e., performed acts of kindness] to one of the least of these my children, you did it to me. . . . [And] as you did it not to one of the least of these, you did it not to me."[8] the main point, in other words, is a profound observation about the nature of love, one that will play an essential role in my own argument *against* the traditional doctrine of hell.

My aim in this paper, however, is not to assess the biblical warrant, or lack of same, for a doctrine of everlasting punishment; it is to assess the philosophical merits of such a doctrine.[9] I shall argue that, when the doctrine of everlasting punishment is conjoined with other doctrines essential to the Christian faith, a logical paradox arises that proponents of the doctrine have failed to appreciate; as a consequence, a Christian theist must either reject the doctrine as incompatible with Christianity or else admit that Christianity is itself logically inconsistent.

II. Some Varieties of Theism

I shall begin with some distinctions. Anyone who holds the following set of beliefs I shall call a theist:

1   God exists.
2   God is both omniscient and omnipotent.
3   God loves every created person.
4   Evil exists.

And anyone who, in addition to the above set of beliefs, also holds the following belief I shall call a *conservative* theist:

5   God will irrevocably reject some persons and subject those persons to everlasting punishment.

I choose the term "conservative theist" for this reason: though universalism, the belief that God will eventually reconcile all persons to himself, had many proponents in the early Christian church, the Fifth General Council, held in Constantinople in A.D. 553, officially condemned it; as a result, the confessional statements of most Christian denominations now endorse (5) much more clearly than they do (3). It is conservative theism, then, not theism in general, that contains, I shall argue, an *implicit* contradiction;[10] that is, from the above set of five propositions together with certain necessary truths one can deduce, I believe, an *explicit* contradiction. A reasonable theist who accepts propositions (1) and (2), therefore, must reject either (3) or (5).

Now an interesting point about much of the theological discussion concerning hell is this. In a variety of subtle ways, many theologians do reject one of these propositions, either (3) or (5), sometimes without even realizing it, and they are often especially deceptive about their rejection of (3). Consider the following passage from Aquinas:

> God loves every man, and every creature also, in that he wills some good for every one of them. But he does not will every good for every one, and is said to hate some in so far as he does not will for them the good of eternal life.[11]

Does God love every human being, according to Aquinas? It would seem not. That God should will *some* good for each of them during, say, seventy years of life on earth is hardly evidence of love, not when that seventy years is followed by an eternity of separation or, as Aquinas calls it, an eternity of hatred. At the very least Aquinas seems reluctant to commit himself clearly, in this passage, to the truth of (3). And what is true of Aquinas is also true of Augustine, Calvin, and many other proponents of everlasting punishment; so far as I can tell, very few mainline theologians are prepared to embrace (3) with any degree of clarity. Many do, it is true, argue that a final rejection of some persons is compatible with God's *justice* and *moral perfection*, but they then simply ignore the implications of such rejection for divine love. Augustine thus writes:

> Now, who but a fool would think God unfair either when he imposes penal judgment on the deserving or when he shows mercy to the undeserving? . . . the whole human race was condemned in its apostate head by a divine judgment so just that not even if a single member of the race were ever saved from it (sic), no one could rail against God's justice.[12]

Throughout the Enchiridion Augustine also says a good deal more in defense of God's justice and moral perfection; he even argues that God can justly condemn those who die in infancy because they are all drawn from a corrupt mass.[13] Nowhere does he even raise the question, however, of how God could possibly love an infant and still condemn (or reject) that infant for an eternity. At least some theologians in the tradition of Augustine and Calvin, moreover, have explicitly denied that God loves all created persons. According to one such theologian, Herman Hoeksema, God restricts his love to a limited elect; the non-elect, those predestined to hell, are subject to the "sovereign hatred of God's good pleasure."[14] Though Hoeksema no doubt accepts the doctrine of God's moral perfection (however confusedly), he does not accept (3); he is at most committed to

3′   God loves *some* created persons but not all.

Accordingly, anyone who, like Hoeksema, accepts all of the above propositions except (3) I shall call a *hard hearted* theist.

Of course relatively few of those who call themselves Christians today could justifiably be called hard hearted theists; most, even those who may wonder about Satan and other fallen angels, would insist that, because the essence of God is love, God truly loves every person that exists. So for them the question is acute: How could a loving God reject *forever* some of those he loves, however evil they may have become, and subject them to *everlasting* punishment? In the face of such a question, some of the more able defenders of everlasting separation modify the traditional doctrine slightly and do indeed reject (5), in effect conceding that conservative theism is inconsistent. According to C. S. Lewis, for example, a loving God would never reject anyone forever, but some sinners do reject God forever and do so of their own free will; according to Lewis, therefore, the gates of hell are always closed from the inside and hell is populated by those free persons (or those formerly free persons) who have chosen to separate themselves from the loving God forever.[15] Richard Swinburne and Eleonore Stump also seem to hold a similar view, which would replace (5) with

5′ Some persons will, despite God's best efforts to save them, finally reject God and separate themselves from God forever.

Accordingly, anyone who accepts propositions (1), (2), (3), and (4) and replaces (5) with (5′) I shall call a *moderately conservative* theist.

Finally, I should perhaps also mention those Christians who take quite literally a teaching found in the New Testament: the teaching that Christ will continue to reign until he overcomes all opposition and all separation from God—until, that is, every opposing will voluntarily place itself in subjection to him, even as he places himself in subjection to the Father.[16] Such theists reject both (5) and (5′) and affirm instead

5″ All persons will eventually be reconciled to God and will therefore experience everlasting happiness.

Accordingly, anyone who accepts (1), (2), (3), (4), and (5″) I shall call, as a concession to my own biases, a *biblical* theist.

Now in what follows I shall argue that, though biblical theism is possibly true, each of the other specific forms of theism outlined above involves a logical impossibility of one kind or another. But I shall not, despite the title of my paper, have much to say about the idea of punishment or about theories of punishment; the evil of everlasting separation is itself, I shall argue, inconsistent with the existence of God. Some may regard such separation as *punishment* for sin; others may regard it as a natural *consequence* of sin; and still others may regard it as both. Some may even believe that, as punishment for sin, God will subject the lost to various forms of "physical" torment, as if *separation* from God would not be torment enough. But we must finally reject all such views if, as I shall argue, everlasting separation is itself inconsistent with the existence of God.[17] In an effort to show that it is inconsistent with the existence of God, I shall examine conservative theism, hard hearted

theism, and moderately conservative theism in that order.

III. Conservative Theism

According to conservative theists, God's grace has a built in time limit, which they usually think of as the moment of physical death. At that moment one's eternal fate is sealed; if one has sinned and has died in a state of rebellion, God then withdraws his grace forever and all hope for one's redemption passes away. Peter Geach even imagines that, after the final judgment, the line of time will split into two branches neither of which will bear any temporal relation to the other, and so "The damned will know that there is no conceivable restitution for them."[18] Here the difference between (5), which says that God will irrevocably reject some persons, and (5′), which says that some persons will finally reject God forever, is crucial. Conservative theists, as I have defined their position, are committed to more than (5′); they are committed to the idea that God actually *rejects* some sinners (not merely their sin) and thus no longer seeks to bring about their redemption.

But what does it mean to say that God rejects some sinners? Suppose (a) that Rameses freely and forever refuses to be reconciled to God (assuming, for a moment, that this is possible), (b) that nothing God could do would bring it about (in Plantinga's broad or weak sense)[19] that Rameses freely repents of his sin, and (c) that the following subjunctive conditionals are true:

6 If God *could* do something to bring it about that Rameses freely repents of his sin, then God would do it.

7 If Rameses *were* to repent of his sin freely, then God would accept him back as a prodigal son.

Given these conditions, we can perhaps say that Rameses freely rejects God but not that God *irrevocably* rejects Rameses; we could hardly say that God irrevocably rejects someone whom he is always prepared to accept back as a prodigal son. But suppose now that God could induce repentance in Rameses only in the following way: if God were to act immorally or to act contrary to the interest of some other loved one—perhaps some Israelite—then and only then would Rameses repent of his sin. Though the supposition here is, I believe, deeply incoherent, the point I want to make about rejection does not require us to challenge it. If God is always prepared to accept Rameses back as a prodigal son but refuses to act contrary to the interest of others in his effort to win back a lost loved one, it still follows only that Rameses has rejected God, not that God has irrevocably rejected Rameses. Perhaps, then, we can distinguish between (5) and (5′) by adopting the following definitions:

(D₁) For any sinner S and time t, S finally rejects God forever at t if, and only if, (a) S freely resolves at t never to be reconciled to God and (b) there is nothing both within God's power to do and consistent with the interest of all other created persons that would (weakly) bring it about, either at t or at some moment subsequent to t, that S freely repents of S's sin and is thereby reconciled to God.

(D₂) For any sinner S and time t, God irrevocably rejects S at t if, and only if, either (a) at t and every moment subsequent to t God would refuse to be reconciled to S even on the condition that S freely repents of S's sin or (b) at neither t nor any moment subsequent to t does S freely repent of S's sin and the following conditions are met: (i) at t God knows of something both within his power to do and consistent with the interest of all other created persons that would (weakly) bring it about, either at t or at some moment subsequent to t, that S freely repents of S's sin, and (ii)

God's immutable intention at t is not to exercise his power in this way.

The idea behind (D₁) is that if, despite God's best efforts to save him, Rameses finally rejects God forever, then he must sustain a commitment to such rejection in the face of all that omnipotent love might do; and the idea behind (D₂) is that divine rejection must involve something more than a sinner's rejection of God. These definitions do, I take it, permit the possibility that God and some sinner might mutually reject each other. If God could do nothing to induce Rameses to repent of his sin freely and (7) were false anyway, then we could say both that Rameses rejects God and that God rejects Rameses. But these definitions also permit the possibility that God and some sinner might, so to speak, reject the other unilaterally, and that is presumably as it should be. Given (D₂), moreover, (5) has serious implications for the doctrine of God's love; in particular, (5) seems to imply that God is prepared to act contrary to the interest of some of those whom he supposedly loves. And that, I contend, is self-contradictory.

Consider first what it might mean to say that God loves a given person. We may be unable to give a complete account, but we can, perhaps, identify some necessary conditions. It would seem, for example, that God truly loves someone only if he desires the good for, and seeks to promote the interest of, that person. This suggests:

(P₁) Necessarily, God loves a person S (with a perfect form of love) at a time t only if God's intention at t and every moment subsequent to t is to do everything within his power to promote the best interest of S.

Is (P₁) acceptable as it stands? One might object, in the first place, that love for another need not be everlasting; if a person were to die (and cease to exist) or simply to become demented in one way or another, the time may come when that person no longer loves someone whom he or she had previously loved. But that rather obvious point must be set beside another. One very good reason for denying that Johnnie ever truly cared for Suzie is that, at some later time, he consistently acts in unloving ways towards her. Under such conditions, we are apt to say that Johnnie *thought* he had loved Suzie but his love was less than genuine; it was selfish or immature and not true love at all. Even when hatred for another —not anger, but the desire to do irrevocable harm to another—develops at some later time and a genuine offense triggers it, such hatred is incompatible with the kind of love of which the New Testament speaks so clearly. The command that we love our enemies and do good to those who do evil to us implies a kind of love that endures even in the face of great offense. In the case of an omnipotent and omniscient being, moreover, the claim that such a being loves a person for awhile and then ceases to love that person makes no sense at all. Suppose that for fifty years God were to act towards Smith in exactly the way he would act towards someone he loves, and suppose that God were to do so in the full knowledge that forever afterwards he would act towards Smith in unloving ways. Could we then say that God loved Smith for awhile?—that for awhile he intended to promote the best interest of Smith? Surely not. In the case of God, it surely is a necessary truth that God loves a person at one time (in the New Testament sense of *agape* love) only if he loves that person at all subsequent times.

Another possible objection to (P_1) is this. It is not in general true, one might observe, that a loving person does *everything* in his or her power to promote the interest of a particular loved one; most of us are, after all, limited in both knowledge and power. Because we are limited in knowledge, we cannot always distinguish "a helping hand" from harmful interference; and because we are limited in power, we must parcel out our limited supply of energy, perhaps in equal portions, to all of our loved ones (including

ourselves). We cannot devote all of our attention, in other words, to any single individual. But these considerations have no relevance in the case of God, who faces no limits but logical limits and whose responsibility includes the providential control of the entire created order. The only conceivable problem of this kind that God might face would be something like this: If the best interest of one person were logically inconsistent with that of another, then God himself would be powerless to promote the interest of both loved ones and would then be forced to resolve the conflict in accordance with some principle of justice. My own view is that no such conflicts are possible; but for those who think they are, we can alter (P_1) in the following way:

(P_2) Necessarily, God loves a person S at a time t only if God's intention at t and every moment subsequent to t is to do everything within his power to promote the best interest of S, provided that the interest of S is consistent with that of all others whom God also loves.

My own view, I repeat, is that the proviso in (P_2) is unnecessary because (P_1) and (P_2) are logically equivalent, but in any event the main point stands: There must be *some* connection between God's loving a person and his willingness to exercise his power in the interest of that person.

It stands to reason that a loving God would want to promote the best interest of his loved ones, but that may tell us less than we would like to know. A lot also depends upon how we construe a person's best interest. How should we do that? We might note, initially, that a person's best interest must have *some* connection, however difficult it may be to specify, with the conditions of a happy life. But again, we might not agree on what those conditions are; and as Swinburne points out, not just anything that someone happens to call "happiness" will qualify as the relevant kind of happiness. So what *is* the relevant kind of happiness, the kind that a loving God would seek to promote? Though it may include "the absence of unpleasant sensations," it is not, says Swinburne, essentially "a matter of having pleasant sensations."

> There are no pleasant sensations had by the man who is happy in reading a good book or playing a round of golf with a friend, or by a man who is happy because his son is making a success of the business which the father founded. Basically a man's happiness consists in doing what he wants to be doing and having happen what he wants to have happen.[20]

Nor can the relevant kind of happiness, what Swinburne calls "supremely worthwhile happiness,"[21] arise from a false belief or from an action that is morally wrong.

> However, although someone may be fully happy doing some action or having something happen, this happiness may arise from a false factual belief or from doing an action or being in a situation which, objectively, is not really a very good one. Happiness is surely more to be prized according as the happy man has true beliefs about what is happening and according as what is happening is in fact of great value. . . .[22]

Nor can the relevant kind of happiness quickly lead to boredom or quickly fade with the mere passage of time. It must be, I think, the kind of contentment and sense of well-being that could quite literally endure forever; the kind of happiness which, according to the New Testament, can exist only when one is loved by others and is likewise filled with love for others. If that is true, if a community of love is a condition of the highest form of human happiness, then that is why, according to the New Testament, God must first purge us of all the selfishness and arrogance and lust for power that separates us from others, the theological name for which is sin. If love, and only love, makes life worth living forever, then

we can achieve happiness that is supremely worthwhile only if we repent of our sin and turn away from everything that separates us from others.

One could, perhaps, enumerate many more conditions of the kind of happiness that is supremely worthwhile, and some may want to quibble over one or more of the conditions mentioned above. But whatever is to qualify as such happiness, it must clearly be the kind of happiness that God would seek to promote in those he loves. And this suggests:

> (P₃)   Necessarily, God loves a person S at a time t only if God's intention at t and every moment subsequent to t is to do everything within his power to promote supremely worthwhile happiness in S, provided that the actions taken are consistent with his promoting the same kind of happiness in all others whom he also loves.

Once again, the proviso is probably unnecessary, but I include it in order to emphasize the point that God would never promote the happiness of one loved one at the expense of another. So long as God's intention is to do everything he can to promote supremely worthwhile happiness in S—that is, everything that is both within his power to do and consistent with his promoting the same kind of happiness in others—I shall say that his intention is to do *everything he properly can* to promote such happiness in S. Similarly, so long as God meets the condition set forth in (P₂), I shall say that his intention is to do everything he properly can to promote the best interest of S. And that should make the contradiction in conservative theism readily apparent. If God loves all created persons, his intention is to do all that he properly can to promote the best interest of and to cultivate supremely worthwhile happiness in all of them; but if he irrevocably rejects some created persons, it is *not* his intention to do all that he properly can to promote the best interest of or to cultivate supremely worthwhile happiness in all of them. More specifically, conservative theism, as I have defined it, includes both

3   God loves every created person

and

5   God will irrevocably reject some persons and subject those persons to everlasting punishment.

But given (P_2), (3) entails

8   For any created person S and time t subsequent to the creation of S, God's intention at t is to do all that he properly can to promote the best interest of S;

and given (P_3), (3) entails

9   For any created person S and time t subsequent to the creation of S, God's intention at t is to do all that he properly can to promote supremely worthwhile happiness in S.

But unfortunately for conservative theists, (5) at least *appears* to entail

10   There is a person S and a time t subsequent to the creation of S such that it is not God's intention at t to do all that he properly can to promote the best interest of S;

(5) also *appears* to entail

11   There is a person S and a time t subsequent to the creation of S such that it is not God's intention at t to do all that he properly can to promote supremely worthwhile happiness in S.

Since, moreover, (8) and (10) are flatly contra-dictory, as are (9) and (11), conservative theism appears to be self-contradictory as well.

Some, however, may want to challenge both the claim that (5) entails (10) and the claim that (5) entails (11). Such persons may concede that everlasting separation from God is in no one's best interest, and that such separation is obviously inconsistent with supremely worthwhile happiness. But the issue, they will point out, is whether God's intention is to do *all that he properly can* to promote the best interest of created persons, or to promote supremely worthwhile happiness in them; and that is a different matter altogether. But here we must remind ourselves of our definition of divine rejection, (D_2) above. (5) obviously entails

5a   There is a person S and a time t subsequent to the creation of S such that God's intention at t is to reject S irrevocably;

and according to (D_2), God rejects a sinner S irrevocably only if either (a) God does *less than* he properly can to bring it about that S freely repents of S's sin or (b) the following subjunctive conditional is true: *Even if S were to repent of S's sin, God would refuse to be reconciled to S*. In neither case is it God's intention to do all that he properly can to promote the best interest of S or to cultivate supremely worthwhile happiness in S. No conservative theist would deny, I presume, that for any sinner S, *genuine* repentance is in the best interest of S and consistent with the best interest of all other created persons; nor would any such theist deny that repentance is (logically) required if a sinner is to achieve supremely worthwhile happiness. So if God does less than he properly can to bring it about that S freely repents of S's sin, he also does less than he properly can to promote the best interest of S and to cultivate supremely worthwhile happiness in S; and if God refuses to be reconciled to S even on the condition that S freely repents of S's sin, then again it is not God's intention to do all that he properly can to promote the best interest of S or to promote supremely worthwhile happiness in S.[23]

I conclude, therefore, that conservative theism is indeed self-contradictory, and that is why, I believe, that so many theologians have tried to achieve consistency by taking steps in the direction of either hard hearted theism or moderately conservative theism. Those who hold out for a doctrine of divine rejection inevitably back away from the claim that God loves all created persons, and those who insist that God loves all created persons inevitably back away from a doctrine of divine rejection. In the following sections, however, I shall argue that nothing short of an explicit universalism will satisfy the demands of logical consistency.

IV. Hard Hearted Theism

It is unfortunate that, like many traditional theologians, recent philosophers who have defended the doctrine of everlasting separation have had little to say about the nature of divine love; neither Swinburne nor Geach, for example, finally makes it clear whether he is prepared to endorse

3   God loves every created person.

The purpose of Swinburne's discussion is "to investigate whether the permanent separation of the good and bad is consonant with the supposed *goodness* of God,"[24] and the purpose of Geach's is "to show that God is not *unjust* in respect of Hell"[25] (emphases are mine); but neither confronts directly the question of whether God's goodness or justice implies that his love extends to all created persons. Geach is especially fuzzy on this point, as the following passage illustrates:

What I want to emphasize is the moral that if a world perished thus, and all its inhabitants were as if they had never been, it would be nothing against the glory of God. For God a billion rational creatures are as dust in the balance; if a billion perish, God suffers no loss, who can create what he wills with no effort or cost by merely thinking of it. . . .[26]

Though himself a Christian, Geach here articulates an altogether pagan conception of God. A God such as Geach has imagined, one who is utterly indifferent to the fate of billions of rational creatures, is as far removed from the God of the New Testament as heaven is from hell itself. For of course indifference is the very opposite of love. Picture a loving father who sees his son gradually corrupted to the point where the son becomes a vicious murderer, one who is finally apprehended, convicted, and executed. Could the father experience this as anything but a loss? We might even imagine that the father finds it necessary to kill his son, perhaps in order to protect other loved ones; but if the father truly loves his son, or even at one time loved him, he can experience the final separation, the absence of reconciliation, only as a terrible loss. And similarly for God. A loving God could no more watch a billion *loved ones* perish forever and experience no sense of loss than a loving father could suffer the death of a child and experience no sense of loss. Evidently, then, Geach does not take the metaphor of God as a loving father very seriously.

Nonetheless, the harsh tone of Geach's discussion could be deceiving, and he does make one point altogether clear: he rejects as unjust any suggestion that God, having hated some "from the foundation of the world," has *predestined* them to eternal perdition.

some forms of the dogma of Hell really are incredible. Predestinarian theories like those of Jonathan Edwards would be an example. It would be unspeakably wicked to make men's performance of certain actions causally necessary, and then torment the men everlastingly as a punishment for having performed them.[27]

I doubt that many theistic philosophers writing today would challenge Geach's assessment of such predestinarian theories; such theories are fortunately not as popular today as they once were. But the moral argument against such theories, the claim that they are "unspeakably wicked," is not the one I want to stress here. What I want to stress here are reasons for thinking that all forms of hard hearted theism, whether based upon a predestinarian theory or not, are implicitly self-contradictory because.

3′   God loves some created persons but not all

is itself necessarily false.

The first question to ask is whether loving-kindness is an essential or an accidental property of God. If it is an essential property, then it is logically impossible for God to act in an unloving way or for him to bear ill-will towards anyone; it is logically necessary, in other words, that God should love all created persons. So if loving-kindness is an essential property of God, (3′) is indeed necessarily false; that, I take it, hardly requires an argument. But suppose now that lovingkindness were merely an accidental property of God, that indifference towards others, or even hatred of them, were at least logically possible for God. Powerful reasons still remain, I shall argue, for denying that God could love *some* created persons without loving *all* of them and for thinking, therefore, that (3′) is necessarily false.

Consider again the claim, expressed in (P₃) above, that God loves a person only if God's intention is to do all that he properly can to promote supremely worthwhile happiness in that person. In the preceding section, we mentioned several conditions of such happiness, two of which are critical for our present discussion: first, that the beliefs upon which supremely worthwhile happiness depends must be true, and second, that one cannot possess such happiness unless one is filled with love for others. These are, as I have said, necessary conditions, not sufficient conditions; but as such, they also

have some surprising implications and pose some serious difficulties for God. For one thing, if a condition of supremely worthwhile happiness is that one be willing to give of oneself freely in love, then as moderately conservative theists sometimes point out, God cannot simply impose such happiness upon a rational agent by an act of creation; and that difficulty will occupy our attention in the following section. A more relevant difficulty for our present concern is this: A disposition to love, though a necessary condition of supremely worthwhile happiness, can also be an instrumental evil, making a person more miserable, not less; indeed, the more one is filled with love for others, the more one's own happiness is jeopardized by the unhappiness of others. If I should love my daughter as myself, for example, I simply cannot be happy knowing that she is suffering or that she is otherwise miserable—unless, of course, I can somehow believe that, in the end, all will be well for her.[28] But if I cannot believe this, if I were to believe instead that she would be lost to me forever—even if I were to believe that, by her own will, she would become intolerably evil—my own happiness could never be complete, not so long as I continue to love her and to yearn for her redemption. I would always know what *could* have been, and I would always experience that as a terrible, unacceptable loss, one for which there could be no conceivable compensation. Given the right circumstances, therefore, love can render happiness utterly impossible; and herein lies a paradox that hard hearted theists would do well to contemplate.

According to hard hearted theists, God loves some created persons but not all. But that, it seems to me, is impossible, because God's love for one person logically requires that he love all persons. God cannot, first of all, love me without loving all of those whom I love; for if two persons are bound together in love, their purposes and interests, even the conditions of their happiness, are so logically intertwined as to be inseparable. That is why Jesus can say, "as you did it to one of the least of these my children, you did it to me," and the letter known as First John can say, "If any one say, 'I love God,' and hates his brother, he is a liar. . . ."[29] Just as I cannot truly love God and, at the same time, hate those whom God loves, neither can God truly love me and, at the same time, hate those whom I love. If God acts contrary to the interest of my loved ones, then he acts contrary to my own interest; and if he fails to do all that he properly can to promote the happiness of my loved ones, then he also fails to do all that he properly can to promote my own happiness. Here we might try, as a thought experiment, to imagine the impossible: what it would be like for God to love me without loving one of my loved ones. If God were to deceive me concerning his indifference toward, or hatred of, one of my loved ones, my blissful ignorance, being based upon a false belief, would not be the kind of happiness that is supremely worthwhile; and if he were to bring it about that I no longer love this person, that my attitude towards this former loved one is as callused as his, he would again destroy the very possibility of happiness that is supremely worthwhile. In either case, he would be acting in unloving ways not only towards my loved one but towards me as well.

But what about those who are not loved ones of mine? Surely God can love me without loving them, can he not? But even that is by no means clear. For if a person S is not an object of my love, it will be for one of three reasons: either I am ignorant of S's existence, or I know S but not very well, or my capacity for love is not yet perfected. Now if I am ignorant of S's existence and thus do not know that God despises this miserable person, then either my blissful ignorance arises from the false belief that there are no such persons whom God despises or my capacity for love is not yet perfected; if I am not ignorant of S's existence but just do not know S very well, then either I will continue to desire the good for S—just as, for instance, I might desire the good for starving children in Ethiopia—or

my capacity for love is not yet perfected; and finally, if my capacity for love is not yet perfected, as it certainly is not, and God wants me to experience happiness that is supremely worthwhile, then he must continue to teach me the lessons of love until it is perfected. Is it not precisely for this reason that, according to Christian teaching, God commands us to love our enemies as well as our friends? Of course love for a cruel and vicious person is difficult (perhaps impossible apart from the grace of God), and we must always express such love in appropriate ways; such love may even require that, like Jonah, we preach repentance to one whom we regard as an enemy. Indeed, the story of Jonah is most illuminating in this regard. According to the story, Jonah's initial refusal to preach to the Ninevites was an expression of his hatred for them, of his desire to see them literally damned by God; the last thing he wanted was for his enemies to repent of their evil ways. Such hatred is often understandable. I would imagine that many Jews who suffered in Nazi concentration camps would find themselves unable, for a period of time anyway, to forgive their tormentors or to desire the good of repentance for them. But if, as the Christian religion has always taught, the highest forms of human happiness require the ability to love even those who wrong us, and wrong us badly, then God cannot truly love us without loving our enemies, those whom he has commanded us to love, as well.

Let us now review the logic of the situation and try to express the argument more precisely. I contend that

3′   God loves some created persons but not all

is necessarily false. If lovingkindness is an essential property of God, then it is clear that (3′) is necessarily false; but even if lovingkindness is an accidental property of God, we still must do justice to this fact: There can be no exclusiveness in love. If God loves some of us, therefore, he wills the good for at least some of us; but he can will the good for even one of us only if he also wills the good for all of us. A principle, already suggested, that points in this direction is the following:

(P$_4$) It is necessary that, for any two persons, S and S', if S wills the good for S', then God wills the good for S only if God also wills the good for S'.

And (P$_4$) is clearly incompatible with the kind of exclusiveness that we find in Jonathan Edwards and other Protestant theologians. If God truly loves us, then we need have no fear that he will reject some of our loved ones. But (P$_4$) is at least *compatible* with this possibility: a nonempty class of persons who are loved neither by God nor by any of God's own loved ones. So two additional principles are required to rule out that possibility:

(P$_5$) It is necessary that, for any two persons, S and S', God wills the good for S only if God wills that S be the kind of person such that, were S to know of the existence of S', S would will the good for S' as well.

(P$_6$) It is necessary that, for any two persons, S and S', if (a) God wills that S be the kind of person such that, were S to know of the existence of S', S would will the good for S' and (b) God himself wills the good for S, then God wills the good for S' as well.[30]

These three principles illustrate nicely, it seems to me, the sense in which love, willing the good for another, differs from the kind of grasping, possessiveness that we so easily confuse with love. Love is inclusive. If God loves us, then according to (P$_5$) he wills that we become the kind of persons who in turn will the good for all others; and if that is his will for us, then according to (P$_6$) he himself must will the good for all others as well. Accordingly, if God loves

one created person, he also loves all created persons.

My claim for this argument is that, even on the assumption that loving kindness is an accidental property of God, it provides powerful reasons for thinking that (3') is necessarily false. Of course a hard hearted theist may want to challenge either (P$_4$) or (P$_5$) or (P$_6$), but it is difficult to see how; it is even more difficult to see how any Christian could challenge these principles without rejecting some of the clearest teachings of the New Testament. It seems to me, at any rate, that these principles are true and that hard hearted theism is not only morally repugnant: it is implicitly self-contradictory as well.

V. Moderately Conservative Theism

So far I have argued that conservative theism and hard hearted theism are both implicitly self-contradictory, because a doctrine of divine rejection is inconsistent with the love of God. If the argument of the previous two sections is sound, therefore, a doctrine of hell is defensible only if modified in one of two ways: One must either deny that hell is *everlasting* or deny that it is a place of *punishment*. My own view, for what it is worth, is that the language of the Bible is compatible with the first alternative but not the second. Though there is (so far as I can tell) no doctrine of rejection in the Bible, the possibility of punishment in the next life is set forth clearly, and the image of fire, so often associated with hell, makes it clear that God himself is the author of the punishment. But those who insist that the Bible teaches *everlasting* punishment would do well to ask how, for example, the main character in the story of Jonah can lament concerning his punishment in "the belly of Sheol": "I went down to the land whose bars closed upon me for *ever*" [my emphasis], and then speak of deliverance in the very next sentence: "yet thou didst bring up my life from the Pit, O Lord my God."[31]

Be that as it may, moderately conservative theists insist that hell is indeed everlasting for this reason:

5′   Some persons will, despite God's best efforts to save them, finally reject God and separate themselves from God forever.

Essential to such view is, of course, a libertarian conception of free will according to which an action cannot be both free and causally determined by antecedent sufficient conditions. Neither, on this view, can God simply impose a moral character upon someone by a simple act of creation. So if a person continues to make wrong choices, continues to cultivate a rebellious spirit, and continues to reject God's grace for an eternity, then God is quite literally powerless to save that person. In the words of Eleanor Stump, "it is not within God's power to ensure that all human beings will be in heaven, because it is not within the power even of an omnipotent entity to *make* a person freely will anything."[32] And in the words of Richard Swinburne, "Free will is a good thing, and for God to override it for whatever cause is to all appearances a bad thing."[33] Moderately conservative theists need not, moreover, *prove* that human beings have the required free will or that (5′) is true (or even plausible); if (5′) is even possibly true, then everlasting separation of one kind or another is at least *consistent* with the existence of God.

But is (5′) even possibly true? Neither Stump nor Swinburne has much to say about the nature of the choice in question, except to deny that it is causally determined. But a sinner of the kind described in (5′) must make a fully conscious decision to reject God, and not only that: the sinner must sustain a commitment to such rejection for an eternity. Indeed, given (D_1) of section III, (5′) entails

12   There exists at least one sinner S such that nothing God can properly do would bring it about that S freely repents of S's sin;

that is, no action God might perform, no punishment he might administer, no revelation he might impart (concerning, for example, the consequences of rejection) would bring about repentance in S. And nothing weaker than (12) will prevent moderately conservative theism from collapsing into conservative theism, which we have already shown to be self-contradictory. According to Swinburne, "God might well allow a man to put himself beyond the possibility of salvation, even without revealing to him the depth of eternal happiness which he was losing";[34] but a *loving* God would do that only if he already knew that such a revelation would be ineffective anyway. If God could *effectively* do more than he in fact does to save a sinner—without, at the same time, harming others whom he also loves—then God has indeed rejected that sinner; and we are back with conservative theism again.

In support of the claim that (5′) is possibly true, Swinburne also gives a quasi-empirical argument that seems to me beside the point altogether. He points out that our choices tend to "shift the range of possible choice,"[35] so that a series of wrong choices often makes it more difficult to make the right choice in the future. He thus concludes:

it is a possibility that a man will let himself be so mastered by his desires that he will lose all ability to resist them. It is the extreme case of what we have all too often seen: people increasingly mastered by desires, so that they lose some of their ability to resist them. The less we impose our order on our desires, the more they impose their order on us.[36]

But as an argument for the possibility that (5′) is true, that will never do. In the first place, if experience provides examples of persons who gradually become "a prisoner of bad desires,"[37] it provides just as many of those who sink to the depths just prior to a dramatic conversion. So the view that a dramatic conversion is more and more likely the deeper one sinks into sin and rebellion is no less consistent with the empirical evidence than Swinburne's view that such a conversion is less and less likely. But such empirical arguments are beside the point anyway. If through a series of wrong choices some persons become prisoners of bad desires, it is always open to a loving God to release them from their bondage. Is it not precisely the function of the Holy Spirit, according to Christian theology, to release sinners from their bondage to sin?—and if a loving God can do this once, can he not do it again and again? The argument that a loving God would not interfere with human freedom has no relevance in a context where, by *hypothesis*, we are speaking of those who have already lost their freedom, who are prisoners of bad desires. A benevolent physician who treats her patient for his addiction to heroin by readjusting the balance of chemicals in his brain is in no way interfering with his freedom, not even if the patient is incapable of consenting freely to treatment; the man is, after all, already in bondage to the drug. The aim of the physician is to release her patient from his bondage and to restore the possibility of free choice. Similarly, if those in hell are already in bondage to their desires and have already lost their freedom, in what sense would God be *interfering* with their freedom when he releases them from their bondage?

Now Swinburne does have an answer of sorts to this question, and his answer brings us to the crux of the matter:

> It might be urged that no man would be allowed by God to reach such a state of depravity that he was no longer capable of choosing to do an action because of its overall worth. But in that case God would have prevented people from opting for a certain alternative; however hard a man tried to damn himself, God would stop him.[38]

But here, it seems to me, Swinburne has confused two quite distinct matters. It is one thing to deny, as I do, that God would permit someone to slide, inch by inch and through a series of choices made at least partly in ignorance, into a state of irreversible corruption; or to say that God is always prepared to release from bondage those who are imprisoned by their desires. It is quite another to say that "however hard a man tried to damn himself, God would stop him." The difficulty with the latter expression is that of understanding what it is supposed to *mean*. We all have some idea of what it means to fall into evil or to choose wrongly on a particular occasion. But what could it possibly mean to say that some sinners are trying as hard as they can to damn themselves? What sort of choice does Swinburne have in mind here? The picture I get is something like this. Though a sinner, Belial, has learned, perhaps through bitter experience, that evil is always destructive, always contrary to his own interest as well as to the interest of others; and though he sees clearly that God is the ultimate source of all happiness and that disobedience can produce only greater and greater misery in his own life as well as in the life of others, Belial *freely* chooses eternal misery (or perhaps eternal oblivion) for himself nonetheless. The question that immediately arises here is: What could possibly qualify as a motive for such a choice? As long as any ignorance, or deception, or bondage to desire remains, it is open to God to transform a sinner without interfering with human freedom; but once all ignorance and deception and bondage to desire is removed, so that a person is truly "free" to choose, there can no longer be any motive for choosing eternal misery for oneself.

Perhaps we are now in a position to see why those who depict the damnation of a soul so often depict it happening in small increments. A rational agent must lose a good deal of its rationality and its ability to choose freely *before* such a choice is even imaginable. But that also makes it clear why a *free* choice of the relevant kind is logically impossible. However *responsible* one might be for one's ignorance and one's bondage to desire, no choice that such ignorance or bondage determines is truly free (in the libertarian sense); and if one is free from the kind of ignorance and bondage that is incompatible with free choice, one could never have a motive to choose eternal misery for oneself. Accordingly, though wrong free choices are no doubt possible on specific occasions, a free choice of the kind described in (5′) is not.

But suppose now that the idea of a rational agent freely choosing damnation for itself were not, as I have suggested, deeply incoherent. It still does not follow either that (5′) is consistent with other doctrines essential to theism or even that (5′) is itself possibly true. Quite the contrary. We still have every reason to believe that everlasting separation is the kind of evil that a loving God would prevent even if it meant interfering with human freedom in certain ways. Consider the two kinds of conditions under which we human beings feel justified in interfering with the freedom of others. We feel justified, first of all, in preventing one person from doing irreparable harm, or what may appear to us as irreparable harm, to another; a loving father may thus report his own son to the police in an effort to prevent the son from committing murder. We also feel justified in preventing others from doing irreparable harm to themselves; a loving father may also physically overpower his daughter in an effort to prevent her from committing suicide. Now people sometimes draw all kinds of faulty inference from such examples as these, in part because we humans tend to think of irreparable harm within the context of a very limited time-frame, a person's life on earth. It does not follow that a loving God, whose goal is the reconciliation of the world, would prevent every suicide and every murder; it follows only that over the long run he would prevent his loved ones from doing irreparable harm either to themselves or to others, and neither suicide nor murder is necessarily an instance of such irreparable harm. So even if a loving God can sometimes permit murder, he could never permit one

person to destroy the very possibility of future happiness in another; and even if he can sometimes permit suicide, he could never permit his loved ones to destroy the very possibility of future happiness in themselves. Just as loving parents are prepared to restrict the freedom of the children they love, so a loving God would be prepared to restrict the freedom of the children he loves; the only difference is that God deals with a much larger picture than that with which human parents are immediately concerned.

Now I expect that many moderately conservative theists would accept at least part of what I have just argued; namely, that a loving God must prevent one person from destroying the very possibility of future happiness in another. Indeed that, according to Eleonore Stump, is one reason for the creation of hell: to prevent bad people from harming the innocent.[39] But if one accepts that part of the argument, one must, it seems to me, accept the rest of the argument as well. Why? Because it is simply not possible for one to destroy the possibility of future happiness in one-self without, at the same time, undermining the future happiness of other persons as well, perhaps even of all other persons. Consider again the case of my own daughter. If I love my daughter as myself, her damnation would be an intolerable loss to me and would undermine the very possibility of my own happiness, as I have said. Nor will it do to say, as Peter Geach does, that "someone confronted with the damned would find it impossible to wish that things so evil should be happy—particularly when the misery is seen as the direct and natural consequence of the guilt."[40] That misses the point altogether. From the premise that I could not wish to see my daughter both morally corrupt and happy, it simply does not follow that I would not wish to see her happy. Indeed, if my own daughter should become as corrupt and miserable as Geach describes, that would only increase the sense of loss and the yearning for what could have been, the desire to see her both redeemed and happy. And if supremely worthwhile happiness requires that I learn to love my enemies even as I love my own daughter, then the damnation of single person is incompatible with such happiness in me.

I conclude, therefore, that an omnipotent and perfectly loving God would never permit sinners to damn themselves; his love would require him to prevent each of them from undermining the possibility of supremely worthwhile happiness in others. What we need at this point is a picture of how the end of reconciliation could be fore-ordained even though each of us is free in the libertarian sense. And the New Testament does, it seems to me, present such a picture, namely this: The more one freely rebels against God, the more miserable and tormented one becomes; and the more miserable and tormented one becomes, the more incentive one has to repent of one's sin and to give up one's rebellious atti-tudes. But more than that, the consequences of sin are themselves a means of revelation; they reveal the true meaning of separation and enable us to see through the very self-deception that makes evil choices possible in the first place. We may think we can promote our own interest at the expense of others or that our selfish attitudes are compatible with enduring happiness, but we cannot act upon such an illusion, at least not for a long period of time, without shattering it to pieces. So in a sense, all roads have the same destination, the end of reconciliation, but some are longer and windier than others. Because our choice of roads at any given instant is truly free in the libertarian sense, we are genu-inely responsible for the choices we make; but because no illusion can endure forever, the end is foreordained. We are all, says the Apostle Paul, predestined to be conformed to the image of Christ; that part is a matter of grace, not human will or effort.[41]

VII. Conclusion

In this paper I have argued that conservative theism is necessarily false because

3   God loves every created person

and

5   God will finally reject some persons and subject those persons to everlasting punishment

are inconsistent; that hard hearted theism is necessarily false because, even on the assumption that lovingkindness is an accidental property of God,

3′   God loves some created persons but not all

is necessarily false; and that moderately con-servative theism is necessarily false because the kind of choice described in

5′   Some persons will, despite God's best efforts to save them, finally reject God and separate themselves from God forever

is deeply incoherent. Even if such a choice were perfectly coherent, moreover, it would be the kind of evil that a loving God would be required to prevent; his failure to do so would be inconsis-tent not only with his love for the person who might make such a choice, but with his love for all other persons as well. Whether it follows from these considerations, however, that (5′) is necessarily false will depend upon the view of divine omniscience adopted. If a choice of the kind described in (5′) were indeed coherent, and if God had no middle knowledge and no knowledge of future contingencies because the relevant propositions about the future are nei-ther true nor false, then (5′) might likewise be neither true nor false. But in any event, (5′) would be either necessarily false or else neither true nor false.[42]

We are thus left with two alternatives. A theist might adopt, on the one hand, the following nonbiblical idea: Though God loves all persons and wills the redemption of all those who have estranged themselves from him, it is not now certain and not now even true that he will be successful. (Neither, of course, is it now true that he will be unsuccessful.) Or, a theist might adopt, on the other hand, the biblical idea that God will eventually destroy all evil and will therefore destroy all evil-doers in the only way possible short of annihilation: by redeeming the evil-doers themselves. According to the Apostle Paul, the very same "all things" created in Christ will eventually be reconciled in Christ;[43] hence Christ will continue to reign until every opposing will voluntarily places itself in subjection to him. A Christian theist who accepts that view, which I have called biblical theism, can avoid the logical impossibilities present in the more popular forms of theism; that view, at least, is possibly true.

Notes

1   See Alvin Plantinga, The Nature of Necessity (London: Oxford University Press, 1974), Chapter IX.

2   John Hick, Evil and the God of Love (New York: Harper and Row, 1966), p. 377.

3   Peter Geach, Providence and Evil (Cambridge: Cambridge University Press, 1977), p. 123.

4   Ibid.

5   Richard Swinburne, "A Theodicy of Heaven and Hell," in Alfred J. Freddoso, The Existence of God (Notre Dame: University of Notre Dame Press, 1983), p. 52.

6   William Barclay, A Spiritual Biography (Grand Rapids: Erdmans, 1977), p. 66.

7   Swinburne, op. cit., p. 52.

8   Matthew 25:40 and 45.

9   I have tried to set forth some of the biblical grounds for an explicit universalism in the manuscript for a book, which I propose to call, Inescapable Love: Reflection on the Nature of God. See also "God's Unconditional Mercy: A Reply to John Piper," The Reformed Journal (September, 1983), pp. 09–13; and "Vessels of Wrath and the Unpardonable Sin," The Reformed Journal (September, 1983), pp. 10–15.

10   I here use the term "implicit contradiction" in the sense defined by Plantinga. See God, Freedom, and Evil (Grand Rapids: Eerdmans, 1977), p. 16.

11   Aquinas, Summa Theologica, I, Q. 23, Article 3.

12   Augustine, Enchiridion, XXV.

13   Enchiridion, XXIV and XXV.

14   Quoted in G. C. Berkouwer, Divine Election (Grand Rapids, Erdmans, 1960), p. 224.

15   See, for example, C. S. Lewis, The Great Divorce (New York: Macmillan, 1946).

16   See I Corinthians 15: 20–28.

17   A stricter statement would be this. The truth of the proposition: Some created persons will never be reconciled to God, is inconsistent with the existence of God.

18   Geach, op. cit., p. 145.

19   For Plantinga's broader or weaker sense of "bring it about that," see The Nature of Necessity, pp. 171–73.

20   Swinburne, op. cit., p. 39.

21   Ibid., p. 39.

22   Ibid., p. 40.

23   I know of no theologian who actually claims that, for some sinner S, God would refuse to be reconciled to S even on the condition that S freely repents of S's sin.

24   Swinburne, op. cit., p. 37.

25   Geach, op. cit., p. 147.

26   Ibid., p. 128.

27   Ibid., p. 136.

28   That seems to be what the Apostle Paul has in mind when he comments concerning his fellow worker, Epaphroditus: "Indeed he was ill, near to death. But God had mercy on him, and not only on him but on me also, lest I should have sorrow upon sorrow" (Philippines 2:27). Anything bad that might happen to one of Paul's loved ones would inevitably be a source of sorrow for Paul himself.

29   I John 4: 20.

30   The reason for condition (b) is this. If lovingkindness were not an essential property of God and God were in fact malicious and cruel, then God might want S to have a disposition to love S' so that God could torment S with the knowledge that S' is suffering. Condition (b) enables us to rule out that possibility; and given condition (b), the argument for (P_6) is the same as that already given. Suppose that God does not will the good for some person S'. If S has a disposition to love S' nonetheless, then S cannot be happy knowing that God does not will the good for S'; and if ignorance of this fact is essential to the happiness of S, then such blissful ignorance is again not the kind of happiness that is supremely

worthwhile. So even if S is unaware of the existence of S′, God cannot will the good for S without willing the good for S′ as well.

31 Jonah 2:6.

32 "Dante's Hell, Aquinas' Moral Theory, and the Love of God," *The Canadian Journal of Philosophy*, June, 1986, pp. 194–95.

33 Swinburne, *op. cit.*, p. 49.

34 *Ibid.*, p. 51.

35 *Ibid.*, p. 47.

36 *Ibid.*, pp. 48–49.

37 *Ibid.*, p. 49.

38 *Ibid.*

39 Stump, *op. cit.*, pp. 196–97.

40 Geach, *op. cit.*, p. 139.

41 See Romans 8: 29.

42 In another paper I hope to reinforce this conclusion by examining, in somewhat more detail, the kinds of providential control that might be compatible with libertarian free will; in particular, I hope to examine further the options that an omnipotent and omniscient being might have had and how a loving God could be expected to deal with those options.

43 See Colossians 1: 15–20. Though some reputable scholars deny that Paul was the author of Colossians, this pre-Pauline hymn or creedal statement is one to which the apostle would surely have assented even if he were not the author of the letter as a whole.

Chapter 36

Eleonore Stump

DANTE'S HELL, AQUINAS'S MORAL THEORY, AND THE LOVE OF GOD

'Abandon all hope, ye who enter here' is, as we all recognize, the inscription over the gate of Dante's hell; but we perhaps forget what precedes that memorable line.[1] Hell, the inscription says, was built by divine power, by the highest wisdom, and by primordial love. Those of us who remember Dante's vivid picture of Farinata in the perpetually burning tombs or Ulysses in the unending and yet unconsuming flames may be able to credit Dante's idea that Hell was constructed by divine power; and if we understand 'wisdom' in this context as denoting an intellectual virtue only (and not as connoting a mixed moral and intellectual one), then we might agree that only divine wisdom is capable of making something like Dante's hell. But many of us would balk at the claim that love, God's great, pure, 'primordial' love, might play a part in producing a Dantean hell. Consider, for example, Dante's description of the wrathful, and their punishment:

This gloomy stream, when it has reached the foot of the . . . grey slopes, enters the marsh which is called Styx; and I, who had stopped to gaze intently, saw muddy people in that bog, all naked and with looks of rage. They were smiting each other not only with their hands but with their heads and chests and feet and tearing each other to pieces with their teeth. My good Master said, "Son, you see now the souls of those whom wrath overcame."[2]

One of those in this group is Filippo Argenti, a proud and quarrelsome Florentine noble.

While we were running through the stagnant channel there rose up before me a man covered with mud who said, "Who are you who come before your time?" And I said to him, "If I come, I do not stay. But you, who have become so foul, who are you?" He answered, "You see that I am one who weeps." And I said to him. "In weeping and in misery remain, accursed spirit, for I know you in spite of all your filth." Then he reached out to the boat with both hands; but my wary Master shoved him back, saying "Back down with the other dogs!" Then he flung his arms around my neck and kissed me, saying, ". . . blessed be the womb that bore thee!" . . . And I said, "Master, I should like to see him drubbed down into the marsh before we leave this lake." . . . Soon after I saw such a rending of him by the muddy crowd that I still give praise and thanks to God for it; all cried: "At Filippo Argenti!" and the passionate Florentine spirit turned on himself with his teeth.[3]

What we see in the case of Filippo Argenti, then, is a man who was given to wrath during his lifetime and who no doubt caused a significant amount of trouble in consequence, but who is punished for that finite fault and finite trouble with an unending torment of beatings and attacks in the swamp of the Styx. How is love, divine love, supposed to be shown to Filippo Argenti?

Now the problem concerning Dante's hell presupposes a certain notion of goodness. If we did not believe, for example, that inflicting pain is on the face of it evil, we would not wonder how to reconcile belief in a loving God with the claim that Filippo Argenti is perpetually tormented at God's command. But, of course, if this concern over evil is to be the basis for a serious objection to Christianity, it must be founded on the same concept of goodness as that employed by Christians. If we can prove, for example, that the existence of hell is incompatible with the existence of a good God, where by 'good' we mean 'pleasure-maximizing,' the result will hardly distress the Christians at whom it is aimed, because they never thought there was such a God. So before we ponder the problems raised by Dante's conception of hell, we need to consider Christian accounts of the nature of goodness.

There seem to be two main sorts of competing Christian theories concerning what is to count as good.[4] Either God's will is taken to create morality, so that whatever God wills is good just because he wills it: consequently, (TS) right actions are right just because God approves of them and wrong actions are wrong just because God disapproves of them. Or morality is taken to be grounded independently of God, so that God frames his will in accordance with those independently existing standards of goodness: consequently, (TO) God approves of right actions just because they are right and disapproves of wrong actions just because they are wrong. The problem with (TS) is that it constitutes a theological subjectivism in which, apparently, anything at all could turn out to be moral. So although (TS) makes a consideration of God essential to an evaluation of human actions, it does so at the cost of depriving that evaluation of its moral character; because it cannot rule out anything as absolutely immoral, (TS) seems to

be a theory of religious morality which has dropped *morality* as we commonly understand it out of the theory. There have been some interesting attempts to resuscitate one or another version of (TS) in recent years;[5] but despite these promising efforts versions of (TS) are, I think, still more widely known for their faults than for their virtues, and so I will leave such theories to one side. (TO), on the other hand, obviously is a candidate for an *objective* theory of morality, since it does not make moral standards dependent on God's will; but it is commonly criticized on the grounds that it does not establish any essential connection between God and the standards for moral values. It seems to presuppose moral standards which exist apart from God and which God may promulgate but certainly does not produce. Furthermore, it appears as if on (TO) the standards to which God looks for deciding what is moral somehow exist independently of him in a way which seems to be dubious or mysterious and which seems to detract from God's sovereignty.

In the work of Thomas Aquinas, however, there is a philosophically interesting version of (TO) which is able to meet these criticism. I want to show briefly what that version is and how it works, and then consider the results of bringing Aquinas's theory to bear on the problem raised by Dante's hell.

Aquinas's theory of morality relies first of all on the claim that God is simple.[6] The doctrine of God's simplicity is notoriously complicated and controversial, but it sometimes seems more implausible than it really is because the doctrine has been misunderstood.[7] Basically, the doctrine of simplicity is the notion of God's radical oneness, and it is comprised in three claims. First, it is impossible that God have any spatial or temporal parts that could be distinguished from one another as here rather than there or as now rather than then. Hence, God cannot be a physical entity. Secondly, the standard distinction between an entity's essential and accidental intrinsic characteristics cannot apply to God; it is impossible that God have any intrinsic accidental characteristics. And thirdly, even when we have recognized that all God's intrinsic characteristics must be essential, we have to acknowledge as well that it is impossible for there to be any real, metaphysical distinction between one essential characteristic and another in God; whatever can be correctly attributed to God must in reality be identical with the unity that is his essence. Furthermore, for all things other than God, there is a difference between what they are and that they are, between their essence and their existence; to be characterized by a human nature is one thing, actually to exist as a human person is another. But on the doctrine of simplicity the essence which God is is not different from his existence. Unlike all other entities, God is his own being.

Clarification of these claims significantly reduces their counter-intuitive character, I think. In the first place, these claims are limited to God's intrinsic characteristics. The distinction between intrinsic and extrinsic characteristics – or between real and "Cambridge" properties – is a familiar one which is widely recognized although not always easy to draw. I do not know of a satisfactory set of criteria for making the distinction with precision, but perhaps an example will be sufficient here. Ronald Reagan's belief that he is of Irish descent is one of his intrinsic accidental characteristics; his being mentioned in this paper is an extrinsic accidental characteristic of his. Some entities, like numbers or like God in the doctrine of divine simplicity, have no intrinsic accidental characteristics; but no entity, not even a mathematical or a divine entity, can be exempted from having extrinsic accidental characteristics.

Secondly, by 'essential' and 'accidental' here Thomas does not mean what we today usually mean. We tend to understand an essential characteristic as one which a thing has in every possible world in which it exists. This is not what Thomas means by the term, at least not when he applies it to God. Instead what he means is something more like 'ineluctable – or

invariant – within a possible world.'[8] For example, if we think about God as he creates the actual world, at the first moment of its existence, and if we think of the future of that world from that moment on as a branching tree with alternative futures as the branches, then a characteristic of God is essential in Aquinas's sense if God has it on every branch of the tree. According to the doctrine of simplicity, from God's first creating, his nature cannot vary from one branch to another of the world he chooses to create, although he might have chosen to create a different world with which he would have had different relations.

And finally the claim that there are no real distinctions among divine attributes such as omnipotence and omniscience should not be read as saying that the property of being omnipotent is identical with the property of being omniscient. On the contrary, Aquinas is careful to claim that terms referring to standard divine attributes are not synonymous.[9] Rather, on the doctrine of simplicity, God is identical with just one indivisible thing, but that one thing has different effects and appearances. God's talking to Cain is not the same as his talking to Abraham; but that undoubted distinction does not compromise God's simplicity, because these events are to be understood just as various temporal effects of the single eternal act which is God. Similarly, what we call God's omnipotence or God's omniscience is the single eternal action viewed under different descriptions or picked out with reference to different kinds of manifestations of it. Thus, what simplicity requires one to understand about all designations for the divine attributes is that they are identical in reference but different in sense; they refer in differing ways to the single thing in act which is God.

So on the doctrine of simplicity there are in reality no distinctions within the divine nature, and God is in some sense identical with whatever can be really attributed to him. But the respect in which God is devoid of real distinctions does not preclude our distinguishing God's actions in the world from one another and does not require our taking the terms for divine attributes as synonymous. On the doctrine of simplicity, then, there is something inaccurate in saying that God is omnipotent. It is more nearly correct to say that he is identical with omnipotence, but even that statement is misleading. Perhaps the best available formulation is that God is identical with the single indivisible act which he is, one of whose manifestations or partial descriptions is omnipotence.

In this much too brief exposition of a complicated idea, I have given just enough of Aquinas's idea to be able to show one of the uses to which he puts it. To begin with, on Aquinas's view, because God is simple, he is identical with his goodness; that is, in some sense it is true to say that the divine nature itself is preeminent goodness. Thus there is an essential relationship between God and the standard by which he judges. The goodness for the sake of which and in accordance with which he wills only certain things to be moral is identical with his nature. Hence, his sovereignty is not impugned by supposing that he judges in accordance with some objective standard, because the standard is his nature. And by the same token the existence of this standard is not something peculiar or mysterious, as the earlier objection to (TO) supposed, because the existence of the standard just is the existence of God. On the other hand, because it is God's whole nature and not his will alone which constitutes the standard for goodness, not just anything could theoretically be moral but only those things which are consonant with God's nature; and hence the dangers and drawbacks of theological subjectivism are avoided. So, on the doctrine of simplicity, God has an essential connection to morality; and yet that connection constitutes an objective rather than a subjective moral standard.

The doctrine of divine simplicity is one of the pillars on which Aquinas's moral theory is based. The other is Aquinas's identification of goodness and being,[10] an identification which serves to turn what would otherwise be a vague and sketchy metaethics into a functioning moral system.[11] On Aquinas's view, the terms 'goodness' and 'being' are the same in reference but different in sense. 'Being' refers to being, with the sense of something's being actual or being existent; 'goodness' refers to being also, but under the description and with the sense of something's being desirable. (Aquinas, in fact, frequently quotes with approval Aristotle's dictum that the good is what all desire.[12]) The terms 'being' and 'goodness,' then, like the terms 'the morning star' and 'the evening star,' refer to the same thing in reality; both "being" and 'goodness' pick out the actualization of something. But they refer to it under different descriptions and with different senses; and so they are not synonymous, just as the terms 'the morning star' and 'the evening star' are not synonymous although they both refer to Venus.

This identification of being and goodness sounds initially more than a little implausible. It seems to follow from this claim, for example, that the more there is of Ronald Reagan, the *better* he is, so that he should be prevented from dieting as a service to the nation. And it also seems to entail that whatever is is good, and is good solely in virtue of being; but it is our common intuition that many of the things which are are bad. To understand why these and the many other apparent objections which could be raised against Aquinas's theory are not in fact effective against it, we need to understand better what Aquinas means by 'being.'

Put very roughly, the relevant parts of Aquinas's metaphysics are these. On Aquinas's view, everything has a nature; that nature is essential to the thing in question and is necessarily shared by all members of its kind.[13] A description of such a nature is not a complete specification of the characteristics of the thing which has it, but it is a complete specification of the species or genus to which the thing belongs. The standard example given by the scholastics is for human nature. On medieval views, a human being – say,

Nathan — is a rational animal. The description *rational animal* is not enough to pick out Nathan, but it does specify the kind to which Nathan belongs. Anything which is human is a rational animal, and anything which is a rational animal is human. Now on Aquinas's view anything that comes into existence comes into existence as a thing of some species, and for something to be is for it to be a thing of a certain kind. For a human being such as Nathan to be is for a particular instance of the species *rational animal* to be actual. 'Being' in this sense typically means *existence*; and the ordinary sense of the term 'being' is the existence of an instance of some species.

To understand the ordinary sense of the term 'goodness' we need to look more carefully at the description of a thing's essential nature. For Aquinas, human nature is specified by two words, 'rational' and 'animal.'[14] 'Animal' picks out the broader group or genus to which human beings belong. 'Rational,' on the other hand, indicates a capacity peculiar to and definitive of the species. And on Aquinas's view, the nature of anything will always be correctly described in the same sort of way; it will be picked out by a genus and a capacity characterizing a particular species.[15]

As the specific capacity of anything is actualized by being exercised, the nature of that thing is progressively completed or perfected, according to Aquinas.[16] Such a completing or fulfilling of a thing's nature can be thought of in two ways. On the one hand, to the degree to which a thing's nature is perfected or fulfilled, it is a good instance of the kind of thing it is. And so the goodness of a thing is tied fundamentally to its fulfillment of its nature.[17] A thing x of a kind K is a good K primarily to the extent to which it has actualized the capacity specific to that kind. Nathan is good as a human being to the extent to which he has actualized the capacity specific to human nature.[18] On the other hand, as any capacity is actualized, something which was not in fact in being but was only potential becomes actual. Hence, by the actualization of a capacity, being is increased. And it is to such an increase of being recognized or conceived of as desirable that the term 'goodness' refers. In this way, then, the terms 'goodness' and "being" both refer to being, on Aquinas's account; but the ordinary sense of 'being' is the existence of an instance of some species, and the ordinary sense of 'goodness' is the fulfillment of a thing's nature, which is brought about by the actualization of its specific capacity.[19]

On this theory, what makes a human being good as a human being (as distinct from good as a politician or good as a poet) is the exercise and actualization of rationality, which is the capacity specific to human beings.[20] And that the actualization of the capacity for reason makes one good as a human being is explained, on Aquinas's metaethical theory, by the fact that such an actualization constitutes an increase of being, and that the term 'goodness' refers to being. So, to return to the objections I raised initially, Aquinas's theory does not entail that an increase in Ronald Reagan's weight is an increase in his goodness, because his added weight does not constitute any actualization of his capacity for reason. On the contrary, if Reagan's weight gain would make him overweight for his height and build, it would be against reason since being overweight jeopardizes health by increasing the likelihood of premature death from heart attacks (among other things). A person who dies prematurely diminishes his being by losing years of his life; but to diminish being is bad, and to do something bad without an overriding good end which justifies it is irrational. Aquinas's theory also easily meets the other objection, that some things exist but are not good. Because Aquinas takes 'being' and 'goodness' to refer to the same thing, he is committed to the claim that everything which is is good, on a certain interpretation of this claim; but the interpretation warranted by his theory is compatible with the claim that some existent things are bad. For Aquinas anything which exists has goodness in some degree or in some respect, but that degree of goodness is not sufficient to merit calling the thing as a whole good because the ordinary sense of the term 'good' is the actualization of that thing's specific capacity. And so a thing may exist and still be correctly considered bad on Aquinas's theory, because although it has a certain amount of being just in virtue of existing, it falls far short of the degree of being it would have if it had completely actualized the capacity comprised in its essential nature.[21]

Insofar as a good human being is a moral one, for Aquinas a rational action is always a moral action. And the system of values on which one determines which act is rational will also involve the identification of being and goodness. To take a very simple-minded example, it is wrong gratuitously to kill a dog, because it is irrational or against reason to do so. It is irrational to do so because killing the dog is the destruction of some being; the destruction of being is by definition bad; and choosing something bad in the absence of some overriding good which justifies it is against reason.[22]

If we return to the instance of moral evil with which this paper began, the wrathfulness of those punished in the Styx in Dante's hell, we are now in a position to provide the analysis of wrath entailed by Aquinas's moral theory. What is striking about Filippo Argenti is the violence of his reaction to Virgil and Dante; there is an obvious disproportion between what they say or do to him and his reaction to them. And insofar as the strength of his negative reaction is greatly mismatched to the events which provoke it, his reaction is against reason. In general, on Aquinas's view, what makes wrath wrong and what distinguishes it from righteous indignation is that the wrathful reaction fails to be commensurate with the events to which it is a response.[23]

But, of course, the seeming incommensurability of *God's* response to human wrong-doing was the problem with which this paper began. Does Aquinas's theory require us to say that God is irrational in his treatment of sinners as Dante

understands it? I don't think so. On the contrary, I think the claim that God is both rational and loving in the sort of punishment afforded sinners described in Dante's hell is consistent with the rest of Aquinas's moral theory. To see that this is the case, we need to look more closely at Aquinas's notion of God's love.

Put roughly, according to Aquinas, love is a passion that stimulates the lover to desire the good of what he loves and recognizes as good and that results in some sort of oneness between the lover and the object of his love.[24] A full analysis of Aquinas's view of love is beyond the scope of this paper, but the gist of his view can perhaps be appreciated by focusing on his own abbreviated formula: to love a person is to will that person good.[25] Although much more needs to be said about love between human beings, even human love on Aquinas's view has as its main characteristic a desire for the good of the person loved. For God to love a human being, then, involves his doing what it is open to him to do to ensure the most good for that person;[26] but the goodness of anything is the actualization of the capacity specific to that thing's nature, and so to desire the good of anything is to desire the fulfillment of its nature. We can perhaps circumvent some of these clumsy locutions by saying in summary fashion that, for Aquinas, to love something is to treat it according to its nature. Thus God's love for human persons consists essentially in treating them according to their nature; and so, given Aquinas's account of human nature, God's love for a person involves helping to maximize that person's capacity for reason.

Now this account may sound like a cold, even a hateful, notion of God's love; but that is entirely a misimpression. Aquinas's view of love is in fact much more in harmony with our ordinary sense of what love should be than it at first appears to be. To begin with, we should remember that on Aquinas's view to actualize one's capacity for reason is to be a good human being and hence a moral human being. For

Aquinas, a wrong action is an action done contrary to reason, and an action done in accordance with reason is a right action. That is why Aquinas describes a human virtue basically as a stable disposition to act in accordance with one's nature;[27] it is a settled tendency to act rationally, that is, to act morally. There is no denigration of emotion in this elevation of reason, as there sometimes is in later periods among those who glorify reason. On Aquinas's view, for example, anger, unlike wrath, is an emotion in accordance with reason.[28] Wrath is an emotion out of proportion to the events arousing it and so is neither rational nor moral. But anger is an emotion which is appropriate in its degree and intensity for the actions and individuals to which it is directed. That is why when Dante gets angry with Filippo Argenti, he is not himself in danger of remaining in the circle of the wrathful. On the contrary, Virgil, the personification of reason, praises him for his anger in the highest terms, because Dante's anger, unlike Filippo Argenti's wrath, is in accordance with reason.

So to treat human beings according to their nature consists of promoting in them moral actions, emotions not contrary to reason, and in general virtuous states of character. At this stage Aquinas's account should begin to look less cold and more in line with our common notions. We do not, after all, commonly take the best mother to be the one who maximizes pleasure for her children or who clings to them with the most emotion, for example; rather we generally assume that true maternal love involves a mother's trying hard to help her children develop into the best people they can be.

But, of course, disinterested promotion of a child's development into a good human being still falls far short of constituting maternal love; and in the same way, for the same sorts of reasons, we might still be quite dissatisfied with Aquinas's account of love. To find in Aquinas's theory what we sense is still needed, we should remember that, on Aquinas's view, the recognition of the beloved as good and the desire for the beloved's good effect a union between the lover and his beloved.[29] Aquinas dwells at length on the nature and causes of such a union. The lover is moved to seek the presence of his beloved, and the beloved is desired by the lover as another self.[30] Because of his love, the lover seeks an intimate knowledge of the person he loves, and he strives to possess the beloved perfectly by knowing the heart and soul of the beloved. In the resulting union the lover and his beloved come to dwell in each other in that each abides continually in the apprehension and affections of the other.[31] For this reason, Aquinas says, love is called the uniting force.[32] With this part of Aquinas's view of love brought to the fore, the last suspicions that his account is hatefully cold should be stilled.

Now insofar as things can be ranked in terms of goodness, to act rationally is to love more the things which are better; and so since God is preeminent goodness, on Aquinas's view he should be loved most of all.[33] Of course, we may wonder how God can be loved if loving a thing includes promoting its goodness, because God's goodness is perfect and so cannot be promoted. But here it helps, I think, to remember the doctrine of simplicity. God is identical with goodness on that doctrine. So we could perhaps say that the love of God is constituted in part by the desire for and the promotion of goodness; to act out of love for God includes desiring and doing good just for the sake of goodness. If a person does will to do good for the sake of goodness, it is in some sense true to say that his will is in accord with God's will, and to that extent he is in unity with God. So, for more than one reason, on Aquinas's theory, to love God is to be united with him, to some extent during this life and perfectly in the afterlife.

To summarize this very brief account of a complicated part of Aquinas's philosophy, then, for God to love a person – Monica, for example – is for God to treat Monica according to her nature. That means helping Monica to actualize her capacity for reason, which in turn means helping Monica to develop into a virtuous woman who wills the good for its own sake. But the height of Monica's virtue will consist in the love of God, and her love of God will both sooner and later unite her with what she loves. And so for God to love Monica is for God to do what he can to elicit Monica's love of him and in the end to unite Monica with himself. Understood in this way, Aquinas's account of God's love looks less like the repugnantly cerebral doctrine it initially seemed to be and more clearly in accord with our ordinary feeling of what divine love is and should be.

But this conclusion seems to heighten the perplexity with which this paper began. For the suffering of the damned in hell on the view of Dante and Aquinas (and most other traditional Christian thinkers) never ends and never eventuates in redemption.[34] How, then, is their suffering reconcilable with the love of God? Answering this question requires a somewhat closer look at the Christian notions of heaven and hell. On Christian doctrine, heaven should be understood not as some place with gates of pearl and streets of gold but rather as a spiritual state of union with God; and union with God should be understood to involve as a necessary (but not a sufficient) condition the state of freely willing only what is in accord with the will of God.[35] But if this is an appropriate description of the Christian doctrine of heaven, then it is not within God's power to ensure that all human beings will be in heaven, because it is not within the power even of an omnipotent entity to make a person freely will anything.

What, then, is God to do with those who will not be saved? In general (but with some notable exceptions),[36] on Dante's view these are people who have willed to love some finite good, typically their own pleasure or power, in preference to the highest good which is God. They have been irrational in short, either because like the thieves in the Inferno they employ reason in a defective way, just to find the means to an end which is itself against reason, or because they fail to use

reason to govern their passions, as is the case with Filippo Argenti. In either case, so far from actualizing their capacity for reason during their lives in such a way as to become habituated to a love of goodness, those in Dante's hell have become habituated to irrational acts. They have not acquired virtues during their lifetimes but vices, on Aquinas's understanding of the vices: stable dispositions to act contrary to their nature.[37]

This notion of vice is fruitful for understanding Dante's view of hell. On the one hand, the vices, the habitual actions of the damned, are irrational, destructive of the being of persons habituated to them, and hence bad or immoral; and so both the actions and the character of the damned are contrary to their nature. But, on the other hand, the vicious actions of the damned during their lifetime were habitual. By their own choices, as a result of recurrently willing to act in a way contrary to their nature, the damned while alive acquired stable dispositions to act in one or another irrational manner. Now a stable disposition, a lasting state of character, is itself a kind of nature; and we commonly refer to such a state as a second nature, an acquired cast of character which is produced over a period of time by our free choices and which is difficult to change.

So what God has on his hands in the case of those who eventually end up in Dante's hell is persons who will not will what they need to will in order for God to be able to unite them to himself in heaven[38] and who by their repeated irrational choices violating their nature have produced in themselves a second, vicious nature. It is not possible for God to bring such persons to heaven.[39] Should he then annihilate them? To annihilate them is to eradicate their being; but to eradicate being on Aquinas's theory is a prima facie evil, which an essentially good God could not do unless there were an overriding good which justified it. Given Aquinas's identification of being and goodness, such an overriding good would have to produce or promote being in some way, but it is hard to see how the wholesale annihilation of persons could produce or promote being. In the absence of such an overriding good, however, the annihilation of the damned is not morally justified and thus not an option for a good God. On Aquinas's account, then, it is not open to God either to fulfill the natures of such persons or to eradicate them.

The genius of Dante's idea of hell is that it finds an intermediate between these two extremes.[40] On Dante's view, what God does with the damned is treat them according to their *second* nature, the acquired nature they have chosen for themselves. He confines them within a place where they can do no more harm to the innocent. In this way he recognizes their evil nature and shows that he has a care for it, because by keeping the damned from doing further evil, he prevents their further disintegration, their further loss of goodness and of being. He cannot increase or fulfill the being of the damned; but by putting restraints on the evil they can do, he can maximize their being by keeping them from additional decay. In this way, then, he shows love – Aquinas's sort of love – for the damned.

And in the second place, in hell God provides for the damned a place in which they may still act and will in accordance with their nature, their second, self-chosen nature. It is not just a dramatic device to illustrate the nature of the sin that in his *Inferno* Dante makes the punishment fit the crime; it is a philosophical thought as well. Dante does not present hell as God's torture chamber in which the damned shriek insanely to eternity under the torments imposed by God. In fact, in the case of Filippo Argenti, it hardly seems true to say that his pains are imposed by God at all, for what Filippo suffers by way of physical pain is largely a result of what his companions in the Styx do to him and what he does to himself. Filippo's punishment is in a sense a natural consequence of the way he chooses to act. His wrathful behavior elicits the wrathful behavior of his wrathful companions; and his response to their beating him is to tear himself

with his teeth in wrath. Because of the nature he has given himself, the closest Filippo Argenti can come to the natural functioning of a human being is to act in wrath. By granting him a place in which to exercise his wrathfulness, God allows him as much being, and thus as much goodness, as Filippo is capable of. God does what he can, then, to preserve and maximize Filippo's being and the being of each of the damned. In so doing he treats the damned according to their nature and promotes their good; and because he is goodness itself, by maximizing the good of the damned, he comes as close as he can to uniting them with himself – that is to say, he loves them.

In this short paper I have rushed through one major piece of Thomistic metaphysics or philosophical theology after another; their cogency and philosophical respectability are not to be judged on the basis of the scanty treatment I have given them here. In the same way I have emphasized Dante's treatment of the wrathful, leaving aside the various cases (such as that of the damned in Limbo) which would require exceptions or refinements to the general idea I have been at pains to present here. What all this rushing and simplifying has been in aid of is the presentation of the outlines of an idea of Aquinas and Dante which I take to be philosophically interesting, theologically consistent, and artistically brilliant – that in all the sufferings of his creatures, even in the unending pains of hell, God's love is at work.[41]

Notes

1 This paper is an altered version of a lecture given to the Medieval Guild at the University of Alberta. I am grateful to the members of the Medieval Guild and to the other members of the audience for excellent discussion of the paper.

2 I have taken this translation, with some modification, from *Dante's Inferno*. tr. John D. Sinclair (Oxford: Oxford University Press 1974), Canto VII, 103–5.

3 I have taken this translation, with some modification, from Sinclair, Canto VIII, 113.

4 I have taken the discussion of the two sorts of theories of religious morality from 'Absolute Simplicity,' Eleonore Stump and Norman Kretzmann, *Faith and Philosophy* 2 (1985), 353–82. See also Norman Kretzmann, 'Abraham, Isaac, and Euthyphro: God and the Basis of Morality' in *Hamartia: The Concept of Error in the Western Tradition*, ed. Donald Stump et al. (Toronto: Edwin Mellen Press 1983), 27–50.

5 See, for example, Robert Merrihew Adams, 'A Modified Divine Command Theory of Ethical Wrongness' in *Religion and Morality*, ed. Gene Outka and John P. Reeder, Jr. (New York: Doubleday 1973), 318–47; 'Autonomy and Theological Ethics,' *Religious Studies* 15 (1979) 191–4: 'Divine Command Methaethics Modified Again,' *Journal of Religious Ethics* 7 (1979) 66–79; and Philip Quinn, *Divine Commands and Moral Requirements* (Oxford: Clarendon Press 1978).

6 See, for example, *Summa theologiae* (ST) Ia, q. 3; *De potentia* q. 7; and *Summa contra Gentiles* (SCG), Bk. 1 ch. 21–5.

7 For a fuller discussion and defense of the traditional doctrine of simplicity, see Stump and Kretzmann, 'Absolute Simplicity.' Some of the discussion of simplicity in what follows is taken from that paper.

8 This view is argued for at length in Stump and Kretzmann, 'Absolute Simplicity.'

9 See, e.g., *De potentia* q. 7, a. 6; ST Ia, q. 13, a. 4; and SCG, Bk. 1, ch. 35.

10 See, e.g., ST Ia, q. 5, and *De veritate* q. 21 a 1–2.

11 For a much fuller discussion and defense of Aquinas's theory of the nature of goodness, see 'Being and Goodness.' Norman Kretzmann and Eleonore Stump, *Divine and Human Action: Essays in the Metaphysics of Theism*, ed. Thomas Morris (Ithaca, N.Y.: Cornell University Press, forthcoming). For a study of this theory in the medieval period prior to Aquinas, see Scott MacDonald, 'The Metaphysics of Goodness in Medieval Philosophy Before Aquinas,' Ph.D. dissertation, Cornell University, 1985.

12 See, e.g., ST Ia. q. 5, a. 1.

13 See, e.g., *In XII libros Metaphysicorum Aristotelis expositio*, Bk. V. L. 5; nn. 822–6 and Bk. VIII, L. 2, n. 1697.

14 See, e.g., *In XII libros Metaphysicorum Aristotelis expositio*, Bk. V. L. 5, n. 822; Bk. V. L. 12, nn. 916–17 and 931; and Bk. VII. L. 3, n. 1326.

15 Cf., e.g., *In XII libros Metaphysicorum Aristotelis expositio*, Bk. V. L 5, n. 822 and L. 7, nn. 861–4; and Bk. VII, L. 3, n. 1327. For the view that rationality (and other characteristics which are the differentiae of species) are capacities, cf., e.g., *In XII libros Metaphysicorum Aristotelis expositio*, Bk. V, L. 5, n. 825 and more generally Bk. IX, L. 3 and L. 4.

16 See, e.g., *In XII libros Metaphysicorum Aristotelis expositio*, Bk. IX, L. 8, nn. 1856, 1860, 1865.

17 Cf. *SCG* Bk. I, c. 37–39 and Bk. III, c. 6–7, 11–12, and 38–39; and *De veritate*, q. 21, a. 3.

18 By 'has actualized' here I mean something like 'has acquired the disposition to operate in accordance with reason.' According to Aquinas, the function of anything is derived from its characteristic form, which is its first perfection; its function or operation is its second perfection. In the case of man the function derived from the form is living according to reason, and virtue is a disposition to act in accordance with reason. Cf. *x libros Ethicorum Aristotelis expositio* Bk. I, L. 10. See also ST Ia IIae, q. 55, a. 1, where Aquinas describes a virtue as a habit which is the perfection of the rational power proper to human beings. And in ST Ia IIae q. 49, a. 2, he defines a habit as the determination of a subject in regard to the nature of a thing. Moreover, nothing in the locution 'has actualized its specific capacity' should be taken to mean that a moral human being is so solely in virtue of his essence. On Aquinas's view, the disposition to act in accordance with reason is accidental to a person (because it is a habit and thus a quality) and added to his essence. Cf. *De veritate* q. 21, a. 5 and ST Ia IIae, q. 49, a. 2.

19 For more of Aquinas's discussion connecting a thing's goodness and its species, cf. ST Ia. q. 5, a. 5 and *De veritate*, q. 21, a. 6.

20 Cf. ST Ia IIae, q. 71, a. 2.

21 Cf., e.g., ST Ia, q. 5, a. 3, esp. ad 2.

22 This example is misleading because, of course, in any ordinary case killing a dog involves in fact a transformation of being: something inanimate is produced in place of something animate. To show that there is a destruction of being in such a case requires arguing that there is a hierarchy of being such that in the transition from animate to inanimate being is lost. Aquinas clearly does hold such a view; see, e.g., SCG Bk. III, c. 22.

23 Cf., e.g., ST Ia IIae, q. 46, a. 4 and q. 48, a. 3. and esp. Ia IIae, q. 158, a. 1 and a. 2.

24 Cf. ST Ia, q. 20, a. 1 and Ia IIae, q. 27, a. 2.

25 Cf. ST Ia, q. 20, a. 1, a. 2, and a. 3.

26 Cf. ST Ia. q. 20, a. 1 ad 3, and a. 2.

27 ST Ia IIae, q. 71, a. 1 and a. 2. Cf. also ST Ia IIae. q. 58, a. 1, ad 3; Ia IIae, q. 55, a. 1 and a. 2 ad 1 and q. 56 a. 1 and a. 4.

28 ST Ia IIae, q. 158, a. 1 and a. 2.

29 ST. Ia, q. 20, a. 1 ad 3; Ia IIae, q. 26. a. 2.

30 ST Ia IIae, q. 28. a. 1 and q. 26, a. 2; and Ia, q. 20, a. 1.

31 ST Ia IIae, q. 28, a. 2.

32 ST Ia. q. 20, a. 1.

33 ST Ia IIae, q. 26, a. 2 ad 1 and q. 27, a. 3; cf. also Ia, q. 20, a. 4 and la llae, q. 27. a. 1.

34 ST. Ia, q. 64, a 2.

35 Cf. ST Ia IIae, q. 3, a. 1, a. 2 ad 4, and a. 4 ad 5.

36 The exceptions include, for example, the virtuous pagans and unbaptized babies.

37 ST Ia IIae, q. 71. a. 1. and a. 2. and a. 3.

38 For Aquinas, what a person needs to will in order for God to save him is, in general, just the free act of will cooperating with God's grace, which does the work of sanctifying him. For a discussion of Aquinas's views on the role of grace and free will in God's redemptive work, see my 'Atonement According to Aquinas,' in *Philosophy and the Christian Faith*, ed. Thomas Morris (Notre Dame: Notre Dame University Press, 1988: 61–9).

39 This position will be disputed by those Thomists who believe Aquinas sees God only as determining and never determined. For some argument against the attitude of such Thomists, see my "Atonement According to Aquinas."

40 To explicate Dante's idea fully would go beyond the scope of this paper, because it would require a consideration of retributive punishment in hell and its compatibility with divine justice, as well as an evaluation of the doctrine that the damned in hell never repent of their evil and so never leave hell for heaven. As far as I understand it, Dante's idea seems to be that the *retributive* punishment the damned endure is a positive good for them, contributing to whatever spiritual health and well-being they have, and that something in the nature of the human state after death rules out the possibility of any spiritual alteration on the part of the damned. But to do justice to either part of this Dantean idea would require at least another paper; and furthermore, no matter how the evaluation of these doctrines turns out, Dante could, I think, abandon either doctrine and still preserve the essence of his idea of hell. So in the brief discussion of Dante which follows I will leave these other considerations to one side and focus just on the ways in which the Thomistic theory of morality and account of love support Dante's claim that his hell is founded on God's love.

41 I am grateful to Diogenes Allen, Mohan Matthen, Scott MacDonald, and Peter van Inwagen for thoughtful comments and questions on an earlier draft of this paper. I'm especially grateful to Norman Kretzmann for numerous helpful suggestions, and I'm indebted to John Crossett, whose efforts on my behalf made this paper possible.

Chapter 37

James F. Sennett

IS THERE FREEDOM IN HEAVEN?

1. The Dilemma of Heavenly Freedom

Is there freedom in heaven? Regardless of how this question is answered, it seems to lead to problems for traditional theism. These problems arise, in part, because of the standard theistic response to the problem of evil known as the "free will defense." The crux of this argument is the claim that it is impossible for God to create a world in which there is both human freedom and a guarantee of no evil.[1] So, according to the free will defense, human freedom makes logical room for the existence of evil, even if God exists.[2] Therefore, if agents in heaven are free, then either there is the possibility of evil in heaven or the free will defense fails (since it is possible that there be freedom and a guarantee of no evil).[3]

However, traditional theism regards heaven as a place in which evil is completely eradicated – it is not even *possible* that any should arise.[4] The difference between heaven and earth is not simply that earth contains evil while heaven does not. It has been concluded by the best free will defenders that it is possible that there be no evil, even with the presence of free agents.[5] It is only the *guarantee* of no evil that the presence of freedom eliminates. If heaven is nothing more than a place where the possibility of freedom and no evil is realized, then the absence of evil in heaven is purely contingent on the choices of human

beings, and not a matter of God's sovereignty or the nature of heaven at all. But the traditional view of heaven is that it owes its purity to the unmediated presence of God. Heaven is *essentially* pristine, grounded in divine immanence, not contingently so due to the fortunate choices of humans.

Furthermore, if heaven is only evil-free contingent on the choices of its human occupants, then it is constantly in danger of losing its evil-free status, since it is always in the power of those occupants to introduce evil into heaven. But certainly the idea that heaven might yet become a place of sin and rebellion is contrary to traditional theism. In order for heaven to be essentially pristine and free from future corruption, it must be necessarily evil-free – it cannot be possible for there to be evil.[6]

The second option for those affirming freedom in heaven – that the free will defense fails – is conceptually unproblematic. However, it is certainly dialectically undesirable. It is arguable that the free will defense is the most promising philosophical response to the so-called "logical argument from evil" available. At the very least, the free will defense is an extremely important theistic tool. It should be surrendered, if at all, only with great fear and trepidation. If there is any way to avoid its loss, that way is *prima facie* preferable.

So it seems that the theist should answer the question, "Is there freedom in heaven?" with a resounding and unequivocal "No." Neither of the consequences of an affirmative answer – the possibility of evil in heaven nor the failure of the free will defense – is desirable. But a negative answer leads to disturbing consequences of its own. First, it can be argued that traditional theism is committed to the claim that agents in heaven are free. It is clear that the tradition assumes that we will be basically the same people in heaven that we are on earth. Though we may have resurrection bodies, be transformed into the likeness of Christ, and the like, none of this will cause us to lose our specific identities or divorce us in any important metaphysical sense from the people we are on earth. But certainly being free is an important metaphysical property. Therefore, if we will not be free in heaven we will indeed be divorced in some important metaphysical sense from the people we are on earth. So, while it may not be obvious that the Western theistic tradition explicitly endorses the view that agents in heaven are free, it seems that the tradition is committed to such a view. At the very least, the tradition would require some serious rethinking if we were to accept the view that there is no freedom in heaven.

But a more important problem, from a philosophical standpoint at least, awaits the one claiming that there is no freedom in heaven. Free will defenders most often bolster the defense by arguing that human freedom manifests a moral good significant enough to outweigh the evil that occurs if it is permitted.[7] Call this morally significant good the "freedom good." If there is no freedom in heaven, then heaven is lacking the freedom good. Now, if God can justifiably withhold the freedom good from heaven by withholding freedom, then why could he not do so on earth? If he could have justifiably withheld the freedom good from earth and thus avoided the possibility of moral evil, then he is morally culpable for not doing so, and the free will defense fails. Therefore, an answer of "no" to the question of heavenly freedom causes as serious a problem for the free will defense as does an answer of "yes."

So there is a dilemma – what I will call *the dilemma of heavenly freedom*. If there is freedom in heaven, then there are serious philosophical problems. If there is no freedom in heaven, then there are serious philosophical problems. However, I believe that a path can be successfully navigated between the horns of this dilemma. Furthermore, the solution I propose involves some significant theses concerning the conception of human freedom in general, and is therefore of interest beyond the confines of this dilemma. I will say a word or two concerning these theses at the close of this paper.

2. Compatibilism and the Dilemma

The dilemma of heavenly freedom results from the fact that freedom is interpreted in a *libertarian* sense – whether or not an agent performs a free action is causally undetermined. Hence, whether or not evil will result from those actions is causally undetermined, and no one – not even God – can guarantee that freedom will not result in evil.

So perhaps one could escape the dilemma by opting for a *compatibilist* or *soft determinist* view of freedom.[8] On this view, all that is required for an action to be free is that there be no coercion, artificial manipulation, or any other interference with the agent's normal decision-making processes. Such a view of freedom is consistent with determinism. Free actions must simply be determined *in the right sort of way*. Hence, it is consistent with the claim that heaven contains free agents who cause no evil. All that is required is that the appropriate causal structures be sufficient to result in all agents in heaven freely choosing good on all occasions.

Unfortunately, this solution also affords unsavory consequences. If God can avoid evil in heaven with compatibilist freedom, it seems that he could exercise the same option on earth, thereby avoiding evil all together. I argued a few years ago in this same journal that the free will defense entails a libertarian view of freedom – if it is true, or even possible, that all free actions are determined, then God bears some moral responsibility for the evil there is.[9] So an attempt to resolve the dilemma of heavenly freedom by adopting compatibilism encounters the same problem as the original dilemma; *viz.*, it wreaks havoc with the free will defense.

Despite this difficulty, however, I will argue that there is a compatibilist conception of freedom that can solve the dilemma of heavenly freedom. The problems just alluded to come about only if one insists that freedom is compatibilist both in heaven and on earth – that is, that *all* free actions are determined. But if there is a way to argue that heaven has only compatibilist freedom while earth includes at least some libertarian freedom, then the pitfalls can be avoided.[10] This is my strategy.

Such a strategy will strike many as obviously incoherent. Compatibilism and libertarianism are, it is most often supposed, conceptual contradictories. Freedom is either one or the other. It cannot be both, or sometimes one and sometimes the other. Besides, even if it could be, it is unclear how this solves any problems. God would still have had the option of making all freedom compatibilist, and thus avoiding evil while retaining freedom. Nonetheless, I will argue that the most plausible notion of compatibilist freedom is not only one with which libertarian freedom is consistent, but one for which libertarian freedom is a necessary condition. Hence, while God can have only compatibilist freedom in heaven, with its guarantee of no evil, he can do only by surrendering such luxury on earth.

3. The Consequence Argument and Proximate Determinism

I begin with a standard argument against a popular conception of compatibilism – an argument best articulated and defended by Peter van Inwagen. Following van Inwagen, I will call it the *Consequence Argument*. He summarizes the argument thus: "If determinism is true, then our actions are the consequences of laws of nature and events in the remote past. But it is not up to us what went on before we were born, neither is it up to us what the laws of nature are. Therefore, the consequence of these things are not up to us."[11]

I find this argument compelling and will, for the balance of this paper, assume that it is sound. However, I think there has been confusion over exactly what the argument proves if it is sound. It is very natural to see it as an argument to the conclusion that the notions *free action* and *determined event* are incompatible – no event can bear both properties. But the notion *determined event* is ambiguous. To clear up this ambiguity, I introduce the concepts of *proximate* determination and *remote* determination.

An event is *remotely determined* just in case the laws of nature and the state of the world *at any given time prior* to the event entail that the event will occur. (That is, for every time t prior to time t* at which the event occurs, the laws of nature and the state of the world at t entail the occurrence of the event at t*.) An event is *proximately determined* just in case the laws of nature and the state of the world at some time *immediately prior* to the event entail that the event will occur. (For the sake of simplicity, I will ignore the technical difficulties inherent in specifying a notion such as *time t immediately prior to time t*. The intuitive notion is clear enough for my purposes – that there is a time t prior to t* such that t is sufficiently close in time to t* to render any identification of times after t and before t* irrelevant.) An event is *remotely undetermined* just in case there is some time in the past such that the laws of nature and the state of the world at that time do not entail that the event will occur. An event is *proximately undetermined* just in case there is no time in the past such that the laws of nature and the state of the world at that time entail that the event will occur.[12]

Any remotely determined event is proximately determined. However, there is conceptual room for an event that is proximately determined and remotely undetermined. The Consequence Argument entails only that no free action is *remotely* determined. It does not entail that there are no *proximately* determined free actions. More specifically, the Consequence Argument entails that

For every free action A, either

(i)   A is proximately undetermined; or
(ii) A has in its causal history some proximately undetermined event such that it is up to the agent in question whether or not the undetermined event occurs (i.e., a libertarian free action).

The proximately undetermined events referred to in (ii) above may have occurred quite far back in the past. The Consequence Argument entails absurdity only in the notion of a free action with no agent control (in the libertarian sense that the agent is not determined to perform the action) *at any time in the past.* Therefore, the notion of a free action over which there is no agent control at the time it is performed, but which is such that there must be agent controlled events in the past that led to the determination of the event, is not ruled absurd.[13] That is, the argument allows for proximately determined free actions whose causal histories contain proximately undetermined free actions by the same agent.[14]

4. The Proximate Conception of Freedom

It is standard compatibilist procedure to insist that free actions are those that are determined by relevant intentional states of the agent – by some appropriate combination of or interaction among her volitions, desires, goals, etc. For the sake of simplicity I will refer to such a phenomenon as an action being determined by the agent's *character*. It is important to note, however, that I am not committing to any particular psychological or mental states comprising the char-

acter. Any compatibilist view that appeals to an intentional criterion for free action (a feature shared by virtually all significant views) is susceptible to the kinds of points I will raise. Therefore, any of these criteria can be subsumed under the notion of acting "from character."

For all such theories, it is *how* an action is determined that specifies it as free. It must be determined by the agent's character, and not by any illegitimate interference from external forces. It must not be the handiwork of a Cartesian demon, evil neurosurgeon, or brain washing interrogator. It must not be performed at gun point or under any other threat of danger. The agent's character must determine what the agent will do at the time she acts freely – not any factors independent of that character. But, the story goes, it is perfectly acceptable that one's character itself be causally determined to be what it is. The facts and events of one's heritage, environment, upbringing, etc., may together necessitate the character from which she freely acts. So when an agent claims to have done something "of her own free will," she need not be claiming that it was causally contingent that she do what she did. It need only be the case that no causal structures independent of her character determined her action. She and she alone (i.e., her character) provided the causal structure sufficient to determine her action.

I will concede the coherence of the notion of free actions determined by character. In fact, I find such a notion quite compelling at times. When I think of Martin Luther declaring before the Diet at Worms, "Here I stand; I cannot do otherwise," I sense the power of an immovable spirit bound to act from character in the face of great external pressures to do otherwise.[15] I understand the action to be free, though so bound – indeed, I understand it to be free, in part, *because* it is so bound. I can, with little reservation, agree to the claim that there is a coherent notion of determined freedom, and that something like acting from character is a necessary condition for such freedom.

But this cannot be a *sufficient* condition for a determined action's being free. Even if an action is determined by character, it will not be free if the character by which it was determined has been illegitimately influenced by coercion or manipulation. If Luther's refusal to recant is true to his character, but his character was formed through brain washing or Cartesian demonic influence, his action is not free.

In Aldous Huxley's anti-utopian novel *Brave New World*, genetic manipulation was used to lead to character formation for virtually all citizens. Because of this manipulation, the people chose the lifestyles the government intended them to choose, no matter how menial, and desired no others. It is canonical to view these people – and it was certainly Huxley's intention that we view them – as quintessentially unfree. The manipulation of their characters, over which they had no control, disqualified their actions as free – even though the actions were determined by the agents' characters. It is not enough that an action be *caused* appropriately; it must also be determined by a character that has been *formed* appropriately.[16]

What does it take for a character to be formed appropriately? There are many possible suggestions, and it is not my intention to name, defend, or refute any of them. I wish here only to note that we have begun a causal regression that should remind us of the dangers signaled by the Consequence Argument. Any suggestions for appropriate character formation will invoke either all determined events or some undetermined events. If the latter are invoked, the determinist thesis is compromised. If the former are invoked, it could then be argued that those events alone are not sufficient for appropriate character formation. The circumstances in which those events occurred could have been different in such a way as to constitute illegitimate character formation. This contingency could be accommodated only by moving further back in time to specify conditions necessary to assure that the future events leading to character forma-

tion are appropriate. Thus, a regressive pattern is established that must either end in undetermined events under the control of the original agent (i.e., libertarian free actions) or take us back to events occurring before the birth of the agent (as in the case of the *Brave New World* citizens), in which case we run into the Consequence Argument.[17]

So those moved by the Consequence Argument will conclude that determination by character is insufficient to make a determined action free. And the missing necessary condition must involve undetermined free actions by the same agent in order to avoid the incoherence outlined in the Consequence Argument. The most natural explanation for this is that an agent must be responsible for his character formation – *choosing* it by performing certain undetermined free actions at certain points in his life. A character that is libertarian freely chosen is the only kind of character that can determine compatibilist free actions.[18]

What I have in mind is this: many of the character traits we display – honesty, for example, or courage or rudeness or punctuality – were formed in us as a result of consistent behavior patterns that developed into habit. These behaviors were not always habitual, but began as overt, deliberate actions, perhaps taken after not a little pondering and soul searching. So one may be an honest and dependable person today because at critical points earlier in her life she decided to behave in honest and dependable ways, Perhaps she now is so practiced in the art of probity that she responds with ingenuousness and veracity without hesitation or forethought. Her character demands and determines that she do so. But she could not have reached such a state had she not deliberately chosen honestly from among genuine alternatives in the past. My assertion here is that her current determined acts of honesty can be labeled "free" without running afoul of the Consequence Argument only provided that they have in their causal past certain libertarian free actions – *viz*, the deliberately chosen acts of honesty that led to the development of the character trait.[19]

Of course, this scenario is open to the charge that these precedent deliberate actions were themselves the determinate product of her character as it stood at that time, and so the standard compatibilist position would insist. But again such a response would suggest a regression that will inevitably lead back to before her birth, and the Consequence Argument again threatens. I will call this conception of compatibilist freedom – under which compatibilist free actions are causally dependent on libertarian free actions – the *Proximate Conception*. Therefore, there is a consistent ontology of free actions under which there are compatibilist free actions that do not violate the Consequence Argument.

5. The Resolution of the Dilemma

I have made two substantive philosophical claims. First, there is a conception of compatibilist freedom that is consistent with – indeed entails – libertarian freedom: compatibilist free actions are *proximately* determined actions whose causal histories include proximately undetermined free actions by the same agent. Second, the standard compatibilist doctrine of free actions as those determined by the agent's character escapes the Consequence Argument only if the agent's character was formed, at least in part, by proximately undetermined free actions by the same agent. I submit that the most plausible way to think about compatibilist free actions is as those proximately determined by the agent's character, but remotely undetermined, since the character is remotely undetermined. In this section I will outline how the Proximate Conception resolves the dilemma of heavenly freedom.

First, the Proximate Conception allows for freedom in heaven with no possibility of evil. If all free actions in heaven are proximately determined, all that is required is that the characters determining them be formed in such a way as to

determine no actions that cause evil. Nevertheless, the danger in the suggestion of compatibilist freedom rehearsed in the second section of this paper is avoided. Since proximately determined actions are free only if the agent performed some libertarian free actions in the past, there must be the possibility of evil at some time in the past in order for there to be any compatibilist free actions in the present. The dilemma of heavenly freedom is resolved if all libertarian free actions contributing to the characters of agents in heaven were performed while those agents were on earth. That is, the characters are formed on earth, but those characters determine only actions for good once the agents enter heaven.[20]

The Proximate Conception can also avoid the charge that the lack of possibility of evil in heaven entails that heaven lacks the freedom good – the kind of moral good critical to the freer will defense. Consider the conception of *general freedom*. A world segment includes general freedom just in case that segment includes libertarian freedom or (proximate) compatibilist freedom. It can be argued, consistent with the free will defense, that it is general freedom, not libertarian freedom *per se*, that manifests the freedom good. Either libertarian freedom or (proximate) compatibilist freedom is sufficient for general freedom. Thus, any world segment excluding libertarian freedom but including (proximate) compatibilist freedom is a world segment manifesting the freedom good.

One way to argue this would be to suggest that the freedom good is the potential or actual possession of character formed by the self – the ability to become and be the person we choose to be. If this is the freedom good, it is clearly manifested by both libertarian and proximate compatibilist freedom. Hence, the freedom good is not absent from heaven, though libertarian freedom is. One might also suggest that the freedom good is the potential for or actual possession of a certain God-like quality – the quality of self-determined righteousness. Again, this good is manifested by both libertarian and proximate compatibilist freedom, and hence is also present in heaven though libertarian freedom is absent. I believe that either of these goods (and they are not unrelated) is a prime candidate for the freedom good, and can certainly play the role called for by the free will defense.[21]

So any world segment in which conditions for general freedom are satisfied is a segment that includes the freedom good. Since heaven is such a world segment, it does not lack the freedom good. Since the presence of proximate compatibilist freedom entails only that there be libertarian free actions in the same world, and not in the same world segment, there need be no libertarian free actions in heaven in order for the freedom good to be manifest.[22]

The last point to note concerning the dilemma of heavenly freedom is that the Proximate Conception leaves room for the success of the free will defense. Proximate compatibilist freedom in heaven necessitates libertarian freedom at some time in the past. Given the provision mentioned above that all libertarian free actions determining the characters of agents in heaven are performed on earth, it follows that the presence of freedom at any time requires the possibility of evil at some time, which is what the free will defense requires.

6. Responses to a Few Objections

In this section I will address several important objections that have been raised against the points of this paper. First, it has been suggested that the threatened absence of some significant good in heaven does not necessarily forebode a dilemma.[23] After all, unless all significant goods are logically compatible, they cannot all be present anywhere – even in heaven. Furthermore, it may well be that certain sensory pleasures would not be present in heaven, as well as goods dependent on the presence of suffering want, or some other evil – compassion, sympathy, sacrifice, and the like.

I concede all of these points. However, the point generating the dilemma of heavenly freedom is not simply that there is some significant good lacking in heaven.[24] Rather, the point is that the significant good lacking is one such that, according to the free will defense, God is relieved of moral blame for the evil in the world because he could not avoid the possibility of the evil without removing the source of the good (human freedom). The problem then, is this: if God could justifiably remove the good from heaven by removing freedom, then why could he not do so on earth? If he could have, then he is morally culpable for not doing so, and the free will defense fails. The Proximate Conception allows that the good manifested by libertarian freedom be present in heaven, though there is no libertarian freedom there. Yet the problem just elucidated does not arise, because even though God has the option to avoid libertarian freedom in heaven, he does not have that option on earth. If there is to be an essentially evil-free heaven at all, there must be a pre-heaven segment of the same world containing the possibility of evil.

Second, I have been asked if it even makes sense to call proximately determined actions free at all. After all, the agent could not have done otherwise, at least in the sense that vindicates libertarianism and gives rise to the Consequence Argument. Hence, those sympathetic to libertarianism and the Consequence Argument, to whom my paper allegedly appeals, will not be inclined to accept the Proximate Conception.[25]

This objection raises a fascinating point concerning proximately determined actions, especially in light of the kinds of issues that normally surround the free will/determinism debate. While it is true that the agent could not have done otherwise in the relevant sense, it is also true that the agent can nonetheless be held morally responsible for proximately determined actions – even in the sense that libertarians claim soft determinism cannot account for. If agent S is determined by his character to do A, and the relevant part of his character was formed by the performance of libertarian free actions by S in the past, then it makes sense to charge that the moral responsibility accruing to those libertarian free actions transfers through the character to A. S can legitimately be rewarded or punished for A, even though it was proximately determined. For example, if I am rude or dishonest literally by "force of habit," so that I no longer have libertarian control over my obnoxious or larcenous behavior, I can nonetheless be held morally (and criminally) responsible for it, because I developed these habits through libertarian free choices I made throughout my life. But given the standard assumption that I am morally responsible for actions only if I am free in performing them, it follows that my actions are free, even though I could not have done otherwise in the sense that motivates libertarianism.[26]

Finally, I have been asked repeatedly if my position entails a rather stringent doctrine of salvation; viz., that only those who have lived long enough and worked hard enough to develop a character that fully determines actions for the good will be allowed into heaven. I do not believe it does. There is room for some kind of doctrine of sanctification, whereby God supplies upon our deaths whatever is lacking in our character formations to bring us to the state of compatibilist free perfection. I believe this can be worked out consistently by insisting that it is the pattern we establish throughout a life of persistent intentional character building that is critical – not our actually attaining the desired character itself in our lifetimes. By establishing such a pattern we are, in effect, giving God permission to fill in the gap. This is a highly complex matter, and one that must await a fully developed theological encounter with the Proximate Conception for complete explication. For the time being, however, I will claim only that it is not apparent to me that it cannot be made consistent with standard Christian views of salvation and sanctification.

7. The Proximate Conception in Broader Context

I wish in closing to point out two further advantages to the Proximate Conception – one philosophical and one theological. The theological advantage is that the Proximate Conception is compatible with and suggestive of a traditional line of thinking regarding the relationship between life on earth and life in heaven. In theistic circles life on earth is often viewed as a proving and training ground for life in heaven. The choices made for good or evil are directly relevant to the eternal destinies they determine for us. As we form our characters, we set our spiritual compass for that location in which the lives we desire for ourselves are most fully and naturally realized. Furthermore, for those who "choose life," earthly living is a time of training and honing of our benevolent and aretaic skills, so that upon entering heaven we are prepared for a life of compatibilist moral perfection, where our very natures compel us to choose only the good – infallibly *and* freely. Such a state is attainable, but only if we choose, free from any compulsion, to develop that character that will guarantee such a state.

The philosophical advantage of the Proximate Conception I wish to mention is wholly independent of the dilemma of heavenly freedom. The Proximate Conception provides a link between compatibilism and libertarianism that softens the hard line commonly perceived to divide the two doctrines. Earlier I noted that libertarianism and compatibilism are traditionally thought of as conceptual contradictories – if one is true, the other must be false. The Proximate Conception removes this incompatibility and replaces it with a significant conceptual dependence.

I believe that the Proximate Conception can help to account for many of the conflicting intuitions that make both compatibilism and libertarianism appealing in the right conceptual contexts. Of course, a driving intuition behind many compatibilist arguments is a desire to retain complete physical determinism. The Proximate Conception will do nothing to alleviate the fears of those unwilling to allow the universe some elbow room. Neither will it steady the nerves of those motivated to compatibilism by what I take to be the false dilemma of determinism and randomness – the Humean charge that undetermined actions are sheerly random, and hence cannot qualify as free. For those haunted by this bugbear, I can only urge reconsideration of the libertarian alternatives. However, for libertarians who, like me, are struck by the plausibility of many of the points made by the compatibilist camp, the Proximate Conception offers hope for squaring the intuitions stirred by such suggestions with the undeniable – though undeniably puzzling – fact of undetermined freedom.[27]

Notes

1   The literature on this subject is, of course, enormous. A collection of much of the most important material recently produced is provided in Robert M. and Marilyn M. Adams, editors, *The Problem of Evil* (Oxford University Press, 1990). For an excellent survey of the debate from an atheistic perspective, see Michael Martin, *Atheism: A Philosophical Justification* (Philadelphia: Temple University Press 1990), pp. 363–391. Perhaps the finest and most sophisticated development of the free will defense to date is offered by Alvin Plantinga in *The Nature of Necessity* (Oxford: Clarendon Press, 1974), ch. 9, and *God, Freedom, and Evil* (New York: Harper and Row, 1974), pp. 7–64. See also my *Modality, Probability, and Rationality: A Critical Examination of Alvin Plantinga's Philosophy* (New York: Peter Lang, 1992), ch. 3.

2   It only *allows* for evil, however. It is logically consistent to assume that free agents always choose the good, hence never engender any evil. It is this assertion that fuels J. L. Mackie's important criticism of the free will defense in "Evil and Omnipotence," *Mind* 64 (1955); reprinted in Nelson Pike, ed., *God and Evil* (Englewood Cliffs, NJ: Prentice Hall, 1964), pp. 41–67. (Though Mackie assumes a compatibilist

conception of free will, the claim is consistent even with libertarianism.) It is a special strength of Plantinga's free will defense (see n. 1 above) that it succeeds in spite of Mackie's objection. See *Modality, Probability, and Rationality*, pp. 53–62, for a critical analysis of the debate between Mackie and Plantinga.

3   It has become canonical in the literature to distinguish between defense and theodicy in the problem of evil. While the latter attempts to present a genuine explanation for God's allowing evil, the former has a much more modest task. A defense attempts only to show that it is possible that God and evil coexist by sketching out a coherent scenario under which both do exist. A defense makes no claim that the scenario is actual – its possibility is enough to accomplish the task at hand.

So construed, the free will defense does not assume that the actions of free beings actually do explain the evil in the world, or even that there are any free beings at all. It is clear, however, that traditional Christianity does assume that there are free moral beings, and that they are responsible for at least some of the evil in the world. Hence it is easy in discussions of the free will defense for the line between the mere possibility of freedom-produced evil and its actuality to become blurred. I have taken precautions to keep this line distinct, but discover on practically every rereading another technical inaccuracy. This is due, in part, to the fact that I am raising the question of whether or not there can be any freedom in heaven, given that there is freedom on earth. This causes me to dance very close to the line and even occasionally step across it. Nevertheless, it should be clear from the discussion that it is not simply free will as a theodicy that is stake here, but the free will defense itself – the dilemma threatens that it may not even be possible for God justifiably to permit free will and the evil it threatens. I beg the reader's indulgence as the line between defense and theodicy alternately blurs and sharpens throughout the paper. I am certain that there is no place where any blurring of the line compromises the central arguments of the paper.

4   Some theists claim that evil did once arise in heaven, when Satan and his armies rebelled against God and were cast out. At least two responses are available. First, traditional theism in no way *entails* the story of

a Satanic fall, and there are serious questions about whether or not it even represents good biblical exegesis. (A seminary professor of mine once remarked that we owe our conception of Satan much more to John Milton than to any biblical sources.) Second, one might accept the story, yet maintain that the fall of Satan constitutes the final eradication of evil from heaven, so that, consequent to his expulsion, no evil can ever arise again. This line is perhaps representative of most theists who accept the story of the fall of Satan, and still leads to the dilemma that will be explicated.

5 See note 2 above.

6 It would be more accurate to say that it cannot be within the ability of any non-divine occupants of heaven to bring it about that there is evil in heaven. This claim is still consistent with the modal claim that it is metaphysically possible that there be evil in heaven, yet gives rise to the dilemma. However, this is a level of precision that would unduly complicate a secondary point. In a paper that will virtually swim in technicalities, I will take advantage of this one opportunity to sacrifice accuracy for the sake of clarity.

7 While this claim is not, strictly speaking, necessary to the success of the defense, free will defenders most often see the need to go beyond the bare bones claim that the existence of God and the existence of evil are shown to be consistent by the possibility of free will. This need arises because of the rejoinder that God could never make such free beings, since they might cause evil, and he would bear some moral responsibility for any such evil. This rejoinder is usually met by claims concerning the moral value of freedom similar to those presented in the text. Without such development, the free will defense lacks the dialectically essential element that God would, in some possible world, allow the possibility of evil by creating free beings.

This move is prominent throughout Plantinga's treatment. Plantinga focuses on the moral good that can only be done if people freely choose to perform certain actions. Early in his defense, Plantinga gives "a preliminary statement of the Free Will Defense" thus: "A world containing creatures who are sometimes significantly free (and freely prefer more good than evil actions) is more

valuable, all else being equal, than a world containing no free creatures at all" (Nature of Necessity, p. 166). Later in his discussion he characterizes the free will defense claim as "God is omnipotent and it was not within his power to create a world containing moral good but no moral evil" (p. 184). Finally, at the end of his discussion, he notes, "Of course, it is up to God whether to create free creatures at all; but if he aims to produce moral good, then he must create significantly free creatures upon whose cooperation he must depend" (p. 190, emphasis mine).

8 In "The Free Will Defense and Determinism," Faith and Philosophy 8 (1991): 341, I make a modal distinction between soft determinism and compatibilism. While both assert the compatibility of determinism and freedom, only the soft determinist commits to the actuality of either. Hence it is possible to be a compatibilist, yet hold that determinism is in fact false, or that there are in fact no free actions, or even that there are in fact free actions that are not determined. I also distinguish between weak and strong compatibilism. The former has all these options open, while the latter commits to the necessary truth of If there are any free actions, they are determined, and thus does not have the final option open. As will be seen, the present paper is, in part, a presentation of a weak compatibilist conception that entails that there are some undetermined free actions.

9 "The Free Will Defense and Determinism," pp. 340–353.

10 This conclusion is still consistent with my argument in "The Free Will Defense and Determinism," though the conclusion of the latter needs to be stated more specifically: the free will defense entails that there are some libertarian free actions if there are any free actions at all. But the compatibilist conception I will argue for here also entails this claim.

11 An Essay on Free Will (Oxford: Clarendon Press, 1984), p. 16. Van Inwagen offers three highly sophisticated versions of this argument in chapter three of his book, and defends them against many objections. For substantive rejoinders to this argument, see John Fischer, "Van Inwagen on Free Will," Philosophical Quarterly 36 (1986): 252–260 and Terrance Horgan, "Compatibilism and the

Consequence Argument," *Philosophical Studies* 47 (1985): 339–356.

12 I take it as obvious that, if there is a time t prior to t*, such that the laws of nature and the state of the world at t entail that E occurs at time t*, then the laws of nature and the state of the world at every time subsequent to t and prior to t* entail that E occurs at t*. Therefore, if there is no time in the *immediate* past at which the event is determined to occur, then there is no time in the past *at all* at which the event is determined to occur.

13 Libertarian *extraordinaire* Robert Kane argues for just such a conception of free will. (*The Significance of Free Will*, New York: Oxford University Press, 1996; see, e.g., pp. 73–78.) While I developed the ideas of this paper before examining Kane's work, it is quite reassuring to find so important a voice in the free will/determinism debate agreeing with me.

14 Note that it is necessary that at least some of the undetermined events in the action's causal history be free actions performed *by the same agent*. If a proximately determined action could have only indeterminate causal elements that are either not free actions or free actions performed by some other agent, then it could be easily argued – analogous to the Consequence Argument – that such an action is no more "up to" the agent than a remotely determined action.

15 According to church historian Roland Bainton, this famous saying of Luther's is missing from the transcription of the trial at Worms, and it is questionable whether or not Luther actually said it. Like Bogart's "Play it again, Sam," or Mae West's "Why don't you come up and see me sometime?" Luther may have become identified with an epithet for which he was not responsible. Nevertheless, the remark undoubtedly reflects Luther's sentiments, and its rhetorical force remains for the purposes of this paper. (Qualifications such as this are the price we inevitably pay for allowing historians access to so precious a commodity as cultural myth.)

16 The *Brave New World* brand of control is what Kane labels "covert, non-constraining control." He sites Huxley in his explication, but concentrates on the control exerted in B. F. Skinner's novel *Walden Two* (Kane, pp. 64f). Kane acknowledges that there is a brand of freedom that the inhabitants of the brave new world and Walden colony possess, but argues that it is not the kind of freedom that allows for ultimate moral responsibility.

17 Needless to say, this argument is far too brief and assumes far too much. However, fleshing it out is well beyond the scope of this paper. Suffice it to say that this paper is addressed primarily to those who share my affinity for the Consequence Argument, yet who find the implications of a strictly libertarian doctrine of freedom bothersome when they consider either the Luther-type cases of apparently determined freedom or the implications of libertarianism and the free will defense for the question of freedom in heaven. In short, the paper is for those who believe the dilemma is real, and this would rule out compatibilists unmoved by the Consequence Argument.

18 Kane develops a similar notion in great detail in chapter five of *The Significance of Free Will*. He argues that a condition he calls "Ultimate Responsibility" is necessary in the causal history of my free actions, and an agent is ultimately responsible for an action only if the action is undetermined.

19 Kane calls these "Self-Forming Actions," and holds that they are the actions for which Ultimate Responsibility is a necessary condition (see above note).

20 Notice, incidentally, that it is a consequence of this position that heaven *per se* cannot be a possible world. It can only be a part, or segment, of some world in which there is libertarian freedom in some other segment that does not include heaven. However, this consequence holds little danger for traditional theism, since heaven in normally thought of as a segment of the actual world, and not a possible world in itself. For an argument to the conclusion that heaven is not a possible world and implications of such a conclusion for theism, see Donald Erlandson and Charles Sayward, "Is Heaven a Possible World?" *International Journal for Philosophy of Religion* 12 (1981): 55–58.

21 Even more to the point is Plantinga's suggestion that the existence of any moral good at all is dependent on the existence of "significant" freedom. In this case the freedom good would simply be the conglomeration of all moral good. Under the Proximate Conception, moral good can be accomplished even through proximately

522 James F. Sennett

determined actions, provided they are remotely undetermined.

Note, by the way, that Plantinga's conception of the freedom good makes the case that there must be freedom in heaven even stronger. If there is no freedom in heaven, then there is no moral good in heaven – a suggestion bordering on the ludicrous.

22 One might object that my use of the notion of *manifestation* of good won't do. Libertarian freedom *just is* a significant good, and if it is missing, so is the good. My only reply to this position is that it gives rise to the dilemma of heavenly freedom, while my approach resolves it. Furthermore, my approach does not seem to sacrifice any of the philosophical import of the identification of libertarian freedom with good – most notably, it still supplies the necessary philosophical fuel to power the free will defense.

Michael Gorman has suggested a rather clever alternative response to this objection. Perhaps, though libertarian freedom is a significant good, proximate compatibilist freedom is even better. So, if God (*per impossible*) could create earth with only the latter, he would. Since proximate compatibilist freedom requires libertarian freedom at some prior time, the best world God could create would contain not a heaven and earth with libertarian freedom, but an earth with libertarian freedom and a heaven with proximate compatibilist freedom. Thus, God permits libertarian freedom on earth not only to provide a significant good on earth, but also to make a greater good possible in heaven.

23 This objection was raised by Philip Quinn in written comments.

24 In fairness to Quinn (see above note), I must point out that in earlier drafts I equivocated on this point. I cleared up the ambiguity and developed the position that follows as a result of pondering Quinn's original objection.

25 This objection was raised in conversation by Tim O'Connor, and subsequent discussion with him aided greatly in my proposed solution.

26 So, interestingly enough, if the Proximate Conception of freedom is coherent, then it is indeed possible for S to be free in performing A, even though S could not have done other than A – a conclusion quite significant for the general debate over free will and determinism. Robert Kane argues that it is the matter of ultimate responsibility, not simply of "could have done otherwise," that is at stake in the Consequence Argument (pp. 75–78).

27 I thank Keith Cooper, Timothy O'Connor, and Mel Stewart for very helpful discussions on previous drafts of this paper. Previous versions were read and discussed before the philosophy department at Pacific Lutheran University, at the 1992 Intermountain Meetings of the Society of Christian Philosophers at Brigham Young University, at a colloquy sponsored by the Palm Beach Atlantic College philosophy club, and at the 1992 American Philosophical Association Eastern Division Meetings in Washington, D.C. I thank participants in all of these forums for their helpful comments and questions. I offer special thanks to Philip Quinn for characteristically helpful and lucid prepared comments at the APA meetings. Finally, I thank Bill Wainwright and two anonymous referees for *Faith and Philosophy* for final refining comments that helped bring this paper (at long last!) to publishable form.

PART 6

Religion and Contemporary Life

INTRODUCTION TO PART 6

PHILOSOPHICAL OPPOSITION TO RELIGIOUS BELIEF is nothing new, and can be found throughout the history of western philosophy. For example, while Epicurus did not explicitly deny the existence of the gods, he argued that even if they did exist they would be unconcerned with human affairs, and thus irrelevant to human life. The philosophical attacks on religion by Hume, Nietzsche, Marx, and others are well known. But in recent years, religion has been brought to the forefront of contemporary life in novel ways. This final section focuses on some of the roles that religion plays in contemporary debates regarding science, education, and politics. While these issues are varied, they all highlight ways in which religion is being debated in the public sphere.

One reason for the resurgence of attention to religion in the public sphere is the highly visible work of a number of leading philosophers who actively, and often quite aggressively, argue for atheism in works aimed at the general public, many of which have become best-sellers. Included in this set are not only Daniel Dennett's *Breaking the Spell* and Sam Harris' *Letters to a Christian Nation*, but also the more confrontationally titled *The God Delusion* by Richard Dawkins and *God is Not Great: How Religion Poisons Everything* by Christopher Hitchens. In an article in the November 2006 issue of *Wired* magazine, Gary Wolf titled these authors "the New Atheists": "The New Atheists will not let us off the hook simply because we are not doctrinaire believers. They condemn not just belief in God but respect for belief in God. Religion is not only wrong; it's evil." Given the visibility of the New Atheists, the concluding section on religion and public life begins with them.

Dennett describes his book *Breaking the Spell* as a scientific study of religion. As the subtitle *Religion as a Natural Phenomenon* makes clear, Dennett understands religion not as the result of supernatural revelation, but rather as an evolutionary byproduct of human culture. He is aware that many religious believers will object to such an examination of religion as impertinent, or perhaps even sacrilegious. In the current selection from *Breaking the Spell*, Dennett turns his attention to the factors at work in the historical transition from folk religions to organized religions. Drawing on a Darwinian understanding of the domestication of plants and animal, Dennett argues that religion also underwent a process by which folk religions gradually became domesticated and then employed for intentional purposes by stewards of that religion. The institutionalizing of religion within a culture serves two related purposes. First, it provides a bond beyond kinship by which individuals in growing communities are able to live peaceably in community. Second, it also encourages subordination to authority via fear of divine retaliation for disobedience and divine reward for submission to that authority. But such an evolutionary account of religion does not mean that religious beliefs are either true or good for us. And here is where further study is needed, Dennett thinks, for it is far from obvious that religion, and religious belief, are actually on the whole good for us.

The selection from Richard Dawkins' *The God Delusion* takes aim at the social impact of religious belief, and is even more provocative. Dawkins begins by claiming that in contemporary society, religious beliefs are treated differently than are other beliefs. More specifically, religious beliefs are claimed to be disproportionately privileged, belonging to a special class of beliefs which are deserving of unparalleled respect and are immune from criticism. While it is acceptable to ask for the rational justification one has for holding certain beliefs, such as political beliefs, this is not true of religious beliefs. Religion is rather, as he puts it, "a trump card" that stops the processes of debate and justification. In fact, the point of religious faith is that it does not depend upon rational justification, and religious freedom prevents one from having to justify one's religious faith. Dawkins takes particular aim at fundamentalism, contrasting fundamentalist religious belief with scientific beliefs. Scientific beliefs are held on the basis of publicly available evidence, and are susceptible to revision in light of further or conflicting evidence. In stark contrast, fundamentalist religious beliefs are held without supporting evidence and often directly in the face of conflicting evidence. Fundamentalist religious beliefs, Dawkins claims, thus undermine the entire scientific enterprise by rejecting the need for justification and support: "it subverts science and saps the intellect." But the dangers of religion are not simply confined to fundamentalist forms. Even mild and moderate forms of religion are damaging to society and its members insofar as they regard the holding of important beliefs without, or even in the face of, justification for those beliefs as a virtue. They thus provide the climate in which fundamentalism can flourish. Religion *per se*, and not just religious extremism, is perilous to contemporary society.

The third reading in this section is taken from Alister McGrath's *Dawkins' God*. Although *Dawkins' God* was published prior to both *Breaking the Spell* and *The God Delusion* and thus does not directly address either of the two previous readings, it does address the dichotomy of science versus religion that is presupposed by them. McGrath begins by addressing the role science plays in Dawkins' argument for atheism. Dawkins' emphasis on and use of Darwin's theory of evolution, McGrath claims, are not merely as a descriptive scientific theory. Rather they are used as part of a meta-narrative in which God has no role. But the scientific method in general is incapable of addressing the question of God's existence insofar as God (if He does exist) is not part of the domain of scientific investigation: the natural world. Thus, science by itself is incapable of establishing the truth of atheism over-against theism or agnosticism. Dawkins must thus supplement his scientific arguments with additional arguments of a non-scientific nature if he is to be justified in his atheism. Next, McGrath investigates the role of proof, or evidence, in both science and religion. As seen above, Dawkins contrasts evidence-based scientific belief with religious faith, which is belief in spite of the lack of evidence for such a belief. McGrath agrees that some religious individuals are unwilling to examine the justification for their religious beliefs; but such a refusal is not an essential part of religious belief, nor is it the understanding of faith at work in most religious belief throughout history. Third, McGrath explores the relationship between science and religion, arguing that the common view that the two disciplines are at war is a socially constructed myth. This view came to prominence in the second half of the nineteenth century when professional scientists sought to distance themselves from religious authorities.

The next two readings further explore the supposed conflict between science and religion by examining the relationship between religious accounts of creation and evolution. Philip Kitcher's "Born-Again Creationism" begins by differentiating literalist creationists from what he calls "born-again creationists." The former think that the Biblical account of creation is literally true, that the earth is only a few thousand years old, and that evolution is false. Such a view faces considerable challenge from science with respect to biodiversity, anatomical structure, etc. In contrast, born-again creationists are willing to grant that biodiversity is the result of millions of years of evolutionary change. What makes this latter group creationists is that natural selection by itself, apart from the operations of a God who directs and guides the evolutionary process, is unable to account for the diversity of living organisms. Kitcher's primary aim in this reading is to criticize the born-again creationist projects of two of its leading advocates: Michael Behe and Phillip Johnson. Behe's work focuses on the idea of irreducible complexity. An irreducibly complex object is an object composed of several interacting parts, all of which contribute to the basic function of that object, and where the removal of any one of the parts causes the system to effectively cease functioning. According to Behe, many biological features are irreducibly complex, and thus cannot be accounted for by evolutionary theory. In contrast, Johnson seeks to defend the existence of an intelligent designer on the bases of distinguishing the fact of evolution from theories of the mechanisms of evolutionary change. That is, while he thinks that evolution is true in that biodiversity is the result of descent with modification, evolutionary theory is not able to account for the process by which such modification has occurred. Kitcher agrees that both biochemistry and evolutionary biology are currently unable to explain all aspects of their domain, but this is no reason to think that a supernatural designer is required. According to Kitcher, the problems raised by Behe and Johnson for evolutionary theory are "wildly overblown." Kitcher ends his article by arguing that even if this were not the case, the problems alleged to plague evolutionary theory cannot be solved by an appeal to creative design. Born-again creationism, like its literalist cousin, is a sham.

In "Evolution as Dogma: The Establishment of Naturalism," Phillip Johnson argues that what many teach evolution to be is not simply a scientific truth, but rather a highly controversial philosophical position. Creationism is, Johnson explains, simply the view which holds that there is a supernatural God who creates. What Darwinism proposes as true is rather *naturalistic* evolution—the conjunction of evolution and naturalism. Naturalism denies that there are any non-natural features of the world, thus leaving no room for either creation or design by a supernatural being. If science is wedded with naturalism, then of course there will be no scientific room for creation. But such a wedding goes beyond science insofar as naturalism is not a scientific claim, but rather a philosophical claim. Darwinism thus rests not upon science but *scientism*, the philosophical claim that knowledge can be found via the methods of investigation available to the natural sciences. And science is itself incapable of proving the truth of scientism.

Johnson's article also touches on legal issues involved in teaching evolution and creationism in school as part of public policy, a theme which is explored in greater detail in the next pair of articles. Robert Pennock's position is apparent from his title: "Why Creationism Should Not Be Taught in the Public Schools." Pennock begins by discussing the difference between teaching creationism in other educational settings—such as private and parochial schools, home schooling, and higher education—but focuses his article on publicly funded schools, since such settings tend to be the focus of the present controversy. Like Kitcher and Johnson, Pennock notes that creationism is a set of related positions rather than a monolithic view, and that there are myriad ways that creationism could be taught in public schools. Nevertheless, he focuses primarily on the teaching of intelligent design, or "creation science," as an alternative to evolutionary theory in science classes. Pennock then addresses the plethora of arguments given in favor of teaching creationism in public schools. Beginning with legal arguments, Pennock canvases a number of recent court cases in the United States that have consistently found that there is no legal basis for teaching creationism. In fact, the U.S. Supreme Court concluded that laws requiring the teaching of creationism in addition to evolution impermissibly legislated the teaching of religion. Pennock then turns to extralegal arguments, including arguments based on fairness, parental rights, academic freedom, and religious protection. He concludes that none of these arguments succeeds in grounding the teaching of creationism in public schools as an alternative to evolution, and there are many reasons for excluding creationism from the curriculum.

Alvin Plantinga responds to Pennock's arguments in his "Creation and Evolution: A Modest Proposal." Plantinga focuses on the role that beliefs in creationism and evolution have in what John Rawls has called "comprehensive beliefs." Given the importance people attach to their comprehensive beliefs, Plantinga thinks that every citizen has a *prima facie* right not to have her children taught materials that contradict her own comprehensive beliefs. If this is the case, then barring overridding reasons, no particular set of comprehensive beliefs can be taught in public schools without infringing on this basic right. While this right can be overridden in certain circumstances, Plantinga thinks that the unpopularity, falsity, or irrationality of a belief does not by itself take away the basic right under consideration. Justice is thus violated when citizens who, for example, believe in creationism as part of their comprehensive beliefs have their children taught a conflicting belief such as the truth of naturalistic evolution. Plantinga then considers a specific objection that scientific consensus overrides this basic right insofar as science is the best bet with respect to the discovery of truth. Such a claim, however, itself rests on contestable philosophical grounds in need of defense. Plantinga is willing for evolution to be taught conditionally, but not as the settled truth.

The final article considers the impact of religion more broadly for politics. Given the importance of religion for many individuals and cultures throughout the modern world, it is not surprising that it is having a significant impact on political matters. Paul Weithman's "Theism, Law, and Politics" explores religion's impact primarily on liberalism, a family of political views which dominates political philosophy in the English-speaking world. Weithman shows how liberalism itself began largely as a response to the increasing religious pluralism brought about by the Protestant Reformation, as political leaders were faced with the challenge of stable and effective government when religious agreement no longer unified much of Europe. Liberal theory is thus largely a response to the problems rooted in religious diversity and the accompanying need for toleration. Weithman also differentiates comprehensive and political versions of liberalism, highlighting differences each version faces with respect to religious and moral diversity. Weithman then considers questions surrounding roles that religious beliefs could play with respect to political motivation and public justification, concluding with a brief treatment of challenges to liberalism raised by contemporary political philosophers.

Further Reading

Brooke, J. H. *Science and Religion: Some Historical Perspectives* (Cambridge: Cambridge University Press, 1991).

Dawkins, Richard. *The God Delusion* (New York: First Mariner Books, 2006).

Dennett, Daniel. *Breaking the Spell: Religion as a Natural Phenomenon* (New York: Penguin Books, 2006).

Hitchens, Christopher. *God is Not Great: How Religion Poisons Everything* (New York: Hachette Book Group, 2007).

Pennock, Robert, ed. *Intelligent Design, Creationism and Its Critics* (Cambridge, MA: MIT Press, 2001).

Polkinghorne, J. *Science and Creation: The Search for Understanding* (Boston: New Science Library; New York: Random House, 1989).

Quinn, Phillip. "Political Liberalisms and Their Exclusions of the Religious," in Christian Miller, ed., *Essays in Philosophy of Religion* (New York: Oxford University Press, 2006), pp. 165–186.

Rawls, John. *Political Liberalism*, 2nd ed. (New York: Columbia University Press, 2005).

Rea, Michael. *World Without Design: The Ontological Consequences of Naturalism* (Oxford: Clarendon Press, 2002).

Wilson, D. S. *Darwin's Cathedral: Evolution, Religion and the Nature of Society* (Chicago: University of Chicago Press, 2002).

Witte, John Jr. *God's Joust, God's Justice: Law and Religion in Western Tradition* (Grand Rapids, MI: Wm. B. Eerdmans, 2006).

Chapter 38

Daniel Dennett

BREAKING THE SPELL

It is high time that we subject religion as a global phenomenon to the most intensive multidisciplinary research we can muster, calling on the best minds on the planet. Why? Because religion is too important for us to remain ignorant about. It affects not just our social, political, and economic conflicts, but the very meanings we find in our lives. For many people, probably a majority of the people on Earth, nothing matters more than religion. For this very reason, it is imperative that we learn as much as we can about it. . . .

Wouldn't such an exhaustive and invasive examination damage the phenomenon itself? Mightn't it *break the spell?* That is a good question, and I don't know the answer. *Nobody knows the answer.* That is why I raise the question, to explore it carefully now, so that we (1) don't rush headlong into inquiries we would all be much better off not undertaking, and yet (2) don't hide facts from ourselves that could guide us to better lives for all. The people on this planet confront a terrible array of problems—poverty, hunger, disease, oppression, the violence of war and crime, and many more—and in the twenty-first century we have unparalleled powers for doing something about all these problems. But what shall we do?

Good intentions are not enough. If we learned anything in the twentieth century, we learned this, for we made some colossal mistakes with the best of intentions. In the early decades of the

century, communism seemed to many millions of thoughtful, well-intentioned people to be a beautiful and even obvious solution to the terrible unfairness that all can see, but they were wrong. An obscenely costly mistake. Prohibition also seemed like a good idea at the time, not just to power-hungry prudes intent on imposing their taste on their fellow citizens, but to many decent people who could see the terrible toll of alcoholism and figured that nothing short of a total ban would suffice. They were proven wrong, and we still haven't recovered from all the bad effects that well-intentioned policy set in motion. There was a time, not so long ago, when the idea of keeping blacks and whites in separate communities, with separate facilities, seemed to many sincere people to be a reasonable solution to pressing problems of interracial strife. It took the civil-rights movement in the United States, and the painful and humiliating experience of Apartheid and its eventual dismantling in South Africa, to show how wrong those well-intentioned people were to have ever believed this. Shame on them, you may say. They should have known better. That is my point. We *can* come to know better if we try our best to find out, and we have no excuse for not trying. Or do we? Are some topics off limits, no matter what the consequences?

Today, billions of people pray for peace, and I wouldn't be surprised if most of them believe with all their hearts that the best path to follow to peace throughout the world is a path that runs through their particular religious institution, whether it is Christianity, Judaism, Islam, Hinduism, Buddhism, or any of hundreds of other systems of religion. Indeed, many people think that the best hope for humankind is that we can bring together all of the religions of the world in a mutually respectful conversation and ultimate agreement on how to treat one another. They may be right, but *they don't know*. The fervor of their belief is no substitute for good hard evidence, and the evidence in favor of this beautiful hope is hardly overwhelming. In fact, it is not persuasive at all, since just as many people, apparently, sincerely believe that world peace is less important, in both the short run and the long, than the global triumph of their particular religion over its competition. Some see religion as the best hope for peace, a lifeboat we dare not rock lest we overturn it and all of us perish, and others see religious self-identification as the main source of conflict and violence in the world, and believe just as fervently that religious conviction is a terrible substitute for calm, informed reasoning. Good intentions pave both roads.

Who is right? I don't know. Neither do the billions of people with their passionate religious convictions. Neither do those atheists who are sure the world would be a much better place if all religion went extinct. There is an asymmetry: atheists in general welcome the most intensive and objective examination of their views, practices, and reasons. (In fact, their incessant demand for self-examination can become quite tedious.) The religious, in contrast, often bristle at the impertinence, the lack of respect, the *sacrilege*, implied by anybody who wants to investigate their views. I respectfully demur: there is indeed an ancient tradition to which they are appealing here, but it is mistaken and should not be permitted to continue. This spell must be broken, and broken now. Those who are religious and believe religion to be the best hope of humankind cannot reasonably expect those of

us who are skeptical to refrain from expressing our doubts if they themselves are unwilling to put their convictions under the microscope. If they are right—especially if they are obviously right, on further reflection—we skeptics will not only concede this but enthusiastically join the cause. We want what they (mostly) say they want: a world at peace, with as little suffering as we can manage, with freedom and justice and well-being and meaning for all. If the case for their path cannot be made, *this is something that they themselves should want to know*. It is as simple as that. They claim the moral high ground; maybe they deserve it and maybe they don't. Let's find out. [. . .]

Should Science Study Religion?

The question is not whether good science of religion as a natural phenomenon is possible: it is. The question is whether we should do it. Research is expensive and sometimes has harmful side effects. One of the lessons of the twentieth century is that scientists are not above confabulating justifications for the work they want to do, driven by insatiable curiosity. Are there in fact good reasons, aside from sheer curiosity, to try to develop the natural science of religion? Do we need this for anything? Would it help us choose policies, respond to problems, improve our world? What do we know about the future of religion? Consider five wildly different hypotheses:

1. *The Enlightenment is long gone; the creeping "secularization" of modern societies that has been anticipated for two centuries is evaporating before our eyes.* The tide is turning and religion is becoming more important than ever. In this scenario, religion soon resumes something like the dominant social and moral role it had before the rise of modern science in the seventeenth century. As people recover from their infatuation with technology and material comforts, spiritual identity becomes a person's most valued attribute, and populations

come to be ever more sharply divided among Christianity, Islam, Judaism, Hinduism, and a few other major multinational religious organizations. Eventually—it might take another millennium, or it might be hastened by catastrophe—one major faith sweeps the planet.

2. *Religion is in its death throes; today's outbursts of fervor and fanaticism are but a brief and awkward transition to a truly modern society in which religion plays at most a ceremonial role.* In this scenario, although there may be some local and temporary revivals and even some violent catastrophes, the major religions of the world soon go just as extinct as the hundreds of minor religions that are vanishing faster than anthropologists can record them. Within the lifetimes of our grandchildren, Vatican City becomes the European Museum of Roman Catholicism, and Mecca is turned into Disney's Magic Kingdom of Allah.

3. *Religions transform themselves into institutions unlike anything seen before on the planet: basically creedless associations selling self-help and enabling moral teamwork, using ceremony and tradition to cement relationships and build "long-term fan loyalty."* In this scenario, being a member of a religion becomes more and more like being a Boston Red Sox fan, or a Dallas Cowboys fan. Different colors, different songs and cheers, different symbols, and vigorous competition—would you want your daughter to marry a Yankees fan?—but aside from a rabid few, everybody appreciates the importance of peaceful coexistence in a Global League of Religions. Religious art and music flourish, and friendly rivalry leads to a degree of specialization, with one religion priding itself on its environmental stewardship, providing clean water for the world's billions, while another becomes duly famous for its concerted defense of social justice and economic equality.

4. *Religion diminishes in prestige and visibility, rather like smoking; it is tolerated, since there are those who say they can't live without it, but it is discouraged, and teaching religion to impressionable young children is frowned upon in most societies and actually outlawed in others.* In this scenario, politicians who still practice religion can be elected if they prove themselves worthy in other regards, but few would advertise their religious affiliation—or affliction, as the politically incorrect insist on calling it. It is considered as rude to draw attention to the religion of somebody as it is to comment in public about his sexuality or whether she has been divorced.

5. *Judgment Day arrives. The blessed ascend bodily into heaven, and the rest are left behind to suffer the agonies of the damned, as the Antichrist is vanquished.* As the Bible prophecies foretold, the rebirth of the nation of Israel in 1948 and the ongoing conflict over Palestine are clear signs of the End Times, when the Second Coming of Christ sweeps all the other hypotheses into oblivion.

Other possibilities are describable, of course, but these five hypotheses highlight the extremes that are taken seriously. What is remarkable about the set is that just about anybody would find at least one of them preposterous, or troubling, or even deeply offensive, but every one of them is not just anticipated but yearned for. People act on what they yearn for. We are at cross-purposes about religion, to say the least, so we can anticipate problems, ranging from wasted effort and counterproductive campaigns if we are lucky to all-out war and genocidal catastrophe if we are not.

Only one of these hypotheses (at most) will turn out to be true; the rest are not just wrong but wildly wrong. Many people think they know which is true, but nobody does. Isn't that fact, all by itself, enough reason to study religion scientifically? Whether you want religion to flourish or perish, whether you think it should transform itself or stay just as it is, you can hardly deny that whatever happens will be of tremendous significance to the planet. It would be useful to your hopes, whatever they are, to know more about what is likely to happen and why. In this regard, it is worth noting how assiduously those who firmly believe in number 5 scan the world news for evidence of prophecies fulfilled. They sort and evaluate their sources, debating the pros and cons of various interpretations of those prophecies. They think there is a reason to investigate the future of religion, and they don't even think the course of future events lies within human power to determine. The rest of us have all the more reason to investigate the phenomena, since it is quite obvious that complacency and ignorance could lead us to squander our opportunities to steer the phenomena in what we take to be the benign directions.

Looking ahead, anticipating the future, is the crowning achievement of our species. We have managed in a few short millennia of human culture to multiply the planet's supply of look-ahead by many orders of magnitude. We know when eclipses will occur centuries in advance; we can predict the effects on the atmosphere of adjustments in how we generate electricity; we can anticipate in broad outline what will happen as our petroleum reserves dwindle in the next decades. We do this not with miraculous prophecy but with basic perception. We gather information from the environment, using our senses, and then we use science to cobble together anticipations based on that information. We mine the ore, and then refine it, again and again, and it lets us see into the future—dimly, with lots of uncertainty, but much better than a coin toss. In every area of human concern, we have learned how to anticipate and then avoid catastrophes that used to blindside us. We have recently forestalled a global disaster due to a growing hole in the ozone layer because some far-seeing chemists were able to prove that some of our manufactured compounds were causing the problem. We have avoided economic collapses in recent years because our economic models have shown us impending problems.

A catastrophe averted is an anticlimax, obviously, so we tend not to appreciate how valuable our powers of look-ahead are. "See?" we complain. "It wasn't going to happen after all." The flu season in the winter of 2003–2004 was predicted to be severe, since it arrived earlier than usual, but the broadcast recommendations for inoculation were so widely heeded that the epidemic collapsed as rapidly as it began. Ho-hum. It has become something of a tradition in recent years for the meteorologists on television to hype an oncoming hurricane or other storm, and then for the public to be underwhelmed by the actual storm. But sober evaluations show that many lives are saved, destruction is minimized. We accept the value of intensely studying El Niño and the other cycles in ocean currents so that we can do better meteorological forecasting. We keep exhaustive records of many economic events so that we can do better economic forecasting. We should extend the same intense scrutiny, for the same reasons, to religious phenomena. Few forces in the world are as potent, as influential, as religion. As we struggle to resolve the terrible economic and social inequities that currently disfigure our planet, and minimize the violence and degradation we see, we have to recognize that if we have a blind spot about religion our efforts will almost certainly fail, and may make matters much worse. We wouldn't permit the world's food-producing interests to deflect us from studying human agriculture and nutrition, and we have learned not to exempt the banking-and-insurance world from intense and continuous scrutiny. Their effects are too important to take on faith. So what I am calling for is a concerted effort to achieve a mutual agreement under which religion—all religion—becomes a proper object of scientific study.

Here I find that opinion is divided among those who are already convinced that this would be a good idea, those who are dubious and inclined to doubt that it would be of much value, and those who find the proposal evil—offensive, dangerous, and stupid. Not wanting to preach to the converted, I am particularly concerned to address those who hate this idea, in hopes of persuading them that their repugnance is misplaced. This is a daunting task, like trying to persuade your friend with the cancer symptoms that she really ought to see a doctor now, since her anxiety may be misplaced and the sooner she learns that the sooner she can get on with her life, and if she does have cancer, timely intervention may make all the difference. Friends can get quite annoyed when you interfere with their denial at times like that, but perseverance is called for. Yes, I want to put religion on the examination table. If it is fundamentally benign, as many of its devotees insist, it should emerge just fine; suspicions will be put to rest and we can then concentrate on the few peripheral pathologies that religion, like every other natural phenomenon, falls prey to. If it is not, the sooner we identify the problems clearly the better. Will the inquiry itself generate some discomfort and embarrassment? Almost certainly, but that is a small price to pay. Is there a risk that such an invasive examination will make a healthy religion ill, or even disable it? Of course. There are always risks. Are they worth taking? Perhaps not, but I haven't yet seen an argument that persuades me of this, and we will soon consider the best of them. The only arguments worth attending to will have to demonstrate that (1) religion provides net benefits to humankind, and (2) these benefits would be unlikely to survive such an investigation. I, for one, fear that if we *don't* subject religion to such scrutiny now, and work out together whatever revisions and reforms are called for, we will pass on a legacy of ever more toxic forms of religion to our descendants. I can't prove that, and those who are dead sure that this will not happen are encouraged to say what supports their conviction, aside from loyalty to their tradition, which goes without saying and doesn't count for anything here.

In general, knowing more improves your chances of getting what you value. That's not quite a truth of logic, since uncertainty is not the only factor that can lower the probability of achieving one's goals. The costs of knowing (such as the cost of *coming* to know) must be factored in, and these costs may be high, which is why "Wing it!" is sometimes good advice. Suppose there is a limit on how much

knowledge about some topic is good for us. If so, then, whenever that limit is reached (if that is possible—the limit may be unreachable for one reason or another), we should prohibit or at least strongly discourage any further seeking of knowledge on that topic, as antisocial activity. This may be a principle that never comes into play, but we don't know that, and we should certainly accept the principle. It may be, then, that some of our major disagreements in the world today are about whether we've reached such a limit. This reflection puts the Islamist conviction that Western science is a bad thing in a different light: it may not be an ignorant mistake so much as a profoundly different view of where the threshold is. Sometimes ignorance *is* bliss. We need to consider such possibilities carefully. [. . .]

The Domestication of Religions

[. . .]

Folk religions emerge out of the daily lives of people living in small groups, and share common features the world over. How and when did these metamorphose into organized religions? There is a general consensus among researchers that the big shift responsible was the emergence of agriculture and the larger settlements that this made both possible and necessary. Researchers disagree, however, on what to emphasize in this major transition. The creation of non-portable food stockpiles, and the resultant shift to fixed residence, permitted the emergence of an unprecedented division of labor (Seabright, 2004, is especially clear about this), and this in turn gave rise to *markets*, and opportunities for ever more specialized occupations. These new ways for people to interact created novel opportunities and novel needs. When you find that you have to deal on a daily basis with people *who are not your close kin*, the prospect of a few like-minded people forming a coalition that is quite different from an extended family must almost always present itself, and often be an attractive option. Boyer (2001) is not alone in arguing that the transition from folk religion to organized religion was primarily one of these market phenomena.

> Throughout history, guilds and other groups of craftsmen and specialists have tried to establish common prices and common standards and to stop non-guild members from delivering comparable services. By establishing a quasi monopoly, they make sure that all the custom comes their way. By maintaining common prices and common standards, they make it difficult for a particularly skilled or efficient member to undersell the others. So most people pay a small price for being members of a group that guarantees a minimal share of the market to each of its members. [p. 275]

The first step to such organization is the big one, but the next steps, from a guild of priests or shamans to what are, in effect, firms (and *franchises* and *brand names*), are an almost inevitable consequence of the growing self-consciousness and market savvy of those individuals who joined to form the guilds in the first place. *Cui bono?* When individuals start asking themselves how best to enhance and preserve the organizations they have created, they radically change the focus of the question, bringing new selective pressures into existence.

   Darwin appreciated this, and used the transition from what he called "unconscious" selection to "methodical" selection as a pedagogical bridge to explain his great idea of natural selection in the opening chapter of his masterpiece. (*On the Origin of Species* is a great read, by the way. Just as atheists often read "the Bible as literature" and come away deeply moved by the poetry and insight without being converted, creationists and others who cannot bring themselves to believe in evolution can still be thrilled by reading the founding document of modern evolutionary theory—whether or not it changes their minds about evolution.)

At the present time, eminent breeders try by methodical selection, with a distinct object in view, to make a new strain or subbreed, superior to any existing in the country. But for our purpose, a kind of Selection, which may be called Unconscious, and which results from every one trying to possess and breed from the best individual animals, is more important. Thus a man who intends keeping pointers naturally tries to get as good dogs as he can, and afterwards breeds from his own best dogs, but he has no wish or expectation of permanently altering the breed. Nevertheless I cannot doubt that this process, continued during centuries, would improve and modify any breed. . . . There is reason to believe that King Charles's spaniel has been unconsciously modified to a large extent since the time of that monarch. [pp. 34–35]

Domestication of both plants and animals occurred without any farseeing intention or invention on the part of the stewards of the seeds and studs. But what a stroke of good fortune for those lineages that became domesticated! All that remains of the ancestors of today's grains are small scattered patches of wild-grass cousins, and the nearest surviving relatives of all the domesticated animals could be carried off in a few arks. How clever of wild sheep to have acquired that most versatile adaptation, the shepherd! By forming a symbiotic alliance with *Homo sapiens*, sheep could *outsource* their chief survival tasks: food finding and predator avoidance. They even got shelter and emergency medical care thrown in as a bonus. The price they paid—losing the freedom of mate selection and being slaughtered instead of being killed by predators (if that is a cost)—was a pittance compared with the gain in offspring survival it purchased. But of course it wasn't *their* cleverness that explains the good bargain. It was the blind, foresightless cleverness of Mother Nature, evolution, which ratified the free-floating rationale of this arrangement. Sheep and other domesticated animals are, in fact, significantly more stupid than their wild relatives—because they can be. Their brains are smaller (relative to body size and weight), and this is not just due to their having been bred for muscle mass (meat). Since both the domesticated animals and their domesticators have enjoyed huge population explosions (going from less than 1 percent of the terrestrial vertebrate biomass ten thousand years ago to over 98 percent today), there can be no doubt that this symbiosis was mutualistic—fitness-enhancing to both parties.

What I now want to suggest is that, alongside the domestication of animals and plants, there was a gradual process in which the wild (self-sustaining) memes of folk religion became thoroughly domesticated. They acquired stewards. Memes that are fortunate enough to have stewards, people who will work hard and use their intelligence to foster their propagation and protect them from their enemies, are relieved of much of the burden of keeping their own lineages going. In extreme cases, they no longer need to be particularly catchy, or appeal to our sensual instincts at all. The multiplication-table memes, for instance, to say nothing of the calculus memes, are hardly crowd-pleasers, and yet they are duly propagated by hardworking teachers—meme shepherds—whose responsibility it is to keep these lineages strong. The wild memes of language and folk religion, in other words, are like rats and squirrels, pigeons and cold viruses—magnificently adapted to living with us and exploiting us whether we like them or not. The domesticated memes, in contrast, depend on help from human guardians to keep going.

People have been poring over their religious practices and institutions for almost as long as they have been refining their agricultural practices and institutions, and these reflective examiners have all had agendas—individual or shared *conceptions* of what was valuable and why. Some have been wise and some foolish, some widely informed and some naïve, some pure and saintly, and some venal and vicious. Jared Diamond's

hypothesis about the practically exhaustive search by our ancestors for domesticatable species in their neighborhoods can be extended. Curious practitioners will also have uncovered whatever Good Tricks are in the nearest neighborhoods in the Design Space of possible religions. Diamond sees the transition from bands of fewer than a hundred people to tribes of hundreds to chiefdoms of thousands to states of over fifty thousand people as an inexorable march "from egalitarianism to kleptocracy," government by thieves. Speaking of chiefdoms, he remarks:

> At best, they do good by providing expensive services impossible to contract for on an individual basis. At worst, they function unabashedly as kleptocracies, transferring net wealth from commoners to upper classes. . . . Why do the commoners tolerate the transfer of the fruits of their hard labor to kleptocrats? This question, raised by political theorists from Plato to Marx, is raised anew by voters in every modern election. [1997, p. 276]

There are four ways, he suggests, that kleptocrats have tried to maintain their power: (1) disarm the populace and arm the elite, (2) make the masses happy by redistributing much of the tribute received, (3) use the monopoly of force to promote happiness, by maintaining public order and curbing violence, or (4) construct an ideology or religion justifying kleptocracy (p. 277).

How might a religion support a kleptocracy? By an alliance between the political leader and the priests, of course, in which, first of all, the leader is declared to be divine, or descended from the gods, or, as Diamond puts it, at least having "a hotline to the gods."

> Besides justifying the transfer of wealth to kleptocrats, institutionalized religion brings two other important benefits to centralized societies. First, shared ideology or religion helps solve the problem of how unrelated

individuals are to live together without killing each other—by providing them with a bond not based on kinship. Second, it gives people a motive, other than genetic self-interest, for sacrificing their lives on behalf of others. At the cost of a few society members who die in battle as soldiers, the whole society becomes much more effective at conquering other societies or resisting attacks. [p. 278]

So we find the same devices invented over and over again, in just about every religion, and many nonreligious organizations as well. None of this is new today—as Lord Acton said more than a century ago, "All power tends to corrupt; absolute power corrupts absolutely"—but it was new once upon a time, when our ancestors were first exploring design revisions to our most potent institutions.

For instance, *accepting inferior status to an invisible god* is a cunning stratagem, whether or not its cunning is consciously recognized by those who stumble upon it. Those who rely on it will thrive, wittingly or otherwise. As every subordinate knows, one's commands are more effective than they might otherwise be if one can accompany them with a threat to tell the bigger boss if disobedience ensues. (Variations on this stratagem are well known to Mafia underlings and used-car salesmen, among others—"I myself am not authorized to make such an offer, so I'll have to check with my boss. Excuse me for a minute.")

This helps to explain what is otherwise a bit of a puzzle. Any dictator depends on the fidelity of his immediate staff—in the simple sense that any two or three of them could easily overpower him (he can't go around with dagger drawn all his life). How do you, as a dictator, ensure that your immediate staff puts its fidelity to you above any thoughts they may very well have about replacing you? Putting the fear of a higher power in their heads is a pretty good move. There is often, no doubt, an unspoken détente between chief priest and king—each needs the other for his power, and together they need

the gods above. Walter Burkert is particularly Machiavellian in his account of how this stratagem brings the institution of ritual praise in its wake, and notes some of its useful complexity:

> By the force of his verbal competence [the priest] not only rises to a superior level in imagination but succeeds in reversing the attention structure: it is the superior who is made to pay heed to the inferior's song or speech of praise. Praise is the recognized form of making noise in the presence of superiors; in a well-structured form, it tends to become music. Praise ascends to the heights like incense. Thus the tension between high and low is both stressed and relaxed, as the lower one establishes his place within a system he accepts emphatically. [1996, p. 91]

The gods will get you if you try to cross either one of us. We have already noted the role of rituals, both individual rehearsals and unison error-absorption sessions, in enhancing the fidelity of memetic transmission, and noted that these are enforced by making nonparticipation costly in one way or another. Moreover, as Joseph Bulbulia suggests, "It may be that religious rituals put on display the natural power of a religious community, an awesome show to potential defectors of what they are up against" (2004, p. 40). But what drives the community spirit in the first place? [. . .]

The Growth Market in Religion

[. . .]

Why make great sacrifices in order to further the prospects of a religious organization? Why, for instance, might one choose loyalty to a religion when one is also, perhaps, a contributing member of a labor union, a political party, and a social club? These "why" questions start by being neutral between two quite different types of answers: they could be asking *why it is rational* to choose loyalty to a religion, or they could be asking *why it is natural* (somehow) for people to be drawn into a religion which then commands their loyalty. (Consider the question *Why do so many people fear heights?* One answer is: because it is rational to fear heights; you can fall and hurt yourself! Another is: we have evolved an instinctual caution triggered by the perception that we are exposed at a great height; in some people this anxiety is exaggerated beyond what is useful; *their* fear is natural—we can explain its existence without residual mystery—but *irrational*.) If we take a good hard look at the first answer regarding religion, as proposed by rational choice theory, it will help us see the forces and constraints that shape the alternatives.

Over the last two decades, Rodney Stark and his colleagues have done a remarkable job of articulating the rational choice answer, and they claim that, thanks to their efforts, "it now is impossible to do credible work in the social scientific study of religion based on the assumption that religiousness is a sign of stupidity, neurosis, poverty, ignorance, or false consciousness, or represents a flight from modernity" (Stark and Finke, 2000, p. 18). They concentrate on religion in the U.S.A., and their basic model is a straightforward application of economic theory:

Indeed, having now had more than two centuries to develop under free market conditions, the American religious economy surpasses Adam Smith's wildest dreams about the creative forces of a free market (Moore, 1994). There are more than 1,500 separate religious "denominations" (Melton, 1998), many of them very sizable—24 have more than 1 million members each. Each of these bodies is entirely dependent on voluntary contributions, and American religious donations currently total more than $60 billion per year or more than $330 per person over age 18. These totals omit many contributions to church construction funds (new church construction amounted to $3 billion in 1993), as well as most donations to religious

schools, hospitals, and foreign missions. In 1996, more than $2.3 billion was donated to support missionaries and a significant amount of this was spent on missionaries to Europe. [p. 223]

H. L. Mencken once opined: "The only really respectable Protestants are the Fundamentalists. Unfortunately, they are also palpable idiots." Many share that opinion, especially in academia, but not Stark and Finke. They are particularly eager to dispel the familiar idea that the more fundamentalist or evangelical the denomination is, the less rational it is:

Among the more common suggestions as to why evangelical churches grow are repressed sexuality, divorce, urbanization, racism, sexism, status anxieties, and rapid social change. Never do proponents of the old paradigm even explore possible religious explanations: for example, that people are drawn to the evangelical churches by a superior product. [p. 30]

People bear the heavy expenses of church membership, and the church in return contracts "to support and supervise their exchanges with a god or gods" (p. 103). Stark and Finke have worked this out carefully, and their driving premise is their Proposition 6, "In pursuit of rewards, humans will seek to utilize and manipulate the supernatural" (p. 90). Some people go it alone, but most think they need help, and that is what churches provide. (Do churches *actually* manipulate the supernatural? Are Stark and Finke committed to the claim that exchanges with a god or gods really occur? No, they are studiously agnostic—or so they claim—on this score. They often point out that it can be perfectly rational to invest in a stock that turns out to be worthless, after all.)

In a later book, *One True God: Historical Consequences of Monotheism* (2001), Stark takes on the role of memetic engineer, analyzing the pros and cons of doctrine as if he were an advertising consultant. "What sorts of Gods have the greatest appeal?" (p. 2). Here he distinguishes two strategies: *God as essence* (such as Tillich's God as the Ground of All Being, entirely nonanthropomorphic, not in time and space, abstract) and *God as conscious supernatural being* (a God who listens to and answers prayers in real time, for instance). "There is no more profound religious difference than that between faiths involving divine beings and those limited to divine essences," he says, and the latter he judges to be hopeless, because "only divine beings *do* anything" (p. 10). Supernatural conscious beings are much better sellers because "the supernatural is the only plausible source of many benefits we greatly desire" (p. 12).

> People care about Gods because, if they exist, they are potential exchange partners possessed of immense resources. Furthermore, untold billions of people are certain that Gods do exist, precisely because they believe they have experienced long and satisfying exchange relations with them [p. 13]. . . . Because Gods are conscious beings, they are potential exchange partners because all beings are assumed to want something for which they might be induced to give something valuable. [p. 15]

He adds that a responsive, fatherly God "makes an extremely attractive exchange partner who can be counted on to maximize human benefits" (p. 21), and he even proposes that a God without a counterbalancing Satan is an unstable concept—"*irrational and perverse.*" Why? Because "one God of infinite scope must be responsible for *everything*, evil as well as good, and thus must be dangerously capricious, shifting intentions unpredictably and without reason" (p. 24). This is pretty much the same *raison d'être* that Jerry Siegel and Joe Shuster, the creators of *Superman*, appreciated when they invented kryptonite as something to counteract the Man of Steel: there is no drama possible—no defeats to

overcome, no cliff-hangers—if your hero is too powerful! But, unlike the concept of kryptonite, these concepts of God and Satan have free-floating rationales, and are not the brainchildren of any particular authors:

> I do not mean to suggest that this portrait of the Gods is the product of conscious human "creation." No one sat down and decided, Let's believe in a supreme God, surround him/her with some subordinate beings, and postulate an inferior evil being on whom we can blame evil. Rather, this view tends to evolve over time because it is the most reasonable and satisfying conclusion from the available religious culture. [pp. 25–26]

Stark's footnote on this passage is not to be missed: "Nor am I prepared to deny that this evolution reflects progressive human discovery of the truth." Ah, that's the ticket! The story doesn't just get better; it *happens* to get closer to the truth. A lucky break? Maybe not. Wouldn't a really good God arrange things that way? Maybe, but the fact that dramatic considerations so conveniently dictate the details of the story does provide an explanation of why the details are what they are that rivals the traditional supposition that they are simply "the God's honest truth." [. . .]

Now What Do We Do?

[. . .]

Since 2002, schools in Cobb County, Georgia, have put stickers in some of their biology textbooks saying "Evolution is a theory, not a fact," but a judge recently ruled that these must be removed, since they may convey the message of endorsement of religion "in violation of First Amendment separation of church and state and the Georgia Constitution's prohibition against using public money to aid religion" (*New York Times*, January 14, 2005). This makes sense, since the only motivations for singling out evolution for this treatment are religious. Nobody is putting stickers in chemistry or geology books saying that the theories explained therein are theories, not facts. There are still plenty of controversies in chemistry and geology, but these rival theories are contested within the securely established background theories of each field, which are not just theory but fact. There are lots of controversial theories within biology, too, but the background theory that is not contested is evolution. There are rival theories of vertebrate flight, and the role of migration in speciation, and, closer to human home, theories about the evolution of language, bipedality, concealed ovulation, and schizophrenia, to name just a few particularly vigorous controversies. Eventually, these will all get sorted out, and some of the theories will prove to be not just theories but facts.

My description of the evolution of various features of religion is definitely "just a theory"— or, rather, a family of proto-theories, in need of further development. In a nutshell, this is what it says: Religion evolved, but it doesn't have to be good for us in order to evolve. (Tobacco isn't good for us, but it survives just fine.) We don't all learn language because we think it's good for us; we all learn language because we cannot do otherwise (if we have normal nervous systems). In the case of religion, there is a lot more teaching and drill, a lot more deliberate social pressure, than there is in language learning. In this regard, religion is more like reading than talking. There are tremendous benefits to being able to read, and perhaps there are similar or greater benefits to being religious. But people may well love religion independently of any benefits it provides them. (I am delighted to learn that red wine in moderation is good for my health, since, whether or not it is good for me, I like it, and I want to go on drinking it. Religion could be like that.) It is not surprising that religion survives. It has been pruned and revised and edited for thousands of years, with millions of variants extinguished in the process, so it has plenty of

features that appeal to people, and plenty of features that preserve the identity of its recipes for these very features, features that ward off or confound enemies and competitors, and secure allegiance. Only gradually have people come to have any appreciation of the reasons—the heretofore free-floating rationales—for these features. Religion is many things to many people. For some, the memes of religion are mutualists, providing undeniable benefits of sorts that cannot be found elsewhere. These people may well depend for their very lives on religion, the way we all depend on the bacteria in our guts that help us digest our food. Religion provides some people with a motivated organization for doing great things—working for social justice, education, political action, economic reform, and so forth. For others, the memes of religion are more toxic, exploiting less savory aspects of their psychology, playing on guilt, loneliness, the longing for self-esteem and importance. Only when we can frame a comprehensive view of the many aspects of religion can we formulate defensible policies for how to respond to religions in the future.

Some aspects of this theory sketch are pretty well established, but getting down to specifics and generating further testable hypotheses is work for the future. I wanted to give readers a good idea of what a testable theory would be like, what sorts of questions it would raise, and what sorts of explanatory principles it could invoke. My theory sketch may well be false in many regards, but if so, this will be shown by confirming some alternative theory of the same sort. In science, the tactic is to put forward something that can be either fixed or refuted by something better. A century ago, it was just a theory that powered fixed-wing flight was possible; now it is fact. A few decades ago, it was just a theory that the cause of AIDS was a virus, but the reality of HIV is not just a theory today.

Since my proto-theory is not yet established and may prove to be wrong, it shouldn't be used yet to guide our policies. Having insisted at the outset that we need to do much more research so that we can make well-informed decisions, I would be contradicting myself if I now proceeded to prescribe courses of action on the basis of my initial foray. Recall the moral that Taubes drew in his history of the misguided activism that led us on the low-fat crusade: "It's a story of what can happen when the demands of public health policy—and the demands of the public for simple advice—run up against the confusing ambiguity of real science." There is pressure on us all to act decisively today, on the basis of the little we already (think we) know, but I am counseling patience. The current situation is scary—one religious fanaticism or another could produce a global catastrophe, after all—but we should resist rash "remedies" and other overreactions. It is possible, however, to discuss *options* today, and to think *hypothetically* of what the sound policies *would be* if something like my account of religion is correct. Such a consideration of possible policies can help motivate the further research, giving us pressing reasons for finding out which hypotheses are really true.

If somebody wants to put a sticker in this book, saying that it presents a theory, not a fact, I would happily concur. *Caution!* it should say. *Assuming that these propositions are true without further research could lead to calamitous results.* But I would insist that we also put the stickers on any books or articles that maintain or presuppose that religion is the lifeboat of the world, which we dare not upset. The proposition that God exists is *not even* a theory. That assertion is so prodigiously ambiguous that it expresses, at best, an unorganized set of dozens or hundreds—or billions—of quite *different* possible theories, most of them disqualified as theories in any case, because they are systematically immune to confirmation or disconfirmation. The refutable versions of the claim that God exists have life cycles like mayflies, being born and dying within a matter of weeks, if not minutes, as predictions fail to come true. (Every athlete who prays to God for victory in the big game and then wins is happy to thank

God for taking his side, and chalks up some "evidence" in favor of his theory of God—but quietly revises his theory of God whenever he loses in spite of his prayers.) Even the secular and nonpartisan proposition that religion *in general* does more good than harm, either to the individual believer or to society as a whole, has hardly begun to be properly tested.

So here is the only prescription I will make categorically and without reservation: Do more research. There is an alternative, and I am sure it is still hugely appealing to many people: Let's just close our eyes, trust to tradition, and wing it. Let's just *take it on faith* that religion is the key—or one of the keys—to our salvation. How can I quarrel with faith (for heaven's sake)? *Blind* faith? Please. Think. This is where we began. My task was to demonstrate that there was enough reason to question the tradition of faith so that you could not in good conscience turn your back on the available or discoverable relevant facts. I am quite prepared to roll up my sleeves and get down to examining the evidence and considering alternative scientific theories of religion, but I think I have already made my case that it would be indefensibly reckless *not* to do this research.

My survey has highlighted a small fraction of the work that has already been done, using it to tell one of the possible stories of how religion became what it is today, leaving other stories unmentioned. I told what I think is the best current version, but perhaps I have overlooked some contributions that will eventually be recognized retrospectively to be more important. This is a risk that a project like mine takes: if, by drawing attention to one avenue of research, it helps bury some better avenue in oblivion, I will have done a disservice. I am acutely aware of this prospect, so I have shared drafts of this book with researchers who have their own vision of how to make progress in the field. My network of informants inevitably has its own bias, however, and I would like nothing better than for this book to provoke a challenge—a reasoned and evidence-rich scientific challenge—from researchers with opposing viewpoints.

References

Boyer, Peter. *Religion Explained: The Evolutionary Origins of Religious Thought* (New York: Basic Books, 2001).

Bulbulia, Joseph. "Religious Costs as Adaptations that Signal Altruistic Intention," *Evolution and Cognition 19* (2004): 19–42.

Burkert, Walter. *Creation of the Sacred: Tracks of Biology in Early Religions* (Cambridge, MA: Harvard University Press, 1996).

Darwin, Charles. *On the Origin of Species by Means of Natural Selection* (London, Murray, 1859).

Diamond, Jared. *Guns, Germs, and Steel: The Fates of Human Societies* (New York: Norton, 1997).

Starke, Rodney. *One True God: Historical Consequences of Monotheism* (Princeton: Princeton University Press, 2001).

Stark, Rodney and Roger Finke. *Acts of Faith: Explaining the Human Side of Religion* (Berkeley: University of California Press, 2000).

Chapter 39

Richard Dawkins

THE GOD DELUSION

Undeserved Respect

My title, "The God Delusion," does not refer to the God of Einstein and the other enlightened scientists of the previous section. That is why I needed to get Einsteinian religion out of the way to begin with: it has a proven capacity to confuse. In the rest of this book I am talking only about *supernatural* gods, of which the most familiar to the majority of my readers will be Yahweh, the God of the Old Testament. I shall come to him in a moment. But before leaving this preliminary chapter I need to deal with one more matter that would otherwise bedevil the whole book. This time it is a matter of etiquette. It is possible that religious readers will be offended by what I have to say, and will find in these pages insufficient *respect* for their own particular beliefs (if not the beliefs that others treasure). It would be a shame if such offence prevented them from reading on, so I want to sort it out here, at the outset.

A widespread assumption, which nearly everybody in our society accepts – the non-religious included – is that religious faith is especially vulnerable to offence and should be protected by an abnormally thick wall of respect, in a different class from the respect that any human being should pay to any other. Douglas Adams put it so well, in an impromptu speech made in Cambridge shortly before his death,[1] that I never tire of sharing his words:

Religion . . . has certain ideas at the heart of it which we call sacred or holy or whatever. What it means is, 'Here is an idea or a notion that you're not allowed to say anything bad about; you're just not. Why not? – because you're not!' If somebody votes for a party that you don't agree with, you're free to argue about it as much as you like; everybody will have an argument but nobody feels aggrieved by it. If somebody thinks taxes should go up or down you are free to have an argument about it. But on the other hand if somebody says 'I mustn't move a light switch on a Saturday', you say, 'I *respect* that'.

Why should it be that it's perfectly legitimate to support the Labour party or the Conservative party, Republicans or Democrats, this model of economics versus that, Macintosh instead of Windows – but to have an opinion about how the Universe began, about who created the Universe . . . no, that's holy? . . . We are used to not challenging religious ideas but it's very interesting how much of a furore Richard creates when he does it! Everybody gets absolutely frantic about it because you're not allowed to say these things. Yet when you look at it rationally there is no reason why those ideas shouldn't be as open to debate as any other, except that we have agreed somehow between us that they shouldn't be.

Here's a particular example of our society's overweening respect for religion, one that really matters. By far the easiest grounds for gaining conscientious objector status in wartime are religious. You can be a brilliant moral philosopher with a prizewinning doctoral thesis expounding the evils of war, and still be given a hard time by a draft board evaluating your claim to be a conscientious objector. Yet if you can say that one or both of your parents is a Quaker you sail through like a breeze, no matter how inarticulate and illiterate you may be on the theory of pacifism or, indeed, Quakerism itself.

At the opposite end of the spectrum from pacifism, we have a pusillanimous reluctance to use religious names for warring factions. In Northern Ireland, Catholics and Protestants are euphemized to 'Nationalists' and 'Loyalists' respectively. The very word 'religions' is bowdlerized to 'communities', as in 'inter-community warfare'. Iraq, as a consequence of the Anglo-American invasion of 2003, degenerated into sectarian civil war between Sunni and Shia Muslims. Clearly a religious conflict – yet in the *Independent* of 20 May 2006 the front-page headline and first leading article both described it as 'ethnic cleansing'. 'Ethnic' in this context is yet another euphemism. What we are seeing in Iraq is religious cleansing. The original usage of 'ethnic cleansing' in the former Yugoslavia is also arguably a euphemism for religious cleansing, involving Orthodox Serbs, Catholic Croats and Muslim Bosnians.[2]

I have previously drawn attention to the privileging of religion in public discussions of ethics in the media and in government.[3] Whenever a controversy arises over sexual or reproductive morals, you can bet that religious leaders from several different faith groups will be prominently represented on influential committees, or on panel discussions on radio or television. I'm not suggesting that we should go out of our way to censor the views of these people. But why does our society beat a path to their door, as though they had some expertise comparable to that of, say, a moral philosopher, a family lawyer or a doctor?

Here's another weird example of the privileging of religion. On 21 February 2006 the United States Supreme Court ruled that a church in New Mexico should be exempt from the law, which everybody else has to obey, against the taking of hallucinogenic drugs.[4] Faithful members of the Centro Espirita Beneficiente Uniao do Vegetal believe that they can understand God only by drinking hoasca tea, which contains the illegal hallucinogenic drug dimethyltryptamine. Note that it is sufficient that they *believe* that the drug enhances their understanding. They do not have to produce evidence. Conversely, there is plenty of evidence that cannabis eases the nausea and discomfort of cancer sufferers undergoing chemotherapy. Yet the Supreme Court ruled, in 2005, that all patients who use cannabis for medicinal purposes are vulnerable to federal prosecution (even in the minority of states where such specialist use is legalized). Religion, as ever, is the trump card. Imagine members of an art appreciation society pleading in court that they 'believe' they need a hallucinogenic drug in order to enhance their understanding of Impressionist or Surrealist paintings. Yet, when a church claims an equivalent need, it is backed by the highest court in the land. Such is the power of religion as a talisman.

Seventeen years ago, I was one of thirty-six writers and artists commissioned by the magazine *New Statesman* to write in support of the distinguished author Salman Rushdie,[5] then under sentence of death for writing a novel. Incensed by the 'sympathy' for Muslim 'hurt' and 'offence' expressed by Christian leaders and even some secular opinion-formers, I drew the following parallel:

> If the advocates of apartheid had their wits about them they would claim – for all I know truthfully – that allowing mixed races is against their religion. A good part of the opposition would respectfully tiptoe away.

And it is no use claiming that this is an unfair parallel because apartheid has no rational justification. The whole point of religious faith, its strength and chief glory, is that it does not depend on rational justification. The rest of us are expected to defend our prejudices. But ask a religious person to justify their faith and you infringe 'religious liberty'.

Little did I know that something pretty similar would come to pass in the twenty-first century. The *Los Angeles Times* (10 April 2006) reported that numerous Christian groups on campuses around the United States were suing their universities for enforcing anti-discrimination rules, including prohibitions against harassing or abusing homosexuals. As a typical example, in 2004 James Nixon, a twelve-year-old boy in Ohio, won the right in court to wear a T-shirt to school bearing the words 'Homosexuality is a sin, Islam is a lie, abortion is murder. Some issues are just black and white!'[6] The school told him not to wear the T-shirt – and the boy's parents sued the school. The parents might have had a conscionable case if they had based it on the First Amendment's guarantee of freedom of speech. But they didn't: indeed, they couldn't, because free speech is deemed not to include 'hate speech'. But hate only has to prove it is *religious*, and it no longer counts as hate. So, instead of freedom of speech, the Nixons' lawyers appealed to the constitutional right to freedom of *religion*. Their victorious lawsuit was supported by the Alliance Defense Fund of Arizona, whose business it is to 'press the legal battle for religious freedom'.

The Reverend Rick Scarborough, supporting the wave of similar Christian lawsuits brought to establish religion as a legal justification for discrimination against homosexuals and other groups, has named it the civil rights struggle of the twenty-first century: 'Christians are going to have to take a stand for the right to be Christian.'[7] Once again, if such people took their stand on the right to free speech, one might reluctantly sympathize. But that isn't what it is about. The legal case in favour of discrimination against homosexuals is being mounted as a counter-suit against alleged religious discrimination! And the law seems to respect this. You can't get away with saying, 'If you try to stop me from insulting homosexuals it violates my freedom of prejudice.' But you can get away with saying, 'It violates my freedom of religion.' What, when you think about it, is the difference? Yet again, religion trumps all.

I'll end with a particular case study, which tellingly illuminates society's exaggerated respect for religion, over and above ordinary human respect. The case flared up in February 2006 – a ludicrous episode, which veered wildly between the extremes of comedy and tragedy. The previous September, the Danish newspaper *Jyllands-Posten* published twelve cartoons depicting the prophet Muhammad. Over the next three months, indignation was carefully and systematically nurtured throughout the Islamic world by a small group of Muslims living in Denmark, led by two imams who had been granted sanctuary there.[8] In late 2005 these malevolent exiles travelled from Denmark to Egypt bearing a dossier, which was copied and circulated from there to the whole Islamic world, including, importantly, Indonesia. The dossier contained falsehoods about alleged maltreatment of Muslims in Denmark, and the tendentious lie that *Jyllands-Posten* was a government-run newspaper. It also contained the twelve cartoons which, crucially, the imams had supplemented with three additional images whose origin was mysterious but which certainly had no connection with Denmark. Unlike the original twelve, these three add-ons were genuinely offensive – or would have been if they had, as the zealous propagandists alleged, depicted Muhammad. A particularly damaging one of these three was not a cartoon at all but a faxed photograph of a bearded man wearing a fake pig's snout held on with elastic. It has subsequently turned out that this was an Associated Press photograph of a

Frenchman entered for a pig-squealing contest at a country fair in France.[9] The photograph had no connection whatsoever with the prophet Muhammad, no connection with Islam, and no connection with Denmark. But the Muslim activists, on their mischief-stirring hike to Cairo, implied all three connections . . . with predictable results.

The carefully cultivated 'hurt' and 'offence' was brought to an explosive head five months after the twelve cartoons were originally published. Demonstrators in Pakistan and Indonesia burned Danish flags (where did they get them from?) and hysterical demands were made for the Danish government to apologize. (Apologize for what? They didn't draw the cartoons, or publish them. Danes just live in a country with a free press, something that people in many Islamic countries might have a hard time understanding.) Newspapers in Norway, Germany, France and even the United States (but, conspicuously, not Britain) reprinted the cartoons in gestures of solidarity with *Jyllands-Posten*, which added fuel to the flames. Embassies and consulates were trashed, Danish goods were boycotted, Danish citizens and, indeed, Westerners generally, were physically threatened; Christian churches in Pakistan, with no Danish or European connections at all, were burned. Nine people were killed when Libyan rioters attacked and burned the Italian consulate in Benghazi. As Germaine Greer wrote, what these people really love and do best is pandemonium.[10]

A bounty of $1 million was placed on the head of 'the Danish cartoonist' by a Pakistani imam – who was apparently unaware that there were twelve different Danish cartoonists, and almost certainly unaware that the three most offensive pictures had never appeared in Denmark at all (and, by the way, where was that million going to come from?). In Nigeria, Muslim protesters against the Danish cartoons burned down several Christian churches, and used machetes to attack and kill (black Nigerian) Christians in the streets. One Christian was put inside a rubber tyre, doused with petrol and set alight. Demonstrators were photographed in Britain bearing banners saying 'Slay those who insult Islam', 'Butcher those who mock Islam', 'Europe you will pay: Demolition is on its way' and, apparently without irony, 'Behead those who say Islam is a violent religion'.

In the aftermath of all this, the journalist Andrew Mueller interviewed Britain's leading 'moderate' Muslim, Sir Iqbal Sacranie.[11] Moderate he may be by today's Islamic standards, but in Andrew Mueller's account he still stands by the remark he made when Salman Rushdie was condemned to death for writing a novel: 'Death is perhaps too easy for him' – a remark that sets him in ignominious contrast to his courageous predecessor as Britain's most influential Muslim, the late Dr Zaki Badawi, who offered Salman Rushdie sanctuary in his own home. Sacranie told Mueller how concerned he was about the Danish cartoons. Mueller was concerned too, but for a different reason: 'I am concerned that the ridiculous, disproportionate reaction to some unfunny sketches in an obscure Scandinavian newspaper may confirm that . . . Islam and the west are fundamentally irreconcilable.' Sacranie, on the other hand, praised British newspapers for not reprinting the cartoons, to which Mueller voiced the suspicion of most of the nation that 'the restraint of British newspapers derived less from sensitivity to Muslim discontent than it did from a desire not to have their windows broken'.

Sacranie explained that 'The person of the Prophet, peace be upon him, is revered so profoundly in the Muslim world, with a love and affection that cannot be explained in words. It goes beyond your parents, your loved ones, your children. That is part of the faith. There is also an Islamic teaching that one does not depict the Prophet.' This rather assumes, as Mueller observed,

that the values of Islam trump anyone else's – which is what any follower of Islam does assume, just as any follower of any religion believes that theirs is the sole way, truth and light. If people wish to love a 7th century preacher more than their own families, that's up to them, but nobody else is obliged to take it seriously . . .

Except that if you don't take it seriously and accord it proper respect you are physically threatened, on a scale that no other religion has aspired to since the Middle Ages. One can't help wondering why such violence is necessary, given that, as Mueller notes: 'If any of you clowns are right about anything, the cartoonists are going to hell anyway – won't that do? In the meantime, if you want to get excited about affronts to Muslims, read the Amnesty International reports on Syria and Saudi Arabia.'

Many people have noted the contrast between the hysterical 'hurt' professed by Muslims and the readiness with which Arab media publish stereotypical anti-Jewish cartoons. At a demonstration in Pakistan against the Danish cartoons, a woman in a black burka was photographed carrying a banner reading 'God Bless Hitler'.

In response to all this frenzied pandemonium, decent liberal newspapers deplored the violence and made token noises about free speech. But at the same time they expressed 'respect' and 'sympathy' for the deep 'offence' and 'hurt' that Muslims had 'suffered'. The 'hurt' and 'suffering' consisted, remember, not in any person enduring violence or real pain of any kind: nothing more than a few daubs of printing ink in a newspaper that nobody outside Denmark would ever have heard of but for a deliberate campaign of incitement to mayhem.

I am not in favour of offending or hurting anyone just for the sake of it. But I am intrigued and mystified by the disproportionate privileging of religion in our otherwise secular societies. All politicians must get used to disrespectful cartoons of their faces, and nobody riots in their defence. What is so special about religion that we grant it such uniquely privileged respect? As H. L. Mencken said: 'We must respect the other

fellow's religion, but only in the sense and to the extent that we respect his theory that his wife is beautiful and his children smart.'

It is in the light of the unparalleled presumption of respect for religion that I make my own disclaimer. I shall not go out of my way to offend, but nor shall I don kid gloves to handle religion any more gently than I would handle anything else. [. . .]

I do not, by nature, thrive on confrontation. I don't think the adversarial format is well designed to get at the truth, and I regularly refuse invitations to take part in formal debates. I was once invited to debate with the then Archbishop of York, in Edinburgh. I felt honoured by this, and accepted. After the debate, the religious physicist Russell Stannard reproduced in his book *Doing Away with God?* a letter that he wrote to the *Observer*:

> Sir, Under the gleeful headline 'God comes a poor Second before the Majesty of Science', your science correspondent reported (on Easter Sunday of all days) how Richard Dawkins 'inflicted grievous intellectual harm' on the Archbishop of York in a debate on science and religion. We were told of 'smugly smiling atheists' and 'Lions 10; Christians nil'.

Stannard went on to chide the *Observer* for failing to report a subsequent encounter between him and me, together with the Bishop of Birmingham and the distinguished cosmologist Sir Hermann Bondi, at the Royal Society, which had *not* been staged as an adversarial debate, and which had been a lot more constructive as a result. I can only agree with his implied condemnation of the adversarial debate format. In particular, for reasons explained in *A Devil's Chaplain*, I never take part in debates with creationists.[12]

Despite my dislike of gladiatorial contests, I seem somehow to have acquired a reputation for pugnacity towards religion. Colleagues who agree that there is no God, who agree that we do not need religion to be moral, and agree that we can explain the roots of religion and of morality in non-religious terms, nevertheless come back at me in gentle puzzlement. Why are you so hostile? What is actually wrong with religion? Does it really do so much harm that we should actively fight against it? Why not live and let live, as one does with Taurus and Scorpio, crystal energy and ley lines? Isn't it all just harmless nonsense?

I might retort that such hostility as I or other atheists occasionally voice towards religion is limited to words. I am not going to bomb anybody, behead them, stone them, burn them at the stake, crucify them, or fly planes into their skyscrapers, just because of a theological disagreement. But my interlocutor usually doesn't leave it at that. He may go on to say something like this: 'Doesn't your hostility mark you out as a fundamentalist atheist, just as fundamentalist in your own way as the wingnuts of the Bible Belt in theirs?' I need to dispose of this accusation of fundamentalism, for it is distressingly common.

Fundamentalism and the Subversion of Science

Fundamentalists know they are right because they have read the truth in a holy book and they know, in advance, that nothing will budge them from their belief. The truth of the holy book is an axiom, not the end product of a process of reasoning. The book is true, and if the evidence seems to contradict it, it is the evidence that must be thrown out, not the book. By contrast, what I, as a scientist, believe (for example, evolution) I believe not because of reading a holy book but because I have studied the evidence. It really is a very different matter. Books about evolution are believed not because they are holy. They are believed because they present overwhelming quantities of mutually buttressed evidence. In principle, any reader can go and check that evidence. When a science book is wrong, somebody

eventually discovers the mistake and it is corrected in subsequent books. That conspicuously doesn't happen with holy books.

Philosophers, especially amateurs with a little philosophical learning, and even more especially those infected with 'cultural relativism', may raise a tiresome red herring at this point: a scientist's belief in *evidence* is itself a matter of fundamentalist faith. I have dealt with this elsewhere, and will only briefly repeat myself here. All of us believe in evidence in our own lives, whatever we may profess with our amateur philosophical hats on. If I am accused of murder, and prosecuting counsel sternly asks me whether it is true that I was in Chicago on the night of the crime, I cannot get away with a philosophical evasion: 'It depends what you mean by "true".' Nor with an anthropological, relativist plea: 'It is only in your Western scientific sense of 'in' that I was in Chicago. The Bongolese have a completely different concept of "in", according to which you are only truly "in" a place if you are an anointed elder entitled to take snuff from the dried scrotum of a goat.'[13]

Maybe scientists are fundamentalist when it comes to defining in some abstract way what is meant by 'truth'. But so is everybody else. I am no more fundamentalist when I say evolution is true than when I say it is true that New Zealand is in the southern hemisphere. We believe in evolution because the evidence supports it, and we would abandon it overnight if new evidence arose to disprove it. No real fundamentalist would ever say anything like that.

It is all too easy to confuse fundamentalism with passion. I may well appear passionate when I defend evolution against a fundamentalist creationist, but this is not because of a rival fundamentalism of my own. It is because the evidence for evolution is overwhelmingly strong and I am passionately distressed that my opponent can't see it – or, more usually, refuses to look at it because it contradicts his holy book. My passion is increased when I think about how much the poor fundamentalists, and those whom they influence, are *missing*. The truths of evolution, along with many other scientific truths, are so engrossingly fascinating and beautiful; how truly tragic to die having missed out on all that! Of course that makes me passionate. How could it not? But my belief in evolution is not fundamentalism, and it is not faith, because I know what it would take to change my mind, and I would gladly do so if the necessary evidence were forthcoming.

It does happen. I have previously told the story of a respected elder statesman of the Zoology Department at Oxford when I was an undergraduate. For years he had passionately believed, and taught, that the Golgi Apparatus (a microscopic feature of the interior of cells) was not real: an artefact, an illusion. Every Monday afternoon it was the custom for the whole department to listen to a research talk by a visiting lecturer. One Monday, the visitor was an American cell biologist who presented completely convincing evidence that the Golgi Apparatus was real. At the end of the lecture, the old man strode to the front of the hall, shook the American by the hand and said – with passion – 'My dear fellow, I wish to thank you. I have been wrong these fifteen years.' We clapped our hands red. No fundamentalist would ever say that. In practice, not all scientists would. But all scientists pay lip service to it as an ideal – unlike, say, politicians who would probably condemn it as flip-flopping. The memory of the incident I have described still brings a lump to my throat.

As a scientist, I am hostile to fundamentalist religion because it actively debauches the scientific enterprise. It teaches us not to change our minds, and not to want to know exciting things that are available to be known. It subverts science and saps the intellect. The saddest example I know is that of the American geologist Kurt Wise, who now directs the Center for Origins Research at Bryan College, Dayton, Tennessee. It is no accident that Bryan College is named after William Jennings Bryan, prosecutor of the science teacher John Scopes in the Dayton 'Monkey

Trial' of 1925. Wise could have fulfilled his boyhood ambition to become a professor of geology at a real university, a university whose motto might have been 'Think critically' rather than the oxymoronic one displayed on the Bryan website: 'Think critically and biblically'. Indeed, he obtained a real degree in geology at the University of Chicago, followed by two higher degrees in geology and paleontology at Harvard (no less) where he studied under Stephen Jay Gould (no less). He was a highly qualified and genuinely promising young scientist, well on his way to achieving his dream of teaching science and doing research at a proper university.

Then tragedy struck. It came, not from outside but from within his own mind, a mind fatally subverted and weakened by a fundamentalist religious upbringing that required him to believe that the Earth – the subject of his Chicago and Harvard geological education – was less than ten thousand years old. He was too intelligent not to recognize the head-on collision between his religion and his science, and the conflict in his mind made him increasingly uneasy. One day, he could bear the strain no more, and he clinched the matter with a pair of scissors. He took a bible and went right through it, literally cutting out every verse that would have to go if the scientific world-view were true. At the end of this ruthlessly honest and labour-intensive exercise, there was so little left of his bible that,

> try as I might, and even with the benefit of intact margins throughout the pages of Scripture, I found it impossible to pick up the Bible without it being rent in two. I had to make a decision between evolution and Scripture. Either the Scripture was true and evolution was wrong or evolution was true and I must toss out the Bible . . . It was there that night that I accepted the Word of God and rejected all that would ever counter it, including evolution. With that, in great sorrow, I tossed into the fire all my dreams and hopes in science.

I find that terribly sad; but whereas the Golgi Apparatus story moved me to tears of admiration and exultation, the Kurt Wise story is just plain pathetic – pathetic and contemptible. The wound, to his career and his life's happiness, was self-inflicted, so unnecessary, so easy to escape. All he had to do was toss out the bible. Or interpret it symbolically, or allegorically, as the theologians do. Instead, he did the fundamentalist thing and tossed out science, evidence and reason, along with all his dreams and hopes.

Perhaps uniquely among fundamentalists, Kurt Wise is honest – devastatingly, painfully, shockingly honest. Give him the Templeton Prize; he might be the first really sincere recipient. Wise brings to the surface what is secretly going on underneath, in the minds of fundamentalists generally, when they encounter scientific evidence that contradicts their beliefs. Listen to his peroration:

> Although there are scientific reasons for accepting a young earth, I am a young-age creationist because that is my understanding of the Scripture. As I shared with my professors years ago when I was in college, if all the evidence in the universe turns against creationism, I would be the first to admit it, but I would still be a creationist because that is what the Word of God seems to indicate. Here I must stand.[14]

He seems to be quoting Luther as he nailed his theses to the door of the church in Wittenberg, but poor Kurt Wise reminds me more of Winston Smith in 1984 – struggling desperately to believe that two plus two equals five if Big Brother says it does. Winston, however, was being tortured. Wise's doublethink comes not from the imperative of physical torture but from the imperative – apparently just as undeniable to some people – of religious faith: arguably a form of mental torture. I am hostile to religion because of what it did to Kurt Wise. And if it did that to a Harvard-educated geologist, just think

what it can do to others less gifted and less well armed.

Fundamentalist religion is hell-bent on ruining the scientific education of countless thousands of innocent, well-meaning, eager young minds. Non-fundamentalist, 'sensible' religion may not be doing that. But it is making the world safe for fundamentalism by teaching children, from their earliest years, that unquestioning faith is a virtue. [. . .]

How 'Moderation' in Faith Fosters Fanaticism

In illustration of the dark side of absolutism, I mentioned the Christians in America who blow up abortion clinics, and the Taliban of Afghanistan, whose list of cruelties, especially to women, I find too painful to recount. I could have expanded upon Iran under the ayatollahs, or Saudi Arabia under the Saud princes, where women cannot drive, and are in trouble if they even leave their homes without a male relative (who may, as a generous concession, be a small male child). See Jan Goodwin's *Price of Honour* for a devastating exposé of the treatment of women in Saudi Arabia and other present-day theocracies. Johann Hari, one of the (London) *Independent*'s liveliest columnists, wrote an article whose title speaks for itself: 'The best way to undermine the jihadists is to trigger a rebellion of Muslim women.'[15]

Or, switching to Christianity, I could have cited those American 'rapture' Christians whose powerful influence on American Middle Eastern policy is governed by their biblical belief that Israel has a God-given right to all the lands of Palestine.[16] Some rapture Christians go further and actually yearn for nuclear war because they interpret it as the 'Armageddon' which, according to their bizarre but disturbingly popular interpretation of the book of Revelation, will hasten the Second Coming. I cannot improve on Sam Harris's chilling comment, in his *Letter to a Christian Nation*:

It is, therefore, not an exaggeration to say that if the city of New York were suddenly replaced by a ball of fire, some significant percentage of the American population would see a silver-lining in the subsequent mushroom cloud, as it would suggest to them that the best thing that is ever going to happen was about to happen: the return of Christ. It should be blindingly obvious that beliefs of this sort will do little to help us create a durable future for ourselves – socially, economically, environmentally, or geopolitically. Imagine the consequences if any significant component of the U.S. government actually believed that the world was about to end and that its ending would be *glorious*. The fact that nearly half of the American population apparently believes this, purely on the basis of religious dogma, should be considered a moral and intellectual emergency.

There are, then, people whose religious faith takes them right outside the enlightened consensus of my "moral *Zeitgeist*". They represent what I have called the dark side of religious absolutism, and they are often called extremists. But my point in this section is that even mild and moderate religion helps to provide the climate of faith in which extremism naturally flourishes.

In July 2005, London was the victim of a concerted suicide bomb attack: three bombs in the subway and one in a bus. Not as bad as the 2001 attack on the World Trade Center, and certainly not as unexpected (indeed, London had been braced for just such an event ever since Blair volunteered us as unwilling side-kicks in Bush's invasion of Iraq), nevertheless the London explosions horrified Britain. The newspapers were filled with agonized appraisals of what drove four young men to blow themselves up and take a lot of innocent people with them. The murderers were British citizens, cricket-loving, well-mannered, just the sort of young men whose company one might have enjoyed.

Why did these cricket-loving young men do it? Unlike their Palestinian counterparts, or their kamikaze counterparts in Japan, or their Tamil Tiger counterparts in Sri Lanka, these human bombs had no expectation that their bereaved families would be lionized, looked after or supported on martyrs' pensions. On the contrary, their relatives in some cases had to go into hiding. One of the men wantonly widowed his pregnant wife and orphaned his toddler. The action of these four young men has been nothing short of a disaster not just for themselves and their victims, but for their families and for the whole Muslim community in Britain, which now faces a backlash. Only religious faith is a strong enough force to motivate such utter madness in otherwise sane and decent people. Once again, Sam Harris put the point with percipient bluntness, taking the example of the Al-Qaida leader Osama bin Laden (who had nothing to do with the London bombings, by the way). Why would anyone want to destroy the World Trade Center and everybody in it? To call bin Laden 'evil' is to evade our responsibility to give a proper answer to such an important question.

> The answer to this question is obvious – if only because it has been patiently articulated ad nauseam by bin Laden himself. The answer is that men like bin Laden *actually* believe what they say they believe. They believe in the literal truth of the Koran. Why did nineteen well-educated middle-class men trade their lives in this world for the privilege of killing thousands of our neighbors? Because they believed that they would go straight to paradise for doing so. It is rare to find the behavior of humans so fully and satisfactorily explained. Why have we been so reluctant to accept this explanation?[17]

The respected journalist Muriel Gray, writing in the (Glasgow) *Herald* on 24 July 2005, made a similar point, in this case with reference to the London bombings.

Everyone is being blamed, from the obvious villainous duo of George W. Bush and Tony Blair, to the inaction of Muslim 'communities'. But it has never been clearer that there is only one place to lay the blame and it has ever been thus. The cause of all this misery, mayhem, violence, terror and ignorance is of course religion itself, and if it seems ludicrous to have to state such an obvious reality, the fact is that the government and the media are doing a pretty good job of pretending that it isn't so.

Our Western politicians avoid mentioning the R word (religion), and instead characterize their battle as a war against 'terror', as though terror were a kind of spirit or force, with a will and a mind of its own. Or they characterize terrorists as motivated by pure 'evil'. But they are not motivated by evil. However misguided we may think them, they are motivated, like the Christian murderers of abortion doctors, by what they perceive to be righteousness, faithfully pursuing what their religion tells them. They are not psychotic; they are religious idealists who, by their own lights, are rational. They perceive their acts to be good, not because of some warped personal idiosyncrasy, and not because they have been possessed by Satan, but because they have been brought up, from the cradle, to have total and unquestioning *faith*. Sam Harris quotes a failed Palestinian suicide bomber who said that what drove him to kill Israelis was 'the love of martyrdom . . . I didn't want revenge for anything. I just wanted to be a martyr.' On 19 November 2001 *The New Yorker* carried an interview by Nasra Hassan of another failed suicide bomber, a polite young Palestinian aged twenty-seven known as 'S'. It is so poetically eloquent of the lure of paradise, as preached by moderate religious leaders and teachers, that I think it is worth giving at some length:

'What is the attraction of martyrdom?' I asked.

'The power of the spirit pulls us upward, while the power of material things pulls us downward,' he said. 'Someone bent on martyrdom becomes immune to the material pull. Our planner asked, "What if the operation fails?" We told him, "In any case, we get to meet the Prophet and his companions, inshallah."

'We were floating, swimming, in the feeling that we were about to enter eternity. We had no doubts. We made an oath on the Koran, in the presence of Allah – a pledge not to waver. This jihad pledge is called *bayt al-ridwan*, after the garden in Paradise that is reserved for the prophets and the martyrs. I know that there are other ways to do jihad. But this one is sweet – the sweetest. All martyrdom operations, if done for Allah's sake, hurt less than a gnat's bite!'

S showed me a video that documented the final planning for the operation. In the grainy footage, I saw him and two other young men engaging in a ritualistic dialogue of questions and answers about the glory of martyrdom . . .

The young men and the planner then knelt and placed their right hands on the Koran. The planner said: 'Are you ready? Tomorrow, you will be in Paradise.'[18]

If I had been 'S', I'd have been tempted to say to the planner, 'Well, in that case, why don't you put *your* neck where your mouth is? Why don't *you* do the suicide mission and take the fast track to Paradise?' But what is so hard for us to understand is that – to repeat the point because it is so important – *these people actually believe what they say they believe*. The take-home message is that we should blame religion itself, not religious *extremism* – as though that were some kind of terrible perversion of real, decent religion. Voltaire got it right long ago: 'Those who can make you believe absurdities can make you commit atrocities.' So did Bertrand Russell: 'Many people would sooner die than think. In fact they do.'

As long as we accept the principle that religious faith must be respected simply because it is religious faith, it is hard to withhold respect from the faith of Osama bin Laden and the suicide bombers. The alternative, one so transparent that it should need no urging, is to abandon the principle of automatic respect for religious faith. This is one reason why I do everything in my power to warn people against faith itself, not just against so-called 'extremist' faith. The teachings of 'moderate' religion, though not extremist in themselves, are an open invitation to extremism.

It might be said that there is nothing special about religious faith here. Patriotic love of country or ethnic group can also make the world safe for its own version of extremism, can't it? Yes it can, as with the kamikazes in Japan and the Tamil Tigers in Sri Lanka. But religious faith is an especially potent silencer of rational calculation, which usually seems to trump all others. This is mostly, I suspect, because of the easy and beguiling promise that death is not the end, and that a martyr's heaven is especially glorious. But it is also partly because it discourages questioning, by its very nature.

Christianity, just as much as Islam, teaches children that unquestioned faith is a virtue. You don't have to make the case for what you believe. If somebody announces that it is part of his faith, the rest of society, whether of the same faith, or another, or of none, is obliged, by ingrained custom, to 'respect' it without question; respect it until the day it manifests itself in a horrible massacre like the destruction of the World Trade Center, or the London or Madrid bombings. Then there is a great chorus of disownings, as clerics and 'community leaders' (who elected them, by the way?) line up to explain that this extremism is a perversion of the 'true' faith. But how can there be a perversion of faith, if faith, lacking objective justification, doesn't have any demonstrable standard to pervert?

Ten years ago, Ibn Warraq, in his excellent book *Why I Am Not a Muslim*, made a similar point from the standpoint of a deeply knowledgeable scholar of Islam. Indeed, a good alternative title for Warraq's book might have been *The Myth of Moderate Islam*, which is the actual title of a more recent article in the (London) *Spectator* (30 July 2005) by another scholar, Patrick Sookhdeo, director of the Institute for the Study of Islam and Christianity. 'By far the majority of Muslims today live their lives without recourse to violence, for the Koran is like a pick-and-mix selection. If you want peace, you can find peaceable verses. If you want war, you can find bellicose verses.'

Sookhdeo goes on to explain how Islamic scholars, in order to cope with the many contradictions that they found in the Qur'an, developed the principle of abrogation, whereby later texts trump earlier ones. Unfortunately, the peaceable passages in the Qur'an are mostly early, dating from Muhammad's time in Mecca. The more belligerent verses tend to date from later, after his flight to Medina. The result is that

the mantra 'Islam is peace' is almost 1,400 years out of date. It was only for about 13 years that Islam was peace and nothing but peace . . . For today's radical Muslims – just as for the mediaeval jurists who developed classical Islam – it would be truer to say 'Islam is war'. One of the most radical Islamic groups in Britain, al-Ghurabaa, stated in the wake of the two London bombings, 'Any Muslim that denies that terror is a part of Islam is kafir.' A kafir is an unbeliever (i.e. a non-Muslim), a term of gross insult . . .

Could it be that the young men who committed suicide were neither on the fringes of Muslim society in Britain, nor following an eccentric and extremist interpretation of their faith, but rather that they came from the very core of the Muslim community and were motivated by a mainstream interpretation of Islam?

More generally (and this applies to Christianity no less than to Islam), what is really pernicious is the practice of teaching children that faith itself is a virtue. Faith is an evil precisely because it requires no justification and brooks no argument. Teaching children that unquestioned faith is a virtue primes them – given certain other ingredients that are not hard to come by – to grow up into potentially lethal weapons for future jihads or crusades. Immunized against fear by the promise of a martyr's paradise, the authentic faith-head deserves a high place in the history of armaments, alongside the longbow, the warhorse, the tank and the cluster bomb. If children were taught to question and think through their beliefs, instead of being taught the superior virtue of faith without question, it is a good bet that there would be no suicide bombers. Suicide bombers do what they do because they really believe what they were taught in their religious schools: that duty to God exceeds all other priorities, and that martyrdom in his service will be rewarded in the gardens of Paradise. And they were taught that lesson not necessarily by extremist fanatics but by decent, gentle, mainstream religious instructors, who lined them up in their madrasas, sitting in rows, rhythmically nodding their innocent little heads up and down while they learned every word of the holy book like demented parrots. Faith can be very very dangerous, and deliberately to implant it into the vulnerable mind of an innocent child is a grievous wrong. It is to childhood itself, and the violation of childhood by religion, that we turn in the next chapter.

Notes

1 The full speech is transcribed in Adams (2003) as 'Is there an artificial God?'
2 Perica (2002). See also http://www.historycooperative.org/journals/ahr/108.5/br_151.html.
3 'Dolly and the cloth heads', in Dawkins (2003).
4 http://scotus.ap.org/scotus/04–1084p.zo.pdf.
5 R. Dawkins, 'The irrationality of faith', *New Statesman* (London), 31 March 1989.

6 *Columbus Dispatch*, 19 Aug. 2005.
7 *Los Angeles Times*, 10 April 2006.
8 http://gatewaypundit.blogspot.com/2006/02/islamic-society-of-denmark-used-fake.html.
9 http://news.bbc.co.uk/2/hi/south_asia/4686536.stm; http://www.neandernews.com/?cat=6.
10 *Independent*, 5 Feb. 2006.
11 Andrew Mueller, 'An argument with Sir Iqbal', *Independent on Sunday*, 2 April 2006, Sunday Review section, 12–16.
12 I do not have the *chutzpah* to refuse on the grounds offered by one of my most distinguished scientific colleagues, whenever a creationist tries to stage a formal debate with him (I shall not name him, but his words should be read in an Australian accent): 'That would look great on your CV; but not so great on mine.'
13 From 'What is true?', ch. 1.2 of Dawkins (2003).
14 Both my quotations from Wise come from his contribution to the 1999 book *In Six Days*, an anthology of essays by young-Earth creationists (Ashton 1999).
15 Johann Hari's article, originally published in the *Independent*, 15 July 2005, can be found at http://www.johannhari.com/archive/article.php?id=640.
16 *Village Voice*, 18 May 2004: http://www.villagevoice.com/news/0420,perlstein,53582,1.html.
17 Harris (2004: 29).
18 Nasra Hassan, 'An arsenal of believers', *New Yorker*, 19 Nov. 2001. See also http://www.bintjbeil.com/articles/en/011119_hassan.html.

References

Adams, D. *The Salmon of Doubt* (London: Pan, 2003).
Ashton, J. F., ed. *In Six Days: Why 50 Scientists Choose to Believe in Creation* (Sydney: New Holland, 1999).
Dawkins, R. *A Devil's Chaplain: Selected Essays* (London: Weidenfeld & Nicolson, 2003).
Harris, S. *The End of Faith: Religion, Terror, and the Future of Reason* (New York: Norton, 2004).
Perica, V. *Balkan Idols: Religion and Nationalism in Yugoslav States* (New York: Oxford University Press, 2002).

Chapter 40

Alister McGrath

DAWKINS' GOD

River out of Eden: Exploring a Darwinian World

For Dawkins, Darwin's theory of evolution – as developed in the light of Mendelian genetics and our understanding of the place of DNA in the transmission of inherited information – is more than a scientific theory. It is a worldview, a total account of reality. Darwinism is a "universal and timeless" principle, capable of being applied throughout the universe. In comparison, worldviews such as Marxism are "parochial and ephemeral."[1]

Where most evolutionary biologists would argue that Darwinism offers a *description* of reality, Dawkins insists that it offers more than this – it is an *explanation*.[2] Darwinism is a worldview, a *grand récit*, a metanarrative – a totalizing framework, by which the great questions of life are to be evaluated and answered. [. . .]

Natural Science Leads Neither to Atheism Nor Christianity

The scientific method is incapable of delivering a decisive adjudication of the God question. Those who believe that it proves or disproves the existence of God press that method beyond its legitimate limits, and run the risk of abusing or discrediting it. Some distinguished biologists (such as Francis S. Collins, director of the Human Genome Project) argue that the natural sciences create a positive presumption of faith; others (such as the evolutionary biologist Stephen Jay Gould) that they have negative implications for theistic belief. But they *prove* nothing, either way. If the God question is to be settled, it must be settled on other grounds.

This is not a new idea. Indeed, the recognition of the religious limits of the scientific method was well understood around the time of Darwin himself. As none other than "Darwin's Bulldog," T. H. Huxley, wrote in 1880:[3]

> Some twenty years ago, or thereabouts, I invented the word "Agnostic" to denote people who, like myself, confess themselves to be hopelessly ignorant concerning a variety of matters, about which metaphysicians and theologians, both orthodox and heterodox, dogmatize with utmost confidence.

Fed up with both theists and atheists making hopelessly dogmatic statements on the basis of inadequate empirical evidence, Huxley declared that the God question could not be settled on the basis of the scientific method.

> Agnosticism is of the essence of science, whether ancient or modern. It simply means that a man shall not say he knows or believes that which he has no scientific grounds for professing to know or believe . . . Consequently Agnosticism puts aside not only the

greater part of popular theology, but also the greater part of anti-theology.

Huxley's arguments are as valid today as they were in the late nineteenth century, despite the protestations of those on both sides of the great debate about God.

In a 1992 critique of an anti-evolutionary work which posited that Darwinism was *necessarily* atheistic,[4] Stephen Jay Gould invoked the memory of Mrs. McInerney, his third grade teacher, who was in the habit of rapping young knuckles when their owners said or did particularly stupid things:

> To say it for all my colleagues and for the umpteenth millionth time (from college bull sessions to learned treatises): science simply cannot (by its legitimate methods) adjudicate the issue of God's possible superintendence of nature. We neither affirm nor deny it; we simply can't comment on it as scientists. If some of our crowd have made untoward statements claiming that Darwinism disproves God, then I will find Mrs. McInerney and have their knuckles rapped for it (as long as she can equally treat those members of our crowd who have argued that Darwinism must be God's method of action).

Gould rightly insists that science can work only with naturalistic explanations; it can neither affirm nor deny the existence of God. The bottom line for Gould is that Darwinism actually has no bearing on the existence or nature of God. If Darwinians choose to dogmatize on matters of religion, they stray beyond the straight and narrow way of the scientific method, and end up in the philosophical badlands. Either a conclusion cannot be reached at all on such matters, or it is to be reached on other grounds.

Now Dawkins knows perfectly well that "science has no way to disprove the existence of a supreme being."[5] This, he argues, cannot be allowed to lead to the conclusion that "belief (or disbelief) in a supreme being is a matter of pure individual inclination." But who said anything about "pure individual inclination"? Where does this idea come from? Dawkins seems to imply that, where the scientific method cannot be properly applied, there is only epistemological anarchy. Without the scientific method, we are reduced to the pure subjectivity of individual opinion.

This misleading gloss on a perfectly serious and legitimate debate about the limits of the scientific method allows Dawkins to evade the point at issue. If the scientific method can neither prove nor disprove the existence or nature of God, then either we abandon the question as unanswerable (something Dawkins certainly does not choose to do) or we answer it on other grounds.

But the point at issue cannot be sidestepped in this way. If an answer is to be given, it is not a matter of "pure individual inclination," but of reasoned and principled argument on the basis of whatever criteria of judgment apply to this debate. This is not an arbitrary or whimsical matter, but a matter of intellectual integrity, in which all sides to the debate – whether atheist, theist, or Christian – seek to offer the "best explanation" of the available evidence.[6] This is basic philosophy of science, and it is not going to go away because Dawkins ignores it.

The issue emerges as important on account of the problem of "underdetermination of theory by evidence." At times, it is impossible to adjudicate between rival theories precisely because they seem to offer equally good accounts of observation. Two quite different theories may turn out to be "empirically equivalent," forcing the scientific community to suspend judgment until the issue is resolved by evidence, or reaching a decision on other grounds. An excellent example is provided by two rival schools of quantum mechanics: the "Copenhagen school," based on the approach of Niels Bohr and Werner Heisenberg, and that of David Bohm.[7] The two are empirically equivalent, and arguably equally elegant and simple.

In practice, the Copenhagen approach has achieved dominance – but largely on account of issues of historical contingency, not theoretical superiority. The two theories are associated with quite different worldviews, with the Copenhagen approach favoring an essentially indeterminist universe, and the Bohmian approach a more determinist model. Much depends on the theory choice made; yet the choice cannot be made with conviction. As James Cushing points out, this hasn't stopped people from making choices. Yet the scientific legitimacy of such decisions is open to question. Either we cannot reach a decision, or we must reach that decision on other grounds.

Yet if the scientific method cannot settle an issue, it does not mean that all answers have to be regarded as equally valid, or that we abandon rationality in order to deal with them. It simply means that the discussion shifts to another level, using different criteria of evidence and argumentation. As it happens, that is precisely what Dawkins does himself – develop arguments for atheism which are ultimately non-scientific in character. The key point for the moment is simply this: the scientific method *alone* cannot ultimately determine the God question, even though it has some important contributions to make to the debate. [. . .]

Proof and Faith: The Place of Evidence in Science and Religion

One of the central themes of the human quest for knowledge is the need to be able to distinguish mere "opinion" from "knowledge." How can we distinguish a belief that is warranted and rigorously reasoned from mere unsubstantiated opinion? The debate goes back to Plato, and continues today. The key question – whether in the natural sciences, philosophy, or theology – is this: what conditions must be fulfilled before we can conclude that a given belief is justified? For

Dawkins, the only reliable knowledge we may hope to have of the world is scientific. Philosophers, lawyers, theologians, and others may make spurious claims to secure knowledge. In the end, however, it is only the natural sciences that can provide a true understanding of the world.

There is no doubt that the debate over how we generate and justify our beliefs is immensely important, and Dawkins' contribution to this debate must be welcomed, and – along with its rivals – taken seriously. In recent years, considerable attention has been paid to the way in which people sustain their belief systems. The evidence is disturbing, especially for those who continue to believe in the Enlightenment vision of complete objectivity of judgment in all things. Yet there is a growing body of evidence that belief systems – whether theistic or atheistic – are neither generated nor sustained in this way.

Cognitive psychological research has demonstrated repeatedly that people "tend to seek out, recall, and interpret evidence in a manner that sustains beliefs."[8] The interpretation of data is often deeply shaped by the beliefs of the researcher. These implicit beliefs are often so deeply held that they affect the way in which people process information and arrive at judgments. Both religious and anti-religious belief systems are often resistant to anything that threatens to undermine, challenge, qualify, or disconfirm them. Deeply held assumptions often render these implicit theories "almost impervious to data."[9]

Some Christian and Islamic writers seem unwilling to examine their deeply held beliefs, presumably because they are afraid that this kind of thing is bad news for faith. Well, maybe it is – for intellectually deficient and half-baked ideas. But it doesn't need to be like this. There are intellectually robust forms of faith – the kind of thing we find in writers such as Augustine of Hippo, Thomas Aquinas, and C. S. Lewis. They weren't afraid to think about their faith, and ask hard questions about its evidential basis, its internal consistency, or the adequacy of its theories.

Yet the problem is not limited to those who believe in God. As I discovered while researching my book *The Twilight of Atheism*, an atheist worldview can be just as detached from empirical evidence as a religious one. Dawkins has his own views of what religious people believe, and proceeds to rubbish these ideas with enthusiasm. Anyone who was theologically illiterate would doubtless be impressed by such a performance, and come to the conclusion that religion had been judged and found wanting at the most profound level. Well, it has certainly been judged. But whether that judgment can be sustained on the basis of the evidence is quite another matter.

To put it bluntly, Dawkins' engagement with theology is superficial and inaccurate, often amounting to little more than cheap point scoring. My Oxford colleague Keith Ward has made this point repeatedly, noting in particular Dawkins' "systematic mockery and demonizing of competing views, which are always presented in the most naive light."[10] His tendency to misrepresent the views of his opponents is the least attractive aspect of his writings. It simply reinforces the perception that he inhabits a hermetically sealed conceptual world, impervious to a genuine engagement with religion. Dawkins tends to seek out, recall, and interpret evidence in a manner that sustains his atheist beliefs. To illustrate this, we may open our discussion of the place of evidence in Dawkins' take on reality by exploring his approach to the idea of "faith."

Faith as Blind Trust?

Faith "means blind trust, in the absence of evidence, even in the teeth of evidence."[11] This view, set out for the first time in 1976, is an expression of one of the "core beliefs" that determine Dawkins' attitude to religion. In 1989 he hardened his views: faith now qualified "as a kind of mental illness."[12] This non-negotiable

core conviction surfaces again in 1992, when Dawkins delivered a lecture at the Edinburgh International Science Festival, in which he set out his views on the relation of faith and evidence. Dawkins was scathing over the intellectual irresponsibility of faith:

> Faith is the great cop-out, the great excuse to evade the need to think and evaluate evidence. Faith is belief in spite of, even perhaps because of, the lack of evidence . . . Faith is not allowed to justify itself by argument.[13]

Four years later, Dawkins was named "Humanist of the Year." In his acceptance speech, published the following year in the journal *The Humanist*, Dawkins set out his agenda for the eradication of what he regarded as the greatest evil of our age.

> It is fashionable to wax apocalyptic about the threat to humanity posed by the AIDS virus, "mad cow" disease, and many others, but I think a case can be made that faith is one of the world's great evils, comparable to the smallpox virus but harder to eradicate. Faith, being belief that isn't based on evidence, is the principal vice of any religion.

This is to be contrasted with the natural sciences, which offer an evidence-based approach to the world. "As a lover of truth, I am suspicious of strongly held beliefs that are unsupported by evidence."[14] And quite rightly so. But does this suspicion extend to his own strongly held atheist views, which to his critics seem surprisingly unsupported by the evidence he adduces?

Dawkins here opens up the whole question of the place of proof, evidence, and faith in both science and religion. It is a fascinating topic, and we must be grateful to him for so doing. In this chapter, we shall explore some of the issues raised by the history and philosophy of science for this debate, and ask if it really is quite as simple as Dawkins suggests. I certainly thought so during my atheist phase, and would have regarded Dawkins' arguments as decisive. But not now.

Let's begin by looking at that definition of faith, and ask where it comes from. Faith "means blind trust, in the absence of evidence, even in the teeth of evidence." But why should anyone accept this ludicrous definition? In his "Prayer for my Daughter" Dawkins makes an important point, which is clearly relevant here:

> Next time somebody tells you that something is true, why not say to them: "What kind of evidence is there for that?" And if they can't give you a good answer, I hope you'll think very carefully before you believe a word they say.[15]

So what is the evidence that anyone – let alone religious people – defines "faith" in this absurd way?

The simple fact is that Dawkins offers no defense of this definition, which bears little relation to any religious (or any other) sense of the word. No evidence is offered that it is representative of religious opinion. No authority is cited in its support. I don't accept this idea of faith, and I have yet to meet a theologian who takes it seriously. It cannot be defended from any official declaration of faith from any Christian denomination. It is Dawkins' own definition, constructed with his own agenda in mind, being represented as if it were characteristic of those he wishes to criticize.

What is really worrying is that Dawkins genuinely seems to believe that faith actually is "blind trust," despite the fact that no major Christian writer adopts such a definition. This is a core belief for Dawkins, which determines more or less every aspect of his attitude to religion and religious people. Yet core beliefs often need to be challenged. For, as Dawkins once remarked of Paley's ideas on design, this belief is "gloriously and utterly wrong."

Faith, Dawkins tells us, "means blind trust, in the absence of evidence, even in the teeth of

evidence." This may be what Dawkins thinks; it is not what Christians think. Let me provide a definition of faith offered by W. H. Griffith-Thomas (1861–1924), a noted Anglican theologian who was one of my predecessors as Principal of Wycliffe Hall, Oxford. The definition of faith that he offers is typical of any Christian writer:

> [Faith] affects the whole of man's nature. It commences with the conviction of the mind based on adequate evidence; it continues in the confidence of the heart or emotions based on conviction, and it is crowned in the consent of the will, by means of which the conviction and confidence are expressed in conduct.[16]

It's a good and reliable definition, synthesizing the core elements of the characteristic Christian understanding of faith. And this faith "commences with the conviction of the mind based on adequate evidence." I see no point in wearying readers with other quotations from Christian writers down the ages in support of this point. In any case, it is Dawkins' responsibility to demonstrate that his skewed and nonsensical definition of "faith" is characteristic of Christianity through evidence-based argument.

Having set up his straw man, Dawkins knocks it down. It is not an unduly difficult or demanding intellectual feat. Faith is infantile, we are told – just fine for cramming into the minds of impressionable young children, but outrageously immoral and intellectually risible in the case of adults. We've grown up now, and need to move on. Why should we believe things that can't be scientifically proved? Faith in God, Dawkins argues, is just like believing in Santa Claus and the Tooth Fairy. When you grow up, you grow out of it.

This is a schoolboy argument that has accidentally found its way into a grown-up discussion. It is as amateurish as it is unconvincing. There is no serious empirical evidence that people regard God, Santa Claus, and the Tooth Fairy as being in the same category. I stopped believing in Santa Claus and the Tooth Fairy when I was about six years old. After being an atheist for some years, I discovered God when I was eighteen, and have never regarded this as some kind of infantile regression. As I noticed while researching *The Twilight of Atheism*, a large number of people come to believe in God in later life – when they are "grown up." I have yet to meet anyone who came to believe in Santa Claus or the Tooth Fairy late in life.

If Dawkins' rather simplistic argument has any plausibility, it requires a real analogy between God and Santa Claus to exist – which it clearly does not. Everyone knows that people do not regard belief in God as belonging to the same category as these childish beliefs. Dawkins, of course, argues that they both represent belief in non-existent entities. But this represents a very elementary confusion over which is the conclusion and which the presupposition of an argument. [. . .]

Is Atheism Itself a Faith?

Is science a religion? Dawkins is often asked this question, and has a standard answer: No. The sciences, he argues, have all the good points of religious belief, and none of their bad points. They evoke a sense of wonder at reality, and offer humanity uplift and inspiration. And they are immune from the problems of faith. Atheism is the only option for today's thinking person, whose ideas are grounded in the only valid mode of encounter with reality – that of the natural sciences. It's a splendidly simple account of things.

It all starts to unravel very quickly, however. We have already noted Dawkins' belief that religious faith is "blind trust, in the absence of evidence, even in the teeth of evidence."[17] This arbitrary and idiosyncratic definition simply does not stand up to serious investigation. In fact, it is itself an excellent example of a belief

tenaciously held and defended "in the absence of evidence, even in the teeth of evidence." Dawkins doggedly holds on to his own hopelessly muddled idea of what "faith" is, and assumes that others share that confusion. But what of atheism itself?

Dawkins presents agnosticism as an intellectual soft option, offering a rhetorical dismissal of the notion. In his Edinburgh Lecture of 1992 he argued that, like faith, agnosticism is a "cop-out" – an argument that can be applied to anything. "There is an infinite number of hypothetical beliefs we could hold which we can't positively disprove." Now there is unquestionably some truth in this. But the real difficulty is that Dawkins' biological arguments – to the extent that they *are* genuine arguments, rather than blunt dogmatic assertions – lead only to agnosticism. He is obliged to supplement them with additional arguments of a non-scientific nature to get to his intended conceptual destination. And these are often rhetorical, rather than analytical, in nature. In the end, Dawkins' atheism does not really rest on his science at all, but on an unstated and largely unexamined cluster of hidden nonscientific values and beliefs. As this point is so important, we shall explore it further.

The debate between atheism and religious belief has gone on for centuries, and just about every aspect of it has been explored to the point where even philosophers seem bored with it. The outcome is a stalemate. Nobody can prove God's existence, and nobody can disprove it. Dawkins, following G. G. Simpson, argues that everything changed with the publication of Darwin's *Origin of Species* in 1859.[18] So just what is the impact of Darwin on religious belief? That question has been explored in detail.

The basic conclusion, as we have seen, is that Darwinism neither proves nor disproves the existence of God (unless, of course, God is defined by his critics in precisely such a manner that his existence is defeated by some central presupposition of Darwinian theory). If the great debate about God were to be determined solely on Darwinian grounds, the outcome is agnosticism – a principled, scrupulous insistence that the evidence is insufficient to allow a safe verdict to be reached.

This does not suit Dawkins at all. His efforts to force an atheist conclusion upon a Darwinian description of the world are the least convincing, not to mention the least attractive, aspects of his writings. As an example, we may consider Dawkins' refutation of theism in *Climbing Mount Improbable*. Here, he argues that the very idea of a "designing God" is intellectually self-defeating:

> Any designer capable of constructing the dazzling array of living things would have to be intelligent and complicated beyond all imagining. And complicated is just another word for improbable – and therefore demanding of explanation . . . Either your god is capable of designing worlds and doing all the other godlike things, in which case he *needs* an explanation in his own right. Or he is not, in which case he cannot *provide* an explanation.[19]

These are just assertions – bold, brash, confident statements, linked to the absolute dichotomist patterns of thought that Dawkins enjoys.

Let's begin with his first point about God being a "complicated" and hence "improbable" entity, on account of the richness of the biosphere. What does Dawkins mean when he makes the extraordinary statement that "any designer capable of constructing the dazzling array of living things would have to be intelligent and complicated beyond all imagining"? It's a bold assertion, made without the customary process of careful argument necessary to lead to such a conclusion, including the fair and thorough evaluation of alternative proposals.

It is far from clear what force this point has. Dawkins himself has devoted much of his career as a scientific popularizer to demonstrating that "the dazzling array of living things" could have arisen quite simply, over long periods of time,

through a process of neo-Darwinian evolution. His point would have some merit as a critique of theism – though how much can be disputed – if he were to propose a doctrine of special, individual creation, similar to that proposed by William Paley. But there is no reason to do so. A theologian might respond by arguing that God created an environment within which incredibly complex entities could develop from quite simple beginnings by quite simple processes. Dawkins seems to think that believing in God commits one to this late eighteenth-century way of thinking about creation. But as the history of the Christian tradition up to, and since, that point makes clear, this is simply not the case.

Dawkins argues that, since God is "complicated," he is "improbable." These notions are not equivalent; nor is the latter entailed by the former. They are connected by a Kierkegaardian leap of faith, buttressed by an aggressive rhetoric rather than a rigorous, evidence-based argument. Yet, once more, it is quite unclear why this has any relevance. To reiterate the fundamental point made in the previous section: it does not matter whether God is improbable (setting to one side the fact that Dawkins neither quantifies this probability, nor offers us a method for determining that probability in the first place); improbable things happen. That, after all, is the point Dawkins makes in *Climbing Mount Improbable*. Improbabilities exist.

Anyway, why does God need to be *explained*? Which of the several diverging theories of scientific explanation is Dawkins basing this assertion upon? Carl Hempel's inferential model? Wesley Salmon's causal approach? Or one of the many other models which attempt to clarify whether an "explanation" actually explains *anything*? There is a singular lack of conceptual clarity in Dawkins' analysis, centering on the problematic yet critically important notion of explanation. As is well known, the philosophy of science has considered a variety of meaningful, yet quite different, concepts of scientific explanation,[20] none of which possess quite the reductive sense that Dawkins appears to presuppose. As Paul Kitcher points out, the most fundamental issue is the reduction of phenomena to as few "ultimates" as possible:

> Science advances our understanding of nature by showing us how to derive descriptions of many phenomena, using the same pattern of derivation again and again, and in demonstrating this, it teaches us how to reduce the number of facts we have to accept as ultimate.[21]

So what's the problem with God, exactly? Why should God require an explanation at all? He might just be an "ultimate," to use Kitcher's term – one of those things we have to accept as given, and is thus amenable to description, rather than explanation. Dawkins needs to do a lot more work on what he means here before his point can be understood, and subjected to rigorous scrutiny.

One of the most striking things about Dawkins' atheism is the confidence with which he asserts its inevitability. It is a curious confidence, which seems curiously out of place – perhaps even out of order – to those familiar with the philosophy of science. As Richard Feynman (1918–88), who won the Nobel Prize for physics in 1965 for his work on quantum electrodynamics, often pointed out, scientific knowledge is a body of statements of varying degrees of certainty – some most unsure, some nearly sure, but none absolutely certain.[22] Yet Dawkins seems to deduce atheism from the "book of nature" as if it were a pure matter of logic. Atheism is asserted as if it was the only conclusion possible from a series of axioms. [. . .]

Science and Religion: Dialogue or Intellectual Appeasement?

It is widely agreed that in recent years there has been a growing interest in exploring the relation of science and religion. Many are openly speaking about "a new convergence" in the disciplines, opening the way to new insights and understandings.[23] Dawkins has an admirably robust response to this: "To an honest judge," he writes – perhaps with himself modestly in mind? – "the alleged convergence between religion and science is a shallow, empty, hollow, spin-doctored sham."[24]

It's an interesting point of view, but it belongs to another century. In recent years, the scholarly understanding of the historical relationship of science and religion has undergone an intellectual revolution no less than that occasioned by Darwin's *Origin of Species*. Intensive historical scholarly research has demonstrated that the popular notion of a protracted war between church and science which continues to this day is a piece of Victorian propaganda, completely at odds with the facts.[25] Sure, there were individual conflicts, often reflecting institutional politics and personal agendas – such as the Galileo affair – or simply misunderstandings on either or both sides of the debate. But these conflicts are neither typical nor defining.

Dawkins takes a strongly positivist view of science, and links this with the idea that science and religion are necessarily at war with each other. To talk of a rapprochement or convergence between these is therefore for him nothing less than crude "intellectual appeasement."[26] It is thus important to note that this belief is firmly located in the social world of nineteenth-century England, and that both have become severely, even fatally, eroded and discredited with the passing of time. It is understandable that they should still linger in some works of popular science – after all, academic historical scholarship takes a long time to filter down. Yet a serious review of the popular myth of the "warfare of science and religion," so vigorously defended by Dawkins, is long overdue. His popular science has a lot of catching up to do.

To begin our exploration of these issues, we may consider the myth of the permanent "warfare" of science and religion in more detail.

The "Warfare" of Science and Religion

The history of science makes it clear here that the natural sciences have often found themselves pitted against authoritarianism of any kind. As Freeman Dyson points out in his important essay "The Scientist as Rebel," science often finds itself in "rebellion against the restrictions imposed by the local prevailing culture."[27] Science is thus a subversive activity, almost by definition. For the Arab mathematician and astronomer Omar Khayyam, science was a rebellion against the intellectual constraints of Islam; for nineteenth-century Japanese scientists, science was a rebellion against the lingering feudalism of their culture. In that the West has been dominated by Christianity, it is thus unsurprising that a general tension between science and Western culture could be seen specifically as a confrontation between science and Christianity.

Yet most historians regard religion as having had a generally benign and constructive relationship with the natural sciences in the West. Tensions and conflicts, such as the Galileo controversy, often turned out on closer examination to have more to do with papal politics, ecclesiastical power struggles, and personality issues than with any fundamental tensions between faith and science.[28] Leading historians of science regularly point out that the interaction of science and religion is determined primarily by the specifics of their historical circumstances, and only secondarily by their respective subject matters. There is no universal paradigm for the relation of science and religion, either theoretically or historically. The case of Christian attitudes to evolutionary theory in the late nineteenth century makes this point particularly evident. As the Irish geographer and intellectual historian David Livingstone makes clear in a groundbreaking study of the reception of Darwinism in two very different contexts – Belfast and Princeton – local issues and personalities were often of decisive importance in determining the outcome.[29]

In the eighteenth century, a remarkable synergy developed between religion and the sciences in England. Newton's "celestial mechanics" was widely regarded as at worst consistent with, and at best a glorious confirmation of, the Christian view of God as creator of a harmonious universe. Many members of the Royal Society of London – founded to advance scientific understanding and research – were strongly religious in their outlooks, and saw this as enhancing their commitment to scientific advancement.

Yet all this changed in the second half of the nineteenth century. The general tone of the later nineteenth-century encounter between religion (especially Christianity) and the natural sciences was set by two works: John William Draper's *History of the Conflict between Religion and Science* (1874) and Andrew Dickson White's *The Warfare of Science with Theology in Christendom* (1896). The crystallization of the "warfare" metaphor in the popular mind was unquestionably catalyzed by such vigorously polemical writings.

As a generation of historians has now pointed out, the notion of an endemic conflict between science and religion, so aggressively advocated by White and Draper, is itself socially determined, created in the lengthening shadows of hostility towards individual clergy and church institutions. The interaction of science and religion has been influenced more by their social circumstances than by their specific ideas.[30] The Victorian period itself gave rise to the social pressures and tensions which engendered the myth of permanent warfare between science and religion.

A significant social shift can be discerned behind the emergence of this "conflict" model. From a sociological perspective, scientific knowledge was advocated by particular social groups to advance their own specific goals and interests. There was growing competition between two specific groups within English society in the nineteenth century: the clergy and the scientific professionals. The clergy were widely regarded as an elite at the beginning of the century, with the "scientific parson" a well-established social stereotype. With the appearance of the professional scientist, however, a struggle for supremacy began, to determine who would gain the cultural ascendancy within British culture in the second half of the nineteenth century. The "conflict" model has its origins in the specific conditions of the Victorian era, in which an emerging professional intellectual group sought to displace a group which had hitherto occupied the place of honor.

The "conflict" model of science and religion thus came to prominence at a time when professional scientists wished to distance themselves from their amateur colleagues, and when changing patterns in academic culture necessitated demonstrating its independence from the church and other bastions of the establishment. Academic freedom demanded a break with the church; it was a small step towards depicting the church as the opponent of learning and scientific advance in the late nineteenth century, and the natural sciences as its strongest advocates.

Today, this stereotype of the "warfare of science and religion" lingers on in the backwaters of Western culture. Yet the idea that the natural sciences and religion have been permanently at war with each other is now no longer taken seriously by any historian of science. It is generally accepted that the "warfare" model was developed by religiously alienated individuals in the nineteenth century to help the professional group of natural scientists to break free from ecclesiastical control – a major issue in the intellectual life of Victorian England.[31] Detailed historical analysis of the origins of the "warfare" model have demonstrated that it is historically located. It does not reflect the fundamental natures or themes of either the natural sciences or Christian theology; it is specifically linked with the social situation of science and religion in Victorian England. With the passing of that particular set of circumstances, that conflict receded.

It is certainly true that some have taken the view that the relation between science and Christian theology is permanently defined, at least in its fundamental respects, by the essential nature of the two disciplines – and, on Dawkins' unsatisfactory reading of the history and philosophy of science, that they are therefore locked into mortal combat, from which science must emerge as the ultimate victor. Underlying these "essentialist" accounts of the interaction of science and religion is the unchallenged assumption that each of these terms designates something fixed, permanent, and essential, so that their mutual relationship is determined by something fundamental to each of the disciplines, unaffected by the specifics of time, place, or culture. But it is simply not so. The relation of science and religion is historically conditioned, bound to the social and intellectual conditions of the age.[32] What we are seeing at present is a growing interest, on both sides of the divide, in seeing how the two disciplines can illuminate and even assist each other's efforts.

The twentieth century has witnessed a vast revision of the simplistic views of the nineteenth century on the nature and limits of the scientific method, and the relation of faith and science. The huge scholarly process of subjecting these traditional views to minute examination has forged a new awareness of possibilities for positive and constructive dialogue and engagement, at a time in the history of Western culture which is showing a new interest in spirituality at every level.

I do wish Dawkins would join in this dialogue, instead of firing off inaccurate, wildly rhetorical salvoes, and lampooning those who disagree with him.

Notes

1 For the exploration of this point, see the essay "Darwin Triumphant: Darwinism as Universal Truth," in *A Devil's Chaplain*. London: Weidenfeld & Nicolson, 2003.

2 For the difference between the two, see Karl-Otto Apel, "The Erklären-Verstehen Controversy in the

Philosophy of the Natural and Human Sciences."
In *Contemporary Philosophy: A New Survey*, edited by G.
Floistad, 19–49. The Hague: Nijhof, 1982.

3   See his 1883 letter to Charles A. Watts, publisher
of the *Agnostic Annual*. For further comment, see Alan
Willard Brown, *The Metaphysical Society: Victorian Minds
in Crisis, 1869–1880*. Oxford: Oxford University
Press, 1947.

4   Stephen Jay Gould, "Impeaching a Self-
Appointed Judge." *Scientific American* 267, 1 (1992):
118–121.

5   *A Devil's Chaplain*, 149.

6   For the issues, which apply equally well to natural
and social sciences, see the classic study of Gilbert
Harman, "The Inference to the Best Explanation,"
Philosophical Review 74 (1965): 88–95. A more recent
and extended discussion worth noting is Ernan
McMullin, *The Inference That Makes Science*. Milwaukee,
WI: Marquette University Press, 1992.

7   See James T. Cushing, *Quantum Mechanics: Historical
Contingency and the Copenhagen Hegemony*. Chicago: University of Chicago Press, 1994.

8   Richard E. Nisbett and Lee D. Ross, *Human Inference:
Strategies and Shortcoming of Social Judgement*. Englewood
Cliffs, NJ: Prentice-Hall, 1980, 192.

9   Nisbett and Ross, *Human Inference*, 169.

10 Keith Ward, *Chance and Necessity*. Oxford: One World,
1996, 99–100.

11 Richard Dawkins, *The Selfish Gene*, 2nd edition.
Oxford: Oxford University Press, 1989.

12 *The Selfish Gene*, 220 (this passage was added to the
second edition).

13 The lecture has no agreed title, and was published
under the title "Lions 10, Christians Nil" in Volume
1, Number 8 (December 1994) of an electronic
journal entitled "The Nullafidian," which describes
itself as "The E-Zine of Atheistic Secular Humanism
and Freethought," formerly known as "Lucifer's
Echo." There is no pagination. The journal appears
to have ceased publication in March 1996.

14 *A Devil's Chaplain*, 117.

15 *A Devil's Chaplain*, 248.

16 W. H. Griffith-Thomas, *The Principles of Theology*. London: Longmans, Green, 1930, xviii. Faith thus
includes "the certainty of evidence" and the "certainty of adherence"; it is "not blind, but intelligent" (xviii–xix).

17 *The Selfish Gene*, 198.

18 *The Selfish Gene*, 1.

19 *Climbing Mount Improbable*. London: Viking, 1996, 68.

20 See, for example, Wesley C. Salmon, *Scientific Explanation and the Causal Structure of the World*. Princeton, NJ:
Princeton University Press, 1984.

21 Paul Kitcher, "Explanatory Unification and the
Causal Structure of the World." In *Scientific Explanation*, edited by P. Kitcher and W. Salmon, 410–505.
Minneapolis: University of Minnesota Press,
1989.

22 See especially Richard P. Feynman, *What Do You Care
What Other People Think?* London: Unwin Hyman,
1989; Richard P. Feynman, *The Meaning of It All*,
London: Penguin Books, 1999.

23 See, for example, Michael Ruse, *Can a Darwinian
Be a Christian? The Relationship Between Science and
Religion*. Cambridge: Cambridge University Press,
2001.

24 *A Devil's Chaplain*, 151.

25 Two publications have been especially important
in forcing this radical review of the popular literature: David C. Lindberg and Ronald L. Numbers,
*God and Nature: Historical Essays on the Encounter Between
Christianity and Science*, Berkeley: University of California Press, 1986; Edward Grant, *The Foundations
of Modern Science in the Middle Ages: Their Religious,
Institutional, and Intellectual Contexts*, Cambridge:
Cambridge University Press, 1996.

26 *A Devil's Chaplain*, 149.

27 Freeman Dyson, "The Scientist as Rebel." In *Nature's
Imagination: The Frontiers of Scientific Vision*, edited by
John Cornwell, 1–11. Oxford: Oxford University
Press, 1995.

28 Mario Biagioli, *Galileo, Courtier: The Practice of Science in
the Culture of Absolutism*. Chicago: Chicago University
Press, 1993.

29 David N. Livingstone, "Darwinism and Calvinism:
The Belfast–Princeton Connection." *Isis* 83
(1992): 404–428.

30 Colin A. Russell, "The Conflict Metaphor and Its
Social Origins." *Science and Christian Faith* 1 (1989):
3–26.

31 Frank M. Turner, "The Victorian Conflict Between
Science and Religion: A Professional Dimension."
Isis 69 (1978): 356–376.

32 For a sustained critique of this position, richly
illustrated with historical case studies, see John
Brooke and Geoffrey Canton, *Reconstructing Nature:
The Engagement of Science and Religion*. Edinburgh: T. & T.
Clarke, 1998.

Chapter 41

Philip Kitcher

BORN-AGAIN CREATIONISM

1. The Creationist Reformation

In the beginning, creationists believed that the world was young. But creation "science" was without form and void. A deluge of objections drowned the idea that major kinds of plants and animals had been fashioned a few thousand years ago and been hardly modified since. Then the spirit of piety brooded on the waters and brought forth something new. "Let there be design!" exclaimed the reformers—and lo! there was born-again creationism.

Out in Santee, California, about twenty miles from where I used to live, the old movement, dedicated to the possibility of interpreting *Genesis* literally, continues to ply its wares. Its spokesmen still peddle the familiar fallacies, their misunderstandings of the second law of thermo-dynamics, their curious views about radiometric dating with apparently revolutionary implications for microphysics, the plundering of debates in evolutionary theory for lines that can be usefully separated from their context, and so forth. But the most prominent creationists on the current intellectual scene are a new species, much smoother and more savvy. Not for them the commitment to a literal interpretation of *Genesis* with all the attendant difficulties. Some of them even veer close to accepting the so-called fact of evolution, the claim, adopted by most scientists within a dozen years of the publication of Darwin's *Origin*, that living things are

related and that the history of life has been a process of descent with modification. The sticking point for the born-again creationists, as it was for many late-nineteenth-century thinkers, is the mechanism of evolutionary change. They want to argue that natural selection is inadequate, indeed that no natural process could have produced the diversity of organisms, and thus that there must be some designing agent, who didn't just start the process but who has intervened throughout the history of life.

From the viewpoint of religious fundamentalists the creationist Reformation is something of a cop-out. Yet for many believers, the new movement delivers everything they want—particularly the vision of a personal God who supervises the history of life and nudges it to fulfill His purposes—and even militant evangelicals may come to appreciate the virtues of discretion. Moreover the high priests of the Reformation are clad in academic respectability, Professors of Law at University of California-Berkeley and of Biochemistry at Lehigh, and two of the movement's main cheerleaders are highly respected philosophers who teach at Notre Dame. Creationism is no longer hick, but chic.

2. Why Literalism Failed

In understanding the motivations for, and the shortcomings of, born-again creationism, it's helpful to begin by seeing why the movement had to retreat. The early days of the old-style "creation-science" campaign were highly successfully. Duane Gish, debating champion for the original movement, crafted a brilliant strategy. He threw together a smorgasbord of apparent problems for evolutionary biology, displayed them very quickly before his audiences, and challenged his opponents to respond. At first, the biologists who debated him laboriously offered details to show that one or two of the problems Gish had raised could be solved, but then their time would run out and the audience would leave thinking that most of the objections were unanswerable. In the middle 1980s, however, two important changes took place: first, defenders of evolutionary theory began to take the same care in formulating answers as Gish had given to posing the problems, and there were quick, and elegant, ways of responding to the commonly reiterated challenges; second, and more important, debaters began to fight back, asking how the observable features of the distribution and characteristics of plants and organisms, both those alive and those fossilized, could be rendered compatible with a literal interpretation of *Genesis*.

Suppose that the earth really was created about ten thousand years ago, with the major kinds fashioned then, and diversifying only a little since. How are we to account for the distributions of isotopes in the earth's crust? How are we to explain the regular, worldwide, ordering of the fossils? The only creationist response to the latter question has been to invoke the Noachian deluge: the order is as it is because of the relative positions of the organisms at the time the flood struck. Take this suggestion seriously, and you face some obvious puzzles: sharks and dolphins are found at the same depths, but, of course, the sharks occur much, much lower in the fossil record; pine trees, fir trees, and deciduous trees are mixed in forests around the globe, and yet the deciduous trees are latecomers in the worldwide fossil record. Maybe we should suppose that the oaks and beeches saw the waters rising and outran their ever-green rivals?

Far from being a solution to creationism's problems, the Flood is a real disaster. Consider biogeography. The ark lands on Ararat, say eight thousand years ago, and out pop the animals (let's be kind and forget the plants). We now have eight thousand years for the marsupials to find their way to Australia, crossing several large bodies of water in the process. Perhaps you can imagine a few energetic kangaroos making it— but the wombats? Moreover, creationists think that while the animals were sorting themselves out, there was diversification of species within the "basic kinds"; jackals, coyotes, foxes, and dogs descend, so the story goes, from a common "dog kind." Now despite all the sarcasm that they have lavished on orthodox evolutionary theory's allegedly high rates of speciation, a simple calculation shows that the rates of speciation "creation-science" would require to manage the supposed amount of species diversification are truly breathtaking, orders of magnitude greater than any that have been dreamed of in evolutionary theory. Finally, to touch on just one more problem, creationists have to account for the survival of thousands of parasites that are specific to our species. During the days on the ark, these would have had to be carried by less than ten people. One can only speculate about the degree of ill-health that Noah and his crew must have suffered.

A major difficulty for old-style creationism has always been the fact that very similar anatomical structures are co-opted to different ends in species whose ways of life diverge radically. Moles, bats, whales, and dogs have forelimbs based on the same bone architecture that has to be adapted to their methods of locomotion. Not only is it highly implausible that the common blueprint reflects an especially bright idea from a designer who saw the best ways to fashion a burrowing tool, a wing, a flipper, and a leg, but the obvious explanation is that shared bone structure reflects shared ancestry. That explanation has only been deepened as studies of chromosome banding patterns have revealed common patterns among species evolutionists take to be related, as comparisons of proteins have exposed common sequences of amino acids, and, most recently, as genomic sequencing has shown the affinities in the ordering of bases in the DNA of organisms. Two points are especially noteworthy. First, like the anatomical residues of previously functional structures (such as the rudimentary pelvis found in whales), parts of our junk DNA have an uncanny resemblance to truncated, or mutilated, versions of genes found in other mammals, other vertebrates, or other animals. Second, the genetic kinship even among distantly related organisms is so great that a human sequence was identified as implicated in colon cancer by recognizing its similarity to a gene coding for a DNA repair enzyme in yeast. The evidence for common ancestry is so overwhelming that even the born-again creationist, Michael Behe is moved to admit that it is "fairly convincing" and that he has "no particular reason to doubt it" (DBB 5).[1] [. . .]

Imagine creationists becoming aware, at some level, of this little piece of history, and retreating to the bunker in which they plot strategy. What would they come up with? First, the familiar idea that the best defense is a good offense: they need to return to the tried-and-true, give-'em-hell, Duane Gish fire and brimstone attack on evolutionary theory. Second, they need to expose less to counterattack, and that means giving up on the disastrous "creation model" with all the absurdities that Genesis-as-literal-truth brings in its train; better to make biology safe for the central tenets of religion by talking about a design model so softly focused that nobody can raise nasty questions about parasites on the ark or the wombats' dash for the Antipodes. Third, they should do something to mute the evolutionists' most successful arguments, those that draw on the vast number of cross-species comparisons at all levels to establish common descent; this last is a matter of some delicacy, since too blatant a commitment to descent with modification might seem incompatible with creative design.

So the best tactic here is a carefully choreographed waltz—advance a little toward accepting the "fact of evolution" here, back away there; as we shall see, some protagonists have an exquisite mastery of the steps.

Surprise, surprise. Born-again creationism has arrived at just this strategy. I'm going to look at the two most influential versions.

3. The Hedgehog and the Fox

Isaiah Berlin's famous division that contrasts hedgehogs (people with one big idea) and foxes (people with lots of little ideas) applies not only to thinkers but to creationists as well. The two most prominent figures on the neo-creo scene are Michael Behe (a hedgehog) and Phillip Johnson (a fox), both of whom receive plaudits from such distinguished philosophers as Alvin Plantinga and Peter van Inwagen. (Since Plantinga and van Inwagen have displayed considerable skill in articulating and analyzing philosophical arguments, the only charitable interpretation of their fulsome blurbs is that a combination of Schwärmerei for creationist doctrine and profound ignorance of relevant bits of biology has induced them to put their brains in cold storage.) Johnson, a lawyer by training, is a far more subtle rhetorician than Gish, and he moves from topic to topic smoothly, discreetly making up the rules of evidence to suit his case as he goes. Many of his attack strategies refine those of country-bumpkin creationism, although, like the White Knight in Alice, he has a few masterpieces of his own invention.

Behe, by contrast, mounts his case for born-again creationism by taking one large problem, and posing it again and again. The problem isn't particularly new: it's the old issue of "complex organs" that Darwin tried to confront in the Origin. Behe gives it a new twist by drawing on his background as a biochemist, and describing the minute details of mechanisms in organisms so as to make it seem impossible that they could ever have emerged from a stepwise natural process.

4. Behe's Big Idea

Here's the general form of the problem. Given our increased knowledge of the molecular structures in cells and the chemical reactions that go on within and among cells, it's possible to describe structures and processes in exceptionally fine detail. Many structures have large numbers of constituent molecules and the precise details of their fit together are essential for them to fulfill their functions. Similarly, many biochemical pathways require numerous enzymes to interact with one another, in appropriate relative concentrations, so that some important process can occur. Faced with either of these situations, you can pose an obvious question: how could organisms with the pertinent structures or processes have evolved from organisms that lacked them? That question is an explicit invitation to describe an ancestral sequence of organisms that culminated in one with the structures or processes at the end, where each change in the sequence is supposed to carry some selective advantage. If you now pose the question many times over, canvass various possibilities, and conclude that not only has no evolutionist proposed any satisfactory sequences, but that there are systematic reasons for thinking that the structure or process could not have been built up gradually, you have an attack strategy that appears very convincing.

That, in outline, is Behe's big idea. Here's a typical passage, summarizing his quite lucid and accessible description of the structures of cilia and flagella:

> . . . as biochemists have begun to examine apparently simple structures like cilia and flagella, they have discovered staggering complexity, with dozens or even hundreds of precisely tailored parts. It is very likely that many of the parts we have not considered here are required for any cilium to function in a cell. As the number of required parts increases, the difficulty of gradually putting the system together skyrockets, and the likelihood of indirect scenarios plummets. Darwin looks more and more forlorn. (DBB 73)

This sounds like a completely recalcitrant problem for evolutionists, but it's worth asking just why precisely Darwin should look more and more forlorn.

Notice first that lots of sciences face all sorts of unresolved questions. To take an example close to hand, Behe's own discussions of cilia frankly acknowledge that there's a lot still to learn about molecular structure and its contributions to function. So the fact that evolutionary biologists haven't yet come up with a sequence of organisms culminating in bacteria with flagella or cilia might be regarded as signaling a need for further research on the important open problem of how such bacteria evolved. Not so! declares Behe. We have here "irreducible complexity," and it's just impossible to imagine a sequence of organisms adding component molecules to build the structures up gradually.

What does this mean? Is Behe supposing that his examples point to a failure of natural selection as a mechanism for evolution? If so, then perhaps he believes that there was a sequence of organisms that ended up with a bacterium with a flagellum (say), but that the intermediates in this sequence added molecules to no immediate purpose, presumably being at a selective disadvantage because of this. (Maybe the Good Lord tempers the wind to the shorn bacterium.) Or does he just dispense with intermediates entirely, thinking that the Creator simply introduced all the right molecules *de novo*? In that case, despite his claims, he really does doubt common descent. Behe's actual position is impossible to discern because he has learned Duane Gish's lesson (Always attack! Never explain!). I'll return at the very end to the cloudiness of Behe's account of the history of life.

Clearly, Behe thinks that Darwinian evolutionary theory requires some sequence of precursors for bacteria with flagella and that no appropriate sequence could exist. But why does he believe this? Here's a simple-minded version of the argument. Assume that the flagellum needs 137 proteins. Then Darwinians are required to produce a sequence of 138 organisms, the first having none of the proteins and each one having one more protein than its predecessor. Now, we're supposed to be moved by the plight of organisms numbers 2 to 137, each of which contains proteins that can't serve any function, and is therefore, presumably, a target of selection. Only number 1, the ancestor, and number 138, in which all the protein constituents come together to form the flagellum, have just what it takes to function. The intermediates would wither in the struggle for existence. Hence evolution under natural selection couldn't have brought the bacterium from there to here.[2]

But this story is just plain silly, and Darwinians ought to disavow any commitment to it. After all, it's a common theme of evolutionary biology that constituents of a cell, a tissue, or an organism, are put to new uses because of some modification of the genotype. So maybe the immediate precursor of the proud possessor of the flagellum is a bacterium in which all the protein constituents were already present, but in which some other feature of the cell chemistry interferes with the reaction that builds the flagellum. A genetic change removes the interference (maybe a protein assumes a slightly different configuration, binding to something that would have bound to one of the constituents of the flagellum, preventing the assembly). "But, Professor Kitcher [creos always try to be polite], do you have any evidence for this scenario?" Of course not. That is to shift the question. We were offered a proof of the impossibility of a particular sequence, and when one tries to show that the proof is invalid by inventing possible instances, it's not pertinent to ask for reasons to think that those instances exist. If they genuinely reveal that what was was declared to be impossible isn't, then we no longer have a claim that the Darwinian sequence couldn't have occurred,

but simply an open problem of the kind that spurs scientists in any field to engage in research.

Behe has made it look as though there's something more here by inviting us to think about the sequence of precursors in a very particular way. He doesn't actually say that proteins have to be added one at a time—he surely knows very well that that would provoke the reaction I've offered—but his defense of the idea that there just couldn't be a sequence of organisms leading up to bacteria with flagella insinuates, again and again, that the problem is that the alleged intermediates would have to have lots of the components lying around like so many monkey-wrenches in the intracellular works. This strategy is hardly unprecedented. Country-bumpkin creos offered a cruder version when they dictated to evolutionists what fossil intermediates would have to be like: the transitional forms on the way to birds would have to have had half-scales and half-feathers, halfway wings—or so we are told.[3] Behe has made up his own ideas about what transitional organisms must have been like, and then argued that such organisms couldn't have existed.

In fact, we don't need to compare my guess-work with his. What Darwinism is committed to (at most) is the idea that modifications of DNA sequence (insertions, deletions, base changes, translocations) could yield a sequence of organisms culminating in a bacterium with a flagellum, with selective advantages for the later member of each adjacent pair. To work out what the members of this sequence of organisms might have been like, our ideas should be educated by the details of how the flagellum is actually assembled and the loci in the bacterial genome that are involved. Until we know these things, it's quite likely that any efforts to describe precursors or intermediates will be whistling in the dark. Behe's examples cunningly exploit our ability to give a molecular analysis of the end product and our ignorance of the molecular details of how it is produced.

Throughout his book, Behe repeats the same

story. He describes, often charmingly, the complexities of molecular structures and processes. There would be nothing to complain of if he stopped here and said: "Here are some interesting problems for molecularly minded evolutionists to work on, and, in a few decades time, perhaps, in light of increased knowledge of how development works at the molecular level, we may be able to see what the precursors were like." But he doesn't. He tries to argue that the precursors and intermediates required by Darwinian evolutionary theory couldn't have existed. This strategy has to fail because Behe himself is just as ignorant about the molecular basis of development as his Darwinian opponents. Hence he hasn't a clue what kinds of precursors and intermediates the Darwinian account is actually committed to—so it's impossible to demonstrate that the commitment can't be honored. However, again and again, Behe disguises his ignorance by suggesting to the reader that the Darwinian story must take a very particular form—that it has to consist in something like the simple addition of components, for example—and on that basis he can manufacture the illusion of giving an impossibility proof.

Although this is the main rhetorical trick of the book, there are some important subsidiary bits of legerdemain. Like pre-Reformation creationists, Behe loves to flash probability calculations, offering spurious precision to his criticisms. Here's his attack on a scenario for the evolution of a blood-clotting mechanism, tentatively proposed by Russell Doolittle:

> . . . let's do our own quick calculation. Consider that animals with blood-clotting cascades have roughly 10,000 genes, each of which is divided into an average of three pieces. This gives a total of about 30,000 gene pieces. TPA [Tissue Plasminogen Activator] has four different types of domains. By "variously shuffling," the odds of getting those four domains together is 30,000 to the fourth power, which is approximately one-tenth to the eighteenth power. Now, if the Irish Sweepstakes had odds of winning of one-tenth to the eighteenth power, and if a million people played the lottery each year, it would take an average of about a thousand billion years before *anyone* (not just a particular person) won the lottery. . . . Doolittle apparently needs to shuffle and deal himself a number of perfect bridge hands to win the game. (DBB 94)

This sounds quite powerful, and Behe drives home the point by noting that Doolittle provides no quantitative estimates, adding that "without numbers, there is no science" (DBB 95)—presumably to emphasize that born-again creationists are better scientists than the distinguished figures they attack. But consider a humdrum phenomenon suggested by Behe's analogy to bridge. Imagine that you take a standard deck of cards and deal yourself thirteen. What's the probability that you got exactly those cards in exactly that order? The answer is 1 in 4×10^{21}. Suppose you repeat this process ten times. You'll now have received ten standard bridge hands, ten sets of thirteen cards, each one delivered in a particular order. The chance of getting just those cards in just that order is 1 in $4^{10} \times 10^{210}$. This is approximately 1 in 10^{222}. Notice that the denominator is far larger than that of Behe's trifling 10^{18}. So it must be *really* improbable that you (or anyone else) would ever receive just those cards in just that order in the entire history of the universe. But, whatever the cards were, you did.

What my analogy shows is that, if you describe events that actually occur from a particular perspective, you can make them look improbable. Thus, given a description of the steps in Doolittle's scenario for the evolution of TPA, the fact that you can make the probability look small doesn't mean that that isn't (or couldn't) have been the way things happened. One possibility is that the evolution of blood-clotting was genuinely improbable. But there are others.

Return to your experiment with the deck of cards. Let's suppose that all the hands you were dealt were pretty mundane—fairly evenly distributed among the suits, with a scattering of high cards in each. If you calculated the probability of receiving ten mundane hands in succession, it would of course be much higher than the priority of being dealt those very particular mundane hands with the cards arriving in just that sequence (although it wouldn't be as large as you might expect). There might be an analogue for blood-clotting, depending on how many candidates there are among the 3,000 "gene pieces" to which Behe alludes that would yield a protein product able to play the necessary role. Suppose that there are a hundred acceptable candidates for each position. That means that the chance of success on any particular draw is $(1/30)^4$, which is about 1 in 2.5 million. Now, if there were 10,000 tries per year, it would take, on average, two or three centuries to arrive at the right combination, a flicker of an instant in evolutionary time.

Of course, neither Behe nor I knows how tolerant the blood-clotting system is, how many different molecular ways it allows to get the job done. Thus we can't say if the right way to look at the problem is to think of the situation as the analogue to being dealt a very particular sequence of cards in a very particular order, or whether the right comparison is with cases in which a more general type of sequence occurs. But these two suggestions don't exhaust the relevant cases.

Suppose you knew the exact order of cards in the deck prior to each deal. Then the probability that the particular sequence would occur would be extremely high (barring fumbling or sleight of hand, the probability would be 1). The sequence only *looks* improbable because we don't know the order. Perhaps that's true for the Doolittle shuffling process as well. Given the initial distribution of pieces of DNA, plus the details of the biochemical milieu, principles of chemical recombination might actually make it very

probable that the cascade Doolittle hypothesizes would ensue. Once again, nobody knows whether this is so. Behe simply assumes that it isn't.

Let me sum up. There are two questions to pose: What is the probability that the Doolittle sequence would occur? What is the significance of a low value for that probability? The answer to the first question is that we haven't a clue: it might be close to 1, it might be small but significant enough to make it likely that the sequence would occur in a flicker of evolutionary time, or it might be truly tiny (as Behe suggests). The answer to the second question is that genuinely improbable things sometimes happen, and one shouldn't confuse improbability with impossibility. Once these points are recognized, it's clear that, for all its rhetorical force, Behe's appeal to numbers smacks more of numerology than of science. As with his main line of argument, it turns out to be an attempt to parlay ignorance of molecular details into an impossibility proof.

I postpone until the very end another fundamental difficulty with Behe's argument for design, to wit his fuzzy faith that appeal to a creator will make all these "difficulties" evaporate. As we shall see, both he and Johnson try to hide any positive views. With good reason.

5. Johnson's Kangaroo Court

Darwin on Trial is a bravura performance by a formidable prosecutor, able to assemble nuggets of evidence and to present them in the most damning fashion. The defense lawyer isn't even court-appointed, and is simply absent or asleep. I'm going to argue that, when the defense actually shows up, Johnson's apparently devastating attacks turn out to be slick versions of old sophisms.

Unlike Behe, who officially admits the universal relatedness of organisms, Johnson takes some trouble to blur the distinction between the process of descent with modification (the "fact of evolution"), and the mechanism that drives the process. Here are some typical passages:

> The arguments among the experts are said to be matters of detail, such as the precise time-scale and mechanism of evolutionary trans-formations. These disagreements are signs not of crisis but of healthy creative ferment within the field, and in any case there is no room for doubt about something called the "fact" of evolution.

But consider Colin Patterson's point that a fact of evolution is vacuous unless it comes with a supporting theory. Absent an explanation of how fundamental transitions can occur, the bare statement that "humans evolved from fish" is not impressive. What makes the fish story impressive, and credible, is that scientists think they know how a fish can be changed into a human without miraculous intervention. (DOT 12)

> We observe directly that apples fall when dropped, but we do not observe a common ancestor for modern apes and humans. What we *do* observe is that apes and humans are physically and biochemically more like each other than they are like rabbits, snakes, or trees. The ape-like common ancestor is a hypothesis in a *theory*, which purports to explain how these greater and lesser similar-ities came about. The theory is plausible, especially to a philosophical materialist, but it may nonetheless be false. The true explanation for natural relationships may be something much more mysterious. (DOT 67)

> Paleontologists now report that a *Basilosaurus* skeleton recently discovered in Egypt has appendages which appear to be vestigial hind legs and feet. The function these could have served is obscure. They are too small even to have been much assistance in swimming, and could not conceivably have supported the huge body on land. (DOT 84)

Here, and in other places, Johnson confuses the question of whether the history of life shows a process of descent with modification with problems about evolutionary mechanisms, as well as cleverly raising the standards of evidence appropriate for calling something a "fact."

Contemporary evolutionary theorists, notably Stephen Jay Gould, have wanted to distinguish the "fact" of evolution (the universal relatedness of life, the process of descent with modification) from theories about the mechanisms of evo-lutionary change, precisely because creationists have exploited debate on the latter issue to cast doubt on the former. The distinction was already clear in the late nineteenth century, when the claim that organisms are related by descent with modification became virtually universally accepted, even though naturalists continued to debate Darwin's preferred account of the causes of evolutionary change. Johnson wants to turn the clock back. His first sally charges that facts are "vacuous" unless they come with supporting theories—and, of course, there's an appeal to authority thrown in. The word choice is interest-ing. Does Johnson think that the claim that organisms are related isn't true? Or that it's equivalent to some elementary logical truth (such as "All fish are fish")? The latter is com-pletely implausible. Of course, Johnson would like to say that the claim of descent with modifi-cation is incorrect, but, since he can't defend that, he insinuates it by using a negative term.

In fact, scientific claims are often made with-out "supporting theories." Consider Kepler's laws about planetary orbits. Prior to the articula-tion of Newtonian theory, were these "vacu-ous"? Were chemists' proposals about chemical composition "vacuous" before we had detailed accounts of molecules and valences? Or Mende-lian claims about hereditary factors in the absence of knowledge that genes are made of DNA? The point derived from Patterson seems straightforwardly false, since it often seems a sci-entific advance to establish *that* something is the case without being able to say why or how it is so. But Johnson cleverly buttresses his argument by misformulating the claim of common descent—instead of "Humans evolved from fishes," we should have "All living things in the history of life on earth are related through a process of descent with modification."

The next step is to offer an appraisal. Johnson opines that the doctrine he dislikes isn't "impressive." Again, it's not obvious that the ability to wow Johnson or his creo friends is the appropriate criterion—shouldn't we be concerned with whether or not the doctrine is *true*? But, of course, it's been made to *seem* less impressive because of the pathetically reduced formulation. Only as an afterthought does Johnson link the irrelevant "impressiveness" to the pertinent criterion, credibility, and then he garbles the relations of evidence. What makes claims about common descent credible is a variety of evidence drawn from comparative anatomy and physiology, comparative embryology, and biogeography—the kind of evidence that clinched the case in the post-Darwinian decades, and that has been extended ever since (most notably in recent biochemical studies)—not any embedding in a theory about the causes of evolutionary change. Precisely the point made by defenders of evolutionary theory like Gould is that we have overwhelming evidence for common descent even though we may debate the mechanisms of evolutionary change.

On to the second version. Here Johnson starts by pouncing on an analogy used by Gould, the comparison of relations of descent to the falling of apples. Of course, it's perfectly correct to point out that we don't *observe* all the intermediates hypothesized by the claim that all organisms are related through descent with modification. However, the fundamental point was to differentiate between parts of science that are so firmly accepted that they are classified as "facts" from parts of science that are more controversial. It's not obvious to me that the fact/theory terminology is the best way of marking this distinction—so Johnson may be justified in criticizing

the rhetoric of his opponents. But that's just a preliminary point, and the main issue is whether the evidence for claims of descent is much stronger than that for causal explanations of the processes of modification.

Of course, there are plenty of parts of science that are not directly established by observation in the way that statements about falling apples are, but which nevertheless are counted as so firmly in place that scientists see themselves as building on them, rather than disputing them. Consider the claim that water molecules consist of two hydrogen atoms and one oxygen atom, or the identification of DNA as the molecular basis of heredity. Gould's characterization of common descent as a "fact" is meant to assimilate the thesis of universal relatedness to these scientific claims, to point out that its status is equally secure. If Johnson means to dispute this point, it's useless to note that one can't observe hypothetical intermediates—observation is just as inept to confirm molecular composition as it is to disclose ancestral organisms. What must be done is to show that the evidence in favor of common descent is far flimsier than evolutionary theorists have taken it to be, that it is nowhere near as strong as the support that has been garnered for the proposal that water is H_2O. To do that he has to explain why all those anatomical and physiological similarities, ranging from matters of gross morphology all the way down to molecular minutiae and including the apparently useless and nonfunctional residues of past structures, have been misinterpreted or overinterpreted by the defenders of evolution.

Johnson's half-hearted attempts to do just that are typified by the third passage I've quoted. As he notes, *Basilosaurus* is a sea-dwelling mammal related to whales, and it appears to retain rudimentary limbs. Evolutionary theorists account for the presence of these limbs by supposing that *Basilosaurus* is a modified descendant of some land-dwelling mammal, in whom the limbs were functional. The genetic changes that have taken place along the lineage have modified the body considerably, but the developmental program continues to produce vestigial versions of the structures present in the ancestors: they proclaim the animal's relatedness to land-dwelling forebears.

What neo-creos have to do at this point is explain that the vestiges don't signal any relationship to other mammals. So why are they there? What's the nonevolutionary explanation? Johnson doesn't tell us. Instead, he changes the subject, pointing out that the limbs aren't functional. But that wasn't the point at issue—indeed, the nonfunctionality was an indication that the limbs had been carried over from ancestral forms! Johnson has let the argument evolve from a dispute about descent with modification to a debate about the *causes* of evolutionary change, and he irrelevantly chides his opponents for not being able to tell a Darwinian selectionist story for these particular features of *Basilosaurus* and its immediate ancestors (DOT 85).

In the end, then, Johnson's attempt to dispute the "fact of evolution" is an exercise in evasion. When the rhetorical tricks are unmasked, it's clear that he's failed to answer the big question: if organisms aren't related by descent with modification, what's the explanation for all the detailed similarities we find among living things? Yes, indeed, the true explanation for observed relationships might be "more mysterious"—as might the true explanation for the data from which chemists justify their views about the composition of water or of genes—but the mysteries are, apparently, to remain the strict property of Johnson and his cronies.

As a lawyer, Johnson has an excellent understanding of ways in which burdens of proof can be shifted, and standards of evidence raised. Here are some samples of his skill:

> The question I want to investigate is whether Darwinism is based upon a fair assessment of the scientific evidence, or whether it is another kind of fundamentalism.
>
> Do we really know for certain that there

exists some natural process by which human beings and all other living beings could have evolved from microbial ancestors, and eventually from non-living matter? (DOT 14)

> *Archaeopteryx* is on the whole a point for the Darwinists, but how important is it? Persons who come to the fossil evidence as convinced Darwinists will see a stunning confirmation, but skeptics will see only a lonely exception to a consistent pattern of fossil disconfirmation. If we are testing Darwinism rather than merely looking for a confirming example or two, then a single good candidate for ancestor status is not enough to save a theory that posits a worldwide history of continual evolutionary transformation. (DOT 79)

The first passage frames the issues so as to impose unnecessarily stringent requirements on defenders of evolutionary theory. We start with two options: either the acceptance of evolutionary theory rests on "a fair assessment of the evidence" or it's a "kind of fundamentalism." Strictly speaking, that doesn't exhaust the possibilities, but let that pass. In the very next sentence Johnson transmutes the first option, reformulating it as the requirement that we know for *certain* that some natural process produced people out of microbes. Now, of course, this is focused directly on the issue of the mechanism of evolutionary change, and explicitly demands knowledge of the mechanisms that have operated over the entire sweep of evolutionary history, but the most glaring distortion occurs in the talk of certainty. In effect, the choices have been reduced to either knowing all the details with certainty or being a fundamentalist, so that no space is left for the thoughtful evolutionary theorist who wants to say "The evidence for the universal relatedness of life is compelling. Further, we know of a number of natural processes that have produced evolutionary change. We can't always say for sure which of these has been operative at which stage of the history of life, nor do we know that our inventory of possible mechanisms is complete, but, on the evidence we have, there's no reason to think that any supernatural process was needed in the evolution of organisms." That type of response is analogous to that of the chemist who declares "The evidence for our views about the kinds of bonds that occur between molecules in a vast number of substances is compelling. Further, we know in principle how the distributions of electrons in bonds result from basic principles of quantum mechanics. But we don't know how to solve the Schrödinger equation for any complex molecule, and it may be that our understanding of the microphysics is limited in various respects. Given the evidence we have, however, there's no reason to think that supernatural processes are needed to keep the constituents of large molecules together." In chemistry, as in evolutionary biology, there are open problems, and, while some parts of the science are quite firmly established (on the basis of compelling evidence), the idea that we should claim certainty überhaupt is as absurd as the thought that, if we can't do so, we've relapsed into fundamentalism.

The second passage occurs in the middle of a discussion of the fossil record (a discussion I'll treat from a different perspective shortly). After clouding the issues about the reptile-bird transition—mainly by claiming that evolutionists ought to produce fine-grained transitional sequences linking ancestral organisms to all the different species of birds—Johnson concedes, grudgingly, that the existence of *Archaeopteryx* is "on the whole a point for the Darwinists." Indeed, since the explicit challenge was to find transitional forms linking major groups, it's hard to see how the production of an intermediate, such as *Archaeopteryx*, could fail to meet the challenge: Johnson's strategy is like that of the child who bets his friend that she can't juggle three balls for a minute and then, when she does it successfully, welshes on the bet on the grounds that she didn't do it with her eyes shut. But, after magnanimously conceding that *Archaeopteryx* is

confirming evidence for the view that reptiles and birds are related by descent, he pooh-poohs the significance of this by suggesting that it's a "lonely exception to a consistent pattern of fossil disconfirmation." Let's formulate Johnson's implicit requirement explicitly: it's the demand that the fossil record would confirm evolutionary theory only if we could discover intermediate forms for every major transition (with Johnson reserving the right to decide which transitions count as "major" and also to demand the fineness of grain of the intermediate sequences). This is as arrogant as a counterdemand to be shown the fingerprint of the Creator in specified domains of the living world. As Darwin well knew, and as our improved understanding of the physics and chemistry of fossilization has shown us ever more clearly, the chances that any given species will be represented in the fossil record is extremely low. Our estimates of those chances are not, as Johnson likes to insinuate, specially cooked to favor evolutionary theory; they are based on independent parts of science. Given those estimates, we'd expect that for many major transitions the hypothesized intermediates would not be found in the fossil record, but, when the transitional fossils do occur, they provide striking confirmation of the claim of descent with modification because, if that claim were not true, the existence of such fossils would be highly improbable.

To see this more clearly, consider an analogy. In building the case against the notorious Moriarty, specifically in order to justify the conclusion that Moriarty visited the scene of the crime, the prosecution appeals to the fact that he was observed, just before the crime was committed, halfway between his lair and the crime scene. The defense responds that there has been no evidence of Moriarty's footprints on the pavement throughout the hundred-yard walk, that nobody saw Moriarty within ten yards of the crime scene, and so forth. The defense lawyer is a studious disciple of Phillip Johnson.

In fact, Johnson is sufficiently uneasy about

the fossil evidence to go to considerable lengths to respond to examples on which evolutionary theorists (rightly) place special emphasis. He cites the reptile-mammal transition as the "crown jewel of the fossil evidence for Darwinism" (DOT 75). He continues with one of his most accurate condensations of the biology:

> At the boundary, fossil reptiles and mammals are difficult to tell apart. The usual criterion is that a fossil is considered reptile if its jaw contains several bones, of which one, the articular, connects to the quadrate bone of the skull. If the lower jaw consists of a single dentary bone, connecting to the squamosal bone of the skull, the fossil is classified as a mammal. (DOT 75)

It might initially appear very difficult for an animal to be "intermediate" between reptiles and mammals, given this criterion in terms of jaw morphology. However, there's a very rich set of fossils showing reduction of the reptilian features and development of the mammalian traits; particularly remarkable are fossils, most famously *Diarthrognathus*, in which both types of jaw-joint are present.

After quoting Stephen Jay Gould's description of the advanced mammal-like reptiles, distinguished by the reduction in the quadrate and articular, Johnson comments:

> We may concede Gould's narrow point, but his more general claim that the mammal-reptile transition is thereby established is another matter. Creatures have existed with a skull bone structure intermediate between that of reptiles and mammals, and so the transition with respect to this feature is possible. On the other hand, there are many important features by which mammals differ from reptiles besides the jaw and ear bones, including the all-important reproductive systems. (DOT 76)

Well, when you can't argue the facts, argue the law. The existence of *Diarthrognathus* and friends shows that transitional forms with respect to jaw morphology *actually appeared* (not just [sniff!] that they were "possible"). So Johnson has to contend that these are irrelevant to the case. He reaches into the creationist bag of debating tricks for a well-known tactic, that of specifying just the intermediate forms that would satisfy him— he wants to see transitions in the "reproductive system." Clever indeed! For what he wants are the soft bits, the parts that don't have a prayer of being represented in the fossil record.

Now in fact, as Johnson ought to know, there isn't a single mammalian reproductive system— there are monotremes (egg-laying mammals), marsupials, and, most familiar, the placental mammals. So what is actually happening is that the question is being shifted. Instead of asking for an account of the reptile-mammal transition, Johnson is making a much more sweeping demand for a fine-grained sequence of transitional forms *within* Mammalia to show the gradual emergence of the placental mammals. What Gould actually claimed to be able to do was to show how a feature shared by all mammals (monotremes and marsupials as well as placentals), the structure of the jaw joint, emerges in the fossil record in a fine-grained transition from the structure found in living and extinct reptiles. However much Johnson might like to invoke the character of the reproductive system as a way of separating the mammals from the reptiles, the criterion of jaw morphology is taxonomically fundamental: mammals are animals that have one jaw structure, reptiles are animals that have a different jaw structure, and the mammal-like reptiles are those in which the bones involved in the reptilian jaw are being reduced, the most advanced of them being double-jointed. These criteria aren't pressed into service to save evolutionary theory. They are demanded by the diversity of the mammals with respect to other features. Johnson's revisionary taxonomy would sweep away some of the Antipodean mammals.

There are signs that Johnson recognizes that all is not well with his first line of argument, for he follows it up with an alternative. After noting that the fossil record for the reptile-mammal transition is so rich that a prominent evolutionary biologist (Douglas Futuyma) suggests that it's impossible to tell which species were the ancestors of modern mammals, Johnson continues:

> But large numbers of eligible candidates are a plus only to the extent that they can be placed in a single line of descent that could conceivably lead from a particular reptile species to a particular early mammal species. The presence of similiarities in many different species that are outside of any possible ancestral line only draws attention to the fact that skeletal similarities do not necessarily imply ancestry. The notion that mammals-in-general evolved from reptiles-in-general through a broad clump of diverse therapsid lines is not Darwinism. Darwinian transformation requires a single line of ancestral descent. (DOT 76)

The claim of common descent is, apparently, to be defeated by an *embarras de richesse*.

Plainly, Johnson hasn't been reading contemporary evolutionary theory very carefully, for he seems to have overlooked the modern emphasis on a theme (already present in Darwin) that the tree of life turns out to be a bush. Well-documented cases of anagenesis (in which a single lineage is gradually transformed) are quite rare. Paleontological reconstructions typically show modifications associated with (branching) speciation. Hence, in studying the mammal-like reptiles, there's no surprise in finding lots of closely related species, not just parents and daughters but sisters and cousins and aunts. Futuyma's point is that there are so many relatives in this family that it's hard to sort out the relationships, and, in particular, hard to tell which mammal-like reptiles are ancestral to the mammals.

So Johnson is quite wrong in thinking that there has to be a linear sequence linking all these fossils by ancestor-descendant relations: evolutionists would be quite surprised if that were so. But the rhetoric of his case depends on a skillful ambiguity. He insinuates doubts about whether jaw morphology is a reliable guide to relationship by talking of "species outside of any possible ancestral line." The suggestion, of course, is that evolutionists are committed to thinking of some of these species as *unrelated*, and that this undermines their claims that anatomical features (like the size and positioning of bones) are a good indicator of evolutionary relationships. But that's completely false. Those who study this transition don't believe that the fossils can be fitted into a single line of ancestors and descendants, but they do think of all of them as related. To repeat, there are daughters and sisters and cousins and aunts. The difficulty lies in assigning particular fossils particular degrees of relationship. But that difficulty doesn't interfere with the enterprise of revealing the reptile-mammal transition in the fossil record. Once again, a legal analogy may prove helpful. If the defense denies that any member of the Crebozo gang could have done the dirty deed, and the prosecution shows how Phil, Al, Pete, and Mike (Crebozos all) had motive, means, and access, the general claim that one of the Crebozos is guilty may be established without the prosecution's being able to tell which of the individual thugs delivered the decisive blow.

Johnson's entire book is filled with the sophistries I've been exposing, as he distorts the positions he opposes, shifts standards of evidence, quotes people out of context, and uses ambiguity to cover his argumentative gaps. Any well-trained philosopher with no particular axe to grind and a modest knowledge about evolutionary biology could hardly fail to see that rhetoric substitutes for sound argument on virtually every page—which is why the endorsements of Johnson by Plantinga and van Inwagen are so revealing. [. . .]

6. Where's the Beef?

I come at last to the most basic difficulty with the neo-creo attack, its dim suggestions that the scientific world needs a shot of supernaturalism. The born-again creationists tread different paths to a common destination. Whether hedgehogs or foxes, they conclude that evolutionary theory is beset by problems—one very deep and systematic problem for Michael Behe, a whole scatter of troubles for Phillip Johnson—and they portray the establishment as dogmatic in its insistence on excluding creative design: given that the going story of life and its history is such a shambles, why are these evolutionists so obstinate in thinking that some "purely naturalistic process" produced people? When this conclusion is made explicit, there's a natural question to pose to the neo-creos. How exactly is the appeal to creative design supposed to help?

I've been contending throughout that the charges of "insoluble problems" are wildly overblown. But let's play along for a bit. Consider the difficulties that Behe and Johnson cite, and suppose that they really do need to be addressed. Why should we think that invoking creative design, with all its theological resonances, is just the ticket for solving them? Behe and Johnson don't say. They've learned from the failures of pre-Reformation creationism, and they know much, much better than to put their literalist cards out on the table. Fine. But we ought to be a little curious about what sort of magic a creative design model might be able to work.

Let's start with Behe, and concede to him that we haven't a clue about how you can produce the bacterial flagellum or the clotting cascade in small steps. We might think we'd get some clues once developmental molecular genetics has developed a bit, but maybe Behe has a plausible proposal that will save us the wait and the trouble. What could it be? Well, it has to involve creative design, so we can assume that the unbridgeable gaps between the bacteria sans flagella and their fully equipped successors are

transcended through the activities of some Creator or "creative force." Continuing to be generous, let's give Behe the personalized version.

So what does the Creator do? Option 1: He (we'll throw in patriarchy as well) arranges the selection regime for the hapless intermediates, directs the mutations, and so forth; so, in accord with a doctrine Behe has "no particular reason to doubt," organisms are linked by descent, and the Creator's work is devoted to making sure that just the right mutations arise in the right order and that the organisms on the way to the complex final state are protected against the consequences of having lots of useless spare parts that will be assembled at some final stage. Option 2: the Creator dispenses with a lot of the intermediate steps by cunningly arranging for lots of mutations to happen at once; if 183 new proteins are needed for the new structure, then zap! He strikes the appropriate loci with his magical mutating finger; or maybe he does it in two goes of 92 and 91 (with a protective environmental regime for the halfway stages); or in three interventions of 61 mutations a trick. . . . Here, again, organisms are related by descent with modification, although the "descent" and the "modifications" are a bit abnormal. Option 3: the Creator gives up on mutation and selection entirely, simply creating a bunch of organisms with the right molecular stuff *de novo*; of course, if Behe thinks that this is the way things worked, then he really does have doubts about descent with modification.

The first point to note is that there's absolutely no evidence in favor of any of these options—they are the kinds of things to which one would be driven only if one thought that Behe's Big Problem was so intractable that there was no alternative. But matters are actually much worse than that, as one can see by posing questions about the Creator's psychology. Why should anyone think that the kind of Creator for whom Behe and Johnson both want to make room would undertake any of these projects? In Option 1, we envisage a Creator with the power to direct mutations and contrive protective environments who prefers simulating natural selection with gerrymandered selection pressures to directing all the needed mutations at once. In Option 2, we envisage a Creator who has the power to create organisms, but who prefers to simulate descent by the magic of mass mutation rather than simply producing the kinds of organisms He wants (either successively or simultaneously). In Option 3, we envisage a Creator who creates all the kinds of organisms He wants, as He wants them, but equips them with the genomic junk found in organisms He's created earlier. I am no engineer, but these visions inspire me to echo Alfonso X on the complexities of the Ptolemaic account of the solar system—had the Creator consulted me at the Creation, I think I could have given him useful advice.

Perhaps I am being unfair. Maybe the project of design looks ludicrous because I have selected the wrong options for Creative intervention. Behe could easily answer my concerns by coming up with an alternative, one that would explain how creative design has figured in the history of life on our planet and how that creative design is part of a project worthy of his favorite Creator. I'm inclined to think that he won't do that, that the silence in neo-creo positive proposals will continue to be deafening. After all, positive doctrines and explanations have always been creationism's Achilles Heel.

Notice that the line of argument in which I'm now engaged isn't a defense of evolutionary theory. For the sake of argument, I've conceded that evolutionary theory faces deep and intractable problems, although I've spent most of my time arguing that that's totally false. To show that the problems alleged to face evolutionary theory can't be solved by appealing to creative design isn't to rehabilitate the theory, for one doesn't always have to adopt the better of two alternatives. But in demonstrating that evolutionary theory is clearly superior to the imaginable

members of the creationist family I ought to sap the motivation of those who are drawn to creationism. Attacking evolutionary theory was supposed to make room for God, but, as we've seen, there's not much hope for an active role for the Deity in any successor to evolutionary theory.

Although it's hard to see just which of my three options Behe would choose, his position is less indefinite than Johnson's. What Johnson thinks actually happened in the history of life is deeply obscure. All he tells us is that the hallmark of creationism is the idea that "a supernatural Creator not only initiated the process but in some meaningful sense *controls* it in furtherance of a purpose" (DOT 4 n. 1). Controls it how and when? With what purpose? Johnson doesn't say. For one so enthusiastic about canonizing Sir Karl, Johnson's "creation model" is rather short on "risky predictions."

Suppose we were to concede Johnson's claims about the difficulties for evolutionary theory. It would be natural to expect, as his book puffs to its conclusion, that he would say something about how those difficulties vanish once one invokes the activities of the designing Creator. Consider those puzzles about the fossil record. What exactly do they indicate? Does Johnson believe that organisms whose fossilized remains are lower in the geological column were around long before those higher up? Which organisms does he think are related to which? And, if he denies the descent of major groups from the organisms evolutionary theorists identify as their ancestors, how does he think the later organisms were formed?

Here are the possibilities. Option 1: Johnson might claim that the fossil record is profoundly misleading, that there's been no succession of organisms; this would be to take over part of old-style creationism, claiming that the major kinds of organisms were all formed at once, and have inhabited the earth since the creation (except, of course, for those that have gone extinct); it would, however, remain uncommitted to whether or not the earth is old or young. Option 2: Johnson might claim that the fossil record really does show a sequence of organisms, with some appearing later in earth's history than others, claiming that the major kinds are created as they appear, and are not modified descendants of earlier organisms. Option 3: Johnson might propose that the history of life is one of descent with modification, but that the Creator has guided the processes (perhaps in the ways signaled in Behe's first two options, considered previously).

Now option 1 is highly problematic because it offers no account of the worldwide ordering of the fossils in geological strata and no account of the anatomical, physiological, developmental, and molecular affinities among organisms. The first of these is the familiar difficulty that led people early in the nineteenth century—including extremely devout naturalists—to abandon the idea of a single fixed creation in favor of a sequence of creations. Option 2 founders on the need to understand why later organisms take over features at all levels from earlier organisms, features that are often no longer functional. Are we to assume that the junk in our genomes and the vestigial bits and pieces of anatomy are just signs of the Creator's whimsy? Option 3 is of course an evolutionary account of life, one widely adopted in the later decades of the nineteenth century by theists who thought that there had to be a supernatural component to mechanisms of evolutionary change. It would require Johnson, like Behe, to explain just what it is that the Creator does, and why he does things that way. All three schematic creation models face large and familiar problems, which is why all the detailed versions of all of them have been abandoned by thinkers whose knowledge and intellectual integrity greatly exceed Johnson's.

But wait! Maybe Johnson has some gleaming new version that will put the general worries to rest? Alas, any reader who expected that would be disappointed. Toward the end of his book, he confesses

> I am not interested in any claims that are based upon a literal reading of the Bible, nor do I understand the concept of creation as narrowly as Duane Gish does. If an omnipotent Creator exists He might have created things instantaneously in a single week or through gradual evolution over billions of years. He might have employed means wholly inaccessible to science, or mechanisms that are at least in part understandable through scientific investigation.
>
> The essential point of creation has nothing to do with the timing or the mechanism the Creator chose to employ, but with the element of design or purpose. In the broadest sense, a "creationist" is simply a person who believes that the world (and especially mankind) was *designed*, and exists for a *purpose*. With the issue defined that way, the question becomes: Is mainstream science opposed to the possibility that the natural world was designed by a Creator for a purpose? If so, on what basis? (DOT 113)

Not only is no creation model offered here, but the definition of "creationism" is modified to make it compatible with orthodox Darwinism!

Johnson's original formulation of the position required that the Creator not merely set things up and let 'em roll, but that He actively intervene in the history of life. In this later passage, the commitment to continued intervention has been abandoned. Some Darwinians would be prepared to allow that the Creator fixed the initial conditions for the universe, although they'd contend that everything that has occurred since can be understood as the outcome of natural processes. For those theistically inclined, a view like this has often seemed superior to one on which the universe requires continual janitorial work—Leibniz chided Newton for hypothesizing that the Creator might have to tinker with His handiwork. Of course, there's a residual cluster of worries centering around the motivations of an omnipotent Creator for proceeding in so indirect a fashion.

Johnson's official line is that we ought not second-guess the Almighty. Confronting concerns about the apparent policy of letting later organisms inherit the junk of their ancestors, he chides evolutionary theorists for "speculating" about what a "proper Creator" would do. But, if the creation model is to be taken seriously as an account of life and its history, the character of processes and products must be full of clues to the attitudes of the Creator, and, on the basis of our observations, it's clear that the motivations of a Creator who let the evolutionary process unfold in the ways that it has in order to produce our own species are quite baffling. The more intimately the Creator becomes involved in the adjustments of the process, the greater the bafflement.

So Johnson leaves everything vague, hoping that nobody will notice that he's either committing himself to an extremely implausible hands-on Creator with purposes for which his means seem singularly ill designed or a slightly more credible hands-off Creator who produced the current world in just the ways cosmologists and Darwinian evolutionary theorists suggest. But his final question reveals his blindness to the historical fate of his options. Unless he does come forward with a new proposal for understanding the role of the Creator in the history of life, we're entitled to suppose that the only ways of articulating a creationist view are those that have been tried from the late eighteenth century to the present. Those are just the options I've canvassed, successively explored by ingenious, pious, but honest thinkers who rejected them because they were at odds with the record of historical and contemporary life. Coffin nails are driven deeper with the advance of fossil discoveries, the dissection of molecular relationships, our increased understanding of biogeography, and all the rest. In the end, the only answer one can give to Johnson's question— presumably intended as rhetorical—is that the best mainstream science can allow him is a Creator who set things up and let them unfold by natural processes. Whether this does more than pay lip service to the yearning for purpose and design is a matter I leave to theists.

The neo-creo model factory is strikingly out of new resources. For all the fancy rhetoric, all the academic respectability, all the accusations and gesticulations, born-again creationism is just what its country cousin was. A sham.

Notes

I am extremely grateful to Dan Dennett and Ed Curley for sharing with me their unpublished discussions of the creationist writers I discuss here. I have also learned much from an illuminating essay by Niall Shanks and Karl Joplin, "Redundant Complexity: A Critical Analysis of Intelligent Design in Biochemistry," *Philosophy of Science*. 66, 1999, 268–282. Finally, I'd like to thank Robert Pennock for his editorial encouragement and for the insights of his own excellent treatment of the neo-creos in *Tower of Babel*.

1   I'll be quoting extensively from two creationist works, Michael Behe, *Darwin's Black Box: The Biochemical Challenge to Evolution*, New York: The Free Press, 1996 (cited as DBB) and Phillip Johnson, *Darwin on Trial*, Washington D.C.: Regnery Gateway, 1993 (cited as DOT).

2   I borrow this pithy formulation from Dan Dennett.

3   For further discussion of this issue, see my *Abusing Science: The Case against Creationism*, Cambridge MA.: MIT Press, p. 117.

Chapter 42

Phillip E. Johnson

EVOLUTION AS DOGMA: THE ESTABLISHMENT OF NATURALISM

The orthodox explanation of what is wrong with creationism goes something like this:

Science has accumulated overwhelming evidence for evolution. Although there are controversies among scientists regarding the precise mechanism of evolution, and Darwin's particular theory of natural selection may have to be modified or at least supplemented, there is no doubt whatsoever about the *fact* of evolution. All of today's living organisms including humans are the product of descent with modification from common ancestors, and ultimately in all likelihood from a single microorganism that itself evolved from nonliving chemicals. The only persons who reject the fact of evolution are biblical fundamentalists, who say that each species was separately created by God about 6,000 years ago, and that all the fossils are the products of Noah's Flood. The fundamentalists claim to be able to make a scientific case for their position, but "scientific creationism" is a contradiction in terms. Creation is inherently a religious doctrine, and there is no scientific evidence for it. This does not mean that science and religion are necessarily incompatible, because science limits itself to facts, hypotheses, and theories and does not intrude into questions of value, such as whether the universe or mankind has a purpose. Reasonable persons need have no fear that scientific *knowledge* conflicts with religious *belief.*

Like many other official stories, the preceding description contains just enough truth to mislead persuasively. In fact, there is a great deal more to the creation-evolution controversy than meets the eye, or rather than meets the carefully cultivated media stereotype of "creationists" as Bible-quoting know-nothings who refuse to face up to the scientific evidence. The creationists may be wrong about many things, but they have at least one very important point to argue, a point that has been thoroughly obscured by all the attention paid to Noah's Flood and other side issues. What the science educators propose to teach as "evolution," and label as fact, is based not upon any incontrovertible empirical evidence, but upon a highly controversial philosophical presupposition. The controversy over evolution is therefore not going to go away as people become better educated on the subject. On the contrary, the more people learn about the philosophical content of what scientists are calling the "fact of evolution," the less they are going to like it.

To understand why this is so, we have to define the issue properly, which means that we will have to redefine some terms. Nobody doubts that evolution occurs, in the narrow sense that certain changes happen naturally. The most famous piece of evidence for Darwinism is a study of an English peppered-moth population consisting of both dark- and light-colored moths. When industrial smoke darkened the trees, the percentage of dark moths increased, due to their relative advantage in hiding from predators. When the air pollution was reduced, the trees became lighter and more light moths survived. Both colors were present throughout, and so no new characteristics emerged, but the percentage of dark moths in the population went up and down as changing conditions affected their relative ability to survive and produce offspring.

Examples of this kind allow Darwinists to assert as beyond question that "evolution is a fact," and that natural selection is an important directing force in evolution. If they mean only that evolution of a sort has been known to occur, and that natural selection has observable effects upon the distribution of characteristics in a population, then there really is nothing to dispute. The important claim of "evolution," however, is not that limited changes occur in populations due to differences in survival rates. It is that we can extrapolate from the very modest amount of evolution that can actually be observed to a grand theory that explains how moths, trees, and scientific observers came to exist in the first place.

Orthodox science insists that we can make the extrapolation. The "neo-Darwinian synthesis" (hereafter Darwinism) begins with the assumption that small random genetic changes (mutations) occasionally have positive survival value. Organisms possessing these favorable variations should have a relative advantage in survival and reproduction, and they will tend to pass their characteristics on to their descendants. By differential survival a favorable characteristic spreads through a population, and the population becomes different from what it was. If sufficient favorable mutations show up when and where they are needed, and if natural selection allows them to accumulate in a population, then it is conceivable that by tiny steps over vast amounts of time a bacterial ancestor might produce descendants as complex and varied as trees, moths, and human beings.

That is only a rough description of the theory, of course, and there are all sorts of arguments about the details. Some Darwinists, such as Harvard Professor Steven Jay Gould, say that new mechanisms are about to be discovered that will produce a more complicated theory, in which strictly Darwinian selection of individual organisms will play a reduced role. There is also a continuing debate about whether it is necessary to "decouple macroevolution from microevolution." Some experts do not believe that major changes and the appearance of new forms (i.e., macro-evolution) can be explained as the products of an accumulation of tiny mutations through natural selection of individual organisms (microevolution). If classical Darwinism isn't the explanation for macroevolution, however, there is only speculation as to what sort of alternative mechanisms might have been responsible. In science, as in other fields, you can't beat something with nothing, and so the Darwinist paradigm remains in place.

For all the controversies over these issues, however, there is a basic philosophical point on which the evolutionary biologists all agree. Some say new mechanisms have to be introduced and others say the old mechanisms are adequate, but nobody with a reputation to lose proposes to invoke a supernatural creator or a mystical "life force" to help out with the difficulties. The theory in question is a theory of *naturalistic* evolution, which means that it absolutely rules out any miraculous or supernatural intervention at any point. Everything is conclusively presumed to have happened through purely material mechanisms that are in principle accessible to scientific investigation, whether they have yet been discovered or not.

That there is a controversy over how macroevolution could have occurred is largely due to the increasing awareness in scientific circles that the fossil evidence is very difficult to reconcile with the Darwinist scenario. If all living species descended from common ancestors by an accumulation of tiny steps, then there once must have existed a veritable universe of transitional intermediate forms linking the vastly different organisms of today (e.g., moths, trees, and humans) with their hypothetical common ancestors. From Darwin's time to the present, paleontologists have hoped to find the ancestors and transitional intermediates and trace the course of macroevolution. Despite claims of success in some areas, however, the results have been on the whole disappointing. That the fossil record is in important respects hostile to a Darwinist interpretation has long been known to insiders as the "trade secret of paleontology," and the secret is now coming out in the open. New forms of life tend to be fully formed at their first appearance as fossils in the rocks. If these new forms actually evolved in gradual steps from preexisting forms, as Darwinist science insists, the numerous intermediate forms that once must have existed have not been preserved.

To illustrate the fossil problem, here is what a particularly vigorous advocate of Darwinism, Oxford Zoology Professor (and popular author) Richard Dawkins, says in *The Blind Watchmaker* about the "Cambrian explosion," i.e., the apparently sudden appearance of the major animal forms at the beginning of the Cambrian era:

> The Cambrian strata of rocks, vintage about 600 million years, are the oldest ones in which we find most of the major invertebrate groups. And we find many of them in an advanced state of evolution, the very first time they appear. It is as though they were just planted there, without any evolutionary history. Needless to say, this appearance of sudden planting has delighted creationists. Evolutionists of all stripes believe, however, that this really does represent a very large gap in the fossil record, a gap that is simply due to the fact that, for some reason, very few fossils

have lasted from periods before about 600 million years ago.

The "appearance of sudden planting" in this important instance is not exceptional. There is a general pattern in the fossil record of sudden appearance of new forms followed by "stasis" (i.e., absence of basic evolutionary change). The fossil evidence in Darwin's time was so discouraging to his theory that he ruefully conceded: "Nature may almost be said to have guarded against the frequent discovery of her transitional or linking forms." Leading contemporary paleontologists such as David Raup and Niles Eldredge say that the fossil problem is as serious now as it was then, despite the most determined efforts of scientists to find the missing links. This situation (along with other problems I am passing over) explains why many scientist would dearly love to confirm the existence of natural mechanisms that can produce basically new forms of life from earlier and simpler organisms without going through all the hypothetical intermediate steps that classical Darwinism requires.

Some readers may wonder why the scientists won't admit that there are mysteries beyond our comprehension, and that one of them may be how those complex animal groups could have evolved directly from preexisting bacteria and algae without leaving any evidence of the transition. The reason that such an admission is out of the question is that it would open the door to creationism, which in this context means not simply biblical fundamentalism, but *any* invocation of a creative intelligence or purpose outside the natural order. Scientists committed to philosophical naturalism do not claim to have found the precise answer to every problem, but they characteristically insist that they have the important problems sufficiently well in hand that they can narrow the field of possibilities to a set of naturalistic alternatives. Absent that insistence, they would have to concede that their commitment to naturalism is based upon faith rather than proof. Such a concession could be exploited by promoters of rival sources of knowledge, such as philosophy and religion, who would be quick to point out that faith in naturalism is no more "scientific" (i.e. empirically based) than any other kind of faith.

Immediately after the passage above about the Cambrian explosion, Dawkins adds the remark that, whatever their disagreements about the tempo and mechanism of evolution, scientific evolutionists all "despise" the creationists who take delight in pointing out the absence of fossil transitional intermediates. That word "despise" is well chosen. Darwinists do not regard creationist as sincere doubters but as dishonest propagandists, persons who probably only pretend to disbelieve what they must know in their hearts to be the truth of naturalistic evolution. The greater their apparent intelligence and education, the greater their fault in refusing to acknowledge the truth that is staring them in the face. These are "dark times," Dawkins noted last year in the *New York Times* because nearly half of the American people, including many "who should know better," refuse to believe in evolution. That such people have any rational basis for their skepticism is out of the question, of course, and Dawkins tells us exactly what to think of them: "It is absolutely safe to say that if you meet somebody who claims not to believe in evolution, that person is ignorant, stupid, or insane (or wicked, but I'd rather not consider that)."

Darwinists disagree with creationists as a matter of definition, of course, but the degree of contempt that they express for creationism in principle requires some explanation beyond the fact that certain creationists have used unfair tactics such as quoting scientists out of context. It is not just the particular things that creationists do that infuriate the Darwinists; the creationists' very existence is infuriating. To understand why this is so, we must understand the powerful assumptions that mainstream scientists find it necessary to make, and the enormous frustration they feel when they are asked to take seriously persons who refuse to accept those assumptions.

What Darwinists like Dawkins despise as "creationism" is something much broader than biblical fundamentalism or even Christianity and what they proclaim as "evolution" is something much narrower than what the word means in common usage. All persons who affirm that "God creates" are in an important sense creationists, even if they believe that the Genesis story is a myth and that God created gradually through evolution over billions of years. This follows from the fact that the theory of evolution in question is *naturalistic* evolution, meaning evolution that involves no intervention or guidance by a creator outside the world of nature.

Naturalistic evolution is consistent with the existence of "God" only if by that term we mean no more than a first cause which retires from further activity after establishing the laws of nature and setting the natural mechanism in motion. Persons who say they believe in evolution, but who have in mind a process guided by an *active* God who purposely intervenes or controls the process to accomplish some end, are using the same term that the Darwinists use, but they mean something very different by it. For example, here is what Douglas Futuyma, the author of a leading college evolutionary biology textbook, finds to be the most important conflict between the theory of evolution and what he thinks of as the "fundamentalist" perspective:

> Perhaps most importantly, if the world and its creatures developed purely by material, physical forces, it could not have been designed and has no purpose or goal. The fundamentalist, in contrast, believes that everything in the world, every species and every characteristic of every species, was designed by an intelligent, purposeful artificer, and that is was made for a purpose. Nowhere does this contrast apply with more force than to the human species. Some shrink from the conclusion that the human species was not designed, has no

purpose, and is the product of mere material mechanisms—but this seems to be the message of evolution.

(Science on Trial: The Case for Evolution)

It is not only "fundamentalists," of course, but theists of any description who believe that an intelligent artificer made humanity for a purpose, whether through evolution or otherwise. Futuyma's doctrinaire naturalism is not just some superfluous philosophical addition to Darwinism that can be discarded without affecting the real "science" of the matter. If some powerful conscious being exists outside the natural order, it might use its power to intervene in nature to accomplish some purpose, such as the production of beings having consciousness and free will. If the possibility of an "outside" intervention is allowed in nature at any point, however, the whole naturalistic worldview quickly unravels.

Occasionally, a scientist discouraged by the consistent failure of theories purporting to explain some problem like the first appearance of life will suggest that perhaps supernatural creation is a tenable hypothesis in this one instance. Sophisticated naturalists instantly recoil with horror, because they know that there is no way to tell God when he has to stop. If God created the first organism, then how do we know he didn't do the same thing to produce all those animal groups that appear so suddenly in the Cambrian rocks? Given the existence of a designer ready and willing to do the work, why should we suppose that random mutations and natural selection are responsible for such marvels of engineering as the eye and the wing?

Because the claims of Darwinism are presented to the public as "science," most people are under the impression that they are supported by direct evidence such as experiments and fossil record studies. This impression is seriously misleading. Scientists cannot observe complex biological structures being created by random mutations and selection in a laboratory or elsewhere. The fossil record, as we have seen, is so unhelpful that the important steps in evolution must be assumed to have occurred within its "gaps." Darwinists believe that the mutation-selection mechanism accomplishes wonders of creativity not because the wonders can be demonstrated, but because they cannot think of a more plausible explanation for the existence of wonders that does not involve an unacceptable *creator*, i.e., a being or force outside the world of nature. According to Gareth Nelson, "evidence, or proof, of origins—of the universe, of life, of all the major groups of life, of all the minor groups of life, indeed of all the species—is weak or nonexistent when measured on an absolute scale." Nelson, a senior zoologist at the American Museum of Natural History, wrote that statement in the preface to a recent book by Wendell Bird, the leading attorney for the creationist organizations. Nelson himself is no creationist, but he is sufficiently disgusted with Darwinist dogmatism that he looks benignly upon unorthodox challengers.

Philosophical naturalism is so deeply ingrained in the thinking of many educated people today, including theologians, that they find it difficult even to imagine any other way of looking at things. To such people, Darwinism seems so logically appealing that only a modest amount of confirming evidence is needed to prove the whole system, and so they point to the peppered-moth example as virtually conclusive. Even if they do develop doubts whether such modest forces can account for large-scale change, their naturalism is undisturbed. Since there is nothing outside of nature, and since *something* must have produced all the kinds of organisms that exist, a satisfactory naturalistic mechanism must be waiting to be discovered.

The same situation looks quite different to people who accept the possibility of a creator outside the natural order. To such people, the peppered-moth observations and similar evidence seem absurdly inadequate to prove that natural selection can make a wing, an eye, or a brain. From their more skeptical perspective, the consistent pattern in the fossil record of sudden appearance followed by stasis tends to prove that there is something wrong with Darwinism, not that there is something wrong with the fossil record. The absence of proof "when measured on an absolute scale" is unimportant to a thoroughgoing naturalist, who feels that science is doing well enough if it has a plausible explanation that maintains the naturalistic worldview. The same absence of proof is highly significant to any person who thinks it possible that there are more things in heaven and earth than are dreamt of in naturalistic philosophy.

Victory in the creation-evolution dispute therefore belongs to the party with the cultural authority to establish the ground rules that govern the discourse. If creation is admitted as a serious possibility, Darwinism cannot win, and if it is excluded *a priori* Darwinism cannot lose. The point is illustrated by the logic which the Natural Academy of Sciences employed to persuade the Supreme Court that "creation-scientists" should not be given an opportunity to present their case against the theory of evolution in science classes. Creation-Science is not science, said the Academy, because

> it fails to display the most basic characteristic of science: reliance upon naturalistic explanations. Instead, proponents of "creation-science" hold that the creation of the universe, the earth, living things, and man was accomplished through supernatural means inaccessible to human understanding.

Besides, the Academy's brief continued, creationists do not perform scientific research to establish the mechanism of supernatural creation, that being by definition impossible. Instead, they seek to discredit the scientific theory of evolution by amassing evidence that is allegedly consistent with the relatively recent, abrupt appearance of the universe, the earth,

living things, and man in substantially the same form as they now have.

> "Creation-science" is thus manifestly a device designed to dilute the persuasiveness of the theory of evolution. The dualistic mode of analysis and the negative argumentation employed to accomplish this dilution is, moreover, antithetical to the scientific method.

The Academy's brief went on to cite evidence for evolution, but evidence was unnecessary. Creationists are disqualified from making a positive case, because science by definition is based upon naturalism. The rules of science also disqualify any purely negative argumentation designed to dilute the persuasiveness of the theory of evolution. Creationism is thus out of court—and out of the classroom—before any consideration of evidence. Put yourself in the place of a creationist who has been silenced by that logic, and you may feel like a criminal defendant who has just been told that the law does not recognize so absurd a concept as "innocence."

With creationist explanations disqualified at the outset, it follows that the evidence will always support the naturalistic alternative. We can be absolutely certain that the Academy will not say, "The evidence on the whole supports the theory of evolution, although we concede that the apparent abrupt appearance of many fully formed animal groups in the Cambrian rocks is in itself a point in favor of the creationists." There are *no* scientific points in favor of creation and there never will be any as long as naturalists control the definition of science, because creationist explanations by definition violate the fundamental commitment of science to naturalism. When the fossil record does not provide the evidence that naturalism would like to see, it is the fossil record, and not the naturalistic explanation, that is judged to be inadequate.

When pressed about the unfairness of disqualifying their opponents *a priori*, naturalists sometimes portray themselves as merely insisting upon a proper definition of "science," and not as making any absolute claims about "truth." By this interpretation, the National Academy of Sciences did not say that it is *untrue* that "the creation of the universe, the earth, living things and man was accomplished through supernatural means inaccessible to human understanding," but only that this statement is *unscientific*. Scientific naturalists who take this line sometimes add that they do not necessarily object to the study of creationism in the public schools, provided it occurs in literature and social science classes rather than in science class.

This naturalist version of balanced treatment is not a genuine attempt at a fair accommodation of competing worldviews, but a rhetorical maneuver. It enables naturalists effectively to label their own product as fact and its rival as fantasy, without having to back up the decision with evidence. The dominant culture assumes that science provides *knowledge*, and so in natural science classes fundamental propositions can be proclaimed as objectively true, regardless of how many dissenters believe them to be false. That is the powerful philosophical meaning of the claim that "evolution is a fact." By contrast, in literature class we read poetry and fiction, and in social science we study the subjective *beliefs* of various cultures from a naturalistic perspective. If you have difficulty seeing just how loaded this knowledge-belief distinction is, try to imagine the reaction of Darwinists to the suggestion that their theory should be removed from the college biology curriculum and studied instead in a course devoted to nineteenth-century intellectual history.

By skillful manipulation of categories and definitions, the Darwinists have established philosophical naturalism as educational orthodoxy in a nation in which the overwhelming majority of people express some form of theistic belief

inconsistent with naturalism. According to a 1982 Gallup poll aimed at measuring nationwide opinion, 44 percent of respondents agreed with the statment that "God created man pretty much in his present form at one time within the last 10,000 years." That would seem to mark those respondents as creationists in a relatively narrow sense. Another 38 percent accepted evolution as a process guided by God. Only 9 percent identified themselves as believers in a naturalistic evolutionary process not guided by God. The philosophy of the 9 percent is now to be taught in the school as unchallengeable truth.

Cornell University Professor William Provine, a leading historian of Darwinism, concluded from Gallup's figures that the American public simply does not understand what the scientists means by evolution. As Provine summarized the matter, "The destructive implications of evolutionary biology extend far beyond the assumptions of organized religion to a much deeper and more pervasive belief, held by the vast majority of people, that non-mechanistic organizing designs or forces are somehow responsible for the visible order of the physical universe, biological organisms, and human moral order." Provine blamed the scientific establishment itself for misleading the public about the absolute incompatibility of contemporary Darwinism with any belief in God, designing forces, or absolute standards of good and evil. Scientific leaders have obscured the conflict for fear of jeopardizing public support for their funding, and also because some of them believe that religion may still play a useful role in maintaining public morality. According to Provine, "These rationalizations are politic but intellectually dishonest."

The organizations that speak officially for science continue to deny that there is a conflict between Darwinism and "religion." This denial is another example of the skillful manipulation of definitions, because there are evolution-based religions that embrace naturalism with enthusiasm. Stephen Jay Gould holds up the geneticist Theodosius Dobzhansky, "the greatest evolutionist of our century and a lifelong Russian Orthodox," as proof that evolution and religion are compatible. The example is instructive, because Dobzhansky made a religion out of evolution. According to a eulogy by Francisco Ayala, "Dobzhansky was a religious man, although he apparently rejected fundamental beliefs of traditional religion, such as the existence of God and of life beyond physical death. His religiosity was grounded on the conviction that there is meaning in the universe. He saw that meaning in the fact that evolution has produced the stupendous diversity of the living world and has progressed from primitive forms of life to mankind. . . . He believed that somehow mankind would eventually evolve into higher levels of harmony and creativity." In short, Dobzhansky was what we would today call a New Age pantheist. Of course evolution is not incompatible with religion when the religion is evolution.

Dobzhansky was one of the principal founders of the neo-Darwinian synthesis. Another was Julian Huxley, who promoted a religion of "evolutionary humanism. A third was the paleontologist George Gaylord Simpson. Simpson explained in his book *The Meaning of Evolution* that "there are some beliefs still current, labeled as religious and involved with religious emotions, that conflict with evolution and are therefore intellectually untenable in spite of their emotional appeal." Simpson added that it is nonetheless "self-evident . . . that evolution and *true* religion are compatible." By true religion he meant naturalistic religion, which accepts that "man is the result of a purposeless and natural process that did not have him in mind." Because efforts have been made to obscure the point, it should be emphasized that Simpson's view is not some personal opinion extraneous to the real "science" of Darwinism. It is an expression of the same naturalism that gives Darwinists confidence that mutation and natural selection, Darwinism's "blind watchmaker," can do all the work of a creator.

Against this background readers may perceive the cruel irony in Justice Brennan's opinion for the Supreme Court majority, holding the Louisiana "balanced treatment" statute unconstitutional because the creationists who promoted it had a "religious purpose." Of course they had a religious purpose, if by that we mean a purpose to try to do something to counter the highly successful efforts of proponents of naturalism to have their philosophy established in the public schools as "fact." If creationists object to naturalistic evolution on religious grounds, they are admonished that it is inappropriate for religion to meddle with science. If they try to state scientific objections, they are disqualified instantly by definitions devised for that purpose by their adversaries. Sisyphys himself, eternally rolling his stone up that hill in Hades, must pity their frustration.

The Darwinists are also frustrated, however, because they find the resurgence of creationism baffling. Why can't these people learn that the evidence for evolution is overwhelming? Why do they persist in denying the obvious? Above all, how can they be so dishonest as to claim that scientific evidence supports their absurd position? Writing the introduction to a collection of polemics titled *Scientists Confront Creationism*, Richard Lewontin attempted to explain why creationism is doomed by its very nature. Because he is a dedicated Marxist as well as a famous geneticist, Lewontin saw the conflict between creation and evolution as a class struggle, with history inevitably awarding the victory to the naturalistic class. The triumph of evolution in the schools in the post-Sputnik era signaled that "the culture of the dominant class had triumphed, and traditional religious values, the only vestige of control that rural people had over their own lives and the lives of their families, had been taken away from them." In fact, many creationists are urban professionals who make their living from technology, but Lewontin's basic point is valid. The "fact of evolution" is an instrument of cultural domination, and it is only to be expected that people who are being consigned to the dustbin of history should make some protest.

Lewontin was satisfied that creationism cannot survive because its acceptance of miracles puts it at odds with the more rational perception of the world as a place where all events have natural causes. Even a creationist "crosses seas not on foot but in machines, finds the pitcher empty when he has poured out its contents, and the cupboard bare when he has eaten the last of the loaf." Lewontin thus saw creationism as falsified not so much by any discoveries of modern science as by universal human experience, a thesis that does little to explain either why so absurd a notion has attracted so many adherents or why we should expect it to lose ground in the near future.

Once again we see how the power to define can be used to distort, especially when the critical definition is implicit rather than exposed to view. (I remind the reader that to Lewontin and myself, a "creationist" is not necessarily a biblical literalist, but rather any person who believes that God creates.) If creationists really were people who live in an imaginary world of continual miracles, there would be very few of them. On the contrary, from a creationist point of view, the very fact that the universe is on the whole orderly, in a manner comprehensible to our intellect, is evidence that we and it were fashioned by a common intelligence. What is truly a miracle, in the pejorative sense of an event having no rational connection with what has gone before, is the emergence of a being with consciousness, free will, and a capacity to understand the laws of nature in a universe which in the beginning contained only matter in mindless motion.

Once we understand that biologists like Lewontin are employing their scientific prestige in support of a philosophical platform, there is no longer any reason to be intimidated by their claims to scientific expertise. On the contrary, the inability of most biologists to make any sense out of creationist criticisms of their presuppositions is evidence of their own philosophical naivete. The "overwhelming evidence for naturalistic evolution" no longer overwhelms when the naturalistic worldview is itself called into question, and that worldview is as problematical as any other set of metaphysical assumptions when it is placed on the table for examination rather than being taken for granted as "the way we think today."

The problem with scientific naturalism as a worldview is that it takes a sound methodological premise of natural science and transforms it into a dogmatic statement about the nature of the universe. Science is committed by definition to empiricism, by which I mean that scientists seek to find truth by observation, experiment, and calculation rather than by studying sacred books or achieving mystical states of mind. It may well be, however, that there are certain questions—important questions, ones to which we desperately want to know the answers—that cannot be answered by the methods available to our science. These may include not only broad philosophical issues such as whether the universe has a purpose, but also questions we have become accustomed to think of as empirical, such as how life first began or how complex biological systems were put together.

Suppose, however, that some people find it intolerable either to be without answers to these questions or to allow the answers to come from anyone but scientists. In that case science must provide answers, but to do this, it must invoke *scientism*, a philosophical doctrine which asserts arbitrarily that knowledge comes only through the methods of investigation available to the natural sciences. The Soviet Cosmonaut who announced upon landing that he had been to the heavens and had not seen God was expressing crudely the basic philosophical premise that underlies Darwinism. Because we cannot examine God in our telescopes or under our microscopes, God is unreal. It is meaningless to say that some entity exists if in principle we can never have knowledge of that entity.

With the methodology of scientism in mind, we can understand what it means to contrast scientific "knowledge" with religious "belief," and what follows from the premise that natural science is not suitable for investigating whether the universe has a purpose. Belief is inherently subjective, and includes elements such as fantasy and preference. Knowledge is in principle objective, and includes elements such as facts and laws. If science does not investigate the purpose of the universe, then the universe effectively has no purpose, because a purpose of which we can have no knowledge is meaningless to us. On the other hand, the universe does exist, and all its features must be explicable in terms of forces and causes accessible to scientific investigation. It follows that the best naturalistic explanation available is effectively true, with the proviso that it may eventually be supplanted by a better or more inclusive theory. Thus naturalistic evolution is a fact, and the fact implies a critical guiding role for natural selection.

Scientism itself is not a fact, however, nor is it attractive as a philosophy once its elements and consequences are made explicit. Persons who want naturalistic evolution to be accepted as unquestioned fact must therefore use their cultural authority to enact rules of discourse that protect the purported fact from the attacks of unbelievers. First, they can identify science with naturalism, which means that they insist as a matter of first principle that no consideration whatever be given to the possibility that mind or spirit preceded matter. Second, they can impose a rule of procedure that disqualifies purely negative argument, so that a theory which obtains some very modest degree of empirical support can become immune to disproof until and unless it is supplanted by a better naturalistic theory. With these rules in place, Darwinists can claim to have proved that natural selection crafted moths, trees, and people, and point to the peppered-moth observation as proof.

The assumption of naturalism is in the realm of speculative philosophy, and the rule against negative argument is arbitrary. It is as if a judge were to tell a defendant that he may not establish his innocence unless he can produce a suitable substitute to be charged with the crime. Such vulnerable rules of discourse need protection from criticism, and two distinct rhetorical strategies have been pursued to provide it. First, we have already seen that the direct conflict between Darwinism and theism has been blurred, so that theists who are not committed to biblical inerrancy are led to believe that they have no reason to be suspicious of Darwinism. The remaining objectors can be marginalized as fundamentalists, whose purportedly scientific objections need not be taken seriously because "everybody knows" that people like that will believe, and say, anything.

The second strategy is to take advantage of the prestige that science enjoys in an age of technology, by asserting that anyone who disputes Darwinism must be an enemy of science, and hence of rationality itself. This argument gains a certain plausibility from the fact that Darwinism is not the only area within the vast realm of science where such practices as extravagant extrapolation, arbitrary assumptions, and metaphysical speculation have been tolerated. The history of scientific efforts to explain human behavior provides many examples, and some aspects of cosmology, such as its Anthropic Principle, invite the label "cosmo-theology." What makes the strategy effective, however, is not the association of Darwinism with the more speculative aspects of cosmology, but its purported link with technology. Donald Johanson put the point effectively, if crudely: "You can't accept one part of science because it brings you good things like electricity and penicillin and throw away another part because it brings you some things you don't like about the origin of life."

But why can't you do exactly that? That scientists can learn a good deal about the behavior of electrons and bacteria does not prove that they know how electrons or bacteria came into existence in the first place. It is also possible that contemporary scientists are insightful upon some matters and, like their predecessors, thoroughly confused about others. Twentieth-century experience demonstrates that scientific technology can work wonders, of course. It also demonstrates that dubious doctrines based upon philosophy can achieve an undeserved respectability by cloaking themselves in the mystique of science. Whether Darwinism is another example of pseudoscience is the question, and this question cannot be answered by a vague appeal to the authority of science.

For now, things are going well for Darwinism in America. The Supreme Court has dealt the creationists a crushing blow, and state boards of education are beginning to adopt "science frameworks." These policy statements are designed to encourage textbook publishers to proclaim boldly the fact of evolution—and therefore the naturalistic philosophy that underlies the fact—instead of minimizing the subject to avoid controversy. Efforts are also under way to bring under control any individual teachers who express creationist sentiments in the classroom, especially if they make use of unapproved materials. As ideological authority collapses in other parts of the world, the Darwinists are successfully swimming against the current.

There will be harder times ahead, however. The Darwinist strategy depends upon a certain blurring of the issues, and in particular upon maintaining the fiction that what is being promoted is an inoffensive "fact of evolution," which is opposed only by a discredited minority of religious fanatics. As the Darwinists move out to convert the nation's school children to a naturalistic outlook, it may become more and more difficult to conceal the religious implications of their system. Plenty of people within the Darwinist camp know what is being concealed, and cannot be relied upon to maintain a discreet silence. William Provine, for example, has been on a crusade to persuade the public that it has to discard either Darwinism or God, and not only God but also such non-materialistic concepts as free will and objective standards of morality. Provine offers this choice in the serene confidence that the biologists have enough evidence to persuade the public to choose Darwinism, and to accept its philosophical consequences.

The establishment of naturalism in the schools is supposedly essential to the improvement of science education, which is in such a dismal state in America that national leaders are truly worried. It is not likely, however, that science education can be improved in the long run by identifying science with a worldview abhorred by a large section of the population, and then hoping that the public never finds out what is being implied. The project requires that the scientific establishment commit itself to a strategy of indoctrination, in which the teachers first tell students what they are supposed to believe and then inform them about any difficulties only later, when it is deemed safe to do so. The weakness that requires such dogmatism is evident in Philip Kitcher's explanation of why it is "insidious" to propose that the creationists be allowed to present their negative case in the classroom:

> There will be ... much dredging up of misguided objections to evolutionary theory. The objections are spurious—but how is the teacher to reveal their errors to students who are at the beginning of their science studies? ... What Creationists really propose is a situation in which people without scientific training—fourteen-year-old students, for example—are asked to decide a complex issue on partial evidence.

A few centuries ago, the defenders of orthodoxy used the same logic to explain why the common people needed to be protected from exposure to the spurious heresies of Galileo. In fairness, the creationists Kitcher had in mind are biblical fundamentalists who want to attack orthodox scientific doctrine on a broad front. I do not myself think that such advocacy groups should be given a platform in the classroom. In my experience, however, Darwinists apply the same contemptuous dismissal to any suggestion, however well-informed and modestly stated, that in constructing their huge theoretical edifice upon a blind commitment to naturalism, they may have been building upon the sand. As long as the media and the courts are quiescent, they may retain the power to marginalize dissent and establish their philosophy as orthodoxy. What they do not have the power to do is to make it true.

Chapter 43

Robert T. Pennock

WHY CREATIONISM SHOULD NOT BE TAUGHT IN THE PUBLIC SCHOOLS

I. The Question

I would like to thank the Association for Philosophy of Education for inviting me to address the question: should creationism be taught in the public schools? The full range of issues that are the subject of debate in the creation/evolution controversy are too numerous to be covered here, so in this first section I begin by analyzing the question so that we might better focus our discussion. I'll take this opportunity to point out related questions that have so far not been considered in the debate, but that deserve the attention of philosophers of education. In subsequent sections I will consider a variety of legal arguments, creationists' extra-legal arguments, epistemological arguments, religious protection arguments, and arguments from educational philosophy that are relevant to our specific question.

(a) The Public Schools

The controversies about educational policies having to do with creationism have almost exclusively involved the teaching of evolution in the public schools, so this is a natural locus for us to consider the problem. However, several key elements of the controversy would be quite different if we looked at the issue in other educational settings, such as private and parochial schools, home schooling, and in higher education.

There has been very little consideration of the issues for private rather than public schools, no doubt because the governance of the former is not subject to public control and review in the same way. However, there is still a measure of external oversight in that private schools must meet certain standards in order to get and maintain accreditation. It is a reasonable question to ask whether a school deserves to be accredited if it teaches creationism rather than evolution in its science classes. In general, however, we tend to take for granted that private schools, if they do not receive public funds or certification, are not subject to public standards and may teach whatever private, esoteric doctrines they choose.

For parochial schools we fully expect that religious views will be taught. Indeed, this is the most natural setting for creationist views, and it is fair to say that it is primarily in parochial schools that we find creationism taught in science classes. This is not to say, of course, that all or even most parochial schools teach creationism. Based on informal assessment of my undergraduate students, those who studied at Catholic high schools typically have had the best education on evolution, often better than their public school counterparts. Fundamentalist and evangelical "Bible schools," on the other hand, often cite the creationist orientation of their science curriculum as a major selling point. As they see it, all true knowledge has a biblical basis. Gil Hansen, of the Fairfax Baptist Temple school, explains his school's educational philosophy, which seems to be representative on this point: "What we do here is base everything on the Bible. This becomes really the foundation, the word of God is the foundation from which all academics really spring" (Duvall 1995). How does the school teach evolutionary theory? Hansen is clear about the school's position on this as well: "We expose it as a false model."

Unless the government begins to significantly fund parochial schools with tax dollars such as through a voucher program, parochial schools can probably expect to remain free to teach creationism or whatever religious doctrines they choose. Moreover, fundamentalist and evangelical schools often choose to forego secular educational accreditation, and may be accredited only within their own independent system. I would argue that there are serious issues of educational philosophy to consider even in this setting. Is it right to teach children that something that is known to be true is false? Is it not bad faith to misrepresent the findings of science in what is purported to be a science class? If the basis for knowledge is taken to be biblical revelation, isn't it intellectually dishonest to put such revelations forward as science?

Most of these same considerations apply if we move to consideration of home schooling. There have always been parents who, for one reason or other, chose to teach their own children at home rather than send them to school, but currently the vast majority of home schoolers consists of religious conservatives who do not want their children to be exposed to what they take to be the evils of the public schools, be it sex education or evolution. Home schooling raises some unique issues, since basic education is compulsory and parents must demonstrate that they are providing their children with an education that meets state standards. Oversight of parents who teach their own children is inconsistent, and it seems to be fairly common that fundamentalist home schoolers teach the bare minimum of what they have to of subjects they object to, and

then regularly supplement the required curriculum with the religious education—in Bible study, creationism, and so on—that they desire. Are parents doing an educational disservice to their children in teaching them creationism on the sly? One might ask whether stricter oversight is necessary in such cases.

Considering the issue in the setting of higher education overlaps some of the previous considerations, but with some relevant differences. One of the most important is the age and maturity of the students. Most undergraduates are at a more advanced developmental stage then they were in high school, so some new educational goals begin to apply. Certainly one of the most significant is that we expect undergraduates to begin to hone their critical and evaluative thinking skills, and to develop (disciplined) independence of mind. At this stage, it can be quite appropriate and instructive to discuss creationist views, so that students can come on their own to see what is wrong with them. Of course, there are any number of other topics that also could serve the same end, but a professor might legitimately choose to dissect creationism in the same way that one might choose to have students dissect a snake rather than a frog in anatomy class. One question we will have to address is whether this might not be a reasonable educational goal in secondary school public education as well.

For the most part, we must leave consideration of these other venues aside, and focus on the public schools, which historically have been (and for the most part remain) the central locus of the controversy. The general causes of the creationism controversy—perceived conflicts between evolution and some Christian views about Creation—have remained fairly constant over the decades, but these have manifested themselves differently in different periods. In the early decades of the public school system in the United States, few textbooks incorporated evolution, and once they did begin to do so many states responded by passing legislation that banned the teaching of evolution altogether. The 1925, antievolutionary Butler Act in Tennessee led to the first legal battle over creation and evolution in the schools—the famous *Scopes* trial. Such antievolutionary laws remained in effect until they were finally overturned by the U.S. Supreme Court in 1968. Creationists countered at first by passing laws in the early 1970s to give "equal emphasis" to the Biblical account. Since these and similar state laws were struck down in the 1980s, creationist activists have turned to other tactics and other venues, getting laws passed that require, for example, "disclaimers" to be read before biology classes in which evolution would be covered. Alabama public school students found a disclaimer pasted in their biology textbooks that began:

> This textbook discusses evolution, a controversial theory some scientists present as a scientific explanation for the origin of living things, such as plants, animals and humans. No human was present when life first appeared on earth. Therefore, any statement about life's origins should be considered as theory, not fact.

In other states, creationist "stealth candidates" got themselves elected to local School Boards and to State Boards of Education and then worked to change science curriculum standards to include creationism or to gut any evolution component. A few go further and require that "evidence against evolution" be presented. Some creationist teachers sometimes simply ignore the law and go ahead and teach their views in their individual classrooms. These and other examples of creationist activism in the public schools keeps this venue at the center of the controversy.

(b) Kinds of Creationism

The next element of the question before us that we need to examine is the notion of creationism itself.

The most common form of "creation-science" is what is known as "young-earth creationism" (YEC). In the law they got passed in 1982 in Arkansas, creationists proposed the following as an outline of what they wanted to have taught:

> (1) Sudden creation of the universe, energy, and life from nothing; (2) The insufficiency of mutation and natural selection in bringing about the development of all living kinds from a single organism; (3) Changes only within fixed limits of originally created kinds of plants and animals; (4) Separate ancestry of humans and apes; (5) Explanation of the earth's geology by catastrophism, including the occurrence of a worldwide flood; and (6) A relatively recent inception of the earth and living kinds.
>
> (La Follette 1983, p. 16)

A more complete outline of the "Creation model" may be found in Aubrey (1998 [1980]). It is also important to understand that creationism does not end with its rejection of biological evolution, though this is the main thesis that so far has been at issue in the public controversy. As we see in the list above, and as I have shown in more detail elsewhere (Pennock 1999, ch. 1), creationism also rejects scientific conclusions of anthropology, archeology, astronomy, chemistry, geology, linguistics, physics, psychology, optics, and so on.

We must also be aware that there is now considerable factionalism among creationists. Disagreements about the details of Christian theology, partial acceptance of scientific views, and different political strategies have given rise to splinter groups that question one or another of the standard views. Old-earth creationists, for example, do not insist that the world is only six to ten thousand years old and accept something closer to the scientific chronology. A few creationists doubt that there was a single, catastrophic worldwide flood, and hold that the

Noachian Deluge may have been local to the Mediterranean, or, if global, then "tranquil" rather than catastrophic. Adherents of the YEC view far out-number members of other factions, but it is important that we recognize that creationism is not a monolithic view and is split by deep divisions.

Though the traditional creationists remain the most active in their political and educational work, there was a significant evolution of creationism in the 1990s, beginning with the publication of *Darwin on Trial*, by Berkeley law professor Phillip Johnson. Johnson neither endorses nor denies the young-earth view, and he argues the we should understand creationism as belief in the process of creation in a more general sense. People are creationists, according to Johnson's definition, "if they believe that a supernatural Creator not only initiated this process but in some meaningful sense *controls* it in furtherance of a purpose" (Johnson 1991, p. 4). Rather than speaking of "creation-science," Johnson and others among these new creationists call their view "intelligent design theory" and advocate a "theistic science." Intelligent design creationists include both young-earth and old-earth creationists, but for the most part they keep their specific commitments hidden and speak only of the generic thesis of "mere creation." As do other creationists, they oppose accommodation to evolution and take it to be fundamentally incompatible with Christian theism. In another way, however, they go further than creationscience does; they reject scientific methodology itself, arguing that scientific naturalism itself must be tossed out and replaced by their theistic science (though they are never clear about what its distinctive methods might be).

Although it has been fundamentalist and evangelical Christian creationists, especially the YECs, who have been the most active in opposing the teaching of evolution in the schools and pressing for the inclusion of their view of Creation, we cannot fairly evaluate the question without also taking into account non-Christian creationist views. For the most part, adherents of these views have not been as politically active in the United States so these have not reached the public attention to the same degree. It is impossible to even begin to canvas these numerous views, but I will mention by way of example two recent cases that have made the news.

In Kennewick, Washington the 1996 discovery of a fossil human skeleton led to a very public legal battle between science and religion. The 9,000-plus-year-old bones were claimed by a coalition of Northwest Indians who wanted to immediately bury them. However, features of the skull seemed to be more Caucasian than Indian, and scientists questioned whether it was really a tribal ancestor and suggested that further analysis could help reveal something of early human history in the area. Armand Minthorn, of Oregon's Umatilla Tribe, said his people were not interested in the scientist's views: "We already know our history. It is passed on to us through our elders and through our religious practices." Their history says that their God created them first in that place. Many Amerindian tribes have origin stories that, on their face, are antithetical to evolutionary theory and other scientific findings. (In parts of northern Canada, an alliance of Native Indians and Christian creationists has formed to oppose teaching evolution in the schools. It is an uneasy union, of course, because the groups differ sharply in what story of Creation they would put in its stead.) The controversy over the Kennewick skeleton also involves another religious group, the Asatru Folk Assembly, an Old Norse pagan group. The members of this pre-Christian faith revere Viking-era Scandinavian gods and goddesses, and believe that their ancestors were the first inhabitants of the region. They expect that scientific study of the skull would support their claim of priority, though their other religious beliefs would certainly put them at odds with other aspects of the scientific picture.

Another religious anti-evolutionary view became newsworthy in 1995, when NBC broadcast a program entitled *Mysterious Origins of Man* that purported to reveal scientific evidence that human beings had lived tens of millions of years ago. Creationists were at first elated by this prime-time repudiation of evolution, but quickly withdrew their endorsement when they learned that the program was based on the 1993 book *Forbidden Archeology* (Cremo and Thompson 1993), which advances purportedly scientific evidence for a position that mirrors a Hindu view of creation and reincarnation.

Finally, let me mention one more type of view that is relevant to the controversy. The Raëlian Movement, which had its start in France in the 1970s, calls itself a "scientific religion." Raëlians reject evolution and believe that life on earth is the result of purposeful, intelligent design, but they also reject creationism, in the sense that they believe that the creator was not supernatural. Instead, they believe that life on earth was genetically engineered from scratch by extraterrestrials. The founder of the Raëlian Movement, Claude Vorilhon, claims that he knows this because the truth was revealed to him by an extraterrestrial, who anointed him as the Guide of Guides for our age. Some 70,000 adherents worldwide, many in the U.S. and Canada, share this faith.

In considering whether creationism should be taught in the public schools, we must always keep in mind that all these (and many more) anti-evolutionary views would have to be included as "alternative theories" to the scientific conclusions.

(c) Taught How?

The third element of the question that requires preliminary discussion involves the kind of academic course in which, and the way in which creationism might be taught.

The issues change dramatically, for instance, if the different forms of creationism were to be taught in a comparative religion class. The Constitution is not taken to bar discussion of religion in a course of this sort. One could imagine a course that surveyed the splendid variety of views of creation of different religions, and could make a good case that such a course might serve a useful educational purpose in fostering an appreciation of American and global cultural diversity. Many opponents of teaching creationism in the schools would be willing to compromise if the topic were to be introduced in such a course. The controversy arises mostly because creationists insist that their view be included as part of the science curriculum, and that it replace or be given equal weight as evolution.

Moreover, creationists want evolution to be revealed as a false model. Creationist textbooks that are used in fundamentalist schools often go further and teach that it is as an evil view as well, promoted by atheist scientists who want to lure people away from God. The textbooks they have lobbied for use in public schools, however, keep the sermonizing about evolutionary evils to a minimum. The most common creationist proposals have followed what is known as the "dual model" approach, whereby "the two theories" are presented and contrasted. The Arkansas "Balanced Treatment" Act specified that the schools should give equal consideration to "creation-science" and "evolution-science." Since all such legislation has been found unconstitutional, creationists now try to argue that science classes should simply present "alternative theories" besides the scientific view. In practice, however, the proposals are essentially unchanged. For example, the textbook *Of Pandas and People* (Davis and Kenyon 1993), which presents intelligent design creationism and is by far the most carefully crafted creationist offering to date, follows the same misleading framework of presenting the views of those who hold "the two" theories of biological origins, natural evolution and intelligent design, neglecting the variety of other views. The terms may have changed, but the dubious strategy it adopts is the same: evolutionary theory is claimed to be riddled with holes, with creationism left as the only alternative. Students are told that the textbook will allow them to do what no other does, namely, let them decide for themselves which theory is true.

One cannot, however, judge simply from such creationist textbooks how creationism would likely be taught were it allowed in the classroom, since these are currently written more for political than for pedagogical purposes, to present an innocent face and get a foot in the door. (*Pandas*, for example, which is offered as a biology text, contains a long section that gives philosophical arguments for why intelligent design should not be disqualified as a scientific hypothesis, and why it purportedly does not violate the court rulings that have found teaching creationism in the public schools to be unconstitutional. This is hardly standard fare for secondary school textbooks.) One can get a more realistic sense of what might happen in classrooms by looking at cases in which teachers have gone ahead and taught creationism despite the laws prohibiting it. In a middle school in Harrah, Oklahoma, a suburb of Oklahoma City, a teacher took away students' textbooks and distributed creationist material, teaching the students that a person who believes in evolution cannot believe in God (RNCSE 1998, vol. 18, no. 2, p. 5).

Finally, let me suggest one further way that creationism might be taught that has not been considered in the literature: creationist views could be used as illustrations of how *not* to do science. Specific creationist tenets could be presented and then the evidence reviewed, showing how scientists came to see that they were false. This might turn out to be a useful educational exercise, in that examination of some of the many errors of so-called creation-science or intelligent design could help teach students how real science is done. As John Dewey pointed out, science education is a failure if it consists of nothing more than the recitation and memorization scientific facts (Dewey 1964 [1910]; 1964 [1938], p. 19). To teach science well is to teach the methods of scientific reasoning, and a critical examination of creationism could serve very well for this purpose. It is because of the possible pedagogic utility of this approach that I actually find myself of two minds about whether teachers should introduce creationism into their science lesson plans. If the courts were to permit the teaching of creation in the public school classrooms I expect that this would soon become a common educational exercise in many science classrooms. Indeed, this is the only intellectually responsible way that it could be taught in a science class.

I'll return to some of these issues shortly, but having delimited the focus of our discussion, let me now turn to the relevant arguments, beginning with a brief review of the legal reasoning that has excluded creationism from the public schools.

II. Legal Arguments

Because our focus is on the public schools, the legal arguments involving the teaching of creationism have been and continue to be the most significant. Both sides have argued that this is primarily a Constitutional question, with some proponents of teaching creationism claiming that it should actually be protected by the First Amendment, under the free exercise of religion clause. Opponents respond that creationists are not being prevented from exercising their beliefs in their churches, homes, or private schools, but that teaching Creation in the public schools would violate the First Amendment's establishment clause. In a long series of cases, the courts have consistently ruled against the antievolutionists' arguments.

Antievolution laws were struck down by the U.S. Supreme Court in the 1968 *Epperson v. Arkansas* case, on the grounds that the Constitution does not permit a state to tailor its requirements for teaching and learning to the principles or prohibitions of any particular religious sect or doctrine. Subsequent rulings have helped define the boundaries of this ruling. In a 1981 case, a parent sued California, claiming that classes in which evolution was taught prohibited his and his children's free exercise of religion. The Sacramento Superior Court ruled (*Segraves v. California*) that teaching evolution did not infringe on religious freedom, and that a 1972 antidogmatism policy of the School Board—which said that statements about origins should be presented conditionally, not dogmatically, and that class discussions on the topic should emphasize that scientific explanations focus on how things occur, not on ultimate causes—was an appropriate compromise between state science teaching and individual religious beliefs.

Creationists next tried to argue that their view should *not* be excluded on grounds of separation of Church and State, because it was not religion but science. The Arkansas legislature passed a bill requiring "balanced treatment" of what they called "creation-science" and "evolution-science." The court struck down the law in the 1982 *McLean v. Arkansas* case, finding that "creation-science" was not a science. The U.S. Supreme Court came to the same conclusion in the 1987 *Edwards v. Aguillard* case, striking down Louisiana's "Creationism Act," which required the teaching of creationism whenever evolution was taught. The court found that, by advancing the religious belief that a supernatural being created humankind, the act impermissibly legislated the teaching of religion, and that a comprehensive science education is undermined when it is forbidden to teach evolution except when creation-science is also taught.

The court has also ruled, as in the 1994 *Peloza v. Capistrano School District* case, that a teacher's First Amendment right to free exercise of religion is not violated by a school district's requirement that evolution be taught in biology classes, rejecting creationists' contention that "evolutionism" is a religion. In another recent case, in Louisiana, the 1997 *Freiler v. Tangipahoa Parish Board of Education* case, the court overturned a policy that would require teachers to read aloud a disclaimer whenever they taught about evolution, and also found that making curriculum proposals in terms of "intelligent design" is no different from the legal standpoint than earlier proposals for teaching creation-science.

When considering questions about what we ought or ought not do, however, philosophers are never content with answers that stop with the law, if only because we may have ethical duties that require more of us than the law does. Moreover, we must always consider the possibility that current law is itself unjust or unwise. In the sections that follow, I'll examine several other sorts of arguments that address these points.

III. Creationist Extralegal Arguments

In pressing for the reintroduction of their views into the schools, creationists most often argue that the legal rulings are themselves unjust in one or another way, appealing to a handful of arguments from fairness, majority rule, parental rights, academic freedom, and censorship. Here I'll briefly review and then respond to these as they have been put forward by creationist lawyer Wendell Bird in a video that creationists air on public access television stations. It was Bird who laid out the legal strategy in the early 1980s of promoting creationism as though it were a science. Bird argued the creationist side in the *Edwards v. Aguillard* case in which the Supreme Court overturned laws that had been based on that strategy. Since that defeat, Bird rarely speaks of "creation-science" and instead uses the term "abrupt appearance theory." Bird's arguments here are representative of the main creationist arguments, but they are not unique to him. Indeed, most of these arguments were originally made by the Great Commoner, William Jennings Bryan, himself in his antievolution crusade that led up to the *Scopes* trial.

By far the most common argument creationists make is to say that it is unfair for the law to exclude their view from the public school science classroom. Isn't it biased and one-sided, they challenge, to teach evolution to the exclusion of creationism? Bird argues that "the only fair approach is to let the children hear all the scientific information and make up their own minds." Phillip Johnson makes the argument in stronger terms, claiming that excluding creationism amounts to "view-point discrimination." Bird tries to bolster the argument by appealing to *majority rule*, saying "The fact is that, contrary to all of the smoke, the great majority of the American public feels that it is unfair to teach just the theory of evolution." He cites polls indicating that a large percentage of Americans believe that "the scientific theory of Creation" should be taught alongside evolution in the schools.[1] This majoritarian argument was the main plank of Bryan's position, and he too cited figures about Americans' beliefs. As Bryan saw it, "The hand that writes the pay check rules the schools" (Larson 1997, p. 44). A related argument involves claimed *parental rights* to determine what one's children will study in the public schools. If it is granted that parents have such a right, then a creationist parent should be able to insist that creationism be taught or that evolution excluded.

Creationists also appeal to what is properly taken to be a prime educational value, *academic freedom*. Bird says: "To me the basic issue is academic freedom, because no one is trying to exclude evolution from public schools while teaching a theory of creation. Instead, the evolutionists are trying to exclude alternatives, while, in general, defending the exclusive teaching of evolutionism." This way of putting the argument is somewhat disingenuous, since creationists have indeed tried to exclude evolution from the public schools, and were very successful in keeping it out until just the past few decades. Moreover, they have subsequently tried to exclude it unless it is taught in conjunction with their view, and they continue to work to diminish or undermine its place in the science curriculum in whatever way they can. Bird is correct, however, that science educators do now usually defend the exclusive teaching of the scientific view, and this leads to his final objection. Mentioning organizations that oppose teaching creationism, he concludes that what they are doing amounts to *censorship*: "They have a very specific desire to preserve the exclusive teaching of evolution and to exclude any teaching of a scientific theory of creation or a scientific theory of abrupt appearance. That's censorship in my view."

We should agree that, at first glance at least, some of these charges exert a powerful pull upon us. No one wants to be seen as engaging in censorship or in unfair, discriminatory exclusion of a popular viewpoint. It is certainly incumbent on professionals to take such charges seriously, and to examine them carefully to see whether they have merit. When we do this, however, we find that the charges do not apply or are irrelevant to the issue before us.

The notion of parental rights to determine what one's children are to be taught may sound attractive at first, but parents typically have no special expertise about specific subject matter, and they certainly do not have a right to demand that teachers teach what is demonstrably false. A recent poll showed that 44 percent believe the creationist view that "humans were created pretty much in their present form about 10,000 years ago," but it is not relevant that a large number of Americans reject the scientific findings and don't believe that evolution occurred.[2] It does not matter what the figures are, because matters of empirical fact are not appropriately decided by majority rule. Nor is it "unfair" to teach what is true even though many people don't want to hear it. Neither are the schools "censoring" creationism; they are simply and properly leaving out what does not belong in the curriculum.

The charge that such a policy violates academic freedom is not so easily dismissed. One might reasonably dispute whether academic freedom applies in the public elementary and secondary schools in the same way that it does in higher education, but prima facie there seems to be no good reason to think that this important protection should be afforded to university professors and not to others of the teaching profession who serve in other educational settings. Isn't this good enough reason to allow teachers to exercise their professional judgment about whether to include creationism or not? However, academic freedom is not a license to teach whatever one wants. Along with that professional freedom come special professional responsibilities, especially of objectivity and intellectual honesty. Neither "creation-science" nor "intelligent design" (nor any of the latest euphemisms) is an actual or viable competitor in the scientific field, and it would be irresponsible and intellectually dishonest to teach them as though they were.[3]

In the previous century, the situation in science with regard to the question of the origin of species was quite different, but it cannot now fairly be said that the basic theses of evolution are scientifically controversial. There currently are no "alternative theories" to evolution that scientists take seriously, since the evidence has gone against previous contenders (including the forms of creationism held by nineteenth-century scientists) and continues to accrue in favor of evolutionary theory. Evolution is in no sense "a theory in crisis," as creationists purport. This is not to say that there are not problems that remain to be solved, but that is true of every science, and such issues are of sufficient complexity that they are properly reserved for consideration at professional meetings, in the primary literature, and in graduate programs. Unresolved issues at the cutting-edge of science are well above the level that would be likely to be included in secondary school textbooks. What is included at these lower levels that concern us here is well confirmed and scientifically uncontroversial.

IV. Epistemological Arguments

Creationists of course refuse to accept the evidence that supports the various hypotheses of evolutionary theory. As they see it, one must look to revelation to determine what is absolutely true, rather than believing the "mere theories" of science. The basic issue, as they see it, is whose truths are to be taught. God help us, they say, if we fail to teach our children God's Truth. Phillip Johnson has outlined a new legal strategy for reintroducing creationism into the public schools, arguing that excluding the religious perspective amounts to "viewpoint discrimination." Citing the 1993 *Lamb's Chapel* case, in which the court found that a school could not bar an evangelical Christian perspective in a class that discussed the subject of family relationships, Johnson claims that it is similarly improper to bar consideration of intelligent design when the topic of biological origins is discussed in science class.

One major problematic assumption behind this kind of argument is thinking that questions about empirical fact are simply a matter of one's peculiar point of view, so that excluding one or another is "discrimination," in the sense of subjective prejudice rather than the sense of objective assessment of differences. But there is a real difference between what is true and what is false, what is well confirmed and what is disconfirmed, and surely it is a good thing for science to discriminate the true empirical hypotheses from the false by empirical tests that can tell which is which. Creationists also are interested in truth, but they believe that they already know what the truths are, indeed, as Johnson puts it, with what the truths "with a capital 'T' " are. However, one cannot ascertain truths except by appropriate methods, and creationists are typically unwilling to even say what their special methods are, let alone show that they are reliable.

A second major questionable assumption is that it makes sense to talk about "the religious" or even "the creationist" viewpoint. Professor Plantinga recognizes that truths must be ascertained by a justifiable method, but he argues that different epistemological assumptions may be taken to be properly basic. On that ground, he argues for what he calls an "Augustinian science," in which scientists pursue their research along parallel epistemological tracks. Christians, he tells us, should do their science starting with "what Christians know" (Plantinga 1997). The problem with this is that there is little that Christians can say univocally that they know.

Christians disagree, sometimes violently, about what it is they supposedly know. With the exception perhaps of Roman Catholicism, Fundamentalist Christianity actually provides perhaps the broadest general consensus to be found, since it traces its roots to a series of publications at the beginning of the twentieth century the explicit purpose of which was to try to distill just "the fundamentals" of the faith. But even our brief view of the factions among creationists reveals the splinters that nevertheless form among even fundamentalists over disagreements about the smallest points of theology. (Intelligent design creationists try to paper over this problem by remaining silent about the details and promoting that minimal positive thesis that God creates for a purpose. Though even this vaguely stated view may resonate with religious meaning, it is devoid of empirical content—it certainly neither opposes nor supports any particular view about the truth of evolutionary theory—and provides no method of investigation.) The problems increase exponentially once we look beyond Christianity, and bring Hindu, Pagan, Amerindian, and other creationist viewpoints into the classroom, taking into account what these other religions take to be properly basic beliefs. If these theologically perspectival epistemologies are taken to stand on a par with ordinary natural science, then what we will be left with is a Balkanized science where specific private revelations that one or another group professes to "know" and take as given will vie with one another with no hope of public resolution.

The knowledge that we should impart in public schools is not this private esoteric "knowledge," but rather public knowledge— knowledge that we acquire by ordinary, natural means. The methodological constraints that science puts on itself serve to provide just this sort of knowledge, and thus it is scientific knowledge that is appropriate to teach in the public schools.[4]

V. Religious Protection Arguments

It is in part a recognition that the esoteric knowledge claims of religions are of a different sort than the conclusions of scientific investigation that the special Constitutional protection of freedom of religion is needed. This leads to several additional arguments for the exclusion of creationism from the public schools.

Probably the main reason typically offered against the teaching of creationism is that it improperly promotes one religious view over others. We need not dig into the theological soils within which creationism is rooted to see that this is so. In their literature, creationists write as though they are defending the Christian faith and that the enemy consists solely of godless evolutionists, but in reality it is the religious who are more often in the forefront of the opposition to seeing creationism taught in the schools. The plaintiffs opposing the "Balanced Treatment" Act in the Arkansas case included Episcopal, Methodist, A.M.E., Presbyterian, Roman Catholic, and Southern Baptist officials, and national Jewish organizations. Though creationists attempt to portray their views as purely scientific and nonsectarian, other religious groups are not taken in by the disguise, and quite understandably argue that to sanction the teaching of creationism would indeed be to privilege one religious view-point over others.

One might argue that this unfair singling out of one view could be avoided by allowing all religious views into the science class. So should we then, following the creationists' pedagogic philosophy, teach them all and let the children decide which is the true one? This is hardly a wise course of action, in that it would make the classroom a place where different religious were inevitably pitted against one another.

Creationists and other conservative Christians often take issue with the Court's interpretation of the Constitution that set up the "wall of separation" between Church and State in the 1947 *Everson v. Board of Education* case. However, the idea of tossing all religions into the science classroom to see which wins would actually violate what some took to be the original intent of the establishment clause of the First Amendment. The influential nineteenth-century Supreme Court Justice, Joseph Story, wrote that the amendment's main object was not just to prevent the exclusive patronage of some particular religion that would result from any national ecclesiastical establishment, but also "to exclude all rivalry among Christian sects . . ." (Larson 1989, p. 93). Religious rivalry and outright persecution was all too common in the American colonies when theocracy was the norm, and it seems reasonable to thank the secularization of the government and the Constitutional policy of religious neutrality in large measure for the fact that the United States has been relatively free of the sectarian violence that continues in other parts of the world. In a comparative religion class, religious differences could be respectfully described and studied, but in the setting of a science class, where the point is to seek the truth by submitting differences to the rigors of crucial tests, it is hard to see how conflict could be avoided.

Creationist law professor Phillip Johnson argues that this rationale of neutrality is "wearing thin" (1995, p. 28) in that teaching evolution is tantamount to governmental endorsement of naturalism, which he says is the "established religion" (ibid. p. 35) of the West. Here he is giving a variation of a complaint that creationists have made over the decades, that "evolutionism" is a religion, but this argument has already been tested in court, and evolution has been properly found not to be a religion. Neither is scientific naturalism religious.[5] Scientific organizations might be tempted to get the religious tax exemptions if the court were to rule otherwise, but they could not in good conscience accept them.

Let me mention one further reason to oppose the introduction of creationism into the schools under this heading that I have not seen discussed before, and that some religious people might find to be compelling, namely, that introducing creationism in the science classroom would necessarily place their religious beliefs under critical scrutiny. Creationists typically teach that Christianity stands or falls with the truth or falsity of each and every specific claim in the Bible interpreted literally, or at least "robustly." Fundamentalist and evangelical Christian parents who are familiar only with creationist literature (which invariably describes evolution as "a theory in crisis," and obviously seen to be false to anyone not "blinded" by "naturalistic biases") have no idea how vast is the amount of evidence that supports evolutionary theory, and how weak are the specific claims of creationists. They also do not recognize that a few of what one might call "missionary atheists" are as eager as creationists to have the "Creation hypothesis" included in the public school curriculum, being confident that a side-by-side examination of the claims and evidence would destroy any student's naïve beliefs in the religious view. In my experience, science teachers who teach evolution currently go out of their way to be respectful of their students' religious views. However, should the curriculum change so that they had to discuss the various "Creation" or "design" hypotheses—the Hindu, Amerindian, Pagan, and Raëlian versions, as well as the multiple Christian ones[6]—as though these were simply "alternative theories," they could not avoid a direct confrontation. Give that we expect the government to neither help nor hinder religion, it does not seem wise policy to open the door to having children's religious beliefs explicitly analyzed and rebutted in the public schools in this way.

VI. Educational Arguments

In this final section, let us set aside the above considerations and simply ask whether it would be a good educational policy to teach creationism if there were no other factors to consider. To answer the question put this way we must turn our attention to philosophy of education more generally.

The choice of what to teach in the public schools must be made in light of the goals of public education. I take it for granted that one of the basic goals of education is to provide students a true picture of the natural world we share. Another is to develop the skills and instill the civic virtues that they will require to function in harmony in society. While there are several common purposes of this kind toward which all public education aims, the more specific goals, of course, will vary depending on, among other things, the age of the student. It makes little sense, for example, to confront students with material that is beyond their developmental level. We also need to ask what is to be included when one teaches a discipline. What should be taught under the particular subject heading of *science?* In particular, does creationism belong within that subject area?

If we think of science in terms of its set of conclusions, then it is clear that creationism does not belong with it. That creationism and science both have things to say about "the subject of origins" is not sufficient to say that the views of former are a part of the subject matter we ought to teach. The specific hypotheses of creation-science have been rejected by science as the evidence accumulated against them, and the general thesis that "God creates" is not a hypothesis that science considers or can treat of at all. Some scientists do discuss their theological musings—some theistic, some atheistic—in their popular writings, but research on the questions of the existence, or possible activities and purposes of a Creator simply is not to be found in the primary scientific literature. The only proper way to treat the specific empirical claims of creation-science in a science textbook is, thus, as an interesting historical footnote about hypotheses that have been long overturned.

But now let me return to Dewey's important contention that to teach science properly is to teach not a collection of facts but a way of thought. Science education that focuses only on scientific conclusions, and omits teaching scientific methods, misrepresents the nature of scientific inquiry and fails in its basic mission of preparing students with the best skills to function in the natural world. "Theistic science," despite its name, rejects science's methodology and therefore does not belong within the subject. "Creation-science," "abrupt appearance theory," "intelligent design theory," and so on are the creationists' cuckoo eggs that they hope will pass unnoticed, enabling them to garner the resources (and cultural prestige) of science and the forum of the science classroom for their own religious ends.

We should not haggle over mere terminology, but it remains the case that neither the conclusions nor the methods of creationism are properly described as "science." Disciplinary boundaries may not be sharply defined, nor should we expect them to be, but they are generally distinguished by a characteristic order. It is because practitioners must adhere to constraints—be they the precedents of (tentatively) accepted conclusions or the procedures of inquiry themselves—that the notion of a "discipline" makes sense at all.

Could creationism could be taught under a different heading, rather than as a science? If "theistic science" were to prove its value as an independent discipline, then educators might have to consider whether it would be worthwhile in relation to the educational goals of the public schools to include in the curriculum. Historically, theistic science had many centuries to prove itself, but in the end scientists concluded that they had no need of that hypothesis, and contemporary creationists have nothing to show for their attempts to revive the view that theology is the queen of the sciences. Intelligent design creationists plead that they are only beginning their researches and ask for patience when asked for concrete results of their approach, and at present there is no sign that they will succeed in developing a fruitful discipline. It does not make sense to create a separate class to teach a discipline that does not exist.

The fact that intelligent design and other versions of creationism have nothing positive to offer accounts for the pattern that we find in all creationist literature and in proposed texts such as *Of Pandas and People*, namely, that they consist almost exclusively of pointing out purported explanatory gaps in evolutionary theory. The "Creation theory" or the "design hypothesis" is supposed to win by default. As we have seen, this dual model strategy has appeared in various forms, but the current favorite is in the creationist proposals to teach their view under the heading of "critical thinking."

As mentioned above, I find some merit in the idea of considering the creation/evolution controversy as a case study to develop critical thinking. At the university level this can work, but there are several practical obstacles to implementing it at lower levels. The main problem is simply that quantity of material that would have to be covered. It takes a semester-long college course just to give undergraduates an introduction to evolutionary theory, and one needs at least that much background to be able to begin to judge the evidence for oneself. It is also questionable whether high school students have developed cognitively to the degree that would make such an exercise worthwhile. Even some honors-level college freshmen are not sufficiently mature intellectually to begin that sort of evaluative project.

But there is a more important reason for not following the creationists' proposal to teach critical thinking by criticizing evolutionary theory in the way they desire. Creationists are ideologues who "know" in advance what is the "absolutely true" answer to the question of origins, and they want the critical tools to be used against evolutionary theory rather than turned on their own views. But it is simply not intellectually honest or professionally responsible to teach as though scientific conclusions were simply a matter of opinion, or that the creationist views of the origin of species are on a par with the findings of evolutionary theory.

Consider what the effect would be if we were to buy into the curricular framework that creationists propose; it would not be only evolutionary biology that would have to be put under critical scrutiny. Take the subject of world history. There are any number of advocacy groups that, for religious, political, or other ideological reasons, advance some idiosyncratic version of history that is at odds with the findings of historians. If we accept the creationists' proposals regarding evolution, we should also be sure to present alternative theories, attach disclaimers to the standard accounts, and give equal time to the "evidence against" the conclusions of historical research so that the students can judge for themselves. In studying the assassination of President Kennedy, for example, we might begin by screening Oliver Stone's movie *JFK*, and then go on to consider the other theories, such as that Vice President Johnson masterminded his death, or that the CIA was behind it. When studying the landing of American astronauts on the moon, we should probably issue a disclaimer and respectfully consider the views of those who believe that the whole event was filmed by the government in a secret Hollywood studio as part of an elaborate charade. When teaching about World War II we would need to give balanced treatment to those who hold that the Holocaust never happened and was just a Zionist propaganda ploy to gain sympathy for Jews.[7] But such a notion of "fairness" and "balance" is absurd. It is certainly not sound educational philosophy.

We should be no less diligent in teaching the results of careful investigation of the history of life on earth as we are in teaching the history of our nation and the other nations of the world. Critical thinking does not mean indiscriminate thinking, but thinking governed by the rules of reason and evidence.

VII. The Answer

In reviewing the arguments, we find many good reasons for excluding creationism from the schools, and few good reasons for not doing so. On balance, it seems the wiser course not to allow the conflict into the classroom. Should creationism be taught in the public schools? The answer is that it should not.

Notes

1 Such a poll question is misleading and biased, however, in that it assumes what is false: that there is just *one* theory of Creation and that it is a science.

2 The 44 percent figure comes from a November 1997 poll. There has been no statistically significant change in the percentage of Americans who accept this creationist view since 1982 (45%), when the Gallup poll began to track beliefs about human origins. The social, political, and demographic breakdown of the poll figures showed that the "those most likely to believe in the *creationist version* were older Americans, the less well-educated, southerners, political conservatives (the New Religious Right?), biblical literalists, and Protestants, particularly in fundamentalist denominations such as Baptists" (Bishop 1998).

3 It should be obvious, but let me nevertheless state explicitly that in making these arguments I am taking it for granted that evolutionary theory is true. I mean this, of course, in the standard scientific sense of approximate, revisable truth; no one thinks that evolutionary theory is complete or that one or another of its specific elements might not have to be modified should new, countervailing evidence be found. Creationism is false in the basic sense that, whatever its specific positive commitments, it by definition rejects evolution. Most of creationists' specific claims about the processes of the origins of cosmological, geological, and biological phenomena (among others) have been shown to be false as

well, provided that we are able to judge these by ordinary scientific means and standards. Note, however, that I do not assume that this means that God does not exist; the larger question of whether a supernatural designer created the world is not answerable simply by appeal to scientific methods. I have discussed some of the evidence for these conclusions elsewhere (Pennock 1999, chs. 2–3) and will not review them here.

4 I previously developed this position in a paper entitled "Creationism in the Science Classroom: Private Faith vs. Public Knowledge," delivered at the 1995 Conference on Value Inquiry, the proceedings of which have yet to be published. I expand the argument in Pennock (1999, ch. 8) and so will not rehearse it here.

5 I have previously rebutted Johnson's claims about scientific naturalism and shown how it is a methodological and not a dogmatic view in Pennock (1996).

6 Creationists want to include only their own view, of course. In 1973, they got the Tennessee legislature to pass a law that would require public school textbooks to give equal emphasis to the Genesis view and to explicitly identify the evolutionary view of human origins as "merely a theory" and not a scientific fact, and attached an amendment so that the Bible did not also have to carry that disclaimer, and another amendment to expressly exclude the "teaching of all occult or satanic beliefs of human origins." In the 1975 *Daniel v. Waters* case Federal Court of Appeals immediately struck down the law as "patently unconstitutional," holding that claims to the contrary would be "obviously frivolous" and did not merit review, citing the amendments in particular and noting that no law could give such preferential treatment to the Biblical view of Creation over "occult" ones (Larson 1989, p. 136).

7 I mention such examples of conspiracy theories intentionally. As one reads creationist literature, from Morris to Johnson and beyond, one is struck by the regularity with which creationists describe scientists as being engaged in a deliberate conspiracy to deceive everyone into accepting evolution so that they might maintain their cultural authority, promote atheism, and spread immorality. Such implicit and explicit accusations are more than irresponsible.

References

Aubrey, Frank. 1998 (1980). Yes, Virginia, There Is a Creation Model. *Reports of the National Center for Science Education* 18 (1): 6.

Bishop, George. 1998. What Americans Believe about Evolution and Religion: A Cross-National Perspective. Paper read at 53rd Annual conference of the *American Association for Public Opinion Research*, at St. Louis, Missouri.

Cremo, Michael A. and Richard L. Thompson. 1993. *Forbidden Archeology: The Hidden History of the Human Race.* Alachua, Fla.: Govardhan Hill Publishing.

Davis, Percival and Dean H. Kenyon. 1993. *Of Pandas and People.* Dallas, Texas: Haughton Publishing Co.

Dewey, John. 1964 (1910). Science as Subject Matter and as Method. In *John Dewey on Education: Selected Writings*, edited by R. D. Archambault. Chicago: University of Chicago Press.

Dewey, John. 1964 (1938). The Relation of Science and Philosophy as a Basis of Education. In *John Dewey on Education: Selected Writings*, edited by R. D. Archambault. Chicago: University of Chicago Press.

Duvall, Jed. 1995. School Board Tackles Creationism Debate. CNN *Interactive (WWW)*, November 5.

Johnson, Phillip E. 1991. *Darwin on Trial.* Washington, D.C.: Regnery Gateway.

Johnson, Phillip E. 1995. *Reason in the Balance: The Case against Naturalism in Science, Law, and Education.* Downers Grove, Ill.: Inter Varsity Press.

La Follette, Marcel Chotkowski, ed. 1983. *Creationism, Science, and the Law: The Arkansas Case.* Cambridge, Mass.: The MIT Press.

Larson, Edward J. 1989. *Trial And Error: The American Controversy over Creation and Evolution.* Updated ed. New York and Oxford: Oxford University Press.

Larson, Edward J. 1997. *Summer for the Gods: The Scopes Trial and America's Continuing Debate over Science and Religion.* New York, NY: Basic Books.

Pennock, Robert T. 1996. Naturalism, Evidence, and Creationism: The Case of Phillip Johnson. *Biology and Philosophy* 11 (4): 543–559.

Pennock, Robert T. 1999. *Tower of Babel: The Evidence against the New Creationism.* Cambridge, Mass.: MIT Press.

Plantinga, Alvin. 1997. Methodological Naturalism? *Perspectives on Science and Christian Faith* 49 (3): 143–154.

Chapter 44

Alvin Plantinga

CREATION AND EVOLUTION:
A MODEST PROPOSAL

The topic of our meeting is the question, should Creationism be taught in the (public) schools? That is an excellent question, and Professor Pennock has interesting things to say about it. I want to begin, however, by asking a complementary question, after which I shall return to this one: should evolution be taught in the public schools? I'm not asking whether it is legally permissible to teach evolution in the public schools; that matter has been long settled. I'm asking instead whether it should be taught. Given that it is permissible, is it also the right thing to do? But why should that even be a question? Daniel Dennett thinks it is a foolish question: "Should evolution be taught in the schools?" he asks? Well, "Should arithmetic? Should history?" Isn't it utterly obvious that evolution should be taught in public schools? I don't think so; the answer isn't nearly so simple. But we must initially specify the question a bit more closely. First, I am asking whether evolution should be taught in the public schools of a country like the United States, one that displays the pluralism and diversity of opinion our country presently displays. And second, I am asking whether evolution should be taught as the sober truth of the matter, rather than as, for example, the best current scientific hypothesis, or what accords best or is most probable (epistemically probable) with respect to the appropriate scientific evidence base. The question is whether evolution should be taught in the way arithmetic and chemistry and geography are taught: as the settled truth.

Still another need for specification: the term "evolution" can expand and contract upon demand: it covers a multitude of sins, as some might put it. First, there is the idea that at least some evolution has occurred, that there have been changes in gene frequencies in populations. I suppose everyone accepts this, so we can put it to one side. Second, there is the claim that the earth is very old—billions of years old, and that life has been present on earth for billions of years. Third, there is the progress thesis, as we humans like to think of it: first there were prokaryotes, then single-celled eukaryotes, then increasingly more complex forms of life of great diversity, achieving a contemporary maximum in us. Fourth, there is the claim of universal common ancestry: the claim that any two living things you pick, you and the poison ivy in your backyard, for example, share a common ancestor. Fifth, there is what I will call "Darwinism," the thesis that the cause of the diversity of forms of life is natural selection working on a source of genetic variation like random genetic mutation. Sixth and finally, there is the idea that life itself arose by way of purely natural means, just by way of the workings of the laws of physics and chemistry on some set of initial conditions, or just by way of the workings of those laws together with what supervenes on their workings; this thesis is part of the contemporary scientific picture of the origin of life, although at present all such accounts of the origin of life are at best enormously problematic.[1] Since the first thesis is accepted by everyone, we can set it aside, and use the term "evolution" or "the theory of evolution" to refer to the conjunction of the remaining five theses, or occasionally to the conjunction of the first four.

So why is there a question as to whether evolution should be taught in the public schools? And if there is such a question, what sort of question is it? I believe there *is* a question here, and it is a question of justice or fairness. First, our society is radically pluralistic; and here I am thinking in particular of the plurality of religious and quasi-religious views our citizenry displays. I say "quasi-religious": that is because I mean the term to cover, not only religious belief, as in Christianity, Islam, Judaism, Hinduism, Buddhism, and the like, but also other deep ways of understanding ourselves and our world, other deep ways of interpreting ourselves and our world to ourselves. Thus consider philosophical naturalism, the idea that there is no such person as God or anything or anyone at all like him: on this use, naturalism is or can be a quasi-religious view. Following John Rawls, let's call beliefs of this sort "comprehensive" beliefs. Now for many, perhaps most citizens, these comprehensive beliefs are of enormous importance; for some they are the most important beliefs of all. And it is natural for these citizens to want their children to be educated into what they take to be the true and correct comprehensive beliefs; they think it is a matter of great importance which comprehensive beliefs their children adopt, some even thinking that one's eternal welfare depends on their accepting the true comprehensive beliefs.

Next, we must think for a moment about the purpose of public schools. This purpose is somehow determined by or supervenes on the purposes of the citizens who support and employ these schools. It is as if we are all party to a sort of implicit contract: we recognize the need

to train and educate our children, but don't have the time or competence to do it individually. We therefore get together to hire teachers to help instruct and educate our children, and together we pay for this service by way of tax money. But what should we tell these teachers to teach? Of course all the citizens party to the contract would prefer that their children be educated into their own comprehensive beliefs—be taught that those comprehensive beliefs are the sober truth. But that isn't feasible, because of the plurality of comprehensive beliefs. It would clearly be unfair, unjust, for the school, which we all support, to teach one set of religious beliefs as opposed to another—to teach that evangelical Christianity, for example, is the truth. This would be unfair to those citizens who are party to the contract and whose comprehensive beliefs—Judaism, naturalism, Islam, whatever—are incompatible with evangelical Christianity. The teacher can't teach all or even more than one of these conflicting sets of beliefs as the truth; therefore it would be unfair to select any particular one and teach *that* one as the truth. More generally, fairness dictates that no belief be taught as the settled truth that conflicts with the comprehensive beliefs of some group of citizens party to the contract. We can put this in terms of what I'll call "the basic right" (BR):

(BR)   Each of the citizens party to the contract has the right not to have comprehensive beliefs taught to her children that contradict her own comprehensive beliefs.

Our society is a pluralistic society; there are many mutually inconsistent sets of comprehensive beliefs. But then no particular set of comprehensive beliefs can be taught without infringing on that basic right. It is therefore unfair and unjust to teach one religious belief as opposed to others in the schools; it is improper and unjust to teach, for example, Protestant beliefs, as opposed to Catholic, or Christian as opposed to Jewish or Hindu, or religious beliefs as opposed to naturalism and atheism. More generally, take any group of citizens who are party to the contract: it would be unfair for the public schools to teach beliefs inconsistent with their religious or comprehensive beliefs: unfair, because it would go against (BR). Of course (BR) is a prima facie right. It is at least possible that special circumstances should arise, perhaps as in wartime, in which this right would be over-ridden by other desiderata, for example national security. The majority might also insist on teaching the denial of certain comprehensive views, Naziism, for example, in which case the fair thing to do would be to exclude the Nazis from the contract (and also exclude them from the tax liability).

But then it is also easy to see how an issue of justice or fairness can arise with respect to the teaching of evolution. As Professor Pennock points out, many American Indian tribes, for example, "have origin stories that, on their face, are antithetical to evolutionary theory and other scientific findings" (this volume, p. 599). Now consider a public school in an Indian village of this sort, one where many or most of the citizens hold and are deeply committed to comprehensive beliefs that are contradicted by contemporary evolutionary theory. Perhaps they believe that the first human beings were specially created by God a hundred miles or so from their village, some thousands of years ago. Would it be fair or just to teach their children, in this public school, that these religious accounts of human origins are false? Would it be right to teach their children that their ancestors emerged on the plains of Serengetti more than a million years ago, and that they were not specially created at all, but descended from earlier, nonhuman forms of life? Would it be just to teach their children accounts of human origins that contradict their religious accounts? I think we can see that this would be unfair and unjust. These citizens are party to the implicit contract by which public education is founded; they support and help finance these schools. By virtue of (BR), then, they have a right not to have their children taught, in public schools, the denials of their cherished religious beliefs. If their children are taught the denials of these beliefs, these citizens' rights are being violated. They are being violated just as surely as if their children were taught, for example, that their religion is merely superstition and evangelical Christianity is the truth of the matter.

Now the fact is there is a substantial segment of the population, at least in certain states and certain parts of our country, whose comprehensive beliefs are indeed contradicted by the theory of evolution. There are fundamentalist Christian, Jewish, and Muslim parents, and quite a few of them, who think the earth is very young, perhaps only 10,000 years old. This is not a casual opinion with them, as might be their opinion that there are mountains on the far side of the moon. It is a part of their comprehensive belief: it is one of their religious beliefs that the Bible (or the Koran) contains the truth on all the matters on which it speaks, and on this matter what it says is that the earth is young. There are others who believe that the first human beings were created specially by God, so that the theory of universal common ancestry is false. We may disagree with their beliefs here, or even think them irrational; but that doesn't change matters. Even if their beliefs are irrational from our point of view, (BR) still applies: they have the right to require that public schools not teach as the settled truths beliefs that are incompatible with their comprehensive beliefs.[2]

So there is therefore a clear prima facie question of justice here: these citizens are party to the implicit contract; they pay their taxes; they support these schools, and send their children to them. But then they have a prima facie right to have their children taught, as settled fact, only what is consistent with their comprehensive beliefs. And this means that it is unfair or unjust to teach evolution—universal common ancestry, for example—in the public schools, at any rate where there is a substantial segment of the population whose comprehensive beliefs are incompatible with evolution. In the very same way, of course, it would be unjust to teach creationism as the settled truth. Both doctrines conflict with the comprehensive beliefs of some of the parties to the contract.

But now for a reply, a reply suggested by some of Professor Pennock's comments. Doesn't truth have any rights here? Perhaps (BR) is a prima facie right, so runs the reply, but this right is overridden by the demands of truth. Pennock "takes it for granted that one of the basic goals of education is to provide students a true picture of the natural world we share" (this vol., p. 607), which seems fair enough; he also takes it for granted that evolutionary theory is true (p. 609); but then he concludes that evolutionary theory ought to be taught in the public schools. "Matters of empirical fact," he says, "are not appropriately decided by majority rule, nor is it unfair to teach what is true, even though many people don't want to hear it" (p. 603). That seems to suggest that if a proposition is true, then it is fair to teach it in public schools, even if it goes contrary to the comprehensive beliefs of the citizens who are party to the contract and support the public schools. But the reasoning seems deeply flawed. Suppose Christianity is in fact true, as indeed I believe it is: would that mean that it is fair to teach it in public schools where most of the citizens, citizens who support those schools, are not Christians and reject Christian comprehensive beliefs? I should think not; that would clearly be unfair, and the fact that the system of beliefs in question is true would not override the unfairness. We can't sensibly just insist that what is true can properly be taught, even if it contradicts the comprehensive beliefs of others party to the contract. After all, *they* also believe that *their* comprehensive beliefs are true: that is why they hold them.[3]

But other things he says suggest a different objection. According to Stephen J. Gould, there is the realm of values, and there is the realm of fact; religion and comprehensive beliefs occupy the realm of values (hence the expression "religious values"); science occupies the realm of fact. Hence when things are done properly there can be no conflict. There are no properly religious beliefs on matters of fact. Of course this is much too strong: clearly *most* religions make factual claims: that there is such a person as God, that the world was created, that Mohammed was God's prophet and spokesman. A slightly (but only slightly) more nuanced view, one that seems to me to be suggested by some of the things Pennock says can be put as follows: when it comes to matters of empirical fact (however that phrase is to be understood) scientific consensus trumps comprehensive belief. These questions of the origin of human beings and of life are factual questions, questions of empirical fact. The proper way to deal with them, then, is by way of science; it is simply a matter of trespass for someone in the name of religion to propose an answer to these factual questions. And this fact of trespass means that (BR) is overridden in some cases. If it's a factual question that's at issue, then the way to deal with it is by way of science. If you happen to have mistaken opinions about algebra or prime numbers (perhaps it is part of your comprehensive belief, somehow, that there is a greatest prime) that is your problem; you can't require the public schools to respect your comprehensive opinion here, and refrain from demonstrating to your children that in fact there is no greatest prime. Citizens do not have the right to object, on the ground of religious or comprehensive beliefs, to any scientific teaching. When it comes to issues that are dealt with by science, the prima facie claims of (BR) are overridden, and it is entirely right to teach the denials of comprehensive beliefs in the public schools, if those comprehensive beliefs are in fact contrary to contemporary scientific consensus.

But again, this seems entirely mistaken. First, why should we think scientific consensus overrides (BR)? Perhaps because we think science is our best bet with respect to the discovery of the truth or the approximate truth on the subjects on which it speaks. But if it is the truth we want taught to our children, then it's far from clear that current science should be treated with this much deference. We all know how often scientific opinion has changed over the years; there is little reason to think that now it has finally arrived at the unrevisable truth, so that its current proposals are like the claim that there is no greatest prime. According to Bryan Appleyard, "At Harvard University in the 1880's John Trowbridge, head of the physics department, was telling his students that it was not worthwhile to major in physics, since all the very important discoveries in the subject had now been made. All that remained was a routine tidying up of loose ends, hardly a heroic task worthy of a Harvard graduate."[4] Twenty years later the same opinion seemed dominant: for example, in 1902 Albert Michelson, of Michelson-Morley fame, declared that "the most important fundamental laws and facts of physical science have all been discovered and these are now so firmly established that the possibility of their ever being supplanted on consequences of new discoveries is remote."[5] And of course we all know of the scientific theories that once enjoyed consensus but are now discarded: caloric theories of heat, effluvial theories of electricity and magnetism, theories involving the existence of phlogiston, vital forces in physiology, theories of spontaneous generation of life, the luminiferous ether, and so on.

But there is another and even more important consideration. Pennock, we are supposing, thinks the way to approach questions of empirical fact is by way of science, not by way of religion; thus scientific consensus trumps religious or comprehensive belief in such a way that the prima facie requirements of (BR) are overridden; and hence it is fair to teach evolution as settled fact, even if it does conflict with the religious beliefs of some of the citizens party to that implicit contract. But now consider this claim, that is:

(PC) The right way to answer questions of empirical fact—for example, questions about the origin of life, the age of the earth, whether human beings have evolved from earlier forms of life—is by way of science, or scientific method.

Note first that (PC) is not, of course, itself a question of empirical fact. Science itself does not decide between (PC) and other possibilities—for example, the claim that the right way to approach certain empirical questions is not by way of scientific inquiry but by way of consulting the Bible, or the elders of the tribe. The question whether the scientific epistemic or evidential base is the right way to settle these issues is not itself to be settled with respect to the scientific epistemic base; this dispute is philosophical or religious rather than scientific. Note second that there are many others, of course, who do not share Pennock's opinion: they do not accept (PC). Indeed, there are many others such that a proposition incompatible with this opinion is part of their religious or comprehensive beliefs. Perhaps (PC) is part of Pennock's comprehensive beliefs; but its denial is part of the comprehensive beliefs of others who are party to the contract. But then clearly it would be unfair to act on (PC), as opposed to these other comprehensive beliefs that are incompatible with it. Suppose in fact fundamentalists are right: the truth is the correct way to determine the age of the earth is by way of consulting Scripture under a certain literal construal of early Genesis: would it follow that it was right in public schools to teach as the settled truth that the age of the earth is some 10,000 years or so? I should think not; and the same goes with respect to (PC). (PC) may be true and (more likely, in my opinion) it may be false; either way it is just one comprehensive belief among others. It would be unfair to teach comprehensive beliefs that entailed the denial of (PC); but by the same token, it would also be unfair to teach (PC).

What we have seen so far, therefore, is that it is

improper, unfair, to teach either creationism or evolution in the schools—that is so, at any rate, for areas where a substantial proportion of the parents hold religious or comprehensive beliefs incompatible with either. But then what *can* be taught, in public schools, about this crucial topic of origins, a topic deeply connected with our sense of ourselves, our sense of where we come from, what our prospects are, what is good for us, and the like? If we can't teach either Creationism or evolutionism, what can we teach in the public schools?

Well, possibly nothing. One answer is to say: in a pluralistic society like ours, there is no fair way to teach anything about origins; hence public schools ought not to teach anything on that subject. They should instead stick to subjects where there isn't disagreement at the level of religious or comprehensive beliefs. This would be just a reflection of a more general difficulty in having public schools of our sort in a pluralistic society. Perhaps, when the citizens get together to found a system of education, what they discover is that there is too much diversity of opinion to make it feasible. But this is a counsel of dispair; I think perhaps we can do better.

We can see a bit more deeply into this question by turning to a bit of epistemology. We have already noted that different people accept different religious or comprehensive beliefs. More generally, for each person P there is an epistemic base, EB_p, with respect to which the probability or acceptability of proposed beliefs is to be evaluated. This epistemic base includes, first, P's current beliefs. Since some beliefs are held more strongly than others, it includes, second, an index of degree of belief. Some beliefs, furthermore, are of the form *probably S*. An epistemic base also includes, third, prescriptions as to how to conduct inquiry, how to learn more about the world, under what conditions to change belief, and the like. And finally, an epistemic base includes comprehensive beliefs. These comprehensive beliefs are not, of course, frozen in stone; nor are they impervious to argument and

reasoning; nor are they irrational just as such, or held in an irrational way. A person's epistemic base is not static, of course; it constantly changes under the pressure of experience, what we are told by others, and the like. An epistemic base can also undergo sudden and drastic revision, as in a religious conversion, for example. A proper characterization of the notion of an epistemic base would take us far afield, and would certainly require an entire paper on its own. But I think the basic idea is fairly clear.

Now what parents want, presumably, is that their children be taught the truth—which, of course, they take to be what is in accord with their own epistemic bases. What is in accord with their own epistemic bases, of course, is not just the propositions they themselves happen to accept. I may know or believe that there are people who hold lots of beliefs I don't hold—about, for example, mathematics; I may also believe that their beliefs, whatever they are, are true, or likely to be true, or more likely to be true than the beliefs I actually hold; and I may therefore want my children taught *those* beliefs, even though they are not parts of my own epistemic base, and even though some may conflict with beliefs in my own epistemic base. These beliefs, we may say, are in accord with my epistemic base, although not contained in it. This can happen with respect to religious or comprehensive beliefs too: I may be an American Indian who holds that the tribal elders know the truth about important matters of origin, or whatever; then I may want my children taught what these elders believe, even if I don't myself know precisely what it is that they do believe.

We must note next that science has its own epistemic base. This base is presumably not identical with that of any of the citizens, although it overlaps in complex ways with those of some of the citizens. It is not important, here, to say precisely what goes into the scientific epistemic base (or how it is related to those of the citizens); presumably logic goes into it, together with prescriptions as to how to conduct various kinds of inquiry, together with a host of common sense beliefs, together with a good bit of firmly established current science. But it is important to note certain beliefs that do *not* go into EB$_p$, at least with respect to science as currently practiced. Among these would be the belief that there is such a person as God, that God has created the world, and that God has created certain forms of life specially—human beings, perhaps, or the original forms of life, or for that matter sparrows and horses. That is because science commonly respects what is often called "methodological naturalism," the policy of avoiding hypotheses that mention or refer to God or special acts on the part of God, or other supernatural phenomena, or hypotheses whose only support is the Bible, or some other alleged divine revelation. There is dispute as to whether science by its very nature involves methodological naturalism, and there is also dispute as to whether science *has a* nature. But as commonly practiced, science does seem to involve methodological naturalism. This means that EB$_p$ does not include any propositions of the above sort. It is not entirely clear whether EB$_p$ includes the *denials* of some propositions about God, or rather just fails to include those propositions. It is also worth noting that a person could think that EB$_p$ is the proper epistemic base from which to conduct scientific inquiry, even if her own epistemic base contains some of those propositions excluded from EB$_p$ by methodological naturalism. Indeed she might hold that a given proposition is a good scientific hypothesis even if it conflicts with one of her comprehensive beliefs and is therefore, as she sees it, false. Thus someone might think that a given scientific hypothesis—Darwinism, for example—is in fact false, but is nevertheless a source of fertile and useful hypotheses.

To return to our subject, then: we can't in fairness teach evolution as the settled truth in public schools in a pluralistic society like ours, and of course we can't in fairness teach creationism either. But there is something else we can do: we can teach evolution *conditionally*. That is, we

can teach, as the sober truth, that from the vantage point of EB$_p$ the most satisfactory hypothesis is the ancient earth thesis, or universal common ancestry, or Darwinism, or even some hypothesis entailing naturalistic origins. We can also distinguish between the likelihoods of these hypotheses, on EB$_p$; the ancient earth thesis is very nearly certain on this basis, universal common ancestry much less certain, but still a very good bet, Darwinism still less certain, and naturalistic origins, or rather any particular current theory of naturalistic origins, unlikely, at least with respect to the current EB$_p$. There is one further complication we must note: given plausible views about EB$_p$, it might be that a hypothesis is the best scientific hypothesis from the point of view of EB$_p$, even though it is not, from that point of view, more probable than not. This might be first just because there are several conflicting hypotheses in the field, all of which enjoy substantial probability with respect to EB$_p$, but none of which enjoys a probability as great as $1/2$. But second, it might be that a conjecture is a fine, fertile hypothesis such that inquiry pursued under its aegis is fruitful and successful, even though the hypothesis in question is unlikely with respect to EB$_p$. Many more questions arise about EB$_p$; there is no time to explore them now.

Now consider the claim that evolution is the best hypothesis (the one most likely to be true), or even that it is much more likely than not with respect to EB$_p$: that claim, I take it, will be compatible with everyone's religious and comprehensive beliefs. There would then be no objection from the point of view of fairness to teaching this claim as the settled truth—while refraining, of course, from teaching evolution itself as the settled truth. Perhaps this is something like what the court had in mind in *Segraves v. California* when it declared that "any speculative statements concerning origins, both in texts and in classes, should be presented conditionally, not dogmatically" (p. 8). And the same would go for creationism: with respect to certain widely shared epistemic bases, the most likely or satis-factory hypothesis will be the claim that God created human beings specially, or even the claim that the earth is only 10,000 years old. Of course the public schools will not, under this proposal, teach that one epistemic base—either that of evangelical Christianity, for example, or scientific naturalism—is in fact the correct or right or true epistemic base. The question of which epistemic base is the correct one is not a question on which public schools should pro-nounce, at least in areas where there is relevant religious disagreement. What the public schools should teach as the sober truth is what is in accord with all the relevant epistemic bases; this is what should be taught unconditionally.

To return to our original question then: should creationism be taught in the public schools? Should evolution? The answer is in each case the same: no, neither should be taught unconditionally; but yes, each should be taught conditionally.[6]

Notes

1 See, e.g., *Origins* by Robert Shapiro (New York: Summit Books, 1986).

2 A slightly different issue: there are still others who believe, as part of their comprehensive belief, that God created the world and humankind one way or another, where one possibility is that he did it by way of an evolutionary process. These parents may very well believe that it is possible (epistemically possible) that human beings are geneologically related to earlier forms of life, but that this sugges-tion is far from certain. They may therefore quite properly resist having it taught as settled truth, on a par with arithmetic and the proposition that there has been an American Civil War.

3 In the same vein, Pennock also holds that "[parents] certainly don't have a right to demand that teachers teach what is false" (this vol., p. 603). But this too seems to me mistaken: didn't parents at the end of the last century have the right to demand that science teachers teach, e.g., Newtonian mechanics, even though as a matter of fact it is false? They also had a right to demand that science teachers teach that there is such a thing as the luminiferous ether, although that too is false, at least by our current lights. Earlier parents had a similar right to demand that science teachers teach the caloric theory of heat, that there is such a thing as phlogiston, that elec-tricity is a kind of fluid, that the sun goes around the earth, and so on.

4 *Understanding the Present* (New York: Doubleday, 1992), p. 110.

5 Quoted in Hanbury Brown, *The Wisdom of Science: Its Relevance to Culture and Religion* (Cambridge: Cambridge University Press, 1986), p. 66.

6 I'm grateful to Tom Crisp, Marie Pannier, and David VanderLaan for comments and criticism.

Reference

Pennock, Robert T. (2000). "Why Creationism Should Not Be Taught in the Public Schools." This volume, chap. 43.

Chapter 45

Paul J. Weithman

THEISM, LAW, AND POLITICS

Religion is among the most potent political forces in the contemporary world and the claims religious believers make on their institutions raise some of today's most pressing political questions. These include whether government can serve explicitly religious purposes, what sort of autonomy religious organizations should enjoy, when claims by religious minorities are unreasonable, and how institutions should accommodate religious diversity. Addressing such questions is the business of practical politics; it is also the task of political philosophy, the normative study of politics.

Contemporary political philosophy in the English-speaking world is dominated by liberalism, a family of political theories which claim that government should insure a significant degree of individual autonomy. This requires, liberals argue, that government guarantee citizens various rights, including freedom of speech, press, assembly, and conscience, and the right to vote. A number of philosophers have contested particular points of liberal theory. Some have developed rival accounts of the nature and purposes of government. But none has dislodged liberalism from its dominant position. When asking about theism's implications for contemporary political philosophy, it is therefore appropriate to begin by querying its implications for liberalism.

Political philosophy's development has been largely independent of Judaism, Byzantine Chris-

tianity, Islam, and the great religions of Asia. I shall therefore construe theism as equivalent to the organized religions descended from Latin Christianity. Focusing on theism so construed illuminates the characteristic motives, strengths, and weaknesses of a number of philosophical views. It casts light on liberalism's motives because liberalism began as an attempt to accommodate the religious diversity consequent on the Protestant Reformation. It also sheds light on the motivations of the other views I will discuss. These developed in reaction to liberalism and, in some instances, in reaction to liberalism's treatment of religion. It spotlights the strengths and weaknesses of various political theories because political philosophy has traditionally assumed both explanatory and normative tasks. Since Plato, political theorists have exploited philosophically compelling accounts of human nature to explain political phenomena. They have relied upon those accounts to defend moral claims about the goods to be realized in political life and the means by which political authorities ought to pursue them. One measure of a political theory's adequacy is its ability to offer compelling explanations of tenable prescriptions for the place of religion in political life.

Liberalism

Before the sixteenth century, it was possible to conceive of Europe as a single spiritual community united by religion. No one denied the reality of Europe's political and ethnic divisions. It was none the less possible to maintain that human beings had common spiritual ends which were to be promoted by diverse political authorities. The advent of Protestantism introduced religious pluralism to Europe on a large scale. Catholicism and the various forms of Protestantism held out different conceptions of human nature and sin, of liturgy and redemption. Their adherents made claims to worship as their religion dictated and urged that those with whom they differed have their rites suppressed. The ensuing conflicts marked the end of a spiritually unified Christendom and posed new philosophical problems. European political theorists had to ask themselves how governmental institutions could remain stable and function effectively in the face of such pluralism.

Some philosophers in the early modern period defended policies of religious suppression. The dominant liberalism of contemporary political philosophy, however, has its origins in the doctrine of religious toleration. John Locke and other champions of toleration argued that religious practice is a legitimate matter of governmental concern only when it is disruptive of public order. Otherwise, Locke argued, religious practice should no more concern the government than should any other private pursuit. Liberal theories descended from the defense of toleration aspire to an even-handed treatment of religious diversity. Government should, their proponents say, neither discourage nor promote various religious and moral views. In the name of individual autonomy, it should guarantee the right to pursue any of them.

Let us say that the scope of a moral doctrine is given by the areas of human life to which its values apply. A moral doctrine is comprehensive in scope if all of human life is covered by its values. Liberalism is itself a moral view. The notion of scope therefore enables us to distinguish, following the American philosopher John Rawls (b. 1921), between *comprehensive* and *political* liberalisms. Comprehensive liberalisms are liberalisms whose normative claims extend to all of human life. According to some comprehensive liberalisms, for example, autonomy is not simply a political value. Its realization is a necessary condition of a well-lived human life; political arrangements which promote it are therefore necessary for human beings to lead the best life of which they are capable. Political liberalisms, by contrast, are moral doctrines of narrow scope: their values and prescriptions apply only to political life and political institutions. They make no claims about the true human good, and present a political morality which purports to be compatible with a variety of philosophical and religious claims about private life.

Many religious believers find comprehensive liberalisms less even-handed than their proponents claim. Critics charge that liberals committed to realizing autonomy in all areas of life are equally committed to government attempts to promote it in ways detrimental to religion. Thus many liberals' commitment to autonomy implies limits on parental control of education. Democratic education, they claim, should be geared to producing citizens capable of critical reflection on all the ways of life available to them. The problem is that some religious believers do not attach high value to critical reflection. Many religious believers conclude that a political theory which purports to treat all religions equally is in fact detrimental to them. Comprehensive liberalisms, framed to accommodate religious and moral diversity, are themselves insufficiently sensitive to it.

Because political liberalism is of more restricted scope, religious citizens in democratic societies might find it more promising. The most sophisticated of the political liberalisms is that recently propounded by Rawls, and critical reaction to it is in a very early stage. It is possible, however, to distinguish two lines of religiously-based criticism.

The first concerns the role political liberalism

accords private associations, including religious associations. The thought of these associations belongs to what Rawls calls "the background culture," which he contrasts with "the public culture," the culture of the political. Some critics have argued that there is no clear distinction between the two. The background culture, including its religious elements, plays an important role in citizens' formation. It is as participants in the background culture, critics argue, that citizens acquire the qualities of character constitutive of good citizenship. A liberalism which ignores the political role of these association therefore ignores an important source of its own stability. The problem with this criticism is that Rawls does not ignore the importance of private associations in moral education. He does argue that democratic citizens should learn to reason about political matters without relying on their religious views. This does not imply that religious associations cannot play a crucial role in teaching them to do this.

Rawls's treatment of public political discussion opens the second line of criticism. He argues that such discussion should proceed on the basis of a common political morality; religious views may be introduced into public discussion only to defend conclusions that can be supported on the basis of that common morality. Some have argued convincingly that these restrictions impose too great a limitation on religious language. Citizens with religious convictions, they say, should be able to introduce them in public argument. Moreover, Kent Greenwalt has argued that any political morality uncontentious enough to be common lacks sufficient content to settle important political issues. Citizens, legislators, and judges have no alternative but to rely upon other views, including religious views.

Theism, Nationalism, and Citizenship

The English political theorist John Gray has argued that what he calls "the new liberalism,"

while ostensibly addressed to all mature democracies, is in fact thoroughly American in its presuppositions and arguments. The charge that contemporary political philosophy is parochially American is an important one for present purposes. Political liberalism's treatment of religion might seem geared to religion's role in American public life and is insensitive to its functions in politics outside the United States. Much contemporary political philosophy might seem insensitive to the ways in which religiously motivated political argument and action result from the combination of religion with the particularities of local, regional, and ethnic culture.

This insensitivity shows itself in the limited explanatory ambitions of contemporary political philosophy. One of the most salient features of politics is the vigor of various forms of religious conservatism. Fundamentalism, the most powerful of these, is too often dismissed as a form of irrationality or wished away by those who hope that the spread of democracy will ameliorate it. Yet the worldwide resurgence of religious fundamentalism and its ability to exacerbate class, ethnic, and national tensions, reveal a deepseated alienation from modernity and liberalism. One of the traditional tasks of political philosophy is to explore moral psychology, drawing out its implications for the stability of regimes; this is as true of the early John Rawls as it was of Plato. Why fundamentalism should be so appealing to so many is in part a question of moral psychology; its popularity has implications for the viability of democratic liberalism. It is therefore problematic that contemporary political philosophers should pay it so little sustained attention.

How might liberals remedy this problem? Focusing on his native Canada, Charles Taylor (b. 1931) has argued that American-style liberalism is unable to conceptualize and accommodate the needs of ethnic and tribal communities. He attributes this inability to the conception of citizenship on which such liberalism is premised.

Crudely put, citizens are conceived of as having moral capacities necessary for social cooperation and for embracing some comprehensive moral view. They are also conceived of as having the rights necessary to protect the exercise of those capacities. Those capacities are, however, characterized without reference to the particular ends and attachments citizens actually have. According to Taylor, political philosophy appropriate to a pluralistic society would begin with a very different conception of citizenship, one which defines citizenship with reference to the sub-communities to which citizens belong, the ties they have, and the goods they pursue in common. Taylor argues that liberals could adopt this conception of citizenship without surrendering their traditional commitment to the most cherished individual rights and liberties.

Philosophers concerned with nationalism and ethnicity are debating the nature of citizenship, and many have put forward variants of Taylor's suggestion. Their proposals are interesting and important, and promise to shed some light on the role of ethnic sub-communities within liberal democracies. They are, however, at a preliminary stage of development. If their details can be worked out, it is possible that philosophers interested in religion's political role could make use of them. It is possible that a theory which defines citizenship with reference to ethnic and national attachments could define it with reference to religious ones as well. This, in turn, raises the possibility that liberalism could more adequately treat religion's role in world politics than it currently does.

Theism and Public Philosophy

As mentioned above, contemporary liberals pay little heed to religious fundamentalism and assume that liberalism is compatible with many forms of theism. In recent years, there has been renewed interest among American religious ethicists in John Courtney Murray's attempt to show the compatibility of Catholicism and American democracy. Murray (1904–67), a Jesuit priest, argued that American democracy depends upon what he called a "public consensus." Among the objects of this consensus are principles of justice, the ideal of civility, and values associated with education and public morality. These norms provide the basis for "the public philosophy," a working philosophy for American public life.

The scope of the public philosophy, while not comprehensive, is considerably broader than that of political liberalism. Civility, for example, is a value that should be realized, not only in public political argument, but in much other interaction among citizens as well. This breadth of scope, Murray thought, is crucial to the transmission of the public philosophy and the maintenance of the American moral consensus. Citizens learn to participate in the moral consensus only if its constitutive values are systematically fostered by and realized in a wide range of institutions. Murray argued that the core values of the American public philosophy can be found in the natural law ethics explicitly embraced by Roman Catholicism and congenial to many other religions as well. It follows that these religions are not merely compatible with liberal democracy, but also supportive of it. Murray concluded that churches and religious schools are among the institutions which form and transmit the American public philosophy.

A generation later, a number of American religious thinkers have returned to Murray's work for inspiration. Religious thought and language, they argue, can inspire innovative policy and help to build political coalitions in support of social justice. Religious ties, they maintain, can rebuild a sense of community eroded by social mobility and an emphasis on autonomy. Religious education can foster the virtues of self-sacrifice and commitment to the common good on which liberal democracy depends. The attempt to update Murray's thought and elucidate its implications for contemporary American politics is among the most exciting projects in religious social ethics. It is not, however, without its critics.

Some criticize Murray for focusing on religious liberty and neglecting economic justice. Others read his defense of rights as an endorsement of modernity's most corrosive ingredient, the element of modern politics that destroys bonds of community. David Hollenbach, one of the most notable thinkers associated with the Murray revival, has replied that human rights should be understood as "the minimum conditions for life in community." Among these conditions, Hollenbach argues, are a guaranteed standard of living and the opportunity to use one's gifts in community life. Hollenbach's theory of rights is therefore sensitive to the distribution of wealth and opportunity. Because human rights have an irreducibly communitarian element, Hollenbach argues, their defense is not a commitment to the individualism that weakens communal bonds.

The Murray revival faces other serious difficulties. First, recall that consensus on a public philosophy is consensus on a moral view with broad though not comprehensive scope. Such consensus requires agreement on the values to be fostered in public education and media of communication; important among these values, Murray thought, were values connected with human sexuality. The diversity of mores in the contemporary United States poses serious obstacles to such a consensus. Second, organized religions in the United States exercise looser control over their members in the 1990s than they did in Murray's time. This diversity of opinion within churches extends to the very issues on which Murray thought there should be a public consensus among religions. The Catholic Church, for example, has been unable to build consensus on sexual morality among its American members despite vigorous efforts. This suggests that even if there were moral consensus among the official representatives of various organized American religions, religious organizations would be incapable of building a consensus that includes most of their members.

Anti-Liberalism

I have so far focused on political philosophers sympathetic to liberalism in some form. There are, however, many thinkers who are unsympathetic to it because of the moral culture fostered by liberal democratic politics. In the name of toleration, these thinkers claim, citizens of liberal democracies come to believe that virtually any way of life is as morally worthy as any other, and that matters of public morality should be left to individuals. As a consequence, they say, liberal democratic societies are insufficiently respectful of inviolable moral norms like those forbidding euthanasia, abortion, and assisted suicide, and insufficiently committed to traditional values.

Many of these critics are religious, spanning the doctrinal spectrum. Pope John Paul II (b. 1920) of the Roman Catholic Church has written a series of public letters called "encyclicals" that have been sharply critical of the capitalist and democratic West. The culture of the West, John Paul argues, inclines increasingly to materialism, moral relativism, and the worship of technology. It thereby neglects the essential spirituality of humankind and leaves human beings spiritually hungry. Culture can be renewed, John Paul says, only by turning to God and returning to the moral absolutes articulated in scripture, the Christian tradition, and the natural law. The evangelical Protestant Stanley Hauerwas argues that the cultures of liberal democracies like the United States systematically misunderstand and trivialize religion. In response, Hauerwas calls on religious citizens to maintain a separatist and critical attitude toward secular liberal society. He urges them to dedicate themselves to communities animated by religious faith where traditional values are nourished.

The most philosophically powerful of liberalism's critics is Alasdair MacIntyre (b. 1929). MacIntyre recognizes the pluralism of large industrial democracies, but argues that liberals have drawn the wrong conclusion from it. While liberals hope to build on a common political morality, MacIntyre argues that any such morality relies upon what he calls "essentially contested concepts." Even concepts like "justice" and "equality" on which liberals like Rawls hope to secure agreement are, MacIntyre contends, used differently by those who endorse different moral views. Some might hope to settle this disagreement by looking at paradigmatic cases in which the demands of justice are satisfied. MacIntyre argues in reply that agreement on the requisite paradigms is impossible to secure. Liberalism presents itself as a moral view neutral among various contending theories. MacIntyre concludes that, as a view committed to its own ways of life and paradigms of justice, it is but one more contender in a series of deep moral disagreements.

MacIntyre argues that the human good consists in a life characterized by the cultivation and harmonious exercise of the moral virtues. From this claim, plus MacIntyre's analysis of moral disagreement, three consequences follow. First, in large and pluralistic societies, there can at present be no meaningful and terminable debate about how those societies might promote the true human good. Second, different and incompatible values regulate the public life of liberal societies on the one hand, and smaller communities, including religious communities, within such societies on the other. Consider, for example, MacIntyre's penetrating studies of truth-telling, written in the early 1990s. Truth-telling, he argued, imposes different requirements and admits of different exceptions in different spheres of life. It is therefore extremely difficult for citizens to develop consistent attitudes toward truth-telling, to exercise the virtue of veracity consistently or to combine that virtue with others. Similar claims are, he says, true of the other virtues. Third, because of the impossibility of realizing and combining the virtues under modern conditions, it follows that the true human good is unavailable, or available with great difficulty, in the most developed societies. MacIntyre echoes Aristotle in claiming that a life of virtue is most easily led in relatively small communities with a high degree of moral consensus. Since the modern state is far from being such a community, MacIntyre like Hauerwas counsels withdrawal to what cultural, religious, and intellectual enclaves persist in liberal societies.

MacIntyre is more interested in the question of what communities are necessary for realizing the true human good than he is in the reform of practical politics. This distance from politics is both a strength and a weakness of anti-liberalism generally. The anti-liberals are at their best as religiously-motivated social critics. They very effectively point out that, from the vantage point of various religious traditions, there appear to be deep human needs unfilled by liberal politics and deep moral problems with the culture it fosters. Political philosophy should, however, play a constructive as well as a critical role. The prevalence of theism and its profound impact on contemporary politics pose powerful challenges to political philosophers. Religion challenges them to explain the persistence of fundamentalism and the alienation from liberal politics experienced by many religious believers. It challenges philosophers to develop new ways of thinking about human rights and the distribution of wealth, about the political promise and spiritual limitations of liberal democracy. In sum, the challenges of theism for politics, and the problems with contemporary political philosophy, show how much remains to be done.

Bibliography

Douglass, R. B., and Hollenbach, D., SJ: *Catholicism and Liberalism* (Cambridge: Cambridge University Press, 1993).

Greenawalt, K.: *Religious Conviction and Political Choice* (New York: Oxford University Press, 1988).

Hauerwas, S.: *A Community of Character* (Notre Dame: University of Notre Dame Press, 1981).

John Paul II: *Evangelium Vitae* [*The Gospel of Life*] (New York: Random House, 1995).

MacIntyre, A.: *After Virtue* (Notre Dame: University of Notre Dame Press, 1981).

Murray, J. C., SJ: *We Hold These Truths* (New York: Sheed & Ward, 1960).

Rawls, J.: *Political Liberalism* (New York: Columbia University Press, 1993).

Taylor, C.: *Reconciling the Solitudes* (Montreal and Kingston: McGill-Queen's University Press, 1993).

Glossary

Annihilationism—the view that either there is no hell or that those who are in hell or deserving of hell cease to exist at some point in the future, and that as a result hell is not eternal.

Compatibilism—the view that it is logically possible for an individual to be free and fully determined, either by God or the conjunction of the past and the laws of nature. Though who affirm truth of compatibilism are called compatibilists. Compatibilists need not think that determinism is true nor that humans have free will.

Cosmological arguments—a family of *a posteriori* arguments for the existence of God which include a premise about a general feature of the world, such as that a contingent universe exists, and argues that the best explanation for that feature is the existence of God.

Design arguments—a family of *a posteriori* arguments for the existence of God which begin by identifying some particular or specific property of the universe, such as the apparent fine-tuning of the laws of nature for life, and conclude that God's existence is the best explanation for the feature in question. Design arguments are also sometimes called teleological arguments for the existence of God.

Divine hiddenness, argument from—a family of arguments which aim to show either that God doesn't exist or that it is not rational to believe in the existence of God on the basis of the fact that God's existence is not obvious to all individuals, and thus that God's existence is "hidden" from them.

Evil, evidential problem of—a family of arguments which aim to show that the existence of evil gives us reason or evidence to believe that an omnipotent, omniscient, omnibenevolent God does not exist. Evidential versions of the problem of evil are thus weaker than the logical problem of evil.

Evil, logical problem of—a family of arguments which aim to show a logical inconsistency between the existence of evil and the existence of an omnipotent, omniscient, omnibenevolent God. Insofar as evil exists, such arguments would, if sound, prove that an omnipotent, omniscient, omnibenevolent God does not exist.

Hell, traditional doctrine—the view of hell according to which (a) hell is not empty, (b) hell is a place of unending torment or punishment, and (c) the damned are not able to escape from hell.

Incompatibilism—the view that it is logically impossible for an individual to be free and fully determined, either by God or the conjunction of the past and the laws of nature. Incompatibilists who believe humans are free, and thus not determined, are libertarians; incompatibilists who think that determinism is true are hard determinists.

Kalam cosmological argument—a version of cosmological argument which takes as a key premise that the universe began to exist at a certain point in time and concludes that there exists a being, such as God, who brought the universe into existence.

Middle knowledge—God's pre-volitional knowledge of contingent truths. According to Molinists, God has middle knowledge as well as natural knowledge (God's pre-volitional knowledge of necessary truths) and free knowledge (God's post-volitional knowledge of contingent truths).

Molinism—named after the sixteenth-century Spanish Jesuit Luis de Molina, Molinism is a view of divine providence which affirms both the truth of libertarianism and that God exercises providential control over every event through His middle knowledge.

Moral evil—evils that are the result of the misuse of free will by free creatures.

Natural evil—evils that are not the result of the misuse of free will by free creatures, but instead are caused by natural processes. Examples include the suffering caused by earthquakes, plagues, or famine.

Natural theology—the enterprise of providing support for religious beliefs, such as the existence of God or claims about God's nature, solely on the basis of human reason and without the aid of divine revelation.

Ontological arguments—a family of arguments for the existence of God on the basis of necessary and *a priori* premises.

Open theism—a philosophical view about the nature of God on which God does not have foreknowledge of what free agents will freely do in the future, either because there are no truths about future free actions to be known or that such truths are in principle unknowable. Open theists are libertarians and affirm that God exists in time.

Providence—God's control over or directing of all the events that occur in creation.

Religious pluralism—generally focuses on the diversity of religious belief, but it is important to differentiate two different versions of religious pluralism. Descriptive, religious pluralism merely points out that there are numerous, and often competing, religious claims. Evaluative religious pluralism, on the other hand, makes the stronger claim that not only are there competing religious claims, but that these competing claims are all equally good in some important philosophical sense (e.g., equally true).

Resurrection—the raising to eternal life of a physical body or organism that has previously been dead. Belief in the resurrection is central to Christianity, Islam, some forms of Judaism, as well as other religions throughout the world.

Revealed theology—the enterprise of making and defending claims about the existence, nature, or actions of God which are based upon revelation. Revealed theology is contrasted with natural theology.

Simple foreknowledge—God's foreknowledge of future events (or atemporal knowledge of events which for us are in the future) which is not based on middle knowledge.

Theological determinism—the view that God's willing an event or causing that event to happen is necessary and sufficient for the event's occurring. In other words, (a) events only occur if God wills them to and (b) if God wills a particular event, nothing else can prevent that event from occurring.

Theological fatalism—the view that divine foreknowledge is incompatible with the existence of free will.

Universalism—the view that while hell may exist, all individuals will ultimately be redeemed and thus that hell will be empty. There are two main types of universalism. According to contingent universalism it is logically possible that some are eternally damned, but all will be saved as a matter of contingent fact. According to necessary universalism, it is a necessary truth that none are eternally damned.

Index